The Local Politics of Rural Development

Published by University Press of New England

Hanover, New Hampshire and London, England   1980

*The Local Politics
of Rural Development*

peasant and party-state in

ZAMBIA

MICHAEL BRATTON

Copyright © 1980 by Trustees of Dartmouth College
All rights reserved
Library of Congress Catalog Card Number 79-56775
International Standard Book Number 0-87451-178-X
Printed in the United States of America

Library of Congress Cataloging in Publication data
will be found on the last printed page of this book.

University Press of New England
Sponsoring Institutions
Brandeis University
Clark University
Dartmouth College
University of New Hampshire
University of Rhode Island
Tufts University
University of Vermont

For Anne

Contents

Tables

Maps

Acknowledgments

This study has consumed my attention for more than five years, and during that time I have accumulated more debts, personal and professional, than I can adequately acknowledge. I first began to study peasant politics and rural development in Africa while a graduate student at Brandeis University in the early 1970's. The Graduate School of that institution provided me with a research fellowship to conduct field work in Zambia. The Institute of African Studies at the University of Zambia granted me research affiliate status during 1973 and 1974. I taught in the Department of Political and Administrative Studies, University of Zambia, from 1974 to 1976, and my research funds were supplemented during this period by a grant from the Research and Higher Degrees Committee. On returning to the United States, I joined the Department of Political Science and the African Studies Center at Michigan State University. Here, generous provisions of released time from teaching permitted me to turn a dissertation into, I hope, a book. I am very grateful to all donors and sponsors.

A large number of people contributed time and support. Thanks are first and foremost due my hosts, the people of Kasama District, Northern Province, Zambia, without whose warm welcome no study would have been possible. Only a few can be mentioned by name. Elijah Chilufya and Safeli Mutengo of Nseluka village regrouping center were unstinting in cooperation and hospitality. Councillors Tennyson Siame, Luka Mutale, Vincent Mwamba, and Simon Mpundu, among others, repeatedly gave hours to answering what must have seemed endless questions. I should stress that any opinions or interpretations offered in this study are mine and not theirs; undoubtedly, too, this outsider will have misunderstood some aspects of the accounts of local politics that were offered me. Benedict Sekwila and Stubbs Mofya, who worked as research assistants and translators, showed imagination and diligence in helping to gather data from the field.

The influence of a number of colleagues must surely show in the pages that follow. Ruth Morgenthau provided intellectual stimulation and guidance from beginning to end. Lionel Cliffe helped me to ask questions relevant to rural development and to make fresh theoretical sense of my data. For reading various versions of the entire manuscript and helping me to synthesize my thoughts, great thanks are owed Larry Bowman, Robert Cancel, Mubanga Kashoki, and Ralph Thaxton. Others, including Jankees van Donge, Manenga Ndulo, Ian Scott, Brian Silver, and William Tordoff, read bits and pieces here and there and made many useful suggestions. The maps were drawn by the Cartographic Research and Spatial Analysis Center, Michigan State University. The final manuscript was typed by Katherine Lehman and Iris Richardson with such speed and accuracy that my deadlines were attainable.

To Lammert de Jong go my very special thanks not only for sharing his detailed knowledge of administrative procedure in rural Zambia but, more than that, for sharing his home in Lusaka. Finally I wish to acknowledge the fourth-year students of the University of Zambia who participated in Development Administration seminars in 1974 and 1975. Our lively discussions, in the classroom and out, saved me from many errors of judgment and gave me confidence in the future leadership of Zambia. I alone bear responsibility for errors that remain.

East Lansing, Michigan   *Michael Bratton*
April 1980

Acronyms and Abbreviations

AA	Agricultural Assistant
AFC	Agricultural Finance Company
ANC	African National Congress
CDA	Community Development Assistant
COZ	Credit Organization of Zambia
DDC	District Development Committee
DC	District Commissioner
DG	District Governor
DS	District Secretary
FNDP	First National Development Plan
GRZ	Government of the Republic of Zambia
IAS	Institute for African Studies
IDZ	Intensive Development Zones
ILO	International Labor Office
K	Kwacha: unit of Zambian currency (average exchange rate, 1974–75: K1 = U.S. $1.56)
KRC	Kasama Rural Council
KTC	Kasama Township Council
MCC	Member of the Central Committee
MP	Member of Parliament
NAMBOARD	National Agricultural Marketing Board
NIPA	National Institute for Public Administration
NPCMU	Northern Province Cooperative Marketing Union
PCDO	Provincial Community Development Officer
PDC	Provincial Development Committee
PPS	Provincial Political Secretary
PTA	Parent Teachers Association
PWD	Public Works Department
RC	Rural Council
RS	Regional Secretary
SNDP	Second National Development Plan
TANZAM	Tanzania-Zambia Railroad
UNIP	United National Independence Party
UNZA	University of Zambia
UPP	United Progressive Party
VPC	Village Productivity Committee
WC	Ward Council
WDC	Ward Development Committee
WRS	Women's Regional Secretary
YRS	Youth Regional Secretary
ZANC	Zambia African National Congress
ZNS	Zambia National Service

INTRODUCTION

1

The Local Politics of Rural Development

The advent of political independence in Africa has had a limited but occasionally advantageous effect on the quality of life in the rural areas of the continent. The posture of the postcolonial African state toward peasant populations, while continuing to reflect colonial preoccupations with political control and economic extraction, has come also to include new commitments to goals of rural development. These goals have in some cases been met. Inhabitants of previously remote communities have gained access for the first time to such basic social services as piped water, feeder roads, and primary education. African governments have boosted public expenditures in the rural sector well beyond colonial levels, and have extended programs in agriculture and community development to unprecedented numbers of peasants. Opportunities for political participation have even been provided in some African states through such institutions as one-party elections, production and marketing cooperatives, and local-level planning and development committees. The way would seem open to what Mabogunje has described as "real development"—that is, "Africans themselves improving or transforming the social and economic structure of their societ(ies)."[1]

Yet all is not well. The delivery of social services, where it has occurred, has usually been directed from above and financed from sources external to rural economies. In other words, the social improvements and political reforms that have accompanied decolonization have been incongruously tacked on to an underdeveloped and untransformed economic base. Rural poverty remains an intractable and growing problem beyond the capacity of African states to comprehensively reduce. From 60 to 95 percent of the population of individual countries derives livelihood from the land, yet rural economies are growing slowly, if at all. National self-sufficiency in food production eludes states in diverse parts of the continent. Rural unemployment remains high, rural incomes remain low, outward labor migration persists. Increases in agricultural production and productivity, prerequisites for self-reliant local development, have been the exception rather than the rule. The difficulties of relieving rural underdevelopment at the fundamental level of agricultural production has hindered rural communities from amassing the investable resources necessary to provide social services for themselves.

Although underdevelopment takes different forms in different parts of the African continent, the persistence of rural poverty can in most cases be traced to political and economic arrangements made in the period of colonial rule. International trade and investment in this period disrupted the structural integrity of traditional African political economies. Subsistence agriculture was weakened and partially superseded by such alien production arrangements as cash-cropping for export or urban labor migration.[2] Traditional polities were dismantled, as under direct rule, or absorbed, as under indirect rule, by a coercive colonial state. Communal solidarities of kinship were fractured and rearranged by forces of the marketplace into new solidarities of region or education or wealth. Although a small stratum of the rural population may have been elevated into advantaged social positions, the overwhelming majority of peasants were relegated to subordinate positions in the realms of production, status, and power. In time, declining economic output and increasing social stratification characterized once integral political economies.

Rural development is understood in this study to involve the reintegration of disrupted rural political economies. This implies not so much an uncritical return to traditional arrangements of the distant past, as if that were even possible, but rather a reconstruction of rural life according to contemporary principles of economic self-reliance, social equality, and popular participation. Rural development is an holistic process in which transformation in the economic, social, and political spheres are interwoven. Rural development requires at minimum that the provision of social services be fueled by increases in production and productivity. Rural development can only be achieved where the productive capacity of rural economies is revived and expanded to a point where peasants provide for, and control the allocation of, the social services they have chosen for themselves.

Rural development can be broken down for purposes of elaboration into its economic, social, and political components. In purely economic terms, rural development requires that rural communities reduce reliance on productive investments from outside and increase the generation and investment of resources within the locality. Rural development can be said to have taken root when economic growth based on local resources becomes self-sustaining. Under these circumstances the economic relationship of the locality to the center, if not one of complete independence, is at least one of healthy interdependence.

Rural development necessitates the redress of unevenness and dependence not only in the economic sphere but also in the social sphere. Few social scientists today dispute that development has qualitative dimensions of redistribution as well as quantitative dimensions of growth. Most contemporary definitions of development explicitly call for the simultaneous expansion of material production and the achievement of goals of social equality.[3] By definition, then, rural development runs counter to the social stratification that is often present and growing in rural African societies in the aftermath of colonial rule. In practice, rural development becomes a matter of spreading employment opportunities and social services to those in rural society who have been historically disadvantaged, subordinated, or excluded.

Finally, rural development has a political component which requires the establishment of a political and administrative apparatus through which development activities can be organized at the local level. The likelihood that economic mobilization and wide diffusion of development will occur in rural areas depends in large part on whether peasants enjoy a meaningful share of political power. Popular participation in drawing up development plans and putting them into effect is not an optional extra but a necessary component of an integrated approach to rural development. Neglect of organization-building at the local level can account for the failure of otherwise worthy strategies to generate self-sustaining and self-reliant rural development.[4]

THE LOCAL POLITICS OF RURAL DEVELOPMENT

The general aim of the present study is to examine the contribution of local-level political organizations to the achievement, or lack of achievement, of rural development. The local-level organizations in question are those of the African party-state. The aspects of rural development to which most attention is directed are the distributive aspects. An attempt is made to describe how the African party-state operates in rural settings, and to analyze the determinants and consequences of party-state performance.

It seems reasonable to suppose that a relationship exists between the way political organizations are built at the local level and the way that development resources are allocated and distributed. On the one hand, the organizational forms assumed by the state can be critical in constraining or facilitating productive allocation and wide distribution. Much depends, for example, on the balance struck between organizational arrangements for local participation and those for central control. On the other hand, local-level political organizations, particularly if the center is weak, may be readily subject to adaptation to the prevailing structure of rural economy and society. As Saul says, "institutions cannot be viewed or assessed independently of the structure that maintains them and influences their activities."[5] In sum, the state may be able to mold the rural environment, but it may also be molded by it. The performance of the local-level organizations of the African party-state must therefore be viewed contextually.

The method of inquiry used here is the case study. The performance of the local-level organizations of one African party-state, that of Zambia, is examined in one context, that of Kasama District in the Northern Province. The research intention, however, is not purely idiographic. The Zambian case offers an opportunity to confirm propositions about relationships between political organization and resource distribution derived from other studies. If existing propositions are found wanting, the Zambian case offers an opportunity to formulate new propositions for subsequent appraisal among a larger number of similar cases.[6]

There is a category of African country, to which Zambia belongs, in which a state apparatus has been built and power consolidated around a civilian one-party regime. Contrary to the popular image of African politics as unstable and institutionless, more than half of the independent black African states, or 24 out of 42, had by 1976 withstood or remained free of military intervention. In most cases the same nationalist leadership was at the helm as at the time of decolonization, and the preferred mode of political institutionalization was unipartism.

Of five typical paths of political change in Africa proposed in one recent study, three resulted in political stability, and two of these three were types of civilian one-party state.[7] Markovitz goes so far as to indulge in a novel heresy: "in contemporary African states . . . the most striking political development since independence . . . is not the lack of stability but indeed, from any long-range historical perspective, the rapidity with which stability has been achieved."[8] The consolidation of political power, such as that attained by the African party-state, is a prerequisite of sustained and effective intervention in development tasks. On this ground alone the relationship between political organization and rural development in the African party-state is a topic worthy of study.

An issue that arises at the outset is whether the African party-state has what Schurmann calls the ideology and organization to sustain a broad and deep strategy of rural development.[9] The survival of the African party-state does not, in and of itself, mean that rural development performance is either predictable or strong. The will of African nationalist leaderships to adopt ambitious social and economic programs is not often matched by a capacity to implement. Ideology has never been an adequate guide to political and administrative performance in Africa. Growth and distribution of development resources typically occur in rural localities in patterns different from those articulated by leadership at the center. Party-state institutions typically perform at the local level in patterns different from the formal organizational blueprint laid down in the capital city. To repeat, achievement rarely matches aspiration; development trajectories can be expected to diverge from development strategies. Further incantation of these commonplace assertions, however, is no longer necessary. Instead, identification is required of the factors that determine the actual allocation and distribution of development resources at the local level.

The principal theme of this study is that rural development in practice is the result of the interaction of the political interests of local leaders on the intended strategies of the state. The actual impact of state intervention in rural areas is not comprehensible without reference to what might be described as the local politics of rural development. For the most part, local politics in rural Africa are comprised of competition over access to scarce development resources. Individuals, groups, or strata who are politically powerful in the local arena are able to make their preferences felt during the development process. Local leaders are particularly well placed to monitor and direct the flow of resources where conditions of rural underdevelopment prevail. Under these conditions, resources for investment in local projects and programs are not generated from self-reliant and self-sustaining rural economies. They are derived elsewhere, in national or international arenas. The flow of development resources, such as it is, is predominantly from center to locality. While leaders at the political center are well placed to determine the size and availability of development resources, local leaders, acting as gatekeepers, are well placed to have decisive influence over actual patterns of distribution.

If the political interests of local leaders are an important factor in determining rural development outcomes, more needs to be known about the nature of these interests. Are they, for instance, the personal interests of ambitious individuals, the shifting interests of temporary coalitions, or the corporate interests of social strata? Do local leaders represent only themselves or do they act as patrons in the interests of client followers? Do the interests of local leaders reflect the formation of social classes as a consequence of the unfolding of rural underdevelopment? This study cannot conclusively answer all these questions for all rural localities in Africa. An attempt will be made, however, to show that regular patterns are likely to emerge in the competition over and distribution of scarce development resources. For example, local leaders are able to reward followers regularly by diverting resources from one locality to another, or from productive projects to social service projects. Local leaders may also regularly intervene in the distribution of resources to the advantage of themselves and their kind and to the detriment of those who are politically weak or economically poor. Of special concern in the present inquiry is whether, over time, a cleavage of interest develops between those who regularly benefit from development and those who are regularly excluded. Of related concern is whether patterns of resource distribution follow ethnic, patronage, or class lines, or some combination thereof. Patterns are likely to vary from locality to locality.

The key questions asked in this study are of the following kind: "Who participates in the planning of rural development?" "Who funds development and who implements it?" "Who benefits from development resources and who is excluded?" Answers are discernible in the performance of the local-level political organizations of party and state. The party-state in Africa provides an organizational framework within which competition over scarce development resources is played out and within which patterns of resource distribution are decided. Political organization has a certain prominence in rural Africa precisely because it provides the channels through which the bulk, or even the monopoly, of central resources are made available in the locality. This argument will be elaborated below. But, to repeat an earlier point, the prominence of political organization does not mean that organization and performance cohere to formal bureaucratic ideals. On the contrary, the party-state may be expected, at least in part, to internalize within its local-level organization the clusters of political interest that are salient in the locality. Conceivably the party-state at the local level may be captured by a coalition of powerful local patrons or a stratum of salaried functionaries. The performance of the party-state at tasks of production and distribution may even contribute to the formation of social classes in the locality along lines already emerging at the center. In these eventualities, political organization can become not so much an instrument of rural development as a block on it.

No deterministic thesis is intended. The African party-state is not merely a passive reflection of structures of underdevelopment in the social and economic spheres. The relationship between center and locality in the African party-state can be said to manifest a two-way dynamic. There is give and take in the local politics of rural development. On the one hand, the center does not generally have the ideological or organizational capacity to penetrate rural localities comprehensively with legions of mobilizing cadres. It has no alternative than to rely for a modicum of policy implementation at the grass roots on leaders recruited in the locality. These leaders may or may not share the resource allocation priorities laid down in the national plan. If the interests of central or local leaders are not coincident, or if the center is particularly weak, a rural development strategy is susceptible to distortion.

But, to repeat, the dynamic is not one-way. The locally powerful, for their part, need the state as much as the state needs them. In order to gain and maintain power, local leaders must bring home development resources, the bulk of which come from the center and are controlled by the state. There is strong pressure on local leaders to align their interests and support with those of national leaders and to become local agents of the center. Indeed, the center may use its scarce resources to purchase political control by recruiting and rewarding local leaders. These leaders, in return for material reward, manage and contain peasant demands. Center-locality relations in Africa are often marked by the tension between the commitment of the center to political control and demands from the locality for rapid rural development. It is in the resolution of such tensions between center and locality that actual development paths are charted. The relationship between state-building and rural development is thus unlikely to be exclusively determined at either center or locality alone.

CENTER-LOCALITY RELATIONS

That center-locality relations in Africa have a two-way dynamic is not a common theme in the social science literature. Studies of the role of the state in development at the local level have tended to adopt either the viewpoint of the center or the viewpoint of the locality. Yet neither a top-down nor a bottom-up perspective can alone reveal the subtlety and complexity of the local politics of rural development.

The *viewpoint of the center* was originally expressed in the work of scholars—mostly American political scientists—who conceived of politics in terms of whole systems. They sought to construct macropolitical theory relevant to politics in all places and all times by the application to empirical cases of such overarching notions as "modernization." Within the modernization schema, political development was defined by these theorists as the enhancement of the capacity of political organization to perform the functions for which it was intended. Huntington's well-known book opens with the assertion that "the most important distinction among countries concerns not their form of government but their degree of government."[10] The test of political development was whether the organization of the state was effective throughout a territory or society. In LaPalombara's words "the widespread impulse to national development . . . require[s] that central governmental authority be capable of ruling."[11] Modernization theorists thus conceived of center-locality relations as the penetration of a distant locality from above for the purpose of building an authoritative state.

The viewpoint of the center expressed by these theorists was that state-building is done unilaterally *by* a polity *to* a society. Almond and Powell, for example, considered that "state-building occurs when the political elite creates new structures and organization designed to penetrate society." [12] Unlike nation-building, a cultural problem, state-building was seen essentially as an organizational problem, graphically described by Doornbos as a matter of "creating the bone structure of a viable body politic." [13] Modernization theorists minced no words in revealing the intimate connection between state-building and the establishment of central political control. LaPalombara stated that political penetration aimed at eliciting "conformance to the public policy enunciated by central government authority." [14] According to Binder political penetration involved "growth in depth and extent of central political control into structures that were previously insulated from society." [15] Almond and Powell again: "State-building is commonly associated with significant increases in the extractive and regulative capabilities of the political system." [16]

A valuable aspect of the viewpoint of the center was the stress laid upon the establishment of some minimum kind of organizational framework as a precondition for the conduct of development activities. Another contribution was to remind analysts of the need for linkage and communication within "whole systems" between organizations of the center and organizations of the locality. But a general weakness of this approach was the conception of state-building as a process whereby a central organization extends its control outward and downward. There was little room for state-building as a process of accretion by local participation from below. Local interests and allegiances were usually interpreted as "parochial" or "traditional" and were categorized as obstacles to development. Local politics was conceived primarily as an arena for the testing of the penetrative capacity of the central state. Thus the viewpoint of the center could never fully illuminate the multiple ways in which local-level political organizations were assembled as a consequence of a complex interaction between center and locality, or between state and society.

A second general weakness was that the viewpoint of the center had strong normative overtones with potentially negative policy implications for rural development. The close theoretical symbiosis between political penetration and political control reflected, in part, the preoccupation among modernization theorists with, in Zolberg's phrase, "creating political order." O'Brien has eloquently argued that from the standpoints of both theory and policy, the key political values of the modernization approach are the maintenance of order and survival of regimes.[17] Markovitz concurs: "'Instability' preoccupies social scientists concerned with developing countries in the same way that 'law and order' concerns establishment politicians."[18] The point here is not that political control is not a resource regularly used by the center in Africa but that modernization theory predisposes observers of African politics not only to expect political control, but to favor its use. Modernization theory addresses only the question of the strength or effectiveness of political organizations and does not further ask "effective at what?" and "effective for whom?"

Cliffe has argued the opposing view that state-building initiatives should be appraised not just by the yardstick of capacity to rule but by their development implications.[19] The proposition that state-building is always associated with other indexes of "modernization," like popular decision-making and wide distribution of development resources, does not necessarily hold. Local-level organizations created by the state can be effective in stimulating self-reliant local development but can also be effective in institutionalizing inappropriate production techniques and dependence on central development funding. Political penetration can lead to a wide or narrow diffusion of development resources; political penetration can even freeze existing inequalities in place or instigate new and deeper patterns of social stratification. It can facilitate local political participation, but it can also, perhaps with greater likelihood, facilitate central control. Thus the questions of "who benefits, and how?" are as pertinent to the building of local-level political organizations as to any other aspect of rural development. But from the viewpoint of the center these were not questions of high priority.

Alternatives to the viewpoint of the center came from several quarters and can be summarized under the general rubric of *the viewpoint of the locality*. The inadequacy of grand theory as a guide to actual political performance precipitated a shift to subsystemic levels of inquiry among political scientists interested in Africa. Micropolitical research was seen to hold the promise of a more intimate understanding of the ways that center meets locality. In the late 1960's and early 1970's, researchers in political science began to forsake the capital cities for the villages and small towns of the hinterland.[20] They undertook to observe *in situ* the concrete realities of political penetration and state-building. In the shift from macropolitics to micropolitics the applicability of the conceptual tools and methods of social anthropology became apparent.[21]

Anthropologists had been critical of the misinformed depictions of the state and its performance in rural localities to which the viewpoint of the center had led. They drew attention to the fact that institution-building at the local level was not simply a matter of initiatives taken from above. In Vincent's words: "Whereas, in the past, the political scientists tended to work downwards . . . dealing with vertical structures, anthropologists have always been concerned to work outwards from any point within an arena, dealing with horizontal structures . . . political scientists focus on integration *per se*, anthropologists on all that precedes and flows in the wake of integration."[22] Simultaneously, anthropologists sought to redefine the terms of reference of their own research. A narrow focus on small communities in isolation was obsolete for societies subject to incorporation by national states and international economies. Weingrod therefore argued that the scope of anthropological research should expand to embrace "larger aggregates, to persons linked to one another by interest rather than by kinship and residence."[23] For Fallers, anthropologists should "conceptualize the place of local institutions they study within larger political wholes so that the results of their work may articulate fruitfully with the macroscopic research of political scientists."[24]

Anthropologists and political scientists thus came to occupy a shared research terrain, an eventuality with significant implications for the study of center-locality relations in Africa. First, the resilience of traditional institutions to political reform from the center was revealed. Empirical studies showed that the traditional institutions did not dissolve when confronted by a penetrative central state but adapted themselves into new and complex constellations.[25] Whitaker was led to the unorthodox proposition that the incorporation of localities does not proceed smoothly from the center downward but is "dysrhythmic" according to the degree of adaptation incurred by the center.[26] Eisenstadt even presented a strong case for the replacement of the concept "modern" with the concept "post-traditional" on the basis of the survival and reconstruction of traditional institutions.[27] Second, anthropologists and political scientists alike found that not all political competition occurred in the locality along institutional lines sanctioned by the center. Instead, both within the state apparatus and without, informal patterns of personalism, factionalism, and patronage prevailed.[28] Empirical studies came to be conceived in terms of the instrumental behavior of ambitious leaders, in particular the mediating behavior of middlemen or brokers who intervened between peasant and state. Many researchers took as their point of departure the individual political actor and the rational pursuit of personal goals.[29] The only major study to date of center-locality relations in Zambia was informed by the underlying premise that the economic and political behavior of peasants is explicable in terms of rational individual choice.[30] Barrows went as far as to suggest that in the context of African localities a politics based on utility is the most serviceable theoretical paradigm.[31]

The viewpoint of the locality helped to explode the myth of the expanding center and to show that local leaders could influence relations between state and peasant. But this approach too was not without its drawbacks. The replacement of grand theory applicable to whole systems with rational actor models applicable to individuals tended to divert attention from the collective bases of local politics in Africa. Second, the replacement of a top-down with a bottom-up perspective implied a notion of center-locality relations in which the local tail wags the central dog. Upcountry political leaders and organizations were often assumed to be insulated from weak centers and able to perform development tasks autonomously, in open affront to central control. Here state-building was seen as something done *by* a society *to* a polity. At minimum a discontinuity rather than a linkage was postulated between political organizations of the center and of the locality. Whether the imbalance between macropolitics and micropolitics could be redressed by emphasizing the latter beyond their true worth is, however, doubtful. Like the viewpoint of the center, the viewpoint of the locality underestimated the bilateral nature of center-locality relations.

THE PROMINENCE OF POLITICAL ORGANIZATION

Divergent approaches to the study of center-locality relations shared one basic assumption, namely that local-level political organization was marginal to local politics. From the viewpoint of the locality this was so because formal organizational arrangements made from the center did not match the informal patterns of political competition and reward by which anthropologists conceived local politics. From the viewpoint of the center this was so because, over time and in reversal of original perceptions, political scientists came to perceive African party-states as organizationally impotent. This latter point requires elaboration.

In the early days of party-state formation, political scientists entertained an idealized image of the capacity of central political organizations to penetrate rural localities. The inflated public claims of African nationalist leaders, and the construction by scholars of neat typologies of African party systems, made plausible the proposition that, in at least some parts of the continent, coherent, disciplined, mass-based "mobilization systems" were to be found.[32] The widespread acceptance of this proposition led to the reification of nonexistent local organizations. Misunderstandings of local realities were an inherent hazard of what has been dubbed the "center-focussed integration-modernization paradigm."[33] With the publication of the influential revisionist interpretations of Zolberg and Bienen, however, conventional wisdom swung to the opposite extreme.[34] Research in the field revealed that the performance of African party-states was meager and ineffective. Hence researchers came to expect not institutional strength but institutional weakness. The notion of the "decline of the one-party-state" entered academic and popular parlance;[35] acceptance was also widely accorded to notions like "the myth of the potent political organization" and "the crisis of penetration."[36] It was assumed that governments rarely governed. Indeed political scientists began to withdraw from the study of state-building in Africa on the basis of Zolberg's pessimistic assertion that African politics was "an almost institution-*less* arena with conflict and disorder as its most prominent features."[37] A new orthodoxy arose that political organization and political performance were unworthy of scholarly attention. As Decalo has said, "the previously fashionable discourse on the merits of unipartism, mass *vis-à-vis* elite parties, pan-Africanism and African socialism in all its varieties has largely petered out."[38] Few studies have been devoted in recent years to the performance of party and state in Africa.

The position taken in this study is that glib dismissal of the relevance of political organization to issues of overall development is mistaken. Unquestionably, "studies focused on incipient central institutions almost necessarily exaggerate their importance in relation to society as a whole."[39] Unquestionably too, "for most developing countries a highly centralized administrative apparatus is neither desireable nor possible."[40] The difficulty of effecting two-way center-locality ties is an established fact with which I take no fundamental issue. Nevertheless, African leaders still try to consolidate center-locality ties even though academic observers happen to be looking the other way. Indeed, the history of postcolonial Africa has been one of attempted state centralization in the face of particularistic local demands. The numerous stable civilian regimes that have survived have done so in part because organizational accommodations have been found to the tensions inherent in center-locality relations. The apparatus of one-party states at the local level, and the organizational linkages between center and locality, have become institutionalized in these cases. The assertions that African regimes universally face a "penetration crisis" or that African politics is an "institutionless arena" are not theoretical givens but hypotheses to be tested. The challenge facing political scientists is not only to generalize about institutional decay and instability but to explain the resilience of states that are stable. An initial determination is required, then, of degrees and forms of institutionalization of unipartism.

The performance of local-level political organizations is a useful guide to the way the local politics of rural development actually occur. An African party-state may have had an historically brief local presence or may not comprehensively exist in all rural areas of a territory, but even limited instances of political performance can depict the outlines of an institutionalized politics. Two related reasons can be given. First, political performance, far from being disorderly and unpredictable, displays a regularity to which all participants in the local political process are attuned. Recurrent patterns of resource allocation and distribution are evident to peasant and party-state functionary alike. Local political actors learn from experience that the state does not always operate according to the ideological or organizational blueprints of the center. They also learn that local-level political organizations are permeable to the clusters of political interest that prevail in the locality. These clusters of political interest cannot be hidden: local people know who gets what—when, where, and how. The actual performance of the party-state thus becomes fairly predictable, as much for the political scientist as for the local political actor. The state *is* what the state *does*. Local politics only appear "institutionless" if rigid formal-legal standards are applied to political performance or if local political interests are taken to lack structure or form.

The second reason not to belittle political organization is that it usually constitutes the main channel through which development resources are made available from center to locality. The disbursement of development resources is conducted through organizations which the center wishes to institutionalize in the locality. Examples of these local-level organizations are cooperatives, settlement schemes, development committees, and party branches. These organizations are typically provided by the center with small development budgets and with an ideology for mobilizing local resources. The penetration of the central state with a program of rural development introduces into the locality extensive and unprecedented opportunities for political competition. As argued earlier, in the context of rural underdevelopment, few material resources are produced locally over which political competition is likely to occur. Given a concentration of resources, the state undertakes more than a small "portion of allocative activity."[41] Local-level political organizations that dispense development become significant arenas for the expression and resolution of conflicting political interests. Control of state power at the local level thus becomes a key concern of political leaders who wish to influence or dominate the development process in rural Africa.

This is not to suggest that political organizations have primacy in the local politics of rural development but only that they have a greater prominence than often acknowledged. Rehabilitation of institutional performance as a theoretically relevant research topic does not imply an uncritical relapse to the early viewpoint of the center. Nor does emphasis on social and contextual analysis indicate whole-hearted approval of the viewpoint of the locality. An integration of the best of both schools would seem to proffer the most valuable approach. The theoretical choice facing political scientists is not solely between the local politics of formal-legal institutions and the local politics of the disorderly institutionless vacuum. Instead, a middle ground exists. Party-states are built in Africa, and competition and allocation unfold, on ground where political organization and socioeconomic structure meet and mutually adapt. Political scientists should thus locate themselves at the crossroads where center meets locality and state meets society. Such a theoretical perspective leads the researcher to an immediate empirical task—namely, the discovery of the exact extent to which the apparatus of the central state penetrates and survives in local society. Where does the center end and locality begin? Where does, and how does, party-state meet peasant? It is with inquiry into the depth, strength, and form of political organization in one local context that I am initially concerned.

PATTERNS OF RESOURCE DISTRIBUTION

This study begins with the performance of political organizations, but it does not end there. The performance of the African party-state can be used as a prism through which patterns of resource distribution within local societies can be observed. The character of these patterns, however, has yet to be described. In the literature on the interpenetration of state and society in rural Africa, two basic patterns of resource distribution have been proposed: *patronage* and *class*. On one hand, researchers who take the individual political leader and the rational pursuit of goals as their point of departure, propose a pattern of resource distribution marked by personal ambition of patrons and shifting factional alliances of mercenary clients. On the other hand, researchers equipped with the tools of class analysis emphasize the collective bases of political action at the local level. Intermediate leaders, according to the dependency and neo-Marxist schools, represent not only themselves as individuals, but the corporate interests of emergent social strata.

Before the relationship between patronage and class can be explored, a brief summary of the conceptual underpinnings of the two perspectives is required. The concept of patronage is widely used in empirical studies at the local level in Africa and has also been generalized into an explanatory framework applicable to African politics in general. Patronage is understood to mean a "personalized relationship between actors, or sets of actors, commanding unequal wealth, status or influence, based on conditional loyalties and involving mutually beneficial transactions."[42] Transactions between patrons and followers are reciprocal in that a patron offers material rewards and opportunities for social mobility in return for political support, particularly at the polls. Powell notes the pervasiveness of patronage patterns of resource distribution in underdeveloped peasant societies "characterized by extreme scarcity."[43] Hyden and Leys posit a "political culture," common to but not bounded by the region of East-Central Africa, which "accepts inequality as natural and sees politics as a means of solving individual and local problems through the provision of support for the 'right' patron."[44] Lemarchand develops a typology of forms of patronage relationship in terms of which, he argues, a wide range of African societies can be classified.[45]

Some scholars acknowledge that patronage politics inherent in African societies are reproduced within the formal political and administrative organizations of the postcolonial period. Thus party-states become "political machines."[46] Political machines manufacture votes at election time and are maintained not by rules or ideology but by the distribution of material resources within the organization. Scott has argued that machine politics presupposes electoral competition.[47] Sandbrook has responded that "machine-like" organizations can form even in non-electoral systems, though the reach of patronage here may be limited to leadership groups alone.[48] In Africa machine politics has arisen as a consequence of expanded opportunities for new leadership groups to acquire benefits during and since colonial rule. Characteristically, "party politicians distribute public jobs and special favors [and] seek to turn public institutions and public resources to their own ends."[49] Bienen has argued that machine politics can substitute for a lack of mobilization capacity on the part of the political center by integrating diverse local leaders and their followers into a spoils system.[50] The thrust of the patronage argument, for our purposes, is that in rural localities peasants benefit from rural development at least some of the time.

An alternative account of patterns of resource distribution at the local level has been given by writers who apply class analysis—or variations upon it—to Africa. Dependency theorists and neo-Marxists do not agree on the weight to be given class formation and class conflict in the analysis of rural underdevelopment. Both schools of thought nevertheless accept the notion that the fundamental social cleavages of underdevelopment are horizontal rather than vertical, and that the poorest peasants are usually frozen out of the distribution of resources. Both also employ an explanatory model of center-locality relations that is not confined to the nation-state but embraces the international economy. The expansion of capitalism, they argue, has created global relationships between the developed and underdeveloped worlds in which the "primary linkages are economic, not political or cultural."[51] Dependency theorists argue that rural underdevelopment is "a product of the single historical process of capitalist development"; neo-Marxists insist that it is rooted in the partial preservation of precapitalist modes of production.[52] Yet both would concur that the effects of capitalism are felt in remote rural localities by the transformation of production and social relationships and by the construction of a state apparatus that protects the interest of emergent middle classes.

In rural African localities, so goes the argument, peasant producers become differentiated from, and exploited by, a class alliance of national and local leaders. The composition of rural classes is a matter of dispute. Some scholars see the major line of stratification as between rich peasants and capitalist farmers on the one hand and, on the other, poor peasants, who may be landless or "semi-proletarianized" by labor migration.[53] Others point to the division between the peasantry as a whole and the state; here "the major source of differentiation within rural communities lies in the relation of rich peasants to the bureaucracy, through which they can control access to material resources and political influence within rural society."[54] The critical issue is whether the state is the formative factor in fostering uneven patterns of resource distribution. Under a capitalist modernization strategy for rural development, emergent farmers, who are already relatively well-to-do, are usually identified as the target group for official development projects. Even under an attempted transition to socialism, discontinuities and distortions in the planned redistribution of central resources regularly occur when the political interests of rich farmers and party-state leaders coincide. Whether these discontinuities give rise to changes in the organization and social relations of production and to the polarization of political interests into conflicting classes is an inquiry with which neo-Marxists are particularly concerned.

The patronage perspective and the class perspective appear to be incompatible, insofar as each assumes the existence of a different set of social identities. The vertical social ties of competing factions assumed from the patronage perspective cut across the horizontal social ties of social strata assumed from a class perspective. In practice, patterns of resource distribution based on patronage would seem likely to prevent the differentiation of local societies into antagonistic classes. Patronage is one method by which the benefits of development can "trickle down" to peasants. Because patrons are able to reach down into local society and reward clients, some scholars argue, even the most marginal social elements are integrated into the resource distribution process. Van den Berghe suggests, for example, that patron-client ties "create a vast and extremely diffuse network of personal relationships which often supersede 'class' loyalties."[55] Sandbrook adds that "where class consciousness is weak, individuals may improve their situation by means of individual action through the mechanisms of patron-clientship. . . . class conflict will be forestalled by the creation of patron-client structures linking the 'have nots' to the 'haves'."[56]

On the other hand, patronage and class may not be as incompatible as is sometimes assumed. Both patterns of resource distribution are sustained, after all, by inequality between social collectivities. Patronage, no less than class, rests on social relationships of *"sets of actors* commanding *unequal* wealth, status and influence."[57] In this regard Barker suggests that the "trickle down" view of patronage overlooks two important considerations: first, the "real inequality on which the factional system depends and which it perpetuates"; and, second, the possibility that the evolution of rural society under the influence of government policy may "create conditions for a class-based politics cutting across and potentially transforming the factional system."[58] Berman makes the interesting observation that "patron-client relationships are strikingly similar to the external imperial linkages of neocolonialism" in the asymmetry of the exchanges between superior and subordinate. Moreover, "patrons have a vested interest . . . in widening the inequalities between themselves and their clients . . . in order to increas[e] the cost of a withdrawal of support."[59] In similar vein, Alavi criticizes the methodological individualism that social anthropology brought to the study of local-level politics. Complex peasant societies, he argues, can be best understood by the study of intermediate local leadership, not simply as isolated individual patrons, but in a wider social, economic and historical context. Patrons can be agents of an emerging class or class alliance. In his words, "the factional model of politics in peasant societies is not a repudiation of the model of class conflict . . . primordial loyalties (including patron-client relationships) which precede manifestations of class solidarity do not rule out the latter; rather they mediate complex political processes through which the latter are crystallized."[60]

The data in this study cannot conclusively support the proposition that patronage and class may coexist. Yet it does seem likely that as ideal types, patronage and class are less distinct in empirical situations than theoretically. In certain empirical situations a mix of the two patterns can be expected. A related proposition is that the relationship between patronage and class is dynamic, incorporating the possibility of ebbs and flows between the two patterns. There is, in other words, no theoretical obstacle to the transformation of the politics of patronage into the politics of social class. Indeed, in certain empirical situations, the former pattern of resource distribution may be expected to lead to the latter. The task facing future research is to specify the conditions under which coexistence arises and the conditions under which the politics of patronage may be transformed into the politics of class.

The conditions considered here are those of an underdeveloped rural economy in which limited penetration of a central party-state apparatus has occurred. These conditions are common not only in much of rural Africa but throughout the periphery of the postcolonial world. The principal argument is as follows. Where a state monopolizes scarce development resources and where local patrons gain preferential access to the state, few peasants regularly benefit. Far from blocking social stratification, patronage here breeds objective wealth disparities. As a consequence, the interests of patrons and clients, once mutual, become bifurcated. Local leaders, dependent for material reward on the state, come to identify their interests with those of political leadership at the center. Peasants, for their part, come to recognize that the reciprocity of patronage relationships is breaking down and that local leaders keep scarce rewards to themselves. Peasants also perceive that limited resource distribution is accompanied by increased political control from the center and that opportunities for more than symbolic local participation are absent. Therefore peasants either withdraw political support from the state or become ready recruits for opposition political movements. Despite real wealth disparities, however, opposition movements seldom take on a class character. Instead peasants remain weakly organized and continue to rely for political expression not on one another, but on alternative patrons with access to the center. In sum, social stratification may be deepened by the playing out of a patronage pattern of resource distribution in rural Africa, but a local politics based primarily on class considerations has yet to emerge.

POLITICAL ORGANIZATION AND RESOURCE DISTRIBUTION

The case study examined in the following chapters suggests three propositions about the local politics of rural development in the African party-state. Each proposition addresses an aspect of the relationship between the form of political organization and patterns of resource distribution.

First, the local politics of rural development are not institutionless. The African party-state has a presence, even a prominence, in rural localities that academics and administrators often underestimate. Although political penetration is incomplete in the African party-state, organizations that use central resources for rural development can still be found in relatively remote localities. Local-level political organizations are not always lifeless paper structures. The type of institutionalization occurring at the local level is likely to reflect not only the organizational designs of the center but also the political interests derived from the structure of local society and economy. If political interests are those of patrons and their clients, the party-state becomes institutionalized as a political machine; if political interests are class-based, the party-state becomes an instrument of a bureaucratic bourgeoisie. The initial proposition is not that one form of state-building is more likely than another; indeed the notion that the organization of the African party-state in principle can reflect the coexistence of patron-

age and class is explicitly entertained. Rather, the initial proposition
is that state-building *does* occur in the locality, and along lines partly
determined in the locality.

Second, the depth in the locality at which state-building occurs is
determined in large part by the extent of the material resources available at the center. In other words, central political penetration is possible to the point that scarce resources permit. As Bienen and others
have shown, the African party-state is maintained in large part by the
distribution of patronage rewards. The proposition presented from
this study is the limits of patronage rewards available to political leaders define the limits of central penetration and control. The notion that
patronage can substitute for a lack of organizational capacity at the
center falls away once patronage is seen to define the limits of capacity.
As noted earlier, state-building, while often remarkably extensive, is
also likely to be incomplete. My argument is that this is so because
of the scarcity of resources available to the state under conditions of
underdevelopment. Scarce resources can stretch so far and no far-
ther. There is usually a gap between development demands and development resources at the local level which even patronage cannot plug.
Empirical inquiry into the patterns of resource distribution in the locality reveals the size and nature of this gap. It may also simultaneously reveal the limits of state-building; it may identify the point where
the state stops and local society begins.

Finally, leadership at the center may seek to remedy the scarcity
of material resources by applying nonmaterial resources to rural development. Two types of nonmaterial resource spring to mind: political
ideology and political control. If the leaders of the African party-state
cannot spread the benefits of rural development to all peasants, they
may try either to persuade or to force peasants to limit demands for
development or to engage in unpopular development measures. Williams and Turner simplify the options open to the center: "Popular
tolerance of the system of appropriating and allocating rewards must
be secured, by *coercion* and by the spread of opportunities and *rewards* among constituents."[61] The use of political control and the distribution of patronage rewards may be complementary rather than
alternative modes of interaction between peasant and party-state. The
proposition arising from the Zambian case is that material resources
are used by the leadership of the African party-state at the center to

purchase political control in the locality. Patronage rewards from the center are concentrated in the hands of selected local leaders who in return ensure that the participation of peasants in local-level political organizations is held to manageable proportions. Moreover, the scarcity of development resources and the reinforcement of social inequalities may induce political leaders to protect their own political positions by substituting political participation with political control. Notwithstanding a commitment to rural development in official ideology, the African party-state may thus continue to confront the peasant in a posture reminiscent of the administrative state of the colonial period.

Far from reversing historical underdevelopment, the African party-state may prove to be unequal to the task of reviving local economic production and ending the exclusion of the rural poor. Indeed, through selective recruitment and reward of prominent local leaders, the African party-state may become the principal organization in the locality through which uneven patterns of resource distribution are institutionalized. Yet my intention is not to attribute blame to the new nationalist leaders of Africa for failure to fill the tall order of structural transformation in economy, society, and polity. Rural development and state-building take place in a context not of their making. As Rothchild and Curry put it: "in the light of poverty and inequalities inherited from the past, it would be a mistake to evaluate Third World peformances in terms of brief post-colonial timespans."[62] My intention is to contribute to the identification of structural impediments that have so far blocked the path to self-reliant rural development in Africa, particularly impediments of political interest and political organization. My hope is that identification of impediments will help in a modest way when rural development strategies are designed for the future.

2

Center and Locality: The Zambian Context

Like many other African countries, Zambia exhibits a political economy marked by stark unevenness. A modern urban industrial sector stands in a dominant relationship to a depressed rural subsistence sector. Zambia is singular, however, because the degree of unevenness between town and countryside is arguably greater than in any other black African country south of the Sahara.[1]

At the core of the development prospects and development problems of Zambia lies copper. Zambia is endowed with rich deposits of the mineral which, at the time of political independence in 1964, accounted for 14 percent of world production. From the onset of the colonial period copper was exploited as an export commodity for use in the industrialized economies of the West by multinational corporations of American and South African origin. In 1969 the Zambian government took a 51 percent share in the copper mines but maintained much the same production and trade arrangements as before. The importance of copper to the contemporary Zambian economy and state is critical. Until the mid-1970's it accounted for over nine tenths of annual export earnings, between one third and one half of gross domestic product, and over one half of public revenues. Income from copper thus determines the capacity of the Zambian state to import goods for purposes of consumption and production. It also determines the levels of resources domestically available for investment in development, including rural development. Without copper Zambia would be a backward agricultural country, in the opinion of Harvey, "probably even poorer in financial terms than Malawi and Tanzania."[2] To Sklar, "despite the great prosperity of her copper industry Zambia was born with exaggerated features of underdevelopment."[3]

The backwardness of the rural areas of Zambia cannot be under-

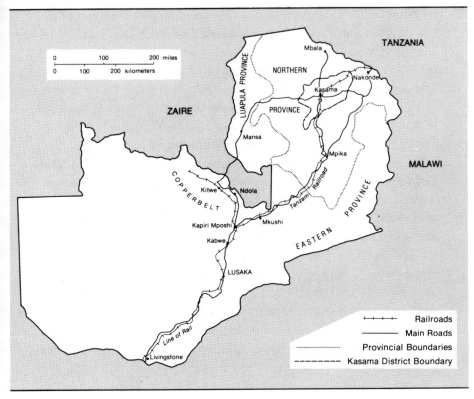

1   The location of Kasama District in the Republic of Zambia.

stood in isolation from the forwardness of the urban areas. The expansion of the large-scale externally oriented copper industry has been associated with levels of urban population drift and urbanization more typical of Latin America than of Africa. Zambian peasants have left the rural areas in search of employment opportunities and improved social services to a point where almost 40 percent of the population lives in town. Urban centers are clustered on the so-called Copperbelt or along the line of rail laid down by the colonial administration as an export route for copper (Map 1). A precedent was set in colonial times for investments in development to be concentrated along the line of rail.[4] This precedent was respected after 1964, when the Zambian government continued to allocate public expenditures in favor of the high-growth urban and industrial enclaves. A pattern of differential access to opportunities and services for urban and rural populations was thus entrenched. For example, in 1969 the line of rail provinces accounted

for 84 percent of the opportunities for wage employment and 91 percent of the total wage earnings.[5] About nine out of ten rural households remained in the small-scale subsistence sector, even by the mid-
1970's, producing primarily for their own consumption and earning
only marginal and sporadic incomes from cash sales.[6] The delivery
of rural social services was far below the levels of urban areas; in
1974, for example, 82 percent of urban households had access to clean
drinking water, compared with 56 percent of rural households.[7]

Yet unevenness and lopsidedness in the Zambian economy is as
much a social phenomenon as a spatial one. President Kaunda has recognized that spatial disparities between urban and rural areas interact
with social disparities between rich and poor. On the one hand, he
warned in 1969 of the danger of "creating two nations within one . . .
not always along the capitalist pattern . . . but between rural and
urban areas."[8] On the other hand, he modified his "two nation" formula by 1975: "at the national level the greedy upper and middle
classes continue to demand more and more without paying due regard
to the have-nots . . . Humanism cannot be reconciled with a class system."[9] Inequalities of income distribution exist within the urban areas
of Zambia, as well as between town and countryside.[10] The main African beneficiaries of public expenditures in the first decade of Zambian
independence were bureaucrats and mineworkers. These groups were
sufficiently well organized and articulate to have their political interests met—for example in the form of substantial salary and wage increases. Employees of the state and parastatal apparatus were able
to adopt the incomes, tastes, and life styles of their colonial predecessors. They came to constitute an emergent Zambian bourgeoisie with
political interests more closely identified with a transnational middle
class than with the urban and rural poor of their own country.[11] A
fairly extensive literature analyzing the postcolonial development path
of Zambia in terms of class formation and class conflict now exists.[12]
A full account of underdevelopment in Zambia must make reference
to what Shaw calls "the domestic class formation [that is] one result
of Zambia's status as a part of the periphery of the world capitalist
economy."[13]

It is against the background of uneven development, between town
and countryside and among emergent social strata, that policies of
rural development in Zambia must be examined.

POLICIES OF RURAL DEVELOPMENT:
THE ZAMBIAN APPROACH

Three characteristics can be discerned in the Zambian approach to the formulation and implementation of public policies of rural development up to 1975. First, investments in rural development were decided primarily at the center and financed out of revenues from copper. Because the state relied for public revenues on one export commodity, the availability of resources for rural development tended to vary with the fortunes of copper on the world market. Two periods are distinguishable in postcolonial Zambia: the period of economic surfeit from 1964 to 1974 when copper prices were generally high and resources for rural development were at their peak, and the period of economic stringency, beginning in 1975, when, because of a combination of international and domestic factors, copper prices and exports declined and, with them, public revenues for rural development. Field work for this study was conducted in 1974 and 1975, during which time the first intimations of the copper crisis reached rural localities though before the full impact of reduced revenues was felt.

Second, rural development was generally granted low priority. Public investments in rural development were never large, either in absolute terms or relative to investments in urban development or industrial infrastructure. The resources made available for rural development were "residual" in a double sense. They were residual not only to resources for urban and industrial development but also to resources for large-scale projects concentrated in rural market towns or special agricultural schemes. Little was left over for rural development as conceived to include mass popular mobilization and attention to the needs of subsistence peasants. Thus even during the period of economic surfeit a scarcity of development resources prevailed in the villages of the rural hinterland.

Third, the policies devised by the party-state to stimulate rural development never amounted to a coherent or integrated strategy. Various approaches were introduced simultaneously. By the mid-1970's Zambia had attempted to encourage cooperatives alongside family farms, state farms alongside private commercial estates, and small-scale self-help social service schemes alongside heavily capitalized "intensive development" schemes. At best this multifaceted strategy reflected the mixed nature of the Zambian economy; at worst it amounted to an array of mutually contradictory policies. Yet the no-choice approach has been defended as appropriate to Zambia, given the strong and irreconcilable political interests exerted on policy-makers under conditions of social stratification and regional diversity. It has also been defended as affordable because of the ability of a comparatively wealthy country like Zambia simultaneously to choose and fund more than one development path.[14] As a consequence of the no-choice approach, however, Zambia came to possess a set of policies that charted no clear direction for rural development. As of mid-1970's Zambia had no ready alternative to copper in terms of either short-term crisis or long-term development.

Yet Zambia has not lacked an ideology of rural development. Party-state ideology has repeatedly stressed the need to raise agricultural productivity in order to lessen structural dependence on copper. More-over, President Kaunda's philosophy of Zambian Humanism explicitly extols the cooperative and egalitarian values of traditional village life. Traditional values are considered applicable in the national realm: in a man-centered society no individual, however impoverished, is to be excluded from the benefits of development. Rural development to Kaunda necessarily involves the reintegration of disrupted village communities and the fulfillment of the basic human needs of peasants: "Humanism in Zambia is a decision in favour of the rural areas."[15] Although the egalitarian and antimaterialist ethos of Humanism has not been warmly embraced by the privileged groups in Zambian state and society, some of its principles did form part of the planning en-vironment for successive National Development Plans. Among the goals announced by politicians and planners were the diversification of production away from mining and into agriculture, and the upgrading of rural standards of living by the reallocation of wealth from the line of rail into rural programs and projects. The First National Devel-opment Plan (FNDP), 1966 to 1970, aimed in part to "minimize the in-herited economic imbalance between urban and rural sectors." The Second National Development Plan (SNDP) was presented as the plan that would give top priority to agricultural and rural development.

The FNDP fell squarely into the period of economic surfeit, the SNDP only partly so. The unbroken trend of rising copper prices be-tween 1964 and 1970 initially permitted lavish public investment in all sectors of the economy. Popular expectations were raised, and the rewards of political independence came to be seen by peasants and political leaders alike in largely economic terms. Public investment in this period was a matter of central "promotion, dispensation and handouts," and a practice grew for party and state officials to "concentrate on expenditure rather than revenue."[16] The government poured more money into the rural areas than could be efficiently used for productive purposes, and allocations for rural expenditures were often returned to Lusaka unspent. Administrative reforms in 1968 and 1969—under which, for example, a consolidated ministry of Rural Development was established—addressed the necessity for an organizational framework for implementing rural development policies. By the end of the SNDP period, however, the problem facing the Zambian government was not how to spend money but how to raise it. The price of copper on the world market declined by half between early 1974 and early 1975. The Zambian state was able to maintain planned levels of spending through 1974; national income in real terms slumped 30 percent in 1975; severe cuts in public spending in all sectors were introduced in the January 1976 budget.

Even before the impact of reduced revenues was felt, however, public allocations and expenditures did not reflect a high priority for rural development. The bulk of expenditures during the FNDP period, which was extended to 1971, was on infrastructure for export-oriented or manufacturing industry. Fifty-five percent of state capital expenditures was devoted to projects like the upgrading of the railroad system, the establishment of a national road transport fleet, the construction of an oil pipeline to the coast, and new generating facilities for hydroelectricity.[17] The illegal declaration of independence by Rhodesia in 1965 and the subsequent adherence by Zambia to international trade sanctions necessitated costlier outlays on infrastructure, especially alternate transport routes, than planners could have foreseen. Some benefits from social infrastructure—for example those resulting from the national drive to build primary and secondary schools—did accrue to rural areas. Nevertheless, by the end of the FNDP period, over two thirds of actual development expenditures had been concentrated in the urban provinces on the line of rail.[18] Nor was official ideology translated into rural development action any more effectively during the Second National Development Plan. Direct allocations to the rural sector did rise from K88 million to K152 million, as did indirect allocations to the rural sector through technical ministries of health, education, and water affairs. It is by no means clear, however, that rural allocations rose as a percentage of total allocations; the SNDP document did not include a breakdown of planned expenditures according to urban and rural provinces. Only nominal resources were allocated to the decentralized Provincial Investment Program. According to plan projections, the share of gross domestic product of the agricultural sector was actually intended to decline at the same time that the share of manufacturing was to rise.[19] Moreover, according to one estimate, public expenditures in the first two plan periods on subsidies for basic foodstuffs, which is a subsidy to urban dwellers, "could hardly have cost less than the entire capital allocation to agriculture."[20] By 1974 the performance of the SNDP in all sectors had begun to fall "far short of set targets";[21] and in the end the results of the plan, notably where agriculture was concerned, were "less than encouraging."[22]

Rural development policies, as designed and implemented up to the end of 1975, did not redress the imbalance between town and countryside in Zambia. Instead, the relative position of the rural sector deteriorated. The contribution of agriculture to gross domestic product declined from 8.2 percent in 1964 to 7.6 percent in 1973; agricultural exports shrank from 2.3 percent of total exports to 1.9 percent during the same period.[23] A group of small-scale emergent farmers, perhaps 50,000 strong and concentrated in the line of rail provinces, did make good much of the loss in maize production created by the departure of white commercial farmers. But the marketed production of such cash crops as tobacco and groundnuts declined. Zambia was unable to reach the goal of national food self-sufficiency by 1975; indeed the value of food imports stood at double that of the time of independence. Food production per capita fell in the subsistence sector and, equally important, agriculture failed to provide a source of increased rural incomes. Per capita income in the subsistence sector was only a fraction of urban income, perhaps as low as one tenth.[24] In 1973 Zambian farmers could purchase only two thirds of the consumption goods that could be purchased with the same amount of production in 1964.[25] In the 1960's and 1970's the urban worker fared better economically than the rural peasant. One observer has noted that "despite enormous expenditures, the majority of Zambians . . . and most of the rural population have not benefitted very much."[26] The urban-rural gap widened. The flow of urban migrants was not stemmed.

LOCAL-LEVEL ORGANIZATIONS: THE ZAMBIAN APPROACH

One of the intentions of the Zambian government toward rural development was the construction of a framework of political and administrative institutions to link center and locality. There was a need not only to consolidate the hold of the state on ethnically and linguistically diverse periphery but to increase and spread development benefits that had not reached the countryside under colonial rule. Insofar as rural development received attention under the first two development plans, it was predicated on the creation of local-level political and administrative organizations. Ideologically the new regime was committed to mass participation and mass mobilization. A "participatory-democratic" rather than a "bureaucratic-authoritarian" mode of political penetration was favored in official ideology.

The difficult question was how to translate ideology into organization. Creating an organization to link center and locality completely *de novo* was a difficult task, given the vastness of the rural periphery and scattered peasant populations. One alternative to creating an organization from scratch was to adapt existing organizations to new functions. But a striking feature of the rural areas in 1964 was the absence of any viable organization that could be used for political participation or political control.

One possibility might have been for the center to use the apparatus of the colonial administration as the Kenyan government had chosen to do. The dissolution of the colonial Provincial Administration and the reduction in the number of field-level administrators after independence, however, had left Zambia with an "institutional vacuum" at district level and below.[27] Linkages between the district *bomas* (headquarters) and the villages were severed by the abolition of the colonial Native Authorities and the withdrawal of powers from the traditional chiefs. In other words the organization used by the colonial administration was largely dismantled at the grass roots level. Severe shortages of personnel trained in administrative skills also rendered the civil service option problematic. Alternatively, there was the Tanzanian strategy of using the dominant political party as the prime organizational link to the locality. In 1964 the United National Independence Party (UNIP) was the only noncolonial national institution with a significant grass roots presence. UNIP suffered, however, from an uncontrolled membership and an organization and ethos better suited to national liberation than national construction. With the advent of independence UNIP began to lose peasant support and UNIP branch organization began to wither (see below, Chapter 8). Moreover, by the early 1970's the penetration of the dominant party was in doubt in those areas of rural Zambia, especially the South, West, and North, where opposition parties were able to garner support.

The new regime thus lacked the capacity to build afresh a top-to-bottom organization, and existing organizations were unsuitable or inadequate for adoption. National leaders set out to piece together from old and new organizations a party-state apparatus that approximated the requirements of rural development in postcolonial Zambia as they saw it. For the most part the process of state-building was undertaken from the top down, perhaps because central political power was easier to consolidate in a sectionally fractious situation than was local power. A number of political and administrative reforms were introduced before and during the First Republic, 1964–73. Together these reforms amounted to a strategy for state-building in which the tension between central control and local participation was never resolved. The problem was how to integrate rural participatory institutions into an increasingly centralized party-state. The unresolved tension was well summarized in the description coined by President Kaunda of the Zambian strategy as one of "decentralization in centralism."[28]

A brief account of the major administrative reforms and the formal organizational structure of party and state is necessary to acquaint the reader with the institutional landmarks in the locality.[29] Just prior to independence, elected local authorities, the Rural Councils (RC's), were established, and the first comprehensive elections were held in 1966. The bulk of Rural Council finance was provided through central government grants for local development and maintenance purposes.[30] Later, in 1965, development committees were set up in provinces and districts in order to assist in the implementation, but not the formulation, of rural projects and programs in the First National Development Plan.[31] Provincial Development Committees (PDC's) were initially given token "block votes" for local spending, but these were later withdrawn and thus rendered PDC's ineffective. In 1969, a comprehensive administrative reform was introduced with the stated aim being to decentralize and politicize the Zambian civil service. A Cabinet Minister was appointed as the political head of each province and a District Governor to each district.[32] Although these political functionaries were charged with responsibility for coordinating development activities in rural localities, few decision-making and spending powers were actually vested with them. In 1971 the administrative reform with the greatest import for this study took place. The development committee idea was carried down to the lowest levels in the locality. Ward Development Committees (WDC's) and Village Productivity Committees (VPC's) were established for the purpose of inducing peasant participation in agricultural production and the provision of social services.[33]

At the point in the locality where state met peasant, development committees were to be augmented with political party organization. The First Republic of Zambia came to an end in 1973 when a one-party state was declared. Opposition parties were outlawed and UNIP was vested with "supremacy" over the state apparatus at all levels.[34] These constitutional reforms ushered in the Second Republic of Zambia and a governmental system described by leaders at the center as "Zambian one-party participatory democracy." The reforms were designed, as far as rural localities were concerned, to fill the institutional vacuum with a cohesive and coordinated phalanx of party and state organizations. Ideally, the party would "mobilize" and the state would "implement."

At the time of research, 1974–75, the formal organization in the locality of the sole political party, UNIP, comprised four levels: the region, the constituency, the branch, and the village (see Chart 1). Under provisions of the Constitution of UNIP (1973), the region was to be headed by a Regional Committee, appointed from the center, of which the District Governor (DG) was chairman and the Regional Secretary (RS) was secretary. The RS deputized for the DG in the latter's absence from the district. Officials, representing the women's and youth wings of UNIP, and two trustees made up the Regional Committee, often known as the Regional Cabinet. The Region was supposed to hold an annual conference attended by representatives of

Chart 1   Organization of party and state in Zambia.

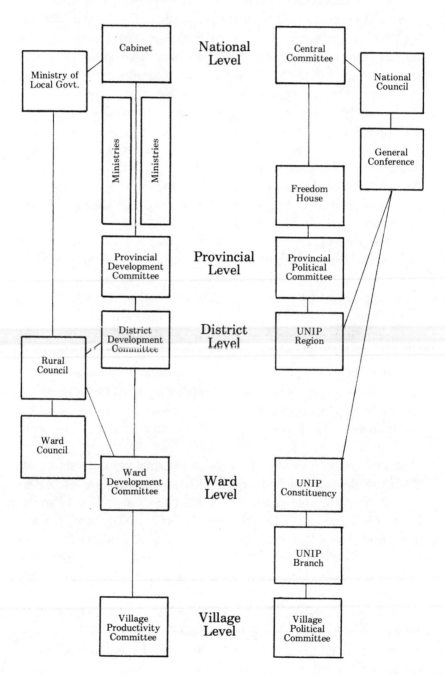

every UNIP constituency and branch. At constituency level there were to be eight officials for each wing of the party, making a total of twenty-four, all of whom were elected for three-year terms. This organization was duplicated at the branch level, with the exception that elections were annual. All officials were expected to be paid-up party members, and requirements were laid down by UNIP head-quarters for the holding of regular meetings of constituency and branch executives. Branch executives were to supervise village political committees, known in urban areas as section political committees, the smallest units of party organization. The main tasks of this organization at all levels was the recruitment of members and the mobilization of support for party candidates in national and local elections. The political party was also to be used to supervise the implementation of policy established by the party-state at the center.

Parallel to this party organization was an administrative organization comprised of development committees (Chart 1). These committees were intended to provide horizontal linkage among government agencies in the locality as well as vertical linkage between administrative center and periphery. As mentioned above, development committees for village and ward were established under the Registration and Development of Villages Act (1971), and a Pocket Manual was distributed in order to provide rural peasants with the details and intent of the new organizations. Together these documents represented a blue-print for the building of a state apparatus in the locality which would involve every adult in Zambia. Every village would have a Village Productivity Committee and every local government ward a Ward Development Committee. These committees would provide a forum both for the expression of local demands and for the enforcement of central policies.

At the base of the structure was the "village," which was to be the fundamental unit of political and administrative organization in the rural areas. Headmen of villages were supposed to prepare and maintain village registers in which the particulars of inhabitants over the age of fourteen were recorded. For the purposes of the Act a "village" was assumed to be a settlement of a minimum of twenty households and each village was to be administered by a Village Productivity Committee (VPC). Where villages were smaller than the statutory minimum, several villages, but not more than five, would be combined under a single VPC. The membership of the Village Productivity Committee was also clearly laid down for the first time. Villagers should meet to elect six to ten of their number as VPC members for three-year terms. The village headman, "by virtue of his traditional status," was automatically the chairman of the VPC. The chairman was responsible for convening meetings of the VPC and, as the last link in the political communication chain between center and locality, was responsible for reporting on development issues to and from the ward level. One VPC member was also chosen secretary-treasurer; his functions included keeping VPC records and supervising development projects in the village.

Immediately above the VPC in the local-level committee organization was the Ward Council (WC), so named because its jurisdiction covered one local government electoral ward. Each VPC was to send two representatives to the WC, namely the VPC chairman and one other. Since the WC was a plenary body containing representatives of every village in the ward, it was designed to act as a sort of ward parliament. At the WC the VPC chairmen were supposed to raise problems or project proposals from their village meetings for discussion and decision by the ward as a whole. According to the Act, the WC was to meet twice annually and to be chaired by the elected councilor for the ward.

Since the WC was often a large, and therefore potentially unwieldy institution, the detailed day-to-day business of the ward was to be handed over to an executive body, the WDC, members of which were elected by and from the WC. They were to serve for a three-year term, and each WDC should contain ten members. As with the WC, the chairman of the WDC was the ward councilor. He was to be assisted by an elected secretary-treasurer who also doubled as secretary-treasurer of the WC. The ward councilor, as chairman of both WC and WDC, occupied the key linkage position in the committee structure between the center and the locality. Not only was he responsible for calling meetings of the WDC and WC and exercising a casting vote over their deliberations, but he was to keep the committees informed of the decisions of the Rural Council and the District Governor. He was also the sole elected representative of the people of the ward at the district level by virtue of his seat on the RC. It was through the ward councilor that most of the political communication and economic resources of the ward were to be channeled.

The central government, charged with standardizing the organization of village and ward committees in 1971, also attempted to standardize a definitive set of committee functions. The first formulation of what the committees should do had centered on expanding the agricultural output of village cultivators and effecting a transition from subsistence to market-oriented agriculture. By 1971 the scope of the local committees was dramatically widened. The Pocket Manual listed a wide range of tasks for a VPC, ninety in all. These tasks covered such diverse fields as setting up an administrative center in the village, teaching Humanism, maintaining security, fighting crime, controlling drinking (mentioned twice!), supplying water for agricultural and domestic uses, ordering farm requisites, repairing farm equipment, arranging for the marketing of produce, designing "school-leaver" projects, and building roads, schools, clinics, and community centers. In short, a village should run itself. According to this ideal picture, a VPC would be a multipurpose development unit with commitments to social, political, security, and administrative matters as well as a basic production brigade at the grass roots. The economic resources available to the VPC for the execution of this ambitious array of projects were to be the resources of self-help. "The Government cannot do everything for every individual in the village because its own resources are limited. [Only] the practical and active participation of the village people . . . improves their social and economic welfare."[35]

The multipurpose nature of VPC's was echoed in the functions laid down for WC's and WDC's. These committees were made responsible for the provision of social infrastructure in all dimensions of education, health, and social welfare. They were also charged with control of the local economy; because the WC and WDC were to supervise and coordinate the work of the VPC, their functions were more those of rural development planning than of actual production. The WDC in particular was to engage in planning for all the villages in the ward, in the sense of choosing development projects according to criteria of social need and available resources. The WDC also planned the raising and allocation of resources by determining from the ward point of view whether projects were best met through self-help or government assistance. In addition, the WDC was supposed to convert government agricultural policy into a production strategy suitable for the ward; this involved choosing suitable cash crops or other productive enterprises, setting ward production targets, and mobilizing people to meet them. For the WDC planning did not stop with the identification of projects but continued through implementation. For example, the WDC might be called upon to ensure that building materials were produced or farm requisites transported for the completion of a project by a village in the ward. It might also be called upon to administer a locally subscribed ward fund or credit union. As the Act described it, the Ward Development Committee was a powerful executive body at the local level. Members of the WC were urged not to "interfere in the day-to-day running" of the WDC; the Ward Council was endowed with fewer powers and was therefore likely to be merely a rubber stamp for decisions taken in the WDC.

The design finally adopted in the Zambian strategy for local level state-building was a compromise, resembling both the Kenyan and Tanzanian models. The strategy called for an integration of party, administrative, and traditional institutions; it called for the performance of political as well as developmental tasks; it called for the balancing of central control with local participation. Cliffe and Saul have pointed to the difficulties inherent in implementing a coherent rural development approach when the machinery for implementation is an uncoordinated array of ill-matched organizations.[36] In those terms Zambia lacked a coherent "development front" in the rural areas; a no-choice approach characterized the mode of implementation as well as the content of rural development policies. At district level, responsibility for rural development was divided among the office of the DG, field ministries of central government, local government authorities, and cooperative unions. Each had different emphases with reference to the overall tasks of inducing mass participation and economic mobilization, and each had a different measure of contact and linkage with peasants at village level. At the village and ward levels the vanguard of the development front was comprised of development committees and party organs. Within WDC's and VPC's, leaders from party, state, and traditional sectors were supposed to reconcile the political interests of their diverse constituencies. The potential for a conflict was high. Moreover, each set of leaders was supposed to provide a measure of linkage between center and locality. Chiefs and headmen would link village to ward; ward councilors, elected through party channels, would link ward to district; finally, state employees would provide the technical and administrative component in local rural development activities. Because there was no consistent line of command or representation, the likelihood that some of the links between center and locality would be missing was also high.

Needless to say, the formal blueprint for state-building and center-locality relations offered a poor guide to actual performance. The mixed organizations of the local-level development front were intended by the center to be woven into the social fabric of rural life, to become "institutionalized." As such, the design of political organization in Zambia was accommodated to, and did not confront, distributions of power in local society. To a certain extent such accommodation was indispensable to enlisting local support for central goals. By the same token, however, local institutions became susceptible to capture by traditional or emergent groups of local power brokers with interests at odds with national ideology.

KASAMA DISTRICT: PROFILE OF A LOCALITY

Kasama District, the Northern Province, occupies a peripheral location on the plateau near the northern border of Zambia with Tanzania (see Map 1, above). Kasama township lies a distant 864 kilometers from Lusaka. Historically, the district was the heartland of the centralized Bemba empire, and the village of the Bemba paramount, Chitimukulu, is located within its boundaries. The Northern Province is the largest province in Zambia in terms of land area and has the third lowest population density. Ninety-two percent of the 103,000 people of Kasama District live in scattered village communities. Writing in 1958, Audrey Richards considered that "the country of the Bemba of northeastern Rhodesia is remote, without transport, and agriculturally backward, and might be considered one of the toughest propositions [an] administration has to deal with from the economic point of view."[37] Geographic isolation and economic underdevelopment remained identifying characteristics of Kasama District almost two decades later.

The economic relationship of the Kasama locality to the center is that of a labor reserve for the copper mining industry. From the peasant perspective the copper mining industry represents the prospect of paid urban employment and the ultimate source of funding for rural development projects. The peasant subsistence economy stands in a dependent relationship to the copper enclave, and its own underdevelopment continues to unfold by virtue of ongoing labor migration.

Labor migration is perhaps the single most important socioeconomic fact about Kasama. The district has a long history of rural-urban population movement, because of low economic potential of its land and its relative proximity to the copper mines. Roberts shows that by 1912, 3957 of the 7290 taxable males in Kasama had been forced to take up wage labor in order to pay taxes imposed by the British South Africa Company.[38] Richards estimates that male absenteeism had settled at about 48–60 percent by 1933.[39] The figure later rose; Richards estimates 70 percent for 1957, and Kay 63 percent for 1962.[40] The 1969 census, the first conducted by the Zambian government, revealed a remarkable trend of population decline in Kasama and other districts in the Northern Province in the context of a nationwide population increase of 2.5 percent per annum (Table 1). One planning report stated bluntly that "the province is declining in population at an alarming rate and this is likely to continue into the foreseeable future."[41] Some reversal of outmigration occurred when job opportunities on the Tanzam railroad became available in the early 1970's, but this reversal primarily affected the urban centers within the Northern Province and

TABLE 1.   Northern Province, Population Trends by District, 1963–1979

District	1963	1969	1974	1979
Chinsali	71,282	58,014	48,000	40,000
Isoka	81,851	77,000	74,000	71,000
Kasama	113,614	107,817	103,000	99,000
Luwingu	80,644	79,164	78,000	77,000
Mbala	91,136	95,633	100,000	105,000
Mpika	60,263	59,378	64,000	70,000
Mporokoso	65,205	67,390	69,000	72,000

Sources: 1963 and 1969 Censuses, and estimates made by the Intensive Development Zone Team, Northern Province.

not the outlying villages. For the main part, outmigration became a standard peasant response to low rural employment opportunities and to piecemeal and ineffective central initiatives to raise rural incomes.[42] Peasants in Kasama have voted with their feet.

Rural exodus on the scale experienced in Kasama points to significant shifts in the population structure of Zambia.[43] Urban population grew by 9 percent in the 1960's and 7 percent in the 1970's; the 1969 census demonstrated that of the people born in the Northern Province, 25.4 percent resided permanently outside. An urban sojourn came to be regarded as a rite of passage for young rural males in Bemba society, and the Copperbelt has been described as "an extension of their own [Bemba] society."[44] Migration of women into permanent urban residence has become increasingly common, to the point where, for all age groups taken together, women in Kasama now outnumber men at the relatively low ratio of 3:2.[45] More significantly, migration, whether permanent or temporary, occurs most regularly among those aged 20 to 49, the group in the rural population with the greatest potential for economic productivity. Fifty-seven percent of the district population is under the age of twenty. Moreover, the tendency of educated people to migrate further depletes the locality's reserve of productive human resources. Thus the demographic profile of Kasama villages in a pattern reminiscent of other labor-exporting rural areas of Africa, is tilted heavily toward the elderly, the very young, and the female. The Kasama case is compelling by any standard because the history of labor migration has been particularly long and the effects on rural development particularly deep.

The toll taken by labor migration is manifest in numerous ways. Most basic is the impact of male absenteeism on agricultural production. Peasants in Kasama traditionally practiced "large-circle" *chitemene* cultivation whereby a staple crop of millet was grown in an ash circle created by the burning of lopped tree branches.[46] The cutting of trees for chitemene was exclusively men's work, as was fence-building and the sowing of millet, but male absenteeism inevitably necessitated modification in traditional practices by the adoption of hoe cultivation by women and of new dietary habits by all. By 1974–75, semi-permanent *mabala* gardens (hoe-cultivated patches devoted to the production of cassava, maize, beans, groundnuts, sweet potatoes, and vegetables), had begun to replace chitemene as the main food source.

Tree-lopping had been replaced by the felling of whole trees and the burning of grass for fertilizer. Fencing of gardens was rare. As a consequence, by 1957 diet "was definitely worse [because] fewer millet gardens were made and the standard of efficiency in gardening [had] gone down with so many young men away."[47] A further drop in nutritional standards was evident by 1974–75 as cassava, an easily cultivated but starchy crop, continued to replace millet as the most readily available staple. One estimate put cassava at 70 percent of the meal consumed in the district.[48]

Subsistence production not only diversified into easier-to-grow crops but also declined per head to village population. In 1974–75 many villages in Kasama were no longer self-sufficient in the production of food; purchases of processed foods formed an integral part of the new subsistence. This applied both to luxury goods, like salt, sugar, oil, tea, and milk powder, and to staple foods, like maize meal. Within a 40- to 50-kilometer radius of Kasama town, peasants with money readily quit the effort involved in maize cultivation in favor of purchase. Nutritional foods, notably groundnuts and beans, were sold for money while children were malnourished. Peasants sold crops even without having a surplus, and three quarters of the malnutrition cases at Kasama General Hospital came from families with cash income.[49] The inclusion of processed maize meal in Bemba diets illustrated several aspects of rural underdevelopment and dependence—for example, adoption of the tastes and preferences of urban wage-earners. It indicated also the availability of cash in the rural economy, primarily remitted from relatives in urban wage employment. And it indicated reliance on food imported from other parts of Zambia and the outside world, since neither Kasama District nor the Northern Province produced enough maize to meet local needs.

Central government policy toward agricultural development after 1966 stressed the introduction of maize as a cash crop. Good soils were found in only 10 percent of the land area of the Northern Province, however, and nowhere in Kasama District. Most soils overlay acidic rock types and had been subjected to long periods of weathering and leaching.[50] Kasama was thus poorly suited to the production of food and such cash crops as maize, tobacco, groundnuts, and cotton associated with other parts of Zambia. Small increases in agricultural production were achieved at high cost to government in terms of direct subsidies and seasonal credit. In the 1960's, for example, considerable sums were expended on mechanization, a technical innovation later conceded to be premature. Policy emphasis shifted in the 1970's to hoe and ox-drawn cultivation, but the presence of tsetse fly constrained the latter in all but the border districts of the Northern Province. Because of the unfavorable environmental conditions and depopulation, the production of maize in Kasama and the Northern Province did not keep pace with rapidly rising consumption (Table 2). At the time of research, and apart from the bumper harvest in the 1969–70 season, Kasama District had never produced a food surplus.

This is not to say that increases in marketed maize production did not occur in Kasama District in the early 1970's; however, production increases cannot be attributed to a mass mobilization of peasants. The bulk of subsistence cultivators received little attention in official rural development policy. Most of the agricultural cooperatives formed in the immediate postindependence period, which had incorporated peasants with proven party loyalties, were defunct by the mid 1970's. The "agrarian revolution" campaign of UNIP in 1974 and 1975 was targeted principally toward party leaders. The Department of Agriculture tended throughout to favor a small group of "emergent" farmers on individual farms and on special commodity settlement schemes far from the village. Increases in maize production in Kasama District in

TABLE 2. Northern Province, Maize Production and Consumption, 1965–1975

Agricultural Season	Marketed Maize Production (no. of bags)	Maize Consumption (no. of bags)
1965/66	28,300	
1966/67	70,300	
1967/68	75,000	
1968/69	113,800	90,000
1969/70	56,800	
1970/71	63,600	102,000
1971/72	72,200	
1972/73	58,500	120,000
1973/74	60,000	
1974/75	96,000	130,000

Source: Department of Agriculture, Kasama.

the 1974–75 season were limited to the approximately 1100 "emergent" farm families, while the output of 18,000 subsistence families did not improve.[51] The purchasing power of rural incomes declined after 1964, yet at the same time peasants were drawn further into the cash economy. Community group labor was undermined in favor of labor for payment in money; peasant families became burdened with large debts to government agencies and private businesses as a result of a scramble to find credit; shortages of vital commodities produced by state enterprises began to affect peasants on a wide scale. Thus while the poorest of peasants were excluded from the benefits of agricultural innovation, they were not necessarily shielded from the effects of disruption elsewhere in the Zambian economy.

Rural underdevelopment has often been depicted in the literature on Zambia in terms of the "decline of the village" at the root of which is the shrinkage of village populations. The Kasama District Notebook records that "in earlier times villages were generally much larger and far more concentrated."[52] Labor migration, the establishment of individual farm homesteads, and the dwindling of traditional authority have interacted to reduce and disperse village populations in Kasama. But a trend toward voluntary regrouping of villages after 1964 was notable. Two model forms of settlement could be discerned, only one of which could be described as a "decline of the village."

First, there were small scattered villages, which comprised the majority in the District, containing between 40 and 80 people, or about fifteen to twenty houses.[53] There were over five hundred small villages in the district; they were usually situated at remote locations and rarely enjoyed such development benefits as roads, wells, and schools. They were distributed around natural water supplies and shifted site every five to ten years according to the availability of trees for chitemene. Round semipermanent houses of "pole and dagga" predominated. Many of the smallest villages were made up of a headman and immediate matrilineal kin. Some lacked the statutory minimum of 20 residents as defined in the Registration and Development of Villages Act.

In contrast to small settlements, another type of village was discernable, with 200 or more residents and 40 or 50 houses. There were 71 such villages in Kasama in 1975. This type was frequently serviced by the state infrastructure, most often in the form of roads and schools.

Primary schools provided the focus for many of the new settlements, as did, to a lesser extent, clinics and supplies of clean domestic water. Other facilities like general stores and churches tended also to be located there. Square houses of burnt brick or "kimberley" (sun-dried) brick were common and sometimes predominated. These large communities were commonly known in Kasama as "regrouped" villages, whether or not they were so designated by government, and were distinguishable from small shifting villages by permanency of settlement and fixed-plot farming. Settlement patterns in Kasama combined the historical trend of village dispersal and decline with isolated cases of population consolidation at points where central state resources were concentrated.

There is little doubt that peasants in Kasama and in Zambia as a whole experienced marked improvements in the availability of essential social services during the period of the first two developmental plans. By 1975 Kasama District had 68 primary schools, up 80 percent from 1964, and 9 rural clinics, more than twice the number at independence. Yet in absolute terms peasants were still poorly served. Forty percent of the population of the Northern Province lived over fifteen kilometers from a basic health facility, the highest figure for any province in Zambia.[54] One quarter of the villages in the province were over five kilometers from even the most rudimentary road.[55] The delivery of social services was tied in government policy to the resettlement and consolidation of rural population. This policy made rational use of scarce development resources but resulted in the exclusion of peasants in the smallest and remotest villages. Schools, health centers, and water installations were concentrated in the large regrouped villages and had low diffusion effects. A distinction was evident by 1975 between communities that had benefited from central development resources and communities that had not. The concentration of development resources in regrouped villages tended to result in the transplantation of patterns of unevenness from the central to the local level (see below, Chapter 6).

The development path of Kasama District was in general conditioned by central planning decisions to concentrate resources at selected development nodes. The most dramatic example was the Chinese-built Tanzam railroad line, which was routed through the district on its course between Lusaka and Dar es Salaam, Tanzania (Map 2). The

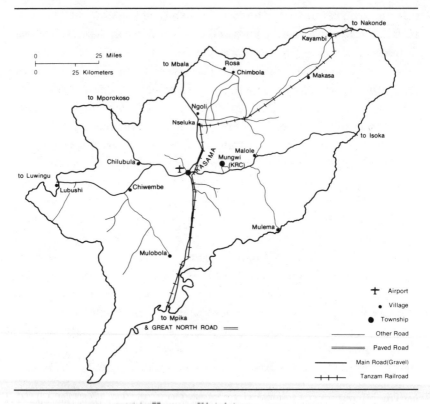

2   Communication within Kasama District.

overriding economic purpose of the railroad was to provide an alternative to routes through Rhodesia for Zambian copper exports. The
stimulation of peasant agriculture in the north was always a secondary
consideration. At the time of research, Tanzam had had little impact
on the peasant economy in Kasama save to provide temporary employment opportunities outside the village during the construction phase
and to ease passenger travel to some parts of the district. Indeed the
general impact of Tanzam was to speed up urbanization. Central resources that flowed in the wake of investment in the railroad were
concentrated in Kasama township. In 1974–75 plans for government
spending included new provincial administrative offices, a luxury
hotel, a sports stadium, a microwave telephone station, and a modern
airport. In addition, a truck assembly plant financed with West German and Japanese capital was in the offing. The assembly plant was

expected to provide approximately 500 jobs, yet many times that number had migrated to the township in hope of employment. None of the state or international projects was of direct or immediate benefit to the poorest strata of the rural population. The projects were aimed at servicing a minority urban population of government employees and other earners of income. The Zambian approach to rural development was thus unlikely to halt the decline of the village or to reverse the migration of labor from rural to urban areas. It was likely instead to reproduce, at the local level, patterns of uneven development which already characterized the nation as a whole.

The reconstruction of rural life along lines of self-reliance and self-sustaining growth was addressed ideologically in Zambia, but adequate material support from the state was never forthcoming. Rural localities were relegated to a residual position in the distribution of development resources. Peasant preferences were addressed only after national priorities for basic infrastructure and the needs of wealthy urban social strata had been met. The reasons, of course, were often beyond the control of central government. The slump in copper prices, the need to divert resources from rural development to the construction of new trade routes, and the appetite for wage and salary increases among the politically powerful mineworkers and bureaucrats, together acted to tie the hands of leaders at the center.

But neglect of the poorest peasants also resulted from a set of conscious central priorities. The resources that were available for rural development were usually designated for emergent farm families on government settlement schemes. Within the subsistence sector, emphasis was placed on carefully selected and closely supervised village regrouping schemes and intensive development zones. There was little "trust for the masses" displayed in the Zambian approach to rural development in the 1960's and 1970's. Resources for a style of rural development founded on the broad-based mobilization of peasants— that is, resources administered not directly by the center but by elected organizations embodying participation from below—were extremely scarce. One estimate put the amount of development expenditure controlled by Lusaka at 90 percent of the national budget, and the percentage controlled by local authorities at less than one quarter of one percent.[56] During the SNDP period, 1972 to 1976, the Kasama Ru-

ral Council had an average annual development budget of K461,000,*
or about K4 for every rural dweller in the district.[57] Since local-level
participatory organizations like the WDC's and VPC's had to rely for
funding primarily on local authorities, in this case the RC, their impact on rural development was constrained from the outset by the
residual nature of the available development resources.

Nevertheless, WDC's and VPC's constitute a useful starting point
for this study. In the first place, WDC's and VPC's are located at the
juncture in the locality where party-state was intended to most directly and most regularly meet peasant. From a peasant perspective, the
district capital, let alone the national capital, is a distant and often
alien center; WDC's and VPC's are more immediate. Second, the resources that WDC's and VPC's bring to the locality, however slim,
represent an unprecedent infusion of opportunities in the context of
rural impoverishment. Peasants and local leaders compete among
themselves for access to any development resources, even the residual
resources of WDC's and VPC's. Finally, precisely because of extreme
scarcity, it matters more whether peasants and leaders are able to gain
access to development resources. To fail is to risk being excluded completely. Hence the dynamics of the local politics of rural development
are laid barest at the grassroots level of rural village and rural ward.

---

*K = Kwacha: a unit of Zambian currency (average exchange rate, 1974–75: K1 =
US $1.56).

The power to prepare detailed plans, to make meaningful decisions, and to commit development funds must be delegated to effective local units of Government in order to develop local communities as total entities.—*Republic of Zambia, Second National Development Plan.*

The low level of living conditions that afflicts most of Africa makes provision of basic amenities one of the central themes of life. Consequently, demands for roads, housing, water, electricity, schools, and medical dispensaries create vast new opportunities for accrual of power to those who dispense these blessings.—*Henry Bretton*, Power and Politics in Africa

I

VILLAGE AND WARD COMMITTEES

3

Village Productivity Committees

It has been estimated that a total of 25,000 Village Productivity and 1,500 Ward Development Committees are needed for the task of linking center and locality in Zambia.[1] The conventional wisdom concerning these committees was that most of them were "not working." An editorial in a national newspaper stated, for example, that "there are signs that in some areas, perhaps the larger part of the country, the productivity committees exist on paper only."[2] This researcher sought to determine the empirical accuracy of this statement in one locality. Research in Kasama began at the level of the "basic administrative unit" of the village with an inquiry into the activation and performance of VPC's to 1975.

This chapter describes the depth and extent to which the Zambian party-state had a presence among peasants at the extreme grassroots. A second purpose is to assess how far the formation and early performance of VPC's was influenced by local political interests. In 1971 President Kaunda expressed the view that the "administrative machinery must become one with the people so that they can see it as their own and as part and parcel of them." This chapter analyzes recruitment to and performance of VPC's from a perspective consistent with the view expressed by the Zambian President. The outcome of policies to build a party-state at the local level cannot be understood in terms of organizational considerations alone but must be related to the social context of implementation. The key question however, is whether VPC's, where active, are part and parcel of the whole peasantry or of some smaller and more particular group interest.

To account for the performance of an African party-state at rural development tasks, a number of explanatory schemes are possible.

The first focuses on the machinery of the party-state itself, in this case on the internal organization of local development committees. Key issues in explaining organizational performance might be, for example, the overburdening of VPC's with too many unspecified functions, or the duplication of development tasks between WDC and WC.[3] The second explanation focuses on the linkages between local development committees and other organizations in the development front. Key issues here might be, for example, the frequency and content of communications between WDC and Rural Council, the integration of VPC's with UNIP party branches, or the impact of central state responses to popular development initiatives.[4] Studies in Zambia to date have been based on one or the other of these points of view.

The explanation of the performance of local-level political organization in this study will refer only marginally to matters of internal organization and linkage. The main explanation will be sought in the social context of organizational performance. More specifically, attention will be directed to the political interests that derive from local social and economic structure. An argument was made in introducing this study that the social composition and political interests of local leaders have a profound effect on the way that rural development policies are put into practice. Analysis of leadership recruitment to local-level organizations therefore logically precedes analysis of organizational performance. WDC's are located in a local context marked by the conflict of social groups for leadership position. WDC's and VPC's are used by groups representing party, state, and traditional interests as an arena in which to conduct local leadership struggles. The accession of different groups to committee leadership has potentially different outcomes in terms of development performance. It might be expected, for example, that committees run by local party activists would be more likely to mobilize peasants and to distribute resources on a wider basis than committees composed of chiefs and headmen. Or it might be expected that committees dominated by administrative personnel would pursue a technical approach to development and a hierarchical style of organization and distribution. The supposition on which much of this study is based is that patterns of resource allocation and distribution can be traced to patterns of recruitment in local-level political organizations. This contextual approach has not, to my knowledge, been applied before to the study of ward and village committees in Zambia.

REGISTRATION OF VILLAGES IN KASAMA

There were 496 VPC's in Kasama District by the end of 1974 (Table 3). The vast majority, over four hundred, were created during the registration of villages in 1972. This registration exercise in Kasama affords an opportunity to begin to describe and evaluate the strategy of Zambian leaders of the center for state-building at the extreme periphery.

According to interviews with ward councilors from the Kasama Rural Council, VPC's existed in six of the twenty three wards before village registration in 1972; several mentioned the Mulungushi UNIP General Conference of 1970 as the source of central directives to form VPC's. These early committees were not distinguishable in membership or function from village "political" committees of UNIP and seem to have existed in only a few villages. Mass village registration and VPC formation did not occur until 1972, when the District Secretary (DS), under the requirements of the 1971 Registration and Development of Villages Act, assembled registration teams to tour every village in the district.

The composition of these teams in part determined who were the "penetrators" in the crucial tasks of organizing the villages and mobilizing peasant participation. The chief of the area, the ward councilor, and regional party officials were accompanied on tour by students from the University of Zambia who were recruited as registering officers.[5] In other words, a patchwork organization for penetration was stitched together from traditional, administrative, and party interests. The political party was directed to educate the people on the purposes of registration and to mobilize them to attend the registration meeting. The touring team would then arrive in the village to prepare the register of inhabitants, and the chief would summon a village meeting in order to elect the VPC. The headman would be declared chairman and other members would be drawn from the village community. The newly elected VPC would in turn choose one of its members as secretary, who would accompany the headman to future meetings of the WC. Having recruited a VPC and recorded its membership, the touring team would then leave for the next village.

The way that village registration was conducted in Kasama District had an important influence on the makeup of village and ward com-

TABLE 3.   Kasama District, Number of Village Productivity Committees, 1971–1974

Ward	Number of VPC's				Number of Villages
	1971[1]	1972[2]	1973[3]	1974[4]	1974[4]
1. Kayambi/Makasa North	7	26	28	29	31
2. Makasa East/Makasa Central	14	12	12	18	23
3. Kafusha/Mpange	20	20	20	22	22
4. Chimbola/Chisangaponde	11	16	16	27	27
5. Rosa/Makasa West	23	11	11	11	11
6. Ngoli/Sume/Kapata	11	32	32	33	33
7. Nseluka/Mangwata	7	15	32	32	48
8. Chitimukulu/Chandawayaya	25	35	47	44	44
9. Chisali/Ndasa	17	32	36	37	38
10. Mumba/Malole South	15	30	30	30	30
11. Mulema/Kanyanta	10	12	12	12	12
12. Malole North/Machemba	11	22	22	17	17
13. Mungwi	4	5	5	5	5
14. Lukashya	3	18	21	21	21
15. Chitambi/Kasonde	6	35	38	40	40
16. Milima/Ntema/Itamena	9	18	18	17	29
17. Mwamba/Ngoma	6	25	25	15	28
18. Chilubula/Mutoba	6	8	8	9	9
19. Munkonge North/Chilongoshi	4	0	9	10	10
20. Munkonge South/Kashinka	7	25	25	26	51
21. Muchila/Chilufya	10	18	18	18	23
22. Mulobola/Chandamukulu/ Nkolemfumu	9	14	14	14	27
23. Musa/Mulanshi	7	9	9	9	20
Totals	242	447	488	496	599

Sources:

[1] Kasama Rural Council, Minutes of the Council Chairman, August 31, 1971, pp. 11–15.

[2] Office of the District Governor, Kasama, "Registration and Development of Villages and Establishment of WC's and WDC's, 1972," compiled by E. B. Chituta. Chituta's total figure for VPC's in 1972 is 404. The discrepancy with my figure of 447 is that the *boma* was missing data on Wards 10, 18, and 23 (total 43 VPC's). Correction was made with the assistance of KRC file LB/KA/1/23, Vol. 1.

[3] Letters, Secretary Kasama Rural Council to District Secretary, Kasama, October 16, 1973 and November 21, 1973.

[4] Councilor interviews, 1974 and 1975. The discrepancy between the number of villages that councilors claim for their wards (599) and the number of villages claimed in official records (746) (Table 4) can probably be put down to (a) the hazy knowledge of some councilors of their own wards, and (b) the lack of distinction in the minds of both councilors and registering officials between villages and individual settlements.

mittees. The most striking feature of registration there was the extent to which it was a purely administrative exercise. The political party was only marginally involved. Ward councilors, who were usually UNIP constituency officials, did little mobilizing on behalf of the registration. Indeed the intent of the operation does not seem to have been appreciated or accepted by party officials at the local level. At a briefing on registration for councilors and chiefs, the only questions asked by councilors related to their own political interests; they requested subsistence allowances and transport to move around the locality during registration.[6] Of the 23 ward councilors in Kasama District, only two eventually agreed to accompany the registration teams on the tours of the villages; the remaining 21 did not assist in registration or the formation of VPC's.[7] One ward councilor stated clearly that "we never made VPC's ourselves; this is something that the District Secretary organized."[8] It is possible of course that the purposes of the new Act were poorly understood by the councilors. More likely, however, their lukewarm response was attributable to their unwillingness to share local leadership with nonparty elements, and to the condition of local party organization in 1972. The previous year had witnessed the formation and banning of an opposition party, the United Progressive Party (UPP), led by Simon Kapwepwe, which had drawn support from the grass roots membership of UNIP in the Northern Province as well as among Bemba-speakers in other provinces (see below, Chapter 7). Molteno has commented that "the chances of [village registration] achieving its intended aim [were] reduced if UNIP, and to some extent the civil service, became divided and preoccupied with combatting the political power of UPP . . . Northern Province members of UNIP, in particular, [came] under suspicion."[9] The loyalties of UNIP members and local party officials were put to the test in 1971 and 1972 and, though few came out openly in support of UPP, significant numbers at branch and constituency levels, including ward councilors, harbored sympathies for the new party. In the highly charged atmosphere of the aftermath of the banning of UPP, people in Kasama were suspicious of any registration that required the disclosure of personal information. Moreover, councilors were probably reluctant to associate themselves with any such national project at a time when popular support for the center was at a low ebb.

In the absence of the party, the path was cleared for other leader-

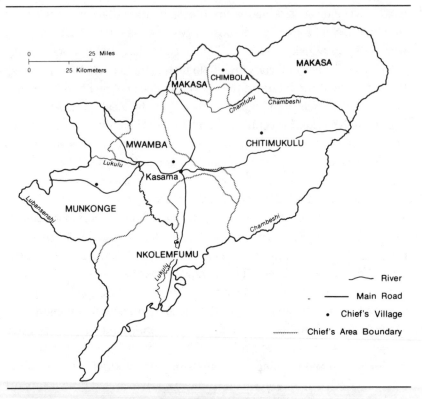

3   Chief's area boundaries of Kasama District.

ship groups to influence the formation of village and ward committees. In contrast to local party officials, traditional leaders,* particularly chiefs, were active in promoting village registration in Kasama. The Provincial Supervisor of registration was able to report that the exercise "progressed smoothly thanks to the chiefs who have played a major part . . . inclusion of the traditional leaders on tour made it possible to meet no opposition from the villages."[10] Apart from Chief Munkonge, who vigorously supervised registration in his own area (Map 3), and Nkolemfumu and Chimbola, who did some touring, most chiefs were too aged and infirm for a heavy program of personal appearances. They ensured, however, that when they could not be per-

---

*The term "traditional leaders" should not be taken to imply that chiefs and headmen represented a pristine precolonial order. From the time of colonial occupation the procedures for appointing local leaders were mediated and supervised by the colonial state. Many "traditional" Bemba chiefs and headmen were appointees of the center who did not necessarily enjoy popular support.

sonally present, their *kapasus* (messengers) were. Peasants, when asked about the procedure for village registration and VPC formation, consistently recalled that the kapasu and the university student were in their village, but only rarely did they mention the district messenger or the party officials. Some even spoke of the register as the "chief's register." And one village secretary from Chitimukulu expressed the view that the Paramount Chief had brought the idea of VPC's to the area.[11]

Traditional leaders were thus able to capitalize on the opportunity presented by the registration of villages to enhance their own positions of authority. Under the Chiefs Act of 1965, which had decapitated the traditional social structure by removing the judicial powers of the chief, the government reserved the right to delegate new powers to the chiefs as and when it saw fit.[12] The first of these powers was delegated to chiefs in 1971 under the Registration and Development of Villages Act; the powers included granting recognition to villages for purposes of registration, calling the village together to elect a VPC, attending VPC and WDC meetings, and providing a communications link from village to the House of Chiefs and District Governor.[13] Chiefs therefore had an interest in making themselves visible during the registration procedure. To fail to assert their interests was to face further reductions in power. Like headmen, they stood to be the immediate beneficiaries of the government's mixed strategy for penetrating the rural areas. They stood to regain some of the power lost to UNIP ward councilors when RC's were set up to replace the colonial Native Authorities in 1963. Thus from the very outset the strategy of the center for state-building was captured by the most socially entrenched and politically conservative group at the village level. Party cadres were not the "penetrators." Far from maintaining a balanced frontal approach, in practice the party deferred to a working alliance between the state on one hand and chiefs and headmen on the other. Under these circumstances VPC's were likely to become rapidly interlocked with a traditional social structure, and in part this was the intention of a central state with a sparse presence in rural localities.

Registration of villages, after a promising start, proved to be a difficult policy for the center to implement in Kasama. In the first month of registration, when touring teams were visiting Paramount Chief Chitimukulu's area, "Northern Province registered more villages and

TABLE 4. Village Registration and Village Productivity Committee Formation in the Northern Province, 1972

District	Villages Registered		VPC's	WDC's
	First Phase	Second Phase		
Chinsali	274	23 (297)	251	18
Isoka	538	15 (553)	254	18
Kaputa	145	— (145)	139	10
Kasama	616	130 (746)	404	23
Luwingu	763	— (763)	622	20
Mbala	402	47 (449)	449	20
Mpika	539	4 (543)	443	18
Mporokoso	297	— (297)	218	13
Total (Northern Province)	3874	219 (4093)	2780	140

Source: Letter, Permanent Secretary, Northern Province, to Secretary to Government, January 16, 1973: Kasama Rural Council, file LG/KA/5/9/ p. 93.

formed more VPC's than any other province in the Republic."[14] By the end of the three-month registration period, however, villages were registered and VPC's formed in only three of the six chief's areas (Munkonge, Nkolemfumu, and Chimbola). Blame was attributed to the scattered settlement pattern in the district, although undoubtedly the low enthusiasm of party officials was also an important factor. As a result, a supplementary phase of registration had to be set up for Kasama and four other districts in the Northern Province (Table 4). Extra administrative staff were recruited from government departments in Mporokoso, Luwingu, and Kaputa, where registration had been completed on schedule. After an extra three months of village touring in late 1972, a halt was called to registration in Kasama, with a total of nearly 600 villages registered and 447 VPC's formed on paper (Table 3).

Yet additional VPC's continued to be formed unofficially after the departure of the registration teams: 41 during 1973 and 8 during 1974 (Table 3). A letter from the Cabinet Office in Lusaka in late 1972 reminded those responsible for committee formation in Kasama that "the Party and Government have given top priority to these committees," and inquired dryly "why they are [still] being formed when they are supposed to be functioning at the moment."[15] In some wards, for example Ward 7, the majority of VPC's actually declined over time, because of the regrouping or breakup of small villages. In other wards, for example Wards 16 and 20, villages remained without VPC's because they were never registered; villages in flood plains which could not be reached during village registration were in this category. Many individual settlers residing outside recognized villages in Kasama also escaped registration. A dispute arose, for example, over Matoka village, which consisted of one man, his three wives and their offspring and which was residentially discrete; was it entitled to a VPC unless recognized as a separate village by Chief Makasa? Other villages escaped registration because their members refused to amalgamate into larger units in order to form VPC's. Kashishi and Kalembwe villages near Kayambi had not complied by mid-1974, despite a resolution by the Ward 1 WDC to take the dispute to "those who began registration, the chief and the District Secretary."[16] In Ward 11 the councilor was unable to form VPC's because of the small populations at Chalekakoba, Chibangu, and Katongokabula villages. Adherents of the Watchtower religious sect in unnamed villages throughout Kasama District were also reported to be resisting VPC formation.[17] Thus some spots in the locality remained unlinked to the center even after village registration.

Yet appearances were to the contrary. The District Secretary's office in Kasama was able to report that a large number of VPC's had been set up; he provided VPC membership lists to prove it. The task of enumeration was complete. After a record had been compiled on paper, civil servants for the most part withdrew from further contact with VPC's. An impression could be gained by an observer of official records that nearly every village in Kasama was connected to the political center by a new grassroots political and administrative framework. Whether these committees were active in development tasks, however, depended not on administrative action from above but on the outcome of political competition in the locality.

RECRUITMENT TO VILLAGE PRODUCTIVITY COMMITTEES

The performance of VPC's is in large part explicable in terms of their adaptation from traditional forms of social and political organization. In the absence of other local leadership cadres, the state in Zambia had no alternative to making village headmen chairmen of VPC's. If VPC's had been established in 1964 in the heyday of UNIP in Kasama, sufficient party branch cadres would probably have been available to accede to village leadership positions. By 1971, however, UNIP fortunes were in serious decline. An organized and widespread campaign for VPC leadership by UNIP against traditional leaders was no longer feasible. Thus both the strategy of the state and the existing balance of power between leadership groups at village level pointed toward reliance on traditional leaders to staff VPC's. The colonial precedent of exercising central authority in the locality indirectly through chiefs and headmen was interrupted briefly after 1964 but largely restored by 1972. The danger inherent in the pragmatic choice of village headmen as grass roots leaders and mobilizers was that VPC's would be used to buttress traditional interests. It was unclear from the outset whether the adaptation of political institutions from the past would facilitate, block, or distort rural development.

The recruitment of VPC members did not disturb existing power relationships at the village level. Since elections were conducted by means of a public show of hands at a village meeting, peasants were subject by social pressures to defer to the headman's choice of VPC members. Almost invariably village elders or the headman's *bakabilo* (advisers) were chosen. All village headmen interviewed who knew the composition of their VPC's said that village elders were useful members. It was commonly said that *bakabilo* were invaluable because "they knew the customs."[18] The pattern of VPC recruitment reinforcing the traditional social structure was most evident in the small, remote villages that were still predominantly kinship units, a majority of the villages in Kasama. One headman admitted that he had not yet chosen his VPC because he was "waiting for (his) sons to come back"; one nuclear family would therefore make up the VPC because "we do not want to lose our own history."[19]

The general rule throughout the district was that older males acceded to the VPC, but there were some exceptions. Any person with literacy skills, regardless of sex or age—even a young "school-leaver" —was included in the VPC, if there was no adult male with similar qualifications. For example, the secretary to the Paul Nseluka VPC was a young man in his early twenties. Often, as at Kasonde Chisuna and Namponda villages, the VPC secretary was the local store-owner; education and occupation in petty trade went together to provide access to the VPC. Mwamba VPC in Ward 15 had a woman secretary and in some cases women were included as ordinary members. Headmen asserted that women were present to supervise chores of village cleanliness and communicating instructions to other women in the village. In sum, however, the makeup of the VPC's did not represent a radical break with the social leadership patterns of the past. And since statutory elections had not been held after three years in more than a handful of VPC's in Kasama, the power arrangements that were established in 1972 had a strong propensity to survive. The headman and his advisers were able to use VPC formation as a means of preventing the erosion of the traditional distribution of power at village level. They were sometimes challenged by educated youths or UNIP branch officials or women, but these were not changes that were directly attributable to the introduction of VPC's and the recruitment of VPC members.

Continuity with the past was evident in the decision-making procedures at VPC meetings as well as in committee composition. As one headman said, "there is no difference between the old way and the new way; we have always sat together to discuss things."[20] At VPC meetings I observed, the headman permitted extensive discussion; in the end, however, he, with the assistance of his advisers, interpreted the popular consensus and announced a decision. I never saw a vote taken at a VPC meeting, though VPC chairmen at Nseluka reported that voting was used there. National leaders argued that consensus rather than voting was suited to the Zambian political culture: "a skillful chairman is able to weigh the feeling of the meeting; the idea of consensus is to create unity whereas a vote is divisive; in Cabinet and Central Committee consensus works well and the system is used from the villages up to the highest organs of state."[21] The consensus approach, however, tended to solidify a tradition of patriarchal decision-making by older males in VPC's. Headmen and elders were sometimes the only people to speak at VPC meetings, though if party officials or government officials were present, they, too, would speak. Peasant participation was often limited to confirming what traditional or party-state leaders proposed. I did observe, however, that women were more influential in village decision-making than headmen would have had me believe. For example, at Namponda in Ward 6, the three women members of the VPC were most vocal. At Chipamba in Ward 7 the main VPC spokesperson was the daughter of the infirm village headman. The assertion of political participation by some women occurred despite the customary opinion that "women cannot speak; their husbands speak for them."[22] Adherence to models of decision-making from the past, in which village discussion, however limited, preceded the announcement of a decision, allowed for at least an illusion of participation. All VPC meetings observed by me were well attended; all had many more than the statutory ten members present, and some had as many as forty.

Insight into recruitment of VPC's and the relationship of recruitment to VPC performance is available from interviews conducted with 44 village headmen in Kasama District in 1974 and 1975. Villages were selected in terms of the access and rapport the researcher was able to establish with certain headmen rather than according to a formula of random sampling. Interviews at village level were conducted as an adjunct to the systematic surveys undertaken at ward level (see below, Chapter 4) rather than as an independent research priority. Nevertheless, an attempt was made to obtain a fairly representative spread of villages according to criteria of size, remoteness, and level of development. The proportion of interviews conducted in large regrouped villages, 8 out of 44, was slightly higher than the distribution of this type of settlement in the district. Interviews with headmen were conducted in 20 of the 23 rural wards in Kasama, thus assuring a reasonable geographic spread (Map 4).

One interesting result from the interviews was that only 25 of 44 headmen said that they had a VPC (Table 5). A significant number, 13 of 44, said they were unaware of the legal requirement to have such a committee. And many of those who said they were aware of the requirement had never seen the green Pocket Manual on ward and village committees. Either that or a headman could not read or understand the complex language of the manual and was often unaware of what a VPC was supposed to do. Even if a headman said that he had a VPC and could produce a list of members, there was no guarantee that the committee was active.

Indeed, in 1975 *fewer than 10 percent* of the 496 VPC's in Kasama District could be called active. That is, fewer than 10 percent fulfilled

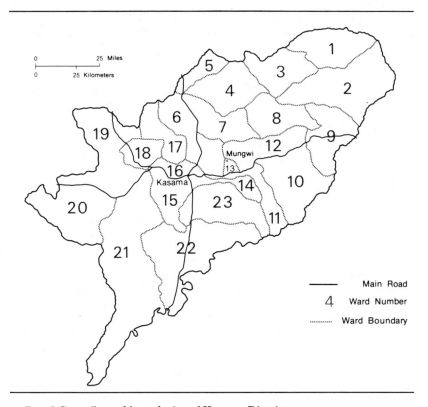

4 Rural Council ward boundaries of Kasama District.

a minimum of the functions of popular participation and rural development for which they were intended. The remaining 90 percent very likely had not met since 1972, when villages were registered and VPC members first elected. A VPC was deemed active if it fulfilled three criteria beyond the headman's assertion that the VPC existed: the VPC met at least once a year; minutes were recorded and communicated to the WDC; a village development project using communal labor was in progress in 1974 or 1975. Only four villages in the sample of 44 fulfilled all three criteria (Table 5). Information on VPC activeness for individual villages was derived initially from headman interviews and later cross-checked with councilors and peasants in the wards and villages concerned. The aggregate estimate of 10 percent was further confirmed by the knowledge of well informed party officials and civil servants at district and subdistrict levels. I am reasonably confident of the accuracy of the 10 percent estimate for the 44

TABLE 5.   Kasama District, Activeness of Village Productivity Committees, 1974–1975

	Large "Regrouped" Villages (n = 8)	Small Villages (n = 36)	Total (n = 44)
Headman said village had a VPC	8 (100%)	17 (47%)	25
VPC met regularly	6 (75%)	12 (33%)	18
VPC recorded minutes in writing	4 (50%)	1 (3%)	5
VPC undertook village development projects	5 (63%)	2 (6%)	7
Active VPC's	4	0	4 (less than 10%)

villages concerned, but caution is urged when results are extrapolated to the district as a whole, given the small number of active cases and the limitations of the sample. Moreover, no implication is intended that the 10 percent figure applies to all regions of Zambia. More research is needed.

The activeness of VPC's in Kasama was associated with patterns of human settlement and patterns of political recruitment. As for the first, VPC's in large regrouped villages were clearly distinguishable from VPC's in small remote villages (Table 5). The four active VPC's were all located in large regrouped villages, namely Bwembya, Kabwibwi, James Mwilwa, and Paul Nseluka, which were already minor development nodes. With the exception of Kabwibwi, each was located close to Kasama township and main communications arteries. As for political recruitment, VPC's that were exclusively composed of traditional leaders tended to be dormant, whereas VPC's in which relatively "well-to-do" earners of income were prominent were more likely to be active. When asked to describe the composition of VPC's, only 20 of 44 headmen could list five names or more. Among the 136 names and characteristics of VPC members provided by headmen, several features were evident. VPC members in general were predominantly male (94 percent) and their average age was above fifty. A small minority (11 percent) were said to gain income from the market or from a salary: the bulk of VPC members were subsistence cultivators, or had been when younger. Most of the income earners, 8 of 14, were members of the minority of VPC's that were active.

The impact of traditional leaders on VPC performance was not simply that this group constituted an obstacle to development. Some traditional leaders did mobilize VPC's, either to recapture political influence for themselves (see below, pp. 76–78), or to pursue rural development according to local preferences (below, Chapter 6). But an initial relationship was evident, based on my limited observations, between recruitment patterns and settlement patterns on the one hand and the activeness of VPC's on the other. Small, remote villages with a VPC based on traditional social structure and political interests were the least active; large, regrouped villages, especially those proximate to the urban center of the district and with "well-to-do" VPC members, were the most active. This relationship was probably in part attributable to opportunities for paid employment near large villages on the outskirts of town. Paid employment among VPC members brought resources in the form of incomes and skills from center to locality that could be applied to self-help activities. It should not be forgotten, however, that active VPC's were exceptional. Most VPC's were not dynamic instruments of development; most members were recruited not by virtue of their skill, education, or employment but because of traditional status. VPC activeness appeared to be connected to patterns of local leadership recruitment.

PERFORMANCE OF VILLAGE PRODUCTIVITY COMMITTEES

A notable number of villages in Kasama, whether large or small and regardless of whether development actually resulted, did hold village meetings. These were considered by both headmen and peasants to be meetings of the VPC. Their frequency and content were determined more by the occurrence of disputes than by the need to plan rural development. In most VPC's there was no regular schedule for meetings; they were held in response to the ebb and flow of village life. On average an active VPC met once every three or four months when a village problem became too aggravated to ignore. As one headman put it, "we meet when there is a complaint or a quarrel" and gave as examples the straying of chickens, a bar brawl, or a disagreement over the rights to land for chitemene cutting.[23] Legal cases covered by customary law were common. Cases of marriage and divorce predominated. One VPC reported that it had met to consider the case of a Bernard Bwalya, a VPC member, who was "found insulting an innocent person on the road to the tsetse camp when he was drunk." The offender was suspended from membership in the VPC and threatened with legal action if his trespasses recurred.[24] The tendency for VPC's to place social disputes above economic development was reinforced by ward councilors who referred back to VPC's personal matters brought to WDC's by constituents.

Much VPC time was also devoted to accusations of witchcraft. The minor cases were settled in the village, but the most serious were conveyed to the chief in accordance with traditional practice. One headman gave the case of a peasant in his village who was accused of plotting to kill a small boy as an example of an accusation that the VPC immediately referred to the chief. VPC's in Kasama were also involved in other customary matters. For example, a headman of one village used his VPC as a forum to remind his followers of their lapsed social responsibilities by asking "anyone who has enough food" to share it with a bedridden old man without relatives, "even though he is not from around here."[25] Another headman urged villagers at a VPC to buy home-made beer from widows who had no other means of earning an income. Where headmen still performed such ritual functions as choosing a site for a new village or constructing ancestral shrines, these matters were also aired at village meetings. Such meetings, while nominally called meetings of the VPC, were little different from meetings that social practice had always required. The settlement of disputes and vigilance for the welfare of the village community were always the responsibility of the village headman. The survival of these aspects of the headman's role was reinforced by the introduction of VPC's.

At minimum, then, VPC's conducted the customary social business of the village. That is all that many VPC's did. Headmen and ward councilors agreed, 22 of 25 in the case of headmen and 16 of 23 in the case of councilors, that VPC's still concerned themselves with traditional legal cases. One councilor said they didn't, and six councilors and nineteen headmen had no idea what VPC's did, if anything.

Nevertheless, some VPC's, notably those in large regrouped villages, began to make the transition from exclusive concern with customary matters to the functions of social and economic innovation for which they were intended. For example, the following items were discussed at a meeting of the James Mwilwa VPC, one of the active VPC's in Kasama District in mid-1974:

1. The headman/chairman announced that now that the dry season had arrived, and in accordance with instructions from the Rural Council, fire breaks should be burned around the village, and bush fires controlled;
2. The headman/chairman requested that trees not be cut for the purposes of chitemene cultivation on a certain side of the village because all villages in the region were experiencing a shortage of construction timber;
3. Every household must have a pit latrine;
4. People should come together to widen the road to the village bar on a self-help basis "so that we don't have to walk along (in single file) like women in the forest";
5. Every household must have a vegetable garden. Those with seeds should share them with their neighbors.
6. The village must be "organized." Rather than quarreling among themselves, villagers should "be of one mother." One man, the UNIP branch chairman, had been acting arrogantly and ignoring the greetings of his fellows. The headman would have a word with him.[26]

Some VPC's were therefore beginning to take on a multipurpose rural development orientation. Village social disputes continued to receive attention (item 6), but the above VPC meeting was largely devoted to village development (items 1, 2, 3, 4, and 5). Not all these items were followed up. For example, few households began growing more than the familiar dietary items of beans and spinach despite the headman's remonstrations; VPC minutes revealed that this was not the first time the chairman had appealed for vegetable growing. The timber shortage and bar road items illustrated a VPC devising local solutions to local problems, and in the active VPC's, self-reliance was increasingly common.

The case of James Mwilwa village also shows that active VPC's were integrated into the administrative apparatus of the state and acted as control agencies at the local level. The concern of active VPC's with such measures as bush fires, pit latrines, and vegetable gardens represented the communication downward to peasants of government policies. Headmen who sought to enforce these measures acted as agents for the center. At James Mwilwa the headman spoke with an authoritarian style, evidently relishing the opportunity to display command as a state functionary. Other headmen too interpreted the functions of VPC's in the light of central control rather than local participation. The headman of Bwembya village, a subchief, when asked what VPC's do, replied that VPC's "teach villagers how to bring about development" and "prevent troublemakers from doing their business here." [27] He equated the VPC with *buteko* (government). This headman was particularly fastidious in registering visitors and new settlers as a means of maintaining control of his large village. He insisted that no resettlement should be allowed in the district beyond that permitted by traditional leaders in consultation with VPC's. [28] The interests of traditional leaders and the state at the center coincided on the issue of the maintenance of village registers. Both wished to control the influx of unauthorized migrants from neighboring states, to monitor and discourage the movement of people to town, and to determine the whereabouts of known opponents of the government. Active VPC's thus provided a control mechanism for the center.

As far as the achievement of rural development objectives were concerned, active VPC's in Kasama had greatest impact in the construction and maintenance of villages. Screened and roofed pit latrines became a common sight, and the majority of villages had a clean well-swept appearance. The exact contribution of VPC's was hard to gauge, since both these aspects of village maintenance were encouraged in precolonial and colonial times. And some headmen in Kasama seemed to think that the task of village development was simply a matter of maintaining cleanliness and nothing more. The mass construction of permanent housing with sun-dried or burnt brick was, however, a postcolonial phenomenon, and credit can be given to active

VPC's for disseminating information and encouragement on house-building. In the four villages where this researcher could confirm that a VPC was working, burnt-brick houses were a prominent feature of the village landscape. Beyond house and latrine-building, few projects were initiated by Kasama VPC's. Isolated cases were found of VPC's undertaking community development projects, but this was by no means a widespread phenomenon. For example, Kabwibwi VPC constructed a building of burnt bricks to serve as church and community hall. Several VPC's in Ward 14 established ponds and stocked them with fish. Fele and Misengo villages dug water-furrows. On occasion VPC's combined forces to undertake projects that affected more than one village. For example, peasants from Kanchule and Andele Chipata formed joint work teams to clear a five-mile stretch of road between their villages and the Lukulu River. Other projects such as wooden bridges and wells were built with cooperative VPC labor in Kasama in response to calls from the center to upgrade rural social facilities. Large-scale projects, however, such as schools and clinics, proved to be beyond the scope of VPC's in Kasama and were left to WDC's or state ministries to plan and implement.

Yet VPC's did not contribute to the expansion of village production and productivity. With the exception of encouraging larger fruit orchards and vegetable gardens, which sometimes yielded a surplus for sale, VPC's had little impact on the transformation of subsistence economies into market economies. Agricultural innovation in the form of maize production for market was undertaken for the main part by individual farmers living outside village settlements. Village gardens contained mostly cassava, as a staple, and millet, for the production of beer, and were generally smaller than gardens at individual settlements. Peasants who did grow maize in village gardens did so without fertilizer or improved seed, and yields were low. The problem in part was peasant resistance to agricultural innovation but bureaucratic bottlenecks and state transport shortages also hindered efficient distribution of farm requisites at village level. Of the 44 VPC chairmen interviewed, only two said their village had no problem obtaining fertilizer and seed. Another common complaint concerned agricultural credit, which, one headman suggested, "went only to those people on the WDC" and not to VPC members.[29] Additionally, villages outside the peri-urban environs of Kasama Township were unable to gain access to a market of sufficient size to support commercial venture.

The reality of subsistence agriculture in the locality contrasted starkly with the intentions of the central state. The pocket manual emphasized that, first and foremost, VPC's were to aim at "organizing for higher productivity" and at the transformation of local communities into "effective production units."[30] In 1975 the Kasama DG advised all committee members to have two hectares each under cultivation: "If our brothers in Mwinilunga [Northwestern Province] and Chipata [Eastern Province] can grow enough to run factories [for canning pineapples and extracting oil from groundnuts] why not ourselves?" Of 44 headmen interviewed, only five claimed to cultivate the requisite two hectares. No VPC in Kasama remotely approached the target of "K600 in the pocket" proposed in 1976 as a target for each village family in Mkushi District.[31] Indeed agricultural production targets were unheard of by all VPC chairmen in Kasama, despite the September 1974 directive from the Ministry of Rural Development that WDC's and VPC's be organized for production on a target system.

As for planning village development, one councilor hazarded the opinion that VPC's "have not got the hang of it; they are forced to accept the plans of the central government."[32] For the most part his assessment was accurate, since most VPC's in Kasama were dormant, and could not undertake even the most basic task of requesting needed developments. Decisions on the location of projects were not in their hands. But in the active VPC's, signs of systematic, if simple, priority formulation could be found. Some active VPC's evolved differentiated organization to handle village tasks. At Lwabwe VPC, for example, responsibility for supervising brickmaking, water supply, cleanliness, and agriculture was distributed among VPC members.[33] Regular weekly meetings were held, with progress reports from each of the members. Joint VPC meetings, embracing four villages, were also held. A similar arrangement was reflected in the following minutes from Munkonge VPC:

1. The Committee proposes that one of its members should be appointed to look over the village health activities. He should see that all houses have got toilet rooms, well-kept wells and houses.
2. Other members will have duties of encouraging people to have burnt brick houses before the end of this year.

3. Other members will be able to arrange with Natural Resources . . . (about controlling) bush fires. When time to burn *fitemene* comes, people will be going in groups in order to stop fires from destroying large parts of the bush. They should inspect bush fires from the month of August.
4. The committee prays our government to extend building of an isolation section at Munkonge Health Centre.[34]

In other cases VPC's were encouraged to embark on planning by ward councilors who held regular Ward Council meetings to hear village reports and requests. This researcher observed WC meetings in Wards 7, 14, and 15, for example, in which VPC chairmen stood in turn and spelled out problems and occasionally priorities, for roads, schools, and wells. The conception of planning held by active VPC's, however, was generally that of a shopping list of state-funded projects; the formation of local capital and the establishment of priorities were not widely seen as part of the planning task. Without an expansion of the productive base of rural villages, the likelihood of VPC's becoming more effective instruments of planned rural development seemed remote.

THE LOCAL POLITICS OF TRADITION

The record of VPC performance in Kasama District was not encouraging. Villages with active VPC's remained the exception rather than the rule. Undoubtedly there are considerations of formal organization and procedure which partly account for poor VPC performance, and some will be briefly reviewed; but the main consideration is the central state decision to entrust development tasks to leadership elements from traditional society. An attempt was made in Zambia to effect political penetration without social transformation.

The scarcity of resources for a broad-based strategy of rural development in part accounts for poor VPC performance. Much initial peasant enthusiasm for participation in VPC activities seems to have been undermined by refusals to fund projects from a central state that had limited resources and better short-term investment prospects than village development. The following letter received by the Secretary of Kasonde Chisuna VPC from the Ministry of Health in Kasama was not untypical: "Received your request for children clinic at your place. Regret to inform you that transport difficulties cannot permit us to increase any more sub-clinics on our pending list. Whenever favourable circumstances arise will inform you."[35] As one councilor told me, "my VPC's lose interest every time I tell them there is no money, no money, no money."[36] Responses from the center were not only negative but sometimes patronizing, as the following letter from the Secretary of the Kasama Rural Council to the Secretary of Mutale VPC illustrates:

Your argument that your VPC will not ask for more things [is] perhaps a personal opinion and does not worry [this] office. I should emphasize that this Council does not deal with one village but the District which is very large. If your VPC feels that all its suggestions would be dealt with in a matter of hours certainly you are making a big mistake.[37]

In addition to resource scarcity, VPC performance was impaired by the intermittence of political communication with the center. Minutes of each VPC meeting were supposed to be recorded and submitted to the RC and District Governor. All parties agreed that this bureaucratic procedure did not work; as has been shown above, only four out of forty-four headmen could produce an example of VPC minutes. At Kasonde Chisuna the VPC Secretary wrote minutes only "if the matter was important"; at Songolo village "minutes are made but we do not send them anywhere; [the headman] speaks to the councillor personally"; at Kabwibwi the headman claimed "to give the VPC minutes to the councillor but nothing happens." In a review of VPC minutes on file at the Office of the District Governor, I could find only two examples on file for the entire period between 1971 and 1974. There were, however, fourteen letters containing requests from VPC secretaries for the same period.[38] A letter on a specific village development was more likely to gain a response from the political center than a minute submitted as a matter of routine.[39] In general, the boma did not rely on the local-level committee organization for regular contact with villages but depended instead on district messengers, as had the colonial state. For 1971–74 there were over five times more district messengers' reports on file at the boma than communications with VPC's. Political communication between state center and village periphery was never regularly established through the development committee chain in Kasama. As early as 1973 the Secretary-General to the Government endeavored to make monthly progress reports on VPC performance routine but was scotched by DC's in the Northern Province, who as a group protested that regular contact and inspection of VPC's was impossible.[40]

An argument often made by civil servants in Zambia was that the performance of development committees was constrained by the paucity of administrative expertise at village level. A lack of functional literacy on the part of VPC chairmen made the performance of VPC tasks difficult. A nonliterate headman could not consult the Pocket Manual or other government documents, was unlikely to ensure that village meetings were recorded in writing, and was unlikely to update the village register. In Kasama village registers were generally not kept up to date after the registration of villages in 1972, in part because there was no administrative follow-up to the first main effort at penetration. For example, one headman admitted that 8 new people had come to his village in the two years after 1972 and 15 children had passed the age of 14, but none had been registered.[41] Some headmen, 33 of 44, were able to produce a register, but others had lost it. Many registers were damaged by rain or pests, and the flimsy pages had proven ideal for rolling tobacco and other smoking substances. Peasants who failed to report a change of residence to the headman involved were liable to a ten kwacha fine or a month's imprisonment,[42] but no one had been prosecuted in Kasama because, as an Assistant District Secretary said, "we would just be punishing ignorance."[43] Nonetheless, the argument that villagers could not handle their own affairs was open to dispute. First, headmen were not without formal education. Of 44 headmen surveyed in Kasama, over half had been to school, though the literacy of many had deteriorated; 19 had no formal education; 23 had some primary education; and two had some secondary education. Second, where a village had a literate VPC Secretary, he or she was able to deputize for and assist the headman. The problem lay perhaps as much with the overly ambitious and formally bureaucratic conception of VPC development activity handed down from above as with the caliber of local leaders.

Tradition should not be seen simply as an obstacle to development. It was used by local leaders as a means of reshaping development. Coherent explanation for the performance of local-level organizations requires reference to the political interests of local leadership groups.

In particular, chiefs and headmen used VPC's in Kasama as vehicles for pursuing their interests as a group. As shown above, the membership and functions of VPC's were tilted toward reinforcing the status of traditional leaders. A further feature of VPC activities in Kasama District was the attempt by traditional leaders to exceed the limited authority granted them in the committee organization and to bolster their own political positions.

Chiefs and headmen endeavored to use VPC's to regain lost powers —for example of legal arbitration. Village meetings called to discuss local disputes ended with the headman imposing a fine on the guilty party in the name of the VPC.[44] Fines were imposed not only for a variety of civil cases, such as adultery and violation of the demarcation of plots for village gardens, but even for criminal cases, such as theft of livestock. All cases should have been handed over to the local courts for arbitration. One headman argued that instead of salary, he wanted the power to fine peasants; fines would be kept by the VPC treasurer in a village development fund.[45] In the most celebrated case of this kind in Kasama, Chief Nkolemfumu used the VPC in his village to impose a one-year prison sentence on a peasant with whom he had a personal dispute. The luckless peasant was transported to the boma for internment, only to be released by the DS after one night in jail. The chief was reportedly agitated at this affront to his authority, and further intervention by the DS was required to find the peasant a place on an agricultural settlement scheme far from the chief's *musumba* (palace). In the precolonial Bemba state, the authority of local leaders rested squarely on the sanctions they were able to impose on their followers. Chiefs and headmen were permitted to impose fines on behalf of Native Authorities in colonial times, a power that was sometimes misused to the personal advantage of traditional leaders. The removal after independence of all judicial functions into the hands of government officers in the Ministry of Legal Affairs damaged the already dwindling credibility of chiefs and headmen among their own people. But the resolution of the Nkolemfumu case shows clearly that the formal requirements of the law had to be accommodated with the interests of powerful traditional groups. In Kasama the VPC's became one of the only arenas available to traditional leaders who wished to assure themselves a place in the process of rural development.

A second indicator of the way in which the committee organization benefited traditional leaders as a group was in the location of development projects. From the point of view of peasants, one of the most urgent development problems was the provision of a reliable and clean supply of water for household purposes. A communal well with a windlass or hand pump was acceptable, but a piped water system with a motor pump and individual standpipes was most desired. Of the six piped water schemes in Kasama District, three were located at the headquarters of a chief. Of the seven government (nonmission) health centers in the district, four were located at the headquarters of a chief. The same held true for three of the first seven villages selected by the DDC for "intensive village regrouping." In part this pattern of project location was attributable to the concentration of population at these places, but it also indicated the ability of traditional elements to use the committee organization to secure first option on the limited central resources that percolated down to the local level.

Third, certain chiefs and headmen benefited from the performance of VPC's not simply by virtue of traditional group membership, but as individuals, or by virtue of new group criteria. Richards noted as early as 1957 that certain "go-ahead" chiefs had used their government allowances to pay traditional tribute laborers, and to buy trucks and thereby become "successful market gardeners."[46] Two examples from Kasama, one of a chief, the other of a headman, can be given to corroborate and extend the Richards account.

The chief in question was an appointed councilor on Kasama RC. His brother was a UNIP Regional Trustee. His area covered three local government wards and, notwithstanding the presence of three elected UNIP councilors, was considered by peasants to be "king of that place anyway."[47] The chief led the mobilization of scattered villages into regrouped settlements and reaped the credit for the provision of government services that followed. He was also able to enlarge his following, and thereby his prestige, by attracting settlers, some even from neighboring Mporokoso District, to his own regrouped village. Thus the chief skilfully used the state apparatus (development committees) and a national rural development policy (village regrouping) to entrench his own power position. Significantly, the chief was also a successful farmer who hired agricultural labor and marketed sufficient surplus to afford to run a private motor vehicle. His area was chosen by the Tobacco Board of Zambia as the site of a virginia tobacco settlement scheme. The scheme began in the colonial period, and the chief was coopted to "encourage recruitment" of peasant farmers.[48] The chief maintained the informal right of screening all applicants from prospective settlers before they reached the manager of the scheme. In addition he secured for himself one of the first plots on the scheme on which construction of his second private house was underway.

Another illustration of the possibilities for personal gain inherent in the committee organization can be drawn from the village cited as a model of an active VPC (see above, page 69, item 4). Villagers were asked by the headman to widen the road to the village bar on a self-help basis. It happened that the bar in question was privately owned by the headman himself. The widening of the road would connect the bar with—and put it in direct line of sight of—the main thoroughfare in a densely settled area just outside Kasama township. The headman, and not the village as a whole, stood to gain from the increased *chibuku* (beer) sales that the new access road would permit. Yet the headman had used his position as chairman of the VPC to control the labor of the peasants in his village. In so doing he was also able to distort to his own purposes the policy of self-help as a tactic for local development. His was not an isolated case; 6 headmen of 44 interviewed had business interests in general stores or bars.

The social background of this type of leader, however, was not generally typical of traditional elements. Both this chief and this headman had some secondary education and a history of paid employment. If there was any group interest to be discerned from these two examples, it was not an uncomplicated case of tradition asserting itself. On the one hand the chief and the headman in question could have been isolated patrons acting alone. On the other hand, their emergence could have reflected deeper changes in social structure in which a bourgeois stratum in the locality had begun to form. Full discussion of this issue is reserved for later. What can be stated firmly about the performance of VPC's at this point is that the dominant voices at VPC meetings were invariably those of the better educated elements of the village, be they headmen, emergent farmers, or party officials. VPC secretaries, as the best educated people in the village, were often able to dominate VPC's, especially if the headman was infirm or disinterested. In large regrouped villages and in villages close to the urban township headmen had to battle hard to maintain control of VPC's. As argued, the most active VPC's were those with a low proportion of traditional leaders among the VPC membership. Chiefs and headmen who did gain control of active VPC's tended to use them in their own interests and to have close associations with other leadership elements from party and state. Yet there was no evidence whatever that traditional leaders as a group had benefited from VPC performance and had come to constitute a privileged stratum in the locality. The Bemba chief or headman was no *emir* or *marabout*. On the contrary, most of this group was not differentiated from other poor peasants in terms of income or living standard. With few exceptions, traditional leaders and their followers among subsistence peasants were not the beneficiaries of rural development.

The Kasama case shows that apparatus of the state at the village level was captured by traditional leaders. The composition and performance of VPC's reflected an attempt on the part of traditional leaders to reassert lost functions and powers. But because VPC's remained largely inactive or otherwise powerless, the decline in traditional authority, first noted by Richards, was not thereby stemmed.[49] Chiefs in general were more effective than headmen in grasping opportunities offered by committee formation. The great majority of headmen either had no VPC or were unable to use a VPC to attract central resources or initiate self-help projects. The state had only sparse presence at the village level.

Notwithstanding the relative powerlessness of traditional leaders and their VPC's, chiefs and headmen still enjoyed a more institutionalized following at village level in Kasama than did the UNIP machine (see below, Chapter 7). The only practical choice open to the Zambian government in 1971 was to rely on the leadership structure of the past and thereby provide a partial continuity with the colonial strategy for linking center and locality. By recruiting traditional patrons to formal leadership positions, the state stood to garner the support of at least some peasant followers too. Older peasants and women still held esteem for traditional leaders, and these groups were prominent in Zambia's rural demographic profile. If anything, after 1971 the central government placed even greater reliance on traditional leaders than before for the implementation of policies like village regrouping, voter registration, and the recovery of agricultural loans.[50] Yet there was an inherent contradiction in the choice of traditional leaders as local development agents. The performance of VPC's showed chiefs and headmen to be disinclined to promote changes that undermined their own positions of authority. At most, this group of village level leaders gained some of the control functions of the state but did not open village political organization to mass peasant participation. In choosing chiefs and headmen as its grass roots allies, the Zambian state acknowledged a low capacity to replace even severely weakened traditional institutions, and accepted the likelihood of minimal village-level socioeconomic transformation.

4

Ward Development Committees

At the level of the local government ward the formation and operation of development committees had proceeded further by 1975 than at the village level. A higher percentage of WDC's than VPC's had survived, and their activities had concrete results in the form of actual rural development projects. The claim that WDC's existed on paper only was decidedly untrue for Kasama. Compared to VPC's, WDC's in Kasama were relatively effective and institutionalized.

At the same time, however, WDC performance in Kasama also illustrated the continued dependence of local-level organizations on central government resources, the bureaucratized nature of the local decision-making process, and the emergence of powerful local interests. Like VPC's, WDC's had not brought about a mass mobilization of local resources for local development or even a fairly equitable diffusion of central resources to the mass of the peasant population. Like VPC's, WDC's were melded into the social structure of the locality and provided an opportunity for ambitious interests to dominate the resource distribution process. The principal beneficiaries of participation in development committees at ward level were necessarily different from those at village level. Above the village, traditional leaders gave way to new leadership groups. The nature of the new rural social structure and its relation to the local-level apparatus of the state is the main concern of the present analysis of WDC performance in Kasama.

Some WDC's were established before 1971—that is, before the strategy for linking center and localities was formalized under an Act of Parliament. At least seven wards in Kasama had meetings of what were called Ward Cooperative Coordinating Committees.[1] Some of these first committees were adapted to all-purpose functions from com-

mittees established to supervise group housing projects and village regrouping under the Department of Community Development.[2] In 1967
President Kaunda called for the creation of ward committees to engage
in such basic economic functions as allocating and enforcing agricultural production targets, supplying farmers with fertilizer, credit and
marketing facilities, and planning future economic investment for the
ward. They were urged to meet monthly and "in terms of the policy
of self-help . . . should as far as possible, resolve most of their [own]
problems."[3]

RECRUITMENT FOR WARD DEVELOPMENT COMMITTEES

Patterns of recruitment for WDC's were established during the period 1967–71 and were not disrupted by the enactment of legislation
on committee formation. From the outset, the ward councilor was permitted wide discretion in forming a committee. The only guideline provided for WDC formation was that the councilor would be chairman of
the committee; the makeup of other members would vary according to
local circumstances and would include "representatives of all sections
of the community," by which was meant farmers, businessmen, headmen, and field-level civil servants.[4] Recruitment to ward committees
was thus an ad hoc affair that vested extensive powers in ward councilors to act as local patrons. Even when responsibility for committee
formation was formally vested in DG's in 1969, central supervision and
standardization of committee formation proved difficult to enforce.
DG's were preoccupied with the problem of carving out positions of
authority for themselves from the preserves of DS's and UNIP RS's.
The DG in Kasama abdicated all responsibility for committee formation to councilors, who were advised to pick "ten people in your ward
as your henchmen" [sic].[5] Thus recruitment to local-level office was,
in 1969—and remained, in 1975—a matter of predominantly local concern. The central state in Zambia never enjoyed the capacity to supervise fully the building of local-level political organizations.

The first group recruited for WDC's were prominent party men.
UNIP councilors used their freedom of selection to assemble committees of compatriots from the party with whom they were accustomed
to working. As one rural councilor put it, "in those days ward com-

mittees were the same as our party security committees"; in the words of another, "committees were just like a party constituency." This is not to say that ward committees were immediately and fully integrated with a vigorous party organization, but rather that UNIP office afforded an easy criterion for claiming membership on a WDC. Automatic accession of party officials to WDC office was part of the process whereby UNIP at the local level made the transition from protest party to ruling party. Furthermore, the first Humanism document held the promise that the new committees would oversee the distribution of development resources in the locality. Hence councilors and other local party leaders perceived an opportunity to gain patronage rewards both for themselves and for their party followers. UNIP "freedom fighters" from the days of the nationalist struggle felt that first option on the fruits of political independence was rightfully theirs. In practice, WDC formation detracted from UNIP branch and constituency organization because development committees appeared to herald the arrival of rural development benefits which, by the late 1960's, the party had patently failed to provide.

Along with local party officials, a second group made itself visible early in the committee formation process. Ambitious farmers pressed councilors for places on the WDC, "because they wanted credit from government."[6] To some extent the two groups, party officials and emergent farmers, overlapped. But the bulk of UNIP's early support in Northern Province had come from subsistence peasants working in the setting of the village. Individual market-oriented farmers working outside the village had been attracted to the Watchtower or Lenshina movements, both of which withheld support from UNIP. In other parts of the country emergent farmers had supported the African National Congress against UNIP. With the advent of WDC's in Kasama, emergent farmers found for the first time a common interest with local party officials in using the new committees to extract resources from the center. Those emergent farmers who had no other means of access to agricultural credit or other development resources were drawn to local institutions previously dominated by local party officials. The recruitment base of WDC's was widened, but not so far as to admit representation of the poorest subsistence stratum. WDC's were grafted onto the UNIP patronage machine as the agricultural cooperative and credit programs had been before.[7] A precedent was set that membership and resources of WDC's were open to control by patrons within the local-level party.

Against this historical background the nature of the local power structure in Kasama District in 1974–75 can be more readily appreciated. The patronage pattern of recruitment to WDC office and of distribution of development resources at the ward level was not fundamentally altered when the framework of local-level organizations was formalized into law. This was the finding of a social background survey that I conducted among the members of WDC's in Kasama District in 1974. With 23 wards in the RC area of Kasama District and a formal membership of 10 on each WDC, there were 230 potential respondents. Rather than taking a sample, the total population of 230 was surveyed. The survey was conducted by means of a self-administered questionnaire. A satisfactory response rate was achieved: of 230 questionnaires circulated, 204 were recovered, a response rate of 89 percent (see below, Appendix). The target population was chosen on the assumption that any local leadership group seeking access to state resources was likely to find its way onto the local-level state apparatus, that is, the WDC. It was further assumed that from a survey of this population a social profile of local leadership could be drawn. In other words, the question "Who are local leaders?" could be tentatively answered. The following general characteristics, then, described local leadership at ward level in Kasama District.

WDC membership was predominantly *middle-aged and male*. The average age of members was 46.8 years in a range from youngest to oldest of 23 to 85. WDC members were mostly men in their forties. These men were the same generation, and in many cases the same individuals, as the "freedom fighters" of 15 years earlier. There had been little refreshment of local-level cadres since the nationalist phase. The few young WDC members were educated men brought to the WDC for their literacy skills or as a reward for service to the youth wing of the party. Only three WDC members were women, who scarcely enjoyed token representation. Even at WC meetings, where attendance was often thrown open, fewer than 15 percent of those attending were women.[8] Decision-making by men was evident at the ward level, where women were less influential than in the villages. The marginality of women to WDC activity was surprising, given the demographic profile of Kasama District, in which females predominated in middle-age categories. Women were first recruited into active political office during the anticolonial struggle, but the decline of the party tended to exclude women again from formal decision-making positions. Given the large economic role played by women in the subsistence economy, exclusion of women from WDC membership may be part of the explanation for the noneconomic orientation of local-level committees.

WDC membership in Kasama was also *ethnically homogeneous*, being 96.3 percent Bemba. An even higher percentage (97.3) took Chi-Bemba to be their mother tongue. This striking homogeneity was an indication partly of the location of Kasama District at the heart of the traditional Bemba state, but also of ethnic and sectional solidarity in Kasama that made Bembaness a sine qua non of election to local or national office. This characteristic of WDC membership can also be interpreted not as a sign of ethnic consciousness but as a sign of marked *localism*. Eighty-one percent of WDC members lived and were elected to leadership positions in the same chief's area in which they were born. To have oneself and one's family known in the locality was an asset in achieving a position of local leadership.

Nevertheless, localism was a disadvantage for recruitment to WDC's unless accompanied by experience outside the rural areas, usually in *labor migration*. Four out of five WDC members (79.9 percent) had been labor migrants during at least one period in their lives. On the average, local leaders had spent 6.7 years in urban employment outside the district. One member of the Ward 8 WDC reported being employed as a plumber on the Copperbelt for 26 years before returning to Chilungu village in Chitimukulu's area. Of those who gained urban employment, only 35 percent claimed to be miners; the remaining 65 percent were engaged in service occupations, lower civil-service jobs, or non-mine industrial work. Significant numbers reported obtaining skills as artisans, particularly as bricklayers (13 percent) and carpenters (10 percent), skills that were applicable to rural development activities. Other useful experience with clerical work and machine operation was also reported.[9] Some former labor migrants, notably those from wards in the northern part of Kasama District, had sought work in Tanzania rather than on the Zambian Copperbelt. In Wards 1–5 over half the WDC members, 28 out of 51, had traveled out of the country to Tanzania. Others reported working in Southern Rhodesia. Labor migration experience, including experience gained by those recruited to fight in the Second World War, was a key aspect of a typical WDC member in Kasama. By the same token, labor migration continued to reduce drastically the pool of able-bodied men and women, especially men, available in the locality for recruitment to activist roles on WDC's in Kasama. Over half of the males in the 15–49 age group were absent from the rural areas of Kasama in 1975.

Relatively few WDC members were drawn from among *traditional leaders*, in distinct contrast to the dominance of those elements at village level. There was less continuity in WDC's with customary social and political institutions than in VPC's. Only 19.1 percent of WDC members claimed to be headmen. The usual pattern was for VPC secretaries rather than VPC chairmen to be elected or appointed to WDC office. In most wards there were only one or two headmen on the WDC. In some wards, however—for example, Wards 1, 16, and 17, where party organization was weak and there were few branch officials —headmen formed up to half the committee. Only 2.4 percent of WDC members claimed to have occupied positions in the colonial Bemba Native Authority. Of the Bemba clans, none had undue representation on WDC's, an indication both of the declining importance of clan to politics and of the inability of members of the royal *bena n'gandu* (crocodile clan) to continue to claim office ascriptively. The general finding was that at the ward level, unlike the village level, a break had occurred with the leadership patterns of the past.

At first glance WDC members appeared to be characterized by relatively *low formal education*. The average length of primary schooling was four years; a mere 10.7 percent had the advantage of post-primary education. This educational pattern was also partly reflected in the one third (34.8 percent) of WDC members who spoke English, the official language of government and business in Zambia. Nevertheless in a predominantly nonliterate society even minimal formal education was an important criterion for recruitment to leadership position. Kasama WDC members did, therefore, represent an advantaged group who had had access to the limited educational resources of a district where the overall literacy rate was low. The great majority of educated WDC members received primary schooling at mission schools before independence. As a result, 93 percent of WDC members regarded Roman Catholicism as their *religious affiliation* and 21.5 percent held church office.

TABLE 6.   Kasama District, Membership of Ward Development Committees
by Occupation (n = 204)

	Well-to-do		Subsistence Peasants
Salaried Employees	*Businessmen*	*Emergent Farmers*	
40	18	77	
(18.7%)	(9.9%)	(37.4%)	
	135		69
	(66.0%)		(34.0%)

In terms of other socioeconomic indicators, WDC membership was
seen to be drawn from a relatively privileged stratum of income earners in the locality. The majority of WDC members engaged in relatively *well-to-do* occupations (Table 6). Of them, 18.7 percent had
paid employment. This category included state functionaries like primary school teachers or agricultural demonstrators. It also included
carpenters or bricklayers who enjoyed a regular income from hiring
themselves out to private individuals and to cooperatives. But 9.9 percent described themselves as businessmen, usually in the petty retail
trade; 37.8 percent, by far the largest group, were emergent farmers
in the sense that their farming activities were oriented toward production of a marketable surplus. Together, the three well-to-do groups
of salaried employees, businessmen, and emergent farmers accounted
for two thirds of WDC membership. Only one third was drawn from
the largest stratum of the rural population—the subsistence peasants.

The impression that economic advantage and local leadership position went together was confirmed by the distribution of *consumption
goods*. In all cases ownership by WDC leaders of selected consumer
items was above the district average. For example, 40 percent of WDC
members owned radios where the average was 24 percent[10]; 10 percent had motor vehicles where the district average was just over one
percent[11]; 22 percent lived in burnt brick houses where the average
for the rural part of the district was approximately 10 percent.[12]

Almost without exception WDC members claimed *UNIP membership* (99.5 percent). Only one man, in Ward 23, answered "no" to the
survey question on this topic. This high response, however, must be
scrutinized carefully. WDC members had nothing to lose and much to

gain by claiming party membership in a single-party state. If party membership were to be measured by the payment of annual party dues, the figure would likely be far lower (see below, Chapter 8). The majority of WDC members (64.4 percent) said that they joined UNIP before 1960—a date which, if accurate, would confirm the popular notion that the party drew considerable support in the North in the initial stages of the independence struggle. Party office-holding by WDC members pointed to a relatively high integration of local-level organizations in the ward. In the first place, party organization and committee organization were well integrated. Almost half (45.1 percent) of WDC members held a *party office* within UNIP; some were constituency officials, some were branch officials (Table 7). Secondly, there was a similarly high crossover between WDC leadership and leadership in *other local institutions*. Again, nearly half (45.9 percent) were members of a cooperative, a credit union, or a parent-teachers association, and 17.1 percent held office in these institutions. This crossover of leaders pointed to a recruitment pattern in which leadership to all local-level institutions was limited to a rather small local elite.

   In sum, recruitment to local leadership at ward level in Kasama was a closed rather than an open affair. Two sets of recruitment criteria were distinguishable. First, there were certain minimum social attributes, such as age, sex, ethnicity, religion, and localism, without

---

TABLE 7.   Kasama District, Membership of Ward Development Committees by Party Office (n = 203)

	UNIP Office Holders			*UNIP Ordinary Members*
	UNIP Constituency	*UNIP Branch*	*Total*	
Main Body	19	63	82	
Women's Brigade	1	0	1	
Youth Brigade	1	8	9	
	21	71	92 (45.1%)	111 (54.9%)

TABLE 8.   Kasama District, Membership of Ward Development
Committees, by Education and Occupation

	Well to do (n = 135)			Subsistence Peasants
	Salaried Employees (n = 40)	Businessmen (n = 18)	Emergent Farmers (n = 77)	
No formal education	2	0	10	25
1–4 years education	7	8	33	32
5 or more years education	31 (78%)	10 (56%)	34 (46%)	12 (17%)

which candidacy for leadership was virtually impossible. But these
minimum criteria were widely shared and alone did not discriminate
between leaders and nonleaders; many locally born middle-aged Bemba men, for example, did not accede to the WDC. Primary recruitment
criteria served only to define the "recruiting ground" from which local
leadership was invariably drawn. Other secondary criteria, which
were unevenly distributed in the locality and which endowed particular groups with advantage in leadership recruitment, had also to be
present. These key secondary recruitment criteria for access to WDC
position in Kasama were *well-to-do occupation* and *UNIP party office*.
Each will be examined in turn.

To repeat, the occupational categories that were taken to comprise
"well-to-do" were salaried employees, petty traders, and emergent
farmers. The annual per capita income of this group on local-level committees in Kasama was K358.00 compared with about K23.0 for subsistence peasants, a differential of 16:1.[13] Not unexpectedly, the well-
to-do also predominated in access to such benefits as education, which
partly accounted for their occupational status (Table 8). Those receiving salaries also engaged in the highest levels of personal consumption,
followed by businessmen (Table 9). Emergent farmers, however,
tended to commit available surplus elsewhere, such as into the hiring
of labor (Table 10). Not all the salaried and entrepreneurial elements
in Kasama District found their way into the local leadership structure.

TABLE 9.   Kasama District, Membership of Ward Development Committees, by Consumption Goods and Occupation

	Well-to-do (n = 135)			Subsistence Peasants (n = 69)
	Salaried Employees (n = 40)	Businessmen (n = 18)	Emergent Farmers (n = 77)	
Burnt brick house	12 (30%)	4 (22%)	13 (17%)	12 (17%)
Motor vehicle	11 (28%)	4 (22%)	5 (7%)	0 (0%)
Radio	24 (60%)	8 (45%)	27 (35%)	28 (26%)

TABLE 10.   Kasama District, Membership of Ward Development Committees, by Employers of Labor and Occupation

	Well-to-do (n = 135)			Subsistence Peasants (n = 69)
	Salaried Employees (n = 40)	Businessmen (n = 18)	Emergent Farmers (n = 77)	
Employ Labor	2 (5%)	3 (16%)	59 (77%)	0 (0%)

Indeed significant numbers of civil servants, traders, and emergent farmers were excluded or held themselves aloof from the activities of the development committees. This may have been because they were outsiders from other provinces in the case of civil servants, or because they were envied for their material success in the case of businessmen. The emergent farmers outside the village on individual land holdings already had a point of access to development benefits through the Department of Agriculture and did not need the WDC. Yet emergent farmers within the village were the largest category among the well-to-do on WDC's. It was to this category that the committee organization offered a major channel for access to development resources.

The term "emergent farmer" requires some explanation in the context of Kasama. The Bemba do not have a long-standing agricultural tradition; in the precolonial period farming was neglected in preference to raiding neighboring states. In the colonial period the Northern Province was transformed into a labor pool for the Copperbelt mines. Shifting chitemene cultivation supplemented by small-scale hoe cultivation remained the predominant form of agriculture up to 1975. The definition of "emergent farmer" under these circumstances was necessarily different from that in highly productive areas like the Central and Southern Provinces. The 1973–74 Farm Register for Kasama District listed only two medium-scale farmers (20–40 hectares cultivated) and 13 small-scale farmers (5–20 hectares). Thus for the purposes of this study a survey respondent was assumed to be an emergent farmer if he described himself as a farmer as opposed to a villager, and if he satisfied either the criterion of selling more agricultural surplus than he retained for home use (31.3 percent), or the criterion of cultivating two hectares of land or more (46.0 percent).[14] Such a farmer did stand out in local society. He was more likely than those at the subsistence level to have introduced fertilizer, improved seed, and chemical insecticides and to have accepted credit from the government. He was likely to share cultivation methods with subsistence peasants, to the extent of using a hand-held hoe rather than a plough drawn by oxen or tractor, but not to the extent of having a chitemene garden. He might grow maize, beans and groundnuts, or vegetables for market as opposed to the subsistence staples of cassava and millet alone.

Of great significance to rural social differentiation and class formation was the growing acceptance among emergent farmers of the employment of labor; 15 percent of WDC members paid others to work for them. The vast majority of these employers (77.3 percent) were emergent farmers (Table 10). Peasants in the subsistence sector sold labor to emergent farmers when they had no other means of earning a cash income. Hired labor was applied to seasonal agricultural tasks, like cultivation, planting, and harvesting, for which family labor was insufficient on a farm of over three or four hectares. By contrast, small-scale businessmen rarely required extra workers for the operation of their retail outlets, so were less important than emergent farmers as employers of labor. Emergent farmers were a notable new element in the local social structure, and they made their presence felt through membership on WDC's. One councilor announced that he made a point of trying to attract "good farmers" to the WDC in order, in his opinion, to "help the agricultural revolution."[15] That emergent farmers were recruited to local political organization in a nonagricultural district like Kasama suggests that for agricultural districts elsewhere in Zambia the accession of this group to local political power was likely to be even more advanced.

The second key determinant of access to local leadership at ward level was service to the political party, particularly the holding of party office. The local government councilors for each ward, who were automatically the chairmen of the WDC's, gained positions by virtue of party office. Almost all councilors in Kasama, 19 of 23, were UNIP constituency officials. Typical of ward leaders were men who were simultaneously ward councilors, chairmen of WDC's, and UNIP constituency secretaries; they often also chaired a PTA or cooperative. They were important mediators of center-local relations by virtue of their linkage positions in the local government and administrative and party organizations. A clear distinction existed in Kasama between the constituency and branch levels of the party. The only UNIP constituency officials on WDC's were WDC chairmen who received payment by virtue of their work as ward councilors; by contrast UNIP branch officials acceded only to ordinary membership of WDC's and were unpaid in any capacity. The most numerous of UNIP officials on Kasama WDC's were branch secretaries (32 percent), followed by branch chairmen (22 percent). The bulk of the party officials on Kasama WDC's (89 percent) were drawn from the main body of the party; only small proportions were drawn from youth (10 percent) and women's (one percent) brigades (Table 7). Without exception all party officials on WDC's had a long history as organizers for UNIP and its predecessors. Some party officials claimed to have belonged to the party for 16 years, that is, since the formation of UNIP; one branch chairman traced his membership back to ANC in 1953. These were the people who in the late 1950's cycled the long miles between Kasama's scattered villages to spread the anticolonial political message and to enroll party members. In the early 1960's they had burnt their identification certificates and organized sabotage campaigns to obstruct the work of the colonial government (see below, Chapter 7).

By way of reward, UNIP endeavored after independence to provide salaried positions for active and loyal cadres. Some UNIP stalwarts from Kasama rose to highly responsible and prestigious posts,[16] but there were never enough jobs to go around. With the creation of WDC's, the local party was supplied with patronage posts for large numbers of previously unrewarded but loyal branch officials. Although these posts carried no salary, they held out the promise of early access to the development resources, such as agricultural credit or housing grants, which WDC's came to administer. At ward level, the party was able to oversee committee recruitment in most wards, and naturally favored its own.

One finding of the social background survey of WDC's in Kasama was that subsistence peasants were not well represented; relatively well-to-do elements had grasped WDC membership. Another finding was that affiliation to the political party was a key avenue of recruitment. A commonly expressed belief in Zambia was that UNIP was a party of the underprivileged. One might therefore expect UNIP in the rural areas to provide a channel of upward mobility for subsistence peasants. The Kasama data did not bear this expectation out. Only 10 percent were subsistence peasants who relied on party affiliation alone to boost them onto the WDC. The majority of members relied upon well-to-do occupation or a combination of occupation and party office to ensure election (Table 11). In other words, the two key recruitment criteria of occupation and party office tended to reinforce rather than cross-cut each other. The relationship between occupation and party office was not perfect; there were still significant numbers of subsistence peasants who were party officials and significant numbers of income earners who were not. Nevertheless, there was some evidence

---

TABLE 11. Kasama District, Membership of Ward Development Committees, by Occupation and Party Position (n = 204)

	Well-to-do	Subsistence Peasants	Totals
Party officials	71 (34.8%)	21 (10.3%)	92 (45.1%)
Not party officials	64 (31.4%)	48 (23.5%)	112 (54.9%)
Totals	135 (66.2%)	69 (33.8%)	204

in the Kasama data for the inception of a community of interest between the party and the privileged.

Two conclusions concerning the political party can be drawn from the importance of party record to local leadership recruitment. First, UNIP's local organization was maintained by the distribution of patronage posts, of which WDC membership was one. There was a continuity of recruitment procedures from the early days of informal committee formation despite the formal electoral requirements of the 1971 Act. In some wards in Kasama, WDC elections did not seem to have been formally conducted; nor were fresh elections held in any rural ward after the three-year statutory limit. Selection of WDC members was done either in party circles or in small, unrepresentative WC meetings. Even where elections were held according to the law, the councilor was often able to influence voters in favor of his own slate, and the membership of existing party-based committees was not altered.[17] The second conclusion follows from the first. Notwithstanding the transformation of a mass-based UNIP into a selective patronage machine, the party still had insufficient resources at its disposal to maintain permanent organization below the level of the party constituency or local government ward. At ward level the party did have a permanent constituency organization that was integrated into a reasonably coherent development front with development committees. This ward-level integration was effected by UNIP control of political recruitment of WDC's. At the village level, by contrast, the party was not able to control recruitment and composition of VPC's and deferred in this task to traditional leaders. The capacity of the party-state apparatus to penetrate to the ward level and no further had major implications for the performance of WDC's as opposed to VPC's, and for the diffusion of development benefits to the poorest peasants.

PERFORMANCE OF WARD DEVELOPMENT COMMITTEES

Social background data on leadership are an insufficient guide to resource distribution patterns in the locality. In order to determine who benefits, the social structure of leadership must be shown to be linked to the performance of WDC's in actual decision-making and actual project implementation.

Of 23 WDC's in Kasama rural area, 12, or about half, were active in 1975 (Table 12). This was above average for the Northern Province; in 1975 Kasama ranked third out of eight districts in activating WDC's (Table 13). Information available to the state at the center on the WDC situation in the locality was of poor quality. On the one hand, the Kasama Rural Council tended to overemphasize the institutionalization and effectiveness of WDC's in order to justify its budget. One estimate from the KRC was for 18 active WDC's out of 23.[18] Patently false claims were made by ward councilors; for example, one claimed a monthly WDC meeting when none was held, with "the average number of 1000 people attending."[19] On the other hand, district administrators were also out of touch with WDC performance, but tended to minimize rather than overemphasize their effectiveness. One 1975 report from the Ministry of Rural Development admitted little knowledge of how WDC's in Kasama were working, on the incorrect assumption that "committees last submitted their reports in 1973."[20] I therefore visited each of the 23 wards in Kasama to conduct in-depth interviews with ward councilors and others in an attempt to achieve a more accurate picture of WDC performance (see Appendix).

An active WDC was one that held regular meetings and undertook self-help projects involving the participation of residents of more than one village. Specifically, to be deemed active for the purposes of this study a WDC must have met at least once in 1973 or 1974, recorded the proceedings in writing, forwarded minutes to the RC, and had a ward project underway at the time of my visit in 1974 or 1975. The figure of 12 active WDC's was based on these criteria.

For the most part, scheduling of WDC meetings was haphazard. WDC's were supposed to meet every three months, but few in Kasama did so. Most met on the VPC pattern—that is, when a local issue arose. A seasonal water shortage, the nonavailability of farm requisites, or an impending visit of the District Governor were events that triggered WDC meetings in Kasama. In half the wards in Kasama there was no written record of WDC's ever having met. In some cases this was a result of poor record-keeping by the WDC secretary, but in some cases the WDC did not in fact meet. Despite the assertions of councilors to the contrary, I could find no person who remembered any meetings in Wards 11, 17, 18, and 22. By contrast, active WDC's had begun to move toward systematic scheduling of four WDC meet-

TABLE 12.   Kasama District, Development Projects of Ward Development Committees, 1973–1974

Ward No.	WDC Active[a]	Capital Projects Using Central Resources[b]	Self-Help Projects Using Local Resources[c]
1.		piped water scheme	village regrouping; school
2.	yes	piped water scheme; health center	group housing; bridge
3.			
4.			
5.			
6.		settlement scheme (coffee)	school; group housing
7.	yes	piped water scheme; settlement scheme; health center	village regrouping; school; group housing
8.	yes	piped water scheme; health center; post office	group housing; maize production
9.	yes	piped water scheme; health center	school; rest house
10.			
11.		IDZ rice scheme	Note: no schools in this ward!
12.	yes	secondary school	schools; maize production
13.	yes	Rural Council HQ; settlement scheme; Farm Training Institute; secondary school; health center	schools; maize production
14.	yes	brickfield	school
15.	yes	Rural Reconstruction Camp; bridge	schools; bridge
16.	yes	piped water scheme (for township)	
17.			bridge
18.		hydro-electric scheme (for township); ZNS camp	group housing
19.	yes		group housing
20.	yes		group housing
21.		bridge; settlement scheme (tobacco)	schools
22.			group housing
23.	yes	dairy	sewing project

[a] Based on evidence independent of the ward councilor's account, i.e., minutes of meetings, observation of WDC meetings, and accounts from third parties.

[b] This category includes projects financed and executed under supervision of the KRC or central ministries and in which the planning decisions were usually out of the hands of the WDC. It excludes wells and roads, built by the central government, which can be found in almost all wards. It also excludes mission-aided projects.

[c] This category includes projects implemented by communal peasant labor, projects financed by village collections, and projects financed by central government grants-in-aid with a local self-help component.

TABLE 13. Northern Province, Activeness of Ward Development Committees

	No. of Rural Council Wards	No. of Active Committees	% Active
Kasama[1]	23	12	52%
Mpika[2]	20	8	40%
Chinsali	18	9	50%
Mbala	20	5	25%
Mporokoso	13	8	62%
Luwingu	20	11	55%
Isoka	18	6	33%
Kaputa	18	5	43%
Total	140	64	46%

Sources:
[1] Figure based on own research.
[2] Ministry of Rural Development: "Productivity Committees at Lower Levels of Administration," letter from PRDO Kasama to Permanent Secretary, Ministry of Rural Development, Lusaka, NP/MRD/COM 5, May 9, 1975. These figures were derived from a survey hastily conducted by District Agricultural Officers in May 1975 and were rough and impressionistic.

ings per year in accordance with requirements from the center. In Wards 2, 7, 13, and 15, for example, councilors publicized WDC meetings well in advance and scheduled them to follow meetings of the RC immediately, so that instructions from the state at the center could be reported to WDC's. In Wards 2 and 12 WDC's met regularly as early as 1971, but the majority of WDC's were activated in the period after village registration—that is, in 1973 and 1974.

Active WDC's in Kasama underwent adaptation of organization and performance to fit local circumstance. A WDC was supposed to perform as the executive body in the ward by implementing policy decisions taken by the WC. In practice the WDC's both formulated and implemented local plans. The distinction between WC and WDC was not rigorously observed in the day-to-day operations of these committees in Kasama. Instead one general-purpose ward-level committee tended to emerge with a regular attendance of anywhere between 8 and 80 persons. That this committee was popularly acknowledged to be a "ward development committee" did not necessarily mean that it conformed in membership and functions to the WDC as laid down in the Pocket Manual. One councilor volunteered that the "WC and WDC do the same work" and therefore the WC should be abolished.[21]

Other modifications to ward-level committee organization were initiated by ward councilors. In Ward 25 the councilor set up two WDC's with two secretaries in different corners of the ward, partly to administer a large ward more efficiently, but also to maximize the number of patronage posts at his disposal. At the same time as pacifying competing ward factions of rural peasants and urban employees, he was able to maintain his own position as patron. In Ward 12 the councilor lived outside the ward and delegated many of his powers to party allies among the WDC membership. The councilor ultimately had to beat off a challenge from subordinates who, buoyed by the success of their active WDC, nurtured aspirations to the councilorship of their own. The main point, however, was that the WDC's in Wards 15 and 12 met regularly and were among the best endowed in the district with school and road projects. The most active WDC's, therefore, were not, necessarily, those that operated by the book but those best adapted to local peculiarities of leadership and social structure.

An active ward meeting in Kasama had some or all of the following features:

WDC Meeting at Chitambi
The meeting was held in a village with a school which, like all such villages, had the advantages of central location in the ward and large population concentration. At the time the meeting was due to commence, few peasants were present but the assurances of the councilor that his constituents would eventually assemble proved correct. Eighty-eight people came. The meeting was not limited to WDC members alone. VPC chairmen and secretaries were welcome, as were peasants who came "because they want to know what is being done." VPC secretaries were distinguishable from village headmen by their relative youth and literacy skills and the fact that the two groups sat in separate clusters in the schoolroom where the meeting was held. At a top table sat the ward councilor and the ward secretary plus the UNIP branch treasurer, a businessman. Visitors to the meeting, in this case the chairman of the KRC and myself, were also seated at the top table. No representatives of

central state administrative departments were present. Respects were paid to the councilor in the form of traditional hand-clap and bow as ward members entered; only when a sub-chief arrived did the councilor rise and offer his respects in return.

The meeting opened with the singing of the Zambian national anthem, the Bemba words of which were not familiar to all, and the shouting of the "One Zambia – One Nation" slogan. The minutes of the previous meeting were read by the WDC Secretary, a meeting to which the District Governor had been invited but which he did not attend. Announcements followed from the WDC Chairman, the Ward Councilor. Much of his speech was devoted to elucidating central policy on the 1971 Act, that is, the proper relationship among and activities of ward and village committees. He also commended the ward on the collection of self-help funds and announced, to applause, the initiation of a Rural Council road project in the ward. He concluded with a stern reminder on the President's call to curb excessive drinking and asked VPC chairmen to ensure that brewers of beer confine their sales to one communal place rather than "every house." The Ward Councilor established himself as a representative of the policies and interests of the political center and maintained this role throughout the meeting.

Motions from VPC's were then invited, as if a Ward Council meeting were underway. Motions were presented by village headmen in their capacity as VPC chairmen. Notably the presentation of formal VPC motions was the only time that headmen spoke; the parry and thrust of argument fell to the more literate and urbane VPC secretaries who were the local element most adept at dealing with the center in its own bureaucratic terms. One VPC secretary had the Councilor give a detailed village-by-village accounting of the expenditure of K10,000 of state funds for wells and boreholes in the ward.

The following is a partial list of VPC motions raised: Chaiwila wanted two wells and a bus service to Kasama; Chisanga Mwamba wanted a school, piped water and market; Kalimuka called for a "proper road to our place"; Bwembya demanded a Rural Council revenue office in or around the township as traveling to distant Mungwi to pay license fees was imposing hardship; and, to the great hilarity of the assembly, Mwanga Mubanga VPC complained that wild pigs had eaten their cassava crop and pleaded for "someone from the government to come and shoot them." Loud laughter also supported the Chitambi VPC Secretary who, dissatisfied with the ward councilor's reply that bridges were too unsafe to provide a bus service, replied that trucks carrying beer could get through so why not buses; "after all, which is heavier, people or *chibuku?*" Indeed the meeting was so boisterous that the Chairman had to use slogan-shouting as an ordering device on no fewer than eleven occasions. There were many more demands from below than the WDC could reasonably accommodate and the Ward Councilor unilaterally blocked the majority of VPC motions on the spot. He was forced to repeatedly explain that projects for which SNDP funds had not been allocated could not be realized. Out of 37 local motions raised he committed himself to following up on only three at the center, that is with government departments or Rural Council.

Voting on VPC projects did not occur at this meeting. The Councillor instead reserved for himself the patronage right of allocating ward resources as he saw fit and resorted to central government policy as support to his own position when challenged. The meeting dispersed after three hours with a final rendition of *"Lumba Nyeni Zambia."*[22]

Thus WDC meetings, properly constituted or not, began to perform tasks of political communication and economic planning for the locality. The dynamics of center-periphery relations in Zambia were well illustrated by the proceedings of WDC meetings; WDC's constituted a forum where local demands and central policy and resource shortages collided. As well as meeting regularly, active WDC's in Kasama undertook concrete development projects. Two examples of effective WDC action will be given:

Case 1: The Mulilansolo Bridge
The Mulilansolo River was a perennial stream that, in 1974, marked the boundary between Kasama Township Council and Ward 15 of the Rural Council. Part of Ward 15 covered a heavily populated semi-urban area. The growth of employment opportunities in Kasama township since independence attracted large numbers of work-seekers from all rural districts in the Northern Province. Like other residential places near the township, the Chitamba-Bwembya part of Ward 15 was beginning to lose its identity as several large, well-established but discrete villages, as more temporary "shanty" dwellings made their appearance and the boundaries between villages became blurred. The councilor for Ward 15 described it as a "difficult place to govern . . . full of drinkers, boxers and funny men who always think that they know best."[23] WDC meetings in Ward 15 were marked by a multiplicity of demands for government assistance and vociferous bargaining over the distribution of resources. Most of the people who lived in this area gained livelihood in the formal or informal sectors of the township economy. Traveling to town required crossing the Mulilansolo River. Always a litter-strewn and muddy ravine, the river was almost impassable once the rains arrived. Hence the WDC for Ward 15 resolved to build a bridge on a self-help basis. Residents of Chitamba-Bwembya and surrounding villages widened the access road by group labor and gathered stone and other materials to begin bridge construction. A self-help fund was started with a levy by each VPC of K2 per family on villagers who would use the bridge. Chitamba VPC alone, for example, collected K171 by this method. Bricks were bought from a local brickmaker at a price below that of the bricks sold by the nearby RUCOM government brickfield. Most important, a grant of K3000 was secured by the councillor from the Rural Council. Once this grant was made, daily-paid hired labor replaced self-help labor in the construction work. Within three months in 1974 a permanent stone and concrete bridge was completed, capable of carrying heavy motor traffic and providing easy all-weather access to the township.

In this case the WDC was able to mobilize a diverse community into action on a common local development problem. When local resources proved inadequate for a relatively large-scale project, the WDC was successful, through the representations of the councilor, in attracting central resources. Once the bridge became an RC project, the self-help element tended to fall away. The WDC did gain institutional credibility among the residents of Ward 15 for initiating the project, but in the final analysis most credit seemed to accrue to the councilor as the "patron" who secured the Rural Council grant.

Case 2: Namponda Village Water Supply

Namponda village was situated seventeen kilometers north of Kasama township on the main gravel road to Mbala. The Tanzam railway line passed nearby. The village moved to its present site in 1966 to take advantage of road access to Kasama and the plentiful supply of edible caterpillars. The main disadvantage of the site was water shortage. In 1972 the Department of Water Affairs sank a 73-ft. open well, deep by local standards, but it proved to be dry for half the year. For domestic supplies women and children from Namponda were forced in the dry season to resume their habit of walking to the well at Kapata Church, four miles away. The seriousness of the water supply issue led at one point to a split in the village and a number of families left to settle elsewhere. The village head, Namponda, sister of Chitimukulu, was unable to control or improve the situation. She was elderly and, in formal terms, uneducated: "she does not understand what committees are supposed to do and she has failed to mobilize the people."[24] The VPC in Namponda rarely met. In addition, the councilor for the ward in 1974 was both lax and unpopular. Peasants from Ward 6 complained that "nothing happens to requests we give to the councilor; he has not visited for two years; we are not satisfied."[25] The DG and Chairman of the KRC had in 1971 been forced to discipline the councilor "for not having met (your constituents) since you were elected."[26] For two years the WDC had sent letters on the water supply issue to the DG, RS, and RC, also without gaining satisfaction. Action was finally initiated in mid-1974 by the UNIP Women's Secretary, Chilunga Constituency, who summoned the councillor and other WDC members to a meeting at Namponda village itself. The upshot of this meeting was a successful WDC application for well reconstruction to the Water Affairs Department. The Community Development Assistant from the area backed the WDC request. The Namponda well was deepened and a hand pump installed. Funding was almost entirely provided by central government although a self-help fund of K9 and labor from several villages were used. Namponda then had year-round "good clean water" for domestic purposes, although there was still insufficient water for brick-making. Peasants from surrounding villages use the well and in 1975 settlers began to return to Namponda.

This was a case of a weak WDC initiating action. Apart from the Namponda peasants themselves, the main beneficiary was the party official who, partly on the strength of her performance in invigorating the WDC and solving the water problem, nudged out the lax councilor for Ward 6 for the nomination and backing of the UNIP Region in the 1975 Local Government Elections. She subsequently won the election and became ward councilor. It remained to be seen whether she could continue to mobilize peasants into active local committees and whether she could maintain patron status by attracting further development benefits to the ward.

ANALYSIS OF WDC PERFORMANCE

These two cases of WDC action should not be viewed in isolation. Not all WDC's in Kasama were "one issue" institutions like the WDC that was organized around a water problem; nor were WDC's always as effective in getting things done as the bridge builders in Ward 15. An attempt will be made to draw a representative picture of WDC activity in Kasama, first by analyzing the performance of one typical active WDC and, second, by analyzing the content of demands made by all WDC's in the district. Finally analysis will be directed toward the identification of factors that explain why some WDC's were active and some were not.

The WDC in Ward 13 was typical of active WDC's in Kasama District. It engaged in a wide range of health, education, and welfare matters and become institutionalized as an agency of innovation at the local level. The following matters were discussed at a WDC meeting in Ward 13 in 1973:

1. The councilor/chairman explained to the members of the WDC that they would be meeting three more times in the year and reminded them of the necessity of full attendance and of the duties of WDC members.
2. The committee discussed the increase of maternity cases in the ward and called on the Ministry of Health to station a midwife permanently at Mungwi Clinic. They also requested the building of an extension to the clinic, or alternatively, the conversion of a government office into a maternity wing.
3. The committee considered requests from the VPC's of James village, Kabula village and Fundiboma village for piped water extensions. The WDC instructed the residents of the villages to start a

self-help fund and, if sufficient money was collected, then an approach to the Rural Council would be made.

4. The councilor/chairman and visiting works officer from the KRC advised that agricultural loans would not be given unless farmers managed to find fertilizer on their own.

5. Complaints concerning the poor condition of bridges at Chisapa and Kananda over the flooded Chibile stream were brought to the committee's attention. In both cases people from the ward had begun repair work but were hampered by the lack of heavy transport to bring logs and gravel to the bridge sites. The WDC resolved to ask the KRC to provide a truck to do this work once the rainy season had ended.

6. The VPC at White Chiti village reported that 126 children were unable to gain primary school enrollment. The councilor advised that government policy forbade the building of a new school within two miles of an existing school. He also told WDC members that elsewhere in the ward there were 513 children without school places. The WDC resolved that the only solution was to request a doubling of classes at all schools in Ward 13 and a letter was written to the Local Council of Education to this effect.

7. A petition was presented from several villagers alleging abusive and arrogant behavior on the part of the Senior Medical Assistant at Mungwi Clinic. The WDC decided to report this government officer to the DG, Kasama, for discipline or removal.[27]

Analysis of WDC performance based on the Ward 13 meeting and its aftermath points to both strengths and weaknesses of local-level organizations. First, the majority of upward demands from WDC's were unsuccessful. For example, peasants from Kabula and White Chiti villages (items 3 and 6) made identical demands for piped water and double-stream primary schools at a WDC meeting sixteen months later.[28] At a public meeting in Mungwi in April 1975 a speaker in the crowd was still able to elicit cheers for a demand to "remove these incompetent people at the clinic."[29] Indeed by early 1975 not one of the requests for central intervention made at the above meeting had been met.

Second, WDC's like VPC's, performed as part of the control apparatus of the state. Although the two "control" issues raised at the above meeting (items 1 and 4) also held development benefits for the locality, issues could nevertheless be found where central and local interests came into conflict. The most common issue was chitemene cultivation, which from a local viewpoint was a rational response to a poor agricultural environment but from a central viewpoint was a malignant cancer on the nation's forest resources.[30] Chitemene continued to be practiced in every ward in Kasama, including Ward 13, against the expressed control attempts of councilors and government officials. These latter officials used WDC's primarily as a forum for implementation of state policy. WDC's did offer an opportunity for rapid communication in otherwise isolated rural areas but also permitted the extension from center to locality of a bureaucratic-authoritarian mode of policy implementation.

Third, the conception of planning in WDC's was merely that of demanding resources from the center. According to this shopping-list conception of planning, as many projects as possible were demanded in the hope that one or two would prove acceptable at the center. No consideration was given to the practicability or priority of implementation or the availability of resources. At the Ward 13 meeting, of the five items that concerned pressing local problems, only two (items 3 and 5) were deemed soluble by self-help techniques and even these two items also involved requests for assistance from central or local government.

I conducted a general survey of the demands occurring at meetings of active WDC's in Kasama and found that the pattern of WDC performance in Ward 13 held true throughout the district. WDC demands on file at the Kasama RC were classified according to the development orientation displayed, the degree to which local self-help activity was stimulated, and the extent to which local political participation was encouraged. The results are reported below.

First, the type of local development strategy envisioned by WDC's emphasized *social welfare above economic productivity*. According to reports submitted to the RC by ward councilors, the items discussed and demands made by the WDC's were biased strongly toward the improvement of rural social facilities (Table 14). Over three quarters of the items discussed (78.5 percent) fell into this category. WDC's were concerned above all, and in order of peasant preference, with the construction of roads, schools, water supplies, and health facilities. With

TABLE 14.   Kasama District, Ward Development Committees, Analysis of Items Requested in Councilor Reports, 1973–1974 (n = 103)

Item Requested	Rank	No. of Requests	%	Economic Productivity or Social Welfare	
Roads and Bridges	1	23	22%	SW/EP	
Schools	2	22	21%	SW	
Water Supply	3	19	18%	SW	
Clinics	4	14	14%	SW	SW = 78.5%
Bus Service	5	9	9%	SW	EP = 21.5%
Fertilizer	5	9	9%	EP	
Village Regrouping	6	4	4%	SW	
Postal Service	7	2	2%	SW	
Cooperatives	8	1	1%	EP	

Source: Kasama Rural Council, Ward Councilor Reports, November 1973 to May 1974; KRC file LG/KA/1/4, p. 78.

the exception of roads, all items bore a tangential relationship to economic productivity. Improvements in village standards of living were sought by WDC members but were not linked to the growth of local economic surplus. Items directly concerned with economic productivity, such as the formation of marketing cooperatives and the provision of fertilizer, accounted for less than one quarter (21.5 percent) of WDC demands. Significantly, other items concerning agricultural innovation, such as provision of seeds, insecticides, and other requisites, and of tractor hire or oxen-training, did not appear in councilor reports. Only three wards in Kasama District (12, 13, and 8) had large marketable maize surpluses, although production in other wards was slowly rising. Exhortations by WDC leaders for each family to cultivate two hectares or more according to state policy were not widely heeded. Only 323 farm families in Kasama met this requirement in the 1973–74 farming season, with approximately 1000 hectares under cultivation.[31] This is not to say that WDC's were not oriented toward rural development, but rural development was conceived in terms of social welfare. Otherwise, WDC's were highly developmental. Of the items discussed at WDC meetings, 70 percent were concerned with the initiation of new projects and 30 percent with care and maintenance of existing projects or other routine matters (Table 14), a reasonable balance for rapid but sustainable innovation.

TABLE 15.   Kasama District, Content of Selected Ward Development
Committee Meetings, 1972–1975

Ward	Date	Development Item	Care & Maintenance Item	Self-Help Resources	Government Resources	Communication Up	Communication Down
7	9.23.72	1	—	2	1	2	2
13	1.31.73	8	2	4	5	9	2
2	2.25.73	1	—	—	1	1	1
2	5. 8.73	2	—	—	2	2	2
15	5.19.73	4	3	3	4	4	4
7	1. 9.74	6	—	2	6	4	5
14	2. 2.74	3	2	2	2	2	—
2	3.30.74	8	2	—	8	6	8
7	4. 8.74	2	4	1	3	2	5
13	4.17.74	7	—	—	7	10	5
15	4.18.74	25	7	7	22	29	2
7	5.19.74	3	2	—	3	3	2
14	6. 8.74	7	2	2	7	8	2
15	7.13.74	9	1	2	6	9	3
2	7.24.74	1	1	—	3	3	4
7	8.25.74	5	1	2	4	4	2
4	10. 5.74	—	3	1	—	—	3
2	10.12.74	4	4	3	4	6	5
16	11.17.74	4	1	3	2	3	3
7	3.26.75	3	1	—	3	3	1
Total		103	36	34	93	110	61
Percentage		(70%)	(30%)	(27%)	(73%)	(64%)	(36%)

Source: Based on items discussed at 20 WDC meetings between September 23, 1972,
and March 26, 1975, as filed in minutes with Kasama Rural Council, or as recorded by
me.

Second, the solutions to problems of local development devised by
active WDC's in the first two years of their operation in Kasama displayed a heavy *reliance on central resources*. Almost three quarters
(73 percent) of the items proposed by WDC's were accompanied by a
request for central government funding: only one quarter (27 percent)
explicitly designated self-help resources (Table 15). Ward councilors
claimed a larger proportion (44 percent) of self-help projects actually
underway,[32] but several of these projects were never completed. Self-
help in most cases was a matter of the provision of unpaid community

labor rather than the provision of community capital. WDC's were poorly placed to sustain capital formation on a self-help basis. Of 23 councilors interviewed, 16 reported that their wards had no self-help fund; of the remaining 7, only 3 had small amounts available which were not tied to specific projects. Amounts of capital accumulated through self-help funds were infinitesimal and accounted for little in the implementation of development projects (Table 16). Even though

TABLE 16. Kasama District, Sources of Capital, Ward Development Committees, 1972–1976

Ward	Self-Held WDC Funds 1972–1975[1]		Rural Council SNDP Allocation 1972–1976[2]	
1	Kwacha	300	Kwacha	101,500
2		600		71,600
3		—		36,928
4		—		57,600
5		—		77,400
6		—		77,900
7		200		88,500
8		—		52,100
9		700		148,900
10		—		95,120
11		—		44,000
12		—		74,300
13		400		267,800
14		400		100,700
15		1,200		27,000
16		—		101,200
17		—		77,200
18		—		42,800
19		—		39,000
20		—		102,600
21		—		21,200
22		—		122,000
23		—		18,000
Totals		3,800		1,845,348

[1] Based on councilor estimates and rounded out; excluding funds raised for such non-community projects as house construction.

[2] Kasama Rural Council, Capital Estimates, 1972; excluding expenditure made in wards by government departments. These funds would be administered not directly by WDC's but by the Rural Council on the behalf of WDC's.

central resources were scarce, they were sufficient to dwarf self-help resources. For the most part WDC's collected contributions from peasants only for specific bridges, clinics or schools and nothing was left over for productive investment. Parent-Teacher Associations were often more successful than WDC's in raising self-help funds for the building of village schools, because of their ability to levy compulsory charges on the families of each schoolchild. Moreover, the specificity of function of PTA's gave an advantage over WDC's in achieving concrete results. The burdening of WDC's with an overwhelming array of development responsibilities led WDC leaders to attempt to extract resources from the state rather than from peasants. Dependence on central resources was a feature of WDC performance from their inception.

The third aspect of performance confirmed by review of the proceedings of active WDC's in Kasama was that WDC's functioned to implement *central political control* as well as local political participation. A two-way dynamic was built into the local-level committee organization by planners at the center who sought "to establish effective channels of communication between the man in the village and his Government leaders in Lusaka."[33] Analysis of WDC demands showed that upward communication predominated over downward communication in a ratio of two to one (Table 15). Nevertheless, this ratio reflected in part the sheer numerical majority of peasants over representatives of the central state at WDC meetings. Representatives of the center took more than a fair share of WDC time for the purpose of explaining central government policy. Ward councilors exercised this control function whether or not other state functionaries from government departments were present. In the words of the Kasama DG, "it is not only the DG, the RS and the Chairman of the Rural Council who explain Government policy, but councilors too."[34] The best example of a councilor in this role was the one from Ward 2, who was also the RC chairman. The minutes of the Ward 2 WDC were predominantly composed of "chairman's announcements." The KRC Chairman also attended WDC meetings throughout the district and consistently took the government line, even against councilors who were inclined to express local grievances. When asked what the job of WDC Chairman entailed, he replied, "to represent the government to the people."[35]

This analysis would not be complete without mention of factors that impinge upon WDC activeness and performance. These factors are inherent in the tensions of center-locality contact and in the structure of political interests in the locality. I rejected a number of plausible factors which were found to have no bearing on WDC activeness in the Kasama case; examples were ward population density, formal party position of the ward councilor, and level of SNDP development-resource allocations. I recognized the influence of village regrouping in animating local-level political organizations but reserved detailed analysis until later (see below, Chapter 6).

Three factors remained which were found to have an effect on whether WDC's were active. First, WDC activeness was related to the geographical *location of the ward*—that is, the distance of the locality from the center. Wards in the Kasama rural area were classified according to whether they were central or peripheral in terms of the development nodes and axes of communications in the district. Thus the location of the ward was not a crude measure of distance from the boma but a measure of whether contact between center and locality was easy and regular. Wards that abutted Kasama township and those with direct main road links from the ward core to the township tended to have active WDC's; of the 13 central wards, 10 had active WDC's (Table 17). Conversely, 8 of the 10 "peripheral" wards had inactive WDC's.

The second factor that accounted for the activation of WDC's was the *patronage position* of the ward councilor. In contrast to the weak explanatory power of formal party position, the councilor's access to the center through the informal political machine of UNIP counted for much. A prestige rating study of ward councilors provided a ranked list of "influentials" on the Kasama Rural Council (see below, Chapter

---

TABLE 17. Kasama District, Activeness of Ward Development Committees, by Location of Ward

	WDC Active	WDC Inactive	Totals
Central location	10	3	13
Peripheral location	2	8	10
Totals	12	11	23

TABLE 18.   Kasama District, Activeness of Ward Development Committees, by Prestige Rating of Ward Councilor

	WDC Active	WDC Inactive	Totals
Influential councilor	9	1	10
Noninfluential councilor	3	10	13
Totals	12	11	23

TABLE 19.   Kasama District, Activeness of Ward Development Committees, by Occupation and Party Position of WDC Members

	Active WDC	Inactive WDC	Totals
Well-to-do party officials (minimum 3 per WDC)	9	5	14
No well-to-do party officials (less than 3 per WDC)	3	6	9
Totals	12	11	23

8, Table 35). The relationship between party influence and WDC activeness was almost perfect for the top ten influentials (Table 18). The ward councilors who led active WDC's were also the key party patrons in the local resource distribution process. This relationship between "big men" and WDC activity tended to confirm the proposition that WDC's had been grafted onto a pre-existing party patronage network.

Finally a third factor in WDC activation was the *social composition* of the WDC. The presence of party officials or well-to-do elements among the WDC members alone had no effect on whether the WDC was active or dormant. This finding changed slightly, however, when WDC members were present who were simultaneously party officials and well-to-do (Table 11). The relationship between social composition and WDC activity was not as strong as with other factors (Table 19). Well-to-do UNIP officials were found in small numbers on all WDC's in Kasama. This stratum of leadership thus had some (though slight) influence on the activeness of local-level organizations. The argument presented below is that although their influence was slight on activeness—that is, if a WDC worked at all—their influence on performance —how a WDC worked—was much greater. The rural development performance of active WDC's did bend to the interests of newly emerged strata in the locality.

THE DISTRIBUTION OF WDC RESOURCES

WDC performance has so far been examined with little reference to a social context. As argued earlier, patterns of resource distribution are determined by the interaction of the organizational and developmental designs of the state with the interests of local leadership groups. Rural underdevelopment and dependence may be institutionalized if agencies of the development front do not diffuse development benefits equitably throughout the locality. For this reason it is necessary to ask the questions "Who decides on" and "Who benefits from" WDC activity? Three local leadership groups take decisive part in the process of resource distribution through local-level committees in Kasama: field-level civil servants, ward councilors, and WDC members who are well-to-do or have party patronage access. The impact of the interests of each of these groups on WDC performance will be examined in turn. These groups in Kasama were the chief beneficiaries of the distribution of state development resources and as such aligned themselves with the state and became the spokesmen for the center. As a result, WDC's did not evolve into participatory institutions controlled from below.

Civil servants in Kasama blocked devolution of decision-making power to WDC's. Most WDC requests for social facilities were turned down at higher levels of the state apparatus. The rejection of projects or the delay of projects was a result not only of unrealistic WDC planning but of poor civil service implementation. At financial year end 1972, Northern Province returned to Lusaka K60,000 in development funds that provincial and district-level civil servants had failed to spend.[36] Until 1974, when all development funds were spent on time, because of the vigilance of the Provincial Cabinet Minister, inefficiency in the implementation of projects made the return of unspent funds from Northern Province a regular occurrence. The Ministry of Local Government and Housing, which funded the bulk of WDC projects through the RC, had spent none of its K14 million allocation by October 1974 and had to scramble to complete the task by year end. This was attributed by the Minister to "a slip-up in the bureaucratic system."[37] Numerous cases can be cited where WDC projects in Kasama suffered from nonperformance or delays on the part of field-level bureaucrats. In Ward 20, for example, the Ministry of Rural Development estimates for 1972 provided funds for a village water supply. The funds were not used by the Department of Water Affairs in that year, and their benefit was lost to villagers. In 1974 the councilor reported this dereliction of duty to a touring member of the Central Committee, who reportedly instructed the DG to rectify the matter.[38] Other cases of this kind included a primary school without a roof in Ward 15 and a health center in Ward 12 planned for by the DDC but delayed by the slow provision of funds from the Ministry of Health.

The best known case of bureaucratic nonperformance in Kasama concerned the pollution of the water supply at Soft Katongo village. A sewage drain from a camp of Tanzam railway construction workers had been built at the headwaters of the stream from which the peasants at Soft Katongo and three other villages drew water. The first record of VPC/WDC action was a request by the four affected villages in March 1971 for urgent intervention by the DG. Seven months later the DG convened a meeting at which he promised to try to mobilize emergency funds, but nothing resulted. In early 1972 the councillor announced at a WDC meeting that K35,000 had been set aside in the Second National Development Plan for the provision of a borehole and piped water system for the four villages. By early 1974, three years after the problem arose, "people are still suffering from water [shortage] and we are still requesting the government to solve this boring problem [sic]."[39] By the end of 1974 the only money spent by the government was a small amount on a well and hand-operated windlass pump, which broke down soon after installation. The K35,000 allocation was apparently withdrawn. Because the problem of the Soft Katongo water was not resolved, peasants in Ward 14 became skeptical that the WDC could do anything for them. Attendance at WDC meetings declined. Other active WDC's became dormant because of bureaucratic immobility. The councilor for another ward offered the opinion that "people have changed . . . they are not the same as in the [nationalist] struggle . . . they are reluctant to attend meetings because they think their problems are not understood by anyone . . . the WDC is refusing to send new motions [to RC and DDC] because they have sent so many and nothing has been done." [40]

A charge of obstructing development was leveled at state bureaucrats by WDC secretaries at a meeting at Mungwi in 1973. Low agricultural productivity was attributed not to the performance of local-level development committees but to state managers of NPCMU and NAMboard, who were responsible for supplying essential farm requisites. [41] It was said that WDC's could not plan and VPC's could not expand production if seed, fertilizer, and insecticides were unavailable on time. A survey of the farm requisites in the 1973/74 agricultural season revealed that "agricultural development in [the Northern] Province [was] severely hampered by the inefficient marketing of farm requisites." [42] In Kasama District fewer than one third (31.5 percent) of the 26 NPCMU agricultural depots had a sufficient supply of fertilizer, and at the remaining depots fertilizer "was only available for a few farmers to buy or it was not available at all." Even fewer (20.6 percent) of the depots had sufficient hybrid maize seed. Political intervention by the DG improved the distribution record in subsequent seasons. Yet officials of the state and the marketing union were unwilling to acknowledge responsibility for low maize output; they sought what one commentator has called in another context "bureaucratic immunity in a situation where peasants and their ignorance provide a convenient scapegoat." [43]

Bureaucratic bottlenecks were in part traceable to the shortages of manpower, transport, and authority experienced by provincial and district offices of government. The logistics of resource distribution at the extreme periphery posed severe challenges to a bureaucracy hamstrung by transport breakdowns and deskbound personnel. There was ample evidence, however, that civil servants regarded a devolution of decision-making power to local-level committees as a threat to their own political interests. Obstructive attitudes and actions of local officials to the growth of WDC's have been documented in Mkushi District. [44] In Kasama, obstruction took numerous forms. To begin with, state officials tried to preserve decision-making for themselves. The Department of Water Affairs, for example, stressed the primacy of technical concerns in the provision of village water supply, and the views of peasants on project type and location were often overlooked.

Provision of water supply in Kasama was not the "self-help" activity it was in other districts in Zambia.[45] Another example of resistance to popular participation was the headmistress of a Kasama school who feared WDC "interference" in school affairs and had to be advised that "VPC's and WDC's are already a national feature in the whole Republic of Zambia and should be treated as such."[46]

State officials were also generally reluctant to tour villages or attend WDC meetings when invited. The Pocket Manual stated that one of the roles of government vis-à-vis local committees was to "extend technical and professional advisory services to WDC's whenever these are required,"[47] yet of 20 WDC meetings (Table 15) only 8 enjoyed the presence of a state official. Of the 23 councilors in Kasama, 12 said that field-level civil servants, such as agricultural assistants and schoolteachers, did not come to WDC meetings, and 19 said the same of bureaucrats from the district capital. Senior party officials, the DG and RS, had a somewhat better record, 10 out of 23. One councilor embarrassed the DS by declaring at a full RC meeting that the latter had ignored all invitations to attend his WDC meetings.[48] One headman obtained shouts of approval from peasants when he stated at a WDC meeting that "no one visits us in the villages . . . in colonial days bicycles were used to tour the district but now *boma* officials will not travel out of Kasama without a car or a Land Rover!"[49]

In addition to admitting low contact with peasants, state bureaucrats readily expressed disdain for the caliber of ward and village leadership. One district official suggested that "only qualified administrators should be allowed to get their hands on government money . . . people in the villages would not know how to use it."[50] An authoritarian or "commandist" style in administrative communication was adopted by district-level officials at WDC meetings. Some Bemba-speaking state officials even indulged in the conceit of addressing peasants in English with the assistance of an interpreter. Moreover, the attitudes of civil servants in Kasama were based on poor information about WDC's; I found many discrepancies between low official estimates on WDC activation and the real world of Kasama WDC's. The solutions proposed by civil servants to problems associated with development committees were bureaucratic rather than participatory. One report of a civil servant from Kasama suggested the appointment of a District Rural Development Officer to "direct the proper functioning" of committees.[51] Another mentioned seminars led by bureaucrats "to bring our WDC members up to the required standard."[52]

The formation of what has been called a bureaucratic bourgeoisie in Zambia since independence finds its expression at the local level in the jealous guarding of administrative power and economic privilege against demands from participatory institutions. Bureaucrats as a self-conscious and self-interested political group have important influence on the manner in which local-level committees perform and are seen to perform.

A second social group whose actions and interests accounted for the performance of WDC's were *ward councilors*. As chairmen of WDC's, these councilors occupied the top formal leadership posts on local committees. The extent to which they used their pivotal positions to link central and local state apparatus determined to a large extent if and how the local committee system performed. In the words of the Kasama District Governor, "a good councilor is one who organizes his ward committees so that they run smoothly."[53] Councilors were often the only link between people in distant villages and the state. A councilor who frequently toured his ward and maintained personal contact with constituents was able to mobilize VPC's into regular meetings. Sometimes he could also ensure that WDC development projects were implemented. But if a councilor neglected to tour, he was likely to be faced with dormant committees. Of the 23 councilors in KRC, only five initiated systematic programs for ward touring and quarterly WDC meetings.

Peasants in Kasama often complained that they did not know their councilor because he did not visit the villages. Complaints of this type were heard even in the wards with the most active councilors, but they were particularly common in large or outlying wards—for example, in Wards 11, 17, 18, 21, and 22. Some councilors were not diligent in touring wards because they had paid employment in Kasama township. In Wards 3, 11, 14, 18, 21, and 23 the councilor lived outside the ward, and in one case, Ward 18, 70 kilometers away. A majority of councilors spoke of the difficulties of touring vast distances by bicycle, especially in swampy, hilly, or tsetse-fly infested wards. As one councilor put it: "I have to prepare a blanket because I know I will be traveling for many days."[54] The councilor for Ward 18 conceded that he had not seen his own WDC Secretary for six months because they lived far apart. The councilor for Ward 20, among others, did not appoint a substitute when he was called for training in the Zambia National Service, and his WDC was neglected for three months. As representatives of the center, councilors personified the state in the eyes of many peasants and consequently shouldered the blame for failures of expected development resources to materialize. One active councilor complained that "although I speak up in the [Rural] Council, the people here do not believe me." [55] A number of councilors expressed fear that their reelection was in doubt because of their inability to attract patronage rewards. The councilor's job was thus a difficult one; like all linkage positions, it created tensions of competing claims from center and locality. Close and regular contact between councilors and peasants was exceptional. As with WDC activation, close contact tended to be limited to wards near the center and with good communications routes.

If the downward communication through councilors was sparse and sporadic, so was upward communication. WDC initiatives were futile if not conveyed by the councilor to appropriate higher authorities, or if the councilor lacked influence at the RC and Regional UNIP headquarters. Part of the routine process of upward communication in Kasama was the submission to the RC of councilor monthly reports. Yet only 3 of the 23 councilors submitted reports with any regularity. In addition, councilors ensured that WDC minutes were written and communicated upward to the RC in only 8 out of 23 wards. WDC minutes for only 2 wards could be found on file at the Office of the DG (Table 20).

Although formal channels of upward communication were underused, councilors relied heavily on informal personal or patronage contacts. Almost all councilors, 21 out of 23, said they personally visited the DG or RS with development requests from their wards. In addition to party contacts, councilors fostered contacts with officials in the state bureaucracy. The consensus among the councilors was that to direct WDC requests through the proper channel of WDC-RC-DDC was to invite inevitable delays. One councilor responded to the referral of a village water problem from the RC to the DDC by saying that he could not tell his people, "for everyone knows that will take two years." [56] Many councilors therefore achieved quicker results by circumventing the RC and DDC, making direct contact with the relevant

TABLE 20. Kasama District, Use of Communication Channels by Ward Development Committees, 1973–1975

Ward	WDC Active	Councilor Monthly Reports at Rural Council[1]	WDC Minutes at Rural Council[2]	WDC Minutes at Boma
1		Yes (?)		
2	Yes	Yes (?)	Yes	Yes
3		Yes (?)		
4				
5				
6		Yes		
7	Yes	Yes (?)	Yes	
8	Yes			
9	Yes	Yes	Yes	
10				
11		Yes (?)		
12	Yes	Yes (?)	Yes	
13	Yes		Yes	Yes
14	Yes	Yes (?)	Yes	
15	Yes	Yes	Yes	
16	Yes		Yes	
17		Yes (?)		
18		Yes (?)		
19	Yes	Yes (?)		
20	Yes	Yes (?)		
21		Yes (?)		
22		Yes (?)		
23	Yes	Yes (?)		
Totals	12	3 14 (?) 17	8	2

[1] Where fewer than three reports were received at the RC over the period October 1973 to April 1975, the "yes" notation is followed by (?).
[2] A minimum of one set of minutes qualified for a "yes" notation.

department of government. The Ministries of Health and Water Affairs were fairly responsive to this approach, but only insofar as maintenance projects and not new projects were concerned. In Ward 12 personal contacts by the councilor, in his role also as secretary of UNIP Kasama Constituency, ensured a "special arrangement" with the Chief Education Officer to bring forward construction plans for two schools.[57] Along with councilor motions at RC meetings, personal contacts were the most common means in Kasama by which local WDC issues were communicated to the central state apparatus. Councilors were key patronage figures in the locality. Party office thus was not only a criterion for recruitment to WDC leadership position, as documented earlier, but also a determinant of the allocation and distribution of development resources. Peasants and WDC members acknowledged that councilors who were the effective party patrons acted as a group to take first option of the central development resources (see below, Chapter 8). There were few councilors who were able to cultivate close contact both with officials of the party-state at the center and with peasants in the locality, and guarantee thereby on even a wide flow of development resources.

The influence of a third and final leadership group was evident in the performance of WDC's in Kasama. As noted previously, WDC's were recruited among *party officials* and *well-to-do elements*, the latter being predominantly emergent farmers. Together this group staked a claim on the development resources that WDC's had at their disposal. WDC members perceived WDC membership as a means of satisfying personal and group interests through preferential access to central largesse. Since WDC's were incorporated into a patronage pattern of resource distribution, opportunities were afforded WDC members to help themselves. Two examples will be given: the first concerns access to agricultural credit afforded WDC members, the second, payment of salaries to WDC officials.

In the 1974–75 farming season the Agricultural Finance Company (AFC) launched an experimental program to decentralize agricultural credit facilities. Consideration of loan applications was no longer to be by a District Advisory Committee composed largely of district civil servants. Instead, loan applicants were to be screened and selected by WDC's meeting in conjunction with field extension workers of the Department of Agriculture. By involving peasant representatives, the AFC hoped to improve its loan repayment record, in the sense that local people could more readily distinguish genuine from fraudulent applicants. In addition, the AFC devised a revolving fund which made financial resources available to the WDC on the basis of the loan recovery in the previous season. This new procedure had the added potential benefit of vitalizing WDC's by giving them something to do, along with the wherewithal to do it.

In Mpika, the neighboring district to Kasama, which was designated as the pilot district for Northern Province, peasants "gained a tremendous momentum to organize the wards."[58] Party and government leaders in other districts were urged to determine whether wards were organized to meet the challenge of the introduction of the new procedure in the 1975–76 season. A central policy decision was taken by the Board of the Rural Development Corporation in Lusaka, however, to delay the nationwide implementation of WDC credit processing until the results on loan recovery were in from the pilot districts. But most wards in Kasama District had already been given the news about the increase in, and local control of, agricultural credit. A grand tour of all wards had been mounted in early 1975 by the DG, RS and Chairman of the RC, among others, all of whom had used the opportunity to consolidate their positions as patrons by promising an imminent inflow of agricultural credit. When the postponement of the new procedure was announced, the AFC received strong protests from these politicians. The protests were sufficiently strong for AFC to make a special exception for Kasama District in the 1975–76 season, whereby WDC's were asked to recommend eligible farmers on an informal basis.

A tentative indication of WDC resource distribution patterns was gained from the first lists of loan applicants that were submitted to AFC Kasama in 1975. Two facts were clear. First, WDC's acted to enforce the selective national strategy of isolating the emergent farmer as the main agent of agricultural innovation in Zambia. AFC instructions to WDC's were replete with references to the farming background, credit-worthiness, "willingness to hire labour," and other measures of the "character, ability and industry" of the applicant.[59] Ward councilors in Kasama unanimously agreed that only the best farmers should get loans, and WDC recommendations did not deviate from the notion of "building on the best." The WDC procedure undoubtedly reached more prospective farmers than before: 353 loans were approved in Kasama for 1975–76, up from 222 in 1974–75. But given government strategy to assist individual family units, as opposed to mobilizing the mass of the peasantry and granting credit cooperatively, WDC involvement in credit distribution was likely to contribute only to socioeconomic stratification. WDC's also assisted in the selection of tenants for the settlement schemes in Kasama District, with the same result.

The second indication of how WDC's distributed resources was the high incidence of WDC members using committee membership to recommend themselves for loans. An analysis of the 1975 lists of WDC-recommended loan applicants shows that the applications of one third (32 percent) of the WDC members in Kasama District were successful.[60] Names of councilors and WDC secretaries were included. The remaining applicants were emergent farmers and local party officials who did not sit on the WDC but who were otherwise close to the center in terms of party patronage. Of the 22 applicants recommended by one WDC, Ward 7, 2 were ward councilors, 4 were members of the WDC, and 15 were branch and constituency officials of the party. As another example, in Ward 18 the councilor and WDC secretary drew up the list of loan applicants themselves; their own names were included, as were those of other WDC members and party officials. The councilor was able to retire from politics and take up farming full time, partly on the strength of the access to credit his political position had afforded him; the WDC secretary, who was also a UNIP branch secretary, was already one of the most well-to-do storeowners in the ward, but he, too, received an AFC loan.

The second example of the benefit of WDC membership concerns the group interest of WDC secretaries in gaining official salaries. In the early stages of the local-level committee experiment, a decision was taken at national level that WDC performance could be improved by offering training workshops to WDC secretaries. The first pilot workshop in the nation was held at the headquarters of the Kasama Rural Council in Mungwi in April 1973. Secretaries from almost all wards attended, to hear lectures from officials of National Institute of Public Administration and the DG's office. The workshop members were permitted to draft a number of recommendations concerning WDC performance. They cited needed improvements in agricultural production, soil conservation, cooperative labor, and social facilities; administrative streamlining of the local-level committee organization was also recommended. For this study, however, the most interesting recommendation read as follows: "In view of the wide responsibilities now being given by government to ward secretary/treasurers they will need to spend more time and energy to carry them out . . . and therefore should receive some allowances from the Rural Councils."[61] Having been trained, WDC secretaries in Kasama regarded themselves as professionals worthy of a salary. On the basis of the demand for salary payment, the state canceled the proposed series of nationwide WDC training workshops. The official explanation was that "formal training to WDC secretary/treasurer has increased their demands for payment [and] has therefore generated negative effects."[62] The state was unwilling to allocate rural development resources for such purposes. From the local perspective the WDC provided a convenient organization for one local leadership group drawn from the membership of WDC's to demand redistribution of wealth in its own favor.

The party-state in Zambia had an institutionalized presence in the form of active WDC's in half of the wards in Kasama District. By 1975 state-building had occurred in Zambia deep in the locality and to an extent not readily acknowledged by administrative and academic observers. But although WDC's existed and undertook development projects, their impact on rural development policy-making and decision-making was negligible. WDC's and VPC's were not consulted about major industrial and infrastructural projects conducted by central government ministries in the locality. The only control that development committees exercised over central expenditure was in the location of certain social service projects and the distribution of some agricultural credit. WDC's and VPC's were able to make few expenditures of their own. Self-help funds were insignificant in comparison with central investments, and the latter were invariably tied to specified projects in the national plan. The meager central resources that did trickle down to the locality were usually allocated by WDC's and to nonproductive social trappings of modernization. Local-level development committees did not embark on investment in productive local enterprises or on the accumulation and reinvestment of local resources. Indeed, peasants tended to use WDC's and VPC's only as a forum for demands to share in national copper wealth.

Under the circumstances of dependence on the center and limited peasant participation, the distribution of development through WDC's in Kasama was readily distorted in favor of a stratum of local patrons.

Whatever central resources were gained by WDC's were incorporated into a patronage pattern of resource distribution in the locality. The primary beneficiaries at ward level were those who were recruited by virtue of emergent farmerhood or party office into positions of WDC leadership. WDC's, where activated, did embark on local development projects; the decentralized agricultural credit procedures were particularly valuable in stimulating WDC activity. In general, however, WDC's failed to obtain more than an uneven and truncated diffusion of benefits. WDC activation was related not only to the distance of the ward from the center but also to the prominence of patrons and privileged social strata among WDC membership. A hierarchical local social structure permitted certain groups of leaders to dominate; some of these groups—namely field-level civil servants, local party officials, and emergent farmers—have been identified. These groups managed and contained peasant demands on behalf of the center through the medium of the party-state apparatus, of which Ward Development Committees became the lowest echelon. Local leaders became, in Saul's words, "those actors—their interests and goals—who define what government actually represents" in the locality.[63]

We want our rural settlements to have a fair share of
national amenities with opportunities for meaningful
employment based on local initiative.—*President
Kenneth Kaunda, Lusaka, February 28, 1976*

When you design and build your own house the final
product rarely resembles the original idea.—
*Commissioner for Community Development, Lusaka,
June 4, 1976*

II

VILLAGE
REGROUPING

5

Two Cases of Regrouping: Nseluka and Kayambi

For the first postcolonial decade, 1964 to 1974, village regrouping was a cornerstone of the ideology of rural development in Zambia. During this period policy speeches of party-state functionaries were replete with exhortations to peasants to "come together" in order to end the economic and social decline of village life. Resettlement of scattered populations into large villages was intended to rationalize and extend the delivery of rural social services by the center. Village regrouping was also supposed to create model islands of development in which agricultural production would be stimulated on the basis of village self-reliance and through which a demonstration of rural development possibilities would be made to surrounding communities. The final and perhaps most important goal was that village regrouping was intended to stem the tide of urban migration by helping to eliminate disparities between rural and urban areas in opportunities for employment, income, and social services.[1]

Village regrouping met with only isolated success.[2] By 1975 the policy was acknowledged within government circles to have failed on a national scale.[3] It was supplemented in 1972 with Intensive Development ment Zones (IDZ), an integrated multisector program aimed at a few promising rural localities.[4] In 1975 village regrouping was shuffled still further aside in favor of a new national emphasis on rural reconstruction camps. These were administered on paramilitary lines by the Zambia National Service (ZNS) to teach agricultural and small-scale industrial skills to resettled urban youths.[5] Thus village regrouping was gradually deemphasized during Zambia's first development decade. This, taken with the impending crisis in rural development revenues in 1975, did not augur well for the future of the policy.

Little has been written about village regrouping in Zambia.[6] The omission is all the more striking in the light of extensive literature on "ujamaa" and "villagization" in neighboring Tanzania.[7] In this study the Zambian approach to rural resettlement is appraised in terms of the implementation of village regrouping policy in Kasama District between 1971 and 1975. During this period the state at the center designated two official regrouping schemes in the district, Nseluka and Kayambi. The former was widely judged to be successful, the latter, unsuccessful. The two schemes are described and compared and possible reasons for success and failure are sought out. In addition, the Nseluka and Kayambi case studies are reviewed against the background of numerous unofficial or voluntary resettlements undertaken in the early 1970's by peasants seeking development resources from the Zambian party-state.

The Zambian approach to rural resettlement raises numerous issues relevant to this study. First, the capacity of the African party-state to penetrate the rural areas and link center to locality by policy implementation can be appraised. The process by which peasants were mobilized to participate in village regrouping, and their subsequent demobilization, will be analyzed to this end. Second, the mechanics of decision-making in Zambian "one-party participatory democracy" can be examined in terms of the performance of village and ward development committees in model growth centers. An opportunity is presented to test and refine further the general proposition that statebuilding at the local level goes together with "regrouped" settlement patterns. Third, basic issues of dependence and underdevelopment in rural localities can be raised by inquiry into the impact of resettlement on agricultural production and social structure in regrouped villages. The growth and distribution of development resources within and around village regrouping schemes reveals in detail the ways in which underdevelopment unfolds in African rural localities.

NSELUKA VILLAGE REGROUPING SCHEME

Settlement at Nseluka had a brief history. The earliest occupants of the northern part of Kasama District were Mambwe, but their ethnic identity was diluted by more than a century of intermarriage with the Bemba. Unlike Kayambi, the other official regrouping site in the

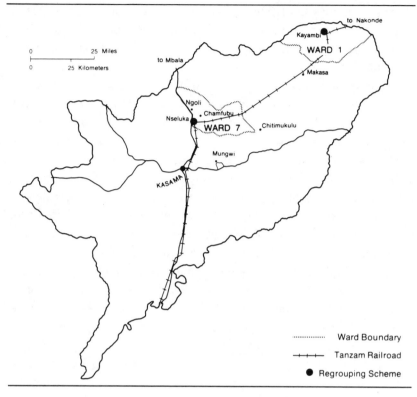

0   25 Miles

0   25 Kilometers

to Nakonde

Kayambi

WARD 1

to Mbala

Makasa

Ngoli

Nseluka   • Chamfubu

WARD 7   • Chitimukulu

Mungwi

KASAMA

··············· Ward Boundary

—+—+—+— Tanzam Railroad

● Regrouping Scheme

5   Official village regrouping schemes in Kasama District.

district, Nseluka historically was never a disputed area. It lay squarely in Lubemba, the territory of Paramount Chief Chitimukulu, and
Bemba control of the territory was unquestioned until the intervention
of the British at the end of the nineteenth century. Nseluka was located at the source of the Kalungu stream, which ran through the
middle of Chitimukulu's area; traditionally it was the domain of
subchief Mutale Mukulu. In 1955 when headman Mubanga Nseluka
brought approximately 25 followers to the present site from a site
further north, he found uninhabited virgin forest.

The site was well-chosen in that it straddled a communications junction; the main north-south road in the district linking Kasama and
Mbala joined the eastward track to Nakonde at Nseluka, providing
convenient access to the urban centers of the province (Map 5). The
location of Nseluka 34 kilometers from Kasama on an all-weather, government-maintained gravel road was a major factor in the expansion

of the regrouped village. The United Bus Company of Zambia operated
a twice-daily bus service between Kasama and Mbala. Nseluka railroad station was also the point at which the Tanzam railroad line swung
south after its southwestward journey from Dar-es-Salaam.

From Kasama, Nseluka was approached by road or rail through
gently undulating woodland. In contrast to the occasional forest cluster
of greyish pole and dagga huts which comprised the small villages en
route, Nseluka presented to the visitor an open vista of rectangular
brick houses aligned neatly around a central array of impressive community buildings. Well-swept pathways and courtyards interspersed
with village vegetable patches, confirmed the initial impression of
Nseluka as a model community. The concentration of population was
also evident, for instead of the half-deserted air of other Bemba villages, Nseluka conveyed an atmosphere of enterprise and bustle. A
group of travelers milled around the bus shelter built by the Rural
Council; a team of carpenters sawed door frames in their "factory"
under a shady tree; the sound of children's voices chanting lessons
in Bemba drifted from the open window of the primary school.

The population of Nseluka was estimated at 700, making it one of
the largest rural villages in Kasama District. The people were ethnically homogeneous; most residents described themselves as Bemba, a
few as Mambwe. One informant suggested that descendants of Aba-
yeke trader-immigrants from East Africa formed part of the village
population, though no one else at Nseluka confirmed this. In any event,
no evidence could be found of ethnic cleavage as a salient factor in local
politics at Nseluka. The influx of people to the regrouping scheme
was at first exclusively from contiguous villages. The settlers came
from six villages lying in an area of five to six kilometers in radius;
the furthest from Nseluka was Mushuka, five kilometers away. At the
outset, "all the settlers knew each other somehow; three-quarters
were related."[8] Headmen of the various village sections within Nseluka agreed that without social cohesion of kinship, regrouping would
have been difficult. Applicants were accepted from distant parts of
Kasama District, up to fifty miles from Nseluka, and notably from
Chief Chimbola's area. Other applicants, some without local relatives,
came to Nseluka to retire after a lifetime in urban wage employment
on the Copperbelt. A popular story in the village was of one such man
who was heading for his home in Mbala District but never got further

than Nseluka; he liked the place so much that he decided to settle there.

The Nseluka regrouping scheme covered an area of about half a square kilometer. In 1975 there were 161 residential housing units in the scheme, excluding temporary dwellings erected by recent arrivals and staff houses erected by government. Of the residential houses, 36 were constructed of burnt brick, 50 of kimberley brick, and the remainder of "pole and dagga." The regrouping project was divided into seven residential groups situated around a central concourse through which the two main roads ran and where most of the community social facilities were located. The commercial sector was represented by five small general stores and two bars. Two of the stores were open year round and were relatively well stocked; in addition to such common commodities as candles, matches, biscuits, sugar, and canned goods, the stores carried clothing, cooking oil and, on rare occasions, maize meal. Bottled beer was a rarity, as the bars sold only chibuku. Many Nseluka peasants took advantage of the proximity of Kasama township to travel to town for major purchases of consumption goods. Expansion of the village commercial sector was outstripped by expansion in the vicinity of the railroad station, where the volume of trade was potentially far higher.

The infrastructure of the state was relatively well developed at Nseluka in the form of government-financed or government-assisted projects. Regrouping schemes were intended, after all, as focal points for the provision of government services in the rural areas. Government buildings were prominently and centrally located. Nseluka Upper Primary School consisted of two long, low brick classrooms, one with a brand-new iron roof, surrounded by several simple teachers' houses. The school was constructed on a self-help basis; peasants burnt bricks communally and provided labor for construction. Metal door and window frames and the iron roof were provided by the Ministry of Education, as was the skilled manpower of bricklayers, carpenters, and, eventually, teachers. The first building was opened in 1968 for Grades 5 to 7, the second in 1974 for Grades 1 to 4. The second and newest building was a source of great pride to the people of Nseluka, and visitors were eagerly invited to admire its sophistication. In addition to the schooling of children, the classrooms were used for a wide range of community purposes such as WDC meetings, adult literacy classes, registration of voters, and polling in national and local elections. The school served a total of 24 villages in the vicinity of Nseluka. The majority of children were local day-scholars, but some weekly boarders walked the 18 kilometers from Chisangaponde village. At the end of 1975 the WDC proposed the burning of bricks for the construction of a large dormitory for weekly boarders. The school had more prospective students than it could accommodate, and the WDC for Ward 7 repeatedly requested the Local Council for Education to permit the doubling of enrollments. In addition to the school, the state was involved in the creation of other social facilities, like piped domestic water and a rural health center. The manner in which these projects were implemented will be described and analyzed in detail later (see below, Chapter 6).

The presence of the state was also evidenced by the number of extension workers permanently stationed at Nseluka. Four government departments were represented. The presence of the Ministry of Education was most pervasive in the persons of three primary school teachers. The Departments of Community Development and Agriculture and the Rural Council each had one extension worker. The RC pump supervisor had the limited and specific job of maintaining the village borehole, storage tank, and reticulation system of the piped water scheme. The Community Development Assistant and Agricultural Assistant had broader tasks of mobilizing peasants in Nseluka and surrounding villages for all aspects of rural reconstruction. These government officials pursued regular tours, but both complained that the absence of motor transport inhibited contact with peasants in the outlying villages.[9]

In addition to transport problems, a shortage of technical staff in rural districts often constrained the attempt of the Zambian party-state to penetrate the most remote of the rural areas. With six extension workers, Nseluka was a well endowed exception. In 1974, for example, two of the four Community Development Assistants in Kasama were stationed there. And in 1976 the complement of extension workers was due to be increased from six to seven with the transfer to Nseluka of a Medical Assistant from the Ministry of Health. In addition to field-level civil servants, ward councilors afforded peasants contact with the party-state. Within the Nseluka project lived the councilors for Wards 7 and 4, and the former kept fairly consistent office hours in the UNIP constituency office in the village. Thus Nseluka enjoyed a concentration of official personnel and service unequaled by any other rural village settlement in Kasama District. The opportunities available to peasants for contact with the party and state and for access to development benefits were therefore potentially greater than in smaller ungrouped villages. By the same token, however, the potential for privileged access and control of resources by a unified local party-state leadership was also high.

The background of Nseluka as a state-approved growth point dated back to 1964, when demonstration teams from the Department Community Development began to visit Henry Kapata village about twenty kilometers to the south. Henry Kapata was upgraded to a Community Development subcenter in 1964. In the first months of independence the Community Development Assistant at this subcenter was urged to "use the usual mode of bicycle transport . . . to acquaint [himself] with the geographical and communities set-up in the whole district . . . Concentrating on one particular area will not help in assessing the people's requirements."[10] Perhaps because of its proximity to the township and easy access to roads, Nseluka was chosen as a target for the attention of the extension worker. The first activity to be established was a women's club for teaching home crafts. On the basis of the quick response of Nseluka women, Nseluka in 1968 was upgraded to a subcenter of the Community Development Department. In that year a staff house and a community building were constructed and a Community Development Assistant took up residence in the village. Almost at once Nseluka was used by central government as a place to train prospective extension workers in community development work, so there was usually more than one government worker on the spot.

The Community Development Department in 1969 and 1970 continued to demonstrate a conviction that the village had a potential for development. An innovation of major importance was the introduction of grant-aided group housing in 1969. Ten peasants from Mubanga Nseluka were each given K20 cash for the purchase of brick molds and door frames in order to upgrade their houses. A group housing project committee was established from among the participants and included the sons of headman Mubanga Nseluka. The chairman of the committee was the Community Development Assistant. The molding of bricks and the further development of village social facilities were hindered in 1969 by the drying up of the well that had been sunk only one year previously.[11]

The turning point in the establishment of the village came in 1970 with the designation of Nseluka by the District Development Committee as one of the two official centers in Kasama District for "intensive village regrouping." Government experts on soils, water, and agriculture determined the site to be suitable for expansion and Nseluka thus became eligible for increased state expenditure as a rural social service center. The house construction program was expanded. In 1970 forty grants were approved for peasants from Mubanga Nseluka, Fundiboma, Songa, Kutunkana, and Mushuka villages who were willing to build houses at the Nseluka site.[12] At this time houses were built of kimberley brick rather than burnt brick, and thatch was exclusively used as a roofing material. But the square design and carpentered fittings of the houses were based on standardized plans provided by the Community Development Department. The Department's building supervisor marked out the foundations and assisted in the laying of bricks at the corners of the houses. The houses were arranged in straight lines. Most of the houses built in 1970 were located separately on the other side of the main road from Mubanga Nseluka in the new Fundiboma and Paul Nseluka sections of the scheme. These two sections, which received 25 of the 40 original housing grants, were at the time of research the most populous and best serviced on the scheme. The distribution of housing grants proceeded without mishap, and "everyone was happy about it."[13] The only exception was the disappearance of K80 of the K260 allocated in housing grants in the Fundiboma section of the village. An investigation was conducted by the Community Development Assistant, but no record of a conclusive finding exists. The money must ultimately have been traced, however, because by the end of 1970 forty new houses had been erected.[14]

The year 1971 was marked by a call to peasants from President Kaunda for the burning of bricks, a central policy directive aimed at a general upgrading of rural housing standards. In April 1971 four Nseluka peasants began brick-burning with the modest output of 300 bricks per person. By May fifteen people had joined in: "since intensive village regrouping is the news of the day, the people in Nseluka, Fundiboma and Kasosomena do not want to remain behind."[15] Not all brick burners were able to accumulate the 2500 bricks required to build a house, and by the end of 1971 only eight had been completed. In 1972 eleven burnt-brick houses were put up and nine and eight in 1974 and 1975 respectively.

Peasants and party-state officials at Nseluka agreed that the regrouping experiment succeeded and pointed to the availability of urban-style housing and social facilities as evidence. Local officials used Nseluka as a showpiece to impress visitors from the center with rural development in the district. The visitor's book at the Community Development subcenter contained an accolade of congratulation from District Governors, Cabinet Ministers, and Members of the Central Committee. Brief national recognition was accorded to the village by President Kaunda, who reported rosily on Nseluka after a tour of the Northern Province:

Here we see a Ward Development Committee and a Village Development committee [sic] coming together and planning for the development of the people, by the people and for the people. They have got burnt brick houses. In other words they have responded to my call . . . they have built a dispensary, they have built a village community hall for women . . . It is fantastic to see this and it is not only in Kasama District but it is being repeated everywhere in the country.[16]

KAYAMBI VILLAGE REGROUPING SCHEME

Kayambi was located in the most peripheral region of Kasama District, Ward 1, over 160 kilometers from the district capital (Map 5). Local party officials and White Father missionaries, among others, expressed the view that Kayambi was very isolated. The center for this locality was not Kasama township at all, but more proximate townships in other districts. Peasants regarded a trip to town as a trip to Mbala or Nakonde. Indeed, there were senses in which Kayambi was not really a part of Kasama District: Ward 1 fell into Kasama District for local government purposes but into Mbala District for postal purposes and Isoka District for Parliamentary electoral purposes. Labor migrants from Kayambi in the first half of the century were as likely to go to Tanzania to seek work as they were to go to the Copperbelt.

Nor was Kayambi easily accessible. Until the opening of the northern Zambian section of the Tanzam railroad in early 1975, the sole link to Kasama was a single-lane unpaved track. This road was first opened by the British during the First World War as a passage for troops and supply wagons in the East African campaign. During field work I found the road impassable in the rainy season except to vehicles with four-wheel drive. There was no bus service. The geographical isolation of Kayambi compared with Nseluka in part accounted for the different paths of development that occurred at each place.

Two other factors distinguished Kayambi from Nseluka: first, the multi-ethnic composition of the people, and second, the permanency of settlement, long before the regrouping policy was introduced. Kayambi was a border region even under the traditional Bemba state and in 1975 continued to abut the territory of the Mambwe Paramount Chief Nsokolo. The region had a rich history of ethnic interaction and conflict. Until 1800 the Mambwe occupied land to within ten miles north of the Bemba capital but were subject to little more than occasional cattle raids. In the early nineteenth century the sons of Chitimukulu took the title Makasa and annexed the preserve of the southern Mambwe chief Mpande II. Those Mambwe who remained in the area after conquest did not readily lose their ethnic identity. Roberts notes that "the patrilineal and semi-pastoral Mambwe and Namwanga differ far more from the Bemba than do the Bisa and other peoples to the south and west who were also conquered by the Bemba. They were thus less easily assimilated into a uniform pattern of Bemba authority and custom. In part of Mpanda [i.e., around Kayambi] there remain to this day distinct non-Bemba villages under Makasa."[17]

Chief Makasa established his capital on the site that over a century later became the Kayambi regrouping scheme. The village, known as Mipini, was the target of Catholic White Fathers in their endeavor to penetrate Bemba territory at the end of the nineteenth century.[18] Missionaries were at first unable to obtain permission to establish a mission in Mpanda province of Lubemba because of the opposition of Paramount Chief Chitimukulu Sampa Kapalakasha. The determination of the missionaries to prohibit slave-trading directly threatened the economic base of slave-trading Bemba chiefs. Nevertheless Makasa was willing to tolerate the presence of missionaries in his area, partly because of the material benefits he hoped to secure, and partly in order to strengthen his position against a relatively weak Chitimukulu. Thus Makasa agreed to the building of the first mission within the borders of Bemba country, on land originally conquered from the Mambwe. On July 23, 1895, Father Dupont founded Kayambi mission.

Not wishing to live among the Europeans and their Mambwe wards, Makasa moved his capital to the south. Makasa's village was subsequently shifted five times before resting at its present location on the Mifunsu stream in Ward 2. As a powerful chief Makasa Mukuka was able to attract most of his followers away from Kayambi, though some did elect to remain behind. According to one aged informant, "Makasa did not care about those who stayed with the missionaries"; once the objections of the chief were withdrawn, peasants converged on Kayambi.[19] Among the Bemba settlers were large numbers of Mambwe who, as freed slaves and Catholic converts, were encouraged to return to their traditional lands. Land ceded back to the Mambwe by Makasa was the site of most resettlement.[20] Peaceful coexistence between Bemba and Mambwe was negotiated, partly by intermarriage and partly by the establishment of discrete villages that maintained a predominant ethnic identity. The establishment of a mission station and the imposition of colonial order served to stabilize a multi-ethnic settlement pattern in the Kayambi area.

There seem to have been two main motives behind the influx of peasants to Kayambi. For the Mambwe in particular, the mission offered protection from incessant conflict with stronger peoples. The mission fence provided a safeguard for Mambwe cattle and crops, first against Bemba raiders and later against German invaders during the First World War. A second motive which in time became increasingly important was the access to development resources which proximity to the mission afforded. The White Fathers introduced Western methods of education, health care, and water supply, all of which proved attractive to peasants. According to Mpashi, "Kayambi became so famous that people from as far as Changala, about forty miles away were coming to be cured by the medicine of the White Fathers."[21] Missions formed the nuclei of large permanent settlements in other parts of the district at Rosa, Mulobola, and Chilubula. Gouldsberry and Sheane noted in 1911 that "square or rectangular houses are found near [mission and government] stations and where East Coast influence has made itself felt."[22] A precedent was established that large settlements emerged as a response to the provision by a central agency of rural social services. Kayambi was the nucleus of a sizable permanent settlement almost 75 years before such settlement began at Nseluka.

The Kayambi village regrouping scheme was approachable in 1975 by road or rail through some of the hilliest and most heavily forested terrain in Kasama District. Kayambi lay on one of a series of ridges that formed the western boundary of the vast and swampy Luchewe flood plain. A tributary of the upper Luchewe River flowed through Kayambi and provided the regrouped village with its water supply. The area surrounding Kayambi was not heavily populated; only 2660 lived in the Kayambi polling district;[23] with few exceptions, villages clustered on high ground. The most striking aspect of Kayambi which set it apart from surrounding villages was the presence of the mission station. The mission buildings, most of which were constructed in the early twentieth century, were designed in the Mediterranean style of North African Catholic stations, with whitewashed walls and orange clay tiles. The buildings stood symbolically apart from the rest of the regrouped village and were separated by a road and a river. The rectory was surrounded by high walls. Parts of the village had the formal layout of Nseluka, with carefully aligned and well constructed houses, notably in the vicinity of the primary school and the staff houses of the Departments of Education and Agriculture. Other parts of the village, near the mission and further from the school, retained the circular settlement pattern and mixed housing styles of older villages. Unlike Nseluka, Kayambi did not impress the visitor with its economic and social vibrancy. There was little evidence of ongoing house construction or of productive backyard vegetable gardens. Fewer community self-help projects occupied pride of place in the village layout. Small groups of people sat conversing in the shade; beer sales boomed; thin chickens pecked in the dust.

The estimated population of the regrouping scheme at Kayambi in 1975 was 450.[24] The population was comprised of long-time residents. Peasants were not attracted from outlying villages to a new site as at Nseluka, but a large settled target population for regrouping already existed in discrete but adjacent villages around Kayambi mission. The Community Development Department estimated that eleven villages were involved in the Kayambi regrouping exercise.[25] This was a somewhat generous estimate because although as many as eleven villages were recruited for regrouping, as few as three actually moved site, built approved houses, or attained access to piped water. Most regrouping activity occurred to the immediate north of the mission and covered the village sections now known as Kaminsa and Kaputa. Before 1964 both villages had moved from more distant sites in order to be close to the mission. Kaminsa was a well established village at the beginning of the regrouping exercise, whereas settlers were still drifting into Kaputa in the early and mid-1970's. As at Nseluka, there were few new settlers; according to one informant, "people were known to us; they just came from the old village."[26]

In 1975 several houses were under construction. If regrouping at Kayambi was taken to be limited to the area where approved house construction occurred, Kayambi regrouping center was far smaller than Nseluka. Kaminsa and Kaputa villages scarcely covered one eighth of a square kilometer. Outlying villages, originally intended for regrouping, remained scattered on their original sites as far as Gregorio, almost fifteen kilometers distant. There were far fewer self-help grant-aided houses at Kayambi (29 in all) than at Nseluka, which had 86. None was burnt brick; all were kimberley.

As with Nseluka, the infrastructure of the state was relatively well developed at Kayambi. Kayambi Upper Primary School formed a natural locus for community activity, situated as it was on a large, sloping, open space between the housing project and the mission complex. The school consisted of an old thatched classroom block surviving from the pre-independence mission school, with two burnt-brick, iron-roofed classroom blocks. Grades 5 to 7 were introduced in 1967, far earlier than at Nseluka. The school served a large catchment area and was annually overenrolled to the tune of 400 children. The need for a doubling of enrollment capacity at the primary school was a major political issue among Kayambi peasants, as it was at Nseluka. There were three schoolteachers permanently stationed at the regrouping scheme, and the head teacher took a keen interest in community affairs. The state was also represented by an Agricultural Assistant, who had a house in the village and two depots nearby, and by a Rural Council pump supervisor for the piped water project. The total number of extension workers at Kayambi was five, one less than Nseluka. A significant difference between the two regrouping centers with regard to state penetration was that Kayambi never had a Community Development Assistant. The absence of coordinating and mobilizing cadres to devote time and effort to village regrouping goes part way in explaining the relative failure of Kayambi regrouping.

Another significant difference between Kayambi and Nseluka was the impact of the Kayambi mission in providing a range of social services comparable to those of the state at Nseluka. After 1966 the Kayambi hospital was officially a mission-aided government hospital, but for all practical purposes, staffing and operation were still in the hands of the missionaries. The hospital was the largest and best-equipped rural hospital facility in the district and continued to attract patients from most northern and western parts of Kasama. Its water supply was used by peasants from Illondola and other proximate villages. The White Sisters also offered home-craft training to the women of Kayambi, and the White Fathers instituted a credit union[27] and a service to local consumers for the grinding of maize.[28] In short, the mission provided many essential services, but in doing so tended to preempt and discourage state intervention and self-help development initiatives.

Private commercial activity was developed at Kayambi to a slightly greater extent than at Nseluka, perhaps because Kayambi peasants were without ready access to town. Many of the dozen stores in the vicinity sprang up in response to the construction of the railroad, and some were likely to close with the exodus of temporary railroad workers. The isolated geographical position of Kayambi was exploited by petty traders who overcharged for luxuries and staples alike.[29] Kayambi had neither chibuku nor bottled beer pubs, because the roads to Kayambi were too treacherous for the trucks of the state brewery to negotiate.

Kayambi had a shorter and less salubrious history than Nseluka as a state-approved growth point. It was never designated as a Community Development subcenter. The first signal that Kayambi was to become a diffusion point for state development resources came with the award in 1968 of five K20 self-help housing grants to village residents. There was an administrative delay of more than a year; at the end of 1969 the group housing committee was still awaiting the processing of grants.[30] In August 1969 top party officials, namely the DG's of Kasama and Isoka and the Chairmen of the Kasama Rural and Township Councils, visited Kayambi as part of a tour to promote village regrouping. The response from peasants was favorable, and in

1970, after a survey of the economic potential of the area, the Kasama DDC declared Kayambi as one of its two official regrouping sites.

Official designation brought development resources in the form of funding for domestic water supply and self-help housing. A well was sunk at Kaminsa village in 1971, but within a year it ran dry. The well was superseded by a borehole and reticulation system, installed by the Water Affairs Department at a capital outlay of K10,000. The site chosen by officials of the Water Affairs Department for the water system was at the top of the hill above the school. Although this site was technically the most suitable in terms of supplying water, it was not the most popular with local residents. The VPC's and WDC's were not consulted, but had they been, a different locus for social services, and thus the regrouping scheme as a whole, would probably have been selected. As it happened, twenty standpipes were provided, but to Kaminsa and Kaputa villages only. The Community Development Department followed the lead of the Water Affairs Department and marked out housing lines at Kaminsa-Kaputa. Housing grants were raised to K40; by the end of 1971, fourteen kimberley brick houses were completed and fifteen more were under construction. All grant-in-aid house construction—that is, construction with official state blessing—took place at Kaminsa and Kaputa villages at the location of the piped water system. No other site was formally sanctioned by the party-state for regrouping activity.

And there's the rub. Prospective settlers from villages in the Kayambi catchment area were unwilling to move their families and build houses at the officially demarcated site at Kaminsa-Kaputa. Peasants from Illondola, Londe Musendamene, Chale, Chipunsa, and other villages elected to forego access to development resources and remain behind. Moreover, despite policy directives on permanent housing, new settlers at Kaminsa-Kaputa refused to undertake the arduous communal work of brick burning. The group-housing committee ceased to function after the initial selection of housing-loan recipients, and by the end of 1971 only three members were still at Kayambi. As a result of these problems in gaining peasant support for regrouping, the state announced that housing grants would be curtailed at Kayambi after 1971. Recognition of Kayambi as an official regrouping center was also withdrawn by the District Development Committee. With it went central capital resources. Only two years after Kayambi had been

TABLE 21. Kasama District, Development Characteristics of Official
Village Regrouping Schemes, 1975

Characteristic	Nseluka	Kayambi
Distance from district capital	34 kms.	160 kms.
Date of first settlement	1955	1890's
Population	700	450
Area (of planned housing)	½ sq. km.	⅛ sq. km.
Number of villages regrouped	6	3
Grant-in-aid housing units	86	29
(Burnt brick)	(36)	(0)
(Kimberley brick)	(50)	(29)
Commercial outlets	7	12
Self-help schools	1	1
Self-help clinics	1	0
Self-help church	1	0
Government water schemes	1 (K16,000)	1 (K10,000)
Government extension worker	6	5
Central grants-in-aid 1975	K1700	—

selected as a diffusion point and in the year that it first became eligible
for K1000 in housing grants, Kayambi was officially dead. The funds
and building materials that would have permitted a large-scale transformation of village housing conditions at Kayambi were transferred
to Nseluka and other group housing schemes.[31]

REGROUPING AND VILLAGE IDENTITY

Nseluka was a larger village than Kayambi, located closer to the
district capital and without a long history of permanent settlement
(Table 21). Each village was designated an official regrouping scheme
in 1970 and initially awarded equal amounts of development resources
by the center in the form of funding and extension personnel. Over
the next five years, however, Nseluka outshone Kayambi in terms of
the influx of settlers and the construction of permanent burnt-brick
houses. Though Kayambi peasants managed to build a self-help school
during this period, Nseluka peasants built a school, a clinic, and a
church. From 1972 to 1975 Nseluka was the only scheme of the two to
receive development resources for village regrouping from the center.

Factors that account for the divergent development paths of the two regrouping schemes will be examined in this and the next chapter.

The explanation provided by the Department of Community Development for the failure of the Kayambi experiment was that applicants for housing grants left the regrouping center to seek work on the Tanzam railroad.[32] Construction began on the Kasama portion of the line and portions north in 1972. Peasants from all parts of Kasama District migrated to railroad camps in search of wage employment, and Kayambi peasants were no exception. The extent to which labor migration disrupted regrouping at Kayambi was, however, overestimated in official reports. At Kaminsa, where most regrouping activity was centered, a village elder could recall only four young men who had left in search of work on Tanzam. More peasants seem to have left for railroad work from Nseluka than from Kayambi, and regrouping was not disrupted there. In any event, by 1974 or 1975 those who did leave Kayambi had returned after short contracts on the railroad; few found permanent jobs.

Peasants cited other reasons for the demise of regrouping. Everyone agreed, from the Ward Councilor down, that social conflict was at the root of the Kayambi problem: "people failed to work together."[33] This stood in stark contrast to the extensive application of self-help labor to community projects at Nseluka. The causes and dimensions of conflict at Kayambi were difficult to ascertain, for peasants were reluctant to discuss the issues directly. My first notion, that conflict between Kayambi villages was ethnically based, could not be confirmed. Ethnic differences between Bemba and Mambwe were not obliterated at Kayambi by interaction and intermarriage, but they were reduced to the point where they were not of key political relevance. Mambwe people predominated in such mission programs as home-craft training classes, but this seemed to be more a cause of central concern than of local resentment.[34] Certain headmen were known as Mambwe headmen, including the headman at Kaputa, but no peasants interviewed cited "tribe" as a reason to resist joining a particular village.[35] In terms of the salience of ethnicity to local political conflicts, Kayambi was indistinguishable from ethnically homogeneous Nseluka.

The salient factor in noncooperation at Kayambi was not ethnic identity but *village identity*, by which is meant a sense of belonging to a particular residential community and of owing political allegiance to a particular headman. President Kaunda recognized its importance when he declared that although the party-state could not effectively combat "hunger, poverty, ignorance and disease without some re-grouping of our villages, I am not proposing that villages should lose their identities completely."[36] The headman of Illondola village put it differently: "this is our place; most of these people were born here and most of their fathers were born here; our ancestors have died here; why should we be willing to leave this place?"[37] Like most villages in the Kayambi vicinity, Illondola had not moved from its present location alongside the mission since its establishment more than 75 years before. There was a sense of natural community that headman and villagers alike were unwilling to violate by amalgamation with strangers. The headman sought to avoid a disintegration of village identity with which his own status was inextricably bound: "why should Illondola village be prepared to become Illondola compound [i.e. within a larger settlement]?"[38] There was a consensus at Illondola that the headman of Kaminsa, in whose village the party-state ex-pected new houses to be built, was a "lazy man who was not suitable to be headman." The original headman had died, and his widow had taken a new husband who was not deemed a worthy successor. In the opinion of one peasant, "it is a weak headman who leaves his village dirty." For this reason, resettlement occurred on only a small scale at Kayambi. The few new settlers at Kaminsa-Kaputa originated not from the government target area—that is, the large, old sedentary vil-lages around Kayambi mission, but from small, distant, shifting vil-lages to the east.

Village identity at Kayambi seems to have been the standard for distinguishing ally from stranger. Conflicts that emerged over re-grouping between peasants from different villages at Kayambi readily escalated into witchcraft disputes. Conventional wisdom had it that "big villages breed witchcraft" and "around here there is fear of each other."[39] Some peasants at Illondola conceded that fear of witchcraft was uppermost in their decision not to move. Missionaries and local party officials agreed that a major influence on the paucity of local political organization at Kayambi was fear by aspiring leaders of be-coming susceptible to witchcraft attacks. The Ward Councilor claimed that when he proposed regrouping, "at first they [his constituents] tried to witch me but now that I have brought development they believe me." For many months of 1974 a well known diviner from the Copperbelt was plying his trade in the area, and he found much of his business in the villages around Kayambi, notably Pupwe and Tambatamba. Information on actual cases was hard to come by because informants tended to be secretive. Nevertheless, Kayambi had a long history of witchcraft, and suspicions were engendered among local people that hindered the amalgamation of villages. Not only between villages, but within villages, people were unwilling to work together. For instance, the main reason behind the failure of Kaminsa-Kaputa peasants to convert from kimberley to burnt brick techniques was the difficulty of organizing communal work parties. Brick-burning required a large contribution of labor in gathering and chopping wood for the kilns. Settlers were unwilling to join hands on this kind of work, in the opinion of nearly every local leader, because of mutual suspicion.

From 1972 onward, after the party-state withdrew resources from Kayambi, the settlement continued to expand, though at a slower rate than before. Settlers from outlying villages, attracted by existing social services, still drifted into Kaminsa and Kaputa. Illondola village went its own way under an active headman and in 1975 had more kimberley brick houses than the official regrouping site.

In no sense, however, did village regrouping at Kayambi create a socially cohesive community with promising growth prospects on the lines of Nseluka. A comparison of the patterns of settlement at the two regrouping schemes holds part of the answer. The Kayambi villages did not coexist and integrate as readily as Nseluka villages because of the entrenchment of village identity. At Kayambi, peasants could trace permanent and discrete village settlement back to the 1890's, when the mission was founded. At Nseluka, the first settlement occurred at the site in 1955, and most settlements occurred over a decade later. Regrouping was easier where boundaries between villages were recent creations and where the influx of new settlers created fluid boundaries. A comparison of settlement patterns at Kayambi and Nseluka suggests that only at new sites and with new settlers was village regrouping a viable proposition.

The importance of village identity at Kayambi was connected with the survival of traditional leaders and the expression of their political interests. As will be shown in the next chapter, conflict between the political interests of traditional leaders and party-state leaders was not resolved at Kayambi, whereas at Nseluka it was resolved decisively in favor of the latter. The existence of a powerful front of party-state leaders at Nseluka helped to subordinate village identity to the identity of the regrouping scheme as a whole. It is to the relationships between political organization, social structure, and economic innovation at regrouped villages that this study now turns.

6

Village Regrouping: A Policy in Practice

Problems with the regrouping of villages could be anticipated from the history of center-locality relations in Zambia. Numerous fruitless attempts had been made by the colonial government to impose a uniform settlement pattern on the rural areas of Northern Rhodesia (Table 22). The thrust of the colonial approach was to reverse the fragmentation of large villages for reasons of administrative convenience, notably the collection of taxes and recruitment of labor for the mines. Only in the final years of colonial rule was attention paid to issues of village development. For example, development resources were distributed through the Northern Province Development Commission, established in 1957 in an attempt to quell the stirrings of African nationalism in Kasama and other districts in the north. The "rural township" of Mungwi in Kasama, now the headquarters of the Kasama Rural Council, was the largest scheme in this program. Kay has observed that settlements established for purposes of administrative control seldom become communities in the sense of being socially cohesive or economically self-sufficient. Indeed, he described Mungwi as no more than "outlier of Kasama [township]" because of the predominance of administrative activities over economically productive activities pursued there.[1] I suggest that Kay's observations are relevant not only to colonial but to postcolonial resettlement measures in Zambia.

Colonial experience also showed that the growth of large rural settlements could not be legislated from above. For the mass movement of people to take hold on a national scale and for development to result, the allegiance of peasants was required. Village regrouping could not succeed if it remained merely a government program; it had also to be a spontaneous grassroots movement. The local-level apparatus

TABLE 22.   Northern Rhodesia, Colonial Village Regrouping Policies, 1906–1964

Policy Introduced		Policy Abandoned
1906	BSAC amalgamation instructions	1915
1930	ten-taxpayer rule	1937[1]
1945	parish system	1964
1957	rural townships	1964

[1] The ten-taxpayer rule was not formally abolished until 1945, but administrators ceased to enforce it with vigor almost a decade earlier.

of the party-state could be deployed to mobilize peasant support—to prod a spontaneous movement into being through political education. This was attempted at Nseluka, Kayambi, and other rural locations in Kasama District from the late 1960's onward. All institutions in the local development front—namely, the party, the administration, and the traditional leadership—were drafted into a program to convince peasants that a change in rural settlement patterns was essential.

Peasants in Kasama responded by showing an initial recognition of the development potential inherent in village regrouping. In many cases a promise of improved social services and employment opportunities was sufficient to stimulate a commitment to resettle. Some regrouping schemes were even oversubscribed with applicants for housing grants. Ultimately, however, the state was unable to live up to promises hastily made. Social services at regrouping schemes were not forthcoming on the scale expected by peasants. Moreover, services that were provided went to local leaders first. Finally, village regrouping was not accompanied by the economic transformation necessary to provide employment and raise rural incomes on a permanent basis. As a consequence, mass support for village regrouping was, in all but a few cases, ultimately withdrawn. Peasants became demobilized. Mass mobilization for permanent resettlement proved to be a long-term logistical endeavor, the resources and organization for which the Zambian party-state possessed in only a few rural localities. The party-state was able to capture but not to sustain the interest of peasants in village regrouping.

PEASANT MOBILIZATION FOR VILLAGE REGROUPING

Responsibility for spreading the word about village regrouping was assigned at the local level primarily to cadres of UNIP. In parts of Kasama where UNIP organization was strong, they did an enthusiastic, even over-enthusiastic, job. Tours were undertaken by DG's in 1969 to familiarize peasants with the regrouping program and to organize party constituency and branch officials to sustain the mobilization effort. At the Rural Council, in council meetings, and in party caucuses, councilors were urged to disseminate information on resettlement through the party constituency and branch apparatus. Councilors announced the new program with a flourish: in one ward the councilor "promised everyone a brick house with running water" and in another "the constituency secretary said that the government would soon employ everyone in building towns in the bush."[2] In 1969 the DG of Kasama went on record that "if people agreed to regroup, they would find it possible to have schools, clinics and markets provided by the government."[3] In 1972 the DG was reported in the national press as publicizing the difficulties of "building a road or a school where there are very few people" and guaranteeing to people in Wards 9 and 10 that "development will be easy if villages regroup and form Village Productivity Committees."[4]

In all cases the idea of village regrouping seems to have been sold to peasants on the basis of pledges of material advantage. Local-level party leaders throughout the district favored regrouping for the same reason they favored other government programs: they regarded them as an opportunity to make patronage rewards. In addition, where party organization was sufficiently strong, coercive tactics were authorized to ensure peasant compliance. The youth wing of the party circulated in some villages with their own heavy-handed interpretation of the regrouping call. At Nseluka an elderly family confessed that they did not know why they had resettled, but they had feared repercussions from UNIP if they did not.[5] Sometimes all that was required was a firm instruction from the UNIP Region; a letter addressed to one headman stated that "we have received the words that you tell your people not to go to regrouping because of the river crossing but making policy does not concern you; go to your friends who have regrouped; only the boatman should stay behind to do his job."[6] For the most part, however, regrouping did not require pressure or coercion, as peasants were willing to move voluntarily on the basis of expected benefits from development. In any event, the party was not organizationally equipped to exert force on a wide scale.

The planning of regrouped villages was supposed to be a participatory affair with a high degree of peasant involvement. The official position was that "the process [of planning] is long and involved but no plan which lacks the people's support can ever stand . . . Local leaders must be allowed to receive the credit and the blame. Field officers must not appear to supervise. In this way projects will be popularly appreciated."[7] The new village settlements were intended to be not government townships but "symbols of the degree of local development and resourcefulness." The planning procedure was designed to combine planning from above with planning from below through WDC's and VPC's.[8] But the actual process of planning village regrouping in Kasama neglected local opinion in favor of decisions made by functionaries of the party-state. Consultation with peasants consisted solely of seminars conducted late in the day by DG's; these meetings were dominated almost exclusively by policy speeches and were held at three villages previously selected for regrouping and nowhere else.[9] Peasants thus had little voice in the location of regrouping centers. The decision on location was pushed through hurriedly in the Rural Council at the same meeting where the policy was announced to councilors for the first time, thereby precluding councilor contact with constituents. The lowest level at which any consultation on the location of regrouping schemes took place was therefore at the Rural Council; VPC's and WDC's were excluded. In the bargaining about location among councilors, the influence of powerful party figures was felt. This was reinforced by pressure brought to bear by the UNIP Regional Office on the Community Development Department both in the DDC and by letter; the Community Development Department was instructed by UNIP to "start working on these [regrouping] places very soon."[10]

Apart from location, other planning decisions about regrouping were kept from popular control. The principal local planning body in Kasama was a regrouping subcommittee of the DDC, consisting of district officers of the party and state agencies.[11] Their task was to "investigate, survey and plan any village regrouping site after it had been chosen by the villagers and councillor of the ward." The only direct contact between these planners and peasants was one tour of regrouping sites conducted in 1971. The DDC subcommittee interpreted planning as a technical task and concentrated purely on questions of the physical resource base of the proposed sites. The sole conclusion drawn about human resources was that "people did not appear to like village regrouping" and thereafter the subcommittee deemed it unnecessary to reconsult the people or adapt its plans accordingly.[12]

Government officials, as well as dominating the planning process, joined the mobilization drive. Again, the approach of local bureaucrats was to give orders rather than to engender participation. The District Agricultural Officer, on tour with the DG, warned that extension services, particularly fertilizer supplies, would not reach people unless they lived together. The Credit Officer of the Credit Organization of Zambia declared that he would grant credit only to villagers who were living and working in one place. Bureaucrats were less generous in their promises than local UNIP officials, however, for upon the shoulders of the former fell much of the burden of implementation.

Upon Community Development Assistants (CDA's) in particular fell the work of channeling into constructive activity the aroused energies of new settlers. Of all the districts in the Northern Province, Kasama and Mbala were the best serviced with a Community Development staff. Nevertheless, eight extension workers were too small a force to reach a scattered population in a large district, especially when four were permanently stationed in the urban centers of Kasama and Mungwi. Since the administration was understaffed with experienced personnel at the village level, many regrouping exercises began with enthusiasm but soon ran into problems. Only one building organizer was available to the Community Development Department to supervise construction at all group housing and village regrouping schemes in the district. A CDA felt compelled to write his superior in Kasama: "on the housing scheme it will be a good thing if one day you send a building organizer to come and work with me so that the problems the participants are facing can be solved in practice rather than in theory."[13] From Nseluka the CDA reported that he had been "beaten to death because of the [non-arrival of] doors meant for village regrouping purposes. You are asked to come and find out what went wrong for yourself. I can't say much. I am longing for your presence."[14] Administrative officials often had to bear the brunt of criticism when village regrouping failed to live up to the expectations of peasants. Relations between party and government in Kasama were sorely strained by the excessive zeal of local party cadres on the regrouping issue. A senior district official from one government department offered the opinion that "the party destroyed our only chance at regrouping because now the people have no reason to trust us."[15]

Some traditional leaders supplemented the party-state mobilization drive by endorsing village regrouping. Chief Nkolemfumu of Kasama made a two-week tour of his area to introduce the idea to his followers, and received for his efforts commendation from the Regional UNIP Office.[16] Chief Munkonge made village regrouping a platform from which to reassert traditional power in the western part of Kasama District. As appointed councilors, Munkonge and Nkolemfumu were able to push the Rural Council for the allocation of regrouping resources to their home areas. Both directly lobbied the District Community Development Officer.[17] The UNIP Region instructed that "encouragement [to regroup] must only be done in conjunction with constituency officials"[18] but often chiefs acted alone, perceiving concentrated settlements as a means of boosting their own following at the expense of local party leaders. Headmen were more reluctant to join the mobilization drive, since regrouping involved the relocation of villages and the merging of members into larger communities, a process in which headmen stood to lose authority. One headman felt that he would no longer be respected in a regrouped village; another offered the view that "there is only room for one big man in each village."[19] In general the support that the party-state enjoyed from traditional leaders in Kasama was from chiefs rather than headmen. Historically, chiefs enjoyed a prerogative of allocating settlements in their own areas, and during mobilization for regrouping reasserted their interest in this aspect of rural life.

All categories of local leadership were enjoined to take part in the regrouping drive as a coordinated "development front," but the activeness of leaders from state, party, and traditional sectors varied from one part of the district to another. This in turn affected the extent of peasant mobilization and the success of regrouping. In places where all categories of leadership favored regrouping, a strong positive response to the policy was evoked from peasants. In places where, say, chiefs and headmen were unwilling to sanction resettlement, there was little that the party-state could do to induce the peasants to move. Or if the state ministries were unable to maintain sufficient technical advice and building materials for village reconstruction, mobilized peasant energies soon dissipated. A comparison of the mix of active leadership groups at Nseluka and Kayambi illustrates the importance of a unified development front when peasant mobilization was the goal. At Nseluka there was a unified front; at Kayambi there was not.

At Nseluka, party, government, and traditional leaders were able from the outset of the scheme to establish a complementary working relationship. The CDA, who was perhaps the single most influential leader of regrouping at Nseluka, stressed that the first step in organizing for any development project was contact with the party officials and headmen of the locality: "if the party works against you you have had it."[20] The Community Development Department recommended close cooperation with UNIP as an appropriate tactic for government field workers in a single-party state. Unlike most of his colleagues in the Community Development Department, the Nseluka CDA was well prepared for close cooperation with the party, having himself been a party constituency chairman in Chinsali in the days of the nationalist struggle.[21] Early suspicions of this CDA as a "big talker from government" and an "outsider" were allayed when the Ward Councilor introduced the newcomer around the villages in the ward. The councilor, for his part, had close ties with the UNIP Region and with government departments in the district. He had involved himself with such party-state programs as fertilizer delivery and registration of voters. The two key local leaders at Nseluka were thus well suited to work together and were active in a village-to-village campaign to promote regrouping. Indeed, they occasionally substituted for one another. In 1974 the CDA was elected secretary of the Ward 7 WDC. Moreover, for three months in 1975 he acted as the councilor of the ward for all practical purposes, while the councilor went to train in the Zambia National Service. Ultimately the relationship between the CDA and councilor soured and the former was transferred to another regrouping center in Chinsali in late 1975. But, especially in early days, united leadership boosted the Nseluka regrouping drive.

The CDA estimated that 85 percent of the peasants in the Nseluka catchment area were mobilized to resettle. Of the remaining 15 percent, most were young men on individual farms, and even they "changed their minds one by one."[22] One approach adopted by the CDA-councilor team was to put regrouping appeals directly to women; as the hewers of wood and drawers of water they stood to benefit first from improved social facilities like piped water. Nseluka women often urged doubtful menfolk to join the scheme. An important victory in the struggle to win over the people of Nseluka was achieved when sub-chief Mutale Mukulu agreed to build his home at the new site. As the senior traditional leader in the immediate area, he was able to bring twenty families to his own section of the Nseluka scheme and to influence many others in favor of resettlement. The early fulfillment of promises about providing social facilities at the regrouping site was all that was required to ensure a regular inflow of settlers.

By contrast to the united development front at Nseluka, the Kayambi experiment suffered throughout from division and conflict between local leadership groups. The only leader wholeheartedly committed to regrouping was the UNIP constituency secretary, who was also the councilor for Ward 1. The branch and constituency apparatus of the party was defunct; hence the burden of spreading the word about party-state policy on regrouping fell solely upon the ward councilor, once the DG's touring team had departed. This official did take his task seriously, because his mobilization efforts were remembered in villages throughout the Kayambi area. He organized a UNIP meeting to which he brought the KRC chairman (his political ally) and "others from Mungwi" to discuss regrouping. This meeting seems, however, to have reinforced the idea among Kayambi peasants that the party was a central, not a local, institution and that village regrouping was a central initiative.

Not only were party cadres poorly organized, but the councilor did not enjoy the cooperation of a Community Development Assistant, as his counterpart at Nseluka had done. No CDA was ever posted to Kayambi. The only state official who contributed was the head teacher of the primary school, who encouraged his pupils to convey the advantages of regrouping to their parents. On other issues the head-teacher was openly opposed to the councilor.

In addition, relations between the party and traditional leaders were poor. The councilor had a low opinion of the competence of headmen and held them responsible for perpetuating a climate of beliefs at Kayambi in which witchcraft thrived. Headmen were successful in holding on to a large measure of authority and were drawn into repeated clashes with the party. One incident, remembered with bitterness, involved a public meeting conducted by a senior party official, in which headmen and village elders were required to stand up "like school children" and explain why they hadn't complied with a government directive for each of them to grow one hectare of maize. Certain headmen therefore used the regrouping issue as an opportunity for retaliation by discouraging followers from compliance with party-state policy. Chief Makasa also withheld support for the Kayambi scheme, except when party-state officials from the center were present. He did publicly encourage peasants from Kashishi village to join Kaminsa-Kaputa at Kayambi but did not move to discipline them when they later refused. Peasants at Kashishi even went so far as to claim that Makasa had instructed them not to move.[23] Makasa also pressured the councilor from his area, who was chairman of the Rural Council, to provide as much in the way of social facilities at his own capital as at Kayambi. Peasants at Kayambi were therefore faced not with a coherent leadership push for regrouping, but with contradictory arguments for and against the idea. Ultimately the majority sided with traditional leaders who opposed resettlement.

Kayambi was not the only place in Kasama where regrouping was not accepted by peasants; in sum, however, the response to the regrouping drive among peasants in Kasama was, with a few notable exceptions, favorable. The DG's publicity tour on regrouping was marked everywhere with high turnouts. At Nseluka he addressed a crowd of two hundred, large by local standards. In the most peripheral regions of the district the outlines of the policy of village regrouping came to be roughly understood. I found that even village headmen who did not understand the functions of VPC's and their own roles as VPC chairmen were able to present a reasoned argument for or against the official move to create large settlements.

Peasants demonstrated not only an understanding of the policy, but in most cases a willingness to offer tangible support. In twenty-two wards out of twenty-three in Kasama there was resettlement of one kind or another which councilors described as "regrouping." Voluntary regrouping was estimated to have occurred at 66 different locations in the district (Table 23). Voluntary regrouping covered a broad range of resettlement patterns. It meant in one local interpretation the simple relocation of small shifting villages at a single site in accordance with the twenty-household guideline of the Village Registration Act. An example of this type of voluntary regrouping was Katampa-Kabansa in Ward 17, which retained traditional housing and dual headmanship. According to another peasant interpretation, voluntary regrouping meant the growth of substantial communities with privately financed permanent housing and with settlers from up to a dozen surrounding villages. An example of this type was Fele-Mulala village near Malole in Ward 12. The significant fact about both these types of so-called regrouping was the absence of party-state assistance. Of the 66 voluntary regrouping villages in Kasama District, only 21 ever received self-help housing grants from the center and only 2 were officially designated as regrouping schemes (Table 23).

Thus to some extent village regrouping in Kasama was a voluntary process conducted by a momentarily mobilized peasantry without the benefit of recognition or development resources from the party-state. Many peasants in Kasama responded to the initial overtures of party-state cadres by agreeing to test the advantages of resettlement. There had always been a spontaneous movement of people toward rural social facilities like missions, schools, and health centers, and the largest villages were usually found around these landmarks. Voluntary resettlement, fueled by the promises of local party leaders, reinforced this tendency for the five years following the inception of official regrouping policy. On occasion eager peasants even took the initiative. One district messenger reported that "when I was touring Chief Chitimukulu's area many people were asking about this government policy of village regrouping"; one councilor suggested that voluntary regrouping was "true self-help because people were coming together without government pressure."[24] An index of commitment to regrouping was the common practice—usually among the relatively well-to-do—of building permanent houses in large villages at personal expense. For example, Kabwibwi village, of Ward 22 in Chief Nkolemfumu's area, had a stable population of over 200, including children, and comprised about 50 to 60 houses. The two burnt-brick and three kimberley-brick houses in the village were constructed without housing grants. A

TABLE 23. Kasama District, Types of Village Regrouping, 1968–1975

Ward	Instances of "Voluntary Regrouping"[1]	Housing Grants Made for Village Reconstruction[2]	Village Regrouping Scheme Designated
1	1	1	1 (Kayambi)
2	4		
3	2	1	
4	2		
5	3	1	
6	5	2	
7	2	2	1 (Nseluka)
8	1	1	
9	2	1	
10	1	1	
11			
12	3		
13	4	1	
14	5	1	
15	5	1	
16	5	2	
17	4		
18	2	1	
19	2	2	
20	4	1	
21	5		
22	3	2	
23	1		
Totals	66	21	2

Sources:
[1] Councilor interviews, 1974 and 1975.
[2] Report from District Community Development Officer to District Secretary Kasama, February 24, 1975.

farmer at Kabwibwi estimated his personal housing expenses at K75 for the hiring of a bricklayer and carpenter and the purchase of wood, cement, paint, and nails. At Mutale Mutimba in Ward 2, twenty permanent houses were constructed with private resources.

Wherever regrouping took place voluntarily, it was on the assumption by peasants that compliance with government policy would be rewarded by the provision of village services such as water, schools, and clinics. If development benefits were not forthcoming and peasant expectations were unfulfilled, mass mobilization backfired, turning potential support for the state into political opposition. Peasants in Kasama came to perceive that the state had let them down for a number of reasons.

First, the programs to which the state was committed by local party leaders were sometimes unrealistic. Ambitious leaders promised a wide range of social facilities for purposes of their own aggrandisement as patrons. Second, the state was often tardy in the fulfillment of genuine programs and projects. The slow dispatch of the sole building organizer in the Department of Community Development to the various group housing schemes in the District was the cause of delays in house construction of up to eighteen months.[25] Construction was held up at Ngoli, Namponda, and Nseluka villages, among others, because administrators failed to provide brickmolds or drums for the storage of water required in brickmaking. Third, the most serious cause of peasant disaffection arose when the party-state appeared to retract firm commitments to provide development benefits. Sometimes peasants confused nonperformance with delay or false promises, but there undoubtedly were instances in Kasama where peasants were misled.

Case 1: Lukulu Village Regrouping: Village regrouping was suggested in KRC and DDC for Lukulu, to the south of the district. Local party officials were urged by the UNIP Region to whip up support for the idea, which they did to the extent of publicly promising a health center at the proposed regrouping site. Of 189 families interviewed by the Community Development Department in 17 villages around Lukulu, 158 agreed to move. All were reportedly "behind the scheme."[26] A formal survey of development potential was made by several government departments. Ultimately, however, the Provincial Agricultural Officer reported that the soil in the area was poor and that the distance from Kasama posed insuperable marketing problems for commercial agriculture. The Lukulu village regrouping center was abandoned before it was begun on the basis of a decision at the center. Yet the people were "still willing to come and very much disappointed to have lost their health center."

Case 2: Mulobola Village Regrouping: Large settlements had existed at Mulobola since the establishment there of a Catholic mission station at the turn of the century, but a notable expansion of the community took place between 1971 and 1974 on the specific understanding that the government intended to install a clinic and a piped-water scheme. The mission had offered limited medical help but because of the shortage of staff had only token effect, and by 1976 the last White Father was withdrawn from Mulobola. People from the villages surrounding Mulobola had embarked on a spate of brick-burning and house-building in preparation for state intervention. Settlers at Mwango-

Kapopo, Kashoki, and Chisoka villages singled out the ward councilor, who at that time was also the UNIP branch chairman, as the source of the promises of government assistance. On the basis of these promises fourteen families relocated in Mwango-Kapopo village alone during 1971 and 1972 and the total for Mulobola as a whole was probably near forty families. The Department of Community Development added credence to the piped-water story by pegging out house sites in straight lines and by giving housing grants to ten families. Nevertheless, by 1975 neither the clinic staff nor the piped-water supply had appeared. The Department of Water Affairs did have Mulobola listed as one of seven priority sites for piped-water installation during the Third National Development Plan period. But at the time of my research, falling government revenues due to the copper crisis cast the implementation of the Third Plan and this sort of project into serious doubt. In 1975 the Ministry of Health provided only sporadic mobile health facilities and had no plans or funds for upgrading its service to Mulobola. As a result of what they perceived to be a severe case of nonperformance, peasants expressed anger at the party and state. In 1975 no party official at Mulobola was willing to admit that facilities had ever been promised. The councilor was the chief scapegoat of the debacle; he lost the support not only of his constituents but also of the UNIP Region and was unable to run for reelection. Significantly, Mulobola became noted throughout Kasama as an area of minimal support for UNIP and of low turnout for voter registration and elections.

For the party-state the danger inherent in failing to meet rising peasant expectations was that of creating a permanent class that was conscious of itself as collectively deprived. People in Kasama long knew that essential social services were more readily accessible in urban areas, and this had been a major factor in outward migration. By 1975 peasants in Kasama were beginning to suspect that the rural-urban gap was not going to be closed in the foreseeable future. Ironically, village regrouping, which was originally designed to close the rural-urban gap and alleviate perceptions of deprivation, contributed in Kasama to disaffection among peasants. Because high expectations engendered by the mobilization campaign for regrouping were not met, and because peasants who came together into larger communities in good faith were disappointed, isolated perceptions of deprivation were combined with a shared perception of deprivation. The deprivation of a whole stratum of people was not necessarily visible when population was sparse and scattered, but was difficult to ignore when large numbers of people were gathered. For example, water shortages were exacerbated when the demand for water increased with a concentrated population. The shortage of school places was more obvious for all to see when crowds of unoccupied children roamed regrouped villages. Even the model village of Nseluka had not wholly escaped this problem; at Kayambi 40 percent of school-age children failed to obtain places in Grade One; at the Mutale Mutimba voluntary regrouping scheme in 1972 there were 244 children but no nearby school. Thus where the state was unable to follow through on the mobilization drive with the actual provision of social services at village regrouping sites, village regrouping served to alienate rather than convert peasants to party-state goals for rural development. Village regrouping also served to foster solidarity in peasant political interests and to create a politically mobilized community that could be as easily organized against as for the party-state.

VILLAGE REGROUPING AND DEVELOPMENT COMMITTEES

Party-state officials and peasants may have disagreed on the exact meaning of "participatory democracy," but both parties expressed an awareness that Village Productivity and Ward Development Committees held the key to getting rural development under way. The building of WDC's and VPC's was part of the general mobilization process for village regrouping. Village regrouping and village registration were begun at approximately the same time, 1972, and Community Development officials were given a special brief to stimulate committee activity at regrouping sites. Like other villages, each regrouped village was supposed to have a VPC, and in practice most had several. Moreover, because regrouped villages comprised the main, sometimes only, diffusion point of development benefits in a ward, WDC activity was usually centered there. WDC meetings were held at regrouped villages where population and facilities were concentrated; most WDC business concerned the affairs of the regrouped village. Because the regrouped villages were intended to be the model for rural growth, the performance of VPC's and WDC's in these communities was critical to the overall Zambian strategy for rural development.

Local-level committees were more active in regrouped villages in Kasama District than in scattered villages. A relationship between VPC activation and large settlement has already been suggested (see above, Chapter 3); WDC activation will be shown to follow suit. The relationship is reciprocal: regrouping is both the cause and the effect of VPC and WDC activeness. At Nseluka, for example, the WDC for Ward 7 took upon itself the work of overseeing the planning and implementation of community projects at the regrouping site. In this way the work of a local committee contributed to the regrouping exercise. By the same token, the WDC at Nseluka, at one time dormant, was resuscitated and provided with a *raison d'être* by the designation of Nseluka as a regrouping center. Of the twelve active WDC's in Kasama District, eight were in wards where substantial village regrouping was under way between 1971 and 1975 (Table 24). That is, two thirds of the politically organized wards in Kasama were engaged in group housing or in voluntary or official resettlement. Officials of the Community Development Department in Kasama argued to a man that local-level committees worked better in regrouped villages. For the most part, village regrouping and state-building at the local level proved to be compatible enterprises. Together, party-state policies on these matters comprised a sound basis for the permanent political and administrative organization of a mobilized peasantry.

Village Productivity Committees were well organized in regrouped villages. First, a higher level of political information about VPC's existed among regrouped peasants than among other village dwellers. Sixty peasants were asked a short schedule of questions pertaining to knowledge of VPC's and attendance at VPC meetings. All these interviews were conducted in a group setting of a formal or informal village gathering of between 3 and 10 people. Answers were given verbally or by show of hands. The group setting probably contaminated some of the responses, but I felt that results were nevertheless valid and interesting enough to report. Of 30 peasants in regrouped villages, 24 said they had heard of VPC's and 22 said they had been to a VPC meeting in their own village. Of 30 peasants in nonregrouped villages, only 16 had heard of VPC's and only 7 said they had attended a meeting. And only in regrouped villages were peasants heard to refer to headmen by the title of chairman of the VPC.

Second, meetings of VPC's were held with greater regularity in regrouped than in nonregrouped villages. Even though the regularity of VPC meetings was difficult to confirm, I found little reason to disbelieve the numerous reports in regrouped villages that VPC's met "ev-

TABLE 24. Kasama District, Activeness of Ward Development Committees by Type of Village Regrouping, 1971–1975

	Types of Regrouping				
Ward	Substantial Voluntary Regrouping[1]	Substantial Village Reconstruction[2]	Official Village Regrouping	Substantial Regrouping in Ward[3]	Active WDC[4]
1			X	X	
2	X			X	X
3					
4					
5					
6	X	X		X	
7		X	X	X	X
8					X
9					X
10					
11					
12					X
13	X			X	X
14	X			X	X
15	X			X	X
16	X	X		X	X
17	X			X	
18					
19		X		X	X
20	X			X	X
21	X			X	
22		X		X	
23					X
Totals	9	5	2	13	12

Notes:
[1] "Substantial" means more than three instances of voluntary regrouping in the ward.
[2] "Substantial" means more than one instance of group housing projects in the ward.
[3] "Substantial" means a ward that scored on any of the three types of regrouping.
[4] From Table 12.

ery month" or "every two or three months." These responses stood in marked contrast to the responses of peasants in outlying villages where the VPC was not institutionalized as a forum for social interaction and the organization of community labor. Third, I expected to find in VPC's with regular meetings and a well informed membership a greater adherence to bureaucratic procedures as laid down by the center for local-level committees. Even in regrouped villages, however, the convention of recording meetings in writing was not readily accepted. At Illondola and Ndasa, headmen explained the absence of VPC minutes as due to the shortage of stationery, an expensive item which they felt should be provided by the government. Another reason was the patronage culture in which development demands were conveyed upward verbally by individual leaders or delegations. During field work in Kasama District I unearthed only fifteen instances of VPC minutes covering only five villages; it appears that in this regard, regrouped villages were also lax.

Generally, the larger the population of a village, the more likely that the VPC was active. Regrouped villages such as Nseluka, Mutale Mutimba, and Misengo with populations of 700, 480, and 250 respectively, had well organized and productive VPC's. Indeed the 10 percent figure for VPC activation (see above, Chapter 3) could well be revised upward if peasant population rather than VPC's were counted. By rough estimate, between 20 and 30 percent of the population of the rural areas of Kasama fell under the jurisdiction of active VPC's. A large population in a village represented an important development resource in the form of communal labor on major projects. A minority of active VPC's did succeed in substituting central capital with local labor, and sometimes even with local capital. At Misengo, for example, a voluntary regrouping scheme in Ward 19, the VPC mobilized peasants to contribute to large communal projects. The VPC organized a K100 self-help fund matched by a K100 grant from the mission to put an iron roof on the village church; the VPC joined with the PTA in providing labor and funds for the construction of a self-help school and dormitory; and the VPC was instrumental in attracting group housing grants and mobilizing peasant energies for the construction of 34 brick houses by 1975.[27] It is interesting that headmen at Misengo were willing to delegate authority to the most senior of their number, subchief Mutale Misengo, thus sidestepping the issue of village identity. The villages of Nsanka, Kakosa, and Mutale Misengo were merged to the full, and a single VPC was set up for all three villages, with the subchief as chairman. Mutale Misengo also sat on the Ward 19 WDC in order to represent the interests of the regrouped village. The unity that a single VPC brought to bear on this larger-than-average community was a major factor in its impressive development record.

Another exemplary case, dating back to an earlier period, was summarized in the following letter to the District Governor from a VPC secretary:

We have the honour of writing this notice to let you know more about our village. Mutale Mutimba is a community village and at the same time is a polling district known as Makasa East. This is a regrouping village with a population of 480 people and there are still more coming in. We have made our own road which is nine miles in distance. It was started in 1966. There are two clubs for poultry and handicraft which started in 1965. We have 28 kimberley brick houses already built. Still some bricks are being made. We have classes of adult literacy with ninety men and women. We have started collecting some money for our first-aid clinic and also some money for a grinding mill. There are more works to do for ourselves but we are asking the government to help us with some of these works.[28]

The letter went on to stress that every project was undertaken on a self-help basis and that requests for government assistance on every project had been turned down. By 1975 the government had contributed to the building of a school in the area. A noteworthy sidelight is that instead of receiving a response to the substance of the letter, the VPC was rebuked for the procedural error of writing directly to the DG rather than through the correct bureaucratic channel of the Ward Councilor. Despite the inappropriate and unfavorable governmental response, the Mutale Mutimba VPC was self-sufficient enough to organize local skills and labor from among the population that had voluntarily converged on the regrouping site.

Large VPC's in Kasama resembled WDC's in terms of the scale of projects undertaken and the size of the population mobilized. In no case was this more evident than with the VPC of Nseluka village. The organizational form taken by VPC's there was different from that in any other rural village in Kasama. Nseluka provided a likely model for the evolution of local committee organization as villages grew. The Nseluka VPC was subdivided into sections and each section had its own mini-VPC. The term "section" was derived from the urban townships in Zambia in which fifty houses were demarcated for local government electoral purposes according to population distribution and street plans rather than according to "natural" communities. Sections in the Nseluka scheme retained some village identity insofar as ties of matrilineal kinship were inherited from the home villages of settlers. Precolonial antecedents existed in the division of large Bemba villages into sections, each with a subchief or headman. But the use of "section" by settlers at Nseluka and large villages near Kasama township indicated the extent to which they considered themselves townspeople-in-the-making. At Nseluka there were seven sections, each headed by its own committee. Most sections and their VPC's retained the names of the villages from which the settlers originated: Fundiboma, Mutale Mukulu, Chipamba, Kasusomena, Mulaya, and Mubanga Nseluka, in addition to Paul Nseluka, recently established. Each section was regarded by residents as part of a new entity called Nseluka Village or Nseluka Regrouping Scheme. The purpose behind subdividing Nseluka VPC into a number of mini-VPC's was, in the words of a community leader, "to keep respect for the headmen."[29] Without some token guarantee that their traditional status would be upheld, headmen would not have supported resettlement. Headmen at Nseluka were even unwilling to give up authority to a single subchief, as headmen had done at Misengo.

Despite guarantees, regrouping undoubtedly reduced the powers of headmen at Nseluka, and this also distinguished Nseluka from Kayambi. In the Mubanga Nseluka section the VPC chairmanship was removed from Mubanga Nseluka himself and vested in a younger brother who "knows more about development" and was a party branch official and WDC member. In the Chipamba section the headman was aged and infirm, failed to hold regular VPC meetings for his section, and yielded leadership to a younger female relative. In the opinion of the Ward Councilor, "VPC's do not work too well because the headmen want money or something that will please them."[30] Subchief Mutale Mukulu held a special position. He was consulted on issues that involved the allocation of land and the admission of new settlers, and he was the only noneducated traditional leader to hold a seat on the WDC for the ward. Deference to Mutale Mukulu was, however, largely a gesture, because the important decisions at Nseluka were not made in his section VPC but in the Nseluka VPC or Ward 7 WDC.

As a group, traditional leaders at Nseluka were used by the local party-state when the support of their followers was needed, but for most important decision-making they were bypassed. For example, headmen were invited to a special meeting of the Ward 7 WDC and instructed by the Ward Councilor to ensure that "all men and women in our ward come forward to register as voters and there must be peace and discipline [during registration]."[31] Otherwise a headman's day-to-day tasks were limited by Nseluka VPC to social arbitration and to care and maintenance of village buildings and environs. Thus even though villages were not "mingled" at Nseluka[32] and each had a measure of village identity, the mini-VPC's that represented them were relatively subordinate institutions. They had little autonomy from the parent Nseluka VPC or from the Ward 7 WDC. In the eyes of peasant and state alike "Nseluka" was a single unit for political and administrative purposes. The work of all VPC's at Nseluka was regularly supervised and coordinated by the WDC in accordance with the relationship stipulated for local-level committees in the Pocket Manual.[33] The large Nseluka VPC became the main organizational force for social cohesion by making the important decisions about community social facilities and community labor projects for the regrouping center as a whole.

Kayambi contrasted sharply with Nseluka as far as Village Productivity Committees were concerned. There was no single VPC to administer the Kayambi community as a whole. Instead each of the villages originally recruited for the resettlement scheme retained its own VPC. These VPC's were responsible for settlements of approximately the same size as the mini-VPC's that existed in each section of Nseluka, but they acted autonomously from one another and from the weak Ward 1 WDC.

For example, Illondola village, one of the villages that refused to resettle at the Kayambi site, independently undertook the task of upgrading domestic water supplies. Because of the unwillingness of Illondola peasants to join Kaminsa village, access to the piped water facility at Kaminsa was never gained. Illondola VPC made repeated efforts to convince the RC and Water Affairs Department to extend water pipes to their side of Kayambi. When these appeals bore no fruit, the VPC secretary, who was also the owner of a village store, traveled to Mungwi with a personal appeal to the chairman of the RC. The VPC secretary claimed to have secured a promise of Council support provided peasants raised a self-help fund to meet half the cost of the extension pipe. But by mid-1975 only K6.95 had been raised, and Illondola women were still drawing water from the stream and the mission spigot. The actions of the VPC, interestingly enough, were not mediated by either a Kayambi VPC or the WDC for the ward. The

VPC acted alone and—partly because its requests were not coordinated with a larger community plan, and partly because its requests were not backed by a larger committee—it was unsuccessful.

Illondola was one of the more active of the eleven VPC's formally supposed to exist in the vicinity of Kayambi. Others, such as Kaputa and Chale-Chipunsu were wracked by headmanship disputes that seriously undermined the ability of VPC's to conduct work.[34] The Kaminsa VPC, in the village that benefited most from regrouping at Kayambi, met "every few months if we are lucky," but "the people do not know what it is supposed to do."[35] The VPC secretary was rarely present because he did not reside in the village but on a distant farm. Of VPC's in the Kayambi area, the Ward Councilor said, "They waste my time because they are not well organized; I get few invitations and I do not often go [to VPC meetings]."[36] Nor was the councilor willing to acknowledge that part of the responsibility for VPC formation rested with himself. Thus the isolated VPC's at Kayambi operated poorly if at all, lacked resources to conduct lone development projects, and were not integrated into a well-organized local committee apparatus. There was no overall regrouped VPC, and the WDC for Ward 1 did not coordinate the work of a large VPC for the community as a whole, as at Misengo or Nseluka. Its absence was sorely felt. In sum the form that the organization of VPC's took at Kayambi vividly reflected the lack of social cohesion in the community and the failure there of the regrouping experiment.

As with VPC's, the *Ward Development Committees* for Nseluka and Kayambi were strikingly divergent in composition and performance. The Ward 7 WDC, which was responsible for Nseluka, embodied the working alliance of party, state, and traditional leadership first established during the mobilization drive. By contrast, the Ward 1 WDC, which was responsible for Kayambi, reflected the political interests of traditional leaders and openly conflicted with the interests of leaders representing the party-state. Because of its social composition, the Ward 1 WDC was regularly bypassed in favor of a patronage network organized by the ward councilor. The recruitment of WDC members and the social composition of the WDC's distinguished Kayambi from Nseluka (Table 25). Kayambi was dominated by traditional leaders, Nseluka by new patrons from the party-state development front.

Headmen were the largest single leadership group on the Kayambi

TABLE 25. Kasama District, Social Composition of Ward Development Committees at Village Regrouping Schemes, 1971–1975

	Ward 7 WDC (Nseluka)			Ward 1 WDC (Kayambi)		
	Occupation	*UNIP Office*	*VPC Secretary*	*Occupation*	*UNIP Office*	*VPC Secretary*
Chairman	Ward Councilor	x		Ward Councilor	x	
Secretary	Community Development Assistant			Businessman		
Members	Carpenter	x		Headman		
	Farmer			Headman		
	Farmer	x		Farmer	x	
	Headman			Headman		
	Carpenter	x	x	Headman		
	Bricklayer			Headman		
	Farmer	x	x	Agricultural Demonstrator		
	Businessman	x	x	Primary School Teacher		

WDC, they occupied five of the ten seats. Election of headmen to WDC positions, including headmen opposed to regrouping, was evidence of a survival of traditional authority among Kayambi peasants and a weakness of alternative institutions like UNIP branches. The Ward Councilor complained that "people here still believe in the elders" and suggested that "if we had leaders with more education this place would not be so far behind."[37] Only one of the headmen could read and write in English. The Agricultural Assistant said that he did not work through the WDC because "the members are not active; they are old men."[38] There were originally more than five headmen on the WDC, but two were unilaterally ousted by the Ward Councilor and replaced by the head teacher and Agricultural Assistant on the grounds that civil servants were "better qualified" to understand complex development issues. The councilor also illegally dismissed the original elected Ward Secretary, a White Father from the mission, perhaps because he was inclined to sympathize with the headmen. At the one WDC meeting in Ward 1 which I attended, only headmen were present.

At Nseluka, WDC membership passed to a new stratum of local leadership. The bulk of the membership was composed of comparatively well-to-do elements who earned income from local trades or market agriculture. The relationship this group held to the mini-VPC's from which they were elected was not that of headman/chairman but often of VPC secretary. Four of the ten read and wrote English. Eight of the ten sat on the large VPC for Nseluka as a whole. In addition, some WDC members held WDC membership by virtue of party office; only two WDC members held party office at Kayambi, whereas six held party office at Nseluka. Most of the latter were branch officials of UNIP, although one was a constituency chairman. Nseluka enjoyed the vigorous local party organization that Kayambi lacked. The integration of party organization through shared memberships gave the Ward 7 WDC an added advantage in getting people to work together on development projects.

WDC members from the two regrouping centers also differed widely in levels of political information. At Kayambi members had scant knowledge of the purposes of the WDC and their own roles within it. One member, a headman, hoped that "we will be taught our work but so far nothing has been done"; another confused the WDC with the VPC when he suggested that the function of the WDC was to "sweep the villages"; a third said he was unsure why he was at a WDC meeting and that he had come simply in response to a summons from the councilor.[39] Few peasants in surrounding villages knew of the existence of a WDC for the ward or could name the chairman. Indeed "Ward 1" was not a unit of organization widely acknowledged by anyone other than the Ward Councilor himself. The situation at Nseluka was quite the reverse. The WDC was not only acknowledged as an effective demand forum by Nseluka residents and its members widely recognized, but the WDC members had a sophisticated understanding of WDC structure and function. I recall a lucid debate with two young members of the Nseluka WDC on a proposal, mooted in central government circles in 1974, to abolish Ward Councils. These two heatedly defended the nonselective plenary nature of large ward gatherings and the opportunities presented therein for direct contact of peasant with state. Sensitivity to the intricacies of local-level committee organization appeared to have emerged only at Nseluka and other wards where extensive voluntary regrouping had occurred. The Nseluka

WDC, guided by the Ward Councilor and Community Development Assistant, met without fail on a quarterly cycle. Yet at Kayambi the WDC met for the first time in mid-1974, two years after committee formation, and then only because the councilor knew that I was coming to observe it.

The achievements of the Ward 7 WDC, which were manifested principally at Nseluka Regrouping Center, were most impressive. Three projects, and the part played in them by the WDC, deserve mention.

Case 1: Nseluka Church. A small church of sun-dried brick was built at Mubanga Nseluka in 1956 which withstood the elements for almost fifteen years. Eventually, after numerous rethatching repairs and during a particularly heavy rainy season, the structure crumbled under the weight of a sodden roof. The Ward 7 WDC resolved to construct the edifice anew on a grander scale. In mid-1974 a work party was organized among peasants from Nseluka and other outlying villages in the ward for the purpose of burning bricks. Approximately 60 people were involved over a six-day period of clay-digging, brick-molding and firewood-collecting under the direction of WDC members. Twenty-seven thousand bricks were burned. Bricklayers from Nseluka contributed their skills in succeeding weeks, and by November 1974 the walls of the church had risen to roof height. At this point construction was stalled for want of iron sheets for the church roof. Self-help collections were taken up by the WDC and by Catholic church leaders in 1975, and the church, equipped with wooden benches but open to the sky, was put into use until such time as enough could be accumulated. Throughout the project the WDC acted entirely alone, it identified a local need, devised and implemented a local solution, and used local resources throughout. The WDC substituted labor for capital wherever feasible and did not depend on a subsidy from central government or mission bodies.

Case 2: Nseluka Clinic. One of the first projects launched by the Ward 7 WDC was to construct a clinic and dispensary to meet the routine health needs of peasants in Nseluka and other nearby villages. On the understanding that state assistance would be forthcoming, peasants erected on a self-help basis a modest three-room kimberley brick structure with an iron roof. In 1971, however, an inspector from the central government Public Works Department declared the building unsound and instructed the builders to mold more bricks and this time to burn them. On the basis of this government appraisal, the RC reneged on a commitment to take over maintenance of the clinic and the Ministry of Health withdrew a promise of clinic staff. Government departments were perceived by the WDC to be evasive and uncoordinated in implementing regrouping projects; the WDC was unable to find any state or local agency that would accept responsibility for the clinic. Thus peasants at Nseluka retaliated by refusing to burn more bricks. In the words of one UNIP branch official "they fear that the government will do the same thing and that their work will be wasted again." WDC leaders felt they had a strong case because the Minister of Health had personally committed himself in November 1972 to "allocate a Stage I Rural Health Centre next year [and] all will be done to speed up work."[40] Between 1971 and 1975 scarcely a meeting of the WDC passed without some reference to the clinic problem. For example, WDC members asked that the PWD take over maintenance chores from the KRC or that the DG intervene on behalf of Nseluka with the Provincial Medical Officer; both requests were initially turned down.[41] Angry allegations were made against government officials, accompanied by racial slurs against one senior medical officer in particular who happened to be an Asian. Correspondence between WDC and government departments was extensive. Because of the constant and widely aimed pressure brought by the WDC, a compromise on the Nseluka clinic problem was achieved by late 1975. Senior medical officials visited the site. The people of Nseluka agreed to begin brick burning for a new building if, and only if, a Medical Assistant and medical equipment began operating at once from the old building. The central government agreed, and a Medical Assistant was due to arrive several days after my last visit to Nseluka. In addition, the permanent building, once constructed, would be upgraded to the status of a Rural Health Center—that is, a more sophisticated facility than the clinic or dispensary originally requested. This case illustrated not only the concrete results of participation from below by an effective and persistent WDC working through official channels; it illustrated also the instrumental attitudes of well organized peasants in Kasama who would not commit themselves to self-help until hard evidence of promised state assistance was provided.

Case 3: Nseluka Water Supply. The original settlers of Mubanga Nseluka relied upon a *dambo* (swamp) for household water. The RC provided wells and hand-pumps after 1966 as part of the effort to upgrade Nseluka to a Community Development subcenter. Regular hand-pump breakdowns forced a return to the dambo supply. This original source was inadequate to the demands of an expanding population, as it dried up during October and water could only be reached by digging. That many new residents required extra water for the molding of bricks served to aggravate the problem. Thus one of the first tasks undertaken by the WDC was to start a self-help water fund in 1972. Only K34.00 had been mustered when state intervention, in the person of the President of the Republic of Zambia, rescued the village from its plight. President Kaunda was on tour in Northern Province in October 1972 and, impressed by the progress in group housing at Nseluka, ordered the self-help water scheme converted into a government project. The Department of Water Affairs was thus directed from the center to allocate K16,000 for the construction of a borehole, water tower and storage tank, pump house and engine, piping, and spigots. As a result of the first of a series of delays on the part of this government department, only half the allocation was actually spent in 1973, and the remainder was presumably returned to Lusaka. Toward the end of 1974, two years after the executive order from the President, vital portions of the scheme, including the storage tank and reticulation pipes, were incomplete. The WDC response, prompted by persistent peasant complaints at ward and village meetings, was unconventional but effective. Five

WDC leaders, including the councilor, CDA, and the subchief, constituted themselves a delegation and, in the name of the WDC, traveled to Kasama to protest directly to the Permanent Secretary, Northern Province. The protest was evidently successful, for the Permanent Secretary was able to prod Water Affairs into completion of the scheme before the year was up. In this case the WDC was again faced with the problem of cooperating with a tardy central government department. Instead of using conventional channels, however, and perhaps emboldened by the partisanship of the President in their cause, WDC leaders went personally to the top of the provincial administrative hierarchy. The WDC devised an innovative solution in a case where massive capital resources were at stake by enlisting the assistance of the authority whose principal role was to oversee the efficient and correct expenditure of central government funds in the province.

The WDC at Nseluka, encouraged by success at attracting central resources for social facilities, was looking ahead at the end of 1975 to projects that would further extend the façade of modernization in the community. Some WDC members enthusiastically advocated the electrification of the village by extending power lines from the generators at Nseluka station on the Tanzam railroad. Others tabled motions at WDC meetings for the state to install a post office, a police station, and a telephone. The expectations engendered by an active WDC in a successful regrouping scheme were high. In the wistful words of the CDA, "our work is never done."[42]

Predictably, the performance of the WDC at Kayambi contrasted sharply with the success story of Nseluka. The WDC did not spearhead a wide range of social development projects. One explanation hinges on the presence of the mission at Kayambi and the provision by missionaries of the very social facilities of clinics, water, and churches, around which organization for development took place at Nseluka. But a full explanation must also take into consideration patterns of organization, formal and informal, which distinguished Kayambi from Nseluka. Note has already been made of the low institutionalization of the Ward 1 WDC at Kayambi in the form of infrequent meetings and the low level of political information of its members. The most important reason for the lack of impact of the Ward 1 WDC, however, was its rare use to resolve local issues or undertake local projects. Peasants and local party-state leaders alike used other channels for these tasks.

Resource distribution at Kayambi was characterized by personalism and patronage. All political transactions were mediated by the powerful Ward Councilor, and his methods of conducting ward business discouraged the participation of peasants and the growth of participatory institutions. The councilor was the prime mover and chief beneficiary of the regrouping exercise. He was described by Kayambi residents as "hungry for power" and "interested only in his own village."[43] One informant suggested that the councilor was "unpopular with the people and lacks their confidence because he is always attacking them." Yet he had "taken a second wife to show that he is a big man." The consensus among peasants was that as far as affairs concerning the community's relation with the state are concerned, the situation at Kayambi was "a one-man show."[44] Instead of channeling development and other requests through the WDC, the ward councilor undertook to use personal influence at KRC headquarters and with the UNIP Region. From numerous examples available, three will be briefly cited.

Case 1: Kayambi Dormitory. The completion of the dormitory for Kayambi upper primary school was facilitated by a personal appeal from the councilor to the Kasama DG, in 1973. No record existed of the WDC's involvement in this project, for if any local organization was active, it was the parent-teachers association and not the WDC. The PTA did collect K310 in self-help funds through a "one-man-one-kwacha" levy. But the DG's intervention was required for the provision of iron roofing and the truck transport to make delivery to distant Kayambi. This would not have been possible without the action of the councilor acting as local patron.

Case 2: Kayambi Water Supply. The piped water system at Kaminsa was widely rumored at Kayambi and at Mungwi to have been the fruit of a close relationship between the councilor and a previous Rural Council Secretary. The home of this latter official was near Kayambi, and he was himself planning to run for Parliament in 1973 from a popular base in the Kayambi area. Whether or not the rumors were accurate, there was no doubt that the water-supply project emanated from the personal representations of local patrons and not, as at Nseluka, from a concerted popular action on the part of the WDC. The councilor freely advertised himself as "the main who brought piped water." He was also able, by virtue of his control of the project, to ensure that the sought-after patronage post of pump supervisor went to a party colleague from a neighboring village.

Case 3: Kayambi School Fence. A dispute arose between the peasants of Kaminsa and the headteacher of the upper primary school involving the building of a school fence which interfered with traffic to and from the village. Normally a WDC would have been able to dispatch such a local problem, but the WDC was never called or consulted at Kayambi. Instead the councilor intervened. But because of prickly relations of long standing with the head teacher, he was unable to reach an agreement. Ultimately a more senior patron, the Minister of State for National Guidance, was called upon, in his role of Member of Parliament for Kayambi, to cool the hostilities.

The outstanding feature of these cases of the resolution of local problems was the exclusion of the WDC from all three. The councilor preferred to rely on patronage rather than on participatory organizational channels. Functions of the WDC were arrogated by an ambitious local party leader or, in a few cases, were transferred to other functionally specific local organizations, such as the PTA or the credit union. And since Kayambi did not enjoy the presence of a vibrant local party organization, peasants there had few choices in channels of access to the state. Thus from quite opposite standpoints, Nseluka and Kayambi gave substance to the notion that success at local-level committee-building and success at village regrouping went together.

VILLAGE REGROUPING AND ECONOMIC TRANSFORMATION

The decline of the village in Kasama District was attributable in large part to the lack of opportunities for generating development resources in a subsistence peasant economy. Village regrouping was designed to provide employment at nodes of rural growth and was a key element in the strategy to promote self-reliant commercial agriculture. The Kasama experience with village regrouping emphasized, however, the difficulty of cutting the ties of village dependence on the urban industrial center. Social services at regrouping centers were usually financed with state revenues derived from copper. Indeed the provision of social facilities was the only substantive mark of development in regrouped villages. In economic terms regrouped villages remained untransformed. Growth in agricultural output at regrouping sites was piecemeal at best, and benefited subsistence peasants least and last.

Resettlement usually has a disruptive effect on peasant economies.[45] In Kasama economic considerations were paramount in peasant decisions on whether to resettle. Peasants responded rationally to party-state initiatives on regrouping by questioning the advisability of abandoning economically viable villages. Peasants at Chitango village in Chief Makasa's area refused to move on the basis that "demolishing old houses and gardens was a sheer waste of time and resources."[46]

The existence of established fruit orchards, cassava plots and other productive gardens made peasants disinclined to quit scattered villages. Many felt that to ask a family to start new gardens in the same year that they built a new house was to ask too much. The subsistence that most peasants eked from the land was too precarious to permit radical interruptions in the agricultural cycle. At Mutale Kabwe village and in many others disgruntled subsistence cultivators decided to "stay put in their nearby chitemene gardens."[47] And wherever individual emergent farmers established farms or outlying gardens, the directive for regrouping was ignored. As one independent farmer put it, "How can you ask a man with a big plot of maize to move to another place?"[48]

At Kayambi, where there was a substantial number of individual farmers, this response to regrouping was especially prevalent. Individuals were actually leaving the regrouping site at Kayambi in 1974 and 1975 to set up farms on their own. At Nseluka, careful attention was paid by WDC leaders to the problem of economic readjustment during resettlement. Prospective settlers were discouraged from building houses in their first year at the village; instead they lived in a transit section of the village where temporary dwellings were permitted in order to devote energies to the establishment of new gardens. The otherwise successful mobilization at Nseluka failed to induce peasants from Katilungu to join Nseluka; significantly, Katilungu was populated by individual farm families producing for market.

The fear of losing the fruits of agricultural labor was not the only factor in convincing peasants to favor well-tested patterns of settlement above regrouping, but it was the most important factor. I recorded a wide variety of responses to the question "Is there anything you do not like about village regrouping?" (Table 26). The question was put to 60 peasants, half of whom lived in regrouped villages, half of whom did not. Loss of productive gardens (28 percent) was cited as the major reason and was connected by the peasants to the difficulty of finding sufficient quantities of land and forest around new villages for the practice of chitemene (15 percent). Others worried that cohabitation in one village with "strangers" would lead to a proliferation of social disputes. Some (20 percent) felt that these disputes would inevitably give rise to accusations of witchcraft, and they feared both for personal safety and for the destructive effect of witchcraft on the

TABLE 26.   Kasama District, Resistance to Regrouping, Reasons Cited by Peasants[1]

Rank	Reason Cited	Citations in Regrouped Villages	Citations in non-Regrouped Villages	Total Citations
1	loss of productive gardens	16	13	29 (28%)
2	fear of witchcraft accusations	8	13	21 (20%)
3	shortage of culti- vable land	11	4	15 (15%)
4	ownership disputes	4	10	14 (14%)
5	breakdown of traditional authority	2	8	10 (10%)
6	separation from ancestors	2	3	5 (4%)
7	other	3	6	9 (9%)
	Totals	46	57	103 (100%)

[1]N = 60; 30 from regrouped and 30 from non-regrouped villages. Total citations exceed 60 because respondents were encouraged to offer more than one reason.

social cohesion of the community. A smaller group (14 percent) saw disputes in more individualistic terms as a threat to property. They predicted, for example, an increase in claims for reparation in connection with disputes over land and livestock; the straying of hungry chickens, dogs, or goats among household gardens was regularly cited. Largely because of the presence of twelve headmen in the sample, a sizable proportion of responses (10 percent) concerned the contribution of village regrouping to the further decline of traditional authority. A smaller group (4 percent) expressed concern over the abandonment of village sites inhabited by the spirits of ancestors. There were, finally, several idiosyncratic reasons offered for resisting regrouping (9 percent). Among them: hunting would be curtailed because wild game would move away from a large human settlement; the noise from the village school would disturb the peace; people would be "bossed around" by party officials; and men with beautiful wives would lose them to other suitors.

Two conclusions arise from the survey of peasant attitudes to regrouping. First, contrary to the popular depiction of peasants as bound by irrational tradition, those in Kasama were motivated primarily out of a rational perception of economic advantage. If peasants had reservations about regrouping or chose to resist regrouping, they did so on the basis of a sound calculation of the best way to preserve the means of family subsistence. If the reasons cited for resisting regrouping were divided into "economic" and "noneconomic" categories, then by far the greater proportion (57 percent as opposed to 35 percent) fell into the first category (Table 27). Whereas witchcraft and other customary beliefs did figure in peasant calculations concerning resettlement, they did not constitute a primary obstacle to change. Second, there was a greater predominance of economic reasons given by peasants who had tried regrouping (72 percent) than those who had not (53 percent). In other words the experiences of new settlers *reinforced* the idea that the type of problems likely to be encountered in re-

TABLE 27.   Kasama District, Resistance to Regrouping, Economic and Noneconomic Reasons

		Regrouped Villages	Non-regrouped Villages	Totals
Economic Reasons	loss of productive gardens	16	13	29
	shortage of cultivable land	11	4	15
	ownership disputes	4	10	14
	Totals	31 (72%)	27 (53%)	58 (57%)
Noneconomic Reasons	fear of witchcraft accusations	8	13	21
	breakdown of traditional authority	2	8	10
	separation from ancestors	2	3	5
	Totals	12 (28%)	24 (47%)	36 (35%)
Other		3	6	9
	Totals			103 (100%)

grouped villages were those of household food production. A prima facie case can be made that the agricultural economies of regrouped villages were less well adapted to the environment of the northern Zambian plateau than the economies of traditional forms of settlement.

The nature of economic dislocation in regrouped villages can be seen clearly by examining agricultural and other production in Nseluka and Kayambi. Ironically, the more successful the regrouping, the greater the economic dislocation. Because Kayambi had a long history of permanent settlement and because there was less mass movement of peasants, agricultural production at Kayambi was not disrupted to the extent experienced at Nseluka. By Kasama standards the Kayambi area was relatively productive. The farm register compiled by the Agricultural Assistant at the Kayambi Agricultural Camp listed 42 farmers with more than two hectares of maize and 36 farmers with between one and two hectares. Virtually all of this number resided in individual settlements or villages in the regrouping catchment area. One prominent farmer was the headman of Illondola village and WDC member who had an acre each of beans and millet in addition to two and a half acres of maize. The Agricultural Assistant also claimed to have contacted over one hundred "starting farmers" who were eager for his advice. The Kayambi Agricultural Camp produced a minimum surplus of 1000 bags of maize annually, but an increase, possibly up to 2000 bags, was predicted for the good 1975 harvest.[49]

One stimulant to economic productivity at Kayambi was the arrival of the Tanzam railroad line. Production for market had not previously been profitable because the isolated location of Kayambi rendered uncertain the arrival on time of fertilizer and seed and the access to market necessary for sale.[50] Attempts to grow maize, beans, and groundnuts without fertilizer had uneconomic yields. Bags of harvested maize often became spoiled before collection was made by the marketing cooperative from Kasama. Thus peasants were attracted by the improved marketing opportunities offered by the railway, and land along the line, particularly around stations, was in high demand. There were reports that Chinese railroad technicians cleared land for family farms with heavy earth-moving equipment, though I could not confirm these. Nor could the impact of Tanzam on agricultural productivity and marketing be assessed accurately, because the full operating capacity of the line had not been reached by the end of 1975. The initial impact, however, was to encourage individual family farm settlements at the expense of village regrouping.

By the end of 1975 Kayambi was beginning to take on the characteristics of other maize surplus areas in the district, such as Malole and Ngulula. A small group of emergent farmers, the majority of whom committed themselves to state assistance for capital, fertilizer, pesticides, and seeds, produced a small surplus for market on individual farms. Meanwhile, the bulk of the peasant population proceeded with familiar methods of subsistence cultivation in village settlements. Chitemene and mabala gardens still predominated. Because of the failure of village regrouping, which resulted in a comparatively dispersed population pattern in the greater Kayambi area, land and tree shortages did not pose a major obstacle to the survival of traditional agricultural practices.

By contrast, Nseluka was a recent settlement, with a concentrated population. The pressure made subsistence agriculture even more economically precarious than usual, and fixed-plot, market-oriented agriculture had only just begun. The Agricultural Assistant at Nseluka was unable to cite figures on maize production, but a local estimate by the CDA was two to three hundred bags annually for the agricultural camp area. The Ward Councilor suggested that there were 57 "farmers" in the locality, but it was unclear what criteria were used to identify them. The use of fertilizer was slightly more widespread at Nseluka than at Kayambi because of closer access to supplies in Kasama town and the demonstration effect of farming schemes at Ngulula just to the south of the Ward 7 border.

As with Kayambi, most emergent farmers lived on their own homesteads; only a handful were found at the regrouping site. Peasants at the Nseluku project continued to rely primarily on ash-circle cultivation supplemented by small hand-hoed household gardens. Besides maize, millet, beans, and groundnuts, peasants favored cassava for its ease of cultivation. As at Kayambi, there was a flourishing market exchange of agricultural commodities independent of the national agricultural marketing institutions. Beans, groundnuts, and fruit were traded by the handful for a few *ngwee* (cents) at a time, and a brisk business was done at both regrouping centers in home-brewed millet

beer. Fruit trees were beginning to bear at Nseluka in 1975, and peasants still made periodic return visits to old orchards at abandoned
villages.

The main problem with food production at Nseluka was the shortage
of land for cultivation and of trees for cutting and burning. Chitemene
gardens at Nseluka began four miles from the village and stretched
away to distances of up to twenty miles. Either peasants were tired
by the time they reached the gardens, or they were forced to camp out
at the gardens, thus depriving the village of their labor and other social
contributions for extended periods. Some older men lived almost permanently in outlying encampments to protect the crops from maraud-
ing birds and other supervisory purposes. At peak moments in the
agricultural cycle, Nseluka became deserted as men, women, and
children migrated en masse to the distant fields. The disjunction of
food production from other social activities in regrouped settlements
was a result of the concentration of peasant populations without sufficient regard for the carrying capacities of local environments. The
party-state endeavored to discourage shifting agriculture in favor of
fixed farming but did not build adequate support for small farmers
into the policy of village regrouping.

At Nseluka there were two state programs aimed at modernizing
agricultural production. The first, functional literacy, was administered primarily by the Community Development Department. Selected peasants were taught to read and write in the vernacular by
means of a course of instruction on small-scale maize growing with
improved agricultural inputs. Each student was expected to produce
half an acre of hybrid maize during the year-long course. Recruitment
to the functional literacy course at Nseluka was at first slow, but once
concrete results were achieved in the 1974/75 season, there were more
applicants than places for them. The provision of fertilizer and seed
by the state and crop yields of up to fifteen bags per half acre, as opposed to eight bags under traditional methods, were incentives to recruitment. Some functional literacy students sold surplus maize to
NPCMU and yielded a small profit. Part of the aim of the functional
literacy program at Nseluka was to demarcate gardens closer to the
village. Many half-acre plots were in the backyards of Nseluka houses.
The program was thus contributing to the adjustment of agricultural
techniques to settlement patterns. In early 1976, however, the func-

tional literacy program was running into trouble at the national level; the costs of preparing manuals in the vernacular and subsidizing agricultural inputs were proving too much for a government faced with falling copper prices.[51] The possibility existed that functional literacy students would in future have to pay for fertilizer and seed—a policy shift which, if effected, would discriminate against poor peasants.

The second state program aimed at restructuring local agriculture was the farm settlement scheme at Chamfubu, twelve kilometers northeast of Nseluka. The scheme was opened in 1974 when 21 plots of 25 hectares each were reportedly cleared, out of a projected scheme of 1800 hectares.[52] Promising farmers were encouraged to join from Nseluka and other villages to undertake mixed farming and to learn ox ploughing. By the end of 1975 farmers at Chamfubu had not begun to produce a marketable surplus. The arrival of oxen was overdue, the government stumping and clearing program had fallen behind schedule, and new water furrows proved to be dry for three months of the year.[53] Only seven farmers were working small plots of land. Apart from attracting a few individuals away from Nseluka, the settlement scheme therefore had little impact on the economic transformation of the regrouped village by 1975. For many peasants the prospect of undertaking maize farming on fixed plots was less attractive than using remittances from relatives in the cash sector to buy processed maize-meal from Kasama. The grinding mill in the Paul Nseluka section was underused. Although Nseluka was a model scheme in terms of social services in 1975—in agriculture, at least—the task of rural reconstruction had only just begun.

Agriculture was not the only economic activity envisaged by the center for regrouped villages. According to official intention, regrouping was intended to be the crucible of cottage industry. Here the record of Nseluka was more encouraging. A sawyer's cooperative had sprung up in response to the demand for construction timbers at Nseluka and other group housing schemes. The cooperative began with five members in 1966, but by 1975 had almost seventy. The work of the cooperative involved the felling of trees at a site near Ngoli, some 25 kilometers from the regrouping center, and sawing them into planks and finished carpentry products. In dramatic exception to the rule of local dependence on the center, the main customer of the sawyers' cooperative was the central government. Roofing timbers were pur-

chased by the Ministry of Education and the Public Works Department
in Kasama for schools and other government buildings throughout the
district. Doors and window frames were purchased by the Community
Development Department on behalf of the recipients of grand-in-aid
housing. In a deal proudly acclaimed in the WDC in 1975, the sawyers
contracted for the first time to supply doors and frames to the village
regrouping scheme at Misengo. The state assisted with the provision
of truck transport from one side of the district to the other. Although
the sawyers did not keep detailed financial records, profits were said
to be divided among participants according to work done. The two
sawyer/carpenters on the Ward 7 WDC reported earning K50 and
K200 per year respectively.

The work of this self-sufficient cooperative enterprise contrasted
with the work of carpenters at Kayambi. There three men produced
many of the same construction items plus furniture in independent
workshops. There was no cooperative. The one carpenter interviewed
said he bought his wood from a sawyer at Makasa and transported
it by bicycle to Kayambi. He sold to individuals rather than by contract
to a government department and had very few customers. Not only
were fewer improved houses being built at Kayambi but only salary-
earners, such as teachers, could afford to buy tables and cupboards.
The scale of operation and diffusion of benefits were far lower from
small-scale rural industry at Kayambi than at the more successful regrouping scheme.

The productivity profiles of Nseluka and Kayambi suggest that village regrouping and the generation of marketable surplus from agriculture have not gone together. One factor explaining persistent economic stagnation was the way in which the strategy of the party-state
was distorted by local leaders in mobilizing peasants for regrouping.
Little emphasis was placed on the need for agricultural innovation and
economic reorganization; instead, regrouping was presented by party-
state leaders as an exercise in social reorganization, with emphasis
on the benefits from improved social facilities. Peasants consequently
came to adopt a noneconomic perception of regrouping. In response to
the question "Is there anything that you like about village regrouping?" 48 out of 60 (80 percent) replied that social facilities were desired. Responses included "productivity means clean water" and "the
government must first of all build us a school." There was a wide con-

sensus at both Nseluka and Kayambi that government-sponsored piped water was the most important factor in attracting settlers. The non-economic orientation of peasants to regrouping was shared by those in and out of regrouping centers: 25 out of 30 and 23 out of 30 respectively. Only a small minority (12 percent) thought that regrouping would lead to "more paid work" or "better gardens."

The question of economic transformation involves not only an analysis of the growth in production but also an analysis of distribution of development resources. The Kasama experience suggested that benefits of regrouping do not diffuse widely throughout the locality. Rather, the distribution of resources was distorted in favor of prominent local leadership groups. That local leadership jelled into a coherent front at Nseluka meant that limited diffusion was particularly evident there. Inequality in diffusion had two important dimensions. First, it reflected the selective recruitment of WDC's and the use by members of WDC's to control resources from the center. Second, it reflected the salience of private wealth in the achievement of access to development.

At Nseluka the WDC, and at Kayambi the Ward Councilor, monitored the flow of resources and made major distributive decisions. They controlled or significantly influenced access to state programs like group housing, agricultural credit and agricultural settlement schemes. For example, at Nseluka a limited number of housing grants was available each year. The WDC, acting in conjunction with the mini-VPC of the section concerned in a "project committee," chose from among many applicants. The first criterion for acceptance was possession of a party card; initial screening for party membership was sometimes done by a Village Political Committee of UNIP. In this process a party official had a better chance of recommendation for a grant than an ordinary UNIP member. The second criterion for acceptance was whether the applicant would work hard for himself. "We live with them and we know them." One WDC member suggested that the ideal applicant was one who had proven "he could stand alone," and another member suggested one "who had the skill and the money to maintain his own house."[54] Invariably the successful applicant chosen by the WDC was an individual who already occupied some kind of leadership position, either as a party official or an emergent farmer. WDC members tended to reward those most like themselves and to neglect the poorer peasants.

Applications for the Chamfubu settlement scheme were processed through the WDC at Nseluka in 1974, and an estimated three quarters of successful applicants came from the regrouping scheme itself and included members of the Ward 7 WDC.[55] Ultimately most applicants dropped their claims to a place on the settlement scheme when they realized how little of the work of clearing the bush and starting productive gardens was to be done by the state and how much they would be required to do themselves; eventually only one of the first seven farmers was from the Nseluka WDC. Nevertheless, the rush to secure access to expected benefits by WDC members and their clients and the ease with which access was gained were well illustrated by the Chamfubu case.[56] The monopolization of agricultural credit by Ward 7 WDC members has already been documented (see above, Chapter 4).

At Kayambi applications for housing grants and agricultural credit were not formally channeled through the WDC, but the social structure that the distribution of rewards revealed was much the same. Ward 1 was one of the few wards in Kasama District not to take advantage of powers to grant credit devolved to WDC's by the Agricultural Finance Company; farmers were recommended instead by the Ward Councilor and Agricultural Assistant conferring privately. And the procedure for securing a plot of land near the piped water at Kaminsa involved an applicant in personal consultation with the Ward Councilor and the headman rather than with the WDC.

As well as considering applicants for projects, local leaders at ward level were often able to determine the location of physical improvements within large villages, and so control the diffusion of benefits. The Nseluka WDC decided which sections of the village would receive piped water. The three sections chosen first were geographically the most central but were also the sections with the highest number of representatives on the WDC. These representatives also had the greatest seniority in the local party-state hierarchy. The selective allocation of standpipes was a source of acrimony and dissension in the village. The Mutale Mukulu section clamored for an extension of the reticulation system, but their headman was the only representative on the WDC and was unable to override local party-state leaders. In any event Nseluka by 1975 was beginning to experience the disadvantages of a large scale, as the carrying capacity of the existing borehole was reached and no further benefits from the initial water project were available for distribution to the more disadvantaged sections of the village.

It was striking that at both Nseluka and Kayambi the senior local party-state leaders were themselves personal beneficiaries of state projects. At Kayambi, for example, the water reticulation system was located in Kaminsa village, the village of the Ward Councilor. At Nseluka it was located in the Fundiboma section, where the Ward Councilor, several UNIP branch officials, and state extension workers lived. At Kayambi, too, the first recipient of a housing grant was the Ward Councilor; the councilor for Ward 7 waited for a more seemly interval to elapse before accepting a housing grant approved by his own WDC in 1975.

A formal position in party-state leadership was not the only criterion of access to the development resources associated with village regrouping. Relatively well-to-do groups secured preferential access to Nseluka and Kayambi, and state policy on regrouping came to increasingly favor these groups. Selective diffusion was well illustrated by the history of group housing at Nseluka. More than half the grant-aided houses at Nseluka were constructed before 1971 in the first two years of the group housing scheme (Table 28). Forty houses were built in 1970 alone, yet for the succeeding five years an average of only nine per year were built. At the same time, however, the number of applicants rose rapidly to a peak of sixty in 1975.

Technical and political factors were responsible for the selective turn taken in the house-building program. In part, water shortages and delays in the transport of building materials were at fault. More important than technical hitches, however, was the central party-state decision in 1971 to opt for burnt bricks rather than kimberley bricks in group housing. This slowed the house-building program and limited benefits to the relatively wealthy. On one hand, the technology of brick-burning was new and required large amounts of hard labor; many Nseluka applicants dropped out, and in 1973 no houses were built while an intensive effort was made to accumulate enough bricks for the schoolhouse, church, and 1974 houses. On the other hand, the brick-burning policy led to a stratification of Nseluka peasants into those who could afford and those who could not afford a burnt-brick house. Grants-in-aid doubled from K20 to K40 at the inception of brick-

TABLE 28.   Nseluka Regrouping Scheme, Number of Grant-Aided Housing Starts, 1969–1975

Year	Number of Applicants	Number of Grant-Aided Houses Built	Housing Materials Used
1969	10	10	kimberley bricks/thatch
1970		40	kimberley bricks/thatch
1971		8	burnt bricks/thatch
1972		11	burnt bricks/thatch
1973[2]		—	
1974	27	9	burnt bricks/iron sheets
1975	60	8	burnt bricks/iron sheets

[1] Sources compiled from various letters and reports in files at Kasama Rural Council and Provincial Community Development Office, Northern Province, and checked against field observation.

[2] "In 1973 there was much preparatory work done for houses in 1974," report, Assistant Community Development Officer, Kasama, to District Secretary, Kasama, February 25, 1975.

burning, but given a fixed budget for Community Development, grants could then be made to fewer people. The trend toward corrugated, galvanized iron roofs at Nseluka also meant that grants could not be used for doors and windows and that recipients had to meet carpentry and other expenses from their own pockets. I calculated that a recipient of a K40 ($60) housing grant required an additional K68 ($102) to complete a simple three-room house.[57] Many house-builders at Nseluka were building larger than standard-size houses, and these houses required an even higher personal contribution. When figures were compared with the K23 annual cash income of a subsistence peasant in Kasama, the tendency of the group housing program to service mainly the well-to-do became apparent.

The party-state sanctioned the increasingly selective nature of the program by endorsing the use of iron roofs. From 1974 onward at Nseluka, housing grants were made in the form of K40 worth of corrugated iron sheets, and any previous recipient willing to convert a thatched roof could receive a state subsidy for half the cost. The Community Development Department openly encouraged people to undertake the expenses of house-building themselves. As a consequence of the reorientation of this "self-help" program, only 12 out of 60 applicants received state assistance for house-building in 1975. The CDA at Nseluka asserted that the emphasis on iron roofs was popular, but both successful and unsuccessful grant applicants agreed that grants of more than K40 were necessary. Recipients of housing grants at Nseluka, Misengo, and other group housing schemes were people with private incomes from government, farming or petty retail trade, many of whom could finance a personal dwelling without state assistance. The remainder were local party officials who, while undoubtedly needy, received preferential treatment ahead of the other poor elements in rural society. In Kasama the iron roof was a mark of status and wealth. The "self-help" policy of group housing, which aimed at leveling social disparities in rural villages, in Kasama was distorted to favor those who needed it least.

Among the local well-to-do who benefited from group housing at village regrouping centers in Kasama were those who accumulated private wealth from long periods of wage employment in urban areas. Two reasons have been noted for housing improvements in Zambia: increased cash remissions from labor migration and a transition to fixed-plot farming.[58] In Kasama the former reason accounts for almost all private house-building. An identifiable subgroup of returned migrants from the Copperbelt emerged at Nseluka; they were partly responsible for the high standard of housing in the village. Some had relatives at Nseluka. Even though no grants were given to prospective settlers while still in urban residence, grants were not difficult to obtain after a nominal period at Nseluka if the applicant had the ability to pay for other building expenses.

This type of settler, whether state-assisted or not, had a detrimental effect on the self-help component of house-building. The group-housing program was originally aimed at owner-builders who would provide their own manual labor. Returned labor migrants, however, tended to use private capital to hire labor for brick-burning, bricklaying, and other construction chores. One Nseluka resident established a small brick-making business which was supported entirely by payments from prospective settlers from the towns. Alternatively, these settlers, who were rarely present in Nseluka themselves, induced relatives with wages or promises of future reward to construct buildings on their behalf. During 1975 one man, who had an administrative post elsewhere in Zambia, hired relatives to build a store as well as a house in the village. Another case, which embodied all the elements of the distortion of the group-housing policy, concerned a WDC member who was also employed as an artisan for a government department at Nseluka. This prominent local leader was constructing a grand six-room house for his son, then a schoolteacher on the Copperbelt. Metal window frames, cement, and money for employing bricklayers was sent home from Luanshya. No self-help resources were used; yet the teacher intended to apply for state assistance with roofing materials, and given the close personal ties of his father with WDC leadership, the application was likely to be successful.

Absentee owners constituted a minority at Nseluka, and their presence could be interpreted as a promising portent of reverse migration to the rural areas. Nevertheless, village regrouping was intended to alleviate conditions of rural poverty for subsistence families and not to provide rural retirement communities for the relatively wealthy. The emergence of a stratum of absentee owners among other house-owning groups pointed to increasing differentiation in the social structure of regrouped villages. Above all, the reliance of absentee owners on wages from the industrialized sector emphasized the paucity of local resources for reinvestment in housing and other facilities.

PEASANT, PARTY-STATE, AND VILLAGE REGROUPING

The intent of the Zambian party-state, like the intent of the colonial government before it, was to prevent urban migration by keeping peasants on the land. Unlike the colonialists, the new government opted not for compulsory restrictions on population movement but for voluntary "back to the land" measures. They sought to build rural growth poles to provide an attractive alternative to wage employment in towns. To this end village regrouping met with only limited success. Migration continued unabated. Alone, voluntary village regrouping could not stem the tide. A significant finding on relations between peasant and party-state which emerged from the Kasama experience was that contrary to the myth widely circulated in bureaucratic circles in Zambia, peasants were not generally averse to village regrouping. Like people anywhere, they responded to the promise of economic opportunities and social services and took risks to improve their standard of living. The Kasama experience showed that traditional orientations of peasants could not be blamed for regrouping failures. Instead, their chief detractors, the party-state bureaucracy, were at least partly responsible. Poor planning was one example: had the people of Kayambi been consulted in advance, the regrouping scheme probably would have been canceled or modified. Poor implementation in the form of lack of logistical support from the state for regrouped peasants was catalogued for Nseluka, Mulobola, and elsewhere. Peasants showed a willingness to attempt new forms of settlement and to use local-level committees to attack development problems. And at places like Nseluka, the signs of success, such as schools, clinics, and water supplies, were abundant.

But insofar as regrouping proved attractive to peasants, it was because of the provision of social services associated with an urban life style. Party-state officials, recognizing the power of this incentive, emphasized social above economic goals. Successful regrouped villages came to stand out as islands of social modernization amidst subsistence patterns of agricultural production. Regrouped villages, no less than other development projects in Kasama, were mere rural appendages of the urban industrialized sector. All major investment in social services in regrouped villages was derived from central state resources. The bulk of the private investment in family housing came from remissions from labor migrants in the cash sector. Notwithstanding isolated instances of self-sufficiency, like the Nseluka sawyers cooperative and the productive farmers of Kayambi, opportunities for earning a cash income were still far greater in town than in the countryside. Most regrouped villages in Kasama had not achieved self-reliance in the production of basic foodstuffs, let alone the production of a marketable agricultural surplus. The social development of regrouped villages preceded economic development; the modern facilities boasted by villages like Nseluka were a false indicator of rural prosperity. Local bases for permanent self-sustained innovation and investment were not established, and the dependence of the locality on the center was not ended by village regrouping.

Finally, village regrouping contributed to social and spatial differentiation among peasants. Not only were development resources concentrated at regrouping sites with little diffusion effect to surrounding villages, but development resources were concentrated in the hands of a few beneficiaries within regrouped villages. Regrouped villages represented a microcosm of the patterns of resource distribution which prevailed under the Zambian rural development strategy. The early promise held by regrouping policy to improve the lot of all peasants was not realized. What first looked like a grass roots mobilization campaign has turned into a selective social-betterment program for local leaders. Village regrouping did not win for the Zambian party-state the mass allegiance of peasants.

Only a mobilized party can achieve rural reconstruction and agrarian revolution.—*Kenneth Kaunda*

In Kasama we have too many hyenas in the party.—*Ward Councilor, Kasama*

III

THE LOCAL-LEVEL POLITICAL PARTY

7

The Rise and Fall of UNIP

In terms of capacity to engender political allegiance to the center, most commentators have depicted Zambia's United National Independence Party (UNIP) in uncritical terms. Mulford speaks of UNIP in 1964 as having "both mobilized and controlled [a] substantial following in the country and maintained [a] prodigious party organization."[1] Official ideology in Zambia has UNIP "a revolutionary mass organization" and a "vanguard of the Zambian people."[2] And writers like Pettman have promoted the image of UNIP in the 1970's as an "increasingly centralized . . . mass political party" and an "emerging mobilization system."[3] The evidence from Kasama District suggests, however, that at no time in its history did UNIP approximate a "mobilization system." On the contrary, the party was characterized, even during its heyday between 1961 and 1964, by loose organizational ties between center and locality. Later, between 1971 and 1975, after the formation and banning of the opposition United Progressive Party, large segments of the party in Kasama became openly disaffected from the UNIP center. The waywardness of the local-level party organization in Kasama illustrates not "the decline of the one-party state" but significant continuities in center-locality relations from colonial to postcolonial eras.[4]

The rise and fall of UNIP support and organization in Kasama District will be documented within a framework of persistent looseness of center-locality ties. Two periods will be compared: UNIP's zenith from 1961 to 1964 and its nadir from 1971 to 1975. Emphasis will not be placed on the changing internal structure of the party, since this subject has been admirably covered elsewhere.[5] Instead I will concentrate on the relationship between party and peasant, the interaction between a nationalist political organization and a subsistence social structure. The issues of recruitment to UNIP and participation and control within the party will be raised. Previously unpublished evidence will be used to support an argument that during the anticolonial struggle UNIP was more of a movement than a political party.[6] Popular sentiment in favor of UNIP was once high, but institutionalization of grass roots party organization was always low. Centralized control from party headquarters was always weak and intermittent.

The nationalist struggle in Zambia was an amalgam of elite bargaining at the center and anomic local uprisings at the periphery.[7] The nationalist political party had little control over the latter. The local-level party that emerged in the nationalist phase was more a reflection of the accession to power of new social categories of local leadership, with strong political interests, than a manifestation of organizational directives transmitted from party headquarters at the center. Yet during the anticolonial nationalist struggle, UNIP was unchallenged in the north by other political parties; Kasama was a de facto one-party district. Ironically, party dominance became a liability in the post-colonial era. Elections consisted of routine endorsement of unopposed UNIP candidates. Kasama District afforded a number of safe seats from which national leaders were sent to the National Assembly in the 1964 and 1968 elections. Competition within the party was not encouraged. Candidates for national office from Kasama were often outsiders selected by the political center rather than representatives of local interests.

During the first decade of political independence, peasants were thus unable to exercise their newly won votes for unopposed candidates in national and local elections. Moreover, perceptions grew among peasants and UNIP officials in Kasama that the benefits of independence, for which the North had fought so hard, were not forthcoming. Like the colonial government before, the party and state was seen to be insufficiently responsive to local grievances concerning rural development. This led to receptivity by peasants, and some local party officials, to the appeals of political opposition. The deleterious impact on UNIP support of the Lumpa Church rebellion led by Alice Lenshina in 1965 has been well documented.[8] The impact of the United Progressive Party (UPP) on UNIP support has been documented for part of Luapula Province but not for the Northern Province.[9] Kapwepwe's UPP promised to promote the sectional interests of Bemba-speakers and, I will argue, received a large measure of support in Kasama District. Its banning in 1971, the declaration of a UNIP one-party state in the following year, and the introduction of electoral competition within the party did little to win back the district. From being a local stronghold of support for the UNIP center during the nationalist struggle, Kasama District became within ten years a local stronghold of opposition. Decline in support was accompanied by atrophy in party branch activity and a tightening of central control at UNIP Regional and constituency levels. UNIP in Kasama underwent a transition between 1961 and 1975 from a popular movement without an organization to an organization without a popular base.

ANTICOLONIAL PEASANT RESISTANCE, 1961–1964

The ascent to power of the United National Independence Party was rooted in a firm foundation of popular support in the Northern Province. The region contributed early, consistently, and strongly to the anticolonial nationalist struggle. African Welfare Societies, the precursors of a nationalist political organization, were first formed in the North.[10] The Copperbelt strikes in 1935 and 1940 were led by Bemba-speaking labor migrants.[11] The African National Congress (ANC), formed in opposition to the settler-dominated Federation of the Rhodesias and Nyasaland, had branches in the Northern Province organized by Kenneth Kaunda. Boycotts of butcheries and other white-owned businesses occurred in Kasama township as well as on the "line-of-rail." The Zambia African National Congress (ZANC), which under Kaunda's leadership broke away from ANC in 1958, drew support from urban workers on the Copperbelt and from peasants from the rural North. When ZANC was banned in 1959, UNIP rose immediately from its ashes; in the Northern Province "UNIP was able to build on the remnants of ZANC's organization which remained strongest in Kasama District."[12]

According to Hall, by 1960 "the party had almost total control of the Northern and Luapula provinces, and a large following on the Copperbelt [but] it was by no means territory-wide."[13] Party officials in Kasama in 1975 recalled the period of 1961 to 1964 as the zenith of party popularity in the district. In the opinion of a schoolteacher who had been an early UNIP supporter, Kasama in the early 1960's was "the real headquarters of the party."[14] The violent peasant uprising in 1961, known as cha cha cha, or positive action, indicated the widespread appeal of the anticolonial message of the party. The success of cha cha cha spelled the end of British control of the rural periphery and, ultimately, the end of British control of Northern Rhodesia. In the wake of peasant resistance the British government reopened negotiations for a constitution for the colony and cleared the way for majority rule. In Mulford's opinion "the negotiations leading up [to] the Northern Rhodesia's 1961 constitution, the Constitution itself and the elections held under it, brought Northern Rhodesia to the most crucial stage of its transition of African government."[15] The rapidity with which political independence was ultimately achieved was due in no small part to cha cha cha. African nationalism in Zambia was as much a rural as urban phenomenon, and peasant resistance was centered in the provinces of the North.

Cha cha cha began in July 1961. Amendments to the 1961 Northern Rhodesian constitution, which would have locked Africans into underrepresentation in national affairs, were rejected by a UNIP General Conference at Mulungushi. Kaunda told the 4000 conference delegates, most of whom were UNIP officials from rural localities, that African political advancement was being sacrificed to save the Federation. He pledged to "strike at the very roots of the British Government in this country" and to wage "practical, nonviolent" war until independence was secured.[16] He called for and was granted party approval for the implementation of a five-point "master plan." Though Kaunda was careful to disguise the content of this plan and to maintain a public commitment to nonviolence, UNIP cadres at the grass roots were left in little doubt that a systematic campaign of sabotage and disruption had been condoned by national leadership. Delegates on returning to their villages began to organize such a campaign within days of the Mulungushi conference.

Kasama District was a hotbed of cha cha cha activities. Peasants, often but not always under local UNIP leadership, attacked the installations of the colonial state in localities throughout the district. The principal targets were government schools, bridges, and roads as well as offices and projects of the Native Authorities. One effective tactic was the felling of trees across main roads in order to bring government communications in the district to a standstill; the road links from Ka-

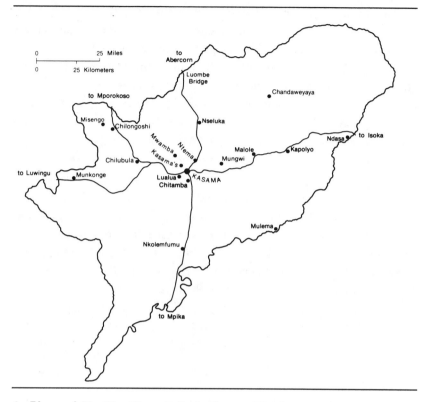

6   Places of *Cha Cha Cha* activity in Kasama District.

sama to the Abercorn, Mporokoso, and Isoka bomas were repeatedly
severed (Map 6). Roadblocks were accompanied by the destruction of
bridges. Party officials from Nseluka and Misengo branches of UNIP
were sentenced to imprisonment for attacks on the Luombe and Ka-
fubu bridges.[17] Twenty-four bridges were destroyed in the province
as a whole. The Munkonge Native Authority suffered the destruction
of a church, courthouse, and treasury office at the hands of UNIP
arsonists. In addition, UNIP had plans to close all government schools.
Schools were burned, as at Ndasa in Kasama, and in neighboring Chinsali District eleven schools were razed in a two-month period. Students
and teachers were urged to boycott classes. The government and the
missions attempted to win the sympathies of schoolteachers by offering protection from what they interpreted as intimidation from UNIP
agitators; but schoolteachers generally refused to act on behalf of the

center. Even though some were armed by the state to protect government property, they "looked the other way when UNIP came to burn
and destroy."[18] Other ambitious plots were hatched by UNIP but
never executed. For example, a plot to burn the hydroelectric power
station at Chilubula was discovered by mission informers before it
could be carried out;[19] and the projected destruction of the District's
largest bridge at Chambeshi on the route linking Kasama with Lusaka
was scotched when an Administrative Assistant from the Nkolemfumu
Native Authority reported the plot to the District Commissioner.[20]

Cha cha cha also took the form of open resistance to the policies of
the colonial state. Taxes went unpaid, as did Native Authority court
fines. The work of colonial officials, such as District Messengers and
chiefs' *kapasus* (messengers), met with obstruction from peasants. As
the "penetrators" of the locality and the "eyes and ears" of the state,
these officials faced protest and threat of violence. The following incident was reported by a Senior District Messenger:

We were sent to go and collect certain people from Kafula Mununga, Chief
Chitimukulu, near Chambeshi. These people refused to go and attend a meeting which was called by [the] Paramount Chief . . . When we arrived at
[Pwemu] village [with arrested persons in tow] we saw people picking sticks,
one picked a hoe. I asked them what these sticks were for. They answered
"why is it that yourself has got a short baton on your waist?" . . . We saw
people coming from the bush in all directions with spears and axes and they
put us in the center . . . They started pushing us with sticks in our stomachs
and cursing at us. They told us that if we shall take these [arrested] people
we would also not go safe and they would even burn the motorcar. Because
the people were many more than we were, we thought of not using force.
There were 89 people present at the scene.[21]

In this case, the District Messenger was forced by a crowd of peasants
from eight villages to release prisoners wanted by the Lubemba Native Authority Court. Spears were thrown at government personnel in
the same area during Kaunda's tour of the Northern Province in June
and July 1960. Violent confrontation between peasant and colonial
state was common in late 1961 in Kasama. At Filaule village, District
Messengers were confronted by an angry mob when they tried to prevent the construction of a UNIP branch office. District Messengers
regularly refused to sleep overnight in certain UNIP villages for fear
of their lives. At Kasama's village, District Messengers met scornful
diatribes from party officials and shouts of "kwacha" ("dawn," loosely

translated to mean "independence"). The Court President to Paramount Chief Chitimukulu reported that:

All UNIP followers between Kanyanta and Mumena villages when they heard I was on tour gathered at Kapolyo's village waiting for me and my party. I talked to them peacefully because I had only five *kapasus* . . . I asked all the tax defaulters to come with me to my camp but Boniface Chewe Mukusao [then UNIP Branch Chairman, later Rural Councilor] stopped them . . . It is also plainly known that people from Malole, Kapolyo and Chambeshi areas are now planning to attack the Chitimukulu's village during the night time to destroy my life and my family.[22]

The response of the colonial state to organized peasant resistance was military force. A state of emergency was declared in July 1961, troops were sent to the North, and in August UNIP was declared illegal. UNIP branches were proscribed. Mobile units of Federal soldiers were dispatched on patrols to outlying regions where attacks on the personnel and property of the state occurred. Most cha cha cha activity took place far from the district boma for, as one informant pointed out, "the people knew that the mobile units were prepared and could move fast."[23] Nevertheless the mobile units occasionally surprised peasants in the act of sabotage or pursued them into the countryside on raids of retribution. Bitter fighting in which lives were lost took place in several parts of the district. Mwitwa village on the road to Mporokoso was remembered as the site of heavy UNIP losses. At Mukolwe a headman, who was also a party official, was killed and a school in his name was erected after independence. The area around Malole mission bred many of the most militant UNIP cadres and was heavily patrolled by the mobile units. According to UNIP documentation, women were raped at Kalikoni's village in Chief Munkonge's area, and houses burned at Shombo's village in Chief Mwamba's area.[24] Granaries and gardens were burned in other parts of the district. Since the identification and apprehension of protesters was difficult, the state applied sanctions indiscriminately. Kasama District was subject to fewer acts of central retribution than Chinsali or Luwingu Districts, but, as one Kasama informant observed, "it was the people in the bush who did all the fighting and they were the ones who died for UNIP."[25]

The northern provinces produced most of the militant "freedom fighters" of the nationalist phase. The role in which Kasama peasants cast themselves accorded closely with the militarist tradition of the Bemba. Of those who died in the entire nationalist struggle, between twenty and fifty, almost all on the UNIP side, were peasants from the northern provinces. Bemba-speakers also formed the majority of the 3000 arrested and 2691 convicted for antigovernment actions.[26] UNIP victory had a special significance to Bemba-speaking people in the northern provinces and on the Copperbelt. A political myth was born and has been nurtured that without them the struggle for independence would not have been won. The pride of Bemba-speakers in their role in the struggle was the basis of strong sectional claims made on the center for development resources after independence.

EARLY RECRUITMENT IN UNIP

The nature and extent of UNIP's organization during cha cha cha and immediately thereafter are important matters for this study. The period 1961–64 represented the zenith of party support and organization in Kasama District and as such affords a baseline against which subsequent party performance in the region can be measured. The extent of peasant recruitment to the party, and the social composition of local party leadership, should both be examined. We also need to know the strength of formal party organizational machinery and the relationship between party center and party locality during and after cha cha cha. Each will be considered in turn. Analysis shows how a nationalist organization attempted to incorporate an uprising in a remote locality into a wider political struggle. In the locality the peasant uprising was an expression of local grievances concerning the lack of rural development under colonial rule, while at the center it was used by nationalist leaders to bolster the drive for political rights for the black majority.

Although the authority of traditional leaders had been in decline for decades, UNIP was the first alternative to traditional political organization to emerge at the grass roots. Tweedie sees 1961 as the date marking "the final functioning of the old system, in which the chiefs were the prime political leaders of the people, and the first functioning of the new, in which people entrusted their political interests to a national political party."[27] This transition was marked by the recruitment of new social groups to positions of local political leadership. The embryonic UNIP organization confronted existing political arrangements for insofar as chiefs and headmen associated themselves with the colonial Native Authority administration, UNIP stood in direct opposition to them.

Party leaders were drawn from strata in Bemba society previously ineligible for leadership. Tweedie credits UNIP with recruiting women and youths into positions of political leadership for the first time.[28] Women were active at UNIP meetings at branch level and were the "mainstay of the movement" when men were imprisoned during cha cha cha. Women had most impact at the lowest levels of the party even though leaders of the UNIP Women's Brigade made symbolic appearances at all party events. The Youth Brigade of young unmarried men and boys acted as messengers and "freedom fighters" for the local party. For the most part the youth wing lacked political sophistication and experience but as one party official said, "the sons sometimes teach the fathers how to fight."[29] UNIP recruitment practices undercut customary respect for age in the main body of the party, as well as in women's and youth wings. As Mulford notes, "the leadership of both ZANC and UNIP was notable for its youthfulness and both organizations placed heavy emphasis on recruiting young people."[30] The average age of main body branch officials in Kasama in 1961 was thirty-two, and some were teenagers.[31]

The most noteworthy experience shared by local UNIP leaders was labor migration to the urban areas in the north. Labor migration created special conditions for the transfer of nationalism between center and locality that were not reproduced to the same extent anywhere else in Zambia. Of the twenty-three UNIP leaders who went on to be ward councilors, twenty had spent time in urban employment in the 1950's; the average time away was eight-and-a-half years. Many had gained political experience in trade unions or in ANC party cells in the boycotts of European butcheries on the Copperbelt. Some had worked as urban party officials: for example, one councilor had been a leader of UNIP Youth in Ndola and another had been a "regional driver" in Kitwe. Another prominent local official attributed his political radicalization to the experience of helping to build Kenneth Kaunda's UNIP office at Chilenje in Lusaka. All said that they transferred techniques of agitation and organization back to the villages in Kasama. One ward councilor boasted that "it was us who taught politics" to peasants. Others picked up characteristics during their urban sojourn—characteristics sufficient to set UNIP leaders apart from ordinary UNIP members. As Tweedie comments, a branch chairman was often "a richer man who works in Kasama but lives in his village, or the leader of a group of farmers on a government-improved farming scheme, or a carpenter from another area."[32] Rasmussen also found that "in the rural areas, anti-colonial sentiments were voiced particularly by cash-crop farmers and returned labor migrants."[33] UNIP appealed to a wide cross-section of the rural population including the poorest subsistence peasants. But from the outset leaders in UNIP were distinguishable from ordinary members according to criteria of education, skills, and wealth. This cleavage is relevant to understanding the decline of strength and appeal of UNIP after the early 1960's.

Traditional leaders found themselves in an awkward position vis-à-vis the party during and immediately after the uprising. The Native Authority system of local government, of which the chiefs were the principal local agents, had been established by the colonial state in order to control peripheral areas. Native Authorities had power to make rules and orders on such important matters as the movement of peasants between villages and the assembly of peasants in public meetings or processions. UNIP activities were an obvious target for regulation by Native Authorities. Most chiefs lacked autonomous authority from the Provincial Administration on which they were dependent for material support and often even for their appointment. Yet chiefs and headmen also sought to retain the support of peasants against the attractions of UNIP. Tweedie argues that in order to retain popular support, traditional leaders therefore had to align themselves, secretly if not openly, with UNIP aspirations. Although UNIP did regard the winning over of traditional leaders as an aspect of the nationalist strategy, the extent to which chiefs became covert supporters of the party should not be overemphasized. Because they were caught between conflicting demands from the colonial state and the nationalist party, traditional leaders wholeheartedly supported neither. Instead, they tried to preserve an independent position that would secure their own interests as a group. Ideally their preference was for a formula of gradual African advancement that would have preserved important powers to the chiefs.

The middle path trodden by traditional leaders can be illustrated as follows. On the one hand, chiefs incurred the displeasure of the Kasama District Commissioner at a Northern Province Chiefs' meeting at Mungwi in July 1961 by rejecting Federal constitutional proposals. One chief, probably Chikwanda of Chinsali, remarked on the acceptability of "bloodshed in preference to the new constitution," and two others "adopted a certain political line as they hoped for ministerial rank under a UNIP-controlled government."[34] Chief Munkonge of Kasama wrote that "he quite agree[d] with the policy and principles of the top party leaders."[35] On the other hand, colonial officials repeatedly warned that the precedent of Ghana, where traditional authority was abolished, awaited chiefs who supported UNIP. Chiefs in Kasama responded by assisting the DC in the apprehension of UNIP activitists and the quashing of party branches. To be sure, some collaboration was explicable in terms of pressure brought to bear upon chiefs by the colonial state, but the zeal with which witchhunts were conducted suggests that opposition to the party among traditional leaders was genuine. For example, the Chitimukulu Native Authority reported on unauthorized UNIP meetings in the Mushimwa Hills near Ngoli and complied with the DC's request to investigate the building of UNIP offices on the Chambeshi.[36] The Chitimukulu Court President also took it upon himself to report the UNIP activities of a man named Pius Kasutu and his family—a man who later became UNIP Regional Secretary for Kasama and then Cabinet Minister for the Northern Province.[37] In October 1961 Chiefs Nkolemfumu, Chimbola, and Makasa jointly signed a letter refusing to allow Kaunda to visit or organize in their areas because:

he taught people to start disturbances in our country, to burn schools, churches, cattle kraals, and destroying roads, things that we use, we whom he says he loves. The same people, UNIP have broken the Native Authority Rules and Orders. They have burnt the offices of Chiefs and caused many deaths among our people.[38]

Until January 1962 Chief Chitimukulu also repeatedly refused to meet Kaunda, and gave his letters of denial wide circulation in the Chi-

Bemba newspaper *Lyashi*. Even Chiefs Mwamba and Munkonge expressed concern that the lifting of the ban on UNIP might cause renewed violence, further undermining the power of the chiefs.[39]

Village headmen were also torn during the nationalist struggle between the competing political organizations of nationalist party and colonial state. Like chiefs, they opted for compromises that best preserved their own interests as a leadership group. UNIP constituted a threat to the existing distribution of power and status in the locality. For the most part headmen, especially the more elderly, did not wish to surrender authority to "young men who do not respect their fathers; they say that freedom fighters have no parents to respect, all are equal."[40] Mutale Mukulu of Nseluka was in this category of headman; in July 1961 he provided information on a meeting at Nseluka school that resulted in the arrest of a branch official. Headmen Kabwibwi and Chinyimba from Mulobola area gave evidence to District Messengers on the collection of identity cards by UNIP.[41] In Tweedie's estimation the normal arrangement in Bemba villages in the early 1960's was for the headmanship and the branch or village chairmanship of UNIP to be vested in separate leaders.[42] Headmen took out party membership or party office only if they calculated that their authority would thereby be maintained. In general, then, the welcome given to UNIP by headmen in Kasama was not enthusiastic. They followed rather than led the nationalist movement and in some cases openly worked against it. Hostility between traditional leaders and local party officials persisted as a feature of local politics in Kasama from the early 1960's to the time of research in 1974–75.

Recruitment of UNIP members took place along the same lines as recruitment of local UNIP officials. Young peasants readily bought party cards while older peasants tended to look to traditional leaders for guidance on how to proceed. But as a whole the population of the district swung convincingly to UNIP. The District Commissioner for Kasama conceded that "the party obtained a high degree of cooperation from the village people who turned out in astonishingly high numbers to take their share of cha cha cha."[43] The Bishop of Kasama complained to the Northern Divisional President of UNIP that "not only some but many members" of the Catholic faith were abandoning the church in favor of the party.[44] UNIP organizers regularly found hospitality from peasants in the villages they visited. Large numbers of peasants participated in risky acts of political sabotage. Tweedie mentions the high incidence among peasants of muscle-strain from tree-felling, which were treated during cha cha cha.[45] Peasant mobilization by UNIP was widespread, as the following account indicates:

[A letter was received by the chairman of Chilanga UNIP branch from the chairman of Machanshi UNIP branch.] He said that our friends were calling us. They wanted us to come and destroy the bridge and put roadblocks at Luombe. We would leave in the evening and arrive in the night time. Many people left at 8 P.M. and arrived at 2 A.M. near Luombe bridge where we found our friends from Chipili village, Chikulu farm, Chilangwa village and Musuku village. All had gathered near Luombe bridge. Some had already started cutting trees and putting them on the road.[46]

UNIP in 1961 was a popular movement with a wide base of support among the poorest of subsistence peasants; yet the emergence of such a movement was as much a consequence of shifts in the economic and social structure in the locality as of mobilization and organization from the center. UNIP offered the prospect of political power to previously disenfranchised elements in rural society. UNIP's initial identification with the underprivileged is made clear by the rapid accession of subsistence peasants, among them young people and women, to party branch office. Despite UNIP's appearance as a mass party, however, the seeds of future stratification between party leaders and party members were present as early as 1961. Once the anticolonial struggle was over, only a limited number of local officials were elevated into positions of power and reward within the permanent organization of the party. In particular the Youth Brigade and Women's Brigade were never integrated into the UNIP spoils system but were relegated instead to auxiliary roles. Most rewards of independence were made on the basis of party hierarchy to those who held official positions in the UNIP main body at constituency level (see below, Chapter 8). And, as will be shown, the situation where peasant mobilization in Kasama constituted the cutting edge of local-level party activity was never recaptured after 1961.

EARLY CONTROL IN UNIP

The degree of control exercised by the party at the center over up-country party organizations has been a subject of debate among analysts of Zambian politics. Tordoff and Scott recognize that "a variety of constraints results in only partial fulfillment of the party's aims to retain a centralized and disciplined machine . . . [these constraints] work against control from the center and increase the power of the local party official."[47] Mulford considers that "UNIP's rapid growth outstripped its capacity to maintain effective internal communication and coordination of party policy."[48] And Rasmussen applies the notion of a "dilemma of scale" to an expanding UNIP, according to which "as the boundaries of a political unit expand, it becomes more difficult to maintain effective control and to accommodate divergent interests successfully within it."[49]

The performance of the local party in Kasama District during cha cha cha illustrates the spontaneity of peasant political action and the looseness of central control. An MP from Kasama, who was a delegate at the July 1961 UNIP conference, recalled that "both the strategy and the time" of the uprising were set by the party center at Mulungushi.[50] Yet all other evidence suggests that the center was caught unawares by the rapidity and enthusiasm of the response to the master plan from northern localities. Tweedie mentions that in mid-1961 "Mr. Kaunda was told to go home at a meeting in which he appealed for patience [in adopting tactics of violence] in spite of failure so far."[51] When asked at the end of July 1061 whether outbreaks of violence were part of UNIP's master plan, Mainza Chona, UNIP Secretary General, replied that he did not know.[52] Local representatives of UNIP failed to exert discipline over the rank and file in the planning of sabotage strikes:

On the night of 13 July 1961 there was a meeting of approximately twenty persons near Kasama's village school, Chief Mwamba. It was presided over by Rodgers Mubanga, Kasama (UNIP) Constituency Chairman. Rodgers Mubanga said he had been informed that the Mobile Unit and Army were leaving Kasama on 15 August and therefore did not want anything to happen before then. Freedom fighters argued with Mubanga saying they wanted to commence activities immediately. They discussed the digging of trenches, roadblocks on all roads in the District.[53]

Against the advice of the constituency chairman, the Luombe bridge action, detailed above, took place on the following day. The constituency chairman acted as a representative of the political center but was unable to restrain local party activists. Some branch officials claimed to be "taking their orders from Kaunda," by which they meant they felt free to implement the UNIP master plan as they saw fit.

The UNIP center was thus forced to react to initiatives prematurely taken in the boisterous North. Kaunda at first called for an end to the uprising but reversed his position by mid-August by publicly burning his own identity certificate and claiming the onset of the first stage of UNIP's master plan in the Northern Province. Looseness of central control may in the end have suited the strategic calculations of top party leadership. The struggle for independence had both local militant and international diplomatic dimensions and Kaunda was careful to maintain a balance between the two. His international image as a Ghandian moderate was reassuring to the British Colonial Office, yet he was also capable of warning, as he did in February 1961, that frustration of legitimate political aspirations would lead to an uprising "which by contrast would make Mau Mau look like a child's picnic." During his numerous tours of the Northern Province, four from June 1961 to January 1962, Kaunda trod a delicate path between endorsing cha cha cha violence and dissociating himself and his party from it. The purpose of Kaunda's tours was to make direct contact between center and locality and to whip up support for UNIP at the local level. Tactics of violent confrontation were presumably discussed in private. Yet at public meetings in Kasama, Kaunda referred only to legitimate means for African advancement and the achievement of self-government, perhaps because of the pervasive presence of District Messengers and other informers. For example, at Nkolemfumu's musumba, Kaunda "condemned acts of violence [which] are generally committed by bad people who do not understand anything."[54] The center-locality dynamic in Kasama during cha cha cha seems to have been that violence was approved and condoned by leaders of the center even if they did not direct it in detail at the periphery or take credit for it in public.

The difficulty that UNIP headquarters encountered in controlling local party-branches in Kasama was partly a consequence of early patterns of political recruitment. The influx of untrained militants at the local level and the ambiguous position of the Youth Brigade within local party organization created severe disciplinary problems. In Kasama "the youths were too independent in the struggle," according to one senior party official.[55] According to another informant, "the youth and the publicity secretaries were the ones who wanted violence. The leaders from Lusaka always talked the other way."[56] Many rural party branches seem to have consisted predominantly of youths. A large proportion of party officials arrested in Kasama on charges related to the uprising were from the UNIP Youth Brigade, despite the fact that the colonial government was systematically aiming to harass the most important senior party organizers. Most of the accusations of political intimidation in the district were laid at the door of the youth wing of the party.[57] Thus while young males were the most enthusiastic of UNIP's new recruits, they were also the least predictable and least controllable. Looseness of control in 1961 was also attributable to other factors, such as a shortage of funds, equipment, transport, and organizational skills within the party. Because of difficulties with center-locality communication, day-to-day matters of local party organization were beyond the purview of UNIP in Lusaka.

Moreover, the center had little control over the way that peasants were introduced to the aims and ideology of the party. From the outset, UNIP's program was presented to peasants by local party leaders in terms of local grievances and in terms of the prospect of material reward. Branch officials in Kasama often made wild and misinformed promises about the impact of independence. Up to a point, local offi cials were able to follow a centrally determined party line, as when appeals to peasants were made on the basis of racial discrimination and the use of force by the colonial regime. Popular slogans like "Kwacha" and "cha cha cha Zambia—majority Kaunda" focused loosely on the achievement of political rights. Issues of economic deprivation took the form of promises of free education, adequate roads and transport, improved clothing, and housing of a European standard. Although none of this departed from national party policy, UNIP officials often asserted an autonomous line. One branch secretary grandly promised that "all Europeans will soon go back to their homes, also messengers and constables; they shall leave all their motor cars and we shall buy them at very cheap prices."[58] Rumors were spread by officials that India, Russia, and the United States were about to intervene on UNIP's behalf and that allied armies were being assembled in Mali and Senegal.[59] Peasants were also led to believe that central government would cease to interfere in their lives if they supported a UNIP victory: "when you get self-government no one will force you to build a good house, to dig a pit-latri [sic], to follow good methods of farming in order to have good food, or compelling you to pay taxes."[60] UNIP officials also indicated that creation of employment opportunities on agricultural and industrial schemes would be forthcoming. Numerous interviewees in Kasama in 1975 confirmed that peasant expectations of rapid rural development were engendered by UNIP during cha cha cha and the 1962 and 1964 election campaigns, and that peasant support for the party was tendered on the basis of these expectations.

Many of the promises made by local leaders did not have the blessing of party superiors. Nor did promises match the capacity of the center to provide. A precedent was established that local party leaders projected themselves to peasants as bountiful patrons, a precedent perpetuated in the postcolonial era. The UNIP center never fully controlled local leaders and peasant followers in Kasama. UNIP and the independence campaign simply provided convenient channels through which dissatisfaction with rural underdevelopment could be expressed. The center rode a wave of peasant resistance, the initiative for which was largely local and unilateral. As late as February 1964, that is after a UNIP government was in power, cars continued to be stoned by peasants on the roads to Luwingu and Mporokoso within Kasama District.[61]

EARLY ORGANIZATION IN UNIP

The party marshaled peasant support with public meetings by day and secret meetings by night. During the ban on UNIP, from August to November 1961, all party organizing activity was proscribed and UNIP operated exclusively underground. Even under normal circumstances public meetings in Kasama required approval from the District Commissioner, but local UNIP leaders proceeded regardless. Meetings consisted of speeches of agitation by party officials, the singing of UNIP songs, and the burning of identification cards. At a meeting in Kasama township the UNIP Constituency Chairman for Kasama declared:

We do not want this government at all; it is a bad one. As you may see, at Mungwi, my people were inside the house singing UNIP songs and for that they were arrested and sent to prison . . . This government is mischievous; if there is no tendency of it being in exile, then we shall just kick it off very hard.[62]

Public meetings took place in the outlying rural areas of the District as well as in the township. In order to avoid prosecution for the holding of outdoor meetings UNIP officials would speak from the doorway of a house while a large crowd of peasants would gather outside.

UNIP organization in Kasama District flourished in places where population was concentrated. The workers' "location" in Kasama township was a key target for UNIP agitation and a stronghold of support. Large rural villages near the township—such as Kasama's village and Chitamba, Lualua, and Ntema villages—had active UNIP branches and sizable UNIP memberships. In peripheral rural areas, too, large villages or clusters of villages, notably Nseluka, Mumba, Mulema, and Kapolyo in the Chambeshi area, were UNIP strongholds, as were villages around mission stations at Malole, Mulobola, and Chilubula (Map 6).[63] At Nseluka, for example, members of the Cairo branch were arrested for holding indoor meetings and for organizing a successful boycott of a mobile government film show.[64]

Kasama's village, a large settlement three kilometers north of the township, was one of the most politically active rural settlements in the district. During the nationalist phase, Kasama's village was not only home to the powerful Milungu branch of UNIP, but a base of UNIP regional operations, with direct access to the large population in the township. Local party officials from all parts of the district and beyond converged on Kasama's village for strategy sessions and briefing on cha cha cha actions. Executive sessions of UNIP were held there when Kaunda and other national leaders visited the District. Encampments of "freedom fighters" were established along the Lukupa river between Kasama's village and Nseluka. These temporary camps were "guarded at night by sentries, and certain noises and whistles [were used] as passwords." The entire locality was described by the colonial authorities as a "concentration area at which [UNIP cadres] would give instructions to UNIP supporters." Up to 5000 identification cards were alleged to have been gathered and burned there.[65]

Party members who were wanted on charges resulting from the uprising left the villages and sought refuge in the countryside. The colonial administration penetrated only to the village level and then only sporadically. Detection by the authorities was avoidable by hiding in the forest, and UNIP was the only organization to penetrate that far. For example, officials of the Misengo-Chipopo branch of UNIP were known to be hiding with "six muzzle guns," and the only recourse open to the state was to try their wives in the Munkonge Native Court on charges of providing food and comfort to guerrillas.[66] One Ward Councilor recounted that along with a future Youth Regional Secretary of Kasama, he hid for "nine months in the hills while the DC was looking to kill me with a gun."[67]

The organizational apparatus of the local party during the peasant uprising had two elements. One was a fairly limited formal network of party branches located at places where population was concentrated. The other was an informal network of freedom fighters from various party branches who were organized into "action groups," operating outside the villages. Formal party branches were presumably subject to tighter central control than were action groups. The latter organizations operated independently, according to tactical considerations determined exclusively in the locality.[68]

The institutionalization of formal party organization in Kasama followed rather than preceded the popular uprising. Before 1964 UNIP was more of a populist social movement than a fully fledged political party. In 1960 and 1961 the UNIP Secretary-General directed an effort to register UNIP branches. The rural areas received most attention, since between July and November 1960 UNIP was proscribed on the Copperbelt. The UNIP Kasama Constituency Chairman claimed a UNIP membership of 14,780 in 1961, but in all likelihood this figure was guesswork. By the end of 1960, seventy-seven branches were registered in the Northern Province, though many more unregistered branches existed.[69] UNIP action groups and branches within the youth and women's wings of the party avoided registration, both to prevent full disclosure of UNIP strength and to maintain a shadow organization in the locality in the event of a ban on registered UNIP branches. Fewer branches of UNIP were registered in Kasama before cha cha cha than in other neighboring districts, and the ban on the party in late 1961 put a temporary end to registration.

The lifting of the ban after cha cha cha signaled the onset of a period of intense party branch organizing, lasting from 1962 through 1964. Clandestine UNIP organization popped up above ground as soon as the ban was lifted; within three days of the Governor's announcement, Kasama UNIP Constituency sent a delegation to the DC's office to discuss registration. Chief Mwamba was informed soon after by the constituency office that branches were reforming in his area at Ntema. The Kasama DC continued to devise ways to block the legal institutionalization of UNIP. Registration was refused wherever a UNIP branch had office bearers who had been arrested or convicted during the uprising. The DC also arrested UNIP officials at the time that applications for registration were lodged, a fate suffered by the chairman of the Kasama Youth Brigade.[70] The DC also twice refused Kaunda's application to hold a public meeting in the township, on the grounds that violence was a likely outcome. On the second occasion a crowd assembled to hear Kaunda and were dispersed with force. An anonymous UNIP official wrote to the DC: "you wanted to see whether UNIP had still some support in the Northern Province after [you] shot sympathizers. What did you see: thousands of people turning up."[71]

Despite obstruction, UNIP's organizing boomed. Tweedie comments on UNIP branch activities in Kasama villages in 1962.

Branch committee members seemed to be active on UNIP business practically the whole time but for most members the UNIP branch meetings on Sunday after Church were the main function. These branch meetings were important instruments in the dissemination and discussion of news. This chiefly came from higher up in the hierarchy, but any member who had been elsewhere, perhaps to a branch meeting at a different branch, perhaps to a public meeting in Kasama, could say what he had to say . . . Both through the organization of the nationalist movement and through their concern with the national news it disseminates, villagers as individuals are integrated into an important national institution.[72]

An informant from Kasama considered that "1961 was the height of UNIP. Everyone shouted *kwacha* at bus stations; many teachers lost employment for participating. There were meetings in all villages, even chiefs' villages."[73] The focal point of branch organization and registration was preparation for the elections of 1962. Interest in the elections was widespread, and from April to October politics was the main topic of conversation in the villages.[74] Peasant solidarity behind UNIP was confirmed when in June 1962 Chilufya and Mangatashi peasants from Munkonge's area refused to register as voters without approval from the UNIP Region; they had assumed a boycott of the 1962 election until the party position on participation was clarified.[75] Moreover, peasants throughout Kasama continued almost universally to refuse payment of taxes, which necessitated the imposition of a ten-shilling levy as one of the first actions of the newly created Kasama District Rural Council in 1963.[76]

The party was restructured on the occasion of the elections, ostensibly to bring top leadership into closer contact with peasants. The eight provincial divisions of the party were replaced with twenty-four regions; Kasama-Luwingu became a region, and Kasama replaced Mpika as the locus of UNIP organizing activity in the Northern Province. Regional party personnel were posted to Kasama township and given professional training and salaries. The Women's and Youth Brigades were integrated more closely with the main body for purposes of central control, a move unfavorably received by local officials in Northern Province.[77] By the end of 1962, UNIP had begun to be consolidated from a powerful movement into a structured organization. The party was able to mobilize peasant political participation in favor of its own candidates in the 1962 election. UNIP was the only political party to mount a registration campaign to attract first-time peasant voters and to teach them the complex voting procedures of the 1962 constitution. Instructions on registration and other organizational matters written in local languages were circulated to all UNIP branches in the District. Regional UNIP officials toured extensively, attacking the opportunistic electoral alliance of ANC with the white United Federal Party.

Ultimately UNIP swept the lower "black" voters' roll in Northern, Muchinga, and Bangweulu seats and even captured the upper "white" roll Northern Rural seat, the only upper roll seat in the country won by UNIP. The opposition to UNIP, the ANC-UFP alliance, miscalculated by assuming that well educated Africans on the upper roll in Kasama had been distressed by UNIP tactics in cha cha cha and would therefore vote for a white trader with a local reputation for racism. Nationally, UNIP captured 78 percent of the vote on the lower roll and 19 percent on the upper roll. UNIP formed the territory's first

African government in a coalition with ANC, which had won heavily in the Southern Province. UNIP's superior organization and nation-wide following, however, ensured the attainment of a strong working majority in the next election. Zambia became politically independent under a UNIP government on October 24, 1964.

THE UPP CHALLENGE

Within ten years peasant support had deserted UNIP in Kasama, and control of the district was maintainable only by the declaration of a single-party state. As Bates well summarizes, "The demands for public amelioration of rural poverty affected the party system in Zambia, both promoting conflict within the ruling party and intensifying the competition between ruling and opposition parties."[78] The genesis of the United Progressive Party can be traced back to disputes over the allocation of development resources, particularly among rural provinces, disputes that were first manifest within the ruling party at the center. Conflict at the center hinged on a widespread perception of Bemba domination of the party and state apparatus. The opening volley in the conflict was the flagrant sectional contest for UNIP Central Committee seats at the general conference of the party held at Mulungushi in 1967. Sectional infighting prompted Kaunda's temporary resignation from the Presidency in 1968 and his dissolution of a meeting of the UNIP National Council in 1969. Strong pressures within the party forced Simon Kapwepwe, spokesman of Bemba-speaking interests, to resign his position as Vice-President of the party. President Kaunda then dissolved the Central Committee and appointed a commission to bring far-reaching changes to the UNIP constitution and to equalize sectional representation within the party.[79]

The resignation of Kapwepwe marked the end of the period when leaders from the Northern Province could be said to dominate the party and national affairs. At one point in 1968 they had held the top positions of President and Vice President of the Republic, Secretary to the Cabinet, Commissioner of Police, and Chairman to the Public Service Commission,[80] as well as five of the eleven elected UNIP Central Committee posts. After 1969 the balance tipped, and was perceived from Kasama as tipped, in favor of Nyanja-speakers from the Eastern Province. Allegations of a plot to give provincial administrative posts in the Northern Province to Easterners could be heard from peasants in Kasama as late as 1975. Because of their fall from favor, UNIP leaders from Northern Province became more vocal in their criticisms on the UNIP center. Members of Parliament attacked Kaunda's policies in the National Assembly, and a Cabinet Minister was dismissed for making unsubstantiated accusations of corruption and anti-Bemba tribalism.[81] The dismissal of Chimba triggered the formation of the United Progressive Party in August 1971. Led by Kapwepwe and Chimba, UPP attracted three other former Cabinet Ministers, six UNIP MP's, and a number of regional-level officials who had lost party posts on disciplinary charges.

Leaders of UPP endeavored to exploit perceptions of sectional deprivation among Bemba-speakers. The party posed no programmatic alternative to UNIP, stressing only, as Gertzel puts it, "the need for a more efficient implementation of the same basic policies that UNIP had initiated."[82] UPP's policies, insofar as any were articulated, were to the right of UNIP policies; as Molteno warns, "the UPP's pretensions of radicalism must be viewed with the gravest caution."[83] Indeed, businessmen were prominent among UPP's leadership at both national and local levels, and in no sense was UPP a party of peasants and workers.[84] The struggle for power between UNIP and UPP did not reflect a struggle between social classes but an attempt to effect a "circulation of elites" within a formative Zambian ruling class. Except on the campaign trail, UPP leaders did not address themselves to the needs of the rural poor. Instead this elite fanned sectional identifications among peasants and other groups in order to create a base for a grab at state power.

Popular support for the new party was induced among three groups: mineworkers on the Copperbelt, Bemba-speaking university students, and local-level UNIP officials and peasants in rural districts of the Northern and Luapula Provinces. Most commentators have assumed that UPP was an urban party; in Gertzel's words, "potentially a Copperbelt party; this was the main thrust of its challenge to UNIP and the government."[85] Tordoff and Scott suggest that UPP "quickly showed considerable organizational competence, especially on the

Copperbelt," where it exploited existing industrial disputes between rank and file miners and leaders of the mineworkers union and government.[86] It has been assumed that the appeal of UPP in the rural areas was slight. Gertzel claims that "notwithstanding local grievances, [UPP] failed to break a basic loyalty to UNIP" and that "dissatisfaction in the rural north seems to have been expressed by abstention rather than by a change of party allegiance."[87] As late as 1974, Tordoff and Molteno could write that the Northern Province remained a "backbone of UNIP."[88]

The conclusion that UPP did not break UNIP hegemony in the North has been based on the results of the 1971 by-elections held as a consequence of the defections of MP's from UNIP to UPP. Kapwepwe won his Copperbelt seat in Mufulira West. But in Mpika East and Mporokoso South, constituencies of the Northern Province, UPP candidates were convincingly defeated, garnering only 4 percent and 15 percent of the vote respectively. Yet the magnitude of these defeats inaccurately reflected the strength of UPP in the North, and because of the following factors. First, five of the six MP's who crossed the floor in August 1971 were detained in September and were ineligible for reelection in the December 1971 by-elections. In both northern seats the party had difficulty finding candidates willing to risk detention. Neither who eventually stood was well known locally. Second, local UPP agents and supporters found difficulty in campaigning openly in an atmosphere of strong control from the UNIP center. Public campaign meetings were not held, and virtually all UPP campaigning in the rural areas was conducted on an interpersonal basis or behind closed doors. Third, the by-elections were held within three months of the formation of UPP, which precluded the establishment of a strong rural organization to replicate the organization of the party on the Copperbelt. By contrast UNIP disbursed K1000 in election funds for each district, and Regional and central party officials were dispatched to ensure that the challenge from Kapwepwe was crushed. Fourth, the turnout of Mpika East was only 41.4 percent and in Mporokoso South a mere 45.2 percent. Only a minority of potential voters in these rural constituencies actually bothered to come out and endorse UNIP. Finally, Mpika and Mporokoso were not in the heartland of UPP support in the North. A senior UNIP official in the Northern Province identified Kasama, Chinsali, and Luwingu Districts as being far stronger in terms of UPP's support.[89] Certain ward councilors from Kasama, admittedly UPP partisans, offered the view that UNIP would have been defeated in any by-election in the District in 1971. Thus it is not possible to conclude on the basis of the December 1971 by-elections alone that UPP was solely a party of urbanites.

UPP enjoyed considerable grass roots support in Kasama in late 1971, even though this support was never marshalled into a coherent organization. In other words, UPP in Kasama in 1971 was analogous to UNIP in 1961. Both were loose, decentralized movements that attracted support initially on the basis of local grievances. Ultimately each was incorporated into a struggle for national power by means of an ideology articulated from the center. Where UNIP's ideology was expressly nationalist, UPP's was expressly sectionalist. Both ideologies, however, emphasized the distribution of material reward in the form of rural development resources party supporters among the poor.

The local grievance of which UPP took most advantage was the shortage of employment and income opportunities in the district, specifically from agricultural projects. For example, the area to the south of the district near the Chambeshi river was strongly pro-UPP. Peasants there held that more tractors had been allocated to other provinces than to the Northern Province and that the government had failed to make good on a promise to provide motorboats for local fishermen. The presence of large numbers of followers of the Emilio and Mutima religious sects, who saw in UPP an opportunity to resist state harassment of their organizations, also had an effect, as did residual loyalties to the Lumpa church. UPP also made appeals on the basis of the low maize harvest of 1971 and the tightening of agricultural credit, especially to peasant cooperatives, in the wake of the dissolution of the Credit Organization of Zambia. The real standard of living of peasants had not risen since 1964, and Kapwepwe was quick to exploit this grievance: he promised industrial projects in the rural areas and free universal education, promises that UNIP had not at the time fulfilled.

Another similarity between the two parties was the strength of UPP in previous UNIP strongholds. Interviews with councilors revealed UPP strength to be concentrated in Kasama township, suburban villages, and large villages in the Malole, Mumba, Mulema, Nseluka, and Mulobola areas. These were the precise locations where UNIP had thrived during the nationalist struggle. Chambeshi constituency, for example, was extremely active during cha cha cha but underwent a dramatic switch of allegiance from UNIP to UPP. Local party officials confirmed in 1975 that "UNIP branches in Chambeshi [were] still privately strong for UPP."[90] Mass membership defections from UNIP constituencies in 1971 also occurred at Ituna and Kasama in Chief Mwamba's area, at Chilunga in Chief Chitimukulu's area, and at Mulobola in Chief Nkolemfumu's area.

Another example of UPP's strength in former UNIP bulwarks was that of Kasama's village. In 1971 this village was the site of frequent secret UPP organizational meetings. Kapwepwe himself often stopped there overnight. Meetings were attended by "other high-ranking officials from party and government in Lusaka, but Freedom House did not know about this."[91] Kasama's village was the headquarters of the UPP organizational network in the District, to which local organizers would come for instruction on party policy and strategy. The stealth and subterfuge of the UPP organization at this time echoed the approach of UNIP ten years earlier, and the proximity of Kasama's village to the urban settlement, where the workers' "location" was reportedly solid for the new party, proved an asset to UPP as it had before to UNIP. The suburban village of Chitamba on the southern side of Kasama township was also a source of opposition support, though this village was later reconverted to the UNIP camp.[92] A senior UNIP official in Kasama described UPP as "a rural party, but with ideas that came from the township and the Copperbelt."[93]

The network of support enjoyed by UPP in these places seems never to have been consolidated into a permanent political apparatus. The UPP interim constitution laid down a party organization on the model of UNIP, except that "unlike UNIP which organized from Region down to branch, UPP would organize divisions based at provincial headquarters to control district branches down to unit councils, comprising ten households of every village."[94] This organizational plan, drawn up by national leaders, was never implemented in Kasama. Few membership cards were distributed, although some subscriptions and donations from businessmen were collected, and party pamphlets were circulated in the township. For the most part UPP's organization in Kasama was personalistic, based on peasant identification with Kapwepwe and the intermediate and local-level leaders who followed him.

Factional disputes within UNIP at the national center were reproduced in the locality. Local-level leaders in Kasama were in quandary regarding a declared allegiance to UPP. The majority of ward councilors and branch and constituency officials in the district seem to have been sympathetic to the new party but could not afford to express sympathy for fear of losing livelihood provided by the UNIP political machine. However much UNIP had failed to provide expected development benefits at the locality, it was still the sole reliable source of income and prestige for local political leaders. Hence support for UPP was covert.

According to interviews conducted by me, three fifths of the members of the Kasama Rural Council, or approximately thirteen out of twenty-three councilors, could be identified as UPP supporters between August and December 1971.[95] Of this number only two councilors openly declared allegiance to UPP. As a consequence, each suffered severe material and prestige losses. Dominic Kacholi, councilor for Ward 8 and a branch official from Chambeshi constituency, was dismissed from both party and Rural Council. The Council refused in 1972 to renew his trading license for a general store at Malole. The store was taken over by an elder brother of the Kasama UNIP Youth Regional Secretary, and Kacholi was forced to take up business elsewhere. Councilor Abel Kasama, councilor for Ward 15 from 1964 to 1971, was detained without trial as a member of UPP and was castigated by the DG "for rebuking the electorate who through UNIP elected him."[96] The deputy chairman of the Kasama Township Council also came out for UPP but was somehow able to hold on to his position. Significantly, the two Rural Councilors who openly joined the ranks of UPP were businessmen with means of support independent of the UNIP patronage machine. Other councilors who secretly supported UPP maintained a façade of UNIP loyalty for reasons as simple as keeping their monthly councilor's allowance.

Commitment to UNIP in public masked quiet but active private campaigning for UPP in the home areas of most councilors. Campaigning for UPP among peasants consisted of disseminationg a crude and exaggerated analysis of Bemba exclusion from national party and state office, and an exploitation of peasant perceptions of deprivation on the subject of rural development. Other campaign issues, such as the abolition of civil service examinations, were used by UPP in appealing to nonpeasant groups, like teachers and state bureaucrats. Before the

December 1971 by-elections and the subsequent banning of the party, there was widespread expectation among councilors that UPP would become a force in national politics. When this expectation did not materialize, councilors who had not openly broken with UNIP were able to slip back into the ruling party fold.

If ward councilors were circumspect about declaring opposition affiliation, lower party officials were not. This group constituted the bulk of the freedom fighters who had been the first young activist recruits of UNIP. They had never been rewarded with patronage posts for their role in the nationalist struggle (see below, Chapter 8), hence had little to lose by openly supporting UPP. Chambeshi UNIP constituency was again an example; only the constituency chairman, secretary, treasurer, and one trustee retained any semblance of support for the center. The remaining twenty constituency officials went over to the other side, taking with them the 43 branches in the constituency. The publicity secretary and his deputy and the constituency vice-chairman were reported to the UNIP Regional Office for UPP organizing.[97] At one point in Kasama township the constituency secretary stood alone among local officials from Chambeshi a reliable representative of the UNIP center.

Divisions within the ruling party on how to deal with the crisis were manifest in the Kasama UNIP Regional Office. The Regional Secretary wished to "use intimidation" against UPP separatists but the District Governor, a former Commissioner of Police, insisted on adherence to legal methods. The UNIP Region in Kasama sent a message to President Kaunda "assuring him that the party [was] solidly behind him" and stating, "we want more development and not confusion in the nation."[98] The telegram seems to have been largely motivated by the desire of the DG and RS to preserve good standing with the UNIP center. Ultimately the entire Regional leadership was dismissed for having lost control of Kasama District. The UNIP Central Committee endeavored to use pro-UNIP Bemba in national office as agents of central political control during the UPP crisis. Lewis Changufu, MP from Malole in Kasama and Minister of Home Affairs, and Andrew Mutemba from Mungwi, Minister for the Southern Province, were put under heavy pressure to calm their restive home district. As a result both were disparaged by peasants and party officials on their visits to Kasama. Mutemba could not be risked in election again and was appointed to the Central Committee in 1972; Changufu was defeated in his first attempt to gain popular election to Parliament in 1973 from his previously unopposed seat in Kasama North.

UPP was banned in February 1972. Kapwepwe and the remaining leaders of UPP were detained. Three weeks later President Kaunda announced that a "one party participatory democracy" would be established in Zambia in which UNIP would become the sole legal political party. To outward appearances UPP was crushed before it could take root as an effective organizational alternative to UNIP. But UPP did enlist extensive support among peasants and left behind in districts like Kasama a reservoir of opposition to the dominant party. A provincial manager of a state corporation offered the opinion that "party loyalty is better in other parts of the country because in Kasama people are UNIP by day but by night they put on black suits."[99] A Regional UNIP Trustee used much the same metaphor when he spoke of "outsiders who sow rotten seeds at night on the pretext of friendship."[100] In 1974 the Kasama Regional Secretary spoke of "fear that some [UPP] might be working inside against the party; we cannot allow squabbles in one house; it can break."[101] Another senior party official commented that the need for the UNIP Region to be constantly concerned with internal security matters "interferes with development."[102]

In 1975 Kapwepwe was still regarded in Kasama by large numbers of subsistence peasants, lower party echelons, and some field-level civil servants as the district's rightful political leader. His detention and subsequent banishment from national politics served to confirm perceptions of discrimination against Bemba-speakers as a group. His periodic visits to Kasama from his Chinsali farm excited more interest and favorable gossip than the visits of President Kaunda. Rumors were heard regularly that Kapwepwe was awaiting the right opportunity to launch a political comeback. In the words of one ward councilor, "Kapwepwe is more popular here than any member of the [UNIP] Central Committee or any [Cabinet] Minister and many people think he would make a good President."[103] Tordoff and Scott's conclusion that "it is questionable whether the threat which UPP posed to UNIP was as great as the leaders of the ruling party feared" did not stand in Kasama.[104] In 1975 Kasama District had reasserted itself as a locality of peasant resistance to the center. Although weakly organized before, during, and after UPP, peasant resistance still posed problems of penetration and control to the newly created single-party state.

THE 1973 GENERAL ELECTIONS

The results of the 1973 parliamentary and presidential elections provide better evidence than the by-elections of 1971 of the decline of UNIP fortunes in Kasama District and the North. Those 1973 elections, the first held under the constitution of the one-party Second Republic, represented an important test of UNIP strength in hostile regions of the country. The UNIP strategy of electoral control and the difficulties faced in effecting it will be considered in the next chapter. Suffice it to say now that candidates favored by the UNIP center went down to severe defeat in Kasama District in 1973. In other northern districts where UPP had had support, candidates backed by the UNIP center were also defeated, such as in neighboring Shiwa N'gandu in Chinsali, where a former deputy speaker of the National Assembly lost his seat. The declaration of a one-party state in 1972 was timed in part because of the impending 1973 election and the recognition on the part of the UNIP center that control of the North and the Copperbelt might be lost. This, coupled with a repetition of the 1968 electoral victories of ANC in Southern and Western Provinces, would have been fatal to UNIP. For all practical purposes the UNIP center did lose the 1973 election in the north, but the party managed to embrace the conflict of UPP within its own ranks under the provisions of the new single-party electoral laws.

Intraparty electoral competition was established in the Second Republic on the Tanzanian model, with the exception that primary elections as well as general elections were to be competitive within the party. After 1973 peasants were able to participate in the election of Members of Parliament instead of having to accept silently a single unopposed candidate. Although both candidates in each National Assembly constituency ran nominally on a UNIP ticket, a very clear distinction was apparent to voters between *candidates of the center* and *candidates of the locality*. Candidates of the locality in Kasama accepted the UNIP label as a matter of convenience—as acceptance was the sole means of gaining election to Parliament; yet they worked for election outside UNIP. The support of the UNIP electoral machine was not extended to them, and indeed, as will be shown later, central resources were deployed against them.

Nevertheless, Kasama voters supported candidates of the locality and in 1973 ejected from office three important national leaders, two of them Cabinet Ministers. Since only three Cabinet Ministers were defeated nation-wide, the role of Kasama voters in upsetting the electoral calculations of the party-state was significant.[105] In Lukashya constituency, the Minister of Home Affairs, Lewis Changufu, was narrowly beaten by nineteen votes by newcomer Joel Kapilikisha (Table 29). In Kasama constituency, the boundaries of which enclosed most of the township, Pius Kasutu, the Minister for the Northern Province, went down before Frederick Walinkonde by a wide margin. Lastly, the Minister of State for the Eastern Province, J. C. Sinyangwe, lost his safe seat in Malole constituency and managed to obtain only one third of the votes cast in an election against another newcomer, Abel Mulanshoka. Votes in the district for candidates backed by the UNIP center amounted to only 42 percent of the total votes cast. In all three cases candidates of the center were defeated by relatively unknown candidates of the locality.

Perceived party affiliations of candidates seem to have been the

---

TABLE 29. Kasama District, Results of Parliamentary Elections, 1973

Constituency	Candidate of the Center	Candidate of the Locality
Lukashya	L. Changufu 1850 (49.9%)	J. Kapilikisha 1869 (50.1%)
Kasama	P. Kasutu 2530 (44.5%)	F. Walinkonde 3159 (55.5%)
Malole	J. Sinyangwe 1666 (34.3%)	A. Mulanshoka 3189 (65.7%)
Totals	6046 (42.4%)	8217 (57.6%)

determining factor in peasant voting patterns in 1973. Candidates of
the center had long associations with the ruling party and were the
official representatives of the center in the locality; for example, Kasutu, defeated Minister for the Northern Province, was the principal
and personal appointee of the President. All candidates of the center
had remained loyal to UNIP during the UPP crisis, and voters knew
their records. By contrast, candidates of the locality were not encum-
bered by affiliation to a ruling party which in the eyes of peasants had
brought only state control and little in the way of development resources to the locality. Theirs were fresh faces. They arrived on the
electoral scene in a year when peasants were ready for change and
were armed with a vote for the first time in almost a decade. The unwillingness of the UNIP region to endorse new candidates reinforced
the impression that the candidates were "non-UNIP" or "anti-UNIP."

Although none of the three candidates of the locality claimed relationship to UPP, all were able to capitalize on a reservoir of support
for the banned party. Evidence of a connection between candidates of
the locality and the skeletal remnants of UPP was circumstantial. In
the National Assembly MP's from Kasama were met with jibes about
being UPP members. At least one of the victorious MP's was popularly known in Kasama as a former UPP organizer, and he continued
throughout and after the election to keep the company of men who had
lost government jobs as a result of UPP affiliation. The other two candidates had established local reputations as educationists: Kapilikisha
had been Chief Education Officer in Kasama, and Walinkonde, after a
career as a schoolteacher in the Northern Province, was a senior civil
servant in the Ministry of Education. They were thus able to draw
upon support from schoolteachers in the district who, as a group, had
favored UPP. During the election campaign UNIP Regional officials
attempted to tar nonfavored candidates with the brush of UPP affiliation, but this probably worked to the advantage of these candidates
in Kasama. The message brought by newcomers to local electoral politics included the familiar litany of deprivation of the rural North at the
expense of other, more urban provinces. Thus while the connection between candidates of the locality in 1973 and former UPP organization
was murky at best, opposition to the UNIP center was seen by peasants in the context of the recent party history of the district.

TABLE 30.   Kasama District, Results of Presidential Elections, 1973

Constituency	Yes	No
Lukashya	2383 (62.9%)	1404 (37.1%)
Kasama	3594 (61.8%)	2220 (38.2%)
Malole	2390 (47.1%)	2676 (52.9%)
Totals	8367 (57.0%)	6300 (43.0%)

Patterns of UNIP support and opposition in Kasama were also evident from the results of the presidential elections in 1973. In general the results were slightly more favorable to UNIP than the results of the parliamentary elections (Table 30). Voters were faced with the choice of voting "yes" or "no" for Kenneth Kaunda as the sole candidate for President of the Republic. A majority of "yesses" was registered in the district. Nevertheless, a substantial number of "no" votes was cast (43 percent), double the national average (under 20 percent). And in the Malole constituency of Kasama a majority of "no" votes (52.9 percent) was registered. Outside of certain constituencies in the Southern Province, which historically were associated with ANC, Malole was the only constituency in the country which failed to reconfirm Kaunda as President. Even Chinsali and the Copperbelt districts, which were usually assumed to be the strongest UPP bases, did not equal this act of electoral resistance from peasants at Malole.[106] A breakdown of electoral figures in Kasama constituencies revealed that "no" votes came from areas identified in this study as UPP strongholds. Within Malole constituency, Makasa, Ngoli, and Malole areas amassed the bulk of the "no" votes. Within Lukashya constituency, which as a whole voted "yes", pockets where "no" votes were in the majority could be found at Mulema-Kanyanta in the Chambeshi area. Here "no" votes outnumbered "yes" votes by 630 to 34, the highest margin in the district.[107] This was probably the least developed area of the district, including as it did the only ward without a school (Table 12) and the area where the entire party apparatus had gone over to UPP in 1971.

Over the district as a whole, a connection was evident between pockets of "no" votes and peasant dissatisfaction with the rural development performance of the center. As argued earlier, village regrouping, as a prominent element in rural development strategy, did not win for the center the mass allegiance of peasants (see below, Chapter 6). It tended, rather, to awaken expectations that could not be fulfilled among settlers at both voluntary and official regrouping sites. This argument was confirmed, though not conclusively, by the relationship between the incidence of "no" votes and the incidence of substantial village regrouping. Of the eleven wards with pockets of "no" votes, eight were sites for substantial regrouping (Table 31). This suggests that peasants, mobilized for rural development in the drive for village regrouping, did not benefit on the scale expected; they translated their dissatisfaction into support for UPP and later a "no" vote against the President. Kaunda's victory in the presidential election in Kasama was thus tempered by overall narrowness and by the existence of pockets of resistance. Had there been another candidate in the Presidential election in 1973, particularly Kapwepwe, Kasama District might have asserted its autonomy from all candidates of the center.

Finally, the 1973 elections were characterized by the lowest voter turnout in a decade (Table 32). In Kasama only 36.6 percent of the eligible voters came to the polls, as compared with 95.2 percent in 1964; this decline in turnout was part of a general trend nation-wide;

TABLE 31.   Kasama District, Village Regrouping and "No" Votes, 1973

	Wards with Substantial Regrouping[1]	Wards without Substantial Regrouping	Totals
Wards with polling districts reporting "no"[2]	8	3	11
Wards without polling districts reporting "no"	5	7	12
Totals	13	10	23

[1] See Table 21.
[2] This category includes any ward in which one polling district showed a majority of "no" votes. It also includes Chandamukulu (Ward 8) and Mungwi (Ward 13), in which "no" votes were 4 and 2 votes, respectively, short of a majority. Polling-district breakdowns were available to me for Kasama and Lukashya constituencies; the designation of areas voting "no" in the disputed Malole constituency were derived from councilor interviews.

TABLE 32. Zambia Electoral Turnout, General Elections, 1964–1973

	Number of Registered Voters (National)	National % Turnout	Kasama District % Turnout
1964	1,379,804	94.3%	95.2%
1968	1,587,966	77.0%	(no voting: all candidates unopposed)
1973	1,700,000	39.8%	36.6%

in 1968 only 77 percent had gone to the polls. Peasants expressed apathy or opposition to UNIP policies by refusing to affirm the legitimacy of the ruling party. In 1973 UNIP candidates were able to capture the support of only 15.5 percent of the registered voters in Kasama district in the parliamentary election and 20.9 percent in the presidential election. This represented an extremely low level of voter affirmation for the one-party state. It stood in marked contrast to the 92.8 percent affirmation of UNIP candidates in Kasama District in 1964.

A decline of this magnitude in electoral participation and affirmation was explicable in large part by the weakness of the political party as an agent of peasant political mobilization. As will be shown in the next chapter, UNIP at the local level was unable to deliver the vote to candidates of the center because of the atrophy of local party organization. Electoral mobilization has usually been assumed to be UNIP's strong point. But the Kasama case points to a severely weakened local party in an area of the country that was once UNIP's heartland. Precisely because UNIP had not institutionalized a "revolutionary-centralizing" or "mass-mobilizing" influence over the course of the nationalist struggle in Kasama, it was ill-equipped to exert such an influence later. The UPP interlude and the withdrawl of electoral support were instances of the weakness of the center. In 1961 the grassroots branch leadership of the party delivered peasant support to the center; by 1971 the self-same party officials were organizing branches of UPP. With the loss of its branches, UNIP lost the capacity to link center and locality by means of mass peasant participation. After 1973 party leadership at the center moved to replace declining mass participation with limited elite competition within a single-party framework.

A tendency, latent in UNIP from the outset, for center-locality relations to be conducted through a stratum of local patrons was thereby institutionalized. This mode of linking center and locality emphasized central control above mass local participation and laid bare the organizational principles of the party in practice. An analysis of these principles is the aim of the next chapter.

8

Patronage and Control in UNIP

By 1975 UNIP had been transformed from a party of participation to a party of control. The transformation was gradual, beginning with party reforms in 1962 which sought to bring upcountry regions under central party direction, and culminating in the massive system changes that accompanied the introduction of the single-party state. The history of UNIP in the postcolonial phase was a history of attempts to centralize authority within the party. UNIP constitutional reforms, of which there were four between 1962 and 1973, progressively concentrated power in the hands of the President, Secretary-General, and Central Committee of the party.[1] By 1975 the UNIP center had for the most part succeeded in disciplining the Regional level of the party and eliciting conformance to the party line. An argument will be made that by 1975 the center, from the point of view of peasant and party-state alike, penetrated and exercised control at least as far down as the UNIP Region.

By the same token, however, political control below the Regional level of the party was sparse and sporadic. First, the strength of any political party depends in part on the size and commitment of membership, and by 1975 in Kasama the period of enthusiastic, voluntary, mass membership in UNIP was over. Party organization at the branch level had atrophied, and active peasant members of UNIP were few and far between. Second, at the constituency level of the party, the maintenance of party organization depended heavily on the availability of patronage rewards for constituency officials. Where development resources were available for local party patrons and their followers, the center had a presence in the locality and a modicum of political control. Where resources were lacking, so was central control. Finally, the place of the UNIP Region in the local politics of rural development underwent transformation from the 1960's to the 1970's. Tordoff and Scott argued that the UNIP Regional Secretary (RS) had "a strong local base [which] gives [him] a greater degree of independence of the center than the method of his appointment [from the center] might suggest."[2] This did not hold for Kasama in 1974–75. In the Zambian single-party state, the RS, far from being a spokesman for local interests, acted almost exclusively as an agent of the center. Without a reliable party organization below the Region, however, the ability of the RS to effect central control was limited.

A wide range of mechanisms for central control of the locality are available to a ruling party. Formal constitutional arrangements can be made in a one-party state for party supervision of elections and development projects. Informal mechanisms for control of party functionaries and party members can be made that are either ideological, coercive, or material. In Zambia the last predominated. The ideology of Zambian Humanism was poorly understood and seldom accepted by party-state functionaries at the local level as a guideline for peasant participation in party affairs. The party was principally maintained not by mass mobilization but by the machine politics of patronage and material reward.

The connection between patronage and control was evident in UNIP in Kasama by the party's use of development resources to buy the loyalty and discipline of local leaders. The shifting social structure in Kasama threw up what Bretton calls "a tight inner circle of middle-level functionaries who make use of the party . . . for their own ends [but who] will always be captive of whoever controls patronage . . . only to the extent that the supreme dispenser of patronage allows freedom of action can the lesser leaders and functionaries pursue their own interests . . . high on the list of demands are retention of privileges and perquisites, income, legitimate and other, and beyond that preservation of the system that brought them their good fortune."[3]

THE ATROPHY OF UNIP BRANCHES

Evidence of growing peasant apathy to the party can be gleaned from figures on UNIP branch registration and membership in Kasama from 1964 to 1974 (Table 33). Claims of party membership made by

TABLE 33.   Kasama District, Estimates of Party Membership and Party
Branches, 1964–1974

Year	Main Body UNIP Branches	Membership
1964	110 (estimated, including unregistered)	11,000
1965	n/a[1]	n/a
1966	22 (registered only)	n/a
1967	26 (registered only)	25,000
1968	55 (registered only)	n/a
1969	15 (registered only)	n/a
1970	n/a	n/a
1971	n/a	n/a
1972	n/a	n/a
1973	n/a	n/a/
1974	87 (estimated, including unregistered)	5,000

[1]n/a = not available.

Regional party officials were difficult to substantiate. For example,
the round figures of 35,000 UNIP members for the Kasama-Luwingu
Region in July 1965, and 25,000 for the Kasama Region in June 1967
were provided without documentation to the Registrar of Societies
and appear to be inflated.[4] High membership claims contrasted with a
marked decline in UNIP branch registration. Before independence
in 1964, 110 main body UNIP branches were registered; in 1966 only
22 and in 1967 only 26 renewed registration.[5] An appeal was launched
by the Registrar of Societies to identify and revive 117 UNIP branches
from previous lists, including youth and women's branches. In response to the appeal, registration of UNIP branches in Kasama was
stepped up to 55 in 1968 but had dropped again to a new low of 15 in
the year after the 1968 election. By 1969 regional UNIP officials had
ceased to submit annual returns to the state on regional membership.
Card sales were dramatically down. When asked about the apparent
decline in branch level party organization and support in the late
1960's, one ward councilor remarked that "people here had done their
work for the party and they were waiting for the party to do something
for them."[6] A farmer said that apart from a few zealous local officials,
"people were too busy getting food to worry about the party; the party
is just politics anyway."[7]

Branch political activity in Kasama in 1974 and 1975 was found by this researcher to be low and in the most peripheral rural areas party branches were generally defunct. The formal provisions for the formation of party branches were flexible. According to the UNIP Constitution, "a branch may cover a big village, a local government area of a ward . . . provided that no branch shall consist of less than thirty paid-up members."[8] The formation of a branch required approval by the UNIP Central Committee and registration with the constituency, Regional, and national party headquarters. In 1974 the UNIP RS estimated the number of party branches in Kasama District at 153, but in 1975 his successor commented that this was "just guesswork."[9] Indeed by late 1974 Regional records had fallen into such disarray that the new RS had no way of precisely determining branch organizational strength. And an incoming DG in 1974 was unable to present to the Provincial Political Committee a report of party activities, or even a confirmable list of UNIP constituency officials. From the late 1960's onward, branch and constituency secretaries were notoriously lax in forwarding to the Region such records as monthly membership returns, minutes of meetings, and branch annual reports. Funds from the sale of party membership cards were not accounted for, and misappropriation of funds led to the suspension from the party of minor officials in 1974. In 1975 a new RS envisaged branch reorganization in Kasama and spoke of establishing branches of roughly one thousand members, encompassing whole wards in areas of low population. This would make for 107 potential UNIP branches in the district as a whole, which would restore the high registration of 110 branches in 1964.

Interviews and observations by this researcher revealed that far fewer UNIP branches existed in 1974–75 than in 1964. The decline in the number of active branches during the mid-sixties, noted above, can be extrapolated to the mid-seventies. All branches were decaying to a greater or lesser extent. Ward Councilors who were constituency officials were asked how many party branches existed in their constituencies. Only 87 branches, most of them unregistered, were revealed in interviews. This figure was probably overestimated because it included defunct branches existing only on paper. For example, Mpanda UNIP constituency in the northeast corner of the district around Kayambi and Makasa was said to have 14 UNIP branches. Peasants at Kayambi reported, however, that no party branch activity was currently under way. On paper Mipini branch of UNIP was supposed to serve all villages of the Kayambi area, but no peasant could recall a branch meeting held in recent times. One peasant remarked that "these branch leaders are invisible." Although the name of the branch chairman was known to a few headmen, peasants could not name the branch secretary; in an embarrassing moment at a VPC meeting in Illondola village, he had to raise his hand when a question arose about his identity. This branch secretary candidly admitted that no branch elections had been held from 1964 to 1974 and that lower-party cadres at Kayambi had been silent in the drive for village regrouping. He claimed that party officials of the branch executive did meet periodically, but that ordinary party members were not invited.[10]

Another example of branch atrophy was found at Mulobola. Armed with a list of branch officials dating from 1968, I was able to determine the whereabouts of fewer than half. Some claimed no longer to be officials because meetings were not held; this explanation was given even by branch chairmen whose duty it was to call the meetings. Others had migrated to other parts of the district or to the line of rail, and with their departure branch activity had lapsed. In any event no new branch officials had been recruited for ten years; those who remained were the freedom fighters whose hour of glory was long gone. That the older generation of party officials was held in low esteem by peasants was evidenced by the treatment accorded one branch chairman at Milenge in Ward 16. He was not invited to a WDC meeting; midway through the proceedings he burst in, loudly disclaiming the legitimacy of a meeting held "without the permission of the party." The branch chairman's argument suffered in authority and coherence because of his noticeable intoxication, and he was jeered out of the meeting. His closing threats about "the power of the party" were apparently not convincing to the assembled crowd.

The situation at Kayambi, Mulobola, and Milenge could be generalized to the whole district. To a man, ward councilors agreed that branch organization in Kasama was past its peak. One commented that "now we have no branch chairmen to help the headmen; we used to have office bearers and youths in every village and the youths got people to come to meetings but now the youths have gone to town."[11] Another said that "there are by this time no branches in my ward; I invite branch officials but they don't come; I never see a branch official helping me; they don't reply to my letters; other councilors have the same problem."[12] The decline of local branches was confirmed at the highest level of district administration by an incoming DG; in August 1974 he declared that he did not regard as legitimate the present holders of branch and constituency office, because no party elections had been held for "the past five or six years."[13] When branch and constituency posts had fallen vacant, local party patrons simply appointed their colleagues, even though the party constitution stipulated election. This state of affairs was hidden from the political center by Regional officials who continued throughout the period to submit rosy reports of constituency and branch organizational strength. With extreme candor the new DG remarked: "I must admit to you we will have to reorganize the party in Kasama."[14]

The general picture of UNIP branch atrophy was disturbed by the few areas in Kasama District where evidence of local party activism was found. Again, large villages provided the locus for political organization. In Luapula, Bates found "the continued functioning and acceptance of the party" and "regular and meaningful competitive [party] elections,"[15] though these findings were based primarily on research in Kasumpa, an atypically large and accessible village. In Kasama, surburban Chitamba and surrounding villages had a full roster of local UNIP officials, and pressure brought to bear by party branches helped to stimulate VPC and WDC activity. The successful mobilization of peasants for development projects at Nseluka was also attributable in part to the work of UNIP branch cadres. Nseluka peasants still acknowledged local party organization to be strong by Kasama standards; branch meetings were still held and branch officials participated on local-level development committees. The performance of UNIP in inducing turnout for elections or symbolic events like independence celebrations at Nseluka was testimony also to the survival of the party. Nseluka peasants even donated a building next to the village clinic for use of UNIP as a constituency and branch office. Yet even at Nseluka the only people to refer regularly to UNIP's role in local development were branch officials themselves. Peasants said that the behavior of party officials was cliquish; for example, party leaders sat with local civil servants while drinking beer, rather than with peasants. As mentioned previously, cooperation between party and state leaders at Nseluka was good, but this did tend to separate party leaders from ordinary party members. The domination over decision-making of a united front of leaders at Nseluka led to a dissociation of UNIP from the people who had originally provided its popular base.

The only minutes of a recent UNIP branch meeting that I was able to uncover referred to a meeting held in 1974 by Malama Branch, Kasama Constituency, in the house of the branch chairman in Chitamba village. The meeting was attended by the Kasama constituency secretary and was marked by the endeavors of officials to revive membership and support. The branch secretary complained that "official members don't come when they are told to do so. That is why all new members have taken the same way." He resolved "to try and organize [members] again to make the party be strong enough." The constituency secretary added that "it was very shameful to see many people with 'no' votes last time. People did not think well by voting *ichimbwe* [hyena, the electoral symbol for a "no" vote]. This must end now as we are grown up people." The meeting adjourned with homilies about hard work and party card-selling and a warning by senior to junior party officials to "remember to interrogate all newcomers" to the branch.[16] In a separate interview the Kasama constituency secretary remarked that UNIP organization in suburban villages was good only because "constant supervision" was possible.[17]

Party organization at subbranch or village level was for all practical purposes nonexistent. Technically UNIP branches supervised the activities of UNIP Village Political Committees, known in urban areas as Section Committees, which were the smallest units of the party.[18] Village Political Committees were not the same as Village Productivity Committees (VPC's); the former were supposedly concerned with political affairs and the latter with developmental affairs, though ward councilors were often hard-pressed to explain the difference. The intent of the center was for close integration of political and productivity committees at village level, with a high crossover of membership and assertion at the grass-roots of the national principle of party supremacy.[19] In Kasama, reality diverged from the ideal plan in two ways. First, few Village Political Committees survived; only at Bwembya village and Nseluka village did I hear any reference to their activities, though presumably more than two are at work in the district as a whole. Only ten out of forty-four headmen could recall village committees of UNIP, as distinct from branches, existing in their vil-

lages at any time. Second, Village Political Committees did not necessarily integrate with VPC's and oversee their work: at Bwembya
only a few of the members of the UNIP Committee sat on the VPC,
and the headman offered the observation that "they do different work
anyway."[20] The Village Political Committee at Bwembya consisted of
a few active officials who used UNIP as a means of gaining personal
status but who lacked a broad following among residents of this large
village. In sum, integration between party and state at village level
was low. The claim made by a senior Regional party official that "chairmen of Village Productivity Committees are always UNIP Chairmen
or other UNIP officials"[21] did not stand empirical test. Of the 44 VPC
chairmen interviewed, only 13 claimed to hold party office and only 7
said they were UNIP branch chairmen.

Insofar as party branches survived, they consisted of party officials
alone. The loss of the mass base of the party among peasants can be
catalogued by declining party membership in Kasama. Exact membership figures were not made available to me, but it can be said with
certainty that until the end of 1974 party membership in the district
was in a serious slump. For example, there were no paid-up UNIP
members in the Chilufya-Mulobola area of the district, among other
areas, in 1974. One peasant was heard to say that "the time when
UNIP was here is difficult to remember." The councilor for the ward
laid blame at the door of the UNIP Region "who have not visited us
for one year and have not brought us party cards to sell; we have no
one to conduct us and everything is going astray."[22] The UNIP constituency office at Mulobola was abandoned and the kimberley bricks
of which it was constructed had begun to crumble. At Mulobola, too,
a peasant commented that the UNIP office was "always closed," and
the broken windows and deserted interior of the building lent mute
corroboration to his testimony.

Two UNIP Central Committee members toured Mulobola and Chi-
longoshi areas in Kasama in 1974 and reported on a lack of party cards;
their report was published in a national newspaper under the headline
"Kasama Party Machinery 'Bad'." One MCC reportedly "told the people that they were not members of UNIP . . . [and] that if any kind of
election was held today people there could not contest or vote"; he
added that he "was worried because the masses there could easily be
disorganized by disgruntled leaders."[23] This researcher saw 1973

cards and stamps that had been sold in 1974 at Munkonge and Chi-tamba. Legitimate updated party card sales in 1974 were limited to Kasama township, and sales were low.[24] Legitimate updated party card sales were not restored to the district as a whole until the follow-ing year. In 1975 cards and stamps to the value of K2548 were sold in Kasama District to a maximum of 5000 members.[25] This figure was less than half of the claimed UNIP membership for the 1961–64 pe-riod, and represented only 9 percent of the present adult population of the District.[26] Coincidentally, the same low magnitude of party sup-port was officially reported in 1975 for the Copperbelt Province, one of the other main Bemba-speaking areas of the country. A national newspaper declared that "only nine percent belong to UNIP on the Copperbelt" and reported a statement by a member of the Central Committee about the "great need for Party officials to review the organization of the Party in the Region."[27]

Nor was party strength necessarily related to formal membership. Membership figures failed to distinguish between an active, committed local party and a local party that maintained support through coercion or the distribution of spoils. Party branch activities in Kasama sug-gested that UNIP was a local party of the latter type. A popular depic-tion of the party among peasants was that card-selling, card-checking, and card-carrying had become its main *raison d'être*. One councilor said that the only reason the UNIP Regional Secretary came to his ward was "to collect party fees."[28] Peasants themselves came to real-ize that the best means to retain access to development resources was to carry a party card. Party activity in early 1975 in Kasama was domi-nated by a card-selling campaign in preparation for party branch elec-tions and local government elections for Town and Rural Councils. UNIP's card-selling approach was to move door-to-door in large set-tlements or to circulate among crowds of peasants gathered at public places. UNIP Youth, in violation of directives from the center but probably with the tacit approval of the Region, were able to deny ac-cess to such state facilities as buses, markets, and clinics to peasants who could not prove paid-up party membership. Ferry passengers in neighboring districts were faced with similar controls. Workers on the Tanzam railroad projects in the district were warned by UNIP branch officials that retention of jobs was conditional on proof of party mem-bership. Peasants at Kasonde Chisuna mentioned that the UNIP special constables were overly assertive in their auxiliary police duties during the election period. The carrying of a UNIP party card along with a voter registration card became a legal requirement for participation in elections in 1975. On balance, the local party tactic of making access to development benefits conditional on proof of party membership tended to generate peasant alienation rather than peasant support. Authoritarian tactics bespoke a party organization without a popular base. The commitment of peasants to the UNIP political machine was instrumental rather than moral or ideological, as illustrated by the farmer from Ngulula who referred to his party card as his "passport for fertilizer."

DAY-TO-DAY POLITICAL CONTROL

The extent to which the UNIP Region was subject to political control from the center and to which the Region itself exercised political control in Kasama District in 1974–75 will be examined below. Day-to-day control was distinguishable from electoral control. Control between elections was facilitated by a party organization that located the making of party policy and key party appointments at the center.

Party policy was made almost exclusively by the President and UNIP Central Committee. The UNIP National Council, nominally the sovereign body for policy formulation in the party, functioned in practice as a rubber stamp. The National Council was used by President Kaunda to announce landmark decisions of national development strategy, like the nationalization of mines and the decentralization of administration. Regional officials of UNIP throughout the country attended the National Council, but delegates had little control over the agenda. For example, a motion by the Kasama delegation to extend payment of party salaries to constituency officials never reached the floor at the April 1974 National Council.[29] Another unsuccessful motion was presented by the Kasama delegation at the National Council on December 1974 to increase and professionalize the Regional bureaucracy of the party.[30] By contrast, Regional officials returned from National Council meetings at the center laden with policy directives for implementation in the locality.

Other central executive functions of Regional party officials included

sharing with civil servants in the DDC the management of development projects, particularly ensuring completion of projects during fis-
cal or plan periods. Regional officials were often faced with a hostile
reception when they functioned as spokesmen for central policy. For
example, the Regional Secretary in Kasama was faced at Milima with
angry questions that he could not answer about the temporary doubling of bread prices during November 1974. On another occasion the
RS was called to Mungwi to settle an ugly dispute concerning the
failure of the state breweries to keep district bars stocked with bottled beer. The local-level party was thus called upon to perform as a
control appendage of the central state and to defend policy made outside the locality.

Central control was also exercised through *key appointments*. The
two top party officials in each district, the DG and the RS, were central
appointees. They were responsible ultimately to the President and
the UNIP Central Committee rather than to a peasant electorate. The
main task of these officials was to make the presence of the party felt
by politicizing all affairs of state in the locality. If they failed to implement party control of local policy and practice, they were subject to
dismissal by the center. For example, after candidates of the center
lost the 1973 election in Kasama, the entire Regional party leadership
was purged. The DG was sent into political obscurity as the Zambian
Ambassador to the United Arab Republic. The RS and Women's RS
were demoted to Mporokoso District, away from the provincial capital. The Youth RS was given the unenviable task of organizing party
activities in Kaputa District, a newly created administrative unit on
the Zambian border with Zaire where, one wag quipped, "his only
party members will be elephants and mosquitoes." Not only had these
leaders allowed branch registration to lapse and party cards to go un-
sold but had engendered resentment from branch and constituency
cadres whom they had failed to support against peasant criticism. By
1973 there were parts of Kasama District where the Regional Secretary did not "dare to go."[31]

The clean sweep by the center of personnel in the Kasama UNIP
Region was aimed at a thorough reorganization of the local party. In
late 1974 branch officials expressed high hopes that an infusion of new
leadership at the Regional level would revitalize branch organization.
Just one year later the same officials expressed disappointment that

"the Region only tells us to work harder but doesn't come out and help us."[32] The new party appointees had no previous relationship with Kasama District. The DG, appointed May 1974, was an experienced party organizer from Kitwe Urban Region on the Copperbelt; the RS had served as YRS in Mbala and Kaputa Regions as well as in Samfya, Luapula, his home province.[33] Both were UNIP careerists whose appointments were made on the basis of considerations of loyalty to the central party and not because they represented local interests.

As part of the attempt to revive central control in rural localities, a new appointive party post was created after the 1973 election. In April 1974 a Provincial Political Secretary was designated for each province to act as deputy to the Minister for the Province with special responsibility for party organization. The creation of the post was attributed at the center to a need "for someone to supervise meetings at Region, constituency and branch level in the absence of the party."[34] The fact that the first two Provincial Political Secretaries appointed to Kasama came from the Eastern Province, at a time when the Provincial Permanent Secretary, the DG, and other heads of government departments were also Easterners, generated much critical comment about outside domination from people of all social strata in the district.

The most sensational case of central control by political appointment in Kasama concerned Pius Kasutu, the Minister for Northern Province defeated in the 1973 elections. Immediately after his defeat, Kasutu was designated Permanent Secretary for the Northern Province, the second most prestigious post in the Province. Opposition was extensive to the reappearance of this leader in an appointed civil service position within a month of his defeat at the hands of the Kasama electorate. He was unable to tour the district or appear in public without pointed questions being raised as to his continued occupancy of a leadership position. Ultimately, in response to local protest, Kasutu was withdrawn by the center and sent overseas for further education.

Day-to-day control was exercised over and through elected officials as well as appointed officials, as was clear from the relationships of the party Region and Members of Parliament in Kasama. In the First Republic "the party regard[ed] the parliamentary constituency as party property rather than the domain of the M.P." and this held true for the Second Republic, too.[35] After the 1973 elections the MP's in Kasama were all candidates of the locality who had acceded to office against the wishes of the UNIP center. On orders from the UNIP Central Committee, the party Region in Kasama monitored the movements of MP's while in office, and controlled access to constituents by granting or withholding permission for MP's to visit the villages. A Central Committee directive in 1974 required MP's to clear all public meetings with the UNIP Region and to permit a party official to accompany them on constituency tours. Sometimes the RS would conduct such supervision; more often a reliable UNIP constituency secretary would be delegated the task.

The case of the MP for Kasama shows the method of UNIP control of non-favored MP's. He applied to hold a public meeting at Mungwi in January 1975 but was refused by the DG. He then had to attend sessions of the National Assembly and National Council in Lusaka and was unable to return to Kasama until three months later. His attempts to secure Regional approval and accompaniment on tour were met again with explanations that the RS was too busy or out of town. "There was not a good understanding between us and the Regional officials," the MP said by way of public account when the meeting was finally held, with the UNIP constituency secretary present, at Mungwi in late April.[36] Nor did the UNIP Region assist the MP for Malole with party transport for constituency touring when his private vehicle was stolen later in the same year.

Indeed the new MP's had difficulty maintaining the support of the peasants who elected them as candidates of the locality in 1973. One councilor said "our M.P. does not wish to pander the people by coming to visit us; we have just heard on the radio that he exists."[37] By the end of 1975, complaints were voiced by peasants, particularly in Kasama and Lukashya constituencies, that "these M.P.'s will not go through [in election] again." One interviewee commented that "they are not enjoying their membership [of Parliament] except for drawing allowances; they do not feel at home in district and just meet friends when they are in Kasama."[38] The endemic conflict between MP's and the UNIP Region in Kasama was well illustrated by arguments over the question of MP's having offices in the district. All MP's were in favor of having independent local headquarters, but the RS would only countenance the idea if the MP's offices were in the same building as the UNIP Region. Local development suffered, in the opinion of one disaffected councilor, because "M.P.'s find it difficult to start schemes because party organizers don't cooperate."[39] From the viewpoint of the center it was "difficult to start projects with [opposition] M.P.'s like this."[40]

The transformation of the UNIP Region from a predominantly local to a predominantly central political institution in Kasama was accompanied by a shift in the social composition of the party. By 1975 recruitment to party office leaned away from peasant agitators and toward educated administrators. In order to compete effectively with the Zambian civil service, whose resources of trained manpower dwarfed the resources of the party, UNIP attempted to professionalize its cadres and bureaucratize its internal procedures.[41] This showed up in numerous ways at the local level. For example, the salaries of Regional officials were increased in 1974 to place them closer to par with the salaries of district-level civil servants.[42] Posts in the party bureaucracy requiring special qualifications were publicly advertised for the first time in 1974, and a large increase in the party subsidy was voted through the National Assembly. Greater selectivity in party membership was exercised by Provincial and Regional officials in Kasama during the party reorganization of 1974 and 1975. Some potential members and branch officials were screened for formal educational background and required to fill out complex applications in quintuplicate, three of which were forwarded for central approval at Freedom House in Lusaka. The Provincial Political Secretary for the Northern Province said that he hoped qualified civil servants would stand in branch elections and that henceforth the party would recruit from among the best and brightest in the locality: "because you threw a stone in 1960 doesn't mean that you are still important; we ask what you are capable of doing now."[43] Another senior party official commented that "reading and writing good English is now the thing we are looking for in our leaders."[44]

Along with the closing of the ranks of local party leadership to former activists from the nationalist era, emphasis continued to be placed by the UNIP Region on wooing support from wealthy African businessmen in Kasama. The two UNIP Regional Trustees, honorary members of the Regional Cabinet appointed by the Central Committee to advise and work with the DG, were the two most prominent African businessmen in the district. One was the owner of a large private hotel and a construction company and had been appointed by UNIP as

Chairman of the Kasama Township Council. The other was the owner of the Kasama Modern Bakery and had good connections with the Bemba royal family. By 1975 UNIP recruitment policies, centrally determined, had deemphasized the original source of party strength among peasants in favor of elements with education or wealth.

The distancing of peasants from the party was amplified by an authoritarian and elitist style of interaction adopted by party leaders. At a public meeting in Kasama township featuring two speakers from the UNIP Central Committee, greater interest was shown by the audience in the American limousine in which the party leaders arrived than in exhortations about improving maize yields. This MCC asserted that "we are all common men underneath" and that "we can learn simplicity from the Chinese railway camp where the doctors are not distinguishable from the sweepers."[45] But the bulk of the meeting was devoted to a lengthy explication from above of government directives on agricultural methods and party reorganization. Regional party officials, and even some constituency officials adopted a similar style in relating to peasants. The Regional Secretary offered the patronizing opinion that party organizing was easy in a rural district because "people in the villages do not know much; there are no intellectuals to shout 'bwana, we know that subject'."[46]

On a campaign tour during the 1975 Local Government elections, the following examples were observed of the maintenance of social distance and political control by party-state leaders. The Regional party officials were easily distinguishable from peasants by fashionable Western dress. The RS shouted angrily at a worker from a Rural Reconstruction Camp who asked for a ride out of Kasama; he made another hitch-hiker, an old man, run toward the UNIP Landrover before driving off at the last minute in a cloud of dust. He ordered the UNIP driver not to stop to pay reparation when a village chicken was run over. Indeed, the RS conducted much party business from the front seat of the Landrover by driving through villages shouting announcements of a campaign meeting or stopping peasants on the road and ordering them to put up campaign posters. Even after stepping down from his vehicle, his manner was no more considerate; headmen were expected to gather to greet the UNIP touring party and to sit on the ground while he sat on a chair with his feet on a table; he ordered children to bring a bowl of sweet masuku fruit when food was pointedly not offered. Most important, he was concerned only in communicating downward the government expectation that electoral turnout would be high; when the time came for questions by peasants, he openly ignored the questioners and engaged the candidates in private discussion. The Youth RS was somewhat more responsive to upward communication, but the general impression of the party projected to peasants was of an alien central institution. The authoritarian style of Regional cadres in asserting central party control was confirmed by one powerful party figure: "the people want to be forced," he suggested. "They won't do farming unless the party gives orders." [47]

ELECTORAL CONTROL: 1973 AND 1975

The extent to which the UNIP center was able to institutionalize political control was most apparent during elections. The 1973 General Elections and the 1975 Local Government Elections in Kasama showed that the relative roles of center and locality under one-party electoral arrangements were fluid. [48] The outcome of elections was still uncertain from the point of view of the center and susceptible to the influence of local political interests. The ruling party had not succeeded by 1975 in correctly gauging the extent of popular opposition to its candidates or in fully controlling the electoral process. The rout of the UNIP center in 1973 was not repeated in all respects in 1975 because the UNIP center had gained experience in preempting opposition electoral victories. Nonetheless, peasants continued to express dissatisfaction with UNIP performance in the locality by partially upsetting UNIP's routine assumption of control of the Rural Council in the Local Government Elections. In the main, interparty competition between UNIP and UPP by 1975 had been replaced by intraparty competition within UNIP, an arrangement that tended to enhance, but not guarantee, central control of elections.

The events surrounding the defeat of candidates of the center in Kasama in the *1973 General Elections*, the first elections under the one-party state, are a useful starting point for analysis. The results of the elections have been given (see above, Chapter 7). The pre-election portents were not favorable from the point of view of the center. Bemba militants had been the first to call for a one-party state during the time they dominated UNIP in the 1960's. By 1972, however, unipartism spelled exclusion of former UPP areas from the distribution of resources. Local opinion in Kasama was thus solidly against the declaration of a one-party state and the hearings conducted by a government commission on the unipartist constitution were by all accounts fiery in Kasama township.[49] The audience at the hearings was predominantly composed of townsfolk, although many ward councilors from the RC and some peasants from villages as distant as Nseluka were present. Numerous questions from the audience about the advisability of unipartism were not accepted, because they exceeded the terms of reference of the Commission. Questions on the low level of employment opportunities and stalled development projects were also not accepted. In general the tone of the questions was hostile, and more than half the questions were ruled out of order.[50] In order to counteract the effects of the hearings, the UNIP Regional Office arranged to send supportive telegrams to Lusaka from villages in Kasama. Most of these messages, however, seem to have emanated from the constituency level of the party rather than from the branch or village levels.

The report of the Chona Commission was accepted by the Government only after considerable alterations had been made to centralize executive power in the presidency and to introduce party supremacy at all levels of the state apparatus.[51] Party supremacy was to be ensured at the local level in part through UNIP control of elections. The Commission recommended that "in a One Party Participatory Democracy, elections should be completely free and the Party should have no role in vetting or selecting candidates."[52] The Commission dismissed the idea of primary elections as too expensive to the state and too confusing to the voter. The Government overturned the Chona proposals, arguing instead that all election campaigns should "be conducted under Party supervision and control; to this end it was essential to hold primaries" and to have central screening of candidates.[53] Henceforth, primary elections would be held in each parliamentary constituency for the purpose of selecting candidates, but voting in primaries would be restricted to Regional, constituency, and branch officials of UNIP. If a candidate unacceptable to the center slipped through the primary net, the UNIP Central Committee was empowered to disqualify such a candidate "on the grounds that his nomination

would be inimical to the interests of the State."[54] Thus the selection
of candidates, rather than actual voting, became the key moment in
the electoral process when the struggle between center and locality
was to be fought out.

The UNIP center was outmaneuvered in its first attempt, in the
1973 General Elections, to use primary elections as a control measure
in Kasama. In Kasama's three parliamentary constituencies at least
three candidates gained approval from the Provincial Political Committee and Regional Party Conference for nomination in the primary
election.[55] In the Lukashya and Kasama parliamentary constituencies,
the Region placed pressure on minor UNIP candidates to step down
in order to clear the field for the incumbents, Cabinet Ministers Changufu and Kasutu. The center sought to avoid primary elections because
in the aftermath of UPP, branch officials in Kasama could not be relied
upon to vote for candidates of the center. Minor candidates complied
with the pressure to withdraw, not all with good grace, and the candidates of the center appeared to be headed for unopposed primary
races.[56]

Forced withdrawal proved, however, to be a tactical error, for two
fresh candidates, Kapilikisha and Walinkonde, stepped forward just
before primary nominations closed. They sailed through to the general
election because with only two candidates there was no necessity to
hold a primary election. Had UNIP retained minor candidates until
after the primary, the latecomers might well have been lost in the
primary shuffle. UNIP could then have induced its own minor candidates to step down—that is, after, rather than before, the primary—
and ensured the unopposed election of candidates of the center. A
party official confided that "our lesson has been learnt; we are preparing for next time when the ones who are not wanted can be squashed
out."[57] In Malole constituency two of the four primary nominees
bowed to party pressure and withdrew early, but the third, Abel Mulanshoka, refused to step down despite a direct personal appeal from
the Prime Minister. Thus in all three constituencies in the district
the UNIP center was forced to contest the general election against
candidates of the locality who, the election results showed, had decisive support.

Because control of the selection of candidates had been bungled in

Kasama, special emphasis was placed by the UNIP center on control of the campaign for the 1973 elections. Throughout Zambia restrictions were placed on the movements and public statements of candidates on the basis of a central directive that "private" campaigning was not permissible. During campaign tours in Kasama all candidates were urged to lodge at the government rest house and to accept the accompaniment of party officials when visiting their constituencies. Public meetings were permitted only if supervised by a senior party official, usually the RS. Candidates could speak only about bland subjects provided by the Region shortly beforehand, such as "Humanism" or "one-party participatory democracy." Divergence from set topics, particularly if it involved promise of development resources for the locality, brought an on-the-spot public reprimand from UNIP.

The real campaign in November 1973, however, went beyond the confines of staged events: much "private" campaigning by both sides took place. Despite the notion that all candidates were UNIP, the Region campaigned vigorously for candidates of the center and endeavored to block the candidacies of outsiders from the locality. The UNIP Region put the bulk of its campaign effort into publicity aimed at teaching peasants to recognize the presidential electoral symbol (the eagle). The DG commented shortly before the election that "the top priority is to get a massive vote for His Excellency the President and only secondly to elect experienced parliamentary candidates."[58] Nevertheless, the local-level party was also mobilized to promote support for the incumbent MP's. Door-to-door reminders of the national stature of incumbents were made in the township and large villages by branch officials and UNIP Youth. Transport was provided by the party to villages known to be sympathetic to incumbents. At a formal campaign meeting at Mwamba one peasant asked why the candidates were making speeches when the RS had already told them who to vote for.[59] One candidate revealed that "all party officials were directed to oppose me [but] some party officials wanted their own choice and supported me."[60]

Allegations of illegitimate campaign tactics were leveled at the UNIP center during and after the 1973 election. One candidate of the center purportedly sent a crate of bottled beer to a senior chief on the eve of the election; the chief responded that "all this time he has refused to acknowledge me as his grandfather . . . and anyway I don't drink this kind of beer."[61] One prospective MP was refused housing for his family in the Kasama location, the allocation of which was in the hands of the UNIP Township Council. Finally, the candidacy of another nonfavored candidate was disrupted when his polling agent, an employee of the Public Works Department, was transferred out of Kasama District one week before the election, apparently under pressure from the party.[62] Illegal private campaigns were also conducted by candidates of the locality. Faced with noncooperation and obstruction from the UNIP Region, these candidates pieced together electoral counter-organizations. A number of informants suggested that private funds were used to pay transport expenses and to hold beer parties. Election agents for candidates of the locality would gather local leaders in village bars, order drinks all around, then begin electioneering. Since candidates were often unable to engage personally in this type of activity, youths were hired for the purpose. One ward councilor said that although the "opposition did not have the support of the DG and RS [they] did have money."[63]

The social composition of opposition organizations was mixed—drawing, like UPP before it, on a loose alliance of disaffected civil servants, party branch officials, and peasants who had not benefited from UNIP machine politics. Many opposition election agents were drawn from the ranks of teachers in the district. The organizational network of primary schools which, through schoolchildren, reached into every village had been used to advantage by UNIP in the early 1960's, by UPP in 1971, and again by candidates of the locality in 1973. One successful candidate bought football jerseys for a school to thank teachers for "whatever they might have done." At Chafwa school on the road to Mwamba at a campaign meeting, the head teacher introduced the candidate of the locality by referring to his long career in education, but introduced the Minister by asking, "Who has ever seen the Minister here before?" The fact that no one in the audience could recall the Minister visiting them in his capacity as MP for the area created for him a grave disadvantage at that meeting, a disadvantage that the teachers present had, in fact, cultivated.[64] In the nationalist phase schoolteaching had provided a route of upward social mobility and a recruiting ground for political leadership, but after 1964 schoolteachers had suffered loss of prestige and become poorly paid in comparison with other civil servants. As a group with a grievance they constituted an important element in the electoral organizations of non-favored candidates in 1973.

The three candidates of the locality in Kasama shared an informal electoral alliance and a uniform socioeconomic background. Each was associated with preindependence nationalist politics and held salaried positions in the state bureaucracy. The social backgrounds of MP's in the Second Republic were generally more middle-class than in the First Republic.[65] The successful candidates of the locality from Kasama were no exception. Although they campaigned on the basis of peasant grievances, they were recruited not from among peasants but from a disaffected faction of relatively educated and privileged stratum. They were able to mobilize sufficient peasant support to wrest the 1973 elections from the control of the UNIP center, but electoral victory was not organized on the basis of an uprising of peasants as a class. Electoral victory by candidates of the locality represented only a circulation of local patrons and a challenge to central control from a local faction within the ruling party.

After the 1973 electoral debacle, the center gained experience at electoral control in the locality. In the *1975 Local Government Elections* in Kasama, the UNIP Region, revived with newly appointed leadership, was more successful in maintaining candidates of the center in office, but was still unable to induce widespread peasant electoral participation.

Before the 1975 local government elections could be held, party organization had to be renewed with the holding of branch and constituency elections. The Provincial Political Secretary had interpreted internal party elections as "the road back" for party organization, but in reality the UNIP Region had to sidestep this explosive issue. Had party elections been held in 1974 or 1975, large numbers of branch and constituency posts would have likely fallen to local leaders with hostile stances to the political center. The UNIP Region would have been stranded without sympathetic incumbent candidates to promote to the Township and Rural Councils. This could have marked the potential loss of central control over the elected local government apparatus of the district. Thus party elections were postponed until after the

1975 local government elections. When faced with a choice between encouraging peasant participation and maintaining central party control, UNIP opted for the latter.

Ultimately, peasant participation in the 1975 Local Government elections was low. Since the inception of the Rural Council in 1963, peasants had not been asked to go to the polls to elect ward councilors; in 1963, 1967, and 1970 all councilorships went unopposed to appointees of the UNIP Region. In the words of one aspirant: "people do not know the polls in this district."[66] Even when internal party competition was introduced under the one-party constitution, peasants did not readily come forward to register as voters. Perhaps they were discouraged by the fact that local government elections were long overdue and had been twice delayed in 1973 and 1974.[67] The official rationale given by the UNIP center for delays was that details of the new electoral law were incomplete, but privately, party officials in Kasama conceded that another electoral setback for UNIP in the North could not be risked so soon after the 1973 elections. When registration of voters was begun in April 1974, high registrations were achieved only in Chilunga and Kasama UNIP constituencies, around Nseluka and the township respectively, areas of sound UNIP branch organization. Over the district as a whole, however, the local-level party was uninvolved and incapable of inducing peasant registration; the task of mobilization fell to nonparty officials. At Kayambi the head teacher, and at Munkonge the CDA, toured villages with registration materials. Despite a last minute show of strength from the center with tours by members of the UNIP Central Committee, the final voter registration figures were low. Fourteen percent fewer peasants registered to vote in Kasama in 1975 than in 1973.[68] Thus it was soon evident that turnout would be low in the first local government election in which peasants could exercise a vote.

As in 1973, the selection of candidates was the kernel of the electoral process. Because the competition for elected office was more parochial, control functions were delegated in 1975 to lower party organs, particularly the UNIP Region. But the UNIP Region in Kasama had come to represent the interests of the party-state at the center and the impact was much the same as if the Central Committee had been directly involved. Candidates were again distinguishable in terms of whether they enjoyed the backing of the center. The aim of the center was to come up with one name in each ward with which UNIP could associate itself. Selection of favored candidates was done by the officials of the UNIP Region sitting together as the Regional Cabinet. As one senior official described the process, "we drew up a strategy of the candidates we favored," and a list was passed up to the Provincial Political Committee for ratification.[69] An additional right of candidate disqualification was reserved for the UNIP Central Committee as in the general elections. In Kasama in 1975 it was exercised against three candidates. In two cases the candidates were prominent former UPP sympathizers, one of whom had been ejected from the Kasama Rural Council in 1971. The third was disqualified on technical grounds in that the signatories on his nomination form came from a ward other than the one he was contesting. Of singular interest to the question of the place of the UNIP Region in effecting central control was the process by which Central Committee screening was actually done in local government elections. In 1975 in Kasama the Central Committee acted on recommendations from the UNIP Region and blank Central Committee disqualification certificates were sent to the Region for completion at the Region's discretion.[70]

In general the party again organized for incumbents and against outsiders. The candidates for fifteen of the twenty-three UNIP councilorships were endorsed by the UNIP Region in 1975. Three councilors decided not to run again for reasons of old age or ill health.[71] One found a better opportunity for earning a cash income.[72] The remainder had fallen out of favor with the party Region during their terms as councilors; the councilors from Wards 18, 21, and 22 were deemed to have no popular support among peasants and were dropped from the party slate; councilors from Wards 6 and 14 had a record of persistent flirtations with opposition politics and were also dropped. UNIP was left with a slate of party faithful drawn predominantly from among officials of the constituency level of the party. As the Regional Secretary said, "we support councilors who work hard for the party."[73] At least six of the incumbent councilors were regarded by peasants as too closely associated with the center, and serious popularity problems in their wards placed their reelection in doubt.[74] The UNIP Region was able to discourage opposition candidates from running in two of these wards. Before the campaign proper began, the RS and YRS "moved around telling people how the opposition serve only their own interests."[75] At a public meeting in the township before candidates were selected, the DG and PPS announced that they wished to continue with "experienced" councilors and that challengers would be "dealt with severely."[76] A large field of enthusiastic runners was thus whittled down, and a familiar pattern of limited competition re-emerged. Nine Rural Council seats out of twenty-three were unopposed, and Ward 12 went vacant for lack of any candidate.

Peasants were poorly informed of the 1975 local government elections. Campaign meetings were not held in every ward in the district, and peasants were not given the opportunity to meet or question candidates. Regional officials, who were supposed to supervise campaign meetings in person, argued that they lacked the resources to cover every ward. In Wards 9, 11, and 19, where campaign meetings were not held, candidates illegally campaigned on a private basis as the only means of disseminating information about their voting symbols. The RS did hold a campaign meeting at Mungwi, but he arrived late after most of the crowd had dispersed. Most campaign meetings, like the ones I observed at Mbusa and Chilufya villages, proceeded stiffly, with the candidates unable to diverge from narrow guidelines laid down by the RS. Information on the elections seems also to have been denied some candidates of the locality. Councilors were only advised of election dates by the DG on the day that primary nominations opened, which left only four days to gather signatures and posed severe problems for candidates in outlying wards.[77] Some prospective candidates who were not councilors and who lacked access to a national newspaper only learned of primary nominations after nominations had closed. In addition, primary nominations had to be lodged at Mungwi, which, for Ward 20 and other outlying wards, gave an unfair advantage to the incumbent who had "a salary and a car."[78] UNIP effectively used monopoly over electoral information as one more means of electoral control in Kasama District.

The turnout on election day in the thirteen wards in Kasama where polling was held was 44.2 percent, somewhat higher than predicted and above the national average. Since voter registration was low, however, the actual number of voters who turned out was approximately the same as the all-time low of 1973. UNIP's electoral strategy succeeded in that the party was able to retain control of the Rural Council, losing only one of its incumbents to a candidate of the locality.

The overturned seat, however, belonged to the senior representative of the center in rural local government, the Chairman of the Rural Council. This official, whose career indicated prospects of promotion to the UNIP Region, was rejected by peasants from Makasa over the issue of maintaining contact with his local constituency. The opponent, a farmer and chief's retainer from Makasa, successfully overturned a UNIP constituency attempt to disqualify him. About one third of the council was replaced by new faces. The presence of alternatives to party faithful in at least some wards partly explained the high voter turnout, for turnout was highest where newcomers stood. Thus even though electoral control was maintained by a now experienced UNIP Region in 1975, it was accompanied by lukewarm peasant support and a single major upset.

In sum, by 1975 central control had replaced local participation as the distinguishing characteristic of UNIP at the local level. Peasant participation dwindled: party branch organization lapsed, and active branches came to serve the interests of party leaders alone. Declining local participation was accompanied by increased central control, marked principally by the emergence of the UNIP Region as an agency of the center. Central control took numerous forms: the appointment of Regional officials, the centralization of party policy-making, the bureaucratization of local party recruitment procedures, and the adoption of an authoritarian style of interaction with peasants. Particularly significant was party control of all phases of election procedure in the one-party state, especially candidate selection, coupled with party control over the work of such elected officials as MP's and ward councilors. What party control failed to do, however, was to maintain the allegiance of peasants enjoyed by UNIP in the 1961–64 phase. UNIP in 1975 was no longer a peasant party riding a wave of demands from below but a political machine responsive mainly to commands and rewards from above.

PATRONAGE IN THE LOCAL-LEVEL PARTY

Three general points can be made about patronage. First, all political parties engage in the distribution of rewards as a means of maintaining party organization and support. The important question is whether patronage is the only or predominant means of maintenance at the disposal of the party or whether other resources such as ideology or coercion are also employed. Second, patronage is a legitimate goal of political competition; the distribution of political office through an elected political party is clearly distinguishable from corruption, which involves abuse of political office. Finally, patronage is usually assumed to establish reciprocal relations between giver and receiver; in return for material reward, the latter is supposed to perform services such as providing votes or ensuring party discipline. One argument presented below is that in return for party patronage rewards, local officials of UNIP were expected to enforce party control below the level of the UNIP Region.

Patronage rewards usually take the form of positions of paid employment, or goods and services, controlled by a party in power. Although the rapid postcolonial expansion of public expenditures was drawing to a close in the mid 1970's in Zambia, a diverse range of resources was still available to the UNIP center for distribution to cadres at the local level. These included paid employment, development plan funds, trade licences and transport, as well as nonmaterial symbolic rewards. Examples of each will be given in order to document the purposes and processes of Zambian machine politics at the local level. Thereafter, a clear relationship can be shown to exist between the occupancy by local leaders of party office and accessibility to patronage rewards. Initial evidence also suggests a relationship between the dispensation of patronage and the performance by local leaders of control functions on behalf of the central state. Finally, an argument can be made that the limits of patronage are coincident with the limits of central control.

In Kasama the party distributed *employment* in the form of paid offices in the party bureaucracy, the state bureaucracy, and elected local authorities. To begin, UNIP had at its disposal a number of offices within the *party bureaucracy*. The UNIP constitution provided for 24 officebearers in every Region, constituency, and branch of the party, eight in each of the women's, youth, and main bodies.[79] Assuming a potential party apparatus in Kasama UNIP Region of nine constituencies and 110 branches, the party would have had the distribution of 2880 party offices at its disposal. In practice, because of decay of UNIP branches, far fewer than this number were actually distributed. In addition, party offices became devalued in the eyes of UNIP members because salaries were not paid to officials at branch and constituency levels. Party office was not a patronage reward of great material value, but it was a reward nonetheless. Although UNIP branch chairmanship, for example, did not ensure a regular salary, it did ensure preferential access to occasional development projects funded from the center. One branch chairman said that "it is better not to forget the party or else the party will forget you."[80] The party was likewise able to bestow a handful of office jobs at Regional headquarters. The Kasama Region employed a salaried driver, a typist, and an office orderly who were recruited on the basis of party experience and who continued to hold branch office in the Youth and Women's wings of township UNIP branches. The Regional Secretary added that "the wish of the party is to upgrade these salaries (of K55) to the level of civil service salaries." He also argued that the Region needed a qualified accountant and an office manager.[81] For the most part, however, patronage posts in the party bureaucracy were not plentiful or well remunerated.

In addition to party posts, UNIP in the locality had influence over hiring and firing from the lowest grades in the *state bureaucracy*. One councilor commented that "the party is a ladder; if you want to get ahead in government you must be an active party member."[82] The state was the largest employer in Kasama District, accounting for the bulk of the approximately 5000 jobs in the district.[83] Even before unipartism was legalized, UNIP in Kasama acted as if it were the legitimate distributor of state employment resources. UNIP's influence was particularly strong over casual or daily-paid labor; the higher the civil service grading or the greater the formal qualifications required for the job, the less party influence could be exercised.

Party membership as shown by the possession of a UNIP card was a minimum condition for employment in Kasama in state, parastatal, or local authority sectors. Party office-holding was an added advantage. The hiring of daily-paid workers for Rural Council projects— road- or bridge-building—serves as an example. Hiring was formally reserved for an administrative official of the Council, the Works Officer. In practice, the councilor for the ward in which the Council project was located, particularly if he was well-placed in the party hierarchy of the Region, was able to influence the procedure in favor of branch officials. Laborers on the Rural Council Bridge on the Chilufya road "were only UNIP officials" according to the councilor for the ward.[84] The UNIP caucus at the Rural Council openly advocated the hiring of UNIP constituency chairmen as road construction *capitaos* (foremen). The Chairman of the KRC interceded on behalf of party officials in the hiring of barmen, barmaids, cleaners, and watchmen at the council rest house in Mungwi, an action which the Council Secretary regarded as "undue party interference."[85]

Employment on the basis of party record also occurred in government departments employing artisans; many party officials were carpenters and laborers in the school-building program of the Ministry of Education; others were drivers, mechanics, and messengers in provincial and district administration. The department of the state bureaucracy which had the greatest number of skilled and semi-skilled jobs to offer—namely, the Public Works Department of the Ministry of Power, Transport, and Works—was staffed heavily in its lower echelons by party faithful. The PWD depot in Kasama employed branch officials from Kasama UNIP constituency, including one ward councilor, two WDC secretaries, and numerous VPC secretaries. The UNIP RS paid frequent supervisory visits to the Kasama employment exchange of the Ministry of Labour and Social Services, presumably to lobby for party appointments. In general, party officials in urban and suburban locations benefited from employment more readily than colleagues in outlying villages. But this form of patronage also operated far from the boma or Council headquarters, where government employment opportunities were few. The peasant hired as tsetse-fly barrier inspector, or pump mechanic for a government-piped water scheme, or building organizer for a group housing project, was invariably a local party leader of long standing. In 1974 President Kaunda gave formal sanction to the existing fact of party patronage by announcing the state's intention of making party activism the prime criterion for civil service promotion. In Kasama in 1974 the nationalist slogan "It pays to belong to UNIP" was revived by local officials.

Given a shortage of resources for mass redistribution of wealth, paid offices themselves became a resource around which political competition occurred. This was evident in Kasama in the manner in which elected offices on *local authorities* were the focus for intraparty competition and attempts at central control. In the Local Government

Elections of 1975, a number of peasants were prepared to declare candidacy solely on the grounds that "the present councillor has been paid for doing nothing" or that "he has been paid long enough; let another have a chance."[86] Ward Councilors on the Kasama Rural Council received no salary per se, only an allowance of K32 per month to cover expenses involved with Council work. This amount more than compensated a councilor for expenses and amounted to a relatively handsome patronage reward by rural subsistence standards. Consequently, Ward Councilors were able to enjoy a slightly higher standard of living than their constituents; the visible rewards of office were manifest in burnt brick houses, iron roofs, radios and, in a few cases, motor vehicles. Councilorship also carried with it perquisites such as paid tours of Councils in other parts of the country, and preferential access to trades licenses. Councilors thus developed a vested interest in elected office. For this reason the announcement of the postponement of Local Government elections at the Local Government Association conference in 1974 was met with loud applause from assembled Ward Councilors. In 1975 in Kasama pressure to avoid holding UNIP branch and constituency elections prior to the Local Government elections came primarily from constituency officials who were Ward Councilors. This group was concerned to ensure its own candidacy for paid councilorships, which party elections under conditions of peasant disaffection in Kasama would surely have upset.

The UNIP center was aware of the utility of patronage as a cement for a disintegrating party organization. Nowhere were central intentions clearer than with party control over the distribution of elected local authority office among local party leaders. A senior Regional official allowed that "we make councillors in order to help our brothers who are party members; there is no other way we can pay them."[87] Part of the task of the Provincial Political Secretary was to maintain files on councilors "so we know which ones were workers and which ones were wasters."[88] The UNIP center extended control into the locality by awarding unopposed or safe Council seats to party officials willing to represent actively the point of view of the center among peasants. Almost without exception UNIP councilors were recruited from the level of the party directly below the Region, that is, the UNIP constituency. In Kasama 19 out of 23 ward councilors were UNIP constituency officials; the remainder were prominent branch

TABLE 34.   Kasama Rural Council, Party Position of Councilors, 1970–1975

Ward	UNIP Party Office	Name of Party Constituency
1	Constituency Secretary	Mpanda
2	Constituency Vice-Secretary	Mpanda
3	Constituency Secretary	Chambeshi
4	Constituency Chairman[1]	Chilunga
5	Branch Secretary	Chilunga
6	Constituency Secretary[2]	Chilunga
7	Constituency Publicity Secretary	Chilunga
8	Constituency Treasurer	Chambeshi
9	Branch Secretary	Chambeshi
10	Constituency Vice-Treasurer	Chambeshi
11	Constituency Chairman	Chambeshi
12	Constituency Secretary	Kasama
13	Constituency Secretary	Mungwi
14	(ex-) Constituency Secretary[3]	Kasama
15	Constituency Youth Chairman	Kasama
16	Branch Secretary[2]	Kasama
17	Constituency Treasurer	Ituna
18	Constituency Publicity Secretary	Mulobola
19	Constituency Chairman	Kalundu
20	Constituency Secretary	Kalundu
21	Constituency Secretary	Mulobola
22	Branch Chairman[2]	Mulobola
23	Constituency Vice-Chairman[2]	Kasama

Source. Social background questionnaire and in-depth councilor interviews.
[1] Elected councilor in by-election, January 1975.
[2] Deposed by UNIP Regional Office in late 1974.
[3] Deposed by UNIP Regional Office in 1972.

officials (Table 34). The office most commonly represented was that of constituency secretary, the office in which day-to-day constituency power was concentrated. All councilors interviewed agreed that the office of constituency secretary was more powerful than the honorary office of constituency chairman.

One example of the manner in which party maneuvers favored party officials for (paid) elected posts was the by-elections held in Ward 4 of the Kasama Rural Council in January 1975. Approximately five peasants from Ward 4 declared candidacy for a vacant post, including a man who had been a councilor in the 1960's. However, a decision was taken by the UNIP Region to reward one of the oldest freedom fighters in the area, a sixty-one-year-old UNIP branch secretary who had been imprisoned for his part in cha cha cha. UNIP branch and constituency officials were consulted on candidate selection, but peasants and ordinary UNIP members were not. The RS at first argued that this candidate had "the right background" but later conceded that old age, nonliteracy, and lack of knowledge of English would disincline the candidate "to stand up and represent his people strongly in Council."[89] The candidate of the center thus received UNIP backing as repayment for services rendered to the party and not because he was otherwise qualified for councilorship. The YRS toured Ward 4 and discouraged peasants from supporting other contenders, who, as a consequence, were unable to find the requisite nine signatories for nomination. The main contender, the former councilor, was disqualified by the UNIP Region because he did not have a 1974 party stamp on his UNIP card, even though he argued vehemently that no stamps had been available for sale. The UNIP candidate sailed through the election unopposed and began drawing his councilor's allowance in February 1975.

The same procedure of patronage awards from UNIP held for local government elections in general. For example, the councilor for Ward 12 lived outside the ward; he owed his councilorship to his work for urban party branches rather than to a strong base of peasant support in Ward 12. Yet having won his seat in the 1975 election, he was promoted by the Region to the position of Chairman of the Rural Council. Another councilor, when asked whether he would be a candidate in the 1975 Local Government elections, commented, "It is up to the Governor whether I can keep this job."[90] Councilor emoluments were withdrawn on the recommendation of the party Region from councilors who allowed local political organization and support to lapse. This fate befell five councilors in Wards 6, 11, 18, 22, and 23, and party support was withheld from all but one of them in the subsequent elections. The connection was plain between the councilor's role in the maintenance of party-state control over the locality and the distribution of patronage reward in the form of paid office.

The distribution of trades and liquor *licenses* as a patronage reward followed a similar pattern to the distribution of employment. Licenses for general stores and chibuku pubs in the rural areas were awarded through the Rural Council and often afforded livelihood to those favored by the party. UNIP ward councilors had the opportunity to act as local patrons in recommending applicants to the Council and in approving Council license recommendations to the DDC or Provincial Liquor Board. Licence applications were supposed to be directed through VPC and WDC channels. Often VPC's in Kasama did conduct the initial UNIP card check and, along with the chief, provided the applicant with a letter of recommendation. In practice, however, the ward councilor represented the application to Council and was able to exercise discretion on whether to actively push it. Ward councilors were asked how many unsolicited visits from constituents were received in a week: the average figure was two per week, but councilors were virtually unanimous that those with licence applications paid the most frequent visits.[91] One councilor said, "They all want recommendations; I finish one and another comes; they don't come with development problems."[92] Paid-up party membership was a sine qua non for a successful license application, and party office-holding was a virtual guarantee. At Nseluka village, for example, businessmen found their way to the offices of UNIP branch and constituency executives or to the WDC. Several ward councilors were themselves holders of trades licenses; perhaps the best example was that of the Chairman of the Rural Council, who owned grocery stores at Mungwi and Makasa and who encountered no difficulty in obtaining and renewing licenses. His successor as KRC chairman in 1976 was the owner of a large bar in the suburban area of Kasama township.

As trades and liquor licenses were used by the representatives of the UNIP center to reward party faithful, so were they used to exclude party opponents from the distribution of patronage rewards. A meeting of WDC secretaries at Mungwi reported "some differences between the people and councilors over the grant[ing] of various licenses."[93] Two cases will be cited from Kasama. A former Federal civil servant and Assistant District Secretary for Kasama retired to his home village fifteen kilometers south of the township. He invested his savings in the construction of a grocery and bottled beer outlet, but from 1972 to 1975 was unable to secure a license to sell anything other than chibuku. In his perception the license applications had been blocked by the councilor for the ward and by the UNIP Region. He attributed the rejected license application to activities as an "election sergeant" for Joel Kapilikisha, the non-favored but victorious candidate in the 1973 parliamentary elections. "We were seen together with him by everyone around here: some people in the party made bad names against us."[94] The second case concerned a businessman who sought to open a bar and general store at Mungwi but because of his blacklisting as a former UPP supporter, repeatedly failed to obtain recommendations from the local UNIP branch and constituency. His appeals to the Regional Secretary were sidetracked. So he took out party membership in 1974 and planned to run for party office at the next branch elections, as the only means of gaining access to the party patronage machine.[95]

Paid employment and trades licenses were part of a long list of patronage goods in which the UNIP political machine dealt. *Development plan funds* for a wide variety of projects were also traded in return for solidarity with the ruling party. Agricultural credit serves as a good example. The first postcolonial credit agency established, the Credit Organization of Zambia (COZ), was founded expressly "in order to make good some of the promises made during the independence struggle."[96] The COZ District Advisory Committees, which decided on loan applications, were heavily staffed with local party officials.[97] In Kasama the appointed district supervisor of COZ was a UNIP constituency secretary who went on to become Kasama RS. He interpreted the distribution of agricultural credit as a means "to make our best party men into farmers; we cannot stand anyone who is not UNIP."[98] Cooperative societies, eligible for loans under the COZ program, were also made up primarily of branch and constituency leaders. COZ failed to implement rigorous precautions in dispensing funds; "they gave credit to anyone who walked in the door," without regard to ability to repay.[99] In Kasama cases of credit awards to peasants from neighboring districts and of party officials with more than one loan were recorded. My interviews in Kasama revealed that COZ loans were used not only for agricultural purposes but also for the purchase of prestige consumer items, like iron roofs, bicycles, stock for rural stores, or, in one case, a second wife. The COZ repayment record was poor, with over one thousand outstanding debts per district in Northern Province at the time COZ was declared bankrupt in 1970. Out of a total loss of K14 million, the Northern Province accounted for over

K2 million.[100] The repayment rate in the Northern Province was the worst of all provinces.[101] (Access by party officials to agricultural credit through revised WDC credit procedures in 1975 has been documented above, Chapter 4.)

One of the main findings of the study of patronage in Kasama was that access to national development plan funds was determined by the relative standing of party officials in the hierarchy of the local party machine. To be a successful patron a Ward Councilor had to bring home the bacon. He had to ensure that central resources reached his locality in the form of rural development projects. In order to gain an allocation of development resources, the Councilor had to be well placed relative to the UNIP Region. The Region had its own priorities in terms of making patronage awards. A Councilor had to prove his worth to the Region by ardently advocating the policies of the center, both in the Council and in the rural constituency. In Kasama, Councilors with the highest standing in the Regional party organization were able to obtain the most development resources for their wards. UNIP constituency secretaries with long ties to the party and with Ward Councilorships were particularly adept at diverting central resources towards themselves and their followers.

A *prestige-rating study* was conducted in order to establish a ranking of councilors on the Kasama Rural Council according to position in the party patronage hierarchy.[102] All councilors in Kasama were asked to name "the big men in the party" from among their colleagues on the KRC (Table 35). Councilors agreed that ten out of twenty-three could be distinguished as having close ties to the UNIP Region. At the top of the list was the Chairman of the Rural Council who had been appointed to his post by the center against opposition with the Council in 1971.[103] He was accompanied in the top spot by a long-time party ally: not only were these councilors from neighboring wards, Wards 1 and 2, but they occupied the positions of Vice-Secretary and Secretary respectively of the same UNIP constituency. Other councilors rated as having a close patronage relationship to the center were those from UNIP constituencies where UNIP membership remained relatively strong (Kasama and Chilunga constituencies) or where the UNIP organization had been established early in the independence struggle (Kalundu and Chambeshi constituencies). The

TABLE 35. Kasama Rural Council, Prestige Rating Study of Party Influentials, 1974–1975

Cllr. Interviewed	1	2	3	4	5	6	7	8	9	10	11	12	13	14	15	16	17	18	19	20	21	22	23
						Councilor Named as Party Influential[1]																	
1	X	X				X						X	X	X	X								
2	X	X					X						X			X							
3	X	X				X	X							X						X			
4[2]																							
5																							
6																							
7	X	X	X			X						X	X	X						X			
8	X	X				X	X		X			X	X							X			
9	X	X												X									
10																							
11																							
12	X	X				X	X					X		X						X			
13	X	X				X	X					X	X	X	X	X				X			
14	X	X				X	X						X	X	X	X				X			
15																							
16	X	X				X						X	X	X		X				X		X	
17	X	X																					
18	X	X												X									
19	X	X					X					X	X	X				X		X			
20	X	X				X	X					X		X		X				X			
21																							
22	X	X					X					X		X									
23																							
Total Citations[3]	15	15				9	9					9	8	12	3	5				9			
Prestige Ranking	1	1				4	4					4	8	3	10	9				4			

[1] Based on councilor interviews conducted in 1974–75; all councilors were asked, "Who are the big men in the party?" from among their colleagues on the KRC.

[2] Councilors from Wards 4, 5, 6, 10, 10, 13, 21, and 23 were unwilling to make responses to the interview question.

[3] Where a councilor received fewer than 3 citations from his colleagues, he was not counted as a "party influential."

patronage hierarchy in the local-level party in Kasama did not necessarily bear any relationship to the actual strength of party organization in different parts of the district, but it *was* related to personal ties and party records of UNIP officeholders.

A clear relationship existed between prestige in the party and preferential access to development-plan funds at the local level. In Kasama allocations under the Second National Development Plan to the wards of the ten most influential party men was on the average 50 percent higher than in the wards of the other thirteen councilors. The SNDP allocations voted by the KRC to the wards of these ten councilors were K987,300, and to the remaining thirteen wards K858,000, for the period 1972–1976 (Table 16).

This group of party influentials was able to oversee and influence the resources distributed by the Rural Council because of their occupancy of key decision-making positions in local-level organizations. Together they comprised the UNIP caucus within the Council which met to ensure unanimity to the party line on issues up for Council decision. The caucus was led by the Chairman of the RC and occasionally the Regional Secretary sat in. When asked which institution in the "development front" provided most assistance to their work as councilors, the nine most influential councilors unanimously cited the UNIP Region. One such patron commented that the party machine provided more lucrative access to development resources than did the state apparatus: "with the Council or a Ministry when they say there is no money it is the end of the matter; with the party it can go as high as the Central Committee."[104] Out of the Council as a whole, only fourteen out of twenty-three cited the UNIP Region. As well as comprising the UNIP caucus, party influentials dominated the Finance and General Purposes Committee of the KRC, in which actual decisions on development fund allocations were made for later ratification by the Council sitting as a whole. Seven of the influential councilors sat on the eight-man Finance and General Purposes Committee of the KRC in 1974–75. The other two influential councilors were Chairman and member, respectively, of the second most important committee of the KRC, the Works Committee. As such the party was able to monopolize Council decision-making on the KRC, in return for which the power as local patrons of influentials within the party was boosted. They were able to favor their own wards in the allocation of development projects. Indeed, several of the less influential councilors expressed the opinion that Wards 1 and 2 received undue favor from the party.

THE LIMITS OF PATRONAGE

The political party had sufficient resources to reach into the locality and anoint certain local leaders as representatives of the center. In Kasama, the UNIP Region was secured as an outpost of the center by the payment of salaries and by the prospects of promotion held out to party officials. Below the Region, central penetration and control occasionally stretched to the constituency level of the party, though the party-state had no permanent or inviolable presence there. Party-state presence below the Region depended on the availability of development resources for distribution by local patrons, or on the incidence of an election, at which time debts to the party were called in. The distribution of development resources was limited to the extent that the UNIP political machine operated intermittently at the party constituency level and not at all at the level of the party branch. The lack of central capacity to widely distribute rural development resources at the extreme periphery was connected in a fundamental way to the atrophy of party branch organization.

Only a very small percentage of branch officials received direct party patronage rewards. In interviews, UNIP branch officials in Kasama depicted themselves as a group excluded and repudiated by party leadership at the center. Since the material benefits of development had not reached the village, branch officials in Kasama tended to share political interests with other subsistence peasants and to resent the conspicuous privilege of party leaders from the Region upward. At the core of this grass roots resentment was the issue of payment for party service. The issue was well summarized by a party branch official at Mulobola:

I joined the party in 1953 when it was still ANC and I was one of the first in Kasama. I organized for the party for all this time. I cycled from this village to that village selling cards and when my bicycle was broken I walked. All this time I got no money from UNIP. My children suffered because I could not buy them school uniforms. My wife suffered because I was imprisoned [in 1961]. We thought everything would change with independence.[105]

Other responses in similar vein from party officials were as follows: "I am a big man [in the party] but I cannot support my family"; "Where is my pension to come from when I am too old for party work?"; "From the struggle to now we [branch officials] have been expecting payment, and this is the only thing that keeps us going"; "My friends are leaving the party because of [lack of] pay, but when you neglect the party the whole country can be on fire."[106]

The decline of branch organization was linked directly to the payment issue. Outdated party membership lists in Kasama were attributable to the migration of branch officials to the urban industrial enclave in search of paid employment. In many cases the only party branch official remaining behind was the branch chairman, who was often an older man whose working days were over. Younger branch officials, according to one councilor, had "grown tired of waiting for party or government jobs and [were] now on the Copperbelt."[107] Migration was on-going, as evidenced by the absence of VPC members (first listed in 1971) by 1974 and 1975. The perception shared by branch officials of exclusion from party patronage was shared by the majority of constituency officials who distinguished between payment for party work and other patronage rewards such as councilors' allowances. When asked, "Is there anything you don't like about your work for party and government?" nineteen out of twenty-three mentioned the party salaries issue, thirteen without prompting from the interviewer.

The intensity with which the issue of payment of party cadres was held in the locality had repercussions on the ability of the party-state to exercise political control. A distinct difference in attitude and behavior of party officials prevailed in Kasama between the beneficiaries of the party patronage machine and the outsiders. The former were publicly willing to explain party-state policy, defend the state against charges of nonperformance and delay, conduct such party business as card-selling, and engage in symbolic support activity, like introducing officials from the center at public meetings. By contrast, the latter were often absent from party duties or joined public criticism of the party center. For example, I observed an unrewarded branch secretary at Mulobola castigate the UNIP Region at a VPC meeting for failing to visit and assist in the maintenance of a UNIP constituency office that had been built with the labor of peasants.[108] At a Ward

Committee meeting, an unpaid branch official of UNIP Youth argued firmly against a state Agricultural Assistant who attempted to pin the blame for low agricultural yields at Mungwi on peasant conservatism rather than poor state marketing facilities.[109]

The political center was made aware of the potential for resistance and opposition that the payment issue harbored for the party. Scarcely a UNIP National Council meeting or National UNIP Councilors Conference passed without a resolution from the floor for the payment of cadres. Councilors in particular were vocal as a group in pushing the material interests of local party officials, themselves included. The political center, however, discouraged the open airing of the payment issue: for example, at the same WDC meeting cited above, the KRC Chairman, acting as a visiting representative of the center, ruled a discussion of party salaries out of order, perhaps because of my presence with a notebook.[110] In any event, UNIP lacked the resources to pay salaries to all party officials and, local protests notwithstanding, was unlikely to institute the practice in the foreseeable future.[111] As a result, central party control in a disaffected district was tenuous at party constituency level and virtually nonexistent at party branch level.

Widespread distribution of development resources was no easy task. Yet the failure of expected development to materialize led quickly to the alienation of once strong support for the center among poor peasants. Opposition to the central state was expressed also by grass roots branch officials of the party, themselves recruited from among poor peasants, many of whom experienced no economic benefit or social mobility after independence. A few local party officials from the constituency level of the party were able to gain limited access to development resources in return for acting as agents of the center in the locality. The party maintained its organization almost exclusively by the distribution of material reward. Under conditions of resource shortage, party presence in the locality was therefore bound to be limited. Below the party constituency level, in the villages of the rural hinterland, the United National Independence Party did not induce regular participation from peasants in politics or rural development. The local party, like other organizations in the apparatus of the single-party state, did not represent the interests of the poorest elements in rural localities. This is not to say that UNIP had no presence at the local level, only that UNIP was institutionalized as a selective "political machine" rather than as the mass mobilizing element in a "development front." In addition, the local party was increasingly associated in peasant perceptions, and in fact, with the interests of party-state managers at the political center. All that was left of the local party was a cluster of patronage beneficiaries. Party organizational adaptation to the form of political machine reflected a general process of stratification of peasant society between those who had benefited from state resources and those who had not.

CONCLUSION

9

Political Organization and Resource Distribution

Throughout the first years of Zambian independence the government was, in the words of one commentator, "primarily concerned with its own survival, (and) with the extension of its control over the people and the area of the state."[1] A quest for rural development was undertaken only insofar as it contributed to the immediate exigency of guaranteeing the political and economic security of the party-state. The search for stability encompassed "not so much the defense of existing political arrangements as the creation of new ones."[2] Local-level organizations of "one-party participatory democracy" were established within an ideological framework of decentralized decision-making. After more than a decade of postcolonial rule the Zambian party-state was intact under a civilian regime. This fact at least attested to the effectiveness of the center at recruiting support among key local leaders and at maintaining order among disaffected peasantries. New political arrangements were aimed not so much at mobilizing peasant political and economic activity as at containing it. The institutionalization of party patronage and unipartist elections at the local level must be counted as key contributions to the survival of the party-state.

Apart from Zambia, there are other atypical African states which do not exhibit patterns of coup and countercoup and which survive by retaining support among selective but powerful elements in society.[3] African party-states have evolved distinct and durable patterns of political organization and resource distribution. Stability is, in itself, however, little cause for rejoicing without "first determining who in fact is in charge."[4] A feature of African politics is that political stability at the center is compatible with the deepening of social stratification and the persistent unfolding of rural underdevelopment in the locality.

Center-locality relations in African party-states are marked by a tension between the commitment of the center to political control and demands from the locality for rapid rural development. Although the center can achieve a modicum of penetration and control over the politics of the outlying areas, control has distinct limitations and varies from locality to locality. Some localities may be infused with central development resources in the form of social facilities like roads, schools, and clinics. Because of the concern of national leadership to centralize control, politically volatile localities, like Kasama District in the Northern Province in Zambia, usually receive a greater share of development resources than politically quiescent localities. From the perspective of the peasant however, patterns of resource distribution appear uneven both within the locality and between the locality and the center. Within the locality, development resources become concentrated in the hands of leadership groups who are willing to represent the center by managing and containing peasant demands. The stability of African party-states thus rests on the following factors: first, the magnitude of patronage resources available to the center and, second, the extent to which local leaders are able to use patronage to prevent the hardening of peasant disaffections into the consciousness of a permanently excluded social class.

The present study has been aimed at illuminating the local politics of rural development in Zambia by examining the patterns of resource distribution that actually prevail in the performance of central political organizations in one rural district. A couple of related assumptions have underpinned this study.

The first assumption is that center-locality relations display a two-way dynamic. Development paths are determined by the interplay of centrally planned and locally expressed priorities. Stated differently, patterns of resource distribution are decided by the extent to which local political interests find expression within organizations designed for central control. The manner in which resources are distributed will diverge, often quite widely, from the organizational blueprint of the center. The type of leadership that emerges locally, and the use it makes of central initiatives, will often be the key determinants of the path taken by rural development. Secondly, divergences from the strategy of the center do not imply that there is no pattern to politics at the local level, only that a pattern cannot be unilaterally enforced from above. Nor do divergences imply that political organization is irrelevant to the distribution of development resources, only that it is one element determining rural development outcomes. African politics is not an institutionless arena. The local politics of rural development are institutionalized insofar as they display a regularity and predictability to which all participants are attuned, and insofar as they are played out, at least in part, within formal organizations of the African party-state.

PATTERNS OF POLITICAL ORGANIZATION

The tension between party-state control and peasant demands was sharpened rather than resolved in Zambia between independence and 1975. In the case of Kasama District, center-locality relations shifted dramatically from those of mutual support to those of overt conflict. Over the first postcolonial decade the center was able to enhance formal political control over the district through pliant local leadership groups, but this was accompanied, ironically, at the expense of grassroots party organization and peasant support for the center. Peasant willingness to support the Kaunda government declined as the anticipated economic benefits of independence failed to diffuse rapidly through the locality. The organizational apparatus of the state became less a forum for the fulfillment of peasant demands than a mechanism for the distribution of rewards to the locally powerful. Hence peasants were readily attracted to political movements that promised a change of government at the center and a redistribution of development resources in the locality.

The creation of a local-level "development front," that is, a set of integrated political organizations in the locality, remained by 1975 an unfinished task for the center. Historically, state-building throughout the rural periphery of present-day Zambia was an incessant problem for the center. Organizational weakness was not a new aspect of center-locality relations. The colonial rulers of Northern Rhodesia had to rely on extant traditional institutions to make their presence indirectly felt in the villages. In the nationalist phase of Zambian history, UNIP became the first organization to link center directly with locality, but local UNIP branches were generally unresponsive to central initiatives. That the present Zambian party-state has any kind of organizational presence at the grass roots in the postcolonial phase thus represents a considerable achievement. But like the colonial state before it, the Zambian party-state has no choice but to rely on chiefs and headmen at village level. Zambian "one-party participatory democracy" may not have fulfilled the ideological promise of inducing political and economic participation from "the common man," but the local appendages of the party-state, notably ward development committees, did partially fill the institutional vacuum with which the state was faced in 1964.

The presence of political organization in the locality can be summarized as follows. The party in Kasama District atrophied from its zenith in the nationalist phase. Its place was in part usurped by a framework of local-level development committees which were oriented more toward tasks of rural development than pure political mobilization. As such, development committees proved better suited than the remnants of the nationalist protest party to the requirements of the postcolonial period. Even though development committees performed at variance to the designs of the center, they enjoyed a relatively institutionalized presence at the ward level. One of the main empirical findings of this study was that one half of the WDC's in Kasama District were engaged in planning and implementing development projects, a higher proportion than is popularly acknowledged in Zambia. Peasant demands that were previously addressed to UNIP were referred to WDC's and VPC's, and many party branch and constituency officials showed up as activists on the new committees. WDC's were widely regarded as a ready channel of access to the center and were used by local leaders for purposes of material gain and social mobility. WDC's tended to replace the UNIP constituency as the focal political organization at the level below the district boma but above the village. This was so in large part because the development committees had more development resources at their disposal than did the party.

At the village level, by contrast, the presence of the political organization of the state was rarely felt. Much peasant political activity at the extreme periphery consisted of avoidance of directives emanating from the center. Only during such national campaigns as voter registration or village registration was direct contact made between peasant and party-state. The fact that the district boma or central ministries used primarily their own personnel for these campaigns was testimony to the patchiness of the framework of party branches and development committees at village level. The institutionalization of development committees did not occur at the village level to the same extent as at ward level. Only one tenth of VPC's were activated, but about 20 to 30 percent of the population lived in villages with active VPC's. Only at large regrouped villages did VPC activity accord in any way with the intentions of the center. In all other locales VPC's, if active at all, were used as vehicles for the reassertion of the authority of chiefs and headmen. Indeed, at Kayambi the use of VPC's by headmen to organize against regrouping was a principal reason for the failure of the scheme. Unlike WDC's, VPC's for the most part failed to plug the organizational gaps left by the decline of party branches in the villages of Kasama after the 1960–64 period.

The organization of the Zambian party-state thus penetrated so far but no further. Both party organization and committee organization were firm at district level; they were partial at the level of the local government ward or party constituency; and they petered out almost completely at the village or party branch level. A general pattern was found: the organizations of the party-state were more active and effective in localities geographically close to the center and in localities where population was concentrated. It is interesting that when the opposition UPP party had a brief moment of organized popularity, the same pattern held.

That state-building declined with distance from the center can be related to the organizational transformation of a popular nationalist movement into a selective political machine. In postcolonial Zambia the center was seeking to consolidate support at the precise time when peasant demands were rising dramatically. Because regime survival was a higher priority for national leadership than rural development, peasant participation and the accommodation of peasant demands came to be traded off against central control. The center opted for an organization that would obtain unipartist hegemony over all outlying regions through the medium of sympathetic and powerful local leaders. The glue for this organization was not ideology but the material resources of patronage. Patronage resources were in short supply, due partly to the government's own development strategy, which placed urban industrialization above rural development. The limits of party-state organization and the limits of central control thus came to be defined in terms of the limits of scarce patronage.

Central control in Kasama could be guaranteed only to the level in the party-state organization that patronage continued to reach local leaders. This applied to WDC's as well as to the UNIP apparatus, because the former were incorporated into prevailing patterns of machine politics. An important research finding from the prestige rating study I conducted in Kasama was that the most active WDC's were led by prominent party figures with the greatest access to patronage. Active WDC's were also used to constrain and turn back peasant demands to the center; well-rewarded patrons were active spokesmen for party-state policy. The connection between patronage and central control was clear in even the lowest of the local organizations of the party-state. Below the level of WDC and party constituency little patronage permeated and little central control was enjoyed.

The local party-state organization can be said to be predominantly the preserve of local leadership groups. Research revealed that the party was little more than a set of office-holders without followers, and that membership of WDC's was never open to mass political competition. The possibility therefore exists that forms of political organization introduced by a center from above can reinforce, or even create afresh, stratification in local society. An attempt will be made, in closing this study, to discuss the ways in which machine politics interacts with changes in social structure in a rural locality.

PATTERNS OF RESOURCE DISTRIBUTION

In order to account fully for the relationship between peasant and party-state, a return must be made to the simple distinction between two patterns of resource distribution with which this study began. To repeat, analyses of "who benefits" and "who is excluded" from development in African localities usually postulate either a patronage or a class pattern. The potential for compatibility of the two patterns of resource distribution is rarely made explicit in the literature. In the case of Kasama District the existence of patronage did not prevent the emergence of marked stratifications in local society. Indeed, it helped to create and reinforce them. Whether such stratifications amounted to nascent class divisions, however, was open to serious question. The possibility of patronage providing a breeding ground for a politics of class, however, is by no means remote and may well apply empirically to parts of rural Africa other than Kasama.

Before considering these issues, however, a few words are needed about the relevance of ethnicity as a pattern of resource distribution at the local-level in Kasama. An extensive literature is devoted to the proposition that ethnic identity is the key social factor in political conflict and competition in Africa.[5] Ethnic identity is not necessarily primordial but can be stimulated and politicized by contemporary leaders in search of a power base.[6] An interpretation of the UPP interlude in Kasama in these terms is certainly tempting. Perception of deprivation among Bemba-speakers as a group were kindled by Kapwepwe, though his appeals were more broadly "sectionalist" than explicitly "tribalist."[7] Bemba political activity at the national level was for the most part organized in terms of a language group or bloc of provinces, rather than in terms of tribe. Peasants were undoubtedly prone to attribute the underdevelopment of the rural districts to sectional discrimination in the division of the national pie. In Kasama non-Bemba party-state officials, particularly those from the Eastern Province, were received suspiciously. It is correct to say that "the rural population of Zambia has contributed to the rise of patterns characteristic of postindependence politics in Africa: provincialism and the growth of sectionalism."[8]

But ethnicity and sectionalism in Zambia are more relevant to politics at the national level than at the local level, and more relevant to urban politics than to rural politics. Neither was found to be of primary relevance to the local politics of rural development *within* the Kasama locality. As Young has observed, cultural identities are fluid, and their adoption by political actors depends on the settings in which political competition occurs.[9] Ethnicity is situational, and the situation within Kasama did not require the mobilization of Bemba identities. In general, the population of localities tends to be more ethnically homogeneous than national populations; this was true of Kasama District, where ethnic homogeneity was found in the composition of the population as a whole and in local-level WDC and party leadership. Local leaders competed with one another along lines other than ethnic identity. No evidence either was found that subethnic identities, such as clan, were important in local politics. Second, where diverse people do mingle, political competition does not necessarily take ethnic form. At Kayambi in Kasama, for example, I found that political competition did not pit Bemba against Mambwe. Third, ethnic identity does not necessarily link center to locality through the presence of ethnic leaders in the apparatus of the central party-state. National Bemba leaders, even if they were born in Kasama District, were not guaranteed electoral and other support from Kasama peasants. Cabinet Ministers and Members of the UNIP Central Committee were generally unwelcome in the district as successful men who had forgotten their humble origins.

For these reasons, analysis of patterns of resource distribution in the locality in this study was turned away from ethnicity and toward other patterns. The principal pattern of resource distribution found in Kasama was patronage. According to anthropological studies of the Bemba, patron client-networks were characteristic of precolonial political organization.[10] Prestige and power were accumulated traditionally according to the number of followers attracted to the village of each chief or headman. In the postcolonial period the recruitment of personal followings and the distribution of patronage rewards was manifest through the political machine of the party-state. The local-level party and the development committees provided arenas for local "big men" to compete over development resources. The party-state machine as a whole was maintained by the disbursement of material benefits.

Perhaps the best indicator of the persistent importance of patronage was the connection found in this study between the activation of WDC's and the presence of a councilor who was close to the party machine. Patrons sought to attract state resources to their localities, not only for direct personal gain, but also to reward peasant followers. Competition *among* local leaders benefited at least some poor peasants some of the time. Patrons in Kasama who were able to win funding for local projects found little difficulty in amassing support at election time. For example, of the nine councilors reelected in the 1975 Local Government elections, all but one was from the "big-man" category as determined by the prestige rating study. Patrons who were unable to "bring home the bacon" were not reelected in 1973 or 1975. The imposition of one-party electoral procedures did not ensure permanency of tenure for unpopular or unsuccessful patrons. Opposition factions continued to be recruited at the local level, both within the ruling party—for example, among disaffected lower cadres, and outside the party—for example, among school teachers. Some competition persisted too, as Scott noted for the First Republic, between patrons from UNIP and patrons from the state bureaucracy.[11] The most common form of competition was the making of rival claims of prowess in attracting development resources.[12] Thus the local politics of rural development in Kasama occurred at least in part among patronage factions delineated by vertical lines of social cleavage. A conventional conclusion can be drawn that the Zambian political machine linked center to locality, even if selectively and intermittently, by vertical ties between patrons and followers.

A second pattern of resource distribution, however, was discernible from the Kasama data; it attracts attention away from the vertical ties and intra-elite competition of the patronage model. The performance of the Zambian party-state gave rise to a stark horizontal cleavage between those who benefited and those who were excluded from development. The Kasama case suggests that social stratification was by no means incompatible with patronage. On the contrary, social stratification was the logical outcome of the performance of a political machine in conditions of rural underdevelopment and dependence.

The question then arises whether the social groups that are differentiated as the result of the performance of an African party-state can be described as social classes. The Kasama case suggests a tentative answer in the negative. Peasants in Kasama have become differentiated among themselves, and from officials of the party-state during the rural development process. But I can present little evidence that rural social strata had evolved into conscious social classes.

In part, the tentativeness of the answer is a consequence of the methodology of this study. A methodology focusing on the distribution of resources rather than the production of resources is not fully capable of eliciting an account of local politics in class terms. In order to reveal the dynamics of rural class formation and rural class conflict, research would have to start with a designation of the ownership and control of the means of production and the relations of production that subsequently arise. More would need to be known about arrangements for agricultural production in the locality and industrial production at the center. These were not inquiries on which the present study was based; studies in the future might well begin here.

Nevertheless a conventional class analysis cannot be imposed willy-nilly. The sharpness of rural class formation in the parts of Africa that resemble Kasama District was blurred by two related factors. The first was that the basic means of production, namely land, remained relatively plentiful. Unlike other parts of Southern Africa large numbers of peasants in Kasama were not forced into over-crowded reserves for purposes of white colonial settlement. Nor had land distribution among peasants become markedly uneven. Land tenure remained communal, with the exception of areas designated for state rural development schemes. The allocation of rural land remained in the hands of chiefs, who, as argued in this study, in no sense constituted a social class apart from subsistence peasants. A second factor blurred class formation in rural localities like Kasama, where extensive labor migration had taken place. Outmigration for temporary work in towns did not fully sever the connection of peasants to the land. Migrants were only "semiproletariarized"—they kept one foot in the countryside and one in the towns. Even laborers who worked for wages paid by the rural well-to-do retained access to a plot of their own. The absence of permanent landless or wage-earning classes among the peasantry complicated attempts to undertake class analysis. Although there may be other parts of rural Zambia and Africa where the process of class formation has proceeded further because of land shortage and landlessness, in Kasama the process was merely embryonic.

Even the data derived by the limited methodology of this study pointed only to social stratification, not to class formation. To be sure, the distributive performance of the African party-state did give rise to objective discrepancies in wealth at the local-level. The distribution of development resources from the center was monopolized by a small minority. The local leaders whom the center rewarded and helped to maintain in power were clearly distinguishable from subsistence peasants by the earning of a regular income. This income may have been from business or a farm, or a patronage reward bestowed by the party. At minimum, a regular income permitted a level of personal consumption which set local leaders apart. At most, the earning of a regular income permitted local leaders to employ peasants for agricultural labor on nonvillage farms or for house construction in village regrouping schemes. The earning of income was sufficient, in the context of a subsistence economy, to make local leaders stand out as relatively well-to-do. A pattern of resource distribution in which limited political power and scarce economic wealth were concentrated in the same hands tended to prevail in Kasama.

Although objective criteria of social stratification were observable in the locality, subjective criteria—that is, manifestations of "class consciousness," were not. The evidence for class consciousness was extremely sketchy. To some extent local leaders did seem to exhibit a shared awareness of privilege and on occasion did act in concert to protect and expand it. Several examples can be given. First, a single group of "big men" regularly met together in a UNIP caucus at the behest of the RS and voted together in a bloc in the Rural Council. This group held official positions in all institutions of the party-state "development front"—that is, in UNIP, the Rural Council, WDC's, and producer and marketing cooperatives. Their solidarity was most evident at the time of national campaigns like village regrouping, when development resources appeared to be in the offing; solidarity was notably absent, however, at the time of village registration and during elections. Second, at the ward level the well-to-do and party leaders acted in concert to monopolize central development resources, such as agricultural credit. Housing grants at village regrouping centers were captured by the privately wealthy or those with party patronage connections. The same group also operated together, in and around WDC's, to gain preferential access to plots on agricultural settlement schemes; these schemes were a main element in the government strategy to transform rural production. Third, local leaders endeavored to use the political organization of the party-state to expand the pool of available resources. For example, in 1973 WDC secretaries presented a joint demand for "professional" salaries; WDC leaders in Kasama also pushed, sometimes successfully, for the right to award contracts for the construction of local development projects. The degree of cohesiveness among local leaders seemed to vary widely from issue to issue, and cohesiveness was not always present. No argument can be made that the behavior of local leaders amounted to the consistent expression of the political interests of a coherent or conscious social class.

As for the attitudes and behavior of poor peasants, even fewer manifestations of class consciousness were evident. Although poor peasants in Kasama recognized that local leadership sometimes attempted to act as a cohesive group, they did not react in kind. They did, however, perceive party and state as one. My interviews found peasants unable or unwilling to draw distinctions between party and state, or between political and administrative affairs. To them all leadership seemed to represent *buteko* (government). The emphasis placed by Scott on the vertical cleavages between party leaders and civil servants in Zambia requires reconsideration in the light of peasant perceptions of an undifferentiated party-state.[13] More work needs to be done on the issue of horizontal cleavage between a frontal party-state leadership on the one hand and an unrewarded subsistence peasantry on the other. There was widespread acknowledgment among peasants that urban-rural wage differentials were wide and widening, and that subsistence was an increasingly difficult standard to maintain. Peasants were also aware that *apamwamba* (a privileged westernized class) existed in towns. The outmigration of young men was seen as a drain of the local economy. A rudimentary connection was made by peasants between outmigration and rural underdevelopment, but as much in terms of town versus country as in terms of rich versus poor.

The political activity of subsistence cultivators in Kasama did not indicate a shared perception of deprivation or the cohesion of a class of poor peasants. Rather, it reflected the persistent relevance of patronage ties. Up to 1975, powerful patrons in the locality and at the center were able to capitalize on peasant disaffection for personal ends. The breakaway opposition party, the United Progressive Party, was popular in Kasama largely because of the peasant expectation that Simon Kapwepwe would actively promote local demands for rural development. UPP was little more than a conservative sectionalist party and a vehicle for a leadership bid by Kapwepwe. In 1973 peasant voters in Kasama District ejected all three incumbent members of Parliament, including two UNIP Cabinet Ministers. But electoral resistance in the locality did not augur a class conscious peasantry on the rise. UNIP patrons, who were perceived to have performed poorly, were simply replaced by patrons from outside UNIP. The new patrons were decidedly middle-class in social background, and by the end of 1975, had begun to lose peasant support because of their own inability to attract and distribute development resources. The political response of subsistence cultivators to exclusion from the rural development process was not to organize among themselves, but to seek new patrons. The self-help activities in which Kasama peasant engaged, particularly around the policy of village regrouping, were confined to small and isolated communities. Nor did self-help give rise to a permanent political organization to articulate the interests of the rural poor. In their powerlessness, poor peasants depended on patrons.

As Dresang has observed, "Zambia represents a case of class formation without a high level of class consciousness."[14] Bates concurs that Zambian peasants compete for public resources on a sectional or factional basis but "appear unable to act out of a sense of class consciousness."[15] Whether this means that the politics of patronage cannot in theory or practice make way for the politics of class is open to question. Patronage does not necessarily crosscut or preclude class formation. Even at the best of times patronage provides upward social mobility for no more than a select few. Under conditions of scarce or declining resources, machine politics is likely to become frozen in a defensive posture, and the interests of existing patrons are likely to be jealously guarded. The performance of the African party-state under these conditions assists in the creation of the objective, if not the subjective, conditions for class formation. The underdeveloped rural periphery is in a transitional stage; its development path, regardless of government strategy, may be summarized in terms of the superimposition of class on patronage.

The choice of a class or patronage perspective on the local politics of rural development is not an either-or proposition. As Murray has argued for Africa, "class structure is diffuse and politics is a complex criss-crossing interaction of horizontal (class, status group, economic group) and vertical (regional, ethnic [and patronage]) allegiances and interests."[16] Zambia is no exception. The Zambian party-state is maintained through what has been described as "a process of conventional bargaining in which the brokers are class, sectional and ethnic units and where tangible rewards are exchanged for political support."[17] Political leaders get power by various means, and a subtle conceptual formulation is required to capture the variety of ways in which they distribute resources and attract support. We need to know in specific cases exactly how ethnicity, patronage, and class interact.

At a minimum, the Kasama case suggests that the local politics of the patronage machine should not be analyzed in isolation from the phenomenon of growing social inequality.

More research is needed on the relationship between the performance of African party-states and the differentiation of rural societies. An argument presented in this study is that the limit of party-state penetration is determined by the extent of patronage resources available to the center. A plausible proposition for further examination is that the limit of party-state penetration coincides with the principal line of horizontal cleavage in a stratified local society. The notion that political organization and social structure interact in this way is not new. Indeed, much of the literature on class formation in postcolonial Africa defines class in terms of differential access enjoyed by social groups to the apparatus of the state. The definition of class in terms of political organization is reflected in the labels of "managerial," "bureaucratic," or "organizational" bourgeoisie, which are often applied in analyses of the Zambian and other African cases.[18] Ownership and control of the means of production by this type of ruling class is indirect, effected through the medium of government departments and state corporations, and often shared with foreign partners. Most studies have concentrated on the manifestation of class formation at the political center. Yet a potentially fruitful avenue for further research would be the role of political organization in fostering a "bourgeoisie of the party-state" in rural localities. To do full justice to the complex relations between peasant and party-state in Africa, however, class analysis cannot be abstracted from the context of patronage politics.

The role of political organization is also crucial to a full account of both local politics and rural development. Poor peasants in rural Africa are disorganized and powerless because they have been unable to capture the local-level organizations of the African party-state and make them their own. Even where formal arrangements for political participation appear to exist, actual participation has been limited or ineffective. Neither political parties nor development committees have been built from below. Autonomous institutions for rural development have not emerged that would permit peasants to revive and control productive local economies. As far as rural development policy-making is concerned, the interests of the rural poor are weakly represented at the center relative to the interests of the party-state bureaucracy.

In Zambia peasants compete for development resources not only with a powerful bureaucracy but with vocal and well-organized urban groups, such as mine workers. Throughout much of Africa, development planning has tended to favor urban and industrial development above rural development. The relative neglect of rural development has come about, at least in part, because the rural poor have yet to find a collective organizational voice.

Appendix

Data for this study were derived from four sources:

(1) *Interviews* were conducted with approximately 135 people on an individual face-to-face basis during the course of field work. Key informants, who consented to repeated visits and many hours of conversation, numbered about two dozen. Some interview information (Chapter 6) was elicited in a group setting when I was permitted to ask questions at formal and informal village gatherings. The majority of respondents were people who lived and worked in Kasama District. I toured the rural areas of Kasama in an effort to speak with peasants and traditional leaders in remote as well as easily accessible parts of the district. My motorcycle took me beyond points where even four-wheel-drive government vehicles regularly reached. In addition to talking to people who lived off the land, I also spoke to representatives of the party and state at subdistrict, district, provincial, and national levels.

Because of my beginner's knowledge of ChiBemba, I was unable to complete every interview without resort to English. I was aided for about one third of the fieldwork time, however, by Bemba-speaking research assistants from the University of Zambia. Interviews were conducted personally by me with the exception of two or three occasions when my assistants worked alone. During regular interview post-mortems, these assistants provided valuable insights that an outsider missed and as such were themselves useful informants.

Interviews took two forms: *structured* and *nonstructured*. Structured interviews with the same schedule of questions being asked of each respondent, were used with all twenty-three ward councilors (Chapters 4 and 8) and with a sample of forty-four village headmen (Chapter 3). An attempt was also made to question systematically the peasants living on and off regrouping sites, but the sample here was very small, only thirty of each, and the schedule of questions was very short (Chapter 6). Structured interviews provided the basis of much of the hard data on number and type of rural development projects quoted here. Structured interviews were also the basis of the prestige rating study (Chapter 8).

As for nonstructured interviews, no attempt was made to hold to a fixed schedule of questions from one interview to another. Length and depth of interview varied with the rapport established and the expertise and volubility of the respondent. I was often surprised at how much vital information would be revealed in the course of an unstructured one- or two-hour chat. Informants were assured of confidentiality whenever a sensitive matter was discussed. Interviews were recorded by hand in rough note form in the presence of the respondent and transcribed in full later on the same day. Special attention was paid to the exact phrasing of significant responses, and many of these responses are reproduced verbatim in the body of the study. Interviews were my main research tool.

(2) *A social survey* with written questionnaires provided a substantial amount of information on the social background of local leadership groups. The survey was conducted among the 230 members of Ward Development Committees in Kasama District (Chapter 4).

The dimensions selected for study by this technique were purely descriptive of the social characteristics of respondents—for example, age, education, ethnicity, class, party, and other affiliations. No attempt was made to elicit attitudinal data. I felt that the validity and reliability of attitudes elicited by questionnaire techniques in a politically disaffected district of rural Zambia would have been dubious. Attitudinal data were collected instead by the interview techniques outlined above. I also felt that objective criteria of political recruitment were more germane than political attitudes to a study of patterns of group interest and resource distribution, and should therefore be the focus of study. Finally, I decided to keep the manipulation of survey questionnaire data in this study to a minimum. To subject the data to precise statistical tests of association and significance would impart to findings an unwarranted, perhaps even spurious, specificity.

The social survey questionnaires were self-administered and contained fifty-five items. In most cases ten questionnaire forms were handed personally to the councilor for each ward with a set of instructions for administering them. A Bemba translation was included in the questionnaire kit. A few councilors could not be reached personally but were contacted by mail. On occasion the researcher was invited by the councilor to attend a WDC meeting to explain publicly the purpose of the questionnaire. In all cases doubts or suspicions held by the respondents seem to have been allayed, because ultimately no one explicitly refused to answer. In one ward the respondents thought they were filling out applications for the Zambian National Service, so the questionnaire had to be readministered after the confusion was resolved.

A very satisfactory response rate of 88.7 percent was achieved (Chapter 4). A few items seem to have been widely misunderstood, and some were misconceived and misdirected by myself. Generally speaking, however, the social composition revealed by the questionnaire survey can be taken as representative of the social structure of local leadership. The picture of local leaders which emerged from the survey was strongly confirmed by other, more casual observations. The cooperation of WDC members and the conscientious assistance of most of the councilors made for a successful outcome. In less than half the wards was a follow-up necessary in the form of a letter or a personal visit, although follow-ups in noncooperative wards were rigorously pursued. Given the unfamiliarity of self-administered questionnaires in Kasama, a less encouraging rate of response than 88.7 percent might have been expected.

(3) *Written records* provided a third source of data. An immediate caveat is required about the reliability of written records in the setting of rural Kasama, which is a nonliterate peasant society only recently overlaid by a bureaucratic party-state. The study of the activities of grass-roots institutions like village and ward committees and party branches and constituencies had to proceed primarily without benefit of accurate, regular, and up-to-date correspondence and minute-keeping. Political communication flowed along less formal, more personal channels. Even though I was granted access to files at the Kasama Rural Council, the Office of the District Governor, and certain government departments, I found records in all cases to be far from complete. I used what I found in the knowledge that the story revealed may be sketchy in spots. I was refused access to files of the United

National Independence Party, Kasama Region, which proved to be a major obstacle to research (Chapter 7 and 8). Other written sources relevant to this study are as follows: books, pamphlets, and articles about Zambia published by the academic presses; official documents produced by the Government Printer, Lusaka, and the Zambian Information Service; unpublished research materials held by the Institute for African Studies, the University of Zambia Library, and the Centre for Continuing Education at the University of Zambia; and press clippings from the *Times of Zambia* and the *Daily Mail* (see below, bibliography). Special mention should be made of two studies of rural Zambia that proved invaluable: George Kay's *Social Aspects of Village Regrouping* (1967) and Ann Tweedie's "Ritual and Political Change in Bembaland" (1970) were drawn upon extensively in the text and helped to fill empirical gaps in my data.

(4) *Participant observation* was also used to gather data. Over the course of eight months in the field in 1974 and four months in the field in 1975, I attended more than a comfortable number of meetings in Kasama District. These included meetings of the Provincial and District Development Committees, or Village and Ward Committees, of parent-teachers association, literacy groups, and group housing committees, not to mention UNIP election campaign and voter registration meetings. I also attended a number of political education seminars conducted by members of the UNIP Central Committee in both Lusaka and Kasama. In addition to formal meetings I had the opportunity to take part in social gatherings in bars, dancehalls, and family homes in both town and country. I spent many days at a time at Nseluka village regrouping center, and paid two extended visits to Kayambi. My experiences in the villages of Kasama taught me as much about the realities of rural underdevelopment as any book I read or speech I heard.

Bibliography

BOOKS

Administration for Rural Development Research Project. *Organization for Participation in Rural Development in Zambia*. Lusaka: National Institute of Public Administration, 1976.

Allan, William. *The African Husbandman*. Edinburgh: Oliver and Boyd, 1965.

Arrighi, Giovanni, and John Saul. *Essays on the Political Economy of Africa*. New York: Monthly Review Press, 1973.

Bailey, F. G. *Stratagems and Spoils: A Social Anthropology of Politics*. Oxford: Blackwell, 1969.

Bailey, Martin. *Freedom Railway*. London: Rex Collings, 1976.

Baldwin, Robert. *Economic Development and Export Growth: A Study of Northern Rhodesia, 1920–1960*. Berkeley: University of California Press, 1966.

Bates, Robert. *Rural Responses to Industrialization: A Study of Village Zambia*. New Haven: Yale University Press, 1976.

———. *Unions, Parties, and Political Development: A Study of Mineworkers in Zambia*. New Haven: Yale University Press, 1971.

Bienen, Henry. *Kenya: The Politics of Participation and Control*. Princeton: Princeton University Press, 1974.

———. *Tanzania: Party Transformation and Economic Development*. Princeton: Princeton University Press, 1967.

Binder, Leonard, et al. *Crises and Sequences in Political Development*. Princeton: Princeton University Press, 1971.

Bond, George. *The Politics of Change in a Zambian Community*. Chicago: University of Chicago Press, 1976.

Bratton, Michael. *Beyond Community Development: The Political Economy of Rural Administration in Zimbabwe*. London: Catholic Institute for International Relations, 1978.

Bretton, Henry. *Power and Politics in Africa*. Chicago: Aldine, 1973.

Burawoy, Michael. *The Colour of Class on the Copper Mines*. Manchester: Manchester University Press, 1972.

Cliffe, Lionel, et al. *Rural Cooperation in Tanzania*. Dar es Salaam: Tanzania Publishing House, 1975.

———. *Government and Rural Development in East Africa: Essays on Political Penetration*. The Hague: Martinus Nijhoff, 1977.

——— and John Saul, eds. *Socialism in Tanzania*. 2 vols. Dar es Salaam: East African Publishing House, 1972–73.

Coleman, James, and Carl Rosberg. *Political Parties and National Integration in Tropical Africa*. Berkeley: University of California Press, 1964.

Colson, Elizabeth. *The Social Consequences of Resettlement: The Impact of the Kariba Resettlement on the Gwembe Tonga*. Manchester: Manchester University Press, 1971.

Dodge, Doris. *Agricultural Policy and Performance in Zambia: History, Prospects, and Proposals for Change*. Berkeley: Institute of International Studies, University of California, 1977.

Dresang, Dennis. *The Zambian Civil Service: Entrepreneurialism and Development Administration*. Nairobi: East African Publishing House, 1974.

Elections Study Committee (University of Dar es Salaam). *Socialism and Participation: Tanzania's 1970 National Elections*. Dar es Salaam: Tanzania Publishing House, 1974.

Epstein, A. L. *Politics in an Urban African Community*. Manchester: Manchester University Press, 1958.

Finucane, James. *Rural Development and Bureaucracy in Tanzania: The Case of Mwanza Region*. Uppsala: Scandinavian Institute of African Studies, 1974.

Gaay Fortman, Bastian de, ed. *After Mulungushi: The Economics of Zambian Humanism*. Nairobi: East African Publishing House, 1969.

Gann, Lewis. *A History of Northern Rhodesia: Early Days to 1953*. London: Chatto and Windus, 1964.

Gouldsbury, Cullen, and Hubert Sheane. *The Great Plateau of Northern Rhodesia*. London: Edward Arnold, 1911.

Gutkind, Peter, and Immanuel Wallerstein, eds. *The Political Economy of Contemporary Africa*. Los Angeles: Sage Publications, 1976.

Hall, Richard. *Zambia*. London: Pall Mall Press, 1965.

———. *The High Price of Principles*. London: Hodder and Stoughton, 1969.

Hall, Richard, and Hugh Peyman. *The Great Uhuru Railway*. London: Victor Gollancz, 1976.

Harries-Jones, Peter. *Freedom and Labour: Mobilization and Political Control on the Zambian Copperbelt*. Oxford: Blackwell, 1975.

Heisler, Helmuth. *Urbanisation and the Government of Migration: The Interrelation of Urban and Rural Life in Zambia*. London: Hurst, 1974.

Hellen, John A. *Rural Economic Development in Zambia: 1890–1964*. Afrika-Studien 32. Munich: Weltforum Verlag, 1968.

Hill, Polly. *Studies in Rural Capitalism in West Africa*. Cambridge: Cambridge University Press, 1970.

Honeybone, David, and Alan Marter. *An Evaluation Study of Zambia's Farm Institutes and Farmer Training Centers*. Lusaka: Rural Development Studies Bureau, University of Zambia, 1975.

Hopkins, Nicholas. *Popular Government in an African Town: Kita, Mali*. Chicago: University of Chicago Press, 1972.

Huntington, Samuel. *Political Order in Changing Societies*. New Haven: Yale University Press, 1968.

Hyden, Göran, Robert Jackson, and John Okumu, eds. *Development Administration: The Kenyan Experience*. Nairobi: Oxford University Press, 1970.

Ingle, Clyde. *From Village to State in Tanzania: The Politics of Rural Development*. Ithaca: Cornell University Press, 1972.

International Labour Office. *Narrowing the Gaps: Planning for Basic Needs and Productive Employment in Zambia*. Addis Ababa: International Labour Office, 1977.

Jackman, Mary. *Recent Population Movements in Zambia*. Zambian Papers, 8. Manchester: Manchester University Press, 1973.

Kapferer, Bruce. *Cooperation, Leadership and Village Structure.* Zambian Papers, 1. Manchester: Manchester University Press, 1967.

Kay, George. *Social Aspects of Village Regrouping in Zambia.* Lusaka: Institute for African Studies, University of Zambia, 1967, 1974.

Kuper, Leo, and M. G. Smith, eds. *Pluralism in Africa.* Berkeley: University of California Press, 1969.

Lamb, Geoff. *Peasant Politics: Conflict and Development in Muranga.* Lewes, Sussex: Julian Friedmann, 1974.

Leys, Colin. *Underdevelopment in Kenya: The Political Economy of Neo-Colonialism, 1964–1971.* London: Heinemann, 1975.

Lombard, C. S., and A. H. C. Tweedie. *Agriculture in Zambia since Independence.* Lusaka: Neczam, 1974.

Long, Norman. *Social Change and the Individual.* Manchester: Manchester University Press, 1968.

Luhring, J. *Rural Development Planning in Zambia.* Tangier: CAFRAD, 1975.

Markovitz, Irving. *Power and Class in Africa.* Englewood Cliffs, N.J.: Prentice-Hall, 1977.

Martin, Antony. *Minding Their Own Business: Zambia's Struggle against Western Control.* London: Hutchinson, 1972.

Meebelo, Henry. *Main Currents of Zambian Humanist Thought.* Lusaka: Oxford University Press, 1973.

———. *Reaction to Colonialism: A Prelude to the Politics of Independence in Northern Zambia, 1893–1939.* Manchester: Manchester University Press, 1971.

Molteno, Robert. *The Zambian Community and Its Government.* Lusaka: Neczam, 1974.

———. *Studies in Zambian Government and Administration.* Lusaka: University of Zambia Department of Correspondence Studies, 1973.

Morgenthau, Ruth. *Political Parties in French-Speaking West Africa.* Oxford: Clarendon Press, 1964.

Mpashi, Stephen. *Abapatili Bafika ku Lubemba* (The White Fathers Arrive in Bembaland). Lusaka: Nedcoz, 1968.

Mulford, David. *Zambia: The Politics of Independence, 1957–1964.* London: Oxford University Press, 1967.

———. *The Northern Rhodesia General Election, 1962.* Nairobi: Oxford University Press, 1964.

Nellis, John. *A Theory of Ideology: The Tanzanian Example.* Nairobi: Oxford University Press, 1972.

Ohadike, Patrick. *Development of and Factors in the Employment of African Migrants in the Copper Mines of Zambia, 1940–66.* Lusaka: Institute for African Studies, Zambian Papers, 4, 1969.

Ollawa, Patrick. *Rural Development Policies and Performance in Zambia.* Occasional Paper, 59. The Hague: Institute of Social Studies, 1977.

Palmer, Robin, and Neil Parsons, eds. *The Roots of Rural Poverty in Central and Southern Africa.* Berkeley: University of California Press, 1977.

Pettman, Jan. *Zambia: Security and Conflict.* Lewes, Sussex: Julian Friedmann, 1974.

Proctor, J. H. *The Cell System of the Tanganyika African National Union.* Dar es Salaam: Tanzania Publishing House, 1971.

Ranger, Terence. *The Agricultural History of Zambia.* Lusaka: Nedcoz, 1971.

Richards, Audrey. *Land, Labour and Diet in Northern Rhodesia*. London: Oxford University Press, 1939; 2nd ed., 1967.
———, ed. *Economic Development and Tribal Change*. Cambridge: W. Heffer, 1954.
Roberts, Andrew. *A Political History of the Bemba*. London: Longmans, 1973.
———. *The Lumpa Church of Alice Lenshina*. Lusaka: Oxford University Press, 1972.
———. *A History of Zambia*. New York: Africana Publishing Company, 1976.
Rotberg, Robert. *The Rise of Nationalism in Central Africa: The Making of Malawi and Zambia, 1873–1964*. Cambridge, Mass.: Harvard University Press, 1965.
Rothchild, Donald, and Robert Curry. *Scarcity, Choice and Public Policy in Middle Africa*. Berkeley: University of California Press, 1978.
Schumacher, Edward. *Politics, Bureaucracy and Rural Development in Senegal*. Berkeley: University of California Press, 1974.
Schurmann, Franz. *Ideology and Organization in Communist China*. Berkeley: University of California Press, 2nd ed., 1968.
Shaw, Timothy. *Dependence and Underdevelopment: The Development and Foreign Policies of Zambia*. Athens, Ohio: Center for International Studies, Africa Program, 1976.
Simmance, Alan. *Urbanization in Zambia*. New York: Ford Foundation, 1972.
Sklar, Richard. *Corporate Power in an African State: The Political Impact of Multinational Mining Companies in Zambia*. Berkeley: University of California Press, 1975.
Swartz, Marc, ed. *Local-Level Politics: Social and Cultural Perspectives*. Chicago: Aldine, 1968.
Tanguy, François. *Imilandu Ya Babemba*. Lusaka: Oxford University Press, 1966.
Tordoff, William, ed. *Politics in Zambia*. Manchester: Manchester University Press, 1974.
Turner, Victor. *Schism and Continuity in an African Society—A Study of Ndembu Village Life*. Manchester: Manchester University Press, 1957.
Uphoff, Norman, and Milton Esman. *Local Organization for Rural Development: Analysis of Asian Experience*. Ithaca, New York: Rural Development Committee, Cornell University, 1974.
Vergroff, Richard. *Botswana: Rural Development in the Shadow of Apartheid*. London: Associated University Press, 1977.
Watson, William. *Tribal Cohesion in a Money Economy: A Study of the Mambwe People of Northern Rhodesia*. Manchester: Manchester University Press, 1958.
Whitaker, Cyril. *The Politics of Tradition*. Princeton: Princeton University Press, 1970.
Widstrand, Carl Gösta, ed. *African Co-operatives and Efficiency*. Uppsala: Scandinavian Institute of African Studies, 1972.
Young, Crawford. *The Politics of Cultural Pluralism*. Madison, Wisconsin: University of Wisconsin Press, 1976.
Zolberg, Aristide. *Creating Political Order: The Party-States of West Africa*. Chicago: Rand McNally, 1966.

ARTICLES

Alavi, Hamza, "Peasant Classes and Primordial Loyalties," *Journal of Peasant Studies*, 1 (1973), 23–62.

Barker, Jonathan, "Local-Central Relations: A Perspective on the Politics of Development in Africa," *Canadian Journal of African Studies*, 4 (1970), 3–16.

———, "Political Factionalism in Senegal," *Canadian Journal of African Studies*, 7 (1973), 287–303.

Barrows, Walter, "Comparative Grassroots Politics in Africa," *World Politics*, 26 (1974), 283–297.

Bates, Robert, "Input Structures, Output Functions and Systems Capacity: A Study of the Mineworkers' Union of Zambia," *Journal of Politics*, 32 (1970), 898–929.

———, "Ethnic Competition and Modernization in Contemporary Africa," *Comparative Political Studies*, 6 (1974), 457–484.

———, "Rural Development in Kasumpa Village, Zambia," *Journal of African Studies*, 2 (1975), 333–362.

———, "People in Villages: Micro-Level Studies in Political Economy," *World Politics*, 31 (1978), 129–149.

Berger, Elena L., "Government Policy towards Migrant Labour on the Copperbelt, 1930–1945," *Transafrican Journal of History*, 2 (1972), 83–102.

Berman, Bruce, "Clientelism and Neocolonialism: Center-Periphery Relations and Political Development in African States," *Studies in Comparative International Development*, 9 (1974), 3–25.

Bienen, Henry, "Political Parties and Political Machines in Africa," in M. Lofchie, ed., *The State of the Nations: Constraints on Development in Independent Africa*, Berkeley: University of California Press, (1971), 195–213.

Bratton, Michael, "Zambia: Security and Conflict," *African Social Research*, 21 (1976), 69–73.

Brelsford, Vernon, "Aspects of Bemba Chieftainship," *Rhodes-Livingstone Communication*, No. 2 (1944).

Brooks, Elizabeth, "Village Productivity Committees and Social Development in Zambia," *International Social Work*, 18 (1974), 71–89.

Cliffe, Lionel, "Tanzania—Socialist Transformation and Party Development," *African Review*, 1 (1971), 119–135.

Cohen, Michael, "The Myth of the Expanding Centre: Politics in the Ivory Coast," *Journal of Modern African Studies*, 11 (1973), 227–246.

Collier, Ruth, "Parties, Coups and Authoritarian Rule: Patterns of Political Change in Tropical Africa," *Comparative Political Studies*, 11 (1978), 62–93.

Cottingham, C., "Political Consolidation and Centre-Local Relations in Senegal," *Canadian Journal of African Studies*, 4 (1970), 101–120.

Coulson, Andrew, "Peasants and Bureaucrats," *Review of African Political Economy*, 3 (1975), 53–58.

Cross, Sholto, "Politics and Criticism in Zambia: A Review Article," *Journal of Southern African Studies*, 1 (1974), 109–115.

Doornbos, Martin, "Concept-Making: The Case of Political Penetration," *Development and Change*, 2 (1971), 98–106.

Dresang, Dennis, "Entrepreneuralism and Development Administration in Zambia," *African Review*, 1 (1972), 91–117.

———, "Ethnic Politics, Representative Bureaucracy and Development Administration: The Zambian Case," *American Political Science Review*, 68 (1974), 1605–1617.

———, "The Political Economy of Zambia," in Richard Harris, *The Political Economy of Africa*, Cambridge, Mass.: Schenkman (1975), 187–226.

Eisenstadt, Shmuel, "Post-Traditional Societies and the Continuity and Reconstruction of Tradition," *Daedalus*, 102 (1973), 1–27.

Fourth International, "Zambia: Humanist Rhetoric, Capitalist Reality," *Africa in Struggle*, Occasional Publication, 1, London: Red Books, 1976.

Gertzel, Cherry, et al., "Zambia's Final Experience of Inter-Party Elections: The By-Elections of December 1971," *Kroniek van Afrika*, 12 (1972), 57–77.

Gluckman, Max, "How the Bemba Make their Living: An Appreciation of Richards' 'Land, Labour and Diet in Northern Rhodesia,'" *Rhodes-Livingstone Journal*, 3 (1945), 55–75.

———, et al., "The Village Headman in British Central Africa," *Africa*, 19 (1949), 89–106.

Hanna, William, "Influence and Influentials in Two Urban-Centered African Communities," *Comparative Politics*, 2 (1969), 17–40.

Harries-Jones, P., and J. C. Chiwale, "Kasaka: A Case Study in Succession and Dynamics of a Bemba Village," *Rhodes-Livingstone Journal*, 33 (1963), 1–67.

Harvey, Charles, "The Control of Credit in Zambia," *Journal of Modern African Studies*, 11 (1973), 383–392.

———, "Rural Credit in Zambia: Access and Exit," *Development and Change*, 6 (1975), 89–105.

———, "The Structure of Zambian Development," in Ukandi Damachi, et al., *Development Paths in Africa and China*, London: Macmillan, 1976, pp. 136–151.

Heisler, Helmuth, "Continuity and Change in Zambian Administration," *Journal of Local Administration Overseas*, 4 (1965), 183–193.

Hudson, W. J. S., "Local Government Reorganization in the Isoka District, Zambia," *Journal of Local Administration Overseas*, 4 (1965), 47–50.

Hyden, Goran, and Colin Leys, "Elections and Politics in Single-Party Systems: The Case of Kenya and Tanzania," *British Journal of Political Science*, 2 (1972), 389–420.

Kaufmann, Robert R., "The Patron-Client Concept and Macro-Politics," *Comparative Studies in Society and History*, 16 (1974), 284–308.

Kay, George, "Agricultural Change in the Luitikila Basin Development Area, Mpika District, Northern Rhodesia," *Rhodes-Livingstone Journal*, 31 (1962), 21–49.

Lemarchand, René, "Political Clientelism and Ethnicity in Tropical Africa: Competing Solidarities in Nation-Building," *American Political Science Review*, 66 (1972), 68–90.

———, and Keith Legg, "Political Clientelism and Development," *Comparative Politics*, 4 (1972), 149–178.

Leys, Colin, "Politics in Kenya: The Development of Peasant Society," *British Journal of Political Science*, 1 (1971), 307–337.

McKown, Roberta, and Robert E. Kauffman, "Party System as a Comparative Analytic Concept in African Politics," *Comparative Politics*, 6 (1973), 47–72.

Makoni, Tonderai, "The Economic Appraisal of the Tanzania-Zambia Railway," *African Review*, 2 (1972), 599–616.

Markakis, John, and Robert Curry, "The Global Economy's Impact on Recent Budgetary Politics in Zambia," *Journal of African Studies*, 3 (1976), 403–427.

Meillassoux, Claude, "A Class Analysis of the Bureaucratic Process in Mali," *Journal of Development Studies*, 6 (1970), 97–110.

Miller, Norman, "The Political Survival of Traditional Leadership," *Journal of Modern African Studies*, 6 (1968), 183–201.

———, "The Rural African Party: Political Participation in Tanzania," *American Political Science Review*, 64 (1970), 548–571.

Morrison, D. G. and H. M. Stevenson, "Integration and Instability: Patterns of African Political Development," *American Political Science Review*, 66 (1972), 902–927.

Mubako, Simbi, "Zambia's Single Party Constitution: A Search for Unity and Development," *Zambia Law Review*, 5 (1973), 67–85.

O'Brien, Donal, "Co-operators and Bureaucrats: Class Formation in a Senegalese Peasant Society," *Africa*, 41 (1971), 263–278.

———, "Modernization, Order, and the Erosion of a Democratic Ideal: American Political Science 1960–70," *Journal of Development Studies*, 8 (1972), 351–378.

Pettman, Jan, "Zambia's Second Republic: The Establishment of a One-Party State," *Journal of Modern African Studies*, 12 (1974), 231–244.

Powell, J. D., "Peasant Society and Clientelist Politics," *American Political Science Review*, 64 (1970), 411–425.

Quick, Stephen, "Bureaucracy and Rural Socialism in Zambia," *Journal of Modern African Studies*, 15 (1977), 379–400.

Raikes, P. L., "Ujamaa and Rural Socialism," *Review of African Political Economy*, 3 (1975), 33–52.

Rainford, R. G., "Provincial Development Committees in Zambia," *Journal of Administration Overseas*, 10 (1971), 178–191.

Rasmussen, T. E., "Political Competition and One-Party Dominance in Zambia," *Journal of Modern African Studies*, 7 (1969), 407–424.

Richards, Audrey, "African Kings and their Royal Relatives," *Journal of the Royal African Institute*, 91 (1961), 135–149.

———, "The Bemba of North-Eastern Rhodesia," in E. Colson and M. Gluckman, eds., *Seven Tribes of British Central Africa*, London: Oxford University Press, 1951.

———, "A Changing Pattern of Agriculture in East Africa: The Bemba of Northern Rhodesia," *Geographical Journal*, 124 (1958), 302–314.

———, "The Political System of the Bemba Tribe," in M. Fortes and E. E. Evans-Pritchard, eds., *African Political Systems*, London: Oxford University Press, 1940.

———, "The Story of Bwembya," in M. Perham, ed., *Ten Africans*, London: Faber and Faber, 1963.

Rothchild, Donald, "Rural-Urban Inequities and Resource Allocation in Zambia," *Journal of Commonwealth Political Studies*, 10 (1972), 222–242.

Sandbrook, Richard, "Patrons, Clients, and Factions: New Dimensions of Conflict Analysis in Africa," *Canadian Journal of Political Science*, 5 (1972), 104–119.

———, "Patrons, Clients, and Unions: The Labour Movement and Political Conflict in Kenya," *Journal of Commonwealth Political Studies*, 10 (1972), 3–27.

Scarritt, James, "Elite Values, Ideology, and Power in Post-Independence Zambia," *African Studies Review*, 14 (1971), 31–54.

Scott, Ian, "Party Functions and Capabilities: The Local-Level UNIP Orga-
nisation during the First Zambian Republic (1964–73)," *African Social
Research*, 22 (1976), 107–129.
Scott, James, "Corruption, Machine Politics, and Political Change," *American
Political Science Review*, 63 (1969), 1142–1158.
———, "Exploitation in Rural Class Relations: A Victim's Perspective,"
Comparative Politics, 7 (1975), 489–532.
Shaw, Timothy, "Zambia: Dependence and Underdevelopment," *Canadian
Journal of African Studies*, 10 (1976), 3–22.
Shivji, Issa, "Peasants and Class Alliances," *Review of African Political
Economy*, 3 (1975), 10–18.
Siddle, D. J., "Rural Development in Zambia: A Spatial Analysis," *Journal
of Modern African Studies*, 8 (1970), 271–284.
Sklar, Richard, "Political Science and National Integration: A Radical Ap-
proach," *Journal of Modern African Studies*, 5 (1967), 1–11.
Staniland, Martin, "The Rhetoric of Centre-Periphery Relations," *Journal of
Modern African Studies*, 8 (1970), 617–636.
Tordoff, William, "Provincial and District Government in Zambia," *Journal
of Administration Overseas*, 7 (1968), 425–433 (Part 1), 538–545
(Part 2).
Wallerstein, Immanuel, "The State and Social Transformation: Will and Pos-
sibility," *Politics and Society*, 1 (1971), 359–364.
Weingrod, Alex, "Patrons, Patronage and Political Parties," *Comparative
Studies in Society and History*, 10 (1968), 377–400.
Werbner, R., "Federal Administration, Rank and Civil Strife among Bemba
Royals and Nobles," *Africa*, 37 (1967), 22–49.
Whitaker, Cyril, "A Dysrhythmic Process of Political Change," *World Politics*,
19 (1967), 190–217.
Zolberg, Aristide, "The Structure of Political Conflict in the New States of
Tropical Africa," *American Political Science Review*, 62 (1968), 70–87.

UNPUBLISHED PAPERS

Bates, Robert, "UNIP and Labour Policy: A Study of the Local Party in the
Mine Townships of Nkana," University of Zambia, Department of Po-
litical and Administrative Studies, mimeo., 1971.
Baylies, Carolyn, "Class Formation and the Role of the State in the Zambian
Economy," University of Zambia, Department of Social Development
Studies, seminar paper, 1974.
Chikwanda, W. M., "Problems of Village Regrouping for Northern Province
and How to Overcome Them," Lusaka, National Institute of Public
Administration, mimeo., 1971.
Dore, M. H., and T. Warke, "Report on a Preliminary Market Survey of
Kasama," University of Zambia, Department of Economics, 1972.
Due, Jean, "Agricultural Credit in Zambia by Level of Development," Ur-
bana-Champaign, University of Illinois, Agricultural Economics Staff
Paper, 1978.
Fielder, R. J., "Government and Politics in Namwala District," University
of Zambia, Centre for Continuing Education, 1971.
Gertzel, Cherry, ed., *The Political Process in Zambia: Documents and Read-
ings*, 2 vols., University of Zambia, School of Humanities and Social
Sciences, Correspondence School, undated.

————, "Communication between Government and People," University of Zambia, Department of Extra-Mural Studies, 1970.

————, "Institutional Development at the District Level in Independent Zambia," University of Zambia, Political Science Workshop, 1972.

————, "Tradition, Economic Deprivation and Political Alienation in Rural Zambia, The 1973 General Elections in Western Province," University of Zambia, unpublished paper, 1974.

Harris, Belle, "The Nature of Leadership and Institutional Structure for Rural Development: A Case Study of Nsega District (Tanzania)," Leiden, Afrika Studiocentrum, 1970.

Hesse, Chris, "Some Aspects of Development Planning and Implementation in Zambia with Particular Reference to Eastern and Luapula Provinces," University of Dar es Salaam, African Social Science Conference Paper, 1968.

Kamina, H. C., "The Establishment of Area, Ward and Village Committees in Mkushi District," Lusaka, National Institute of Public Administration, 1971.

Kapteyn, R. C. E., "Local Government in Solwezi District: A Case Study in Development Administration," Free University of Amsterdam, Institute for Social Sciences, mimeo., 691105/KL/192, 1969.

Lof, Gerard and Louise, "The Impact of Modern Changes on Food and Nutrition in the Rural Areas of Zambia: Two Case Studies in Kasama District, Northern Province," Wageningen, Holland, Agricultural University, 1974.

Lombard, Stephen, "Farming Co-operatives in the Development of Zambian Agriculture," University of Zambia, Centre for Continuing Education, 1974.

McEnery, Hugh, "The Village Productivity Committee System and Production Targets as Set Up in Mkushi District," Lusaka, Ministry of Rural Development, August 1974.

Mpaisha, Chisepo, "Agricultural Extension Service in Chipata District: A Preliminary Survey of the Work and Difficulties of Village Workers," University of Zambia, Humanities and Social Sciences Research Project, Working Paper No. 4, 1975.

————, "The Policy and Practice of Rural Self-Help Group Housing in Chipata District: A Comparative Study of Chipungo and Chambwa Group Housing Projects," Lusaka, National Institute of Public Administration, Administrative Studies in Development, No. 10, 1973.

Mushota, Robert, "Conflict between the Centre and Locality: The Nansala-Nalubi Case (Central Province, Zambia)," University of Zambia, Political Science Workshop, 1972.

Muyoba, Godfrey, "Governmental Machinery at the Grass Root Level: An Area Study of Ward 19 of Serenje District," Lusaka, National Institute of Public Administration, Administrative Studies in Development No. 11, 1974.

Nadeau, E. G., "A Comparison of Two Cooperative Farming Unions in Northern Zambia," University of Zambia, Rural Development Studies Bureau, Research Seminar Paper, 1973.

National Food and Nutrition Commission, "Food Consumption in the Northern Province," Lusaka, mimeo., undated.

Quick, Stephen, "Aspects of Cooperative Development in Eastern Province," University of Zambia, Department of Political and Administrative Studies, Seminar Paper, 1973.

Rasmussen, Thomas, "Administrative Change and Rural Development in Zambia," African Studies Association Conference Paper, 1972.
——, "Provincial and District Development Committees," University of Zambia, Department of Political Science, 1969.
——, "The District Secretary and District Governor as Coordinators of Development," University of Zambia, Department of Political Science, 1969.
Rau, William, "Rural Underdevelopment in Zambia's Northern Province, 1900–1964," University of Zambia, Extra-Mural Studies, 1975.
Ray, Donald, "Settlement Schemes and Rural Development in Zambia with Special Reference to Chifwile and Musuma Settlements," Lusaka, Institute for African Studies Seminar Paper, 1974.
Samoff, Joel and Rachel, "The Local Politics of Underdevelopment," University of Zambia, Interdisciplinary Seminar Paper, 1974.
Scott, Ian, "Party-Bureaucratic Relations and the Process of Development in Zambia," University of Zambia, Department of Political and Administrative Studies, 1971.
Taylor, Laurence, "Decentralization for Coordinated Rural Development," Lusaka, National Institute for Public Administration, 1971.
Tschannerl, G., "Rural Water Supply in Tanzania: Is 'Politics' or 'Technique' in Command?" Dar es Salaam, Annual Social Science Conference of East African Universities, 1973.
Tweedie, Ann, "Ritual and Political Change in Bembaland," Lusaka, Institute for African Studies, 1970.
Van Ruller, Henk, "Ward Development Committees and Village Productivity Committees in Chipata District," Lusaka, National Institute for Public Administration, Administrative Studies in Development No. 5, 1973.
——, "Administrative Boundaries of Chiefs' Areas and Wards in Chipata District," Lusaka, National Institute for Public Administration, Administration Studies in Development, No. 13, 1973.

DOCUMENTS

Government of the Republic of Zambia, *The Constitution of Zambia Act, 1973*. Lusaka: Government Printer, 1973.
——, *Local Government Act, 1965*. Lusaka: Government Printer, 1965.
——, *Local Government (Amendment) Act, 1975*. Lusaka: Government Printer, 1975.
——, *Local Government Elections Act*. Lusaka: Government Printer, undated.
——, *The Registration and Development of Villages Act, 1971*. Lusaka: Government Printer, 1971.
——, *Report of the Commission of Inquiry into the Allegations Made by Mr. Justin Chimba and Mr. John Chisata*. Lusaka: Government Printer, 1971.
——, *Report of the National Commission on the Establishment of a One-Party Participatory Democracy in Zambia* (Chona Commission). Lusaka: Government Printer, 1972.
——, *Report of the National Commission on the Establishment of a One-Party Participatory Democracy in Zambia: Summary of Recommendations Accepted by Government* (Chona Commission White Paper). Lusaka: Government Printer, 1972.

————, *Report and Recommendations on Rural Agricultural Credit in Zambia* (Crisco Report). Lusaka: Government Printer, 1969.

Government of the Republic of Zambia: *Report of the Working Party Appointed to Review the System of Decentralised Administration* (Simmance Commission Report). Lusaka: Government Printer, 1972.

————, *Village Productivity and Ward Development Committees* (Pocket Manual). Lusaka: Government Printer, 1971.

Government of the Republic of Zambia, Central Statistical Office, *Census of Population and Housing, 1969*, Preliminary Report. Lusaka: Government Printer, 1970.

————, *Census of Population and Housing, 1969*, Final Report, Vol. IIe, Northern Province. Lusaka: Government Printer, 1975.

————, *Census of Population and Housing, 1969*, Final Report, Vol. IV(e3), Kasama District (Polling District Populations). Lusaka: Government Printer, 1974.

————, *Sample Census of Population 1974*, Preliminary Report. Lusaka: Government Printer, 1975.

Government of the Republic of Zambia, Department of Agriculture, "Farming in Northern Province: Report on 1972/73 Farm Register," Kasama, 1973.

————, "Farming in Northern Province: 1973/74 Season," Kasama, 1974.

————, *Kasama District Farm Register*, Kasama, 1975.

Government of the Republic of Zambia, Department of Community Development, *Government Policy: Village Regrouping*, Lusaka, mimeo., 1968.

————, *Manual for Functional Literacy Work*. Lusaka: Government Printer, 1975.

Government of the Republic of Zambia, Ministry of Local Government and Housing, Kasama Rural Council, File LA/KA/1/4, Councillor Reports.

————, Kasama Rural Council, File LA/KA/1/23, Vols. 1 and 2, VPC's and WDC's.

————, Kasama Rural Council, File LS/KA/5/9, Village Regrouping.

————, *The Councillor's Handbook*. Lusaka: Government Printer, 1966.

Government of the Republic of Zambia, Ministry of Rural Development, File MRD/COM/5, Village Regrouping.

Government of the Republic of Zambia, National Archives of Zambia, *Calendars of the District Notebooks (Northern Province) 1862–1963*, Vol. 2. Lusaka: Government Printer, 1973.

Government of the Republic of Zambia, Office of the District Governor, Kasama, File AGR/13, Productivity Committees.

————, File COR/1/1, District Messengers Reports.

Kaunda, Kenneth, *Humanism in Zambia and a Guide to Its Implementation, Part I*. Lusaka: Government Printer, 1967.

————, *Humanism in Zambia and a Guide to its Implementation, Part II*. Lusaka: Government Printer, 1975.

————, *Zambia's Guideline for the Next Decade*. Address to National Council of UNIP, 9 November 1968. Lusaka: Government Printer, 1968.

Mansfield, J. E., et al., *Land Resources in Northern and Luapula Provinces, Zambia: A Reconnaissance Assessment*, Vols. 1–4. British Government Foreign and Commonwealth Office, Overseas Development Administration, 1973.

Mytton, Graham, *Report on the National Mass Media Audience Survey, 1970–71*. Lusaka: Zambia Broadcasting Service Research Project, 1972.

Northern Rhodesian Government, *An Account of the Disturbances in North-ern Rhodesia, July-October 1961*. Lusaka: Government Printer, 1961.

——, *Annual Report on African Affairs for Northern Province, 1963*. Lusaka: Government Printer, 1963.

——, Development Commissioner, Kasama. *Progress at Mungwi*. Ndola: Rhodesian Printers, 1959.

——, Provincial Administration. *Kasama District Notebook*, Vols. 1 and 2. Lusaka, National Archives of Zambia, 1898–1963.

——, Provincial Administration, File C/SOC/3/5, United National Independence Party, July 1961 to July 1962.

——, Provincial Administration File SOC/3/3, Vol. 1. UNIP Registration of Societies/Change of Office Bearers, 1961–1964.

United National Independence Party, "Grim Peep into the North." Lusaka: *Voice of UNIP*, 1961.

——, *National Policies for the Next Decade, 1974–1984*. Lusaka: Government Printer, 1973.

Notes

INTRODUCTION
1. THE LOCAL POLITICS OF RURAL DEVELOPMENT

1. Cited by William A. Hance, *Black Africa Develops* (Waltham, Mass., Crossroads Press, 1977), p. 1.

2. Samir Amin, "Underdevelopment and Dependence in Black Africa—Origins and Contemporary Forms," *Journal of Modern African Studies*, 10 (1972), 503–24. Robin Palmer and Neil Parsons, *The Roots of Rural Poverty in Central and Southern Africa* (Berkeley, University of California Press, 1977); E. A. Brett, *Colonialism and Underdevelopment in East Africa: The Politics of Economic Change, 1919–1939* (London, Heinemann, 1973).

3. Dudley Seers, "The Meaning of Development," in Norman Uphoff and Warren Ilchman, *The Political Economy of Development* (Berkeley, University of California Press, 1972), pp. 123–129. Everett Rogers, "Communication and Development: The Passing of the Dominant Paradigm," *Communication Research*, 3 (1976), 213–240.

4. Albert Waterston, "A Viable Model for Rural Development," *Finance and Development* (December 1974), 22–25, reprinted with an addendum stressing the organizational imperative of rural development in Charles Wilber, *The Political Economy of Development and Underdevelopment* (New York, Random House, 1978), p. 240. Reginald Green, "Basic Human Needs, Collective Self-Reliance and Development Strategy: Some Reflections on Power, Periphery and Poverty," University of Sussex, Institute of Development Studies, mimeo. (1976), p. 24. Norman Uphoff and Milton Esman, *Local Organization for Rural Development: Analysis of Asian Experience* (Ithaca, New York, Rural Development Committee, Cornell University, 1974).

5. John Saul, "Class and Penetration," in Lionel Cliffe and John Saul, eds., *Socialism in Tanzania* (Dar es Salaam, East African Publishing House, 1973), Vol. 2, p. 122.

6. On the methodological status of case studies and their relationship to the construction of general statements, see Arend Lijphart, "Comparative Politics and the Comparative Method," *American Political Science Review*, 65 (1971), 682–693. Harry Eckstein, "Case Study and Theory in Political Science," in F. I. Greenstein and N. W. Polsby, eds., *The Handbook of Political Science*, Vol. 9 (Reading, Mass., Addison-Wesley, 1975).

7. Ruth Berins Collier, "Parties, Coups and Authoritarian Rule: Patterns of Political Change in Tropical Africa," *Comparative Political Studies*, 11 (1978), 62–93.

8. Irving Leonard Markovitz, *Power and Class in Africa* (Englewood Cliffs, New Jersey, Prentice-Hall, 1977), p. 5.

9. Franz Schurmann, *Ideology and Organization in Communist China* (Berkeley, University of California Press, 1971).

10. Samuel Huntington, *Political Order in Changing Societies* (New Haven, Yale University Press, 2nd ed., 1968), p. 1.

11. Joseph LaPalombara, "Penetration: A Crisis of Government Capacity" in Leonard Binder, et al., *Crises and Sequences in Political Development* (Princeton, Princeton University Press, 1971), p. 219.

12. Gabriel Almond and G. Bingham Powell, *Comparative Politics: A Developmental Approach* (Boston, Little, Brown, 1966), p. 35.

13. Martin Doornbos, "Concept-Making: The Case of Political Penetration," in *Development and Change*, 2 (1971), 98.

14. LaPalombara, p. 207. Lucian Pye echoes this definition when he conceives of political penetration as "the state reaching down into society and effecting basic policies": *Aspects of Political Development* (Boston, Little, Brown, 1966), p. 64.

15. Binder, L., "The Crises of Political Development," in Binder, p. 62.

16. Almond and Powell, p. 35.

17. Donal Cruise O'Brien, "Modernization, Order, and the Erosion of a Democratic Ideal—American Political Science, 1960–70," *Journal of Development Studies*, 8 (1972), 351–378.

18. Markovitz, p. 3.

19. Lionel Cliffe, et al., *Government and Rural Development in East Africa: Essays on Political Penetration* (The Hague, Martinus Nijhoff, 1977), introduction.

20. Walter Barrows, "Comparative Grassroots Politics in Africa," *World Politics*, 26 (1974), 284.

21. Martin Staniland, "The Rhetoric of Centre-Periphery Relations," *Journal of Modern African Studies*, 8 (1970), 617–636.

22. Joan Vincent, "Anthropology and Political Development," in Colin Leys, ed., *Politics and Change in Developing Countries* (Cambridge, Cambridge University Press, 1960), pp. 46–47.

23. Alex Weingrod, "Patrons, Patronage, and Political Parties," *Comparative Studies in Society and History*, 10 (1968), 377–400.

24. Lloyd Fallers, "Political Sociology and the Anthropological Study of African Politics," *Archives Européens de Sociologie*, 4 (1963), 328.

25. Norman Miller, "The Political Survival of Traditional Leadership," *Journal of Modern African Studies*, 6 (1968), 183–201. Nicholas Hopkins, *Popular Government in an African Town: Kita, Mali* (Chicago, University of Chicago Press, 1972). C. S. Whitaker, *The Politics of Tradition* (Princeton, Princeton University Press, 1970).

26. C. S. Whitaker, "A Dysrhythmic Process of Political Change," *World Politics*, 19 (1967), 190–217.

27. Shmuel Eisenstadt, "Post-Traditional Societies and the Continuity and Reconstruction of Tradition," *Daedalus*, 102 (1973), 1–27.

28. Marc Swartz, ed., *Local-Level Politics: Social and Cultural Perspectives* (Chicago, Aldine, 1968). F. G. Bailey, *Stratagems and Spoils: A Social Anthropology of Politics* (Oxford, Blackwell, 1969).

29. Maxwell Owusu, *Uses and Abuses of Political Power: A Case Study of Continuity and Change in the Politics of Ghana* (Chicago, University of Chicago Press, 1970). Joan Vincent, *African Elite: The Big Men of a Small Town* (New York, Columbia University Press, 1971).

30. Robert Bates, *Rural Responses to Industrialization: A Study of Village Zambia* (New Haven, Yale University Press, 1976).

31. Barrows, p. 284.

32. James Coleman and Carl Rosberg, *Political Parties and National Inte-*

gration in Tropical Africa (Berkeley, University of California Press, 1964), drew the distinction between "revolutionary-centralizing" and "pragmatic-pluralist" parties. David Apter proposed the "mobilization system" to cover the former category, in his *Ghana in Transition* (Princeton, Princeton University Press, 1964). Ruth Morgenthau contrasted the concepts of "mass" and "patron" parties, in *Political Parties in French-Speaking West Africa* (Oxford, Clarendon Press, 1964) and "Single-Party Systems in West Africa" in *American Political Science Review*, 55 (1961), 294–307.

33. Jonathan Barker, "Local-Central Relations: A Perspective on the Politics of Development in Africa," *Canadian Journal of African Studies*, 4 (1970), 3.

34. Henry Bienen, *Tanzania: Party Transformation and Economic Development* (Princeton, Princeton University Press, 1967). Aristide Zolberg, *Creating Political Order: The Party-States of West Africa* (Chicago, Rand McNally, 1966).

35. Immanuel Wallerstein, "The Decline of the Party in African Single-Party States," in Myron Weiner and Joseph LaPalombara, *Political Parties and Political Development* (Princeton, Princeton University Press, 1966).

36. Henry Bretton, *Power and Politics in Africa* (Chicago, Aldine, 1973), p. 3. See also Michael Cohen, "The Myth of the Expanding Centre: Politics in the Ivory Coast," *Journal of Modern African Studies*, 11 (1973), 227–246. LaPalombara, pp. 205–232.

37. Aristide Zolberg, "The Structure of Political Conflict in the New States of Tropical Africa," *American Political Science Review*, 62 (1968), 70; my emphasis.

38. Samuel Decalo, *Coups and Army Rule in Africa: Studies in Military Style* (New Haven, Yale University Press, 1976), p. 1.

39. Zolberg (1968), p. 86.

40. LaPalombara, p. 230.

41. Zolberg, (1968), p. 71.

42. René Lemarchand, "Political Clientelism and Ethnicity in Tropical Africa: Competing Solidarities in Nation-Building," *American Political Science Review*, 66 (1972), 69; my emphasis. For an earlier theoretical formulation, see Lemarchand and Legg, "Political Clientelism and Development: A Preliminary Analysis," *Comparative Politics*, 4 (1972), 149–178.

43. J. D. Powell, "Peasant Society and Clientelist Politics," *American Political Science Review*, 64 (1970), 411.

44. Goran Hyden and Colin Leys, "Elections and Politics in Single-Party Systems," *British Journal of Political Science*, 2 (1972), 389–420; quoted by Henry Bienen, *Kenya: The Politics of Participation and Control* (Princeton, Princeton University Press, 1974), 109–110.

45. Lemarchand, p. 69.

46. Henry Bienen, "One Party Systems in Africa," in Samuel P. Huntington and Clement H. Moore, eds., *Authoritarian Politics in Modern Society* (New York, Basic Books, 1970), pp. 99–127.

47. James C. Scott, "Corruption, Machine Politics, and Political Change," *American Political Science Review*, 63 (1969), 1143.

48. Ibid., p. 109.

49. Weingrod (above, n. 23).

50. Bienen (above, n. 46) and "Political Parties and Political Machines in Africa," in Michael F. Lofchie, ed., *The State of the Nations: Constraints on Development in Independent Africa* (Berkeley, University of California Press, 1971).

51. Immanuel Wallerstein, *The Modern World-System: Capitalist Agriculture and the Origins of the European World-Economy in the Sixteenth Century* (New York, Academic Press, 1974), p. 15.

52. Compare Andre Gunder Frank, "The Development of Underdevelopment," in J. Cockroft, A. G. Frank, and D. Johnson, *Dependence and Underdevelopment: Latin America's Political Economy* (Garden City, N.Y., Doubleday, 1972), p. 4, with Ernesto Laclau, "Feudalism and Capitalism in Latin America," *New Left Review*, 67 (1971), 19–38.

53. Colin Leys, "Politics in Kenya: The Development of a Peasant Society," *British Journal of Political Science*, 1 (1971), 307–337, and *Underdevelopment in Kenya: The Political Economy of Neo-Colonialism, 1964–1971* (London, Heinemann, 1975). Lionel Cliffe, "The Policy of Ujamaa Vijijini and the Class Struggle in Tanzania," in Cliffe and Saul, eds., *Socialism in Tanzania* (Dar es Salaam, East African Publishing House, 1972–73).

54. Gavin Williams, "Taking the Part of Peasants: Rural Development in Nigeria and Tanzania" in Peter Gutkind and Immanuel Wallerstein, eds., *The Political Economy of Contemporary Africa* (Beverly Hills, Sage, 1976), p. 139. See also Theo Van Velzen, "Staff, Kulaks and Peasants: Study of a Political Field," in Cliffe and Saul, pp. 153–168. Donal C. O'Brien, "Co-operators and Bureaucrats: Class Formation in a Senegalese Peasant Society," *Africa*, 41 (1971), 263–278. Claude Meillassoux, "A Class Analysis of the Bureaucratic Process in Mali," *Journal of Development Studies*, 6 (1970), 97–110. Issa Shivji, "Peasants and Class Alliances," *Review of African Political Economy*, 3 (1975), 10–18. *Class Struggles in Tanzania* (London, Heinemann, 1976).

55. Pierre Van den Berghe, *Power and Privilege at an African University* (Cambridge, Mass., Schenkman Publishing Company, 1973), p. 92.

56. Richard Sandbrook, "Patrons, Clients and Factions," *Canadian Journal of Political Science*, 5 (1972), 119.

57. Lemarchand, p. 972; my emphasis.

58. Jonathan Barker, "Political Factionalism in Senegal," *Canadian Journal of African Studies*, 7 (1973), 289.

59. Bruce Berman, "Clientelism and Neocolonialism: Center-Periphery Relations and Political Development in African States," *Studies in Comparative International Development*, 9 (1974), 15, 13.

60. Hamza Alavi, "Peasant Classes and Primordial Loyalties," *Journal of Peasant Studies*, 1 (1973), 59.

61. Gavin Williams and Terisa Turner, "Nigeria," in John Dunn, *West African States: Failure and Promise* (Cambridge, Cambridge University Press, 1978), pp. 136–137; my emphasis.

62. Donald Rothchild and Robert Curry, *Scarcity, Choice and Public Policy in Middle Africa* (Berkeley, University of California Press, 1978), p. 8.

2. CENTER AND LOCALITY: THE ZAMBIAN CONTEXT

1. Helmuth Heisler, *Urbanisation and the Government of Migration: The Interrelation of Urban and Rural Life in Zambia* (London, Hurst, 1974), p. 2.

2. Charles Harvey, "The Structure of Zambian Development," in Ukandi Damachi, et al., *Development Paths in Africa and China* (London, Macmillan, 1976), p. 139.

3. Richard Sklar, *Corporate Power in an African State: The Political*

Impact of Multinational Mining Companies in Zambia (Berkeley, University of California Press, 1975), p. 19.

4. Robert Baldwin, *Economic Development and Export Growth: A Study of Northern Rhodesia, 1920–1960* (Berkeley, University of California Press, 1966). J. A. Hellen, *Rural Economic Development in Zambia: 1890–1964*, Afrika-Studien, 32 (Munich, Weltforum Verlag, 1968).

5. Donald Rothchild, "Rural-Urban Inequities and Resource Allocation in Zambia," *Journal of Commonwealth Political Studies*, 10 (1972), 224.

6. International Labour Office, *Narrowing the Gaps: Planning for Basic Needs and Productive Employment in Zambia* (Addis Ababa, ILO Jobs and Skills Program for Africa, 1977), p. 42.

7. Ibid., p. 58.

8. Republic of Zambia, *Towards Complete Independence*, an address by President Kaunda to the UNIP National Council, Matero, August 11, 1969 (Lusaka, Government Printer, 1969), p. 44.

9. Kenneth Kaunda, *Humanism in Zambia and a Guide to Its Implementation, Part II* (Lusaka, Government Printer, 1975), p. 19.

10. Ann Seidman, "The Haves and Have Nots in Zambia," *Africa Institute Bulletin*, 12 (1974), 168–170.

11. Osvaldo Sunkel, "Transnational Capitalism and National Disintegration in Latin America," *Social and Economic Studies*, 22 (1973), 132–176.

12. Karen Eriksen, "Zambia: Class Formation and Detente," *Review of African Political Economy*, 9 (1978), 4–26. Michael Burawoy, *The Colour of Class on the Copper Mines*, Institute for African Studies, Zambian Papers, 7 (Manchester, Manchester University Press, 1972). Carolyn Baylies, "Class Formation and the Role of the State in Zambian Economy," unpublished paper, Department of Social Development Studies, UNZA, 1974. Fourth International, "Zambia: Humanist Rhetoric, Capitalist Reality," *Africa in Struggle*, Occasional Publications, 1 (London, Red Books, 1976).

13. Timothy Shaw, "Zambia: Dependence and Underdevelopment," *Canadian Journal of African Studies*, 10 (1976), 4.

14. Jankees van Donge, "Planning in Chaos or Chaos in Planning?" (Lusaka, Department of Political and Administrative Studies, UNZA, mimeo., 1975), pp. 5–10.

15. Republic of Zambia, *Zambia's Economic Revolution*, an address by President Kaunda to the UNIP National Council, Mulungushi, April 19, 1968 (Lusaka, Government Printer, 1968), p. 14.

16. John Markakis and Robert Curry, "The Global Economy's Impact on Recent Budgetary Politics in Zambia," *Journal of African Studies*, 3 (1976), 424.

17. Calculated by Dennis Dresang, *The Zambian Civil Service: Entrepreneurialism and Development Administration* (Nairobi, East African Publishing House, 1974), p. 109.

18. Republic of Zambia, *Estimates of Revenue and Expenditure for the Year(s) 1961–1968*, cited by Bates, ibid., p. 105.

19. Republic of Zambia, *Second National Development Plan, January 1972 – December 1976* (Lusaka, Government Printer, 1972), Table 1–4, p. 41; subsistence and commercial agriculture together were to decline from 15.1% of GDP in 1971 to 13.7% in 1976, while manufacturing was to rise from 9.4% to 13%.

20. Alan Simmance, *Urbanization in Zambia* (New York, Ford Foundation, 1972), p. 15.

21. Republic of Zambia, *Mid-Term Review of the Second National Development Plan (Performance of the Zambian Economy, 1972–1974)* (Lusaka, Development Planning Division, 1975).

22. Doris Dodge, *Agricultural Policy and Performance in Zambia: History, Prospects and Proposals for Change* (Berkeley, Institute of International Studies, 1977), p. 3, pp. 68–78.

23. Ibid., p. 2.

24. Markakis and Curry, p. 425.

25. James Fry, "An Analysis of Employment and Income Distribution in Zambia" (Oxford University, unpublished doctoral dissertation, 1974). Fabian Maimbo and James Fry, "An Investigation into the Change in the Terms of Trade between the Rural and Urban Sectors of Zambia," *African Social Research*, 12 (1971), pp. 95–110. Dodge, pp. 130–137.

26. ILO, p. 2.

27. Cherry Gertzel, "Institutional Developments at the District Level in Independent Zambia," UNZA, Political Science Workshop, mimeo., 1972.

28. Kenneth Kaunda, *Zambia's Guideline for the Next Decade* (Lusaka, Government Printer, 1969).

29. For a complete account, see William Tordoff, "Provincial and Local Government in Zambia," *Journal of Administration Overseas*, 9 (1970), pp. 23–36. Thomas Rasmussen, "Provincial and District Development Committees," UNZA, mimeo., 1969. Laurence Taylor, "Decentralization for Coordinated Rural Development," NIPA, mimeo., 1971.

30. Republic of Zambia, *The Local Government Act, 1965*, No. 69 of 1965.

31. Republic of Zambia, *First National Development Plan, 1966–70* (Lusaka, Government Printer, 1966), p. 18.

32. Republic of Zambia, *Report of the Working Party Appointed to Review the System of Decentralised Administration* (Simmance Commission) (Lusaka, Government Printer, 1972), p. 24.

33. Republic of Zambia, *Registration and Development of Villages Act, 1971*, No. 30 of 1971 (Lusaka, Government Printer, 1971).

34. Republic of Zambia, *The Constitution of Zambia Act, 1973*, No. 27 of 1973 (Lusaka, Government Printer, 1973). For an account of the political events surrounding the declaration of a one-party state, see above, pp. 212–222; also Jan Pettman, "Zambia's Second Republic: The Establishment of a One-Party State," *Journal of Modern African Studies*, 12 (1974), pp. 231–244; Simbi Mubako, "Zambia's Single Party Constitution: A Search for Unity and Development," *Zambia Law Review*, 5 (1973), 67–85.

35. Republic of Zambia, *Village Productivity and Ward Development Committees* (Pocket Manual) (Lusaka, Government Printer, 1971).

36. Lionel Cliffe and John Saul, "The District Development Front," in Cliffe and Saul, eds., *Socialism in Tanzania*, Vol. 2, pp. 302–328.

37. Audrey Richards, "A Changing Pattern of Agriculture in East Africa: The Bemba of Northern Rhodesia," *Geographical Journal*, 124 (1958), p. 304.

38. Andrew Roberts, *A Political History of the Bemba: Political Growth and Change in Northeastern Zambia Before 1900* (London, Longmans, 1973), p. 343.

39. Audrey Richards, *Land, Labour and Diet in Northern Rhodesia: An Economic Study of the Bemba Tribe* (London, Oxford University Press, 1939).

40. Ibid., 2nd ed. (1967), p. xiv. George Kay, *A Social Geography of Zambia* (London, University of London Press, 1967), p. 78.

41. Ministry of Rural Development, "Recommendations for the Selection of

an Intensive Development Zone in the Northern Province" (Lusaka, mimeo., 1973), p. 5.

42. For an analysis of the connection between state rural development performance and outmigration in the Luapula Province, see Bates, *Rural Responses*, (above, p. 14, n. 30), chapters 6–9.

43. Mary Jackman, *Recent Population Movements in Zambia* (Manchester, Manchester University Press, 1973).

44. J. E. Mansfield, et al., *Land Resources in Northern and Luapula Provinces, Zambia: A Reconnaissance Assessment* (British Foreign and Commonwealth Office, Overseas Development Administration, 1973), Vol. 1, p. 188.

45. Calculated from *Census of Population and Housing, 1969* Final Report Vol. II(e), Northern Province (1975), Table 7, pp. 17–19.

46. For technical descriptions of chitemene and regional variants upon it, see W. Allan, *The African Husbandman* (Edinburgh, Oliver and Boyd, 1965). The best descriptions of the Bemba variant can be found in C. G. Trapnell, *The Soils, Vegetation and Agriculture of Northeastern Rhodesia* (Lusaka, Government Printer, 1953), and Richards (1939). For recent innovations, see George Kay, "Agricultural Change in the Luitikila Basin Development Area, Mpika District," *Rhodes-Livingstone Journal*, 31 (1962), 21–49.

47. Richards (1958), p. 310.

48. Gerard and Louise-Fresco Lof, "The Impact of Modern Changes in Food and Nutrition in the Rural Area of Zambia: A Case Study of Two Villages in Kasama District," (Wageningen, Holland, Agricultural University, mimeo., 1974).

49. Ibid.

50. Mansfield, et al., Vol. 1, p. 6.

51. Calculations based on Department of Agriculture, Kasama, *Farm Register* (1975) and *Census of Population and Housing 1969* Final Report, Vol II(e), 1975.

52. Northern Rhodesian Government, *Kasama District Notebook*, Vol. II, Chapter I, 1959. See also George Kay, *Social Aspects of Village Regrouping* (Lusaka, Institute for African Studies, 1967 and 1974), and P. Harries-Jones and J. C. Chiwale, "Kasaka: A Case Study in Succession and Dynamics of a Bemba Village," *Rhodes-Livingstone Journal*, 33 (1963), p. 1–67.

53. Office of the District Governor, Kasama District, *Master Village Register*, lists all villages in the District together with their populations; all figures are drawn from this source.

54. Estimates prepared by the National Council for Scientific Research, Cartographic and Locational Analysis Unit 1972; cited by ILO, p. 69.

55. Estimates prepared by the National Food and Nutrition Commission, Survey of Northern Province, 1969–70; cited by Rothchild, p. 223.

56. Administration for Rural Development Research Project, *Organization for Participation in Rural Development in Zambia* (Lusaka, National Institute for Public Administration, draft report, 1976) p. 6.

57. Calculated from Kasama Rural Council, Capital Estimates, Second National Development Plan, 1972–76, File LG/KA/5/5, p. 51; the entire capital budget of the KRC was funded from the state at the center, as was 55% of the K204,000 average recurrent budget.

VILLAGE AND WARD COMMITTEES

3. VILLAGE PRODUCTIVITY COMMITTEES IN KASAMA

1. Republic of Zambia, *Report of the Working Party Appointed to Review the System of Decentralised Administration* (Lusaka, Government Printer, 1972), p. 107.

2. *Times of Zambia*, April 23, 1975. See also "Village Groups Are a Failure," ibid., March 17, 1975.

3. See Cherry Gertzel, 1971. R. Kapteyn and C. Emery, *District Administration in Zambia* (Lusaka, first report, NIPA-Administration for Rural Development Project, 1971). C. K. Kaindu, "Rural Reconstruction: Problems and Prospects," in Robert Molteno, ed., *Studies in Zambian Government and Administration* (Lusaka, UNZA, 1973), pp. 3–14. *Report of the Working Party*, pp. 105–113.

4. See Hugh McEnery, "The Village Productivity Committee System and Production Targets as Set Up in Mkushi District" (Lusaka, Ministry of Rural Development, mimeo., 1974). *Organization for Participation in Rural Development*, 1976. Elizabeth Brooks, "Village Productivity Committees and Social Development in Zambia," *International Social Work*, 18, (1974), 35–42.

5. Office of the Permanent Secretary, Northern Province, Circular No. 5, 1972.

6. Letter from Permanent Secretary, Northern Province, to the Secretary General to the Government; Monthly Progress Report on Registration of Villages, September 21, 1972.

7. Office of the District Secretary, Kasama, *Registration and Development of Villages* (report compiled by E. B. Chituta), p. 2.

8. Interview, councilor for Ward 12, November 17, 1974.

9. Robert Molteno, "Zambia and the One Party State," *East Africa Journal*, 9 (1972), 6–18.

10. Office of the Permanent Secretary, Northern Province, Monthly Progress Report on Registration of Villages, April 31, 1972.

11. Interview, Namponda village, June 17, 1974.

12. Republic of Zambia, *Chiefs Act*, No. 67 of 1965, Section 10(b).

13. Republic of Zambia, *Registration and Development of Villages Act*, 1971, Part VI.

14. Office of the Permanent Secretary, Northern Province, Circular No. 7 of 1972.

15. Letter, Secretary General to the Government to the Permanent Secretary, Northern Province, November 25, 1972.

16. WDC meeting, Ward 1, Kayambi, July 24, 1974.

17. Letter, UNIP Youth Regional Secretary to Secretary, Kasama Rural Council, undated (1973).

18. Interview, Mungwi, April 24, 1975.

19. Interview, headman, Songolo's village, June 13, 1974.

20. Interview, headman, Kasonde Chisuna village, July 22, 1974.

21. Elijah Mudenda, MCC, Seminar on One-Party Participatory Democracy (Lusaka, UNZA, September 4, 1974).

22. Interview, headman, Bwembya village, July 27, 1974.

23. Interview, headman, James Mwilwa village, June 22, 1974.

24. VPC Minutes, Lwabwe village, March 15, 1972.

25. Songolo's village, June 13, 1974.

26. Recorded at VPC meeting, James Mwilwa Village, June 11, 1974.

27. Interview, headman, Bwembya village, July 27, 1974.
28. This issue was discussed in the House of Chiefs on September 28, 1971, as one of the means of maintaining traditional authority.
29. Interview, headman, Kasonde Chisuna village, July 22, 1974.
30. Pocket Manual, pp. ix–xv.
31. Hugh McEnery, "The Village Productivity Committee System and Production Targets as Set Up in Mkushi District," p. 5.
32. Interview, councilor for Ward 3, April 24, 1975.
33. Minutes of Lwabwe VPC, March 15, 1972, KRC file LG/KA/1/23, p. 1.
34. Minutes of Munkonge VPC meeting, January 19, 1974. Ibid., Vol. II, p. 93.
35. March 15, 1974.
36. Interview, councilor for Ward 14, June 26, 1974.
37. KRC file LG/KA/1/23, p. 33.
38. Office of the District Governor, Kasama, file AGR/13.
39. I am indebted to Lammert de Jong for this and many other insights based on his research in Serenje and Chipata Districts.
40. Office of the District Governor, Kasama, file AGR/13, series of letters, pp. 142–145.
41. Interview, headman, Chisoka village, July 18, 1974.
42. Republic of Zambia, *Registration and Development of Villages Act*, No. 30 of 1971, Sec. 19.
43. Interview, Assistant District Secretary, Kasama, May 15, 1975.
44. Kasama Rural Council, Minutes of Ward Council Secretaries' meeting, Mungwi, October 1, 1974, confirmed in interviews with District Governor, Assistant District Secretary, and numerous headmen and councilors. Reference to cases of VPC fines were found in the minutes of WDC's in Ward 4 (Chimbola, October 5, 1974) and Ward 16 (Ntema, November 17, 1974).
45. Interview, headman, Bwembya village, July 27, 1974.
46. Audrey Richards, "A Changing Pattern of Agriculture in East Africa," p. 311.
47. Interview, Kasakula village, July 17, 1974. UNIP organization was noticeably weak in this area. During the 1975 registration of voters campaign, the task of mobilizing the people as well as administering the campaign fell to the chief and the field-level civil servants. The councilor for Ward 20, who was also the UNIP constituency secretary, was at the time away on the Copperbelt having his Landrover repaired.
48. District Commissioner, Kasama; minutes of District Team, November 11, 1961, p. 2.
49. Audrey Richards, "The Political System of the Bemba Tribe" in Fortes and Evans-Pritchard, *African Political Systems* (London, Oxford University Press, 1940).
50. "Help Us Recover Loans," report on address of Minister of Rural Development to House of Chiefs, *Times of Zambia*, September 25, 1975.

4. WARD DEVELOPMENT COMMITTEES IN KASAMA

1. Wards 1, 2, 4, 8, 14, 18, 20, and 22. Evidence of early committee meetings was gathered from diverse files at the Rural Council, Office of the District Governor, and Department of Community Development.

2. Ministry of Cooperatives, Youth, and Development: Department of Community Development, Northern Province, *Annual Report* (1967), p. 9.

3. Kenneth Kaunda, *Humanism in Zambia and a Guide to Its Implementation, Part I* (Lusaka, Government Printer, 1967), p. 43.

4. Ministry of Local Government and Housing, *The Councillor's Handbook* (Lusaka, Government Printer, 1966).

5. Kasama Rural Council, address by District Governor, minutes of 30th ordinary meeting, September 22, 1971, File C/40/71.

6. Interview, councilor for Ward 17, November 25, 1974.

7. See Charles Harvey, "Rural Credit in Zambia: Access and Exit," *Development and Change*, 6, no. 2 (1975), 89–105. Stephen Quick, "Bureaucracy and Rural Socialism in Zambia," *Journal of Modern African Studies*, 15 (1977), 379–400.

8. This figure was based on counts made at seven Ward Council meetings.

9. Urban occupations mentioned by WDC labor migrants were, in descending order of frequency: miner, bricklayer, carpenter, house servant, laborer, clerk, teacher, driver, and policeman.

10. Graham Mytton, Zambia Broadcasting Service Research Project, *Report on the National Mass Media Audience Survey, 1970–71*, Report No. 3 (Lusaka, Institute for African Studies, 1972), table XIV, p. 27. The figure of 24% is for all Northern Province; no district breakdown is provided.

11. Estimated from Kasama Rural Council, *Register of Motor Vehicles*, 1975.

12. Central Statistical Office, *Final Report, 1969, Census of Population and Housing*, Vol. IIe (Lusaka, Government Printer, August 1973); table 97 gives a figure of 6.5%. This figure was adjusted upward to take into account the flurry of house-building that took place after 1969 and for which no updated figures were available.

13. Source: estimate from my own survey data; see also Seidman (1974).

14. The Department of Agriculture, Kasama, employed a "two hectare" criterion in compiling a register of emergent farmers. The farm register was used to select a target group to whom most extension advice and assistance was directed. The Provincial Crop Husbandry Officer, Northern Province, estimated that emergent farmers thus defined accounted for "over 70%" of the marketable maize surplus in Kasama District (interview, May 20, 1974).

15. Interview, councilor for Ward 8, Malole, November 25, 1974.

16. For example, Pius Kasonde Kasutu rose from branch official in the Malole area to Regional Secretary, Kasama, to Cabinet Minister for Northern Province. Andrew Bwalya Mutemba, for the same part of the district, rose to Chairman of the Youth and Sports Committee in the UNIP Central Committee. Robert Makasa rose to Zambia's Ambassador to Tanzania.

17. Research in Kabwe Rural District confirmed that WDC's and WC's "do not draw membership from VPC's; we learned that members are chosen . . . by the councillor": H. A. Mwankanye and J. M. Nyambonza: "Report on Field Work Experiences, Mutakwa, Chief Mungule's Area" (UNZA, Department of Social Development Studies, mimeo., 1975), p. 3.

18. Kasama Rural Council, "Compiled Report of WDC Minutes of the Kasama Rural Council, Northern Province" (Mungwi, mimeo., April 4, 1975).

19. Ibid., p. 1.

20. Ministry of Rural Development: "Productivity Committees at Lower Levels of Administration," letter from PRDO Kasama to Permanent Secretary MRD, Lusaka, May 9, 1975.

21. Interview, councilor for Ward 6, Ngoli School, July 11, 1974.

22. Source: notes taken during WDC meeting, Chitambi village, April 18, 1974.

23. Interview, Chitamba village, July 13, 1974.

24. Interview, Nseluka Community Development Assistant, Namponda village, August 10, 1974.

25. Interview, Secretary, Namponda VPC, Namponda village, August 17, 1974.

26. Office of the District Governor: letter, Chairman KRC to councilor for Ward 6, November 22, 1971, file AGR/13, p. 35.

27. Minutes of WDC meeting, Ward 13, Rural Council Welfare Hall, Mungwi, January 31, 1973.

28. Noted at WDC meeting, Ward 13, Council Chamber, Mungwi, April 17, 1974.

29. Meeting for Members of Parliament for Kasama, Mungwi, April 25, 1975.

30. See President Kaunda's speech commemorating World Forestry Day as reported in *Times of Zambia*, March 22, 1976.

31. Department of Agriculture, *Farming in Northern Province, 1973/74 Season*, (Kasama, mimeo., 1974), p. 1.

32. Kasama Rural Council, Councillor Annual Reports at December 31, 1973, file LGKA/1/4; only ten councilors submitted reports.

33. *Pocket Manual*, p. xii.

34. Interview, April 23, 1974.

35. Interview, Mungwi, April 24, 1975.

36. Solomon Kalulu, Member of the Central Committee, public meeting at Buseko Hall, Kasama, May 24, 1974.

37. *Daily Mail*, October 19, 1974: "Mystery of the Missing K14m."

38. Interview, councilor for Ward 20, November 27, 1974.

39. Minutes of WDC meeting, Ward 14, February 2, 1974.

40. Interview, councilor for Ward 16, November 26, 1974.

41. Minutes of Seminar of WDC Secretaries, Mungwi, April 16–20, 1973.

42. Department of Agriculture, Kasama: memorandum, Farm Management Officer to Provincial Agricultural Officer, February 4, 1974.

43. Shem Mighot-Adholla: "The Politics of Mechanization in Sukumaland," in Carl Gösta Widstrand, ed., *African Co-operatives and Efficiency* (Uppsala, Scandinavian Institute of African Studies, 1972).

44. McEnery (1974).

45. Interview, Senior Engineering Assistant, Department of Water Affairs, Kasama, November 20, 1975. See also G. Tschannerl, "Rural Water Supplies: Is Politics or Technique in Command?" (University of Dar es Salaam, mimeo., 1974).

46. Office of the District Governor, Letter, Chief Education Officer to Headmistress, Kasama Girls' Secondary School, 1971, File AGR/13, p. 23.

47. Ibid., p. 33.

48. Interview, councilor for Ward 14, June 27, 1974.

49. Ward 14, June 8, 1974.

50. Seminar, University of Zambia, Extra-Mural Department, Kasama, 1975. For further research on the attitudes of Zambia Civil Servants, see James Scarritt, "Elite Values, Ideology, and Power in Post-Independence Zambia," *African Studies Review*, 14 (1971), 31–54.

51. Ministry of Rural Development, "Productivity Committees at Lower Levels," p. 12.

52. Kasama Rural Council, "Compiled Report of WDC Minutes . . ." (1975), p. 6.
53. Address to Kasama Rural Council, September 22, 1971.
54. Interview, councilor for Ward 21, July 18, 1974.
55. Interview, councilor for Ward 15, May 22, 1975.
56. Ward Council meeting, Ward 13, April 14, 1974.
57. Interview, councilor for Ward 12, November 17, 1974.
58. Agricultural Finance Company, Kasama, circular, AFC Provincial Manager, August 27, 1974. For an account of AFC procedures and evaluation of the WDC credit program in pilot districts, see Administration for Rural Development Research Project, NIPA (1976), chapter 7.
59. Agricultural Finance Company, Kasama: Instructions Nos. 410 1A and 1B, April 8 and 19, 1974.
60. Based on provisional figures for new and existing customers for 1975–76. The sample excludes Wards 18 and 21 which had not submitted lists. The percentage may well be higher, given that loan applicants may use more than one name. Moreover, research in Mpika, Mumbwa, and Mazabuka districts revealed a higher preponderance of WDC members among successful applicants than in Kasama. In Kasama only 20% of local applicants were WDC members, as opposed to an average of 40% in the other three districts. Also, in the other three districts 83% were members of either the committees or the party: Jean Due, "Agricultural Credit in Zambia by Level of Development" (Urbana-Champaign, University of Illinois: Agricultural Economics Staff Paper, mimeo., 1978), p. 26.
61. Kasama Rural Council, Report of the first seminar of WDC secretaries of Kasama District, Mungwi, April 16–20, 1973, p. 8.
62. Office of the District Governor: Circular, Secretary to the Cabinet to all Permanent Secretaries: "Workshops for WDC Officials," September 3, 1973, file LG/KA/1/23, p. 81.
63. Saul, p. 119.

VILLAGE REGROUPING

5. TWO CASES OF REGROUPING: NSELUKA AND KAYAMBI

1. Government of the Republic of Zambia, *Government Policy: Village Regrouping*, mimeo., 1968.
2. "Village Regrouping is a Big Success in Solwezi," *Times of Zambia*, January 4, 1974.
3. Interview, Minister of State for National Guidance, March 26, 1975, and interview, Commissioner for Community Development, June 4, 1976.
4. Republic of Zambia, *Second National Development Plan 1972–1976* (Lusaka, Government Printer, 1972), pp. 177–181, 201.
5. *Times of Zambia*, February 5, 1975. ILO (above, p. 28, n. 6), pp. 339–341.
6. J. J. C. Mpaisha, "The Policy and Practice of Rural Self-Help Group Housing in Chipata District" (Lusaka, NIPA-ARD Research mimeo., No. 10, 1973). W. M. Chikwanda: "Problems of Village Regrouping for Northern Province and How to Overcome Them" (Lusaka, NIPA mimeo., 1971).
7. The extensive literature on Tanzania results in large part from the centrality of rural development to the Tanzanian development strategy since 1967. Recent additions include Jannik Boesen, *Ujamaa: Socialism from Above*

(New York, Africana Publications, 1978); P. L. Raikes, "Ujamaa and Rural Socialism," *Review of African Political Economy*, 3 (1975), 33–52; Michael Lofchie, "Agrarian Socialism in the Third World: The Tanzanian Case," *Comparative Politics*, 8 (1976), 479–499; Goran Hyden, "Ujamaa Villagization and Rural Development in Tanzania," *ODI Review* (Sussex) 1 (1975), 53–72; Helge Kjekshus, "The Tanzanian Villagization Policy: Implementational Lessons and Ecological Dimensions," *Canadian Journal of African Studies*, 11 (1977), 269–282.

8. Interview, Community Development Assistant, Nseluka Regrouping Scheme, June 20, 1974.

9. At the time of my first visit to Nseluka in June 1974 the Department of Community Development had three Landrovers for the entire Northern Province, and two of these were off the road with serious mechanical faults. For two days the Nseluka CDA relied on rides on my motorcycle to visit villages in his jurisdiction.

10. Department of Community Development, Kasama, Letter, PCDO to CDA, Henry Kapata Subcenter, November 9, 1964, Office file EXT/6, p. 17.

11. Ibid., letter, CDA to PCDO September 29, 1969, p. 36.

12. Kasama Rural Council, Report, PCDO to District Governor (undated), file LG/KA/5/9, p. 28.

13. Ibid.

14. Kasama Rural Council, Report, Assistant Community Development Officer, Kasama, "Village Regrouping and Village Reconstruction," February 28, 1975, file LG/KA/5/9, p. 103.

15. Department of Community Development, Kasama, letter, CDA to PCDO, May 13, 1971, file EXT/6, p. 52.

16. Interview by K. Chibesakunda, *Enterprise: The INDECO Journal* (Lusaka) 4th quarter, 1972, p. 3.

17. Roberts, *History of the Bemba*, p. 99.

18. Henry Meebelo, *Reaction to Colonialism* (Manchester, Manchester University Press, 1971) pp. 34–43. Roberts, pp. 246–252. Stephen Mpashi, *Abapatili Bafika ku Lubemba* [The White Fathers Arrive in Bembaland] (Lusaka, NEDCOZ, 1968), pp. 2–3.

19. Interview, Mr. Sangweni (aged 90+), Illondola village, May 7, 1975.

20. Roberts says that "Makasa appears to have returned his conquests north of Kayambi to the Mambwe of Nsokolo. . . . In the early 1900's the Mambwe chief Mpande had regained authority over his people at the expense of Makasa's 'son' Changala who withdrew to the western party of Mpanda" (p. 291).

21. Mpashi, chapter 4.

22. Cullen Gouldsbury and Hubert Sheane, *The Great Plateau of Northern Rhodesia* (London, Edward Arnold, 1911).

23. Central Statistical Office, 1969 Census Report by Polling District (Lusaka, mimeo., undated).

24. Office of the District Governor, *Master Village Register, Kasama District*; and estimate for children under 16.

25. Department of Community Development, Kasama DCDO to District Secretary, February 24, 1975. It is unclear where the figure came from, but at a minimum, nine villages were urged to regroup at Kayambi: Illondola, Gregorio, Tambatamba, Chale Buyala, Pupwe, Chipunsu, Kaminsa, Mulola, and Kaputa.

26. Interview, Mr. Kalunga (aged 60) Kaminsa village, May 7, 1975.

27. Interview, Kayambi Mission, May 4, 1975. In 1975 the credit union had 102 paid-up members and a working capital of K2000. The first loans were about to be made to credit-worthy members for the purchase of agricultural capital equipment, such as grain hammer mills. Cooperative groups were favored. The Kayambi Credit Union was modeled on the Chilonga Union in Mpika District, whose working capital stood at K30,000 in 1975. The missionaries at Kayambi, however, expressed concern that the Chilonga pattern of giving loans primarily to salaried outsiders, such as school-teachers, should be avoided.

28. The cooperative purchased maize at K4.50 per bag, 50 ngwee above the national price, ground it, and re-sold it at 50 ngwee below the national price. Kayambi farmers and consumers naturally favored this arrangement, but in early 1975 were blocked from transacting business outside national price guidelines by the manager of the Northern Province Cooperative Marketing Union.

29. In 1975 a 5-liter can of cooking oil that sold in Kasama for K4.44 sold in Kayambi for K6.00; a 50-kg. sack of maize meal that sold in Kasama for K3.50 sold in Kayambi for between K4.50 and K5.50. Cigarettes, when available, regularly sold for 25–50% above town prices. Transportation costs did account for some but not all of this markup. Rural stores were beyond the reach of state price control inspectors, so little prospect of relief from high prices was at hand for Kayambi peasants.

30. Kasama Rural Council, file LG/KA/5/9, p. 17.

31. Department of Community Development, Kasama, Letter, PCDO to Commissioner for Community Development, Lusaka, March 3, 1974.

32. Department of Community Development, Lusaka, *Annual Report*, 1972, p. 6.

33. Interview, Councilor for Ward 1, Kayambi, July 25, 1974.

34. Public meeting, MP for Nakonde, Kayambi, April 16, 1974. Mr. Arnold Simuchimba, MP and Minister of State for National Guidance, urged Bemba girls to join the classes.

35. Interviews, Mr. Sangweni (aged 90+) and others, Illondola village, May 7, 1975.

36. Kaunda, *Humanism in Zambia, Part I*, p. 31.

37. Interview, Illondola village, May 8, 1975.

38. Ibid.

39. Various interviews, Kayambi, May 7–9, 1975.

6. VILLAGE REGROUPING: A POLICY IN PRACTICE

1. Kay, *Social Aspects of Village Regrouping in Zambia*, p. 19.

2. Interview, Kabwibwi village, July 19, 1974. Interview, Misengo village, April 14, 1975.

3. Kasama Rural Council, Minutes of Seminar on Village Regrouping, Kayambi, August 22–23, 1969.

4. Zambia News Agency, press release, August 22, 1972.

5. Interview, Nseluka village, September 3, 1974.

6. United National Independence Party, Kasama, letter, UNIP Youth Publicity Secretary to Andele Makumba, Abene village, Mulobola, no date.

7. Republic of Zambia, *Government Policy: Village Regrouping*, mimeo., 1968.

8. Peasants were to be consulted by local councilors, through VPC's and

WDC's when they existed, and from there requests for social and economic services were to be conveyed to the Rural Council. The chairman of the Rural Council, having received technical planning clearance from the District and Provincial Land Settlement Committees, was to present his Council's requests for village regrouping to the Provincial Development Committee. The PDC would consider requests in the light of regional development priorities. If the Land Settlement Board in Lusaka agreed to the PDC's slate of approved requests, then a village plan was to be drawn up at national level by the Town and Country Planning Department. The village plan would then be passed back to the Rural Council for implementation.

9. Kasama Rural Council, Minutes of Seminar on Village Regrouping, Kayambi, August 22, 1969, file LG/KA/5/9, p. 2.

10. Kasama Rural Council, minutes of Council meeting, June 26, 1969. Kasama Rural Council, letter from Secretary, KRC to Provincial Agricultural Officer, Kasama, undated, LG/KA/5/9, p. 4. Letter, UNIP Regional Secretary to District Community Development Officer, Mungwi, July 10, 1969, p. 10.

11. Membership of the DDC subcommittee was as follows: District Governor, UNIP Regional Secretary, District Health Officer, District Education Officer, District Water Affairs Officer, District Secretary, Secretary of Rural Council, plus representatives of planning and survey offices.

12. Kasama Rural Council, LG/KA/5/9, pp. 30, 34.

13. Department of Community Development, Kasama, Report from CDA, Munkonge group housing project, to PCDO, January 1975.

14. Department of Community Development, Kasama, letter from CDA Nseluka to PCDO, Kasama, December 27, 1972.

15. Interview, anonymous source, March 27, 1975.

16. United National Independence Party, Kasama, circular, Regional Youth and Publicity Secretary to "All Chiefs and People of Kasama District," March 3, 1970.

17. Kasama Rural Council, LG/KA/5/9, p. 7.

18. Ibid.

19. Interview, Fele village, November 18, 1974; interview, Nkole Mwankulya village, November 25, 1974.

20. Interview, Community Development Assistant, Nseluka village, July 10, 1974.

21. Ibid. He had worked in the Ministry of Health in the Federal period, during which time he secretly held ANC membership. He resigned in 1961 and from then until 1964 did party organizational work in Chinsali. After independence he returned to government service in the Department of Community Development, in his words, "in order to work with the people." He had been at Nseluka since its inception and was proud that, in part through his efforts, it would become "a town."

22. Ibid.

23. Office of the District Governor, Kasama, District Messengers Reports, File COR/1/1, confirmed by interviews, Kaminsa-Kaputa village, May 9, 1975.

24. Office of the District Governor, Kasama, District Messengers Reports, file COR/1/1, p. iii. Interview, councilor for Ward 2, April 24, 1975.

25. For example, complaints were recorded by me in 1974 from prospective house-builders at Chimangulu, Misengo, Munkonge, and Namutimba villages, who were awaiting technical assistance in the form of plot demarcation or bricklaying.

26. Details of the Lukulu and Mulobola cases are drawn from two sources: Kasama Rural Council, file LG/KA/5/9, pp. 7 and 11; and discussions with party officials, Mulobola UNIP constituency.

27. Interview, councilor for Ward 19, April 14, 1975. The Misengo VPC was in the one village in the headman survey that had development projects under-way but which was not deemed "active" because VPC minutes were not writ-ten and communicated upward (see Table 5).

28. Office of the District Governor, Kasama, letter from Secretary, Mutale Mutimba VPC to District Governor, September 5, 1971, file AGR/13, p. 29.

29. Interview, CDA, Nseluka village, June 20, 1974.

30. Interview, Nseluka, April 26, 1975.

31. Minutes, Ward 7 WDC, Nseluka, March 26, 1975.

32. Interview, CDA, Nseluka village, June 20, 1974.

33. Pocket Manual, pp. 20–21.

34. The dispute at Kaputa had a history dating back 80 years to the estab-lishment of Kayambi Mission. Headman Kaputa was accused by a certain Mr. "Makarios" of wrongfully occupying the headmanship. Makarios alleged that Kaputa's father had bought the headmanship from Father Dupont, the missionary. An accusation of adultery was also involved. The missionaries at Kayambi refused to handle the case when brought to them and handed it back to the Kaputa VPC. In 1975, when I visited Kaputa, the dispute was still the main item on VPC business. The committee had attempted to eject "Maka-rios" from the village, but the latter and his followers were resisting by ac-cusing headman Kaputa of "special medicine." No evidence of other VPC business was found.

35. Interview, Kaminsa village, May 7, 1975.

36. Interview, Ward Councilor, Ward 1, Kayambi, July 23, 1974.

37. Ibid.

38. Interview, Kayambi village, May 8, 1975.

39. Interviews, Ward 1 WDC meeting, Kayambi, July 23, 1974.

40. Entry in Nseluka Visitors' Book, signed by A. B. Chikwanda, Novem-ber 24, 1972.

41. Minutes of WDC meetings, Ward 7, April 18, 1974, and August 25, 1974.

42. Interview, Nseluka, November 25, 1975.

43. Interviews, Kayambi, May 9, 1975.

44. Ibid.

45. Elizabeth Colson, *The Social Consequences of Resettlement: The Im-pact of the Kariba Resettlement on the Gwembe Tonga* (Manchester, Man-chester University Press, 1971), chapter 6.

46. Office of the District Governor, Kasama, Report, District Messenger, file COR/1/1, p. 104.

47. Kasama Rural Council, Letter from Secretary, Mutale Kabwe VPC to Secretary KRC, January 25, 1975.

48. Interview, Ward 16, June 2, 1975.

49. Interview, Agricultural Assistant, Kayambi, May 8, 1975.

50. In December 1973, two weeks after the onset of the rains, fertilizer had not been delivered by NPCMU to its depot at Kayambi. The Depot cap-tain managed, however, to secure eight bags of fertilizer for himself. The situation was partially alleviated by the Ward Councilor who, acting in his accustomed role of local patron, approached the KRC Secretary for the loan of a truck and personally collected 70 bags of fertilizer and several bags of

Kayambi, peasants were discussing the prospect, announced by the MP, of an enlarged depot being established at Kayambi. The WDC, which at Kayambi meant the Ward Councilor, would be in charge of disbursements.

51. Interview, Commissioner for Community Development, May 4, 1976.

52. Ministry of Rural Development, Northern Province, *Annual Report*, 1974, p. 12.

53. Interview, Chamfubu settlement, April 22, 1975.

54. Interviews, WDC members, Nseluka, November 23, 1974.

55. Estimate provided by CDA, Nseluka.

56. One schoolteacher from Nseluka was at first turned down because of his government job. He then had his father-in-law apply, was successful, and received a grant "for making mounds" before finally repudiating his stake.

57. Figures based on interviews with house-builders at Misengo and Nseluka regrouping schemes:

Door	K12
Frames	K16
Nails/Hinges/Paint	K 8
Iron Roofing (24 sheets)	K72
	108
minus K40 grant	− 40
	K68.

58. David Siddle, in J. Hywel Davies, *Zambia in Maps* (London, University of London Press, 1971), p. 60.

THE LOCAL-LEVEL POLITICAL PARTY

7. THE RISE AND FALL OF UNIP

1. David Mulford, *The Politics of Independence, 1957–1964* (Oxford, Oxford University Press, 1967), p. 327.

2. Republic of Zambia, *The Constitution of the United National Independence Party* (1973), preamble, p. 4.

3. Jan Pettman, "Zambia's Second Republic: The Establishment of a One-Party State," *Journal of Modern African Studies*, 12 (1974), 231.

4. Edward Schumacher, *Politics, Bureaucracy and Rural Development in Senegal* (Berkeley, University of California Press, 1974), p. 225.

5. Ian Scott, "Party Politics in Zambia: A Study of the Organization of the United National Independence Party" (University of Toronto, Ph.D. dissertation, 1976).

6. Northern Rhodesia Government, Provincial Administration, *Kasama UNIP*, file C/SOC/3/5 vol. III, July 1961, to July 1962, marked "secret" and "confidential," Kasama District Archives. Much of the account of the peasant uprising of 1961 is based on this previously unpublished source.

7. Thomas Rasmussen, "The Popular Basis of Anticolonial Protest," in William Tordoff, ed., *Politics in Zambia* (Manchester, Manchester University Press, 1974), pp. 40–61. Other studies which conceive of nationalism as a mass populist phenomenon as opposed to an elite leadership phenomenon are Martin Kilson, *Political Change in a West African State* (Cambridge, Mass.,

Harvard University Press, 1966), and H. F. Weiss, *Political Protest in the Congo* (Princeton, Princeton University Press, 1967).

8. Andrew Roberts, *The Lumpa Church of Alice Lenshina* (Lusaka, Oxford University Press, 1972). Robert Rotberg, "The Lenshina Movement of Northern Rhodesia," *Rhodes-Livingstone Journal*, 29 (1961), pp. 63–78.

9. Robert Bates, *Rural Responses to Industrialization*, pp. 242–251.

10. Robert Rotberg, *The Rise of Nationalism in Central Africa: The Making of Malawi and Zambia, 1873–1964* (Cambridge, Mass., Harvard University Press, 1965).

11. Lewis Gann, *A History of Northern Rhodesia: Early Days to 1953* (London, Chatto and Windus, 1964), p. 301.

12. Office of District Governor, Kasama, Kasama District Archives, file ADM/14/1 reference 2849, 1959.

13. Richard Hall, *Zambia* (London, Pall Mall Press, 1965), p. 196.

14. Interview, Headteacher, Ituna Government School, Kasama, November 30, 1974.

15. Mulford, p. 337.

16. *Northern News*, July 10, 1961.

17. File C/SOC/3/5, pp. 53 and 61.

18. Interview, headteacher, Ituna Government School, Kasama, November 30, 1974.

19. File C/SOC/3/5, p. 20.

20. Ibid., p. 35.

21. Ibid., p. 27.

22. Ibid., p. 51/1.

23. Interview, headteacher, Ituna Government School, Kasama, November 30, 1974.

24. United National Independence Party, "Grim Peep into the North" (Lusaka, Voice of UNIP pamphlet, 1961), p. 3.

25. Interview, Member of Parliament for Malole, Malole, November 26, 1974.

26. Northern Rhodesia Government, *An Account of the Disturbances in Northern Rhodesia, July to October 1961* (Lusaka, Government Printer, 1961).

27. Ann Tweedie, "Ritual and Political Change in Bembaland" (Lusaka, Institute for African Studies, unpublished paper, 1970). To my knowledge, Tweedie's excellent paper is the only first-hand account of local UNIP organization in Northern Province in the 1962–63 period.

28. Ibid., pp. 11–14.

29. Interview, UNIP branch vice-chairman, Nseluka, April 21, 1975.

30. Mulford, p. 238.

31. This figure was arrived at by averaging the ages of all Ward Councilors in Kasama District who were UNIP branch officials in 1961.

32. Tweedie, p. 13.
33. Rasmussen (1974), p. 51.
34. File C/SOC/3/5, p. 33.
35. Ibid., p. 196.
36. Ibid., p. 10.
37. Ibid., p. 194.
38. Ibid., p. 81.

39. Ibid., p. 100.
40. Ibid., p. 196.
41. Ibid., pp. 25 and 62.
42. Tweedie, p. 13.
43. Ibid., p. 115.
44. Ibid., p. 156.
45. Ibid., p. 6.

46. Ibid., pp. 61 and 69.

47. William Tordoff and Ian Scott, "Political Parties: Structures and Poli-

cies," in Tordoff, ed., *Politics in Zambia* (Manchester, Manchester University Press, 1974), p. 110.

48. Mulford, p. 163.

49. Thomas Rasmussen, "Political Competition and One-Party Dominance in Zambia," *Journal of Modern African Studies*, 7 (1969), 407–424.

50. Interview, MP for Malole, November 26, 1974.

51. Tweedie, p. 6.

52. Quoted by Mulford, p. 201.

53. File C/SOC/3/5, p. 60.

54. Ibid., p. 90/1.

55. Interview, UNIP Regional Secretary, Kasama, November 19, 1974.

56. Interview, head teacher, Ituna Government School, Kasama, November 30, 1974.

57. File C/SOC/3/5, p. 125.

58. Ibid., p. 44.

59. Ibid., p. 26/2.

60. Ibid., p. 196.

61. I am indebted to Ian Scott for this information.

62. District Messenger's report on UNIP meeting, Kasama township, August 5, 1961. File C/SOC/3/5, p. 4.

63. A letter, District Commissioner, Kasama to Provincial Commissioner, Northern Province, August 14, 1961, identifies the "Mulema-Mumba-Nseluka area" as places where the ban on UNIP was particularly ill-received. File C/SOC/3/5, p. 64.

64. Ibid., pp. 5 and 46.

65. Ibid., pp. 60 and 61.

66. Ibid., p. 65/1.

67. Interview, councilor for Ward 11, Kapolyo's village, November 25, 1974.

68. File C/SOC/3/5, p. 4.

69. Mulford, p. 162.

70. File C/SOC/3/5, p. 143.

71. Ibid., p. 172.

72. Tweedie, p. 9.

73. Interview, headteacher, Ituna Government School, Kasama, November 30, 1974.

74. Tweedie, p. 9.

75. File C/SOC/3/5, p. 209/2.

76. Northern Rhodesia Government, *Annual Report on African Affairs for the Northern Province* (1963), p. 4.

77. Tordoff and Scott, p. 111. The Regional Secretary in Kasama at first tried to resist responsibility for the Youth Wing: see Mulford, p. 237.

78. Bates, *Rural Responses to Industrialization*, p. 226.

79. For a fuller account of the intrigue surrounding the formation of UPP, see Robert Rotberg, "Tribalism and Politics in Zambia" *Africa Report* (December 1967), pp. 29–35. Robert Molteno, "Cleavage and Conflict in Zambian Politics," in William Tordoff, *Politics in Zambia*, pp. 62–106. Dennis Dresang, "Ethnic Politics, Representative Bureaucracy, and Development Administration," esp. pp. 1615–16; and Robert Bates, *Rural Responses to Industrialization*, pp. 226–239.

80. Tordoff, ibid., p. 157.

81. Republic of Zambia, *Report of the Commission of Inquiry into the Al-*

legations Made by Mr. Justin Chimba and Mr. John Chisata (Lusaka, Government Printer, May 1971).

82. Cherry Gertzel, et al., "Zambia's Final Experience of Inter-Party Elections: The By-Elections of December 1971," *Kroniek von Afrika*, 12 (1972), p. 73.

83. Robert Molteno, "Zambia and the One Party State," *East Africa Journal*, 9 (1972), 8.

84. Ibid. Molteno gives details on the private investments of national UPP leaders and notes that among them were the President and Secretary General of the Zambia National Council for Commerce and Industry.

85. Gertzel, et al. (1972), p. 77.

86. Tordoff, p. 138.

87. Gertzel, p. 74.

88. Tordoff, p. 375.

89. Interview, UNIP Provincial Political Secretary, Kasama, July 28, 1974.

90. Interviews, chairman and treasurer, Chambeshi UNIP constituency, November 25, 1974.

91. Interview, anonymous source, Kasama, November 1975.

92. Interview, councilor of Ward 15, Kasama, April 23, 1975.

93. Interview, UNIP Regional Secretary, May 22, 1975.

94. *Times of Zambia*, August 26, 1971.

95. This figure must be viewed with caution, considering the difficulty of eliciting reliable information in 1974 and 1975 on a subject as sensitive as opposition to the one legal party in Zambia. I am confident, however, that the rough order of magnitude of UPP support among Kasama councilors is correct.

96. Kasama Rural Council, minutes of 30th Ordinary meeting, September 22–23, 1971.

97. Interviews, chairman and treasurer, Chambeshi UNIP constituency, November 25, 1974.

98. *Times of Zambia*, September 3, 1971.

99. Interview, anonymous source, Kasama, April 28, 1975.

100. Interview, Kasama, November 27, 1973; I am indebted to Donald Ray for this interview.

101. Interview, Kasama, November 19, 1974.

102. Interview, Minister of State for National Guidance, April 1, 1975.

103. Interview, Mungwi, November 27, 1975.

104. Tordoff, p. 139.

105. The third defeated Cabinet Minister, Wilson Chakulya, went down in Mansa constituency, Luapula Province, which had also been a rural base of UPP.

106. For several days after the election, the Elections Office held in doubt the accuracy of the count from Malole constituency, because of a discrepancy of approximately 200 votes between the votes cast in the Presidential and Parliamentary elections. The figures used in this study of 2476 "noes," 2390 "yesses," and 269 rejected ballots are taken from the final official published listings.

107. The Elections Office was not permitted to provide polling district breakdowns, but this information was in the possession of, and was made available by, electoral agents of parliamentary candidates.

8. PATRONAGE AND CONTROL IN UNIP

1. Ian Scott, "Party Politics in Zambia: A Study of the Organization of the United National Independence Party" (University of Toronto, Ph.D. dissertation, 1976).
2. Tordoff, p. 128.
3. Bretton, *Power and Politics in Africa*, p. 281.
4. Office of the District Governor, Kasama, file SOC/3/3, Vol. 1, pp. 40 and 102. Only main body UNIP branches were counted; the number of registered women's and youth branches fluctuated greatly over time and were the first to become defunct.
5. Ibid., pp. 37, 62, 103.
6. Interview, councilor for Ward 14, Lualua, September 30, 1974.
7. Interview, farmer, Lualua, September 30, 1974.
8. Republic of Zambia, *Constitution of UNIP*, p. 13.
9. Interviews, Kasama, April 16, 1974, and November 19, 1975.
10. Interview, Kayambi, May 7, 1975.
11. Interview, councilor for Ward 1, Kayambi, July 23, 1974.
12. Interview, councilor for Ward 6, Razuru village, July 11, 1974.
13. Interview, District Governor, Kasama, August 26, 1974.
14. Ibid.
15. Bates, p. 209.
16. Minutes, Malama Branch meeting, misfiled at Office of District Governor, Kasama, file AGR/13, p. 184.
17. Interview, councilor for Ward 12, Kasama, May 28, 1975.
18. Republic of Zambia, *Constitution of UNIP*, p. 22.
19. United National Independence Party, *Circular on Party Supremacy* (Lusaka, Freedom House, mimeo., 1973).
20. Interview, Bwembya village, July 27, 1974.
21. Interview, UNIP Regional Secretary, Kasama, April 16, 1974.
22. Interview, Mulobola, July 18, 1974.
23. *Daily Mail*, September 6, 1974.
24. The only branch party membership records to which I gained access were for Kasama township in 1974, and low membership was in evidence: Location Branch, 59; Chibote, 20; Kanyanta, 30; Mulilansolo, 30; Malama 28. Interview, councilor for Ward 12, November 17, 1974.
25. United National Independence Party, *Report to the UNIP National Council, Northern Province, 1975*. Party card renewals cost 50n and new membership cost K1.50. The figure of 5000 new members was based on the assumption that all sales in 1975 were renewals. If a significant number of new members were recruited, the membership figure was lower than 5000. The K2548 may also contain larger contributions by businessmen, but the UNIP Region did not provide a financial breakdown.
26. The adult population of the district was taken to be 55,651. *Census of Population and Housing, Final Report, Vol. II*. (Lusaka, Government Printer, 1973) Tables 6 and 7.
27. *Times of Zambia*, January 19, 1975. It was unclear from the newspaper report whether the Copperbelt 9 percent was based on adult population or total population.
28. Interview, councilor for Ward 17, November 25, 1974.
29. Interview, UNIP Regional Secretary, May 16, 1974.
30. Ibid.
31. Interview, councilor for Ward 14, Kasama, August 23, 1974.

32. Interviews, councilors for Wards 21 and 22, 1974 and 1975.

33. Interview, Regional Secretary, Kasama, May 22, 1975.

34. Elijah Mudenda, then MCC, UNIP-UNZA Seminar on One-Party Democracy, Lusaka, September 4, 1974.

35. Molteno and Scott, in Tordoff, p. 177.

36. Public meeting, Mungwi, April 25, 1975.

37. Interview, councilor for Ward 21, July 18, 1974.

38. Interview, former Secretary of KRC, Kasama, May 22, 1975.

39. Interview, councilor for Ward 14, Kasama, November 15, 1974.

40. Interview, UNIP Regional Secretary, Kasama, November 19, 1974.

41. Michael Bratton, "Zambia: Security and Conflict," *African Social Research*, 21 (1976), 71.

42. UNIP Regional Secretaries received K250 per month, as opposed to K120 before. Salaries of WRS's and YRS's were raised to K200.

43. Interview, Provincial Political Secretary, Kasama, August 25, 1974.

44. Interview, Chairman of Kasama Rural Council, Mungwi, April 24, 1975.

45. UNIP public meeting, Buseko Hall, Kasama, May 24, 1974.

46. Interview, Kasama, November 19, 1974.

47. Interview, councilor for Ward 13, Mungwi, May 29, 1974.

48. I was in the field for the 1975 Local Government Elections and observed them first-hand in Kasama. I was in Zambia, but not in the field, at the time of the 1973 General Elections. Thus the data for 1973 was based on ex post facto interviews and statistics, plus materials provided by Donald Ray, researcher for the Northern Province portion of the 1973 University of Zambia Election Study.

49. Republic of Zambia, *Report of the National Commission on the Establishment of a One-Party Participatory Democracy in Zambia*, chaired by Mainza Chona, then Vice President of the Republic (Lusaka, Government Printer, 1972).

50. Interview, teacher, Kasama Girls' Secondary School, September 26, 1974. The proceedings of the Chona Commission have never been released to the public, so I had to rely on the above first-hand account.

51. Republic of Zambia, Government Paper No. 1 of 1972, *Summary of Recommendations Accepted by the Government* (Lusaka, Government Printer, 1972).

52. Chona Commission Report, p. 22.

53. Government White Paper No. 1 of 1972, p. 11.

54. Republic of Zambia, *The Constitution of Zambia*, Act No. 27 of 1973, part VI, para. 75, secs. 1–5.

55. United National Independence Party, Kasama constituency "Elections" file, interview, UNIP Constituency Secretary, Kasama Constituency, November 17, 1974.

56. The minor candidates who stepped down in Lukashya were J. Mulenga, a head teacher, and A. Mucheleka, the UNIP Regional Secretary. In Kasama they were H. Mutale, schools inspector, and Mr. Nsabashi, Secretary of the Township Council. Messrs. Njelesani and Jim were their counterparts in Malole constituency. Potential loss of civil service jobs seems to have been a key consideration in the decision to step down.

57. Interview, Constituency Secretary, UNIP Kasama Constituency, November 17, 1974.

58. Interview conducted by Donald Ray, Kasama, November 19, 1973.

59. Interview, member of Ward 16 WDC, November 17, 1974.

60. Interview, MP for Malole, November 26, 1974.

61. This story was heard from three separate sources but could not be confirmed further. But it gained circulation in the district and was therefore influential in the campaign.

62. Interview, MP for Kasama, conducted by Donald Ray, November 22, 1973.

63. Interview, councilor for Ward 16, November 26, 1974.

64. Interview, head teacher, Ituna Government Primary School, Kasama, November 13, 1974.

65. Based on unpublished data collected by Ian Scott, 1975.

66. Interview, candidate for Ward 7, Mungwi, November 28, 1975.

67. Announcement by Minister of Local Government and Housing, Local Government Association of Zambia meeting, May 4, 1974.

68. Elections Office, Lusaka; 41,069 voters were registered in Kasama in 1973, and 36,257 in 1975; in addition, a registering officer from the Provincial Information Office, Kasama, intimated that the 1975 voter registration figures were selectively overinflated.

69. Interview, Chairman of the Rural Council, November 24, 1975.

70. Interviews, councilor for Ward 14, November 24, 1975, and Member of Parliament for Malole, November 27, 1975.

71. Councilors for Wards 23, 17, and 4.

72. Councilor for Ward 8.

73. Interview, Kasama, May 22, 1975.

74. Councilors for Wards 1, 2, 3, 13, 16, and 19.

75. Interview, Regional Secretary, Kasama, May 22, 1975.

76. Interview, former Rural Council Secretary, May 22, 1975.

77. Kasama Rural Council, minutes of Council meeting, October 7, 1975.

78. Interview, Community Development Assistant, Munkonge, November 26, 1975.

79. The eight officials were Chairman, Secretary, Treasurer, and Publicity Secretary and the deputies for each.

80. Interview, Misengo village, April 14, 1975.

81. Interview, Kasama, May 22, 1975.

82. Interview, councilor for Ward 14, Lualua, August 23, 1974.

83. Estimate based on total employment figure for the Northern Province in June 1974 of 29,500: Central Statistical Office, *Monthly Digest of Statistics* (Lusaka, Government Printer, 1976), 12, pp. 3–4, table 4(c), p. 4.

84. Interview, Chikosa village, July 18, 1974.

85. Interview, Kasama, May 22, 1975.

86. Interviews, Rural Council candidates, Mungwi, November 29, 1975.

87. Interview, UNIP Regional Secretary, Kasama, November 19, 1974.

88. Interview, PPS, Kasama, August 26, 1974.

89. Interview, Kasama, May 22, 1975.

90. Interview, councilor for Ward 13, November 27, 1975.

91. The average figure of two unsolicited visits per week blurs a sharp distinction between suburban and outlying wards. Councilors in suburban wards reported up to ten visits per week, and many councilors in outlying wards reported zero.

92. Interview, councilor for Ward 15, Chitamba village, July 13, 1974.

93. Minutes, Ward Council (sic) Secretaries meeting, Mungwi, October 1, 1974.

94. Interview, James Mwilwa village, June 11, 1974.

95. Interview, Kasama, November 21, 1975.

96. Charles Harvey, "Rural Credit in Zambia: Access and Exit," *Development and Change*, 6, no. 2 (1975), 93–94.

97. Ian Scott, "Party Functions and Capabilities: The Local-Level UNIP Organisation during the First Zambian Republic (1964–73)," *African Social Research*, 22 (1976), 107–129.

98. Interview, Kasama, April 16, 1974.

99. Interview, Provincial Manager, Agricultural Finance Corporation, November 25, 1975.

100. The K14 million figure was quoted by the Minister of Finance, Economics Club meeting, Ridgeway Hotel, Lusaka, February 18, 1975. Bates cites a higher figure for total COZ debts of K22m. The K2 million figure was quoted by the Minister of State for National Guidance, public meeting, Kayambi, May 7, 1975.

101. Republic of Zambia, *Report and Recommendations on Rural Agricultural Credit in Zambia* (Crisco Report), Lusaka, Government Printer, 1969.

102. Prestige rating studies have been used by other researchers in Zambia: J. C. Mitchell and A. L. Epstein, "Occupational Prestige and Social Status among Urban Africans in Northern Rhodesia," *Africa*, 29 (1959), pp. 22–40. Norman Long, *Social Change and the Individual* (Manchester, Manchester University Press, 1968), pp. 145–151.

103. Republic of Zambia, *The Local Government (Amendment) Act, 1970*; this empowered central government to appoint council chairmen and mayors. The councilor from Ward 2 in Kasama gained the chairmanship, because of the intervention on his behalf of the Kasama UNIP Regional Office and against the popular will of the Council as a whole; see Kasama Rural Council: Minutes of 29th Ordinary Meeting, 1971.

104. Interview, councilor for Ward 1, Kayambi, July 27, 1974.

105. Interview, Chairman of UNIP Lion branch, Mulobola, July 18, 1974.

106. Interviews, various, Kasama District, 1974–75.

107. Interview, councilor for Ward 13, Mungwi, August 26, 1974.

108. VPC meeting, Chisoka village, July 18, 1974.

109. Ward Council meeting, Ward 13, Mungwi, April 17, 1974.

110. Ibid.

111. A rough calculation was made by a senior party official in Lusaka on the cost to UNIP of paying constituency officials alone. At an estimated salary of K150 per month, assuming 200 constituency officials for each of UNIP's 53 Regions, the annual cost to UNIP would be K19 million. This figure did *not* include branch officials.

9. POLITICAL ORGANIZATION AND RESOURCE DISTRIBUTION

1. Jan Pettman, *Zambia: Security and Conflict* (Lewes, Sussex, Julian Friedmann, 1974), p. 235.

2. Ibid., p. 7.

3. Henry Bienen, *Kenya: The Politics of Participation and Control* (Princeton, Princeton University Press, 1974), p. 195.

4. Irving Markovitz, *Power and Class in Africa* (Englewood Cliffs, N.J., Prentice-Hall, 1977), p. 5.

5. See, for example, Colin Legum, "Tribal Survival in the Modern African Political System," *Journal of Asian and African Studies*, 5 (1970), 102–112; Ali Mazrui, "Violent Contiguity and the Politics of Retribalization in Africa,"

Journal of International Affairs, 23 (1969), 89–105; Donald Rothchild, "Ethnicity and Conflict Resolution," *World Politics*, 22 (1970), 597–616; Robert Bates, "Ethnic Competition and Modernization in Contemporary Africa," *Comparative Political Studies*, 6 (1974), 457–484; Walter Barrows, "Ethnic Diversity and Political Instability in Black Africa," *Comparative Political Studies*, 9 (1976), 139–170.

6. Richard Sklar, "Political Science and National Integration—A Radical Approach," *Journal of Modern African Studies*, 5 (1967), 1–11; Archie Mafeje, "The Ideology of 'Tribalism,'" *Journal of Modern African Studies*, 9 (1971), 253–261.

7. Robert Molteno, "Cleavage and Conflict in Zambian Politics: A Study of Sectionalism," in William Tordoff, ed., *Politics in Zambia* (Manchester, Manchester University Press, 1974), pp. 62–106.

8. Robert Bates, *Rural Responses to Industrialization: A Study of Village Zambia* (New Haven, Yale University Press, 1976), p. 5.

9. Crawford Young, *The Politics of Cultural Pluralism* (Madison, University of Wisconsin Press, 1976), pp. 41–44, 98, 164.

10. Morris Simon, "Political Processes among the Bemba of Zambia" (Cornell University, Ph.D. dissertation, 1970).

11. Ian Scott, "Party-Bureaucratic Relations and the Process of Development in Zambia," unpublished paper, Political and Administrative Studies Department, UNZA, 1971.

12. For example, an angry public altercation was observed by me between a UNIP ward councilor and an official from the provincial cooperative marketing board, about who deserved congratulation for an emergency delivery of fertilizer and seed to a remote part of the district: meeting of Kasama Rural Council, Mungwi, April 17, 1974.

13. Scott (1971).

14. Dennis Dresang, "Ethnic Politics, Representative Bureaucracy and Development Administration: The Zambian Case," *American Political Science Review*, 68 (1974), 1608.

15. Bates, p. 260.

16. Roger Murray, "The Ghanaian Road" *New Left Review*, 32 (1965), 63–71.

17. John Markakis and Robert Curry, "The Global Economy's Impact on Recent Budgetary Politics in Zambia," *Journal of African Studies*, 3 (1976), 427.

18. The term "bureaucratic bourgeoisie" is derived in African context from René Dumont, *False Start in Africa* (London, Deutsch, 1966), chapter 6. For Zambia see Richard Sklar, *Corporate Power in an African State: The Political Impact of Multinational Mining Companies in Zambia* (Berkeley, University of California Press, 1975), esp. pp. 108–109; Timothy Shaw, "Zambia: Dependence and Underdevelopment," *Canadian Journal of African Studies*, 10 (1976), esp. 5–6. The terms "managerial" (Sklar) and "organizational" (Markovitz) are sufficiently broad also to include class allies of state functionaries whose base of wealth, status, and power is in the private sector.

Index

AA. *See* Agricultural Assistant.

Administration, colonial, 3, 4, 25, 33, 200, 271. *See also* District Commissioner; Native Authorities.

AFC. *See* Agricultural Finance Company.

Africa, Southern, 278

African National Congress (ANC), 83, 92, 193, 199, 211, 212, 220, 223

African Welfare Societies, 193

Agricultural Assistant (AA), 130, 137, 166, 176, 177, 182, 265

Agricultural cooperatives, 3, 29, 45, 83, 88, 92, 105; sawyers' cooperative, 180

Agricultural credit, 83, 93, 118–122, 148, 181, 182, 215, 259, 279

Agricultural Finance Company (AFC), 118–120, 182. *See also* Agricultural credit; Credit Organization of Zambia.

Agricultural production: low levels of, 3–4, 32, 40–44, 113; in Kasama District, 43–46; Zambian government policies, 44, 119; by VPC's, 71–72; by WDC's, 105; and village regrouping, 125, 126, 173, 178; and class formation, 277. *See also* Economic transformation; Food production.

Agricultural settlement schemes, 45, 77–78, 179, 181, 182, 279

Agriculture, Department of, 45, 90, 130, 136

Alavi, Hamza, 22

Almond, Gabriel, 11

ANC. *See* African National Congress.

Bakabilo (elders; advisers), 62

Barker, Jonathan, 21

Barrows, Walter, 14

Bates, Robert, 14, 212, 232, 281

Bemba: ethnic group, 41, 85, 126, 127, 141, 163, 198, 212, 276; Bemba-speakers, 192, 193, 198, 212, 213, 217, 219, 275. *See also* Ethnicity.

Berman, Bruce, 21

Bienen, Henry, 15, 19, 24

Binder, Leonard, 11

Brick-making, 47, 143, 162, 168, 169. *See also* Housing.

Bureaucracy: class formation, 20, 28, 49, 115, 282 (*see also* Class); decision-making, 81, 113; and delay, 112–114; "bureaucratic style," 114, 149, 241–242

Businessmen, 87, 89, 91, 138, 240

Candidates, electoral: "of the center," 221–222, 244, 249; "of the locality," 221–222, 244, 249. *See also* Elections.

CDA. *See* Community Development Assistant.

Center-locality relations: two-way dynamic, 9–10, 270; "viewpoint of the center," 10–12; in Africa, 10–25, 126; "viewpoint of the locality," 12–14; prominence of political organization in, 15–18; and patterns of resource distribution, 18–23; and political organization, 33, 37, 41, 79 (*see also main entry*); and development committees, 41, 53, 61, 74 (*see also main entry*); and village regrouping, 145; in UNIP, 191, 203–207, 242 (*see also main entry*)

Central African Federation. *See* Federation of the Rhodesias and Nyasaland.

Cha cha cha (anti-colonial peasant resistance, 1960–1961), 194–198, 202, 203, 204, 205, 209, 210, 216

Changufu, Lewis, 218, 221, 244

Chiefs: and village registration, 58–59 (*see also* Villages); reassertion of authority, 76–77, 79; and village regrouping, 77, 150–151, 152; anticolonial resistance, 201; *See also* Native Authorities; Traditional leaders.

Chiefs Act (1965), 59

Chimba, Justin, 213

Chimbola, Chief, 58, 128, 201

Chitemene cultivation, 43, 91, 104, 173, 177, 178

Chitimukulu, Paramount Chief, 41, 59, 127, 134, 154, 201

Chona, Mainza, 204, 243

Church, 168. *See also* Religion.

Civil Service: reform of, 35, 240; political interests in, 111–115; and village regrouping, 149

"Well-to-do," 66, 93, 110, 111, 118, 167, 183–185, 279
Western Province, 220
Whitaker, Cyril, 13
White Fathers. *See* Missionaries; Roman Catholicism.
Witchcraft, 142–143, 153, 173–175
Women. *See* Females, political roles.
Women's Regional Secretary (WRS) (UNIP), 237
WRS. *See* Women's Regional Secretary.
Workers. *See* Mineworkers.

Young, Crawford, 275
Youth Regional Secretary (YRS) (UNIP), 237, 238, 242, 257

YRS. *See* Youth Regional Secretary.

Zambia, Republic of, 6, 27, 269, 281; uneven development in, 26–28, 32, 49; First Republic (*1964–1973*), 34, 35, 238; Second Republic, 35, 220; independence (*1964*), 194, 212, 271. *See also* Rhodesia, Northern.
Zambia African National Congress (ZANC), 193, 199
Zambia National Service (ZNS), 116, 151; rural reconstruction camps, 125
ZANC. *See* Zambia African National Congress.
ZNS. *See* Zambia National Service.
Zolberg, Aristide, 12, 15

Library of Congress Cataloging in Publication Data

Bratton, Michael.
   The local politics of rural development.

   Bibliography: p.
   Includes index.
   1. Rural development—Zambia—Kasama District.
2. Kasama District, Zambia—Politics and government.
3. Zambia—Politics and government.   4. United National Independence Party (Zambia)
I. Title.
HN803.K37B7   307.7'2'096894   79-56775
ISBN 0-87451-178-X

T5-CQA-395

Super Keys

TO MOVE THE CURSOR TO:	PRESS:
Beginning of a document	Home, Home, ↑
Beginning of a document	Home, Home, Home, ↑
Beginning of a line	Home, Home, ←
Beginning of a line	Home, Home, Home, ←
Bottom of the screen	Home, ↓
End of the document	Home, Home, ↓
End of the line	Home, Home, → or End
Bottom of the current page	Ctrl+Home, ↓
Next instance of that character	Ctrl+Home, character
Page [number]	Ctrl+Home, #
Top of the current page	Ctrl+Home, ↑
Next character	→
Next line down	↓
Next outline family at same level	Alt+↓
Next outline heading (any level)	Alt+→
Next page	PgDn
Next paragraph	Ctrl+↓
Next word	Ctrl+→
Other document window	Home+(window #)
Previous character	←
Previous line up	↑
Previous outline family at same level	Alt+↑
Previous outline heading (any level)	Alt+←
Previous page	PgUp
Previous paragraph	Ctrl+↑
Previous word	Ctrl+←
Specified page	Ctrl+Home
Top of the screen	Home, ↑

TO INSERT:	PRESS:
Back tab (margin release)	Shift+Tab
Cancel hyphenation	Home, forward slash
Hard page break	Ctrl+Enter
Hard return	Enter
Hard space	Home, Space
Hyphen, hard	Home+-
Hyphen, soft	Ctrl+-
Hyphen, soft return	Home, Enter
Space	Spacebar
Tab	Tab

TO DELETE:	PRESS:
Character to the left	Backspace
Current character	Delete
Delete block	[Block on] Backspace
Delete block	[Block on] Del
Delete current word	Ctrl+Backspace
Delete from cursor position to the beginning of the word	Home, Backspace
Delete from cursor position to the end of the word (including the space)	Home, Del
Delete to the end of current page	Ctrl+PgDn
Delete to the end of line	Ctrl+End

OTHER EDITING KEYSTROKES:	PRESS:
Cancel or Repeat (Version 5.1)	Esc
Copies text to the clipboard	Ctrl+Insert
Cuts text to the clipboard	Ctrl+Delete
Force Typeover mode (useful in macros)	Home, Insert
Force Insert mode	Home, Home, Insert
Typeover/insert toggle	Insert

WHILE IN A DIALOG BOX, TO:	PRESS:
Decrement a dialog box counter	Alt+↓
Increment a dialog box counter	Alt+↑
Move to the next control	Tab
Move to the previous control	Shift+Tab
Select the default action	Enter

WHILE IN AN OUTLINE, TO:	PRESS:
Insert the next level	Tab
Return to the previous level	Shift+Tab

Control Combinations

CONTROL KEY	FUNCTION
Ctrl+a	Compose
Ctrl+b	Bold
Ctrl+c	Copy
Ctrl+d	Record sound clip
Ctrl+f	Find Quickmark
Ctrl+i	Italics
Ctrl+n	Normal font

CONTROL KEY	FUNCTION
Ctrl+o	Outline edit
Ctrl+p	Insert formatted page number
Ctrl+q	Set Quickmark
Ctrl+r	Repeat
Ctrl+s	Play sound clip
Ctrl+t	Toggle text or paragraph number

CONTROL KEY	FUNCTION
Ctrl+v	Paste
Ctrl+w	WP characters
Ctrl+x	Cut
Ctrl+y	Cycle through windows
Ctrl+z	Undo

Special Combinations

PRESS:	TO:
Home, F7	Exit to main editing screen (in a dialog box)
Home, F7	Exit all open documents (main editing screen)
Shift+Tab	Backtab (previous tab)
Ctrl+A	Compose (special characters) dialog box
Ctrl+2	Compose (special characters) "quiet" mode (no prompt)
Ctrl+A, Tab	Tab code (useful in a table or search)
Ctrl+A, Shift+Tab	Backtab (useful in a table or search)
Ctrl+Enter	Insert hard page, hard column, or hard row break
Home, F3 or Home, 0	Switch to Document dialog box
Home, (Doc #)	Switch to Doc #
Home, PageUp	When in a footnote, endnote, textbox, comment, header or footer window, watermark or comment, go to the previous item of the same type.
Home, PageUp	When in a footnote, endnote, textbox, comment, header or footer window, watermark or comment, go to the next substructure of the same type.
Ctrl+6	Toggle between alternate and regular keyboard

(Note: WordPerfect doesn't give any visual feedback when you switch back to the regular keyboard, but it does display a message when you switch back to the alternate keyboard.)

Column Keystrokes

TO MOVE TO:	PRESS:
Bottom of column	Ctrl+Home, ↓
Leftmost column	Ctrl+Home, Home, ←
Next column	Ctrl+Home, → or Alt+→ (dedicated key)
Previous column	Ctrl+Home, ← or Alt+← (dedicated key)
Rightmost column	Ctrl+Home, Home, →
Top of column	Ctrl+Home, ↑

Navigating Tables

TO INSERT (IN TABLES):	PRESS:
Append a new row	Tab (when in the last cell)
Back Tab	Ctrl+a, Shift+Tab
Center Tab	Home, Shift+F6
Decimal Tab	Home, Ctrl+F6
Delete current row	Ctrl+Delete
New row (and move the insertion point)	Ctrl+Ins
Left Tab (hard)	Home, Tab
Left Tab (regular)	Ctrl+A, Tab
Right Tab	Home, Alt+F6

TO MOVE (IN TABLES):	PRESS:
Beginning of Text	Ctrl+Home, ↑
First Cell	Ctrl+Home, Home, Home, ↑, or Alt+Home, Home, ↑
First Cell in Column	Ctrl+Home, Home, ↑, or Alt+Home, ↑
First Cell in Row	Ctrl+Home, Home, ←, or Home, Home, Home, ←, or Alt+Home, ←
Last Cell	Ctrl+Home, Home, Home, ↓
Last Cell in Column	Ctrl+Home, Home, ↓, or Alt+Home, ↓
Last Cell in Row	Ctrl+Home, Home, →, or Home, Home, Home, →, or Alt+Home, →, or Ctrl+Home, End
Last Line of Text	Ctrl+Home, ↓
One Cell Down	Alt+↓
One Cell Left	Shift+Tab, or Alt+←, or Ctrl+Home, ←
One Cell Right	Tab, or Alt+→ Ctrl+Home, →
One Cell Up	Alt+↑

Outlining Keys

PRESS:	TO HIGHLIGHT:
↑	The previous outline family
↓	The next outline family
Alt+↑	The previous family on the same or a preceding level
Alt+↓	The next family on the same or a preceding level
Home, ↑	The first outline family
Home, ↓	The last outline family
Ctrl+↑	Move the selected family up
Ctrl+↓	Move the selected family down

What Makes This Book Super

Synopsis of project

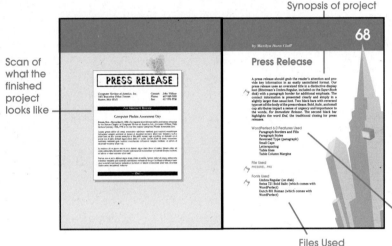

Scan of what the finished project looks like

Projects Workshop

Workshop XIII, "Projects," contains projects that can be used as templates or they can teach you how to strengthen future projects of your own.

WordPerfect 6.0 Features Used

Files Used

What's on the *Super Book* Disk

▲ 5 decorative fonts from the **Bitstream™ WordPerfect 6.0 Font Pack**

▲ More than 40 pieces of color clip art from the **Masterclips— The Art of Business** collection

▲ A special version of **QwkScreen™**, the program that makes WordPerfect 6.0 easier and faster to use

▲ **!Bang**, the utility that searches for and performs actions on WordPerfect 6.0, 5.1, and 5.0 files

▲ **WPReveal**, the WordPerfect 6.0 file inspection utility

▲ All example projects from the book

▲ A variety of useful macros

▲ 8 foreign language keyboards

The Command Reference Card

The tear-out card in the front of this book is designed to give you a convenient reference to many of WordPerfect's functions and control-key sequences.

WordPerfect® 6.0
Super Book

WordPerfect® 6.0
Super Book

Marilyn Horn Claff, et al.

SAMS
PUBLISHING

A Division of Prentice Hall Computer Publishing
11711 North College, Carmel, Indiana 46032

International Standard Book Number: 0-672-30260-8

Library of Congress Catalog Card Number: 93-85100

96   95   94   93   4   3   2   1

Interpretation of the printing code: the rightmost double-digit number is the year of the book's printing; the rightmost single-digit, the number of the book's printing. For example, a printing code of 93-1 shows that the first printing of the book occurred in 1993.

Trademarks

Composed in MCPdigital by Prentice Hall Computer Publishing.

Printed in the United States of America.

Contents

Wokshop II Writing Tools

Workshop III   Formatting

Workshop VII   Graphics, Lines, Borders, and Fills

Workshop X   Merge

Contents

Workshop XIII   Projects

Acknowledgments

A great many people contributed to this book, many of them unknowingly. I would like to thank:

▲ My co-sysops on the WordPerfect Users Forum on CompuServe who devoted a tremendous amount of time and energy into helping WordPerfect users with tough questions.

▲ The Forum members whose questions and answers continually challenged me.

▲ My clients who taught me how WordPerfect works in the real world.

▲ All the folks at WordPerfect Corporation who made WordPerfect 6.0 the great program that it is. Among the people at WordPerfect Corporation who stand out:

Tracy Goden, beta coordinator for WordPerfect 6.0, for her support.

Roxanne Weir, director of enhancements, who never gives away a secret and never forgets an enhancement request.

Carlos Ferron, WordPerfect features support operator, who tracked down all sorts of obscure information for me and called me back with the answers.

▲ A special thanks to all of the *Super Book* contributors, a clever, dedicated, and fun group of people.

▲ The editorial and production staff at Sams for doing a superb job under impossible deadlines, especially Rosemarie Graham, development editor; Grant Fairchild, senior editor; Wayne Blankenbeckler, software development editor; and Bill Whitmer, editorial coordinator.

Most of all, I would like to thank:

▲ Gregg Bushyeager, acquisitions editor at Sams, who cheerfully worked around the clock to make this book happen.

▲ Dr. Henry Mankin, my back surgeon, without whom this book would have been unthinkable.

▲ My husband, Bill Claff, who was supportive in every possible way, from writing two of the programs on the *Super Book* disk to cooking dinner every night for the duration of this project.

About the Authors

Bob Boeri, a technology consultant at Factory Mutual Engineering, lives in Westboro, Massachusetts. He specializes in evaluating text retrieval, hypertext, and SGML software. Bob is also SGML editor for *New Media News*, a publication of the Boston Computer Society. He has written articles about SGML and text retrieval for *New Media News* and *Desktop Communications*. Off hours, Bob loves to garden, sing in a local church choir, and consult for his wife, Judy, who manages a home-based desktop publishing business named WordPower Associates.

Bill Bruck, Ph.D., is a WordPerfect certified instructor. Bill has his own training and consulting business in the Washington, D.C. area. He specializes in designing, developing, and conducting training programs for large-scale conversions and consulting with firms regarding office automation. He works mostly with law firms, scientific and engineering companies, and government agencies. His courseware for WordPerfect Corporation products is used by trainers and certified instructors nationwide. A counseling psychologist by profession, Bill comes from academia, having taught at Seattle University and West Georgia College. He is a tenured professor of psychology at Marymount University in Arlington, Virginia.

Marilyn Horn Claff, President, pc techniques, was the first WordPerfect certified instructor in the Boston area. A co-author of the best-selling Que title *Using WordPerfect 5.1* and its successor *Using WordPerfect 6*, Marilyn has been an assistant sysop on the WordPerfect Users Forum on CompuServe since 1988. She is highly regarded as one of the world's leading experts on WordPerfect. Marilyn is the principal trainer and consultant for pc techniques, a company specializing in WordPerfect training, support, and macro/merge programming. Marilyn is the director of the Boston Computer Society WordPerfect Special Interest Group (SIG), the WordPerfect for Windows SIG, and the Destop Publishing for Windows SIG. She keeps abreast of new developments by participating in several of the WordPerfect beta programs. Marilyn holds an M.A. in Italian literature from Middlebury College.

Diane Clayton, a WordPerfect certified instructor, has been a WordPerfect user since 1987. When Diane become Idaho's first WordPerfect certified instructor, she promptly purchased a license plate that reads WDPRFCT. Diane has worked with data processing and adult education for more than 30 years. She is a computer consultant at Boise State University, where she provides PC and WordPerfect training and support for faculty and staff and teaches WordPerfect classes for students in the evening. Diane also does private consulting and training, writing and editing, and document preparation/design. She has three adult children and two grandsons, is active in community theater, and has done volunteer work with foreign exchange students for 16 years.

Susan Hafer, Instructional Technology Specialist, has been working with IBM and IBM-compatible computers in a college setting for more than a decade and with WordPerfect since Version 4.1. While her primary focus these days is designing instructional technology, she continues to learn, use, and teach WordPerfect to college staff, faculty, and students and work closely with the Boston Computer Society WordPerfect User Group. She has collaborated on several other WordPerfect books. And, to prove she is more than a computer nerd, she worked as a country music disc jockey and published a short story (having nothing to do with computers) in a college magazine when she was a student.

Milan Keeney has worked as a furniture mover, a stable hand, a Mormon missionary, and a WordPerfect employee. Currently, Milan works as a freelance computer consultant. While at WordPerfect, he worked in PC Testing, Problem Resolution for WordPerfect 5.1, and WordPerfect customer support. He is married with one child and a dog named Rover (no kidding). Known to crash parties at computer conventions, Milan once got thrown out of a Microsoft party for bragging about the benefits of WordPerfect over Word. He has also been seen on Internet and CompuServe in the WordPerfect and Lotus forums. His ambition is to one day write a book on the history of WordPerfect.

Paul McFedries, WordPerfect pinch hitter, is a computer consultant and freelance writer. He has written a number of books for Sams, including *DOS 6 for the Guru Wanna-Be* and the *Excel Superbook* (as a co-author). Paul lives in Toronto (yes, the one in Canada) and is a diehard Leafs fan.

Ted Pedersen began his professional career as a programmer-analyst for Boeing, Seattle Community College, and the University of Southern California. When the bright lights of Hollywood beckoned, he began to write with a computer rather than for a computer. Paul is the author of more than 100 produced television episodes for "Batman: The Animated Series," "X-Men," "Captain Planet," "Teenage Mutant Ninja Turtles," and the upcoming "Cadillacs & Dinosaurs" series. In addition to scriptwriting, Paul works as computer consultant to several production companies. Currently he is writing a *Deep Space Nine* novel, which will be published in 1994. He and his wife, Phyllis, share their Venice, California, home with several computers and cats.

Beth Pickett Fitzherbert is a technical writer, network administrator, and systems analyst with six years of experience supporting WordPerfect users in private industry and the federal government. She has worked with, written about, and trained people in every version of WordPerfect since Version 4.2 in a variety of stand-alone and network environments. Beth is also a freelance technical writer and editor and a member of the Society for Technical Communication.

William Robertson, President, SoftWise (Staten Island, New York), specializes in consulting systems integration and support services for clients in the legal and medical markets. SoftWise's primary focus is customization and integration of commerial PC/LAN software such as WordPerfect and WordPerfect Office to enhance productivity throughout the organization. William has been working with WordPerfect

Corporation products since 1985, and he has extensive experience with WordPerfect macro programming on both the DOS and Windows platforms. (You can reach William on CompuServe at 70314,2352.)

Art Schaak, a word processing specialist at Stonefield Josephson Accountancy Corporation, a business consulting and accounting firm in Santa Monica, California, has been a beta tester for WordPerfect 5.0, 5.1, and 6.0. He has also taught WordPerfect courses, including desktop publishing with WordPerfect, through UCLA Extension since 1989. Art is happily married to the most wonderful woman in the world, has two spectacular daughters, and an enchanting granddaughter.

Esther Schindler, a chocoholic computer consultant, writes and teaches about computers. She is an online junkie who runs a ZiffNet forum on CompuServe and a user group evangelist, currently serving as vice-president of the Phoenix PC Users Group. In real life, she is working on getting a startup software development company off the ground. Esther is married to a brilliant guy who is funnier than she is, and she has a cat whose major contribution to this book is a pound of fur, carefully lodged inside Esther's disk drive. (You can reach Esther on CompuServe at 72241,1417.)

Cathy Wallach is owner and president of Perfect Access, Inc., a New York-based computer training and consulting firm whose clients include Fortune 500 companies in the legal, entertainment and banking industries and many small businesses and individuals. Cathy and her staff provide training and support for PC-based applications ranging from word processing, spreadsheets, databases, and graphics to document management systems and electronic mail. Perfect Access, Inc. also provides installation and configuration assistance and develops customized forms, macros, and styles. Her company is a beta test site for WordPerfect Corporation, and Cathy is one of several WordPerfect certified resources on staff.

Carolyn Woodie, a WordPerfect certified instructor, has been a computer training consultant specializing in WordPerfect software products since 1984 and a WordPerfect certified instructor since 1989. Carolyn is recognized for her ability to communicate technical information in an easy-to-learn, nontechnical manner. For several years, she was the author of a newspaper column, "Bytes & Nibbles," on general computer topics. She is currently the author of a newsletter, *The Wonders of WordPerfect* (*WoW!*), containing WordPerfect tips. A popular conference speaker, Carolyn is well known for her "WordPerfect 101 Tips, Hints, and Shortcuts" seminars.

David Wurmfeld, director of DSP Technology, is a hardware and software engineer specializing in laser printer controllers and controller software. He is currently director of DSP Technology at Aox, Inc., in Waltham, Massachusetts. David was educated at UMass Boston in physics and computer science. His hobbies include glass making, wood working and Greek Classics. Originally from Montebello, California, David lives in Sudbury, Massachusetts, with his wife, Shulamit, and son, Benyamin.

Introduction

The *WordPerfect 6.0 Super Book* is aptly named for several reasons. First of all, WordPerfect 6.0 is a super program, immensely rich and packed with features. The upgrade from WordPerfect 5.1 to 6.0 is without a doubt the greatest upgrade in the history of PC computing. Only WordPerfect Corporation would have the courage and the vision to undertake a project of this magnitude.

Secondly, the *Super Book* required a superhuman effort on the part of everyone involved in the project. Becoming familiar with WordPerfect 6.0 during the beta cycle, with only minimal—and preliminary—documentation, dealing with the software glitches and considerable design changes that inevitably occur in beta, and meeting impossible deadlines was a challenge for the authors, as well as for Sams' skilled editorial and production teams.

Most of the *Super Book* contributors are computer consultants and trainers who are keenly aware of the real needs of real people in the real world. We've tried to give you insight into why features work the way they do and eliminate potential misunderstandings that could keep you from getting the most out of WordPerfect. Most of all, we've tried to demonstrate, through the Workshops, Tips, Cautions, Notes, and especially through the Projects, how you can command, control, and coax WordPerfect 6.0 into producing the kinds of documents you expect it to.

WordPerfect 6.0 has been totally rewritten, and even the most skilled 5.1 users will need some help if they are to master it quickly. Don't be put off by the size of this book or the radical changes to WordPerfect. With the right tools—and we believe that the *Super Book* is one of them—the learning curve is shorter than you might expect.

Moving to WordPerfect 6.0

If you're like most users, you cannot undertake an upgrade of the magnitude of WordPerfect 6.0 on a whim and a promise. You need to know that the new software will provide real benefits, that interruptions to your work will be minimal, and most of all, that the transition will be a smooth and painless one. You're wary because you've have been burned by software bugs, hardware failures, inadequate documentation and support. (You probably have at least one computer nightmare to tell.) Some of you may stay with your current software configuration, no matter how restricting, to avoid living through a another software upgrade!

Most users, however, will look at a broader picture and base their decisions on whether the benefits of the new program will outweigh the inevitable inconveniences. No matter what stage of the upgrade process you are in, the *Super Book* can help you. If you're trying to make an intelligent decision about whether to upgrade or not, the *Super Book* provides an in-depth discussion of the capabilities (and in some cases, limitations) of WordPerfect 6.0. If you've decided to upgrade, but need to get up to speed quickly, this book provides the jump-start to get you on your way. If you've already made the switch and are looking for a way to master the more advanced features, the *Super Book* offers Workshops and Projects that will make you more productive immediately.

We can't guarantee that the WordPerfect 6.0 will always be able to do exactly what you want it to do, or that you won't run into any minor snags or find all the new features easy to understand and apply. We believe, however, that the benefits of WordPerfect 6.0 are so tangible and immense that the *Super Book* will make these benefits more accessible to you, regardless of your current skill level.

Understandably, many users are nervous about upgrading. In talking to users across the country, we've identified the top six concerns users have about upgrading to WordPerfect 6.0.

File Compatibility

Without question, the chief concern for nearly everyone is file compatibility. In the Nineties, few businesses are computerizing for the first time. Most new users are converting from an earlier version of WordPerfect or from another word processor, and they need to be able to access existing files with a minimum of hassle. Many businesses will use WordPerfect 6.0 side-by-side with WordPerfect 5.1 and/or WordPerfect for Windows. They need assurance that their users can exchange WordPerfect 5.x and 6.0 files without difficulty.

File compatibility has been one WordPerfect Corporation's top priorities from the earliest planning stages of WordPerfect 6.0. WordPerfect Corporation recognizes that not all users will be able to upgrade to 6.0, and that users, especially corporate users, must be able to exchange files from different versions easily. In order to provide the new features that users wanted, WordPerfect Corporation was forced to change the file format for WordPerfect 6.0 documents. This means that WordPerfect 6.0 files must be saved in WordPerfect 5.X format in order to be read and edited in earlier versions.

WordPerfect Corporation has addressed this issue by including a full-featured conversion program called ConvertPerfect 2.0 in the WordPerfect package. You can open WordPerfect 5.x and 45 other file formats directly in WordPerfect 6.0, even without knowing where the files came from. From within WordPerfect, you can save your documents easily in any of the supported formats. You can even set up

WordPerfect so that it automatically saves your files in a specific file format if you exchange files with users of other programs on a regular basis.

ConvertPerfect can be run as a stand-alone program from outside WordPerfect. From DOS, you can run ConvertPerfect interactively, using on-screen menus, or you can run it in batch mode using command-line startup options. Whether you need to convert a single file or several hundred files at once, you'll be able to do it easily with ConvertPerfect.

The following tips should help you get the best possible results when converting files:

- ▲ If you plan to import WordPerfect 5.x files, ask the 5.1 users providing the files to turn off the Fast Save feature, or else the 5.1 files will not contain enough formatting information for ConvertPerfect to do a good job.

- ▲ Conversion from WordPerfect 5.1 to WordPerfect 6.0 should be seamless. However, if you are saving a WordPerfect 6.0 file in 5.x format, any WordPerfect 6.0 features that have no 5.1 equivalents are lost.

- ▲ If your WordPerfect 6.0 files contain graphics, the graphics are stored in the WPG 2 format, which is not compatible with WordPerfect 5.x. To convert these files, change the graphics contents for the WordPerfect 6.0 file to "Image on Disk" and make sure that the image is in WPG 1 format (or in another graphics format that WordPerfect 5.x understands). To convert the graphics file from WordPerfect 6.0, use the Save As feature from the Image Editor.

- ▲ For detailed information about file conversion to and from WordPerfect 6.0, see the files WP5X.DOC and RTF.DOC, located in your \WP60 directory.

- ▲ For a nominal charge, WordPerfect Corporation offers additional conversion filters that work with ConvertPerfect 2.0. Additional documentation for specific filters is also available from WordPerfect Corporation.

- ▲ WordPerfect 5.1 users who are not upgrading to 6.0 can purchase ConvertPerfect 2.0 separately from WordPerfect Corporation if they need to convert 6.0 files.

- ▲ Because the choice of fonts affects the number of characters per line and the number of lines per page, converted files won't format exactly the same way as they did in the original program. For most types of documents, this won't be a problem.

- ▲ Documents that are formatted correctly (for example, documents that use tabs instead of spaces for horizontal alignment) always convert better than incorrectly formatted documents, even if the incorrectly formatted documents appear to format and print correctly in the original program.

- ▲ If you run ConvertPerfect as a stand-alone application from DOS, you'll have more options to control how particular features are converted.

Macros

Next to document compatibility, macro conversion is a top priority for most users, especially in corporate environments that have invested heavily in macro development. Fortunately, the news here is excellent. WordPerfect Corporation has worked hard to provide nearly seamless conversion of WordPerfect 5.1 macros, and the results are impressive. Most converted WordPerfect 5.1 macros will work in 6.0 without any manual editing, and if editing is required, it will probably be minor.

If you are nervous about moving to WordPerfect 6.0 because of your investment in WordPerfect 5.x macros, consider the following points:

▲ Many features that required macros in WordPerfect 5.x are now built into the program so you can access them easily from menus and dialog boxes. For example, WordPerfect 6.0 provides a built-in envelope feature, so envelope macros are no longer necessary.

▲ Although macro developers will have to learn a new macro language, WordPerfect 6.0's macro language is actually easier than the language in WordPerfect 5.x.

▲ WordPerfect 6.0 provides more and better tools for developing and debugging macros. For example, when you save a macro, WordPerfect checks the syntax. If it finds an error, it gives you a chance to correct it, and it even moves the insertion point directly to the offending command. You can also set values for variables from the macro control menu, so debugging is easier.

▲ WordPerfect 6.0 gives you the capability to switch between Edit and Record mode, so macros are far easier to modify.

▲ WordPerfect 6.0 macros are regular WordPerfect documents, so you can edit them easily and print them without using a special software program.

▲ WordPerfect 6.0 supports a macro library feature, so you can reuse macro routines easily by referencing the library file.

▲ WordPerfect 6.0 supports shared and personal macro directories, so macros are easier to use and support on a network.

Hardware Requirements

Hardware requirements are an important consideration for nearly everyone. Hardware is ultimately the determining factor in deciding whether to upgrade or not. The minimum requirements for WordPerfect 6.0 are as follows:

▲ A 286-based computer
▲ 480K free conventional memory
▲ DOS 3.0 or higher
▲ 7M free hard disk space

In reality, few users will be satisfied with WordPerfect 6.0's performance with the minimal configuration. Performance is unacceptable and key features such as Graphics mode and spell checking are disabled in low-memory situations. If you can't use the features that make WordPerfect 6.0 great, stay with WordPerfect 5.1. A more reasonable configuration for WordPerfect 6.0 would be as follows:

▲ A 386-based computer (preferably a 486)

▲ 520K conventional memory

▲ Extended or expanded memory

▲ 16M free hard disk space

▲ VGA (preferably a super VGA) graphics card

Essentially, you'll need a system capable of running Windows to use this DOS product. If you're wondering why you should not just make the move to Windows if you have to upgrade your computer system anyway, the best reason for staying with WordPerfect for DOS is that it provides better performance than a Windows word processor run on the same configuration.

File Size

Even if you have the requisite 7-16M to install WordPerfect 6.0, free disk space may influence your decision to upgrade. WordPerfect 6.0 files are considerably larger than equivalent 5.1 files. (My own documents have ranged from 40-100 percent larger than their 5.1 equivalents.) If you need to keep a large number of WordPerfect documents available, this extra overhead could be a problem for you. Not upgrading because of a lack of hard disk space would be a shame, but for many users, file storage requirements will be a compelling reason to stay with WordPerfect 5.1. If your disk situation is borderline, the following tips may help you make the best use you can of your space:

▲ In the long term, the best solution is also the most obvious one: invest in a new hard disk if you possibly can.

▲ Avoid disk compression programs—they're inherently unsafe. If your data is important to you, don't take that risk.

▲ Get in the habit of pruning out files you don't really need. Eliminate duplicates on your hard disk. (The !BANG utility on the *Super Book* disk can help you with this task.)

▲ Do a minimal installation of WordPerfect, or if you do a regular installation, delete unnecessary program files. For example, you probably don't need to keep all of the conversion filters (*.CVX) on your hard disk. (Be sure you know what you are doing, or you'll have to reinstall.)

▲ In WordPerfect 6.0, turn off Fast Save and Undo. Both features cause your files to be larger than necessary.

▲ If you aren't using the new formatting options in WordPerfect 6.0, such as borders and contour text to graphics, save your WordPerfect 6.0 files in 5.1 format. Use the Save Setup dialog to make 5.1 your Default Save Format. When you need to save a file in WordPerfect 6.0 format, you can override the default. This compromise is extreme, but it will enable you to take advantage of many of the benefits of WordPerfect 6.0 without its overhead. This way, you can still enjoy WordPerfect 6.0's WYSIWYG editing, enhancements to speller, multiple-document interface, improved macros, and built-in faxing, to name just a few good reasons to upgrade.

▲ To reduce the size of an individual file, block the entire document, copy it to a free document window, and save it. You'll lose the document summary and initial codes (if they are different from your default settings), but your file will be far smaller.

Relearning

WordPerfect 6.0 is a nearly total rewrite of WordPerfect 5.1. With nearly 700 enhancements and new features, WordPerfect 6.0 is an extraordinarily rich program that satisfies the needs of a wide range of users, from casual home user, to business, legal, and academic users. For many projects, WordPerfect 6.0 provides sufficient desktop publishing power to eliminate the need for a separate desktop publishing program. It's not surprising, then, that even if you're a WordPerfect 5.1 power user, you'll need to spend some time and effort learning to use its new capabilities.

Since WordPerfect 5.0 was released in May 1988, changes to WordPerfect have been incremental and evolutionary. Users who were comfortable with WordPerfect 5.0 had little difficulty learning the new features in WordPerfect 5.1, and many users, probably the majority, were able to make the transition to WordPerfect 5.1 with little or no formal training.

With WordPerfect 6.0, the situation is quite different. Although the program has a familiar feel and major keystroke sequences remain the same, the design of the program is substantially different, and you may find yourself disoriented and frustrated if you attempt to tackle your usual workload without any training or orientation. If you are concerned with the human aspect of transitioning, heed the following advice:

▲ Don't upgrade when you are just about to undertake a major critical project. Try to choose a timeframe when you don't expect to be under heavier work pressure than usual.

▲ Allow yourself some learning time. Your productivity may be lower for the first month or two that you use WordPerfect 6.0, but this is a normal and temporary phenomenon.

▲ Different people have different learning styles. For many people, the best learning tool is a good book (such as this one), for others, hands-on classroom training is the best way to learn a software program. Other users prefer watching a video tape or just experimenting. With a program as popular as WordPerfect 6.0, you'll have a wide choice of learning aids.

▲ Don't overlook the learning tools that come with WordPerfect, including the workbook, tutorial, and the new coaches. Coaches help you learn new features without leaving your current document.

▲ Join a local user group, or form an in-house user group within your company. User groups improve morale and motivate users as well as helping them learn.

▲ When learning WordPerfect, create a plan of attack. There are probably a few key features, such as collapsible outlining or paragraph borders, that influenced you to upgrade, so after becoming comfortable with the basics, concentrate on these features and don't worry about the rest of the program.

▲ If you're in management, be sure your users understand the reasons why you've decided to make the transition. Users resent changing software programs, especially after they have struggled to learn their current one. Letting them know that you've chosen to upgrade to WordPerfect 6.0 to make their jobs easier will do a lot to lessen resistance to upgrading.

▲ Consider setting up a demo session to give users (before you train them) an overview of the new capabilities.

▲ Keep your old software accessible as a fall-back for rush jobs when you can't afford to take the extra time the unfamiliar software will require.

▲ Give your users a cut-off date when their old software will be removed from their systems.

▲ Hire outside help, if necessary, to handle the company support desk during the transition.

▲ Investigate custom training courses. Most independent trainers and some training centers provide customized training, often at little additional cost.

Support

The final critical issue is support. If you can't afford any "down time," you're understandably concerned about getting help if you don't understand a new feature or run into a problem.

Fortunately for you, WordPerfect Corporation provides the best support in the software industry, and they've pledged to continue and expand this support with WordPerfect 6.0. The following points may help reassure you:

▲ WordPerfect Corporation has offloaded its support for previous versions of WordPerfect to another company so they can provide the best possible support for WordPerfect 6.0. All 900 of the WordPerfect support operators in Orem, Utah, have undergone extensive training, and they will be supporting WordPerfect 6.0 exclusively.

▲ WordPerfect offered excellent telephone support on WordPerfect 6.0 during the prerelease period, using this time to prepare and train its support staff on WordPerfect 6.0.

▲ WordPerfect Corporation maintains an enormous database of questions and solutions which help their operators provide support for even the most obscure features. (This database is available on CD-ROM to Customer Advantage Program participants. Talk to your local WordPerfect area manager about how your company can join this program.)

▲ WordPerfect Corporation issues periodic "maintenance releases" or "interim updates" that fix bugs and add enhancements for its software programs. These interim updates are available to registered users through WordPerfect Corporation for a nominal fee.

▲ WordPerfect Croporation has several supplementary disks of drivers for printers, video cards, and fax and sound boards, as well as disks with additional conversion filters and documentation, that are available through it bulletin board system or for a nominal fee.

▲ WordPerfect Corporation offers utility disks (containing programs such as PTR, the printer driver editor) for a nominal fee.

▲ The Support Group, Inc. sponsors an independent forum called WordPerfect Users devoted to WordPerfect on CompuServe (Go WPUSERS). WordPerfect Corporation sponsors a forum called WordPerfect Customer Support (Go WPCS). Both forums are excellent sources of information.

▲ Call WordPerfect Corporation for a list of certified resources, certified instructors, and authorized training centers in your area. All of these groups have passed rigorous exams as well as other requirements. (Most of the contributors to the *Super Book* are either WordPerfect certified resources or certified instructors.)

▲ *WordPerfect Magazine* is an excellent monthly publication devoted exclusively to WordPerfect and WordPerfect add-on products. *WordPerfect Magazine* is aimed primarily at new and intermediate users.

Conventions Used in This Book

The *WordPerfect 6.0 Super Book* employs various conventions to get you up and running with WordPerfect and shorten your learning curve. Understanding these conventions will help you get the most out of the *Super Book* and WordPerfect 6.0 from the very beginning.

> **The Command Reference Card**: The tear-out card in the front of this book is designed to give you a convienient reference to many of WordPerfect's functions and control key sequences.
>
> **Procedures**: All of the step-by-step procedures have been numbered by chapter and in numerical order (for example, Procedure 1.1, 1.2, and so on).
>
> **Commands**: All commands that you must select to do something appear in second color (for example, "select OK"). This should allow you to quickly scan a procedure and focus on the commands required to accomplish that procedure.
>
> **Hot Keys**: If a command has a hot-key equivalent, it appears in a bold type-face (for example, "select Save As" and "to access the **F**ile menu).

Several icons are used throughout the *Super Book* to draw your attention to important information:

Note: The Note icon introduces information related to a topic in the text. Although notes are not required reading, they often provide you with valuable information about why a feature works—or doesn't work—the way it does.

Tip: The Tip icon is intended to draw your attention to information that will make your work easier. These are valuable insights direct from the experts to you.

Caution: Don't miss these! The Caution icon points out potential pitfalls that could potentially cause you big problems. Don't say we didn't warn you!

The disk icon is a free floating icon that you will see used throughout the book. Wherever you see it, you'll know that the author is talking about one of the files or utilities contained on the *Super Book* disk.

With the *Super Book* in hand and all of these resources, you're well on your way to becoming a WordPerfect Super User. Good luck!

Basic Skills

by Susan Hafer

The WordPerfect Environment

WordPerfect 6.0 provides many tools and features that enable you to tailor its "look and feel" to suit your equipment and tastes. Extensive online help is available to help you learn about these options and all the program's features.

Selecting the Right Mode

There are three different interfaces available in WordPerfect 6.0. You can select Text Mode, Graphics Mode, or Page Mode from the View pull-down menu (see Figure 1.1). You will probably find yourself switching between them as you work.

Text Mode

Text mode looks very much like the WordPerfect 5.1 screen. It takes the least amount of memory and works significantly faster than the other modes. Because it is character-based, you see text only (documents with complex formatting are difficult to work with, relative to the other modes). Use Text mode when your computer is low on memory—or *you* are low on patience!

Tip: You can also select the various modes from the Screen dialog box, accessed with Ctrl+F3 (see Figure 1.2).

Text mode is the default when you first install WordPerfect. To switch to Text mode from one of the other modes, follow the steps in Procedure 1.1.

Procedure 1.1. Selecting Text mode.

1. Select View (or press Ctrl+F3) to access the Screen dialog box. Figures 1.1 and 1.2 show the View pull-down menu and the Screen dialog box, respectively.

Figure 1.1. The View pull-down menu.

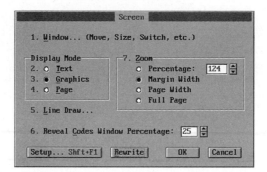

Figure 1.2. The Screen dialog box (Ctrl+F3).

2. Select Text mode from the menu or Text from the dialog box. Figure 1.3 shows the basic Text mode screen; Figure 1.7, found later in this chapter, shows Text mode with some of the optional screen elements active.

 Tip: The default button bar includes a TextMode button for quick access with a click of the mouse.

Menu bar

Page break

Status line

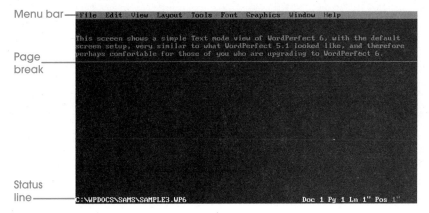

Figure 1.3. Text mode.

Graphics Mode

Figure 1.4 shows a simple Graphics mode screen. Graphics mode requires significantly more resources from your computer than Text mode. If you have an older computer, Text mode is probably your only hope, because Graphics and Page modes will run too slowly.

Procedure 1.2. Selecting Graphics mode.

1. Select View (or press Ctrl+F3) to access the Screen dialog box. Figures 1.1 and 1.2 show the **View** pull-down menu and the Screen dialog box, respectively.
2. Select Graphics Mode from the menu or Graphics from the dialog box. Figure 1.4 shows the basic Graphics mode screen. Figure 1.6, found later in this chapter, shows Graphics mode with some of the optional screen elements active.

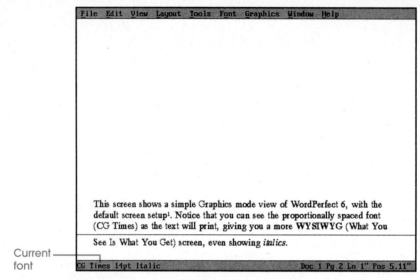

Current font

Figure 1.4. Graphics mode shows the body of the document as it appears when printed.

Tip: The default button bar includes a GrphMode button for quick access with the mouse.

Page Mode

Figure 1.5 shows a Page mode screen. Page mode is identical to Graphics mode except that Page mode shows more than the document's body text—it includes page headers and footers, page numbering, and footnotes and endnotes.

Procedure 1.3. Selecting Page mode.

1. Select View (or press Ctrl+F3) to access the Screen dialog box. Figures 1.1 and 1.2 show the View pull-down menu and the Screen dialog box, respectively.
2. Select Page mode from the menu or Page from the dialog box. Figure 1.5 shows the basic Page mode screen.

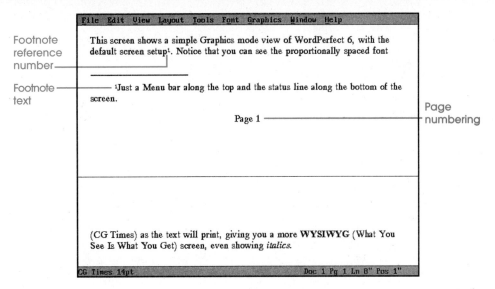

Footnote reference number

Footnote text

Page numbering

Figure 1.5. Page mode shows page headers and footers, page numbering, and footnotes and endnotes on the editing screen.

WordPerfect's Screen

The WordPerfect 6.0 screen varies from one mode to another, as you have seen. It also varies by which options you choose to display on-screen within each mode. You control all these options from the View menu, shown in Figure 1.1.

Changing screen options in Graphics mode affects both Graphics and Page modes. To affect Text mode screen options, go into Text mode and make your selections. For example, turning on the button bar in Graphics mode does not provide a button bar in Text mode, and vice versa.

Tip: The Screen Setup dialog box, described later in this chapter, enables you to select screen options for Text and Graphics modes more quickly, without having to invoke each mode first.

Figures 1.6 and 1.7 show Graphics and Text modes with all the screen elements turned on. You can adjust the button bar, as you will see, to be along the top, left, right, or bottom of your screen. You can choose to have the buttons use the picture and text identifiers for each button (as shown in Figure 1.6), or the text or picture only to fit more buttons on the screen; the button bar in the figures is shown along the left side. You may find the screens in Figures 1.6 and 1.7 cluttered, so use only those elements you find useful.

7

Pull-down menus

Ribbon

Outline bar

Button bar

Vertical scroll bar

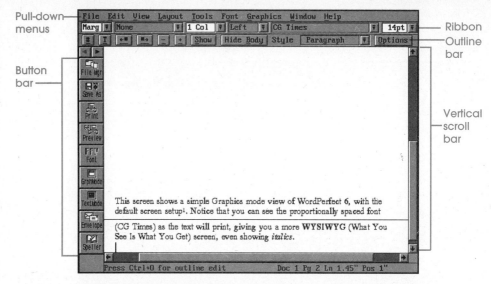

Figure 1.6. Graphics mode with all the screen elements turned on.

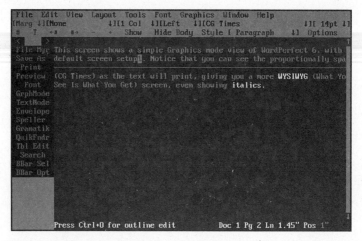

Figure 1.7. Text mode with all the screen elements turned on.

Status Line

As you can see in Figures 1.1 through 1.7, for all three modes—Text, Graphics, and Page—a status line appears along the bottom of the screen. In the left corner is either the current font or, if the document has been saved to disk at any time, the filename. WordPerfect also uses this space to give you brief instructions, as when the outline bar is active and the message `Press Ctrl+) for Outline edit` appears. In the right corner is the Document number (you have up to nine editing screens), the current page, the current line (counted down from the paper's top edge), and the current position (counted from the left edge of the paper). The position number appears in bold or underline when those features are active, and the word *Pos* appears in all caps (*POS*) when Caps Lock is on. If you are using the Columns or Tables feature, the current column or table cell is displayed immediately before the Document number.

Tip: If you double-click the status line, a window frame appears around the current document. See Chapter 6, "Working with Multiple Documents," for more details.

Tip: You can control what displays on the left edge of the status line using View, Screen Setup, Window Options, Status Line.

Pull-Down Menus

As you can see in Figures 1.1 through 1.7, for all three modes—Text, Graphics, and Page—a pull-down menu bar appears along the top of the screen.

Tip: You can turn off the pull-down menu bar by selecting View, Pull-Down Menus (the menu selection will no longer be checked and the pull-down menus will no longer be displayed). To bring back the pull-down menus, press Ctrl+F3 to access the screen dialog box, then Shift+F1 for Screen Setup, then Screen Options, then Pull-Down Menus, then Home, F7 to exit all dialog boxes and return to your document, with the pull-down menu bar reactivated.

In keeping with the industry standard, you access the pull-down menus by clicking the menu you want with the mouse or by using an Alt+*Letter* keystroke (Alt+F for the File menu, for example). Once in menus, you may make selections by clicking menu items with the mouse, using the arrow keys and pressing Enter when on the selection you want, or using the mnemonics (typing the underlined letter within a selection, as in O for Open).

Tip: By default, pressing Alt alone and then releasing it in WordPerfect does nothing. In Windows, this activates the menu bar by selecting the first menu item (the **F**ile menu). You can set up WordPerfect to behave the way Windows does by using View, Screen Setup, Screen Options; Alt key activates menus.

Selecting a menu item may produce an immediate result (selecting **P**aste from the **E**dit menu, for example), a dialog box from which you make more selections (such as when you select Screen Setup from the View menu), or another layer of cascading menus (selecting **Z**oom from the View menu, for example). If a cascading menu is the result, the menu selection appears with an arrow to the right, as shown in Figure 1.8. If a dialog box is the result, the menu selection appears with an ellipsis after the menu item text (Screen Setup).

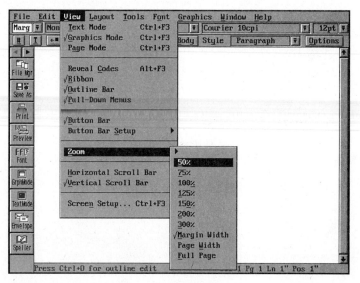

Figure 1.8. Cascading menus.

Tip: If you get into a dialog box or menu unintentionally and want to back out a level, press Escape (alternatively, in a cascading menu, you could press the left arrow).

Tip: If you are many levels deep into menus or dialog boxes and want to get out completely (back to your document), without having to exit each menu or dialog box, use Home, F7.

Ribbon

In Figures 1.6 and 1.7, you see that one optional screen element is the ribbon, which provides quick access to the current settings for Zoom, Paragraph Numbering Level, Number of Columns, Justification, Font, and Point Size. Zoom is discussed here (for details about the other functions, see Chapters 15, "Line Formatting," 16, "Paragraph Formatting," 42, "Using Subdivided Pages," and 43, "Getting Started with Macros," respectively).

The only way to access the ribbon items is by clicking with the mouse on an item or its down arrow button—you cannot access them with the keyboard. If you do not have a mouse, do not use the ribbon. Access the ribbon's items from the pull-down menus or from function keys.

Clicking a ribbon item or the down arrow pulls down a list of your choices. When you make a selection, a code is inserted in your document and all text following the code is affected. See Chapter 12, "Understanding Formatting Codes," for more information about formatting.

In Graphics and Page modes, you can use the Zoom feature to control the size of the document display.

Note: The first item, controlling the Zoom, does not apply to Text mode and is not selectable in that mode.

Marg (the default setting) displays a document from the left margin to the right margin. This generally gives you the most legible screen. Your other choices are Wide, Full, or a percentage of the true size of the page, which is usually 8.5-inches wide by 11-inches high. See Figures 1.9 through 1.13 to compare some of the various Zooms.

Note: If you click the font point size box for a font with more than one point size available, a list is not displayed; the cursor is placed by the number so that you may type in a size or press the down arrow to display the list of available sizes.

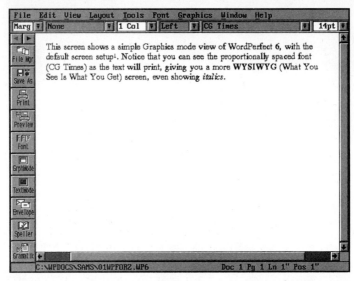

Figure 1.9. A screen in Graphics mode, using a Zoom of Marg (the default).

Figure 1.10. A screen in Graphics mode, using a Zoom of Wide.

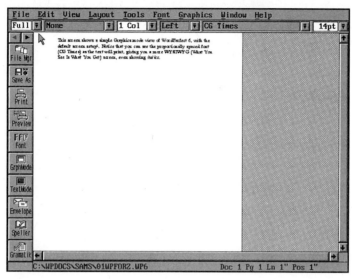

Figure 1.11. A screen in Graphics mode, using a Zoom of Full.

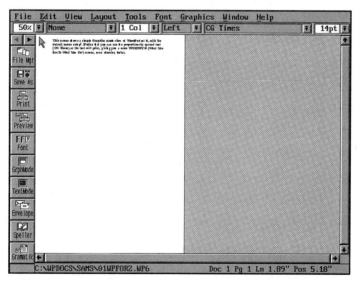

Figure 1.12. A screen in Graphics mode, using a Zoom of 50 percent.

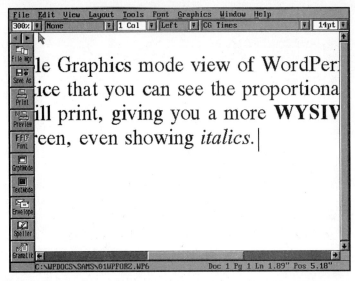

Figure 1.13. A screen in Graphics mode, using a Zoom of 300 percent.

Caution: If you use the mouse to browse through one of the ribbon lists and you don't want to make any changes, be careful to press Escape or highlight the original selection.

Reveal Codes

WordPerfect 6.0's display of your document is referred to as WYSIWYG (pronounced Wissy-wig, for "What You See Is What You Get"). When you ask for underlining, you see your text underlined, rather than commands that turn underlining on and off, as older editing software shows.

Although it is easier to work with your text in WYSIWYG format, it is often helpful when troubleshooting problems to see not only the text and formatting, but also the codes that control the formatting. WordPerfect gives you access to this information with the Reveal Codes feature.

To turn on (or off) Reveal Codes, select View, Reveal Codes (or press Alt+F3). (See Chapter 12 for detailed information about formatting and using Reveal Codes.)

Button Bar and Button Bar Setup

The button bar you see in Figures 1.6 and 1.7 displays along the left edge of the screen. This WordPerfect 6.0 feature gives you instant access to commands you use often. It is particularly useful to have a button for a feature that does not have a convenient short-cut key, or one that is buried deep within menus.

The button bar is only accessible with the mouse. Only a certain number of buttons will fit on the screen at one time. Click the left and right arrows at the top of any side button bar (or up and down arrows at the left of the button bar along the top or bottom of the screen) to scroll through the buttons if there is more than one screenful of buttons.

You can use the Button Bar Setup menu or the [BBar Sel] button to select a different button bar. Use the Button Bar Setup menu or the [BBar Opt] button to control how button bars are displayed. Use the Button Bar Setup menu to edit a button bar, enabling you to quickly and easily delete and add buttons. (For more details, see Appendix B, "Customizing WordPerfect 6.0.")

Scroll Bars

You may activate vertical and horizontal scroll bars, both of which are shown in Figures 1.6 and 1.7. These scroll bars enable mouse-oriented users to easily and quickly scroll through a document. The thumb button in the scroll bar is sized relative to the current screen, giving the user a clear picture of the length of the current document. If the document is very short, the current screen of text is a large percentage of the document as a whole, so the thumb button almost fills the entire scroll bar. If the document is very long, the current screen of text is a small percentage of the document as a whole, so the thumb button is quite small.

You will probably very rarely use a horizontal scroll bar, if at all. Normally you will adust the document's Zoom so you can see the complete width of the text rather than having to scroll to the left or right of the document window.

Table 1.1. Navigating in WordPerfect 6.0 using the keyboard or the scroll bar.

Result	Scroll Bar Action	Keyboard Equivalent
Up one line	Up	Arrow button
Down one line	Down	Arrow button
Scroll up/down continuously	Click and hold	Up/down arrow button

continues

Table 1.1. Continued

Result	Scroll Bar Action	Keyboard Equivalent
Up one screenful/ top of current screen	Click between	Thumb button and up arrow button
Down one screenful/ bottom of current screen	Click between	Thumb button and down arrow button
Top of document	Click and drag	Thumb button to top*
Bottom of document	Click and drag	Thumb button to bottom*

*WordPerfect 6.0 does not scroll the document to match the scroll bar action until you release the thumb button.

(There are many more ways to navigate through WordPerfect documents using the keyboard. See Help (F1), Keystrokes for a detailed list.)

Note: The horizontal scroll bar works the same way (substitute left/ right for up/down in the table). If you use a Zoom of Margins, you do not need a horizontal scroll bar.

Outline Bar

The outline bar is shown in Figures 1.6 and 1.7. If you use WordPerfect 6.0's paragraph numbering or outline feature (explained in detail in Chapter 58, "Page, Chapter, and Volume Numbering"), you may find the outline bar quite useful for quick access to outline functions. To select or deselect the outline bar, select View, Outline Bar.

The Screen Setup Dialog Box

Selections from the View menu and other interesting screen elements are found in the Screen Setup dialog box, shown in Figures 1.14 and 1.15.

Note: WordPerfect 6.0 makes frequent use of dialog boxes where full-screen menus were used in WordPerfect 5.1 and earlier versions.

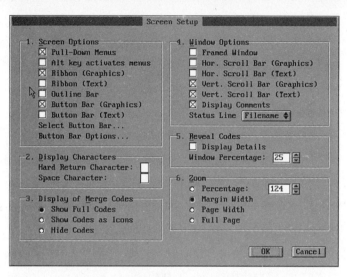

Figure 1.14. The Screen Setup dialog box in Graphics mode.

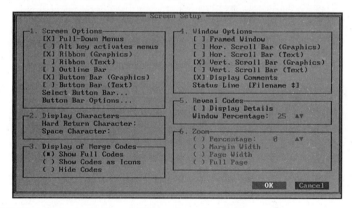

Figure 1.15. The Screen Setup dialog box in Text mode.

Dialog boxes use check boxes, radio buttons, drop-down lists, and buttons. In check boxes, an *X* means that the item is selected and no *X* means it is not selected. Selecting one option from a group of radio buttons disables the others in that group. You can access drop-down lists by clicking the down arrow and pulling down the list of options. (You can continuously scroll through long lists by dragging the mouse in the upper or lower region of the list.)

You can make your selections from dialog boxes in a number of ways. You can click them with the mouse, press the mneumonic key, or use the arrow keys to highlight the selection and press Enter. (You can use the Tab key to move the focus to the next item and the Shift+Tab key combination to move the focus to the previous item when using the arrow key method.)

17

Note: There is no mneumonic key for OK or Cancel, but you can press Escape for Cancel.

To access the Screen Setup dialog box, select View, Screen Setup (or press Ctrl+F3, Shift+F1).

Many of the options in the Screen Setup dialog box are already familiar to you—in particular, the Window Options check boxes for scroll bars, the Screen Options check boxes for pull-down menus, ribbon and button bar selections, the outline bar, and the last section for controlling the Zoom.

 Tip: From this dialog box you can quickly select your preferences for Graphics and Text mode without having to select each mode first.

You may not be as familiar with the other controls in the Screen Setup dialog box:

Display Characters enables you to make hard returns and spaces visible characters.

Display of Merge Codes controls the visibility of codes used for the WordPerfect Merge function (see Chapter 50, "Merge Projects").

Reveal Codes controls how the Reveal Codes screen appears (see Chapter 12, "Understanding Formatting Codes," for details).

Window Options, in addition to providing the scroll bar options, includes Framed Window (see Chapter 6, "Working with Multiple Documents"), Display Comments, and Status Line, which controls whether the filename, the current font, or nothing is displayed in the left corner of the status line.

Getting Help

WordPerfect 6.0 has *context-sensitive help*. If you are in a menu or dialog box and call up Help, you will see help about that menu or dialog box. General help is also available.

To get general Help, choose the **H**elp menu (shown in Figure 1.16) and make your selection: Contents, Index, How do I, Coaches, Macros, Tutorial, and WP Info. Index, How do I, and Coaches are also accessible from the Help Contents dialog box; Macros, Tutorial, and WP Info are only available from this **H**elp menu.

Figure 1.16. The **H**elp menu.

The Help Pull-Down Menu

Some help functions are only available from the **H**elp menu, shown in Figure 1.16.
Some are only available from the Help Contents dialog box (see Figure 1.26). Some
help functions are available from either location. Let's begin with a discussion of
all the help available from the menu.

WP Info

Selecting WP Info from the **H**elp menu calls up a dialog box similar to the one in
Figure 1.17.

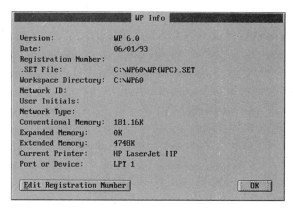

Figure 1.17. The WP Info dialog box.

This information is particularly useful to WordPerfect Corporation when you
have questions about how WordPerfect is working and call their Customer
Support staff.

The button at the bottom of the screen enables you to edit the registration number
for your WordPerfect 6.0 license, in case you didn't have it handy when you
installed WordPerfect.

Tutorial

WordPerfect has an online tutorial to show the basics of using WordPerfect 6.0 (see Procedure 1.4).

Procedure 1.4. Using an online tutorial for a demonstration of basic WordPerfect use.

1. Save your document in case you run into problems with the tutorial and have to reboot the computer.

2. Select Help, Tutorial to access the Screen dialog box. The Welcome dialog box appears, shown in Figure 1.18.

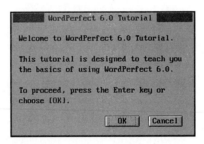

Figure 1.18. The Welcome dialog box in the tutorial.

3. Select OK (or press Enter) to open the tutorial. To cancel out of the tutorial, select Cancel (or press Escape).

Caution: The tutorial opens the next available document-editing screen. If you are using all nine document-editing screens, you will see a dialog box asking you to exit one or more of your documents before running the tutorial.

When you open the tutorial, a dialog box similar to the one shown in Figure 1.19 appears, asking whether you will be using a mouse or just the keyboard in the tutorial.

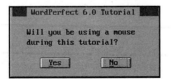

Figure 1.19. The tutorial asks whether you will be using a mouse.

4. Make your selection. Choose Yes if you have a mouse and may want to use it. Choose No if you do not have a mouse or have one but do not wish to use it.

The Tutorial's Main Menu dialog box appears (see Figure 1.20).

```
┌──────────────────────────────────────────────────┐
│ ▓▓▓▓▓▓▓▓   WordPerfect 6.0 Tutorial - Main Menu ▓▓▓▓ │
│          ┌─Lessons──────────────────┐            │
│ To choose a lesson, click │ 1. Starting Out     │ │
│ it using your mouse, or   └──────────────────────┘ │
│ select it using your arrow ┌──────────────────────┐ │
│ keys and then press the   │ 2. Editing Text     │ │
│ Enter key.                └──────────────────────┘ │
│                           ┌──────────────────────┐ │
│                           │ 3. Formatting Text  │ │
│                           └──────────────────────┘ │
│                           ┌──────────────────────┐ │
│                           │ 4. Finishing Up     │ │
│                           └──────────────────────┘ │
│ To go to a topic within   ┌──────────────────────┐ │
│ a lesson, choose          │    Topic List       │ │
│ [Topic List].             └──────────────────────┘ │
│                           ┌──────────────────────┐ │
│ To Exit this tutorial,    │   Exit Tutorial     │ │
│ choose [Exit Tutorial].   └──────────────────────┘ │
└──────────────────────────────────────────────────┘
```

Figure 1.20. The tutorial's Main Menu dialog box.

5. Choose one of the four lessons, or go straight to a particular topic of interest by selecting Topic List and choosing the topic from the list shown.

If you select a lesson, you see an opening screen that tells you approximately how long it will take and how to use the tutorial. At any time you can select Exit to return to the main menu and exit the tutorial.

6. After you finish the part(s) of the tutorial you want, select Exit Tutorial.

Tip: If you have to exit the tutorial before you complete a lesson, note the particular topic. When you return later, rather than going through the entire lesson again, select Topic List and go straight to the topic you left prematurely. Some lessons start by having you modify an existing file, however, so jumping into the middle of a lesson may not work correctly because the sample text file is not open.

Macros

Selecting Macros from the Help menu calls up an extensive help system for WordPerfect's macros facility, which enables you to record and play back keystrokes and automate common tasks. See Workshop IX, "Macros," for information about WordPerfect macros.

Index

The Help Index is an alphabetized list of features and functions in WordPerfect (see Procedure 1.5).

Procedure 1.5. Using the help Index for an alphabetized list of items you can look up.

1. Select Help (or press F1). Select Index. A Help Index dialog box similar to the one in Figure 1.21 appears.

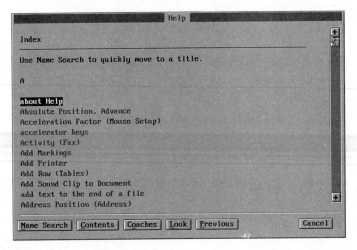

Figure 1.21. The Help Index dialog box.

2. Scroll through the list, or use Name Search to move quickly to the exact feature with which you want help. For example, you might select help about Zoom, pulling up a dialog box similar to the one shown in Figure 1.22.

3. At the end of each help screen, you are likely to find related topics (see Figure 1.23).

4. You can select one of the related topics to delve deeper into the help system or select Previous to go back one level.

5. Press Escape any time in the Help System to exit Help and return to your document.

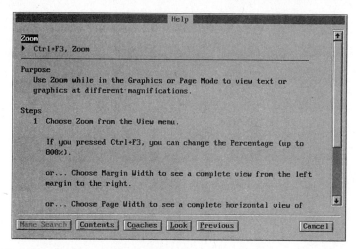

Figure 1.22. A sample help screen for Zoom.

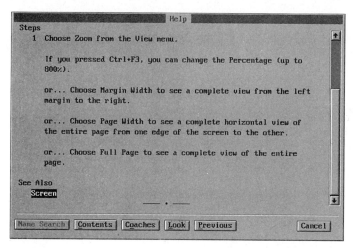

Figure 1.23. Related topics at the end of a help screen.

How Do I

In addition to being able to look up commands and features in an alphabetical list using the Index, you can search the How Do I section for help with Basics, Basic Layout, Advanced Layout, and other categories. Figure 1.24 shows the How Do I dialog box.

Select How Do I from the Help pull-down menu or from Help Contents (F1).

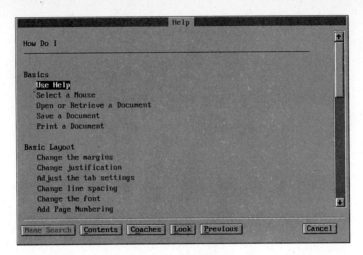

Figure 1.24. The How Do I dialog box in Help.

Coaches

Also available within the WordPerfect 6.0 Help system are "coaches" that interactively walk you through commands (see Procedure 1.6). Unlike the tutorial, the coaches work with you in your own text rather than in sample documents that may be nothing like the documents with which you typically work.

Procedure 1.6. Using Help Coaches for a guiding hand using a specific function within your own document.

1. Select Help and then select Coaches (or press F1) and then select the Coaches button at the bottom of the screen. A dialog box similar to the one shown in Figure 1.25 appears.
2. Highlight the item in the Coaches list you would like to work with.
3. Choose Select (or press Enter).
4. Follow the directions on-screen.

WordPerfect 6.0 has a utility that enables you to create your own coaches. This is particularly useful to people who provide WordPerfect support and consulting to others. The utility can be ordered from WordPerfect Corporation.

Contents

Pressing F1 or selecting Help, Contents calls up the Help Contents dialog box shown in Figure 1.26.

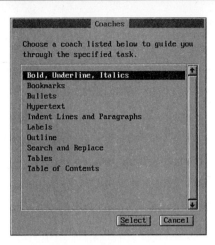

Figure 1.25. The Help Coaches dialog box.

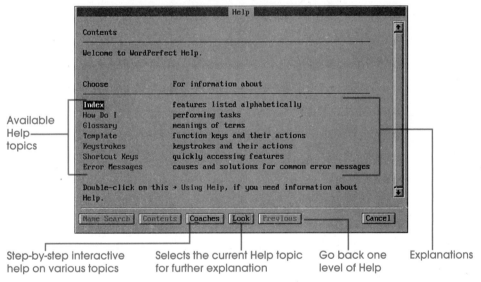

Available Help topics

Step-by-step interactive help on various topics

Selects the current Help topic for further explanation

Go back one level of Help

Explanations

Figure 1.26. The Help Contents dialog box.

Note: F1 is the industry standard help key. If you will be going back and forth between WordPerfect 6.0 and previous versions, you may want to select the WP 5.1 keyboard, setting F1 to be Cancel, F3 to be Help, and Escape to be the Repeat function.

The Help Contents Dialog Box

As you can see in Figure 1.26, the Help Contents dialog box includes some selections available from the Help pull-down menu, as well as other selections.

Glossary

To learn or review WordPerfect-specific and general computer terminology, follow Procedure 1.7.

Procedure 1.7. Using the Help Glossary to look up unfamiliar words and phrases.

1. Select Help and then Contents (or press F1).
2. Highlight Glossary and select Look or press Enter. A dialog box similar to the one in Figure 1.27 appears.

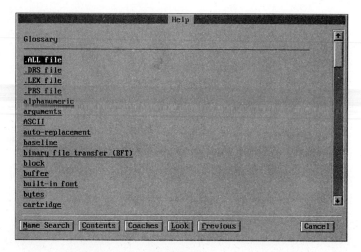

Figure 1.27. The Help Glossary dialog box.

3. Use the arrow keys or the scroll bar to browse through the glossary items, or use Name Search to jump directly to an item in the list.
4. When you have highlighted an item you want to look up, select Look or press Enter. A dialog box with a brief description of the term appears, as shown in Figure 1.28.
5. Continue looking up words as you wish. When you have finished, select Cancel or press Escape to return to your document.

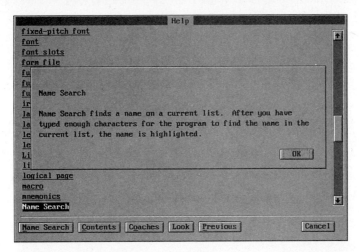

Figure 1.28. A Help Glossary lookup of the word phrase *Name Search*.

Template

Selecting Template from the Help Contents dialog box pulls up a copy of the function key template that comes with WordPerfect 6.0, as shown in Figure 1.29.

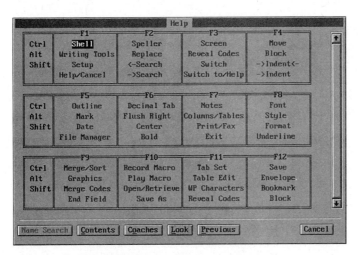

Figure 1.29. The Template dialog box within Help.

Tip: You can also press the Help function key, F1, anywhere within Help to pull up the Template dialog box.

Within this dialog box, you can highlight any of the functions shown on the function keys and select Look to see it, pulling up the same information as when you select that item from the Help Index.

Keystrokes

If you want help with cursor movement, deleting, and other keystrokes, select Keystrokes from the Help Contents dialog box. A Keystrokes dialog box similar to the one shown in Figure 1.30 appears.

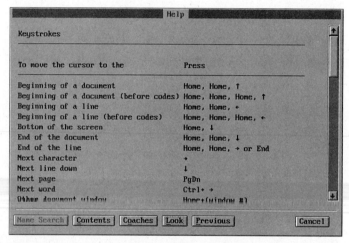

Figure 1.30. The Keystrokes dialog box in Help Contents.

Shortcut Keys

If you want help with shortcut keys, select Shortcut Keys from the Help Contents dialog box. A Shortcut Keys dialog box similar to the one shown in Figure 1.31 appears.

Error Messages

If you want to look up an error message, select Error Messages from the Help Contents dialog box. An Error Messages dialog box similar to the one shown in Figure 1.32 appears.

Looking up an error message pulls up a general, brief explanation of what might cause the message and what you should do if you see that message. For example, selecting Printer Files Not Found shows a screen of information similar to the one shown in Figure 1.33.

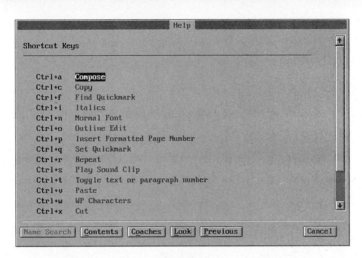

Figure 1.31. The Shortcut Keys dialog box in Help Contents.

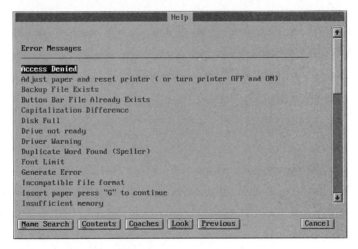

Figure 1.32. The Error Messages help screen.

Tip: Notice that several of the words on the screen are underlined. These are glossary terms that you can look up by highlighting the word and selecting Look or pressing Enter.

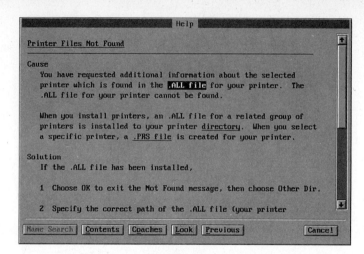

Figure 1.33. Looking up an error message: Printer Files Not Found.

by Susan Hafer

Using the Mouse and the Keyboard

You can use two input devices to interact with WordPerfect: your computer's keyboard and your mouse (if you have one). You can use either to select text, use the menus and dialog boxes, and scroll through the document.

The Mouse

When you install WordPerfect, it guesses what kind of mouse is installed. You can change this at any time using the Setup procedures discussed in this chapter. You may prefer to use the keyboard for most functions and ignore the mouse, but some features, such as the customizable button bars, scroll bars, and the formatting ribbon, are accessible only by using the mouse.

Mouse Setup

WordPerfect has its own built-in mouse drivers, so you can either use the appropriate WordPerfect mouse driver or the one that came with your mouse. If you want to use the mouse with Grammatik or other programs that do not use WordPerfect's setup information, you need to load a mouse driver in your CONFIG.SYS or

AUTOEXEC.BAT startup files. Check your mouse documentation for further information.

You can also make the mouse left-handed (making the right button the primary one and the left one the secondary button), change the mouse double-click interval, or adjust the speed of the mouse's movements.

Procedure 2.1. Setting up the mouse.

1. Select File, Setup (or press Shift+F1).
2. Select Mouse. A dialog box similar to the one shown in Figure 2.1 appears.

You can see which mouse driver is selected in the Type box. If it is set to MOUSE.COM, you must load your mouse driver before invoking WordPerfect (preferably by including it in CONFIG.SYS or AUTOEXEC.BAT).

3. To change the mouse driver selection, choose Type. A dialog box similar to the one shown in Figure 2.2 appears.
4. Select the driver you want (highlight it and choose Select or press Enter), or let WordPerfect make the selection automatically. Or, select Cancel or press Escape to exit the dialog box without making a change.

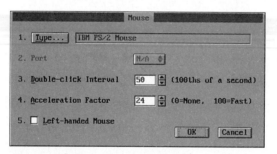

Figure 2.1. The Mouse Setup dialog box.

5. If you want to adjust the double-click speed, select Double-click Interval and edit the number, or use the mouse to click on the up and down arrows to the right of the number. The number is in hundredths of a second. The correct setting depends on your equipment and how fast you like to double-click—raise the number if you're a quick draw; lower it if you double-click at a more leisurely pace—often, however, you'll find your double-click interpreted as two single clicks.

Back in the Mouse Setup dialog box, if you want to adjust how fast the mouse moves around the screen, select Acceleration Factor and edit the number, or use the mouse to click on the up and down arrows to the right of the number. The range of possible numbers is shown to the right: 0 is no acceleration; 100 is the fastest. At 0, you will probably find your mouse moving slower than molasses; at 100, you will probably find yourself equally frustrated because you may lose control of the mouse easily. The correct speed depends on your equipment and your personal preference.

If you want to switch the mouse's left and right mouse button functions, select Left-handed Mouse.

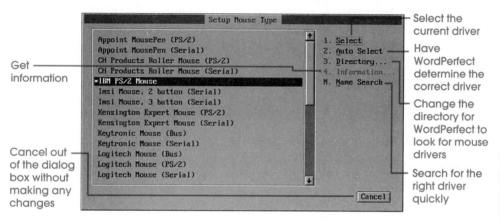

Figure 2.2. The Setup Mouse Type dialog box.

6. Select OK to accept your changes, or select Cancel or press Escape to ignore the changes.

Using the Mouse

To "click" on something with the mouse, use the main, or left, button. If you set up the mouse as left-handed, use the right button. The secondary button behaves much the same as the Escape key from menus and dialog boxes, exiting one or more levels. In the editing screen, clicking the secondary button once highlights the File menu on the menu bar. Clicking it again deselects the menu.

There are several ways you can use the mouse in WordPerfect 6.0. In a text editing screen, clicking once within the text places the insertion point at that point. Clicking twice counts either as two single clicks or as one double-click, depending on how fast you click. Two single clicks count as one: the first moves the insertion point to where you clicked in the text, and the next single click, if in the same place, does the same. A double-click selects the current word. A triple-click selects the current sentence. A quadruple-click selects the current paragraph. You can then copy or move the block of text, change its formatting, delete it, or save it to a file.

You can also use the mouse to scroll through a document if you activate the vertical and, occasionally, horizontal scroll bars. See Table 1.1 in Chapter 1, "The WordPerfect 6.0 Environment," for a description of the mouse functions using a scroll bar.

The Keyboard

The mouse is one way you can interact with WordPerfect, and the keyboard is the other—the one that is essential. You could get along without the mouse, but not without the keyboard! As you type text or commands in WordPerfect, you may find some keystrokes inconvenient. If this is due to the physical construction of your keyboard (laptops with smaller than standard keys), WordPerfect isn't much help, but if reassigning keystrokes would help, WordPerfect enables you to select from existing keyboard designs or create your own.

Setting Up the Keyboard

Although WordPerfect has the keyboard layout already set up when you install the program, you can reassign a wide variety of functions to the keyboard keys. You can change the QWERTY-style layout of the letters to an ABC or Dvorak style, reassign the function keys, and assign macros to any allowed keystroke combination. (For information about customizing the keyboard, see Appendix B, "Customizing WordPerfect 6.0.")

Using the Keyboard

The usual keys (alphabet characters, Shift, and so on) do the usual things, unless you remap them as discussed in Appendix B. The basic arrow keys do what you would expect: move up a line, down a line, and left and right by one character. More advanced cursor movement, using the original keyboard layout, is included in Table 2.1.

You can also use the keyboard to access WordPerfect's menus and dialog boxes. A mouse is required for the button bars, scroll bars, and ribbon, as explained in Chapter 1.

Tip: You can use **R**epeat to do a set of cursor movement keystrokes quickly. For example, select Edit, Repeat, type a number to replace the default of eight, then press Enter. Next, press Ctrl+right arrow to move forward by the number of words you entered (or by eight words if you did not change the number).

To access the menu bar at the top of the screen using the keyboard, press Alt plus the mnemonic letter for the menu you want. Alt+F accesses the **F**ile menu, for example, and Alt+O accesses the F**o**nt menu.

Tip: By default, just pressing the Alt key and releasing it does nothing. If you are accustomed to other programs that activate the File menu when you do this, you can set up WordPerfect that way. Select View, Screen Setup, Screen Options, and, if it is not checked, the Alt key activates menus. Exit the dialog box.

Caution: If you have an older computer, you may find that some of the cursor movement keystrokes (Ctrl+up arrow and Ctrl+down arrow, for example) do not perform as "advertised" in WordPerfect 6.0. If so, you can use the keyboard mapping function described in Appendix B to map these keystrokes for your computer.

Tip: Use the Goto function (Edit, Goto; or Ctrl+Home) to move the insertion point to the beginning of a particular page (Ctrl+Home, 11, Enter goes to page 11); to the next occurrence of a character (for example, Ctrl+Home, e, Enter goes to the next occurrence of the letter e; this feature is case-sensitive), punctuation mark (Ctrl+Home, Enter, for example, moves to the next hard return), or to the previous location of the insertion point (Ctrl+Home, Ctrl+Home).

The Original Keyboard

The original, unmodified keyboard layout consists of the function key layout.

Table 2.1. Cursor movement keystrokes in the original keyboard layout.

To move to:	Press:
Previous character	←
Next line down	↓
Previous line up	↑

continues

Table 2.1. Continued

To move to:	Press:
Top of Next page	`PgDn`
Top Previous page	`PgUp`
Next word	`Ctrl`+`→`
Previous word	`Ctrl`+`←`
Next paragraph	`Ctrl`+`↓`
Previous paragraph	`Ctrl`+`↑`
Top of the screen	`Home`, `↑`
Bottom of the screen	`Home`, `↓`
Beginning of a document (after codes)	`Home`, `Home`, `↑`
End of the document	`Home`, `Home`, `↓`
Beginning of a document (before codes)	`Home`, `Home`, `Home`, `↑`
Left edge of text on screen	`Home`, `←`
Right edge of text on screen	`Home`, `→`
Beginning of a line (after codes)	`Home`, `Home`, `←`
End of the line (before codes)	`Home`, `Home`, `→`
Beginning of a line (before codes)	`Home`, `Home`, `Home`, `←`
End of a line (after codes)	`Home`, `Home`, `Home`, `→`
Other document window	`Home`, (window #)
Specified Page	`Ctrl`+`Home`, page #, `↵Enter`

Tip: If you are a dyed-in-the-wool WordPerfect 5.1 user, you may want to consider using the WordPerfect 5.1 Cursor Movement found in File, Setup, Environment. Activating this selection makes small changes, such as making Ctrl+Up/Down move to the beginning or end of the current paragraph if the insertion point is not already at the beginning or end, then move to the next/previous paragraph.

This selection also causes the insertion point to reflect when you are moving through codes; the insertion point does not move to the next character if a code was just passed. This allows you to delete codes without first having to activate Reveal Codes—you can move the insertion point slowly through your text, noting when the insertion

> insertion point slowly through your text, noting when the insertion point is told to move to the right one character and does not appear to do so. Probably a code was just passed. Press Backspace to delete the code if you so wish. If a code was indeed there, a dialog box opens, asking if you would like to delete the code and telling you which code it is.

If you change to a different keyboard and want to go back to this original layout, use the following steps:

1. Select File, Setup (or press Shift+F1, unless the keyboard you are using redefines Shift+F1). If you use the pull-down menus, you will see something similar to the one shown in Figure 2.3. If you use Shift+F1, you will see something similar to the one shown in Figure 2.4.

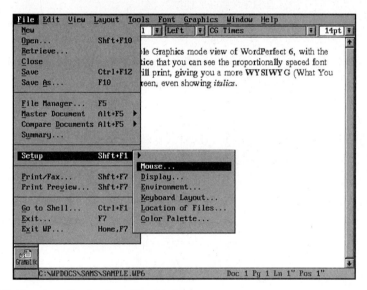

Figure 2.3. The result of using File, Setup.

Notice that the Setup dialog box shows you which keyboard is currently selected (the cascading menus do not).

2. Select Keyboard. The Keyboard Layout dialog box appears, as shown in Figure 2.5. The currently selected keyboard layout is marked with an asterisk.

37

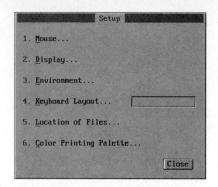

Figure 2.4. The result of using Shift+F1 for Setup.

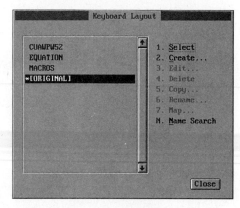

Figure 2.5. The Keyboard Layout dialog box.

3. Use the arrow keys to highlight [Original], and press Enter to select the original keyboard layout. If you used Shift+F1, press Enter again to close the Setup dialog box.

CUA Keyboard

Those who use Windows products may prefer to use the CUA (common user access) keyboard layout. Using the CUA keyboard, Alt+F4 is Close rather than Block, for example, and you can select (block) text by simply pressing Shift at one end of a block and moving the insertion point with the keyboard to the other end.

To select the CUA keyboard, follow the procedure for selecting the original keyboard, but highlight CUAWPW52 (corresponding to WordPerfect for Windows Version 5.2) instead of [Original] in the Keyboard Layout dialog box. To see a complete list of all keystroke assignments, choose Edit rather than Select from the Keyboard Layout dialog box and scroll through the list shown.

WordPerfect 5.1 Keyboard

You can set up WordPerfect 6.0 to revert its function key layout to that of Version 5.1. This changes F1 from Help to Cancel, Escape from Cancel to Repeat, and F3 from Switch To to Help. This is particularly useful for those who use WordPerfect 5.1 and 6.0. For others, it is probably better to get accustomed to using the new layout, which more closely matches the industry standard.

> **Caution:** F3 was the Repeat function using the standard keyboard in WordPerfect 5.1. Using the original keyboard layout, you can use the shortcut key Ctrl+R or the pull-down menu Edit, Repeat. If you use it often, you may want to remap F3 to Repeat, or be aware of the change and get used to the new layout.

1. Select File, Setup (or press Shift+F1, unless your current keyboard layout redefines Shift+F1).
2. Select Environment.
3. If the checkbox for WordPerfect 5.1 Keyboard (F1 = Cancel) is empty, select it.
4. Select OK or press Enter. If you used Shift+F1 to access Setup, select Close or press Enter to return to your document.

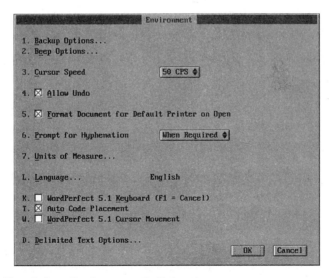

Figure 2.6. The Setup Environment dialog box.

Caution: If you are using the CUA keyboard layout, do not use the 5.1 keyboard. The CUA keyboard overrides these settings and the results are confusing.

Note: You also see available keyboard layouts MACROS, which contains useful shortcuts (Alt+I to capitalize the initial letter in the current word, for example), and EQUATION. (See Workshop X, "Merge," and Workshop XI, "Advanced Features," for more information about macros and WordPerfect's Equation Editor, respectively.)

3

by Susan Hafer

Working with Files

As you type a document, WordPerfect stores it in memory. If there is not enough memory available, WordPerfect uses overflow files to store the parts of your document that don't fit in memory, swapping sections as needed as you move from one part of a long document to another. Sometimes, once you've created a document, you may just want to print it and forget it. Usually, however, you'll want to save it on your hard disk or a floppy disk so you can work with it another time. And, unless you are very short on disk space, you'll want to take advantage of WordPerfect's automatic backups to protect yourself from losing updates to documents (or even entire documents in case of a power failure or other unexpected mishap).

Creating a Basic Document

When you first open WordPerfect 6.0, you may adjust the screen settings to your liking, set up special formatting, and so on—or you may simply begin typing a new document, accepting the default formatting. You can always go back later and change the formatting as you see fit.

By default, you have one-inch margins at the top and bottom of each page and on the left and right sides for 8.5-inch by 11-inch paper, using the default printer definition and its default font you set up when you installed WordPerfect. (See Workshop III, "Formatting," for details about changing the formatting.)

> **Tip:** WordPerfect uses a file header to store these document defaults, along with other information pertinent to the document. As a result, the file's size is larger than you might expect, particularly for short documents. The size of the file header varies, depending on the printer selected, the complexity of the document, and the printer's capabilities.

As you type a paragraph, WordPerfect automatically wraps words that don't fit within the margin to the next line. When WordPerfect wraps text to the next line, it creates a soft return. A soft return automatically changes to a space as you edit text and the end of the line changes.

Automatic page breaks (soft pages) are shown as a single line stretching from the left to right margins. If you force WordPerfect to begin a new page using a hard page (Ctrl+Enter), the line stretching from the left to right margins is a double line. As described in Chapter 1, "The WordPerfect Environment," the status line shows the current position of the insertion point—this is especially helpful when you have trouble finding the insertion point in a screenful of text.

By default, WordPerfect works in Insert mode. Text is automatically inserted before the insertion point with the existing text flowing after. You can switch to an Overwrite mode, called Typeover, by pressing Insert, and you can switch back to Insert mode by pressing Insert again.

Saving Files and Exiting

Now that you know some basics about creating a document, let's look at how to save a document to a file on disk so you can later retrieve the document to edit and print. You will also want to know how to exit WordPerfect back to DOS, the WordPerfect Shell program, or Windows.

> **Tip:** Save your work often, especially for complex documents that would be difficult or impossible to re-create should your computer lose power or crash.

Save

To save a new document or a WordPerfect 6.0 document that you opened or retrieved in WordPerfect 6.0 format, use the Save function.

To save a document, select Save from the File menu, or press Ctrl+F12. If the document already exists on disk when you ask to save it, a dialog box flashes briefly on-screen, saying that WordPerfect is saving and showing the path and filename for the file being saved.

Caution: Users of WordPerfect 5.1 and earlier versions expect the F10 key to correspond to the Save function. Instead, F10 corresponds to Save As, described in the following section. The Save function is now Ctrl+F12.

When you save a new document that has never been saved to disk, you will see a dialog box offering many options for saving your document and a note saying (Document has been modified). The simplest response is to type the name for the new file and press Enter or select OK to have the file stored in the current directory. (For information on the options available, see the next section.)

Caution: If you are saving a document that was in a format other than WordPerfect, it is saved automatically in its original format, not in WordPerfect 6.0 format. (To save it in WordPerfect 6.0 format, see the following section.)

Tip: If you plan to exit the document immediately after saving it, you can save time by using the Exit function rather than the Save function.

Save As

Using Save As rather than Save gives you more flexibility. You can select Directory, for example, or a format other than WordPerfect 6.0.

Procedure 3.1. Using Save As.

1. Select Save As from the File menu, press F10, or click on the Save As button in the WPMAIN button bar. A dialog box similar to the one shown in Figure 3.1 appears.

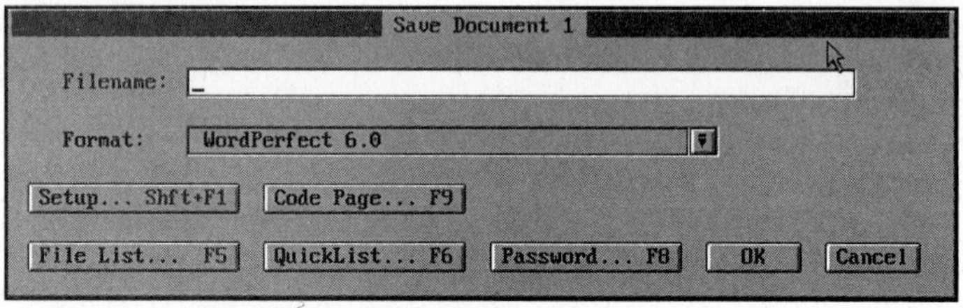

```
┌─────────────────────── Save Document 1 ───────────────────────┐
│                                                               │
│  Filename:  ┌──────────────────────────────────────────┐      │
│             └──────────────────────────────────────────┘      │
│                                                               │
│  Format:    ┌──────────────────────────────────────┐ ┌─┐      │
│             │ WordPerfect 6.0                      │ │▼│      │
│             └──────────────────────────────────────┘ └─┘      │
│                                                               │
│  ┌─ Setup... Shft+F1 ─┐  ┌─ Code Page... F9 ─┐                │
│                                                               │
│  ┌ File List... F5 ┐ ┌ QuickList... F6 ┐ ┌ Password... F8 ┐ ┌ OK ┐ ┌ Cancel ┐ │
└───────────────────────────────────────────────────────────────┘
```

Figure 3.1. The Save As dialog box.

2. Make your selections from the dialog box.

   To change the name of the file being saved, edit the filename.

   To save the document in a format other than WordPerfect 6.0 (Word-Perfect 5.1, for example, or ASCII), select Format to choose from a list of available file formats. Be sure to change the filename if you select a new format.

   If you want to assign or change a password for this document, select Password (F8). (Passwords are discussed in Chapter 26, "File Manager.")

   If you are saving this document in ASCII format and it contains non-English characters, you may want to change the Code Page to match the language; select Code Page (F9).

   To select a different directory for the file, either edit the filename or select a directory from the Quick List (F6) or File List (F5).

   To change the defaults for file saving, select Setup (Shift+F1), then uncheck (or check) the Fast Save box or change the default file format. Select OK when you have finished making changes, or select Cancel to not make any changes.

3. Select OK to accept your changes and save the file.

   If the name of the file or location is not changed, or if there is another file with the name you selected here, a dialog box similar to the one shown in Figure 3.2 appears, asking if you want to replace the existing file with the current document.

   Selecting Yes saves the document, replacing the existing file by the same name. Selecting No, the default, returns you to the Save As dialog box (the file is not saved).

Figure 3.2. The Replace File dialog box.

 Tip: If you plan to exit the document immediately after saving it, save time by using the Exit function rather than the Save **As** function.

Closing and Exiting

When you are finished working with a document or with WordPerfect, close the document or exit the program.

Closing a Document

When you are finished working with a document and want to work on another, close the current document, leaving a cleared editing screen for another document.

Procedure 3.2. Closing the current document.
1. Select Close from the File menu. If the document has not changed since the last save, the document is cleared immediately. If the document has changed, a dialog box similar to the one shown in Figure 3.3 appears.

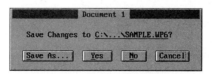

Figure 3.3. The Save dialog box for a File: Close.

2. Select Yes to save the updated file, No to undo any changes, or Cancel (Escape) to return to the document. You can also choose Save As to save the document under another name, perhaps in a different location or format.

45

Exiting a Document

Procedure 3.3. Exiting a document.

1. Select Exit from the **F**ile menu, or press F7. A dialog box similar to the one shown in Figure 3.4 appears.

Figure 3.4. The Exit Document dialog box.

If the document has changed since the last time you saved it, a `Document has been modified` message appears between the save question and the buttons along the bottom of the dialog box.

2. Make your selection:

To save the document under the same name, select Yes.

To save the document under a different name or in a different drive or directory, select Save As. (Refer to the previous section for information about the Save As dialog box.)

If you do not want to save the document, select No.

If you change your mind about Exiting and want to return to the document you are editing, select Cancel or press Escape.

3. If you saved the file or selected No, the next dialog box asks one of two questions: whether you want to exit WordPerfect or the current document editing screen. If you have more than one document open, a dialog box similar to the one shown in Figure 3.5 appears. If you have only one document open, a dialog box similar to the one shown in Figure 3.6 appears.

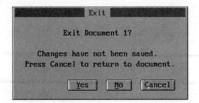

Figure 3.5. The Exit Document dialog box if more than one document is open and you have made changes to the document since the last save.

If you saved the document in Step 2, the dialog box would contain the same information as in Figures 3.5 or 3.6, but without the two lines about changes not having been saved.

4. Select Cancel or press Escape to return to your document. Select Yes to exit WordPerfect or the current document editing screen. Select No to stay in WordPerfect with a blank, new document screen.

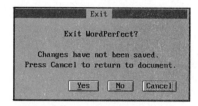

Figure 3.6. The Exit WordPerfect dialog box if only one document is open and you have made changes to the document since the last save.

Exiting WordPerfect

To exit WordPerfect quickly, saving any changes to documents as you do, use the Exit command.

Procedure 3.4. Exiting WordPerfect.

1. Select Exit from the File menu, or press Home, F7. A dialog box similar to the one shown in Figure 3.7 or Figure 3.8 appears.

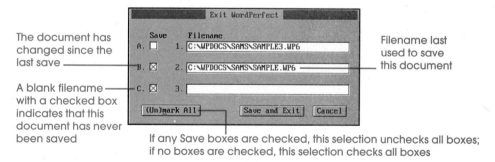

The document has changed since the last save

A blank filename with a checked box indicates that this document has never been saved

Filename last used to save this document

If any Save boxes are checked, this selection unchecks all boxes; if no boxes are checked, this selection checks all boxes

Figure 3.7. The Exit WordPerfect dialog box, showing files that have changed since the last save.

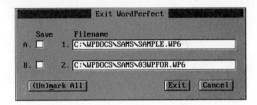

Figure 3.8. The Exit WordPerfect dialog box, showing only files that have not changed since they were last saved.

2. All currently open documents are shown. Normally you will just press Enter to accept the defaults and exit WordPerfect, but you can make changes (changing the filename, for example, for the equivalent of a Save As) before selecting Save and Exit or Exit.

Opening Files

When you first enter WordPerfect or close a document, you can either open an existing document or create a new one.

Creating New Documents

When you first enter WordPerfect, you can begin typing and formatting a new document without a command, because a blank document screen is automatically opened. However, you may work with a document, leave it open, and open a new screen to create a new document.

To open a new document screen, select File, New.

> **Tip:** If you have only one document open and want to open another, you can use Window, Switch (Shift+F3) to switch to a new window. The result is the same as selecting File, New unless you already have more than one document open.

Opening or Retrieving an Existing File

WordPerfect has two functions to open a document that has been stored on disk: Open and Retrieve. Use **O**pen to bring a file onto a blank screen; use **R**etrieve to pull a file into the current document. If the current document screen is unused, **O**pen and **R**etrieve do the same thing.

Procedure 3.5. Opening an existing file.

1. Select File, Open.

2. Tell WordPerfect which file you want to open. You have several options for doing so.

   ▲ Type the filename (including its path, if the file is not in the current directory), then press Enter or select OK.

   ▲ Click on the down arrow just to the right of the Filename box, or press the down arrow key on your keyboard. A list of the last four documents opened in WordPerfect appears. Select one of the files and press Enter.

   ▲ Choose File Manager (F5) for a complete listing of files and directories, or QuickList (F6) for a personalized listing of files and directories, and find the file you want to open. (See Chapters 26 and 27 for information about using the File Manager and the QuickList.)

The document is opened. If no other documents are open, this file is opened into Doc 1, the main editing screen. If there is already a document in Doc 1, this file is opened into the next available editing screen of the nine allowed in Word-Perfect 6.0.

Procedure 3.6. Retrieving one document into another.

1. Place the insertion point in the current document where you want the other file retrieved into the current text.

2. Save the file you are working on (in case you accidentally retrieve one document into another or retrieve the wrong file).

3. Select File, Retrieve.

4. Tell WordPerfect which file to retrieve into the current document. You have several options:

   ▲ Type the filename (including its path, if the file is not in the current directory). Press Enter or select OK.

   ▲ Click on the down arrow just to the right of the Filename box, or press the down arrow key on your keyboard. A list of the last four documents opened in WordPerfect appears. Select one of the files and press Enter.

   ▲ Choose File Manager (F5) for a complete listing of files and directories, or QuickList (F6) for a personalized listing of files and directories, and find the file you want to retrieve. (See Chapters 26 and 27 for information about using the File Manager and the QuickList.)

The file is retrieved into the current document without further prompting or notification.

Tip: If you retrieve the wrong file or retrieved the file in the wrong location, select Edit, Undo (or press Ctrl+Z). If the last editing action you performed was the retrieve, the file retrieved into the current document is removed.

Using QuickMark to Find Your Last Position

When you save or exit a document, WordPerfect 6.0 automatically inserts a bookmark, called a QuickMark, where the insertion point was located when you requested the save or exit. When you open or retrieve an existing document, you can have the insertion point jump to the place where you were last working by finding the Quickmark. This is extremely convenient, especially for large documents.

Procedure 3.7. Using a Quickmark to go immediately to where you were last working in a document.

1. Select Edit, Bookmark (or press Shift+F12). A dialog box similar to the one shown in Figure 3.9 appears.

2. Highlight the Quickmark and select Find from the menu, or select the Find Quickmark button at the bottom of the dialog box.

Tip: All of the above can be accomplished in one keystroke: Ctrl+F.

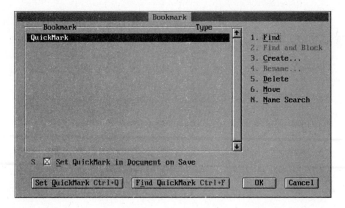

Figure 3.9. The Bookmark dialog box.

The document scrolls to the appropriate screenful of text, and the insertion point returns to its last location when you last saved the document.

 Tip: In the Bookmark dialog box shown in Figure 3.9, you can control whether a Quickmark is automatically inserted every time you save or exit a document with Set Quickmark in Document on Save.

Protecting Your Work Using Backups

Backups, or copies of your files, are a critical process in your everyday work. Perhaps you will never need them, but the likelihood of your making a disastrous mistake (saving an empty screen as a file or getting overzealous in cleaning up your hard drive) or the computer's hard drive crashing goes up significantly as you work under stress (deadlines looming ominously, for example).

There are three types of backups for WordPerfect users:

▲ Automatic backups every few minutes in case of power failure.

▲ Automatic backups of older versions when you save a document.

▲ Backups you make to floppy disk (or another backup media, such as tape) in case your hard disk crashes.

Saving Documents to a Floppy Disk

You should use a backup program to make archival copies of all data stored on your hard drive, but it takes time, and time is often a scarce resource. Many people whose hard disks crash have no recent backups for this very reason. You may want to make a habit of storing all your documents on a floppy disk as you work.

Procedure 3.8. Saving a backup copy of a document to a floppy disk.

1. After finishing your work with a document, save it to the hard disk as usual.

2. Use File, Exit WP or F7, or Home, F7, depending on whether you want to exit the current document and continue using WordPerfect or exit WordPerfect altogether. (See the previous section for details about the Exit commands.)

3. If you used File, Exit (or F7), select Save As from the dialog box that appears. If you used File, Exit (or Home, F7), the Save box for the file in question should not be checked, because you just saved the document to the hard disk.

4. Edit the Filename box to change the path for the filename to be the A: or B: drive.

5. Press Enter.

   If you were in the Save As dialog box, pressing Enter was the same as selecting OK. The document will be saved and you will see the Exit dialog box. (See the previous section if you are not sure which selection to choose.)

If you are in the Exit WordPerfect dialog box rather than the Save As dialog box, pressing Enter moves you to the Save and Exit button and marks the file to be saved. Press Enter to select Save and Exit.

Using Automatic Backups in Case of Power Failure or a Lockup

When you install WordPerfect, Automatic Backups are set to back up your work every 10 minutes. If you find this is not a good interval for your work style, use this procedure to change to whatever interval you want.

An automatic backup file is named WP{WP}.BK1 (for text in the main editing screen—Doc 1) through WP{WP}.BK9 for text in the ninth (and last) editing screen (Doc 9). (See Chapter 6, "Working with Multiple Documents," for more information about the nine editing screens.) These backup files are automatically erased when you exit WordPerfect in the normal manner. However, if your computer locks up or the power fails and a normal exit is not an option, these backup files are available when you start using WordPerfect again.

Procedure 3.9. Adjusting the automatic timed backups.

1. From the document editing screen, select File, Setup (or press Shift+F1).

2. Select Environment, Backup Options.

3. If the Timed Document Backup check box is empty, select it to turn on the automatic backup feature. To turn off automatic backups, uncheck the box and skip the next step.

4. Set Minutes Between Backups to whatever number of minutes you want.

5. Select OK or Close as many times as it takes to return to your document.

If you use automatic backups and experience a power failure or a computer lockup, WordPerfect automatically asks you what you want to do with the backup files, using the dialog box shown in Figure 3.10.

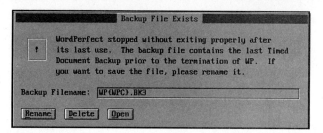

Figure 3.10. The dialog box you see when you invoke WordPerfect if you do not exit WordPerfect normally and use automatic backups.

If you know the backup file is no use to you, choose Delete. Generally, however, it's a good idea to check the file before you make such a decision.

To see the backup file, you need to open or rename it. If you open the file, WordPerfect opens it as an unnamed document. You can exit without saving if you don't want it or save it, replacing the older version of the file by the same name.

If you selected Rename from the dialog box, the insertion point moves to the Backup filename box so you can assign a new name for this file. You can then use List Files to look at the file before deciding what you want to do with it.

Caution: The file is stored in the same location as the original backup file, even if you type a different path as part of the name. WordPerfect ignores the path and uses the filename you specify. To find out where the backup files are stored, look in File, Setup (Shift+F1), Location of Files, Backup Files.

Backing up Original Documents When Saving or Exiting

Whenever you save a document, replacing an existing document by the same name, WordPerfect makes a temporary backup of the existing file under a different name (the same name with a BK! extension) in the same directory as the original file. If the file save is successful, this temporary file is deleted; if the save is not successful for any reason, WordPerfect then has the opportunity to reinstate the original file by renaming the temporary file.

Tip: If you have disk utilities or DOS 5's UNDELETE program, you can often undelete a BK! file to recover a recent version of a file that was lost or damaged.

You can elect to have this temporary backup file not deleted at the end of the save process. The advantage is that you have the two latest copies of a document stored on your disk. The disadvantage is that you use twice as much disk space.

Procedure 3.10. Setting up WordPerfect to make a backup copy of a file before saving a new version of that file.

1. From the document editing screen, select File, Setup (or press Shift+F1).

2. Select Environment, Backup Options.

3. By default, the check box for Backup **O**riginal Document (.BK!) on Save or Exit is blank. Select it to turn it on.

4. Select OK or Close as many times as it takes to return to your document.

Caution: If you have more than one file with the same name, but with different file extenstions (QUIZ.QUE and QUIZ.ANS, for example), only one at a time can have a BK! backup file.

4

by Susan Hafer

Basic Editing Skills

There are many ways to edit a document. As you move from a rough draft to a final copy of a document, you delete text, move it from one location in a document to another (or to another document entirely), and copy the text to more than one location in the document.

Deleting Text

You can delete text one character at a time, one word at a time, or in larger chunks. To delete a character, press Backspace to delete the character just before the cursor, or Delete to erase the character just after the cursor.

You can also delete text by blocking (selecting) it and then erasing the block, as described in Procedure 4.1.

Caution: Pressing Insert in an editing screen toggles between Insert mode (the default) and Typeover mode, where typing text over- writes existing text in your document. If Typeover mode is on, pressing Delete behaves as it does in Insert mode, but Backspace does not. Backspacing in Typeover mode erases characters and leaves a space in its place.

Table 4.1. Deleting more than just one character with a single keystroke.

Press	To Delete
Ctrl+Backspace or Ctrl+Delete	The current word
Ctrl+End	From the current position to the end of the current line
Ctrl+PageDown	From the current position to the end of the current page
Home, Backspace	From the current position to the begin- ning of the current word, but not the space before the word
Home, Delete	From the current position to the end of the current word, including the space after the word

Procedure 4.1. Blocking text and deleting it.

1. Place the insertion point at the beginning or end of the block of text you want to delete.
2. Turn Block on by selecting Edit, Block (or pressing Alt+F4 or F12), using the original keyboard layout. As a reminder, the status line echoes "Block on" in place of the font or filename.
3. Move the insertion point to the other end of the block. The text is high- lighted, as shown in Figure 4.1. (Ignore the Undelete dialog box for now.)
4. Press Backspace or Delete.

Tip: You can extend a block using any of the normal cursor movement keys or key combinations, but it's often faster to press a character (letters are case-sensitive) to extend the block forward to the next occurrence of that character. Pressing Enter while Block is on, for example, blocks to the next hard return, which is normally at the end of the paragraph.

Tip: If you prefer using the mouse rather than the keyboard, block the text by clicking and holding the left mouse button at one end of the block, dragging the mouse to the other end of the block, and releasing the mouse button.

Caution: Users upgrading from an earlier release of WordPerfect may expect a confirmation at this point. However, there is none, WordPerfect 6.0 simply deletes the block. If you made a mistake, you can undelete the block or undo the deletion. (This is described in the next section in this chapter.)

Tip: If you use the keystrokes in Table 4.1 to do several deletes in a row without moving the insertion point between deletions, the deleted text is appended to the text already deleted, rather than each deletion replacing the previous one. Once you move the insertion point, the text thus far deleted is counted as a single unit; further deletions will not be appended, but will instead begin a new block of deletions. This is sometimes quicker than blocking the text to delete.

Undeleting and Undoing

If you accidentally erase some text, WordPerfect 6.0 lets you undelete the last three deletions. WordPerfect 6.0 also has an undo feature that can, among other things, undelete text you just deleted.

Using Undo

The Undo function undoes the last editing action you did in this document. This may be text you entered that will be removed, text you erased that will be undeleted, text you pasted that will be removed, or text you moved using drag and drop that is returned to its original location.

Procedure 4.2. Undoing your last editing action.

1. Select Edit, Undo (or press Ctrl+Z). The last editing action is undone.
2. If the Undo is not what you expected, you can undo the undo by repeating Edit, Undo (or Ctrl+Z).

Using Undelete

If you have deleted text and decide to undelete it either in its original location or in a new one (or both), even in another document, you can use Undelete, provided that the text in question was one of the last three deletions.

Procedure 4.3. Undeleting one of the last three deletions.

1. Place the insertion point where you want to undelete the text.
2. Select Edit, Undelete (or press Escape). The Undelete dialog box appears (see Figure 4.1), and the last deleted text appears, highlighted, at the insertion point.

   If you see the Repeat dialog box, you have the WordPerfect 5.1 keyboard selected. Use F1 for Cancel rather than Escape.
3. If the text you want to undelete is not the text shown, it was not the last text deleted. Select Previous Deletion to see the text deleted before the text now shown. Continue to select Previous Deletion until the text you want appears, or until you have cycled through all three of the last deletions.
4. If the text you want is not one of the last three selections and, therefore, not in the undelete buffer, select Cancel or press Escape to abort the undeletion. Otherwise, select Restore to have the highlighted text restored from the undelete buffer.

Tip: If you cannot undelete text because more recent deletions have cleared it from the undelete buffer, try copying and pasting the text from the last saved version of this file or from the backup file.

Figure 4.1. A blocked section of text and the Undelete dialog box.

When to Use Which

Because there is some overlap between Undo and Undelete, when do you use which function? If you just completed a task (typing text, deleting text, using drag and drop, copying and pasting text), Undo takes care of you. To undelete something after some time has passed, or undelete something in more than one place, use Undelete.

 Caution: You cannot undelete text that was removed using Undo.

Copying and Moving Text

As you may have guessed, one way to copy or move text within your document is to use Undelete, or a combination of Undo and Undelete. To copy text, you could delete it, undo the deletion, then place the cursor where you would like a copy of the text and use Undelete. To move text, do the same but without first using Undo to return the text to its original location. There are simpler, more elegant ways to copy and move text, however.

59

Drag and Drop

For users who prefer to use the mouse rather than the keyboard, WordPerfect 6.0's drag and drop feature is very convenient.

Procedure 4.4. Using drag and drop to move or copy a block of text within a document.

1. Block the text you wish to copy or move. You can do this with either the mouse or the keyboard.

2. With the block of text selected, click and hold down the mouse button.

   As soon as you move the mouse out of the selected block of text, a message is echoed at the bottom of the screen: `Release mouse button to move block`. In Graphics or Page mode (see Chapter 1, "The WordPerfect Environment"), you have another reminder: the mouse pointer changes from a simple arrow to an icon representing the move, as shown in Figure 4.2.

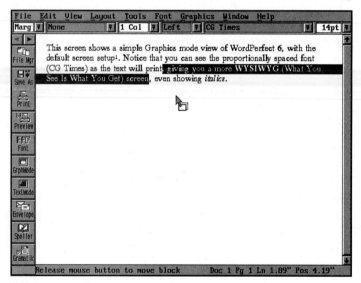

Figure 4.2. The mouse pointer reflects the drag and drop move.

3. Move the mouse pointer to the location where you want the selected text moved or copied to. If that location is not on the current screen, drag the mouse to the top or bottom of the screen to have your document scroll up or down to the desired location.

Caution: You cannot drag and drop text across documents. Use one of the other methods to copy or move text from one document to another.

4. To copy the selected text rather than move it, press and hold the `Ctrl` key at any time while the mouse button is still down. The reminder message in the status line changes to read `copy block` rather than `move block`, and the mouse pointer changes from a drag and drop move icon to a drag and drop copy icon, as shown in Figure 4.3.

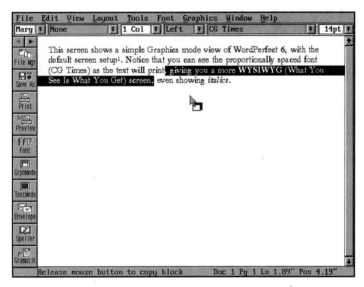

Figure 4.3. The drag and drop mouse pointer reflects the copy request.

5. With the mouse pointer in the new location, release the mouse button. The selected text is moved or copied.

 Tip: If at any point before releasing the mouse button you change your mind about the drag and drop and want to cancel it, place the mouse pointer within the selected text. The reminder in the status line changes to `Block on`. When you release the mouse button, the text will be in its original location and Block will be turned off.

Cut and Paste

You can use Cut and Paste to move text within a document or between documents (see Procedure 4.5).

Procedure 4.5. Using cut and paste to move text within a document or between documents.

1. Block the text you want to cut.
2. Select Edit, Cut and Paste (or press Ctrl+Del). The blocked text disappears, and a reminder note appears in the status line: Move cursor; press Enter to retrieve.
3. Move the insertion point to the location where you want the cut text to appear. Or, if you change your mind about pasting the text now, press Escape. You can later paste the text separately, as long as you have used no other cut or copy commands in the meantime.
4. Press Enter.

Tip: You can paste the text into another document by switching to another document editing window before pressing Enter. (See Chapter 6, "Working with Multiple Documents," for information about using different windows.)

Tip: Pasting the text into the document at this location might create the need to insert a hard return, which is generated by pressing **Enter** to open up space for this new text. However, you must paste the text into the document first. The insertion point is left at the beginning of the pasted text, so when placing the insertion point in Step 3, place it so you can add one or more hard returns before the new text rather than at the end of it.

You may sometimes find that simply pressing Enter to retrieve your copied text is more of a hindrance than a help, because you find you need to insert a hard return but can't without restoring the selected text. For those times, use one of the other methods for moving text, such as the following procedure, which describes using cut and paste separately.

Procedure 4.6. Using cut alone, then using paste later.

1. Block the text you want to cut.

2. Select Edit, Cut (or press Ctrl+X).

3. Move the insertion point to the location where you want the cut text to appear. You may make other editing changes to your document as long as you do not use the Cut or Copy function in the meantime. Only the latest cut can be pasted.

> **Tip:** You can paste the text into another document by switching to another document editing window before pressing Enter. (See Chapter 6 for information about using different windows.)

4. Select Edit, Paste (or press Ctrl+V).

Copy and Paste

Parallel to the cut and paste procedures just described are very similar methods that copy and paste, leaving a block of text in its original location as well as in a new one.

Procedure 4.7. Using copy and paste to copy text within a document or between documents.

1. Block the text you want to copy.

2. Select Edit, Copy and Paste (or press Ctrl+Ins). The blocked text remains unchanged, and a reminder note appears in the status line: `Move cursor; press Enter to retrieve`.

3. Move the insertion point to the location where you want the copied text to appear. Or, if you change your mind about making a copy of the text, press Escape. You can later paste the text separately, as long as you have used no other Cut or Copy commands in the meantime.

4. Press Enter.

> **Tip:** You can paste the text into another document by switching to another document editing window before pressing Enter. (See Chapter 6 for information about using different windows.)

Tip: Pasting the text into the document at this location might create the need to insert a hard return, which is generated by pressing Enter to open up space for this new text. However, you must paste the text into the document first. The insertion point is left at the beginning of the pasted text, so when placing the insertion point in Step 3, place it so you can add one or more hard returns before the new text rather than at the end of it.

You may sometimes find that simply pressing Enter to retrieve your copied text is more of a hindrance than a help, because you find you need to insert a hard return but can't without restoring the selected text. For those times, use one of the other methods for moving text, such as the following procedure, which describes using cut and paste separately.

Procedure 4.8. Using copy alone, then pasting later.

1. Block the text you want to copy.
2. Select Edit, Copy (or press Ctrl+C).
3. Move the insertion point to the location where you want the copied text to appear. You may make other editing changes to your document as long as you do not use the Cut or Copy function in the meantime. Only the latest copy can be pasted.
4. Select Edit, Paste (or press Ctrl+V).

The Move Function

The Move function combines many of the functions available from the Edit menu, adding a few selection options not otherwise available. You can either use the Move function by first blocking the text you want to work with or by beginning with the Move function and instructing it whether you want it to select the current sentence, paragraph, or page.

Procedure 4.9. Using the Move function with Block to copy, move, or delete text.

1. Block the text you want to work with.
2. Press Ctrl+F4 for Move. A dialog box similar to the one in shown in Figure 4.4 appears.
3. The default type of blocked text is a simple block. If you have blocked a tabular column or rectangle of text, select Type and choose the appropriate block type.

64

A tabular column is one in a tabbed table (or parallel or newspaper-style columns); this works best if you have only one tab between columns. If your tabbed columns are regularly spaced, you may prefer using the rectangle option.

4. Choose the action appropriate to the task you want to perform: cut and paste, copy and paste, delete, append, or delete and append. The last two actions are discussed in the next chapter in Procedures 5.4 and 5.6.

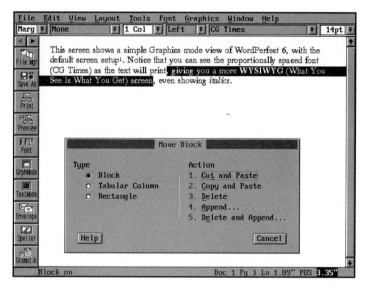

Figure 4.4. The Move dialog box, with a block of text selected.

Procedure 4.10. Using the Move function without first blocking text.

1. Place the insertion point within the sentence, paragraph, or page you want to work with.

2. Press Ctrl+F4 for Move. A dialog box similar to the one shown in Figure 4.5 appears.

3. Select the type of text block you want to work with by selecting the current sentence, paragraph, or page. The text you indicate is highlighted, and the type selection is made unavailable. The action selections are now available.

4. Select the action appropriate to what you want to do with the selected text: cut and paste, copy and paste, delete, append, or delete and append.

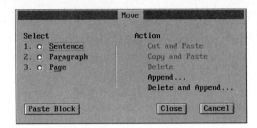

Figure 4.5. The Move dialog box, with no block of text preselected.

Proofing a Document

After you complete a draft of a document, you need to proofread your work. WordPerfect 6.0 has Writing Tools, discussed in detail in Workshop II, that can help with your proofreading. The Speller catches not only misspelled words but many typographical errors as well. The grammar checker, Grammatik, may point out grammar, capitalization, and punctuation errors that you could miss as you proofread the text yourself. Use these writing tools first, letting them catch many of the simpler mistakes, then browse through the text yourself to catch any mistakes the tools missed.

The Thesaurus, another one of the writing tools, can help you spiff up your writing by making it quick and simple to look up alternate words when you have trouble finding exactly the right word or phrase, or when you can only think of the opposite of the word you mean to use.

Tip: Professional editors use a common proofreading trick—reading the text backwards, beginning at the end and scanning back line by line. There are mistakes the eye misses when reading the text as written, instinctively filling in missing letters for words in context. Reading the text in reverse removes the context.

If your document includes graphics, font changes, and other formatting, work in Text mode, because it is fastest. Be sure to proof the document in Graphics or Page mode before you print so you do not waste paper before correcting formatting and layout problems.

5

by Susan Hafer

Advanced Editing

In Chapter 4, "Basic Editing Skills," you learned many basic editing techniques for WordPerfect 6.0. This chapter covers more advanced editing and explores the following topics:

- ▲ Searching for text and codes
- ▲ Replacing text and codes using the Replace feature
- ▲ Working with blocks of selected text
- ▲ Appending text in one document to the end of another, or to a clipboard so that the text can be pasted into another application (other than WordPerfect 6.0)

Using Search and Replace

WordPerfect has a very useful Search function that enables you to search your document for text, codes, or a mix of both. You can limit the search to the body of the document or extend the search to include headers, footers, footnotes, endnotes, captions, and text boxes. The Replace function is a Search with a bonus: you can tell WordPerfect to search for something and, if it finds it, replace it with something else. You can tell WordPerfect to do all replacements with or without confirming each replacement.

Search

You may want to use the Search feature to quickly move to a particular passage in a long document, or as part of a macro. Search begins wherever the insertion point is located and stops when it reaches the end of the document (for a forward search) or the beginning (for a backward search).

Procedure 5.1. Searching for text from the insertion point to the end of the document.

1. Place the insertion point in the document where you want the search to begin. To search the entire document, press Home, Home, Home, up arrow. (Pressing Home three times before the up arrow places the cursor before any codes at the beginning of the document.)

2. Select Edit, Search (or press F2). A dialog box similar to the one in Figure 5.1 appears.

> **Tip:** The default button bar includes a Search button for quick access with the mouse. It's near the end of the button bar, so you may have to scroll to the bar's end to find it.

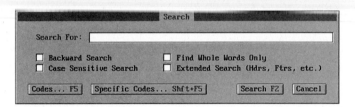

Figure 5.1. The Search dialog box.

3. Type the text you want to find in the search. You can include spaces, but if you want to include a tab or hard return, you need to use the Codes feature discussed in Procedure 5.2. Pressing Tab moves to the next item in the dialog box, and pressing Enter moves to the Search button in the dialog box.

> **Tip:** If you executed a Search earlier in this WordPerfect session, the last item(s) searched for appear highlighted in the Search For box. You may enter new text and/or codes to replace the highlighted item(s) or move the insertion point, which deselects the Search For item(s), at which point you may selectively delete and insert item(s) for the new Search.

Note: WordPerfect's Search function is not incremental. The search does not begin until you complete the text and complete the next step in this procedure.

Tip: The Backward Search checkbox is checked automatically as the dialog box appears if you press Shift+F2 rather than F2 to start the Search process.

4. Select any appropriate check box in the dialog box to modify the search.

    Backward Search reverses the direction of the search, searching from the insertion point to the *beginning* of the document.

    Case Sensitive Search limits the search to a word that matches, letter for letter, the upper- and lowercase of the text you typed. For example, searching for *WordPerfect* with Case Sensitive Search checked does not stop at *WORDPERFECT* in all caps; without this checkbox checked, the search stops, regardless of the capitalization.

    Find Whole Words Only limits the search to a complete word surrounded by word boundaries (spaces, soft and hard returns, and punctuation). Searching for *the* with Find Whole Words Only checked stops at *the* only, not *then* or *therapy* or *lathe*; without this option checked, each of these four are found.

    Extended Search (Hdrs, Ftrs, etc.) extends the search beyond the body of the document to include headers, footers, footnotes, endnotes, captions, text boxes, and comments.

Caution: Hidden text is found only when it is shown; even an extended search fails to find hidden text that is currently hidden.

Tip: The Extended Search checkbox is checked automatically as the dialog box appears if you press Home, F2 rather than F2 to start the search process. You can also combine this with the Backward Search shortcut by pressing Home, Shift+F2.

5. Select Search (or press Enter twice) or press F2.

The insertion point moves to the next occurrence of the text you specified. If the search reaches the end of the document and has not found the text, a Not Found dialog box appears. Select OK or press Enter and the insertion point will be exactly where it was when you requested the search. You can then request a new search, perhaps searching in the opposite direction.

> **Tip:** If the search locates the word, but not the occurrence of the word you want, press F2 (or Shift+F2) twice to find the next occurrence of the word. When you press F2 (or Shift+F2), the last text searched for remains in the Search For box. Pressing F2 from that dialog box activates the search. You do not need to wait for the dialog box to appear if you know that the Search For text is the text for which you want to search.

In addition to searching for text, you can search for formatting codes (see Procedure 5.2).

Procedure 5.2. A simple search for a code within the current document.

1. Place the insertion point in the document where you want the search to begin. To search the entire document, press Home, Home, Home, up arrow.

2. Select Edit, Search (or press F2). A dialog box similar to the one in Figure 5.1 appears.

> **Tip:** The default button bar includes a Search button for quick access with the mouse. It's near the end of the button bar, so you may have to scroll to the bar's end to find it.

3. Enter the code for which you want to search. Press the appropriate function key for that code, or use Codes (F5) or Specific Codes (Shift+F5).

> **Tip:** If you executed a Search earlier in this WordPerfect session, the last item(s) searched for appear, highlighted, in the Search For box. You may enter new text and/or codes to replace the highlighted item(s) or move the insertion point. This deselects the Search For item(s), at which point you may selectively delete and insert item(s) for the new search.

There are a few formatting and other special codes you can search for by pressing the function key that invokes that formatting function. For example, F6 searches for [Bold On], F8 (using the Original keyboard layout) searches for [Und On] (an underline on code), and Home, Space searches for a hard space.

During a search, most codes are not available directly from the keyboard. Instead, you need to use either the Codes (F5) or Specific Codes (Shift+F5) button. Codes searches for general codes, such as a hard return, underlining, or a style code. Specific Codes searches instead for a particular code, such as a specific style (rather than any style) or a left margin code (rather than any margin code).

Tip: If you want to search for a [Bold Off] code, press F6 twice in the Search For box to bring up a [Bold On] followed by a [Bold Off] code. Then delete the [Bold On] code. This also works with the underline codes and any other paired codes accessible from the keyboard.

4. If you selected Codes or Specific Codes, a pop-up list of codes appears (the Search Codes dialog box is shown in Figure 5.2). (Searching for specific codes is covered in Chapter 12, "Understanding Formatting Codes.") Begin typing for the highlight to move to a specific code in the list, or use the cursor movement keystrokes or scroll bar to browse the list. Highlight the code you want to include in the search and then choose Select or press Enter.

Figure 5.2. The Search Codes dialog box.

Tip: The ? (one character) and * (many characters) codes—the typical DOS wildcard characters—are now available in a WordPerfect 6.0 search through the Codes button, as well as in the Speller and File Manager. You can search for *w[?]ll*, which finds *will*, *well*, and *wall*, or *w[*]ll*, which finds those same words, as well as words such as *windmill* and *waterfall*.

 Tip: If you aren't sure what a code is, the WordPerfect manual includes a complete, alphabetical listing of all codes.

5. As in Procedure 5.1, select the appropriate checkbox (if any) items to modify the search.

6. Select Search (or press Enter twice) or press F2.

The insertion point moves to the next occurrence of the code you specified. If the search reaches the end of the document and the code is not found, a Not Found dialog box appears. Select OK or press Enter, and the insertion point will be exactly where it was when you requested the search. You can then request a new search, perhaps searching in the opposite direction.

 Caution: WordPerfect 6.0 does not cycle the search; it does not give you the option of continuing the search from the beginning or end of the document as many other programs do.

 Tip: If the Search locates the code, but not the occurrence of the code you want, press F2 (or Shift+F2) twice to find the next occurrence of the code. When you press F2 (or Shift+F2), the last code that was searched for remains in the Search For box. Pressing F2 from that dialog box activates the search. You do not need to wait for the dialog box to appear if you know that the Search For item is what you want to search for.

 Tip: You can combine codes, or codes and text, for a more sophisticated search.

72

Search and Replace

The Replace function works much the same as the Search function, but with an added entry box for text and/or codes to replace the item(s) for which you want to search (see Procedure 5.3). As you can see in Figure 5.3, the Search and Replace dialog box is quite similar to the Search box.

Procedure 5.3. Automatically replacing text or codes in a document.

1. Save your document, especially if you are new to the Replace function! You could unintentionally request a replace that could be destructive. (For example, replacing all occurences of *HE* with *SHE* could produce some interesting words, like *TSHEY* or *TSHEORY*.)

2. Place the insertion point at the point in the document where you would like the search to begin. To search the entire document, press Home, Home, Home, up arrow.

3. Select Edit, Replace (or press Alt+F2). The Search and Replace dialog box appears, as shown in Figure 5.3. Notice the two checkboxes that were not in the Search dialog box: Confirm Replacement and Limit Number of Matches.

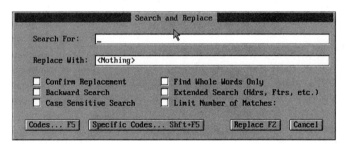

Figure 5.3. The Search and Replace dialog box, which is similar to the Search dialog box.

4. Enter the text or codes you want to replace, just as you entered text or codes in Procedures 5.1 and 5.2. Then press Tab to select the Replace With box.

5. Enter the text or codes that you want to replace the original material you just entered.

6. Check any appropriate checkboxes to modify the Replace. (Most of the items are explained in Procedure 5.1.) The remaining two are unique to Replace. Confirm Replacement, if checked, has the Replace function check with you for each occurrence or, if not checked, has the Replace

function do all replacements without verifying any of them with you. Limit Number of Matches, if checked, has the Replace function stop after a specified number of replacements.

7. Select Replace or press F2.

8. If you checked Confirm Replacement, the insertion point moves to the first occurrence of a potential replacement and a dialog box similar to the one in Figure 5.4 appears. The text will be clearly visible so you can easily decide whether this occurrence should be replaced. Select Yes to replace this one occurrence and move to the next, No to ignore this occurrence and move to the next, Cancel to forget the whole thing, or Replace All to replace this occurrence and all others from this point to the end of this document. If you select Yes or No and another occurence appears, you get the same dialog box, but with the occurrence number incremented.

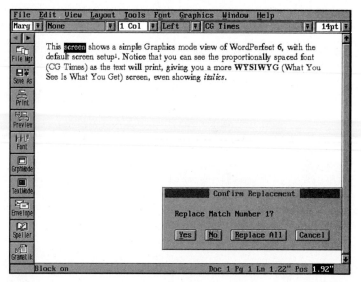

Figure 5.4. Replace requests confirmation from you if you checked Confirm Replacement.

9. If any replacement items were found, a Search and Replace Complete dialog box similar to the one shown in Figure 5.5 appears. Read the summary and then select OK or press Enter.

10. If you did not request confirmation for replacements, go back and skim your document to make sure all replacements were correct. If there were many problems, you probably want to Close or Exit the document and retrieve the version you saved just before doing the Replace.

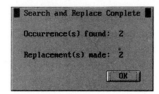

Figure 5.5. If any replacement items are found, a summary appears.

Working with Blocks and Selected Text

In Chapter 4, you learned to do many things with a block of text using the mouse or the keyboard. You can use many other functions with special uses when a block is active, including the following:

▲ Move, Cut, or Copy a block, as discussed in detail in Chapter 4.

▲ Check the spelling or grammar in the block (Tools, Writing Tools; or Alt+F1), described in detail in Chapter 7, "Speller," and Chapter 9, "Grammar Checking."

▲ Create a table from tabbed text, or affect the formatting of a blocked section of a table (Layout, Tables; or Alt+F7), described in detail in Chapter 20, "Formatting Tables."

▲ Print or fax the block (File, Print/Fax; or Shift+F7), described in detail in Chapters 23, "Printing," and 25, "WordPerfect Fax Services," respectively.

▲ Create a comment (Layout, Commment; or Ctrl+F7) or hidden text (Font, Hidden Text; or Alt+F5) with the block.

▲ Mark blocked text for an index, table of contents, list, cross-reference, or table of authorities (Tools or Alt+F5).

▲ Create a Hypertext link from the blocked text (Tools or Alt+F5).

▲ Save the block as a separate file (File, Save or Save As; or F10).

▲ Convert the block to all lowercase, all uppercase, or lowercase with initial capitalization for the first letter of the block (Edit, Convert Case; or Shift+F3).

▲ Limit a Search and Replace function to the blocked section of a document (Edit, Replace; or Alt+F2).

Caution: You might expect WordPerfect 6.0 to enable you to select a block of text and then perform a Search of just that block. However, if you use Search while a block is on, the block is extended to the next occurrence of what you searched for.

▲ Append a block of text to the clipboard, if WordPerfect Shell is running, or to a file (Edit, Append) (see the following section of this chapter).

Appending Text

You can append the current document or block of text to the end of an existing file or a new one (see Procedure 5.4).

Procedure 5.4. Appending a block of text to another file.

1. Block the text you want appended to the end of another file.

Caution: If you do not block the text before selecting Append, the entire current document will be appended.

2. Select Edit; or press Ctrl+F4 for Move. A menu appears, as shown in Figure 5.6.

3. If you used the Edit menu, select Append; a menu appears as shown in Figure 5.6. If you used the Move key (Ctrl+F4), the Move menu appears (see Figure 4.4 in the preceding chapter). Select Append if you want the blocked text to be copied to the end of another file, or select Delete and Append if you want the text moved.

4. If you used the Move key (Ctrl+F4), skip to the next step, otherwise, to append the block of text to an existing or new file, select To File. WordPerfect prompts you for a filename, using the Append To dialog box shown in Figure 5.7.

5. Type the name of an existing file to which the blocked text will be appended, and then type the name of a new file to create a new document with that blocked text. Alternatively, you can use File List (F5) or QuickList (F6) to retrieve the file name rather than having to type it. (See Chapters 26, "File Manager," and 27, "QuickList," for more information about the File Manager and Quick List, respectively.)

Figure 5.6. Appending a block of text to the end of another file.

Figure 5.7. Specifying the filename to which the block will be appended.

The blocked text remains in its original location, and the block is turned off. Next time you **Open** or **Retrieve** the file specified in Step 4, you will find the text blocked in Step 1 at the end.

Tip: If you now want to delete the block from the current file, turn on the block (**Edit**, **Block**; or Alt+F4), press Goto, Goto (Ctrl+Home, Ctrl+Home) to extend the block to the other end of the last blocked text and erase the block (**Edit**, **Cut**; or press Backspace or Delete).

Another use of **Append** is to copy a block (or entire file) to the WordPerfect Shell Clipboard so you can copy that block (or entire file) into another application accessible from the Shell program. The Shell program, which comes with WordPerfect 6.0, allows you to quickly toggle between different application programs (see Appendix B, "Customizing WordPerfect 6.0," for more information about Shell). Procedure 5.5 walks you through a WordPerfect Shell 4.0 setup. If you have already set up Shell 4.0 to your liking, skip to Procedure 5.6 for information about Appending to the Shell Clipboard.

Procedure 5.5. Setting up or running WordPerfect Shell 4.0.

1. Rather than invoking WordPerfect from a DOS prompt by typing WP, type SHELL to invoke WordPerfect Shell 4.0. If you have not already set up Shell, your screen should look something like the one shown in Figure 5.8. If you have already installed Shell 4.0, skip to Step 8 to run a program from Shell.

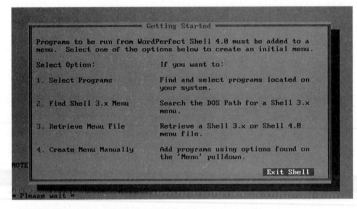

Figure 5.8. The initial Shell 4.0 dialog box.

2. Unless you have used a previous version of Shell on this computer, you will want to choose Select Programs or Create Menu Manually to create a Shell menu. It is easiest to let WordPerfect show you programs from which you can then select, so choose Select Programs. Another dialog box, similar to the one in Figure 5.9, appears.

Figure 5.9. The dialog box Shell responds when you ask it to select programs.

3. Make any changes to the way WordPerfect will search for programs. For this example, we selected Program Type and selected WordPerfect Products rather than Common Programs.

4. From the dialog box in Figure 5.9, select Search or press F2. Shell begins searching the hard drive (or path) for the type of programs you specified. As it searches, you see a dialog box similar to the one shown in Figure 5.10.

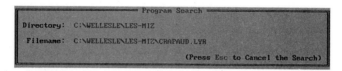

Figure 5.10. Shell searches for programs to include in your Shell menu.

5. When the search is complete, Shell enables you to select the programs for your menu. Press * (asterisk) by each program name you want added. Shell asks you to identify any that have more than one potential program name to match the filename found. For example, in Figure 5.11 you can see that WP.EXE might be WordPerfect, Multimate, or SPC OfficeWriter. As you scroll through the list of programs, note the filename below the Programs box, which includes the pathname for each file and therefore is your clue to which program you are looking at.

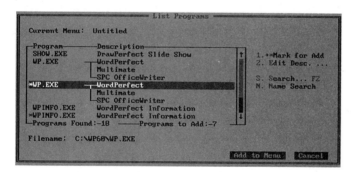

Figure 5.11. Mark and identify the programs you want added to your Shell menu.

6. When you have marked all the programs you want, select Add to Menu. A dialog box appears asking you to name your menu, as shown in Figure 5.12.

Figure 5.12. Enter a name for your Shell 4.0 menu.

7. Type a name for your menu and then select OK or press Enter. Your newly created menu appears in the middle of your Shell 4.0 screen, as shown in Figure 5.13.

8. Scroll through the list of programs in your menu and press Enter when you reach the program you want to run (or press the mnemonic key for the program).

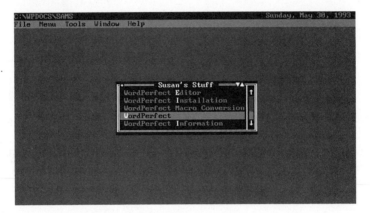

Figure 5.13. The Shell 4.0 menu screen.

If you use WordPerfect's Shell 4.0 program, you can easily copy text between programs (see Procedure 5.6).

Procedure 5.6. Appending a block of text to the WordPerfect Shell Clipboard.

1. Rather than invoking WordPerfect from a DOS prompt by typing WP, type SHELL to invoke WordPerfect Shell 4.0.

2. From the Shell menu, select WordPerfect 6.0.

3. Create, Open, or Retrieve the document containing the text you would like to append to the Clipboard.

4. Block the text you want appended to the Clipboard.

Caution: If you do not block the text before selecting Append, the entire current document will be appended.

5. Select Edit, Append. A menu appears, as shown in Figure 5.6 (see Procedure 5.4).

6. Select To Clipboard. If a dialog box appears saying Shell is not available, you ran WordPerfect from DOS rather than from Shell. Exit WordPerfect and begin from Shell. If nothing seems to happen, the blocked text was successfully appended to the current Clipboard. Each Clipboard is saved to a file named }CLP_{00.CLP, }CLP_{01.CLP, and so on. (WordPerfect uses brackets and braces in reverse order for its temporary files.)

> **Tip:** You can use Cut and Paste or Undelete, as described in Chapter 4, to copy or move text between documents, but only one block at a time (or three, if you are careful with Undelete). You can have up to 80 Clipboards, so you can save blocks to different Clipboards and retrieve the Clipboards as you like. Use File, Go to Shell (or press Ctrl+F1) to change the current Clipboard number, save the current file or block to a Clipboard, or retrieve the contents of the current Clipboard into your current WordPerfect 6.0 document.

by Susan Hafer

Working with Multiple Documents

WordPerfect 6.0 enables you to open up to nine documents simultaneously. This is handy if you have one document as an outline and another document as the actual text, or if you are working on several related documents and need to quickly refer to others as you work on one, or need to copy or move text between documents. Depending on the work involved and your work style, you may want to switch between full-screen versions of each document or have the documents in windows that you can move and resize, showing some or all of the documents at the same time.

Documents Displayed Full-Screen

To open multiple documents, just save the document you are currently working on and use File, Open (or press Shift+F10). Enter the filename of the next file to open, and it is placed in the next available document window. Or, to create a new document, use File, New.

Note: If all nine document windows are being used, a dialog box saying `No empty documents available` appears.

If you have only two documents open, you can quickly switch between them by using Window, Switch (or you can press Shift+F3).

If you have several documents open, you can quickly switch between them by using Window, Switch to (or by pressing F3). A dialog box similar to the one shown in Figure 6.1 appears. Select the document you want to work on by clicking with the mouse, typing the number corresponding to the document on which you want to work, or using the cursor movement arrow keys and then pressing Enter.

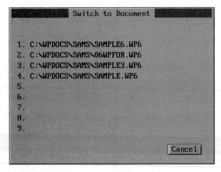

Figure 6.1. The Switch to Document dialog box.

 Tip: Remember from Chapter 3, "Working with Files," that you can use File, Exit (or Home, F7) to exit all open documents at the same time, saving any that have changed since the last time they were saved.

Documents in Windows

There are times when you may prefer working with multiple documents displayed simultaneously on-screen, each in a window. To put the current document into a window, or frame, you can do any of the following:

▲ Double-click the status line

▲ Select Window, Frame

▲ Press Ctrl+F3 and select Window, Frame

The framed window will look something like the one shown in Figure 6.2 if in Graphics mode, or Figure 6.3 if in Text mode.

Note: If this document window was put into a Frame earlier in this WordPerfect session, subsequent Framings will result in the same size and position rather than the system default, shown in Figure 6.2.

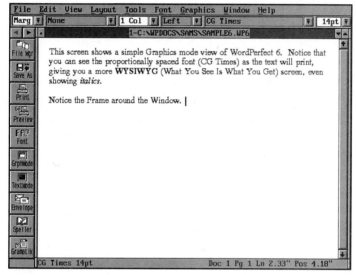

Figure 6.2. A framed window in Graphics mode.

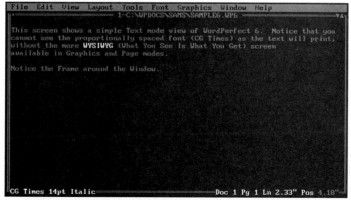

Figure 6.3. A framed window in Text mode.

Tip: You can quickly close a framed document by clicking the Close dot in the upper-left corner of the document window.

Moving and Resizing Windows

To change the size of the current document window, you can use the mouse to do any of the following:

▲ Click and drag corner buttons (or corners in Text mode)

▲ Click and drag side buttons (or side borders in Text mode)

▲ Click and drag the title bar or status line

Notice that when you move the mouse into one of the specified areas in Graphics mode, the mouse pointer changes from the standard arrow to an arrow indicating which way the window corner or edge will be moved, as shown in Figure 6.4.

Note: If your Zoom is set to Margin Width, the text displayed in the window shrinks accordingly to fit within the smaller window, to a point.

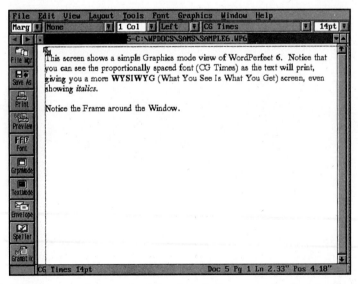

Figure 6.4. Clicking and dragging the top-left corner button in Graphics mode.

```
 File  Edit  View  Layout  Tools  Font  Graphics  Window  Help
                    1-C:\WPDOCS\SAMS\SAMPLE6 .WP6
This screen shows a simple Text mode view of WordPerfect 6. Notice that you
cannot
without the more WYSIWYG (What You See Is What You Get) screen
available in Graphics and Page modes.

Notice the Frame around the Window.




CG Time
```

Figure 6.5. Clicking and dragging the top-left corner in Text mode.

You can also press Ctrl+F3, Window, Size, which adds a dashed line around the window. You can then use arrow keys to move the window's right and bottom borders. Press the up arrow to begin moving the bottom edge up, or press the left arrow to begin moving the right edge inward. Press Enter to complete the job. This method is not as flexible as the click-and-drag methods just listed, but if you do not have a mouse, you need to use this.

Caution: At the time of this writing, if you press the left arrow at least once, you cannot use the right arrow to move the right border of the window all the way back to the edge of the screen. The best you can do once you have moved in several increments is to move the right border about a half inch from the right edge of the screen—about the width of the button bar. There is no problem moving back to the bottom once you begin using the up arrow, however.

Tip: If you use the keyboard method to resize the window, you may want to then use the keyboard method to move the window, because you can only manipulate the right and bottom borders using Size. The previous Caution applies to this keyboard method as well (in Graphics mode with the button bar along the left).

You can also change to the smallest possible window with a single click of the Minimize button. Alternatively, select Window, Minimize.

Caution: You might expect to see some sign of other open windows when you minimize the current document, but this is not necessarily true. None of the full-size windows appear in any form. You may even have minimized windows stacked on top of each other, leaving only the uppermost one visible. Always use Switch To (F3) if you need to see all documents that are open.

Note: Even if your Zoom is set to Margin Width, WordPerfect knows better than to attempt to show the minimized window with text tiny enough to fit between the current window borders.

Caution: You might expect Minimize to temporarily make the document an icon. Instead, it just makes the window very small.

To move the current document window, click and drag the title bar using the mouse, or, if you are using the keyboard, press Ctrl+F3, Window, Move, and then use the arrow keys to move the window. Press Enter to complete the job.

Note: The mouse pointer changes to a four-way arrow as soon as it enters the title bar, indicating that you may click and drag to move the window.

Caution: When moving a window, you may notice at times that WordPerfect will not let you move in certain directions. This is not a bug—all of the window must fit on-screen, so once a window border hits the screen's edge, you can move no further in that direction.

Viewing All Documents Simultaneously

To make all open documents visible on-screen simultaneously, select Window, Tile. The screen will look something like the one shown in Figure 6.6, depending on the number of windows you are using. You can then click any window to make that document the current one. You will want to resize the window or maximize it to make it easy to work with.

To make all open document title bars visible on-screen simultaneously, but have only one document window visible (the current document), select Window, Cascade. The screen will look something like the one shown in Figure 6.7, depending on the number of windows you are using. You can then click any title bar to make that document the current one. You may want to resize the window, Maximize it to make it easier to work with, or leave it as is so you can easily and quickly bounce between all the documents with the click of a mouse.

Caution: The more documents you have open in WordPerfect 6.0, the more memory is required and the slower the program will run.

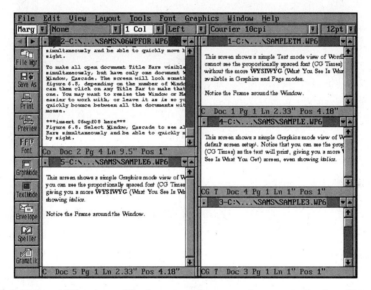

Figure 6.6. Select Window, Tile to see all open documents simultaneously and be able to quickly move between documents by sight.

Figure 6.7. Select Window, Cascade to see all open document title bars simultaneously and be able to quickly move between documents by sight.

Writing Tools

7

by Diane Clayton

Speller

WordPerfect 6.0 comes with an online dictionary as one of its Writing Tools. When you use the Speller feature, each word in your document is compared to this dictionary. If the word is found, the Speller proceeds to the next word. However, if the word is not found, the word is highlighted as a possible error, and you have several options. This chapter discusses the various options and shows you how to use them.

In addition to checking for misspelled words, the Speller also checks for duplicate words and irregular case (capital letters in unexpected places).

Speller lets you create your own supplemental dictionary, which can be attached to a specific document or used in all your documents. This feature lets you add words that fit your own needs, such as your name and address.

The WordPerfect dictionary is available in many different languages. It is also possible to add dictionaries of terms specific to a particular profession, such as medical or legal. The last part of the chapter discusses multiple dictionaries.

Caution: The Speller is not intended to take the place of proofreading your document! If a word is not spelled the proper way for its use in the document, but it is a correct word, it "passes" the Speller. Consider this little poem, which goes through the Speller with flying colors:

> I have a spelling checker,
>
> It came with my PC.
>
> It plainly marks four my revue
>
> Miss takes eye cannot sea.
>
> I've run this poem threw it,
>
> I'm shore your please too no,
>
> Its letter perfect in it's wait,
>
> My checker tolled me sew.
>
> —*author unknown*

Using Speller

You have the option of checking the spelling of a single word or page, the entire document, or a portion of the document. If you want to check a word or page, be sure to position the insertion point (cursor) in that word or page before proceeding.

Caution: Be sure to save your document before using the Spell Check feature!

The procedure for using the Speller includes the following steps, which are discussed in detail later in this chapter.

Procedure 7.1. Using the Speller.

1. The document you want to spell check should be on your screen.
2. Access the **Writing Tools** menu.
3. Choose Speller.
4. Identify the portion of the document to be checked for spelling errors.

5. Accept or correct each word that is highlighted as a possible error.

6. Save the corrected document.

The Writing Tools Menu

First choose Tools from the menu bar. (You can double-click on the word with your mouse, or press Alt+T to retreive the menu shown in Figure 7.1 "Writing Tools" is highlighted. Press Enter to access the Writing Tools menu.)

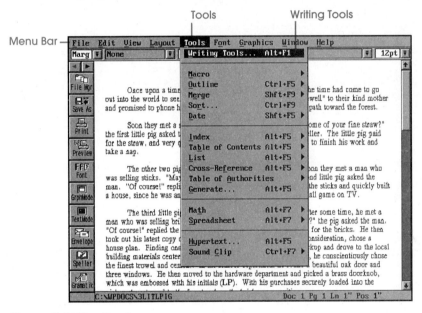

Figure 7.1. The Tools menu.

Tip: A keyboard shortcut to get to the Writing Tools menu is to press Alt+F1.

The Writing Tools menu (shown in Figure 7.2) has five choices. Choose Speller to see the Speller Menu.

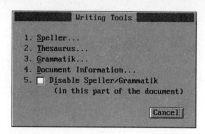

Figure 7.2. The Writing Tools menu.

The Speller Menu

The Speller menu is shown in Figure 7.3.

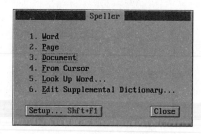

Figure 7.3. The Speller menu.

This menu has several options:

▲ Word—this command checks only the word at the insertion point (cursor). After the word has been checked (and any necessary changes made), the cursor moves to the next word, and the Speller menu returns. Choose another option, or press Close or Escape to return to the document.

▲ Page—this command checks the spelling of only the page that contains the insertion point (cursor). While the spell check is in progress, the message Spell Checking Page appears in a dialog box in the middle of the screen. After the page has been checked (and any necessary changes made), the cursor moves to the following page, and the message Spell Check Completed appears. Press , or OK to return to the document.

▲ Document—this command checks the spelling of the entire document. While the spell check is in progress, the message Spell Checking Document appears in the dialog box. When it is done, the message Spell Check Completed appears. Press Enter to return to the document. The cursor now appears at the bottom of the document.

> **Note:** Speller can be used when creating headers or footers, although the menu looks slightly different. For example, if you are spell checking Header A, the menu lists Header A instead of Document.

▲ From Cursor—this command begins to check spelling from the position of the insertion point (cursor).

> **Note:** The capability to begin Speller at the cursor position is a new feature with WordPerfect 6.0.

▲ Look Up Word—this command allows you to enter a word pattern that may help identify the word. Phonetic patterns are acceptable (for example, *f* finds *ph*).

If you are not sure of the word, you can use the "wild card" characters (* or ?) in your word pattern. A question mark (?) represents any one letter in the word. For example, the word pattern *?at* gives you a list of all the words that have a single letter in front of "at," such as *bat, cat, eat, fat, hat*, and so on. You can use several question marks in a word search. Each one represents any single character. (Looking up the word *m?n?y* lists *mangy, manly, minty*, and *money!*)

You can also use an asterisk (*) to represent any number of letters (including no letters) in the pattern. For example, the word pattern *w*p*t* gives you a list of all words that begin with the letter *w* and end with the letter *t* that have a *p* somewhere in the middle. (The list includes *waterspout, weepiest, wept, whippet, windswept, wispiest*, and *WordPerfect!*)

▲ Edit Supplemental Dictionary—this command allows the user to create or edit personal dictionaries used by the Spell Check in addition to the main WordPerfect dictionary. (Use of this command is discussed in detail in a later section of this chapter.)

In addition, the bottom of the Speller menu includes a button called Setup. (Information about Speller's setup can be found in a separate section of this chapter.)

> **Tip:** You can choose an option from the Speller menu by typing the highlighted letter or number. You can also move the highlight bar through the menu by pressing Tab or Shift+Tab. Pressing Enter activates the highlighted entry. If you prefer, you can double-click on the choice with the mouse.

Choices During the Speller Edit

When the Speller finds a word that is not in any of the available dictionaries, it highlights the word and stops. The screen splits, and the lower half displays a Word Not Found menu. The word in question is shown in a bar at the top, followed by numbers showing how many possible substitutes have been found for the word.

Under this word is a list of suggestions. The first ten suggestions show on-screen—you can use your cursor to move up and down through the list. The letters *A-J* are displayed along the left margin. These letters provide a quick way to replace the highlighted word with a word from the list.

> **Tip:** If suggestions are provided, the default choice is Replace word, as shown by the small arrow. If there are not suggestions, the default is Skip Once. You can move the default arrow up and down by pressing Tab or Shift+Tab.

1: Skip Once

This choice tells the Speller to accept the highlighted word as it is spelled, one time only. If the word appears again in this document, it is highlighted as an error.

2: Skip in this Document

This choice tells the Speller to accept the highlighted word as it is spelled any time it appears in this document. It is added to the Document Specific supplemental dictionary. If the word appears in other documents, it is highlighted as an error.

> **Note:** This is one of the nicest (and newest) features in WordPerfect 6.0! You can now add words to a specific document to be stored with that document. On future spell checks of the document, the words will be accepted.

3: Add to Dictionary

This choice adds the highlighted word to the Supplemental Dictionary. The word is then accepted in all future documents.

4: Edit **W**ord

This choice moves the cursor back to the highlighted word. You can use the left and right arrows to position the cursor and make any needed corrections. You can use backspace or delete to remove any unwanted characters and/or type in any new characters. When you are finished editing the word, press Exit or Enter to return to the document. If you are checking the page or document, the new word is then spell checked.

5: **L**ook Up

This choice takes you to the same menu as Look Up Word on the main Speller menu. It allows you to look for a word that matches a pattern. You can use a question mark (?) to represent a single letter, or an asterisk (*) to represent zero or any number of letters in the pattern. Phonetic patterns are acceptable. (For more information, refer to the section about the Speller menu.)

> **Tip:** When using Look Up, remember that the more specific your word pattern is, the shorter the list of suggestions will be.

6: Ignore **N**umbers

If you check this box, the Speller ignores words that combine numbers and letters in this document. Otherwise, those words are considered to be possible errors.

7: **R**eplace Word

Choosing this option places the highlighted word from the suggestions list in the document, in place of the word that had been highlighted. Because the default choice is Replace Word, pressing Enter activates this choice.

> **Tip:** You can also replace the word by pressing the letter that appears in front of the correct word.

8: Select Dictionary

This choice allows you to choose which supplemental dictionary is used when adding words. The current supplemental dictionary is shown in the box under this choice. (The default supplemental dictionary for the United States is WP{WP}US.SUP.) (More information about dictionaries is found later in this chapter.)

Sample Exercise

The letter shown in Figure 7.4 needs to be spell checked. After choosing Document from the Speller menu, (see Figure 7.3) the speller first stops on the word *Shoup* (see Figure 7.5). Because this word appears to be the writer's home address, it will probably appear in all correspondence. A proper choice would be Add to Dictionary. The word is then added to the Supplemental Dictionary, and it will be accepted on future spell checks of other documents.

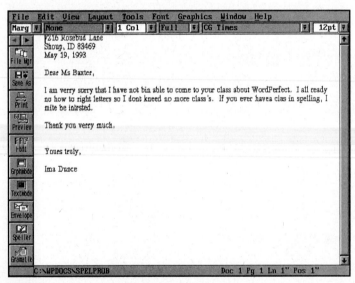

Figure 7.4. A letter containing spelling errors.

Error?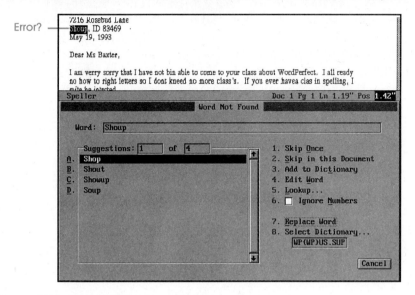

Figure 7.5. A highlighted word: *Shoup*.

The next word to be highlighted is *Baxter* (see Figure 7.6). If the writer knows this word is spelled properly, it can be skipped each time it occurs in the document, so Skip in this Document is the proper choice.

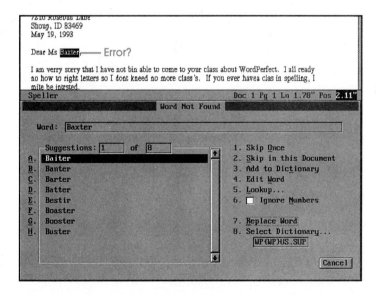

Figure 7.6. A highlighted word: *Baxter*.

101

The next word to be highlighted is *verry* (see Figure 7.7). The proper spelling of the word (*very*) appears as choice 1 of 11. Press Enter to replace the misspelled word with the correct word.

Dont is the next word to be highlighted (see Figure 7.8). The proper word (*don't*) appears in the list of suggestions. Move the cursor and press Enter, or simply press E, which is in front of the word.

Next, the speller stops on *havea* (see Figure 7.9). Choose Edit Word, move the cursor to the space after the word *have*, insert a space before the letter *a* (see Figure 7.10), and press Exit to return to the Speller.

The speller next stops on *clas*, and the proper word is not shown on-screen (see Figure 7.11). However, the screen shows that there are 23 suggested words. Press Page Down and the down arrow, and *class* appears. Press the proper letter to replace the word (see Figure 7.12).

The only suggested word for *intrsted* is *intrusted*, which is not a proper replacement (see Figure 7.13). Choosing Look Up brings up the Look Up Word screen (see Figure 7.14), which includes the Word or Word Pattern menu.

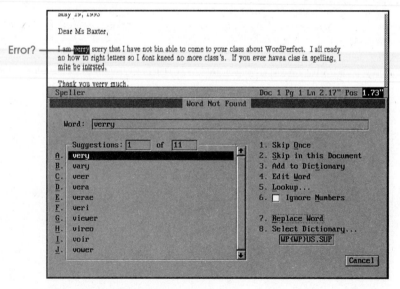

Figure 7.7. A highlighted word: *verry*.

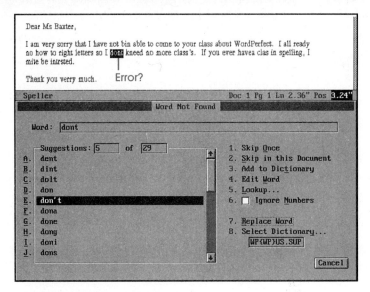

Figure 7.8. A highlighted word: *dont*

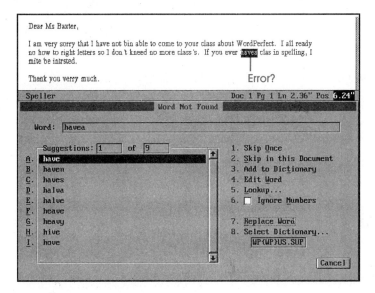

Figure 7.9. A highlighted word: *havea*.

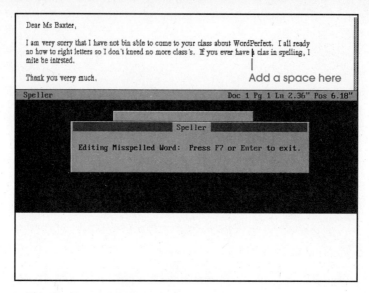

Figure 7.10. The Editing Misspelled Word screen.

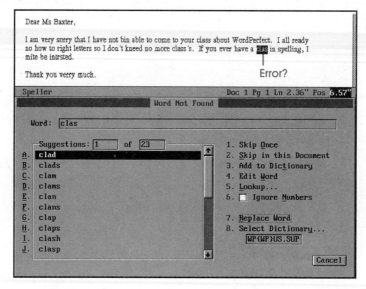

Figure 7.11. A highlighted word: *clas*.

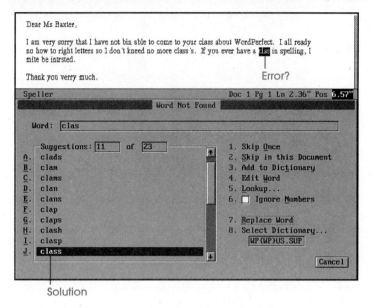

Figure 7.12. The correct word, *class*, is found.

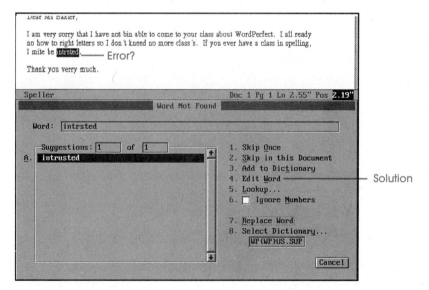

Figure 7.13. A highlighted word: *intrsted*.

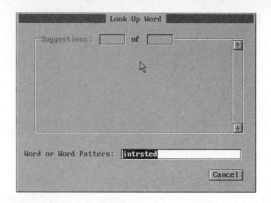

Figure 7.14. The Look Up Word screen.

Using the rules for entering a word pattern, enter some of the letters that occur in the word. However, using the word pattern *in*t*d* give 161 choices (see Figure 7.15)! Press Cancel, then Word or Word Pattern, and enter a more specific word pattern (such as *int*r*s*d*) to see a more useful list! The word *interested* is the first choice. Select Enter to replace the word in the document (see Figure 7.16).

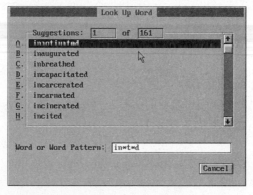

Figure 7.15. The word pattern *in*t*d*.

The last word to be highlighted is *Ima*, which should be added to the **dictionary**, because it is the writer's name (see Figure 7.17). At this point, the message shown in Figure 7.18 appears on-screen. Pressing Enter returns you to the **finished** document, as shown in Figure 7.19.

Notice that correcting *verry* in the first line of the letter also corrected *verry* in the last line of the letter. However, this letter still contains a lot of errors (*bin, no, right, knead, class's,* and *mite*). Remember that you must still proofread!

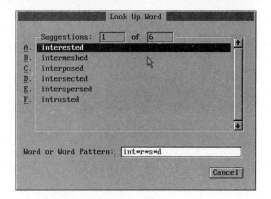

Figure 7.16. The word pattern *int*r*s*d*.

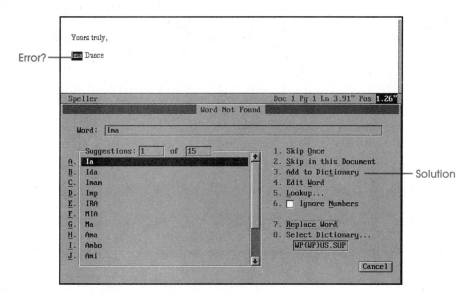

Figure 7.17. A highlighted word: *Ima*.

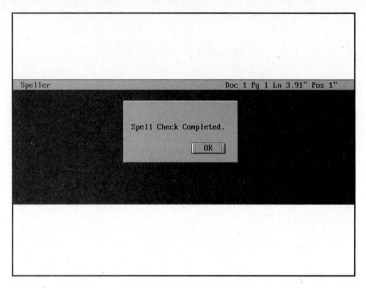

Figure 7.18. The Spell Check Completed screen.

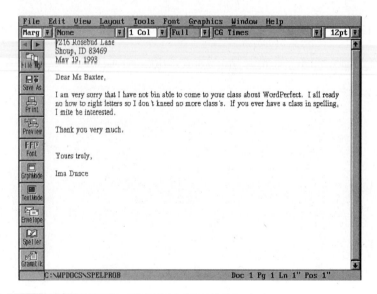

Figure 7.19. The corrected letter.

Double Word Checking

One of the common errors made when entering data is the duplication of words. This is particularly true for the "little" words, such as *is*, *to*, and *and*. If double words are found during the spell check, the second word is highlighted, and the menu shown in Figure 7.20 appears.

The Duplicate Word Menu has four choices:

▲ Skip Duplicate Word—this choice allows both words to remain in the document (in case you live in Walla Walla or Bora Bora).

▲ Delete Duplicate Word—the duplicated word is deleted (this is the most common choice).

▲ Edit Word—this is identical to Edit Word on the main Speller menu. Your cursor moves to the word, and you can make any necessary changes to it. When you are done, press Exit or Enter to return to your document.

▲ Disable Duplicate Word Checking—if you select this option, future occurrences of duplicate words are not highlighted.

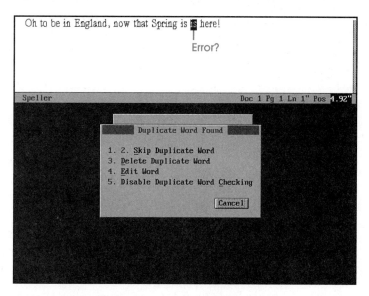

Figure 7.20. The Duplicate Word Found screen.

 Note: Disable Duplicate Word Checking is dependent upon Speller Setup. The default is ON. See "Setup" to disable this feature.

Checking for Irregular Case

During the spell check process, Speller stops when it finds words with uppercase letters placed within a lowercase word. Words such as *AUtomobile* are highlighted as errors.

Figure 7.21 shows the Irregular Case screen. Note that the suggested replacements include the word in all lowercase letters, uppercase letters, and with the initial letter capitalized. The options are Skip Word, Replace Word (after choosing from the suggested list), Edit Word, or Disable Case Checking.

> **Note:** Checking for Irregular Case is dependent upon Speller Setup. The default is ON. See "Setup" to disable this feature.

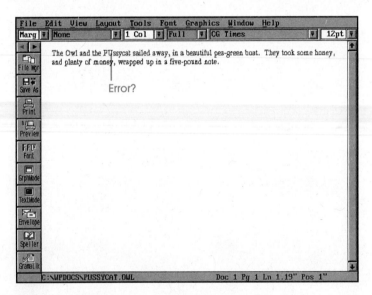

Figure 7.21. The Irregular Case screen.

Words with Irregular Case may be added to either the Supplemental dictionary or the Document Specific dictionary. From the Speller menu, choose Edit Supplemental Dictionary, highlight the desired dictionary, choose Add, Word to Skip, and enter the word with the desired case.

> **Note:** The ability to include irregular case words in the dictionary is a new feature in WordPerfect 6.0.

Capitalization Differences

If you add words containing capital letters to your Supplemental dictionary, and later those words are used without the capitalization, the Capitalization Difference screen appears, as shown in Figure 7.22. In this example, the word *Grammatik* had been added to the Supplemental dictionary.

During a spell check, the word *GRAMMATIK* was accepted. However, when the word was spelled with all lowercase letters (*grammatik*), it was flagged as a capitalization difference error.

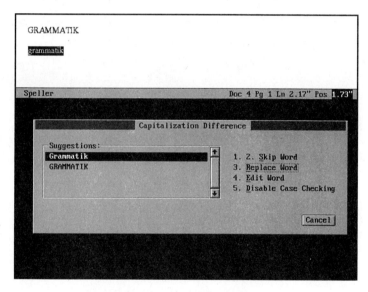

Figure 7.22. The Capitalization Difference screen.

Speller Setup

From the **S**peller menu, press Shift+F1 to see the Speller Setup screen, shown in Figure 7.23. The first two choices on the menu take you to other dialog boxes. The last five choices are off/on switches.

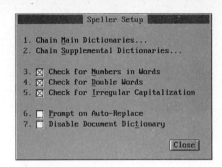

Figure 7.23. The Speller Setup screen.

Chain Main Dictionaries

 Note: Chaining dictionaries is a new feature with WordPerfect 6.0.

Choosing this option from the Speller Setup screen produces the Dictionary Chains screen shown in Figure 7.24. The Chain List shown includes the dictionary for the language you have purchased. In order to chain dictionaries of other languages, you can choose Add Chain from this menu. You are then taken to the Select Language screen, shown in Figure 7.25. Highlight the desired language and press Enter—the dictionary for that language is then chained to your main dictionary list.

Figure 7.24. The Dictionary Chains screen.

Figure 7.25. The Select Language screen.

 Caution: Unless you have a .LEX file for a language, you cannot chain that dictionary. An attempt to do so results in an error message: `Dictionary File Not Found`.

The Dictionary Chains menu, shown in Figure 7.24, can also be used to edit or delete dictionaries from your chain. Selecting Edit from the Dictionary Chains menu takes you to the Main Dictionary Chain dialog box, which is shown in Figure 7.26. From here you can add or remove chains, or edit the path to a chained element.

Figure 7.26. The Main Dictionary Chain screen.

Chain Supplemental Dictionaries

This option is similar to Chain Main Dictionary, and it can be used to edit/add/delete supplemental dictionaries. (See the section on dictionary types for more information about supplemental dictionaries.)

The screens shown in Figures 7.24 and 7.26 also apply to supplemental dictionaries. However, when you choose Edit from the Dictionary Chains menu (see Figure 7.24) you will see the Setup Supplemental Dictionary Chain menu, shown in Figure 7.27.

Check for Numbers in Words

If this switch is on, Speller highlights words that include numbers, such as *12B* or *Ver5*. If this switch is off, numbers are ignored. (The default setting for this switch is ON.)

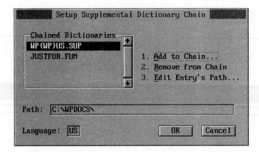

Figure 7.27. The Setup Supplemental Dictionary Chain screen.

Check for Double Words

If this switch is on, Speller stops when it finds duplicate words. If this switch is off, duplicate words are ignored. (The default setting for this switch is ON.) (See the section on double word checking for more information.)

Check for Irregular Capitalization

If this switch is on, Speller stops when it finds words with uppercase letters placed within a lowercase word. If this switch is off, these words are ignored. (The default setting for this switch is ON.) (See the section on checking for irregular case for more information.)

Prompt on Auto Replace

If this switch is off, correcting a word once corrects it every time it occurs in the document. If this switch is on, you are prompted at each occurrence of the word. (The default setting for this switch is OFF.)

Disable Document Dictionary

If this switch is off, words that you choose to skip are placed in a document specific dictionary for each document. If this switch is on, skipped words are not added to the document specific dictionary. (The default setting for this switch is OFF.)

Disable Speller/Grammatik

 Note: The ability to disable Speller for all or a portion of the text is a new feature with WordPerfect 6.0.

On the Writing Tools menu, there is an option called Disable Speller/Grammatik (see Figure 7.2). When this option is selected, text following the insertion point (cursor) is not spell checked.

If you want to disable speller for only part of the document, select the text you wish to have excluded. From the **W**riting Tools menu, choose Disable Speller/Grammatik. If you look in Reveal Codes, you will see that the code [+Speller/Grammatik] has been added at the beginning of the text and the code [-Speller/Grammatik] has been added at the end. Text between these two codes is not spell checked.

 Tip: This option is particularly useful when lists of names and other "unusual" words appear in a document.

Installation and Location of Dictionaries

During a standard installation of WordPerfect 6.0, the dictionary file (WPUS.LEX) is installed in the directory WPC60DOS. The supplemental dictionary (WP{WP}US.SUP) is created in the directory designated for documents in Setup, Location of Files.

Dictionary Types

WordPerfect uses three types of dictionaries when spell checking a document: main dictionaries, supplemental dictionaries, and document specific dictionaries. The following pages describe each of these dictionary types and how they can be used.

Main Dictionaries

WordPerfect word lists (main dictionaries) are available in many different languages. Each dictionary is named WPxx.LEX, with the two letters before ".LEX" indicating the language code of the dictionary. (WPUS.LEX is the version used in the United States.)

Dictionaries that are compatible with WordPerfect may be used to extend your list of acceptable words. Third-party dictionaries are considered main dictionaries, and they can be chained to the WordPerfect main dictionary. Up to six main dictionaries may be chained together. (See "Speller Setup" in this chapter.)

Supplemental Dictionaries

The supplemental dictionary is accessed only if a word is not found in the main dictionary. This dictionary can be edited by choosing Edit Supplemental Dictionary from the Speller menu.

When a word is to be added to the supplemental dictionary, the user has the option (on the Word Not Found menu) to choose which dictionary to use. Up to six supplemental dictionaries may be chained together. (See "Speller Setup" in this chapter.)

To create a new supplemental dictionary, choose Edit Supplemental Dictionary from the Speller menu, then choose Create New Sup. Name the dictionary, and choose Add to add words. Use Edit or Delete to modify the dictionary. (See the section on replacement/alternate word lists for more information.)

The default name used when a supplemental dictionary is created is WP{WP}xx.SUP, with the two letters before ".LEX" indicating the language code of the main dictionary. The .SUP extension is not a requirement of the program—you may use another name.

> **Tip:** In a network environment, you may want to share supplemental dictionaries. These dictionaries can be placed on the network. Selective read/write rights can be assigned, so that each person has access to the appropriate dictionaries.

Document Specific Dictionaries

Each document is stored with a list of words that have been accepted for that document (for example, marked "Skip in this Document"). This list can be edited by choosing Edit Supplemental Dictionary from the Speller menu.

Editing/Creating Supplemental Dictionaries

One of the choices on the Speller menu is Edit Supplemental Dictionary (see Figure 7.28). Choose this option to see the Edit Supplemental Dictionary screen shown in Figure 7.28.

Figure 7.28. The Edit Supplemental Dictionary screen.

You can edit an existing dictionary from the Edit Supplemental Dictionary screen. Choose the dictionary you want to edit and press Enter. You can now edit, add, and delete words. (The next section discusses options for adding words.)

"Document specific" refers to those words that were skipped during the spell check process. Highlight Document Specific and press Enter. For the example shown in the sample exercise on the preceding pages, the document specific dictionary is shown in Figure 7.29.

"WP{WP}US.SUP" refers to the default supplemental dictionary. Words added during the spell check appear in this dictionary and are used for all future spell checks. To edit this dictionary, highlight it and press Enter. For the example shown above, WP{WP}US.SUP is shown in Figure 7.30.

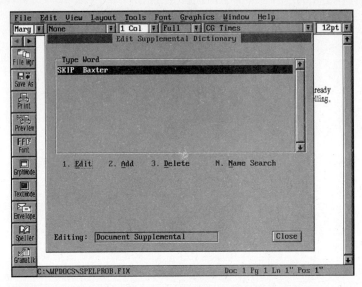

Figure 7.29. Additions to the Document Specific Dictionary screen.

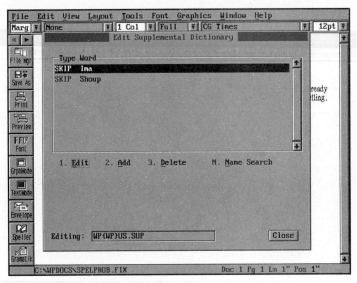

Figure 7.30. Additions to WP{WP}US.SUP.

From the Edit Supplemental Dictionary screen, you can also create a new supplemental dictionary. Choose Create New Sup to go to the Create New Supplemental Dictionary screen (see Figure 7.31). Type the name of your new dictionary and press Enter to go to the screen shown in Figure 7.32. Choose Add and enter the words you want included in this dictionary. (See the following section for information on Add options.)

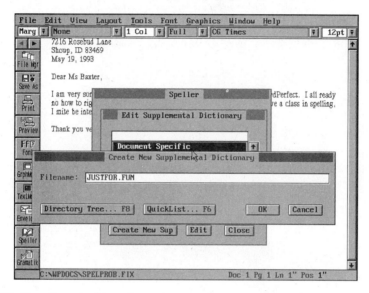

Figure 7.31. The Create New Supplemental Dictionary screen.

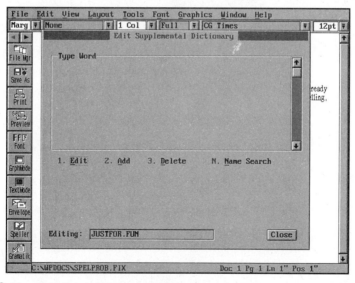

Figure 7.32. The Edit Supplemental Dictionary screen.

Using Replacement/ Alternate Word Lists

 Note: Replacement/alternate word lists are a new feature with WordPerfect 6.0.

You can create one or more supplemental dictionaries to list commonly used abbreviations that you would like to expand, or to alert you to words/phrases that you want to avoid in your writing.

When you choose Add from the Edit Supplemental Dictionary menu, you have three choices, which are shown in Figure 7.33. Word/Phrase to Skip allows you to add words and phrases to your dictionary.

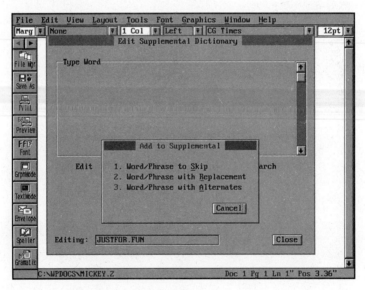

Figure 7.33. The Add to Supplemental screen.

Replacement Lists

Word/Phrase with **Replacement** allows you to enter a word with a replacement string (see Figure 7.34). Whenever Speller encounters that word, it substitutes the replacement you have specified. Using the supplemental dictionary, Speller converts the memo shown in Figure 7.35 to the one shown in Figure 7.36!

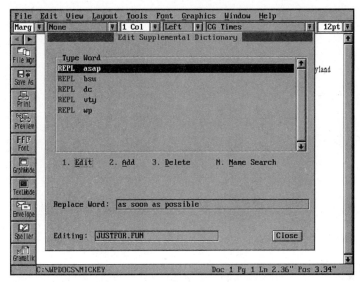

Figure 7.34. The Edit Supplemental Dictionary screen—Replace Word.

Alternate Lists

In addition, you may want to avoid certain words or phrases when you write. If you enter those words/phrases into your supplemental dictionary as Word/Phrase with Alternates, you can create a matching list of more acceptable words/phrases (see Figure 7.37). You also have the option of including a comment on this screen to describe your reasons for using alternate words/phrases.

When Speller encounters one of these words, it presents you with the list of alternate words/phrases (see Figure 7.38). Highlighting the chosen word/phrase and pressing Enter replaces the word, as shown in Figure 7.39.

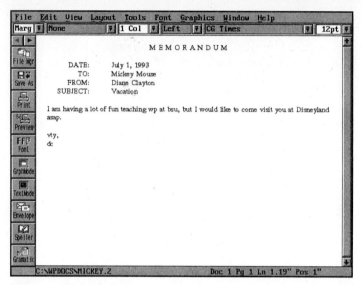

Figure 7.35. The original memo.

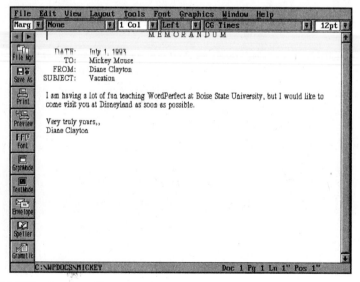

Figure 7.36. The memo after word replacement.

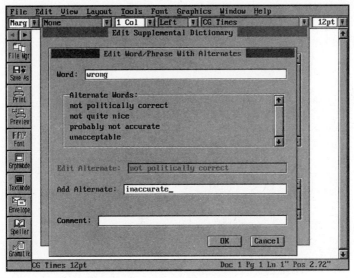

Figure 7.37. The Edit Word/Phrase with Alternate screen.

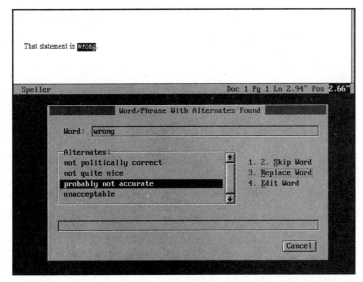

Figure 7.38. The Word/Phrase with Alternate Found screen.

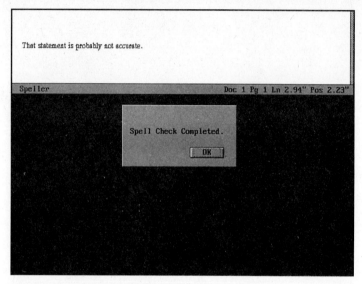

Figure 7.39. A new word inserted in the document.

by Diane Clayton

Thesaurus

One of the Writing Tools provided by WordPerfect 6.0 is an online thesaurus—an extensive list of words cross-referenced to synonyms (words with similar meanings) and antonyms (words with opposite meanings). If you've ever been "stuck" for the perfect word (or if you discover that the word you used was *so* perfect that you used it seven times in one paragraph), WordPerfect's Thesaurus can help streamline your writing. You can easily move from one word list to another, and when you find the word you want, it can be inserted in your document with a single keystroke. This chapter shows you all the details.

Headwords, References, and Subgroups

The WordPerfect Thesaurus identifies the words it displays as *headwords*, *references*, and *subgroups*. It's important to understand the differences between these categories.

A *headword* is a word that can be looked up in the Thesaurus. An attempt to look up a word that is not a headword may result in the message `Word Not Found`. Looking up a headword produces a list of words grouped and identified as nouns (n), verbs (v), adjectives (a), or antonyms (ant).

Some words on the list are preceded by a bullet (•), which identifies them as *references*. References are also headwords. If you look up a reference, you will see another list of words.

A *subgroup* is a group of words that appears under a headword. Words in a subgroup all have the same essential meaning. Words in a subgroup are usually the same category (e.g., all nouns or all verbs).

Using Thesaurus

Because the Thesaurus is concerned with finding a synonym or antonym for a single word, it is necessary to place an insertion point (cursor) in the word you want to look up. Follow the procedure listed below. (The steps in this procedure are listed in detail on the following pages.)

Procedure 8.1. Using the Thesaurus

1. Position the insertion point (the cursor) in the selected word.
2. Access the **Writing Tools** menu under **Tools**.
3. Select Thesaurus.
4. Determine which word on the Thesaurus list you want to use. Move the highlight bar to that word.
5. Press Replace to insert the new word and return to the document screen.

The Writing Tools Menu

Choose Tools from the menu bar by double-clicking on it with your mouse or pressing Alt+T to see the menu shown in Figure 8.1. With Writing Tools highlighted, press Enter to access the **Writing Tools** menu (shown in Figure 8.2), and select Thesaurus. The Thesaurus screen is shown in Figure 8.3.

 Tip: A keyboard shortcut to get to the **Writing Tools** menu is Alt+F1.

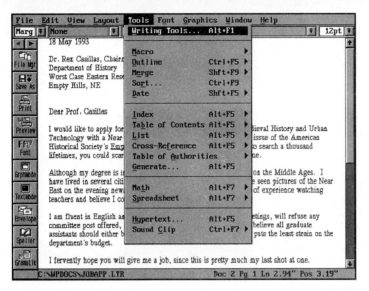

Figure 8.1. The Tools menu.

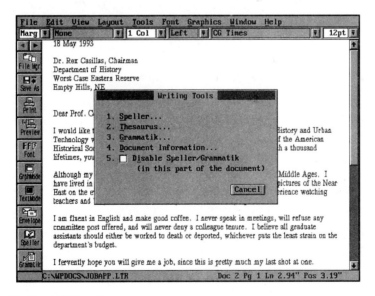

Figure 8.2. The Writing Tools menu.

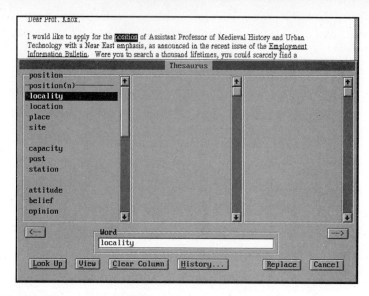

Figure 8.3. The Thesaurus screen.

Replacing a Word

In the example shown in Figure 8.3, the insertion point is on the word *position*. Examine the list of words and choose a replacement. You can move the highlight bar to the word you choose by using the up and down arrows, or by clicking on the word with the mouse. The highlighted word is shown in the Word box at the bottom of the screen.

If the list is longer than can be contained on-screen, not all the words appear on-screen. You can scroll through the list with the up and down arrows or the vertical scroll bar.

 Caution: Be careful! Many words have multiple meanings. Be sure you choose an appropriate word.

The word list shown in Figure 8.3 includes *locality* as a synonym for *position*, and indeed it is, but not as *position* is used in this example. To maintain the meaning of the original word, you must choose a word from the subgroup that has a similar meaning. In this example, *capacity*, *post*, and *station* are appropriate choices. Highlight one of these words (this example used *post*—see Figure 8.4). Now select Replace to make the new word appear in the document (see Figure 8.5).

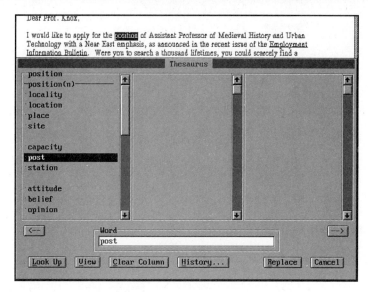

Figure 8.4. Selecting a replacement word.

Word replaced

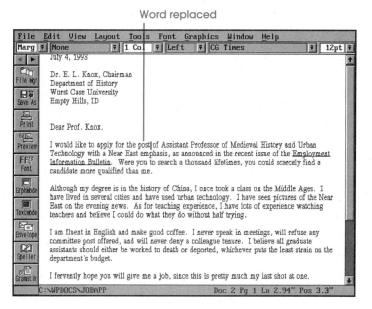

Figure 8.5. The document after replacing a word.

Additional Word Lists

If the "perfect" word you're looking for is not shown on the word list, move your cursor to any reference word (indicated by a bullet) on the list and press Enter. That word now appears at the top of the column to the immediate right, with a new list of words beneath it.

Let's look at an example. With the cursor on the word *history*, the Thesaurus has been called (see Figure 8.6). In this case, the writer may feel that none of the suggested words is exactly right, although *tradition* is close. Highlighting *tradition* and pressing Enter produces a second column of suggested words, as shown in Figure 8.7.

However, the writer is still not satisfied. Highlighting *heritage* and pressing Enter results in a third column (see Figure 8.8). The new column contains the word *background*, which the writer chooses as a replacement for *history* (see Figure 8.9).

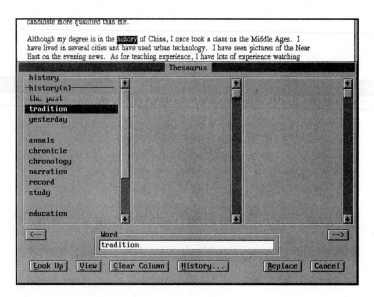

Figure 8.6. The first word list.

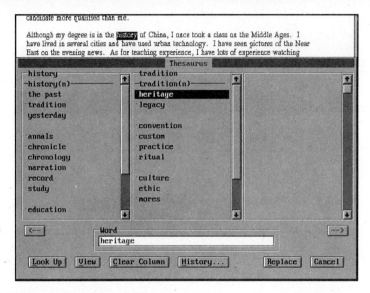

Figure 8.7. The second word list.

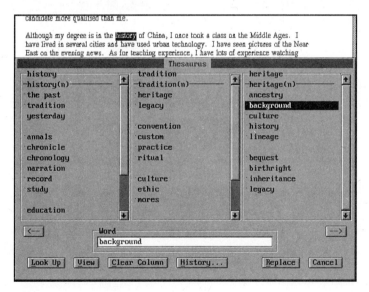

Figure 8.8. The third word list.

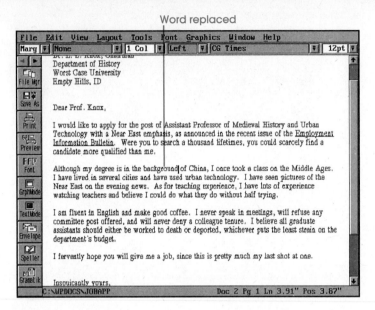

Figure 8.9. The document after word replacement.

History

After you've created several word lists, it is easy to lose track of the path you've followed to get where you are! WordPerfect handles this by keeping a list of all words you have looked at during the current Thesaurus use. You can see this list by selecting History from the bottom of the screen. The History List for the preceding example is illustrated in Figure 8.10.

Highlighting a word on the Thesaurus History List and pressing Enter (to choose Select) takes you to the column with that word as a headword.

Caution: The History List is only available when Thesaurus is active. As soon as you replace a word, the History List is erased.

132

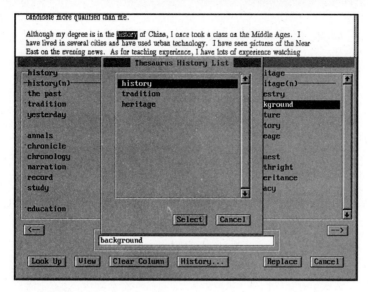

Figure 8.10. The Thesaurus History List.

Moving from One Column to Another

You can continue to search for words by highlighting a word and pressing Enter. As you add additional columns, you may want to move the highlighted bar from one column to another. You can do so by using the left and right arrow keys, or by clicking the mouse on the arrows shown in the lower portion of the Thesaurus dialog box.

Clearing a Column

There are two ways to clear a column of words. If there is already a list of words to the right of the highlighted word, press Enter to delete that column and replace it with a new column based on the highlighted word.

You can also clear a column by placing the highlight bar in the column and selecting Clear Column from the menu at the bottom of the screen. (The cursor moves into the column to the left of the column that has just cleared.)

Suffixes

You need to be aware that when you use the Thesaurus, only the "root" of the word is checked. Suffixes (word endings), such as *-ed* and *-ing*, plurals, such as *-s* and *-es*, and possessives, such as *-'s* are not preserved when a word is replaced. After the replacement is finished, the cursor is positioned at the beginning of the word. Move the cursor to the end of the word (use Ctrl+right arrow, then left arrow) and add the proper suffix.

In the following example, with the cursor on the word *announced*, the writer has chosen *publish* from the Thesaurus list (Figure 8.11). However, replacing *announced* with the word *publish* is still incorrect usage. In order to make the document correct, an *-ed* must be typed at the end of the word (see Figure 8.12).

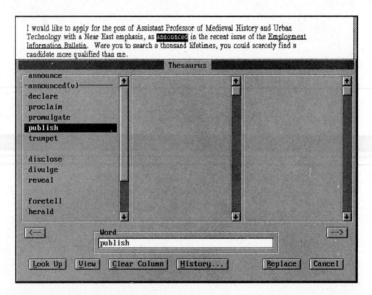

Figure 8.11. Replacing the word *announced*.

View

Sometimes, after working with all the choices offered by the Thesaurus, you may find it necessary to review the document. Selecting View from the menu at the bottom moves the cursor into the document, and the Thesaurus screen is greyed out. You can move the cursor through the document in any direction using the cursor movement keys, but you cannot add or delete text. When you press Exit, you are returned to the Thesaurus screen and the cursor returns to the original word (see Figure 8.14).

Needs suffix

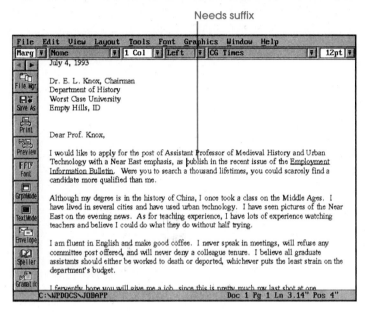

Figure 8.12. The document after the replacement.

Correct word

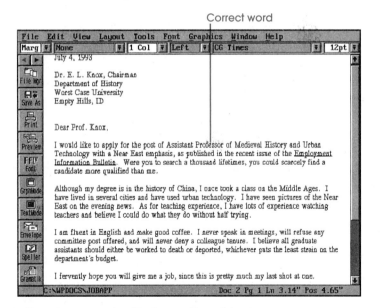

Figure 8.13. The document with the suffix added.

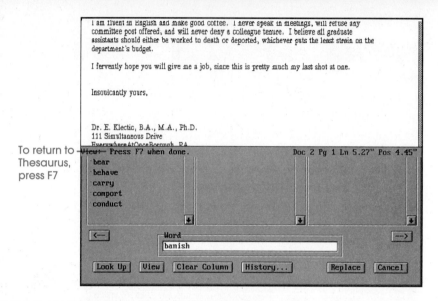

To return to Thesaurus, press F7

Figure 8.14. Returning to the original word.

Look Up

Selecting Look Up from the menu at the bottom of the screen moves the highlighted word into the Word box. Pressing Enter creates a column of words associated with the word you have chosen.

You can also select Look Up and then type a word in the Word box. Pressing Enter creates a column of words associated with the word you enter.

Caution: As of this date, you can't use wild cards during Look Up—but this may change!

Just for Fun

Word game enthusiasts love playing with a Thesaurus, and this is even easier with WordPerfect's online Thesaurus. The idea is to find two words that are exact opposites, and then find a path from one to the other, using synonyms. For example, can you get from *black* to *white* in eight steps?

Type the word *black* on your screen and put the cursor on it. Call the Thesaurus. Pick a synonym for *black*. From the list, pick a synonym for the second word.

Continue to choose a synonym for each word, and see if you can locate the word *white*. (One possible answer is shown in Figure 8.15. Can you do it in fewer steps?)

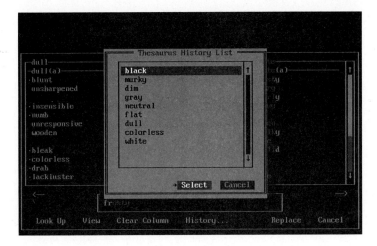

Figure 8.15. *Black* to *white* in eight easy steps!

Thesaurus Files

The Thesaurus files must be properly installed in order for this feature to work. During a basic installation, the file WPUS.THS is installed in a directory named WPC60DOS. If you have done a custom installation, be sure the proper path has been included.

by Diane Clayton

Grammar Checking

Grammatik has been available to PC users since 1981. Now Grammatik 5 is included with WordPerfect 6.0, and it is automatically included during a standard installation. Its purpose is to analyze the grammar and style of a document and to notify the user of possible errors in order to improve the finished document.

Grammatik checks the spelling of each word and analyzes the way it is used. It examines each sentence and assigns parts of speech to each word. It checks the chosen Rule Class list and inspects sentences for grammatical errors (such as proper structure) and mechanical errors (such as punctuation). Finally, it collects statistics about the document and calculates its readability.

Grammatik offers the user the flexibility of choosing which rules to follow (or not follow) based on the type of document. The user also can record personal conventions and rules to preserve individual style.

The Grammatik Opening Screen

With the document on-screen, choose Writing Tools from **Tools** on the menu bar, then select Grammatik (see Figure 9.1) to see the opening screen, shown in Figure 9.2.

Tip: You can go directly to the **Writing Tools** menu by pressing Alt+F1.

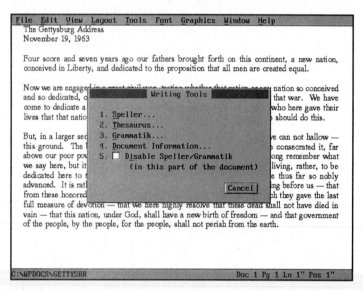

Figure 9.1. The Writing Tools menu.

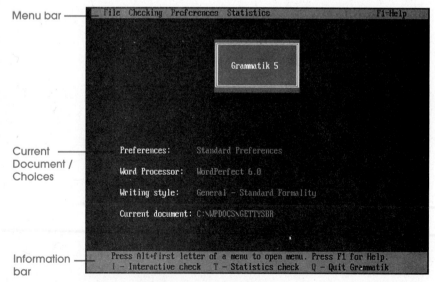

Menu bar

Current Document / Choices

Information bar

Figure 9.2. The Grammatik opening screen.

140

The Menu Bar

In Figure 9.2, the menu bar at the top of the opening screen lists four choices:

▲ File—this option allows you to open a file, to Get or Save a Preferences file, or Quit Grammatik.

▲ Checking—this option allows you to choose one of five modes of proofing:

1. **Interactive**—Grammatik stops at each error and waits for a re sponse before proceeding. (Choosing I from the information bar at the bottom of the screen gives the same results.)

2. **Grammar/Mechanics**—only Grammatical/Mechanical rule classes are used. Style problems are ignored.

3. **Spelling Only**—Grammatik checks for spelling errors. Rules/styles are not checked.

4. **Read-Only**—errors are displayed, but editing is not allowed.

5. **Mark-Only**—errors are marked, and advice for correction is in- serted in the document, preceded by a pipe symbol (¦). You can use WordPerfect's Search feature to find the marked text and make corrections at a later time.

▲ Preferences—details about your word processor and other choices are saved in a Preferences file. Unless otherwise specified, the Preferences file is GK51GK.INI. (Creating custom Preference files is discussed in detail in a later section of this chapter.)

▲ Statistics—this choice allows you to see various statistics about your document. For more information, see the section on Statistics later in this chapter.

All choices on the menu bar may be accessed by holding down Alt while pressing the first letter of the menu item, or by clicking the mouse on the menu name.

Information about
Current Document/Choices

The central portion of the screen gives information about the Preferences currently being used. It also lists the current Word Processor, the Writing Style currently being used, and the name of the Current Document. (Writing Style is discussed in a later section of this chapter.)

The Information Bar

The information bar at the bottom of this screen offers three choices:

▲ I = Interactive check—Grammatik stops at each error and waits for a response before proceeding. (This same choice is offered on the Checking menu.)

▲ T = Statistics check—this choice gives the same information as the first choice offered on the Statistics menu. The results are discussed later in this chapter.

▲ Q = Quit Grammatik—return to document. You can also press Esc to quit Grammatik.

Starting a Grammatik Session

From the opening screen, shown in Figure 9.2, choose I for Interactive (or choose a different mode from the Checking menu as previously described). Accept the Preferences and Style shown in the center of the screen (or choose different preferences/styles as described in other sections of this chapter). At this point, the proofing session begins.

Error Detection and Correction

Each time a possible error is detected in the interactive mode, the Error Detection screen shown in Figure 9.3 appears. This screen has several sections:

▲ The Editing window at the top of the screen shows the current writing problem and the surrounding text.

▲ The Rule Class window identifies the rule class for the current problem.

▲ The Advice line includes suggestions for correcting and/or improving the text.

▲ The Replacement line displays an appropriate replacement for the word or phrase in question. (This may not be available for all errors.) If several possible replacements exist, you are instructed to press F2 for a list from which to choose.

▲ The command buttons listed at the bottom of the screen are options for responding to the problem. These buttons vary with each individual problem. Additional command button options can be listed by opening the Edit menu.

Tip: If you wonder why Grammatik has identified an error, you can press F4 for a parts-of-speech analysis of each word in the problem sentence. This feature is not available for mechanical errors.

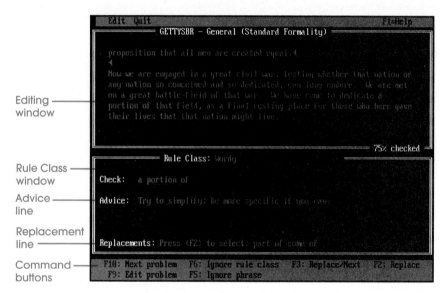

Editing window

Rule Class window

Advice line

Replacement line

Command buttons

Figure 9.3. The Error Detection screen.

Correcting Errors

If, after reading the advice on the Error Detection screen, you choose to correct an error, the Grammatik screen offers several choices.

Pressing F9 allows you to edit the problem. Your cursor moves into the document, and you can add or delete text. When you are finished editing, press Esc to return to Grammatik.

If a replacement is suggested, you can select F2 or F3 to insert that replacement in your document. If more than one replacement is suggested, pressing either F2 or F3 produces a list from which you can select your choice.

Tip: If you select F2, you have to select F10 to move to the next error. Selecting F3 replaces and moves to the next error!

The Learn Word command, F7, adds the word to the Grammatik spelling dictionary.

False Errors

Grammatik tries to prevent "false errors." For example, the program recognizes headings and lists, and it does not flag them as incomplete sentences. You can also identify blocks in your document to keep them from being marked as errors by enclosing those blocks in the special Ignore Block characters—a pipe, hyphen, asterisk, and parentheses. These characters must be placed on either side of the block you want to ignore, with the order reversed after the text. Use no spaces between the Ignore Block characters.

For example, to ignore the title Chapter 9, "Grammar Checking," place Ignore Block characters as follows:

```
|-*(Chapter 9, "Grammar Checking")*-|
```

After using Grammatik to proof your document, use the Search feature to locate the Ignore Block characters, which must be removed manually.

Ignoring Errors

Although Grammatik marks anything it considers to be a writing error, correction is entirely up to you.

During the proofing session, you can choose F10 to skip this error and move to the next problem. You can also instruct Grammatik to Ignore Word or Ignore Phrase. Either of the Ignore commands causes Grammatik to ignore the highlighted word or phrase for the rest of the session.

One of the choices on the Edit menu (and the command button list) is Ignore Rule Class. Choosing this causes Grammatik to ignore all the problems in this class for this proofing session. If you change your mind, return to the Edit menu and choose Restore Rule Class.

> **Note:** If you use Ignore Rule Class, you will see a reminder at the end of the session, and you will be asked to confirm if you want to save these changes permanently by creating a custom writing style.

Preferences

Four choices are listed on the Preferences menu: Writing Styles, Word Processor, Options, and Screen Attributes.

Writing Styles

This option is discussed in detail in the following section.

Word Processor

In the unlikely event that you might use a different word processor than WordPerfect, Grammatik can be run independently. Change to the directory where it is located (usually C:\WPC60DOS), type GMK, and select the appropriate word processor from this screen.

Options

The Options list can be displayed from the Preferences menu. To change an option, select it using the arrow keys, then press the space bar to turn it on ([X]) or off ([ ]). When you are satisfied, press Enter to save the options. Press Esc to cancel the selections.

The following options are available on this menu:

▲ Check for paragraph errors (the default is ON)—this option checks for end-of-paragraph punctuation marks and hard carriage returns.

▲ Ignore periods within words (the default is ON)—this option allows DOS filenames (such as WP.EXE) and other embedded periods.

▲ Print errors on printer (the default is OFF)—if ON, each time you mark an error, the information is routed to your printer.

▲ Show all file warnings (the default is OFF)—if ON, exiting Grammatik produces warnings, such as confirming that saving a file may overwrite an existing file.

▲ Swap left/right mouse button (the default is OFF)—this option allows you to switch the active mouse button for left- and right-hand use.

▲ Write errors to .ERR file (the default is OFF)—if ON, proofreading errors are kept in a file with the same name as your document (plus the extension .ERR).

145

Screen Attributes

You can change the screen colors used by Grammatik with this menu. If you are using a laptop computer with an LCD monitor, choose Black and White or Reverse Black and White as the color scheme.

Creating Custom Preference Files

The following settings are saved in a Preference file:

▲ Default document path and extension

▲ Current writing style

▲ Current formality level

▲ Rule class settings for all custom styles

▲ Writing style thresholds

▲ Options

▲ Screen attributes

▲ Comparison chart statistics

When you make changes to Preference files, they are stored in a file named G51.INI, unless you specify a different filename. It is sometimes helpful to create additional Preference files to save information about custom writing styles or choices you have customized, such as alternate colors or alternate comparison documents.

Save Preferences File

To save a custom Preference file, you must first start Grammatik and choose the options you want to incorporate into that file (different screen colors, custom styles, custom comparison documents, and so on). Then, after selecting those options, open the File menu and choose Save preferences file. Press Tab, and the cursor moves into the box that lists the Current Preference (.INI) file. Type a new name for your custom Preferences file. Be sure the filename ends with .INI!

> **Note:** If you want, you can save your preference file in a different drive and/or directory. Just include the proper path with the filename.

Press Enter, and the following message appears on-screen:

```
Preferences file does not exist, create new one? <Yes> <No>
```

When you respond Yes, you are asked to enter an Identification Message, which can be up to 31 characters long. This ID message appears on Grammatik's opening screen to remind you of the preferences currently in use.

Get Preferences File

Grammatik uses the standard Preferences file unless you specify a custom file. When you begin Grammatik, choose Get Preferences from the File menu. Highlight your desired preference file and press Enter.

More About Writing Styles

Different types of documents have different requirements for format, formality, readability, and so on. Grammatik gives you the capability to choose from ten predefined templates or to create your own custom writing style. The current Writing Style is listed on the Grammatik opening screen. To see the available templates, select Writing Style from the Preferences menu (see Figure 9.4).

The Writing Style templates are shown in Figure 9.5. Each of the templates has a different set of rules to follow and a different threshold for the number of times a situation can occur before it is considered to be an error.

Writing style —

Current writing style —

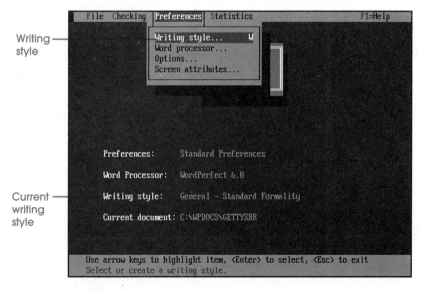

Figure 9.4. The Preferences menu.

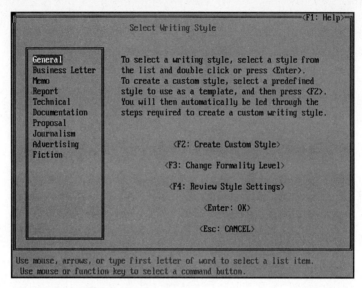

Figure 9.5. The Select Writing Style screen.

Some writing styles require a more formal tone than others. Each style has a default formality style, which is shown in the following list. You can change the level of formality by highlighting a style and pressing F3 Change Formality Level. (The default level is shown.) To change formality level, highlight the desired level and press Enter.

The available templates and their formality level (FL) are shown in the following listing:

Writing Style	Formality Level
▲ General (the default)	Standard
▲ Business Letter	Formal
▲ Memo	Standard
▲ Report	Formal
▲ Technical	Formal
▲ Documentation	Standard
▲ Proposal	Formal
▲ Journalism	Standard
▲ Advertising	Informal
▲ Fiction	Standard

To see the list of rules for a particular style, highlight that style and press F4 Review Style Settings. (Four screens appear in succession.) On each of the first three screens, an [X] indicates that the rule is active for that template. Press Enter to see the next screen; press Backspace to see the previous screen.

Tip: You can't change the settings for a template. If it is not quite what you want, use it as the basis for creating a customized style, which is discussed in a later section of this chapter.

The first screen lists the grammar rules—those that relate to proper use of parts of speech, such as incomplete sentences, subject/verb agreement, pronoun case/number agreement, and split infinitives.

The second screen lists the mechanical rules. These include errors in capitalization, spelling, and unmatched pairs of quotation marks and parenthesis.

The third screen shows style rules, which include use of abbreviations, foreign words and phrases, and gender-specific words.

The fourth screen is slightly different from the first three. It lists the thresholds (number of occurrences) permitted before each of the following items is considered an error:

▲ Consecutive nouns

▲ Consecutive prepositional phrases

▲ Long sentence length

▲ Passive sentences (of the last 10)

▲ Spell numbers below or equal to

▲ Words allowed in split infinitive

Remember, you can't change any of these settings. If you want to alter them, it is necessary to create a custom style, as described in the following section.

Creating a Custom Writing Style

If you want to create your own Writing Style, you can pick the rule classes that it will use. You can create up to three unique Writing Styles.

First, choose Writing Styles from the Preferences menu. Pick a predefined writing style to use as a template. Be sure to choose one that is close to your needs. Then press F2, Create Custom Style.

There are three Writing Style placeholders: [Custom 1], [Custom 2], and [Custom 3]. Select the first available placeholder. Press Enter and type a new name for your style. (You may use up to 23 characters.)

At this point, you are taken to the first of four Review Style Setting screens (as described in the previous section). Set each rule class by moving to it with the arrow keys and pressing the space bar to turn it on ([X]) or off ([ ]). When you finish each screen, press Enter to move to the next screen.

On the threshold screen, after you highlight a choice and press the space bar, you are asked to enter a number and press Enter. The number you enter becomes the new threshold value.

After entering the necessary information on these screens, press Enter to accept the custom changes.

You may want to change the formality level of your new Writing Style. The default formality level is the same as the style you used as a template. You can change it by pressing F3 Change Formality Level.

Statistics

When you select Statistics from the menu bar, you cannot only see various kinds of information about your document, but also how it compares with other documents.

There are six choices listed on the Statistics menu. The first, Show Statistics, is identical to choosing T from the bottom of the opening screen. The statistics screens are shown in Figures 9.6 and 9.7. This screen lists paragraph, sentence, and word statistics. In addition, it gives information about readability, which is discussed in the following section. Pressing Enter produces a second screen showing additional facts about the document readability, plus statistics for average word, sentence, and paragraph length.

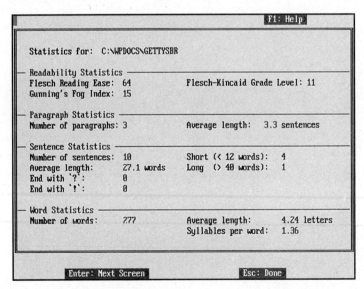

Figure 9.6. Document statistics, screen 1.

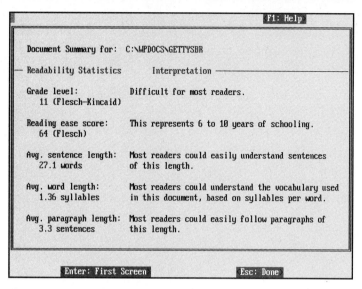

```
                                            F1: Help

    Document Summary for:  C:\WPDOCS\GETTYSBR

  — Readability Statistics         Interpretation ──────────────

    Grade level:            Difficult for most readers.
      11 (Flesch-Kincaid)

    Reading ease score:     This represents 6 to 10 years of schooling.
      64 (Flesch)

    Avg. sentence length:   Most readers could easily understand sentences
      27.1 words            of this length.

    Avg. word length:       Most readers could understand the vocabulary used
      1.36 syllables        in this document, based on syllables per word.

    Avg. paragraph length:  Most readers could easily follow paragraphs of
      3.3 sentences         this length.


         Enter: First Screen              Esc: Done
```

Figure 9.7. Document statistics, screen 2.

The second choice, Historical Profile, produces a list of the most frequently used words in all the documents you have checked with Grammatik, along with the number of times you have used each word. This information is stored in the file GK51US.HST.

The next choice, Single Document Profile, gives similar information about the current document.

If you choose Comparison Charts, your document is compared with three standard documents: the Gettysburg Address (which rates high with Grammatik), a short story by Ernest Hemingway (characterized by short words and simple sentences), and a life insurance policy (typical of business writing).

Restore Default Comparisons is used after Customizing Comparison Documents (see the next section) in order to return to the default comparison standards.

Save Statistics in File allows you to create a file containing the statistics you have just obtained. The default path\filename is \WP60\G51.SUM, but you are given the option to change the name. The file is stored in standard ASCII text format.

Customizing Comparison Documents

If you press the plus sign (+) when the Comparison Charts are on your screen, you can replace any of the standard documents with the document that is on your screen. In this way, you can compare each of your documents to standards you have set for your own personal writing goals.

Caution: Restoring the default comparison standards removes any custom comparisons you have created. If you want to save your custom preferences, see the following sections.

Saving Custom Comparisons

You can save an unlimited number of comparison standards, each in a different custom preferences file. In this way, you can create a set of documents to use when comparing business letters, legal documents, and so on. Each file you create must end with the extension .INI. (See the section on creating custom preferences for more details.)

How Readable is Your Document?

Readability statistics can help you see if your document can be understood by its intended audience. Fiction for a general audience requires a different level of readability than technical documents for specific readers.

Grammatik uses three readability scales, the Flesch Reading Ease score, the Flesch-Kincaid Grade Level score, and the Gunning's Fog Index. All are derived from mathematical formulas based on such factors as number of words per sentence and number of syllables per word. Because they are calculated in different ways, different results may be shown for each method. A chart showing how to interpret these scales is shown at the end of this section.

The Flesch Reading Ease score multiplies the average sentence length by 1.015, then multiplies the number of syllables per 100 words by .846. The two products are added, and the total is subtracted from 206,835. The resulting score is analyzed, as shown below. A low score means the document is difficult to read.

The Flesch-Kincaid Grade level score uses the product of the average number of words per sentence multiplied by .39, and the product of the average number of syllables per word multiplied by 11.8. The two products are added together, and then 15.59 is subtracted from the total. The resulting number indicates the approximate school grade level a reader must have completed in order to understand the sentence. A grade level score between 6 and 10 is considered desirable.

The Gunning's Fog Index also refers to the approximate grade level required for a reader to understand the sentence. It is calculated by adding the average number of words per sentence to the number of words containing three or more syllables, then multiplying the total by .4.

Reading Difficulty	Flesch Reading Ease	Grade Level
Very Easy	90-100	4th
Easy	80-90	5th
Fairly Easy	70-80	6th
Standard	60-70	7th-8th
Fairly Difficult	50-60	Some High School
Difficult	30-50	High School/College
Very Difficult	0-30	College and Up

Ending a Session

As you work with a document in Grammatik, your corrections are written to a temporary copy of the file. At the end of a session, you are returned to the Grammatik screen. Pressing Q or Esc returns you to your word processor.

If you exit Grammatik before the end of an interactive session, (by choosing Quit from the menu bar) you have several options:

Quit, Save work so far—Grammatik returns you to your word processor, and corrections made to this point appear in the document.

> **Tip:** You still have to save the document in WordPerfect in order to make the changes permanent!

Quit, place Bookmark—this option inserts the marker %GMK% in your document. When you resume proofreading, select Resume Interactive from the Checking menu. The session resumes at the place where the marker was inserted, and the marker is deleted.

> **Caution:** If you do not use Resume Interactive, the marker remains in your text and must be manually removed.

Quit, mark rest of document—this option marks all remaining errors and inserts advice on correcting them in the document. (It is similar to the Mark Only mode on the Checking menu.)

Cancel, ignore work so far—if you choose this option, you exit Grammatik and all changes are cancelled. If you choose this option after you have resumed editing, the bookmark remains in the document.

153

Note: You can also exit Grammatik before the end of a session by pressing Esc. However, the only choice you will be offered is Quit, Save work so far.

Using Help

Pressing F1 during a Grammatik session accesses the online help system. In addition to general Help, the feature is context-sensitive, which means it incorporates help specific to the current screen, the selected menu command or list item, or the highlighted Rule Class. The first few items on the help menu vary depending on the context.

The last five Help indexes on each help menu each produce an index of related topics, as shown below:

▲ Rule Classes

▲ Commands—including menus and windows

▲ Word Processors

▲ Writing—tips on improving your writing skills

▲ Glossary—grammatical terms and parts of speech

Grammatik Files

During a Standard installation, the following Grammatik files are installed in c:\WPC60DOS: GK51GK.INI, GK51US.HLP, GK51EN.MOR, GK51US.RUL, GK51US.WPS, GMK.EXE, and GK51US.INI.

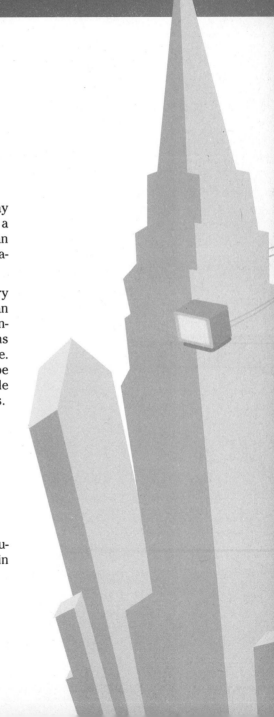

by Ted Pederson

Document Information

Document Information enables you to quickly display statistical information for your entire document or a selected portion of your document. At a glance you can see how many characters, words, lines, sentences, paragraphs, and pages your document contains.

The potential usefulness of this information will vary with the situation. One immediate use is to get an accurate word count at any point in your writing. Another is to compare the statistics for different sections of a long document that was written by several people. Thus, you could see where one section may need to be revised because it uses long, rambling sentences while all the other sections have shorter, snappier phrases.

Displaying Information for the Entire Document

To display statistical information for the entire document you are currently working on, follow the steps in Procedure 10.1.

Procedure 10.1. Displaying information for the entire document.

1. Choose Writing Tools from the Tools menu, then choose Document Information; or press Alt+F1, 4 from the Writing Tools dialog box (see Figure 10.1). The Document Information display box (see Figure 10.2) appears.

2. Choose OK to exit; or press Enter. This returns you to your current document.

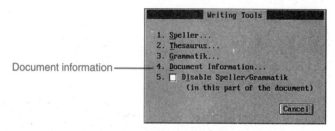

Document information

Figure 10.1. The Writing Tools dialog box.

Displaying Information for Part of the Document

To display statistical information for a selected part of the current document, follow the steps in Procedure 10.2.

Procedure 10.2. Displaying document information for a selected part of the document.

1. Select the text you want.

2. Choose Writing Tools from the Tools menu, then choose Document Information from the Writing Tools dialog box; or press Alt+F1, 4. The Document Information dialog box appears.

3. Choose OK to exit; or press Enter. This returns you to your current document.

The information displayed for the entire document, or a selected part of the document, comprises:

▲ **Characters**. The number of actual characters contained in the document.

▲ **Words**. The number of words contained in the document. The average document usually has 5 characters per word, which is what typographers use as a rule of thumb. You may want to divide the number of characters by 5 and see how it compares to the actual word count.

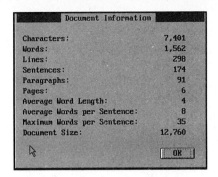

Figure 10.2. The Document Information dialog box.

▲ **Lines**. The number of lines contained in the document, including blank lines, such as between paragraphs.

▲ **Sentences**. The number of sentences contained in the document. A sentence is defined as text that ends with a period, question mark, exclamation point, or hard page break. If you put quotation marks after a period, question mark or exclamation point—like "Help!"—Document Information counts this as a sentence. But if you put two sentences together without a space between them—like "He said.She said."—Document Information counts this as only one sentence.

▲ **Paragraphs**. The number of paragraphs contained in the document. A paragraph is defined as text that ends with a hard return or a hard page break.

▲ **Pages**. The number of pages in the document.

▲ **Average Word Length**. The average length of the words in the document.

▲ **Average Words per Sentence**. The number of words in the typical sentence.

▲ **Maximum Words per Sentence**. The number of words in the longest sentence in the document.

▲ **Document Size**. This is the file of the document and will reflect the entire document (even if you select only a part of the document for a statistical analysis).

Document Information is a simple tool, but one that most users will find to be an invaluable addition to WordPerfect.

Formatting

by Esther Schindler

Default Settings

Each of the codes discussed in this chapter has a default value—a predetermined value that WordPerfect assumes unless you tell it otherwise. For example, when you first install WordPerfect, it assumes that you'll want to use 8.5-inch by 11-inch paper, with 1-inch margins all around and tabs every half inch. You can change any WordPerfect setting to one you prefer using the formatting codes in this or other sections, or by changing the defaults with Document Initial Codes. We will explore Initial Codes in more detail in this chapter, but this should give you the general idea. (The WordPerfect manual provides a complete list of codes starting on page 745 in Appendix B.)

Changing Initial Codes

The default justification setting for WordPerfect, as it comes out of the box, is Left. If you want to change the default to full justification, use the following procedure.

Procedure 11.1. Changing default formatting settings.

1. Choose Layout , then Document , or press Shift+F8 and then choose Document . Choose Initial Codes Setup . WordPerfect shows an empty window.

2. Type the codes you wish to have as your personal default. In this example, you want the default to be full justification, so choose Layout, then Line, or press Shift+F8 and then Line. Select Justification and Full. The [Just:Full] code appears in the Initial Codes window, although you'll only see the abbreviated code unless the cursor is positioned on the code.

3. Click Close or press F7 to close the Initial Codes screen. Press Enter repeatedly until you are returned to the regular WordPerfect screen.

Instead of (or in addition to) the justification codes, you can set the margins, or paper size, or nearly any other code WordPerfect uses. You can include a graphic, or position the text to halfway down the page—though I don't know why you would want to do such a thing in initial codes.

When you first discover the ability to customize your WordPerfect settings, you will probably lose control of yourself and add a setting for every possible code. Don't do this! Instead, begin with WordPerfect's defaults. Pay attention to the formatting codes you use most often. It will become clear, soon enough, which codes you type into every document. When you get tired of changing the codes every time you start a new document, change the initial codes to match what you are already doing.

12

by Esther Schindler

Understanding Formatting Codes

Reveal Codes

One of the reasons for WordPerfect's long popularity is that it keeps the guts of the program from showing, yet it gives you access to the guts when you need it. When WordPerfect was first released, the competing word processors required users to type arcane codes to indicate underline, center, or any of the then-exciting text formatting features the programs supported. WordPerfect, on the other hand, provided the clean screen you explored in earlier chapters, providing access to its fancier features with function keys. Bold text was displayed in bold, centered text was centered on the screen, and so on. The codes that told WordPerfect to "center this text" were hidden to the user's eyes. This enabled WordPerfect users to concentrate on what they were writing, undistracted by the program's how-to machinery.

You may have little need to look at WordPerfect's formatting codes. If your documents stay simple and straightforward, you may never need to see "what's really going on here." But as you explore the immense range of WordPerfect's features—and I encourage you to do so—you'll find that you can create a real mess with formatting codes. The best and easiest way to see what's going on is to look at WordPerfect's Reveal Codes window.

It's much harder to make a mess of your document in WordPerfect 6.0 than it was in earlier versions. Auto Code Placement (discussed a little later in this chapter) moves your formatting codes to a logical location—somewhere you probably intended to place them anyway. WordPerfect now provides some code management, which gets rid of duplicate codes that confused the writer ("Now, I'm sure I changed the tabs in here somewhere!") and slowed down printing (even if a formatting code was duplicated or immediately changed, WordPerfect had to examine every single code when it printed a document).

Nevertheless, situations will arise when you will want to examine or change formatting commands. You may inadvertently pick the wrong formatting code (a mistake your dutiful author—all in the name of research, naturally—discovered is all too easy when trying to learn the program's new features). Or you might want to delete or move some formatting attributes. In any case, as you gain expertise with WordPerfect's formatting, you'll also get more familiar with looking at Reveal Codes.

Fortunately, WordPerfect makes it easy for you to examine the formatting codes when you want to see them, and it keeps them politely out of the way when you don't want to be bothered. As a matter of fact, they're only a keystroke away.

To see the Reveal Codes window (shown in Figure 12.1), choose View, then Reveal Codes, or press either Alt+F3 or F11. WordPerfect displays a small window at the bottom of your screen. Your text is displayed, as well as the codes for special characters and formatting that you typed into your document. The amount of actual text displayed depends on the amount of formatting in your document—many of the formatting codes take up a bit of screen space. You can scroll through your document as usual, and the Reveal Codes screen follows along. To turn the Reveal Codes Window off again, just press Alt+F3 again.

Let's take a look at how these codes work:

▲ Some formatting creates standalone codes. [HRt] is WordPerfect's code for a hard return, or the end of a paragraph. [SRt] is the code for a soft return, the end of a line as WordPerfect figures it, based on your margin size, font, and so on.

▲ Other formatting attributes, and the codes associated with them, are more complex. Many have a value associated with them. Some of these values are like toggle-switches—Bold can be set to bold or not bold. When you change a format value in WordPerfect, the code you see in Reveal Codes reflects the new value. (In this example, you would see [Bold On] or [Bold Off].) The technical term for this kind of code is a *paired code*, because it begins something and, later, ends that something.

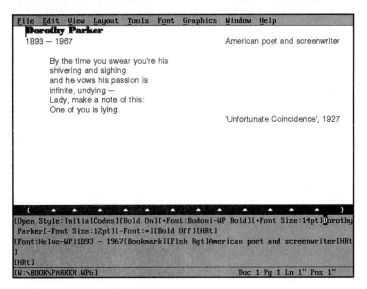

Figure 12.1. The Reveal Codes windows.

▲ Other codes have a finite range of alternatives supplied by WordPerfect: text can be left-, center-, right-, or fully justified. Because these codes can take quite a bit of screen real estate, WordPerfect abbreviates them in Reveal Codes (see Figure 12.2). For example, a line justification code would appear as [Just] in the Reveal Codes screen unless you place the cursor directly on the code. With the cursor placed on the code, the code is expanded, showing [Just:Full,All].

▲ You can also specify some formatting attributes based on an explicit value. For example, tabs can be set at any location. Many of these codes are shown in an abbreviated form even when "expanded" (the code for a footnote, header, text box, or other item containing a large amount of text shows the first 30 characters of the item). This is usually enough to remind you what that code is doing there. If it's not, you have to edit the code to find out.

The codes with finite or explicit values are called *open codes*, because they affect the document from where the code is set forward until you enter another open code of the same type. (You can tell WordPerfect to show full detail in Reveal Codes all the time, but you will probably have very little reason to do so. Look under Setup if you want to do this.)

By default, the Reveal Codes window is 25 percent of your screen size, but you can adjust the size. To change the size of the Reveal Codes window, press Ctrl+F3. Select Reveal Codes Window Percentage and type in the percentage of the screen you want WordPerfect to use to display the codes. You can also adjust the percentage by clicking the arrows next to the numerical entry field.

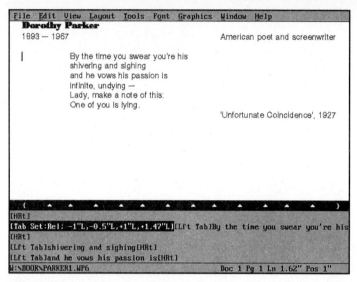

Figure 12.2. Reveal Codes with detail.

Most of the time, the 25 percent allocated to the Reveal Codes screen is just right. However, you might find it useful to change the relative window sizes when you're poring over a complex desktop publishing example full of codes.

Location of Codes

The next few paragraphs describe how codes are placed in WordPerfect with Auto Code Placement turned off. Auto Code Placement, described in the next section, changes how a great deal of this works, but it's important to understand the context.

Many new users of WordPerfect find the placement of formatting codes confounding. Novice users may set a margin and blithely assume that the margin applies to the entire document, or to the selected paragraph. They don't realize that the new margin setting takes effect at the location in the document where the code was entered, or the most reasonable location thereafter, not for the entire document. Grown men and women have shouted with joy when this particular light bulb comes on.

WordPerfect tries to be logical about changing formatting (and other) settings at your command. If you insert a page-numbering code in the middle of a page, on which page should the new page numbering take effect? In the past, WordPerfect assumed that codes not in a specific location would take effect at the next logical juncture. If page formatting commands weren't at the beginning of a page, those commands would take effect at the beginning of the next page.

Thus—Auto Code Placement aside—it's a good idea to get into the habit of putting your page formatting commands at the beginning of a page, your paragraph formatting commands at the beginning of a paragraph, and so on.

Auto Code Placement

One of the most significant new features in WordPerfect 6.0 is Auto Code Placement. Instead of codes collecting haphazardly in your document, wherever you happen to drop them, WordPerfect takes over the management and placement of codes.

When Auto Code Placement is off, all codes remain where they are inserted. In the margin setting change in the last example, the code was entered in the middle of a paragraph, and the margins took effect for the following paragraph.

When Auto Code Placement is on, WordPerfect moves codes to a "sensible" place. In almost all cases, the locations that WordPerfect picks are reasonable. Using the same example, WordPerfect would move the margin code to the beginning of the paragraph in which it was entered. The margins would take effect for that paragraph, rather than the following one.

WordPerfect may move codes to the beginning of a paragraph or page. Auto Code Placement affects page borders, paragraph borders, page centering, columns, delay codes, footers, headers, justification, hyphenation zone, leading adjustment, line height, line numbering, line spacing, all margins (left, right, top, and bottom), page numbering, paper size, paragraph spacing, suppress, tab set, and watermarks.

As you can see from the list, not all codes are affected by Auto Code Placement. Those that are unaffected are codes that are intended to change the text where it stands—font changes, bolding, and so on.

In addition to moving the codes, when Auto Code Placement is on, WordPerfect eliminates duplicate or contradictory codes. For example, if you enter a tab setting change, followed by another tab setting change, WordPerfect deletes the first setting. This is a real boon. Before Auto Code Placement came along, even experienced WordPerfect users had documents full of superfluous codes.

By default, Auto Code Placement is turned on. Under most circumstances, you won't have any reason to change this. If you are accustomed to the old way of doing things, however, you might need to make a conscious adjustment to this feature (you were sure you put this code right here, after all—now where did it go?).

If you do want to change the Auto Code Placement setting, choose File, Setup or press Shift+F1. Select Environment. Change the Auto Code Placement setting to the one you wish and select OK and Close and return to your document.

Delay Codes

The Delay Codes feature enables you to insert codes that take effect a certain number of pages after the beginning of the document (or, in some cases, after a certain page). This means that you can enter formatting codes for subsequent pages on the first page of your document.

Delay Codes is immensely useful for letterhead and other documents where the first page has a different look than the rest of the document. You can use Delay Codes to set up the margins, footers, and so on for the pages that follow a cover page or first sheet.

Delay Codes is very different from Page/Suppress, though experienced WordPerfect users might be confused. Suppress turns off only a limited number of features—page headers, footers, and watermarks. Suppress also assumes that you have already set those features and simply want to turn them off for a given page. On the other hand, Delay Codes lets you enter the formatting for a given page ahead of time.

The most understandable example of using Delay Codes is the one for which it will probably be used most often: letterhead. In many businesses, the margins on the first page needs to be quite different from subsequent pages. Now you can set the initial margins to the letterhead measurements, followed by a Delay Code containing the margins for following pages. The codes are all in one place, and the delayed margin codes aren't hidden somewhere in the document where text insertion or changes can move them elsewhere.

You probably don't want to use Delay Codes unless Auto Code Placement is on. If Auto Code Placement is on, all delayed codes are placed at the top of your document, or right after a hard page break (if your document contains hard page breaks). If Auto Code Placement is turned off, the delay code is placed at the cursor position, and the delay is set to the specified number of pages from that cursor position. This opens up opportunities to create a mess of your document, because your document could contain conflicting delay codes. If you create conflicting delay codes, the delay code that occurs last in your document takes precedence. Also, you cannot edit a delay code created when Auto Code Placement is off. In general, I recommend that you don't use Delay Codes without Auto Code Placement unless you are quite sure of what you're doing, or you want to become close friends with the Reveal Codes function.

Delay Codes can be entered anywhere in the document. Because under most circumstances you will expect those codes to be placed at the beginning of the document, you should check for hard returns. Remember that WordPerfect inserts the `[Delay]` code at the preceding hard page break or at the beginning of the document. The formatting codes you entered appear at the top of the page, the specified number of pages later. The code will show that the formatting code was delayed.

The Delay Codes feature has some limitations. You cannot delay codes that take visible space on your screen, such as Tab, Indent, Center, and Flush Right. You cannot delay paired codes. Paired codes are those with beginning and ending codes, including Underline, Columns, Tables, and Math.

> **Caution:** WordPerfect lets you enter a paired code in the Delayed Codes window, but it removes the code when the delay code is inserted into your document. WordPerfect doesn't warn you that the code you entered is a paired code, so you have to be aware of it. Because there is nothing to stop you from blithely entering paired codes, it's entirely likely that this lack of warning will result in some surprised users. Don't be one of them!

If Auto Code Placement is on, WordPerfect may automatically enter a delay code. If you change the paper type on a specific page, WordPerfect may enter the new paper type code into a delay code at the top of the document, updating the paper change location on the fly. (Although it sounds neat, I think this feature might get on my nerves, but I haven't lived with it long enough to be certain.)

Under certain circumstances, you might want to enter Delay Codes in Initial Codes Setup. Personally, I don't recommend the practice unless the only things you type are letters on letterhead, or other very clear-cut documents that make it an obvious choice, but at least WordPerfect gives you the option. If you are among the users for whom WordPerfect designed this feature, your mind is probably already racing, and you don't need any more suggestions from me.

Procedure 12.1. Creating delay codes.

1. Choose Layout or press Shift+F8. Choose Page, Delay Codes.
2. Type in the number of pages you want the codes delayed and choose OK.
3. WordPerfect displays a window. Type in the formatting codes as if you were entering them into your base document. You can use the function keys or choose formatting codes from the menu. When you are done, choose File and Exit, or press F7.
4. Select OK and Close and return to your document.

To edit Delay Codes, simply repeat the process as if you were entering new codes. If you don't have any Delay Codes for the document (or for the page following the hard return), the window will be empty. If you entered Delay Codes earlier, at that location and for the same number of pages, the Delay Codes window will contain those codes.

Block Marking to Change Attributes

You can put formatting into your text in two basic ways. You can enter the formatting as you type along, or you can add the formatting after the fact. There's no one correct way to do this—choose whichever method is most comfortable for you. Most people combine the two.

If you want to enter codes as you type, the methodology is simple: as you type, select the appropriate formatting commands from the menu or the button bar, or use the function keys. In many cases, you need to turn off a feature that you turned on just a few keystrokes ago, but some shortcuts are available. For font changes, you can select Normal, which sets the text back to the base code font, without any bolding, italicizing, or other fancy embellishments. Ctrl+N is a shortcut back to Normal.

If you are using the WordPerfect 5.1 cursor movement option (see the Setup section for more on this), in some cases you can use the right arrow key to skip past formatting codes, getting you out of the range of paired codes (such as Bold and Math). WordPerfect 6.0 has changed this from previous versions.

Block marking makes adding formatting after you enter your text easy. Most formatting features can be added by block marking the text and choosing the formatting codes. You can block mark a word, phrase, paragraph, or page and italicize the entire thing by choosing Italic from the Font dialog box. Or you can block mark a paragraph and select Paragraph Borders from the Layout/Lines menu to put a border around the selected text. This feature existed in earlier versions of WordPerfect, but it has been expanded in WordPerfect 6.0. (For more information about block marking, refer to Chapter 5, "Advanced Editing.")

After you block mark text and apply an attribute to it, WordPerfect automatically unmarks the text. In many cases, you will want to apply more than one attribute to the same block. There is no single-key solution to this, alas, but there is a shortcut. You can re-mark the block, if you haven't moved your cursor, by pressing Block (F12 or Alt+F4), then pressing Ctrl+Home+Home.

As you'll read throughout this section, block marking is the only pragmatic way to use some features. That's because WordPerfect has added *revertible codes*, which essentially turn a formatting code into a temporary paired code. In other words, you can turn a feature on using block marking, and when the feature turns off (at the end of the block), it returns to its previous value—whatever the previous value was. This is an enormously powerful new ability for WordPerfect, and it requires some focused attention.

Using WordPerfect 6.0, you can mark a block of text and set new tab stops while the text is marked. Those tab stops would be in effect for the text you had marked, but the text after the block would return to the earlier tab settings. WordPerfect doesn't simply put in a code at the end of the block-marked text, indicating what the settings were beforehand—it really reverts to the previous value. A revertible code sets the attribute to what it is at the beginning of the block, not what it was. Even if you back up a page in the document and insert a completely different tab setting (to take effect over the entire document), the revertible code (placed at the end of the block of text you had marked) reflects the newer tab setting.

This single feature avoids situations that were awkward, at best, in earlier versions of WordPerfect. One common annoyance in earlier versions was managing frequent font changes.

Let's explore revertible codes with a simple example using fonts. You can create revertible codes for margins, tabs, or any number of other formatting codes, but you will probably use fonts most often.

1. Type in some text (a few sentences will suffice). Block mark a segment of the text (press Alt+F4 or F12 and use the mouse or arrow keys to select the text).

2. Select Font, then Font..., or press Ctrl+F8 to bring up the font dialog box. Change the font and/or attributes (specific instructions are in the next chapter, but you can experiment for now), and select OK and Close until you return to the document window.

3. To examine what you've done, press F11 or Alt+F3 to display the Reveal Codes window. The code at the beginning of the block will have a plus (+) in front ([+Font:Palantino Italic]), and the code at the end will begin with a minus (-) ([-Font:Times]). Other than the plus and minus signifying that the code is revertible, this doesn't look significantly different than simply changing a font.

4. Here's the difference, though. Move to the beginning of the text, at least a few words before the text marked with the revertible codes. Without block marking the text, change the font to, say, Zapf Chancery. When you display Reveal Codes again, the [+Font] code remains the same, but the [-Font] code reflects the current font—Zapf Chancery ([-Font:Zapf Chancery Medium Italic]).

Codes whose effect is at the location of the code, rather than in subsequent text (such as indents, footnotes, and tabs) are not revertible. That's not a problem, because under most circumstances you wouldn't think of applying any of those as attributes to a block of text. You'll find that almost any attribute is revertible. I encourage you to experiment.

Deleting Codes

You can remove formatting commands by deleting the codes that created them. The easiest and most efficient way to delete a code is by using Reveal Codes. Select View and choose Reveal Codes, or press Alt+F3 or F11. Position the cursor on the code to be deleted and press Delete, or position the cursor to the right of the offending code and press Backspace.

WordPerfect 6.0 changed the way that you delete codes when Reveal Codes is not displayed. Any formatting code that affects how text is displayed on-screen (especially in Graphics mode) is ignored when you press Backspace. WordPerfect does seem to prompt you when you are about to delete some codes, but which ones are included is not clear. By far, you will be safest and least confused if you use Reveal Codes to delete codes.

Some codes can't be deleted. The first code in any document is [Initial Codes], which contains your own default settings. You can't change these without going into Document/Initial Codes, as detailed above—and you can't delete the code at all.

Other codes that can't be deleted include those that WordPerfect generates. When you press Enter, WordPerfect generates a [HRt], called a *hard return*, which shows up in Reveal Codes and can be deleted. But when WordPerfect determines that a line should wrap, based on the size and nature of the font you're using, it generates a *soft return*, shown as [SRt]. You can't delete a [SRt] or similar code. They are there because WordPerfect is doing its job.

Searching for Codes

In earlier versions of WordPerfect, searching for formatting codes was possible, but only in a general sense. For example, when searching for a font, WordPerfect 5.1 finds any font change. In a document of any complexity, with dozens of font changes, that rarely helps matters. WordPerfect 5.1 doesn't replace generic codes, at least not in any useful fashion.

Using WordPerfect 6.0, you can incorporate a code search in any search command, and you can find codes that are set to a specific value. The latter is brand-new. Now you can search for a generic font change, or for a font change to Times Roman.

You can also replace formatting codes. Doing so is still somewhat awkward—there's no easy way to say "change all bolded text to italic"—but it is much improved.

In general, the code search procedure works just the same as searching for text (see Chapter 5).

Procedure 12.2. Searching for a code.
   1. Select Edit and choose Search, or press F2. WordPerfect displays the Search dialog box.

2. Type the text you seek into the Search For box. If your search text needs to include a generic code, such as Font or Footnote, press F5. WordPerfect displays the list of codes. Use the arrow keys or the mouse to select the code you want, or start typing the first few letters of the code (typing Foot leads you to [Footnote]). Press Enter or click Select to accept the code, which displays in the text entry box.

3. If you want to include a specific code in your search, select Specific Codes, or press Shift+F5. WordPerfect displays the list of codes that can have a specific value attached. Select the code you want and press Enter. WordPerfect provides you with an appropriate dialog, giving you the opportunity to enter the value you want to search for. For example, if you select Bottom Margin from the Specific Codes list, WordPerfect asks you for the bottom margin value you seek (e.g., 1").

4. When you are finished creating your search string, press F2 to begin the search.

The procedure for replacing codes (or codes with text) is the same as replacing text (covered in Chapter 5), with a few special notes:

▲ You can replace one specific font with another. You cannot replace any font change with a specific font change. That is, you cannot change all font changes to Times Roman, though you can change all Palatino font changes to Times Roman font changes.

▲ You can change font sizes. You can change fonts from 12 point to 10 point. You can search for and delete font size codes (press F4 from the dialog box that WordPerfect presents when you specify the Font Size code).

▲ Here's the list of Specific Codes you can search and replace: margins, fonts, font size, line spacing, overstrike, horizontal and vertical advance, and justification. Each one permits you to delete the code when found (replacing them with nothing).

▲ You can search for (but not search and replace) styles.

13

by Esther Schindler

Changing Fonts

This chapter discusses fonts. You'll find font installation and setup instructions in Chapter 23, "Printing." Workshop VIII, "Desktop Publishing," covers the theoretical and aesthetic issues concerning fonts, helping you to make the most of your layout.

A *font* is a combination of printer typeface, appearance, and character size.

A *typeface* describes the "picture" of the way a given character set appears on the page. One typeface might be tall and thin; another might be elegant, with flourishes; still another might have a western flavor. Each typeface has a different feel to it and a different mood.

Font appearance or font *attributes* are variations on a typeface. Most typefaces support the "normal" typeface (sometimes called Roman), bold, italic, and bold-and-italic. Every printer comes with at least one typeface. Most printers supply quite a few built-in typefaces, stored in the printer's memory. In many cases, using these fonts can be the fastest way to print a document. If your printer supports graphics (most do), you can also print the graphic fonts included with WordPerfect 6.0, as well as those available from third-party vendors.

You can add more attributes to your text than bold and italic. Text can be outlined, shadowed, printed in small capitals, underlined, double-underlined, struck-out, or redlined. Text can be printed in superscript or subscript. New to WordPerfect 6.0, text can also be printed in color, in superscript, or in subscript.

Your printer may not be able to print every font or attribute, especially if it is an older model or has very limited memory. The easiest way for you to see what your printer can do is to print the document PRINTER.TST, included with WordPerfect.

WordPerfect's Graphics mode or Page mode shows text as it appears on the page, including fonts and their attributes. In Text mode, text appears on the screen in a monospaced font, no matter which printer font is selected. You can change the colors that WordPerfect uses to display text mode font attributes by changing the Setup/Display, Text Mode:Screen Type/Colors.

Tip: If you work in Text mode, Use Print Preview (Shift+F7 ,View) to see how your document will be printed.

Auto Code Placement does not affect font changes. When you insert a font change in your text, all of the text following the insertion is influenced. To change the font, attribute, or size of only a certain range of text, use block before you issue the WordPerfect command. Press Alt+F4 or F12 and move the cursor to encompass the range, then issue the font, attribute, or size change.

Usually, you'll find it much easier to block mark and change fonts and attributes than to type the changes as you go. WordPerfect's new revertible codes feature ensures that text following the block mark automatically returns to the font or attribute you were using previously.

By default, headers, footers, footnotes, and endnotes use the document's initial font. Font changes made within a specific header, footer, footnote, or endnote only affect that text. System header, footer, footnote, and endnote styles override the initial font, but not any specific changes you make.

If you have Format Document for Default Printer selected in your environment setup, when you open a file that was created using a printer that you don't have defined, WordPerfect makes a "best guess" concerning fonts. If your printer doesn't support a given font, Reveal Codes displays the original font with an asterisk ([Font:*Swiss 721 Bold]). WordPerfect chooses the closest available font for printing the document—actually, it does a remarkably good job. Unless you explicitly change or delete the original font code, it remains in the document. Graphics fonts are unaffected.

Changing Base Fonts

There are several ways to establish or change the fonts used in your document.

Each printer definition contains the default font and font size used for new documents. You can change the default font by editing the printer definition, or by modifying the document initial base font (the latter is easier). See Figure 13.1.

When you change the initial base font, you can specify whether the font change should apply to all new documents, or to this document only. If you specify that the font should be used for all new documents, initial fonts for existing documents do not change. When you specify that the initial font should be assigned for this document only, that is just what happens (note that the initial font is not reflected in Reveal Codes).

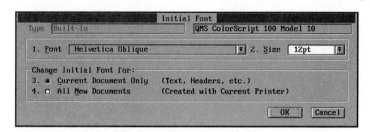

Figure 13.1. Changing the initial base font.

Procedure 13.1. Changing the initial base font.

1. Choose Layout or press Shift+F8 Select Document Select Initial Font (To get a list of the fonts available, click on the down arrow or select Font. Select Size or click on the down arrow next to the font size field.)

2. Select the Font you want to use. Select the font Size

3. Indicate whether this font and font size should be used as the default font for this document only, or for all new documents.

4. Select OK and Close until you return to your document screen.

Font changes are generally made for an overall font change, intended to affect the document from the cursor onward, or a limited font change, intended to apply to specific text only. You can change the base font as often as you wish. If you want to write a ransom note, you can change fonts several times in the same sentence.

Remember that a general font change affects the rest of your document, or until you issue another font change. Make sure that your cursor is positioned where you want the font change to begin.

Procedure 13.2. Changing a base font.

1. Select Font and Font... or press Ctrl+F8 WordPerfect displays the Font dialog box.

2. Choose Font WordPerfect displays a list of the fonts available for the printer you have selected. Select the font you want to use. If you are in Graphics mode or Page mode, WordPerfect displays a sample line of text using the font under the cursor. In Text mode, the preview area lists the name and size of the font that is currently selected.

Font preview is great if you are "shopping" for an appropriate font, and you aren't sure which one to use. However, if you know which font you want, looking at the comparatively slow font preview can become tedious.

> **Tip:** You can speed up font manipulation by choosing fonts while you are in Text mode. Whichever mode you use, if you are familiar with the available fonts, you can find the font faster by using the PageUp and PageDown keys, or by using the Name Search command to find the font as quickly as possible. With the font choices displayed, gradually spell the name of the font. WordPerfect will position the cursor on the font name that fits (see Figure 13.2).

3. Note that you can also change the font size and appearance at this point.

4. Select OK and Close until you return to your document screen.

Often, you will want to change the font for a specific block of text. Block mark the text to be changed and follow the same procedure. The font you select applies to the marked text; the text following the block reverts to the base font in effect before the block began.

You can use the WordPerfect ribbon to change fonts. With the ribbon displayed, click on the font. WordPerfect displays the list of fonts available. Double-click on the font to use.

Figure 13.2. Selecting a font.

When you choose fonts, remember that fonts built into your printer print faster than graphics fonts. If you are using a printer with fixed-size fonts, this can be a difficult trade-off. Graphics fonts are scalable, which means that you can make them nearly any size. Graphics fonts can also be printed in either landscape or portrait orientation—you may have less choice with your printer's defaults. However, graphics fonts take longer to print than the built-in fonts. Because they are (as their name implies) printed as graphics, they use your printer's memory just as a picture would.

Changing Text Attributes

WordPerfect provides a wide variety of text attributes to change the appearance of text. Limited somewhat by what your printer can do, you can print text that is outlined, shadowed, printed in small capitals, underlined, double-underlined, struck-out, redlined, or any combination. If you have a color printer, you can print text in color. Figure 13.3 shows you what the various attributes look like.

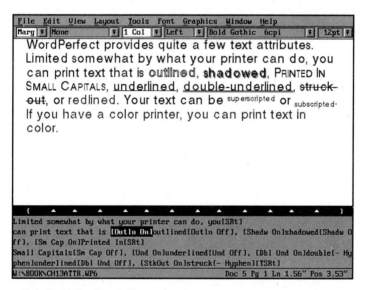

Figure 13.3. Print attribute options.

All text attributes are paired codes. If an attribute (for example, bold) is typed, any text after the code is displayed and printed in bold, until you issue the command to turn bold off. When you insert a text attribute in unmarked text, WordPerfect applies the attribute to the text that follows (you must turn off the attribute manually). When you block mark text and change the text attributes, WordPerfect adds both the *on* code and the *off* code.

Although attributes take effect at the insertion point, Auto Code Placement affects attribute changes. If you assign bold to a marked block that already includes a bolded sentence, WordPerfect moves the [Bold:On] to the beginning of the block and deletes the [Bold:On] that began the sentence. In other cases, WordPerfect displays an [Ignore:Bold:On] command in Reveal Codes.

To change text attributes, choose Font and select the appropriate attribute. Be sure to notice the shortcut keys: Ctrl+I for italics, F6 or Ctrl+B for bold, F8 or Ctrl+U for underline, Ctrl+N for normal. Using Ctrl+N is the fastest way to turn off all special attributes.

Use the font dialog box to make more than one appearance change at once. Select Font, Font..., or press Ctrl+F8. Choose Appearance, and select the attributes you want to use.

You can change the vertical position of text on the line. Under most circumstances, the default of *normal* is adequate, but text can also be assigned to superscript or subscript. From the font dialog box, choose Position and select Normal, Superscript, or Subscript; or select Font, Size/Position, and Normal, Superscript, or Subscript.

WordPerfect 6.0 lets you make use of the color capability of your printer. WordPerfect can print up to 16 million colors, but your printer probably has limitations that will keep you from trying every one!

Procedure 13.3. Printing text in color.

1. To change the color of your text, select Font, Print Color..., or press Ctrl+F8 and Color.
2. Select the color to use for text. In Graphics mode or Page mode, WordPerfect displays an approximation of the colors you are examining. Choose OK and Close until you return to your document window.

WordPerfect supplies predefined colors for the "basic" colors (red, yellow, and so on), as well as a selection of popular alternatives (such as navy, brown, and wild strawberry). Figure 13.4 shows one example. You can change the shade of a given color. You can define additional colors by choosing Custom Color from the Color dialog box and using your mouse or changing the Red, Green, and Blue settings to establish the new color. Select Add to Palette and assign a name to your new color, if you want to use it again.

Font Sizes

Fixed size fonts are measured in *pitch*, a horizontal measurement of the number of characters that print per inch. With pitch, the larger the number, the smaller the character size. Laser printer fonts and scalable fonts are described in *points*, a vertical measurement. There are 72 points in an inch, so the larger the point size, the larger the character.

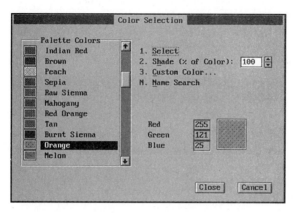

Figure 13.4. Printing text in color.

You can specify the size of a font explicitly, or you can change the size based on a measurement relative to the base font. Font size limitations are limited by your printer and by the nature of the font itself.

If you are using a non-scalable font, you can only select supported font sizes. This applies to most built-in dot-matrix fonts. If you type in a size that isn't supported, WordPerfect chooses the size that is closest.

Procedure 13.4. Changing the font size.

  1. Select Font, Font..., or press Ctrl+F8. Choose Size.
 2.a. Type in the point or pitch size directly.

        or

 2.b. Click on the arrow to the right of the font selection box. WordPerfect displays a pre-selected list of font sizes. In Graphics or Page mode, the font preview box reflects the font size change as you scroll through the pre-selected font sizes. If the typeface selected is a scalable font, you are not limited to these sizes. If the typeface selected is a fixed-size font, these are your only choices.

  3. Select OK and Close until you return to your document screen.

You can also select font size from the ribbon. Click on the font size box. Double-click on the font size to select it, or type in the new size.

Revertible codes apply to font size. If you change the font size of a marked block, the size of the text following the block remains at the size set earlier.

Text size can be adjusted based on *relative size*, wherein WordPerfect picks the font size proportionally larger or smaller than the current font. While you can adjust the ratio that determines *fine*, *small*, *large*, *very large*, and *extra large*, the default ratio is usually adequate. Choose Font, Size/Position, and select the size. Or, press Ctrl+F8 and choose Relative Size. Choosing headings and other emphasis text based on relative size rather than a fixed size is extremely useful, because the size adjusts automatically when you change the size of the base font.

by Esther Schindler

Using Character Formatting

Decimal Align

Decimal tabs align the text on the decimal point, or on the character you have defined as the alignment character. If you type documents with columns of numbers, you will find this feature handy. Without decimal tabs, numbers of different lengths would line up unevenly, making the text hard to read. Here's a very simple example of the difference:

Before:	*After:*
26.374	26.374
556.08	556.08
1,900.0	1,900.0

To align text on a decimal, use Ctrl+F6 or define the tab stop as a decimal tab (see "Tabs" in Chapter 15, "Line Formatting"). Think about the width of the numbers you will use when you set the tab stop; if you have large numbers aligned on the decimal, your numbers could overlap your text.

Setting decimal tabs is an excellent place to make use of revertible codes. If you have only a few lines of text that require decimal tabs, type the numbers without the decimal tabs, block mark the lines with the numbers, and change the tab stops to reflect the decimal tab placement. WordPerfect uses the decimal tabs you specified for the blocked text and returns to the old settings for the following text.

On a statement of cash flows, you might see the following:

Cash	$150,000
Accounts receivable	(500)
Inventory	250,000

There are two tab stops, one for the *$* and one where the number aligns. The *$* location is set to a left tab, and the align tab is a decimal tab. The underline starts at the left tab. Notice that there isn't a decimal in the list of numbers. In this case, the decimal tab character has been changed to a right tab.

Although your most frequent use of decimal tabs will be for numbers, as in the example above, you can use any character, including the WordPerfect Characters (Ctrl+W) as a decimal tab. In the financial statement above, you should use the closing parenthesis as the alignment character, to make the numbers align.

Procedure 14.1. Changing the decimal tab character.

1. Select Layout, or press Shift+F8. Choose Character, and select Decimal/Align Character.
2. Enter the character you want to use as the alignment character. Note that you can use WordPerfect characters (Ctrl+W)
3. Select OK and Close until you return to your document.

Thousands Separator

WordPerfect lets you change the character used to separate large numbers in tables. North Americans use the comma (,) to separate digits in numbers greater than one thousand, but other countries use different characters. You can use any keyboard character or a WordPerfect Character (Ctrl+W).

Procedure 14.2. Changing the thousands separator.

1. Select Layout, or press Shift+F8, and choose Character. Choose Thousands Separator, and type the new value.
2. Choose Exit and Close until you return to your document screen.

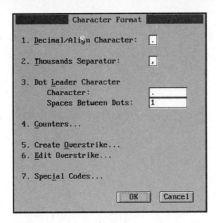

Figure 14.1. The Character Format dialog.

Dot Leader

Leaders provide a row of periods or other characters that make it easy for the eye to follow. Use the tab settings to define where leader characters will be used (see Tabs).

Although WordPerfect calls this feature a dot leader, the leader character can be an underscore or any other character, including a WordPerfect Character. You can also adjust the spacing between the leader characters.

The most frequent use of leaders is in tables of contents and other lists, but you can get creative. For example, you can set the leader character to an underline and use it to create signature lines for legal documents. Experiment with WordPerfect Characters to create interesting leaders (try bullets or iconic symbols). Use the copyright symbol if you really want to get a point across. If you have an older printer that doesn't support graphics, you can use it to make attractive (or at least acceptable . . . okay, not terribly ugly) lines and borders.

Procedure 14.3. Changing the dot leader character.

1. Select Layout, or press Shift+F8, and choose Character.
2. Choose Dot Leader and type in the new dot leader character and the number of spaces you want between each dot.
3. Choose Exit and Close until you return to your document screen.

Tip: If you have only a few lines that need dot leaders, you don't have to go through the exercise of creating tabs with leaders. WordPerfect provides a short-cut. To create centered text with a dot leader, press Shift+F6 twice. To create right-justified text with a leader, press Alt+F6 twice. Both of these work with leader characters as well as they do with the standard dot.

Counters

When I first encountered WordPerfect's new Counters feature, I was confused. I didn't understand its purpose. Sure, the documentation said "you can count or number anything in your document," but what did that mean? Why would you ever want to count or number anything in your document—or, at least, why would you want to number something that WordPerfect didn't supply? Weren't paragraph numbers, figure caption numbers, and all that enough? What else would one want to count or number?

Then the light bulb blinked on.

With counters, you can count and number anything in your document. *Anything.* In writing the chapters for this book, I needed to keep track of figures and procedures. Every item needed to be numbered, but I don't work in a top-to-bottom manner. If I tried to number procedures and figures by hand, the references would always be out of sync.

WordPerfect 6.0's counters solve this kind of problem perfectly, because, like footnotes, equations, and figure boxes, the numbers are continuously updated. Counters are ideal for any job that requires you to keep track of items, in one form or another. If you are writing a technical manual, you can keep separate counters for exhibits, examples, and problems for the student. You can count items in a table. Counters can be used in a macro-based application, keeping track of mailing lists or customers.

In short, this is a truly cool feature. Let's look at counters in detail.

Each counter can have up to five levels. Each level has a separate numbering scheme. You can display the value of a counter anywhere in your document, using numbers, letters, or Roman numerals.

Counters do not work automatically. This is both good and bad. You have control over what happens, but you have to make it happen. It is your responsibility to manage the counter values and remember to insert the counter display codes. Ideally, you will find a way to automate the process (incorporate the way you control counters in a style or a macro).

It's important to remember that the display of counters is separate from the manipulation of their values. You can set the value of any counter, or increment or decrement the value. But WordPerfect won't display the value of the counter until and unless you explicitly tell it to do so. For example, you could keep count of items in a document, and never actually display the value. When you add counter increments, WordPerfect updates any values that follow, similar to the way it keeps track of footnote numbers. (Auto Code Placement does not affect Counters.)

A major difference between counters and other numbering features provided by WordPerfect is the control that counters give you—that they force upon you, actually. Because incrementing and displaying counters are entirely separate functions, you gain much more control. However, they can be confusing.

WordPerfect lets you change the defaults for what it calls the "system counters," the equation box, figure box, table box, text box, and user box. You can change the manner in which these are numbered (make all figures numbered with Roman numerals, for example), or change the number of levels that equations support. I'm not sure why you would want to add levels to any of the system counters, but WordPerfect permits you to do so. On the other hand, there might be good reasons to change the value of a figure box counter. For example, you might include a document or chart from another program, manually added to your report. Manually incrementing the figure counter gives you a way to keep the numbered figures in sync.

You control four things with Counters:

▲ Counter method

▲ Counter display

▲ Counter increment and decrement

▲ Counter value

The *counter method* controls each counter's numbering method. Counters can display using numbers, letters, or Roman numerals. Each level of a counter may use a different numbering method. (When you look at this in Reveal Codes, you'll see [Count Meth].)

You control the *counter display*. Counters are not automatically shown in a document. To display a counter, you must position the cursor where you want the number to appear, and then tell WordPerfect to display the counter value. (When you do so, Reveal Codes shows [Count Disp].)

You can increment or decrement a counter value—add or subtract one to the value—at any time. Each counter level is incremented or decremented separately. When you issue a *counter increment* or *counter decrement*, Reveal Codes shows [Count Inc] or [Count Dec]. You can change the *counter value* at any time, altering the counter to a new number. (Reveal Codes displays the value change as [Count Set].)

If you explicitly change (rather than increment) the value of one level of a counter, the values of other levels will not change. For example, if MyCount counter (with three levels) has a value of 14.5.3, and you explicitly change the counter value for the first level to 15, the rest of the MyCount levels remain the same (i.e., 15.5.3). However, if you increment the value of an upper level counter (e.g., the "14" in 14.5.3), the levels underneath are set to 1; incrementing MyCount level 1 to 15 would result in 15.1.1.

Creating a Counter

Every counter has a name (assigned by you), a numbering scheme, a number of levels (up to five), and a starting value. The default numbering scheme is numbers, the number of default levels is 1, and the default starting value is 1.

Each level of a counter may use a different numbering method. The three levels of a counter called "Exhibit," for example, could be set to Uppercase Roman (first level), Lowercase Roman (second level), and letters (third level). When you create a counter with more than one level, remember that each level needs to be incremented and displayed separately. Selecting *Display in Document* for Exhibit level 3 displays only the value of level 3 (for example, *c*), not the values of levels 1 and 2. Your document would display *c*, not *Xvc*.

You can edit counter settings later in the document. You can change the numbering method of a counter, even after you've manipulated the value and displayed it. WordPerfect lets you display Exhibit:Level 1 with a *Numbers* format one time and *Roman* the next.

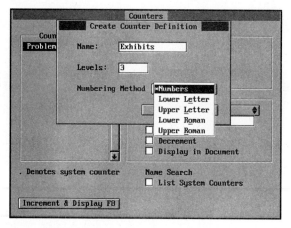

Figure 14.2. Creating the Exhibit counter.

Procedure 14.4. Creating a counter.

1. Select Layout or press Shift+F8. Choose Character, then Counters....

2. Select Create, and type in the name of the new counter.

3. Optional: if you want to change the number of levels from the default of one, select Levels and type in the new value.

4. Optional: if you want to change the numbering method from the default of Numbers, select Numbering Method and choose the method you prefer.

5. Optional: if you want to create the counter with an inital value, other than the default of 1, select Set Value and enter the new value. Note that counters with more than one level require that you position the cursor on a specific level in order to adjust the value.

6. Select OK and Close until you return to your document.

Incrementing and Decrementing Counters

Because incrementing and decrementing counters is completely within your control, you should give some thought to where it makes the most sense to do so. In most situations, you will want to increment a counter right before or after you use it. But should you do so before or afterward? Each method has its benefits and disadvantages.

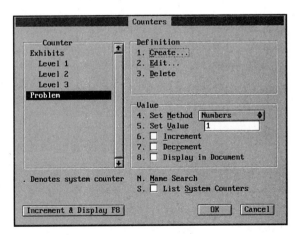

Figure 14.3. Incrementing a simple counter.

One prosaic reason to decrement a counter is in a countdown list: "Here are the Top Ten Reasons: Reason #10, #9, and so on." Macro wizards will find decrementing counters extremely useful. In fact, macros will probably be where counter decrementing finds its popularity.

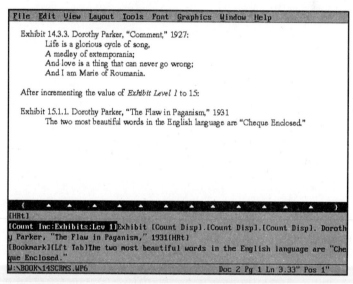

Figure 14.4. Incrementing a multilevel counter.

Usual locations for incrementing counters are at the beginning of sections and chapters. Because the need for incrementing (and displaying) counters at those locations is so predictable, it's an ideal item to include in a paragraph style. For instance, assuming that you have defined a Chapter counter, incorporate `Chapter [Count Disp:Chapter].[Count Inc:Chapter]` in a chapter style to display and increment the chapter number.

Procedure 14.5. Incrementing or decrementing a counter.

1. Position your cursor where you want the counter to be incremented or decremented.

2. Select Layout or press Shift+F8. Choose Character, then Counters....

3. Select the counter that you want to adjust. If the counter has more than one level, be sure to select the level of the counter you want to increment. Select Increment or Decrement.

4. You can insert a code to display the counter at this time, too, or change the values of the counter. Even easier, press F8 to automatically increment and display the code and return to your document.

5. If necessary, select OK and Close until you return to the document.

Changing the Value of a Counter

When you increment, decrement, or set a new value for one level of a counter, the value for all subordinate levels is reset to 1.

If the current value of the Exhibit counter is Xvc:

> Level 1. X (10)
> Level 2. v (5)
> Level 3. c (3)

Incrementing level 2 (to *vi*) sets Level 3 back to 1 (displayed as *a*). After incrementing Exhibit Level 2, displaying the values would look like this:

> Level 1. X (10)
> Level 2. vi (6)
> Level 3. a (1)

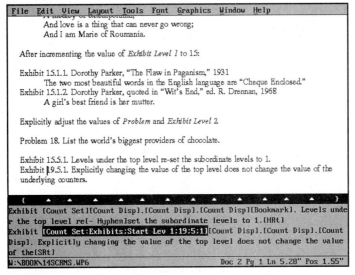

Figure 14.5. Changing the value of a counter.

When you create a counter, its default value is 1. You can change the value of a counter at any time in the document. From the Counters dialog box, select the counter (or counter level) whose value you want to adjust. Choose Set Value and enter the new value. All display, increment, and decrement functions inserted thereafter reflect the new value.

Displaying a Counter

WordPerfect will not automatically display the value of any counter. You can create a counter, manipulate its values, and never display the value in the document.

You explicitly tell WordPerfect to display the value of the counter. Note that displaying the value of one level of a counter doesn't automatically display the value for each level. Selecting Display in Document for ExhibitLlevel 3 displays a simple 5. If you want to see the values for Exhibit Levels 1 and 2, you have to display those explicitly as well. You can issue the display command for each level concurrently, because the Counter dialog box doesn't close until you tell it to do so. Select Display in Document for the first counter level, then use the cursor key to select the next level. Select Display in Document for that one too. When you do finally select OK, all of the levels you selected will display.

To display numbers, you must move your cursor to the place where you want the value to appear, and then tell WordPerfect to display the value. Because the locations where you will want to display counters are often predictable—chapter and section headings, or exhibit numbers, for example—they are ideal for inclusion in paragraph styles.

> **Note:** If you display every counter level number concurrently, you will get a number that looks like 12345. You will probably want to insert punctuation between the level numbers. This is another great use of styles!

Procedure 14.6. Displaying a counter.

1. Select Layout or press Shift+F8. Choose Character, then Counters....
2. Select the counter that you want to display. Select Display in Document.
3. Select OK and Close until you return to the document.

Counters won't do everything, and they aren't the best solution for every problem. You will find that there are times when paragraph numbering or styles or another feature solves the problem better. Nonetheless, they're exciting and useful.

Overstrike

On occasion, you may want to print characters that aren't directly supported by WordPerfect. Sometimes, you can accomplish what you want by using an overstrike character, which creates the same effect that you would get from typing two characters on top of each other with a typewriter.

Because of the interrelationship between overstrike characters, WordPerfect Characters, and Compose characters, an entire chapter has been devoted to the subject. This section provides the basics, but check out Chapter 54, "Special Characters and Foreign Languages," for more details.

Procedure 14.7. Creating an overstrike character.

1. To create an overstrike character, select Layout, then Character, or press Shift+F8, and Character. Choose Create Overstrike.... WordPerfect displays a small window in which you can type the characters you want to be printed on top of each other. Select OK and Close until you return to your document screen.

2. You can set text attributes that apply to the overstrike characters alone. At the Create Overstrike entry window, press Ctrl+F8 to display the choices of character position, size, and appearance. These attributes apply only to the overstrike characters, not to the rest of your document. It's as if you block-marked the overstrike characters and selected that set of character attributes for them.

Figure 14.6. Creating overstrike characters.

Editing overstrike characters uses a similar procedure. Select Layout, then Character, or press Shift+F8, and Character. Choose Edit Overstrike.... WordPerfect searches for the last overstrike character created in your document (looking backward from the cursor position), and displays the overstrike creation window. Make your changes and select OK and Close until you return to the document window.

In WordPerfect's Text mode, you won't be able to see what the overstrike character looks like. Instead, you'll see the last character typed in the overstrike. For example, if your overstrike character is *oe*, the Text mode of WordPerfect displays *e*. Reveal Codes shows the overstrike character as a special code, `[Ovrstrk:oe]`.

by Esther Schindler

Line Formatting

Changing Tab Settings

If you ever used an old-fashioned typewriter, you will remember that pressing the tab key moved the text to the next tab stop, a predefined location on the line. Word processing extends the notion of tab stops, and WordPerfect augments the concept even further.

An important concept in using and defining tabs is that, unlike the typewriter tab stops, a WordPerfect tab is a kind of character. Pressing Tab on the typewriter simply moved the platen; it didn't affect what you had written on the paper. In WordPerfect, tabs are values that tell the cursor to move to a position to a particular location on the line. If you look in Reveal Codes, you will see that the tab has a code all its own.

Kinds of Tabs

WordPerfect supplies several kinds of tab stops. What you might consider to be an "ordinary" tab is called a *left tab* ([Lft Tab]). Text typed after pressing a *right tab* ([Rgt Tab]) is right-justified against the tab stop. Similarly, a *center tab* ([Cntr Tab]) causes text to be centered at the location of the center tab code. Text typed at a *decimal tab* aligns on the *alignment character*, which is usually the decimal point.

In addition, you can set tab stops to have a *dot leader*. When you press the tab key and the tab setting is defined as a dot leader, WordPerfect types a row of dots from the cursor position to the tab setting. The tab setting can be a left, right, centered, or decimal tab—the dots are a visual clue for the reader. You can change the character that WordPerfect uses for the leader character (see Chapter 14, "Using Character Formatting," for instructions).

Tab settings can be measured from the left edge of the page (called *absolute* settings), or from the left margin (called *relative* settings).

Setting Tabs

WordPerfect's default tab settings are left tabs, positioned every half-inch, relative to the left margin. Tab settings are affected by Auto Code Placement. WordPerfect moves a [Tab Set] code to the beginning of the current paragraph. Tab settings take effect from the code placement forward in the document, or until WordPerfect finds another tab setting. Note that revertible codes work extremely well with tab settings.

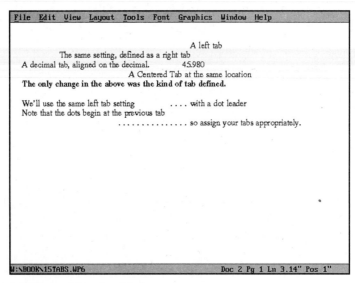

Figure 15.1. Different kinds of tabs.

When you modify tab settings, or create new ones, it can help to erase old settings first. In the Tab Setting dialog box, you can erase an individual setting (select Clear One), clear all tabs (choose Clear All), or clear the tabs to the right of the cursor position by pressing Ctrl+End.

To set repeating tabs (for example, every inch), position the cursor on the paragraph where you want the settings to take effect.

Procedure 15.1. Setting repeating tab stops.

1. Select Layout, or press Shift+F8. Choose Line, and Tab Set....
2. Clear all tabs.
3. Repeating tabs are all the same type, although you can change individual tabs afterward. Select the type of tab to use (left, right, center, or decimal), and whether the tabs should be relative or absolute.

4.a. Enter the spacing between tabs in the Repeat Every box, and press Enter.

or

4.b. Enter the starting tab position in the Set Tab entry field;, a comma;, then the amount of space between the tabs. For example, if you want tabs to begin at 4 inches and repeat every 1.5 inches thereafter, enter 4,1.5. You can enter the starting position in the Set Tab field and the spacing thereafter in the Repeat Every field.

5. Choose OK and Close until you return to your document. (Note that it's easiest to use F7 to exit when you create tabs, especially if you aren't using a mouse.)

> **Tip:** If you aren't sure how much room you will need for tab stops, change the tab settings after you enter the text. The Tab Settings dialog displays a few lines of existing text. As you make changes in the Tab Settings dialog box, WordPerfect adjusts the text to reflect your proposed changes. This feature lets you fine-tune tab stops and saves you time. Use the control keys and arrows to move tab settings. WordPerfect permits you to move a tab as far as the next tab stop.

To create or modify an individual tab, position the cursor on the ruler bar where the tab should appear. Press D for a decimal tab, L for a left tab, R for a right tab, or C for a center tab. Pressing a period (.) at that location adds a dot leader. Alternatively, you can type the exact location in the Set Tab entry box. You can use decimals or fractions in the Set Tab box, which gives you a greater measure of accuracy. Typing a plus sign (+) before entering a tab setting ensures that the tab is a relative tab; including an at-sign (@) ensures an absolute tab.

To delete a tab from the ruler, position the cursor on the tab stop and press the Delete key, or select Clear One.

Justification

WordPerfect can align text in several different ways. You can align text along the left margin (the technical term for what you get if you type on a typewriter is *left justified*). Text can be aligned along the right margin or centered between the margins. It can also have *full justification*, wherein the text is aligned along both right and left margins. In this case, WordPerfect adds space between words and characters to "stretch" the text so that it lines up evenly, with the rightmost character along the right margin. You are most likely to see full justification used in newspapers and formal documents.

With WordPerfect 6.0, you have a choice between two kinds of full justification. *Full Justification* does the text stretch for all lines in a paragraph, except the last line. With *Full Justification, All Lines*, the last line in a paragraph is justified, even if it is only a few letters long.

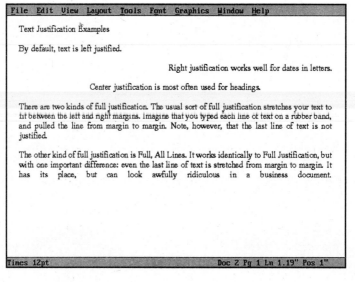

Figure 15.2. Text justification.

The line justification you set applies to the text within your current margins, whatever those margins happen to be. For example, if you have text set to centered while you are working in a 3-column layout, the text is centered in the margins of the current column, not across the overall page. Right-justified text in a text box is justified only in that box (the setting doesn't extend outside of the box).

Justification applies around graphics boxes, too. As you'll read in detail in Workshop VII, "Graphics, Lines, Borders, and Fills," WordPerfect permits graphics with irregular shapes. The justification you set for the text that wraps around that graphic works the same as it does in a normal, rectangular paragraph.

If you want to right-justify or center only one line of text, it isn't necessary to go through the Layout-Line process. WordPerfect lets you center one line of text at a time (Shift+F6) or right-justify a single line (Alt+F6). If your primary purpose is to right-justify a date or to center a heading, these should be more than adequate.

To insert dot leaders around centered text, press Shift+F6 twice. Type the text you want centered, ending with an Enter. The dot leader character (usually the single-spaced period, but adjustable under Layout/Character/Dot Leader Character) fills from the left margin to the centered text.

A similar trick creates a dot leader to the right margin. Press Alt+F6 twice. The dot leader character fills from the left margin to the right-justified text.

You can center text over a specific tab position on a line. This is useful when you want to center text in columns created with tabs or indents. Tab or space to the position on the line where you want to begin centering. Select Layout, then Alignment and Center, or press Shift+F6. Type the text you want centered, and the text is centered at the text position you chose.

If line justification is set to centered or right-justified, WordPerfect ignores tabs, although it records them. (The code that it uses is [Ignore:Lft Tab].) If you change the justification to a form that does accept tabs, the tabs you entered are recognized and used.

WordPerfect tables ignore any justification settings that you use in regular text. Tables use their own justification settings, and these settings are not connected to the line justification described here. If you set the justification for a table to all center, for example, the text justification after the table remains the same as it was before the table.

Procedure 15.2. Changing line justification.

1. Choose Layout, or press Shift+F8. Select Line, and Justification.
2. Choose the justification option you prefer: Left, Right, Center, Full, or Full, All Lines.
3. Select OK and Close until you return to your document window.

If Auto Code placement is on, line justification takes effect at the beginning of the current paragraph. If Auto Code Placement is off, justification changes take effect immediately (WordPerfect may insert an extra line).

Paragraph Borders

This section provides basic instruction in creating paragraph borders. Borders are covered in Workshop VII, in great detail, so look at Chapter 34, "Borders and Fills," if you want to learn more.

WordPerfect predefines several paragraph border styles, with variations on border lines and fills. You can, however, create impressive results using paragraph border customization settings. In addition to picking line styles and fill styles, you can modify the color, spacing, or shadow of a border or border fill. It is so easy to modify paragraph borders, in fact, that it is tempting to go beyond the borders of good taste. Figure 15.3 demonstrates that adding too many borders and fills can make your document difficult to read.

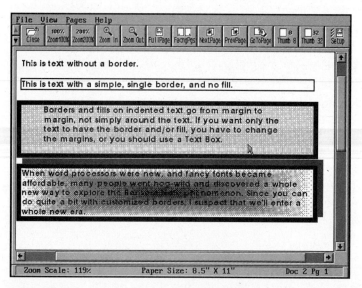

Figure 15.3. Paragraph borders with limited taste.

If Auto Code Placement is on, WordPerfect moves a Paragraph Border code to the beginning of the paragraph.

Border codes are paired codes— once you turn a border on, the border stays on until it is turned off. Even empty paragraphs, the blank lines you might enter between paragraphs, use the border and any fill. Thus, if you want to highlight only a single paragraph, I highly recommend that you use block mark to mark the text before you turn the border settings on. In addition, the process of turning a border off is somewhat cumbersome. Using block mark makes the task a bit easier.

Once you turn on a paragraph border (for example, a single border with a 10 percent fill), any columns or tables you create inherit those border settings. That may or may not be what you had in mind.

Borders and fills apply to the paragraph from margin to margin, not to the text as it is indented. If you want to create an indented text quote, for example, with a text border and fill around the text only, you may find it easier to use a text box. Otherwise, you have to temporarily change the margins to keep the empty "indented" space from being included in the border.

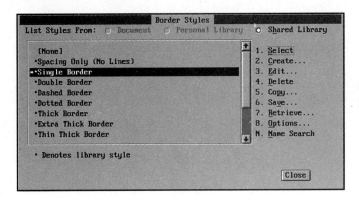

Figure 15.4. Creating a paragraph border.

Procedure 15.3. Defining a paragraph border.

1. Select Layout, or press Shift+F8. Choose Line, Paragraph Borders....
2. Select Border Style.... Select the predefined border you want to use.
3. Optionally, select Fill Style... and choose a border fill.
4. Choose OK and Close until you return to your document window.

To turn off paragraph borders, position the cursor in the paragraph that should have no borders. Choose Layout or press Shift+F8. Choose Line, Paragraph Borders..., and select Off. Choose Select and Close until you return to your document window.

Hyphenation

Hyphenation divides words at the right margin when they are too long to fit on the line. Wordperfect hyphenates words when the feature is turned on, and when a word spans the *hyphenation zone*. The hyphenation zone is normally 10 percent of your current line length (on the left) and 4 percent (on the right), but these values may be modified.

You can control where WordPerfect hyphenates a word, or prevent it from hyphenating a word. Type words that are usually connected (e.g., *top-secret*) using the hyphen (dash) on the keyboard. Use a *soft hyphen* (Ctrl+-) when you want to control where a word should hyphenate, without showing the hyphen in normal text. For example, *Way*[- Soft Hyphen]*Cool* displays as *WayCool* under normal circumstances, but *Way*-[SRt]*Cool* when the word falls in the hyphenation zone. As an alternative method of entering a soft return, you can control where WordPerfect divides a word without using hyphenation with Home+Return. This is useful when a hyphen is inappropriate, such as *either/or* or *Home+Return*.

Use a *hard hyphen* to keep hyphenated text together. For example, you should use a hard hyphen (Home+-) to keep phone numbers (555-1212) from wrapping. Similarly, a *hard space* (Home+space) prevents WordPerfect from separating the words (*OS/2*[HSpace]*2.1*).

The WordPerfect characters for em-dashes (4,34) and en-dashes (4,33) are treated as characters, not hyphens.

To turn hyphenation on, choose Layout or press Shift+F8. Select Line, and Hyphenation.

When hyphenation is on, and a word crosses the hyphenation zone, WordPerfect prompts you for an action. WordPerfect makes a hyphenation suggestion based on the speller dictionary for the language you are using. You can insert a hyphen (a soft hyphen is used), insert a space, insert a soft return, suspend hyphenation temporarily, or ignore the word (move the entire word to the next line).

Line Height

Use the line height adjustment to change the space between text baselines, without regard to the font or font size. Ordinarily, line height is set automatically, but you may want to change it for desktop publishing reasons. Keep the document legible—don't make the line height too small!

Choose Line from the Layout menu, or press Shift+F8. Select Line, and Line Height. Pick Fixed, and modify the height value.

Line Spacing

WordPerfect lets you change the amount of space between lines in your document. By default, line spacing is 1. When line spacing is set to 2, it is called double-spaced. You can change the spacing to any number, including fractions. Auto Code Placement affects line spacing.

Procedure 15.4. Changing line spacing.

1. Select Layout, or press Shift+F8, and choose Line. Choose Line Spacing. Type in the number of lines you want between lines of text, or use the arrows to select the number. Note that this value can be a decimal.

2. Select OK and Close to return to the document window.

Line Numbering

WordPerfect's line numbering feature prints line numbers in the left margin of the page. (If you can't imagine who would use this feature, I congratulate you for your healthy lifestyle, which has kept you far from the domain of lawyers.) WordPerfect provides several ways to customize line numbering features.

The line numbers appear when you print; ordinarily, they are not visible in Text mode, Graphics mode, or Page mode, though you will see them in Print Preview. In Page or Graphics mode, if you set View/Zoom to something other than margin, you'll see the line numbering. Line numbering can be turned on and off anywhere in the document. Line numbering begins on the line that the feature is turned on (choose Layout, Line, or press Shift+F8, and select Line Numbering). Auto Code Placement affects line numbering.

You can select the value of the starting line number, the first line number to print, the interval between line numbers (i.e., print every third or seventh line number), and the numbering method (numbers, letters, or Roman numerals). You can adjust the location on the page where the numbers are printed, as well as select the line number font, attribute, and color. Line numbering can be continuous, or can begin anew on each page. It's up to you if blank lines should be counted. You can also specify if newspaper columns should be numbered.

by Esther Schindler

Paragraph Formatting

Using Tabs and Indents

Why should you use tabs at all? Many novices, comfortable with typewriting and new to word processing, avoid using tabs. Instead, they use the space bar to indent text—it's comfortable to them, and the text seems to line up on-screen. However, even if the untabbed text appears to line up on-screen (in Text mode at least), it probably won't line up on the page. Most modern fonts are proportional, reflecting different character widths. A *w*, for example, is wider than an *i*. As a result, someone who uses the space bar to indent text has a few rude surprises in store. I watched one woman spend three hours converting a document full of spaces to one that used tabs. It was not a pretty sight. Even if you use a monospaced font, using spaces makes it difficult to modify formatting. (If you have reached this point in the book, you are unlikely to make such a mistake, but fate may drop a novice in your lap, and this concept is a shocker to a few of them.)

The tab key will move the cursor to the next predefined tab stop. (See Chapter 15, "Line Formatting," for instructions on defining tabs.) A back-tab (Shift+Tab) indents text to the next tab stop to the *left*. If you set tab settings

every inch, for example, and the cursor is positioned at 4.13 inches, pressing Shift+Tab moves the cursor to the tab stop at 4 inches. This isn't something you would ordinarily want to do in the middle of a paragraph. However, it works well, in conjunction with indent codes, to create hanging indents.

The indent keys (F4 and Shift+F4) affect paragraphs, not single lines. Indenting a paragraph (F4) moves the entire paragraph text in one tab stop ([Lft Indent]). Indenting a paragraph on both sides (Shift+F4) indents the paragraph by one tab stop from each margin ([Lft/Rgt Indent]). WordPerfect uses existing tab stops, regardless of their right, left, centered, or decimal definition. If no tab settings are defined, or if you run out, WordPerfect ignores any tab key presses and does not insert them in the document.

Tabs work well for columns of numbers, or for columns of very short text. But it's awkward, at best, to edit more than a word or two in columns that are formed with tabs. If you change the font or the printer, the tab settings won't change, but the text size may take up more or less room on the line. Thus, your text may wind up in unexpected places. If you need columns of text, use columns or tables. They are easier to manipulate in the long run.

You aren't limited to one indent on a line, just as you aren't limited to one tab. If you press Tab, followed by an Indent, the indent begins at the next tab stop (i.e., the second one). If you press Tab, Indent, Back-Tab, you create a hanging indent—the first line sticks into the left margin, but the rest of the body text indents regularly.

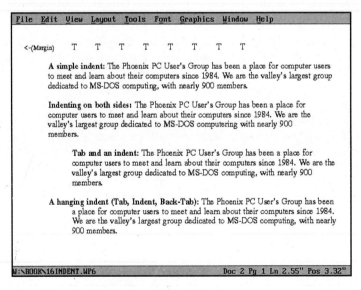

Figure 16.1. Some indenting examples.

The white space between the margin and your indented text is dependent on the tab settings you have defined. If you change the tab settings before the indents, that white space changes. To have more direct control over the measurement from the right and left margins, explore *margin adjustments*, discussed in detail later in this chapter.

When you examine the Reveal Codes screen, you'll notice small triangles in the bar dividing Reveal Codes from your document screen. Those triangles represent tab settings, and they can help you visually line up text.

Once you set your tab settings in a document, you may be loath to modify them. However, you might want to center text on an existing left tab setting, or to right-justify text against a tab that is set to decimal. For example, you may want to create a centered heading for a list of numbers, where the tab setting is decimal. WordPerfect lets you accomplish this with a feature called *hard tabs*. You can create a hard left tab by pressing Home+Tab. When you do, Reveal Codes displays the code in all capitals ([LFT TAB], instead of the usual [Lft Tab]). To create a hard right tab, press Home+Alt+F6; for hard center, press Home+Shift+F6. Generate a hard decimal align tab with Ctrl+F6.

Leader Characters

Use leader characters to create a row of dots (or another character) across a line. Leader characters are most often used in tables of contents or indices, in combination with tabs—the line of periods draws your eye across the page or column. When WordPerfect generates a table of contents or an index, it generates tab settings that are defined as dot leaders. (You'll find more information regarding dot leader tab settings in the section on changing the leader character, in Chapter 14, "Using Character Formatting," and in Chapter 15.)

If only one or two lines require leader characters, you don't have to create a tab setting for that purpose. To create centered text with a dot leader, press Shift+F6 twice (i.e., Shift+F6, Shift+F6). Enter your text. The leader character fills from the left margin (or the end of any existing text, to the centered text). Similarly, create a leader to the right margin by pressing Alt+F6 twice.

Margins

Margins are the white space around your text, the boundary area between your text and the paper edge. You can modify the size of document margins, or, new to WordPerfect 6.0, change paragraph margins and spacing.

Auto Code Placement affects margin settings. It moves any margin codes to the beginning of the paragraph. Block marking text before you set margins enables WordPerfect's revertible codes to adjust the margins before and after the marked block, which can be extremely helpful in styles.

Document Margins

The WordPerfect default is a one-inch margin, all around the page. You can set margins on the top, bottom, left, and right side of the page. Nothing is printed in the margins—the only exceptions are line numbers (optionally), and minor adjustments made if you change the text baseline.

If you write general business documents, WordPerfect's one-inch margin default makes sense. However, that one-inch default can get in the way when you use different paper sizes. In particular, you will probably be surprised the first time you create an envelope that has a one-inch margin. The default is even more awkward when you use a label format, because many labels aren't much wider than the two inches allocated to the margin! Get in the habit of changing the document margin settings whenever you change the paper type to a small sheet format.

All laser printers have an *unprintable zone*. The printer rollers use this part of the paper to grip the page, so it is impossible for WordPerfect (or any other program) to print in that region. The unprintable zone is about 3/10 of an inch, so it rarely causes a problem. With that one exception, you can make the margins as large as the page.

Paragraph Margins

There are four new margin settings in WordPerfect 6.0:

- ▲ Left margin adjustment
- ▲ Right margin adjustment
- ▲ First line indent
- ▲ Paragraph spacing

Margin adjustments adjust text margins relative to the right or left margins, adding a little more margin than provided by the usual left or right margin. At first, this feature can seem a bit confusing (why have two margins at once?), but it gives you greater formatting control.

The new margin adjustments give you more power over paragraph indentation. As you'll recall from the discussion on indenting, indenting is based on tab settings. If you change your tab settings ahead of indented text in your document, you unwittingly change the spacing for the indented block of text. Also, in unpredictable environments, such as creating styles for corporate use, it's not feasible to predict what a user's tab settings will be. Much gnashing of teeth may ensue.

However, if you create a style that turns a margin adjustment on and off, you will know *exactly* what the indenting will look like. A one-inch margin adjustment indents the text one inch from the margin, whether the tabs are set every two inches or every quarter-inch, or whether the page size is 8.5 inches by 11 inches or 3 inches by 4 inches. Using margin adjustments in a style, rather than changing tab settings, requires less knowledge of the user's current document settings. (Note that margin adjustments can use negative numbers.)

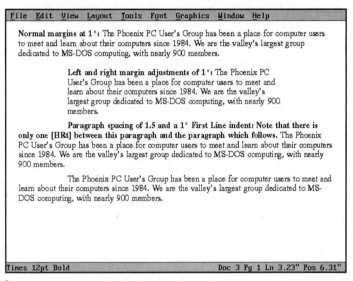

Figure 16.2. Using paragraph margins

WordPerfect's *first line indent* setting indents the first line of a paragraph by the specified amount. For example, you can set all paragraphs to be indented a half inch. If you're really enamored of hanging indents, you can type in a negative number for First Line Indent (i.e., -.5"). WordPerfect won't let you create settings where the margins overlap.

If you are familiar with desktop publishing, you may have wished for a feature desktop publishers call *paragraph leading* (WordPerfect calls it *paragraph spacing*). WordPerfect can insert additional spaces between paragraphs, above and below the paragraph. WordPerfect measures paragraph spacing in number of lines, not inches, although you can use fractions. For example, you can set paragraph spacing to 1.13 lines.

Procedure 16.1. Setting margins.

1. Choose Layout, or press Shift+F8. Select Margins. WordPerfect displays the Margin Format dialog box.

2. Select the document margin you want to change (Left, Right, Top, Bottom) and enter the new margin value. Note that you can use fractions as well as decimals; if you type 1/3", WordPerfect converts it to the correct decimal value.

209

3. Select the paragraph margin you want to change, and enter the new value. If your numbers create overlapping margins, WordPerfect displays an error message and does not permit you to exit the dialog until the margins make sense. If your printer has an unprintable zone and you type a value that falls in the zone, WordPerfect modifies the value. For example, on an HP LaserJet, WordPerfect changes a left margin setting of 0" to 0.3".

4. Select OK and Close until you return to the document window.

Binding Offsets

If your document will be printed on both sides of the page and bound, you need to allow extra room in the margin to account for the binding. The Binding Offset feature works in conjunction with margin settings to let you adjust the text away from the bound edge of the page. WordPerfect increases the size of the margin on the bound side by the distance you specify, as if you had a different margin adjustment for right and left pages.

Previous versions of WordPerfect included binding offset adjustments at print time, as part of the print menu. WordPerfect 6.0 includes it as a kind of paragraph or margin code. Binding offset settings are in effect from the code insertion point (until you turn them off or change them).

Procedure 16.2. Creating binding offsets.
1. Choose Layout, or press Shift-F8. Select Other.
2. Choose Printer functions..., then Binding Offset.
3. In Binding Offset, enter the distance that should be added to the margin.
4. Choose From Edge and indicate the Left, Right, Top, or Bottom margin as the paper edge to which the binding offset should apply.
5. Select OK and Close until you return to the document screen.

Creating a Numbered or Bulleted List

Workshop XII, "Long Documents," later in this book, explains how to use styles, outlines, and numbered lists. Your list needs, however, are usually very simple— a list with bullets, for example, or a numbering of a collection of paragraphs. This section examines the simple methods of accomplishing these aims. Once you become comfortable with these basic techniques, investigate the more advanced ways of using the same features.

The most straightforward way to create a bulleted list is to create one manually. Insert the WordPerfect bullet character of your choice (WordPerfect characters 4,0 through 4,4 are most common), indent the paragraph, and type away.

You can also use WordPerfect's built-in paragraph styles to create a numbered or bulleted list.

Procedure 16.3. Using paragraph styles to create lists.

1. Select **Tools**, **Outline**, or press Ctrl+F5. WordPerfect displays the Outline dialog.

2. Choose **Begin New Outline**. WordPerfect displays the outline style list.

3. Choose the *Bullets* outline style, or the *Numbers* or *Paragraph* styles. (You can also create your own, but try to keep this simple for the moment.) WordPerfect returns to your document automatically.

Until you select **End Outline** from the Outline Dialog, WordPerfect numbers your paragraphs in the designated manner, or inserts bullets and indents. When you press Tab, WordPerfect indents the paragraph and, with most of the styles available, assigns a different kind of number or bullet. You can use Shift+Tab to back up to the previous outline level. You can also backspace over the paragraph number if you don't want a particular paragraph to be numbered (doing so turns off outlining).

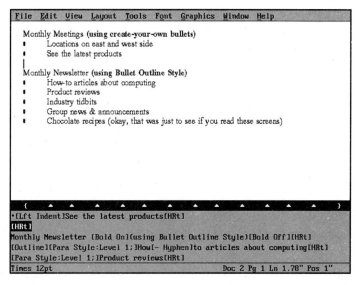

Figure 16.3. Bulleted lists.

The preceding procedure works well under most circumstances. However, there may be times when you want to number paragraphs without using indents. You can customize an outline, but you can also use counters to number paragraphs in a very controlled manner. If you are being that careful, you probably want to maintain the methodology in a style. Define a counter named *Paragraph*, and increment and display it at the beginning of every paragraph that you wish numbered. Using counters, you can refer to and display many-levelled paragraph numbers.

by Esther Schindler

Page Formatting

Basic Page Numbering

WordPerfect 6.0 has expanded the number of ways you can number pages in your document. There are different ways to keep track of pages (chapter and volume) and page numbering (numbers, Roman numerals, and letters), and more extensive formatted numbering styles. As in earlier versions of WordPerfect, page numbering information can be included within headers and footers.

By default, WordPerfect uses the document's Initial Base font for page numbering font and attribute information. Font, attribute, and color information can also be specified in the page number definition.

If you have defined both a page number and a header or footer, their text may overlap. Either include the page number in the header or footer definition (as described below), or pay careful attention to the line formatting of the header and footer. For example, left- or right-justify the footer information, so that it doesn't interfere with the centered page number. To see a WYSIWYG view of page numbering, you must be in Page mode or Print Preview.

Page numbering can be defined for every page, with different options based on even and odd pages. Page numbering can be turned off temporarily using the Format/Page/Suppress feature.

There are an abundant number of ways to customize and manipulate page numbering or its display, but this is the most straightforward method (see Figure 17.1). Chapter 58, "Page, Chapter, and Volume Numbering," discusses more elaborate options.

Procedure 17.1. Numbering pages: the simplest way.

1. Choose **L**ayout, or press Shift+F8. Choose **P**age.

2. Select Page Numbering.... WordPerfect will show the Page Numbering dialog box, with several options.

3. Select Page Number **P**osition. WordPerfect will display a graphical choice of page locations where the page number will appear. Choose the location you prefer. Optionally, choose Font/**A**ttributes/Color to specify the page number's font information.

4. Select OK and Close to return to your document window.

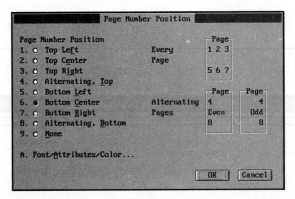

Figure 17.1. Simple page numbering.

Each numbering option (page number, primary and secondary page numbers, chapter and volume numbers) has identical selections. You can change the value of the page number, change the numbering method (numbers, Roman numerals, letters), and increment, decrement, and/or display the number in the document.

The ability to change numbering methods is extremely useful. For instance, you can number the table of contents with lowercase Roman numerals but change the numbering scheme to arabic numbers for the document body.

Page Number Positions

WordPerfect permits you to display formatted page numbers at the top-left, top-center, top-right, bottom-left, bottom-center, or bottom-right of every page. You can also display page numbers that alternate between the top right/left or bottom right/left of the page, depending on whether the pages are even or odd.

Page numbering can be turned off by selecting None from the Page Number Position options.

Page Number

To modify the page number value, select Page Number from the Page Numbering dialog box, and enter a new value. You can set the page number to 1 at the beginning of a document's "real text," after the table of contents, preface, and so on. If you don't do this, the body of your document might begin at page 3 or 4, after the table of contents, confusing your readers.

Page Number Format

Automatic page numbering displays page number information in the format defined in the Page Number Format field. This field can include about 40 characters of text, as well as the codes for page, secondary page, chapter, or volume numbers. The default is [page #], which is WordPerfect's code for the actual page number value. When you select Page Number Format, the Number Codes (F5) box becomes available. By pressing F5, you can insert one mention each of the Secondary Page Number, Chapter Number, and Volume Number in addition to (or instead of) the page number. A typical page number format could be Page [page #], or The Chocolate Book: Chapter [chap #], page [page #]. See Figure 17.2 for an example.

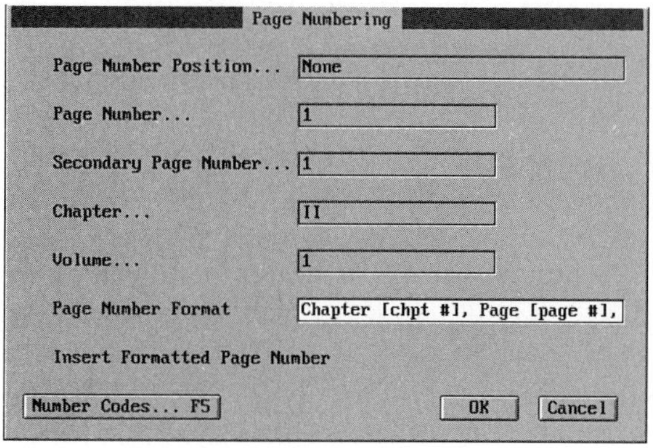

Figure 17.2. Defining a page number code.

To display a page number without the formatting, choose Display in Document from the options for Page Number, Secondary Page Number, Chapter, or Volume.

Inserting Formatted Page Number

You can insert the current page number at any point in your document. Because WordPerfect uses the format defined in the Page Numbering dialog box's Page Number Format field, the displayed number may include chapter or volume numbers as well as text. Select Insert Formatted Page Number from the Page Numbering dialog box, or use the shortcut keystroke Ctrl+P. In Figure 17.3, you can see an example using the formatted page number in both the text and a footer ("Chapter 11, Page 1, of the Great American Novel"), and an unformatted page number (1) in the text.

WordPerfect will insert a [Formatted Pg Num] code in the document. The values in that formatted code will automatically be updated when they change.

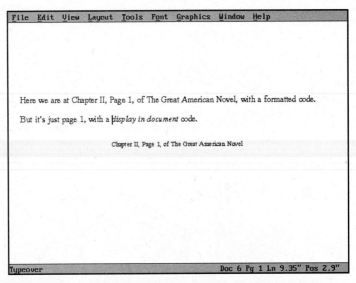

Figure 17.3. Using the page number code, defined above.

Use this feature to include a page number in a header or a footer. To display the unformatted page number only, choose Display in Document from the Page Number options. The same method also works to include the unformatted value of secondary pages, chapters, or volumes.

Force Odd/Even/New Page

Most chapters or document sections begin on an odd, or right-hand page. You have no way to predict the evenness or oddness of a page, so WordPerfect provides this feature to force the page to the one you specify. If the current page is odd when you issue a `Force Odd Page`, or the page is even when you issue a `Force Even Page`, WordPerfect ignores the code. If the page has an odd number when you choose even, or vice versa, WordPerfect will insert a hard page return.

Forcing a new page is similar to a hard page break (Ctrl+Enter), but it avoids the problem where a hard page break bumps into a soft page break. If a hard page code and soft page code are next to one another, you will have an extra, blank page. Using Force Page New ensures that a new page begins, but it doesn't create an extra page.

Procedure 17.2. Forcing Odd/Even/New Page.

1. Choose Layout, or press Shift+F8. Choose Page.
2. Select Force Page, and choose Odd, Even, New, or None.
3. Select OK and Close to return to your document window.

Using Headers, Footers, and Watermarks

Use headers or footers to print text at the top or bottom of the page. Use watermarks to print text or graphics as a page background.

Two headers, two footers, and two watermarks may be active at any time. You can use any number of these items in a document, but only two may be active at one time. Each of these (the A and the B) can print on every page, on alternating (even/odd) pages, or not at all.

To create a header, footer, or watermark, choose Header/Footer/Watermark... from the Layout menu. Whether you choose Header, Footer, or Watermark, you will have identical options: you can Create or Edit the option, or you can turn it Off. Each item can be assigned to Even pages, Odd pages, or All pages.

Note that separate A and B headers, footers, or watermarks must be turned off individually. Turning off Header A will not turn off Header B. Use Reveal Codes to delete header, footer, and watermark codes.

> **Tip:** Here's an undocumented feature that may save you some time. If you are editing a header, footer, or watermark (for example, Header A) and want to edit the next header, footer, or watermark (for example, Header B), pressing Home+Page Up will move you to the next header, footer, or watermark. Pressing Home+Page Down will move you to the previous item.

Headers and Footers

Headers print just above the top margin of a page. Footers print just below the bottom margin. Headers and footers can contain almost anything that you can include in the main text of your document. One new, exciting feature that headers and footers can include is graphics and graphic lines, as well as formatting features such as paragraph borders. Formatting within a header or footer does not affect the document body; i.e., paragraph borders may be turned on within a footer, but the body of your document will not have borders. If a formatting code is not permitted within a header or footer, it will be greyed out on the WordPerfect menu.

When you create a new header or footer, WordPerfect shows you a blank screen that looks similar to a document screen. You type in the text and codes that you want to appear in the header or footer. Common header and footer items include company names, document names (*Annual Report*), page numbers, filenames, and dates.

The fastest way to include a page number within a header or footer is to use the shortcut keystroke Ctrl+P. Doing so will display the formatted page number, as defined in the Page Numbering dialog box. To include the page, secondary page, chapter, or volume number without formatting, choose Display in Document from the matching dialog under Page Numbering. (Choose Page Number, Secondary Page Number, Chapter, or Volume from the Page Numbering dialog box: each has a Display in Document option.)

Editing a header or footer modifies the entire item and does not create a new header or footer code. For instance, imagine that you create a footer on page 1 containing nothing but a title (*The Chocolate Report*). On page 2, you edit the footer to include the page number (*The Chocolate Report, Page 2*). When you examine the footer on page 1, you'll see that the entire footer was changed; page 1's footer now reads *The Chocolate Report, Page 1.*

To make changes to an existing header or footer without changing the original (i.e., to add the page number, in the example above), you must create a new header or footer. WordPerfect will display another blank screen. Because WordPerfect has no way of knowing that you want to make only minor changes, edit the original item before you create the new one, and copy the appropriate text.

You can modify the space above and below footers.

If you have turned on page numbering as well as headers or footers, check carefully to determine that you create no visual interference. If you create a centered heading and also create a top-centered page number, one may print on top of the other. Either include the page number in the heading, or ensure that the heading has enough space that the numbers won't overlap. Because headers and footers can incorporate all the page numbering features, you'll probably want to choose between page numbering or headers/footers.

Watermarks

Watermarks enable you to add text or graphics behind the document text. The text or graphics are automatically lightened so that the main document shows through.

Watermarks work well when you want to distinguish every page in some manner. You can print a company logo, or a background message such as *"Draft Copy—Do Not Distribute!"*

Watermarks look cool, but because the graphics in watermarks are full-page graphics, keep in mind that your documents can take longer to print. With all the formatting features available to you, watermarks could be one of many tools that enable you to give your document the dreaded "ransom note" look, exceeding the bounds of good taste. Use the feature judiciously and conservatively. Too little is better than too much.

Watermarks can include text, graphics, or both; it's simply a page behind your document page. When you use text in watermarks, remember that it will print lighter than usual. Because watermarked text will be important almost by definition (*company confidential*), you should use a larger or more distinctive font to make it stand out. Watermarks, like headers and footers, can include nearly anything that the document would include; menu items that are unavailable are dimmed.

When you include a graphic image within a watermark, WordPerfect will automatically set it to full-page and set the image box style. With the image box style, WordPerfect will automatically lighten the graphic. If you choose to modify the graphic type, you will have to adjust the darkness yourself.

Watermarks do not display in Text, Graphics, or Page modes. The only way to see the document with the watermark image is with Print Preview.

Procedure 17.3. Creating a watermark.

1. Choose Layout, or press Shift+F8.

2. Choose Header/Footer/Watermark. Select Watermark, and choose the A or B watermark.

3. Indicate whether the watermark should appear on All, Even, or Odd pages, and press Enter to select Create. WordPerfect will display a blank screen.

4. Enter the text and formatting codes you wish to appear on the page. If you like, create a graphics box and choose the image you want to use. When you are done creating the watermark, press F7 to exit the Watermark Edit window. WordPerfect will return to the document screen automatically.

Understanding Paper Sizes

WordPerfect needs to know about the size and attributes of the paper you use. For example, to center text on the page, WordPerfect has to understand where the edges are or it can't determine where the center is. If your printer has a sheet feeder, WordPerfect has to know that before it can issue the proper control codes.

The physical aspects of Paper Size/Type features are easy to understand; they are simple descriptions of the different paper sizes, features, and orientations. Many of the description options are for your benefit more than for WordPerfect; for instance, WordPerfect treats documents the same whether they're printed on plain bond or on transparencies.

Envelopes, labels, and subdivided pages are special cases. Envelopes can either be treated as a specific paper type/size (if you're printing a stack of them), or they can be sort of separate but attached to a letter or other document. Labels and subdivided pages are both *logical* pages within pages. An 8.5- by 11-inch sheet may have 30 or more labels; WordPerfect has to treat each label as a kind of page, yet retain an awareness of that 8.5- by 11-inch page.

One major distinction in paper types is paper orientation. In most cases, WordPerfect can print in either portrait (narrow edge up) or landscape (wide edge up). Not every font will be available in both orientations, however.

If Auto Code Placement is off, every time you change the paper size or type in a document, WordPerfect will insert a hard page break—even if you change the paper size to the current size. Although this feature can be disconcerting at first, it makes sense; you couldn't really switch from a 4- by 5-inch page to an 8.5- by 11-inch page without changing the piece of paper. When Auto Code Placement is on, the paper size code is inserted at the top of the current page.

When you work with smaller paper sizes (which includes logical sheet sizes such as labels and subdivided pages), keep WordPerfect's default 1-inch margin in mind. Although a 1-inch margin is the likely choice for a full-sized sheet of paper, it's probably not what you have in mind for a Rolodex card or a mailing label. Most of the predefined label definitions include a margin setting of 0" (new to WordPerfect 6.0), but always verify this. When you work with small sheet sizes, learn to change your margins immediately.

Auto Code Placement moves Paper Size/Type codes to the beginning of the current page. If you have more than one printer defined, choose your printer before you select your paper size. Not all printers support all paper sizes. WordPerfect makes a good "best guess" when you change printers, but there's no point in making it work harder than necessary.

Procedure 17.4. Selecting a paper definition.

1. Choose Layout, or press Shift+F8. Choose Page.

2. Choose Paper Size/Type. WordPerfect will display a dialog box with a scrollable list of paper sizes that have been defined for the current printer.

3. Select the size and type of paper that you will be using, noting carefully whether the orientation is portrait or landscape.

4. Select OK and Close to return to your document window.

You can also create new paper sizes and types. When you add a new paper size, the information is stored in the printer's .PRS file. To use an unusual paper size for this document only, use the [All Others] paper definition, which will prompt you for size and page orientation.

To add a new paper size/type, follow the above procedures for picking a paper size, but select Create from the Page Size/Type dialog box. Fill in the new dialog box, with attention to these page features:

▲ **Paper Name**: The name you assign the paper size. Try to make the name describe the paper itself, or how you use it. *Manila Envelope* is a better name, in the long run, than *Pookie's Favorite Paper*.

▲ **Paper Type**: Most of the choices in this section are for your benefit more than WordPerfect's. WordPerfect makes certain assumptions for Envelope types, but the labels of cardstock, standard, or glossy film are there to help you in paper matching. Try to be accurate, as some printer definitions do make a distinction; for instance, the HP DeskJet printers wait a bit longer before each page when the paper type is Transparency, so that one transparency can dry before the next page drops on top.

▲ **Paper Size**: The actual size of the paper, measured by height and width.

▲ **Paper Location**: Indicate whether the paper is fed manually (i.e., by hand), continuously, or from a sheet feeder. The usual choice for dot-matrix and laser printers is Continuous.

▲ **Prompt to Load**: Select this box if you want to be reminded to change the paper. If so, at print time WordPerfect will beep and require you to tell the printer to Go (from the Control Printer dialog box) before the document will print.

▲ **Orientation**: Select a wide or narrow form, with portrait or landscape fonts.

▲ **Adjust Text**: If all the pages settings seem right, but you can't get text to print where you want it, adjust the settings here.

Using Labels and Subdivided Pages

This section examines the basics of selecting and using labels and subdivided pages. Check the chapter about mail merge for labels (Chapter 50, "Merge Projects"), as well as the chapter concentrating on using subdivided pages (Chapter 42, "Using Subdivided Pages").

Some years ago, a friend asked a waiter in a Chinese restaurant, "What's the difference between the chop suey and the chow mein?" The waiter replied, "No difference. Some people like to order chop suey. Some people like to order chow mein."

Labels and subdivided pages are a lot like chop suey and chow mein. In your mind, they are different because you use them differently. In reality, they work identically. Both labels and subdivided pages are based on the notion of *logical* pages—areas of the physical page that WordPerfect treats as a kind of virtual page. In practice, choose labels when you're working with a page format that is predefined as a label (at least in your own mind); use subdivided pages in all other cases.

You can use subdivided pages for booklets, 3-fold brochures, program listings, or greeting cards. The principles of labels apply equally well to subdivided pages, especially in cases where a physical page has more than one logical page on it.

WordPerfect supplies an abundance of predefined label formats. Under most circumstances, you need only to look for the company name and label number on the box to figure out which label format to use.

In earlier versions of WordPerfect, each printer definition had separate label settings. If you used the same label on two different laser printers, you had to go through label setup for each one. WordPerfect 6.0 makes using labels much easier. Label definitions, including those you add, are stored in a separate file, not in the printer driver (PRS). Label definitions are available no matter what printer you are using, and you don't have to set up new label definitions every time you update your printer driver. You can have more than one label file.

Procedure 17.5. Using a predefined label.

1. Choose Layout, or press Shift+F8. Choose Page.
2. Choose Labels.... WordPerfect will display the Labels dialog box.
3. Scroll through the list of predefined labels to match the description on the label box, as in Figure 17.4. The Label Details window will reflect the settings for each label. Select the label description that fits your labels.
4. WordPerfect will display the Label Printer Information dialog box. Usually the settings here will be correct, but you can modify them. For instance, if you need to add extra space to the margins, modify the settings in Adjust Text. Select OK. WordPerfect will return to the Page dialog box. Notice that both the Paper Size/Type and Labels... fields reflect the label setting you just entered.
5. Select OK and Close to return to the document window.

Working with labels is slightly different from working with regular documents. Because each label is a logical page, remember that page formatting applies to each label. The small page size—a few inches wide by a few inches long—affects layout choices such as font sizes. The print size is generally small, and (even with the best of printers) getting everything to line up perfectly can be a frustrating experience. Experiment with the center page commands, especially the Center All Pages command. Also, although page borders can look contrived in business documents such as letters, they look good on labels.

WordPerfect shows an approximation of the label's appearance on the page. Because the page size is much smaller than usual, even the lines that show page breaks will be shorter on-screen. Even when you have three labels across the page, you will see one label atop another. It helps to look at Print Preview frequently. The page indicator on the status line shows the current logical page (label). Reveal Codes will show you a Paper Size/Type code; when you look at the code in detail, you'll see that it identifies the label you chose. In Figure 17.5, you'll see that WordPerfect displays the proper size for the disk label: three labels to a sheet.

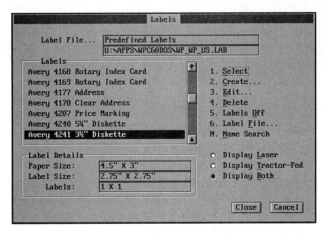

Figure 17.4. Choosing a predefined label.

Procedure 17.6. Defining new labels.

1. Choose Layout, or press Shift+F8. Choose Page.
2. Choose Labels.... WordPerfect will display the Labels dialog box.
3. Choose Create. As Figure 17.6 shows, WordPerfect will display the Create Label dialog box with options for you to fill in:

   ▲ **Label Description**: Try to use a meaningful name that describes the function of the label.

   ▲ **Label Paper Size**: The paper size is the measurement of the single sheet of paper, without regard to the number of labels.

   ▲ **Label Size**: The width and height of individual labels, without regard to the wax paper "margin" separating some labels.

   ▲ **Number of Labels**: The number of labels across (rows) and down (columns) on the physical page.

223

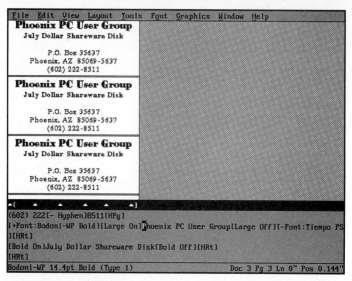

Figure 17.5. Working with labels.

▲ **Top Left Corner**: Measure the distance from the paper edge to the label edge.

▲ **Printer Info**: Different information will be required for each printer that the labels are used with. Here you define whether the printer requires text adjustments, manual feed, prompt to load, and whether the printer supports rotated text.

▲ **Distance Between Labels**: Measure the distance between labels, horizontally and vertically. Some labels bump up against each other; in that case, enter 0".

▲ **Label Margins**: Specify the margins inside the label. On a regular sheet of paper, you would think of these as page margins.

▲ **Label Type**: Indicate whether the labels are laser, tractor-fed, or both. This will determine where the label description shows in the Labels dialog box.

4. Select OK and Close to return to the document window.

In earlier versions of WordPerfect, telling WordPerfect to print one page printed only a single label. In WordPerfect 6.0, when you print a full document or a page, the entire sheet of labels will print. To print an individual label, use Multiple Pages on the print menu and specify the label (page) numbers.

Envelopes

Because envelopes are frequently used in mail-merge operations, be sure to investigate the merge workshop later in this book.

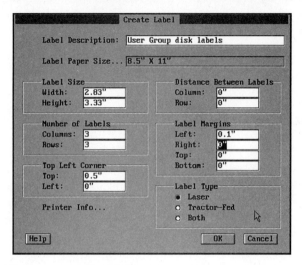

Figure 17.6. Defining a new label type.

Envelopes can be used in two ways: as a standard (if odd-sized) paper size/type, or as a special feature, attached to another document.

To create an envelope, you must first have an envelope definition in the page size/type listing for your selected printer. Most printers come with at least one predefined envelope size, but if necessary you can create one.

Before you print a batch of envelopes, experiment with a few blank sheets of paper. Despite manufacturer claims, some printers seem to require arcane chanting, eyes of newt, and sacrificial sheep entrails before they will print an envelope correctly. WordPerfect supports printing envelopes from either the narrow or wide edge (landscape or rotated), as long as your printer will support it too. You'll have to experiment to find out what works, and what works best. (I favor arcane chanting.)

Nothing is very different about using envelopes as just another paper type. Pay special attention to margins (left margins of 1 inch on envelopes look a little strange). And take note of WordPerfect's new POSTNET code.

The U.S. Post Office uses POSTNET codes to speed mail delivery. If you use presorted mail, using POSTNET codes on your letters can save you money. (Check with your postmaster for details.) POSTNET codes are 5, 9, or 11 digits—the length of a Zip code. WordPerfect can insert POSTNET Zip codes in documents or, in particular, on envelopes.

Procedure 17.7. Inserting a POSTNET Zip code.

1. Choose Layout, or press Shift+F8. Choose Other.

2. Select Bar Code.... Enter the 5-, 9-, or 11-digit Zip code. The code must be 5, 9, or 11 digits; WordPerfect will not accept it otherwise.

3. Select OK and Close to return to your document screen.

The POSTNET code is visible in Graphics and Page modes. In Text mode, it displays as a square block.

WordPerfect 6.0 lets you create an envelope in the current document. It's now easy to keep a letter and its envelope in the same file. This feature is not intended to generate a stack of envelopes from a mail-merge list; for that purpose, use the merge function with envelopes defined as the paper size/type.

When you create an envelope, WordPerfect will pick up anything in the document that it thinks looks like a mailing address. If you have more than one address in the document, block mark the recipient's address to use as the default mailing address before you create the envelope. You can also manually enter the addresses.

WordPerfect can maintain a default return address. A return address is not required, which makes it simple to print on preprinted envelopes.

The envelope feature can automatically or manually include the POSTNET bar code for the Zip code. If you select the POSTNET option, the bar code will print right above the recipient's name; this location cannot be changed.

The envelope can be printed from the Envelope dialog box, or the envelope "document" can be inserted at the end of the current document. If you insert the envelope at the end of your document, WordPerfect will insert a new Page Size/ Type command as well as the appropriate commands to generate the envelope. If you want to keep typing into your document, make sure you position your cursor correctly, or you might have some odd surprises at print time.

Make sure that you have selected the correct printer before you generate the envelope. WordPerfect makes some pretty good best guesses if you change your printer selection after you create the envelope, but there's no point in dealing with surprises that you can avoid.

Procedure 17.8. Creating an envelope for an existing document.

1. Choose Layout or press Shift+F8. Select Page and Envelope....

2. Visually check that the envelope size selected in the Envelope dialog box is the one you want. In most cases, it will be. Optionally, select Envelope Size and select a different envelope shape/size. If no envelopes are listed in the Envelope Size box, refer to the section on creating Paper Size/Type in order to create an Envelope definition.

3. Select Return Address if you wish to include one. Optionally, choose Save Return Address as Default if you expect to use it frequently. If a return

address is present but you don't want to use it, select Omit Return Address. If you do want to include the return address, type it in the space allocated, and press F7 to exit.

4. If WordPerfect did not automatically pick up the correct recipient, choose Mailing Address to enter one or to edit the one present.

5. If you want WordPerfect to print the POSTNET bar code, select POSTNET Bar Code and type in the Zip code. This code will accept only numbers and a hyphen, no letters.

6. You can print the envelope directly from the screen (by choosing Print) or insert the envelope definition into your document (by choosing Insert).

7. Select OK and Close to return to the document window.

To change the envelope setup options, choose Shift+F1 from the Envelope dialog box. The envelope setup options permit you to select or create the default envelope size and type, to indicate what the default bar code use should be (automatic, manual, or none), and to specify the horizontal and vertical address positions on any of the envelopes you have defined. For instance, you might want to indent your return address more than usual because of the nature of your stationery. You can select fonts and attributes for envelope text; if you don't, WordPerfect will use the font specified in Document Initial Font.

Double-Sided Printing

If your printer supports double-sided printing, you can insert a code to tell WordPerfect to take advantage of the feature. Select Double-sided printing from the Page format menu and indicate whether the document will be bound on the long edge or the short edge.

Suppress Page Formatting

Sometimes it makes sense to conceal page numbering, watermarks, headers, or footers. For instance, you may create a page number definition on page 1, but it's considered bad form to show page numbers on the first page. Use Suppress to temporarily turn off features for this page only.

To suppress features for the current page, choose Suppress from the Page Format dialog box. Select the individual items you want to turn off, or choose Suppress All. You can optionally choose to print the page number at the bottom center of the page.

Suppress works with a limited number of codes. See the discussion of delay codes in Chapter 11, "Default Settings," which describes another, possibly more flexible way to control the placement of any formatting code.

Centering Pages

WordPerfect allows you to center pages between the top and bottom margins. Headers, footers, and footnotes are unaffected by centering.

You can center the current page only (useful for title pages and posters). Or, new to WordPerfect 6.0, you can center all pages. Center All Pages is especially valuable for mailing labels, name badges, and other documents that need a balanced look, because you don't have to have a Center Page code at the top of each individual label.

Page centering is visible only in Page mode, not Text mode or Graphics mode. Auto Code Placement moves a Center Page code to the beginning of the page.

To turn Center Page on or off, choose Layout or press Shift+F8, and choose Page. Select Center Current Page or Center Pages. These items work as toggle switches.

Page Borders

A detailed discussion of the use of paragraph and page borders is contained in Chapter 34, "Borders and Fills." This section provides the basic procedures for using page borders. Because they work so similarly to paragraph borders, I recommend that you read that section as well.

WordPerfect lets you define page borders and page fills. You can select any of a number of line or border styles, colors, or shading, or you can create your own border definition. Unlike paragraph borders, you can modify the border shape to square or rounded corners (paragraph corners are always square).

Once you turn Page Borders on, they stay on until explicitly turned off. To mark a single page to have a page border, block mark text on the page where you want the border, and then turn the border on.

Procedure 17.9. Creating a page border.

1. Select Layout or press Shift+F8. Choose Page, and select Page Borders. (You can accomplish the same thing with Graphics or Alt+F9, Borders, Page.)
2. Choose Border Style, highlight the border you want to use, and choose Select.
3. If you want the page to have shading or color, choose Fill Style..., highlight the percentage of shading, and choose Select.
4. Select OK and Close to return to your document window.

Keeping Text Together on a Page

WordPerfect provides several methods for you to keep text together. There are **several times when you might want to do so**: when a single paragraph line wanders alone on the top or bottom of a page, to keep headings together with subsequent text, or to keep related information together.

Widow/Orphan

A single line of a paragraph that stands alone at the top of a page is called a *widow*; the same lonely line at the bottom of a page is called an *orphan*. Having widows and orphans in a document is considered typographically unsanitary, as well as visually confusing. Unless you are strapped for space, there's no reason not to use Widow/Orphan Protect; it's a code I have always included in my own initial codes.

Procedure 17.10. Changing the Widow/Orphan Protect setting.

1. Select Layout or press Shift+F8. Choose Other.
2. Select Widow/Orphan Protect to turn the feature on or off.
3. Select OK and Close to return to your document window.

Conditional End of Page

Use Conditional End of Page to keep a specific number of lines together on one page. This is especially useful for keeping titles and headings together with the body text that follows and is highly recommended for inclusion in a heading style.

Blank lines count against the "number of lines to keep together." If you have set spacing to double- or triple-spacing, remember that the blank lines count as "lines," too.

Procedure 17.11. Selecting Conditional End of Page.

1. Position the cursor on the line ahead of the first line of text you want to include.
2. Select Layout or press Shift+F8, and choose Other.
3. Select Conditional End of Page, and enter the number of lines to keep together.
4. Select OK and Close to return to your document window.

229

Block Protect

Conditional End of Page works to keep lines together. Block protect keeps a block of text together. If you have a table or section of a document that logically should be kept on one page, Block Protect will keep it together.

The block-protected text must be less than a page in length. WordPerfect will treat successive protected blocks as one large block, unless they are separated by at least one soft return or hard return.

Procedure 17.12. Using Block Protect.

1. Block mark the text that should be kept together.
2. Select Layout or press Shift+F8, and choose Other.
3. Select Block Protect.
4. Select OK and Close to return to your document window.

by Esther Schindler

Advanced Formatting Features

The features discussed in this chapter are mainly used for typographic control. Except for Advance, you aren't likely to use them often in general business documents, but they are irreplaceable when you need to fine-tune a document's appearance.

Printer Commands

The Printer Functions dialog, under Layout (Shift+F8), Other, gives you nearly microscopic control over document layout. Some of these features are covered in the desktop publishing chapters, but here is an overview of what each one does.

Word Spacing Justification Limits lets you adjust the compression or expansion of justified text. In contrast, Word Spacing and Letter Spacing adjusts the spacing between individual letters and words without regard to formatting. By default, WordPerfect sets word spacing and letter spacing to what it judges is optimal, based on font definitions. You may find typographic reasons to adjust these, but those occasions will be rare.

Kerning, whether for an entire document or for a specific block of text, adjusts the spacing between specific letters in the document. For instance, if you look at a *W* and an *A*, you'll see that there's some space below the ascender of the *W* and above the left "foot" of the *A*. Kerning moves the characters closer together, so that the left foot of the *A* nestles comfortably under the ascender of the *W*. Doing so makes a document look much more finished.

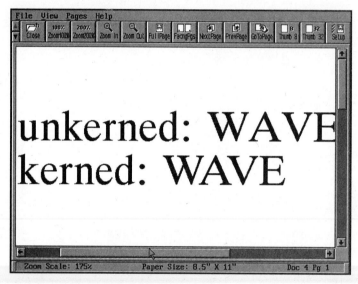

Figure 18.1. Kerning: before and after.

Leading adjustments allow you to change the amount of space between each line of text. Compare this to paragraph spacing, which adds space between each paragraph, and line spacing, which adds extra lines (or fractions thereof) between each line. Paragraph and line spacing add any "extra" amount based on a multiplier of the character height. For instance, double-spacing a line that is in 24-point type will create a 24-point "blank" line. In comparison, adding leading of 8 point will increase the space between each line by 8 points, whether the character point size is 12 point or 24 point.

Under exceptional circumstances, you may find it necessary to get down-and-dirty and send a command to your printer. WordPerfect lets you do so with the Printer Commands... dialog. You can pause the command input as well as save the collected printer commands to a file. Refer to your printer manual for instructions on issuing printer commands.

Baseline Placement

Baseline placement, found in the Document Format menu, makes the character baseline even with the top margin of the page. Ordinarily, the top margin is even with the top of the first line of text, and the baseline—the invisible line on which the characters seem to "sit"—is somewhere below. The baseline for the first line of text will be lower on the page for a bigger font than a smaller one.

When you use Advance (described later in this chapter) and other codes intended to locate text in a precise location, you need a consistent baseline. Using Baseline Placement for Typesetters puts the baseline of the first line at the top margin of the page, moving the text up slightly. Because the measurements are consistent, it is easier to measure exact text placement from the top of the page. This can be important if you're designing forms or being careful about text placement in a newsletter.

To use Baseline Placement for Typesetters, choose the feature from the Document Format dialog.

Redline Methods and Characters

Anyone who has ever had to compare two versions of the same document manually will cherish WordPerfect's capability to compare documents. WordPerfect automatically marks deleted text with the strikeout attribute and redlines text that was added. It also notes text that was moved from one part of the document to another. (Changes in graphics boxes, headers, footers, and comments are not marked.)

Procedure 18.1. Comparing documents.

1. To compare documents, retrieve the newest version.
2. Choose File, and select Compare Documents, or press Alt+F5. Choose Add Markings.
3. Enter the name of the older document, and indicate what level of granularity should be used for comparing the two. Select OK for WordPerfect to begin the comparison.
4. After comparing the two documents, WordPerfect will display the redlined and struck-out text on your screen.

The default redline character is a vertical bar (|), printed in the left margin. You can change the redline method to left, right, alternating, or printer-dependent. An alternating redline method will print the redline character in the right and left margins, depending on whether the page is even or odd. Any character can be assigned as the redline character, including WordPerfect characters (Ctrl-W).

To change the redline method or character, choose Document from the Layout menu, and select Redline Method.

233

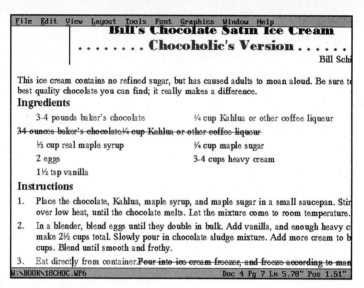

Figure 18.2. A redlined document.

Advance

WordPerfect's Advance commands provide fine-tuned control over the cursor's exact location on the page.

If you use an indented signature block at the end of letters, you may commonly use the Tab key to move over the 4 inches or so before you type `Sincerely`. Then you hit Enter two or three times before you tab over again, and type your name. But if you change the document's tab settings in the letter body, the *Sincerely* may wind up 3 inches, or even 2 inches from the left margin. If you change the line spacing or font size, the standard 1-2 inches between *Sincerely* and the typed name might become unreasonably large. The situation becomes worse when you create or change styles, because you can't predict the user's document settings. If you create a style sheet for another user (even if that user is you), you don't know whether s/he'll be using 1-inch tabs on an 8.5-inch by 11-inch page or .25-inch tabs on a 3-inch by 5-inch card.

Advance lets you position the cursor in an absolute location (4 inches from the top of the page) or a relative position (4 inches to the right of where the cursor is now). You can use Advance in a style to position a letter's date at the exact location appropriate for your stationery. It is excellent for use with preprinted forms. You also can use it to manually kern text or to add text to existing graphics.

You can advance up, down, left, or right from the cursor. You can provide the explicit measurement from the left edge or the top edge of the page. Text cannot be advanced past a page break. If your measurements must be extremely precise, examine the description of Baseline Placement for Typesetters, also in this chapter.

Advance codes don't seem to have any effect when you're in Text mode, though peeking at the status line will show you the change in text position. In Graphics mode or Page mode, however, you'll see that the cursor moved where you commanded.

To use Advance, choose Layout (or press Shift+F8), and select Other. Choose Advance... and enter the distance measurements.

Language

WordPerfect supports dozens of languages other than American English. You can use another language's formatting conventions for dates, sorting, footnotes, and tables. Selecting another language for a document or for a block of text enables WordPerfect to use that language's conventions for dates, or to print a footnote's *Continued...* in the selected language.

Using another language's dictionary for spelling and as a thesaurus requires a separate purchase of the associated language module; contact WordPerfect Corporation for details.

To select another language, select Other from the format dialog and choose Language. Pick the language to use for the document or the blocked text.

Display Pitch

The display pitch value is a measurement that specifies how many character widths something will occupy on the screen. The smaller the value, the more spread-out the text will appear on the screen. The larger the value, the more compressed the text will appear on the screen.

Use Display Pitch when you are stuck in Text mode and, for whatever reason, your text runs off the right side of the screen. (This doesn't bother some people; it makes other people rip out their hair.) By adjusting the display pitch, you can coerce the text to appear on the screen. The only way to do this is by trial and error. It's probably not worth the effort on a short document, but if you are struggling with a large, unwieldy page, or a very wide table, this feature is worth remembering.

The display pitch can be changed anywhere in the document. It affects the entire document, not just the unwieldy part. Remember, too, that it affects the display of the screen only, not the printed document.

Procedure 18.2. Manually adjusting the display pitch.

1. Choose Layout or press Shift+F8. Select Document, and choose Display Pitch.
2. Type in a display pitch value, and select Manual.
3. Select OK and Close to return to the document window.

To return to automatic Display Pitch, repeat the process, but choose Automatic.

Applying Page Formatting Features

In this section, we'll discuss ways to combine formatting features creatively.

A Simple Logo

If a line of text is short, Full Justification, All Lines can look pretty silly. However, you should be able to use the feature creatively for letterhead and other graphic word forms. You can create a text box with narrow margins and create a nifty logo for your company.

Here's an incredibly simple project, combining WordPerfect's new full justification with paragraph borders, to create a basic logo for a computer user group.

Procedure 18.3. Using justification and paragraph formatting for a simple user-group logo.

1. Select Layout or press Shift+F8. Select Line and choose Justification, then Full, All Lines.
2. Choose Paragraph Border. Pick a border, or customize your own.
3. Select a large display font of your choice.
4. Type:

```
Downeast Computer Society
WordPerfect Special Interest Group
```

That's all there is to it. You could add shading or change the borders, but since most small user-group newsletters are photocopied, staying simple is much safer than adding color gradations.

A Sales Flyer

In this exercise, we'll create some sample lines for a sales flyer. The example here borders on the tasteless, but that's only because we're overusing the feature. This example does show you what you can do with a few simple keystrokes.

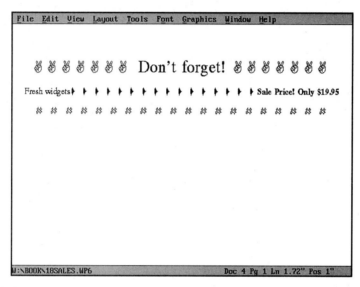

Figure 18.3. Experimentation with the leader character.

In each of these examples, the special character is a modified leader character. The "Don't Forget" character—Is that a peace sign or a sick rabbit?—is 5,44, from WordPerfect's iconic character set (use Ctrl+W, then type 5,44; or select the Iconic set and choose another character). To duplicate the effect, change the leader character from the Character Format dialog. Then press Shift+F6 twice and enter the heading text. Press Alt+F6 twice to fill to the margin with the leader characters again. (Reveal Codes will show [Center on Mar (dot)] and [Flsh Rt (dot)].)

Fresh Widgets was created with the exact same tools. I changed the leader character again, this time to 5,231, and also changed the number of spaces between the leader characters. WordPerfect's iconic symbol set provides quite a few arrow symbols, so you should have fun exploring this feature.

The last line in this example has no text, just another random selection from the WordPerfect character set for dot leaders, followed by a double Alt+F6. You could use this line in both a header and footer to create an unusual, yet simple, border.

A Recipe

The recipe in this example provides food for thought in more than one sense of the term. It demonstrates several of the features introduced in this chapter, and it also gives you a nifty recipe for chocolate ice cream.

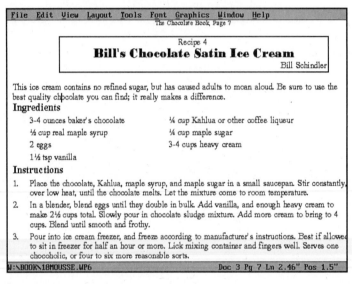

Figure 18.4. A recipe, using a collection of simple formatting commands.

The recipe uses a page number in the header. The title uses revertible fonts and margins, a paragraph border, and a *Recipe* counter. (One presumes that you would have a large collection of chocolate recipes.) Paragraph spacing is set to 1.25, to make the recipe easier to read. The *Ingredients* and *Instructions* subtitles are bolded, and their relative size is set to large. The recipe instructions use paragraph numbering provided by WordPerfect's built-in outline. I used smaller margins and tab settings than I would normally choose to get the entire recipe on one screen; otherwise, you might send me an e-mail asking for directions.

Despite the attractive formatting, it took less time to create the entire document than it did to pry the recipe out of Bill.

Tables and Forms

19

Basic Table Skills

by Bill Bruck

A table is information that is arranged in rows and columns. This "information" can be numbers, text, graphics, or formulas. Formatting options can be set for any part of the table. Font style, justification, or numeric type (currency, percentage, integer, and so on) can be specified. You can use virtually any line, border, or fill that you can imagine to enhance the appearance of your table. Even better, once these options are set, you merely type data into your table. It automatically takes on the formatting options you have specified, and there are no formatting codes that you can accidentally delete!

For example, a common task is to include tabular data in a report. The left (text) column is usually left-justified, and the other (numeric) columns should be decimal- (or right) justified. Using Tables, this is a snap. What's more, it's easy to make the top row of titles bold, large, centered, and with a double-line under them. This row can even be defined as a header that is repeated if the table spans more than one page. If you like, the bottom row and the right column can automatically total rows and columns of data in the table. Data entry becomes a breeze, because everything entered automatically has the correct format.

The table feature may become one of your favorite and most used tools within WordPerfect. Tables can be created quickly and easily, and they can be used for a wide variety of tasks:

▲ To create customized forms with a variety of lines and fonts, for example, a pay request form, which can be printed in-house on a laser printer.

▲ To automate data entry by allowing users to enter information in only specified cells and allow WordPerfect to calculate totals (for example, an invoice).

▲ To create parallel columns (for example, a movie script).

▲ To construct a spreadsheet, complete with calculations, formulas, and named cells.

About Tables

A table is a matrix composed of rows and columns. Rows are identified by numbers (1, 2, 3), and columns are identified by letters (a, b, c). WordPerfect allows you to have tables with up to 64 columns and (in theory) 32,766 rows. In practice, of course, such a table would be very unwieldy!

The intersection of a row and a column is a *cell*. Cells are identified by the letter of the column and the number of the row (e.g., Cell B2 is located at the intersection of Column B and Row 2—see Figure 19.1).

	A	B	C
1	Cell A1	Cell B1	Cell C1
2	Cell A2	Cell B2	Cell C2
3	Cell A3	Cell B3	Cell C3

Figure 19.1. Cell addresses.

Cells are like miniature pages in a document. They have left, right, top, and bottom margins. When you type more text than fits on one line, the cell expands vertically to accommodate it unless you specify that it shouldn't. You can put numbers, text, or even graphics boxes into cells.

You may also put formulas into cells. For example, you can create an invoice in which two columns contain the unit price and quantity and a third column contains a formula that calculates the total price. A cell at the bottom of the invoice can subtotal the entire order or even add sales tax.

In fact, however, WordPerfect 6.0 provides much more powerful formulas than simple addition, subtraction, multiplication, and division. Most of the functionality of PlanPerfect (WordPerfect Corporation's spreadsheet program) has been included in the options available to you within the Tables feature. WordPerfect contains a complete set of mathematical, statistical, financial, and scientific functions that can be included in formulas. (The use of these advanced features is discussed further in Chapter 21, "Advanced Table Skills.")

You may create and edit tables using the function keys, the menu interface, or (if you are in Graphics mode and have a mouse) the Tables button bar.

Table Codes

If you examine a table using Reveal Codes, as in Figure 19.2, you will find four codes that WordPerfect uses to define the table.

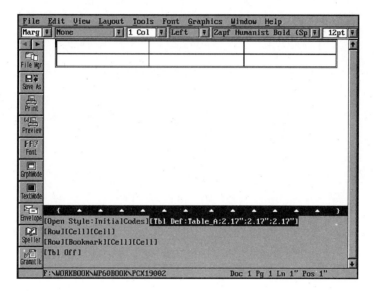

Figure 19.2. Table control codes.

▲ `[Tbl Def]`: This code comes at the beginning of a table. If you place your cursor on this code, it expands to show the name of the table and the column widths (for example: `[Tbl Def:Table_A;2.17"2.17"2.17"]`).

Caution: The `[Tbl Def]` code can be deleted if you are in Reveal Codes. Doing so deletes the table structure. The data in the table remains. Cells are separated by tabs, and rows are separated by hard returns. If you delete a `[Tbl Def]` code inadvertently, you may undo the operation and restore the table's structure by selecting Edit, Undo.

▲ `[Row]`: This code appears at the beginning of every row. It cannot be deleted.

▲ `[Cell]`: This code appears at the beginning of every cell. It cannot be deleted.

▲ `[Tbl Off]`: This code appears at the end of the table, after the last cell. It cannot be deleted.

243

The fact that you cannot delete row and column codes is a great help in data entry. You cannot inadvertently delete a row or column code that defines the table structure while you are editing your data. (This is a common complaint of people who use the parallel columns feature to accomplish tasks that can often be done more easily using tables.)

The Table Editing Window

When you first create a table, WordPerfect is in a special mode that allows you to change the basic format of the table, but not to enter data into it. This is called the Table Editing window. Remember, you enter information in a table from the main editing window. You edit the table's structure and appearance in the Table Editing window. You can switch back and forth between these modes any time you desire.

Table Editing Window Elements

Figure 19.3 displays the important elements of the Table Editing windows.

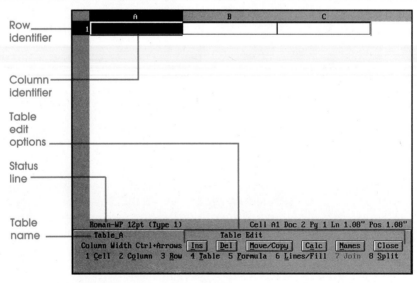

Figure 19.3. The Table Editing window.

Important elements of the Table Editing window include:

▲ Row and column identifiers: rows and columns are identified with numbers and letters. The selected cell is highlighted, as is its row and column identifier.

▲ Status line: this provides information on the base font of the selected cell, the cell address, and page/position information. If the cell contains a formula or function, the formula or function appears instead of the filename on the status line. The cell address also provides information on cell attributes:

B2* Header cell (this row appears on every page)

"B2 Ignored cell (ignored during calculations)

[B2] Locked cell (user cannot enter cell or edit information)

▲ Table name: this specifies the name of the table (if the table has not been assigned a name, this name reflects Table_A, Table_B, and so on).

▲ Table edit options: this allows you to specify various options related to the table formatting, size, and formulas.

Table Editing Window Functions

From the Table Editing window, you can perform functions that affect the appearance or structure of the table as a whole, including:

▲ Changing the number of rows and columns

▲ Joining two or more cells into one cell

▲ Splitting one or more cells into additional, smaller cells

▲ Joining two tables together or splitting a single table into two tables

▲ Specifying lines, borders, fills, and colors for the table

▲ Placing formulas into cells

▲ Moving and copying cells, rows, or columns to other locations in the table or other tables

(These functions are discussed in greater detail in Chapter 20, "Formatting Tables.")

Creating a Table

Creating a table is much easier than you might think, considering the considerable power of tables. The basic strategy is to use the Create Table function to specify the number of rows and columns. You will be in the Table Editing window. You may then enter initial formatting codes or return to the main editing window to enter data and format the table later. To create a table, follow the steps in Procedure 19.1.

Procedure 19.1. Creating a table.

1. Move the cursor to the position of the table.

2. Choose Layout or press Alt+F7. Then choose Tables, Create. The Create Table dialog box appears (see Figure 19.4).

Figure 19.4. The Create Table dialog box.

3. Specify the number of rows and columns for your table.

4. Click OK or press Enter. This closes the Table Create dialog box and creates the table. The desired table appears on the screen.

5. In the Table Editing window, make any desired formatting changes to the table. (See Chapter 20 for details on formatting tables.)

6. Click Close or press F7 to return to the main editing window. You may now enter text or data into your table.

Tip: Use the table button bar to create and edit tables. Many of the table editing features can be accessed through one mouse click that otherwise would require that you go through several menu levels. Select the table button bar by choosing View, Button Bar Setup, Select. Highlight the Table button bar and choose Select. To display the selected button bar (if it is not already displayed), choose View, Button Bar.

Create Tables from Existing Data

You can also create a table from data that is already in a document. The data may be in tabular columns or in parallel columns. This can be helpful to secretaries or editors who need to take draft data or imported ASCII files and insert the data into a table. To create a table from such data, follow the steps in Procedure 19.2.

Procedure 19.2. Creating tables from existing data.

1. If you are using tabular data, reset the tabs if necessary to ensure that there is only one tab between each column of data. This ensures that you have the right number of columns in the table you are creating and that your data is put into the correct column.

2. Make a block of the data to be converted into the table using the mouse or by using either of the block keys: Alt+F4 or F12. The selected data should be highlighted after you block it.

3. Choose Layout or press Alt+F7. Then choose Tables, Create. The Create Table from Block dialog box appears (see Figure 19.5).

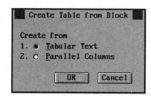

Figure 19.5. The Create Table from Block dialog box.

4. Specify whether you are creating the table from tabular text or parallel columns and click OK. The new table appears, and you are in the Table Editing window.

Tip: You can also import part or all of a spreadsheet into a WordPerfect table. (See Chapter 31, "Exchanging Information Between Applications," for more information.)

Inserting Text in a Table

After you have created your table and returned to the main editing window, you are ready to insert information into your table. Inserting text or other information into tables is both intuitive and simple. It parallels entering text in the main editing window, with a few minor exceptions:

▲ Move the cursor to the next cell. Press the Tab key to move to the next cell when entering data.

▲ Add rows. Press the Tab key from the last cell of the last row to add a new row to the table and advance your cursor into the next cell.

▲ Insert tabs. To insert a hard tab in the table, press one of the following keys (pressing Tab does not insert a tab in a table. Use the keystrokes below to insert tabs in a table):

Left Tab	Home, Tab
Right Tab	Home, Alt+F6
Center Tab	Home, Shift+F6
Decimal Tab	Home, Ctrl+F6

To add a dot leader to any of the tabs above, press Home twice rather than once. The tabs described above are hard tabs. That is, they are left, right, center, or decimal no matter what type of tab is called for in the tab specifications. To insert a soft tab (one that takes on the characteristics defined in the tab specifications), press Ctrl+a, Tab. To insert a back tab, press Ctrl+a, Shift+Tab.

Moving the Cursor Within Tables

The easiest way to move the cursor in a table is to click the mouse pointer in the desired cell. Alternatively, you can use the following keystrokes, which work in both the main editing window and the Table Editing window.

To move	Press
One Cell Down	[Alt]+[↓]
One Cell Left	[⇧Shift]+[Tab⇄], or [Alt]+[←], or [Ctrl]+[Home], [←]
One Cell Right	[Tab⇄], or [Alt]+[→] [Ctrl]+[Home], [→]
One Cell Up	[Alt]+[↑]
Beginning of Text	[Ctrl]+[Home], [↑]
Last Line of Text	[Ctrl]+[Home], [↓]
One Cell Left	[Ctrl]+[Home], [Home], [↑], or [Alt]+[Home], [↑]
Last Cell in Column	[Ctrl]+[Home], [Home], [↓], or [Alt]+[Home], [↓]
First Cell in Row	[Ctrl]+[Home], [Home], [←], or [Home], [Home], [Home], [←], or [Alt]+[Home], [←]
Last Cell in Row	[Ctrl]+[Home], [Home], r[→], or [Home], [Home], [Home], [→], or [Alt]+[Home], [→], or [Ctrl]+[Home], [End]
First Cell	[Ctrl]+[Home], [Home], [Home], [↑], or [Alt]+[Home], [Home], [↑]
Last Cell	[Ctrl]+[Home], [Home], [Home], [↓]

Tip: You can move the cursor from cell to cell with the arrow keys in the main editing window if there is no text in the cells.

You can move the cursor to a named table, cell, row, or column by pressing Ctrl+Home and typing the name. (See Chapter 21 for more table information.)

The Table Editing Window

To edit the structure of the table, you need to switch from the main editing window to the Table Editing window. Switch to the Table Editing window by following the steps in Procedure 19.3.

Procedure 19.3. Entering the Table Editing window.

1. Place the cursor anywhere inside the table to be edited.
2. Choose Layout, Tables, Edit, or press Alt+F11. The Table Editing window appears.
3. Change the table structure and appearance as desired.
4. To return to the main editing window, click Close or press F7. The main editing window appears.

Moving and Copying Table Information

There are many times when you may wish to move or copy information in a table. How you do so depends on whether you wish the action to pertain to blocked text in the table, the entire table, or selected cells, rows, or columns.

Blocked Text

Use the *blocked text* procedures when you want to move or copy part of the contents of a cell, or when you want to move or copy text without moving the cell codes with it.

Moving or copying blocked text in a table is done exactly like it is when blocked text is not in a table. You use the same procedures to select the text, either with keystrokes or by clicking and dragging the mouse pointer to select the text. The text may be part or all of the text in a single cell, it may span cells, or it may include text that is not even part of the table, as shown in Figure 19.6.

Selecting this text and then moving or copying it is accomplished using the same procedures that are discussed in Chapter 4, "Basic Editing Skills." The fact that part or all of the text is in a table is immaterial.

When moving or copying blocks of text in this manner, only the text itself is moved or copied, not the table structure. Any [Cell] codes in the blocked text are replaced by [Lft Tab] codes, and any [Row] codes are replaced with [HRt] codes. Thus, for example, if you blocked the text from an entire row of cells and copied it into the first cell of an empty row, the text from the entire row would be placed into the destination cell. If you wish to place text from several cells into the equivalent destination cells, use the procedures described in the section titled "Moving and Copying Rows, Columns, and Cells" in this chapter.

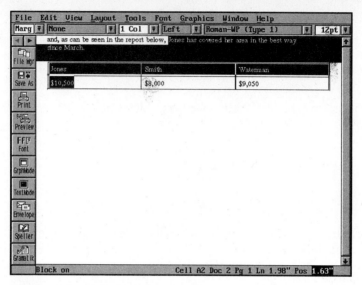

Figure 19.6. Selected text in tables.

Entire Table

To move or copy an entire table, use the same procedure used when moving or copying text. The only difference is that you must be sure that you have included the table definition and table off codes in the text you have selected. To do this, turn Reveal Codes on and make a block of everything from the [Tbl Def] code up to and including the [Tbl Off] code, as shown in Figure 19.7.

Rows, Columns, and Cells

When you start working with tables extensively, you will find that there are many instances in which you wish to move, copy, or delete the entire contents of a cell or a group of cells to another place within the table.

Moving and Copying Rows, Columns, and Cells

When you move or copy cells, the table format is copied as well. You can use this fact in creating tables that have complex formatting specifications. After specifying the necessary format for title or data cells in one part of the table, you can use the Copy Cell (or Row or Column) command to replicate the format for cells in other parts of the table. You may also use this method to move selected cell information from one table to another.

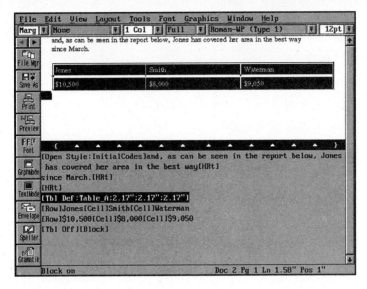

Figure 19.7. Selecting the entire table.

Moving or copying rows, columns, and cells operates on entire cells or groups of cells, not on some of the text in cells. For this reason, it makes sense that this operation is done in the Table Editing window—not at the main editing screen. To move or copy cells, follow the steps in Procedure 19.4.

Note: When text is cut or copied, it is placed in a *buffer*, a special area of memory on the disk. It stays in this buffer until you exit WordPerfect or until other text is cut or copied into the buffer. Thus, you can retrieve multiple copies of text after it is cut or copied.

The buffer used when cutting or copying cells is a separate buffer than that used for cutting or copying blocks of text, tabular columns, or rectangles. Therefore, cutting or copying text that is not in tables does not delete information that is in the move-cell buffer.

Procedure 19.4. Moving and copying cells, rows, and columns.

1. Enter the Table Editing window.
2. If you wish to move or copy a row, column, or single cell, position the cursor anywhere in the row, column, or cell.
3. If, alternatively, you wish to move a block of cells, block the cells using the mouse or either of the block keys: Alt+F4 or F12.
4. Select Move or press Ctrl+F4 to access the Move dialog box (see Figure 19.8).

251

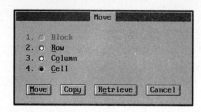

Figure 19.8. The Move dialog box.

5. Select what you want to move. If a block is active, you can select Block, Row, or Column. If no block is active, you can select Row, Column or Cell.

6. Select Move or Copy. If you select Copy, the selected cells are copied to the move-cell buffer, but they are not cut from the table. If you select Move, the result depends on whether you are moving a cell or cells, a row, or a column.

6.1. If you are moving a row, a column, or a block of rows or columns, the selected rows and columns are deleted from the table. That is, the resulting table has that many fewer rows and columns in it. For example, if you block two rows of a five-row table and move these two rows, the resulting table has only three rows remaining until you retrieve the rows again.

6.2. If you are moving a cell or a block of cells, the contents of the selected cells are moved to the move-cell buffer. The information in the cells is thus deleted, but the empty cells remain in the table, and the cell format information is retained. For example, suppose that all the cells in the first two rows of a five-row table have double-lines between them and you block all of these cells and move the block of cells. The resulting table still has five rows. The cells in the first two rows still have double-lines between them, but all the information in them has been cut.

6.3. If you are copying a single cell, you will see the Copy Cell dialog box, as shown in Figure 19.9. If you choose To Cell, follow Steps 7 and 8 to retrieve the information. Otherwise, if you choose Down or Right, you are prompted for the number of times the information should be copied, and it immediately appears in the specified cells. (You will not need to follow Steps 7 or 8.)

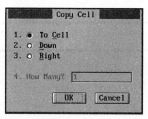

Figure 19.9. The Copy Cell dialog box.

6.4. If you are copying a block of cells, the selected cells are copied to the move-cell buffer. The information in the original cells is retained. When you retrieve the cells, the information in the move-cell buffer overwrites any information in the destination cell(s).

6.5. If you are copying a row or block of rows, or a column or block of columns, the selected rows or columns are copied to the move-cell buffer. The information in the original cells is retained. When you retrieve the row(s) or column(s), the information in the move-cell buffer does not overwrite current cells. Rather, copies of the selected row(s) or column(s) are inserted above or to the left of the cursor position.

7. After you have cut or copied cells, rows or columns, you will see the message `Move cursor, press Enter to retrieve`. At this point, you have two options:

7.1. If you wish to retrieve the cells immediately, move the cursor to the appropriate spot (see Step 7.4) and press Enter.

7.2. If you wish to perform other actions before you retrieve the cells, press the Esc key, then retrieve the cells manually (see Step 8).

7.3. To determine the appropriate spot for your cursor, use the following rules:

   (a) A cell or block of cells in the move-cell buffer are retrieved to cells starting with the cell your cursor is in. Data in those cells is overwritten by the data being retrieved. If there is not enough room—for example, if you cut four cells of information and place the cursor in the second to last cell before retrieving—information in the cells that do not "fit" is lost. It is still retained, however, in the move-cell buffer, until you move another cell or exit WordPerfect.

   (b) Rows in the move-cell buffer are inserted above the row the cursor is on.

   (c) Columns in the move-cell buffer are inserted to the left of the column the cursor is on.

8. You will retrieve information in the move-cell buffer manually in two instances: when the move or copy operation has been interrupted by pressing the Esc key; or when you wish to retrieve the contents of the move-cell buffer more than once. To manually retrieve the contents of the buffer:

   (a) Ensure that you are in the Table Editing window.

   (b) Place the cursor at the appropriate spot in the table.

   (c) Select Move or press Ctrl+F4 to access the Move dialog box. Then select Retrieve.

Tip: You can move or copy rows, columns, or selected cells between tables as well as within a table. Cut or copy the selected cells to the move-cell buffer using Steps 1-6, then press the Esc key to cancel the move or copy operation. Exit from the Table Edit mode and place your cursor in the destination table. Follow Step 8 to manually retrieve the information into the destination cell.

Deleting Contents of Cells

There will be many times when you wish to delete the contents of a specific cell. At other times, you may wish to retain the formatting of a table, but delete all the information in it. When you need to delete the contents of cells, rows, or columns, follow the steps in Procedure 19.5.

This procedure is not used for deleting actual rows and columns (i.e., making the table smaller). (See Chapter 20 for procedures to add and delete rows and columns from a table.)

Procedure 19.5. Deleting contents of cells.

1. Enter the Table Editing window if you are not already in this mode.

2. Move the cursor to the cell whose information you wish to delete, or block the group of cells from which you wish to delete information using the mouse or either of the block keys: Alt+F4 or F12.

3. Press Backspace. If a block of cells is selected, you are asked to confirm the deletion. If only one cell is highlighted, the deletion takes place without confirmation.

4. Return to the main editing window.

Note: Instead of pressing Backspace, you can choose Del, or press Del to access a Delete dialog box. From here you can choose to delete rows, columns, or cell contents. If you choose cell contents, the contents of the blocked cells are deleted in the same way as if you had pressed the Backspace key.

Printing Tables

Printing a document that contains a table is pretty much like printing any other document. There are a few points, however, that may make your printing chores easier:

▲ Table lines, fills, and borders are graphic elements. If your printer cannot print graphics, it will not be able to print table lines.

▲ Many times, tables imported from spreadsheets are wider than can be printed on a page. In these instances, only the portion that will fit on the page will print.

▲ Printing tables with graphics lines can be a slow process. You can speed it up in two ways:

   (a) If you are not using fills, but only graphics lines, if you are not using extended characters that print graphically, and if you are using a laser printer, try setting Graphics Quality to draft. On many laser printers, graphics lines print with the same quality whether you are in draft or high quality, and they print much faster in draft.

   (b) If you are printing multiple copies of a complex table, and do not need the output to be collated, set your print output options to Generated by Printer, rather than Generated by WordPerfect. The job will only be sent to the printer once. The first copy will take as long, but additional copies print very rapidly.

Combining Tables with Other Functions

Tables can become even more powerful when you combine them with other functions—functions you will learn to do in future chapters. Some of these include:

▲ Tables in columns: both parallel and newspaper columns can contain tables. Thus, you easily can include a table in your company newsletter.

▲ Tables in graphics boxes: any type of graphics box can contain a table, combined with any desired text. (Remember, however, that a graphics box cannot contain a table that would span a page.)

▲ Graphics in tables: you may also choose to place a graphic—for example, a piece of clip art—inside the cell of a table. This is often done when creating a form that should include a company logo.

▲ Tables in headers and footers: you can place a table in a header or a footer. This enables you to easily create headers and footers that have graphics lines and shading.

▲ Tables and styles: you can place a style in a table, and you can place a table in a style. If a table is in a style, you must edit the style to edit data in the table, and tables that are not in a style cannot reference tables in a style.

255

Table Limitations

Although tables are very powerful, there are a few things that they cannot do. In most cases, knowing this, you can work around any limitations they impose.

▲ Cells cannot span a page. As a cell lengthens to accommodate the text you put in it, it can only grow to the size of the page it is on.

If you attempt to type more information into a cell than it can hold, the text you type will not appear on-screen. In reveal codes, you will see a `[Hidden Txt]` code. The text you type is not "lost," but it is contained in this control code. Similarly, if you move or copy more text into a cell than it can hold, shorten the page's top/bottom margins, or decrease the cell's fixed row height (excess text becomes hidden). This text reappears if the cell height or margins allow for it to be seen on the page.

For this reason, parallel columns are often used for scripts and other applications in which the text of an individual "cell" may be longer than one page will accommodate. In most instances, however, users will find the table function to be more powerful and easier to use.

▲ There can be nothing to the side of a table. You cannot have text on the side of a table, nor can two tables be parallel to one another.

However, you can place a table in a column, and you can place a table in a graphics box. Either of these methods allows you to get around this inherent limitation in tables. Quite often, if you wish to have text wrap about a small table, the easiest way to accomplish the task is to create a user box (with no lines), and place the table within it, as shown in Figure 19.10.

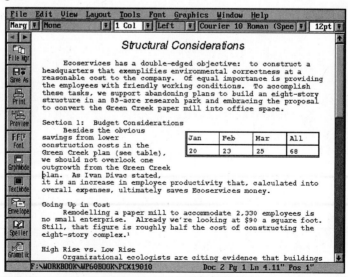

Figure 19.10. A table in a user box.

▲ Tables must have the same number of columns throughout. This can be a limitation when creating some types of forms in which different sections have differing numbers of columns.

There are two workarounds for this problem. The first is to create more columns than needed by either section of the table and join the appropriate cells together to create larger apparent columns. (This technique is described further in Chapter 20.)

The second alternative is to create two tables and leave no space between the `[Tbl Off]` code of the first table and the `[Tbl Def]` code of the second. The two tables print as if they were one table. However, it is more complicated to write formulas that takes data from both tables.

Similarly, when you need to have two or more tables side by side, you can put them in graphics boxes, or you can create columns and place the tables in them. Either method allows you to have side-by-side tables, as shown in Figure 19.11.

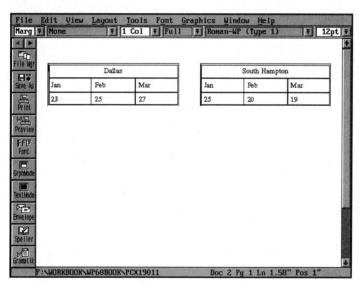

Figure 19.11. Two tables side by side.

by Bill Bruck

Formatting Tables

In the last chapter, you learned how to create a table, enter information into it, and move cells both within and between tables. In this chapter, you will begin to unleash the real power contained in tables. You will learn how to:

▲ Format numbers and text in the table

▲ Specify lines, fills, and shadows to enhance the appearance of your table

▲ Create virtually any form by changing a table's structure

Changing the Table Structure

There are many times when you will want to have a more sophisticated table structure than a simple matrix of rows and columns. You may wish to have a title row that spans the entire table, or a column that is split to show subcategories of data (see Figure 20.1).

In addition, you will probably find that you need to add and delete rows as you use your table for data entry. You can accomplish all of these tasks easily as you learn the basic commands for changing a table's structure.

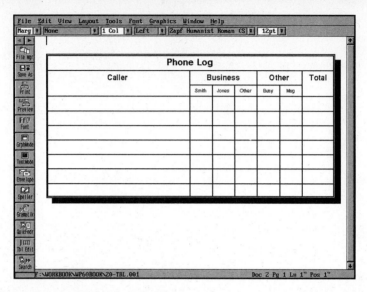

Figure 20.1 A sample form using tables.

Inserting/Deleting Rows and Columns

Usually, you need to insert or delete both rows and columns as you initially create and refine the structure of your table. Once the table is created, you will often find the need to insert extra rows in the table—for additional data—but not extra columns.

Inserting and Deleting Rows from the Main Editing Window

WordPerfect 6.0 provides is a new way to insert a row at the end of the table while you are in the regular editing window. With your cursor in the last cell of the table, press the Tab key. This makes sense, because you usually press the Tab key to move from cell to cell when you are entering data.

Another shortcut for inserting and deleting rows from the main editing window is to press Ctrl+Ins or Ctrl+Del. Ctrl+Ins inserts a new row above the current cursor position. Ctrl+Del deletes the row your cursor is in. You will be asked to confirm this deletion before it occurs. These commands work with most, but not all, enhanced keyboards. Try it with the specific keyboard you use. However, these are by no means the only ways to insert and delete rows and columns.

Inserting and Deleting Rows and Columns from the Table Editing Window

When you are first creating the structure of your table, you are in the Table Editing window. To insert columns or rows from this window, follow the steps in Procedure 20.1.

Procedure 20.1. Inserting columns or rows in a table.

1. Enter the Table Editing window, place the cursor anywhere inside the table to be edited. Choose Layout, Tables, Edit; or press Alt+F11.
2. Choose Ins, or press Insert to see the Insert dialog box.
3. Select whether you wish to insert columns or rows, the number of columns or rows to be inserted, and whether they should be inserted before or after the current cursor position.
4. Choose OK or press Enter.

Note: Users of WordPerfect 5.1 may notice that there is no Table Size command. This command, available in the Table Edit mode of Version 5.1, showed the current number of rows and columns in the table and allowed you to reset either figure. Using this command was the only way to add rows or columns to the end of the table. While the methods provided in Version 6.0 are much easier to use, there is no way to easily ascertain the number of columns or rows in a table without scrolling to the end of it—which can take time in an especially long table.

To delete columns or rows, you will follow similar steps (see Procedure 20.2).

Procedure 20.2. Deleting columns or rows in a table.

1. Enter the Table Editing window.
2. Optionally, you can mark a block of the rows or columns to be deleted.
3. Choose Del, or press Delete to see the Delete dialog box.
4. Select whether you wish to delete columns or rows, and (if a block is not active) the number of columns or rows to be deleted. (Note that you can also delete the contents of blocked cells with this command.)
5. Choose OK, or press Enter.

Tip: You can press Ctrl+Z—the Undo command—immediately after you insert or delete rows or columns, and the table will be restored to its former structure.

Joining and Splitting Cells

Now that you're familiar with the steps needed to change the size of a table, only one more thing is needed in order to create the sophisticated table structures needed to create forms like the phone log shown above. You need to be able to join groups of cells together and split cells apart.

Joining and splitting cells is a very straightforward procedure, and this is done from the Table Editing window. While the technique is easy (see Procedures 20.3 and 20.4), performing the steps does not ensure attractive design. Just as many people who have purchased a laser printer try to see how many different fonts and sizes will fit on a page (and call it desktop publishing), it is easy to create forms which use an overly complex table structure and too many graphic line elements. The best way to start designing forms is by replicating forms that you use at work using WordPerfect. You will find that, by using the Join and Split functions, you can create almost any form that you find in the office.

Procedure 20.3. Joining cells in a table.

1. Enter the Table Editing window.
2. Make a block of cells to be joined.
3. Choose Join. (You will see a confirmation dialog box.)
4. Choose Yes.

Procedure 20.4. Splitting cells in a table.

1. Enter the Table Editing window.
2. Position the cursor inside the cell to be split, or make a block of the group of cells to be split.
3. Choose Split to see a Split Cell dialog box.
4. Select how many columns or rows the cell(s) should be split into and whether to split the selected cell(s) into additional columns or rows.
5. Choose OK or press Enter.

Tip: Remember that joining and splitting cells can be undone by pressing Ctrl+Z immediately after you have joined or split the cells. This can be done from the Table Editing window or the main editing window.

Joining and Splitting Tables

WordPerfect 6.0 offers a new feature that will be a boon to users of Versions 5.1 and earlier: the ability to join two tables together, or split a table into two separate ones.

Splitting Tables

Users occasionally find that they need to split a table into two or more separate tables when they are initially designing the table or form. This is because of one shortcoming inherent in tables—a table must have the same number of (total) columns throughout. Take the following table (see Figure 20.2), for example, with what appears to be two columns at the top, and three at the bottom.

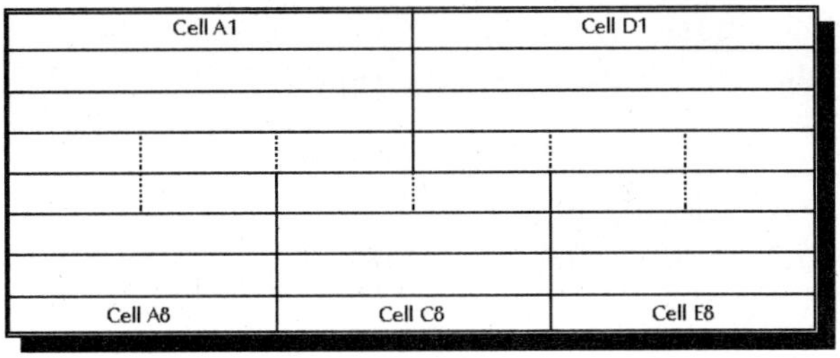

Figure 20.2. A table with an apparently varying number of columns.

As you can see from the dotted lines in the fourth and fifth rows, the entire table actually has six columns (2 x 3). Cells in columns A-C and D-F are joined at the top of the table to produce cells that are three columns wide. Cells in columns A-B, C-D, and E-F are joined in the bottom of the table to produce cells that are two columns wide. Not only is this unwieldy and awkward to do, but as you can see in Figure 20.2, the cell addresses are not consecutive—Cell A1 is next to cell D1 in the top row of the table!

When you are in the middle of designing a form, and have spent a lot of time entering cell formats and text, it is disconcerting to find that you really should have used to separate tables and need to redo your work. In a case like this, you may wish to split the table into two, using the steps defined in Procedure 20.5.

Procedure 20.5. Splitting a table.

1. Ensure that you are in the main editing window (not the Table Editing window).
2. Position the cursor in a cell that is in the top row of what will be the new, second table.

3. Choose Layout, or press Alt+F7. Then select Tables.

4. Select Split.

5. Select Reveal Codes and position the cursor between the [Tbl Off] code of the first table and the [Tbl Def] code of the new table.

6. Press Enter a few times to create some space between the two tables.

Joining Tables

There will be certain times when you wish to split a table into two. Other times, you may wish to combine two tables into one. This can make calculations much easier. For example, employees may use tables for logging time spent on various projects. To obtain totals, you may wish to join the tables together and calculate totals on the combined table.

Tables to be joined must have the same number of columns, and they will take on the formatting of the first (top) table. To join two tables, follow the steps in Procedure 20.6.

Procedure 20.6. Joining two tables.

1. Ensure that you are in the main editing window (not the Table Editing window).

2. Move the two tables to be joined until they are adjacent to each other.

3. Select Reveal Codes and delete any [HRt] or other codes between the tables so the [Tbl Off] code of the first table is immediately before the [Tbl Def] code of the second table.

4. Place the cursor in the first table.

5. Choose Layout or press Alt+F7. Then select Tables.

6. Select Join.

Formatting Text and Numbers

Formatting allows you to change the look and feel of numbers and text in your table. It permits you to define the size of the table's columns and cells, as well as the margins within them.

While you can edit the formatting of an existing table, specifying formats is usually done when the table is first created. Data put into a table takes the format of the cells into which it is entered. Thus, by creating a formatted table with no data, you can provide tables and forms in which users tab from cell to cell, entering data. Each time they tab to a new cell, the data they enter automatically takes on the correct format for its position in the form or table. You can even lock title and calculation cells so the user tabs only between data entry cells. A well-designed table makes data entry easy and attractive.

General Considerations

Formatting tables is accomplished in the Table Editing window. While it is usually done when the table is first created, you can format a table at any time. Formatting controls the look and feel of a table, including the following:

- ▲ Text font and appearance
- ▲ Numeric format
- ▲ Justification and vertical alignment within cells
- ▲ The position of a table on the page
- ▲ Column width and cell margins
- ▲ Keeping text together and splitting it apart
- ▲ The number of lines of text and the vertical size of cells
- ▲ Header rows
- ▲ Locked and non-calculating cells

Formatting Precedence

You may apply table formatting commands to four different table elements:

- ▲ Individual cells or blocks of cells
- ▲ Columns of cells within the table
- ▲ Rows of cells within a table
- ▲ The table as a whole

Some formatting commands are unique to the table element in which they appear. For example, you can only set row height when you format rows. Other formatting commands are common to several table elements. For example, you can set text size for cells, columns, or the table as a whole.

In order to effectively utilize table formatting commands, it is important to understand the concept of *formatting precedence*. Formatting commands for individual cells or groups of cells take precedence over all other formatting commands. Formatting commands for columns or groups of columns and formatting commands for the table as a whole have an equal precedence. The most recent table or column formatting command that applies to a given cell takes precedence if there is no cell formatting command that applies to that cell. (There is no overlap between row formatting commands and other formatting commands, so row formatting does not enter into precedence order.)

The easiest way to work with formatting commands and precedence is to format your table from the largest component to the smallest:

265

▲ First, set the format you want for the table as a whole. For example, in a table containing mostly integer data, most columns will probably be right justified. What lines do you want around most cells?

▲ Second, format specific columns that do not fit into the overall table format. For example, the leftmost column of the table may contain labels, rather than numbers. You can set its justification to left.

▲ Third, format specific cells. For example, the top row of cells might contain titles and need to be center-justified. The bottom-right cell could conceivably contain a summary of all the other numbers, and thus perhaps it should be bold.

Selecting Cells to be Formatted

To apply formatting commands while you are in the Table Editing window, use the following rules to select the appropriate cells:

▲ To format the table as a whole, place the cursor anywhere in the table. Select Table.

▲ To format one column or row, the cursor can be anywhere in the column or row. You need not use the block to select the entire column or row. When the cursor is in the appropriate place, select Column or Row.

▲ To format a group of columns or rows, make a block that includes at least one cell from each column or row that should be formatted. You need not select every cell in the desired column(s) or row(s). Then select Column or Row.

▲ To format one cell, place the cursor in that cell, then select Cell.

▲ To format a group of cells, make a block that includes every cell that should be formatted. Then select Cell.

Specify Text Font, Appearance and Justification

You may specify text formatting attributes for the table as a whole, specific columns, or specific cells. While you cannot change the base font as part of table formatting, you can select the same *font sizes* and *font attributes* as you can within the Font dialog box, as is shown in the Cell Format dialog box—see Figure 20.3. To set text formatting attributes, follow the steps in Procedure 20.7.

Procedure 20.7. Setting text attributes in tables.

1. Ensure that you are in the Table Editing window.
2. Decide whether you wish to format the table as a whole, or specific columns or cells.

3. Select the appropriate cell(s) by positioning the cursor and/or making a block as described above.

4. Select Cell, Column, or Table.

5. If you wish to change attributes, select Appearance, then specify all desired attributes. Note that you can select more than one attribute.

6. If you wish to change text size, select Size, then specify the desired size. You may only select one size, but if desired, you may also specify subscript or superscript.

7. If you wish to remove all size and appearance attributes, select Normal.

8. When you are finished selecting text size and appearance attributes, select OK, or press Enter to return to the Table Editing window.

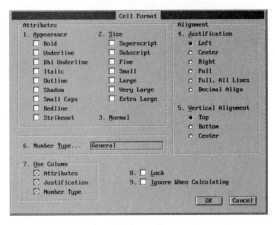

Figure 20.3. The Cell Format dialog box.

Numeric Format

As with text formatting, you may specify the format of numeric display attributes for the table as a whole, specific columns, or specific cells.

Selecting a display format does not change the number itself, but merely the way it is displayed. For example, if a cell contains the number 12.8 and you choose to display it as an integer, it displays as 13 (rounded to the nearest integer). However, if you later change the display format back to general, it again displays as 12.8.

Note: Numbers whose formats do not allow them to be completely displayed are *rounded*, not *truncated*. The actual number is retained in memory and can be displayed if the numeric format is changed.

Standard Numeric Formats

You may choose from several predefined formats for numbers in your tables, as can be seen in Figure 20.4.

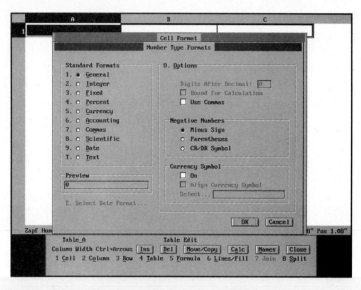

Figure 20.4. The Number Type Formats dialog box.

With each format, several options are set by default, some can be changed, and others cannot. For example, the general format does not display commas by default, but you can choose to display them. You cannot, however, choose how many decimal places will display, because a "general" format does not have a fixed number of decimals displayed. When you select a standard number format in the Number Types Format dialog box, options that are not available to you are dimmed (available options are highlighted). Available formats include the following:

General displays numbers with no trailing zeros. Calculated numbers wider than the cell width are displayed in scientific notation.

Integer displays numbers as whole numbers with no decimal places. Displayed numbers are rounded to the nearest whole number.

Fixed displays numbers rounded to the specified number of decimal places. The specified number of decimal places will display, even if they contain zeros.

Percent displays numbers multiplied by 100 with the percent sign following them. For example, .50 displays as 50%.

268

Currency is like the fixed option, but it displays numbers with the currency sign immediately preceding the number.

Accounting is like the currency option, but with the currency sign aligned to the left of the column.

Commas is like the fixed option, but negative numbers are expressed in parentheses and commas are displayed by default.

Scientific displays numbers in exponential notation.

Date converts integers into the current date format. (Time is formatted under Select Date Format.)

Text displays results of last calculation for formulas as a number. As long as the display mode is text, future recalculations do not affect the number in the cell. Effectively, the formula in the cell has been converted to the results of the last calculation.

Negative Numbers

Negative numbers can be expressed in three ways:

▲ with a minus sign, e.g., -300
▲ with parentheses, e.g., (300)
▲ with CD/DR notations, e.g., 300 DR

Standard formats default to specific ways of expressing number signs. General, integer, fixed, and percent use the minus sign. The other standard formats use parentheses. In any of the standard formats, however, you can opt to use any of the alternative formats for the display of negative numbers.

How Dates Are Calculated

If a cell's format is set to Date, entries are converted into the currently defined date format as soon as you move the cursor to another cell. Points you may wish to note about the way that numbers are converted into dates include:

▲ The earliest date that can be calculated is January 1, 1900.
▲ Positive numbers are converted to the date representing the number of days after January 1, 1900. For example, inputting the number 28 returns the date January 28, 1900; the number 365 results in December 31, 1900; and the number 366 results in January 1, 1901.
▲ Negative numbers are translated to January 1, 1900. Numbers between 1 and 24 are translated as measures of time. For example, 13 converts to 1:00pm.

▲ A shortcut for entering dates is to enter the day and month (e.g., 6.14). This will convert to June 14 of the current year in the currently specified format.

Note: Calculating dates in this way provides several benefits. Date differences can easily be calculated; it is easy to sort by date or calculate a 90-day suspense account.

Rounding for Calculation

By default, WordPerfect uses the actual number, not its rounded values, for calculations. For example, if you add 2.4 and 3.3, the result is 5.7. If you then display all the numbers as integers, the numbers in the cells are 2, 3, and 6 (the rounded numbers). Because the numbers used for the addition were the actual numbers, not the displayed numbers, and the display appears not to add up.

You may choose to use the rounded numbers for calculation when you specify the number type format. If you choose this option, the rounded numbers (rather than the actual numbers) are used for calculation, and the total reflects the sum of the numbers as they appear (see Figure 20.5).

Actual numbers	Rounded numbers	
	Actual total (displayed rounded)	Use rounded numbers for total
2.4	2	2
3.3	3	3
5.7	6	5

Figure 20.5. Rounded and actual numbers in table calculations.

Set Number Type Formats

Number type formats can be set for specified cells, columns, or the table as a whole—just as you can do for text attributes. To set number type formats, follow the steps in Procedure 20.8.

Procedure 20.8. Setting number type formats.

1. Ensure that you are in the Table Editing window.
2. Decide whether you wish to set number type formats for the table as a whole, specified column(s), or specified cell(s).
3. Select the appropriate cell(s) by positioning the cursor, and/or making a block as described above.

4. Select Cell, Column, or Table.

5. Select Number Type.

6. Choose the appropriate standard format.

7. Modify the standard format you have chosen by selecting any option, if desired.

8. When you are finished selecting the number format, select OK, or press Enter to return to the Table Editing window.

Formatting Text Within Cells

Another important aspect of controlling the table's appearance is selecting how the text appears within the cell: its justification, vertical alignment, margins, column width, and row height. In addition, WordPerfect allows you to "lock out" cells that should be skipped over in data entry, specify certain cells not to be used in calculations, and provide ways to keep cells together on a page. The range of options provides total flexibility in customizing the appearance of your table or form, and does so using the intuitive menus found in the Table Edit window.

Justification and Vertical Alignment

WordPerfect allows you to set both horizontal and vertical justification. You can justify cells horizontally with the same options you use to format a line of text. In addition, however, you can specify that text appear at the top, bottom, or middle of the cell. As with text attributes and number type formats, you may apply these formatting commands to the table as a whole, specified columns, or certain cells. The rules of precedence previously discussed apply.

Justifying Text in Cells

You may set the following justification options in tables:

Left (left-justified, ragged right)

Center (all lines centered)

Right (right-justified, ragged left)

Full (left- and right-justified)

Full—all lines (for titles and headers—words and letters spaced evenly between the left and right margins)

Decimal aligned (aligned on the decimal alignment character)

To set justification, follow the steps outlined in Procedure 20.9.

Procedure 20.9. Setting justification.

1. Ensure that you are in the Table Editing window.
2. Decide whether you wish to set justification for the table as a whole, specified column(s), or specified cell(s).
3. Select the appropriate cell(s) by positioning the cursor, and/or making a block as described above.
4. Select Cell, Column, or Table.
5. Select Justification.
6. Choose the desired justification method.
7. Select OK or press Enter to return to the Table Editing window.

Setting Vertical Alignment

Vertical alignment refers to the vertical position of the text within the cell. Normally, cells contain text from their top to bottom margins. However, there are two common instances in which this is not the case. If one cell in a row has several lines of text, and other cells have only one, the text in those other cells appear at the top of the cell. Similarly, if several cells in one row have been joined to form one "tall" vertical cell, text often does not fill the cell and appears at the top.

WordPerfect allows you to display text at the top, center, or bottom of cells. You may only set vertical alignment under the cell options. You cannot set it for the table as a whole or for columns or rows. This is described in Procedure 20.10.

> **Note:** Text appears top aligned in Text and Graphic modes even when center or bottom is chosen. In order to see the proper alignment of text, use Print Preview.

Procedure 20.10. Setting vertical alignment.

1. Ensure that you are in the Table Editing window.
2. Select the appropriate cell(s) by positioning the cursor, and/or making a block as described above.
3. Select Cell.
4. Select Vertical Alignment.
5. Choose the desired alignment method (**t**op, **b**ottom, or **c**enter).
6. Select OK or press Enter to return to the Table Editing window.

Column Width and Cell Margins

WordPerfect creates evenly spaced columns by default. Very often, you may wish to have some columns wider than others. You may use the shortcut noted on this page, or set column width more exactly by following the steps in Procedure 20.11. You may also wish to alter the cell margins—the distance between the text in the cell and the lines around it. The steps for doing so are listed in Procedure 20.12. Note that you may set column width and left/right margins for columns or tables as a whole, but not individual cells or groups of cells. You may set top/bottom margins for rows, but not for cells, columns, or the table as a whole.

Tip: The easiest way to change the column width is to use the Ctrl+right/left arrow keys when you are in the Table Edit mode. The column that the cursor is in gets larger and smaller as you use the right and left arrow. This is often the best way to set the column width—especially if you already have text in the table. You can then see the table reformat and make the column as wide as is needed for the text in the table. While this method is easiest, it is also the least exact. If you need to have columns be an exact measured width, use the steps in Procedure 20.11.

Procedure 20.11. Setting exact column width.

1. Ensure that you are in the Table Editing window.
2. Decide whether you wish to set column width for the table as a whole or specified columns.
3. Select the appropriate columns (if appropriate) by positioning the cursor, and/or making a block as described above.
4. Select Column or Table.
5. Select Width.
6. Specify the desired column width.
7. If desired, select Fixed Width (see the following note).
8. Select OK or press Enter to return to the Table Editing window.

Tip: To obtain even column widths, block the columns whose widths you wish to set. Set column width as described in Procedure 20.11. The default width is the necessary width to evenly space the columns.

Note: Column widths have a precedence order, which must be understood to successfully create a table with the desired appearance. The width of any column to the left takes precedence over the width of any column to its right.

This is best understood by example. As you continue to increase the width of the leftmost column, you will see that when the table width reaches that of the page, the widths of all other columns start to decrease equally.

If you move to the second column from the left and increase its width, the widths of all columns to its right decrease, but the width of the column to its left stays the same. In fact, you may notice that, in this case, if you move to the rightmost column, you cannot increase its width at all—there is no column to its right to "borrow" space from.

There are two implications of this precedence order. The first is that when you set column widths, you should start with the leftmost column. Otherwise, every width you set may be undone if you set widths of columns to the left of the one you set.

Secondly, in Version 6.0, you can "fix" the width of a column, so that changing the widths of other columns does not affect it, even if it is in the "lowly" right position. You can fix a column's width as described in Procedure 20.11.

Procedure 20.12. Setting cell margins.

1. Ensure that you are in the Table Editing window.
2. If you are setting left/right margins, decide whether you wish to set margins for the table as a whole or specified column(s).
3. Select cells in the appropriate columns (for left/right margins) or rows (for top/bottom margins) by positioning the cursor, and/or making a block as described above.
4. Select Column or Table for left/right margins. Alternatively, select Row for top/bottom margins.
5. If you are setting left/right margins, select Column margins. If you are setting top/bottom margins, select Top margin or Bottom margin.
6. Specify the desired margins.
7. Select OK or press Enter to return to the Table Editing window.

Row Height

By default, cells expand vertically to accommodate the amount of text you put into them. This is the way that most people use tables most of the time. However, there are other times when you wish to have a fixed row height. This is especially useful in creating forms where a box should be a specific height and not vary with the amount of text put in it. For this reason, WordPerfect allows you to specify two different settings for row height, as follows:

> **Row Height** Fixed. This option allows you to specify the exact row height in inches. It is especially useful for forms.

> **Row Height** Auto. This option allows the row height to vary depending on the text inside the cell.

> **Number of lines** Single. This option allows for only one line of text. If row height is auto, the row height depends on the largest point size of characters in the one line of allowed text.

> **Number of lines** Multiple. This option allows for as many lines of text as will fit in the specified row height (if it is fixed), or as will fit on one page (if row height is automatic).

To set the row height options, follow the steps in Procedure 20.13 below.

Procedure 20.13. Setting row height.

1. Ensure that you are in the Table Editing window.
2. Select cells in the appropriate rows by positioning the cursor, and/or making a block as described above.
3. Select Row.
4. Select Fixed or Auto row height.
5. Select Single or Multiple lines of text.
6. Select OK or press Enter to return to the Table Editing window.

Locked and Non-Calculating Cells

Two other functions will assist you in creating forms that are easy to fill out and forms that can perform calculations for you. Locked cells are cells a user cannot move the cursor into. In a simple table consisting of three cells, if the middle one is locked, a user tabs directly from the left cell to the right cell, skipping over the locked cell.

Locked cells are very useful in data entry. Often, the creator of the table or form locks cells that contain titles, constants (like sales tax percentage), totals, or calculated amounts. In an invoice, the only cells which might be unlocked, in fact, are the cells for item name, quantity, and unit price. The total column, taxable subtotal, and total after tax may be calculated automatically. Thus, these cells, along with all title cells, may be locked.

You may also specify that a cell's content should not be included for any calculations. The need for this is due to the way the WordPerfect works. If a cell that contains both text and numbers is included in a calculation (like a total), the number in that cell is added to the other cells—the text in the cell is ignored. This can be especially disconcerting when totalling sales figures from columns that have headings like "March 1993" or "FY1993." (The totals will thus be off by 1,993!) To prevent this unfortunate occurrence, you may designate that specific cells (often title cells) should not be included in calculations.

You may lock cells or ignore them when calculating using the steps in Procedure 20.14.

Procedure 20.14. Locking or ignoring cells when calculating.

1. Ensure that you are in the Table Editing window.
2. Select cells in the appropriate rows by positioning the cursor, and/or making a block as described above.
3. Select Cell.
4. Select Lock and/or Ignore cell when calculating.
5. Select OK or press Enter to return to the Table Editing window.

Keeping Text Together

As you have learned, information within a single cell is always on the same page, because cells cannot span page breaks. There are instances, however, in which several cells should always be kept together (when a page break should not separate certain rows). This can easily be accomplished by using WordPerfect's block protect feature.

Make a block that includes some text from each row that should be kept together. With the block active, select Layout, or press Shift+F8. Then select Other, Block protect.

> **Note:** You may force a page break at any row in a table by pressing Ctrl+Enter anywhere in the row which will start the new page. Assuming that auto-code placement is turned on, the [HRow-HPg] code will migrate to the beginning of the first cell in that row. If the text in which a page break is inserted is block protected, the block protection will be turned off by the insertion of the hard page.

Tip: You may force a page break at any row in a table by pressing Ctrl+Enter anywhere in the row that will start the new page. Assuming that auto-code placement is turned on, the [HRow-HPg] code migrates to the beginning of the first cell in that row.

Page Layout of the Table

In creating tables or forms, you will also be concerned about the table's appearance on the page as a whole. Using WordPerfect, you can specify a table's horizontal position or header rows.

Horizontal Position of Table

WordPerfect 6.0 allows you to position a table anywhere on the line that you desire. Although Version 5.1 provided the ability to position a table at the right, left, or center of the page or from margin to margin ("full"), Version 6.0 adds the capability to position the table a specified distance from the left edge of the page. To specify the horizontal position of a table, follow the steps in Procedure 20.15.

Procedure 20.15. Setting horizontal position of table.

1. Ensure that you are in the Table Editing window.
2. Select Table, then choose Position.
3. Select Right, Left, Center, Full, or Set.
4. If you chose Set, specify the distance from the left edge of the page.
5. Choose OK or press Enter to return to the Table Editing window.

Header Rows

You may specify that certain rows of your document are "header rows." This means that they are repeated on the top of every page that the table extends to. To mark a row as a header row, follow the steps in Procedure 20.16.

Procedure 20.16. Marking header rows.

1. Ensure that you are in the Table Editing window.
2. Place your cursor in the appropriate row, or make a block that includes cells from all header rows block as described above.
3. Select Row.

4. Select **Header** Row.

5. Select **OK** or press **Enter** to return to the Table Editing window.

Note: Although in WordPerfect 5.1 you specified the number of header rows, WordPerfect 6.0 allows you to mark any row individually as a header row. This brings up the interesting question of what happens if you mark Row 1 and Row 3 as header rows, but not Row 2.

WordPerfect counts as the header all rows marked as header rows until a row is not marked. Thus, in the case above, only one row would constitute the header. If, however, you later edit the table and mark Row 2 as a header row, all three marked rows will be included in the header.

Lines, Borders, and Fills

The last step in customizing the look of your table or form is to add lines. Although WordPerfect 5.1 offered many attractive line options, Version 6.0 provides a quantum leap in the ability of the user to customize the look of tables. Features include the following:

▲ Stacked lines consisting of multiple lines of varying widths

▲ Table borders that are independent of cell lines

▲ Line and border definitions contained in graphic styles that can be saved in style libraries for use in other documents

▲ A full complement of fill patterns—like those provided in WordPerfect Presentations

▲ Full support for color lines, borders, and fills

Introducing Lines and Borders

WordPerfect 6.0 introduces a new concept: table *borders*. The border for a table is the set of lines that surrounds the table as a whole. Why is this helpful? If, in WordPerfect 5.1, you ever sorted a table, or moved a cell from the bottom row to the middle of the table, you probably found that the double-line that defined the outside of the table moved with the bottom row of cells.

In WordPerfect 6.0, the border surrounding the table is a different entity from the lines that surround cells. This, in fact, is the defining difference: borders surround tables, lines surround cells. Each can be defined and edited separately from the other.

Lines, Borders, and Cell Boundaries

Lines and borders start at the outside boundary of the cell or table, and extend inward. This means that an extra thick line or border reduces the amount of space available for text in cells. This can be seen clearly in Figure 20.6. Notice that the bottom line of Cell A2 and the top line of Cell B3 do not line up. Instead, the extra thick lines take up space that is normally occupied by the cell.

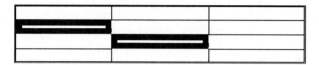

Figure 20.6. Thick lines and cell boundaries.

Table borders work the same way as lines do. They start at the outside edge of the table and take space from the table itself.

Relation Between Lines and Borders

A special condition occurs at the table boundary—the outside line of the outer cells of the table meets the table's border. What happens then? Do they overprint each other? Which takes precedence? The following points define important aspects of the relationship between the table borders and lines:

▲ Table borders mask, but do not erase, table lines. Although you often cannot see them, table lines exist "underneath" the border.

▲ If a table border is turned off, you will see the outer cells' lines.

▲ If a table border is turned to Spacing only (no lines), it continues to mask cell lines, although it masks them with white space.

▲ If the outer lines of a cell are set to the default line for the table, they are masked by the table border. This is true even if the default line for the table has been reset from single lines.

▲ If the outer lines of a cell are set to anything other than the default, they print next to (and inside of) the border line.

How Lines and Borders Are Defined

As you have seen throughout this book, WordPerfect 6.0 saves most default and option settings in styles. (Styles are discussed in detail in Chapter 39, "Styles.") Line and border defaults are saved in a special type of style—graphics style. Like all other styles, graphics styles can be edited, and once edited, all occurrences of that style in the document are changed. Also like other styles, graphics styles can be saved in style libraries so they can be used in other documents.

Thus, you can customize the definition for any lines used in your tables. The customized lines can be used in your current document, or saved for use in others as well. For example, you may change the widths of the lines that constitute a "double-line," along with their color and the spacing between them. All changes are made to the Double Line graphics style and saved with the document—unless you save the style in a style library (see also Workshop VII).

Lines

As stated above, "lines" refers to the lines between and around cells. In order to customize the appearance of your table, you should be able to select the default lines that appear around cells, as well as specifying the lines that appear around any given cell or group of cells. If you work with color, you may also wish to specify the color of these lines.

Custom line definitions that you create can be chosen for your table lines just as easily as the predefined line styles. The procedures for creating and editing these styles are covered in Chapter 39.

Default Line Style

The default line style is the line that appears around each cell, unless you specify otherwise. The system setting for this is single line—just as the default border style is a double line. To select a different default line style, follow the steps in Procedure 20.17.

Procedure 20.17. Selecting the default table line style.

1. Ensure that you are in the Table Editing window. Your cursor can be anywhere in the table.
2. Select Lines/Fill. You will be in the Table Lines dialog box.
3. Select Default Line.... You will see the Default Table Lines dialog box.
4. Select Line Style... You will see the Line Styles dialog box shown in Figure 20.7.
5. Highlight the line style you would like to choose and choose Select, or press Enter.

Note: From the Line Styles dialog box, you can also select other style libraries, including your personal style library or the shared style library. You can also create a new line style or edit a line style. The procedures for working with line styles are discussed in depth in Chapter 39.

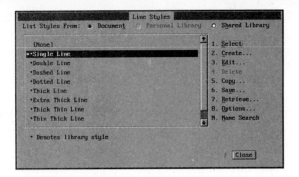

Figure 20.7. The Line Styles dialog box.

6. Press Enter twice to close the Default Table Lines and the Table Lines dialog boxes.
7. You will return to the Table Editing window.

Current Cell Line Style

You may override the default line style for a cell or a group of cells. If you wish to set a line style for a group of cells, you must first block the cells. When you set a line style for a specific cell or block of cells, you are given the option to set lines as follows:

Left/right/top/bottom   Along the left, right, top, or bottom edge of the cell or the entire block of cells (if a block has been defined).

Inside   All lines inside a defined block of cells. This option is not available if only one cell is selected.

Outside   the top, right, left, and bottom edge of the cell or entire block of cells (if a block has been defined).

To select the line style for a cell or group of cells, follow the steps in Procedure 20.18.

Procedure 20.18. Specifying a line style for a cell or group of cells.

1. Ensure that you are in the Table Editing window.
2. Select cells by positioning the cursor, and/or making a block as described above.
3. Select Lines/Fill. You will be in the Table Lines dialog box.
4. Select the line position: Left, Right, Top, Bottom, Inside, or Outside. You will see the Default Table Lines dialog box.
5. Select Line Style... You will see the Line Styles dialog box, shown in Figure 20.7.

281

6. Highlight the line style you would like to choose, and choose Select, or press Enter.

7. Press Enter twice to close the Default Table Lines and the Table Lines dialog boxes.

8. You will return to the Table Editing window.

Tip: Sometimes, the normal editing screen may not show you the exact effect of using several different line styles on adjacent cells. If you use the Print Preview feature, you can use the Zoom command to enlarge one specific portion of the table so that a cell boundary occupies the entire screen. This gives you an accurate representation of the way the table will print.

Choose Line Color

You may choose the color of your lines from more than 50 predefined colors. If these don't meet your needs, you can also customize your color by mixing primary colors, or by selecting from a graphic color palette!

You may set the default line color just as you choose the default line style. This will be the color of all lines in your table, but not the border. You may also set the line color for an individual cell or group of cells by following the steps in Procedures 20.19 and 20.20.

Procedure 20.19. Selecting the default table line color.

1. Ensure that you are in the Table Editing window. Your cursor can be anywhere in the table.

2. Select Lines/Fill. You will be in the Table Lines dialog box.

3. Select Default Line.... You will see the Default Table Lines dialog box.

4. Select Color.

5. If you wish to use the color associated by default with the default line style, choose Use Line Style Color. Then skip to Step 9.

6. If you wish to specify the default line color, select Choose Color.... You will see the Color Selection dialog box, shown in Figure 20.8.

7. Highlight the color you wish to select from the Palette Colors, and choose Select, or press Enter.

8. Press Enter twice to close the Default Table Lines and the Table Lines dialog boxes.

9. You will return to the Table Editing window.

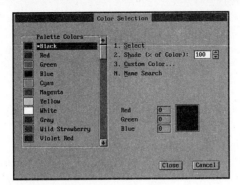

Figure 20.8. The Color selection dialog box.

 Note: The Color Selection dialog box allows you to specify the shade of your selected color or customize the color by specifying the amount of red, green, and blue in it. You may also create a custom color using a color palette. These procedures are discussed further in Appendix B.

Procedure 20.20. Specifying line color for a cell or group of cells.

1. Ensure that you are in the Table Editing window.
2. Select cells by positioning the cursor and/or making a block as described above. The color you choose will be applied to the entire cell or group of cells you select.
3. Select Lines/Fill. You will be in the Table Lines dialog box.
4. Select Line Color. Then select Choose Color. You will see the Color Selection dialog box shown in Figure 20.8.
5. Highlight the color you wish to select from the Palette Colors, and choose Select, or press Enter.
6. Press Enter to close Table Lines dialog boxes.
7. You will return to the Table Editing window.

Fills

A *fill* is a pattern or shading that constitutes the background of a cell or table. In WordPerfect 5.1, you were able to set shading for a cell or group of cells. However, only shading was supported, and the same shading percentage had to be used for all shaded cells.

In Version 6.0, shading has become "fills." Fills, like lines and borders, are saved as graphics styles. By default, WordPerfect ships with fills that are in fact shadings—from 10 percent to 90 percent darkness. But you may create a fill style that uses a pattern or even a gradient between two colors! In addition, you may apply a different fill style to any cell or group of cells. Finally, you may also define a default fill that serves as the background for all table cells that do not have another fill associated with them.

In Procedure 20.21, you will learn to select a default fill style and select a fill style for a cell and a group of cells. To create a fill style incorporating patterns, colors, and gradients that can be used in tables, see Chapter 34, "Borders and Fills."

Procedure 20.21. Selecting the fill style.

1. Ensure that you are in the Table Editing window.
2. To select a default fill style, your cursor can be anywhere in the table. To choose a fill style for a group of cells, select cells by positioning the cursor and/or making a block of the cells.
3. Select Lines/Fill. You will be in the Table Lines dialog box.
4. To specify a default fill, choose Border/Fill. You will be at the Table Border/Fill dialog box. Choose Fill Style and skip to Step 6.
5. Alternatively, to specify a fill style for selected cells, choose Fill from the Table Lines dialog box. You will be at the Fill Style and Color dialog box. Choose Fill Style.
6. You will be at the Fill Styles dialog box (see Figure 20.9).

Figure 20.9. The Fill style dialog box.

7. Highlight the fill style you wish to select and choose Select, or press Enter.

Note: From this dialog box, you can create new fill styles or edit old ones. These procedures are discussed further in Chapter 34.

8. Press Enter twice to return to the Table Editing window.

Table Borders

You can select from fourteen predefined border styles for your table. Some are simple (for example, a single or double line) and some are more complex (a thick and thin line, for example). In addition, you can create or edit a border style, just as you can for line styles. To select a table border, follow the steps in Procedure 20.22.

Procedure 20.22. Selecting a table border.

1. Ensure that you are in the Table Editing window. Your cursor can be anywhere in the table.

2. Select Lines/Fill. You will see the Table Lines dialog box.

3. Choose Border/Fill. You will see the Table Borders/Fill dialog box.

4. Select Borders. You will see the Border Styles dialog box shown in Figure 20.10.

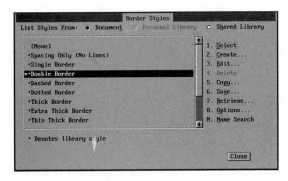

Figure 20.10. The Border Styles dialog box.

5. Highlight the desired border style, then click Close, or press Enter.

6. Press the Enter key twice to return to the Table Edit window.

You may customize this border to change some or all of the lines, change its color, or specify a fill. You can even put an automatic shadow around the table! Use the steps outlined in Procedure 20.23.

Procedure 20.23. Customizing a table border.

1. Ensure that you are in the Table Editing window. Your cursor can be anywhere in the table.
2. Select Lines/Fill. You will see the Table Lines dialog box.
3. Choose Border/Fill. You will see the Table Borders/Fill dialog box.
4. Select Customize. You will see the Customize Table Border/Fill dialog box shown in Figure 20.11.

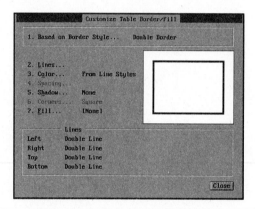

Figure 20.11. The Customize Table Border/Fill dialog box.

5. Select the desired customization options, then click Close, or press Enter.
6. Press the Enter key twice to return to the Table Edit window.

Customization options include the following:

Lines: This option allows you to specify the top, bottom, right, or left line, and for each, select from the available list of line styles.

Color: This option allows you to use the color predefined for each line style, or choose a new color for the entire border.

Shadow: This option allows you to specify a shadow at the upper-left, upper-right, lower-left, or lower-right of the table. You may also specify the color of the shadow and how wide it should be.

Fill: This option allows you to pick from the available list of fill styles (or to create or edit your own). The fill style will apply to the whole table, except for any cells for which a different fill style has been selected.

by Milan Keeney

Advanced Table Skills

Tables can fill a variety of needs. Two of their most powerful applications are as a forms generator and a spreadsheet. In this section, we talk first about how to use the Tables feature to set up a form. The example you'll use is a checkbook register. Next you'll use the form you create to enter sample checks and amounts. Finally, we discuss floating cells and how to pull the information from the table you created into a document.

Formatting the Checkbook Register

Set both the left and right margins to .5". This ensures that you have enough room to display the column descriptions.

Creating the Table

Creating a table is a straightforward process. Procedure 21.1 describes the process of creating the table for a checkbook register.

Procedure 21.1. Creating a table.

1. From the pull-down menu, choose Layout and Tables or press Al+F7 and select Tables to bring up the Table Create option. If you use the pull-down menus, your screen should look like the one shown in Figure 21.1. If you press Alt+F7, a screen that looks like the one shown in Figure 21.2 appears. Both the menu and the dialog box serve the same purpose.

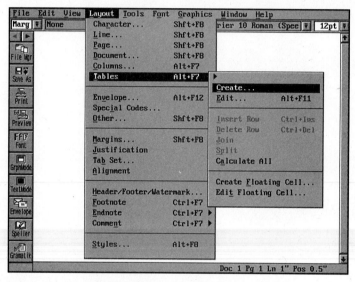

Figure 21.1. The Table Create menu.

Figure 21.2. The Table Create dialog box.

2. Select Create and enter 7 as the number of columns to create.

3. Set the number of rows to 21 and choose OK.

4. The Table Edit screen appears with the insertion point in cell A1 (see Figure 21.3).

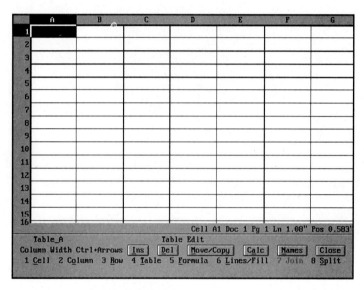

Figure 21.3. The Table Edit screen.

You are ready to start formatting the rows and columns to make this table look like a checkbook register. Use the following steps shown in Procedure 21.2 to format the header row.

Procedure 21.2. Formatting a header row.

1. With the insertion point in Column A1, select 3 or Row to bring up the Row Format screen (see Figure 21.4).

2. Select 7 or Header Row to define Row 1 as a header row and choose OK. A header row appears at the top of each page if the table spans multiple pages.

3. Press Alt+F4 and block Row 1 or hold the left mouse button down and select all the cells in Row 1.

4. Select 6 or Lines/Fill and set the bottom line of the current block to a double line.

5. Position the insertion point in Cell G1 and choose 8 or Split.

6. Split Cell G1 into 2 rows.

7. Position the insertion point in Cell G1 and block all cells in Row 1.

Figure 21.4. The Row Format screen.

8. Choose 1 or Cell to display the Cell Format screen (see Figure 21.5).

9. Any changes made at this screen affect all cells in Row 1. Set the cell Size to Fine, Justification to Center, Number Type to Text, and Ignore when Calculating.

From the Table Edit screen, select Close. Position the insertion point in Cell A1. Use the following steps shown in Procedure 21.3 to set up the column headings.

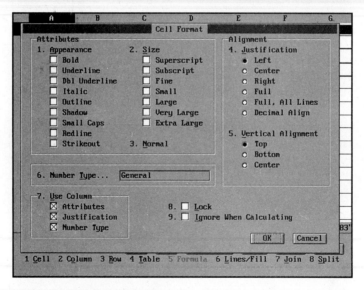

Figure 21.5. The Cell Format screen.

Procedure 21.3. Setting column headings.

1. Enter the word Check and press Tab or move the insertion point to Cell B2.

2. Enter the word Date and move the insertion point to Cell C1.

3. Enter the word Transaction and move the insertion point to Cell D1. (Note: *Transaction* gets split into two lines; don't worry about it at this point. You will be widening this column.)

4. In Cell D1, type Payment/Debit and press Enter. (This will probably wrap to the second line.)

5. Type (-) and move the insertion point to Cell E1.

6. Type the letter T and move the insertion point to Cell F1.

7. Type the words Deposit/Credit and press Enter.

8. Enter (+) and move the insertion point to Cell G1.

9. Enter the word Balance.

As you typed the column headings, several probably wrapped to the second line. Wrapping occurs because all the columns are the same width. Your table should look like the one shown in Figure 21.6.

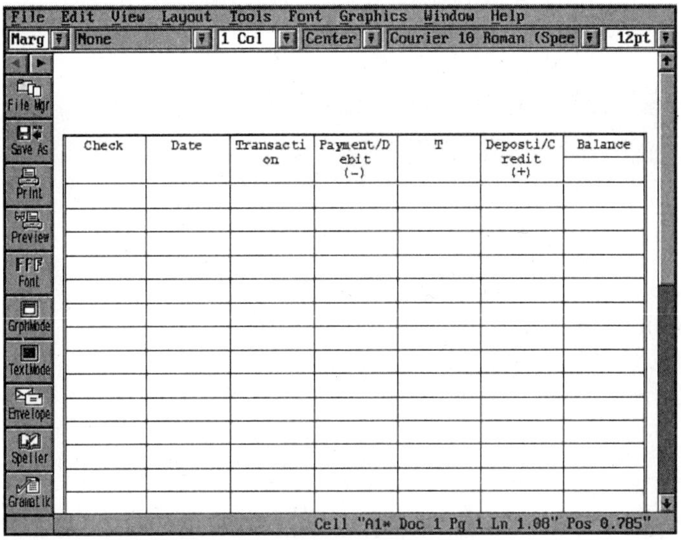

Figure 21.6. A table with column headings.

The next step is to format the columns. This includes sizing them to fit the headings. With the insertion point on one of the cells in the table, choose Layout, Tables, and Edit, or press Alt+F7 and choose Tables, Edit. Use the following steps shown in Procedure 21.4 to format the columns in your checkbook register.

Procedure 21.4. Formatting checkbook columns.

1. Move the insertion point to Column E. Use the Ctrl+left arrow to size Column E to the width of a single character.

2. Move the insertion point to column C. Use the Ctrl+right arrow to widen Column C until the entire word *Transaction* fits on a single line.

3. Move the insertion point to Cell A3 and select 2 or Column. The Column Format screen appears (see Figure 21.7). Column A contains the check numbers.

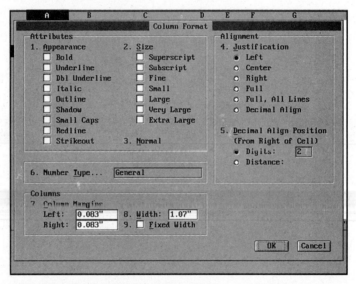

Figure 21.7. The Column Format dialog box.

4. Set the Justification to Center and select OK.

5. Move the insertion point to Cell B3 and access the Column Format screen.

6. Set Justification to Center and change the Number Type to Date. You can leave the date format at the default or change it to a format that is wide enough to contain the dates. Many people prefer to enter dates in the format MM/DD/YY.

7. From the Number Type Formats screen select E or Select Date Format to change the date format. Then return to the Table Edit screen. (If you try to enter a date into a cell that is not formatted to accept a date, WordPerfect tries to evaluate the date as a numeric expression.) For example, if you were to enter the shipping date of WP 6.0 for DOS

(7/28/93) into a column that was not formated as a date or text column, WordPerfect would try to evaluate it as the quotient of the number 7 divided by the number 28 divided by 93.)

8. Move the insertion point to Cell C3 and access the Column Format screen.

9. Change the Size to Small, the Justification to Center, and the Number Type to Text. Select OK to return to the Table Edit screen.

10. The formatting of Column D, Payment/Debit, and column F, Deposit/Credit, will match. Move the insertion point to Cell D3 and access the Column Format screen.

11. Change the Justification to Right and the Number Type to Currency.

12. Select Options and turn off the use of commas.

13. Repeat Steps 11 and 12 for Column F. Then move the insertion point to Cell G2.

14. Select 2 or Column. Change the Appearance to Bold, the Size to Large, the Justification to Right, and Number Type to Currency. Change the Options and turn off the use of Commas. Select OK to return to the Table Edit screen.

15. Select Close or press F7 to exit the Table Edit screen.

You want Column G to display a running total of the current balance. After you enter the beginning balance in Cell G2, the rest of the cells in this column will show the current balance after adding deposits or subtracting withdrawals for each row. Use the following steps shown in Procedure 21.5 to set a formula in Column G to keep a running total.

Procedure 21.5. Setting a formula.

1. Move the insertion point to Cell G3.

2. Select 5 or Formula. The Table Formula dialog box appears (see Figure 21.8).

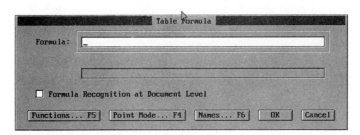

Figure 21.8. The Table Formula dialog box.

3. The insertion point should be in the box next to the word *Formula*. If the insertion point is not in this field, select it.

4. Choose Point Mode or press F4. You can select a single cell by pressing Enter, or a group of cells by pressing F4 again and blocking them. Move the insertion point to Cell G2 and press Enter.

5. The letters *G2* appear in the formula box. You could continue to select each cell to include in the formula, or you could type them all at once. Type -D3+F3 to form the complete formula G2-D3+F3.

6. Select Close or press F7 to exit the Table Edit screen.

This formula takes the current balance from G2, adds anything in Cell F3, Deposit/ Credit, and subtracts anything in Cell D2, Payment/Debit. Although this is a fairly simple formula, WordPerfect can support much more complex formulas and functions.

Formula Recognition at Document Level

On the Table Formula screen is an option for setting Formula Recognition at Document Level. When you select this option, you can type formulas directly into table cells. This is useful if you are planning to include several formulas in your document and feel comfortable with the formula syntax.

Copying a Formula to Multiple Cells

The formula you created resides in Cell G3. You can't define formulas for an entire column. Instead, you need to copy the formula to the cells on which you want the formula to operate.

When you copy the formula to another cell, the formula maintains its relative relationships. In other words, although the original formula pointed to G2 from G3, if you copy it to G4, it still looks to G3 for the balance. Likewise, it looks to F4 and D4 rather than F3 and D3. Use the following steps shown in Procedure 21.6 to copy the formula to all cells in column G.

Procedure 21.6. Copying a formula.

1. While in the Table Edit screen, position the insertion point in Cell G3.

2. Select Move/Copy. The Move dialog box appears with the option defaulting to Cell (see Figure 21.9).

3. Select Copy. The Copy Cell dialog box appcars (see Figure 21.10).

4. Select 2 or Down and enter 19 as the number of times to copy it.

5. Select OK to return to the Table Edit screen.

6. Select Close or press F7 to exit the Table Edit screen.

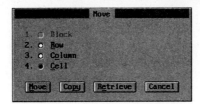

Figure 21.9. The Move dialog box.

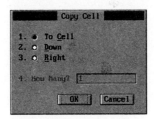

Figure 21.10. The Copy Cell dialog box.

Notice in Figure 21.11 that the formula appears at the bottom of the table whenever the insertion point points to a cell with a formula.

	A	B	C	D	E	F	G
1	Check	Date	Transaction	Payment/ Debit (−)	T	Deposit/ Credit (+)	Balance
2							
3							$0.00
4							$0.00
5							$0.00
6							$0.00
7							$0.00
8							$0.00
9							$0.00
10							$0.00
11							$0.00
12							$0.00
13							$0.00
14							$0.00
15							$0.00
16							$0.00
17							$0.00

=G2-D3+F3   Cell G3 Doc 1 Pg 1 Ln 1.71" Pos 7.31"
Table_A   Table Edit
Column Width Ctrl+Arrows [Ins] [Del] [Move/Copy] [Calc] [Names] [Close]
  1 Cell 2 Column 3 Row 4 Table 5 Formula 6 Lines/Fill 7 Join 8 Split

Figure 21.11. A cropped screen showing a formula below the table.

Adding Values

At this point, your table represents a blank template you could save and retrieve whenever you needed. The next step is to type numbers and see how the table keeps the running balance. Use the following steps shown in Procedure 21.7 to add values to an existing table.

Procedure 21.7. Adding values to a table.

1. Retrieve the previously created table. Position the insertion point in Cell G2.
2. Enter 1000 as the beginning balance.
3. Position the insertion point in Cell A3.
4. Enter 3000 as a beginning check number.
5. Move the insertion point to Cell B3 and enter the date of the check as 7/1/93.
6. Move the insertion point to Cell C3 and enter the description for the transaction, Lotsa Software (Purchased WP 6.0).
7. Move the insertion point to Cell D3 and enter the amount of the transaction as 205.
8. Repeat Steps 3 through 7 using the next open row in the table.
9. Enter Deposits in column F and Withdrawals in column D.

(Note: don't enter any values in the Balance column. This column will be calculated automatically.)

File	Edit	View	Layout	Tools	Font	Graphics	Window	Help

Check	Date	Transaction	Payment/ Debit (−)	T	Deposit/ Credit (+)	Balance
						$1000.00
3000	7/1/93	Lotsa Software (Bought WP 6.0)	$205.00			$0.00
3001	7/1/93	Printers R US	$859.00			$0.00
3002	7/2/93	Joe's Computer Hospital	$165.00			$0.00
	7/2/93	Consultant Work			$475.00	$0.00
						$0.00
						$0.00
						$0.00
						$0.00
						$0.00
						$0.00
						$0.00
						$0.00
						$0.00

Cell F7 Doc 1 Pg 1 Ln 3.2" Pos 6.76"

Figure 21.12. The table before calculating.

Calculating Tables

After you enter the checks and deposits that you've made, your table should look similar to the one shown in Figure 21.12. (Of course, your screen will show the values you entered.) Notice that the balance column still shows $0.00. You need to have WordPerfect calculate the totals. Select Layout, Tables and Calculate All or press Alt+F7, Tables, and 5 or Calculate All. Figure 21.13 shows our sample table after calculation.

File Edit View Layout Tools Font Graphics Window Help							
Marg ▼ None ▼		1 Col ▼	Center ▼	Courier 10 Roman (Spec ▼		12pt ▼	
Check	Date	Transaction	Payment/ Debit (−)	T	Deposit/ Credit (+)	Balance	
						$1000.00	
3000	7/1/93	Lotsa Software (Bought WP 6.0)	$205.00			$795.00	
3001	7/1/93	Printers R US	$859.00			($64.00)	
3002	7/2/93	Joe's Computer Hospital	$165.00			($229.00)	
	7/2/93	Consultant Work			$475.00	$246.00	
						$246.00	
						$246.00	
						$246.00	
						$246.00	
						$246.00	
						$246.00	
						$246.00	
						$246.00	
						$246.00	
						$246.00	
						$246.00	
Cell "A1" Doc 1 Pg 1 Ln 1.08" Pos 0.785"							

Figure 21.13. The table after calculating.

 Note: If the balance or any other numbers display in scientific notation, it is probably because the column is too narrow. If you widen the column it should display as currency.

Notice that the negative numbers are displayed inside parentheses. If you prefer to have negative numbers preceded by a minus sign, make the change in the Column Format screen.

Because the formula you entered in Column G reads the value from the previous row, Column G shows the final balance on any empty rows after the last valid entry. If you aren't going to continue to add information to this table, you can delete the trailing rows.

Using Floating Cells with Tables

Tables are a great way to crunch numbers and display data. Unfortunately, most modern writing is still done in sentence form. Like a checkbook register, a table packs a lot of information into a small space. Most people, though, simply want to know "How much money do I have, anyway?"

WordPerfect 6.0 provides a method for taking information from tables and displaying it in other places in your document. This capability is called *floating cells*. A floating cell is just that: a single cell that can float to any place in your document. Floating cells can be included in the body of your text or made to stand out on their own.

As an example, you can use the checkbook register to show how floating cells work.

Setting Up the Floating Cell

Floating cells have essentially no formatting. You're going to pull the final balance from the table and display it in a paragraph form. Use the following steps shown in Procedure 21.8 to set up a floating cell.

Procedure 21.8. Creating a floating cell

1. Retrieve the document containing the checkbook register. Position the insertion point at the point where you want the floating cell to appear. Figure 21.14 shows a sample piece of text that I hope you'll never have to type.

2. From the pull-down menus, choose Layout, Tables, and Create Floating Cell. The Edit Floating Cell dialog box appears (see Figure 21.15). If this is the first Floating Cell you have created, the default name FloatingCell_A appears.

3. Either leave the default name or choose 1 or Name to change the name of this floating cell to Ending Balance.

4. Select 3 or Number Type to change the number type to Currency. Change the Options to turn off the use of commas.

5. Select OK to return to the Edit Floating Cell dialog box.

6. Choose 2 or Formula to bring up the Table Formula dialog box.

7. From this dialog box, you can type a formula, type the name of a table cell, and access the Function and Names lists (see Figure 21.16).

8. Choose Names or F6. The List Names Table dialog box appears as shown in Figure 21.17. Select Table_A. Table_A appears in the Formula field of the Table Formula dialog box.

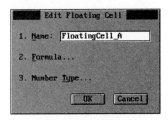

Figure 21.14. Floating cell placement.

```
┌──────────────────────────┐
│     Edit Floating Cell   │
│                          │
│  1. Name: FloatingCell_A │
│                          │
│  2. Formula...           │
│                          │
│  3. Number Type...       │
│                          │
│         [ OK ] [ Cancel ]│
└──────────────────────────┘
```

Figure 21.15. The Edit Floating Cell dialog box.

(Because you can have multiple tables in a single document, every cell reference in a floating cell has to reference a table name.)

9. Place a period after the word *Table_A* and type the cell number you want to reference. In this example, the last cell in Column G is 21. Therefore, type G21 after Table_A to identify the entire cell name.

10. Select OK until you return to the document.

The number $246.00 appears at the insertion point. Anytime the data in the table is changed, the floating cell is updated with the new ending total.

You also can reference cell names in floating cells.

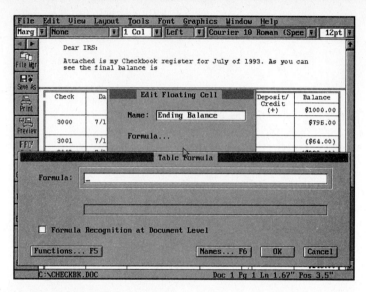

Figure 21.16. The Table Formula box.

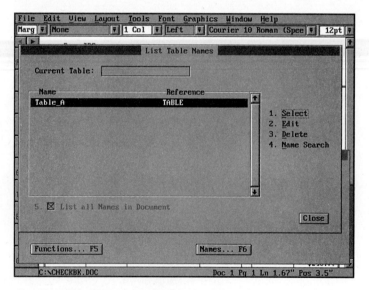

Figure 21.17. The Table Formula dialog box showing Table_A.

by Milan Keeney

Importing Spreadsheet Information

Often, it is desirable to import parts of a spreadsheet into your documents. Whether this is to include the figures that support your statements or to provide greater information to the reader, it can greatly enhance your document.

Using the Import Feature

WordPerfect 6.0 gives you the power to import or link the needed information from your favorite spreadsheet program. You can import or link from the following file formats: PlanPerfect (Versions 3.0 through 5.1), Lotus 1-2-3 (Versions 1A, 2.01, 2.3, 2.4, 3.0, 3.1), Microsoft Excel (Versions 2.1, 3.0, 4.0), Quattro Pro (Versions 3.0, 4.0), Quattro Pro for Windows (1.0), and Spreadsheet DIF.

Procedure 22.1. Importing a spreadsheet.

1. Place your insertion point in your document where you want the spreadsheet information.

2. Choose Tools or press Alt+F7.

3. Choose Spreadsheet and select Import. The dialog box shown in Figure 22.1 appears. Your insertion point is on the line for Filename.

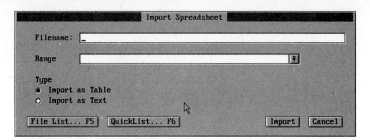

Figure 22.1. The Import Spreadsheet dialog box.

4. Type or select your spreadsheet filename. (See "Specifying the File to Import" in this chapter.)

5. Choose **Range** or press Tab to move your insertion point to the Range option. (See "Setting a Range to Import" in this chapter.)

6. Select the radio button for either "Import as Text" or "Import as Table." (See "Importing as Text or Table" in this chapter.)

7. Select Import or press Enter to perform import.

The following explanations in the sections "Specifying the File to Import," "Setting The Range to Import," and "Importing as Text or Table" apply to both importing and linking a spreadsheet.

Specifying the File to Import

If you are unsure of the filename, at this point you can select F5 or choose File List to go into a list of files to select your spreadsheet filename. If you pressed F5 to go into List Files, a dialog box prompting you with a directory (see Figure 22.2) appears. This is the same directory you specified in Setup under Location of Files for Spreadsheet.

Figure 22.2. The Select List dialog box.

Pressing Enter or selecting OK gives you a directory listing. If you want a different directory, you can type the alternate path you want to look at before you press Enter or select OK. When you have selected the file you want to import, you are returned to the Spreadsheet Import dialog box with the spreadsheet name showing on the filename line.

You also can use the QuickList to select a spreadsheet. With your insertion point on the line for filename, press F6 for QuickList. This gives you a list of specified directories you can choose from. You may have a couple of different spreadsheets that you use. In this case, QuickList enables you to get a listing of the directory used by either program (see Chapter 27, "QuickList").

Setting the Range to Import

A *range* is a block of cells within your spreadsheet. You can manually enter a range by typing the cell references separated by a colon as (A1:C10) or typing the cell references separated by a period (A1.C10).

When you are using 3-D spreadsheets, your range may include multiple spread-sheets. Each cell address may include a letter to designate which spreadsheet it came from (for example, A:B10). In this case, the colon separates the spreadsheet from the cell reference. The range is listed as A:B10.A:D27, with the colon separating the spreadsheet and the cell reference, and a period separating the first cell reference from the second spreadsheet-cell reference.

If the spreadsheet you selected at the filename section of this dialog box has named ranges within it, you can select the down arrow at the end of the Range line. The list of named ranges within your spreadsheet then appears below the Range line. You can highlight one of these ranges and press Enter to select it.

In addition to the named ranges that appear, the entire spreadsheet range appears as <Spreadsheet> with the range of the spreadsheet example (a1:g277) on the right side of the line. This enables you to select the entire spreadsheet as the range to be imported.

Importing as Text or Table

Once you have typed or selected the range, you can choose whether the import is to be a table or text. Under the Line for Range are two radio buttons. One is labeled "Import as Table," and the other is labeled "Import as Text."

If you want to import your spreadsheet in a format closest to the way it displayed in your spreadsheet, import it as a table. With WordPerfect 6.0, you do not need to create a table before you import your spreadsheet. WordPerfect creates a table that matches the spreadsheet's original format as closely as possible. Word-Perfect inserts as much of the spreadsheet as possible (up to 64 columns). Your spreadsheet appears on the screen with its cells enclosed within graphic lines. These lines can be made to disappear by turning Line/Fill type to None in your Table Edit screen.

If you want to specify your table size within WordPerfect before you import your spreadsheet, you can create your table prior to the import. After the table is created, place your insertion point within the table and import or link the data. The spreadsheet fills the table from the insertion point forward, and any cells that exceed the table size are not imported.

All 3-D spreadsheets can be imported in the spreadsheet file, or you can import the spreadsheets of your choice.

Importing a Spreadsheet as Text

When you import a spreadsheet as text, as much of the formatting is preserved as possible. Left and right justification is maintained, and formats are as close as possible. Special tab settings are created, and each of the columns are lined up with the tab settings.

Setting Up a Spreadsheet Link

Linking a spreadsheet to your WordPerfect document is much like importing a spreadsheet, with one difference: a spreadsheet link can be updated in WordPerfect to reflect figures that change within your spreadsheet, automatically. This allows your WordPerfect document always to have the most current figures that you are working with in your spreadsheet.

Procedure 22.2. Creating a spreadsheet link.

1. Place your insertion point in your document where you would like the spreadsheet information.

2. Choose Tools or press Alt+F7.

3. Choose Spreadsheet and select Create Link. The dialog box shown in Figure 22.3 appears. Your insertion point is on the line for Filename.

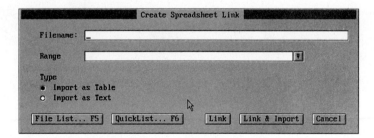

Figure 22.3. The Create Spreadsheet Link dialog box.

4. Type or select your spreadsheet filename. (See "Specifying the File to Import" in this chapter.)

5. Choose Range or press Tab to move your insertion point to the Range option. (See "Setting a Range to Import" in this chapter.)

6. Select the radio button for either "Import as Text" or "Import as Table." (See "Importing as Text or Table" in this chapter.)

7. Select Link to create only the link codes (see "Linking Without Importing" in this chapter) or Link & Import to create the link codes and import the spreadsheet (see "Linking and Importing" in this chapter).

Linking Without Importing

In order to save space within a document, you may, at the time you create a document with spreadsheet links within it, create the link codes, but not have the spreadsheet actually appear on-screen. If this is the case, select the Link button. The beginning and ending link codes appear, but the spreadsheet does not. When you are ready to perform the link, select Perform All Links from the Link Options dialog box.

Linking and Importing

If you want your spreadsheet information to appear in your WordPerfect document at the time of creating the link, Link & Import is the option you want to use. The beginning link code is placed at the insertion point, the spreadsheet is imported, and the ending link code is placed after the spreadsheet table or text. You see your figures immediately after creating the link.

Editing the Link Options

Once you have created a link, you can edit that link in a variety of ways. You can change to another file or to a different range, change the link to Text rather than to Table, and so on. Each of these can be changed from the Link Edit dialog box.

Procedure 22.3. Editing a spreadsheet link.

1. Place your insertion point within the link codes of the link you want to edit.

2. Choose Tools or press Alt+F7.

3. Select Spreadsheet and choose Edit Link. The Edit Link dialog box shown in Figure 22.4 appears.

4. When you have made the desired changes, select Link or Link & Import.

The link then is changed to reflect the changes made within the Link Edit dialog box.

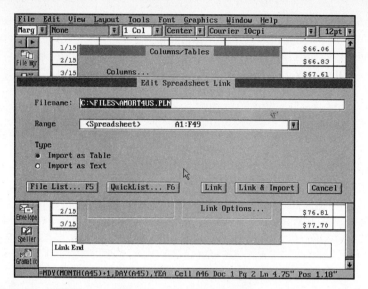

Figure 22.4. The Edit Spreadsheet Link dialog box.

Updating Links on Retrieve

You can set your document to update all links within it on retrieval of the document. This means that every time you open this document, your document is updated to what your spreadsheet file currently has in information.

Follow Procedure 22.4 to set your document to update on retrieval.

Procedure 22.4. Updating on retrieval.
1. Choose Tools or press Alt+F7.
2. Choose Spreadsheet and select Link Options (see Figure 22.5).

Figure 22.5. The Spreadsheet Link Options dialog box.

3. Mark the Box for Update on Retrieve.
4. Close the Link Options dialog box.

Now, after saving this document, your spreadsheet links update when you retrieve this document.

Showing the Link Codes

One option that you have on the Link Options dialog box is the ability to decide whether you want the link codes to display. This enables you to decide whether you want the link codes to appear on the document screen before and after the spreadsheet information. If they don't show on the document screen, the codes still display in Reveal Codes.

Procedure 22.5. Changing the display of link codes.

1. Choose Tools or press Alt+F7.
2. Then, choose Spreadsheet and select Link Options
3. Mark the box for Show Link Codes if you want them to display, and unmark the box if you don't.
4. Close the Link Options dialog box.

The default for this option is to have the codes display. If you prefer to have them not appear on-screen, you can change this.

Printing, Faxing, and E-Mail

by David Wurmfeld

Printing

Regardless of what you may have heard, the real magic of WordPerfect 6.0 happens when you finally get to hold your creation. Hopefully, what you get is what you wanted. In this chapter, you will explore the basic skills needed to print your document. To start with, it is assumed that at least one printer has been selected at installation time, but don't worry, with this new version, you can add or change printers at will, on the fly! (I discuss the more esoteric printer controls in Chapter 24, "Printer Controls.")

Printing Your Document: Where the Ink Flies, the Toner Is Hot and the Pin Hits the Page

In this chapter, I describe in detail how to print all or selected parts of your document. I cover how to produce double-sided pages in a single-sided printer and other nifty formats such as booked pamphlets and envelopes. If you have encountered WordPerfect 5.1, you are in for a treat—printing is a lot easier in 6.0. If you are new to this whole game, don't worry! I'll provide key-by-key (or mouse click-by-click) guidance to printing your document.

The basic skills covered in this chapter include:

▲ Previewing the document to be printed

▲ Printing the current document from the keyboard or menu

▲ Printing a document from disk

▲ Printing a selected block of text

▲ Printing a range of chapters and/or pages

▲ Printing booklets

▲ Printing envelopes

▲ Printing double-sided documents

▲ Printing the document summary

Previewing the Document to be Printed

In this day and age of shrinking forests and depleted natural resources, it is nice to know that you don't have to waste paper, ink, toner, or time anymore printing out "test pages." WordPerfect Corporation has worked hard to produce a WYSIWYG ("What You See Is What You Get") style of text and graphics editing, and even better, an interactive way of previewing the document as it will be printed on the page. The Print Preview also shows you any headers or footers in the document.

This feature lets you get a good feeling for the "color" of the whole document. The *color* of a document is a typesetters term for the overall look and feel of the typeface. With the possibility of many hundreds of fonts available at your fingertips, it is important to step back and see how that particular typeface looks in conjunction with the rest of the document. For example, if I were to use a sans serif font like Ariel-Narrow on this paragraph, it might look okay by itself, but when viewed with the Print Preview, it would appear "darker" (or more dense) than the surrounding text and may not be appropriate. Remember, when working with type, the space around the characters, the "air" if you will, is as important to the overall look of the document as the characters themselves.

The Print Preview option gets the information it needs from the printer driver you selected for the document. If you do not have a printer selected, it will ask you for one (see Chapter 24 for more details). To use the Print Preview feature, choose File, Print Preview; or enter the Print/Fax menu using Shift+F7, then choose 7 for Print Preview. The Print Preview screen will come up, and the previous preview mode will be in effect, or full page mode by default.

Print Preview provides you with all the functions needed to see some, part, or all of the document. Table 23.1 lists the various Print Preview options and actions:

Table 23.1. Print Preview options and actions.

Option	Action
100%	View the current page at the actual printed size
200%	View the current page at twice the actual printed size
Zoom In	Increase the display size of text and graphics by 25 percent
Zoom Out	Decrease the display size of text and graphics by 25 percent
Zoom Area	Increase the display size of a selected area, up to 1000 percent
Select Area	Change the portion of text displayed in the Print Preview window when you Zoom
Reset	Restore the view and size ratio that was in effect when you opened the Print Preview window (when you are playing with the zoom, this is a quick way to get back to normal)
Full Page	Display a complete view of the current page
Facing Pages	Display two consecutive pages, side by side
Thumbnails	Display several pages at once
Button Bar	Display (or hide) the Print Preview button bar
Button Bar Setup	Edit the Print Preview button bar, change the button bar options, or select another button bar

Use the Thumbnails option or button to see all or part of your document laid out, side by side. If you have a VGA screen, it is useful to layout no more than four pages at a time, because any more than that will obscure the type. Of course, if you are just looking at the positioning of text and graphics, eight pages at a time works fine with a normal VGA screen. To use the Thumbnails option, simply choose the Thumb # button from the button bar or View, Thumbnails from the Print Preview menu, and the number of displayed pages or Other and enter the desired number of pages in the Thumbnail Other dialog box.

Tip: For faster screen performance, choose **F**ile, **S**etup, View Text & Graphics in Black & White from the Print Preview menu.

Note: As nice as the Print Preview option is, you cannot edit the document while in this mode. To edit the document, choose Close from the File menu to return to your document.

Printing the Current Document

As in Version 5.1, printing the current document is as simple as choosing Shift+F7 and then Enter or r. With WordPerfect 6.0, the process can also be started with the mouse by choosing File, Print/Fax, Print (see Figure 23.1).

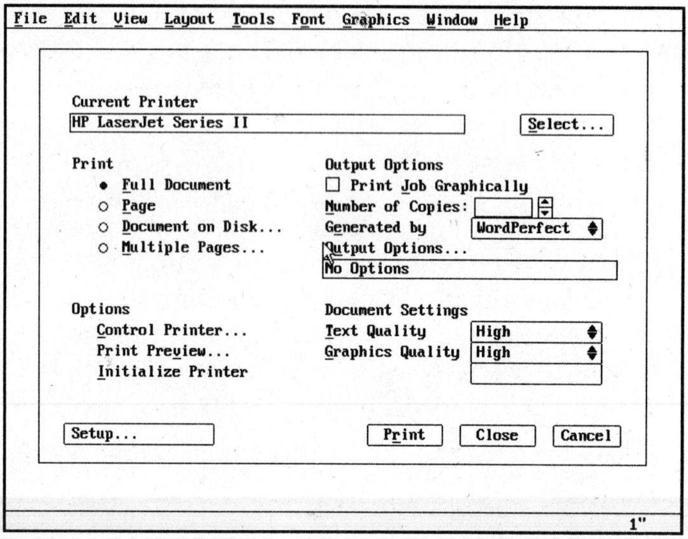

Figure 23.1. The Print/Fax menu.

This prints the full document to the currently selected printer. Before a document can be printed, however, there must be a printer selected. If there is not, you will be told so (see Chapter 24 before proceeding). You will be able to see the name of the currently selected printer in the Current Printer box. If all is well, the Print/Fax screen disappears and you are returned to the document screen. At this point, there is no indication of the printer's progress (or lack of it).

To check on the print job, choose the Print/Fax screen as above, but this time select 6, Control Printer. This brings up the Control Printer screen. Here you will see the status of your print job. A print "job" is any single request for the printer manager part of WordPerfect 6.0 to print. While these jobs are being printed, they are queued up and can be monitored and managed via the Control Printer menu (see Figure 23.2). This menu gives you the current status and alerts you if there is a problem with the printer. At any time, you can close this menu and resume working on your document (WordPerfect 6.0 prints in the background while you are editing).

Tip: To avoid grungy looking output from your laser printer, it is important to maintain the laser engine. Follow your printer's user manual and replace the fuser cleaner bar, wipe the Corona wire on the cartridge with a cotton swab, and replace the used toner bottle as frequently as specified. A dirty Corona wire produces fine spots on the page, giving it an overall crudy look. It can also cause long streaks on the page. A dirty fuser roller (the common culprit) will not fuse the page evenly, and the image can smear.

Caution: I once forgot to empty the used toner bottle, which subsequently overflowed, leaving a mess of toner in the bottom of the printer. Using a vacuum cleaner, I sucked out the toner only to find the toner particles were finer than the vacuum filter, and I sprayed fine, black toner all over the wall and ceiling behind me. I had to replace the ceiling tiles, because I couldn't get the toner off. Learn from my mistake—replace the used toner bottle as specified in the user manual, *not* when you think it is full.

Caution: Laser printer engines produce ozone. Normally it is removed for the most part by the ozone filter. That is, if it was replaced as recommended in the users manual. It is okay to use nonmanufacturer's toner cartridges, but it is very important to purchase at least the ozone filter replacements from the printer manufacturer, to ensure proper filtering. The office air quality is not the place to save money. Improper replacement intervals can cause a build up of ozone, which in turn adds to the indoor air pollution.

There are times, however, when you may want to take advantage of a printer not on the network or a printer attached to a machine without WordPerfect 6.0. It is easy to take advantage of the foreign printer by selecting the foreign printer type from the Print/Fax menu, and printing the document to file (see Chapter 24 for details on selecting printers on the fly). Once you have the "raw" printer file, you can network or "Sneaker Net" the file to the other PC. To print from that PC, use the DOS copy command:

```
copy /b filename.ext [lpt(1/2/3): or com(1/2):]
```

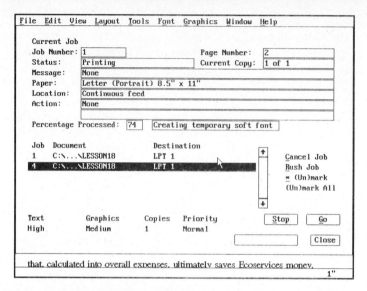

Figure 23.2. The Control Printer menu.

The copy parameter /b is necessary, because DOS sometimes tries to post format what it thinks are ASCII text files before sending them to the lpt or com port, and the /b parameter avoids that problem. Coffee break! Raw printer files are typically very large and can take up to 10 minutes to print, depending on the PC-to-printer interface.

Tip: Many laser printers and most dot matrix printers have both parallel and serial interfaces. If at all possible, use the parallel interface. When printing to file, file sizes tend to be quite large, usually in the order of hundreds of thousands of characters. Usually the fastest a serial printer connection can receive files is around 1,000 characters per second. A parallel connection, however, can average 8,000 to 15,000 characters per second, and in some of the newer printers and computers, as much as a million characters per second. If this cuts into your coffee breaks, please disregard the tip.

Caution: Although it is possible to print from the DOS prompt directly to a properly mapped network printer, it is usually not a good idea to force the network to print a raw printer file, such as the one produced when printing to file. This is especially relevant if there are graphics or embedded fonts. These files can take minutes to print, and with the light blinking and no output for minutes, an impatient networker might try to "reset" the printer with the power switch, causing havoc to the print server, because the print job can leave the printer in an indeterminate state. Over the network, there are printer control programs that optimize the interface between WordPerfect, the network, the spooler, and the printer. Printing raw or "captured" printer files on a local printer is okay, as long as you can wait for it.

Printing a Document from Disk

You can print a document stored on disk without first opening it up as the current document. To do this, choose Print/Fax, Document on disk from the File menu or press Shift+F7, 3. Type the filename of the document to be printed or use the FileList (F5) or QuickList (F6) buttons to select the document on disk to be printed and then choose 1 (Select). The Print multiple pages menu appears. Choose the default range (all) to print the entire document, or select the desired range (explained later) before choosing OK. To begin printing, choose the Print button or ⌐ (see Figure 23.1).

Printing a Selected Block of Text

As in WordPerfect 5.1, you are able to print arbitrary blocks of the current document. This process is started by selecting a block in the normal fashion, then, as above, choosing File, Print/Fax, Print Blocked Text or pressing Shift+F7, r. The neat thing about printing a block of text is that WordPerfect places the block to be printed in the same position on the page that it would normally occupy. This is great for checking the alignment of text and graphics for forms or newsletters.

Printing Selected Pages

WordPerfect 6.0, as in 5.1, has a feature that allows you to print selected chapters and pages, but with 6.0, it is much easier. It is not always necessary to print the entire document. You can select individual pages, ranges of pages, or combinations of the pages and ranges. To selectively print pages of your document, choose the Print Multiple Pages menu and specify the pages to be printed. This is done by choosing File, Print/Fax, Print Multiple Pages and entering the page(s) to be printed in the highlighted box (see Table 23.2). After entering the range(s) of page(s) to be printed, choose OK, then Print to print the list of pages.

Table 23.2. Syntax to specify page range(s).

Type	To Print
3	Page 3
1,5,8	Pages 1, 5, and 8
3 8	Pages 3 and 8
21-	The range of pages starting at 21 and going to the end of the document
-6	The range of pages from the beginning of the document up to and including page 6
27-99	The range of pages from page 27 to page 99
1-9, 11, 14, 99-	The range of pages from page 1 to page 9 *and* the pages 11, 14, *and* the range of pages starting at page 99 to the end of the document

Printing Booklets

It is assumed you have used the Subdivided Page feature to format the document into logical pages. This organizes the printing into leaves that can, when printed, be stapled together to form a booklet. When you use Subdivide Page to create programs and booklet-style documents, you can use the Print as Booklet feature to number and arrange pages for you. If you have a duplexing printer, it can print both sides in the booklet format. To print booklets, use the steps shown in Procedure 23.1. (Refer to Chapter 42, "Using Subdivided Pages," for information on the subdivided pages feature.)

Procedure 23.1. Printing booklets.
1. Choose Print/Fax from the File menu, then select Multiple Pages or Shift+F7, 4.
2. Select Print as Booklet, OK, then Print. If your printer does not support duplex printing, you will be prompted to turn the pages over and insert them into your printer again.

Note: The booklet printing feature is a bit tedious if you do not have a duplexing printer. If there is a paper jam, you will probably have to start the job over, because you have a 75 percent chance that the paper jam crosses logical page boundaries. Also, do not select double-sided printing if you are not hooked up to a duplexing printer.

Printing Envelopes

In many ways, the WordPerfect 6.0 Print/Fax menu is a complete printing control center. Unfortunately, when it comes to printing envelopes, it is not. It is necessary to invoke the Layout menu to create and print an envelope. Although creating merged mailings aren't covered here, I will show you how to create and print a single envelope on the fly. WordPerfect 6.0 has a new feature that converts the mailing address zip code into the postal bar code and prints it in the appropriate place.

Procedure 23.2. Printing an envelope.

1. Choose Envelope from the Layout menu or press Shift+F8, 3, 7 or Alt+F12.
2. Select an envelope from the Envelope Size drop-down list.
3. Select Omit return address or enter the return address in the return address box; finish by pressing F7 or by choosing the F7 on-screen.
4. Enter the mailing address and press F7 as above.
5. Type in the zip code and extension in the POSTNET Bar code entry field.
6. If you have previously selected the Prompt to load option in the envelope paper definition, you are all set to print the envelope. If, however, you have not selected prompt to load, before choosing print, insert the envelope to be printed into the printer manual feed slot. Then choose Print from the menu or press P.

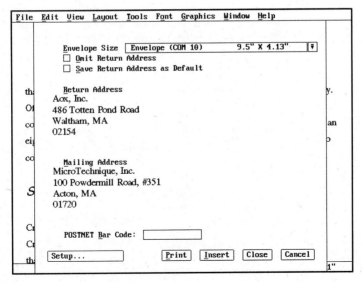

Figure 23.3. The Envelope menu.

Caution: The post office is offering some new prestamped envelopes with holograms for stamps. Do not use them—they tend to melt and bind to the hot fuser roller.

Printing Double-Sided Documents

If your printer is capable of duplex or two-sided printing, then this is a breeze. Choose Page from the Layout menu, then choose Double-sided Printing. Select long edge if the document will be bound on the long edge, short edge if the document will be bound on the top or short edge. WordPerfect 6.0 then adjusts the offset necessary to compensate for the binding. If, however, you do not have a duplex printer, all is not lost.

Let's say you have a HP LaserJet III printer and you want to produce crisp, clear copies of your masters thesis on butterfly - beetle circadian rhythm symbioses. First, before you pop that 15-cent per page bond paper in the tray, do a little experiment. Use Print Preview in the side by side mode to see if you like the typographic feel of how the pages relate to each other. Page through the chapters looking for out of place illustrations, tables, charts, and so on. When all looks symbiotic, print all the odd pages by selecting Odd from the Print Multiple Pages menu of the Print/Fax menu. Once all the pages have printed successfully, carefully joggle the stack of papers, lining them all up into one stack, and Replace them into the printer tray. Make sure the top of the page is the first to enter the printer, and the blank back side is up. At this point, the pages are in reverse order, back side up. Choose the Descending order option in the Print Multiple Pages menu, then the even page selection. Complete your masterpiece by choosing OK, then Print. After the "draft" experiment, put in your bond paper and print away.

Tip: To minimize problems of paper jams using bond or heavy paper, ensure the paper is fairly dry prior to using it in the printer. Keep the paper in its plastic wrapper until it is needed. When stacking it in the paper tray, keep 10 or so sheets of plain copier paper on the bottom—the sheet feed mechanism seems to work better this way. Don't use a paper weight that exceeds the specified weight in the printer users manual. You may get away with paper that is too heavy for a few hundred or so sheets, but you will force the fuser roller shims out of alignment, causing all other jobs to fuse improperly.

Printing the Document Summary

The document summary can be printed separately, or in conjunction with selected ranges of pages. To use this feature, choose File, Print/Fax, Print Multiple Pages, then check off selection 6: Document summary. If you also want to include selected page(s), fill in the page range box. Print by selecting OK, then Print.

24

by David Wurmfeld

Printer Controls

In WordPerfect, the task of printing is broken into several basic parts. I covered the first part (selecting and starting print jobs) in Chapter 23, "Printing." When you have the proper printer selected, WordPerfect, by default, does an excellent job of taking care of the rest. However, to access all the features of your printer, you must let WordPerfect know what parts to activate. In essence, to get the most out of your printer, you need to fine tune WordPerfect to the printer connection.

Controlling Your Printer

In this chapter, I show you how to perform basic printer selection and setup. WordPerfect has drivers for more than 1,000 different printers, but nearly all printers have the same basic control features. It doesn't matter if a printer is a monkey in the corner with a piece of paper and a crayon, or a state of the art 180-page-per-minute magneto-dynamic, nonimpact printer—they share the same basic parts. These parts include:

▲ **Communication link**. This physically connects the printer to the source of the print job. It also sends information back to the sender about the printer's status.

▲ **User's or operator's front panel**. A communication link is not the only way to control the printer. The printer can be unconditionally controlled from a front panel, which is a major annoyance to other printer users on a network. Unlike a communication link (where the network has some control), the network cannot control the user that changes the front panel settings or turns the printer power off.

Note: Network printer etiquette dictates that the user use the network printer utilities to cancel jobs. Print jobs on the network are often held in special locations if the printer jams. The network print queue will keep sending the job until it gets an OK from the printer or until the print job is removed from the queue. Turning off the printer hangs the print queue for that printer and can cause other print jobs to be trashed. Good network users use the proper utility (pconsole in Novell's Netware) to stop their print jobs. While I'm on the subject of good deeds, fill the paper tray while you're there!

▲ **Paper path**. This is the physical path the paper follows from the unprinted paper source to the printed, sorted, stapled, or shredded destination. Printers must control the transport and positioning of the paper to ensure consistency. The printer's paper path controls manage the paper size.

▲ **Imaging mechanism**. Inside the printer, something makes a mark on a medium. Previously, I alluded to printer paper, but a medium can be anything from paper in an ATM machine printer and plastic overhead transparencies to a very sophisticated stainless steel silk-screen stencil. There are many ways to transfer images from the interpreter to the medium. These days, flying ink (ink jet), pounding pins against an inked ribbon (dot matrix), and the Xerographic process ("laser" exposed imaging) are the norm.

▲ **Image control and interpretation**. This is the heart of the printer. En- coded instructions, which tell where to place images (such as text) on the page, are deciphered, interpreted, and executed. This is often called the printer control language (PCL) or the page definition language (PDL). A common language is PostScript (a type of PDL). Another is HP LaserJet's native language (PCL-5), which is with the LaserJet III/4 family of printers and clones.

WordPerfect 6.0's extensive menus control nearly all the things a printer can do. This chapter won't make you a printer expert, but it does show you what choices are important and what selections are intelligent.

Tip: While experimenting with the printer, it's easy to get carried away and get the printer into a "weird" mode. To recover, you must reset both WordPerfect and the printer. To reset the printer, turn it off. While it's off, restore the previous copy of the printer definition in WordPerfect by deleting the printer definition from the Printer selection menu (refer to Procedure 24.1, but choose Remove rather than Edit to remove the printer definition). Then, add the same printer definition back again. Make this the default printer (see Procedure 24.1 for details). This method resets how WordPerfect reads the printer setup. When you turn the power on again, the printer will reset itself into a "sane" state.

The following skills are covered in this chapter:

▲ Selecting a printer

▲ Controlling document options

▲ Controlling output options

▲ Printing documents to disk

▲ Controlling printer defaults using Print Setup

▲ Managing print jobs in the queue

Selecting a Printer

When WordPerfect formats a document on-screen, it makes allowances for the current printer—keeping the graphics view as close to the actual output as possible. WordPerfect can't always account for a printer's nuances, which is why Print Preview exits. WordPerfect also needs to know what printer the document is being formatted for. Often, there is more than one printer in the office or on the network. To print your document in WordPerfect 6.0, you must select at least one printer. However, you can have more than one printer. WordPerfect 6.0 can have many printers loaded and ready to be selected when needed.

Of all the printers available, only one is assigned as the current printer (the printer you commonly use). You can accomplish selection of your current printer in the Print/Fax menu. To select a different printer, use the following procedure (see Figure 24.1).

Procedure 24.1. Selecting a printer and interface.

1. Choose File, Print/Fax.

2. Choose Select, next to the Current Printer box.

3. Using the scroll bar on the left of the Select Printer menu, scroll through the list of available printers. The currently selected printer is indicated with an asterisk. Move the highlighted bar up and down until you find the printer you want to select.

4. Choose menu item 3, Edit.

325

```
File  Edit  View  Layout  Tools  Font  Graphics  Window  Help

     PRS Filename  APLW2NT.PRS
     Printer Name  Apple LaserWriter IINT

     Description:

     Hardware Options
       • Port...                COM1:9600,N,1,8

       Sheet Feeder...          No sheet feeder defined
       □

     Fonts
       Font Setup...            Courier 12pt
       Directory for Soft Fonts:
       (and Printer Command Files)

                                                    OK      Cancel

                                                              1"
```

Figure 24.1. The Edit Printer menu.

5. From the Edit Printer menu, select Port or 2.

6. Choose the printer interface port from the port menu.

7. Choose OK, OK to get back to the Select Printer menu.

8. Choose Select or 1 to select the highlighted printer.

9. Return to the **P**rint/Fax menu by choosing Close.

Whew! You have selected and set up a printer as the new current printer. If you don't select another printer, the one you just selected is saved as your current printer. When you start WordPerfect again, the same printer appears as the current one.

Controlling Document Options

WordPerfect has options that select a *resolution* for the printed document. The resolution describes how many dots of toner, smatterings of ink spots, or number of consecutive pin impacts there are in an inch. The more dots per inch, the better the print quality. Text Quality and Graphics Quality control what printer resolution is used when you print a document.

Note: When printing a document that has lots of graphics, it's a good idea to print test drafts at a lower Text Quality and Graphics Quality. This prints faster than a medium or high text and graphics quality does. Better yet, take advantage of the excellent Print Preview feature to save paper and toner. If characters are missing from the output, there might not be enough memory in your printer. This typically happens with PCL laser printers such as the HP LaserJet series II or III. Lower the print quality or add memory to your printer. If there was enough memory to Page Protect, they would not have run out of it in the first place. Page Protect is a PCLV specific control over font/page buffers, and typically is necessary if using TrueType and asking for letters larger than 36 point.

Procedure 24.2. Changing the print quality.

1. Choose Print/Fax from the File menu.
2. Choose Text Quality or Graphics Quality from the Document Settings area.
3. Select a quality setting by holding down the left mouse button and dragging through the choices.
4. Choose Print to print the document at these settings or choose Close to save these settings.

Changing the print quality doesn't always work, because some printers don't allow the output resolution to be changed. Another selection in the quality list, Do Not Print, controls whether WordPerfect will print the graphic images or text. This selection is useful for draft printing text without graphics.

The next output option is the Print Color option. If you have a color printer, you can choose to use black only for draft views and documents that will be copied later. To choose Black, select the Print Color menu item. Hold down the left button on the mouse and drag the highlighted bar to Black. You can define Black as the default in the Print/Fax, Setup dialog box. See "Controlling Printer Defaults Using Print Setup" in this chapter for instructions on how to use Print Setup.

The last option, Network Options, is available to workstations on a Novell network. A workstation is a personal computer (PC) with a network card, which is not the server. If your workstation is currently attached to the network, Novell provides print job services. The two base services are Banner Pages and Forms. The Banner Page is a page that precedes the print job. This page shows the user name (network login name), the date/time stamp, and the print/file server managing the printer.

The Forms feature of Novell is about as useful as the Banner Page. For each type of printer on the network, Novell maintains a set of predefined Forms that help format raw ASCII (plain text) files that are queued up for printing.

Caution: You can get in a lot of trouble playing with forms on the network. When you change the default form, you ask the network to reformat the document before you print it. WordPerfect does a great job formatting the document and controlling the printer. Let WordPerfect do its job! If you are still interested in changing the form, follow the instructions in the *Novell Netware Print Server* manual. It has information about running the utility programs Printdef and Printcon. Printdef lets you customize the printer form. Printcon lets you select the forms to be applied to printers on print queues. In any case, customizing Novell print forms isn't for the faint of heart. You definitely need a good understanding of how to program your printer, and you need a copy of the printer's programmer's reference manual. It's good network etiquette to work with the network supervisor. It makes network life easier if a temporary print queue is set up and connected to the printer. This excludes others from the queue while you are experimenting. Good luck!

All caveats aside, you can direct the network to print a banner page by selecting Banner Page. The Netware printer form can be changed with the Form Number setting. By default, form "0" is assigned to each printer. To select a customized form, insert the number of the form to be used.

Controlling Printer Output Options

The **P**rint/Fax menu includes option choices for output. These options are:

▲ Print **J**ob Graphically

▲ **N**umber of Copies

▲ Generated By

▲ Output Options

Use the Print **J**ob Graphically option when you want to add background fill or reversed text (white text on a black background). To print background fill or reversed text, choose Print Job Graphically.

The next option, **N**umber of copies, sets the number of copies for each print job. The printed copies are collated.

The Generated By option tells WordPerfect what performs the multiple copies. Some printers, such as PostScript printers, can do multiple copies of a page being generated. In this case, WordPerfect sets the PostScript variable (#ncopies) and lets the printer do the job. However, if WordPerfect is doing the multiple copies,

328

it will generate all the copies separately and send them out one at a time. Although letting PostScript do the copies is faster, it's not always easier. If you select the printer to do the copies, it will print the job uncollated. This means n copies of page 1, n copies of page 2, and so on. Then, you must let your fingers do the walking and manually collate the job.

The last item, Output options, allows you to select the printer dependent path options. Today, printers on the market offer multiple sources for paper (letter head, legal, 11-inch by 17-inch) and multiple destinations (output bins). With the multiple output bins, it's possible to send or sort jobs to separate bins. Some of the newer network page printers have output joggers that separate print jobs by shifting the output paper (jogging) between jobs. This makes separation easier. Most of the time, however, you choose the paper size by which paper tray you insert into the printer. If the current printer has other output capabilities, those options will show up in the Output options box. If the current printer has no host output options, the selection is grey. The standard output options are:

▲ Sort
▲ Group
▲ None
▲ Output Bins
▲ Offset Jogger

Use the Sort option to route copies to separate bins. For example, if the printer supports multiple output bins, and you specify 9 copies in the Number of copies box, the first copy ends up in the first bin, the second copy in the second bin, and so on.

The Group option separates the pages of a multiple copy job into different bins. For example, if you use the same printer with multiple output bins (with the Group option), 9 copies of the first page are sent to bin 1, 9 copies of the second page are sent to bin 2, and so on. This is similar to the behavior of a simple PostScript printer with only one output bin.

The selection None does nothing; it just sends the print jobs (collated or uncollated) to the default output bin—usually bin 1.

Use the Output Bins selection to select the output bin (to which your jobs are going) by name. The collated print job will be sent to the selected bin. WordPerfect's Name Search feature aids in locating a named bin from the bin list.

Last, but not least, is the Offset Jogger option. Most page printers use this option to separate jobs or copies. The output paper bin does an Elvis impression and shimmies from side to side (to the right for one copy and to the left for the next copy). The resulting pile of paper is easily separated into individual copies. The IBM line of 20-page-per-minute duplexing laser page printers features an offset jogger with the output tray.

Tip: When using page printers with offset joggers, it's not a good idea to have more than about 60 pages in the bin at a time. If the paper gets too heavy, the bottom copies start to slip and you'll loose the separation. Empty the bin to avoid slippage. (To see how to change used toner bottles, see the general laser tips in Chapter 23, "Printing.")

Printing Documents to Disk

Sometimes, the printer you want isn't connected to your system or the network. You might also want to have your document made into 35mm slides using an off-site slide service. To accomplish either of these tasks, you must ensure that the document is formatted for the new printer. To print to this "foreign" printer, transport the raw printer information to the new printer by printing the document to a standard DOS file. To do this, follow the directions in Procedure 24.3.

Note: The DOS filename used to capture the raw print output can be specified in one of two ways. I recommend you choose to be prompted for a filename each time you print to disk. This way, you can choose the filename on the fly. I use my own filename to send the file to the floppy. If you choose to use the default filename, WordPerfect saves the raw output file to the same filename, over-writing the last document without warning.

Procedure 24.3. Printing documents to a disk.

1. Choose a printer to be edited using Steps 1 through 5 in Procedure 24.1 (explained previously).

2. In the Port Menu, check the box beside item 9, Prompt For Filename. If you want the same name each time, select menu item 8, Filename. This will become the default filename. To change it, you'll need to repeat Steps 1 and 2 of the previous procedure.

3. Return to the Print/Fax menu to print the job. The current printer will output all jobs to the default or prompted filenames until a different printer or port is selected.

The DOS file is Sneaker Netted (using the Nike Network) to the PC supporting the foreign printer. To print from that PC, use the DOS copy command as follows:

```
copy /b filename.ext [lpt(1/2/3): or com(1/2):].
```

> **Note:** Long ago, there were no cute wires connecting our PCs together, and networking wasn't even a thing MBA's did during lunch. Back then, if you wanted to get a file from point A to point B, you had to copy it onto a floppy, get up out of your chair, and escort it to its destination. As we mostly wore sneakers or "low boys" at work, this came to be known as "Sneaker Net," "Rockport-Net," and so on.

Controlling Printer Defaults Using Print Setup

When working in a document, it's common to change print job parameters, print the results, and change them again as necessary. After the right set of options is determined, you can make those options defaults. However, the changes made "on the fly" live with the current document only and are not automatically invoked with the next document. The Print Setup menu is a type of Printer "style" editor. It sets the printer defaults (see Figure 24.2).

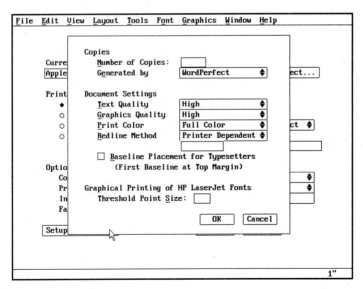

Figure 24.2. The Print Setup menu.

Procedure 24.4 shows how to invoke the Print Setup menu, make selections, and save the new default. All the options available in the Print Setup menu have been described previously in this chapter.

Procedure 24.4. Selecting and saving the initial printer setup.

1. Choose **P**rint/**F**ax from the **F**ile menu.
2. Choose the **S**etup button.
3. Select the default options.
4. Choose OK to save your settings and make them the new default.

Managing the Print Jobs in the Queue

After you select the printer (and select Print), WordPerfect queues the print jobs in a line. The first job in is the first job to be printed. As soon as WordPerfect returns you to the document screen, you can resume editing or start a new document. If you are still in WordPerfect, the document will be printed in the background. WordPerfect does not, however, provide a print progress status. To see how your print job is progressing, you must ask for print queue information from the Control Printer menu. To do this, choose Print/Fax from the File menu, and select **C**ontrol Printer or 6. This will bring up the Control Printer menu. This menu has complete information about the status of the job currently being printed, as well as the other jobs in the print queue. If you are connected to a network, the Control Printer menu provides you with network print queue information.

The Control Printer menu is divided into areas. One area provides information about the print job currently being printed. The other provides print queue information and control. The following information is provided about the current job area:

Job Number: This number corresponds to the job's place in the queue.
Status: The actual status of the job, it can be: blank, preparing print job, printing, and stopped.
Message: The last message from the printer (or information about the last problem). Examples are `Printer not responding, check printer and try again` and `None`.
Paper: The size and orientation of the paper selected for the job.
Location: Information about where the paper is coming from.
Percentage Processed: The percentage of the print job that has been processed.
Page Number: The page that is currently being processed.
Current Copy: Of the copies requested, the number of the copy currently being printed.

The print queue information/control area of the Control Printer menu provides information about print jobs waiting to be printed. Each entry gives the job number, filename of the document, and destination of the print job. The job currently being printed is highlighted. Print quality, number of copies and priority information is also displayed below the print queue box. To the right of the print queue box is a list of print queue controls. These controls are:

Cancel Job: Completely cancels the current job and those jobs in the queue that are marked.
Rush Job: This bumps the selected job up the queue to be the next job printed.
* (un)mark: This selects a job(s) from the queue for control.
(un)mark All: This unselects all selected jobs in the queue.

Below the job control box are the Stop and Go buttons. These provide temporary job control. The Network button opens up the network print queue information box. The following procedures show how to use the print queue control features:

Procedure 24.5. Cancelling the current print job.

1. Choose Print/Fax from the **F**ile menu.
2. Choose Control Printer.
3. Choose Cancel Job.
4. Choose Yes.

Procedure 24.6. Cancelling job(s) in the print queue.

Cancel immediately stops the current print job or job(s) selected from the queue with an asterisk. If you want to print the jobs again, you have to start them again from the Print/Fax menu. To stop a job and not remove it from the queue, use the Stop button (described later).

> **Note:** If WordPerfect wasn't finished printing the job when you stopped it, you might not be able to cancel or stop it immediately. Follow the instructions given in the message area of the Print Control menu. If you do, press I for cancel Immediately. Then, you need to power down or reset your printer to recover.

1. Choose Print/Fax from the **F**ile menu.
2. Choose Control Printer.
3. Choose those print job(s) from the list using "*" or * (un)mark from the list of queue controls.
4. Choose Cancel Job.
5. Choose Yes.

Procedure 24.7. Stopping the current print job.

If you choose to stop a print job while it's printing, restart it. It won't continue where it left off, but it will print the entire document again. You can cancel the job and print it starting at the next page (see Chapter 23).

1. Choose Print/Fax from the File menu.
2. Choose Control Printer.
3. Choose the Stop button.
4. Choose the Go button to restart printing the document.

Procedure 24.8. Rushing a print job.

You can choose to advance the job to be "rushed" to just after the currently printing job. You can also interrupt the current job, print the rushed job, then reprint the interrupted job. As with Stop and Go, the interrupted job will not resume printing where it left off; the entire document is reprinted.

1. Choose Print/Fax from the File menu.
2. Choose Control Printer.
3. Select a print job from the print queue.
4. Choose Rush Job.
5. Choose Yes.

Procedure 24.9. Cancelling a print job on the network.

The Network option on the Printer Control shows all the files queued on that particular print queue. You can only cancel print jobs that you originated.

1. Choose Print/Fax from the File menu.
2. Choose Control Printer.
3. Choose Network.
4. Highlight the job to be cancelled.
5. Choose Yes.
6. Choose OK and close to get back to your document.

Procedure 24.10. Holding/releasing a print job on the network.

Holding a print job on the network stops the job from being printed but doesn't remove it from the queue. Releasing a held job places it in the queue again, as if you were starting it from scratch. Then, you lose your place in line.

1. Choose Print/Fax from the File menu.
2. Choose Control Printer.
3. Choose Network.
4. Highlight the job to be held/released.
5. Choose Yes.
6. Choose OK then close until you are back to your document.

Summary

In Chapter 23, you discovered how to get a print job rolling with the current printer. You also learned how to preview the job before committing toner to paper. In this chapter, you've discovered the basics of printers, print jobs, and some of the controls. These controls can be used to get the highest quality or fastest draft print possible. I have also covered how to choose which printer WordPerfect 6.0 will use to format the output. In the next chapter, I discuss bypassing the printer altogether and sending the document to a fax device.

by David Wurmfeld

WordPerfect Fax Services

Waiting in line for your faxes? Did you see red because your last fax was half done when the machine ran out of paper? Did the text look like bar code underwater? These are the typical complaints of users of the venerable old fax machine. We don't have to put up with it anymore! By installing a fax board on your system or using the fax server on the network, WordPerfect provides fax services to your doorstep. Sound too good to be true? Well, yes and no. This chapter covers how to use the basic WordPerfect fax service. In this chapter, we cover the following basic skills:

▲ WordPerfect's fax feature

▲ Sending a fax

▲ Sending a fax on disk

▲ Using the phone book

▲ Viewing a fax file

▲ Sending a document file

Faxing Your Document

WordPerfect has integrated the fax interface into Version 6.0. Unlike other word processing systems that treat a fax board as just another printer, WordPerfect has given you substantial control over the fax creation process. If this sounds more complex than necessary, be assured that WordPerfect has made the basic fax services easy to use.

Faxing from WordPerfect for DOS involves two separate but necessary components. These are the underlying fax BIOS and the fax rendering software. The fax BIOS is a separate TSR that must be loaded and running before you start WordPerfect. The fax BIOS provides a fax board-independent interface. What this means is that the interface "talks" to the fax through a common interface, and as long as the fax BIOS is properly set up, it isolates WordPerfect from having to provide hundreds of fax board drivers (unlike the 1,000+ printer drivers). If you change your fax board, you don't need to reconfigure WordPerfect, although you may need to change your AUTOEXEC.BAT and CONFIG.SYS files. This board-independent interface ensures compatibility with future fax/modem cards.

The second piece of hardware "lives" within WordPerfect: the fax rendering portion. A fax document is an image of the text, graphics, and bitmaps called for in the document. The fax renderer must convert the document into the requested resolution and write it to a fax file. You select the resolution, which can be from *standard*—100 x 100 dpi—to *fine*—200 x 200 dpi. Of course, you don't get something for nothing: the fine resolution takes longer to send than the standard resolution, but the results are worth the wait. By taking over the job of converting the document into a fax image, WordPerfect can provide font hinting and image screening to give you superior image and text for comparable resolution.

WordPerfect fax services provide a straightforward way of defining, using, grouping, and saving your fax telephone numbers in the fax phone book. We will show you some tricks for "broadcasting" faxes and how to manage your phone book.

Also with WordPerfect 6.0 is an exciting document-file feature. If the modem you're connecting to is a compatible *Class 2* or *CAS* modem, you have the option to send the WordPerfect document file rather than the converted fax file. This means you can send the document you're working on to another site, ready for revision or printing locally. This is fantastic for those documents that have a lot of "parents," and it allows for interactive editing from anywhere in the world. This isn't just another modem connection. This is an integrated feature in WordPerfect that provides a simple-to-use interface and is as easy as sending a regular fax.

To use the fax option, you must have the fax BIOS installed *before* you start WordPerfect 6.0. During the installation procedure, you're asked whether you want fax services installed. When you answer *yes*, the installation program automatically adds the proper lines to your autoexec.bat file, so fax services are invoked each time you boot your PC.

Note: WordPerfect requires at least 480K of conventional memory to start up and at least 520K to utilize the graphics document view or preview features. Adding the fax TSR might take away too much conventional memory and reduce the functionality of WordPerfect or even cause WordPerfect not to start at all. If you see the message `Not enough memory to start WordPerfect` or `Not enough memory to use graphics mode`, you don't have enough conventional memory free. You'll have to manage your memory resources differently. (I have 16M of RAM and it happened to me!) A discussion of DOS memory management is beyond the scope of this chapter, but you can find many good books on the subject. If you get stuck, a call to WordPerfect's customer support line will get your computer up and running in a short time.

Sending a Fax

Sending a fax is as easy as opening the document you want to fax, selecting a person to fax it to from the Phonebook (or manually entering the number), and choosing Send Fax. Refer to the following procedure for explicit details:

1. Open the document you want to fax.
2. Choose Print/Fax from the **F**ile menu.
3. Choose Fax Services from the Print dialog box.
4. Mark the phone book entries you want from the Phonebook or choose Manual Dial if this is a new number or one you don't want to add to the phone book. In the latter case, fill in the required information and choose OK. (See "Manual Dial" in this chapter for more details.)
5. Select the options you want from the Send Fax dialog box, and then choose Send Fax. (See Table 25.1 for details on fax options and actions.)

Table 25.1. Send Fax options.

Option	Actions
Full Document, Page, Document on Disk, Multiple Pages, Blocked Text	Specify how much of a document to fax.

continues

Table 25.1. continued

Option	Actions
Fax on Disk	Send previously converted files that you've saved on disk as an image for fax. (See "Sending a Fax on Disk" in this chapter.)
Save as an image	Save on disk and name converted fax files for fax. (See "Sending a Fax on Disk" in this chapter.)
Coversheet	Create a cover sheet for your document.
Send Time	Specify a delivery date and time.
Resolution	Specify the print quality to which the fax will be converted for transmission.
Priority	Designate the priority of the fax.
Routing	Designate which line it will be routed to.
Billing	Designate how the fax will be billed.

Sending a Fax on Disk

To save time, you can preconvert your fax and save the converted result on disk. This way, you also have a chance to choose the name under which the converted fax file will be saved. Otherwise, WordPerfect chooses a name for you, one that won't be recognizable except for its .fax extension. (WordPerfect uses a file-naming scheme that guarantees there are no two names alike. This is okay for the computer but not very useful to you.) To save a named, preconverted fax file to disk, use the following steps:

1. Choose Print/Fax from the File menu.
2. Choose Fax Services from the Print dialog box.
3. Mark with an asterisk (*) the phone book entries you want. Then choose Send Fax or Manual Dial, type the requested information, and choose OK. (See "Manual Dial" in this chapter for more details.)
4. Choose Fax on Disk.
5. Type the name of the fax file you want to send in the Filename entry field or select it from the File List.
6. For each file, specify a Date to Send. The file will be queued up for sending when the date/time matches that of the system clock and calendar.
7. Use the Coversheet option to specify the cover sheet for the file(s) you're sending.

8. Use the Remove From List option to remove any files you don't want to fax.

9. Choose Send File. You can send as many files as you want. The files sent are listed in the Files to send box.

Using the Phone Book

The phone book mechanism collects all your fax phone numbers and details in one place, a little fax "black book," if you will. From this phone book, you can easily select people or groups of people to fax to by marking the entry with the asterisk (*). To use the phone book, use the following steps:

1. Choose Print/Fax from the File menu.

2. Choose Fax Services.

3. Choose Phonebook.

4. Select the option you want from the Phonebook dialog box. (See Table 25.2 for options and actions.)

Table 25.2. Send Fax options.

Option	Actions
Create Entry	Create a phone book entry. If your system supports more than standard resolution, you can select a resolution from the list in the Destination Fax Machine group box.
Create Group	Create a group from your list of phone book entries. Type a name for the group and then use Add to Group to add the names of the people you want included in the group.
Edit	Edit a phone book entry.
Delete	Delete a phone book entry.
Select Different Phonebook	Select a different phone book.

Note: Some fax programs, such as the Intel SatisFaction program, maintain the phone book outside WordPerfect. To maintain the phone book, you have to exit WordPerfect, use the utility provided, and then re-enter WordPerfect.

Viewing Fax Files

WordPerfect uses the same mechanism for viewing fax files as it does for Print Preview (see Figure 25.1). To view a fax file, use the following steps:

1. Choose Print from the File menu.
2. Choose Fax Services from the Print/Fax dialog box.
3. Choose View Fax File.
4. Type the name of the fax file you want to view and choose View or select it from FileList or QuickList.

View Fax Files offers all the functions you need to see some, part, or all of your fax. Figure 25.2 lists the various View Fax Files options and actions.

Figure 25.1. The Print Preview menu.

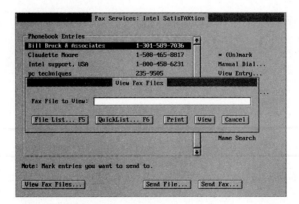

Figure 25.2. The View Fax Files dialog box.

Table 25.3. View Fax Files options and actions.

Option	Action
100 percent	View the current page at the actual printed size.
200 percent	View the current page at twice the actual printed size.
Zoom In	Increase the display size of text and graphics by 25 percent.
Zoom Out	Decrease the display size of text and graphics by 25 percent.
Zoom Area	Increase the display size of a selected area, up to 1,000 percent.
Select Area	Change the portion of text displayed in the Print Preview window when you Zoom.
Reset	Restore the view and size ratio that were in effect when you opened the Print Preview window (a quick way to get back to normal from Zoom).
Full Page	Display a complete view of the current page.
Facing Pages	Display two consecutive pages side by side.
Thumbnails	Display several pages at once.
Button Bar	Display (or hide) the Print Preview button bar.
Button Bar Setup	Edit the Print Preview button bar, change the button bar options, or select another button bar.

Use the Thumbnails option or button to see laid out side by side all or part of your fax. If you have a VGA screen, laying out any more that four pages at a time makes the type illegible. If you're just looking at the positioning of text and graphics, eight pages at a time work fine with a normal VGA screen. To use the Thumbnails option, choose the Thumb # button from the button bar or View, Thumbnails from the Print Preview menu (see Figure 25.3). Enter the number of pages you want displayed or choose Other and enter the desired number of pages in the Thumbnail Other dialog box.

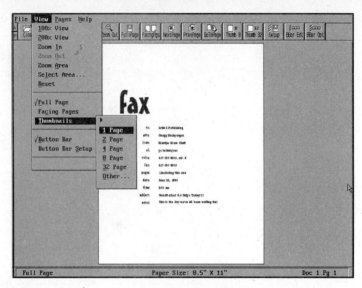

Figure 25.3. The Print Preview Thumbnails menu.

Tip: For faster screen performance, choose the View Text and Graphics in Black & White option from the File menu.

Sending a Document File

To send unconverted (unrasterized) document files to another fax/modem, both fax/modems must have binary file transfer (BFT) capability. BFT is also listed as *CAS* or *Series 2* interface. If both the sender and the receiver are compatible, use the following steps to transfer documents:

1. Choose Print/Fax from the File menu.

2. Choose Fax Services from the Print dialog box.

3. Mark with an asterisk (*) the phone book entries you want. Then choose Send Fax or Manual Dial, type the requested information, and choose OK. (See "Manual Dial" in this chapter for more details.)

4. Choose Send File.

5. Type in the Filename entry field the name of the fax file you want to send or select the file from the File List or QuickList.

6. For each file, specify a Date to Send. The file will be queued up for sending when the date/time matches that of the system clock and calendar.

7. Use the Coversheet option to specify the cover sheet for the file(s) you are sending.

8. Use the Remove From List option to remove any files you don't want to fax.

9. Choose Send File. You can send as many files as you want. The files that will be sent are listed in the Files to send box.

Canceling a Fax

Canceling a fax is a lot easier than sending one on its way.

1. Choose Print/Fax from the File menu.

2. Choose Fax Services from the Print/Fax dialog box.

3. Choose Fax Activity from the Fax Services dialog box.

4. Choose Cancel current fax.

Manual Dial

Use Manual Dial (see Figure 25.4) to send a fax to a number you don't want entered in the Phonebook.

The Manual Dial dialog box shown in Figure 25.4 may not be the same as the one your fax modem supports. In any case, fill in the required information and choose OK or Cancel to abort Manual Dial.

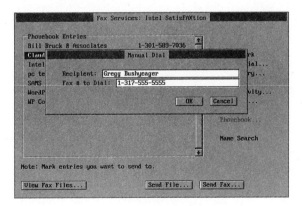

Figure 25.4. The Representative Manual Dial dialog box.

Monitoring Fax Activity

After the fax/modem box or board has squawked its way through the handshake phase (a sort of electronic version of "I'm OK, You're OK"), the fax quiets down and returns you to your document. This is just like the way WordPerfect treats printing. For most of us, however, faith is hard to come by. We like to see some indication of progress (or failure) and not leave everything up to the "trust me and everything will come out fine" school of thought. In other words, to see your fax's progress, you have to ask (see Figure 25.5).

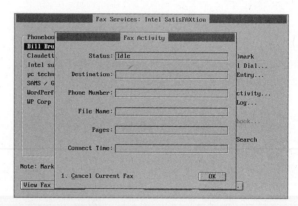

Figure 25.5. The Fax Activity menu.

To ask for your fax's progress, do the following:

1. Choose Print/Fax from the File menu.
2. Choose Fax Services from the Print dialog box.
3. From the following table, choose the fax information desired.

Option	Action
Fax Activity	Gives the status, destination, phone number, filename, progress, and total connect time so far for the current fax
View Log	Gives a log of all sent and received faxes
Send Log	Lists all the faxes you've sent, along with all fax details; provides option to print sent faxes
Receive Log	Lists all the faxes you've received, along with all fax details; provides option to print received faxes
Name Search	Use this to find a specific person's number quickly in the Phonebook.

Printing Faxes

Received or sent faxes can be printed or viewed at any time, provided you haven't removed the fax file from your disk. Use the following steps to view a log:

1. Choose Print/Fax from the File menu.
2. Choose Fax Services.
3. Choose View Log (see Figure 25.6).

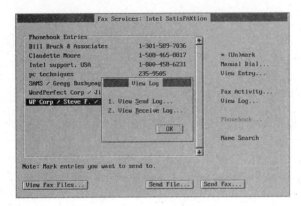

Figure 25.6. The View Log menu.

4. Choose View Send Log (see the Send Log menu in Figure 25.7) or View Receive Log.
5. Highlight fax to be Viewed/Printed.

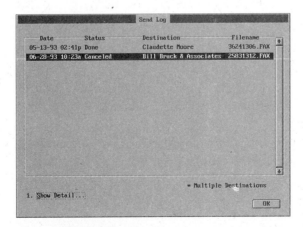

Figure 25.7. The Send Log menu.

347

6. Choose Show Details (see the Log Details menu in Figure 25.8).

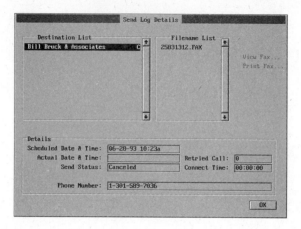

Figure 25.8. The Log Details menu.

7. Choose View or Print Fax. View Fax works as described earlier, Print Fax sends the fax to the current printer. (See Chapter 24, "Printer Controls," for details on controlling and monitoring the printing process.)

File Management and Data Exchange

by Ted Pederson

File Manager

The documents you create in WordPerfect are saved in files on your hard disk. These files accumulate, and it becomes easy to forget which files to retain and which to erase. Of the files you do choose to keep, there will be some you'll need to access on a regular basis and others that can be copied to floppy disks for an occasional reference.

Without a system to organize your files, you may find your hard disk looking like a desktop cluttered with documents. Finding a file might feel like looking for the proverbial needle in a haystack.

About File Manager

WordPerfect's File Manager enables you to quickly navigate through and organize your files. It compliments the DOS file management system by enabling you to sort your file list in a variety of sequences, as well as to mark and manipulate multiple files.

Understanding the Basics of File Management

Before exploring the potential uses of File Manager, I'll review some of the basic concepts of file management.

File Management Terms

You might be familiar with computer terminology, but "technobabble" can be confusing even to experts. I'll define some of the more common terms that are used in file management.

Industry standards generally require referring to file management in the following "office" terms:

> Disk: filing cabinet
> Directory: folders
> Files: contents of the folders (documents)

Disk Drives, Directories, and Subdirectories

Your hard drive and disk drive(s) have one or more directories. The main directory is called the root directory. This is usually indicated as C:\ on your hard drive and A:\ or B:\ on your disk drive(s). Every disk automatically has a root directory. Every other directory is a subdirectory of the root directory and each of these can contain their own subdirectories.

A hard drive structure might look something like this:

```
C:\
    DOS\
    UTILITY\
    WP60\
        DOCS\
            LETTERS\
            MEMOS\
            REPORTS\
        MACROS\
        PICS\
```

Paths and the Default Directory

A path is the full name of the subdirectory. In the preceding example, the location of LETTERS is:

`C:\WP60\DOCS\LETTERS`

If you are in the root directory, and type in the command CD LETTERS to change to that directory, you will get an error message. You need to type the full path: CD C:\WP60\DOCS\LETTERS to get there.

The current directory (which can be a default) is where you are at the moment. If you're in the DOCS subdirectory and type CD LETTERS, you'll go to the LETTERS directory. This is because C:\WP60\DOCS is your current default directory; the

352

computer will use this directory as its reference point until you command otherwise. For example, if you are in the DOCS directory and copy a file from your floppy drive to C:, the file will copy to the DOCS directory.

The failure to type complete paths when moving files is one of the most common causes for misplacing files. A good rule of thumb is to always type the full name of the file—path plus filename—when moving files. While this may take a little more time and effort, it can save you grief later.

Files and Documents

A document, whether it is a few sentences in a memo or a hundred pages in a report, is stored on your hard drive or floppy disk as a file.

Think of your disk as a filing cabinet and a computer file as a file folder inside that cabinet. A document is what you put inside of the folder.

Going to a filing cabinet, removing a file folder, and opening a file is similar to selecting a file, retrieving it into WordPerfect, and opening the document contained inside.

Think of the document (your work) as going back into a file folder when you're done. It's much easier to move a few file folders than to move several hundred individual pages that are contained inside those folders.

File Name and Extension

The disk operating system (DOS) is the structure in which your computer operates. DOS dictates that a file can have a name of up to eight characters and an extension of up to three characters. An example of a filename is FILENAME.EXT. When you name a file, *don't* use the following special characters. They are only used by DOS:

```
* + = [ ] :; < > ? / \ ¦, (space)
```

Use a period only to separate the name from its extension. However, you don't have to use an extension when naming a file. Examples of filenames are as follows:

```
DOCUMENT
FILE-001.EXT
MEMO-13.JUN
JMS-PROP.WP6
$OCT93.RPT
```

Several extensions have special meanings in WordPerfect and DOS. These include .ALL, .BAT, COM, .CON, .CRS, .DRS, .EXE, .FIL, .FRS, .SET, .TUT, .WPK ,.WPM, and .VRS. You shouldn't use these extensions when saving documents unless you do so for the appropriate reasons.

Wildcards and Other Shortcuts

Like the joker in a deck of playing cards, WordPerfect allows you to use *wildcards* to manipulate files.

There are two basic types of wildcards: ? and *. The ? represents a single character. BO?T could stand for BOOT or BOAT. The * represents anything that follows its insertion. BUILD* can mean BUILDS, BUILDER, BUILDING or BUILT.

. signifies all the files in the current directory, but *.wp6 would signify only the files which end in the extension .WP6.

The * wildcard is more powerful than ?, but it might retrieve more files than you want. If you are trying to find documents that reference "TRACY," and can't remember if her name ends in a *Y* or an *I*, typing TRAC? does the trick.

File Organization

"A place for everything, and everything in its place." You may not have to be quite that neat, but how you organize your directories and subdirectories can mean the difference between a well-run operation and total chaos.

Everyone has their own way of structuring their hard disk. The best rule is to organize a system of directories and subdirectories that reflect the way you work. You might have a DOCUMENT directory with subdirectories for LETTERS, MEMOS, NOTES, REPORTS, and so on. If several people are using the same computer, you might have subdirectories called GEORGE, SALLY, and RALPH.

If your business deals with only a few clients, you may choose to allocate the subdirectories under DOCUMENT by client names such as SMITH and JONES.

Tip: WordPerfect enables you to choose a beginning file location for documents. If all your current documents are in directories and subdirectories in one location, it's easier for several people to use the same computer without having to create special setup batch files for each user.

File Backup and Storage

Anyone who has worked on a computer long enough has lost a file, either because of data corruption or error. It's like living in southern California. You know an earthquake will happen—you just don't know when. So the motto for Californians is one that applies to WordPerfectionists: "Be Prepared."

Get into the habit of backing up your current documents on a daily basis. Back your files to floppies or a backup tape. Once a week, back up everything. You should also have a backup copy of WordPerfect. Update your copy when you add macros and keyboards or make other changes.

Caution: Floppy disks can wear out or become damaged. If you have backed up your program to disks, you should make a new backup copy every six months or so. It's a good idea to have two backup copies.

Filenaming Strategies

A rose by any other name may still be a rose, but if you choose to name your rose "George," will you remember it stands for a flower two years from now? Proper filenames are not only crucial to efficient organization, but they are vital to maintaining your personal sanity later on. Anyone who has ever lost their car keys can aptly testify to this.

When you search through a filing cabinet, you identify the contents of each file folder by what is written on the outside. The more information you gain from what is on the outside of the folder, the less you have to determine what is on the inside. For this reason, it's important to name your files appropriately.

Unfortunately, as mentioned previously, DOS limits the choice of names to eight characters and a three character extension. Learn to be creative in your choice of filenames—and follow a system.

You can use extensions to identify different kinds of files: FILENAME.MEM is a memo, FILENAME.DOC is a document, FILENAME.RPT is a report, FILENAME.LET is a letter, and so on. The only problem with this system (and many people do use it quite successfully) is that WordPerfect automatically adds the extension .BK! whenever it makes a backup of your document. So if you open and close the file FILENAME.LET, then open and close the file, FILENAME.MEM, you will have only one FILENAME.BK! file. This can be quite a problem if, because of an error, you need to retrieve a backup file.

One way to limit the system of using the extension as a file type identifier is to make different directories for each file type.

Tip: For critical files, you can reduce the potential of typing mistakes by using characters that are difficult to enter accidentally. For example, type _ or $ as part of the name (for example, FILE_ONE.C$T).

355

Using File Manager

Think of File Manager as your navigator through the maze of DOS files. You don't have to leave WordPerfect either. With File Manager, you can list files in a variety of orders (alphabetic, date sequence, and so on), search for a particular file, change to another directory, and create and delete directories. To open File Manager, follow the steps in Procedure 26.1.

Procedure 26.1. Opening File Manager.

1. Choose **File Manager** from the File menu or press F5. The File Manager dialog box is displayed (see Figure 26.1).

2. To list the contents of the current directory, choose OK or press Enter. You can type the name of a different directory or choose it from QuickList (F6) or Directory Tree (F8). Choose OK.

> **Tip:** To list the same directory you listed last time you opened File Manager, choose Redo (F5). To change the default directory for this WordPerfect session, type = before you type the name of the directory.

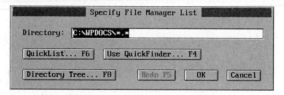

Figure 26.1. The File Manager dialog box.

If the file you need to edit is in a different directory, follow the steps in Procedure 26.2 to change the default directory.

Procedure 26.2. Changing the default directory in File Manager.

1. Choose File Manager from the File menu or press F5. The File Manager dialog box is displayed.

2. Choose OK to list the contents of the current directory. You can type the name of a different directory or choose it from QuickList (F6) or Directory Tree (F8). Choose OK.

3. Choose Change Default Dir. The Change Default Directory dialog box (see Figure 26.2) is displayed.

4. Type the full path and name of the directory or choose it from Directory Tree (F8) or QuickList (F6). Choose OK.

356

5. You can type = or press F5 and type in the name of the new directory.

See Figure 26.3 for an example of a File Manager directory listing.

Figure 26.2. The Change Default Directory dialog box.

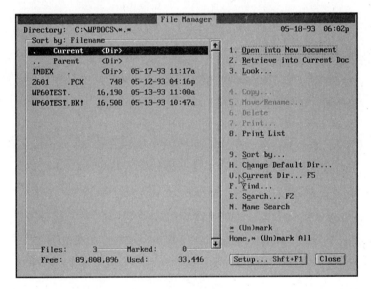

Figure 26.3. A directory listing in File Manager.

Temporarily Change Directories

Sometimes when you are in the middle of a WordPerfect session, you may want to go to another working directory without changing the default directory. To do this, follow the steps in Procedure 26.3.

Procedure 26.3. Temporarily changing to another directory.

1. Choose File Manager from the File menu or press F5. The File Manager dialog box is displayed.

2. Choose OK to list the contents of the current directory. You can also type the name of a different directory or choose it from QuickList (F6) or Directory Tree (F8). Choose OK.

357

3. Choose Current Dir.

4. Type the full path and name of the directory or choose it from QuickList (F6) or Directory Tree (F8).

5. Choose OK.

You can list the contents of any directory in the file by double-clicking its name with a mouse. You can also highlight the name and press Enter. To list the contents of the Parent directory (the directory containing the current directory), highlight .. Parent and press Enter.

Directory Tree

You can use the Directory Tree to display the organization of directories on a drive. This kind of snapshot of directories and subdirectories is very helpful, particularly on a large disk drive. When you use a feature that requires you to specify a directory (such as File Manager), you can select Directory Tree (F8). Then, follow the steps listed in Procedure 26.4.

 Note: The first time you use Directory Tree, it creates an image of your disk in a file called WP{WPC}.TRE. If you make changes to the directories on your disk, you need to choose the rescan option to update that file so it has an accurate image of your disk.

Procedure 26.4. Using Directory Tree.

1. Choose the Directory Tree (F8) button in the dialog box that contains it. The Directory Tree dialog box is displayed (see Figure 26.4).

2. To change to a different drive, choose Other Drive and highlight the drive you want. Then choose Select.

3. To search for a directory or subdirectory in the current directory, choose Name Search. Type the path of the directory (without the drive letter). For example, type WORK\LETTERS. Press Enter when the directory you want is highlighted.

   or

   Choose Search (F2) and specify the directory name (without including its path). If you want to search above the highlighted directory in the tree, select Backward Search. Then choose Search or press F2.

4. When the directory you want is highlighted, choose Select Directory.

   or

   Choose Use as Pattern to insert the path of the directory into the dialog box mentioned in Step 1. For example, suppose you are using File Manager to open a document in a directory named LETTERS. If you choose

Directory Tree, highlight LETTERS and choose Use as Pattern. You will be returned to the Specify File Manager List dialog box, and C:\WORK\LETTERS will be specified in the entry field. Choose OK to list the files in the LETTERS directory and open the one you want.

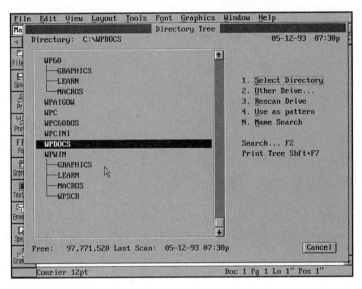

Figure 26.4. The Directory Tree.

Selecting a File

When you select a file, you can open, retrieve, look at, copy, move, rename, delete, or print it.

Select a file by moving the insertion point to the filename and clicking once to highlight it. You can also use the arrow keys to move up and down through the file list.

To perform the same operation on several files, select files by moving to each file and choosing (Un)mark (*). This marks or unmarks the file. The * key works as a toggle to mark and unmark highlighted files.

Tip: If the current directory contains many files, use Find, Search, or Name Search to quickly find the files you want.

Tip: You can quickly mark all the files by pressing Home+* or Alt+F5.

Looking at a File

Look enables you to examine a file before you open it. You can view a document or a graphics file and even listen to a sound file. To do this, follow the steps in Procedure 26.5.

Procedure 26.5. Looking at a file.

1. Choose File Manager from the File menu or press F5. The File Manager dialog box is displayed.

2. Choose OK to list the contents of the current directory. Type the name of a different directory or choose it from QuickList (F6) or Directory Tree (F8). Choose OK.

3. Select the file you want by highlighting it. Choose Look. The contents of the file are displayed (see Figure 26.5). If a Document Summary is attached to the file, the summary is displayed.

4. Now you can perform any of the following tasks:

   ▲ If the Document Summary is displayed, you can choose to view the contents of the document itself.

   ▲ View the Next or Previous files.

   ▲ Open the file to a new document window.

   ▲ Scroll through the file to scan its contents.

   ▲ Delete the file.

   ▲ Mark (*) the file to select it.

   ▲ Search (F2) for a word or phrase in the file.

5. Choose CLOSE when you're finished.

Finding a File

There are two methods to find a file. The first is to find the file by name. If you have been diligent in your naming of files, this search may be the only one you need. Procedures 26.6. and 26.7 are examples of two ways to search for a file by its name.

Procedure 26.6. Finding a file with Search.

1. Choose File Manager from the File menu or press F5. The File Manager dialog box is displayed.

2. Choose Search or press F2. The Search dialog box (see Figure 26.6) is displayed.

3. Enter a filename. You can also enter a filename pattern using a wildcard.

4. If you want to search backward through the list of files, select Backward Search.

5. Choose Search or press F2.

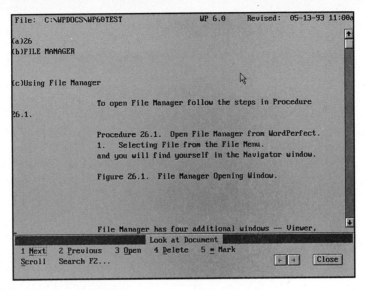

Figure 26.5. File Manager Look.

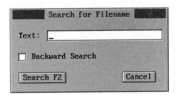

Figure 26.6. The Search for Filename dialog box.

Using Name Search to Find a File

Name Search lets you select a file by typing the first few characters of its name.

Procedure 26.7. Using Name Search.

1. Choose File Manager from the File menu or press F5. The File Manager dialog box is displayed.
2. Choose Name Search. The name search drop down dialog box is displayed.
3. Enter the first few letters of the filename. The filename will be highlighted when you have entered enough characters for File Manager to recognize it.
4. Press Enter to turn off Name Search.

The other way to find a file is by its contents. To find a file by the words contained inside the file, follow the steps in Procedure 26.8.

Procedure 26.8. Finding a file with Find.

1. To search certain files, select those files using (Un)mark (*). By default, Find searches all the files in the current directory.

2. Choose Find. The Find dialog box is displayed (see Figure 26.7).

3. Select one of the following to make your search:

   ▲ Name of the file

   ▲ Document Summary, which allows you to select those elements of the Document Summary to search (see Chapter 29, "Document Summary," for information on document summaries).

   ▲ First Page of the document

   ▲ Entire Document

   ▲ Conditions to search more than one of the above areas

   or

   ▲ Choose QuickFinder for your search (See Chapter 28, "QuickFinder").

4. When you have selected a search area, type a word or phrase in the selected entry field(s) and choose OK.

> **Note:** To search for a pattern of words, enclose the pattern in quotation marks. To search for an exact phrase, include a space between the last letter and the last quotation mark.

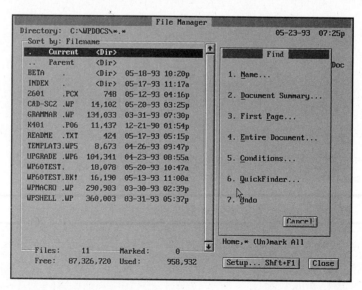

Figure 26.7. The Find dialog box.

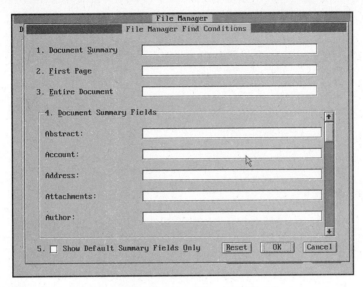

Figure 26.8. The File Manager Find Conditions dialog box.

Opening or Retrieving a File

To open a file into a new window, or to retrieve a file from the current document, follow the steps in Procedure 26.9.

Procedure 26.9. Opening or retrieving a file.

1. To retrieve a file from another document, place an insertion point at the place to which you want the file to be retrieved. (See Figure 26.9 for an example of retrieving a file into an existing document.)

2. Choose File Manager from the File menu or press F5. The File Manager dialog box is displayed.

3. Choose OK to list the contents of the current directory. You can also type the name of a different directory or choose it from QuickList (F6) or Directory Tree (F8). Choose OK.

4. Select the document you want.

5. To open the document into a new document window, choose Open into New Document.

   or

   To retrieve the document into a document you already have on-screen, choose Retrieve into Current Doc. Press Shift+F10 to toggle between the two choices.

363

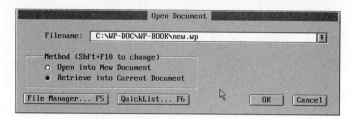

Figure 26.9. Retrieving a file into an existing document.

Copying Files

When you copy a file, it stays in its current place and duplicates to the destination you specify. Therefore, when you back up a file, you'll have a backup copy.

You can copy a file to a different computer (such as from your office machine to the laptop computer you have at home). However, you might find a directory getting full. So, you must divide the files into several different directories. You can use the wildcard options to copy several files with one command.

Copy a File

To copy a file(s), follow the steps in Procedure 26.10.

Procedure 26.10. Copying a file.

1. Choose File Manager from the File menu or press F5. The File Manager dialog box is displayed.

2. Choose OK to list the contents of the current directory. You can also type the name of a different directory or choose it from QuickList (F6) or Directory Tree (F8). Choose OK.

3. Highlight the file you want to copy or use (Un)mark (*) to mark several files you want to copy.

4. Choose Copy. The Copy files dialog box is displayed (see Figure 26.10).

5. Enter the name of the disk drive and/or directory to which you want to copy the files. Choose OK or press Enter.

Tip: If you specify a new filename for a copy, you can rename it when you copy it.

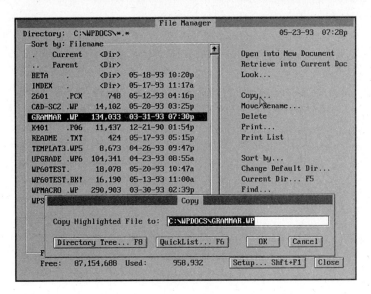

Figure 26.10. The Copy files dialog box.

Moving or Renaming Files

When you move or rename a file, you don't alter its contents. You just change the way to access that file. You can access a file differently by renaming or moving it. Because renaming and moving are so similar, File Manager combines these options under one window.

Move or Rename a Single File

To move or rename a single file, follow the steps in Procedure 26.11.

Procedure 26.11. Moving or renaming a single file.

1. Choose File Manager from the File menu or press F5. The File Manager dialog box is displayed.

2. Choose OK to list the contents of the current directory. You can also type the name of a different directory or choose it from QuickList (F6) or Directory Tree (F8). Choose OK.

3. Select the file and choose Move/Rename. The Move/Rename dialog box (see Figure 26.11) is displayed.

4. To move the file, enter the target directory path and choose OK.

   or

   To rename the file, enter the new filename and choose OK.

365

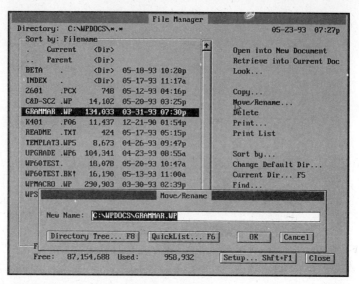

Figure 26.11. The Move/Rename dialog box.

Tip: If you want to move and rename the file, specify a new directory and filename when you choose the rename option.

Move Multiple Files

If you want to move multiple files, follow the steps in Procedure 26.12.

Procedure 26.12. Moving multiple files.

1. Use (Un)mark (*) to mark each of the files you want to move. Choose Move/Rename. The Move/Rename dialog box is displayed.
2. Enter the path of the directory to which you want to move the files. Choose OK.

Delete a File

If you don't need a file anymore, you can delete it—and your hard disk will have more free space. To delete a file with File Manager, follow the steps in Procedure 26.13.

Procedure 26.13. Deleting a file with File Manager.

1. Choose File Manager from the File menu or press F5. The File Manager dialog box will be displayed.

2. Choose OK to list the contents of the current directory. You can also type the name of a different directory or choose it from QuickList (F6) or Directory Tree (F8). Choose OK.

3. Select the file you want to delete and choose Delete.

    or

    Use (Un)Mark (*) to mark the files you want to delete and choose Delete. The Delete dialog box is displayed (see Figure 26.12).

4. Choose Yes if you're sure you want to delete the file. If you make an error, press Escape. Choose No to abort the operation.

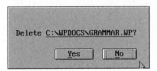

Delete C:\WPDOCS\GRAMMAR.WP?

Yes   No

Figure 26.12. The Delete dialog box.

Caution: You might delete a file and find later that you really needed it. It's always best to backup files before deleting them. You can back up an entire directory, too.

If you delete the wrong file, and don't have a backup, don't panic! There are several utility programs (including one in DOS 5.0 and 6.0) that enable you to recover a deleted file. If you're not sure what to do—stop and get help from someone. When you delete a file, DOS removes that filename from its FAT (file allocation table) and frees up that file's old space. If you continue to save other files, you may not be able to recover your deleted file.

Add a New Directory

You might need to add new directories to store documents. If you organize invoices monthly (by subdirectory), you'll need a new directory for each month. You can create a new directory in File Manager.

To add a directory in File Manager, follow the steps in Procedure 26.14.

Procedure 26.14. Adding a new directory.

1. Choose File Manager from the File menu or press F5. The File Manager dialog box is displayed.

2. Choose OK to list the contents of the current directory. You can also type the name of a different directory or choose it from QuickList (F6) or Directory Tree (F8). Choose OK.

3. Choose Change Default Dir. The Change Default Directory dialog box is displayed.

4. Type the full path and name of the new directory. Choose OK, then Yes to create it.

Saving a File

When you edit a document on disk, the file becomes active in your computer's memory. However, the changes you make are not recorded on disk until you save the file.

You need to use Save to replace the disk copy of a document with the on-screen copy. Use Save As to save the document with a new name, in a different directory, with a new format, as a code page, or as a password.

To save a file, follow the steps in Procedure 26.15. To save the file with a new name or in a new location, follow the steps in Procedure 26.16.

Procedure 26.15. Using Save.

1. Choose Save from the File menu or press Ctl+F12. If the document is named and saved, the current copy replaces the saved copy on disk. If you haven't previously saved the document, WordPerfect prompts you to give it a name.

Procedure 26.16. Using Save As.

1. Choose Save As from the File menu or press F10. The Save Document dialog box is displayed (see Figure 26.13).

2. Select one or more of the following options:
   ▲ Specify a path and filename.
   ▲ Save the document in a different format.
   ▲ Assign or remove a password from the document (see Procedure 26.17 for more information).
   ▲ Change the Code Page for the file (see Chapter 30, "Converting File Formats").
   ▲ Use File List or QuickList to specify a path for the new file.

3. To save the document in the default directory, type a filename for the file.

   or

   To save the document in a directory other than the default directory, enter a path and filename for the file.

4. To save the file in a different format, choose an option from the Format pop-up list (see Chapter 30 for more information).

5. Choose OK.

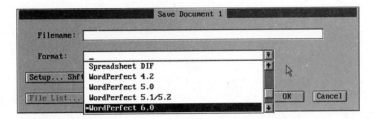

Figure 26.13. The Save Document dialog box.

> **Tip:** To save a portion of your document as a new file, highlight the text you want to save and use Save As.

Assigning a Password to a Document

WordPerfect allows you to lock a file to keep others from viewing or altering the document. Think of Password as the key to locking your desk drawer. It prevents others from snooping where they don't belong. However, it's not intended as a high security safeguard against someone who is really determined.

> **Caution:** Although a password can prevent others from accessing the document, it won't stop someone from deleting the document at the DOS prompt.

To assign a password or change an existing password for a file, follow the steps in Procedure 26.17.

Procedure 26.17. Assigning or changing passwords.

1. Choose Save As from the File menu or press F10. If you haven't already typed a Filename for the document, do so now.
2. Choose Password (F8). The Password dialog box is displayed (see Figure 26.14).
3. Type a password with up to 23 characters. Choose OK. Retype the password to confirm your original entry and choose OK again.
4. Choose OK to accept the password.
5. Choose Yes to save the file with the password.

> **Note:** Passwords are not case sensitive. For example, "MaryAnn" is treated the same as "maryann."

Figure 26.14. The Password dialog box.

> **Caution:** After you assign a password to a document, be sure to remember it. WordPerfect can't open the file if you forget the password.

To remove a password from a document, follow the steps in Procedure 26.18.

Procedure 26.18. Removing a password.

1. Choose Save As from the File menu or press F10. If you choose Save and the document has already been saved, you won't have the opportunity to select the Password option. The Save Document dialog box is displayed.
2. Choose Password (F8) and then select Remove (F6).
3. Choose OK.
4. Save the file with the password removed.

When you protect a document with a password, WordPerfect also protects any associated backup or temporary buffer files.

Note: If you save a password-protected file in a format other than WordPerfect, the password is lost.

Printing a File

To print a file directly from File Manager, follow the steps in Procedure 26.19.

Procedure 26.19. Printing a file from File Manager.

1. Choose File Manager from the File menu or press F5. The File Manager dialog box is displayed.

2. Choose OK to list the contents of the current directory. You can also type the name of a different directory or choose it from QuickList (F6) or Directory Tree (F8). Choose OK.

3. Select the file to print.

   or

   Use (Un)mark (*) to select each of the files in the directory that you want to print.

4. Choose Print and choose Yes. The Print/Fax dialog box is displayed (see Figure 26.15).

5. Specify the settings you want and choose OK.

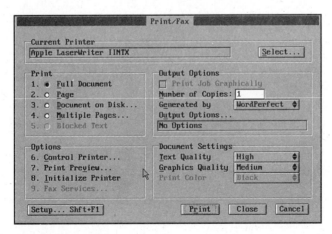

Figure 26.15. The Print/Fax dialog box.

Caution: If you specify a range of pages to print from a document listed in File Manager, you must do so in numerical order. For example, if you want to print pages 3 and 7, you would specify 3 7, not 7, 3.

Printing a File List

Use Print List to print the displayed file list by following the steps in Procedure 26.20.

Procedure 26.20. Printing a File List from File Manager.

1. Choose File Manager from the File menu or press F5. The File Manager dialog box is displayed.
2. Choose OK to list the contents of the current directory. You can also type the name of a different directory or choose it from QuickList (F6) or Directory Tree (F8). Choose OK.
3. Choose Print List.

Setting up File Manager

Normally the file list in File Manager is arranged alphabetically, but you can list the files other ways. To list files differently, follow the steps in Procedure 26.21.

Procedure 26.21. Setting up File Manager.

1. Choose File Manager from the File menu or press F5. The File Manager dialog box is displayed.
2. Choose OK to list the contents of the current directory. You can also type the name of a different directory or choose it from QuickList (F6) or Directory Tree (F8). Choose OK.
3. Choose Setup or press Shift+F1. The File Manager Setup dialog box is displayed (see Figure 26.16).
4. Select one or more of the following options:
   ▲ Sort alphabetically by filename or by extension
   ▲ List filenames only
   ▲ Sort by date and time last saved
   ▲ Sort smallest to largest
   ▲ Sort alphabetically by descriptive names or types you have assigned

▲ List filenames as well as descriptive names and descriptive types

▲ Sort files from bottom to top

▲ List WordPerfect documents only

▲ Display the files in the order in which they reside on disk; this helps File Manager list files faster

▲ Make Print List print the file list in a small font

5. Select the options you want. The choice of one option (for example a sort) may preclude the selection of other options (such as a different sort). When you have selected the appropriate options, choose OK.

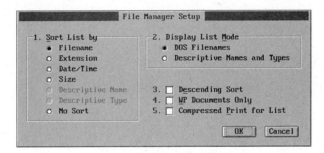

Figure 26.16. The File Manager Setup dialog box.

Using QuickList

File Manager enables you to select the QuickList in the dialog box. Chapter 27, "QuickList," covers QuickList in detail.

Using QuickFinder

File Manager allows you to select the QuickFinder in the main dialog box. Chapter 28 covers QuickFinder in detail.

by Ted Pederson

QuickList

QuickList enables you to define and then access a "plain English" list of the directories and files you use most frequently.

About QuickList

QuickList can be opened from **F**ile Manager or any other menu from which you can open or retrieve a file. You can either click on the QuickList box or press F6 to get to the QuickList dialog box (see Figure 27.1).

You can also use QuickList as a shortcut when you are using Save **As** to save a file. QuickList attaches your selected path to the saved file, eliminating the possibility of making a typing mistake that will cause an error or might save the file to another location.

The following examples illustrate some of the many different ways in which you can specify directories and files. You can use wildcards when defining filenames in your search paths. This way, if you have 200 files in a directory, you can elect to see only those that begin with SAM*.

In these QuickList filename examples, the "plain English" name is followed by the path/filename it references. Note that if only the path is indicated, the filename defaults to *.*, or all the files in that directory.

▲ **Documents:** C:\WPDOCS (This includes all the files in the WPDOCS directory.)

▲ **Documents—Jones Acccount:** C:\WPDOCS\ABC*.* (This includes all the files that begin with ABC.)

▲ **Graphics—WPG:** C:\WP60\GRAPHICS*.WP6 (This includes the .WPG files that are in this directory.)

▲ **Graphics—PCX:** C:\WP60\GRAPHICS*.PCX (This includes the .PCX files in this directory.)

▲ **Letters:** C:\WPDOCS\LETTERS*.WP (This includes all the .WP files in this directory. Note that the .BK! file extension or any other file extensions would not show in this case.)

▲ **Technical Report—May:** C:\WPDOCS\TECH-MAY.WP (This includes only the "Technical Report for May" document. Use this type of entry to quickly access a particular document that you are working on over a period of time.)

Tip: You can use QuickList to quickly access your floppy drives by including an item like Floppy A: or Floppy B: to your list, and refering to A:\ or B:\ directories. When you select this item, you will get a list of the files on that floppy disk. If you use subdirectories on your floppies, consider setting up a common subdirectory (such as WPDOCS or BACKUP) that can be set up in QuickList so you can quickly access the files on any floppy disk.

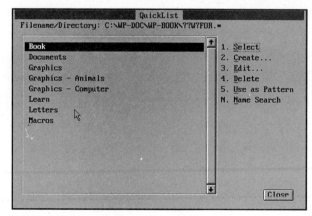

Figure 27.1. The QuickList dialog box.

Creating or Adding Names to QuickList

If you are opening QuickList for the first time, the first thing you need to do is create a QuickList name list. To do this—or to add a new entry or edit an already existing QuickList entry—follow the steps in Procedure 27.1.

Procedure 27.1. Creating or modifying QuickList.
1. Choose File Manager from the File menu and then choose QuickList (or press F5, F6).
2. If you are adding a new entry, choose Create. The Create QuickList Entry dialog box appears (see Figure 27.2). If you want to modify an already existing entry, choose Edit. The Edit QuickList Entry dialog box appears.

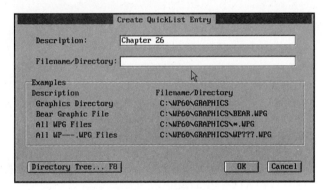

Figure 27.2. The Create QuickList Entry dialog box.

3. Type a description for the directory or filename (for example, Letters or Report) in the Description entry field.
4. If you are adding a directory, type its name in the Filename/Directory entry field, or select it from the Directory Tree by clicking the Directory Tree button or pressing F8. If you are adding a document, type in the path and filename, using wild cards as necessary. Note that if you enter only a path, *.* (all files in that path) is assumed as the filename.
5. Choose OK to add the item to your QuickList.
6. Repeat Steps 2 through 5 to add or modify any other items in the list.
7. When you are done, choose Close and OK, or press Enter until you return to your document.

Tip: QuickList automatically puts items in alphabetic order. One way to order items the way you want is to enter them in the following manner:

```
1. First Item
2. Second Item
3. Third Item
```

Because numbers sort before letters, using this system ensures that these items will be at the top of your QuickList. You can also group similar items together:

```
Document: Letters
Document: Memos
Document: Reports
```

If several people have access, you can list the items in this manner:

```
Paul: Documents
Paul: Letters
Sally: Documents
Sally: Letters
```

Using QuickList

Once you have created a QuickList, you can use it as a shortcut to find and save files by following the steps in Procedure 27.2.

Procedure 27.2. Using QuickList.

1. Choose the QuickList button in a dialog box that contains it, or press F6. Dialog boxes containing this button are available when you use Open, Retrieve, Save As, File Manager, and any other feature that requires you to specify a file or directory.

2. Highlight the item you want. If your list contains many items, you can quickly find the one you want by choosing Name Search and then typing a description of the item.

3. Choose Select. If the item is a directory, its contents will be listed in File Manager. If the item is a single file, you can open, retrieve, or save it.

   Alternatively, you could choose Use as Pattern to insert the item into the dialog box mentioned in Step 1. For example, suppose you want to save a document called SMITH.WP in a directory you have defined

with the description *Letters*. The actual name of this directory is
C:\WPDOCS\LETTERS. By choosing Use as Pattern, you automatically
insert C:\WPDOCS\LETTERS as the path in which to save the file. You are
now saving SMITH in this path, rather than the default document location, which is probably C:\WPDOCS. (See Figure 27.3 for an illustration of
the Save Document dialog box.)

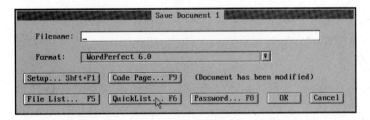

Figure 27.3. Use QuickList to attach the path when saving a file.

Tip: If you have created a long QuickList, you can get to a particular
item quickly by choosing the Name Search option and entering the
first letters of the name you are seeking.

Note: You can create QuickList items for items such as macros,
graphics, and printer files. If you select Update QuickList in the
Location of Files dialog box, when any of these directories are
changed, QuickList is automatically updated to reflect those changes.

by Ted Pederson

QuickFinder

QuickFinder creates a full-text, alphabetical index of every word contained in a group of files and directories, and it can then rapidly search that index to select those documents that match your search criteria.

About QuickFinder

Using QuickFinder is much faster than doing a search, because QuickFinder searches its index and does not have to actually look at every word in every document.

In addition, you can use QuickFinder to group directories and files in special indexes that you can then search for key words to find a specific document or group of documents. For example, for a major project you can index all the files that relate to that project, or you might maintain individual client indexes that could contain all the information relating to a particular client.

Using QuickFinder

Unlike QuickList, which is limited to a single directory path, QuickFinder can include multiple directories and/or filenames in a single index. For example, you can create a MEMOS index that can index all files that end with the extension .MEM, regardless of directory or subdirectory location.

Once you've built a QuickFinder index for a group of files, QuickFinder gives you almost instant gratification.

In a matter of seconds, it can select those few files that contain the words or phrase you are searching for out of a total list of hundreds of files.

 Note: Because QuickFinder indexes are produced in a highly compressed format, you cannot retrieve or edit a QuickFinder index file in WordPerfect or any other word processing program.

When you do a normal search, WordPerfect has to read through every file in your selected group, even if that word is found only in the first file. By contrast, QuickFinder simply refers to its index, selecting only those files that meet the search criteria.

 Note: QuickFinder can index all of the words found in WordPerfect 4.2, 5.0, 5.1, and 6.0 files. QuickFinder will treat any other file formats as ASCII, or plain text, and index only the ASCII words they contain. If you have files in other word processing formats that you want to index, you should first use WordPerfect's conversion program to turn them into WordPerfect files. (See Chapter 30, "Converting File Formats," for information.)

 Tip: You can use QuickFinder to set up an index of all your batch files, enabling you to quickly access and make changes to those files.

If you don't want QuickFinder to index certain files, you can exclude those files, such as those ending in .COM, .EXE or .BK!, when you build a QuickFinder index.

Creating an Index

Before you can use QuickFinder, you must first create one or more indexes. To do this, follow the steps in Procedure 28.1.

Procedure 28.1. Creating your first QuickFinder index.

1. Choose File Manager from the File menu, or press F5.
2. Choose Use QuickFinder, or press F4. The Quickfinder File Indexer dialog box (see Figure 28.1) is displayed.
3. To indicate where to store the Index, choose Setup from the QuickFinder File Indexer, or press Shift+F1. The QuickFinder File Indexes Setup dialog box (see Figure 28.2) is displayed.

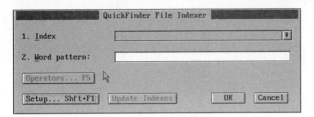

Figure 28.1. The QuickFinder File Indexer dialog box.

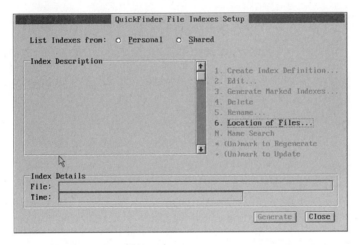

Figure 28.2. The QuickFinder File Indexes Setup dialog box.

4. Choose Location of Files. The QuickFinder File Indexer Setup dialog box (see Figure 28.3) is displayed.

5. Choose Personal Path or Shared Path. This is the location where you will store your index files. A personal path is one that you will use on your computer, while a shared path can apply if you are setting up a common shared index on a network. Now type the path of the directory where you want to store your QuickFinder index; or use Directory Tree (F8) or QuickList (F6) to browse through your available directories.

6. When you have selected where you want to store your QuickFinder index files, choose OK, or press Enter. The QuickFinder Index Files dialog box is displayed.

7. To create your first index, choose Create Index Definition. The Create Index Definition dialog box (see Figure 28.4) is displayed.

8. Type a description to identify the group of files you want to index; for example, "Memos: Jones Project" or "Peter's Documents." When you've done this, press Enter.

383

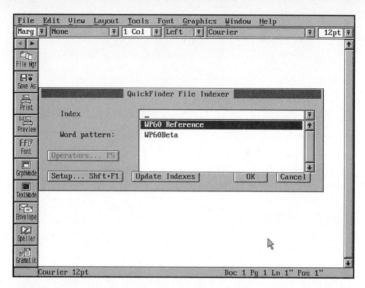

Figure 28.3. The QuickFinder File Indexer Setup dialog box.

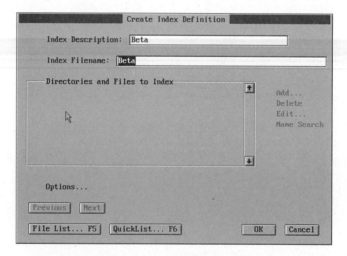

Figure 28.4. The Create Index Definition dialog box.

9. WordPerfect will attempt to create an index name based on your description and will add an .IDX extension. You can accept WordPerfect's name, and press Enter; or manually edit the name and press Enter.

10. Choose Add to begin including the directories that you want to include in this index. The Add QuickFinder Index Directory Pattern dialog box (see Figure 28.5) is displayed.

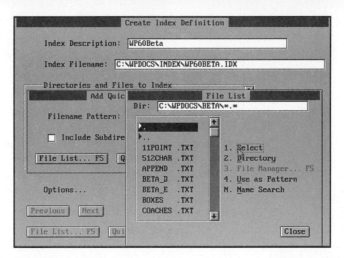

Figure 28.5. Using File List to create a QuickFinder index definition.

11. Type in the directory path that contains the files you want indexed; or select it from the File List (F5) or QuickList (F6).

12. If you want to include the subdirectories of your chosen directory, select Include Subdirectories. For example, you would select this option to index not only the files in C:\WPDOCS, but also those in all of the subdirectories: C:\WPDOCS\LETTERS, C:\WPDOCS\MEMOS, C:\WPDOCS\REPORTS, and so on. If you want to select only certain subdirectories for a parent directory, add each of these individually, as C:\PETER\LETTERS, C:\SUSAN\LETTERS, and so forth, to index the letters files for all users.

13. Choose OK, or press Enter. The Create Index Definition dialog box is displayed.

14. If you want to include additional directories and/or files in your index, repeat Steps 10-13 as many times as necessary.

15. When all directories and/or files are included in your index, click outside of the Directories and Files to Index list box, or press F7.

16. You can choose Options at this point to make any changes to the index options (see Procedure 28.10 for setting QuickFinder index options); or choose OK, or press F7. The QuickFinder File Indexes Setup dialog box is displayed.

17. The new index description will be highlighted, marking it for regeneration.

18. Choose Generate Marked Indexes to begin indexing. An indexing screen is displayed during the indexing progress. When the indexing is complete, the QuickFinder File Indexer dialog box is redisplayed.

19. Choose Close, or press F7 to return to the QuickFinder Files Indexes Setup dialog box. At this point you can create or edit additional indexes; or choose OK, or press F7 to exit QuickFinder and return to your document.

Once you have created an index, you can continue to add directories and files to that index by following the steps in Procedure 28.2.

Procedure 28.2. Adding directories and files to QuickFinder the index.

1. Choose File Manager from the File menu, or press F5. The File Manager dialog box is displayed.

2. Choose Use QuickFinder, or press F4. The QuickFinder File Indexer dialog box is displayed.

3. Choose Setup, or press Shift+F1. The QuickFinder File Indexes Setup dialog box is displayed.

4. Highlight the index you want to change and choose Edit.

5. Choose Add to begin including the directories that you want to include in this index. The Add QuickFinder Index Directory Pattern dialog box is displayed.

6. Type in the directory path that contains the files you want indexed; or select it from the File List (F5) or QuickList (F6).

7. If you also index the subdirectories of your chosen directory, select Include Subdirectories.

8. Choose OK, or press Enter. The Create Index Definition dialog box is displayed.

9. If you want to include additional directories and/or files in your index, repeat Steps 4-7 as many times as necessary.

10. When all directories and/or files are included in your index, click outside of the Directories and Files to Index list box, or press F7.

11. You can choose Options at this point to make any changes to the index options (see "QuickFinder Index Options" later in this chapter for more discussion of the possible options); or choose OK, or press F7. The QuickFinder File Indexes Setup dialog box is displayed.

12. With the new index description highlighted, choose (Un)mark to Regenerate; or enter * to mark it for regeneration; or choose (Un)mark to Update; or enter +. Then choose Generate Marked Indexes to begin the appropriate indexing process. When the indexing is complete, the QuickFinder File Indexer dialog box is displayed.

13. Choose Close, or press F7 to return to the QuickFinder Files Indexes Setup dialog box. At this point you can create or edit additional indexes; or choose OK, or press F7 to exit QuickFinder and return to your document.

Updating and Regenerating Indexes

After you modify the files included in an index, you will want to update or regenerate that index.

It is always faster to update an index than it is to regenerate one, which deletes the old index and rebuilds a new one. However, an updated index requires more disk space, so you will also occasionally want to regenerate the entire index after a major addition of new files or several updates.

You can chose to update or regenerate all your indexes, or you can select certain indexes for updating. You can also choose to update all files in your selected indexes, or you can update only the files that have changed since the last time you updated the index.

To update all files in your selected indexes, follow the steps in Procedure 28.3. To update only the files that have changed since the last update, follow the steps in Procedure 28.4.

Tip: To spare you from having to update indexes that seldom change, the Update Indexes option on the QuickFinder File Indexer dialog box does not apply to indexes which have been edited with the Manual Update Only option.

Procedure 28.3. Updating all indexes.

1. Choose File Manager from the File menu, or press F5. The File Manager dialog box is displayed.
2. Choose Use QuickFinder, or press F4. The QuickFinder dialog box is displayed.
3. Choose Update Indexes. When updating is complete, the QuickFinder File Indexer dialog box is displayed.
4. Choose OK, or press F7 to return to your document.

```
┌─────────── Add QuickFinder Index Directory Pattern ───────────┐
│                                                                │
│   Filename Pattern: [_                                      ]   │
│                                                                │
│      ☐ Include Subdirectories                                  │
│                                                                │
│   [ File List... F5 ] [ QuickList... F6 ]     [ OK ] [ Cancel ] │
└────────────────────────────────────────────────────────────────┘
```

Figure 28.6. Updating QuickFinder indexes.

387

Procedure 28.4. Regenerating or updating individual indexes.

1. Choose File Manager from the File menu, or press F5. The File Manager dialog box is displayed.

2. Choose Use QuickFinder, or press F4. The QuickFinder File Indexer dialog box is displayed.

3. Choose Setup, or press Shift+F1.

4. Select an Index Description in the Index Description list box so that it is highlighted.

5. Choose (Un)mark to Regenerate; or enter * to recreate the index; or choose (Un)mark to Update; or enter + to update the index.

6. Repeat Steps 4 and 5 and mark any other indexes you want to update or regenerate.

7. Choose Generate Marked Indexes to update or regenerate all of the marked indexes.

Editing an Index

You can use Edit to change the directories included in an index. To do this, follow the steps in Procedure 28.5.

Procedure 28.5. Editing QuickFinder.

1. Choose File Manager from the File menu, or press F5. The File Manager dialog box is displayed.

2. Choose Use QuickFinder, or press F4. The QuickFinder dialog box is displayed.

3. Choose Setup, or press Shift+F1. The QuickFinder File Indexes Setup dialog box is displayed.

4. Select an index in the Index Description list box and highlight it.

5. Choose Edit. The QuickFinder Edit Index Definition dialog box (see Figure 28.7) is displayed.

6. You can add, delete, or edit any highlighted directory within the index. Make any changes to the index, then choose OK, or press Enter.

7. Choose OK and Close, or press F7 until you return to your document.

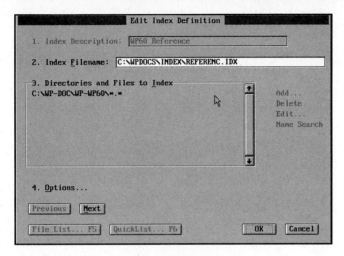

Figure 28.7. The Edit Index Definition dialog box.

Deleting or Renaming an Index

If you created an index for a special project and that project is now complete, you may want to delete that index. Or you may want to rename an index, which also provides the option of moving it to a new directory. To either delete or rename an index, follow the steps in Procedure 28.6.

Procedure 28.6. Deleting or renaming an index.

1. Choose File Manager from the File menu; to press F5. The File Manager dialog box is displayed.

2. Choose Use QuickFinder, or press F4. The QuickFinder dialog box is displayed.

3. Choose Setup, or press Shift+F1. The QuickFinder File Indexer dialog box is displayed.

4. Select an index in the Index Description list box.

5. Choose Delete to delete the index (or Rename if you wish to rename a QuickFinder index), type the new name for the index, then choose OK.

6. Choose Close and OK or press F7 until you return to your document.

389

Searching an Index

Once you have created a QuickFinder index, you can have QuickFinder rapidly scan it and list the files that contain a certain word or pattern. To search a QuickFinder Index, follow the steps in Procedure 28.7.

Procedure 28.7. Searching a QuickFinder index.

1. Choose File Manager from the File menu, or press F5. The File Manager dialog box is displayed.
2. Choose Use QuickFinder, or press F4 to display the QuickFinder File Indexer dialog box.
3. Choose Index, or press an arrow key, then type i.
4. Select the index you want to search from the drop-down list box (see Figure 28.8).

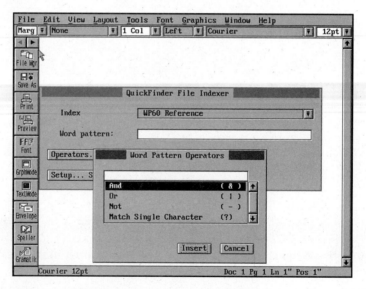

Figure 28.8. The Word Pattern Operators dialog box.

5. Choose Word Pattern.
6. Type a word you want to search for; or, to use a search operator in the word, choose Operators, select an operator, then choose Insert.
7. Choose OK.

Once a successful search is finished, a list of the files that contain the search pattern is displayed (see Figure 28.5). It includes the standard options of the File Manager dialog box.

Using Search Operators

Search operators can be used to create a word pattern in the QuickFinder File Indexer dialog box. To use search operators, follow the steps in Procedure 28.8.

Procedure 28.8. Using search operators.

1. To access these operators, choose Operators from the QuickFinder Files Indexer dialog box, then select one of the following Operators (note that the currently selected level determines where the words must be found). For example, if Line is the level, the words must found in the same line in the document:

   ▲ Word pattern: And (&)

   Example: cat & dog

   Finds: files containing the words *cat* and *dog*.

   ▲ Word pattern: Or (¦)

   Example: cat ¦ dog

   Finds: files that contain the words *cat* or *dog*, or both words.

   ▲ Word pattern: Not (-)

   Example: cat—dog

   Finds: files with the word *cat*, but not *dog*.

   ▲ Word pattern: Match Single Character (?)

   Example: cat?

   Finds: files that contain the word *cat*, plus a single character (for example, *cats*). This is a good way to ensure you have the plurals of the word you are searching for.

   Example: c?n

   Finds: files that contain three-letter words that start with *c* and end with *t* (for example, *cat*, *cot*, and *cut*). Each question mark represents one character. *T??N* would find *town* and *toon*.

   ▲ Word pattern: Match multiple characters (*)

   Example: cat*

   Finds: files containing all variations of words that begin with *cat*, with or without other characters (for example, *cat* and *catastrophe*). As you imagine the possible number of words beginning with *cat*, you can see that care is needed in selecting a wildcard pattern.

Searching an Index that Contains Document Summaries

Additional search operators appear for document summaries if the Index Document Summary or Index Both QuickFinder Index options are selected when the index is generated. An operator is available for every one of the 51 available document summary fields. You can also use the document summary operators to limit a search to a specific document summary field. To use Document Summary search operators, follow the steps in Procedure 28.9.

Procedure 28.9. Using document summary search operators in QuickFinder.

1. Choose File Manager from the File menu, or press F5. The File Manager dialog box is displayed.
2. Choose Use QuickFinder, or press F4. The QuickFinder Files Indexer dialog box is displayed.
3. From the drop-down list box, select an index with the Index Document Summary or Index Both QuickFinder Index options selected.
4. Choose Operators, or press F5.
5. Use the scroll bar or arrow keys to select and highlight the appropriate operator. Then choose Insert to insert it into the Word Pattern box.
6. Type a space in the word pattern box, followed by the text or word pattern you want to find.
7. Choose OK, or press Enter to begin your search.

Tip: If you want to see a list of all of the files in a particular QuickFinder index, use t^* for your word search pattern.

Note: QuickFinder ignores files with .IDX extensions, temporary files, open files, and files with passwords. This speeds up the indexing process. QuickFinder also ignores executable files (for example, those with .EXE and .COM extensions). You can use Exclude Files to specify which files to ignore.

Saving QuickFinder Indexes

QuickFinder indexes are stored as files that use an .IDX extension (for example, MEMOS93.IDX). You can specify the directory where they are stored using the Location of Files option on the QuickFinder File Indexes Setup dialog box. You can also specify a QuickFinder Index directory in Setup: Location of Files.

 Tip: If you back up your documents to floppy disks, you can index those files and place the index itself on the floppy disk.

Speeding Up Indexing

To speed up indexing, you can customize the indexing options, or you can do the following:

▲ Exclude as many file types as you can

▲ Index only document text

▲ Index only WordPerfect documents

▲ Do not include numbers

QuickFinder Setup Options

The QuickFinder Setup Options determine how QuickFinder generates an index. To access the QuickFinder Index Options dialog box, follow the steps in Procedure 28.10.

Procedure 28.10. Setting QuickFinder index options.

1. Choose File Manager from the File menu, or press F5.
2. Choose Use QuickFinder, or press F4 to display the QuickFinder Files Indexer dialog box.
3. Choose Setup, or press Shift+F1 from the QuickFinder File Indexer dialog box. Then choose Create if you are setting options for a new index you are adding; or Edit or set the options for an index you have already created.
4. Now select one or more of the following options:

    ▲ Level. This option controls the level of detail for the indexing. (For example, Line is very specific and takes longer to index; Document is broader and speeds up indexing.)

393

▲ Exclude Files. This option ignores files you specify. (Files with .EXE and .COM extensions are automatically listed.)

▲ Index Document Text. This option indexes only the document text for each document.

▲ Index Document Summary. This option indexes only the Document Summary for each document.

▲ Index Both. This option indexes both the document text and the document summary for all documents.

▲ Index WP Documents Only. This option indexes only WordPerfect documents.

▲ Include Numbers. This option indexes numbers as well as letters.

▲ Manual Update Only. If you select this option, the currently selected index will not be updated when you use the Update Indexes option on the QuickFinder File Indexer dialog box.

5. When you have completed your setup, select OK, or press Enter to return you to your document.

Tip: If you use Document Summary on all or most of your documents, you can index several hundred documents for quick and easy access by setting up a QuickFinder Document Summary that only indexes the document summaries on all of your documents. This way you can quickly search by keywords (author, subject, typist, and so on) in your document summary layout to find almost any file.

by Ted Pederson

Document Summary

When you create document summaries for your files, you don't have to scroll through the text of each file to determine what that file contains. Instead, you are presented with a brief on-screen synopsis of each document.

You can use Document Summary to create a general overview of a document, helping you to organize and quickly locate your documents based on keywords and abstracts.

When you create a document summary, the selected information is saved as part of the document. The summary information is visible in the Document Summary dialog box or in File Manager. A document summary can also be printed, or, if you like, you can save the information in a summary as a separate document file.

At any point when you are in the Document Summary dialog box, you can:

▲ Edit the information in the selected fields

▲ Add or delete fields

▲ Print the Document Summary

▲ Save the Document Summary as a seperate file

▲ Extract information from your current document to automate the process

▲ Change the Document Summary set up

Each of these options is discussed in detail in this chapter.

Note: If you create a summary for a document, that summary is displayed. You can then select an option to look at the contents of the file in File Manager.

Creating a Document Summary

To create a document summary for the current document you are working on, follow the steps in Procedure 29.1.

Procedure 29.1. Creating a document summary.

1. Choose **Summary** from the File menu, or press Shift+F8, 4, 4. The Document Summary dialog box (see Figure 29.1) appears.

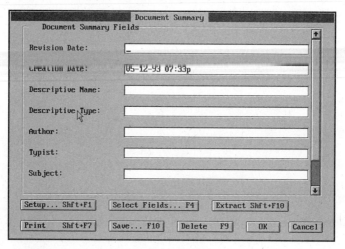

Figure 29.1. The Document Summary dialog box.

2. Choose **Extract**, or press Shift+F10. Then choose **Yes** to automatically fill in some of the summary fields—Author, Typist, Abstract, and Subject—by extracting this information from the document.

3. Use the scroll bar or arrow keys to move through the summary fields. When a field is highlighted, you can enter or edit the information in that field. Repeat this step as often as necessary to make all your changes.

4. Choose **OK** and **Close**, or press **Enter** until you return to your document.

Tip: WordPerfect can search for subject text when it extracts information from your document. For example, many memos or letters include a line that begins with "RE:" or "Subject" to indicate the subject of the document. If you specify "RE:"as the subject text, WordPerfect places the text immediately following "RE:" in the Subject summary field when it extracts information from your document.

Customizing a Document Summary

You can include a wide variety of information in a document summary. The WordPerfect default summary list includes these items:

- ▲ Descriptive Name
- ▲ Descriptive Type
- ▲ Subject
- ▲ Creation Date
- ▲ Revision Date
- ▲ Author
- ▲ Typist
- ▲ Abstract
- ▲ Account
- ▲ Keywords

Tip: You can create macros to automate the process of updating document summaries. For example, if you are responsible for checking documents, you can create a macro that will enter your name and the current date in the Checked By field. If you maintain standard client information in documents (contact person, telephone number, and so on) you can automate the insertion of this information in the document summary by client-oriented macros.

There are 51 possible fields to select from for your documents. While you cannot edit the names of these fields, you can configure them for your own particular needs.

Document Summary Fields:

Abstract	Language
Account	Mail Stop
Address	Matter
Attachments	Office
Author	Owner
Authorization	Project
Bill To	Publisher
Blind Copy	Purpose
Carbon Copy	Received From
Category	Recorded By
Checked By	Recorded Date
Client	Reference
Comments	Revision Date
Creation Date	Revision Notes
Date Completed	Revision Number
Descriptive Name	Section
Descriptive Type	Security
Destination	Sound
Disposition	Status
Division	Subject
Document Number	Telephone Number
Editor	Typist
Forward To	Version Date
Group	Version Notes
Keywords	Version Number

Tip: If you use a few common fields for all your documents (such as subject, author, and abstract) and other fields for only certain types of documents (bill to, security, and so on), it is a good idea to move the common fields to the top of the document summary screen. This way you can quickly fill these in and ignore scrolling down to the less used fields.

To customize the Summary Fields to your own preference, follow the steps in Procedure 29.2.

Procedure 29.2. Customizing document summary fields.

1. Choose Summary from the **F**ile menu or press Shift+F8, 4, 4.

2. Choose Select Fields or press F4. The Select Summary Fields dialog box appears.

3. The Summary Fields on the left are those fields that are currently included in the document summary. The Available Fields on the right list all the possible fields that can be selected. Those marked with an * are the ones that are currently included in the summary fields.

5. If you want to build a new document summary setup from scratch, you can use Clear to clear all of the currently selected summary fields.

6. Click on either list or press Tab to move to the right list and Shift+Tab to move to the left. Use the scroll bar or arrow keys to move through the lists. You can also use Name Search to quickly navigate the lists on either the right or left side by typing in the first letters of the name. When you have selected an item, it will be highlighted and you can peform one of the following tasks:

   ▲ **Add** includes those marked items from the Available Fields list in the Summary.

   ▲ **Move** enables you to rearrange the position of the chosen fields in the summary fields list into any order you want.

   ▲ **Remove** enables you to remove the currently highlighted item from the summary fields list.

Note that if you save this setup, the summaries for all documents created from this point on will use this setup as the default.

Saving a Document Summary as a Document

While you can print out a copy of a Document Summary, there are ocassions when you may want to send a document summary as a separate file. For example, if you have a series of letters dealing with a certain client, you can save the document summaries of those letters (which may be quite lengthy) and then send only the smaller summary files to the appropriate persons by electronic mail (e-mail).

To save a document summary as a separate file, follow the steps in Procedure 29.3.

Procedure 29.3. Saving a summary as a separate document file.

1. Choose Summary from the **F**ile menu, or press Shift+F8, 4, 4.

2. Choose Save, or press F10, then choose Yes.

3. Type a filename in the Filename entry field.
4. Choose OK and Close, or press Enter until you return to your document.

Printing a Document Summary

Sometimes you may simply want to print out a copy of the document summary of the file in which you are working. To print a document summary, follow the steps in Procedure 29.4.

Procedure 29.4. Printing a summary.
1. Choose Summary from the File menu, or press Shift+F8, 4, 4.
2. Choose Print or press Shift+F7. This displays the Print Document Summary dialog box.
3. Choose to begin printing.
4. Choose OK to begin printing. Then choose Close or press Enter until you return to your document.

Deleting a Document Summary

You can delete a document summary entirely, by following the steps in Procedure 29.5.

Procedure 29.5. Deleting a document summary.
1. Choose Summary from the File menu or press Shift+F8, 4, 4.
2. Choose Delete or press F9 then choose Yes.
3. Choose OK and Close or press Enter until you return to your document.

Document Summary Options

You can automate several Document Summary Tasks with Setup Options. To do this, follow the steps in Procedure 29.6.

Procedure 29.6. Document Summary Set Up Options.
1. Choose Summary from the File menu, or press Shift+F8, 4, 4.
2. Choose Setup, or press Shift+F1. The Document Summary Setup dialog box will appear.

3. Choose from the following options as desired:

   ▲ **Subject Search Text**. Specifies text to appear in the Subject summary field. (See "Subject Search Text" later in this section.) RE: is the default, but you can change this to SUBJECT:, TO:, or anthing else. WordPerfect will include the text immediately following the keyword into the summary.

   ▲ **Default Descriptive Type**. Specifies text to appear in the Descriptive Type summary field. If you use the Descriptive Type field in your summary and most of your documents are a certain kind (such as memo, letter, or invoice), you can have WordPerfect fill in the field for you with a default name, such as MEMO, LETTER, or INVOICE.

   ▲ **Create Summary on Exit/Save**. This option will display the Document Summary dialog box when you save or exit a document, which is a way to ensure that a document summary is always created.

4. When you have completed selecting your options, choose OK and Close, or press F7 until you return to your document.

For an author, document summaries are a great method of tracking your submissions by keeping those statistics as a part of the document itself. Similarly, you can use document summaries to maintain an abstract and status of the chapters for a book.

For any user, document summaries provide an excellent indexing tool. For example if you maintain a single floppy disk of document summaries saved as files, you can quickly look through several hundred documents on a single disk—while the actual documents may occupy several boxes of backup disks.

30

by Ted Pederson

Converting File Formats

Documents created in other applications do not share the same file format as WordPerfect 6.0. They are essentially written in a foreign language. Thus, before they can be used in WordPerfect they must translated into WordPerfect 6.0's language.

WordPerfect 6.0 has a built-in translating utility that can convert files that were created in most applications.You can also use this process in reverse to convert the WordPerfect files you create into other popular formats. This is a very handy feature since it is likely that you will occasionally have to work with files that must be imported into other applications.

About Conversion

Conversion is a very powerful tool, but be aware that the imported document will not always look exactly the same as the original. Some features may vary between programs, particularly advanced formatting elements like tables and styles. For the best results, as a general rule of thumb you should keep the formatting in your documents simple.

Tip: If you know you will be converting a document file, try to use only the formatting features that are available in both WordPerfect and the other application. It is a good idea to avoid using Styles and other features that will be difficult to translate successfully into another format.

Converting Files Created in Other Versions of WordPerfect

If you have a document created in WordPerfect 5.0 or 5.1 for DOS or WordPerfect 5.1 or 5.2 for Windows that you want converted into WordPerfect 6.0 for DOS, simply open or retrieve it as you would any other file. It will be automatically converted into a WordPerfect 6.0 document.

Note: WordPerfect 4.2 files cannot be directly opened or retrieved and first must be converted as though they were created in a different application.

Formats WordPerfect Recognizes

WordPerfect 6.0 can convert files that were created in any of these following formats:

AmiPro (Windows Versions 1.2—3.0)
ASCII text (CR/LF or standard)
BMP Graphics (Bitmap)
CGM Graphics
CompuServe GIF
DisplayWrite (Versions 4.0—5.0)
DOS Delimited Text
ESP (Encapsulated Postscript)
Excel (Versions 2.1—4.0)
IBM DCA FFT
IBM DCA RFT
HLPG (Hewlett-Packard Plotter)
Kermit (7-bit transfer)

Lotus PIC Graphics
Lotus 1-2-3 (Versions 1A—3.1)
MacIntosh PICT
Micrographic Graphics
Microsoft Windows Write
Microsoft Word (DOS Versions 4.0—5.5)
Microsoft Word for Windows (Versions 1.0—2.0b)
PCX (PC Paintbrush Graphics)
PlanPerfect (Versions 3.0—5.1)
Quattro Pro (Versions 3.0—4.0)
Quattro Pro for Windows (Version 1.0)
RTF (Rich Text Format)
TIFF (Tagged Image File Format)
Truevision TGA
WMF (Windows MetaFile)
WordPerfect (MacIntosh Versions 2.0—2.1)
WordPerfect (DOS Version 4.2)
WordPerfect Graphics (WPG Versions 1.0—2.0)
WordStar (Versions 3.3—6.0)

Importing a File in a Different Format

If you need to import a file created in another format into a WordPerfect 6.0 document, follow the steps in Procedure 30.1.

Procedure 30.1. Converting a file into WordPerfect 6.0 format.

1. Choose **O**pen or **R**etrieve from the File menu, or press Shift+F10. The Open Document dialog box (see Figure 30.1) is displayed.

2. Type the name of the file you want to convert, or select it from the **File Manager** (F5) or QuickList (F6). Then choose OK or press Enter. If this is not a WordPerfect 5.0, 5.1, or 5.2 document (these are automatically converted as though they were WordPerfect 6.0 files), the File Format dialog box (see Figure 30.2) is displayed.

3. WordPerfect determines the proper format of the document you are trying to import. If the choice is correct, go to Step 4; otherwise, use the scroll bar or arrow keys to move through the list until you highlight the originating format of the file you want to open.

4. With the import file format highlighted, choose **S**elect or press Enter. The document will be converted, and you can then edit the document as usual.

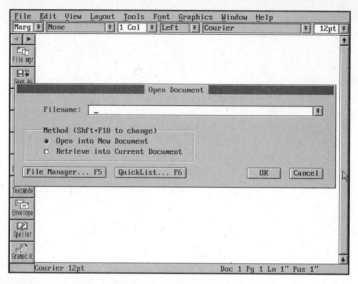

Figure 30.1. The Open Document dialog box.

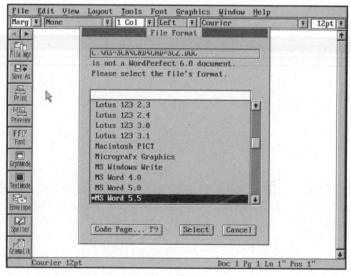

Figure 30.2. The File Format dialog box.

Caution: Converted documents are saved in WordPerfect 6.0 format unless they are converted ASCII files. WordPerfect saves converted ASCII files as ASCII files by default. As soon as you import a document created in another format, it is a good idea to save the file with a new name so that you do not overwrite the original file.

Importing Spreadsheets

Use the DOS Delimited Text format to retrieve spreadsheet or database files into a WordPerfect merge data file. The DOS Delimited Text format contains delimiters, or characters, that mark the beginning and end of each field or record.

Saving Documents in Formats

You can save your documents in WordPerfect 4.2, 5.0, 5.1, or 5.2 format when you want to edit them using a previous version of WordPerfect. In addition, some software applications will accept WordPerfect files only in these older formats. You can also save the file in other formats that can be directly read into a different application that cannot import a WordPerfect document.

Caution: Keep in mind that anything in a WordPerfect 6.0 document that uses features new to WordPerfect 6.0 will be lost when the document is converted to a previous version format. For example, if you use the paragraph first line indent feature, the indent will lost when you go back to WordPerfect 5.1 format.

To convert a WordPerfect file into another format that is supported by WordPerfect's conversion utilities, follow the steps in Procedure 30.2.

Procedure 30.2. Converting a WordPerfect file into Another Format.

1. Choose Save As from the File menu or press F10. The Save Document dialog box (see Figure 30.3) will be displayed.
2. Type a filename for the converted file, or use File List (F5) or QuickList (F6) to select a path for the file, then enter the name.
3. Choose Format. The drop-down format menu will be displayed.
4. Use the scroll bar or arrow keys to highlight the file format you want to use from the drop-down list.

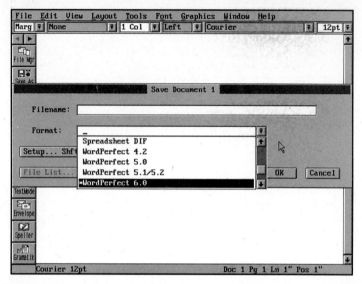

Figure 30.3 The Save Document dialog box.

5. Choose OK or press Enter. The document will be saved in the new name and in the selected format.

Tip: If you use WordPerfect to edit your CONFIG.SYS file or AUTOEXEC.BAT file (or other special files with a .BAT or .TXT extension), save the files in ASCII Text (Standard) format.

Caution: If you save a file as a WordPerfect document, DOS can no longer recognize it as a batch or system file. If you do accidentally save a batch or system file as a WordPerfect file, you can reopen the file back into WordPerfect, then resave it in ASCII Text (Standard) format.

Note: Some of the characters in the WordPerfect character sets are not supported in other applications. If a character is not supported in the file format you are converting your document into, it will be replaced by a space character.

Changing the Code Page

A code page is a table that defines which ASCII character set is used in a document. Different ASCII character sets are used for different languages. Each code page contains the same standard set of ASCII characters (the first 128 characters of each set are the same), but each code will have an additional set of national language characters. When you save a document, WordPerfect gives you the option to change the code page, and thus the character set, for the document for use in another language. Note that changing the code page will not make WordPerfect display or print in these languages, which is determined by your hardware (BIOS) system setup. This is a specialized feature and would only be used if you're translating documents between different foreign languages.

To change the code page when opening a document, follow the steps in Procedure 30.3; to change the code page when saving a document, follow the steps in Procedure 30.4.

Procedure 30.3. Changing the code page while opening a document.

1. From the File Format dialog box, choose Code Page. The Code Page dialog box (Figure 30.4) is displayed.

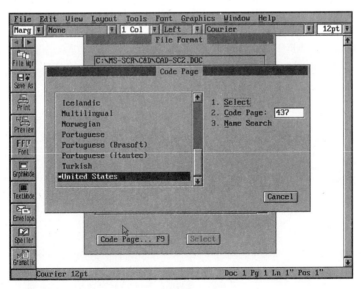

Figure 30.4. The Code Page dialog box.

2. Use the scroll bar or arrow keys to highlight the code page you want, then choose Select.

Procedure 30.4. Changing the code page while saving a document.

1. Choose Save As from the File menu or press F10. The Save Document dialog box is displayed.

2. Choose Code Page, or press F9. The Code Page dialog box is displayed.

3. Highlight the desired code page and choose Select.

Using ConvertPerfect to Convert Several Files at Once

You can convert only one file at a time when using WordPerfect's built-in file conversion. If you want to convert several files at once, use ConvertPerfect, the stand-alone conversion utility that was installed with WordPerfect 6.0. To use ConvertPerfect, follow the steps in Procedure 30.5.

Procedure 30.5. Using ConvertPerfect.

1. From the DOS prompt type CV+Enter. (If WordPerfect is not in your path, you will have to use Change Directory (CD) to change to your WP60 directory.) The ConvertPerfect opening screen (see Figure 30.5) is displayed.

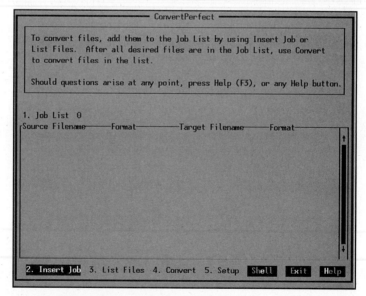

Figure 30.5. ConvertPerfect's opening screen.

2. If this is the first time you are using ConvertPerfect, you should select 5, Setup. The Setup dialog box (see Figure 30.6) is displayed.

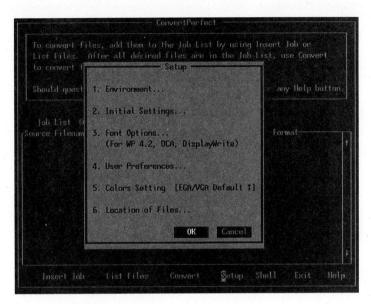

Figure 30.6. The Setup dialog box.

3. From the Setup dialog box, select one or more options:

▲ **Environment** will let you set the several options that determine your standard operating environment: whether you want the computer to beep at you when it completes a task, the default source, and target formats (see Figure 30.7). There is no written documentation with ConvertPerfect, but you can use F1 to get more information on any highlighted item.

▲ **Initial Settings** allows you to set up delimiters for spreadsheets, code page defaults, and operating toggle switches to verify source file format, ask for a confirmation when you are about to overwrite a file, and run all conversions in a batch or stop between each file conversion (see Figure 30.8).

▲ **Font Options** allows you to set your computer to use the WordPerfect 4.2 or DCA/DisplayWrite character sets (see Figure 30.9).

▲ **User Preferences** allows you to set up page layout, margins, decide whether to underline spaces or tabs, and convert soft page breaks and other elements.

▲ **Color Settings** allows you to change the default color settings.

411

▲ **Location of Files** lets you set the default directories for your source or target files. Note that you can change this during conversion by selecting alternate paths for either your source or target files.

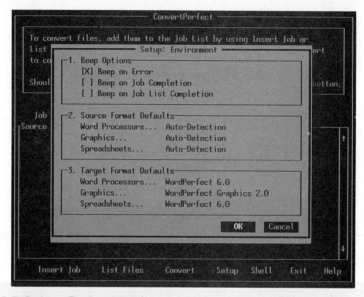

Figure 30.7. Setup: Environment.

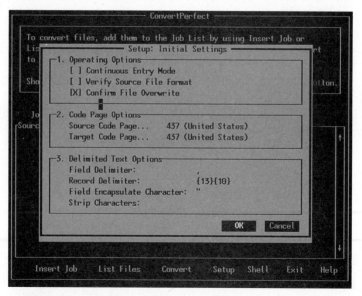

Figure 30.8. Setup: Initial Settings.

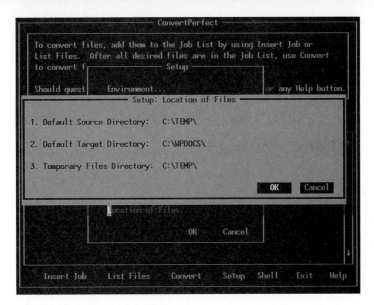

Figure 30.9. Setup: Location of Files.

When you have made any desired changes, select OK or press Enter to return to the Setup menu. Then select OK or press Enter to return to the ConvertPerfect main menu.

4. Choose 2, Insert Job. The Insert Job dialog box (see Figure 30.10) is displayed.

5. Enter the Source Filename, changing the input path if you are not using the default file location.

6. Accept the default Source File Format, or use the scroll bar or arrow keys to highlight and select a different one.

7. Enter the Target Filename, changing the output path if you are not using the default file location.

8. Accept the default Target File Format, or use the scroll bar or arrow keys to highlight and select a different format.

9. Repeat Steps 5-8 to add all the files you want to convert. The Job List count will display the number of files to be converted. When you have selected all your files, select OK to return to the ConvertPerfect main menu.

10. Select 4, Convert to begin the conversion process.

11. When the conversions are complete, select Exit or press F7 to exit the program and return to the DOS prompt.

413

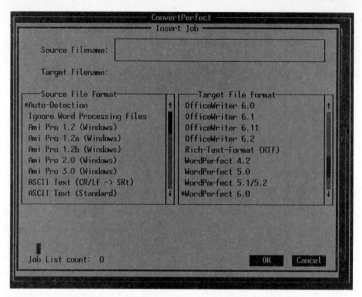

Figure 30.10. The ConvertPerfect Insert Job dialog box.

Tip: If you will be converting a lot of files between WordPerfect 6.0 and another format (for example, WordPerfect 5.1), you may want to use ConvertPerfect to do all of these conversions at the end of a working session.

by Ted Pederson

Exchanging Information Between Applications

Although you may be devoted to WordPerfect, there will be times when you must work with people who are using different applications. In this chapter, we will deal with some of the practical aspects of exchanging information with other word processing programs, spreadsheet programs, and database programs.

Exchanging Information with Another Word Processor

Chapter 30, "Converting File Formats," outlined the steps for importing or exporting a document in another format.

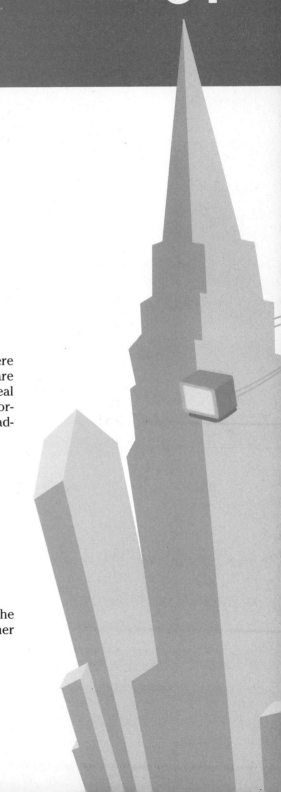

Tip: If you are going to do a lot of work with someone who is using a different word processing program, such as Microsoft Word, you may want to set up a pair of macros that will set the Save as format default to that word processor when you begin your session, then another macro to reset back to your normal default when you end the session.

Exchanging Information with a Spreadsheet

One of the more powerful new features in WordPerfect 6.0 is its ability to dynamically link a document with a spreadsheet created in another application. This allows you to include elements maintained in a spreadsheet program, like an address file, sales figures, or a project timeline. Then, in a WordPerfect status report, you can have that document automatically updated, say on a weekly basis, as new information is entered into the spreadsheet to reflect changes in the projected timeline.

Spreadsheet Import and Link

Spreadsheet Import and Link will copy information from a spreadsheet file into a WordPerfect document. (See Figures 31.2 and 31.3 for an illustration of an example of a spreadsheet imported into a WordPerfect document as a table and as text.)

You can import a spreadsheet into graphics boxes, headers, footers, footnotes, endnotes, text boxes, and other editing windows. In fact, you can import a spreadsheet into everything but a style. WordPerfect imports as much of the spreadsheet as will fit into that box or window.

You can import a complete spreadsheet or select a range in a spreadsheet. A spreadsheet range is defined as a block of cells, and the effect is similar to importing a marked block of text from a word processing document.

In a two-dimensional spreadsheet, a range is defined by an upper-left cell and a lower-right cell. A colon or period is used to separate the two cell names (or addresses). (See Figure 31.1 for an example of a range selected in a spreadsheet; in this instance, the range is the month of February.)

A three-dimensional spreadsheet file can include several separate spreadsheets. Consequently, in a range definition for three-dimensional spreadsheets, each cell address also includes a letter to indicate which sheet the cell is from. A colon is used to separate the spreadsheet letter from the cell address. A period is used to

416

separate the two cell names. You can import all sheets in a three-dimensional spreadsheet file or select only those sheets that you want to import. Each sheet will be imported as a separate table.

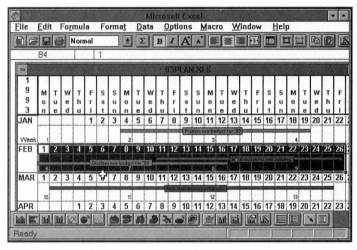

Figure 31.1. Spreadsheet range blocked.

Many spreadsheet programs also let you assign a name to a range. These names can also be used to easily import a range of cells from a spreadsheet.

Importable Spreadsheet Formats

Currently, you can import and link files from the following file formats:

- ▲ PlanPerfect (Versions 3.0 through 5.1)
- ▲ Lotus 1-2-3 (Versions 1A, 2.01, 2.3, 2.4, 3.0, 3.1)
- ▲ Excel (Versions 2.1, 3.0, 4.0)
- ▲ Quattro Pro (Versions 3.0 and 4.0)
- ▲ Quattro Pro for Windows 1.0
- ▲ Spreadsheet DIF

Note: WordPerfect 6.0's spreadsheet import is different from the normal file import, which was discussed in Chapter 30. Anything converted using the file format conversion will be treated only as text and cannot be imported as a table.

Importing and Linking

Importing a spreadsheet copies information from the spreadsheet file only once, whereas linking a spreadsheet lets you update the spreadsheet information in your WordPerfect document to keep it current with any changes in the spreadsheet.

Importing A Spreadsheet as a Table

To match the original spreadsheet as closely as possible, import the spreadsheet as a table. You do not need to create a table in your document before importing the spreadsheet. If you select Import as Table from a Spreadsheet dialog box, WordPerfect creates a WordPerfect table that matches the spreadsheet's format as closely as possible and inserts the spreadsheet into it.

When you import a spreadsheet into an existing table, WordPerfect inserts the spreadsheet down and to the right. WordPerfect inserts as much of the spreadsheet as will fit into the table. (See Figure 31.2 for an example of a spreadsheet imported into a WordPerfect table.)

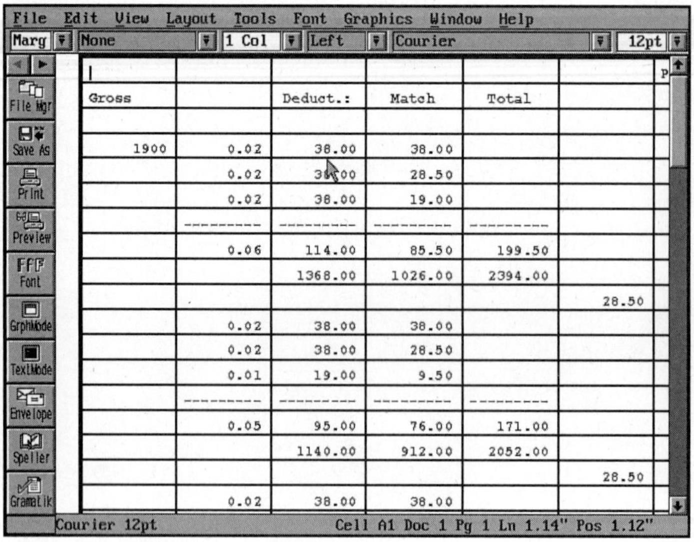

Figure 31.2. A spreadsheet imported into a table.

Caution: WordPerfect only displays as much of the table as can fit in the width of your document. Also, WordPerfect does not import more than 64 columns of a spreadsheet.

 Caution: For spreadsheet links, any changes you make to the table in the WordPerfect file will be overwritten when the link is updated.

Importing A Spreadsheet as Text

When you import a spreadsheet file as text, WordPerfect attempts to preserve left and right justification and to reproduce the original format of the spreadsheet as closely as possible. The cells from the spreadsheet are separated by tabs. Rows are separated by hard returns. WordPerfect creates special tab settings for the table and the cells appear on the page as columns at those tab settings. (See Figure 31.3 for an example of a spreadsheet imported into WordPerfect as text.)

File	Edit	View	Layout	Tools	Font	Graphics	Window	Help
Marg	None		1 Col	Left	Courier			12pt

						P06: K401
Gross			Deduct.:	Match	Total	
	1900		0.02	38.00	38.00	0.06
199.50		2394	0.02	38.00	28.50	0.05
171.00		2052	0.02	38.00	19.00	0.04
142.50		1710				0.03
109.25		1311				
			0.06	114.00	85.50	199.50 0.0276.00
912						
456				1368.00	1026.00	2394.00 0.0138.00
						28.50
			0.02	38.00	38.00	
			0.02	38.00	28.50	
			0.01	19.00	9.50	
			0.05	95.00	76.00	171.00
				1140.00	912.00	2052.00
						28.50
			0.02	38.00	38.00	
			0.02	38.00	28.50	
			0	0.00	0.00	
			0.04	76.00	66.50	142.50
				912.00	798.00	1710.00
						33.25

Courier 12pt   Doc 1 Pg 1 Ln 1" Pos 1"

Figure 31.3. A spreadsheet imported as text.

To import or link a spreadsheet into a WordPerfect document, follow the steps in Procedure 31.1. Whether you choose to import or link a spreadsheet depends on how you intend to use the information. Importing a spreadsheet is a one-time-only

419

process, while linking allows you to update your WordPerfect document as changes are made to the spreadsheet. You might choose to link a spreadsheet that contains budget figures so you can produce a standard weekly report that always contains the latest budget changes. Or, you might link that part of a payroll spreadsheet that contains names and addresses to produce a current office roster.

Procedure 31.1. Importing or linking a spreadsheet.

1. Place the insertion point in your document at the point where you want to import the spreadsheet.

2. Choose Spreadsheet from the Tools menu, or press Alt+F7, 5. The spreadsheet drop down menu is displayed.

3. Choose Import to import the spreadsheet once. By selecting this option, any future changes in the spreadsheet program will not be reflected in your WordPerfect document. Alternatively, you can choose Create Link to create a dynamic link that will enable WordPerfect to update the spreadsheet information, keeping it current with any changes that are made in the spreadsheet.

4. In the Filename entry field, type the filename of the spreadsheet file you want to import or link, then press Enter. Once you have selected a filename, the range is displayed as <Spreadsheet> in the Range entry field and the default is to import the entire spreadsheet. To import only part of the spreadsheet, you can indicate a range of cells in the Range entry field. You can identify the range either by its cell address or by a name.

5. Now choose OK to select the entire spreadsheet; or choose Range to display the Edit Spreadsheet Link dialog box. Type in the range address or range name; or choose Range List to list the names of the ranges in the spreadsheet, select a name from the Range List, then choose Insert. If you select a range by name, WordPerfect displays the range address in the Reference box.

6. Choose OK or press Enter.

7. Select Import as Table or Import as Text to indicate how you want the spreadsheet imported.

8. If you selected Import in Step 3 above, choose Import to import the spreadsheet; or, if you selected Create Link in Step 3, choose Link and Import to import the spreadsheet and create the link; or choose Link to bring in only the link codes. Note that if you choose Link, you will later have to use update to bring in the spreadsheet itself. You might use link only if you are preparing a document and want to include spreadsheet information but know that the spreadsheet will be updated later that day.

When you link a spreadsheet, WordPerfect inserts comment codes, which show information about the link as well as where the link begins and ends. The comments are never printed. You can also choose to hide them on-screen.

Redefining a Link

After you create a link, you can edit the information that determines which part of the spreadsheet is imported, including the filename, range of cells, and type of import (text or table). To redefine a spreadsheet link, follow the steps in Procedure 31.2.

Procedure 31.2. Redefining a spreadsheet link.

1. Place the insertion point inside the link.
2. Choose **S**preadsheet from the **T**ools menu, then choose Edit Link, or press Alt+F7, 5, 3. The Edit Spreadsheet Link dialog box is displayed.
3. Make any changes you want to the dialog information.
4. Choose Link and Import to import the spreadsheet and create the link; or choose Link to bring in only the link codes. You will then have to update to bring in the spreadsheet.

Updating a Linked Spreadsheet Upon Document Retrieval

You can have WordPerfect automatically update the linked spreadsheet to match the original spreadsheet each time you open a document by following the steps in Procedure 31.3.

Procedure 31.3. Automatically updating a linked spreadsheet.

1. Choose **S**preadsheet from the **T**ools menu, then choose Link Options, or press Alt+F7, 5, 4. The Spreadsheet Link Options dialog box is displayed.
2. Select Update on **R**etrieve. Then choose OK or press Enter.

You can also select to manually update the linked spreadsheet by following the steps in Procedure 31.4.

Procedure 31.4. Updating a linked spreadsheet manually.

1. Choose **S**preadsheet from the **T**ools menu, then choose Link Options, or press Alt+F7, 5, 4. The Spreadsheet Link Options dialog box is displayed.
2. Choose Update All Links. WordPerfect updates the linked data throughout the document to match the data in the spreadsheet.

To display or hide the spreadsheet link codes, follow the steps in Procedure 31.5.

Procedure 31.5. Displaying/hiding link codes.

1. Choose **S**preadsheet from the **Tools** menu, then choose Link Options or press Alt+F7, 4.

2. Select or deselect Show Link Codes, then choose OK or press Enter.

(See Figure 31.4 for an example of how link codes appear in your document if they are displayed.)

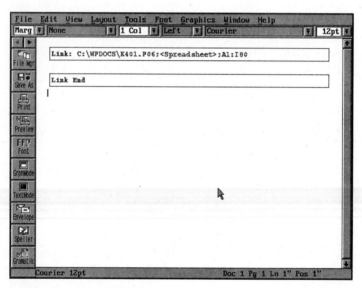

Figure 31.4. Link codes displayed.

 Tip: You can delete a link without removing the spreadsheet by deleting the [Link] or [Link End] code.

 Tip: If you use a spreadsheet application to create a rolodex type of name and address base, you can then link it dynamically to a WordPerfect document, so that any changes you make to the spreadsheet file will update the WordPerfect document. This is an ideal way to maintain an office roster or customer address base.

422

> **Caution:** If you import a password-protected spreadsheet, you must first use the spreadsheet software to remove the password from the spreadsheet file. The only exception to this is the WordPerfect Corporation's PlanPerfect spreadsheet program, which will prompt you for the password during the import process.

Spreadsheet Size Constraints

Because WordPerfect limits the number of table and text columns you can import, you can use the following suggestions to fit a spreadsheet into your document:

▲ Reduce the column widths in the spreadsheet program so that more information will fit onto a page.

▲ Just before the insertion point where you intend to import the spreadsheet, select a smaller font. Again this will allow you to put more information on the page. (Remember to change back to your original font after the spreadsheet has been imported or the rest of your document will be in the smaller typeface.)

▲ Reduce the margins in your WordPerfect document.

▲ If you have imported the spreadsheet file as a table, size the table to fit between the left and right margins.

▲ Choose a landscape paper size for printing (if your printer has that capability).

Exchanging Information with a Database

WordPerfect cannot dynamically link WordPerfect to a database as it can with a spreadsheet.

But most major spreadsheets will allow the import of database files into a spreadsheet. If you do this, you can link the resulting spreadsheet to your WordPerfect document.

Graphics, Lines, Borders, and Fills

by Carolyn Woodie

Retrieving Graphic Images into WordPerfect Documents

After you have mastered text documents in WordPerfect 6.0, you can enhance your documents with graphics. You may want to include some of the WordPerfect graphic images with your text. Or, you may want to use a table of data, a pie chart from your spreadsheet program, or even a scanned drawing. Using graphics in your documents strengthens the message of your text. If you have used WordPerfect 5.0 and 5.1, you will be happy with the ease of retrieving and editing graphics in WordPerfect 6.0.

WordPerfect Images

As with WordPerfect Versions 5.0 and 5.1, WordPerfect 6.0 includes graphic images that may be used in your documents. The graphic image files are usually copied onto your computer when the WordPerfect software is installed. Graphic files end with .WPG. (See Figure 32.1 for a directory of the graphic images included in WordPerfect 6.0.) You can also use graphic files from other programs, scanned files, and other third-party clip art files. (See "Other Graphic Formats" later in this chapter.)

Figure 32.1. WordPerfect 6.0 graphic images.

 Caution: You can use the graphic (.WPG) files from WordPerfect 5.0 and 5.1 in WordPerfect 6.0 with no conversion required. However, at present, you cannot use WordPerfect 6.0 graphics (.WPG) directly in previous versions of WordPerfect or WordPerfect Presentations. The WordPerfect 6.0 graphic files can be converted into the earlier graphics formats. (See "Exporting Into Other Graphic Formats" later in this chapter.)

WordPerfect uses boxes to control and position the graphics. There are eight different predefined box styles:

- ▲ Figure Box—normally used for figures or text.
- ▲ Table Box—normally used for figures or text.
- ▲ Text Box—normally used for figures or text.
- ▲ User Box—normally used for figures or text.
- ▲ Equation Box—normally used to create mathematical equations. (See Chapter 53, "Equation Editor," for more information on this feature.)
- ▲ Button Box—normally used as a Hypertext link.
- ▲ Watermark Image Box—normally used to create a watermark on a page. A watermark creates a grey-shaded figure or text and the text of the document flows overtop of the image.

▲ Inline Equation Box—normally used to create a mathematical equation that would appear in the same line with text in the document. (See Chapter 53 for more information on this feature.)

Although each style of graphic box has a specific name, the use of the box is not confined to the name of the box style. You can use any graphic box style to hold graphic images or text. Since the Equation Box and Inline Equation Box are usually reserved for mathematical equations, we will work with the other six box styles. (See examples of the predefined graphic box styles in Figures 32.2 through 32.7.)

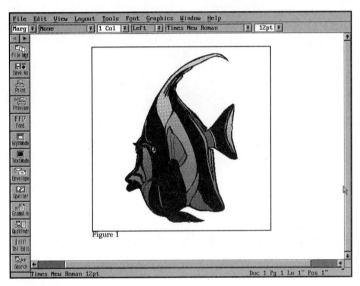

Figure 32.2. The Figure Box.

Note the differences in borders, position of captions, shading, and the spacing between the border and the object within the graphic box. Even though several of the box styles do not have borders, they are still boxes. You can select the box style with the settings you need (see "Creating a Graphics Box" later in this chapter). You may also edit the borders, caption, shading, and many other details of a graphic box to suit your specific needs. (See "Editing a Graphics Box," in Chapter 33, "Editing a Graphics Box," for more information.)

Note: The only time it is necessary to choose one particular box style is if you require a list of the location of the particular boxes in your document. For example, in a large document with many figures, you could provide a list of the page number of each figure. You might call this a table of contents of your figures. WordPerfect produces this list automatically using the List function (see "Creating a List of Graphics Boxes" in Chapter 36, "Graphics Box Captions and Numbering").

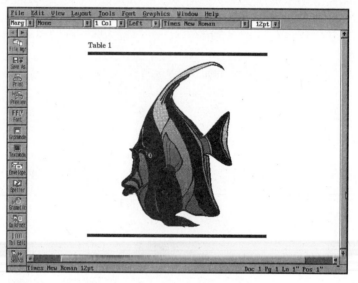

Figure 32.3. The Table Box.

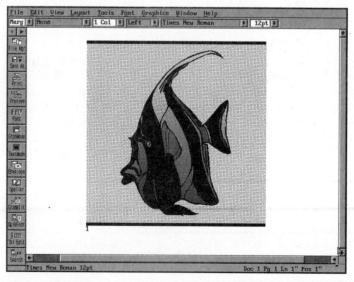

Figure 32.4. The Text Box.

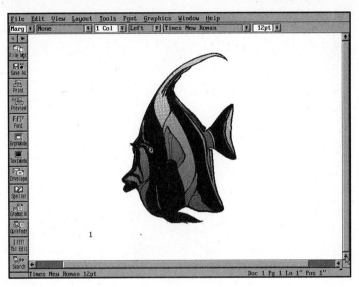

Figure 32.5. The User Box.

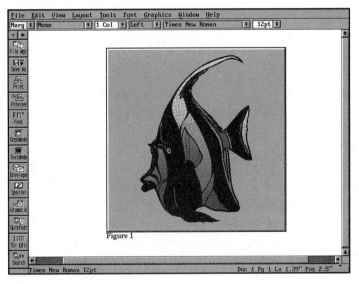

Figure 32.6. The Button Box.

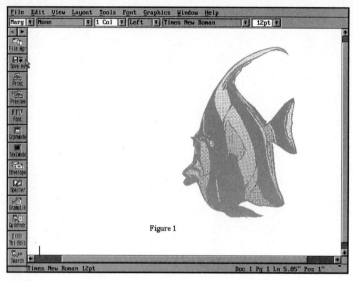

Figure 32.7. The Watermark Box.

Placing an Image into a Document

There are two ways to place a WordPerfect graphic image into your document. The easiest method is to retrieve an image file directly into the document. However, as you become more proficient with graphics, you may want to use the second method, creating a graphics box, so you have creative control over the style and placement of your graphics box before it is created.

Retrieving an Image File

You can easily retrieve an image file into your document. The graphics file may be on your hard drive or a disk.

Procedure 32.1. Retrieving a graphic image file.

1. Choose Graphics or press Alt+F9. Then choose Retrieve Image to access the Retrieve Image File dialog box (see Figure 32.8). Type the name of the graphics image file and click OK or press Enter to continue to Step 3.

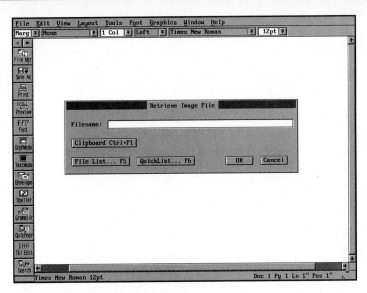

Figure 32.8. The Retrieve Image dialog box.

2. If you do not know the exact name of the graphic image file, click on File List or press F5 to see a list of your graphic image files. Select the graphic image file you want to retrieve and choose Select.

   If no graphic files are listed on the File List, check where the graphic (.WPG) files are located by looking through the various directories on your hard drive. When you find the graphics (.WPG) files, make a note of the path of the subdirectory and check to see that WordPerfect knows in which directory the files are located. From the pull-down menu choose File, Setup or press Shift+F1. Then choose Location of Files. Choose Graphic Files and type in the correct drive and path for the directory where the graphic files are stored.

3. If this is the first graphic image created in this document, the graphic image file appears in your document in a figure box on the right side of the screen. This is the predefined box style and location. If you have previously selected a box style for a graphic in this document, WordPerfect selects the last unedited box style you used.

   Of course, you can easily move and size the box and even change the borders and style of the graphic box. (How to move, size, and edit the graphic box and even modify the image within the box is discussed later.)

Creating a Graphics Box

The second method for retrieving a graphics image file is to create the box first and then retrieve the file into the box.

433

Procedure 32.2. Creating a graphics box.

1. Choose Graphics or press Alt+F9. Select Graphics Boxes. Then choose Create to access the Create Graphics dialog box (see Figure 32.9).

   The current settings for the box border style, attachment, position, and fill style are based on the current box style. Each different box style has different predefined settings. I'll talk about those settings more later in this section.

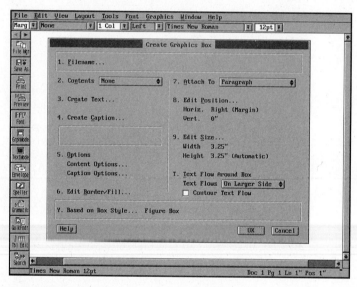

Figure 32.9. The Create Graphics Box dialog box.

2. Choose Filename. When the Retrieve File dialog box appears, type the name of the graphics image file, including the pathname, if appropriate.

3. If you do not know the exact name of the graphic image file, click on File List or press F5 to access the Select List dialog box. Indicate the full pathname of the directory you want to list, then click OK or press Enter to continue. The File List now appears.

4. From the File List, select the graphic image file you want to retrieve, and choose Select. Note that the filename is then listed in the Create Graphics Box and the Contents type has changed from None to Image.

5. If you want to change the graphics box style, Choose Based on Box Style to show a list of the box styles available. Select the style desired and choose Select. The new box style is listed as the new Based on Box Style.

6. Click OK or press Enter to continue. Your graphic image will be placed in the selected box style on your screen.

Of course, you can easily move and size the box and even change the borders and style of the graphic box. Later in this section, how to move, size, and edit the graphic box and even modify the image within the box is discussed (see Chapter 33 and Chapter 35, "Modifying Graphics Images").

> **Tip:** Once you have created a graphic box, the code [Para Box:1;Figure Box] appears in the Reveal Codes. If you want to see the name of the image file in the box, place your Reveal Codes highlight on the code. The code is then expanded to show the name of the image file contained in the box.

Viewing a Graphic Image

You can view a graphic image before retrieving the image. You can look at an image file whether retrieving the file directly into your document or creating a graphic box. From the File List dialog box, choose File Manager or press F5. Select the graphic image file you wish to view. Choose Look. You can also view the next or previous graphic image by choosing the appropriate options at the bottom of the Graphics Look Screen (see Figure 32.10).

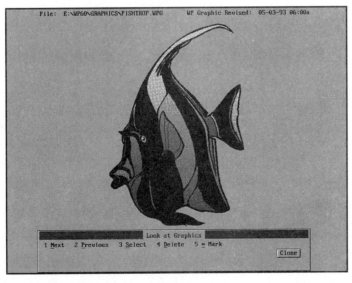

Figure 32.10. The Graphics Look screen.

435

Printing Documents that Contain Graphics

There are a few things to note when printing documents that contain graphics. You should know the memory limits of your printer. If you do not have additional memory in your printer, you may not be able to print very large graphics, very detailed graphics, or print pages with several graphic files. If you intend to print many graphic images, you should consider purchasing additional memory for a laser printer.

You will find that it takes longer to print pages that contain graphic images. In the WordPerfect Print/Fax dialog box, there is an option called Document Settings. The Document Settings option is used to select the quality of printing for both graphics and text. (See Figure 32.11 for an illustration of the Graphics Quality menu.) The default graphics quality setting for printing graphics is Medium.

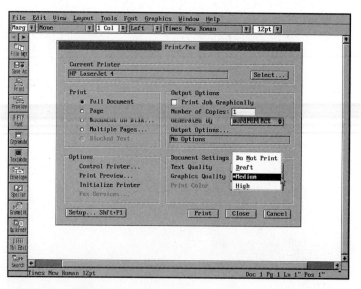

Figure 32.11. The Print/Fax dialog box.

Setting the graphics quality to **D**raft or **M**edium hastens the printing and still allows you to see the layout of your document. However, make certain that the graphics quality setting is set for **H**igh before printing your final copy. This provides the sharpest, clearest graphic possible from your printer.

Tip: Create a graphics box with a graphics image. Print the same image three times—once in **D**raft graphics quality, once in **M**edium, and once in **H**igh graphics quality—to obtain examples of how your particular printer prints the three different graphics quality selections.

To set the graphics quality to High before printing, choose File, Print/Fax, or Shift+F7 to access the Print/Fax dialog box. Under the section Document Settings, in Graphics Quality, click on the arrows to open the menu showing the Graphics Quality options. Select High and continue printing your document.

Tip: If you have printer memory problems when printing graphics, try printing your document text and the graphics separately. To print text only, set the graphics quality to Do **N**ot Print and print the page. Then, to print graphics only, feed the same page through the printer again setting the graphics quality to **H**igh and the text quality to Do **N**ot Print.

Other Graphics Formats

Once you begin using graphic images, you will think of many more creative ways to use graphics in your documents. A lawyer could use a pie chart from a spreadsheet program to visually show the division of property in divorce proceedings. A proposal could include the company logo in a header or footer on each page for a professional touch. Or, you may have a holiday graphic that you want to include in your newsletter. You can import and export other graphics file formats with WordPerfect.

Importing Other Graphics Formats

There are a number of graphics file formats that may be imported directly into a WordPerfect graphics box (no conversion is required). The following list indicates the formats that may be used directly in WordPerfect 6.0:

- ▲ EPS   PostScript and Encapsulated PostScript
- ▲ GIF   A bitmapped color graphics file format for IBM and IBM-compatible computers
- ▲ GRF   Charisma
- ▲ HPGL   Hewlett-Packard Graphics Language Plotter File

437

▲ PCX   Zsoft PC Paintbrush
▲ PIC   Lotus 1-2-3 PIC
▲ PICT   Macintosh for black-and-white images
▲ PICT2   Macintosh for color images
▲ Targa   Truevision
▲ TIFF   Tagged Image File
▲ WMF   Windows metafile

Most graphic programs allow you to export your data into a format that WordPerfect can use. Most image scanners can produce a .PCX file or a .TIF file. Therefore, most scanned images can be brought directly into a WordPerfect 6.0 graphics box. You may have to experiment and save a scanned image into both types of formats. One format may look better than the other once it is used in WordPerfect.

WordPerfect 6.0 also includes a utility program called ConvertPerfect. When you retrieve an image that is in a graphics format not supported directly into WordPerfect, ConvertPerfect automatically converts the other graphics format into a format that WordPerfect can use. So, don't limit yourself to the images WordPerfect provides.

Exporting Other Graphics Formats

As mentioned earlier, although other .WPG files from earlier versions of Word-Perfect, DrawPerfect, and Presentations can be used in WordPerfect 6.0, the WordPerfect 6.0 graphic files may not be used directly in earlier versions of WordPerfect or the Presentations Graphics program. Some of the WordPerfect 6.0 .WPG files can be exported in a format compatible with those programs.

Procedure 32.3. Exporting into other graphics formats.

1. Choose Graphics, Create (or Edit if editing an existing image).
2. Type in the filename and select Image Editor to enter the Image Editor.
3. Choose File, Save As. The Save As dialog box appears.
4. Type a different filename for your converted file.
5. Open the Format menu by clicking on the down arrow.
6. Select the desired format, and the possible exporting formats for that graphic image appear. Choose Bitmapped, Presentation 2.0, or, for earlier versions of WordPerfect, select WordPerfect 1.0. Choose OK or press Enter to convert the file.

Caution: Make certain you type a new filename for your converted file or your current graphics file will be overwritten by the new file when it is converted.

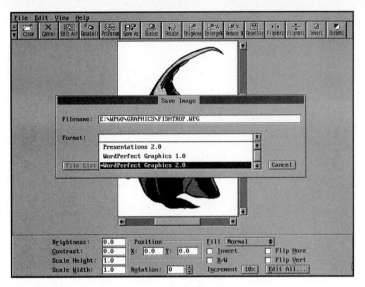

Figure. 32.12. The Save Image dialog box.

by Carolyn Woodie

Editing a Graphics Box

Now that you have created a graphics box, it is probably not exactly the way you want it to appear. There are many different ways that you can customize how your graphic image and graphics box will appear. It is difficult to know just where to begin. First of all, your box may not be just the size you expected it to be. So, you will begin by learning how to change the size of your graphics box and the image in the box.

Sizing a Graphics Box

Basically there are two ways to size the graphics box. The first way is to use the mouse to size the box and visually adjust the size of the box on the document screen. As you become more experienced, you may want to change the size of the box to specific measurements through a dialog box. I'll introduce you to both methods. (One method is not necessarily better than the other.)

Sizing a Graphics Box Using the Mouse

Procedure 33.1. Sizing a graphics box using the mouse.

1. Once you have created a graphics box, the box must be selected in order to edit the size of the box. To select a graphics box using the mouse, place your mouse pointer in the center of the box and click once with the left mouse button.

 Caution: While selecting the box, be careful that you do not move the mouse, or you will move the box. If you do move the box, you can return the box to the original location by selecting Edit, Undo.

Notice that the borders of the box are now dotted and there are definite points at the corners and center of each side of the box. These points are called handles. See Figure 33.1 for an illustration of a selected graphics box indicating the handles.

2. To size the box at the document screen, place your pointer on any one of the handles. Your pointer should change shape and become a double-headed arrow.

3. While the pointer is a double-headed arrow, click and drag the handle to make the box larger or smaller.

4. To adjust the height, click and drag on the top-center or bottom-center handle. To adjust the width, click and drag on the left-center or right-center handle. To adjust both the width and height at the same time, click and drag on one of the corner handles.

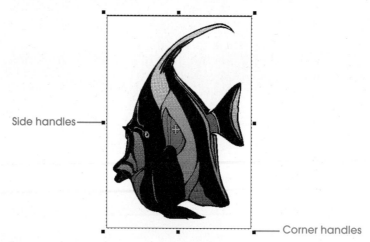

Side handles

Corner handles

Figure 33.1. The selected graphics box.

5. When the box is sized to your liking, release the mouse button.

You have to try sizing with the mouse once or twice before you feel in control. With a few practice efforts, you'll see just how easy it is to change the size of a graphics box using a mouse. Note that the graphic image in the box remains proportional, even though the image may be larger or smaller (see the example in Figure 33.2).

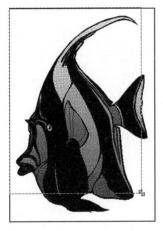

Figure 33.2. Sizing a graphics box.

Tip: If you find that your image changes proportionally when you size the box, from the Edit Graphics Box dialog box, select Content Options. Make certain that the Preserve Image Width/Height Ratio is checked with an *X*.

Sizing a Graphics Box Using the Edit Graphics Box Dialog Box

The second way to size a graphics box is to go into the Edit Graphics Box dialog box. Although there are several methods to access the Edit Graphics Box dialog box, the fastest method is to place the mouse pointer inside the graphics box and double-click the left mouse button. The Edit Graphics Box dialog box should appear (see Figure 33.3). You can control many features of the graphics box from this dialog box. You will use this dialog box to edit the size of the graphics box.

443

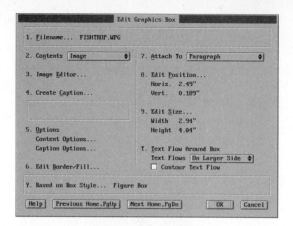

Figure 33.3. The Edit Graphics Box dialog box.

Procedure 33.2. Editing the graphics box size with the Edit Graphics box dialog box.

1. Enter the Edit Graphics Box dialog box by double-clicking on the graphics box in the document, or choose Graphics, Graphics Boxes, Edit, enter box number.

2. Note that the current size of the graphics box is shown in the Edit Size.

3. To change the size of the box, select the Edit Size option to access the Graphics Box Size dialog box (see Figure 33.4).

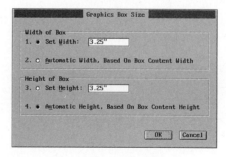

Figure 33.4. The Graphics Box Size dialog box.

4. To change the width, place your mouse pointer on the current width measurement and click (the width is highlighted). Type the new width measurement.

Note: It is not necessary to type the inch marks, because WordPerfect automatically assumes inches unless you indicate otherwise.

5. To change the height, place your mouse pointer on the current height measurement and click (the height is highlighted). Type the new height measurement. Once you have completed the size adjustment of your graphics box, click on OK or press Enter to close the dialog box.

   You also have the choice to ask WordPerfect to automatically adjust the width or height of the box. This way, you only have to enter one measurement, the width or the height, and WordPerfect adjusts the other measurement automatically. To have WordPerfect adjust one of the sizes automatically, select Automatic Width or Automatic Height.

Tip: It is a bit difficult to measure tenths and hundredths of an inch on a regular ruler. You may find it much easier to measure in centimeters. Most rulers also have a centimeter guide. Anytime you want to use a centimeter measurement in WordPerfect, follow the measurement with a c (for example, 3.5c). WordPerfect automatically converts that measurement to inches. The centimeter indicator may be used anywhere you enter a measurement—tabs, margins, graphics lines, and graphics boxes. Other units of measure available are millimeters (m), 1200th of an inch (w), and WP 4.2 units (u).

Moving a Graphics Box

The fastest and easiest method to move a graphics box is to use the mouse. However, you may want to place your graphic image in a specific location, or have several boxes positioned in several paragraphs exactly the same way. If so, you should use the Edit Graphics Box dialog box.

Moving a Graphic Using the Mouse

To move a graphics box with the mouse, you may use the click and drag method.

Procedure 33.3. Moving a graphics box using the mouse.
   1. With the mouse pointer, select the graphics box you wish to move.
   2. Click and drag the graphics box with the pointer to the position desired.

3. Release the mouse button.

4. If you decide to return the graphics box to the original position, select Edit, Undo.

Tip: A shortcut for the Undo function is to press Ctrl+Z.

Caution: A character style graphics box, because it is a box that is treated as a character, may not be dragged into a completely blank area of the document.

Moving a Graphic Using the Edit Graphics Box Dialog Box

In order to move the graphics box using the Edit Graphics Box dialog box options, you must first understand what is meant by the term *attached to*.

Attachment Options

Note in the Edit Graphics Box dialog box (see Figure 33.3) that one of the options is **A**ttach To. In WordPerfect 5.1 for DOS, this option was called *Anchor Type*. I describe this as a "thumbtack option." Consider where you would like to "thumbtack" your graphic image. If you have a paragraph interpreting the graphic, you want to thumbtack or attach the graphic image to the paragraph. Then, if the document is edited and the paragraph is moved, the graphic image moves with the paragraph.

Positioning the graphic image is dependent on the attachment selection. A graphic image can also be attached to a position on a page or considered just like any character and basically not attached to anything. Different graphics box types are predefined as certain attachment type boxes. Of course, any box attachment can be changed. The predefined attachment types are listed below:

Box Type	Attachment
Figure	Paragraph
Table	Paragraph
Text	Paragraph
User	Paragraph
Button	Character
Watermark	Page

Fixed Page Position

The Fixed Page Position attaches the box to a specific position on the page. Even if the text is edited and the text moves to the next page, the graphics box remains on the page.

Think of the Fixed Page Position as thumbtacking the graphics box to a specific spot on the page. Please note that the Fixed Page Position can be set only to specific measurements from the top and left edges of the page (see Figure 33.5). Use this type when you want an exact position horizontally and vertically for your box, regardless of the surrounding text. A good use for a fixed page position graphics box is as a logo used with a title of a newsletter or letterhead.

Figure 33.5. The Fixed Page Position attachment.

Paragraph Attachment

The Paragraph selection attaches the box to the current paragraph (the paragraph where your insertion point is sitting). If the document is edited and the paragraph moves, the graphics box moves with the paragraph.

When you select the Attachment to Paragraph option, you can set the position based on that type. At the Edit Graphics Box dialog box, after setting the Attachment to Paragraph, select Edit Position to access the Paragraph Box Position dialog box (see Figure 33.6).

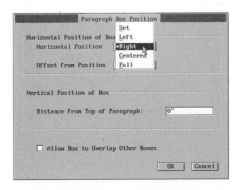

Figure 33.6. The Paragraph Box Position dialog box.

Note that you can change the Horizontal Position to appear at the left margin of the paragraph, the right margin, in the center between the margins, or spread across from margin to margin. The term *Set* appears anywhere you can set a definite measurement in WordPerfect. So, if you knew you wanted your box to appear exactly 3.67 inches from the left edge of the page, you could enter that measurement under the Set option.

The vertical position can only be set in relation to the top of the paragraph. If you want to drop the box .5 inches from the top of the paragraph, enter .5" and your box should appear similar to the one shown in Figure 33.7.

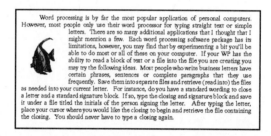

Figure 33.7. The distance from top of the paragraph.

The Offset from Position option allows you to adjust the graphics box to the left, right, or none from the horizontal position. If you have set the horizontal position to be right and the Offset from Position to .75 inches, the box appears .75 inches from the left margin of the paragraph (see Figure 33.8).

 Tip: If you want your text to flow on both sides of your graphics box, you must set Text Flows Around Box to On Both Sides. If it is not set for both sides, the text flows only on one side of your graphics box.

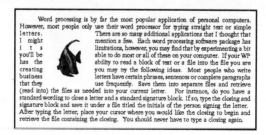

Figure 33.8. The Offset from Position example.

Use the paragraph attachment if you want the graphic image to remain with the surrounding text. This attachment type is also a good type to use for a drop cap (see "Creating Special Effects with Graphics Boxes" later in this chapter).

Page Attachment

The Page selection attaches the box to the current page. At the Edit Graphics Box dialog box, after setting the attachment to Page, select Edit Position to access the Page Box Position dialog box (see Figure 33.9).

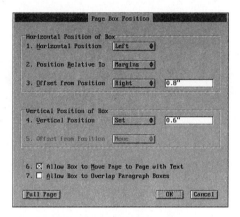

Figure 33.9. The Page Box Position dialog box.

Note that you can indicate both the horizontal and vertical positions of the box. First, note the Position **R**elative To option under Horizontal Position of box. Defining the position of the page box can be done in relationship to the left and right margins, text columns on a page, or a specific text column. See "Paragraph Attachment" earlier in this chapter for an explanation of Offset.

Caution: If you use the mouse to position the graphics box, the attachment type always changes to Page Attachment. A box that was attached to a paragraph when moved with a mouse is no longer attached to a paragraph, but is now attached to the page with definite horizontal and vertical positions set.

The vertical position may be set to a specific measurement at the top, bottom, or centered in relationship to the page.

WordPerfect automatically sets the box to Allow Box to **M**ove Page to Page with Text. However, you may turn that feature off and require that the box remain on the page. You also have the option to overlap the page box over paragraph boxes. This is similar to setting a box to be a transparency so it allows stacking of graphics boxes.

> **Tip:** If you want a graphics box to fill the entire page, select the Full Page button at the bottom of the Page Box Position dialog box— WordPerfect automatically changes all settings to allow your graphics box to fill a full page.

Character Attachment

The Character selection handles the graphics box as a character, and a character box is not attached to anything. If you type text before the graphics box, the box moves to the right. If you press the space bar or Tab, you move the graphics box as if it were a character. At the Edit Graphics Box dialog box, after setting the attachment to Character, select Edit Position to access the Character Box Position dialog box (see Figure 33.10).

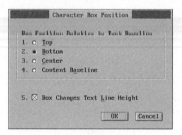

Figure 33.10. The Character Box Position dialog box.

The first option allows you to adjust the character box position in relationship to the surrounding text baseline (the bottom of the characters). The default setting is to set the bottom of the box with the baseline of the surrounding text. However, you can change the box position to top, center, or the content baseline. The content baseline option means that you may align the contents of the graphics box with the baseline of the surrounding text. See Figure 33.11 for examples of the different positions of the character box position relative to the text baseline.

You can also control whether the character graphics box changes the height of the current text line. WordPerfect automatically assumes that you want to change the line height when inserting a character graphics box into the text. However, you turn Box Changes Text Line Height off if you want the line height controlled by the text and not the graphics box.

This character box is positioned with the text at the bottom.

This character box is positioned with the text at the top.

This character box is positioned with the text at the center.

Figure 33.11. Character Box positions.

A good application for the character type attachment would be if you are using a special graphic as a bullet for a presentation. You can then tab the graphic image to the position where you want it to appear. An example of a character type attachment is shown in the bullet chart in Figure 33.12. The vertical position is set for Center.

Figure 33.12. A character attachment example.

Editing Graphics Box Borders

Of course, once you have created the box, you may want to change how the borders appear. WordPerfect 6.0 has many more options for the borders than earlier versions. Not only can you change the thickness of the borders, but you now can change the shape of the corners, the color of the lines, and create a great variety of shadow boxes.

451

Tip: To quickly reset the options to the original box style options, double-click on the box. At the Edit Graphics Box dialog box, select Based on Box Style. Select the button Reset to Style at the bottom. Select the features you want to reset. Click on OK or press ENTER.

Border Line Options

Procedure 33.4. Changing the graphics box borders.

1. To change the border of a graphics box, first enter the Edit Graphics Box dialog box by double-clicking on the graphics box.

2. Select Edit Border/Fill to access the Edit Graphics Box Border/Fill dialog box (see Figure 33.13).

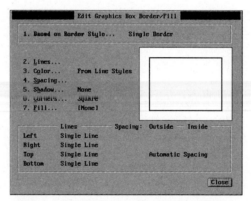

Figure 33.13. The Edit Graphics Box Border/Fill dialog box.

3. Select Lines to access the Border Line Styles dialog box (see Figure 33.14).

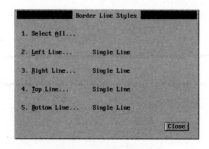

Figure 33.14. The Border Line Styles dialog box.

4. You can choose to change all the sides or just individual sides of a graphics box. Choose one of the sides and the Line Styles dialog box appears (see Figure 33.15).

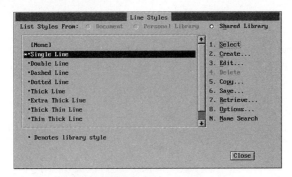

Figure 33.15. The Line Styles dialog box.

5. Make the changes to the borders as desired. Click on Close when done. You should see your changes to the box borders in the sample box in the Edit Graphics Box Border/Fill dialog box. Return to your document. (Samples of the border types are shown in Figure 33.16.)

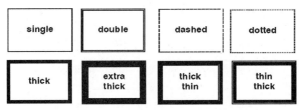

Figure 33.16. Sample box borders.

Tip: To make changes to all of the boxes of a certain style in a document, make the changes to the graphics box style. Select Based on Box Style, select the style of the box you want to change, choose Edit, and make changes using the Edit Graphics Box dialog box for the style.

Color of Box Lines Options

When we see the vivid color choices of the new programs, all of us want a color printer. However, owning a color printer may be just a dream for most of us. Even though you may not have a color printer, changing the color of the box lines also changes how the box is printed in black and shades of grey. So, you may want to experiment with some of the color choices to see just how they print on your printer. For example, magenta prints a grey bordered box, and yellow prints a very light grey border.

Procedure 33.5. Changing the box line color.

1. Double-click on the graphics box to enter the Edit Graphics Box dialog box.
2. Select Edit Border/Fill to enter the Edit Graphics Box Border/Fill dialog box.
3. Select Color to enter the Border Line Color dialog box (see Figure 33.17).

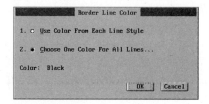

Figure 33.17. The Border Line Color dialog box.

4. Select One Color for All Lines to enter the Color Selection dialog box (see Figure 33.18).

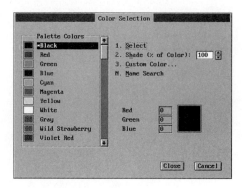

Figure 33.18. The Color Selection dialog box.

5. Highlight a color or mix your custom color for the border lines. Click on the Close button to exit the Color Selection dialog box.

Note: You can see additional colors using the vertical scroll bar on the right.

6. Click on OK or press Enter to exit the Border Line Color dialog box. You should see a sample of your new color selection at the Edit Graphics Box Border/Fill dialog box. Click on the Close button to accept the change to the graphics box. Click on OK or press Enter to return to your document or remain in the Edit Graphics Box dialog box for additional changes.

Tip: Save a few keystrokes by double-clicking to select the color and close the dialog box.

Caution: Make certain that you double-click on the color or choose Select from the menu before closing the dialog box or else you will not change the color.

Controlling Spacing in Boxes

There will be times when you want to make an adjustment to the amount of space between the object or text within the graphics box and the borders of the box. Or, there may be other times when you want to change the amount of space between the border and the text outside of the border of the box. WordPerfect allows you to control that spacing to the thousandth of an inch!

Procedure 33.6. Changing the spacing of a graphics box.

1. Double-click on the graphics box to enter the Edit Graphics Box dialog box.
2. Select Edit Border/Fill to enter the Edit Border/Fill dialog box.
3. Select Spacing to enter the Border Spacing dialog box (see Figure 33.19).
4. Notice that **A**utomatic Spacing is selected and the other options are not available. Turn off the **A**utomatic Spacing to enter specific measurements.
5. To make it easier, you can choose to change all of the outside border spacing by selecting Outside, Set All or the inside spacing by selecting Inside, Set All. Or, you may change just selected spacing. Once you have made the changes desired, click on OK or press Enter to exit the Border Spacing dialog box.

Figure 33.19. The Border Spacing dialog box.

6. Click on the Close button to accept the change to the graphics box. Click on OK or press Enter to return to your document or remain in the Edit Graphics Box dialog box for additional changes.

Creating Shadow Boxes

Special effects may be produced by creating a drop shadow effect to your graphics box. This helps to emphasize whatever is inside the box. Of course, just like any special effect, it can be overdone. So, use this feature sparingly.

Procedure 33.7. Creating shadow boxes.

1. Double-click on the graphics box to enter the Edit Graphics Box dialog box.
2. Select Edit Border/Fill to enter the Edit Border/Fill dialog box.
3. Select Shadow to enter the Shadow dialog box (see Figure 33.20).

Figure 33.20. The Shadow dialog box.

4. Choose the Shadow Type to indicate the direction of the drop shadow.

5. Notice that you may also select a color for the drop shadow by selecting Shadow Color. You may also change the width of the drop shadow to make it thicker or thinner by selecting Shadow Width. Click on OK or press Enter to accept and exit the Shadow dialog box.

6. Note the new drop shadow on sample graphics box. Click on Close to exit the Edit Border/Fill dialog box. Click on OK or press Enter to return to the document or remain in the Edit Graphics Box dialog box for additional changes. (Some examples of drop shadows are shown in Figure 33.21.)

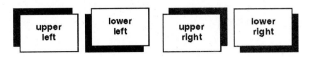

Figure 33.21. Some sample graphics box drop shadows.

Changing the Corners of Graphics Boxes

The corners of the box can be changed in the Edit Border/Fill dialog box from square to rounded. Select Corners and change from square to round. You can even control the roundness of the corners by changing the radius of the rounded corner.

Changing the Fill of a Graphics Box

The fill of a graphics box allows you to fill the box with a color or a pattern and color. You may select a color for the pattern and a different color for the background of the pattern. You may even prepare a box that blends from one color to another color (this is called a gradient fill).

Procedure 33.8. Changing the fill of a graphics box.

1. From the Edit Border/Fill dialog box, select Fill to enter the Fill Style and Color dialog box (see Figure 33.22).

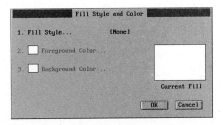

Figure 33.22. The Fill Style and Color dialog box.

2. Select Fill Style to enter the Fill Styles dialog box where you can select the percentage of the fill (darkness) (see Figure 33.23).

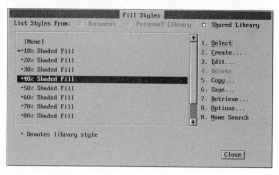

Figure 33.23. The Fill Styles dialog box.

3. If you want to experiment with the gradient fill type, at the Fill Styles dialog box, select Create. Type a new name for this new style and press Enter. The Create Fill Style dialog box appears (see Figure 33.24).

Figure 33.24. The Create Fill Style dialog box.

4. Experiment with the various fill types. You may select pattern or gradient (blending one color into another color) and then experiment with the different fill patterns. You will get many different effects. Once you have determined the fill type and colors, click on OK or press Enter to exit the dialog box. Continue to close dialog boxes until you return to your document.

Tip: Press Home+F7 to immediately return to your document.

458

Note: You will find it helpful to read Chapter 34, "Borders and Fills," which covers using borders and fills in more detail.

Exchanging the Image in the Graphics Box

Once you have created your graphics image in a box, if you decide you want to use a different graphic image, you can replace the image at any time.

Procedure 33.9. Exchanging the image in the graphics box.

1. Double-click on the graphics box to enter the Edit Graphics Box dialog box.

2. Select Filename.

3. Type in the new graphic image filename (including a pathname if required) and press Enter.

4. You will be prompted to confirm "Yes" if you want to delete the current graphic image. Select Yes. Your new filename will be listed at the Filename location.

5. Then click on OK or press Enter to close the Edit Graphics Box dialog box. Your old graphic image should be replaced with your new image.

Using Content Options

The position of the contents of the graphics box can be controlled by going into the **O**ptions, Contents Options dialog box (see Figure 33.25). Note that you can position the image or text horizontally or vertically within the box. (Caption options are covered in Chapter 36, "Graphics Box Captions and Numbering.")

Changing How Text Flows Around the Graphics Box

As mentioned previously, WordPerfect 6.0 now offers many ways to handle how the text will flow around your graphics box. Earlier versions of WordPerfect required you to place the text in columns to allow text to flow on both sides of a graphics box. In WordPerfect 6.0, not only do you have the capability to flow the text on both sides of a graphics box, but you can contour the text around the shape of your graphic image.

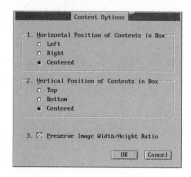

Figure 33.25. Content Options.

At the Edit Graphics Box dialog box, note Text Flow Around Box option. Click on the arrow to show the pop-up menu of text flow options (see Figure 33.26).

To contour the text around the shape of a graphic figure, click on the box next to the Contour Text Flow to turn the feature on. (See Figures 33.27 and 33.28 for text flow examples.)

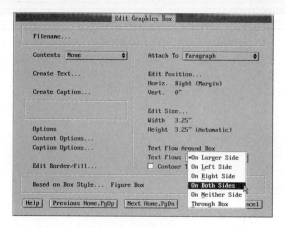

Figure 33.26. Text Flow Around Box options.

Note: When you contour the text around a graphics image, existing borders of your graphics box disappear.

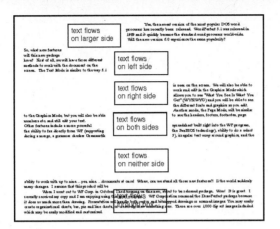

Figure 33.27. Text flow examples.

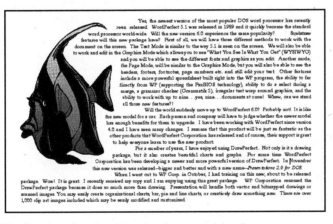

Figure 33.28. Contouring text around a graphics box.

Creating Special Effects with Graphics Boxes

Please see Workshop VIII, "Desktop Publishing," which follows, to learn how you can use WordPerfect 6.0 to publish many types of documents. I hope that this chapter has encouraged you to think of adding graphics to enhance your documents and the message of your text. Here is a different way to use a graphics box which may not be obvious at first glance.

461

Reserving a Space

Sometimes newsletter space is sold to advertisers. The advertiser may send a business card, a photo, or camera-ready artwork to be added to the newsletter. You may find it easier to physically cut and paste some of your artwork than to clean up a scanned image. Consider creating a graphics user box the size of the space allotted for the ad. This allows the text to easily flow around the box while reserving the space for the paste-up of the artwork or business card.

Procedure 33.10. Creating a blank space with a graphics box.

1. Measure the size of the space required and where the box is to be located from the left edge of the page and from the top of the page.
2. Create a graphics box. Choose Graphics, Graphics Boxes, Create.
3. At the Create Graphics Box dialog box, select Based on Box Style and change the style to a User Box.
4. Change the Attachment type to Fixed Page Position. Enter the horizontal position to indicate the measurements from the left of the page and the top of the page, as measured in Step 1.
5. Select Edit Size to change the measurements to the size of the area you measured in Step 1.
6. Click on OK or press Enter to close the Create Graphics Box dialog box.
7. You should have a blank space as shown in the example in Figure 33.29.

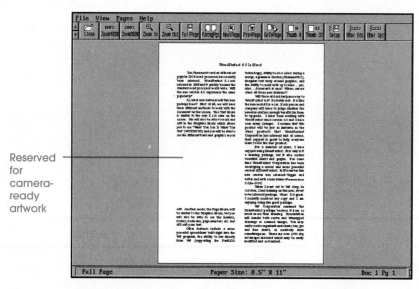

Figure 33.29. Creating a blank space with a graphics box.

by Bob Boeri

Borders and Fills

What Are Borders and Fills?

Borders and fills are two graphics devices that give life to otherwise boring documents. Borders surround various elements such as graphics with visual appeal formerly possible only in desktop publishing systems. The difference between a WordPerfect 5 graphic and a new WordPerfect 6.0 graphic is the difference between a posed, fifties box camera picture of your mother and her aunt Lucy and a dazzling nineties hologram.

A border is a stylized line surrounding paragraphs, pages, columns, graphics, or any other document element that can include a line. Because you can assign many different special variations to lines, you can use each style as a border. In prior versions of WordPerfect, you could add various line borders around graphics boxes, and you even could give a raised effect by selecting thick lines on two sides and normal lines on the other two sides. You now can do that too, but you also can do much more. Your border lines can be rounded, and you can specify different degrees of rounding, for example. The net result can be graphics that look like cameos or dozens of other effects.

You also can add borders around whole pages, paragraphs, and columns. Moreover, border styles can include placement of lines, so you can tailor your graphical effects further and—when appropriate—specify separator lines such as in pull-quotes or sidebars. You can shade border lines to various degrees, and you can specify various thicknesses and styles such as "thick over thin on the top and bottom."

For all their appeal, borders are only half this story. What borders are to the outside of elements, fills are to the inside. What is a fill? A fill is a kind of shading. Unlike earlier versions of WordPerfect where you could obtain percentages of grey shading for elements such as lines, your choices now include patterns of shading and foregrounds or backgrounds. WordPerfect provides several patterns of shading as well as gradient filling, which means a range of shades, light to dark, within the same filled area. If that's not enough, you can modify, shift, and even rotate these shading patterns. We'll discuss the various special effects available in fills shortly.

We no longer live in a black-and-white world, and WordPerfect also now provides color options throughout its many new features. The list of elements you can colorize include lines, borders, and fills. Having used colors, you have several options to show them off:

▲ Print the colors if you have a color printer.

▲ Select a color Postscript printer driver, print to a file, and give that file to someone (perhaps a service bureau) who has a color Postscript printer.

▲ Deliver your documents electronically where they can be viewed on a color screen.

Of course, you can combine borders and fills to add graphics touches easily to entire pages. Alternatively, you still can embed graphics in headers and footers, and you can have both headers/footers and borders with fills. As with many other features of WordPerfect, you will find the hardest part to be selecting the most effective combination of options from this feast of possibilities.

Creating Borders and Fills

Although borders and fill styles can apply to many document elements, let's focus here on the most common choices: paragraphs, columns, and pages. After becoming comfortable applying border and fill styles to these three document elements, it is easy to become more proficient applying them to graphics, tables, and other document elements. When using borders and fills, be sure that you learn the menus and how to navigate them successfully. Moreover, treat borders and fills the way you treat combinations of fonts. Just as some desktop publishers overuse fonts, it is possible to distract rather than dazzle by using too many combinations of borders and fills. As with fonts, simplicity reigns; a little goes a long way.

Paragraph Borders and Fills

Creating borders and fills is a fundamental operation. To apply these to an existing paragraph, you start with the Graphics menu.

Procedure 34.1. Applying a paragraph border and fill.

1. Place the cursor in the paragraph anywhere you want to have this decorative effect, or to apply this to several paragraphs, block any amount of text in several sequential paragraphs.

2. Choose Border from the **G**raphics menu, or press Alt+F9.

3. Choose Paragraph, then Border Style and highlight the style you want; and then choose Select.

4. To add a fill, choose Fill Style, highlight your selection, and then choose Select.

5. Choose OK or press Enter.

The border and fill style you select will be applied to the paragraphs you blocked. Figure 34.1 shows highlighted paragraphs and the borders and subordinate drop-down menu.

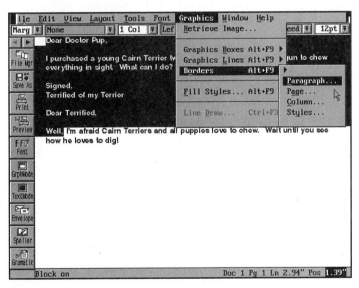

Figure 34.1. Selecting borders for paragraphs.

Note that we needed to block some words from each paragraph, but not all words in each paragraph. Figure 34.2 shows the result of this operation after selecting thick top and bottom borders and a 10 percent fill. We choose thick top and bottom borders to make this section stand out as a pull-quote.

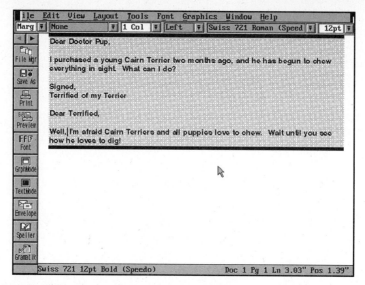

Figure 34.2. Applying top and bottom borders to paragraphs.

Note: If you don't like the result, you can repeat the sequence while the cursor is within the bordered paragraph by selecting Edit. You also can remove the whole border and fill style from the paragraphs by using Reveal Codes; place your cursor on the [Para Border] code at the beginning of the paragraphs and delete it. Note that when you place your cursor on this code, it expands to show you the underlying style settings, "Thick Top and Bottom... ; 10% Shaded Fill."

In this example, we picked system borders and fills that are available by default. A cornucopia of special effects becomes available when we select the Customization option. Reblock the paragraphs, and go to the Edit Paragraph Border as before, but now select the Customize choice. Figure 34.3 shows the Customize Border menu. Note that this is based on the border style "Thick Top and Bottom Border," but we now see a lot more choices: Lines, Color, Spacing, Shadow, Corners, and Fill. "Corners" is greyed because that is not an option for paragraphs.

Note: Cornered border styles are available only for page borders; they are unavailable for column or paragraph borders.

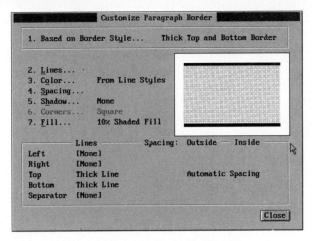

Figure 34.3. The Customize Paragraph Border menu.

This simple example of borders and fills gives you an idea of the impact they can provide to your documents. Now, let's look at each of the style and fill options, plus customization, in detail.

Selecting a Paragraph Border Style

First, let's get to the Border Style option following Procedure 34.1, selecting the Border Style menu. You will see this list of border styles on the left in the Border Styles menu:

> Spacing Only (no lines)
> Single Border
> Double Border
> Dashed Border
> Dotted Border
> Thick Border
> Extra Thick Border
> Thin Thick Border
> Thick Thin Border
> Thick Top and Bottom
> Button Border (can give a solid three-dimensional look)
> Column Border (Between Only)
> Column Border (Outside and Between)

These styles are self-explanatory. The column borders are listed to show border separators you can have for your paragraphs in columns. Simply Select the one you want if you want to choose the system default versions. Of course, as with styles in general, you can Create a new border style, Edit one of those in the list,

Retrieve a graphics style, or select Options to use a style from an existing personal or shared library.

The easiest way to understand your options if you choose to deviate from the default system border styles is to select Edit. Do this, and you will see the categories of border attributes shown previously in Figure 34.3: Lines, Color, Spacing, Shadow, and Corners. Beneath the options, you see the current positions we've chosen for border lines, including optional separators and spacing. In this case, we've chosen "Thick Top and Bottom Border."

You may want something different from the system-specified line width and style, and WordPerfect lets you change these too. You can alter the color of the line, its thickness, and the pattern of characters to appear in a line. The default line width is .013. To make these changes, go to the Line Styles menu. This is the menu that lists all line styles. The list of these is similar to but not exactly the same as the list of border styles presented earlier. The list of line styles, in order, is as follows:

> [None]
> Single Line
> Double Line
> Dashed Line
> Dotted Line
> Thick Line
> Extra Thick Line
> Thin Thick Line
> Thick Thin Line
> Button Top/Left Line
> Button Bottom/Right Line

Let's create a customized thin line based on the style "single line." Follow Procedure 34.1 through Step 3, choose Edit instead of Select. In the Edit Border Style menu, select Lines and pick any choice of border line (e.g., Left). Then, in the Line Styles submenu under Single Line, select Edit. Selecting this will bring you to the Edit Line Style submenu shown in Figure 34.4.

Your choices are Create, select a Pattern Type (custom or predefined), a Pattern, a Color, and a Thickness. There are 16 predefined line styles. In Figure 34.4, we have picked the simple line pattern, the color black, and a thickness of .005 inches for a very thin line.

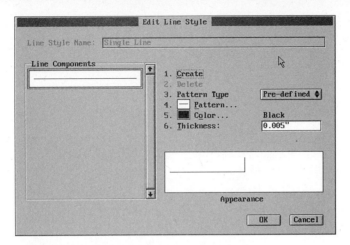

Figure 34.4. The Edit Line Style menu.

Now, let's look at the other options, starting with color. Select Color. There are an unlimited number of colors you can select or edit. Here is a list of 71 predefined colors, starting with Black and ending with Bittersweet:

Black	Apricot
Red	Burnt orange
Green	Raw umber
Blue	Yellow orange
Cyan	Orange yellow
Magenta	Goldenrod
Yellow	Maize
White	Dandelion
Grey	Lemon yellow
Wild strawberry	Spring green
Violet red	Yellow green
Orange red	Green yellow
Vivid tangerine	Green yellow
Indian red	Pine green
Brown	Olive green
Peach	Sea green
Sepia	Forest green
Raw sienna	Jungle green
Mahogany	Aquamarine
Red orange	Periwinkle
Tan	Cadet blue
Burnt sienna	Sky blue
Orange	Blue green
Melon	Green blue

469

Blue grey	Violet (purple)
Teal blue	Orchid
Turquoise blue	Red violet
Navy blue	Thistle
Cornflower	Lavender
Midnight blue	Carnation pink
Cerulean	Mulberry
Royal purple	Maroon
Plum	Brick red
Blue violet	Salmon
Violet blue	Fuchsia
	Bittersweet

These colors are well-named and accurately describe what you will see on-screen. Of course, if you don't find what you want here, WordPerfect provides you a mini-electronic palette for mixing your own. For each color you mix, you can select its shade. Let's create our own custom line color called "Flannel."

Doing this is similar to Procedure 34.1, except now you edit the border line's color.

Procedure 34.2. Creating a custom border line color.

1. Place the cursor in the paragraph wherever you want to have this decorative effect, or if you want this to apply to several paragraphs, block any amount of text in several sequential paragraphs.
2. Choose Borders from the **G**raphics menu or press Alt+F9; select **P**aragraph.
3. Choose **B**order Style, highlight the style you want, and then choose Edit.
4. In the Edit Border Style menu, select Color.
5. Click the bottom radio button, "**C**hoose One Color For All Lines...."
6. Select Custom Color.
7. Move the cursor to "Red."
8. Select the following ratios: Red 200, Green 25, Blue 50.
9. Select Add to Palette.
10. Select Color Name and type Flannel. Select OK.

Flannel is now a custom color available to you for lines, fills, and other styles. During this exercise, you should see the color palette and screen shown in Figure 34.5.

In addition to creating a custom color such as Flannel, or using a system-supplied color such as Fuchsia, you can adjust the color's shading or saturation. Follow the preceeding example through "Choose One Color For All Lines...." Specify a percentage of shading in the S**h**ade box; the extremes are 100 percent (which gives you full saturation) through 0 percent (which gives you none and no color at all).

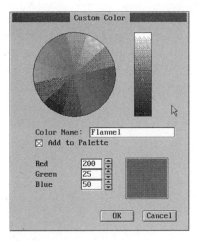

Figure 34.5. The Custom Color menu.

After color, the options for borders are spacing, shadows, and fills. By default, WordPerfect provides preset spacing for borders, but, as with most things in WordPerfect, you can change some or all the spacings inside and outside the borders.

Shadows give borders a 3-D effect, as though a light source is shining above them and casting a shadow. You could provide a similar effect in earlier versions of WordPerfect by specifying lines of varying width around graphics boxes. Now, however, you have more choices and shadows are easier to create.

The choices for shadows include none (the default), upper-left, lower-left, upper-right, and lower-right. Note that you can select only one shadow option. This helps you keep track of the sides to select to simulate a light source. If you select "lower-right," a shadow is cast as though a light source is at the upper-right above the border. Of course, the color style applies to shadows too, and thus you can specify a shadow color. By default, shadows are black and .125 inches. If you specify a shadow color, you are presented with the full color palette selection menu described previously.

Note: Selecting a shadow saturation (percent of shading) can be particularly effective when creating custom shadows. Grey shadows often look less harsh when used with black borders.

Selecting a Paragraph Fill Style

To apply a fill style, get to the Border Style option following Procedure 34.1, stopping at the Fill Style menu. You will see this list of fills on the left of the Fill Styles menu:

> [None]
> 10% Shaded Fill
> 20% Shaded Fill
> 30% Shaded Fill
> 40% Shaded Fill
> 50% Shaded Fill
> 60% Shaded Fill
> 70% Shaded Fill
> 80% Shaded Fill
> 90% Shaded Fill
> 100% Shaded Fill
> Button Fill

Each of these fills is a simple, uniform dot pattern. Figure 34.6 shows the Edit Fill Style menu with percentages and the built-in non-uniform patterns that you can select.

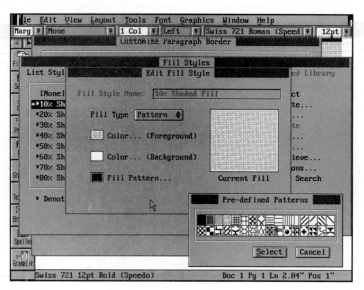

Figure 34.6. The Paragraph Edit Fill Style menu.

Note: If you use standard black printing with a fill, use a lighter fill depending on the font, its weight, and so on. If your printer can print white characters, using a darker shaded fill can be an effective way to grab your reader's attention.

Although one choice for fills is a uniform pattern in various percentages of shaded fill, that is not all. To help us get our bearings, let's show the procedure for selecting and using a special fill pattern.

Procedure 34.3. Applying a customized gradient fill to a paragraph.

1. Place the cursor in the paragraph wherever you want to have this decorative effect; or if you want this to apply to several paragraphs, block any amount of text in several sequential paragraphs.

2. Choose Borders from the **G**raphics menu or press Alt+F9.

3. Choose Paragraph.

4. Choose Fill Style, and in the Fill Styles menu, highlight the percentage of fills you want, then choose Edit.

5. In the Edit Fill Style menu, select Fill Type (**G**radient or **P**attern).

6. Choose Fill Pattern and select the style with the variations that you want.

7. Choose OK or press Enter.

In Step 5, there are four choices: Fill Type, Color Foreground, Color Background, and Fill Pattern. Under Fill Type, the choices are Pattern or Gradient. If you select Pattern, and choose a predefined pattern shown in Figure 34.6, that predefined pattern would be applied. You also can select Fill Gradient. Selecting Gradient presents the Gradient Fill Edit submenu. The Gradient choices are linear, radial, or rectangular. Linear means an even shading from light to dark. Rectangular and Radial give you squared and rounded shades. You can rotate the shaded appearance for rectangular and radial shades. Select the number of degrees to rotate this pattern. The rotation angles can range from 0° (none) through 359°. You also can select horizontal and vertical offsets from 0 through 100. These values indicate percentages to shift the center of the radial or rectangular pattern from the center. Selecting a larger horizontal offset shifts the gradient to the right; selecting a lower one shifts it to the left. A selection of 50 centers the gradient pattern. Finally, you have a choice in the number of shades for a gradient. You can accept the default **C**alculate Number of Shades; WordPerfect will apply its predefined blending of shades. Or, you can deselect that default and specify 1 (solid) through 9,999 shades. Practically speaking, after 100 shades, the effects are similar—a smooth, blended gradient.

Figure 34.7 shows the Gradient Fill Edit menu. In this case, the Gradient Type is Linear with a 45° rotation angle (darker gradient at the upper-left, lighter gradient at the lower-right). WordPerfect is calculating the number of shades for a smooth effect.

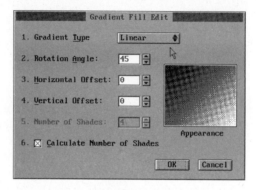

Figure 34.7. Border Fill with 45° linear gradient.

A final note about paragraph borders: you can specify a border to go around a header or footer because they are considered to be paragraphs.

Procedure 34.4. Applying a border and a fill to a header or footer.

1. Choose Header/Footer/Watermark from the **Layout** menu. Then select Headers or Footers, or press Shift+F8, 5, 1, 2.
2. Choose the Header or Footer to which you want to apply a border and fill style. Then, select Edit to enter the Header or Footer editor.
3. Position the cursor anywhere within the header or footer text.
4. Choose Borders from the Graphics menu or press Alt+F9.
5. Choose Paragraph.
6. Select a border style and choose Select.
7. Choose OK and then press F7 to exit the Header/Footer editor.

Similarly, within the Edit Paragraph Border menu, select Fill Style to choose a fill for that header or footer.

Note: There are two ways to turn off a border or fill in a header or footer. One way to do this is to go to the Header or Footer editor and delete the paragraph border code (seen only in Reveal Codes as [Para Border:...]). You then can create a new border and fill for that header or footer. As an alternative, within the Header or

Footer editor, position your cursor anywhere within the header or footer text, choose Borders from the Graphics menu, and then select Paragraph followed by Off.

Borders and Fills for Tables

Tables are essentially lines and borders. If you think you can use borders and fills to dress them up, you're right. Figure 34.8 shows a pet store grooming service price list, one that is really a table spreadsheet but has been dressed up with borders and fills. Using WordPerfect's new full-function spreadsheets in such a price list could make it a "smart" form that enables you to adjust prices according to business formulas. With borders and fills, you then can dress up the price list as well.

Dog Grooming Services and Price List		
Service	**Dog Size**	**Price**
Shampoo	S	$10.00
	M	$15.00
	L	$20.00
Deluxe Grooming	S	$15.00
	M	$25.00
	L	$35.00

Figure 34.8. Table price list with borders and fills.

To apply borders and fills to tables, realize that you can apply two sets of changes: borders and fills for the inside of the table and its cells, and borders and fills for the outside of the table. In Figure 34.8, we see the three-column table (whose top row's cells have been joined). We have a simple pattern fill applied to the inside of these joined cells. To specify borders and fills, press Layout, Tables, Edit, or press Alt+F11. This brings you to a Table Edit menu much like what you would see in WordPerfect 5, except that the "Lines" choice has now become Lines/Fill. Click that, and you will see the Table Lines submenu shown in Figure 34.9.

This menu is divided into two parts: Entire Table—Default Line and Border/Fill—and Current Cell or Block that has the choices **L**eft, **R**ight, **T**op, **B**ottom, **I**nside, **O**utside, Line **C**olor (use Current Color or Choose Color), and **F**ill. You will see that because our cursor is placed in the top row of joined cells, "Fill" is displayed as 40 percent.

Figure 34.9. The Table Lines submenu.

 Note: You can format all the lines in a table at once, or you can block certain cells and specify only their format.

Note, too, that the Entire Table choice of "Default Line" applies to all cell lines except those around the outside of the table. Border choices apply to the outside of the table. Fill choices apply to all cells in the table. As usual, you can override the default settings. In this table, we chose a border style of Button Border that we customized to have the color "Flannel," which we defined earlier in this chapter.

Column and Page Borders and Fills

With few exceptions, selecting and customizing borders and fills for columns and pages works exactly the same as it does with paragraphs. Because WordPerfect's styles work consistently and present you with the same menus for attributes such as colors, learning them once for paragraphs suffices for columns and pages.

Column Borders

By now you should be familiar with adding borders and fills. Adding them to columns works just as you would expect. The only special consideration with columns is that you can select borders occurring only between columns or borders outside *and* between columns. Likewise, you can select a fill for columns. By selecting Customize in the Create Column Border menu, you can fine-tune such things as the spacing of lines and fills. However, you cannot select rounded borders with columns. You can turn off borders and fills by placing your cursor anywhere within the columns and selecting Off in the Create Column Border menu.

Page Borders

We end this chapter on borders and fills by repeating the procedure for applying them and then by showing how to apply them to a simple desktop publishing document. One special feature of page borders is that you can select rounded borders, specifying a radius for rounding the corners. You cannot select rounded corners for either column or paragraph borders.

Procedure 34.5. Applying a border and a fill to a page.

1. Position the cursor where you want borders to begin appearing on the first page.
2. Choose Border from the Graphics menu. Then select Page, or press Alt+F9, 3, 2. Choose Border Style.
3. Choose the style you want from the list of styles on the left of the Border Styles menu, first editing your selection if you want.
4. Choose Select, returning to the Edit Page Border menu.
5. Choose OK to return to your main document screen.

Note that if you wanted to select or edit a fill, you would repeat Steps 2 through 4 except selecting Fill before choosing to exit the Edit Page Border menu.

Now let's use page borders to create a sample certificate. This certificate uses rounded page borders to create a pet store dog obedience graduation certificate, which also contains a 16-level, grey-scale photo of a terrier named Jake. The photo is shown in a graphics box that also has rounded corners to give it a cameo effect. The certificate uses a 10 percent gradient fill background with the color Flannel created earlier. The pet store logo, "Pups & Pals," is a graphics logo stored within a style. Figure 34.10 shows you this certificate as seen in Print Preview. Note that we include this certificate (and the graphics logo for Pups & Pals) as CERTIF. WP6 on the *Super Book* disk.

Note that you can see page borders only in Print Preview or on your finally printed page. If you do not have a color printer, consider dressing up the border by using laser foil, the sort you run through your printer and that adheres to whatever black toner is beneath it. Also, when printing a document containing a grey-scale photo, it generally is better to use the dithered printing option to get crisp lifelike images.

Other particulars about the certificate are that it uses standard 8.5-inch by 11-inch paper (Landscape), with 5-inch margins all around. The page border is a single line border, with rounded corners, and 10 percent gradient colored fill. Body type is Swiss 721 bold italic, and the main heading is 48 point.

Figure 34.10. Print Preview of graduation certificate with gradient fill.

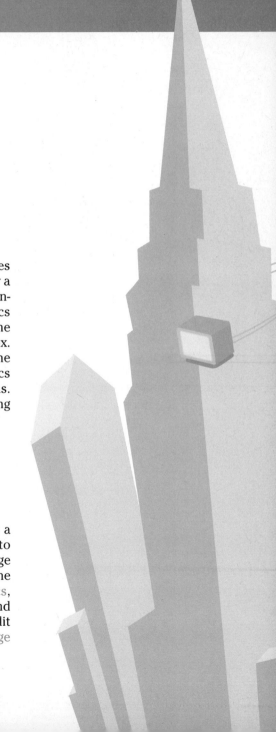

by Carolyn Woodie

Modifying Graphics Images

In previous chapters, making changes to graphics boxes was discussed. Although WordPerfect 6.0 is not truly a graphics design program such as WordPerfect Presentations, you can make certain changes to the graphics image in the box. You have learned how to change the box and borders with a graphics image inside the box. Now you will learn how to change the image inside of the box. You can move, size, rotate, and scale a graphics image, as well as change the colors and fill patterns. WordPerfect can even control many aspects of printing the image.

Moving or Cropping an Image

Once you have created a graphics box that contains a graphics image, you can then use the Image Editor to make changes to the graphics image. To enter the Image Editor, place the mouse pointer in the middle of the graphics box and double-click or choose Graphics, Graphics Boxes, Edit. Type the box number to edit, and click the Edit Box button or press Enter. The Edit Graphics Box dialog box appears. Choose the Image

Editor to enter the Image Editor (see Figure 35.1). Your graphics image should appear on-screen in the Image Editor.

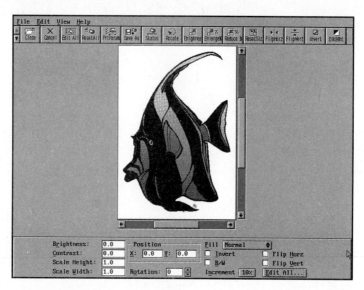

Figure 35.1. The Image Editor screen.

There are several ways to make changes to your graphics image at the editing screen. You can use the pull-down menus at the top of the screen. The button bar at the top of the Image Editor screen has many of the editing options available at the click of a button. There are also places at the bottom of the screen for entering specific measurements for editing changes. The fastest method, however, may be to use the quick editing keys from the keyboard. These quick editing keys make changes to the image in a relative manner—not with specific measurements. Without covering each and every method, this chapter presents you with several methods for making changes and the results to the image.

To move an image using the fast keyboard method, press the right arrow key to move the image to the right, or press the left arrow to move the image to the left. The up arrow and down arrow move the image up or down.

Note: All relative changes from the keyboard are done in increments. The increments of change are 10%, 25%, 1%, and 5%. The default setting is 10%. You may change the increment of change by clicking the Increment button at the bottom of the Image Editor screen.

An absolute way to move an image within a box is to type a measurement for the *x* and *y* position in the boxes at the bottom of the Image Editor screen. You also can use the horizontal and vertical scroll bars to move the graphics image within the box.

Cropping is trimming or cutting off portions of a picture. You can do some limited cropping by moving an image within a graphics box. Any portion of the image not inside the box will not print. For example, if you want to use just one of the hot air balloons from the HOTAIR.WPG graphics file, you can move the image within the box so that only the one balloon is visible (see Figure 35.2).

Tip: Because cropping may leave large blank portions of the graphics box, you may wish to change the size of the graphics box by returning to the Edit Graphics Box dialog box and changing the box size.

Figure 35.2. The original image (*top*) and the cropped image (*bottom*).

Note: All changes at the Image Editor are changes to the image in the graphics box and not changes to the graphics box.

Tip: To reset the image back to the original size and position, just choose Edit, Position, Reset Size and Position.

Sizing an Image

To size an image using the fast keyboard method, press the Page Down key to make the graphics image 10 percent smaller. Each time you press the Page Down key, the image shrinks by 10 percent. To enlarge the image, press Page Up (the image grows by 10 percent).

Tip: If you want to start over because you sized the image incorrectly, click the Reset Size button on the button bar to reset the image to the original size.

Another method for sizing the image is to select the Enlarge Area button from the button bar. When you select this button, you can click and drag your pointer to make a window around the area you want to enlarge. When you release the mouse button, the marked area is enlarged and centered in your graphics box (see Figure 35.3). Notice how this was done to the lighthouse in the LIGHTHS.WPG to use only the lighthouse as the graphic image.

Rotating an Image

To rotate an image using the fast keyboard method, press the + (plus) key on the keyboard (either plus key will work). The image will rotate clockwise by the percentage shown in the Increment box at the bottom of the screen. (See the Note on Increment setting earlier in this chapter.) To rotate an image counter-clockwise, use the – (minus) key.

An easy method for rotating an image with the mouse is to select the Rotate button from the button bar. When you select this, a horizontal axis line appears. Drag the horizontal axis to rotate the image.

For a more specific method for rotating an image, enter the degrees of rotation in the Rotation box at the bottom of the screen.

Figure 35.3. Selecting the area to enlarge (*top*). The resulting enlarged portion of the image (*bottom*).

Distorting an Image

For special effects, you may want to distort an image. You can stretch an image as if it were rubber (see Figure 35.4). You do this using the scaling measure. The scaling measurements for the height and width are usually equal. However, you can change your image by changing the height scale and width scale so they are not equal. Take the figure in the Scale Height box at the bottom of the Image Editor and enter a new number that is double the number in the Scale Width box. You will see the dramatic change to the image in the box. Enlarging the Scale Height stretches the image from top to bottom. Enlarging the Scale Width stretches the image from side to side.

Adjusting the Color of an Image

You can change the image into a negative of the original image by turning on the Invert option. This option changes the colors of the image to the complementary

483

colors (see Figure 35.1 for the original and Figure 35.5 for the changes). If you want to get rid of the shading of colors, you can select the B/W (black-and-white) option. This option converts the image to a black-and-white image.

Figure 35.4. An image prior to scaling (*left*). An image after changing scale height (*middle*). Changing the scale width, stretches the image from side to side (*right*).

Figure 35.5. The results of turning on the Invert option (*left*). The results of turning on the B/W option (*right*).

Changing the Brightness, Contrast, and Fill Type of an Image

The *brightness* of an image is how dark or light the entire image appears. A quick keyboard method to change the brightness of your image is to press the , (comma) key to darken the image or the . (period) key to lighten the image.

The *contrast* of an image is the difference between the light and dark areas of the image. A quick keyboard method to change the contrast of your image is to press the < (less than) key to decrease the contrast and the > (greater than) key to increase the contrast.

You can change the *fill* of an image to white, or even transparent, so the background shows through the image (see Figure 35.6). To change the fill, select the Fill option at the bottom of the Image Editor. This opens a pop-up menu, so you then can choose the type of fill desired.

> **Note:** You can combine many of these image attributes for special effects. It may take some experimenting to get the right combination of attribute modifications.

Mirror Image

You also can reverse the image to provide a mirror image of your original graphics image. You can flip the image horizontally or vertically. The easiest way to flip an image in the Image Editor is to click the Flip Vert or Flip Horiz buttons at the top of the screen. Another way to flip the image is to click the appropriate Flip Horiz or Flip Vert box at the bottom of the Image Editor screen.

> **Caution:** All changes made to the image are saved with the image in the current document. However, if you use the File, Save As command to save the image as a separate file, you will loose your changes to the graphics image.

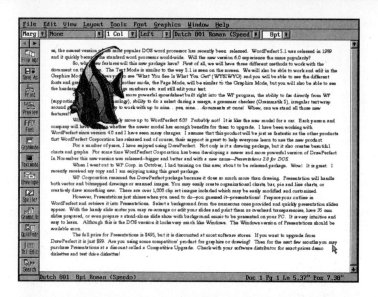

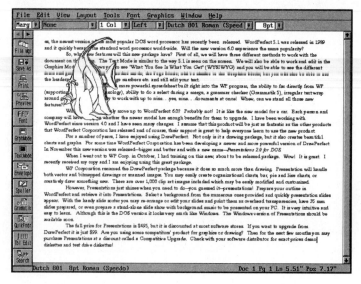

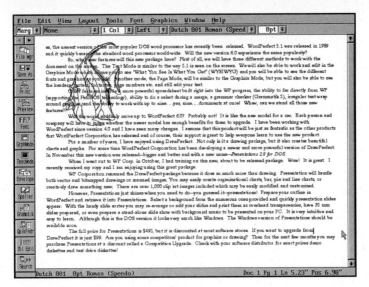

Figure 35.6. The original image (*opposite, top*). A white fill (*opposite, bottom*). A transparent fill (*above*).

Tip: If, after making changes to your image, you want to revert back to the image in its original state, click the Reset All button at the top of the Image Editor screen.

by Carolyn Woodie

Graphics Box Captions and Numbering

WordPerfect 6.0 provides very flexible methods for adding captions to your graphics boxes. Captions may be added when the box is first created, or you may add captions at a later time. Captions may be customized by changing fonts, point sizes, colors, rotating the captions, or even adding additional graphics to the caption. WordPerfect can create lists of your graphics boxes with the page number of each box. Consider using a list of your graphics boxes with the corresponding page numbers. This kind of list provides a very professional finish to your larger documents.

Creating a Caption

You may write a caption while creating the graphics box, or you may edit the box at a later time and add a caption. To create a caption, enter the Create Graphics Box or Edit Graphics Box dialog box. Select Create Caption. The caption editing screen appears.

Note that a caption with an automatic number appears. The caption is set in the box style. (See "Creating a List of Graphics Boxes" in this section for examples of the five different box styles and locations of the captions.) If you reveal the codes (View, Reveal Codes), you will see that the caption with the number is actually contained in a predefined style. WordPerfect provides five predefined automatic counting methods. See "Creating a List of Graphics Boxes" later in this chapter.

If you would like to number the graphics boxes automatically but want to change the style of the number, press Alt+F9 at the caption editing screen. This brings up the Graphics dialog box. Select Caption Number Style, Edit. Here you can edit the style of the automatic number. Press F7 when you're done to return to the caption editing screen.

At the caption editing screen, you may add text before or after the automatic number. If you don't want to use a number, press the Backspace key, which deletes the entire style. Then, you can type your caption without a number.

Note that you can change the font, size, color, and other attributes of the caption at the caption editing screen. If you want to include a graphics logo with every caption, you can even create another graphics box within your caption. You can access the Speller and Thesaurus while creating your caption. Once you have completed your caption, exit the caption editing screen by pressing Exit+F7.

Note: When you run a spell check on a document, the Speller also checks the spelling of any captions in the document.

To edit a caption, select Edit Caption from the Edit Graphics Box dialog box, and you are returned to the caption editing screen to edit your existing caption. Press Exit+F7 when you complete the editing of your caption.

Using Caption Options

Now that you have created your caption, you can change the location of your caption. At the Create Graphics Box or Edit Graphics Box dialog box, select Options, Caption Options. The Caption Options dialog box appears.

Select Side of Box to change the side of the box where the caption appears. You can place the caption at the **B**ottom, **T**op, **L**eft side or **R**ight side of your graphics box (see Figure 36.1).

Select Relation to Border to change how the caption appears with the border. Then, you can select Outside the border, Inside the border, or right On the border (see Figure 36.2).

Select Position to align the caption in the **C**enter, **L**eft, or **R**ight on the caption line. You may also move the caption a definite amount of space by selecting Offset from Position and entering a specific measurement or a percentage of the distance you want the caption adjusted. Indicate the direction of the offset, left or right, by selecting Offset Direction.

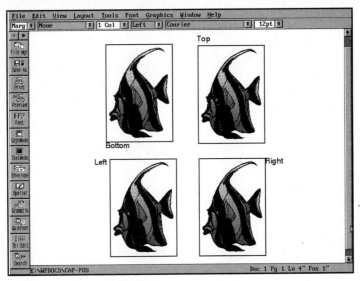

Figure 36.1. Positions of captions.

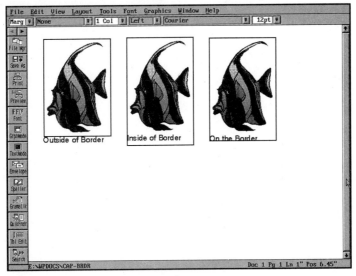

Figure 36.2. Captions relative to borders.

 Tip: If your caption has too much white space, you can adjust the Caption **Width** and set it to a specific measurement at Set, or set it for a percentage of width.

491

If you wish to rotate your caption, select **R**otation and select 90°, 180°, or 270° (see Figure 36.3).

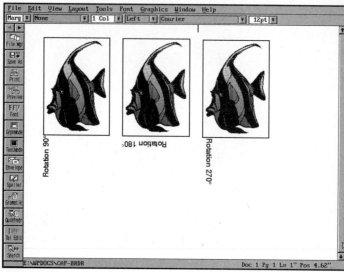

Figure 36.3. Caption rotation.

Creating a List of Graphics Boxes

At times, you may have had a number of graphics boxes in your document and would have liked to provide a list of the graphics boxes with the corresponding page number. WordPerfect provides an easy method to automatically create such a list. Use the List function of WordPerfect. The List function is often used to create an automatic table of contents or index. However, it is also used to create a list of boxes and their captions.

Because WordPerfect lists all of the same style of box, make certain that you have consistently used the same type of box. For example, the List function will produce an automatic list of all of your figure boxes. However, if you have mixed styles and have used user boxes and figure boxes, you would get two separate lists.

Tip: In WordPerfect 6.0, you can produce a list of mixed boxes by using the Counter function.

Use the following steps to create an automatic list of your boxes and captions:

1. Place your insertion point where you want your list to appear. You probably want it to appear on a separate page. Select Tools, List, Define, Create.

2. Enter a reference name, such as *charts*, for your list. This name won't appear in the list produced by WordPerfect, but it will appear as a name for the definition of that particular list.

3. Select Numbering Mode to choose the style of page numbers for the list. If you want your numbers to appear differently than they appear in the document, you can make changes by selecting Page Number Format.

4. Select Include Graphics and select the style of graphics box that you want listed. Click Select to close the dialog box. Then click OK or press Enter to exit the Create List dialog box.

5. Select the name of the captions list you just defined and click Select. This step places a definition mark in your document at the location where you want the list to appear.

> **Note:** You may have many different types of lists in the same document. In addition to a table of contents and index, you might create lists of charts, lists of maps, and lists of examples by using different styles of boxes for each desired list.

6. Generate the list by selecting Tools, Generate, click OK or press Enter. From the keyboard, you also can press Alt+F5, Generate.

> **Tip:** Always generate before the final printing of your document and after each editing session to update the page numbers in any table of contents, cross-referencing, index, counter, or list.

by Carolyn Woodie

Using Graphics Boxes for Text

We have spent a great deal of time describing graphic boxes for graphic images. However, a common use for graphic boxes is to emphasize text. WordPerfect 6.0 provides several ways to emphasize text. One way is to use Graphics, Borders. This feature allows you to place borders around paragraphs, pages, or columns (see Chapter 34, "Borders and Fills"). Another way to emphasize text is to place the text into a graphics box. As mentioned earlier in this book, text may be placed into any of the graphics box styles.

Creating a Graphics Box with Text

Procedure 37.1. Creating a graphics box with text.

1. Place your cursor at the top of the page where you want the text box to appear.
2. Choose Graphics, Graphics Boxes, Create. This takes you to the Create Graphics Box dialog box.
3. Select Create Text. This takes you into the Text Editor screen.

4. At the Text Editor screen, you can type your text or paste text if you are copying it from the document. You may even retrieve a text file into the Text Editor.

 Tip: To copy some text from the document into a graphics box, select the text and choose Edit, Copy, or press Ctrl+C. Create the graphics box, go into the Text Editor and select Edit, Paste, or press Ctrl+V to retrieve a copy of the selected text.

 Note: At the Text Editor screen, you may also use the Speller, Thesaurus, create tables, create graphics lines, or even line draw.

5. You may change the font and change the font appearance at the Text Editor screen. These changes affect the text within the graphics box only.

6. Once you have created and changed the text to the style desired, press F7 when you are done. At the Create Graphics Box dialog box, you can determine the position and size of your graphics box.

7. When all changes have been made, click on OK or press Enter to exit the Create Graphics Box dialog box. Your text box should appear in a graphics box in your document.

Editing Text in a Graphics Box

Once you have created the text graphics box, it is easy to edit the text within the box. Not only can you change the text content, you can change the font, size, or other attributes of the text.

Procedure 37.2. Editing text in a graphics box.

1. Place the mouse pointer in the center of the text box and double-click to enter the Edit Graphics Box dialog box, or choose Graphics, Graphics Boxes, Edit.

2. Type in the Document Box Number, then click on the Edit Box button. The Edit Graphics Box dialog box appears.

3. Choose Edit Text to re-enter the Text Editor.

4. Make the changes in your text and press F7 to exit when completed. Click on OK or press Enter to exit the Create Graphics Box dialog box. The text box with your new changes should appear on-screen.

Changing the Text Size in a Graphics Box

Once in the Text Editor, you may change the text size or appearance of the text.

 Tip: You may find it helpful to reveal the codes while in the Text Editor to see your current codes. To reveal codes, select View, Reveal Codes, or press Alt+F3.

To select a new font for all of the text in the box, place your insertion point at the beginning of the text and select Font, Font. For a list of the fonts available, click on the down arrow next to the current font listing. Select a new font. You will note by looking in Reveal Codes that the old font code has been replaced with a new font code. The font change affects only the text within the box. It does not change the remaining text in your document.

If you want to use any of the appearance or relative size options in the Font dialog box, you must first select the amount of text to change. For example, to double underline a phrase, select the complete phrase and choose Font to access the Font dialog box. Click on the box beside double underline. Click on OK or press Enter.

Rotating Text in a Graphics Box

Procedure 37.3. Rotating text with a graphics box.

1. To rotate text at the Text Editor screen, press Alt+F9 to access the Graphics dialog box.
2. Select Rotate Box Contents to access the Rotate Box Contents dialog box.
3. Select the desired degree of rotation: 90°, 180°, or 270°. Click on OK or press Enter to close the dialog box and return to the Text Editor. Press Exit+F7 to exit the Text Editor screen.

 Note: The Text Editor does not show the text as rotated text.

 Tip: A fast way to return the text to 0° degree rotation is to select Edit, Undo.

4. Click on OK or press Enter to exit the Graphics dialog box and return to your document. Your text should appear in a box rotated to the angle requested.

Moving or Changing the Size of a Graphics Box with Text

Just remember that although this graphic box contains text, it is still a graphics box. You may move or size the graphics box using the mouse or the Edit Graphics Box dialog box.

To move the box using the mouse, click and drag the box to the new location. To move the box using the Edit Graphics Box dialog box, double-click on the box. The Edit Graphics Box dialog box appears and you may then Edit the Position of the box.

To size the box using the mouse, place the mouse pointer inside the box. Click once to select the box, then click and drag on one of the box handles. To size the box using the Edit Graphics Box dialog box, double-click on the box. The Edit Graphics Box dialog box appears, and you may then change the size of the box. Remember, this changes the size of the box, not the size of the text in the box. (For more information on sizing graphics boxes, see Chapter 33, "Editing a Graphics Box.")

Caution: When adjusting your box, if you make your box too small, not all of your text will appear in the box.

Special Effects Using Text in Graphics Boxes

The graphics features of WordPerfect 6.0 are so powerful that it is hard to select just a few examples to show you how to use these features. However, a few of my favorites are discussed in the following sections. First, I'll use a *pull-quote* to show how to use a graphics box with text to emphasize a quotation from an article. The second example uses a table box to create a quick masthead for a newsletter. The last example shows you how to use a graphics box to create a *drop cap*.

Creating a Pull-Quote

A *pull-quote* is usually a box that holds a quotation taken from the adjacent article, and it is usually displayed in a much larger font. Look through a few magazines to find a variety of pull-quotes—they are attention grabbers, enticing you to read the articles (see Figure 37.1).

Procedure 37.4. Creating a pull-quote.

1. At the top of the page where you want the pull-quote to appear, create a table box. Select Graphics or Alt+F9, Graphics Box, Create.

2. Select Based on Box Style and change to a Table Box.

3. Change the Attachment to Page.

4. Set the position of the box. At Edit Position, set Horizontal position to Center with the Position-Relative to Margins. Set the Vertical position to Center with the Position-Relative to Margins. Click on OK or press Enter.

5. Enter the Text Editor by selecting Create Text. Select a larger font and possibly a different typeface than the one selected for the body of the document. (Figure 37.1 uses Swiss Bold 20-point type.)

6. Set the justification to Left. Type your quotation. Press F7 when finished to exit the Text Editor. You may have to adjust the size of the box to fit the quotation. The example in Figure 37.1 was changed to a width of 2.4 inches, and the height was left at automatic.

7. At the Create Graphics Box dialog box, set the Text Flows Around Box on Both Sides. Pull-quotes are very effective in documents displayed in columns. Click OK or press Enter to return to your document.

Figure 37.1. A pull-quote example.

Creating a Masthead

If you do not have desktop publishing experience, one way to begin is to use graphics boxes to easily create elements of desktop publishing. For newsletters, usually the title of the newsletter is placed across the top with any identifying

499

logo. A simple way to create a masthead is to create a table box with the newsletter title in a large font centered within the box. A caption could be created to indicate the issue of the newsletter (see Figure 37.2 for a masthead example).

Procedure 37.5. Creating a masthead.

1. With your insertion point at the top of your document, change your margins. Choose Layout, Margins or press Shift+F8. Change all document margins to .4 inches. Click on OK or press Enter.

2. Create a table box for the masthead. Select Graphics or Alt+F9, Graphics Box, Create.

3. Change the Attach to Page.

4. At the Create Graphics Box dialog box, select Based on Box Style—Table Box.

5. Set the position of the box. At Edit Position, set Horizontal position to Full. The Vertical position should be set to Top.

6. Enter the Text Editor. Select Create Text. At the Text Editor, press Enter. This places an additional amount of space at the top of the text box to balance the text within the box. Select a larger font. The example uses Dutch 801 Bold Italic (Speedo) 50-point type. Center and type the title of your newsletter. Press F7 when finished to exit the Text Editor.

7. To create the caption, at the Create Graphics Box dialog box select Options, Caption Options. Change the Side of Box to Bottom. Change the Position to Center. Click on OK or press Enter to exit the Caption Options dialog box.

8. To type the caption, select Create Caption to enter the Caption Editor. Use Backspace to delete the current caption.

9. Change the font. The example used Helve-WP Bold (Type 1) 12-point type. Type the information that will appear on the left, move to the right margin by pressing Alt+F6, and type the information that will appear on the right. Press F7 to exit the Caption Editor.

10. Click on OK or press Enter to close the Create Graphics Box dialog box. Your masthead is complete!

Neighborhood Newsbits

Harbor Hills Community   Summer 1993

Figure 37.2. A masthead example.

Creating a Drop Cap

Drop caps are often used in newsletters or magazine articles. If you are not familiar with the phrase, just look through a magazine. A drop cap refers to the large letter often found at the beginning of the first paragraph of an article (see Figure 37.3 for an example of a drop cap).

Procedure 37.6. Creating a drop cap.

1. With your text document on the document screen, place your insertion point at the beginning of the paragraph where the drop cap should appear. Make note of the size of the font of the text within your document and multiply this by 2.5 to determine the size of the font to set for the drop cap. Make a note of both numbers—you will need them later.

2. Delete the first character and any Tab or Indent command appearing at the beginning of the paragraph.

3. Create a graphics box for the enlarged letter. Select Graphics or Alt+F9, Graphics Box, Create.

4. Attach To should be set for Paragraph.

5. Select Based on Box Style—User Box.

6. Set the size of the box. At Edit Size, set width for Auto Width, set height to double the font size of your text. For example, if your document appears in a 12-point font, set the height to 24 point.

> **Note:** You may enter any measurement in WordPerfect in points by following the measurement with a *p* (for example, 24p). WordPerfect converts the measurement to inches automatically.

7. Select Edit Border/Fill, Spacing. Turn off Automatic Spacing. Change Outside, Set All to 10 percent of the drop cap size. For example, if your drop cap size in Step 1 is set for 30 point, set the outside measurements to 3 point.

8. Select Edit Position, Horizontal Position to Left.

9. Set Text Flows Around Box to Right Side and set Contour Text Flow to On.

> **Tip:** This is a perfect type of box to create as a box style for future use. (See Chapter 34 for a detailed explanation of styles.)

10. Now you are ready to create the drop cap. Go into the Text Editor by selecting Create Text.
11. Select a font for the drop cap. Set the point size for the drop cap as determined in Step 1. Select a typeface. The example uses Helve-WP Bold (Type 1) 30 point. Often it is more attractive to have a typeface other than the one used as the typeface of the body of the document. Try a few to see which is most attractive. Click on OK or press Enter.
12. Type the drop cap character and press F7 to exit the Text Editor.
13. Click on OK or press Enter to exit the Create Graphics Box dialog box. Your drop cap should appear at the beginning of the paragraph (see Figure 37.3).

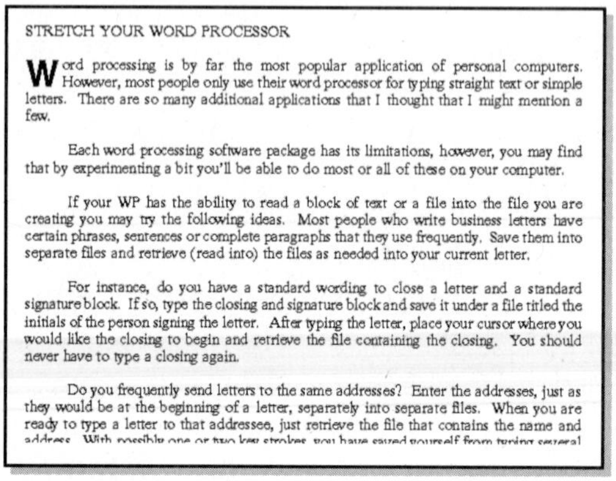
STRETCH YOUR WORD PROCESSOR

Word processing is by far the most popular application of personal computers. However, most people only use their word processor for typing straight text or simple letters. There are so many additional applications that I thought that I might mention a few.

Each word processing software package has its limitations, however, you may find that by experimenting a bit you'll be able to do most or all of these on your computer.

If your WP has the ability to read a block of text or a file into the file you are creating you may try the following ideas. Most people who write business letters have certain phrases, sentences or complete paragraphs that they use frequently. Save them into separate files and retrieve (read into) the files as needed into your current letter.

For instance, do you have a standard wording to close a letter and a standard signature block. If so, type the closing and signature block and save it under a file titled the initials of the person signing the letter. After typing the letter, place your cursor where you would like the closing to begin and retrieve the file containing the closing. You should never have to type a closing again.

Do you frequently send letters to the same addresses? Enter the addresses, just as they would be at the beginning of a letter, separately into separate files. When you are ready to type a letter to that addressee, just retrieve the file that contains the name and address. With possibly one or two key strokes you have saved yourself from typing several

Figure 37.3. A drop cap example.

by Carolyn Woodie

Working with Graphic Lines and Line Draw

Often people will think that they don't need to learn about graphics in WordPerfect because they won't be using pictures; but everyone using WordPerfect should learn how to use the graphics features even if they do not expect to use images in their documents. Most text documents can easily be enhanced by adding graphics boxes with text or graphic lines.

In this chapter we will learn how to create graphic lines, how to alter them with a mouse, and how to create some special effects using graphics lines. We will also introduce you to the Line Draw function. You will be pleased with how a few graphic lines added to a document will give it a professional, finished appearance.

Creating Horizontal Lines

Procedure 38.1. Creating a Horizontal Line.
1. To create a horizontal line, place your insertion point where you want to create the line.
2. Choose Graphics, or Alt+F9. Then choose Graphic Lines and Create. The Create Graphics Line dialog box appears.

3. Choose whether you want to create a horizontal line or a vertical line by selecting Line Orientation to open a pop-up menu. Select Horizontal.

4. Once you have selected horizontal line, you can set the position of the line. The horizontal and vertical position options will vary depending on whether you are creating a horizontal or vertical line. When you select horizontal line, the horizontal position option will allow you to begin the line at the **L**eft margin; **R**ight margin; **C**enter of the line, or **F**ull reaching from margin to margin, or you can **S**et the exact position measured from the left edge of the page where you want to begin the line.

5. The vertical position for a horizontal line indicates where vertically on the page you want the line to appear. You may **S**et the line at any specified position measured from the top edge of the page or you can choose to have the line appear at the **B**aseline of the line where your insertion point is sitting. The Baseline indicates the base or bottom of the line.

6. The thickness of the line can either be set to a particular size or you can choose Auto to use the default thickness of the line.

7. The length of the line may be set by selecting Length. If you have selected the horizontal position as Full, the length is controlled by the margins and you will not be able to set a length for the line.

Tip: You will probably find it hard to measure the thickness or even the length of a line in inches. Centimeters is a much more precise measurement. You can enter the measurement in centimeters by typing the measurement followed by a c (for example, .25c). WordPerfect will convert the centimeters to inches for you.

8. Select the Line style. Figure 38.1 shows examples of the Line styles available; or, you can create a new line style.

9. In addition to selecting the Line Style, you may select the color of the line or even the percentage of the color in order to shade the color. To change the color of the line, choose Color. Select the color and click on OK.

Caution: Make certain that you click on Select after highlighting the desired color. If you just click on OK, you will not be changing the color and the line will remain the original color.

10. If you want to control the spacing above or below the created line, you can set a measurement under Spacing.

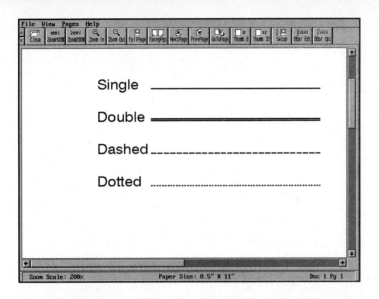

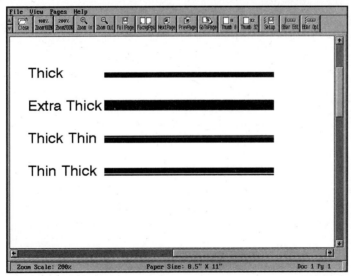

Figure 38.1. Examples of Line Styles.

 Once you have created a graphic line, a code for the line is placed into the document. You may see the codes in the Reveal Codes screen. When you highlight the code in Reveal Codes, you will see the details about the line.

Creating Vertical Lines

Procedure 38.2. Creating a vertical line.

1. To create a vertical line, place your insertion point where you want to create the line. Go to the Create Graphics Line dialog box.

2. Choose whether you want to create a horizontal line or a vertical line by selecting Line Orientation to open a pop-up menu. Select Vertical.

3. When you are creating a vertical line, the horizontal position options will allow you to position the vertical line at the **L**eft margin, **R**ight margin, **C**entered between the left and right margins, or **B**etween Columns; or you can **S**et any position measured from the left edge of the page where you want the vertical line to cross.

4. The vertical position options allow you to begin the vertical line at the **T**op margin, **B**ottom margin, **C**entered between the top and bottom margins, **F**ull stretching the line from the top margin to the bottom margin, or **S**et, which allows you to set the measurement from the top edge of the page.

5. The thickness of the line can be either **A**uto, to let WordPerfect determine the thickness of the line, or **S**et on a particular thickness.

6. The length of the line may be set by selecting Length. If you have selected the vertical position as Full, the length is controlled by the margins and you will not be able to set a length for the line.

Editing Graphic Lines Using a Mouse

You will find it very easy to edit a graphic line with the mouse. Just click with your mouse pointer on the graphic line once to select the line. You will notice that "handles" appear in the center and at the ends of the graphic line (see Figure 38.2).

To edit the thickness of a line, place your pointer at the center handle. Your pointer should change to a double-headed arrow. Click and drag the line down to make the line thicker.

To edit the length of the line, place your pointer at one of the side handles. Your pointer should change to a double-headed arrow. Click and drag the line to the right or left to make the line shorter or longer.

To edit both the length and the thickness at once, click and drag on a corner handle.

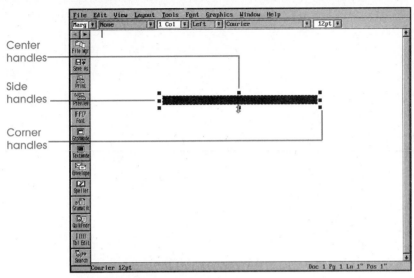

Center handles—

Side handles—

Corner handles—

Figure 38.2. Selected Graphic Lines.

Tip: If you have problems selecting a line to edit it, just choose Graphics, Graphic Lines, Edit, type the number of the line, or indicate the previous graphic line or the next graphic line. You will be placed in the Edit Graphic Line dialog box for the line you indicated.

Editing Graphic Lines Using the Graphic Line Dialog Box

To edit a line using the graphic line dialog box, just double-click with your pointer on the line. You will see the Edit Graphic Line dialog box.

This dialog is exactly like the Create Graphic Line dialog box. Your current settings will be shown in the box. Make the changes to the length, thickness, colors, or other attributes of the graphic line. Click on OK or press Enter to accept your changes and close the dialog box.

Moving Graphic Lines Using a Mouse

To move a graphic line, place your pointer on the line and click once to select the line. Your pointer should change to a four-headed arrow. Click and drag the line to the position desired.

507

Caution: Be aware that when you move a line with the mouse, the horizontal and vertical positions change from relative positions (top, bottom, baseline, and so on) to "set" positions where a specific position measurement is entered. Thereafter, if an adjoining line of text is moved, the graphic line will remain in the same position.

Moving Graphic Lines Using the Graphic Line Dialog Box

To move a graphic line using the Edit Graphic Line dialog box, just double-click on the line to enter the dialog box. Make appropriate changes to the horizontal and vertical positions. Click on OK or press Enter to close the dialog box.

Creating a New Line Style

If you are going to use a specific line design several times within a document, you may want to create a line style. By doing so, you won't have to re-create the line design each time you want to use it in the document. Also, once you become experienced in using lines, you will want to save some of your line combinations for use in other documents. You can save these line designs by creating and saving a new line style. (For more information on the concept and use of styles, see Chapter 39, "Styles.")

Procedure 38.3. Creating a Line Style.

1. At either the Create or Edit Line dialog box, select Line Style. (Or you can go directly to Line Styles by selecting Styles from the Graphics Lines menu.) The Line Styles dialog box will appear. The current listing of Line Styles will be shown.

2. Choose Create from the menu on the right. Type in a descriptive name for your new line style, such as Thick-inside, dotted-outside line. The press Enter. The Create Line Style dialog box will appear.

The window in the Create Line Style dialog box will show you how your design would appear as a vertical line or a horizontal line.

3. You may change the first line by changing its pattern, color, and thickness. To create an additional line, just click on the down scroll arrow. You can then create another line and also adjust the interline spacing.

4. Once your line style has been created, click on OK or press Enter to exit the Create Line Style dialog box. Then click on Close to close the Line Styles dialog box. Your new line style can then be selected for future use in your document.

Caution: Make certain that you save the newly created line styles into a file to use with other documents or your new line styles will just remain with your current document.

Special Effects Using Graphic Lines

Below are a few examples of how lines can be used to enhance your documents. When you use graphic lines to enhance your document, you don't want the emphasis to be on the lines. If the lines distract attention from the body of the text, the lines are too bold.

Tip: One way to keep the lines from overwhelming the text is by changing their color or reducing the shading to below 85 percent. This can lighten the visual impact of the lines.

Using Graphic Lines in a Header or Footer

One very effective way to use lines is to add them to headers or footers. Often lines are used to clearly separate the header or footer from the body of the document (see Figure 38.3).

Chapter titles can be emphasized with graphic lines. The sample below shows a vertical line and a horizontal line in a lighter color (see Figure 38.4). Once a pattern of lines is designed, you may want to put it in a line style for future use. (See the preceding section, "Creating a Line Style.")

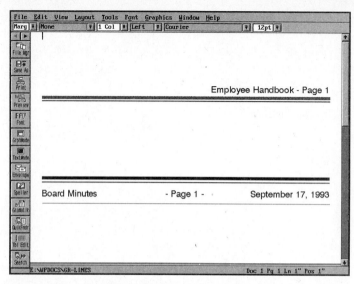

Figure 38.3. Using Graphic Lines in a header or footer.

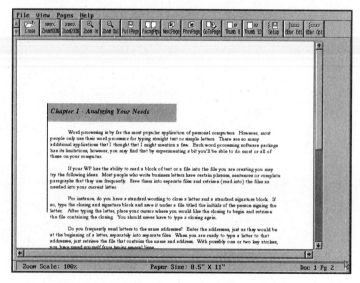

Figure 38.4. Using Graphic lines to enhance chapter titles.

Using Line Draw

The Line Draw function has been with us through various versions of WordPerfect, and before WordPerfect 5.0, the Line Draw function was the only way to produce lines. Although Line Draw is fun to use, you will probably like using graphic lines and boxes better. Often people use Line Draw because they aren't aware of how to use graphic lines and boxes. The Line Draw function is similar to the magnetic drawing screen we used as children.

Tip: If you want to change the color of the character used in Line Draw, it is changed through the Font menu. Select Font, Color, and select the color desired before beginning Line Draw.

Caution: When using Line Draw, you must use a monospace font (sometimes called a fixed space font) such as Courier. Monospaced fonts are indicated on the font list by a number followed by "cpi," which stands for "characters per inch." A proportionally-spaced font such as Times Roman will not work for Line Draw.

Drawing Lines

To create lines using Line Draw, select Graphics and Line Draw, or press Ctrl+F3 and select Line Draw. The Line Draw screen will appear (see Figure 38.5).

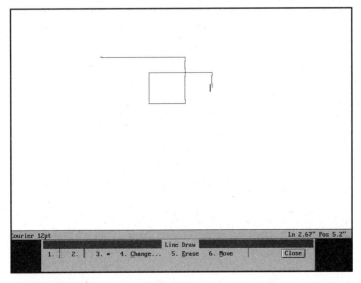

Figure 38.5. The Line Draw screen.

The lines are drawn using the arrow keys on the keyboard rather than the mouse pointer. Move the right arrow to see a single line appear at your insertion point. Experiment with the arrow keys to draw lines on the screen.

Moving the Insertion Point

You can move the insertion point without drawing a line by selecting Move from the options at the bottom of the screen. You can then move your insertion point to another area on the screen without drawing as you move. It will remain in the Move mode until you again select a line type to draw by selecting 1, 2, or 3 at the bottom of the line draw screen.

Erasing Portions of a Line

You can erase portions of a line that you have drawn by selecting Erase from the options at the bottom of the line draw screen. Your insertion point then serves as an eraser and will erase a line as you move over that line.

Changing the Line Draw Character

You can change the line style by selecting line options 1, 2, or 3 at the bottom of the line draw screen. However, you are not limited to those selections. To see what other options are available, select Change. From the options provided, you may select a new line draw style. Note that you can even select a character from the keyboard as your line draw character. For example, this would allow you to draw a box using a string of dollar signs ($). Once you have completed your line drawing, just click on Close and you will return to your document.

> **Tip:** If you are using text with lines drawn in Line Draw, use the Insert mode to insert the text along with your Line Draw. If you do not use Insert and you type text or spaces with lines drawn in Line Draw, you will be inserting characters and inadvertently moving portions of the line.

Desktop Publishing

by Bob Boeri and Marilyn Horn Claff

Styles

WordPerfect styles are a feature that most people have not used, because they found other ways (like macros) to achieve similar effects, because styles made their documents larger, or because they never really understood them. Styles were optional and therefore easy to avoid in earlier versions of WordPerfect. If you wanted to create a drop shadow for a graphics box, you simply specified lines for top and left and thick lines for bottom and right. Styles didn't enter into this operation. In WordPerfect 6.0, avoiding styles is no longer easy, and certainly not recommended. Styles are everywhere, and they have become a fundamental tool for formatting documents. Styles can control all aspects of your documents, from text characteristics to graphics lines, borders, boxes, and fills.

To understand styles it is very important to understand all their fundamental concepts. This chapter will explain those concepts and show some simple applications of styles so you can start using them immediately to design a document and to build a style library.

Even if you've used styles before, you'll find the newly expanded WordPerfect styles unfamiliar. Take the time to learn how to use styles and you will achieve desktop publishing effects never before possible in WordPerfect.

What are Styles?

Styles are primarily a formatting tool. Styles may contain formatting codes, text, graphics, and even other style definitions. The most common usage for styles is to control the formatting that applies to particular document elements. For example, a text style could contain formatting codes for double-spacing, full justification, and italics. Wherever you use that style in a document, those formatting attributes apply. If you modify the style, the appearance of the document changes to reflect the new version of the style.

Styles are a complex topic because there are so many ways to classify styles. On one level, you can divide styles into two main groups, *user-defined styles* and *system styles*. User-defined styles, as you would expect, are styles that you define and apply yourself. System styles are styles that are built into the WordPerfect program and are automatically applied to various document elements, whether you are aware of it or not. To name just three examples, WordPerfect has system styles for footnotes, graphics boxes, and headers that determine the default appearance for each of these items. By redefining a copy of these system styles, you can in effect change your default settings for these items. This design gives you enormous control over nearly all elements of your document.

An another level, you can define styles by the elements to which they apply. For example, there are three basic types of styles that apply to text *(Open, Paragraph,* and *Character)*, and graphics styles that apply to lines, borders, fills, and graphics boxes. Just to make things interesting, most of these types of styles can include other styles. A single *Open* style might include another Open style, a graphics line style, a page border style, and even a graphics, text, or equation box style.

Still another classification refers only to text styles. Text styles can be divided into *Outline* and *Non-Outline* styles. Outline styles are groups of up to eight regular styles that form a hierarchical group, or family. Each outline style in an outline family is assigned an outline level number. You can then manipulate the text to which the outline styles are applied. For example, you can move or copy an outline level head and all of the outline levels beneath it, up to the next outline level head of the same or higher level, without blocking it. You can adjust the level of the outline style attached to a paragraph and all of the outline levels beneath that level with a single command. Like regular text styles, outline style levels are either Open, Paragraph, or Character styles. (See Chapter 55, "Outlining," for more details.)

Why Use Styles?

The most obvious reason is that they are there so pervasive. You can simply accept WordPerfect defaults for all styles—probably a fine idea to get started— but you will still see lists of style choices throughout various menus, and you will need to know what to do with them. You did not need this level of style awareness before, but now it is inescapable.

If the first reason sounds a bit intimidating, there are four commonly attractive reasons why you will want to use styles:

▲ Customization
▲ Control

▲ Ease of use

▲ Consistency

Customization. Styles let you use a wide variety of built-in effects, and if you want something more, you are free to create your own variations. Even for simple elements such as lines, you can create a nearly infinite set of variations in appearance.

Control. If you use styles to format your documents, you can easily reformat your documents by modifying one or more style definitions. When you change a style definition in a document, the changes take effect in your document immediately. By changing your style library, you can reformat groups of documents quickly and easily. By way of contrast, if you use direct formatting in your documents, you would have to search for each individual hidden formatting code and change the format options on a case-by-case basis. In a document of even average complexity, this task will be time-consuming, difficult, and boring; in a complex document, it could be next to impossible.

Ease of Use. Giving you control also makes it easier for you to create and use styles. Instead of having to remember the sequence of keystrokes to put a WordPerfect icon (such as the recycle symbol, WordPerfect character 4,85) into your document, you can create a style palette of your commonly used icons and pick its name from a list. That style palette could also specify making the icon a special size or color. Ease of use flows from control in styles. Ease of use becomes very important for certain powerful features such as defining level headings for a table of contents. Most authors don't want to be bothered learning how to mark a section title so that title can appear in an automatically generated table of contents. Providing a simple menu choice, "level one heading," makes it easier for authors to do that and add considerable extra value to their work.

Consistency. If you or your peers work with groups of documents, it probably is important that they look similar and use similar typographic or page design conventions. By sharing libraries, you guarantee consistency between them. Moreover, if you decide to change a style decision, that style change can be applied instantly to all documents using that style.

There are other strong arguments for using styles to control your formatting. Styles reduce "code clutter" in Reveal Codes. If you use a style, all of the formatting codes that make up that style are treated as a single code. When you look at the style in Reveal Codes, you see the name and type of the style, rather than a jumble of formatting codes. When you move your insertion point onto the style code in Reveal Codes, the style code expands to show you what the style does (see Figure 39.1). Style codes that expand and contract are far easier to work with in Reveal Codes than regular codes.

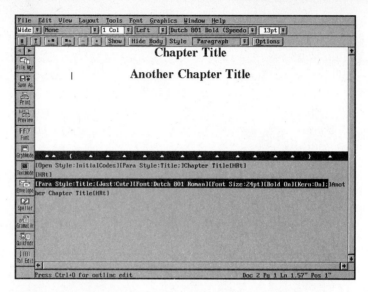

Figure 39.1. The Title paragraph style, shown in its short and expanded forms in Reveal Codes.

Another benefit of styles is that you can only change the styles by editing the style definition in the Edit Style dialog box. Users, especially novice users, cannot inadvertently change the formatting by moving the insertion point between codes or by deleting individual codes at the document level.

In many cases, the sequence in which WordPerfect formatting codes are arranged in your document is important. For example, if you mark text for a table of contents and also apply the bold and large font attributes to that text, your table of contents will pick up the bold and large attributes if the table of contents markers are *outside* the bold and large codes, but not if the markers are *inside* the bold and large codes. If you mark the table of contents headers by hand, you may end up with some table of contents entries that are bold but not large, large but not bold, bold and large, or just normal text, depending on the order of these hidden codes. If, instead, you use a style to apply all of these codes, the order of the codes will be consistent from one table of contents entry to the next.

Speed of formatting is still another important reason for using styles. Once the styles have been defined, it's a cinch to apply them to your text, especially if they are defined as Paragraph styles, which you can apply by choosing from the drop-down style list on the ribbon, or Outline styles, which you can apply by clicking the number symbol or the promote or demote buttons on the outline bar (see Figure 39.2).

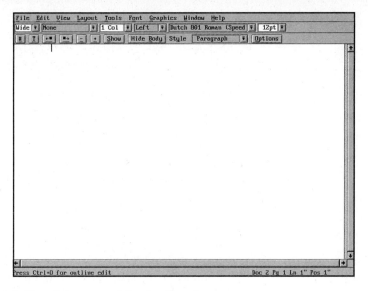

Figure 39.2. The ribbon and the outline bar.

There are two other subtle, little-known, and very persuasive reasons for using styles. These reasons have to do with the fact that books aren't just paper any more. (More about this later in the chapter.)

How Styles Differ From Macros

If you can create a keystroke to insert a happy face icon, why use a style? When should you use styles and when should you use macros? First, sometimes this decision is a matter of choice. You use "Alt+H" and I'll select "happy face" as a library style. Your way is faster, but mine is easier to remember. If I want to change the appearance of a family of documents, I can do that by changing the way I define some style element I call "page design" and use it in several documents. You can effect the same change by writing a macro that does several searches and replacements. Here the choice is not so clear. Writing macros nearly always entails some debugging and testing, and you must remember to use the macros to effect the changes. And after you've applied a macro to change a document, it might not be possible to revert to the earlier version. With styles it would be as simple as using a different style library or making a simple change in the same library.

Of course, styles would be of no help at all for certain complex tasks easily achieved with macros. For example, you could write a macro that interactively guides the user to fill out a form and saves the result to a file. This is beyond the capabilities and purpose of styles.

Style Libraries

Giving you all that power could make it very difficult to keep track of your handcrafted special effects, but fortunately, WordPerfect also gives you ways to control and manage your libraries. You can do the following:

▲ Restrict special style definitions to the current document

▲ Save your style definitions in one or more style libraries

▲ Retrieve another style library into your current document

▲ Copy one or more styles to your personal or shared style library

▲ Share your style libraries with other users by specifying them as "shared libraries"

New Concepts in Style Libraries

There are several major changes in WordPerfect 6.0 styles:

▲ Types of styles

▲ Types and locations of style libraries

▲ Precedence of style libraries

In addition to these categories, there is one other significant change in the way styles work. If you made a change to a style in a WordPerfect Version 5 library, that change would not automatically take effect in documents that had retrieved the earlier version of the library. You had to retrieve the new library into the document (or use Update if the library was defined as your default style library) in order for that library to take effect. In WordPerfect Version 6.0, if you have a personal or shared library defined or if you assign a personal or shared library to a document, then whenever a change is made to that library, your document's styles will reflect those changes automatically, because the document maintains a dynamic link to that library.

> **Note:** If you want to use a style library in a document but do not want it to update if the style library is changed, use the Retrieve feature from the Style List dialog box, or delete the name of the Personal and/or Shared style libraries assigned to the document in the Style Options dialog box.
>
> Style libraries themselves can be "personal" or "shared." Actually these two categories suggest, but do not compel, their use. That is, you may share a personal library or subdivide your personal libraries into the categories called "shared" and "personal." It's best to keep things simple at first, though, and use them as their names suggest.

Note: You can have many personal and shared style libraries.

Open, Character, and Paragraph Styles

In WordPerfect Version 5, there were two primary types of style tags: open and paired. Open styles used open (or unpaired) formatting codes, such as paper size/ type, margin settings, or base font, which didn't need to be closed or turned off. When you turned on an Open style, it remained in effect until you either inserted direct formatting codes in your document that overrode the codes in the style, or until you used a different style.

The other type, paired, was a type which was turned on and off, and had a beginning and an end. One common example would be to apply the large size attribute to a blocked section of text.

In WordPerfect 6.0, the concept of open styles remains, but there are now two types of paired styles: character and paragraph. This new distinction is required because WordPerfect now recognizes the concept of a paragraph—a sequence of characters followed by one or more hard returns. Thus, you can define and apply character styles to sequences of characters (or passages of any length) and paragraph styles to entire paragraphs.

Use Character styles for passages that may be either less than or more than an entire paragraph. Character styles are useful for adding emphasis to words or phrases. For example, you could define a Book Title style that would be bold and italic. Character styles are also useful for extended text passages. You might define a style as French that contains the FR language code and a code to disable the Speller (assuming that you don't own the French language module for WordPerfect). Whenever you wrote a passage in French, you could apply the French style so the English speller would skip over the passage in French.

Because WordPerfect recognizes paragraphs as such, you need not block the paragraph or worry about reblocking it if the size of the paragraph changes. If you need to assign a different paragraph style to a particular paragraph, you don't need to delete the original paragraph style code, because only one paragraph style can be in effect in a paragraph. Typical uses for paragraph styles include paragraphs, titles, lists, and special items such as bibliographic entries.

In many cases, you can define a style as either a paragraph or a character style. Given the choice, you'll probably prefer to use paragraph styles whenever possible, for a number of reasons. First, paragraph styles are easier to apply because you don't have to block the text first. Secondly, you can choose paragraph styles from the ribbon, which also tells you the name of the current paragraph style, if one is in effect, or displays the word *None* if not. Thirdly, paragraph styles are attached to paragraphs, so you don't have to worry about inadvertently extending a paragraph style, or adding text outside the `[Para Style End]` code.

Types and Locations of Style Libraries

Whenever you use a style in a WordPerfect document, the style definition for that style automatically becomes part of the document. This design means that if you give another user a copy of your WordPerfect document on disk, you don't need to make a copy of the style library as well.

In WordPerfect 6.0, as in previous versions of WordPerfect, you can also maintain your style definitions in an external file, called a style library, so that you can use those styles in other documents, not just the document that you were in when you created the styles. A style library is a special kind of WordPerfect document consisting of a document header (also called a file prefix) containing the style definitions, with an empty document area.

WordPerfect 6.0 has greatly enhanced its support for style libraries. In Setup, Location of Files, you can define two directories for storing style libraries, one For Personal Style Libraries and one For Shared Style Libraries, and you can define a default personal and a default shared style library.

> **Note:** The terms *personal* and *shared* are for convenience only. You can make both directories and libraries personal, or both shared, if you prefer.

Unlike previous versions of WordPerfect, WordPerfect 6.0 does not automatically copy the styles in your default style library to your current document. Only when you use a library style in your document is it automatically copied to your document style list. In addition, you can explicitly copy individual or marked styles from a style library to your current document, or vice versa.

If you want to use different style libraries with a particular document, you can assign a Personal and/or Shared style library to that document. The assigned style libraries act for that document just like the default style libraries do for other documents.

Also unlike previous versions of WordPerfect, in WordPerfect 6.0, documents maintain a live one-way link with the default (or assigned) style libraries. If you change the styles in the default or assigned style library, when you retrieve a document to which that library is linked, the styles in the document are automatically updated. (That's why there is no Update option in the Style List dialog box.)

If you do not want the styles in the current document to change if the original style library is changed, you can break the live link by deleting the names of the external style libraries in the Style Options dialog box (choose Layout, Styles or press Alt+F8; then choose Options).

Tip: You can tell if a style in your document is linked to another style of the same name in an external style library because a bullet character appears next to the style in the Type column on the Style List.

System and User Created Styles

There are fundamentally two types of styles: those default styles provided by WordPerfect, called System Styles, and those you define, called User-Created styles. System styles are built into WordPerfect itself. Styles you define may reside either in a single document or they may be contained in style libraries for use by several documents.

System Styles

System styles are built into WordPerfect. Unlike user-created styles, system styles are not normally listed in your Style List. To see a list of the System Styles, choose Layout, Styles; or press Alt+F8. Then choose Options. At the Style Options dialog box, either deselect List User Created Styles to see only the System Styles or select List System Styles (leaving List User Created Styles selected) to see both user created styles and system styles. Then choose OK.

Tip: When you select styles, WordPerfect always displays the list of user-created styles for that document, not the most recently viewed style list (whether system styles or the styles in your personal or shared style library). To display the most recently viewed style list, press Alt+F8 twice.

System styles are predefined for the following document elements:

▲ Borders

▲ BoxText (uses InitialCodes style)

▲ Caption (uses InitialCodes style)

▲ Comment (uses InitialCodes style)

▲ Endnotes (uses InitialCodes style)

▲ Endnote number

▲ Equation box number

▲ Figure number

▲ Footers A and B (uses InitialCodes style)

- ▲ Footnotes (uses InitialCodes style and inserts a tab and superscript footnote number)
- ▲ Footnote number in document
- ▲ Graphic fills
- ▲ Graphic boxes
- ▲ Graphics captions
- ▲ Headers A and B (uses InitialCodes style)
- ▲ Hypertext
- ▲ Indexes (levels one and two)
- ▲ InitialCodes style (initially empty)
- ▲ Levels (including bullets, paragraph numbering, and outline styles)
- ▲ Lines
- ▲ Lists
- ▲ Tables of contents (five levels)
- ▲ Tables of authorities
- ▲ Table box numbers
- ▲ Text box numbers
- ▲ User box numbers
- ▲ Watermarks A and B (uses InitialCodes style)

If you are happy with the default settings for these items, you don't need to do anything; however, if you would like to customize your settings for any of these elements, you must modify a copy of the system style for that element. Note that you cannot actually change the system style itself, because system styles are built into the WordPerfect program. You can, however, modify a copy of any of the system styles in your personal style library. As long as that style library is defined as your personal style library in Setup when you create a document, assigned to the document through the Style Options dialog box, or retrieved into the Style List, the modified copy of the system style takes precedence over the default settings.

 Note: From now on, references to modifying or editing a system style should be interpreted as modifying or editing a copy of the system style.

Unlike regular text styles, which can only be defined through the Style List dialog box, most system styles can be modified in two places. You can edit all of the system styles from the Style List dialog box. Choose Options, then either uncheck List User Created Styles or check List System Styles to display the system styles in the style list. Then edit the style like a regular style. This method is convenient if you want to edit more than one system style at a time, or if you need to edit the Comment style, which can only be edited from the Style List dialog box.

Alternatively, you edit the style from the style option on the dialog box or menu for that feature. For example, from the Footnote menu (choose Layout, Footnote), you can edit the style that controls how the footnote number appears in the document by choosing Edit Style in Doc, or edit the style that controls the footnote itself by choosing Edit Style in Note.

The InitialCodes Style

"Document Initial Codes," a concept familiar to WordPerfect 5 users, is now treated as an open style in WordPerfect 6.0. In addition to selecting Document Initial Codes through the sequence of Layout, Document, Document Initial Codes, you can view or modify an open style called InitialCodes. The InitialCodes style is one of the predefined styles on your Style List. Whenever you create a file, the InitialCodes style is automatically inserted at the beginning of your document. You cannot remove the InitialCodes style from any of the places where WordPerfect inserts it automatically, but you can redefine it or insert other formatting codes or styles after it to override it.

The InitialCodes style is a handy visual reminder of the formatting settings contained in Document Initial Codes. Just move your insertion point to the beginning of the document, turn on Reveal Codes, and move your insertion point onto the InitialCodes style. If you have not changed your InitialCodes style, the InitialCodes style does not contain any formatting codes (see Figure 39.3).

> **Tip:** If you are near the end of a long document, it's faster to view the InitialCodes style from the Style List dialog box or from the Layout, **D**ocument, Document Initial **C**odes option, because you do not need to move your insertion point with either of these methods.

If you have changed your InitialCodes style, as shown in Figure 39.4, the Initial-Codes style displays the new codes when expanded in Reveal Codes.

Looking at Figure 39.4, where the cursor is placed on InitialCodes, you see the initial settings of this document. In this document, the InitialCodes style sets all four margins to 0.5 inches and specifies full justification.

> **Note:** The default settings for WordPerfect 6.0 are 1-inch margins on all four sides and left justification.

525

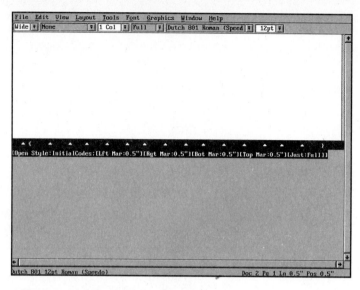

Figure 39.3. The default InitialCodes style.

> **Tip:** To reset your InitialCodes style to the default settings, open the Style List dialog box, move the highlight bar to the InitialCodes style, and press Delete or Backspace. WordPerfect displays a prompt asking Reset to default state? Answer Yes. Notice that a bullet now appears next to the word *Open* in the Type column. The bullet indicates that the InitialCodes style is using WordPerfect's default settings.

The InitialCodes style is special for another reason—the InitialCodes style is nested in the system styles for certain complex document elements such as BoxText, caption, comment, endnote, footers, footnote, headers, and watermarks. If you change your InitialCodes style (or change your Document Initial Codes, which amounts to the same thing), those changes are picked up by all the system styles that include the InitialCodes style as part of their style definition. For this reason, you should get into the habit of changing document settings in the InitialCodes style, rather than at the beginning of your document. If you don't, you may find that your footnotes are left justified when the rest of your document is full justified, that the margins for your headers are different from your document margins, or that your figure captions print in Courier when the rest of your document is printed in Times Roman.

526

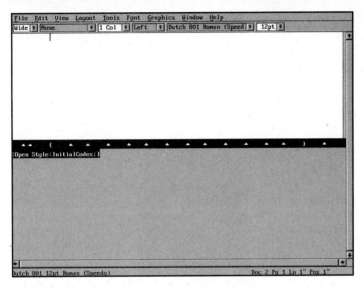

Figure 39.4. Initial Codes style with custom settings.

Tip: The **E**dit option on the Style List dialog box is greyed out when you are in a document substructure, so you cannot edit the InitialCodes style from the Style List. You *can* change your Document Initial Codes by selecting Layout, Document, Document Initial Codes.

Note: You cannot edit any styles, whether user-created or system styles, while you are in a document substructure, such as a footnote, endnote, comment, header, or footer. Either insert direct formatting, turn on another style to override the system style for that particular substructure, or exit to the main editing screen and change the system style for that substructure from the Style List dialog box or from the menu for that substructure.

Precedence of Style Libraries

Styles can exist in up to four places. User-defined styles, and modified copies of system styles, can occur in a document, in a personal library, or in a shared library. System styles are built into the WordPerfect program. What happens if you have two or more styles with the same name in different locations? Which style takes effect?

For user-defined styles, the rules are simple: styles defined or modified in the document take precedence over similarly named styles in a personal or shared library. Styles in your personal library take precedence over styles in your shared library.

For system styles, the situation is a little different. System styles are not normally present in style libraries, unless you copy them from your document to a library. If you have redefined a system style in both your personal and shared style libraries, the style in your personal library has precedence over the style in your shared library. However, if you have redefined a system style in your shared style library, but not in your personal style library, when you use a feature that is based on that system styles, the system style from the shared library is used.

You can, of course, override this by resetting the system setting in your document to its default setting, or by redefining the system style in your document. To reset a system style in a document to its default setting, highlight the style in the style list and choose Delete. WordPerfect prompts you Reset to default state? Answer y to reset the style. A bullet appears in the Type column for that style.

Figure 39.5 shows the basic default Style List screen. Note the bullets beside each style in the list except the Level 1 paragraph style. Bullets only appear in the document style list. If a user-defined item is bulleted, it means that it is a library style. If you modify the copy of the style in the document, the bullet disappears, indicating that the link to the style library has been broken. If a system style is bulleted, it means that the system defaults have not been changed. (In the document shown in Figure 39.5, we modified the Level 1 style by deleting the paragraph number; hence there is no bullet next to this style.)

> **Tip:** To reset a customized style to its default settings, highlight the style name and press Delete or Backspace. Answer Yes when WordPerfect prompts Reset to Default State?

The rule for which style takes effect is this: styles defined in a document override styles (with the same name) defined in a personal library. Personal library styles in turn override styles of the same name in a shared library. You will not be able to list or use styles in personal or shared libraries unless you first specify the location and default name of the personal or shared library you wish to use. See "Using Style Libraries" later in this chapter for more details.

> **Note:** You can tell which styles are being listed by accessing the Styles List dialog box: choose Layout, Styles (or press Alt+F8) and note in the Styles List dialog box which radio button is darkened: Document, Personal Library, or Shared Library. In Figure 39.5, the Document radio button is darkened.

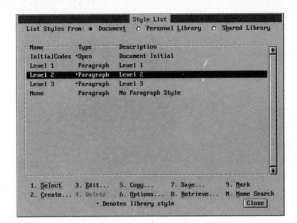

Figure 39.5. The default Style List screen. You can tell that the level 1 style has been customized because the bullet is missing.

Viewing Lists of Styles

Because styles are so pervasive, trying to see what styles are available in any category can be confusing. If you use the most straightforward path to styles, Alt+F8 (see the Note above), you will see any regular styles you may have created (none are shown in Figure 39.5) plus levels one through three and None for paragraph styles and InitialCodes. To see an expanded list containing system styles, temporarily, select the Style List menu (Alt+F8), select Options, and, in the Style Options menu, select List System Styles, then exit this menu. At the Style List dialog box, you will see the expanded list of system styles (arranged alphabetically). However, after you exit the Style List menu, normally you will have to reselect this option to see system styles.

> **Tip:** You can redisplay the last list of styles that you viewed in the same session by pressing Alt+F8 twice from the main editing window, or by pressing Alt+F8 from the Style List dialog box. If the last list that you displayed was the default list of user created styles in the current document, this keystroke sequence appears to have no effect. Alas.

The Styles button bar on the *Super Book* disk contains several macros that make viewing, editing, and creating style definitions easier. One button displays your system styles for the current document, another displays the styles in your personal library, and a third button displays the styles in your shared library. There is also a button to create a paragraph style from the current paragraph.

You cannot see all possible styles in the initial main list of styles (and because there are so many, you would not want to see them here). All of the styles that affect text can be displayed in the main style list, but outline styles only show up if they have been used in the current document. Also, you cannot view or change the outline level assigned to a style from the main Style List. To view or edit outline styles, choose Tools, Outline, Outline Style.

Graphics styles, including line, border, fill, and Graphics box styles, are not displayed in your main Style List. To see a list of styles for these elements, you must go to whatever spot in the menu where you would create or edit that element. For example, to see a list of line styles, you could go to Graphics, Graphic Boxes, Create, Border/Fill, Lines.

Creating, Editing, and Deleting Styles

To create a style for a personal or shared style library, follow the steps in Procedure 39.1.

Procedure 39.1. Creating a style.

1. Select Layout, Styles (or press Alt+F8).

2. In the List Styles menu, select a radio button at the top indicating you want to create a Personal Library or Shared Library. (If these buttons remain greyed, you have not specified a location for your library or given it a name yet; see Procedure 39.3.)

3. Select Create.

4. In the Create Style submenu, in the Style Name box, type a name for this style. Until you become an expert with styles, avoid using names already used for other styles in your libraries or document.

5. In the Style Type box, select a type of style: paragraph, character, or open.

6. Select OK.

7. In the Edit Style submenu, type a description of your style in the Description box.

8. Click on Style Contents, and create your style. Press F7 when done.

9. If your style is a character or paired style, you may want to define the Enter Key Action, which, by default, is set to Off/On. This means that when you press Enter, the current style is turned off and immediately back on.

10. Click OK returning to the Style List menu, select Close, and your new style is created.

Tip: WordPerfect does not require you to name your style libraries with the extension .STY, although that is a common convention. It is advisable to follow that practice for easy identification of libraries.

Now let's create a very small and simple set of open styles. These will be a set of icons, taken from the WordPerfect character set. Although you can use the WordPerfect command Ctrl+W to access the various sets of WordPerfect-defined characters, you could find using styles simpler and quicker than either macros or using the WordPerfect character menus.

Let's start off by naming a personal library (in Location of Files, Styles) named ICONS.STY, which will contain the WordPerfect special characters for the four suits in a deck of cards.

Follow Procedure 39.1, naming the style "Heart" and selecting an open style. Choose OK to display the Edit Style submenu. The name *Heart* is inserted in the Style Name box. For its description, type One of two red suits in a deck of cards. Choose Style Contents. With the insertion point in the Style Contents box, press Ctrl+W to display the WordPerfect Characters dialog box and enter 5,170. Press or click F7 to exit the Style Contents box, then press Enter or choose OK to return to the Style List dialog box. Repeat this procedure for the other three suit icons (press Ctrl+W then 5,168 for club; 5,169 for diamond; and 5,171 for spade). You now have these four styles at your disposal for use within this document.

Linking Styles

Document formatting is often predictable. As you produce a document, you may want to use several styles in a fixed sequence, or switch back and forth between two styles. If you use a title style, you may always, or nearly always, want to follow it immediately with a subtitle style. If you set up a paragraph or character style so that it turns on another style when you turn it off, you have in effect created a chain of linked styles.

See the Résumé styles in the Projects section for an example of linked styles. The RESUME.STY style library and a sample résumé based on that library are included on the *Super Book* disk.

> **Note:** Styles can be linked to themselves as well as to other styles. If you are creating a series of similarly formatted paragraphs, such as a bulleted or numbered list, you might want to use a paragraph style that links to itself, so that each time you press Enter, the style is turned off and back on again.

One possible use of this technique could be to have the appearance of body text change in a series of questions and answers (e.g., question in bold, answer in italics). Figure 39.6 below shows such an alternation. Note in Reveal Codes that after the first hard return, the style changes from question to answer, where the style answer specifies italic text, and the style question—automatically invoked by the hard return—selects bold text.

Tip: You can only link styles to other styles of the same type. For example, you can only link character styles to other character styles, and paragraph styles to other paragraph styles.

Caution: In order to link one style to another, the linked style must already exist. WordPerfect does not allow you to enter the name of a nonexistent style in the **T**urn Style Off and Link to: box. You can, however, change the Enter Key Action option at any time.

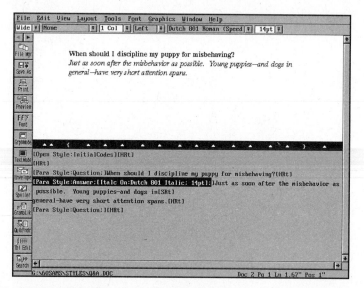

Figure 39.6. Alternating styles by linking them.

Tip: To turn off the last linked paragraph style, choose Styles (Alt+F8); then choose None or press Ctrl+A, Enter.

Basing New Styles on Existing Styles

There are times when it is very convenient to create a style and then use it in one or more other styles. This technique is called *nesting* or *embedding* styles. We have already seen how the InitialCodes style is embedded in several of the system styles. If you modify the InitialCodes style, all of the styles that are based on that style also change.

To nest an existing style definition in a new style definition, use the following steps:

1. From the Style List dialog box, choose Create. Enter the new style name, choose a style type, and choose OK. WordPerfect displays the Edit Style dialog box.

2. Enter a description, then choose Style Contents.

3. Choose the Based on Style option (Alt+F8). WordPerfect displays a list of the styles that are defined for the current document.

4. Select the style that you want from the list. WordPerfect inserts the style code in your new style (see Figure 39.7).

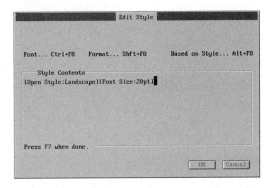

Figure 39.7. The Edit Style dialog box with new style inserted.

For example, if you are creating a new style called Overhead that is based on a style called Landscape, and you later change the Landscape style, the changes are reflected in the Overhead style.

Note: You can only base a style on a style that already exists in your current document. You cannot base a style on a style in your personal or shared style library. If you want to base a style on a style in a library, first copy the style to your current document.

Tip: To use an existing style as a starting point for a new style definition without embedding it in the new style definition, use the Copy option to copy the style to current document, using the name of the style you want to create. Then edit the copy of the new style.

Graphics in Styles

In WordPerfect 6.0, you can use graphics images in styles. In WordPerfect 5.1, if you wanted to use graphics images in styles, you were limited to using the Image on Disk option. The Image on Disk option means that the style contains a reference to the filename and location of a graphics image stored on disk, but not a copy of the image itself. The advantage to using the Graphics on Disk feature is that such externally stored graphics do not take up extra space in your current document. The disadvantages to this technique are twofold:

1. If you change the location of the external graphic, the document can no longer find it.
2. It takes longer when printing a document to go out to disk, get the image, and continue printing.

WordPerfect 6.0 gives you a choice in using graphics with styles. You can continue to use graphics on disk (bearing in mind the advantages as well as the disadvantages). Alternately, you can choose the Image option to bring the graphic into your document via the style. This increases the size of your document but speeds up printing and frees you from the need to make sure that the pathname for the image on disk is correct if you copy or move the document.

> **Tip:** If you are creating a style that you will use frequently, such as a letterhead, choose the Image on Disk option to avoid wasting disk space.

Using Style Libraries

Enough theory. Now let's show some simple, practical things you can do with WordPerfect styles. We'll create a simple style library to show you the basic techniques of using styles and progress to some fancier things. When you've finished with this chapter introducing styles, see Chapter 34, "Borders and Fills," for some detailed examples of their use. Before long you'll wonder how you ever lived without styles.

Getting Started

Before you can start using styles, there are two things you should do. First, make sure that Auto Code Placement is on (this is the default setting) (see Procedure 39.2).

Procedure 39.2. Setting Auto Code Placement on.

1. Select File, Setup (or Shift+F1), Environment.
2. Select Autocode Placement, and click on "On" if the box is not already checked.

Secondly, specify directories for your style libraries, and the names for your default personal and shared libraries, as in Procedure 39.3. Although you can restrict your use of styles to only the current document, you will probably want to begin using a personal library, a shared library, or both.

> **Tip:** Remember that you can use the shared library option to specify another personal library, giving you ready access to two style libraries.

To specify where your libraries will be found, and to specify particular style libraries by name, follow the steps shown in Procedure 39.3.

Procedure 39.3. Specifying style libraries.

1. Select File, Setup (or Shift+F1), Location of Files.
2. In the Location of Files menu, select Style Files.
3. You now see the Style Files menu, which has four entries: two for personal libraries and two for shared libraries. Specify paths in the first and/or third entries to indicate where your personal and/or shared libraries will be found.

> **Tip:** The pathnames for your personal and shared style library files should point to directories where only style libraries will be stored. (They can point to the same directory, if you wish.) That way, when you choose the File List feature from either the Style Options or Retrieve Styles dialog boxes, the list will contain only the names of style library files.

4. Specify default personal and/or shared libraries by name in the second and fourth entries. (See Figure 39.8 for a picture of the Style Files menu.)

Alternatively, you can assign a library as your personal or shared library for the current document. Press Alt+F8, Options, and in the Style Options menu specify the personal or shared libraries in the selection **Libraries Assigned to Document.**

535

Note: If you have already specified personal or shared libraries as your default, and later assign personal or shared libraries to a document, the assigned libraries will take effect and you will not see the styles from your default personal and shared style libraries when you list personal or shared libraries.

In Figure 39.8, we see that the path to our personal style libraries is D:\STYLES, and that our default style library is a library called ICONS.STY.

Of course, we haven't yet told you how to create a style library. If you are anxious to get started, you could practice with the sample style library which WordPerfect supplies and name it as your personal or shared library. Its name is LIBRARY.STY. This library, found in the WordPerfect directory, includes a collection of simple and complex styles for creating headings, bibliographies, and creating legal documents.

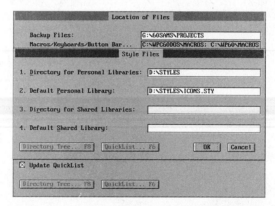

Figure 39.8. Setting default style libraries in the Location of Files menu.

Tip: Before you use or make changes to LIBRARY.STY, it's a good idea to make a copy of it, giving it a name such as MYCOPY.STY, and confine your changes to the copy. If you want to be doubly sure you don't change the original, go to DOS, and in the directory containing LIBRARY.STY issue this DOS command:

```
ATTRIB +R LIBRARY.STY <return>
```

This will make the library "read-only" and prevent any changes until you later remove this restriction by typing

```
ATTRIB -R LIBRARY.STY <return>
```

536

Saving a Set of Styles as a Library

To save styles into a style library, follow the steps shown in Procedure 39.4.

Procedure 39.4. Saving styles to a style library.

1. Select Layout, Styles (or press Alt+F8).
2. In the List Styles menu, mark the style(s) you want to be saved by positioning the highlight bar and pressing M or an asterisk (*). Then click on Save.

> **Tip:** You can also press F10 to save the styles.

3. In the Save Styles submenu, enter the name you want for your style
   library and click OK.

Continuing from the previous example, select each of the four suit styles, follow
Procedure 39.4, and save the four styles to style library ICONS.STY. You have now
created a style library named ICONS.STY. If in the Style List submenu you select
Personal Library, you should see the Style List Menu shown in Figure 39.9.

> **Note:** You cannot mark all the styles in the Style List menu with a
> single key combination, as you can in other WordPerfect lists, such
> as List Files. You must mark the styles individually.

> **Tip:** You can save, copy, or delete marked files.

As an exercise in using styles, let's now try using this simple ICONS.STY library by
selecting each of the four styles and placing them into a document. We assume
that you have followed the steps above to create a library called ICONS.STY and
have put four open styles in it, one corresponding to each of the four suits in a deck
of cards. We also assume that you have named ICONS.STY as a personal or shared
library or assigned it to your current document (after clearing your screen) as a
personal or shared library.

If, after using the style, you decide that you do not want it to be in your list of styles
(and therefore make your document smaller, because each style in your style list
adds some to the invisible overhead of your document), you could simply click on
the style and select Delete.

This is a simple exercise but useful because it familiarizes you with the mechanics
of using styles. Now let's go one step further, defining the "diamond" and "heart"
styles to be red as they would be in playing cards. After you've finished with this

small edit you will see that those styles have become red in your document. In fact, if you had used these styles in any other document (by specifying the ICONS.STY style library as a personal or shared library, or an assigned library), they would automatically become red in those documents, too. This simple exercise shows how the initial mastery of styles can be a powerful tool in applying controlled, efficient change to a collection of documents.

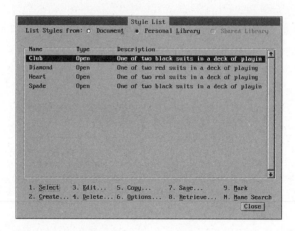

Figure 39.9. The Style List menu.

Procedure 39.5. Changing the color of the heart and diamond styles.

To make this color change in the two style icons of "heart" and "diamond," follow these steps:

1. Press Alt+F8 to get to the Style List dialog box.
2. Select Personal Library (or Shared Library, if that is what you specified earlier for ICONS.STY).
3. Highlight the "heart" style.
4. Select Edit.
5. In the Edit Style menu, select Style Contents.
6. Move your cursor onto the WordPerfect character for "heart."
7. Press Ctrl+F8 to get to the font dialog box, select the Color red, return to the Edit Style menu.
8. Move the insertion point immediately after the heart character and repeat Step 7, choosing Black as the color.
9. Press or click F7 to exit the Style Contents box.
10. Press Home, F7 to return to your main document screen. You will see the heart icon is now red.

Repeat the process for the diamond style. Note that we needed to select the color black after the WordPerfect character, or else every following character (style icon and regular text) would be red. Open styles remain in effect until changed.

 Note: Observe that the Create Style menu has a check box labeled "Create from current paragraph" or "Create from current character," depending on whether you select a paragraph or character style. (There is no such option if you select an Open style.) If you check this box, WordPerfect selects the currently active character formatting (typeface, point size, color, and other font attributes) in the current paragraph or character. If you select a Paragraph style, WordPerfect also picks up other active paragraph formatting information such as margin codes, justification, and line spacing if they are defined in the current paragraph.

 Tip: If you want to create a style from the current paragraph and include text and/or graphics as well as formatting, block the paragraph and choose Delete. Then create a new style and undelete the block in the Style Contents box. (Note: Delete works better than Move because Move does not always capture formatting codes.)

 Tip: The Create from Current Paragraph and Create from Current Character options do not pick up text or graphics. If you want to create a style from the current paragraph and include text and/or graphics as well as formatting, block the paragraph and choose Delete. Then create a new style, and undelete the block in the Style Contents box. (Note: Delete works better than Move because Move does not always capture formatting codes.)

Copying Styles

The Copy feature allows you to perform four types of operations. You can:

1. Copy styles from one library to another
2. Copy styles from a library to your current document
3. Copy styles from your document to a library
4. Copy a style to a style with a different name in the same document or style library

Before we show you how to copy styles, let's discuss why you might want to use this feature. Copying styles between libraries helps you to organize and maintain your style libraries. Copying a style from the current document to a library is necessary if you are to use the style in other documents.

It's less clear why you might want to copy a style from a library to a document, because whenever you select a library style, WordPerfect turns that style on in your document and automatically copies the style definition to the document's style list. One good reason for using Copy is if you want to copy a style definition from a style library to a document without turning it on. For example, if you have a style library that contains several styles that you know you'll need in the course of creating a new document, you can access them more easily if you copy them to your current document. If the files are copied to the current document, you won't have to choose the Personal or Shared style library each time you want to use a new style for the first time, and the paragraph styles will be accessible through the ribbon.

The primary reason for making a copy of a style definition with a new name in the same location is to have a starting point for creating a new style. For example, you may need to create a new version of a letterhead style that is similar to your existing letterhead style. By making a copy of the letterhead style with a new name, you can then modify the copy, rather than creating the style from scratch.

Procedure 39.6. Copying a style.

1. Select Layout, Styles (or press Alt+F8).
2. In the List Styles menu, mark the style(s) you want to copy, and click on Copy.
3. Choose the correct option in the Copy Styles menu to say where you want to save your styles: Document, Personal Library, or Shared Library. Then select OK.

Remember that if you copy your styles to a document, those styles will no longer be "connected" to a style library. Any changes you make to those styles in the document will be localized to that document.

 Note: If you want to copy a style within the same place (Document, Personal, Shared) you can only copy one at a time by highlighting, not marking them.

Now let's create a style from a graphic logo. Here we start with a palette of often-used typographic characters, built as a library of styles containing common typographic characters (such as the cent sign, degree symbol, and trademark symbols). Note that even though you can use macros or go to the WordPerfect Characters character menus to create these directly, it can be a real time saver to create such a personal library. You might even prefer the textual description of a style to be sure you're picking the one you want.

Assume we've already created this personal library, using the procedures you saw above in ICONS.STY. We've already named that library TYPOGRAP.STY. Assume also that we've created a logo for a pet store, Pups & Pals, and that we want that logo to be used consistently on letterheads, newsletters, and the like. Both TYPOGRAP.STY and the Pups & Pals logo can be found on the *Super Book* disk. Because we want to assure consistent use of our logo, this is a perfect application of styles. We've used borders and other graphic editing features (described in Chapter 34) to create this logo shown in Figure 39.10.

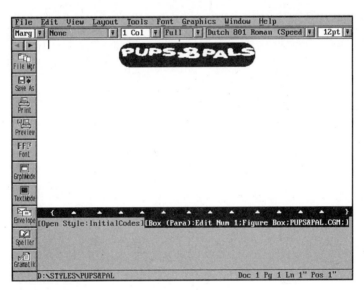

Figure 39.10. Copying a graphic into a style.

We will create a simple paragraph style and copy it into a personal library we've created (and named in our location of files, styles) called TYPOGRAP.STY. Because this will be a paragraph style, there is no need to block the area; simply place the cursor next to the graphics box. Go to the styles list menu (Alt+F8). Next, Create the style, give it the name "pups&pal," select paragraph style from the drop-down menu, check the box "Create from current paragraph," and select OK. This creates the style for our present document.

Now, to copy that style to TYPOGRAP.STY, in the Style List menu use the Copy option, select Personal Library and OK. You will then see a list of styles shown in Figure 39.11, including the often-used typographic characters and our corporate logo.

Using Outline Styles

Although more an author's tool than a desktop publishing tool, outlines can facilitate the process of creating frameworks of writing. WordPerfect now supplies headline, legal, bullet, number, outline, and paragraph outline styles, each in up to eight levels. And as with other style-controlled elements, you can modify the way each level in each outline style is presented. Although the use of WordPerfect's Outline facility is described in greater detail elsewhere in this book, we will show briefly how you can apply style techniques to change and use outline styles.

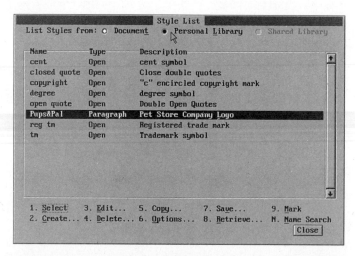

Figure 39.11. The logo copied and shown in a list of personal library styles.

Tip: If you work with outline styles, and have not done so already, consider making the outline bar visible so you can select or switch between the various outline styles. To do this, select View from the main menu, and then select Outline Bar On (a check mark will appear to show it is selected). The outline bar appears beneath your ribbon bar (If the ribbon is displayed), and it is a handy tool for selecting outline styles, promoting and demoting levels, and so forth. The outline bar can only be accessed with a mouse or other pointing device.

> **Note:** There is no equivalent tool for applying non-outline styles, but you can select paragraph styles from the drop-down paragraph style list on the ribbon. Because your most-frequently used styles are likely to be paragraph styles, the ribbon is extremely handy, too.

In this example we will use bullet outline styles and change the top-level bullet from its standard round black dot to a star.

Procedure 39.7. Editing an outline style.

1. Select the Options button of the outline ribbon or select Tools, Outline or press Ctrl+F5; then choose Outline Options.
2. Select the Outline Style menu.
3. Highlight bullets at the Outline Style list.
4. Select Edit at the Outline Style menu.
5. You will now see the default bullet characters for all eight levels of bullets. Select the first level bullet (or whichever level you wish to change).
6. Choose Numbers.
7. Select List Bullets (F5) and you will see a long list of available bullet choices. Select the choice you want, and then click Select. The new bullet character replaces the round black dot.

Figure 39.12 shows the Edit Outline Style menu with the first-level bullet style changed to a star (WordPerfect character 6,112).

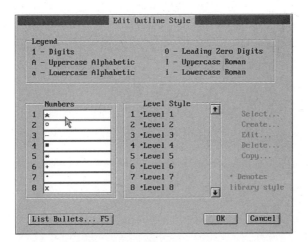

Figure 39.12. The Edit Outline Style menu with a star bullet.

The result of this edit would change the outline we might be writing for a pet newsletter from a bullet to a star (see Figure 39.13).

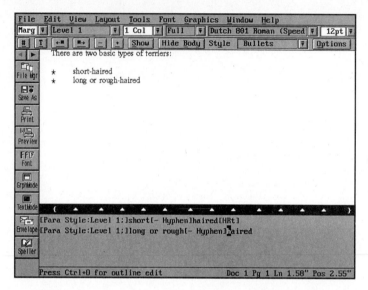

Figure 39.13. The result of changing a first-level bullet to a star.

Even though you may never want to change WordPerfect's default outline styles, WordPerfect gives you this option so you can personalize even the smallest detail of your documents.

Miscellaneous Style Functions

The following sections discuss some miscellaneous style functions and issues that do not speak for themselves:

▲ Turning on and off styles

▲ "Enter Key" actions

▲ Deleting styles

▲ Master and subdocuments

Turning Styles On and Off

The only kinds of styles you can turn off in your document are paragraph and character styles. Open styles, by definition, take effect at the point you use them and stay in effect until you do something to change their effect. Although you cannot turn off an open style, you can override it by turning on a new style or by using direct formatting codes in your document. If you want to undo an open style, delete the style code where it occurs in your document. To do this, simply turn on Reveal Codes, place your cursor on it, and press Delete.

If the Enter Key Action for a character or paragraph style is defined as Turn Style Off, all you need to do to turn that style off is to press Enter.

There are several ways to turn off a paragraph style that uses one of the other Enter Key Actions. The official way is, with your cursor within the paragraph, go to the Style List menu and select the None style. You can also press Ctrl+A, Enter. If the Enter Key Action is set to link to itself or to another style, you can press Enter, and then Backspace to delete the unwanted linked style.

To turn off a character style, move your cursor to the text affected by the character style. Then, go to the Styles menu and choose Off.

Tip: If you are accustomed to using the right arrow key to move past the end of a paired style in earlier versions of WordPerfect, consider selecting WordPerfect 5.1 Cursor Movement in the Environment menu of the Setup options.

Enter Key Actions

One of the more obscure aspects of creating styles is choosing an Enter Key Action for Character and Paragraph style. Simply put, the Enter Key Action determines what happens when that style is active and you press the Enter key. There are four choices:

1. Insert a **H**ard Return
2. Turn Style O**ff**
3. Turn Style Off and Back **O**n
4. **T**urn Style Off and Link To

The first choice, available only for Character styles, allows you to insert a hard return without turning off the style. WordPerfect's normal blocking function also works with this kind of style, allowing you to block a selection of text and apply this style to it alone.

The second choice moves the cursor past the style, and it is most useful for paragraph styles. Typical applications might be titles or headings.

The third choice moves the cursor past the style and then turns the style on again. You would use this to apply the same style appearance to a series of paragraphs. You might use this if, for example, you wanted the first line of each paragraph to be indented, or to create a bulleted list.

When you select the fourth choice and pressed Enter, you end one style and invoke another different style. You specify the different, second style when you select this enter key action defining the first style. You would use this choice if you normally prefer a second style to follow a first style.

 Tip: See the Résumé project for other examples of linked styles.

Styles in Master and Subdocuments

You may wonder which styles take effect in a document when that document consists of a master document expanded with its subdocuments. The answer is that the master document's styles prevail and subdocuments with styles closer to the top of the master document prevail over those subdocuments further from the top.

First, the master document's list of styles combines its own styles and those of all its subdocuments. However, if the master document has a style of the same name as any subdocuments, the master's style overrides the others. Likewise, if a subdocument has a style with the same name as another subdocument, but this style is not one in the master document, the style of the subdocument closest to the top of the master document overrides the styles of the other, lower subdocument(s).

When you condense an expanded master document, and save its subdocument(s), the styles in the master document will replace styles in the subdocuments.

Retrieving Versus Assigning Style Libraries

As noted earlier, if you use a personal or shared style library, when you open a document WordPerfect automatically updates all styles in your document with the current values of those styles. This is true whether you use the personal or style libraries by specifying them in Setup, Location of Files, or whether you use those style libraries by assignment. When you retrieve a style library into a document, your document gets a copy of all the styles from that library and they become "unlinked" from that library. That is, if the styles in that library are changed, they do not affect your version of those styles.

The main value of assigning style libraries is that it gives you a way to override the default personal and shared libraries that you specified in Setup, Location of Styles. WordPerfect accesses the assigned libraries instead of your default libraries.

Keeping Your Documents Trim

Style libraries have always added much overhead and size to documents. How do you use Version 6.0 libraries and yet keep the size of your documents manageable? You must weigh all the pros and cons of retrieving and using personal or shared libraries to decide this. The key consideration is that style libraries, as such, do not add overhead to your documents unless you retrieve those libraries into your documents or modify the default system styles. Your document "gains weight" from style libraries only as you select styles from those libraries or modify the default system styles. And remember, default system styles reside in WordPerfect itself, not in your documents. Considering the benefits of consistency gained from styles, the larger file size is usually a small price to pay.

Converting Style Libraries Between Versions

Strictly speaking, there is no way to convert a WordPerfect Version 5 to a Version 6.0 style library, or vice versa. However, it is possible to retrieve a Version 5 WordPerfect document into a Version 6.0 document, or to save a WordPerfect Version 6.0 document as a Version 5 document. And therein lies the back door to conversion. WordPerfect Version 5 style libraries are retrieved into documents to apply their styles to the documents. When you retrieve a WordPerfect 5 document containing styles into a WordPerfect 6.0 document, the styles remain as document styles: open styles remain as open, and WordPerfect Version 5 paired styles become character styles (with the style names remaining the same).

To save and document your WordPerfect Version 5 style libraries, retrieve each into a separate document, describe what the styles are (or actually use them in the document for illustration's sake), and save each separately (perhaps with an extension to indicate they contain Version 5 libraries, such as "ST5"). When you retrieve these into WordPerfect Version 6.0, you can save the document styles as personal or shared libraries.

Advanced Uses of Styles

Now that you've learned the primary use of styles, here are some unusual reasons you might consider creating and working with styles. Styles could be especially useful if you plan to take your WordPerfect document to a service bureau for typesetting, you are using portions of a document to create electronic HELP files, or you want to lay some of the groundwork to apply an up-and-coming tagging technology called SGML, the Standard Generalized Markup Language, to your documents. Although SGML isn't useful for many desktop publishing pieces, especially those that emphasize form over content, SGML might be something you want to prepare for. Use of SGML is increasing in some industries, such as the telecommunications and aircraft industries. WordPerfect itself is preparing a product called "Intellitag" to facilitate conversion of documents to SGML. As a user of WordPerfect 6.0, with sounds and hyperlinking, you already know that

547

books are more than printed paper. Let me explain how you can get unusual benefits from styles.

First, some service bureaus use typesetting systems that can not only import WordPerfect, but can translate your styles into their own. Some such systems require styles to be only one word, all lowercase, and so on. Check to see if they can use your styles and what their style naming requirements are. It could save you money if they could translate your style tag for "degree symbol" into their own pie character.

Styles can provide a technique for you to redeliver what you've produced in printed form electronically. For example, suppose you are writing a software manual explaining how to print a report. The software developers want to use parts of what you've written in a Help screen. They insist on Courier, and your book uses Century Schoolbook. You plan to give them an electronic version of your book by "printing to a file." The problem with that is that your use of bold text attributes may cause a "doubling" of emboldened words, and your use of underlines may replace underlined text with lines.

The trick here is to create two parallel style libraries. By parallel I mean that each has the same tag names, but different contents depending on use (screen or book). You can simply create a style called "page design" used in two libraries (BOOK.STY and SCREEN.STY) with totally different content: different margins, different fonts, and so on. You get complete control over your paper document (using your BOOK library) and can also deliver the document to them for their use and inspection (using the SCREEN library) as Courier fitting onto an 80-column screen. You might create a style called "emphasize," which becomes bold in your paper document and puts an asterisk at the start and end of blocked text in your screen document.

The trick is to cheat a little. Use the BOOK style library (retrieved into your document) when producing formatted output for your paper document. Then, after producing your paper document, retrieve the SCREEN style library into your document. Respond Yes when warned that style names already exist and asked if you want to replace the styles. Your new styles will be applied to the document and you can "print to file" and produce the electronic copy, suitable for Help screens.

Lastly, you could create a third parallel style library to replace heading styles with tags whose content is something like "<HD1> ... <\HD1>." This would be useful if the set of SGML tags you use specify <HD1> and <\HD1> to mark the beginning and end of a level one head. You'll probably never completely tag a document with SGML using this technique, but it can help. The more style tags you use, the more likely you will facilitate future conversion to SGML.

40

by Art Schaak

Producing Good-Looking Documents

We all share a common goal of wanting to produce the best-looking document possible. But how?

A number of chapters in *The WordPerfect 6.0 Super Book* address this question, each focusing on a particular feature or series of features of WordPerfect 6.0. This chapter examines fonts—getting the most out of both the fonts that ship with WordPerfect, as well as third-party fonts.

Producing good-looking documents really isn't all that difficult. We draw your attention to the simple guidelines that run through every discussion of maximizing your use of whatever microcomputer program you are using (and there are more books than there are programs themselves)—know what you've got, learn how to make the most of what you've got, and learn what the program in question has to offer.

Throughout this book, we look at what you've got (what comes with WordPerfect 6.0), how to make the most of what you've got (in this chapter, the fonts that come with 6.0 and third-party fonts), and how to use 6.0 to achieve the maximum benefit.

The editors would love to assure you that by following the simple steps in these pages you will be able to produce immaculate documents in a minimal amount of time. This, of course, is a familiar promise that you've heard over and over again, usually with the actual results falling short of the promises. The fact is, producing good-looking documents requires an understanding of your tools, the final goals for that particular document, and a healthy amount of time.

What follows, then, is a discussion of fonts and WordPerfect 6.0. Please note that the discussion is not limited to just this one program. Instead, we ask you to look at a particular font and ask yourself why you should use Dutch as opposed to Swiss or Commercial Script (no matter what program).

Producing good-looking documents relies solely on your understanding of what you've got (both in terms of the program and the fonts) and how to use it.

WordPerfect is a word processing program, not a desktop publishing program, and you should be clear about the difference. However, the arsenal of tools at your command in WordPerfect 6.0 is quite robust.

A Brief Inventory

You should know what you've got. Take an inventory of the tools at your disposal before you start to use them.

WordPerfect 6.0

The first item in the inventory is WordPerfect 6.0. This chapter, and this entire book, assumes that you have WordPerfect 6.0. More specifically, this book is written with the underlying assumption that you have a complete package, including manuals and, most importantly, a registration number. If you have not registered your copy of WordPerfect, you should, because there are many benefits that may not otherwise be available to you. Some of the features that weren't quite ready at the time of the initial release of 6.0 will be included with interim releases of 6.0. Those interim releases are available only to registered users of the program, and then only upon request. WordPerfect Corporation has threatened to require a registration number for access to their 800 help line telephone numbers.

Make sure you have installed WordPerfect 6.0 properly. "Properly" means more than simply installing the program. You should understand where the various pieces of the program are located. Where are the fonts, for example, and how are they organized? This topic is so important to controlling fonts that a discussion of font installation is included in this chapter, a discussion that duplicates some of the information in Appendix A, "Installing WordPerfect 6.0."

Fonts from WordPerfect

WordPerfect 6.0 ships with fonts. The installation procedure sets up directories for the fonts that come with the program, and it expects to find the fonts in those directories. You need to install the following fonts included on the *SuperDisk* in a directory where WordPerfect will look for them.

Benefits of WordPerfect Fonts

The fact that WordPerfect is providing a library of fonts with the program is an important change from previous releases of WordPerfect. Before 6.0, fonts were external to the program and considered more a function of the printer than the software. The user that wanted more fonts than what came with their printer had to incur the expense of purchasing those fonts. The connection between the software program, a particular printer, and the font package (read: three different products from three different manufacturers) caused tremendous confusion and difficulty. By including fonts as a part of 6.0, WordPerfect Corporation has taken a great step toward making good-looking documents a much easier goal.

WordPerfect is not the first software package to include fonts. As with dialog boxes and the graphics display mode, 6.0 appears to be following the example of Microsoft Windows in bundling fonts with the rest of the package. There is, however, one major difference: WordPerfect takes advantage of including various font formats and makes the most of these formats.

Windows includes TrueType fonts. Installing additional fonts so Windows recognizes them is relatively simple as long as you follow the instructions and use TrueType fonts. Other font formats (such as Bitstream Speedo fonts or Type 1 fonts) require additional software (Bitstream's FaceLift from Bitstream or Adobe Type Manager).

WordPerfect includes the software to use TrueType, Bitstream Speedo, and Type 1 fonts in 6.0. No additional software is required. WordPerfect includes sample Bitstream Speedo and Type 1 fonts, and it sets these fonts up as a normal part of the installation procedure.

You could use Bitstream Speedo fonts with previous versions of WordPerfect, as well as various other font packages produced by a handful of font foundries. Access to the Speedo fonts, for example, required you to purchase and install the Bitstream FaceLift for WordPerfect package. In order to use WordPerfect and the Speedo fonts, you had to load FaceLift, which in turn would run WordPerfect. Each third-party package worked the same. To use their particular font package you had to load their software, which, in turn, would load WordPerfect. You could use only one font package at a time.

6.0 allows you to use Speedo, True Type, and Type 1 fonts within WordPerfect. No third-party software is required, except the actual fonts.

WordPerfect's Font Library

The scalable font outlines that come with WordPerfect 6.0 are:

Bodoni-WP Bold (Type 1)
CommercialScript-WP (Type 1)
Courier 10 Bold (Speedo)
Courier 10 Bold Italic (Speedo)
Courier 10 Italic (Speedo)
Courier 10 Roman (Speedo)
Courier-WP (Type 1)
Courier-WP Bold (Type 1)
Dutch 801 Bold (Speedo)
Dutch 801 Bold Italic (Speedo)
Dutch 801 Italic (Speedo)
Dutch 801 Roman (Speedo)
Helve-WP (Type 1)
Helve-WP (Type 1)
Roman WP (Type 1)
Roman-WP Bold (Type 1)
Roman-WP Bold Italic (Type 1)
Roman-WP Italic (Type 1)
Swiss 721 Bold (Speedo)
Swiss 721 Roman (Speedo)

Font Formats

The names of the fonts are followed by their formats. Bodoni-WP Bold, CommercialScript-WP, Courier-WP, Helve-WP, and Roman-WP are Type 1 fonts. The Courier 10, Dutch 801, and Swiss 721 fonts are Speedo fonts.

(The screen shots in this chapter show more fonts than these. As this book went to press, WordPerfect Corporation was contemplating the distribution, upon the request of registered users, of certain other Type 1 fonts. Other fonts, such as CG Times and Univers, are resident in the Hewlett Packard LaserJet III, the selected printer.)

Because WordPerfect ships with Type 1 and Speedo fonts, this chapter's discussion of installing third-party fonts looks at True Type fonts, specifically those that ship with Windows 3.1.

Fonts on the Accompanying Disk

The *WordPerfect 6.0 Super Book* includes a disk with Speedo-format scalable font outlines from Bitstream. These font outlines should be copied to the \BTFONTS directory and installed as Speedo fonts. The following fonts are included on the *Super Book* disk:

Davida Bold
Freehand 471
Mister Earl
Monterey
Umbra

Installing Third-Party Fonts

The WordPerfect 6.0 for DOS package includes various utility programs integrated into the program, including the WordPerfect Font Installer, or WPFI for short. There are three associated WPFI files installed in the WPC60DOS subdirectory, all sharing the name WPFI with individual extensions.

Although WPFI can be run from a DOS prompt, it will most likely be accessed from within WordPerfect. The differences between executing the WPFI independent of WordPerfect and installing fonts from within WordPerfect are limited to what it takes to get from 6.0 to the installation program, which will be explained more thoroughly later in this chapter.

Use the following steps to install third-party fonts from within WordPerfect 6.0:

1. Access the **P**rint/Fax dialog box
2. Choose the Select option
3. Select Edit
4. Select Font Setup
5. Select Install Fonts, which jumps you to the WPFI program
6. Select the font format TrueType
7. Indicate the location of the font outlines (those files with a .TTF extension)
8. The location of the WP.DRS file is \WPCGODOS
9. Mark the fonts to be installed by making sure only those fonts have an asterisk
10. Select Install
11. Verify the location of the Graphics Fonts Data Files
12. Watch as WordPerfect updates the WP.DRS file
13. Continue and select OK to get back to the document screen

Installing third-party fonts is not, however, as easy as following the steps in the above list.

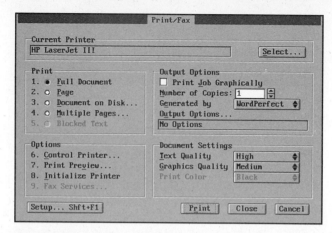

Figure 40.1. The Print/Fax dialog box.

Start at the Print/Fax dialog box (see Figure 40.1). Select the current printer, which brings the Select Printer dialog box to the screen (see Figure 40.2). All the currently installed printers and their respective PRS files are listed. The next step is to edit the selected printer.

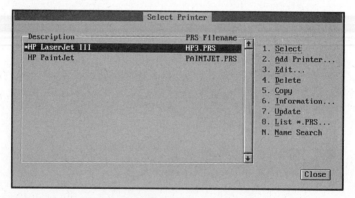

Figure 40.2. The Select Printer dialog box.

What Is the PRS File?

Bear in mind, what you are about to edit is the PRS—the Printer ReSource file. WordPerfect provides disks identified as "printer disks." When you install a printer via the WordPerfect install program, you are telling the program to decompress the information on the printer disk and create a file with an extension of .ALL in the WPC60DOS subdirectory. This ALL file contains the information for various similar printers. WP then takes the information specific to the printer you wish to install and creates a unique PRS file for it. Each PRS file bears a name specific to its printer, and the printers (installed in Figure 40.2) have identifiable, individual names.

Select File, Print/Fax, Select, then Edit, raising the Edit Printer Setup dialog box (see Figure 40.3) to the screen. Select Font Setup, bringing up the Font Setup dialog box (see Figure 40.4).

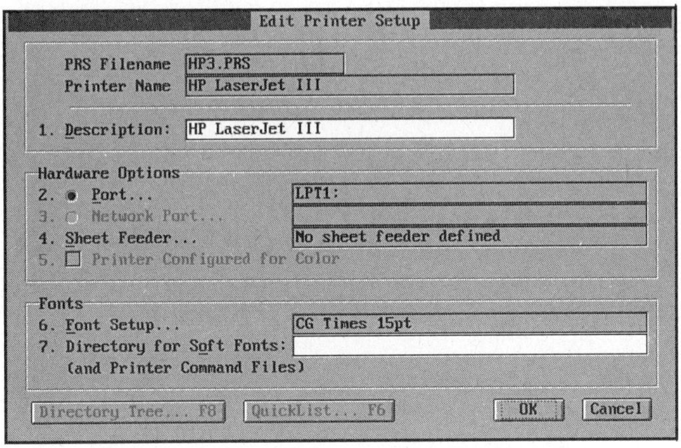

Figure 40.3. The Edit Printer Setup dialog box.

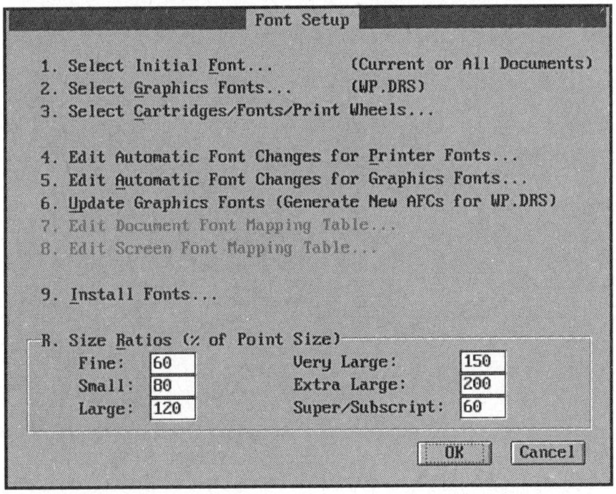

Figure 40.4. The Font Setup dialog box.

The Font Setup dialog box serves as a threshold to a number of important activities. WordPerfect has separated the PTR program from WordPerfect 6.0, requiring the registered user to call and request the PTR program from WordPerfect Corporation the first time the need to edit a PRS file arises. The tradeoff is that many of the controls relegated to the 5.1 PTR program have been moved to Font Setup in 6.0, primarily the capability to edit Automatic Font Changes.

Additionally, the font setup dialog box can be accessed from the font dialog box by holding down the shift key and pressing F1.

Automatic Font Changes

Automatic Font Changes, AFCs for short, are the key to appearance and relative size attributes. When you change the relative size of the font, how large is large? The Size Ratios demonstrated in Figure 40.4 indicate that when you change the relative size of the font to Very Large, the size automatically changes to 150 percent of the current font. When Italics is selected, the program looks to the defined automatic font changes to see what font will actually be used. It is possible, and not all that uncommon, to find the automatic font changed to a completely different font for outline or shadow switching.

From the Font Setup dialog box, select Install Fonts. WordPerfect jumps to the WordPerfect Font Installation program and pauses with the Select Font Type dialog box on the screen (see Figure 40.5).

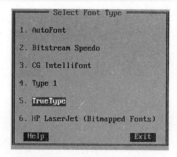

Figure 40.5. The Select Font dialog box.

Font Formats Supported by WordPerfect 6.0

Although WordPerfect includes Type 1 and Speedo fonts within the 6.0 package, the program supports a number of other font formats, including AutoFont, CG Intellifont, TrueType, and the old bitmapped fonts for the HP LaserJet. The Select Font Type dialog box requires you to identify the type of font(s) to be installed.

The TrueType fonts are not currently located in the WP60 directory, which is WordPerfect's default for fonts. Had the program found TrueType fonts in the WP60 directory, the Select Fonts dialog box would be displayed. Because the program did not find any in the default directory, the Select Fonts dialog box is greyed out and over it is the Location of Files dialog box (see Figure 40.6).

Figure 40.6. The Location of Files dialog box.

Location of Files

The Location of Files dialog box includes an explanatory paragraph, as well as an area to identify the location of the TrueType files and the WP.DRS file. In the example illustrated by Figure 40.6, the TrueType fonts are located in the C:\Windows\System subdirectory, specifically those which come with Windows 3.1. (Windows 3.1 automatically installs TrueType fonts in the \Windows\System subdirectory.)

WP.DRS remains in the WPC60DOS directory. The WP.DRS file contains the information WordPerfect needs for graphics printing. WordPerfect 6.0 handles all scalable font outlines graphically (except those resident in the printer). The DRS file must include information about all the fonts WordPerfect recognizes as installed and accessible. (The WP.DRS file is extremely important, and it is discussed in greater detail in Chapter 23, "Printing.")

Identifying What Fonts to Install

Indicate to the program that this information is OK and a list of the TrueType fonts in the C:\Windows\System subdirectory is brought to the screen. At first, all the fonts are selected, as WordPerfect assumes that you will want to install all the fonts. This is not the case. We will install only the Arial and New Times Roman font families (a family consisting of the bold, bold italic, italic and regular faces). The keystroke combination of Home followed by the asterisk (*) unmarks the entire list, thus enabling you to identify only those specific fonts that you want to install in WordPerfect.

Figure 40.7 shows that the four fonts in the Arial family are marked. Notice that each of these fonts is identified as a Graphic font type. (This is more fully explained in Chapter 23.)

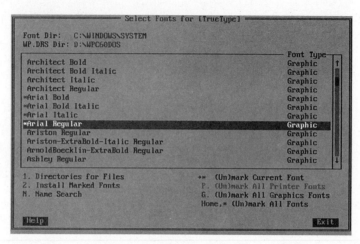

Figure 40.7. The fonts to be installed are marked.

Once all the fonts that are to be installed are marked, select Install Marked Fonts to initiate the process. WordPerfect will require a little more information, as detailed below.

Where Are Font Data Files?

Where WordPerfect expects to find the font files is exceedingly important. If WordPerfect can't find the necessary file, it can't print. Immediately after identifying the fonts to be installed, the program brings to the screen the Verify Locations of Graphics Fonts Data Files dialog box (see Figure 40.8). This dialog box states that the specified directory for the fonts to be installed into WordPerfect is different from where the program expects to find the Graphics Fonts Data Files directory, and offers the user the option to either update the Graphics Fonts Data Files directory, copy the fonts to the Graphics Fonts Data Files directory, or ignore this perceived discrepancy.

There are a number of issues to consider with each choice. If you update the Graphics Fonts Data Files, you run the risk that WordPerfect will not be able to find the other font files. Copying the fonts to the Graphic Fonts Data Files directory means duplicating the fonts on the disk—this alternative could be disastrous if you are low on hard disk space. Ignoring the message and situation means WordPerfect has to resolve the problem it has brought to your attention in some other fashion, and the odds of WordPerfect's resolution not always being what you expected is very high. If disk space allows, you are advised to copy the fonts to the Graphic Fonts Data Files directory.

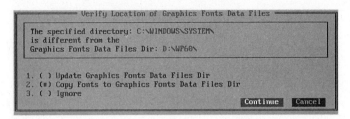

Figure 40.8. The Verify Locations of Graphics Fonts Data Files dialog box.

The fonts are then processed, as indicated by Figure 40.9. They are copied to the directory where WordPerfect expects to find them: the Graphic Fonts Data Files directory. Inasmuch as these are graphics files, the WP.DRS file is updated and saved (see Figure 40.10).

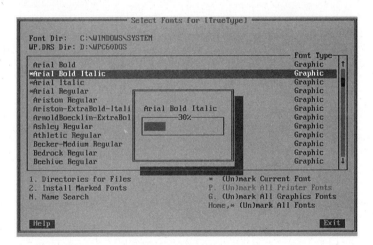

Figure 40.9. WordPerfect informing the user what font is being processed.

Finally, the Font Installation Completed message (see Figure 40.11) appears on-screen. You cannot "exit" this message, you can only continue. Perhaps you would like to install additional fonts? WordPerfect waits for your command.

Pressing F7 four times exits to the Font Setup dialog box. By selecting Initial Font and reviewing the list of available fonts (see Figure 40.12), you can verify that the fonts were properly installed.

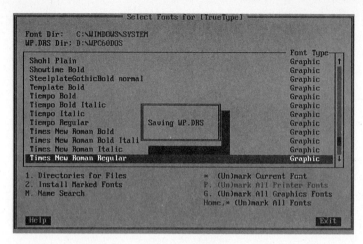

Figure 40.10. WordPerfect updates and saves its WP.DRS file.

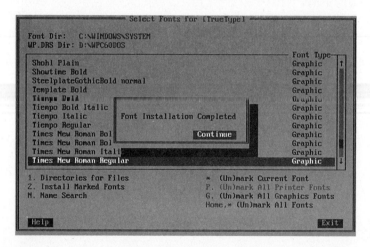

Figure 40.11. The *Font Installation Completed* message appears when WordPerfect has finished its installation of third-party fonts.

WP.DRS File Is Updated

WordPerfect updates the WP.DRS file (see Figure 40.10) as part of the font installation process. All installed printers are dependent upon the WP.DRS file. This means that the graphics fonts that have just been installed in one printer are available in the other printers!

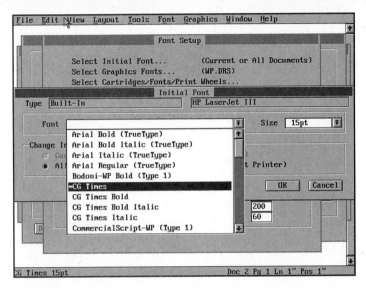

Figure 40.12. The Initial Font list indicates the fonts have been installed into WordPerfect and are ready to use.

Make the Most of What You've Got

The mysteries of typographical aesthetics can be wiped away with three easy guidelines: the fonts should match the message of the document, the fonts should be harmonious, and you should trust your instincts.

What Is a Font?

We have installed two families of fonts: Arial Regular, Bold, Italic, and Bold Italic and New Times Roman Regular, Bold, Italic, and Bold Italic. Many font families include not only these four, but also consider Compressed, Extra Bold, or other variations.

Properly done, each of the four fonts in a family should be independent and unique. Dutch Bold is not just a darker variety of Dutch, it stands on its own as an individual face with separate characteristics. Dutch Italic is considerably different from the Dutch font at an angle. Each font is a little different.

WordPerfect, within the program, has the capability to darken a font. The Automatic Font Changes, which can be edited from the Font Setup dialog box (see

Figure 40.4), controls whether the WordPerfect bolds the font when the bold appearance is marked on the Font Dialog Box or if the program switches to the bold font.

Font and Face

It is very easy to get font and face confused. A font is a specific typeface at a particular size. On the Font dialog box (see Figure 40.13), WordPerfect includes a list identified as "Font." This "Font" list includes both scalable typeface outlines (the TrueType, Type 1, and Speedo faces), as well as those fonts that are resident in the printer.

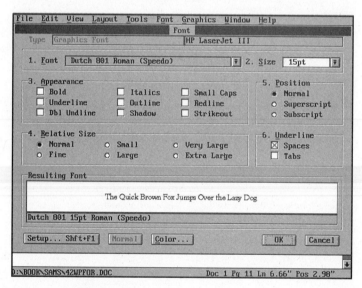

Figure 40.13. The WordPerfect Font dialog box.

A typeface, or face for short, is a set of characters that share a common appearance. Commercial Script-WP is one face and Swiss is another. All the commercial Script-WP faces are bonded together by the way each character looks (and by the personality we anthropomorphically assign it). Compare three characters of Commercial Script-WP with the same characters of Swiss. The characters of the same face visually belong together, whereas the differences between the exact same character of the two individual faces is obvious.

WordPerfect's default font for the Hewlett Packard LaserJet III is Courier 10 cpi, a font resident in the printer. Courier 10 cpi is a font because it is both the face (Courier) and the size (10 cpi—characters per inch).

The "fonts" that are included as part of the WordPerfect 6.0 package and the *Super Book* fonts are scalable font outlines. Courier 10 cpi has one size, 10 characters to the inch. Scalable font outlines can be sized from 1 to 999 points. (A point is a printing measurement, and there are approximately 72 points in an inch.)

The software that manipulates the font outline is incorporated into WordPerfect; you merely indicate the size of the font and the program does the rest.

Names Are Confusing

Typeface names are confusing. What does Dutch mean? What does Swiss mean? What about Arial and New Times Roman?

The fact is, many faces look very similar. Without getting into an analysis of the legal situation, Bitstream's Dutch, HP's CG Times, New Times Roman that comes with Windows 3.1, and WordPerfect's Roman are all based on a font developed for the London *Times* newspaper known as "Times Roman." The names of the faces is an issue for the lawyers, the way they look is very similar. Bitstream's Swiss, HP's Univers, the Arial family that comes with Windows 3.1, and WordPerfect's Helve are all based on "Helvetica."

Times Roman and Helvetica are the most popular typefaces for the world that uses this character set. Times Roman is popular in the United States, while Helvetica is more prominent in Europe. Both, however, are extremely common.

These pretty names—Dutch, Swiss, Arial, Helve—don't have much significance independent of the faces they represent. There are other, more important, considerations when discussing fonts. Is it a display or text face? Serif or sans serif?

Display or Text?

When should one face be used as opposed to another? The popularity of Times Roman and Helvetica over Bodoni-WP Bold or CommercialScript is not an aesthetic issue so much as a question of function. It is easier to read Times Roman or Helvetica than Bodoni-WP Bold or CommercialScript, particularly in large quantities of text, in part because their familiarity causes a certain anonymity. Bodoni-WP Bold and CommercialScript, on the other hand, work especially well in small quantities where the personality of the face is an important tool in communicating the document's message.

A very simple differentiation is made, then, between display and text faces. Times Roman and Helvetica are two text faces, Bodoni-WP Bold and CommercialScript are both display faces. The differentiation is based on the utility of the faces. Figure 40.14 shows the same paragraph at 11 point in Dutch, Bodoni-WP Bold, CommercialScript, and Swiss. The display faces are not as easy to read as the text faces. A full paragraph of CommercialScript might look very pretty, but it is virtually illegible.

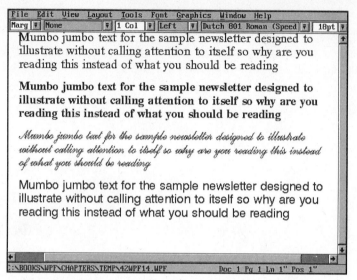

Figure 40.14. A comparison of one paragraph in four faces (Dutch, Bodoni-WP Bold, CommercialScript and Swiss) at 11 point.

The Font display box (see Figure 40.13) includes a sample of the font you have selected, just another wonderful utility incorporated into 6.0. You can see a sample of the font on the screen before accepting the choice.

Serif or Sans Serif

Another differentiation between faces, particularly text faces, is whether it is a serif or sans serif face. Many people like to use two faces on a page, most commonly one serif and one sans serif face.

Serif is a printing term referring to the strokes or flags off the main stroke of the character. Figure 40.15 contains two capital *A*s, one Dutch and one Swiss, both at 200 point. There is a base on the Dutch *A*, feet that jut off from the character. There are no additional lines on the Swiss character.

These lines are serifs. Dutch, and all the faces derived from Times Roman, are serif faces. Swiss, and any face emulating the look and feel of Helvetica, is a sans serif (literally, without serif) face.

Using the Fonts

WordPerfect's Font dialog box (see Figure 40.13) is the key to controlling the fonts in a document. Chapter 13, "Changing Fonts," reviews the Font dialog box in detail. The great thing about the Font dialog box is how it puts all the information about fonts in one place, thus inviting the long-time WordPerfect user to rethink the use of fonts. By centralizing the various menus into one dialog box, WordPerfect gives the user considerable more control over the document's appearance.

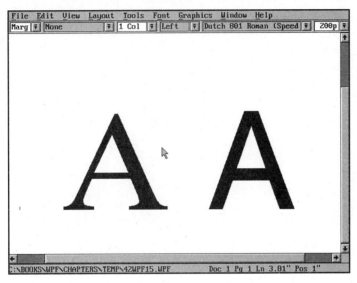

Figure 40.15. A serif *A* and a sans serif *A* at 200 point.

The fonts should match the message of the document. In order to do this, you need to consider the document very carefully. What is the document saying? What tone is the document using? Is it funny? Serious? Formal? The list of adjectives which might describe any document is as large as the nearest dictionary.

Chapter 42, "Using Subdivided Pages," examines subdivided pages by building a series of party place cards. The font is CommercialScript. CommercialScript is a fancy, formal script font that fits the tone the people giving the party want to achieve.

Consider four other examples, all similar in that they are announcements or invitations, yet completely unique—an eight-year-old boy's birthday party, the office moving to a new location, the opening of a car dealership, and a political rally.

The proper font(s) can convey or strengthen information about the function. The eight-year-old boy's birthday party will be fun, so you want to use a font that looks "fun," perhaps Bodoni-WP Bold. The font used to announce a new office location might be described as formal, serious, dignified, and respectable, perhaps CommercialScript. The opening of a new car dealership might mix fun and dignity in an informal but serious sense—consider using Bodoni-WP Bold with a text font. A political rally will be topical. The fact that Courier looks like the fonts commonly associated with a typewriter echoes that topicality.

The message, including the tone, can be conveyed by the face, as the above paragraph demonstrates. Each face has a personality. Ask yourself, with each and every document you produce, whether the face matches the message of the document. Don't get caught wearing weekend grungies to a formal cocktail party.

Just as the right face can strengthen a document's message, the wrong one can be ruinous. Figure 40.16 is the invitation to the eight-year-old's party. What would happen if, instead of Bodoni-WP Bold, the face were CommercialScript (see Figure 40.17)? CommercialScript is a great face for an invitation, but not to a birthday party of an eight-year-old boy. Courier (see Figure 40.18), which is fairly nondescript, doesn't detract from the message as much as CommercialScript, but Bodoni-WP Bold is still the best choice.

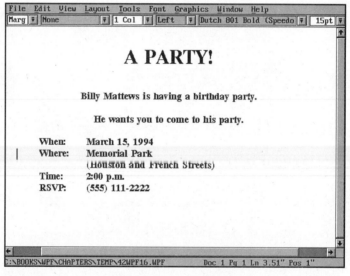

Figure 40.16. A party invitation in Bodoni-WP Bold.

Trust Your Judgment

We are not interested in dictating what face to use with what document. Our concern lies strictly with you, the user. Ask yourself, does the face match the message? If you aren't sure, compare the document in other faces. Turn on Graphics Display Mode and change the font on your screen—you can see the difference right there on the monitor. Trial and error was never so easy!

You choose the font, not the editors of *Super Book*. You determine the message and the tone of the document. You know what other factors might come into play, including secondary messages others might want to communicate without being blatant. In other words, it is your document.

Figure 40.17. The same party invitation in Commercial Script.

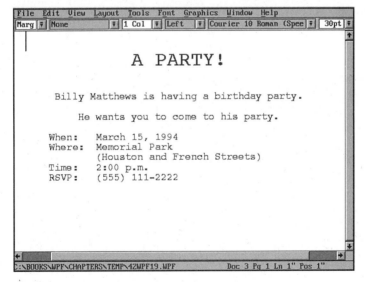

Figure 40.18. The same party invitation in Courier.

Trust yourself. The example of the eight-year-old's birthday party invitation might seem simplistic, but it is representative of the situations you'll probably face. Let's review how we decided to use Bodoni-WP Bold:

567

▲ Does the face match the message? If it does, go no further. Use that face. The odds are against a perfect match, unless you have a huge library of typefaces at your disposal.

▲ Do you have a face that matches the message? The separation of font and size in the Font dialog box makes changing faces simple. Try different faces and compare them.

If you find a face that matches the message, again, go no further. Use that face. However, the odds are still against finding a perfect match.

▲ Can you rule out any faces that clash with or deter from the message? Each face has a personality that has to be considered. CommercialScript, a great face for invitations, simply wouldn't be appropriate for Billy's party.

▲ What remains in your library of typefaces? Is there a tradition to follow? One reason why CommercialScript is a great face for invitations is because script faces have been used for initiations for years and years. It's history! It's tradition! It works!

▲ The point is, use your judgment and trust it. If there's a reason for using the face, do it. There might be better faces than Bodoni-WP Bold for the birthday party invitation, but they aren't available to you. There's something fun about Bodoni-WP Bold, and whatever it is that is "fun" about the face makes it harmonious with the invitation's message.

Mixing Faces

Should the document be in one face, or should you mix faces? Like most other design questions, the answer lies with you and your preference. Design is an art, not a science, and there are no hard and fast rules.

Ask yourself these questions:

▲ Is the document improved by the second face? If so, how?

▲ Does the second face clash with the first? Do they work together to make the document more attractive?

You'll always be safer using just one face, but sometimes safety is the wrong thing. If there's a reason to use the second face, do it.

Display Faces

Display faces are usually so unique that mixing display faces courts disaster. It can be done, but only with the utmost of caution.

Text Faces

Use a serif for headings and a sans serif for text, or vice versa. This adds a visual variety without going overboard.

Do not use two serif faces on a page, or two sans serif faces. There isn't enough contrast between them. If you are going to go to the trouble of using the two different faces, make sure the document gets the benefit.

Font Size

How large should the font be? As with all other questions of how your document should look, the answer is to trust your judgment.

Make reading as easy as possible for the document's audience. Invite them to read the document. There's a definite relationship between font size and how much text the reader's eye can grasp quickly. Line length, particularly in columns, should be the major factor in font size.

A common font size for text is 11 point. Figure 40.14 has four paragraphs in 11 point, albeit different faces. Is this a comfortable size for you?

Establishing Document Organization

The most common cause of font abuse is ill-advised attempts at defining the organization of a document. Here are a few ideas to consider the next time you aren't sure of the best way to communicate the message.

Marry Heading and Text

A heading and its accompanying text should be married. The use of negative space is the best way to ensure that the heading is married to the text. Avoid large jumps in font size between the text and the heading. Take advantage of WordPerfect's font attributes, and always be consistent.

Use Negative Space

Negative space is the most powerful tool you have to control how the reader perceives your document. By simply having more space above the heading than between the heading and the text, you tell the reader that the heading and the text belong together. Marrying the heading to the text is that simple!

No Big Jumps

Having scalable fonts is often seen as an invitation to have a huge heading and small text. Huge jumps in font size are often detrimental to the document, distracting the reader away from the message instead of adding any drama or tension. Limit the change in font size to a small step of two or three points.

There are exceptions to everything, and particularly guidelines to font size changes. The best rule of thumb is to trust yourself. If there is a reason for a dramatic size change, do it.

The point is, don't do it just because you can. Make sure there is a reason behind what you do, and a good reason at that.

Use Font Attributes

Bold, underlining, all caps, and italics can all be used to establish an order to your document. Figure 40.19 illustrates five variations of attributes defining the priority of the headings.

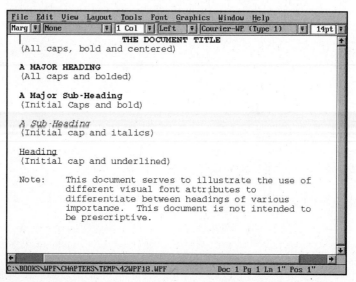

Figure 40.19. An example of using font attributes to prioritize the document headings.

Be Consistent

Above all else, be consistent. This can't be stated too often or followed too closely.

Size and Face

Large fonts can scream at the reader. Consider the word *Hello* at 120 point in various faces, say Swiss, Swiss Bold, Bodoni-WP Bold, CommercialScript, Dutch, and Dutch Bold. The Dutch and Swiss shout to the reader. The Bodoni-WP Bold is quite friendly. CommercialScript almost dances. Dutch Bold and Swiss Bold scream out at the reader.

(Is this a comparison of the face or the size? Try the same word at 12 point and note that the dancing, the screaming, and the shouting stop. A font is both size and face. You need to understand and control both face and size.)

by Art Shaak

Columns and Page Layout

Desktop publishing seems to mean producing newsletters to many people, even though there is much more to desktop publishing than newsletters. A lot of "desktop publishing" is done with word processing programs, including WordPerfect 6.0, that neither are, nor claim to be, desktop publishing packages.

WordPerfect 6.0, however, does have may desktop publishing features. Newsltr.Tem, located in your WPDOCS directory, is a template for the first page of a newsletter template provided by WordPerfect. The template uses a three-column format.

Columns: What Are They?

Columns provide an excellent opportunity to discuss how WordPerfect combines various features to produce one great utility. Columns, labels, and subdivided pages take advantage of what WordPerfect calls *logical pages*, which, simply put, means the program can divide a sheet of paper into parts, each part having the attributes of a page. In order to break the physical page into logical pages (in this case, columns), the program needs to know what type and how many columns are on each page.

Columns and Newsletters

Understanding and controlling columns is paramount to newsletter production. Picture a newsletter with one column on the page. That isn't what you had in mind, is it? Additionally, any discussion of columns and newsletters must cover what a grid is and why the grid is so important.

What's Available?

WordPerfect provides four types of columns:

▲ Newspaper
▲ Balanced Newspaper
▲ Parallel
▲ Parallel with Block Protect

Newspaper Columns

Newspaper Columns and Balanced Newspaper columns are very similar, each snaking the text vertically to the bottom of one column and continuing the text through the next column. Parallel and Parallel with Block Protect present the text in rows horizontally across the page before moving down to the next row of information.

> **Note:** Balanced Newspaper columns "even out" columns. The difference between Balanced Newspaper columns and Newspaper columns may not always be obvious.

Use Newspaper columns in newsletters and similar documents when you want the text to wrap from one vertical column to the next. Balanced Newspaper columns differ from Newspaper columns in that each column on a page of Balanced Newspaper columns ends at the same vertical position, whereas Newspaper columns always start at the same line. Be careful, though, as the initial release of WordPerfect 6.0 has no Dormant Return safety net for the occasional hard return that falls at the bottom of a column.

> **Caution:** Always check Balanced Newspaper columns for stray hard returns at the bottom of the column.

Parallel Columns

Parallel columns are best used to present comparisons such as Figure 41.1, which shows responses to a questionnaire given to three separate demographic groups. A large column for the questions is followed, on the same line, by the answers for each group.

Question	18-25	26-35	35-50
Do you watch more than ten hours of commercial television in a week?			
Yes	85%	75%	60%
No	10%	20%	35%
Does your household receive "premium" cable television stations?			
Yes	95%	95%	95%
No	5%	5%	5%
How many movies did you see in a motion picture theatre last year?	15-20	8-15	10-20
How many movies did you rent on video tape last year?	40-50	20-30	35-60

Figure 41.1. Parallel columns allow comparison of different categories of information.

Parallel columns with Block Protect are the same as Parallel columns with Block Protect added. Parallel columns with Block Protect differ from Parallel columns at the end of the page because Block Protect keeps the horizontal group together on a page. If the whole group won't fit on one page, Parallel columns with Block Protect move the entire portion to the next page.

Tables or Columns?

The introduction of Tables in WordPerfect 5.1 made the future of Parallel columns, with or without Block Protect, questionable. Tables take advantage of many microcomputer users' familiarity with spreadsheets while providing a method to achieve the same results as Parallel columns. Tables appear easier to manipulate and control; it's easier to conceptualize a row for each question, a column for each demographic group, and a cell where the response for a particular group to a specific question appears as opposed to columns holding the same information.

Tip: You might find Tables easier to use than Parallel columns.

The rest of this chapter focuses on newspaper columns.

Defining Columns

The Column feature requires two instructions: defining the columns and turning columns on or off. Both instructions are found in the Text Column dialog box (see Figure 41.2).

Procedure 41.1. Accessing the Text Column dialog box.

1. Move the insertion point to the beginning of the text you wish to format as columns.
2. Choose Layout or press Alt+F7.
3. Select Columns.
4. The Text Column dialog box now appears on your screen.

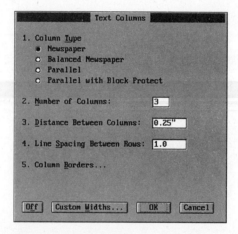

Figure 41.2. The Text Columns dialog box.

Columns On

Turning the columns feature on is simple. Accept the information as it appears on the Text Columns dialog box, and at the same time WordPerfect turns columns on. Turning columns off is even simpler. Select Off at the Text Columns dialog box.

Column Type

Defining columns requires a little more of your attention. The Text Columns dialog box asks that you identify the type of column (Newspaper, Balanced Newspaper, Parallel, or Parallel with Block Protect), the number of columns, the distance between columns, the line spacing between rows, and the borders between each column.

Text columns, as WordPerfect identifies this dialog box, are different from Table columns. A table is a group of cells; a cell is the intersection of horizontal rows and vertical columns. (Workshop IV, "Tables and Forms," discusses tables in great detail.) The term *column* is also used in Math Definition.

 Caution: In WordPerfect, the word *column* has different meanings in different situations.

Number of Columns

The number of columns depends upon the grid and layout you've designed. The number of columns will be affected by the size of each column. Be aware that there is a relationship between the size of a column and the font size used for that column, as demonstrated in Figure 41.3. The width of the column should be no more than the amount the eye can grasp quickly and easily. The wider the column, the larger the font.

Distance Between Columns

The amount of space between columns is defined by indicating the distance between columns.

Line Spacing Between Rows

Line spacing between rows is limited to Parallel columns, providing the capability to alter the spacing between rows of information. WordPerfect offers two features to control vertical spacing: Line Height and Paragraph Spacing. Line Height is controlled from the Line Format dialog box off the Layout pull-down menu (and more fully explained in Chapter 15, "Line Formatting"). Paragraph Spacing, discussed in Chapter 16, "Paragraph Formatting," is located on the Margin Format dialog box off the Layout pull-down menu.

Line Height controls the amount of space between the bottom of the previous row and the top of the characters in the current row. Paragraph Spacing offers the capability to change the amount of vertical space between two paragraphs. Judiciously used, both can make the difference between a document that is just okay and one that is outstanding.

> This is an example of 20 point (Dutch font) text.
>
> This is an example of 15 point (Dutch font) text.
>
> This is an example of 13 point (Dutch font) text.
>
> This is an example of 11 point (Dutch font) text.
>
> This is an example of 9 point (Dutch font) text.
>
> This is an example of 7 point (Dutch font) text.

Figure 41.3. Font size and column size are interrelated. The wider the column, the larger the font should be.

WordPerfect provides two additional border options unique to columns: Column Border (Between Only), which places a border between columns, and Column Border (Outside and Between), which combines a page border outside the column text with borders between columns.

Custom Widths

Unless otherwise specified, WordPerfect makes all columns the same size. Select Custom Widths, at the bottom of the Text Columns dialog box (see Figure 41.2), and see a different perspective on column definition (see Figure 41.4). You can control the size of each column, independent of the other columns. Plus, you can control the size of the space between the columns.

Fixed Width

"Fixed" tells WordPerfect that regardless of what other changes you make regarding allocating the space, this variable should remain the same. On an 8.5-inch by 11-inch sheet of paper formatted with 1-inch margins and three columns with a distance of .5-inches between each column, Custom Widths shows that each column has a width of 1.83 inches. Change the paper size from portrait (8.5-inches by 11-inches) to landscape (11-inches by 8.5-inches), review the custom widths of the column definition without making any change other than the paper size, and see that the column widths have been changed to 2.67 inches. The distance between columns remains .5 inches because Fixed is checked on. If Fixed was not turned on, the same change in orientation would result in the column widths jumping to 2.54 inches and the space between columns increasing to 0.693 inches.

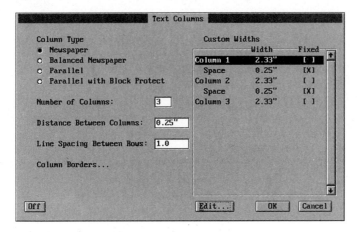

Figure 41.4. A second Text Columns dialog box showing the width of each column and the space between each column.

Unequal Widths

A word of warning: WordPerfect will not prevent you from varying the distance between columns so that the distance between columns 1 and 2 is .5 inches while the distance between columns 2 and 3 is only .25 inches. Please carefully consider the effect before taking advantage of this capability. Most of the time, unequal distances between columns is a bad idea.

On the other hand, unequal column sizes can be quite successful if the columns follow the grid and maintain their proportion. For example, two columns 1.5 inches wide and a third column with a width of 3.0 inches result in a pleasing design that works because the larger column is exactly twice the size of the other two columns.

Introducing the Grid

Any discussion of newspaper columns naturally leads to the topic of page layout. The number of columns created depends on the page design and layout. Many books are devoted solely to page design and page layout. This chapter presents a few guidelines, but it is not intended to be a complete or exhaustive examination of page layout.

A grid is the underlying infrastructure of any page layout. Once you have established a grid for a particular document, you should never stray from it. No, a grid is not a WordPerfect feature, so don't try looking it up in the manual. Grids are a page layout tool that you need to bring to WordPerfect.

A grid is a way of breaking up the page into consistent units of space. There are a number of ways of breaking up the page, and you need to be sure that the grid developed for a document is flexible enough to meet the needs of the document.

The grid is dependent upon the size of the page. What would work quite nicely on an 8-inch by 11-inch sheet may look terrible on the same piece of paper printed sideways. The numbers are different and the final document is different; therefore, the grid must necessarily be different.

Define Your Graphic Elements

Before establishing the grid, you have to consider the size of the various graphic elements you plan to use in the document. The graphic elements of any document, say a newsletter article, might include the title, the text of the article, photographs, headings, charts, tables, illustrations, captions, and supplemental information such as an author's biography. Some of the graphic elements, such as the text of the article, can be adjusted to fit the grid, whereas the size and aspect ratios of other elements—illustrations, photographs, charts, tables, and anything else where manipulation risks distortion—must be considered before finalizing the grid.

Aspect Ratio

Take out a ruler and start measuring. Pay attention to both the size and the aspect ratio of the graphic elements. The aspect ratio is the ratio of horizontal to vertical. A head shot photograph that looks great at its current size of 2-inch by 3-inch will look okay at 1-inch by 1.5-inch. The same photograph would be distorted at 1-inch by 2-inch, because the ratio of horizontal to vertical is corrupted.

Notice that there's been no mention of using WordPerfect or even a microcomputer since starting on grids. Before turning on the computer, before loading WordPerfect, make sure you know what you want to do. Establishing the grid, as well as figuring out the best way to place the graphic elements within that grid, should be done before turning on the computer.

Maintain the Proportion

Columns do not have to be the same size. The size of one column should be tied to the size of the other columns on the page and the grid. The earlier example of unequal columns exemplifies a basic design principle: maintain the proportion. The larger column is twice the size of the smaller column.

One last general comment about the grid, and this applies to the page design throughout a document: be consistent. Always. The path leading away from consistency may be a shortcut straight to a designer's inferno.

Bear in mind one other extremely important fact. Design is not a science, it is an art. While the path leading away from consistency may be a quick slide to Designer's Inferno, it might also be exactly what the document requires. Chapter 40, "Producing Good-Looking Documents," illustrates how the message of the document must be supported by the document's visual appearance.

Building the Grid

Note: A grid is a series of construction lines that serve as the foundation upon which the document is built.

The example in Figure 41.5 has three columns and two alleys (an alley is the space between two columns) on an 8.5-inch by 11-inch sheet of paper. The grid contemplates the left and right margins, of course, as well as the top and bottom margins.

Identifying Spatial Relationships

Some definite spatial relationships exist in the example in Figure 41.5. The alleys between the columns are the smallest layout element. The left and right margins are twice the size of the alleys. The size of the columns is a multiple of the alleys.

Specifically, each alley is a quarter of an inch (.25 inches). The two alleys total .50 inches, leaving 8 inches of unreserved horizontal space.

The left margin is twice the size of an alley, or .50 inches. Left and right margins are balanced. A full inch is given to the margins, leaving 7 inches of unreserved horizontal space.

581

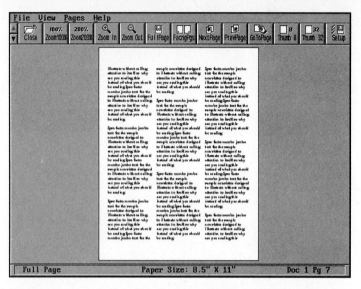

Figure 41.5. Newspaper columns, three columns to the page.

There are three columns of text and 7 inches of available horizontal space, so each column is 2.33 inches wide. (7 inches divided by 3 is 2.33 inches.)

Translating the Grid to WordPerfect

Let's translate this to WordPerfect codes.

Left margin	.5
Right margin	.5
Column Definition:	
Column Type	Newspaper
Number of Columns	3
Distance between columns	.25
Line spacing	1

At this point, click Column **W**idths and check that the numbers match Figure 41.6.

Editing Columnar Text

Finalize your text before turning columns on. Editing text already formatted for columns is a thankless task. Moving around from one column of text to another isn't intuitive, even to the experienced WordPerfect user. It is much easier to navigate through text if you turn off columns before editing.

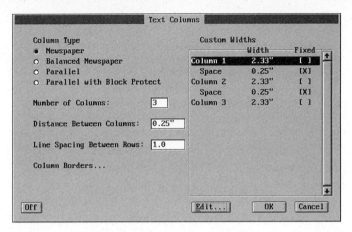

Figure 41.6. The Text Columns dialog box used to define Figure 41.5.

Finalizing the Text

Do as much editing as possible before you turn your attention to the layout of the document. Write the text without columns on. Columns are part of layout, so have your text finished before attacking design issues. If changes are required to the text after you start working on document layout, make those changes with columns off.

Fitting the amount of text to the allocated space is always going to be a problem. You either have too much or too little text, usually too much. Squeezing too much text into a limited area makes the entire document harder to read. Measure the importance of each golden word—and no doubt your words are golden—with the entire document's readability. How golden are the words that cause the document to be passed by?

If, after all the editing is done, you define columns and turn them on and there is still too much text to fit the allocated space, turn the columns off before moving through the text.

Turning Columns Off

Use the following procedure to turn columns off, although you might want to read the "Notice Your Position" section in this chapter first:

1. Select Layout.
2. Choose Columns.
3. Choose Off.

Notice Your Position

Before turning columns off, move the insertion point to the top of the document. The program complies with your instructions: if you tell WordPerfect to turn columns off in the middle of the second paragraph, the program stops formatting columns in the middle of the second paragraph. (Columns on/off does not appear to be affected by Auto Code Placement. For more information on Auto Code Placement, an important feature new to WordPerfect 6.0, see Chapter 12, "Understanding Formatting Codes.") The easiest way to move the insertion point to the top of the document is to press Home twice, followed by the up arrow.

A Way To Save The Definition

Be careful here. If you turn columns off immediately after the column definition code, you cancel the first code and WordPerfect deletes the column definition. Insert a hard return, which is simple enough to remove once editing is complete, and then turn columns off. The program recognizes even a single [HRt] code as text and so preserves the otherwise contradicting codes.

 Caution: Columns codes are not affected by Auto Code Placement.

Codes Inserted by WordPerfect

Between the codes that turn columns on and off are four codes, including the [HRt] resulting from pressing Enter. The other codes are three [THCol] codes, one for each column. WordPerfect inserted these codes to preserve the validity of the column definition before turning columns off. WordPerfect makes sure the column definition code is followed by one complete set of columns before turning columns off.

After editing the document, move the insertion point back to the top of the document and delete the [HRt] and [Col Def: Off] codes. The document is once again formatted in columns.

Editing with Columns On

The hardest part about editing text with columns on is moving around the columns. Let's say the text to be changed is in the third line of the second column. Cursoring through the document means going through the entire first column before getting to the second column. Fortunately, there is an easy way to just jump to the second column.

A combination of Ctrl+Home and the left arrow will move the insertion point to the column to the left. Ctrl+Home followed by the right arrow will move the insertion point to the column to the right.

> **Tip:** Ctrl+Home followed by the left arrow jumps the insertion point to the column immediately on the left.
>
> Ctrl+Home followed by the right arrow jumps the insertion point to the column immediately to the right.

Borders

The ability to add a border around text, a paragraph, or a page is much simpler with 6.0 than with previous editions of WordPerfect. The program even allows borders between and around columns. Figure 41.7 includes borders between the columns.

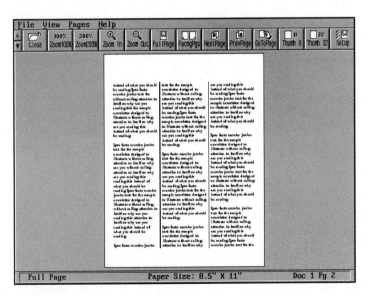

Figure 41.7. Newspaper columns with column borders

Adding Borders

The Create Column Border dialog box can be reached from at least two different approaches, via Columns or Graphics. This makes sense, because Column Borders fit under both Columns and Graphics.

Create Column Border Dialog Box Via Columns

The steps to access the Edit Column border dialog box are:

1. Select Layout.
2. Choose Columns.
3. Choose Column Borders.

You are at the Create/Edit Column border dialog box.

Create Column Border Dialog Box Via Graphics

The steps used to access the Create/Edit Column Border dialog box through Graphics are:

1. Select Graphics.
2. Choose Borders.
3. Choose Columns.

You are at the Create/Edit Column border dialog box.

The Create Column Border Dialog Box

WordPerfect assumes that if you have ventured this far through the dialog boxes to the Create Column Border dialog box, you want borders. The choice initially made by the program is "Column Border (Between Only)," which places a border between the columns. By selecting Border Style, you can choose other borders.

 Caution: If you fail to cancel out of the Create Column Border dialog box, you will insert a border in the text.

Pressing Enter—even the space bar—is interpreted by the program as "OK," accepting the border defined in the Create Column Border dialog box. Only Esc or Cancel moves you away from this box without turning borders on.

A document with columns may or may not have borders. It is even possible to have some pages with column borders and some without borders in the same document. For example, in the document in Figure 41.8, there are borders on pages 2 and 3, but not on pages 1 and 4.

Columns and Auto Code Placement

Auto Code Placement, discussed in much greater detail in Chapter 12, is a major concern. Auto Code Placement is turned on by default. With Auto Code Placement on, turning column borders off will affect the entire document no matter where the code is entered. The Auto Code Placement feature moves the code to its proper position; the proper position for a columns border on or off code is at the beginning of the text formatted as columns.

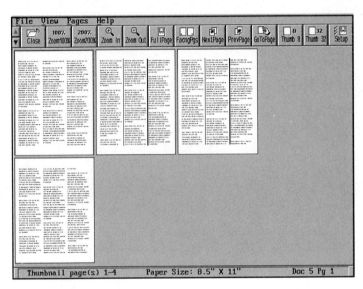

Figure 41.8. This four-page document has column borders on pages 2 and 3, but not on pages 1 or 4.

Turn Auto Code Placement off, however, and the code stays in approximately the same position as it is placed. The first column border code in the document (Figure 41.9) is at the beginning of the text of page 2, turning column borders on starting with page 2. Putting the column borders off code at the very top of page 4 will not turn column borders off until after page 4. However, if the column borders off code is on page 3, the borders will remain on page 3, but not on page 4.

The column borders off code can appear anywhere on page 3 to turn column borders off on page 4, but you need to be very careful about the placement of any columns-related code. If a columns-related code is placed between paragraphs in the middle of the first column on the page, WordPerfect completes the column row by inserting three [THCol] codes and severely alters the appearance of the text. Column-related codes should always be placed at the very top of the page, immediately after the Column Definition code or the preceding page end code.

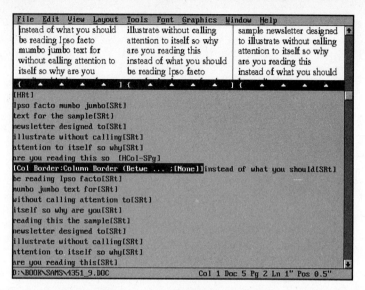

Figure 41.9. Column borders on is the very first code on page 2. Borders between the columns appear on page 2.

Adding Figures to Columns

Newspaper columns are essential for preparing newsletters with WordPerfect 6.0, but four pages of text is boring. The single page of a newsletter template provided as part of the 6.0 package (newsltr.tem in the WPDOCS subdirectory) includes text plus a masthead and space for a figure box (see Figure 41.10).

How you develop a masthead or a graphic is outside the scope of this chapter, and WordPerfect 6.0 is quite possibly not the best program for either. This discussion will borrow the masthead from WordPerfect's newsletter template and use one of the graphics that comes with the program.

Masthead

Open the document newsltr.tem. This file will probably be found in the WPDOCS directory, assuming you did a standard installation of the WordPerfect program. (For more information on installing the program, please see Appendix A, "Installing WordPerfect 6.0.")

Set Reveal Codes to display to be absolutely certain where the insertion point is located. This is tricky but insertion point position is extremely important. Move the insertion point so that it is on the *I* of *Issue*, immediately after the `[-Para Border:[None];[None]]` code (see Figure 41.11).

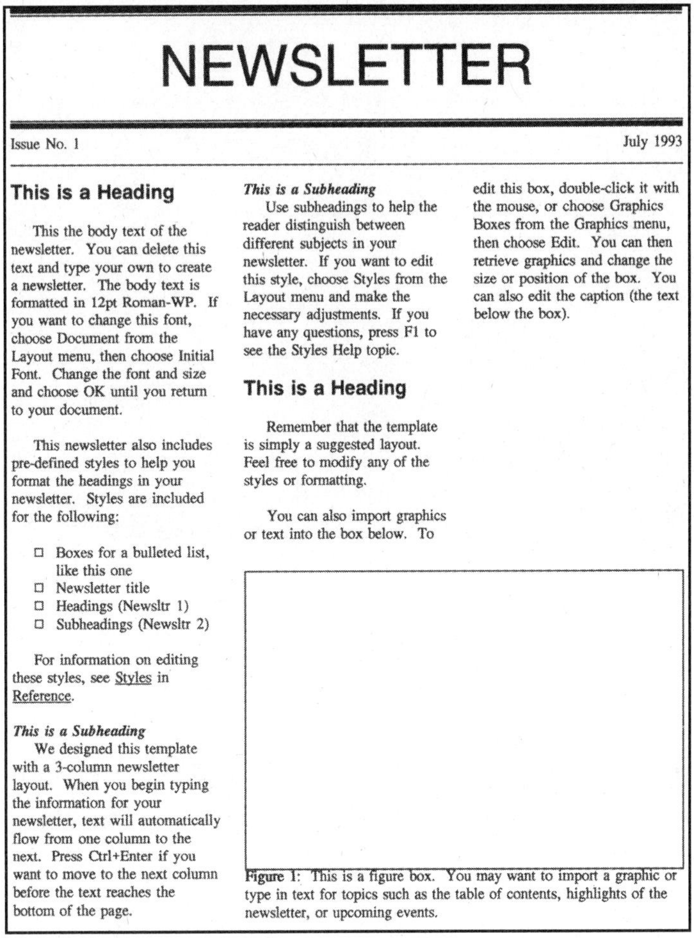

NEWSLETTER

Issue No. 1   July 1993

This is a Heading

This the body text of the newsletter. You can delete this text and type your own to create a newsletter. The body text is formatted in 12pt Roman-WP. If you want to change this font, choose Document from the Layout menu, then choose Initial Font. Change the font and size and choose OK until you return to your document.

This newsletter also includes pre-defined styles to help you format the headings in your newsletter. Styles are included for the following:

☐ Boxes for a bulleted list, like this one
☐ Newsletter title
☐ Headings (Newsltr 1)
☐ Subheadings (Newsltr 2)

For information on editing these styles, see Styles in Reference.

This is a Subheading
We designed this template with a 3-column newsletter layout. When you begin typing the information for your newsletter, text will automatically flow from one column to the next. Press Ctrl+Enter if you want to move to the next column before the text reaches the bottom of the page.

This is a Subheading
Use subheadings to help the reader distinguish between different subjects in your newsletter. If you want to edit this style, choose Styles from the Layout menu and make the necessary adjustments. If you have any questions, press F1 to see the Styles Help topic.

This is a Heading

Remember that the template is simply a suggested layout. Feel free to modify any of the styles or formatting.

You can also import graphics or text into the box below. To

edit this box, double-click it with the mouse, or choose Graphics Boxes from the Graphics menu, then choose Edit. You can then retrieve graphics and change the size or position of the box. You can also edit the caption (the text below the box).

Figure 1: This is a figure box. You may want to import a graphic or type in text for topics such as the table of contents, highlights of the newsletter, or upcoming events.

Figure 41.10. The newsletter template that comes with 6.0.

The `[-Para Border:[None];[None]]` code is an integral part of the double rule at the top and bottom of the masthead. Delete the code by accident and you've deleted both the top and bottom set of lines. The masthead looks much better with these two sets of lines, so leave them in.

With the insertion point properly positioned on the *I* of *Issue*, delete the rest of the page by holding down the Ctrl key while you press Page Down. This removes the rest of the sample from the screen.

Using the Save As feature, save this document under a different name so as not to lose the newsletter template. You never know when you'll want to use the template again.

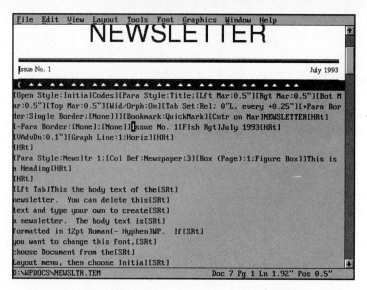

Figure 41.11. Position that insertion point carefully. Display your codes to be absolutely sure of the insertion point's location.

Define three newspaper columns, as done in the earlier section "Translating the Grid to WordPerfect," and then retrieve the file 43sample.txt into the current document. 43sample.txt is on the disk that comes with this book. Make sure you retrieve the file into the current document and not a new document. The NEWSLETTER masthead should be on top of the 43sample.txt text.

Space Between Masthead and Text

Is there enough space between the bottom lines of the masthead and the text? You don't want the text crowding the masthead. How can you tell?

There are really two questions here. First, how can you tell if there's enough space between the masthead and the text? Second, how much space is enough?

The best way to tell if there's enough space between the masthead and the text is to print and check it, but you might waste a lot of paper using this trial and error method. WordPerfect's Print Preview feature (**Print, View**) allows you to "print" the final text to the screen. Unfortunately, Print Preview is not particularly accurate, as you can judge for yourself by noting whether the two lines of the top and bottom border can be distinguished. Only in 200 percent zoom is it possible to differentiate between the top and bottom border, and 200 percent zoom severely limits how much of the document is displayed on the screen.

How much space is enough? Take a look at the sample newsletter template WordPerfect provides. There is 5/8 of an inch between the bottom of the masthead border and the top of the "This is a Heading" characters, and 3/16 of an inch between the top of the heading and the line under the issue and date identification.

Print the first page of the document with the WordPerfect masthead and the 43sample.txt text (see Figure 41.12) (43sample.txt is included on the *Super Book* disk) and compare it with the sample newsletter (see Figure 41.10). The sample newsletter feels more comfortable because it has much more room, putting the reader at ease. The other document feels uncomfortably cramped. There's no room to breathe.

Figure 41.12. Compare this document with WordPerfect's template, shown in Figure 41.10.

Negative Space

The main difference between the two documents is the amount of negative space; the sample newsletter has more. Negative space is an extremely important part of your document, and indubitably the first graphic element to be abused.

All too often, negative space is sacrificed in order to fit in just a little more text. Unfortunately, that "little more text" results in a newsletter (or document) discouraging the reader by inviting the reader *not* to read it. A healthy amount of negative space in any document helps the reader want to read the document. Negative space invites the attention of the reader, and a newsletter that forfeits it sends a clear message to the newsletter's audience: don't read me.

There are no hard and fast rules about how much negative space a document should have, other than it shouldn't look cramped.

Adding Negative Space

Add one blank line between the bottom of the masthead and the beginning of the columnar text. Once again, insertion point position is extremely important. With Reveal Codes displayed, make sure the cursor highlights the Column Definition code. Anything you insert will be placed before the highlighted code.

Where should the blank line be placed, before or after the Column Definition code? If the [HRt] code appears after the Column Definition code, the blank line will appear in the first column but in none of the other columns on the page. The Column Definition code marks where the columnar formatting starts. You want the blank line above all three columns. The [HRt] code, which represents the blank line, should be before the Column Definition code, moving the vertical starting point of all columns on the page down one line.

The final result is shown in Figure 41.13. Notice the improvement just a little negative space makes by contrasting Figures 43.12 and 43.13.

Graphic Box

Workshop VII, "Graphics, Lines, Borders, and Fills," goes into great detail about importing graphics into WordPerfect 6.0, so the focus here will be on using graphics within the established grid.

The fact that WordPerfect allows you to position and size the graphic at the editing screen (assuming you work with Graphics display mode on) makes adding a graphic deceptively simple.

Take a look at Figure 41.14. The globe graphic (GLOBE.WPG), which comes with WordPerfect 6.0, has been sized so that it fits in one column. After the graphic was retrieved, the graphic box was edited to assure it was attached to the page (not the paragraph), and the horizontal position was right (relative to the margins, offset from position left 2.58 inches). The vertical position was set at 2.11 inches, and the width at 2.33 inches. The height, based upon the width, was automatic because the preserve image/width ratio was set.

NEWSLETTER

Ipso facto mumbo jumbo text for the sample newsletter designed to illustrate without calling attention to itself so why are you reading this instead of what you should be reading Ipso facto mumbo jumbo text for the sample newsletter designed to illustrate without calling attention to the sample newsletter designed to illustrate without calling attention to the sample newsletter designed to illustrate without calling attention to itself so why are you reading this instead of what you should be reading

Ipso facto mumbo jumbo text for the sample newsletter designed to illustrate without calling attention to itself so why are you reading this without calling attention to itself so why are you reading this instead of what you should be reading Ipso facto mumbo jumbo text for the sample newsletter designed to illustrate without calling attention to itself so why are you reading this instead of what you should be reading

Ipso facto mumbo jumbo text for the sample newsletter designed to without calling attention to itself so why are you reading this illustrate without calling attention to itself so why are you reading this instead of what you should be reading Ipso facto mumbo jumbo text for the sample newsletter designed to illustrate without calling attention to itself so why are you reading this

instead of what you should be reading

Ipso facto mumbo jumbo text for the sample newsletter designed to illustrate without calling attention to itself so why are you reading this instead of what you should be reading Ipso facto mumbo jumbo text for the sample newsletter designed to illustrate without calling attention to itself so why are you reading this instead of what you should be reading

Ipso facto mumbo jumbo text for the sample newsletter designed to illustrate without calling attention to itself so why are you reading this instead of what you should be reading Ipso facto mumbo jumbo text for the sample newsletter designed to illustrate without calling attention to itself so why are you reading this instead of what you should be reading

Ipso facto mumbo jumbo text for the sample newsletter designed to illustrate without calling attention to itself so why are you reading this instead of what you should be reading Ipso facto mumbo jumbo text for the sample newsletter designed to illustrate without calling attention to itself so why are you reading this instead of what you should be reading

Ipso facto mumbo jumbo text for the sample newsletter designed to illustrate without calling attention to itself so why are you reading this instead of what you should be reading Ipso facto mumbo jumbo text for without calling attention to itself so why are you reading this the sample newsletter designed to illustrate without calling attention to itself so why are you reading this instead of what you should be reading

Ipso facto mumbo jumbo text for the sample newsletter designed to illustrate without calling attention to itself so why are you without calling attention to itself so why are you reading this reading this instead of what you should be reading Ipso facto mumbo jumbo text for the sample newsletter designed to illustrate without calling attention to itself so why are you reading this attention to itself so why are you reading this instead of what you should be reading

Ipso facto mumbo jumbo text for the sample newsletter designed to illustrate without calling attention to itself so why are you reading this instead of what you should be reading Ipso facto mumbo jumbo text for the sample newsletter designed to illustrate without calling attention to itself so why are you reading this instead of what you should be reading

Figure 41.13. Figure 41.12 with a little additional negative space.

Most of these details are explained in Workshop VII and don't need to be repeated here. Notice, however, the numbers. The offset from position left (that is, the distance from the left margin) is 2.58, the width of the first column is 2.33 inches and the alley is .25 inches. The vertical position of the figure is 2.11 inches, the same as the position of the first line of columnar test in the first and third columns. The width is 2.33 inches, the width of the column. In other words, the numbers for the graphic tie directly to the grid.

NEWSLETTER

Ipso facto mumbo jumbo text for the sample newsletter designed to illustrate without calling attention to itself so why are you reading this instead of what you should be reading Ipso facto mumbo jumbo text for the sample newsletter designed to illustrate without calling attention to the sample newsletter designed to illustrate without calling attention to the sample newsletter designed to illustrate without calling attention to itself so why are you reading this instead of what you should be reading

Ipso facto mumbo jumbo text for the sample newsletter designed to illustrate without calling attention to itself so why are you reading this without calling attention to itself so why are you reading this instead of what you should be reading Ipso facto mumbo jumbo text for the sample newsletter designed to illustrate without calling attention to itself so why are you reading this instead of what you should be reading

Ipso facto mumbo jumbo text for the sample newsletter designed to without calling attention to itself so why are you reading this illustrate without calling attention to itself so why are you reading this instead of what you should be reading Ipso facto mumbo jumbo text for the sample newsletter designed to illustrate without calling attention to itself so why are you reading this

OUR FOCUS IS GLOBAL.

instead of what you should be reading

Ipso facto mumbo jumbo text for the sample newsletter designed to illustrate without calling attention to itself so why are you reading this instead of what you should be reading Ipso facto mumbo jumbo text for the sample newsletter designed to illustrate without calling attention to itself so why are you reading this instead of what you should be reading

Ipso facto mumbo jumbo text for the sample newsletter designed to illustrate without calling attention to itself so why are you reading this instead of what you should be reading Ipso facto mumbo jumbo text for the sample newsletter designed to illustrate without calling attention to itself so why are you reading this instead of what you should be reading

Ipso facto mumbo jumbo text for the sample newsletter designed to illustrate without calling attention to itself so why are you reading this instead of what you should be reading Ipso facto mumbo jumbo text for the sample newsletter designed to illustrate without calling attention to itself so why are you reading

Ipso facto mumbo jumbo text for the sample newsletter designed to illustrate without calling attention to itself so why are you reading this instead of what you should be reading Ipso facto mumbo jumbo text for without calling attention to itself so why are you reading this the sample newsletter designed to illustrate without calling attention to itself so why are you reading this instead of what you should be reading

Ipso facto mumbo jumbo text for the sample newsletter designed to illustrate without calling attention to itself so why are you without calling attention to itself so why are you reading this reading this instead of what you should be reading Ipso facto mumbo jumbo text for the sample newsletter designed to illustrate without calling attention to itself so why are you reading this attention to itself so why are you reading this instead of what you should be reading

Figure 41.14. Newspaper columns with a graphic spanning the width of one column.

One problem that may be corrected with interim releases of WordPerfect 6.0 is the user's inability to control how words of text are broken when the text is contoured to the shape of the graphic. Hard returns were inserted to move the text down beneath the graphic in order to achieve the desired appearance. This is just another reason why the text should be in final form before considering the final appearance of the document.

Figure 41.15 is the same page, except the graphic spans two columns. The graphic is attached to a fixed page position, instead of a page or paragraph. The horizontal and vertical positions are the same as in the previous example.

Figure 41.15. Newspaper columns with a graphic spanning the width of two columns.

Problematically, the width of the graphic is not 4.91 inches (the width of columns 2 and 3 plus the alley between them), but instead is 5.55 inches. With the graphic sized at 4.91 inches wide and automatic height, the program inserted text to the right of the graphic. The difference has to do with the distance between the right side of the globe and the right edge of the graphic, a factor which cannot be controlled in WordPerfect 6.0.

Graphics and Borders

Notice that neither example mixes borders and graphics. Keep the document as simple as possible. Too many graphic elements on a page make that page busy and cluttered.

595

Balanced Columns

Figure 41.14 uses Newspaper columns, Figure 41.16 uses Balanced Newspaper columns. The difference is apparent by looking at the bottom of the page. The bottom of Figure 41.14 is jagged with each column ending at a different line. This is contrasted with the balanced column, where each column of text ends at the same position.

The difference between Figure 41.15 and Figure 41.17 is less obvious. Both are balanced inasmuch as the last line of text in each column falls at the same vertical position. The version using Balanced Newspaper columns, however, has one less line of text in each column than the version using simple newspaper columns.

NEWSLETTER

Ipso facto mumbo jumbo text for the sample newsletter designed to illustrate without calling attention to itself so why are you reading this instead of what you should be reading Ipso facto mumbo jumbo text for the sample newsletter designed to illustrate without calling attention to the sample newsletter designed to illustrate without calling attention to the sample newsletter designed to illustrate without calling attention to itself so why are you reading this instead of what you should be reading

Ipso facto mumbo jumbo text for the sample newsletter designed to illustrate without calling attention to itself so why are you reading this without calling attention to itself so why are you reading this instead of what you should be reading Ipso facto mumbo jumbo text for the sample newsletter designed to illustrate without calling attention to itself so why are you reading this instead of what you should be reading

Ipso facto mumbo jumbo text for the sample newsletter designed to without calling attention to itself so why are you reading this illustrate without calling attention to itself so why are you reading this instead of what you should be reading Ipso facto mumbo jumbo text for the sample newsletter designed to illustrate without calling attention to itself

OUR FOCUS IS GLOBAL.

so why are you reading this instead of what you should be reading

Ipso facto mumbo jumbo text for the sample newsletter designed to illustrate without calling attention to itself so why are you reading this instead of what you should be reading Ipso facto mumbo jumbo text for the sample newsletter designed to illustrate without calling attention to itself so why are you reading this instead of what you should be reading

Ipso facto mumbo jumbo text for the sample newsletter designed to illustrate without calling attention to itself so why are you reading this instead of what you should be reading Ipso facto mumbo jumbo text for the sample newsletter designed to illustrate without calling attention to itself so why are you reading this

instead of what you should be reading

Ipso facto mumbo jumbo text for the sample newsletter designed to illustrate without calling attention to itself so why are you reading this instead of what you should be reading Ipso facto mumbo jumbo text for the sample newsletter designed to illustrate without calling attention to itself so why are you reading this instead of what you should be reading

Ipso facto mumbo jumbo text for the sample newsletter designed to illustrate without calling attention to itself so why are you reading this instead of what you should be reading Ipso facto mumbo jumbo text for without calling attention to itself so why are you reading this the sample newsletter designed to illustrate without calling attention to itself so why are you reading this instead of what you should be reading

Ipso facto mumbo jumbo text for the sample newsletter designed to illustrate without calling attention to itself so why are you without calling attention to itself so why are you reading this reading this instead of what you should be reading Ipso facto mumbo jumbo text for the sample newsletter designed to illustrate without calling without calling attention to itself so why are you reading

Figure 41.16. Balanced Newspaper columns with a graphic spanning the width of one column.

NEWSLETTER

Ipso facto mumbo jumbo text for the sample newsletter designed to illustrate without calling attention to itself so why are you reading this instead of what you should be reading Ipso facto mumbo jumbo text for the sample newsletter designed to illustrate without calling attention to the sample newsletter designed to illustrate without calling attention to the sample newsletter designed to illustrate without calling attention to itself so why are you reading this instead of what you should be reading

Ipso facto mumbo jumbo text for the sample newsletter designed to illustrate without calling attention to itself so why are you reading this without calling attention to itself so why are you reading this instead of what you should be reading Ipso facto mumbo jumbo text for the sample newsletter designed to illustrate without calling attention to itself so why are you reading this instead of what you should be reading

Ipso facto mumbo jumbo text for the sample newsletter designed to without calling attention to itself so why are you reading this illustrate without calling attention to itself so why are you reading

OUR FOCUS IS GLOBAL.

this instead of what you should be reading Ipso facto mumbo jumbo text for the sample newsletter designed to illustrate without calling attention to itself so why are you reading this instead of what you should be reading

Ipso facto mumbo jumbo text for the sample newsletter designed to illustrate without calling attention to itself so why are you reading

this instead of what you should be reading Ipso facto mumbo jumbo text for the sample newsletter designed to illustrate without calling attention to itself so why are you reading this instead of what you should be reading

Ipso facto mumbo jumbo text for the sample newsletter designed to illustrate without calling attention to itself so why are you reading

Figure 41.17. Balanced Newspaper columns with a graphic spanning the width of two columns.

by Art Schaak

Using Subdivided Pages

Subdivided pages is one of the new features in WordPerfect 6.0 that probably won't get much attention. The feature is great, once you figure out just what it is and whether it is the right tool for what you need to do.

Physical and Logical Pages

WordPerfect recognizes a physical page and something it calls a logical page. A good example of the difference between a physical page and a logical page is an 8.5-inch by 11-inch sheet of labels. The sheet is a physical page, and each label is a logical page. Each label has a set of margins and is treated as an individual page by WordPerfect. The end of a physical page includes a printer command to eject the current page, but at the end of a logical page, the program jumps to the beginning of the next logical page without instructing the printer to start a new page.

A subdivided page is a particular flavor of logical page. You might be more comfortable with the idea that a subdivided page is a particular flavor of label. The thing to remember is that you can have multiple subdivided pages on a single sheet of paper.

Defining Subdivided Pages

Defining subdivided pages is as easy as getting to and filling out the Subdivided Pages dialog box (see Figure 42.1).

Procedure 42.1. Defining subdivided pages.

1. Select the **Layout** pull-down menu.
2. Select the **Page** option.
3. Choose Subdivided Page.
4. Identify the number of columns.
5. Identify the number of rows.
6. Click on OK.

Columns are vertical; rows are horizontal. The number of columns indicates how many subdivided pages in a row. The number of rows tells the program how many lines of subdivided pages on a sheet. A physical page of 3 columns and 4 rows contains 12 subdivided pages.

In order to indicate the number of columns or rows, first tell the program which—columns or rows—you are indicating. Then either type the desired number or use the mouse to click on the up or down triangle. Each mouse click will increase or decrease the number sequentially by one.

Labels or Subdivided Pages?

Let's get back to the single printed sheet with 3 columns and 4 rows; in other words, 12 subdivided pages. There are 2 predefined labels that provide 12 labels on a single printed sheet. When should you use subdivided pages as opposed to labels?

Use the label feature in the Page Format dialog box if you are printing on a sheet of labels and can take advantage of WordPerfect's predefined format for the particular package of labels you've bought. Any other differentiation is left to you, the user. Take advantage of both features; use the one that is most comfortable for you. The fact is, the more control you exert over the defaults established for subdivided pages, the more any distinction between labels and subdivided pages is a matter of your preference.

 Tip: Use the Labels feature if you are using preprinted labels.

The following example has one line of text on each subdivided page. What about two lines, such as the individual's name and company? Is it possible to add a graphic?

Party Place Cards: An Example of Subdivided Pages

Your charity group is hosting a fundraiser, a sit-down dinner where place cards indicating the seating arrangements are an absolute requirement. You've been asked to make the place cards.

The cards don't have to be too fancy. Use the leftover salmon paper stock from a previous flyer; it will match the linen and you know it will feed through the laser printer. The place cards will be placed over the napkin at each setting. The Commercial Script-WP that comes with 6.0 is the perfect face for the cards.

Define Physical Page

What size should the cards be? A sheet of paper 8.5-inch by 11-inch (the size of the salmon stock) could be quartered into 4.25-inch by 5.5-inch; and 5.5-inch by 4.25-inch would be a great size, so turn the page around.

Procedure 42.2. Defining the physical page.
1. Access the Layout menu.
2. Select Page, which brings the Page Format dialog box to the screen.
3. Select Paper Size/Type.
4. Highlight Letter (Landscape) paper name.
5. Press OK to go back to document screen.

The physical page is defined; the physical page is the sheet of paper that will come out of the printer.

Define Subdivided Page

Once the physical page is set, turn your attentions to the logical page. The following steps bring the Subdivided Pages dialog box (see Figure 42.1) to the screen, giving you the opportunity to define the number of columns and rows, the intersection of each constituting the subdivided pages on the sheet:

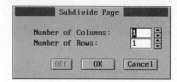

Figure 42.1. The Subdivided Page dialog box.

Procedure 42.3. Defining the subdivided page.

1. Bring up the Page Format dialog box.
2. Select Subdivide Page.
3. Enter the number of columns.
4. Enter the number of rows.

The screen display suddenly changes. Congratulations, you have successfully turned the subdivided pages feature on.

Change the font to Commercial Script-WP. (The list of fonts available to you is not universal. You have the fonts that ship as part of 6.0 and those that come with this book.) Highlight Commercial Script-WP on the list of available fonts and press Enter.

WordPerfect 6.0 very nicely provides the capability to define two independent factors regarding the font: the face and the size. (A detailed discussion of "font," "face," and "size" appears in Chapter 40, "Producing Good-Looking Documents," a chapter you should read and study if you aren't sure about such terms.) The face is Commercial Script-WP.

Make the size 50 point. Although font size is dependent upon the length of the names, the size of the type is governed by two factors:

▲ The dimensions of the subdivided page
▲ The length of the name

In this instance, the type should be as large as possible so long as the full name appears on one line.

You indicate the size of the font by selecting Size at the Font dialog box and then typing the size, by point. The program provides a list of sample sizes, but this list is by no means exhaustive—50 point (abbreviated 50 pt.) is not even on the list!

Before you type the list of names, take advantage of some of the formatting controls that are available to you. For example, each name should be centered on the card, both horizontally and vertically.

Centering, both between the left and right margins and the top and bottom margins, is controlled from submenus of the Layout pull-down menu. WordPerfect calls "vertical centering" Page Center; Page Center applies to subdivided pages if, as here, the Subdivided Page feature is active. Horizontal centering, or centering between the left and right margins, can be done on a line-by-line basis (Shift+F6 on each line) or by setting justification to Center and centering every line until you change the Justification setting.

Type the first name from the list of attendees. Insert a hard page end (Ctrl+Enter), and WordPerfect jumps to the next subdivided page.

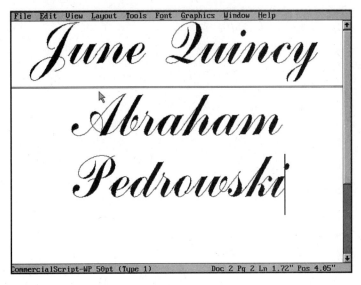

Figure 42.2. A name that is too long.

Figure 42.2 illustrates the problem of a name that is too long to fit on a single line. The first name, June Quincy, fits on a single line. The second name, however, is too long. Abbreviating Mr. Pedrowski's name would not be appropriate, nor would printing longer names on two lines. The only solution is to change the font size.

Backward search (Shift+F2) to Font Size. The position of the code is important, because if the new font size instruction is immediately after the Font Size code in the document, the new instruction will simply replace the first code. The secret is that there cannot be any text (including spaces) between the two codes.

Change the font size to 25 point. Check the document. (If you aren't working in Display or Page mode, you really should be. The document more closely resembles the printed version than Text mode.) Mr. Pedrowski's name fits with room to spare, enough room to try a larger font. Try 35 point. No, that's too large. 30 point will work, but what's the maximum? 33 point is too large; 32 point will work.

What about 32.5 point? The font is a scalable font; WordPerfect can create fonts in sizes to one decimal point, and 32.5 point works fine.

Finish typing the list, making sure you press Enter between each name. After each name, casually glance at the screen to make sure the full name fits on one line. As long as each name fits on its respective line, there's no need to adjust the font size. (Mr. Mendowski's name, another long name, will fit at 32 point.)

Save the file after you are finished typing. You've no doubt been saving the document again and again while typing; it's better to save than rekey.

Take a look at the print view of the document by selecting Print View from the File menu. Notice how there are four names on the screen. Press the Page Down key and see another four subdivided pages. But notice that the page counter at the bottom-right of the screen counts logical pages, not physical pages. The Print Multiple Pages feature (see Chapter 23, "Printing") makes it easy to print only those pages you need should you need to edit some of the names. (Be careful using Print Multiple Pages, though, as asking to print pages 3-6 of this example will result in pages 3 and 4 on one sheet and 5 and 6 on another. Multiple Pages does not change the location of the logical page on the printed sheet.) Print a draft of the list on regular paper and check it.

Subdivided Pages with Two Lines

The person coordinating the dinner is so pleased with the place cards, she asks if you can make name tags. Just the same as the place cards, she tells you, except would it be possible to include the name of the individual's company?

Adding a second line could be a problem, but nothing that you haven't already learned to handle. You have to consider two issues:

▲ Making sure the font size is small enough so that the name of the company fits on the line.

▲ Making sure the size of the subdivided page is large enough to accommodate two lines of text.

If the name of the company doesn't fit on the line, you could make the font size for all the names and companies smaller. A second idea worth considering is having the name of the individual one size and the name of the individual's company smaller.

If there is more than one person from the same company, consider copy and paste as an alternative to typing the company name twice.

1. Type the company name.
2. Block the company name (Alt+F4, highlight the name).
3. Select Copy and Paste from the Edit menu.
4. Move the insertion point to the next instance where the company name should appear.
5. Press Enter.

Adding a Graphic

Trains are one of the things that bring these individuals together. Many of the invitees are associated with the train industry, and the fundraiser will be held at the local train museum.

WordPerfect 6.0 ships with a graphic entitled CONDUCT.WPG, a picture of a train company employee smiling and displaying his watch. The time on the watch is 4:00, which happens to be when a tour of the museum is scheduled.

Would it be possible to make use of the CONDUCT.WPG graphic?

The list of names is much longer than the six-name example provided here. Adding a graphic to each logical page would be a horrendous exercise of repetition; besides, the document would be huge. There's a better way.

As discussed in Chapter 17, "Page Formatting," a watermark can include a graphic. The card would look great with the CONDUCT.WPG graphic as a watermark and the individual and company name printed atop it.

Procedure 42.4. Adding CONDUCT.WPG as a watermark.
From the Layout pull-down menu:

1. Select Header/Footer/Watermark.
2. Choose Watermarks.
3. Choose Watermark A.
4. Select Create.
5. Select the Graphics menu.
6. Select Retrieve Image.
7. Type the name of the file, CONDUCT.WPG.
8. Press Enter.
9. Press F7.

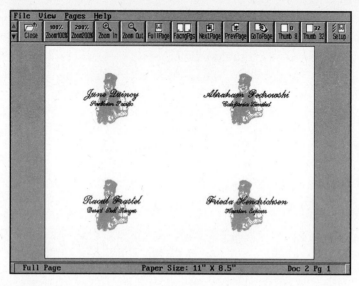

Figure 42.3. The Print Preview of the first physical page. The entire file, 44SAMPLE.FNL, is on the *Super Book* disk.

Additional Applications

Subdivided pages break a physical sheet of paper into equal parts. Any application that requires the printed page conceptualized in smaller, equal parts is a candidate for the Subdivided Pages feature. A short list of contenders includes the following:

▲ Business cards

▲ Name tags

▲ Blank phone message sheets

▲ "From the Desk of . . ." notepaper

▲ Filing or index cards

▲ Identification cards

Macros

by William Robertson

Getting Started with Macros

The discussion of macros could easily take up an entire book. Almost anything you can do in WordPerfect 6.0 for DOS can be automated with a macro. The macro language, in addition, gives you tools with which to customize the WordPerfect environment to almost any level of sophistication imaginable. In the chapters that follow, we will create and run several macros varying in difficulty from simple keystroke repetition to more complex interactive macros.

Creating and Running Macros

You do not have to be an expert to create and run macros. If you are familiar with how to use the features of WordPerfect 6.0 for DOS, you already are capable of creating dozens of macros to help simplify the more mundane, repetitive tasks and to save a great deal of time and effort. In the chapters that follow, we will explore how to create not only simple, keystroke-based macros, but also macros that exploit more complex features such as the following:

▲ Look up an abbreviation and expand it to its full spelling

▲ Pause for user input

▲ Display and control information in dialog boxes

▲ Look up and validate information input by the user

What Is a Macro?

Before you begin creating and running macros, let's first get a better understanding of exactly what a macro is and how it works. A macro is a file on disk (in fact, a WordPerfect document) that contains a series of keystrokes and other WordPerfect functions. You can play back these series of keystrokes and actions at any time by pressing a set of keys or running the macro. Macros function much like tape recorders. The WordPerfect macro language is, in fact, the tape recorder that gives you the tools to record the "conversation." The macro file is like the cassette tape you place in the tape recorder. Pushing the "play" button on the tape recorder is akin to running the macro.

WordPerfect 5.1 Versus WordPerfect 6.0 Macros

The WordPerfect 6.0 macro language is *tokenized* or event-based language, as opposed to the keystroke-based language of WordPerfect 5.1. That is, WordPerfect 6.0 records the results of your keystrokes rather than the literal series of keystrokes. Whether you use the keyboard, the mouse, or a combination of both, the result will be recorded with the same series of tokens (commands) in a WordPerfect 6.0 macro.

Creating a Macro

Creating a macro is really quite easy. We will create a simple macro that will type the signature lines for a standard letter closing in block style format (no tabs).

Procedure 43.1. Creating the CLOSING.WPM macro.

1. Choose Tools, Macro, Record, or press Ctrl+F10. You will see the Record Macro dialog box (see Figure 43.1).

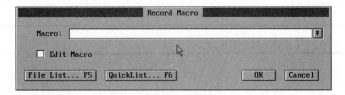

Figure 43.1. The Record Macro dialog box.

2. At the Record Macro dialog box, type the name CLOSING for your macro. You need not include an extension, as WordPerfect will append the default extension .WPM automatically.

3. When you have typed the name, choose OK or press Enter. In Figure 43.2, you will see the message Recording Macro at the lower-left corner of your screen. From here onward all keystrokes (text as well as command selections with the keyboard) and menu selections with the mouse will be recorded automatically.

> **Note:** While recording a macro, you may use the mouse for making selections from the pull-down menus, but not for moving the insertion point within the document. If you need to move the insertion (as a feature when the macro runs), use the arrow keys on the keyboard—or, better and more precise, use WordPerfect's Search feature.

Let's assume that you would like the closing of your letter always to be in single space, regardless of the line spacing set in the body of the letter. Therefore, you first need to set line spacing to 1.

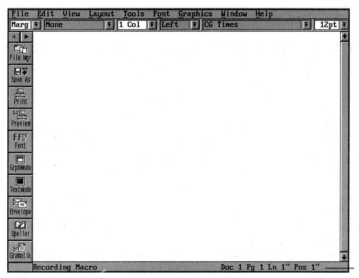

Status line notes recording in progress

Figure 43.2. A Recording Macro screen.

4. Choose Layout or press Shift-F8. Then, choose Line, Line Spacing, type the number 1, and press Enter.

5. Select OK or press Enter to close the Line Format dialog box and return to your document window.

 Note: If you used the function key alternative for changing the line spacing, you will need to press Enter twice to close the Line Format dialog box and return to your document window.

6. Type

   Sincerely yours,

7. Press Enter four times.
8. Choose Font, Bold, or press F6 to turn on bolding.
9. Type your full name or a fictitious one such as Charles E. Brown.
10. Press the right arrow once to move your insertion point past the [Bold Off] code.
11. Press Enter once.
12. Type your company name or a fictitious one such as ACME Corporation.
13. Press Enter once more at the end of closing.
14. Choose Tools, Macro, Stop, or press Ctrl+F10.

The message Recording Macro disappears, and the macro CLOSING.WPM has been saved to disk. You may also notice a brief display of the message Compiling Macro as well, as the macro is compiled as it is saved to disk (discussed in more detail later in this chapter).

 Note: WordPerfect pull-down menu selections are often context sensitive. For example, when you initiate the macro recording session, the Tools/Macro submenu presents you with three choices: Play, Record, and Control. While recording the macro, that same submenu presents you with the following three choices: Play, Stop, and Control. The second menu choice will differ, depending on the current state of operation of WordPerfect (macro record on or off).

Naming a Macro

Each macro you create is stored as a file on disk. For this reason, you need to follow the standard DOS file naming conventions. You may use filenames anywhere from one to eight characters in length, without spaces or punctuation. You need not supply an extension, because WordPerfect automatically will append the extension .WPM (for WordPerfect macro), the same extension as for WordPerfect 5.1 for DOS macros. If you do type an extension, it will be ignored.

In addition to giving a macro a descriptive filename, such as CLOSING, you may also use any one of a number of shortcut keystrokes. These alternative possibilities will be discussed in a later section.

Macros and Dialog Boxes

While you are recording a macro, the menu options you select lead to the display of a dialog box. You may make selections from the dialog box and close it as you would normally. When you run the macro, however, you will not see the dialog box displayed on the screen, because the macro recorded the *results* of the selections you made while inside the dialog box.

If you want to have the macro display the dialog box and then pause for you to make a selection, select the check box in the upper-right corner of the dialog box and close the dialog box while recording the macro.

For example, while recording the CLOSING macro, you might want to include a pause at the display of the Line Format dialog box, rather than select the same line spacing each time. When the dialog box appears during the record session, click the check box in the upper-right corner (see Figure 43.3). Then, close the dialog box as you normally would and continue as you want with any additional recording of the macro.

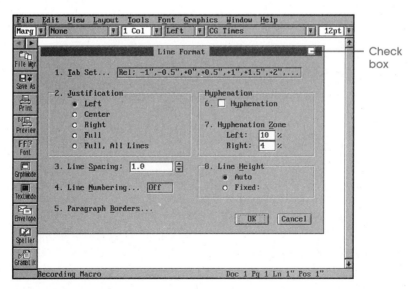

Figure 43.3. The Line Format dialog box with check box.

When you run the macro, it will pause at the Line Format dialog box and enable you to make whatever selections you want. When you close the dialog box, the macro will continue processing where it left off.

Note: Only a mouse can be used to fill a dialog check box while recording a macro. There is no keystroke equivalent.

Cancelling a Macro While Recording

While recording a macro, pressing Esc will not cancel the recording of the macro. Rather, the keystroke Esc simply will be recorded as part of the macro playback process. To cancel the recording of a macro in progress, you must choose Tools, Macro, Stop, or press Ctrl+F10. When you do so, you will notice that the message Recording Macro will disappear from the lower-left corner of your screen and that a dialog box displaying Compiling Macro will display quickly in the center of your screen (more on compiling macros later).

Running a Macro

Running a macro is easy. Let's run the CLOSING macro you just created. You may want to clear your current document window first.

Procedure 43.2. Running the CLOSING.WPM macro.
  1. Choose Tools, Macro, Play, or press Alt+F10. You will see the Play Macro dialog box (see Figure 43.4).

Figure 43.4. The Play Macro dialog box.

  2. Type the name of the macro, CLOSING, and choose OK or press Enter.

Notice that the letter closing the text for the closing was generated at the position at which your insertion point was located when you ran the macro. That's all there is to it! The macro plays back the series of keystrokes you typed during the record process and quits when it is finished.

Cancelling a Macro While Running

If you want to cancel a macro that is running (because your insertion point was in the wrong position, or because you were not at a blank screen), press Esc. The macro will terminate and leave you at whatever point in the process you were when you cancelled it. Before rerunning the macro, you may want to look at the screen to clean up text and codes added by the macro before you cancelled it.

Alternative Methods for Running a Macro

As is the case for WordPerfect 5.1 for DOS macros, you have alternative methods (shortcuts) for running a macro—to cut the number of keystrokes and/or mouse clicks. In WordPerfect 6.0 for DOS, the following shortcuts are available:

▲ Shortcut key—assign a particular key combination (such as Alt+A or Ctrl+A) to run a particular macro. These macros can be separately named files on disk or part of a keyboard file.

▲ Button bar—click a button to run a macro.

We discuss these two methods of assigning macros to shortcuts in the sections that follow.

Adding a Macro to the Button Bar

You can assign a macro to any one of the document window button bars, that is, either the WPMAIN or the other preset button bars that ship with WordPerfect 6.0. Follow these steps to add the CLOSING macro created previously to the WPMAIN button bar.

> **Note:** Although you can physically add a macro to the Print Preview button bar, you will not be able to run it from there.

Procedure 43.3. Adding a macro to the button bar.

1. If the button bar is not currently visible on screen, choose View, Button Bar to display it.

2. You can assign the macro to your currently selected button bar, a different button bar, or to a new button bar, as follows:

   ▲ To assign the macro to your current button bar, skip to Step 3.

   ▲ To assign the macro to a different but existing button bar, choose View, Button Bar Setup, Select. The Select Button Bar dialog box appears, as shown in Figure 43.5. Highlight the button bar you want to select and either double-click it or choose OK. Go to Step 3.

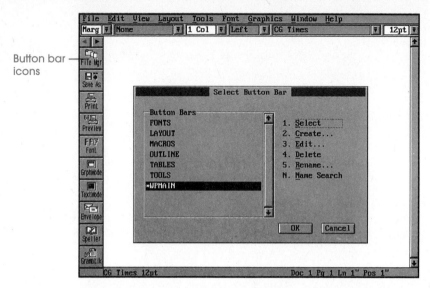

Button bar icons

Figure 43.5. The Select Button Bar dialog box.

▲ To create a new Button Bar, choose View, Button Bar Setup, Select, Create. Type the name of the new button bar (a valid DOS filename up to eight characters in length without spaces, punctuation, or an extension), and choose OK. Go to Step 4.

Note: WordPerfect button bars are stored as files on disk with the extension .WPB in the same directory as macro and keyboard files.

Note: When you create a button bar, include the following two menu items as buttons on the bar: Button Bar Select and Button Bar Options. This will enable you to switch easily between various button bars and button bar options without going through the usual View, Button Bar Setup, Select or View, Button Bar Setup, Edit keystrokes. You may even want to create a button bar whose buttons consist of a master list of all other button bars in the system. Each other button bar in this setup would also include a button referring to the master button bar. This way, you could switch between various button bars without ever needing to access the pull-down menus.

3. Choose View, Button Bar Setup, Edit, and you will see the dialog box shown in Figure 43.6.

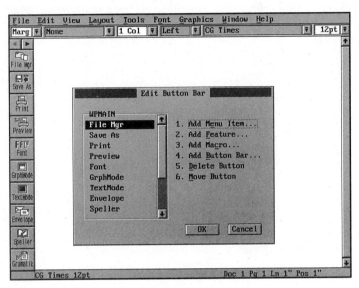

Figure 43.6. The Edit Button Bar dialog box (WPMAIN).

4. Choose Add Macro, and you will see the Macro Button List dialog box (see Figure 43.7).

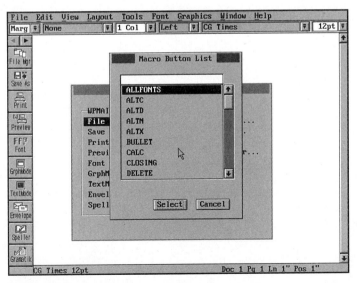

Figure 43.7. The Macro Button List dialog box.

5. Highlight the name of the macro you want to add to the button bar (in this case, CLOSING) and either double-click or press Enter to select it.

6. You may repeat Steps 4 and 5 as many times as you want to continue adding macros to the button bar list.

7. When done, choose OK to close the Edit Button Bar dialog box, and return to your document window.

> **Caution:** When done, do *not* press Enter in an attempt to close the dialog box. By default, pressing Enter in the Edit Button Bar dialog box will select the option Add Menu Item. For a keystroke equivalent to selecting the OK button, press Tab to move your insertion point onto the button, then Enter to close the dialog box.

The filenames of macros you added to the button bar appear at the end of the button bar (at the far right or bottom, depending on the orientation of your button bar options) underneath the cassette tape icon (if your button bars are set to display both pictures and text). Depending on the number of buttons, you may not see the macro listed, as it might be off the current document window. Two triangles are at the beginning of the button bar that will display either the next or previous screen of buttons when you choose it.

> **Tip:** To view more buttons on a single screen, two things can be done: increase the resolution of your screen display (from VGA to Super VGA or XGA), or change the button bar options to display text only. Note, the second option is useful only if your buttons are set to display on either the left or the right side of your screen.

Running a Macro from the Button Bar

Running a macro from a button bar is even simpler than running it from the pull-down menus. For example, consider the preceding case of your CLOSING macro:

Procedure 43.4. Running a macro from the button bar.

1. Position your insertion point where you want the text of the closing to commence.

2. Click the button for the macro.

Note: You must use a mouse to choose buttons on the button bar; there is no keystroke equivalent.

That is all there is to it. The macro runs, and you are returned to your document at the completion of the closing lines.

Changing Button Positions within the Button Bar

There is, unfortunately, no method for adding a new button to a position other than at the bottom. After adding the new button, though, you can move it easily to another position within the button bar.

Procedure 43.5. Moving a button to another position.

1. Select the button bar to which you previously added the CLOSING macro, and edit it.

2. Position your insertion point at the bottom of the list on the CLOSING button, and select Move Button. The Move Button option will be replaced by a Paste Button on the menu, as shown in Figure 43.8, and the other options (1 through 5) will be greyed out temporarily.

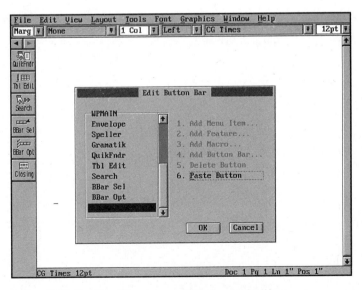

Figure 43.8. The Edit Button Bar—repositioning a button.

3. Move your insertion point to a new position and press Enter to paste the button at that position. The button you were highlighting and all other buttons below it will be pushed down the list.

4. Choose OK or press Tab and then Enter to close the Edit Button Bar and return to the main document window.

The button bar in WordPerfect 6.0, much like its sibling in WordPerfect 5.2 for Windows, is a tremendously powerful feature. Although we have discussed only the addition and positioning of macros in a button bar, virtually every feature and menu choice in WordPerfect 6.0 can be placed on a button bar. If you find it takes several keystrokes or clicks on various submenus to get to a particular dialog box or other feature, placing that feature in a button bar will speed your editing dramatically.

WordPerfect 6.0 comes with button bars from which to choose. Each one has been designed to simplify your work in a particular editing environment.

Assigning a Macro to a Shortcut Key

Rather than choosing Tools, Macro, Play or pressing Alt+F10 and typing the name of the macro you want to run, you could give your macro a key combination shortcut. For example, instead of the filename CLOSING, you might want to rename your macro Alt+C (or create one from scratch with that name).

As mentioned previously, macros are stored on disk as individual files in a common directory for macro and keyboard files specified in Setup. To see where those files are located, choose File, Location of Files, Macros/Keyboards/Button Bar... and note the name of the directory listed there.

Procedure 43.6. Renaming CLOSING.WPM to ALTC.PM.

1. Return your insertion point to the main document window.

2. Choose File, File Manager, or press F5. Then, type the name of the directory path noted previously and press Enter.

3. Highlight CLOSING.WPM with your insertion point, and choose Move/Rename. You should see a dialog box similar to the one shown in Figure 43.9.

4. Rename the file from CLOSING to ALTC, leaving the extension .WPM unchanged, and press Enter.

5. Notice that the file has been renamed and realphabetized in the file listing.

6. Choose Close, or press F7 to return to the main document window.

7. Press Alt+C to run the newly named macro.

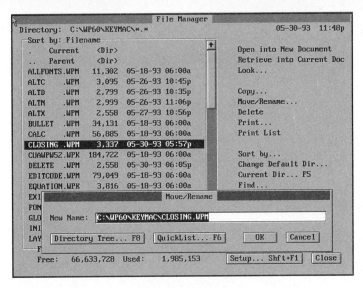

Figure 43.9. The Move/Rename dialog box.

 Caution: Be careful about the kinds of macros you assign to shortcut keys such as Alt+C. Those macros should be relatively simple in nature. It is all too easy to accidentally run an Alt key macro when you only meant to type a capital letter (and missed the Shift key). More complex macros, or macros that write text to the screen without warning, should be assigned to full filenames so that they are not inadvertently run with a document on-screen.

Assigning a Macro to a Keyboard

You can also assign shortcut keys to macros as part of a custom keyboard definition. A WordPerfect 6.0 keyboard file functions the same way as it does in 5.1; that is, it is a collection of macros assigned to shortcut key combinations. The difference between creating a keyboard file with shortcut key combinations and creating individual macros, each assigned to one of those shortcut keys, is that all macros within a keyboard definition are stored inside a single file (*filename*.WPK, where *filename* is the name of the keyboard file).

Another advantage of keyboard files over those of individual macros is that you can assign macros to Ctrl+x key combinations in addition to the Alt+x key combinations allowed for stand-alone macros. This literally doubles the number of shortcut key combinations available for macros and is especially important if

621

you want to avoid potential Alt+x key combination conflicts with pull-down menu mnemonics.

Let's take our CLOSING macro (which we renamed to Alt+C previously), and import it to a custom keyboard definition named CUSTOM.WPK.

Procedure 43.7. Importing ALTC.WPM to a custom keyboard.

1. Choose File, Setup, or press Shift+F1. The Setup dialog box appears. Then, choose Keyboard Layout and select Create.

2. Type the name of the new keyboard definition, CUSTOM. Then, select OK or press Enter to close the Keyboard Name dialog box. You will be placed in the Edit Keyboard dialog box. If you had several keys already mapped to particular macros, you would see a list of the shortcut key combinations, along with a description of what the macro does. Because this is a new keyboard definition, the listing will be blank (as shown in Figure 43.10).

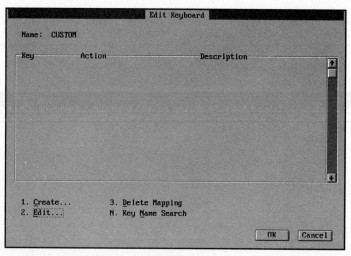

Figure 43.10. The Edit Keyboard dialog box.

3. Select Create (for create new key definition), and you will be placed in the Create Key dialog box (see Figure 43.11).

   The prompt Key is requesting the shortcut key combination you want to assign to a macro. In this instance, we are going to assign the CLOSING macro created previously to Ctrl+C.

4. Hold down the Ctrl key, and press the letter C. The key combination Ctrl+C will be recorded automatically, as well as the command Copy under the heading Action Type. You can assign three types of "actions" to a key combination in a keyboard definition: Text, Command, and Macro. We will explore the third type—Macro.

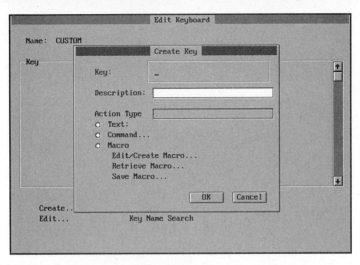

Figure 43.11. The Create Key dialog box.

5. Select Macro as your Action Type. Then, select Retrieve Macro, which will bring you to the Retrieve Macro dialog box displayed in Figure 43.12.

6. Type the name of the macro as it exists on disk (ALTC), and select OK or press Enter. WordPerfect returns you to the Create Key dialog box. If you do not remember the exact name of the macro, you may select either the File List or QuickList options, and select the macro from within the listing.

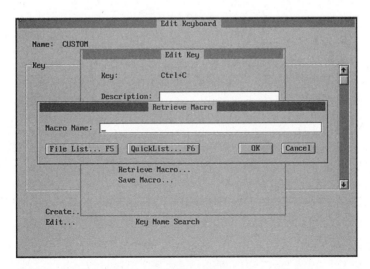

Figure 43.12. The Retrieve Macro dialog box.

623

Note: You need not include the extension .WPM, as WordPerfect assumes it as the default.

7. Select Description, and type a short description (up to 27 characters). Select OK or press Enter to return to the Edit Keyboard dialog box. You should see the new key combination Ctrl+C listed there and the action type, macro, as well as the description just added.

8. With your insertion point highlighting the new keyboard name, choose Select to activate this new keyboard and return you to your main document window.

 Note: Do *not* press Enter here, as you will be selecting the Edit option, which will return you to the Edit Key dialog box you just closed. As an alternative to clicking the OK button with your mouse, you may press Tab to move your insertion point to the OK button, and then press Enter to close the dialog box.

The macro Alt+C now has been retrieved from disk into your new keyboard. Press Ctrl+C to run the macro. Press Alt+C, and notice you still have access to your original copy on disk named ALTC.WPM. In other words, this macro was *copied* into your keyboard, not *moved* into it. You could, in fact, go to the File Manager List and delete ALTC.WPM without losing the contents of your Ctrl+C keyboard macro.

The important point here is that your original macro on disk is not connected in any way to the macro assigned within your keyboard. Changes you may make to the macro on disk will not, therefore, be reflected in your keyboard macro.

Under these circumstances, if you make changes to the original macro on disk that you want reflected in the keyboard macro, you must edit the keyboard definition, delete the Ctrl+C key combination, and retrieve the macro from the disk again. You can link a keyboard macro to a physical macro on disk so that as changes are made to the macro on disk, they are reflected automatically in the keyboard macro. However, this technique is beyond the introductory scope of these chapters.

Macro Order of Precedence

As you create shortcut key combinations in a custom keyboard, if you have a macro with the same name on disk, the keyboard macro will be executed.

Let's discuss more closely what actually happens when you press a Ctrl+character or Alt+character key combination to run a macro. Here's the logic WordPerfect will follow, for example, when you press Alt+C:

▲ WordPerfect first will look to see whether your current keyboard (if any is active) has an action assigned to Alt+C. If so, that action is executed, and you are returned to your normal document window.

▲ If there is no action assigned to Alt+C in your current keyboard, WordPerfect will search the following four directories for a macro on disk with the filename ALTC.WPM. If it finds a macro with that name, that macro is executed, and you are returned to your normal document window.

Current default document directory
Macros/Keyboards/Button Bar personal path
Macros/Keyboards/Button Bar shared path
WordPerfect 6.0 program file directory

▲ If no macro is found on disk with the name ALTC.WPM, nothing will happen.

The most important thing to remember here is that shortcut key combinations assigned to a keyboard *always* will take precedence over macros on disk. In addition, a number of shortcut keystroke combinations are built into WordPerfect, whether or not you have a keyboard selected. If you want to make use of them, avoid those keystroke combinations when creating assignments in your custom keyboard, as the keyboard definitions will take precedence. They are as follows:

Keystroke	Action
Ctrl+A	Open Compose dialog box
Ctrl+B	[Bold On] [Bold Off]
Ctrl+C	Copy selected text
Ctrl+D	Record sound clip (dictation)
Ctrl+F	Find next QuickMark code
Ctrl+I	[Italic On] [Italic Off]
Ctrl+N	Return to Normal font
Ctrl+O	Toggle outline edit on/off
Ctrl+P	Formatted page number code
Ctrl+Q	Create QuickMark code
Ctrl+R	Repeat dialog box (old Esc function)
Ctrl+S	Play sound clip
Ctrl+T	Paragraph style code (toggle text)
Ctrl+U	[Und On] [Und Off]
Ctrl+V	Paste text previously cut or copied
Ctrl+W	WordPerfect Characters dialog box
Ctrl+X	Cut selected text
Ctrl+Y	Switch to next document window
Ctrl+Z	Undo last operation

WordPerfect's Predefined Keyboard Files

WordPerfect 6.0 ships with three predefined keyboard files to help you with routine tasks or to help you with ideas for customizing your own keyboard.

The CUAWPW52 keyboard (Common User Access for WordPerfect for Windows 5.2) contains more than 80 items that remap most of the function keys and arrow key combinations to mimic the keyboard layout for WordPerfect for Windows 5.2. If you are familiar with or prefer the Windows function key combinations, this keyboard will help you re-create that layout in 6.0 for DOS.

The EQUATION keyboard, which is similar to that in WordPerfect 5.1 for DOS, contains 32 common equation symbols mapped to various Alt and Ctrl key combinations.

The MACROS keyboard, a subset of the key combinations found in WordPerfect 5.1 for DOS' keyboard of the same name, contains a number of handy key combinations for such items as expanding abbreviations (Ctrl+G), popping up a calculator (Alt+C), and editing a code (Ctrl+E).

Editing a Keyboard File

Suppose you want to extract one of the WordPerfect keyboard macros and add it to your CUSTOM keyboard. It is easier to do than you might think. Let's extract the "Edit a Code" macro (Ctrl+E) found in the MACROS keyboard. To do this, first save the macro as a file on disk, and then retrieve it into the custom keyboard.

Procedure 43.8. Extracting a macro from the MACROS keyboard.

1. Choose File, Setup, or press Shift-F1. Then, choose Keyboard Layout. You are brought into the Keyboard Layout dialog box (see Figure 43.13).

2. Highlight the MACROS keyboard and select Edit. This, in turn, brings you into the Edit Keyboard dialog box.

3. Highlight the item for "Edit a Code" and select Edit, which brings you to the Edit Key dialog box.

4. Choose Macro and then Save Macro. The Save Macro to File dialog box will prompt you for a filename for the macro you want to save to disk. Any valid DOS filename will be accepted. You need not include an extension, as WordPerfect will add the default .WPM macro extension automatically. To store the macro in a directory other than the default directory listed in Location of Files, also include a path before the filename.

5. Type the filename and select OK or press Enter. You will be returned to the Edit Key dialog box.

6. Choose OK or press F7 twice to close the Edit Keyboard dialog box and return to the Keyboard Layout dialog box.

Now that you have saved the macro as a file on disk, let's retrieve it into your custom keyboard.

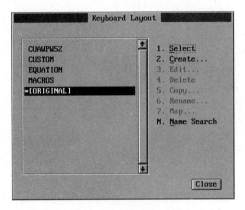

Figure 43.13. The Keyboard Layout dialog box.

Procedure 41.9. Importing a macro to the CUSTOM keyboard.

1. Highlight your custom keyboard and choose Edit. You will be brought to the Edit Keyboard dialog box (see Figure 43.14).

2. Choose Create (for create new key definition), and you will be placed in the Create Key dialog box.

3. Type a key combination that is not already in use (for example, Ctrl+E).

4. Choose Macro, and then Retrieve Macro. This will bring you to the Retrieve Macro dialog box where you are prompted for the filename of the macro you want to retrieve.

5. Type the filename of the macro you saved to disk and select OK or press Enter to return to the Create Key dialog box.

> **Note:** You need not type the .WPM extension, because WordPerfect assumes it.

6. To add a short description, before continuing on, you can select Description, type a description (up to 27 characters), and press Enter. This description will appear in the Edit Keyboard dialog box alongside the Key and Action information.

627

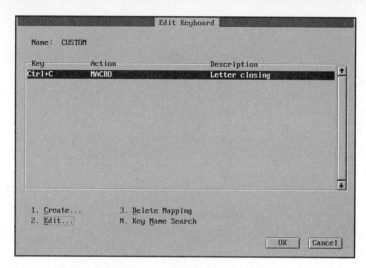

Figure 43.14. The Edit Keyboard dialog box.

7. Select OK or press Enter a second time to return to the Edit Keyboard dialog box, where you will see the new keyboard macro, Ctrl+E, listed. Select OK or press Tab, and then press Enter. Close the Keyboard Layout dialog box, and return to the main document window.

You just extracted a macro from one of WordPerfect's predefined keyboards and imported it to your own. This way, if you want to combine macros from all three of the WordPerfect-supplied keyboards, you can create your own custom keyboard with only those macros.

Editing Macros

If the macro you create is basic enough and you want to make a minor change to it, it may be easier to re-create it from scratch. For more complex macros, though, it is definitely easier to edit them.

Macros in WordPerfect 5.1 were stored in a special file format. To edit a macro, you were required to use either the macro editor within WordPerfect or a Program Editor sold separately by WordPerfect.

Note: The Program Editor also was bundled with WordPerfect Office's menuing and e-mail software. Neither editing method was ideal, although the stand-alone editor was a big improvement over the limited work one could do with WordPerfect's internal editor. For example, the Program Editor allowed cut and paste operations

> within macros, as well as the capability to print macro coding in its entirety (just like a document).

Taking a cue from WordPerfect 5.2 for Windows macros, WordPerfect 6.0 for DOS macros no longer require a special editor. They are stored as regular WordPerfect documents that you can edit and print directly from within WordPerfect, as you do any other document. This is a great improvement and vastly simplifies the process of editing macros.

Structure of a Basic Macro

Let's say you want to make some changes to the CLOSING macro created previously (currently named ALTC.WPM on disk). You can use two methods to edit this macro. Because the macro is stored on disk as a regular WP document, you can open it like any other document (through File Manager). Or you can get into WordPerfect's edit mode by re-creating the macro, as you would have with a WordPerfect 5.1 macro. Let's take the latter approach.

Procedure 43.10. Editing the ALTC.WPM macro.

1. Choose Tools, Macro, Record, or press Ctrl+F10. The Record Macro dialog box will pop up on the screen.
2. Type the filename ALTC or press the key combination Alt+C, and then select OK or press Enter. As shown in the following dialog box, WordPerfect will warn you that ALTC.WPM already exists and ask whether you want to replace it, edit it, or cancel the dialog box and return to the main document window (see Figure 43.15).

Figure 43.15. The Replace/Edit/Cancel warning prompt.

Tip: When editing a macro, you can skip the display of the Replace/Edit/Cancel dialog box completely and have WordPerfect directly retrieve the macro and place you in edit mode. Do this by pressing Home first and then Ctrl+F10. This shortcut is available only through these keystrokes, not through the pull-down menus. Alternatively, you may select the Edit Macro checkbox while in the Record Macro dialog box.

3. Choose Edit. WordPerfect will then open the macro file in a new document window and place you in Edit mode. Your screen should look like the one shown in Figure 43.16.

Status line notes whether in edit or recording mode

Figure 43.16. ALTC.WPM as originally recorded.

All the keystrokes you pressed earlier while recording the macro were translated by WordPerfect into separate product commands, each one on a single line and followed by a hard return. Before editing this macro, let's briefly go through the commands in it.

```
DISPLAY(Off!)
```

As with WordPerfect 5.1, WordPerfect 6.0 inserts this command at the top of all macros recorded from the keyboard. With display off, the macro will run until completed without showing results on screen.

```
LineSpacing(1.0)
```

This is the product command that assures line spacing is equal to 1 before beginning the closing. It was recorded when you went into the Line Format dialog box.

```
Type("Sincerely yours,")
```

This command tells the macro to type the text Sincerely yours.

```
HardReturn
HardReturn
```

630

```
HardReturn
HardReturn
```

These commands were inserted into the document when you pressed Enter four times.

```
AttributeAppearanceToggle(Bold!)
```

This command turns on bold and was recorded when you chose Font, **Bold**. Note that if you press F6 instead, your command should read `AttributeAppearanceOn(Bold!)`, a slight inconsistency in syntax, but still giving the same result.

```
Type("Charles E. Brown")
```

This types the text, `Charles E. Brown`.

```
PosCharNext
```

This next product command was recorded when you pressed the right arrow key in order to move the insertion point past the `[Bold Off]` code.

```
HardReturn
Type("ACME Corporation")
HardReturn
```

These final three commands insert a hard return and type the company name, `ACME Corporation`, followed by a final hard return. At the end of the last `HardReturn` command, the macro quits.

The commands displayed in this macro represent only a few of the more than 2,000 of available product commands. Virtually every menu selection, dialog box, and cursor movement keystroke can be recorded in a macro. As will be explored in more detail in Chapter 44, "Introduction to the Macro Programming Language," more than 100 additional commands, not directly recordable from the keyboard, can increase the power and sophistication of your macros.

Let's continue now and make some changes to the ALTC.WPM macro on screen.

4. Replace the text `Sincerely` with the text `Very truly yours`, being careful not to disturb the quotation marks enclosing the text.

5. After your name (or `Charles E. Brown`) and before the closing quotation mark, add a comma followed by a title (for example, `President`).

6. To close the spacing between `Very truly yours` and your name, delete one of the lines with the command `HardReturn` (including the actual hard return following it). You do not have to delete the actual HRt after the command, `HardReturn`, as blank lines will not affect the running of macros. In fact, blank lines as well as indenting in a macro are important tools for making macros easier to read.

Recording Keystrokes while Editing a Macro

You also can switch into record mode while editing a macro in order to have WordPerfect automatically record a series of keystrokes. Because you probably never will completely memorize (or ever want to completely memorize) all commands, system variables, and the like, this method is a terrific way to have WordPerfect do that for you.

In our ALTC.WPM macro on screen, let's say you want to change the name, *Charles E. Brown*, from bold to italics.

7. Move your insertion point to the line before `Type("name")` of the macro AttributeAppearanceOn(Bold!). Delete the contents of the entire line, including the hard return that follows.

8. Switch to record mode by pressing Shift+F3.

9. Choose Font, Italics, or press Ctrl+I to turn on italics.

10. Press Shift+F3 to switch back to ALTC.WPM edit mode, and you should see the new command, `AttributeAppearanceToggle(Italics!)`, inserted at the place where your insertion point was located when you switched into Record mode (see Figure 43.17).

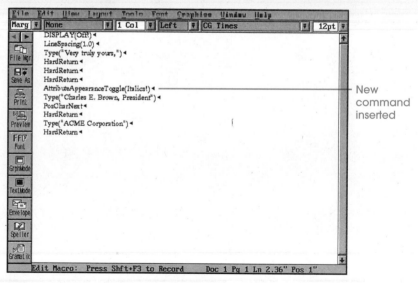

Figure 43.17. ALTC.WPM with italics command.

Let's also add a command at the end of the macro that moves your insertion point back to the top of the document.

11. Move your insertion point to the bottom of the macro document, and press Shift+F3 to switch to record mode.

12. Press Home, Home, up arrow to move your insertion point to the top of the document on-screen, and switch back to ALTC.WPM. The command PosDocTop now is inserted as the last line in the macro (see Figure 43.18).

Because of the capability to tile documents in WordPerfect 6.0 (split-screen feature in WordPerfect 5.1), with tiling you can even record changes to your macro and watch them at the same time! For example, let's tile our documents and add the word *Enclosures* on the line immediately underneath the company name.

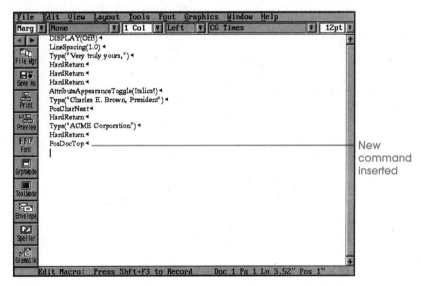

Figure 43.18. ALTC.WPM with *PosDocTop* command.

13. Choose Window, Tile to tile the two active documents. Your screen should look similar to Figure 43.19 with your insertion point at the bottom of the Macro Record window.

14. Move your insertion point to the beginning of the line PosDocTop. Insert the text for "Enclosures" at the beginning of this line, before moving back to the top of the document.

15. Choose Window, Switch, or press Shift+F3 to switch to the record mode document in the lower window.

16. Type the word Enclosures followed by a hard return, and notice that as you do that, these two new commands are inserted in the ALTC.WPM macro in the upper window as you type (see Figure 43.20). What is great is that you did not have to worry about command spellings or syntax to

633

do that! Of course, you always can type any macro command while editing a macro, but the ease with which you can switch to record keystrokes while editing will lure you from directly typing all but the simplest commands in your macros.

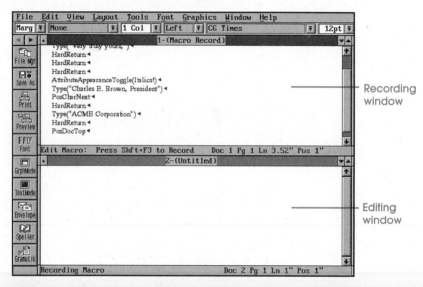

Figure 43.19. ALTC.WPM edit and record documents.

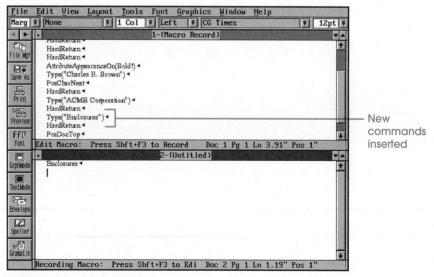

Figure 43.20. ALTC.WPM with "Enclosures."

Tip: This method of viewing the edits in a macro as they happen can be instructive on its own, in terms of helping you become more familiar with the various macro commands and their syntax.

17. Let's end this editing session by switching back to the ALTC.WPM document in the upper window.

18. Choose File, Close, or press F7, and answer Yes to the dialog box prompt Save...\ALTC.WPM?. You will be prompted to exit Document 1. Answer Yes and close Document 2 in the same fashion, this time without saving the changes on-screen.

Note: Depending on which you choose, you will see a slightly different dialog box prompt. The meaning of either is the same; that is, do you want to save the changes you just made to the document on screen?

After you select Yes to save the changes to the macro, a dialog box stating Compiling Macro and displaying a progress bar will appear briefly as the macro is recompiled and checked for errors. Assuming no errors, you have successfully edited the macro, and it is ready to be rerun with the changes in place.

Compilation of Macros

As was mentioned earlier, when you first create a macro or make changes to it, WordPerfect automatically *compiles* it. When a macro is compiled, WordPerfect converts the individual "English-like" commands (called *source code*) into commands more directly recognizable by the computer (called *executable code*). These executable code instructions are stored at the top of the document in a hidden area called the *document prefix*. When you next run the macro, WordPerfect looks only at the executable code in the prefix and ignores the actual source code in the rest of the document.

You may be wondering what the bother of all this compilation is. The answer is very simple—speed. WordPerfect 5.1 for DOS macros are based on an interpretative language (like other programming languages such as BASIC or dBASE). With interpretive languages, execution is performed one line at a time. That is, when you run the macro, the first line is first interpreted and then executed. Then the second line is interpreted and then executed, and so on. Each time you run the macro, the same process takes place. The constant interpretation/execution is what adds a considerable amount of time overhead to the running of the macro, because the software is checking each and every line of the macro for errors every time it is run.

635

With WordPerfect 6.0 for DOS macros (as well as WordPerfect 5.2 for Windows macros and other compiled languages such as C), all lines of the macro are compiled at the outset and checked for errors. This way, when the macro is rerun, there is no need to recompile each command line. The end result is that the macro runs much faster. You never have to worry about how or when you may need to compile a macro. WordPerfect will automatically compile any macro whenever the situation warrants that.

Note: WordPerfect always will compile a macro on initial creation. In addition, if you make changes to a macro while in macro edit mode, compilation will be automatic when you save those changes. Otherwise, compilation will happen when you run the macro for the first time after making those changes.

by William Robertson

Introduction to the Macro Programming Language

The total of all commands available to macros in WordPerfect is called the *macro command language*. This language is broken into three categories: product commands, programming commands, and system variables.

Product Commands

A product command in WordPerfect 6.0 is a *token*, which represents a single function that the word processor would normally do. For example, in the CLOSING macro created in the preceding chapter, the Line Spacing( ) command inserts a line spacing code ([Ln Spacing]) in the document according to the number in parentheses, and the HardReturn command inserts a hard-return code ([HRt]) in the document. These commands are inserted into your document just as if you had done so yourself at the main document window.

Product commands, or tokens, are inherently more efficient and readable than the keystroke-style commands in WordPerfect 5.1. For example, to record a line-spacing change to 1.5 in a WordPerfect 5.1 macro, something similar to the following cryptic series of codes would be required:

```
{Format}161.5{Enter}{Enter}{Enter}
```

In WordPerfect 6.0, the same function is accomplished with a single product command:

```
LineSpacing(1.5)
```

Virtually every keystroke combination, menu selection, or mouse choice can be automatically recorded by WordPerfect 6.0 as a product command and placed in a macro without worry as to the correct syntax or spelling of the command. Of course, you can always type the command directly into a macro on-screen, but the enhanced capability in WordPerfect 6.0 to simultaneously edit and record a macro leaves little reason to do so.

Command Names

Product commands are recorded by WordPerfect in mixed case—for example, `Center`, `PosDocTop`, `HardReturn`, `DeleteCharPrevious`, and so on. However, you can use any combination of uppercase and lowercase letters. Thus, `Center`, `center`, and `CENTER` are all valid versions of the same command. Product commands are *always* spelled as a single word. Although they may actually be composed of several words, there can be no spaces between them. `PosDocTop`, `POSDOCTOP`, and even `pOsDoCtOp( )` are all acceptable commands, but `PosDoc Top` will cause an error to generated when compiled.

Parameters

Many of the product commands require a *parameter* after the command name in order to describe more specifically what action the command should take. A parameter, if required, always appears in parentheses. For example, in the command `MarginLeft(1.5")`, the parameter `1.5"` specifies where the new left margin should begin. As commands such as `Center` and `PosDocTop` don't require a parameter, they also don't require any parentheses.

Note: Although WordPerfect doesn't require parentheses for product commands that don't have parameters (and doesn't record them with parentheses), including parentheses at the end of these commands doesn't cause an error to be generated. Parentheses also don't affect the functioning of that particular product command in any way.

Because more than 2,000 product commands are available — one for almost every action you can perform in WordPerfect — you might wonder why you would need anything else.

Command Abbreviations

When WordPerfect 6.0 records product commands, it spells them out in full. It's possible to record product commands (or to manually type them) in an abbreviated form. To record product command abbreviations rather than their full spellings, follow the steps outlined in the following Procedure.

Procedure 44.1. Changing Macro Recording to Abbreviations mode.

1. Choose Tools/Macro/Control or press Ctrl+Page Up to display the Macro Control dialog box shown in Figure 44.1.
2. Select Record Abbreviations. This puts an *X* inside the checkbox.
3. Select OK or press Enter to return to the main document window.

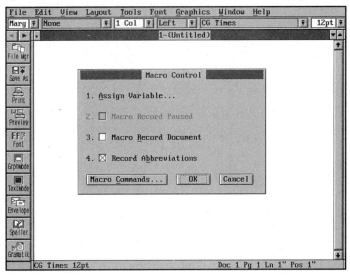

Figure 44.1. The Macro Control dialog box with the Record Abbreviations box checked.

From this point onward, when you turn on Macro Record, WordPerfect 6.0 records all commands in their abbreviated form rather than their long form. This change remains in effect for the rest of your WordPerfect session — that is, until you exit WordPerfect. Whether commands are abbreviated or fully spelled out should have little or no effect on the speed of execution. Your choice of full spelling versus abbreviation is mainly one of style. If you're in the habit of typing product commands, abbreviation might save you typing time. The following is a list of representative commands with both their full spellings and abbreviations:

Spelling	*Abbreviation*
AttributeAppearanceOn(Bold!)	AttrAppearOn(Bold!)
AttributeAppearanceOn(Underline!)	AttrAppearOn(Und!)
ConditionalEndOfPage(3)	CondEndOfPg(3)
BlockOn(CharMode!)	BlkOn(CharMode!)
DeleteCharPrevious	DelCharPrev
DeleteToEndOfLine	DelToEndOfLn
PosLineDown	PosLnDn
PosCharPrevious	PosCharPrev
Undelete(1)	Undel(1)

Note: If you prefer abbreviated command spellings, you need to set WordPerfect to record abbreviations each time you load it. There is no provision (at the time of this writing) for changing its default.

Tip: Stick with the default of long command names. In many instances, the abbreviations are not much shorter. If you attempt to type an abbreviated product command name directly into your macros, you might not be able to guess the abbreviation that WordPerfect assigned to the command, and you will get an error message. Also, WordPerfect's help system shows all commands with their full spellings. There is no list of the abbreviations. Because the only way of knowing what the abbreviations are is to record them automatically, there is little benefit to doing so.

Programming Commands

Although all product commands can be inserted into a macro by simply turning on the recording of keystrokes or mouse actions (select Tools/Macro/Record or press Ctrl+F10), programming commands are nonrecordable and must be inserted into a macro manually. With these additional commands you can build more sophisticated macros, which could include the following features:

▲ Pausing and prompting for user input

▲ Displaying selection choices on a custom menu

▲ Looking up and validating user input according to a predefined list

▲ Handling errors, such as CANCEL key, search strings NOT FOUND, and so on

Command Names

Like product commands, programming commands can be entered in lowercase, uppercase, or mixed case. Also like product commands, they are always spelled out as a single word (with no spaces), even though they can be composed of more than one word. Some examples are CASEOF, DEFAULTUNIT, and SAVESTATE.

Tip: Type all your programming commands in uppercase to better distinguish them from product commands (which are in mixed case). This will make it easier to read your macros.

Parameters

Like product commands, many programming commands require parameters. Some require several parameters as part of the command syntax, some of which may be optional. The FOR command provides a good example of both multiple and optional parameters. Its full syntax is as follows:

```
FOR(var;start;stop[;step])
```

This command has four parameters, the last of which is optional. Parameters are always separated from one another by a semicolon (;). Optional parameters are placed in square brackets. They are optional because WordPerfect usually assumes a certain default condition if they aren't specified. If a parameter isn't optional, it must be included for the command to compile properly.

There are more than 100 programming commands, ranging from the simple BEEP command, which produces a beep from the CPU's speaker, to the DLGCONTROL command, which controls all aspects of the design and functionality of a custom dialog box. Discussion of all of these commands is beyond the scope of this book. The rest of this chapter introduces you to the commands that will be of immediate use to you as you build more intelligence into your macros. These commands are the building blocks of good programming practices (working with variables and prompts, handling multiple-choice prompts, handling errors, and so on) that you can then expand upon.

Chapter 48 integrates these building blocks into several complete sample macros to demonstrate solutions to specific automation needs you might want to tackle with macros.

Command Syntax

One of the most frustrating things about typing programming commands is getting the syntax right, especially because they can't be automatically recorded by WordPerfect with the correct syntax, unlike product commands. However, this doesn't mean that you need to memorize the spelling and syntax for every programming command or even resort to looking up that information in the reference materials that ship with the software.

Note: As of the date of this writing, WordPerfect Corporation does not plan to ship a separate hardcopy reference manual for macros (like the Macros Manual for Windows). Rather, it will provide that information in the form of an electronic infobase accessible through the Help menu.

Macro Command Inserter

As with the 5.1 for DOS and 5.1/5.2 for Windows products, you can add programming commands to your macro through the aid of a *macro command inserter*, rather than typing them from scratch. You can access any of the programming commands or system variables through the Macro Control dialog box (see Figure 44.2) as follows:

Procedure 44.2. Accessing the Macro Commands listing.
1. Choose **Tools/Macro/Control** or press Ctrl+Page Up, then select Macro Commands.

A Macro Commands dialog box (see Figure 44.3) pops up in which you can view a list of all programming commands and system variables. The highlighted bar appears at the top of the list of programming commands. As you move the bar through the list, you will notice that there is listing to the right of the command list box for the command syntax, accompanied by a short description of what the command does.

Tip: Press Ctrl+Page Up twice to move directly into the Macro Commands dialog box without having to select Macro Commands.

Figure 44.2. The Macro Control dialog box.

If you move the bar downward to highlight the command CHAR, for example, you will notice that the syntax for that command consists of one required parameter, variable (in parentheses), and one optional parameter, "prompt" (in square brackets). If you want to insert this command into your macro on-screen, press Enter. Notice that the base command is inserted into an editing window and that the insertion point is between the parentheses so that you can type the text for the required and/or optional parameters (see Figure 44.4). Pressing Enter a second time inserts the command and parameter text into your document at the place where the insertion point was located when you brought up the dialog box.

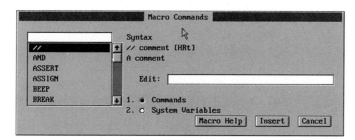

Figure 44.3. The Macro Commands dialog box.

By using the *macro command inserter*, you can easily look up the spelling and syntax of any of the programming commands and insert them directly into your document on-screen. Thus, you should be able to avoid many of the common errors caused by misspelled command names, missing parentheses, semicolons, and so on.

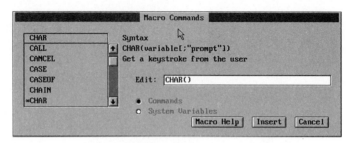

Figure 44.4. The *CHAR( )* command.

Parameter Types or Values

There are four different kinds of information that can be provided as parameters for programming commands: character, numeric, logical, and measurement. The next sections briefly discuss how they differ.

Character Expressions

Character expressions can represent anything from a single character to a complete sentence or paragraph. When incorporated as parameters within commands (either product commands or programming commands), they must be placed in quotation marks, as in the following example:

```
Type("Very truly yours,")
```

All text between the quotation marks is treated as a character expression and is simply typed out in the document. The following command:

```
Type(Very truly yours,)
```

would generate an error message because of the missing quotation marks.

If the character expression you want to use includes quotation marks as a part of the expression itself, use double quotation marks to distinguish between the quotes required by the command syntax and the quotes in the expression. For example, the command:

```
Type("""I am a Berliner,"" he said.")
```

would print the following phrase on-screen:

```
"I am a Berliner," he said.
```

The initial quotation mark denotes the beginning of the character expression. The next two pairs of quotation marks represent individual quotes within the character expression, and the final quotation mark denotes the end of the character expression.

Examples of programming commands that require character expressions as parameters are CHAIN, CHAR, CTON, INPUT, and SUBSTR.

Numeric Expressions

Numeric expressions are composed of numbers or any expression that might result in a number. Numeric expressions can contain numbers (0 through 9), the decimal point, and any of the four mathematical operators (+, -, *, and /). Numeric expressions are *never* enclosed in quotes. The following examples are all representative of numeric expressions:

```
2
2.0
2.123
-5
2+2                    (which is stored as 4)
10-5                   (which is stored as 5)
2*2                    (which is stored as 4)
25/5                   (which is stored as 5)
```

> **Note:** WordPerfect 5.1 can handle only whole numbers, but WordPerfect 6.0 for DOS also can work with fractions. Though as yet undocumented, it seems that the degree of accuracy with decimals is only eight digits. For example, adding 1.44444444 and 1.55555555 in a WordPerfect macro will total 2.99999999, while adding 1.444444444 and 1.555555555 will total 3.

The following LineSpacing product command requires a numeric expression as its parameter. It would be written as follows:

```
LineSpacing(2)
```

Examples of programming commands that require numeric expressions as parameters are FOR, FOREACH, PRESSKEY, and SHOWPOSITION.

Order of Precedence in Numeric Expressions

WordPerfect supports multiple operands in numeric expressions. That is, you can use complex numeric expressions in macros that are composed of several parts. For example, the expression:

```
2*5
```

is a numeric expression with only two operands (2 and 5). The expression:

```
2+5*7
```

is a more complex expression with three operands (2, 5, and 7). In situations where there are more than two operands, WordPerfect evaluates that expression order to a set of rules of precedence generally accepted as a standard in mathematics. Because multiplication (*) in WordPerfect is accorded a higher precedence than addition (+), the expression 2+5*7 would evaluate to 37 (2+35), not to 49 (7*7), the answer you would get by simply calculating the expression from left to right. You can override the operator precedence by placing parentheses around the parts of the expression you want evaluated first. In the expression 2+5*7, if you wanted to add the first two numbers *before* multiplying them by the third number, you would need to type the expression as follows:

```
(2+5)*7
```

Because parentheses are the highest order of precedence, they force calculations within the parentheses before calculations outside the parentheses. The following is a table of precedence and the order of operators:

Precedence	Operators
1	( ), - (unary minus), + (unary plus), ~ (bitwise not), NOT (logical not)
2	* (multiply), / (divide), % (mod), DIV (integer divide)
3	+ (add), - (subtract)
4	<< (shift left), >> (shift right)
5	<? (less than), <= (less than or equal to), > (greater than), >= (greater than or equal to), <> (not equal), = (equal)
6	& (bitwise and), ¦ (bitwise or), ^ (bitwise xor)
7	AND (logical and), XOR (logical xor)
8	OR (logical or)

Tip: When in doubt about how an expression will be evaluated, use parentheses! Errors with orders of precedence can sometimes be quite subtle.

Note: WordPerfect 5.1 for DOS uses a simple left-to-right order of precedence when calculating expressions.

Logical Expressions

Logical expressions are always evaluated as either TRUE or FALSE, depending on the results of a comparison within the parameter itself. This kind of logic often is referred to as *Boolean.* For example, the syntax for the IF command is as follows:

```
IF(expression)
```

Note: The term *Boolean* is taken from George Boole, an English mathematician who was responsible for formulating the system of representing relationships between entities with the logical operators AND, OR, and NOT.

Any valid logical expression can be substituted for this parameter. In the instance:

```
IF(overdue > 90)
```

the IF command tests whether the variable overdue is greater than 90. The command:

```
IF(response="n")
```

tests whether the variable response contains the value of lowercase n.

With logical expressions you can build very powerful macros that can test for certain conditions and then make decisions based on the outcome of those conditions. Examples of programming commands that can use or require logical expressions include CASE, FOR, FOREACH, IF, UNTIL, and WHILE.

Measurement Expressions

A fourth type of expression used in macro commands is the measurement expression. A measurement expression looks similar to a numeric expression, except that it can be followed by, but is not required to be followed by, one of the following unit-of-measurement characters:

c	Centimeters
i	Inches
p	Points
w	WordPerfect units (1/2000 of an inch)
"	Inches

If a unit-of-measurement character isn't used in the expression, the current unit of measurement in effect at the time the macro is run is assumed.

Note: Unless you've changed the system default, WordPerfect assumes inches as a unit of measurement.

For example, the measurement expression:

```
25c / 5c
```

would evaluate to 5 (25 centimeters divided by 5 centimeters). However, the measurement expression:

```
25c / 5
```

would evaluate to 1.968 (25 centimeters divided by 5 inches).

Note: Due to rounding errors, the first expression, 25c / 5c, actually evaluates to 4.99492386! When using the default unit of measurement, inches, WordPerfect uses conversion tables to translate numbers in measurements other than inches. The translations are not as accurate as they could be. For example, 1 centimeter is converted to 0.373 inches, whereas a more precise conversion would be to 0.3737 inches. This is where rounding errors will inevitably occur.

The following Margin commands all require numeric expressions as their parameters. They could be written as follows:

```
MarginLeft(1.5")
MarginRight(1.5c)
MarginBottom(1.5p)
MarginTop(1.5)
```

Enumerated Type Parameters

In addition to character, numeric, measurement, and logical expressions, there is a fifth type of parameter that is different from the others: enumerated type. It must be selected from a finite, enumerated list of accepted values for the parameter of the command in question. An enumerated type parameter always finishes with an exclamation point (!) and should never be placed in quotation marks. Also, each enumerated value has a numeric (shortcut) equivalent that can be used instead of the name.

For example, the DISPLAY command can contain either of two enumerated type values:

```
DISPLAY(Off!)
DISPLAY(On!)
```

or numeric equivalent values:

```
DISPLAY(0)
DISPLAY(1)
```

The product command, AttributeAppearanceToggle(), has a finite list of enumerated parameters, of which the following is a partial list:

Enumerated	*Numeric*
Italics!	8
Bold!	12
SmallCaps!	15
Underline!	16

Either AttributeAppearanceToggle(Italics!) or AttributeAppearance-Toggle(8) would be an acceptable product command in a macro. Although WordPerfect 6.0 records all product and programming commands with enumerated parameters, you could go back and change those parameters to numeric, without affecting their functionality.

Tip: Leave WordPerfect's recording of enumerated parameters alone. Although you may want to put in numeric equivalents and abbreviated product commands in order to shorten the lengths of those commands, you will make your macros much more difficult to decipher afterward.

A number of programming commands, as well as many other product commands, fall into this category—for example, CANCEL, DISPLAY, DLGINPUT, ERROR, and NOTFOUND.

By the way, you will see the DISPLAY(OFF!) command placed at the top of every macro you begin recording from the keyboard. This command hides the actions of the macro from view while it runs. If you turn DISPLAY(On!) on in a macro, from that point onward you will see the actual keystrokes and other operations of the macro acted out step-by-step on-screen.

Tip: Turning DISPLAY(On!) in a macro can slow down the processing of that macro considerably. The more screen activity there is in the macro, the more the speed will be affected. Use DISPLAY(On!) only at various points in the macro where you need to see the results of what has been accomplished so far. Another reason to leave DISPLAY(OFF!) is that it usually confuses the user to see all the individual keystrokes in the macro flying by.

Variables

A variable is a piece of information stored in the computer's memory temporarily. As the name implies, the information within the variable can change. This way, you can use variables to calculate expressions that might change during the process of running a macro. With the adept use of variables, you can add tremendous power and flexibility to your macros. The reason is that a variable can be used to represent any character expression, numeric expression, measurement expression, or logical expression that may exist at the time the macro is running. As with Wordperfect 5.1, WordPerfect 6.0 uses two types of variables: system variables and user-defined variables.

System Variables

System variables are variables that WordPerfect creates and tracks internally while the program is running. These variables contain information about the state of WordPerfect—for example, whether Reveal Codes or Block is active or what the Name or Path is for the current document on-screen. You can't alter either the names or the contents of these system variables, but you can test for what their current contents are and make decisions accordingly. (For example, if Reveal Codes is active, turn it off before beginning the macro.) WordPerfect 5.1 has approximately 40 system and state variables to work with. WordPerfect 6.0 has more than 300 system variables that track virtually every aspect of the current state of WordPerfect.

User-Defined Variables

You create and assign names and values to user-defined variables. You also can manipulate the contents of these variables (if needed) during the course of the macro. There are three types of variables in WordPerfect 6.0: persistent, global, and local.

Persistent Variables

Persistent variables are active and available for use at all times during any macro, FUNCTION, or PROCEDURE. Once defined, these variables remain in memory until you explicitly delete them or until you exit WordPerfect. This is the only variable type available in WordPerfect 5.1.

> **Note:** Alt+# keyboard variables work the same way in WordPerfect 6.0 as they do in WordPerfect 5.1. Once defined, you can access them directly by holding down the Alt key and simultaneously pressing a number from 0 to 9. All Alt+# keyboard variables in WordPerfect 6.0 are automatically classified as persistent.

Global Variables

Global variables are active and available for use at all times during the current macro or FUNCTIONs or PROCEDUREs of the current macro, as well as any other chained or nested macros. When that macro completes, all variables assigned during that macro are automatically deleted from memory.

Local Variables

Local variables are active and available only in the current macro, or in FUNCTIONs or PROCEDUREs of the current macro containing a LOCAL command. When that macro completes, all variables assigned during that macro are automatically deleted from memory.

> **Tip:** In order to conserve memory, try to assign the majority of your variables as local or global. This way, when the macro or macros complete, those variables will be erased from memory and that memory will be returned to the general memory pool. Keep your usage of persistent variables to a minimum.

Assigning a Value to a Variable

Variables may contain either text or numbers and may substitute for all four expression types: character, numeric, measurement, and logical. For the most part, the command you use to assign a value to a variable determines the variable type. The ASSIGN command, however, is different in that you can use it to assign variables of all data types. The ASSIGN command has two possible syntaxes:

```
ASSIGN(variable;expression)
```

and

```
variable=expression
```

Tip: I recommend using the second method of assigning variables, because its syntax is simpler and more readily readable (and therefore understandable). This method is utilized in all further examples.

For example, the following command assigns the value WordPerfect 6.0 (character expression) to the variable name program because that value is enclosed in quotation marks. This variable can then be used with any command that allows a character expression as a parameter:

```
ASSIGN(program;"WordPerfect 6.0")
```

or

```
program="WordPerfect 6.0"
```

The next example assigns a numeric data type to a variable. Any command that allows numeric expressions as parameters can reference this variable:

```
amount=1000
```

Measurement data types can be assigned, as in the following example:

```
fontsize=12p
```

You also can assign a logical expression to the contents of a variable. Keep in mind that logical expressions can have only one of two values: TRUE or FALSE. In the following example:

```
result=("A" > "B")
```

the variable, result, is assigned the Boolean value FALSE because the logical expression "A" > "B" is false. (A is not greater than B, because *B* comes later in the alphabet than *A*.)

Note: The actual value stored in the variable is not the word *TRUE* or *FALSE*, but the Boolean value for TRUE or FALSE, 0 or 1.

Naming Variables

Variable names can include any combination of characters, numbers, and spaces. They can have a maximum of 29 characters. Variables names longer than 29 characters produce a Macro Interpreter error message when you try to run the macro (see Figure 44.5). Like product commands and programming commands, variables are not case-sensitive. Thus, the variable names testvariable, TestVariable, and TESTVARIABLE are all treated by WordPerfect 6.0 as the same variable.

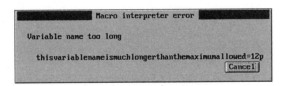

Figure 44.5. This variable name is greater than the 29-character limit.

Tip: I recommend using all-lowercase when naming your variables to distinguish them from product commands (mixed case) and programming commands (uppercase). This will aid in reading and editing more complex macros. In addition, for the sake of readability, keep your variable name lengths to a minimum and use names that indicate what is stored in the variable.

Reserved Words

WordPerfect 6.0 has predefined reserved words for internal use as Macro commands. These words can't be used anywhere within macros as variable, label, procedure, or function names, or you will receive compiler errors or other, more cryptic error messages on compilation.

AND	FRACTION	PROCEDURE
ASSERT	FUNCTION	PROMPT
ASSIGN	GETNUMBER	QUIT
BEEP	GETSTRING	REPEAT
BREAK	GETUNITS	RETURN
CALL	GLOBAL	RUNUNATTENDED

653

CANCEL	GO	SAVESTATE
CASEOF	IF	SHELLASSIGN
CHAIN	INDIRECT	SHELLMACRO
CHAR	INTEGER	SHELLVARIABLE
CONTINUE	LABEL	SHOWATTROFF
CTON	LOCAL	SHOWATTRON
DEFAULT	LOOK	SHOWCODE
DEFAULTUNITS	MENULIST	SHOWCOLOR
DISCARD	NEST	SHOWPOSITION
DISPLAY	NEXT	SHOWTEXT
DIV	NOT	STATUSPROMPT
DLGCONTROL	NOTFOUND	SPEED
DLGCREATE	NTOC	STEP
DLGEND	NUMSTR	STRLEN
DLGINPUT	ONCANCEL	STRUNIT
ELSE	ONERROR	SUBSTR
ENDFOR	ONNOTFOUND	SWITCH
ENDFUNC	OR	TOLOWER
ENDIF	PAUSE	TOUPPER
ENDPROC	PAUSECOMMAND	UNITSTR
ENDSWITCH	PAUSEKEY	UNTIL
ENDWHILE	PAUSESET	VARERRCHK
ERROREXISTS	PERSIST	WAIT
FOREACH	PERSISTALL	WHILE
FORNEXT	PRESSKEY	XOR

Caution: Don't use a variable name that begins with a question mark. Because the more than 300 system variables all have names that begin with a question mark, you probably will run into interference with one of them sooner or later.

Working with Variables and Commands

As mentioned earlier, variables can be substituted for any character expression, numeric expression, measurement expression, or logical expression in any command, subject to the types of expressions the command accepts as a parameter. For example, the product command for typing text to the screen has the following syntax:

```
Type(text)
```

where the variable text can be any expression type. Therefore, the following commands:

```
favorite=blue
Type("My favorite color is "+favorite+"!")
```

type the following text to the screen:

```
My favorite color is blue!
```

In this example, three character expressions are joined to make a sentence. My favorite color is and ! are called *literals*, because they literally are typed character-for-character as they appear within the command. Literals are always enclosed in quotation marks. The actual color referred to as favorite is a variable (favorite). Variables are never enclosed in quotation marks. When the macro is run, the Type command doesn't literally type the word *favorite,* but rather the contents of the variable at that time.

If you prefer, you can use spaces to increase readability without affecting the result of the commands:

```
favorite = blue
Type("My favorite color is " + blue + "!")
```

You can mix and match variables with different expression types within the same command. Because the Type command allows only character expressions as parameters, you would think that the following commands would produce an error (as they would in WordPerfect for Windows):

```
booknum=200
Type("I own over "+booknum+"books.")
```

But the variable booknum is automatically converted by the Type command into a character expression before it is joined with the other literal expressions on either side!

Variables of all expression types can be added to one another. In the following example, the three variables (character expressions) are joined to make a complete sentence:

```
subject="Jane "
verb="runs "
adverb="fast."
Type(subject+verb+adverb)
```

These lines would produce the following screen print-out:

```
Jane runs fast.
```

Likewise, numeric expression variables can be added to one another as a way of obtaining calculations within macros:

```
num1=150
num2=250
num3=num1+num2
```

The value of the variable num3 would be 400 in this example.

Variables can be even added to themselves to produce a kind of counter mechanism:

```
count=1
count=count+1
```

Each time the second command would be processed, the variable count would increase its value by 1. Be sure to assign an initial value to the variable. The following command by itself produces an error message explaining that the variable hasn't been assigned a value (see Figure 44.6):

```
count=count+1
```

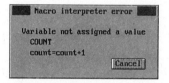

Figure 44.6. The variable wasn't assigned an initial value.

Assigning a Variable from the Keyboard

Variables can be assigned values directly from the keyboard as well as from within macros. To assign a variable from the keyboard, follow these steps:

Procedure 44.3. Assigning a variable.

1. Choose Tools/Macro/Control or press Ctrl+Page Up. The Macro Control dialog box appears.
2. Select Assign Variable, which displays the Assign Variable dialog box (see Figure 44.7).
3. Type the name for your variable and press Enter.
4. Select Content, type the contents of the variable, and press Enter. Choose OK or press Enter twice to return to the main document window.

Note: You need not include quotes with your text, unless the quotes form part of the text itself.

Although you can't directly access the variable's contents from the keyboard, any macro that uses that variable will reference the newly assigned contents. This can be helpful as a development technique when you want to see how assigning the variable different contents affects the functioning of the macro. This way, you don't have to edit the macro and change the contents of the variable each time you want to run a test.

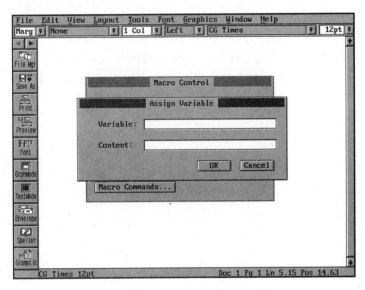

Figure 44.7. The Assign Variable dialog box.

Assigning a Variable from a Block of Text

You also can assign the contents of a block of text to a variable. This is very helpful in cases where you don't know the contents of the variable until a particular document is on-screen. In WordPerfect 5.1, the command/keystroke series:

```
{Macro Commands}3block{Enter}
```

assigns the contents of whatever was blocked at the time to a variable named block.

In WordPerfect 6.0, the steps involved in assigning blocked text to a variable are very similar to the steps for assigning a value to a variable from the keyboard. Once the text is blocked, follow the steps in Procedure 44.4.

Procedure 44.4. Assigning blocked text to a variable.
1. Choose Tools/Macro/Control or press Ctrl+Page Up.
2. Select Assign Variable, type the variable name, and press Enter.
3. Select OK or press Enter twice to return to the main document window.

657

Note: When you assign blocked text to a variable from the keyboard, the Contents window is preset by WordPerfect to Block. You can't change it.

The product command that gets recorded is quite different from the command series in WordPerfect 5.1, shown above, and is much simpler in construction:

```
block=?BlockedText
```

The system variable, ?BlockedText, is one of more than 300 available. This example demonstrates the increased power and simplicity that WordPerfect 6.0's *tokenized* macro language offers. The WordPerfect 5.1 command sequence for assigning a block to a variable hardly resembles the command sequence for assigning values to other variables because it records the keystrokes involved. Because WordPerfect 6.0 records the *end results* of those keystrokes, the command sequence is identical, no matter what keystrokes are involved.

Note: You can access the list of system variables for insertion into macros by going to the Macro Control menu and selecting Macro Commands. The default listing is for macro commands. For a listing and description of each variable, see WordPerfect's help menu on macros, subsection System Variables Index.

Controlling Prompts and Pauses

There may be times when you want a macro to pause at various points while it's being run so that you can insert text. After inserting the text, you would then press Enter to tell the macro to continue where it left off. This technique would be a handy way of filling in the blanks of a master form on-screen.

Suppose you wanted to create a macro that filled out a memo form like the one shown in Figure 44.8. You could record this macro as a simple keystroke macro by turning on Macro Record and then going through the steps necessary to create the memo template. This would involve changing fonts, turning on bold, setting the tabs, spacing between the lines, and so on.

When you were done, you could then run the macro (from a blank screen) whenever you wanted to draft a memo. The macro would re-create the memo template, and you would go back to the various fields of the memo (To:, From:, Re:)

and fill in the blanks. But wouldn't it be better if the macro could pause after typing each of those fields, wait for you to type the particulars, and then continue when you pressed a certain key?

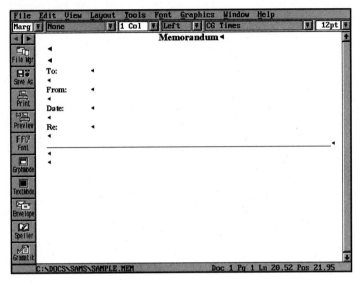

Figure 44.8. Sample memo.

Four commands control pauses within a macro: PAUSE, PAUSECOMMAND, PAUSEKEY, and PAUSESET. The simplest is PAUSE.

PAUSE

The PAUSE command doesn't take any parameters. It pauses a macro until you press Enter. While the macro is paused, you can type text or access menus just as if no macro were running. Listing 44.1 is a printout of a macro, MEMO1.WPM, that retrieves the master memo template, MEMO.FRM, searches for each field to fill in, pauses for input, then continues to the next field. When it is done, it leaves the insertion point at the bottom of the document and quits. MEMO1.WPM utilizes the PAUSE command to stop the macro wherever in the memo input is needed. Pressing Enter causes the macro to move to the next step.

Listing 44.1. MEMO1.WPM, which utilizes the *PAUSE* command.

```
//------------------------------------------------------------
//                        MEMO1.WPM
//------------------------------------------------------------
```

continues

Listing 44.1. continued

```
// Retrieves the template, MEMO.FRM, into a new document window,
// then searches for each field in the memo and pauses for user
// input. NOTE: MEMO.FRM is assumed to be in the current default
// directory. If it isn't, you must add the appropriate path
// statement to the FileOpen command below or you will receive a
// "File Not Found" error when you run the macro.
//-----------------------------------------------------------------
DISPLAY(Off!)                              // turn off display
FileOpen("MEMO.FRM";WordPerfect_60!)       // retrieve master form
SearchString("To:")                        // move to To: section
SearchNext()
PosLineEnd                                 // move to end of line
PAUSE                                      // pause for user input
SearchString("From:")                      // move to FROM: section
SearchNext()
PosLineEnd                                 // move to end of line
PAUSE                                      // pause for user input
SearchString("Date:")                      // move to DATE: section
SearchNext()
PosLineEnd                                 // move to end of line
DateText                                   // input current date
SearchString("Re:")                        // move to RE: section
SearchNext()
PosLineEnd                                 // move to end of line
PAUSE                                      // pause for user input
PosDocBottom                               // move to bottom of doc
// End of macro
```

Tip: Wherever possible, write a macro that retrieves a master form from disk and then continues, rather than actually creating the form from scratch with steps within the macro. This gives you greater flexibility to make changes to the form without having to edit the macro (as long as those changes don't affect anything the macro relies on in the actual form). Also, the macro coding will be easier to read because it won't be cluttered with lines for changing fonts and turning bold on and off.

When it is run, this macro moves the insertion to each section, waits for you to input text and press Enter, then moves to the next section of the memo. One thing noticeably absent, though, is a prompt while the macro is pausing. In fact, while the macro is paused, it's impossible to know whether the macro is still running. The Enter key "awakens" the macro and causes it to continue processing. A prompt would be an improvement for three reasons:

▲ It would help guide you through each section and provide context-sensitive suggestions for what text is needed at that particular section.

▲ It would remind you that the macro is still in progress.

▲ It would tell you how to continue to the next step after the appropriate text has been input.

PROMPT and *STATUSPROMPT*

The PROMPT and STATUSPROMPT commands display a prompt on the status line — that is, the bottom line of the document window. Their formats are as follows:

```
PROMPT("prompt")
STATUSPROMPT("prompt")
```

The text parameter in quotation marks is displayed on the status line until another PROMPT command overwrites it, the macro terminates, or the prompt display is intentionally cleared. To clear either prompt during a macro, use the following command:

```
PROMPT("")
STATUSPROMPT("")
```

The difference between the STATUSPROMPT and PROMPT commands is that the STATUSPROMPT command continues to display its prompt on the status line, even after the macro has terminated, unless it is explicitly cleared. This allows its prompt to remain displayed on the status line during the time text is being input by the user during the actual pause. The PROMPT is automatically erased from the display with the next keystroke after the pause begins, whether it is a keystroke entered from the keyboard or from within the macro.

In Listing 44.2, MEMO1.WPM has been revised to include PROMPT commands paired with each PAUSE command. Notice that the addition of a simple prompt (see Figure 44.9) really helps guide you through filling out the memo. We've made this macro a little more user-friendly!

Listing 44.2. MEMO2.WPM with *PROMPT* commands.

```
//-------------------------------------------------
//                    MEMO2.WPM
//-------------------------------------------------
// Retrieves the template, MEMO.FRM, into a new document window,
// then searches for each field in the memo and pauses for user
// input. NOTE: MEMO.FRM is assumed to be in the current default
// directory. If it isn't, you must add the appropriate path
// statement to the FileOpen command below or you will receive a
// "File Not Found" error when you run the macro.
```

continues

Listing 44.2. continued

```
//-------------------------------------------------------------
DISPLAY(Off!)                                // turn off display
FileOpen("MEMO.FRM";WordPerfect_60!)         // retrieve master form
SearchString("To:")                          // move to To: section
SearchNext()
PosLineEnd                                   // move to end of line
DISPLAY(On!)                                 // must turn on to see
                                             //   prompts
STATUSPROMPT("Recipient's name; Enter to continue")
PAUSE                                        // pause for user input
SearchString("From:")                        // move to FROM: section
SearchNext()
PosLineEnd                                   // move to end of line
STATUSPROMPT("Sender's name; Enter to continue")
PAUSE                                        // pause for user input
SearchString("Date:")                        // move to DATE: section
SearchNext()
PosLineEnd                                   // move to end of line
DateText                                     // input date (text format)
SearchString("Re:")                          // move to RE: section
SearchNext()
PosLineEnd                                   // move to end of line
STATUSPROMPT("Subject; Enter to continue")
PAUSE                                        // wait for user input
PosDocBottom                                 // move to bottom of doc
STATUSPROMPT("")                             // clear prompt from screen
PROMPT("Memo macro has finished; Enter to continue")
PAUSE                                        // pause; Enter to clear
                                             //   prompt

// End of macro
```

Caution: Note the DISPLAY(On!) command just prior to the first STATUSPROMPT command. Unless the display is on, neither PROMPT nor STATUSPROMPT commands will be visible on-screen.

Tip: The PROMPT command is best used for what I call "static" prompts—that is, prompts that don't require user input during their display. They simply display something at the status line and are cleared with the next keystroke.

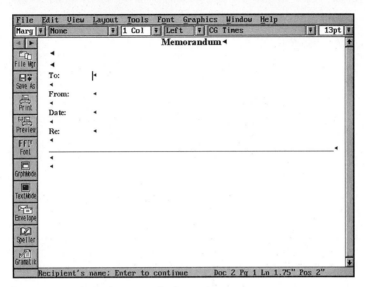

Figure 44.9. A prompt created with the *PROMPT* command.

PAUSEKEY and *PAUSECOMMAND*

What if you want to input more than one recipient name and you want each to be on a separate line? Currently, you can't press Enter to move the insertion point to the next line, because doing so takes you out of the PAUSE and moves you to the next section of the memo. The commands PAUSEKEY, PAUSECOMMAND, and PAUSESET enable you to control the key or command that terminates the pause. PAUSEKEY and PAUSECOMMAND have identical formats:

```
PAUSEKEY(Key Name)
PAUSECOMMAND(Command)
```

Listing 44.3 shows the MEMO macro in which PAUSEKEY and PAUSECOMMAND references replace the PAUSE commands in MEMO2.WPM. By allowing the Enter key to be used for input during the pause, you now can type multiple lines of text before pressing either F7 (in the PAUSEKEY example) or F9 (in the PAUSECOMMAND example) to move to the next section.

Note: For a complete listing of valid key names for use with the PAUSEKEY command, see Appendix B in the WordPerfect Online Macros Macro. Unfortunately, there does not seem to be any listing for the PAUSECOMMAND command.

Listing 44.3. MEMO3.WPM with *PAUSEKEY* and *PAUSECOMMAND.*

```
//-----------------------------------------------------------------
//                     MEMO3.WPM
//-----------------------------------------------------------------
// Retrieves the template, MEMO.FRM, into a new document window,
// then searches for each field in the memo and pauses for user
// input. NOTE: MEMO.FRM is assumed to be in the current default
// directory. If it isn't, you must add the appropriate path
// statement to the FileOpen command below or you will receive a
// "File Not Found" error when you run the macro.
//-----------------------------------------------------------------
DISPLAY(Off!)                           // turn off display
FileOpen("MEMO.FRM";WordPerfect_60!)    // retrieve master form
SearchString("To:")                     // move to To: section
SearchNext()
PosLineEnd                              // move to end of line
DISPLAY(On!)                            // must turn on disp to see
                                        // prompts
STATUSPROMPT("Recipient's name; <F7> to continue")
PAUSEKEY(ExitDlg)                       // pause until <F7> pressed
SearchString("From:")                   // move to FROM: section
SearchNext()
PosLineEnd                              // move to end of line
STATUSPROMPT("Sender's name; <F9> to continue")
PAUSECOMMAND(EndField)                  // pause until <F9> pressed
SearchString("Date:")                   // move to DATE: section
SearchNext()
PosLineEnd                              // move to end of line
DateText                                // input date (in text
                                        // format)
SearchString("Re:")                     // move to RE: section
SearchNext()
PosLineEnd                              // move to end of line
STATUSPROMPT("Subject; <F7> to continue")
PAUSEKEY(ExitDlg)                       // pause until <F7> pressed
PosDocBottom                            // move to bottom of doc
STATUSPROMPT("")                        // clear prompt from screen
PROMPT("Memo macro has finished; Enter to continue")
PAUSE                                   // pause; Enter to clear
                                        // prompt

// End of macro
```

PAUSESET

The PAUSESET command enables you to define the default key used to terminate the PAUSE command. Including the PAUSESET command at the top of the macro redefines the termination key for all PAUSE commands throughout the macro. If you want to have the same key (other than Enter) terminate all your PAUSE commands, this is the most efficient way to do so.

Prompting with Dialog Boxes

Rather than moving the insertion point to a particular position on the memo form and then pausing the macro for user input, you could prompt the user to input text into a dialog box prompt and then place that text at the appropriate position on the memo form. The two principal advantages of this approach are as follows:

▲ Dialog box prompts are much more visible to the user because they're displayed in the center of the screen rather than at the bottom. A user might not notice a prompt at the bottom of the screen.

▲ You have greater control of the macro process. With the PROMPT and STATUSPROMPT techniques just described, the user has free reign to type text, access menus, and even exit WordPerfect while the macro is paused. With dialog boxes, that is not so.

Three principal commands request input from the user with set dialog box styles: GETSTRING, GETNUMBER, and GETUNITS.

GETSTRING

The format of GETSTRING is as follows:

```
GETSTRING(variable[;"prompt";"title";len])
```

where `variable` is the name of the variable that stores the text input, `prompt` is the message displayed inside the dialog box, `title` is the title of the dialog box (top center), and `len` is the character limit of the text to be input.

The `prompt`, `title`, and `len` parameters are optional. If you don't supply a length parameter, the dialog box displays across the full width of the screen and allows a maximum of 127 characters of input. Setting `len = 5` restricts text input to a maximum of five characters and also creates a much thinner dialog box.

Note: When you're filling in the parameters of a command using the Macro Command Inserter dialog box, there is a limit to the number of characters you can type. When this limit has been reached, you can insert the command into the macro and then continue with additional text and parameters.

Listing 44.4 shows revisions to the MEMO.WPM macro that replace the various PAUSE commands with GETSTRING command dialog boxes.

Listing 44.4. MEMO4.WPM with *GETSTRING* commands.

```
//------------------------------------------------------------
//                        MEMO4.WPM
//------------------------------------------------------------
// Retrieves the template, MEMO.FRM, into a new document window,
// then searches for each field in the memo and pauses for user
// input. NOTE: MEMO.FRM is assumed to be in the current default
// directory. If it isn't, you must add the appropriate path
// statement to the FileOpen command below or you will receive a
// "File Not Found" error when you run the macro.
//------------------------------------------------------------
DISPLAY(Off!)                           // turn off display key-
                                        //   strokes
FileOpen("MEMO.FRM";WordPerfect_60!)    // retrieve master form
SearchString("To:")                     // move to To: section
SearchNext()
PosLineEnd                              // move to end of line
DISPLAY(On!)                            // must turn on disp to see
                                        //   prompts
GETSTRING(to;                           // dialog box prompt for To:
     "Enter recipient's name; then choose OK or press Enter";
     "Recipient's Name")
Type(to)                                // type "to" var to screen
SearchString("From:")                   // move to From: section
SearchNext()
PosLineEnd                              // move to end of line
GETSTRING(from;                         // dialog box prompt for
FROM: section
     "Enter sender's name; then choose OK or press Enter";
     "Sender's Name")
Type(from)                              // type "from" var to screen
SearchString("Date:")                   // move to DATE: section
SearchNext()
PosLineEnd                              // move to end of line
DateText                                // input date (in text
                                        //   format)
SearchString("Re:")                     // move to RE: section
SearchNext()
PosLineEnd                              // move to end of line
GETSTRING(re;                           // dialog box prompt for RE:
     "Enter memo subject, then choose OK or press Enter";
     "Subject Line";25)
Type(re)                                // type "re" var to screen
PosDocBottom                            // move to bottom of docu-
                                        //   ment
STATUSPROMPT("")                        // clear prompt from screen
```

```
PROMPT("Memo macro has finished; Enter to continue")
PAUSE                                    // pause; Enter to clear
                                         prompt

// End of macro
```

Note: Keep in mind that the GETSTRING, GETNUMBER, and GETUNITS commands allow input on only a single line. If you need multiple-line input capability, stick with one of the PAUSE commands that has a terminator key other than Enter.

You should take note of several changes to the macro:

▲ The GETSTRING and Type commands have replaced the pair of STATUSPROMPT and PAUSEKEY or PAUSECOMMAND commands. Note that the GETSTRING command is broken over more than one line. Hard returns and tabs have been inserted within the command in order to improve clarity, without affecting the processing of the command.

Note: To learn more about formatting conventions in macros, see the section "Comments and Indents" in the next chapter.

▲ The GETSTRING command places the contents of the user input into a variable. The Type command that follows types the contents of that variable to the screen.

▲ Notice the pair of DISPLAY(On!)/DISPLAY(Off!) commands right after the Type commands. Without DISPLAY(On!), the text is inserted into the form by the Type command but isn't seen by the user. The DISPLAY(Off!) keeps the remaining steps of the macro invisible to the user.

▲ In the first two instances of the GETSTRING command, the optional length parameter is left out. If the parameter is left out, the dialog box is sized to the full width of the screen (see Figure 44.10). The last instance of the GETSTRING command has a length parameter of 25. WordPerfect creates a dialog box that is smaller and restricts the input window to 25 characters (see Figure 44.11).

GETNUMBER

The format for GETNUMBER is identical to that of GETSTRING, except that there is no optional length parameter:

```
GETNUMBER(variable[;"prompt";"title"])
```

667

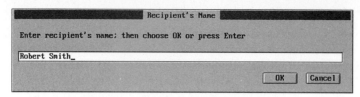

Figure 44.10. *GETSTRING* with no length parameter.

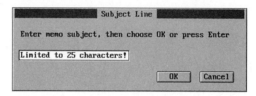

Figure 44.11. *GETSTRING* with a *len = 25* parameter.

The following example displays the dialog box shown in Figure 44.12:

```
GETNUMBER(num;"Type in a number below.";"Number")
```

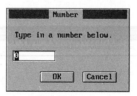

Figure 44.12. The Number dialog box.

The GETNUMBER dialog box accepts only valid numbers. If you enter any text or other unacceptable characters, WordPerfect generates an error message like the one shown in Figure 44.13.

Figure 44.13. A nonnumeric character was entered in the number field.

When you select Retry, you are returned to the dialog box to enter another number. A valid number can contain only numbers (0 through 9) or a leading minus sign (dash). Any other characters, such as currency ($123.45), embedded dashes (123-45-6789), or mixture of numbers and letters (123D 45F), will not be accepted.

> **Caution:** At the time of this writing, invalid number entries won't always produce an error message. If your first character is invalid, but the remaining characters are valid (for example, X12345), the entire entry will be invalid and an error message will result. If you enter valid numbers followed by an invalid character (12345X), you won't receive an error message, and the resulting variable created by the entry will store the numeric portion of the entry up to the point of the first invalid character (12345 only). Apparently, if you type a number with a decimal point (123.45), no error will be displayed, and only the integer portion of the number will be stored in the assigned variable (123).

Prompting with a Menu of Choices

The various prompt commands discussed to date involve different methods for prompting the user for input and then either allowing the user to type directly in the document on-screen (PROMPT, STATUSPROMPT) or having the user type into a variable assigned from a dialog box (GETSTRING, GETNUMBER, GETUNITS). But in many circumstances it would be helpful to prompt the user with a list of preset choices and to ask him or her to select from the list, rather than type the text in full. WordPerfect 5.1 accomplishes this with either the CHAR or TEXT commands for single-line prompts, or with a series of cumbersome positioning codes ({P}) to design a menu of choices to display to the user.

WordPerfect 6.0's MENULIST command is designed to display full-screen menus to the user with a list of items to choose from. It's more powerful and yet considerably simpler than WordPerfect 5.1's capabilities. The format of the command is as follows:

```
MENULIST(variable;{"Item1";"Item2";..."ItemN"};"Title";
    Horizontal Position;Vertical Position)
```

Each item in the list is automatically numbered, and the number of the item selected by the user is assigned to the variable specified in the initial parameter. Once assigned, this variable can be manipulated with other commands such as IF or SWITCH (which are discussed in the section "CASE Command"). The horizontal position and vertical position parameters are optional and control the physical position of the title within the menu. If they are left out, the menu title will be centered at the top of the dialog box.

669

Caution: Because WordPerfect 6.0 uses numbers for the menu selections rather than letter mnemonics (as does WordPerfect for Windows), a maximum of nine selections is allowed on any menu. If you have more than nine items in your command, they will display on the menu but you won't be able to select them!

Let's go back to the CLOSING macro created in Chapter 43. Instead of typing `Sincerely yours`, you will prompt the user with a menu of closings to choose from (see Listing 44.5 and Figure 44.14).

Listing 44.5. CLOSING.WPM with the *MENULIST* command.

```
//-------------------------------------------------------------
//                      CLOSING.WPM
// Sample macro prompting user with a menu list of closings to
// choose from.
//-------------------------------------------------------------
DISPLAY(Off!)                              // turn off display
LineSpacing(1.0)                           // in case not curr
                                           //   default

MENULIST(menu;
    ["Sincerely yours";"Very truly yours";"Best
    regards";"Respectfully submitted"};
    "Closing Styles")                      // 4-choice menu


HardReturn                                 // 4 [HRt]'s for sig
                                           //   space
HardReturn
HardReturn
HardReturn
AttributeAppearanceOn(Bold!)               // turn on bold
Type("Charles E. Brown")                   // type SIGNATORY name
PosCharNext                                // move past bold off
                                           //   code
HardReturn                                 // 1 [HRt]
Type("ACME Corporation")                   // type COMPANY name
HardReturn                                 // 2 [HRt]'s
HardReturn
Type("Enclosures")                         // ENCLOSURES
HardReturn                                 // 1 [HRt]
Type("CEB/wlr")                            // signatory/operator
                                           //   init
HardReturn                                 // 1 last [HRt]
PosDocTop                                  // move to top of doc
// End of macro
```

Figure 44.14. The dialog box from CLOSING.WPM.

With the new MENULIST command added, you are now prompted with a menu of closing selections. The number of the selection you make is then assigned to the variable closing, but nothing is done with that variable yet. You need to create a routine afterward that reasons as follows: "If choice #1 is selected, type...; if choice #2 is selected, type...," and so forth. For each possible selection you would branch off to a different routine that would type the appropriate text for that particular selection. This is what the SWITCH command enables you to do.

SWITCH Command

The SWITCH command is an extremely powerful command that enables you to choose from among a series of possible values (for example, items from a menu list) and take a different action depending on which item is selected. The SWITCH command takes any valid expression as a parameter, although this usually is a variable previously assigned by another command, such as MENULIST, GETSTRING, and so on.

CASEOF Command

A single SWITCH command ends with an ENDSWITCH command (with no parameter for the ENDSWITCH command). Between these two statements is a series of CASEOF statements that evaluate each of the possibilities of the SWITCH scenario. The general format is as follows (you can have as many CASEOF statements as you want):

671

```
SWITCH(expression)
     CASEOF expression: action
     CASEOF expression: action
     CASEOF expression: action
ENDSWITCH
```

Note: The `SWITCH` statement just shown has been simplified some-what. Discussion of its other parameters, such as multiple expres-sions in the `CASEOF` sections, branching to `LABEL`s, and so on, is beyond the scope of this book. At the time of this writing, WordPerfect Corporation couldn't confirm whether it would be shipping any macro documentation in hardcopy format. See your online Macro Commands Index for more details.

Figure 44.15 shows CLOSING.WPM with the additions needed to evaluate each closing selection within the `SWITCH` statement and then act accordingly. When it is run, you are prompted with a list of closings to choose from. When you select a number from 1 to 4, the `SWITCH` command evaluates that number and runs the matching `CASEOF` command, which then types the appropriate text to the screen. Once completed, the macro moves to the next command *after* the `ENDSWITCH` command.

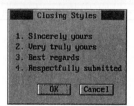

Figure 44.15. The Closing Styles dialog box within CLOSING.WPM.

Listing 44.6. CLOSING.WPM with *SWITCH* statement added.

```
//----------------------------------------------------------------
//                         CLOSING.WPM
// Sample macro prompting user with a menu list of closings to
// choose from.
//----------------------------------------------------------------
DISPLAY(Off!)                              // turn off display
LineSpacing(1.0)                           // in case not current
                                           //    default

MENULIST(menu;
     {"Sincerely yours";"Very truly yours";"Best
     regards";"Respectfully submitted"};
```

```
        "Closing Styles")                       // 4-choice menu
SWITCH(menu)                                     // evaluate the 4 choices
        CASEOF 1: Type("Sincerely yours,")
        CASEOF 2: Type("Very truly yours,")
        CASEOF 3: Type("Best regards,")
        CASEOF 4: Type("Respectfully submitted,")
ENDSWITCH

HardReturn                                       // 4 [HRt]'s for sig
                                                 space

HardReturn
HardReturn
HardReturn
AttributeAppearanceOn(Bold!)                     // turn on bold
Type("Charles E. Brown")                         // type SIGNATORY name
PosCharNext                                      // move past bold off
                                                 code
HardReturn                                       // 1 [HRt]
Type("ACME Corporation")                         // type COMPANY name
HardReturn                                       // 2 [HRt]'s
HardReturn
Type("Enclosures")                               // ENCLOSURES
HardReturn                                       // 1 [HRt]
Type("CEB/wlr")                                  // signatory/operator
                                                 init
HardReturn                                       // 1 last [HRt]
PosDocTop                                        // move to top of doc
// End of macro
```

Note: Keep in mind that the CASE command doesn't have to be coupled with a MENULIST command structure, but it can be used to evaluate any situation where there is more than one possible value to act on. For example, this could be a situation where you need to evaluate what the user typed act and accordingly.

One thing is missing from our SWITCH statement that would be very helpful. Currently, if you run the macro and select nothing from the list of menu items (by choosing OK or pressing Enter), no closing at all is inserted into the document (although the macro will continue and complete the remaining commands).

DEFAULT Command

The DEFAULT command is an optional command that provides for a default action if all previous CASEOF statements are false. In the Listing 44.7, a DEFAULT command has been added to the CLOSING macro just below the final CASEOF command. If the user simply presses the Enter key, bypassing the menu selection, the DEFAULT command will type the default closing style, "Sincerely yours," and continue.

Listing 44.7. Closing WPM with the DEFAULT command added.

```
//-----------------------------------------------------------
//                      CLOSING.WPM
// Sample macro prompting user with a menu list of closings to
// choose from.
//-----------------------------------------------------------
DISPLAY(Off!)                          // turn off display
LineSpacing(1.0)                       // in case not default
                                          current

MENULIST(menu;
    {"Sincerely yours";"Very truly yours";"Best
    regards";"Respectfully submitted"};
    "Closing Styles")                  // 4-choice menu

SWITCH(menu)                           // evaluate the 4 choices
    CASEOF 1: Type("Sincerely yours,")
    CASEOF 2: Type("Very truly yours,")
    CASEOF 3: Type("Best regards,")
    CASEOF 4: Type("Respectfully submitted,")
    DEFAULT: Type(:Sincerly yours,")   // if #1-4 not selected
ENDSWITCH

HardReturn                             // 4 [HRt]'s for sig
                                          space

HardReturn
HardReturn
HardReturn
AttributeAppearanceOn(Bold!)           // turn on bold
Type("Charles E. Brown")               // type SIGNATORY name
PosCharNext                            // move past bold off
                                          code
HardReturn                             // 1 [HRt]
Type("ACME Corporation")               // type COMPANY name
HardReturn                             // 2 [HRt]'s
HardReturn
Type("Enclosures")                     // ENCLOSURES
HardReturn                             // 1 [HRt]
Type("CEB/wlr")                        // signatory/operator
                                          init
HardReturn                             // 1 last [HRt]
PosDocTop                              // move to top of doc
// End of macro
```

There are many more programming commands and principles I haven't covered and which are beyond the scope of the introductory nature of these chapters. Evaluating conditional statements (`IF`/`ENDIF`), looping constructions (`FOR`/`ENDFOR`, `FOREACH`/`ENDFOR`), creating `PROCEDURE`s and `FUNCTION`s, `CHAIN`ing and `NEST`ing other macros from within a macro, creating custom dialog boxes, and a host of other features are all areas within this substantially improved macro programming language that I invite you to explore after you have become proficient in manipulating the basic building blocks discussed in this chapter.

In Chapter 45, "WordPerfect 6.0 Macro Errors and Debugging," I discuss some of the tools available for debugging macros, understanding error messages in macros, and converting macros created in WordPerfect 5.0 or 5.1 to WordPerfect 6.0's format.

by William Robertson

WordPerfect 6.0 Macro Errors and Debugging

Common Macro Error Messages

Bugs are a fact of life in programming. Whether you have recorded a simple keystroke macro or a more complex macro using the programming language, chances are that somewhere along the way, you have encountered problems with a macro that either didn't work at all or didn't work the way you intended it to.

WordPerfect 6.0 provides a much more robust environment for "debugging" or fixing problems than earlier versions. One of the most frustrating parts of the WordPerfect 5.1 macro programming language was a lack of tools for tracking down and eliminating bugs in the coding. You found out there was a problem only upon running the macro, and then you were not given any details about either the nature of the problem or the location of the "offending" code. The more complex your macros (and therefore the greater the number of lines of code it contained), the more difficult it was to ferret out the problem.

Much more intelligence has been built into the WordPerfect 6.0 compiler than was built into the WordPerfect 5.1 interpreter, and it is clear that WordPerfect listened carefully to its macro programmers when they communicated the problems they had debugging macros. But before we go into more detail about the kinds of error reporting the compiler is capable of, let's outline the three basic kinds of errors you may encounter when designing your own macros:

▲ **Syntax** errors, such as missing colons, semicolons and parentheses, and so on, are the simplest kind and are usually caught by the compiler.

▲ **Runtime** errors are errors which surface after a macro has successfully compiled. When run, however, the macro encounters something it cannot interpret for some reason or another. These errors are a little more difficult to catch, because they have escaped the initial pass through the compiler.

▲ **Logic** errors are the most difficult to resolve. The macro compiles and runs without error; but it does not necessarily do what you had intended it to do, or it does not behave consistently under different sets of circumstances.

Syntax Errors

Syntax errors are usually the first to be detected and the easiest to resolve. The compiler almost always catches these errors and notifies you not only of the kind of syntax problem encountered, but also the area of the macro where the problem exists.

Missing Parenthesis

For example, in the CLOSING.WPM macro discussed in the last chapter, I have deleted the closing parenthesis in the opening command DISPLAY(Off!). If you try saving this modification to disk, the compiler will prompt you with an error message that the closing parenthesis is missing (see Figure 45.1). Select the Edit button from the dialog box. Notice that your insertion point is moved to the next occurrence of an opening parenthesis on the second line of the macro.

The compiler detected the error in syntax when it encountered a second opening parenthesis without having encountered a closing parenthesis in between, and it automatically placed you at the point of the second opening parenthesis. Although it may look like the compiler is pointing to the second line of the macro as the location for the error ((LineSpacing(1.0)), it is simply placing your insertion point at the location where it discovered there was a missing closing parenthesis. It cannot pinpoint the exact location for where that parenthesis should be, although it has substantially narrowed the field of view (in this instance, to less than one line of code). After replacing the closing parenthesis in the DISPLAY(Off!) code, you will be able to save and recompile the macro without further incident. Keep in mind, though, that the macro will neither compile nor run at all until you do this.

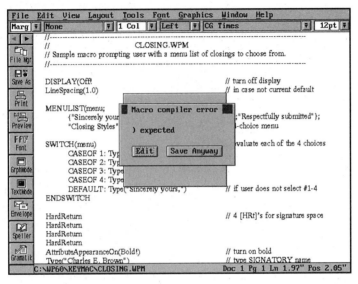

Figure 45.1. Missing parenthesis error.

The Macro compiler error dialog box also presents you with a second option, "Save Anyway." If you select this option, the changes to the macro will be saved to disk along with the error(s) and without the compiler processing the remainder of the macro. When you attempt to run the macro, WordPerfect will recognize that the macro has not been compiled and will attempt to compile it, with the same error message resulting. If you select the option to edit this time, WordPerfect will retrieve the macro from disk and place your cursor at the same location as it did on initial compilation; that is, at the location of the second opening parenthesis.

Command Name Misspelling

Like missing parentheses, a misspelled command name always generates an error. Unfortunately, the compiler does not simply inform you that "command x" was misspelled. The resulting error message varies depending on which command was misspelled. For example, in the CLOSING.WPM example cited above, three different command misspellings produce three different error messages of varying degrees of detail:

▲ Changing the spelling of the command LineSpacing to LineSpacng produces the LABEL name not found error shown in Figure 45.2.

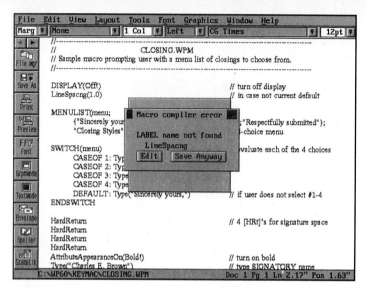

Figure 45.2. The *LineSpacing* command misspelled.

When you select the edit button this time, your insertion point is taken to the bottom of the document because WordPerfect is searching for some fictitious LABEL named LineSpacng. (Of course, you can at least avoid any misspellings of product command names by always using the macro record feature to insert them into your macros, as opposed to typing them directly into the macro.)

▲ Changing the spelling of the CASE command to CAS causes a more generic, and therefore less helpful, Syntax error message and your insertion point is brought inside of the CASE / ENDCASE substructure.

▲ Changing the spelling of the CASEOF statement within the CASE / ENDCASE to another CASE command produces the most specific of the syntax error messages, Bad CASE statement, and your insertion point is brought directly to the offending second CASE command.

Missing Quotation Marks

Missing characters such as quotation marks, colons, semicolons, and French brackets often produce an error message that reports that a particular character is missing, but the error message might not report the correct missing character. As with the error message connected with the missing parenthesis, the compiler knows that something is wrong and generally places your insertion point at thc point where it discovered the problem, which is not necessarily where the problem is.

Using a Reserved Word as a Variable Name

You are guaranteed a syntax error if you create a variable name which is the same as one on the reserved word list cited in the preceding chapter. For example, replacing the variable name menu in the MENULIST command in the CLOSING.WPM macro with the name speed causes the following error message to be displayed (see Figure 45.3).

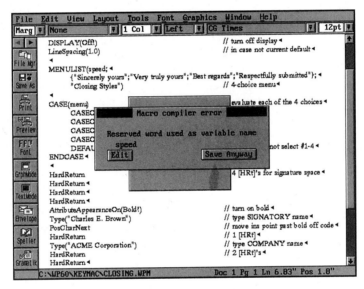

Figure 45.3. Reserved word used as a variable name.

Runtime Errors

Just because your macro has successfully compiled does not necessarily mean that it is free from errors. Runtime errors are those errors which are not discernible to WordPerfect until the macro is actually run.

Variable Not Assigned a Value

All variables used within a macro must be initially assigned a value, even if that value is a null string (for character expressions) or zero (for numeric expressions). If you reference a variable which has not been previously assigned a value in the macro, you will receive an error to that effect. In the MEMO4.WPM macro discussed in the preceding chapter, I intentionally misspelled the variable name from as frm. The wayward command line now reads as follows:

681

```
Type(frm)
```

The macro compiles without a problem, but when it is run, the following error message results (see Figure 45.4).

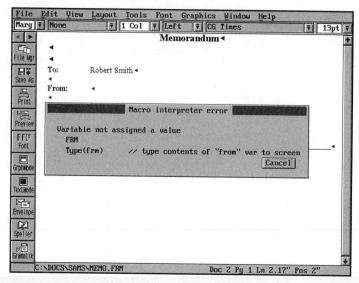

Figure 45.4. Variable not assigned a value error.

When WordPerfect reads this command line, it looks for the value of the variable `frm`. (Remember, variables are never enclosed in quotation marks.) When it cannot find such a variable name in memory, it displays the error message. At this point, you have no choice but to cancel out of the macro. You must retrieve the macro source document and fix the error before you can continue.

Not Found Error Message

The second most frequent runtime error you are likely to encounter is the `Not Found` error message. This error could be caused by an attempt to retrieve a file no longer stored on disk or not stored in the expected directory on disk. For example, in the series of macros MEMO1.WPM through MEMO4.WPM discussed in the preceding chapter, the template retrieved from disk, MEMO.FRM, is assumed to be located in the current default directory. If it is not in the current directory, the following error message results (see Figure 45.5).

Unfortunately, most other `not found` errors are much less helpful. Should a search string fail, the macro will simply quit execution, with no clue whatsoever as to the cause. In such circumstances, you will need to employ some of the troubleshooting suggestions outlined in "Debugging Macros" in this chapter.

Figure 45.5. The *File not found* error message.

Note: The `ONNOTFOUND` command allows you to avoid immediate termination of the macro and to control, in fact, what happens when a `NOT FOUND` error condition occurs. Further explanation of the command is not possible, though, as it is beyond the introductory scope of these chapters.

Logic Errors

Logic errors are the most difficult to pin down because they rarely produce an error message. Instead, the macro runs with inconsistent or unexpected results.

Debugging Macros

You can take a number of steps when you are attempting to track down a logic error.

Turn Display On

The first thing I suggest is to turn on your display mode, if your macro is not already running in `DISPLAY(On!)` mode. Do this at the very top of the macro and then watch it as it runs to see if you can notice anything visibly suspect.

Slow Down the Speed of Execution

Even with the display of keystrokes turned on, the macro may very well go flying by too fast for you to be able to distinguish the individual keystrokes involved. The `SPEED` command lets you specify the speed at which each keystroke is processed by the macro. The single parameter value specifies the length of time in tenths of a second that the macro will pause between each keystroke. For example, the following command

```
SPEED(5)
```

causes the macro to execute one keystroke every .5 of a second.

683

Pause or Quit the Macro

If you are still unsure where the trouble spot is, you need to narrow your focus to the potential area where the error is occurring. One helpful technique is to place a PAUSE command at the beginning or end of various sections of the macro. This way, you can see if the macro is able to complete a particular section without error before moving on to the next one.

Another, similar approach is to place a QUIT command at a point close to where you believe the problem to be. If the macro processes successfully up to that point, move the QUIT command further down in the macro, until the error occurs. Be sure, of course, to go back to the macro and delete the QUIT from it after you have successfully resolved the logic problem.

"Comment Out" Suspect Commands

If you suspect a particular command or series of commands may be causing the logic error in a macro, comment them out by preceding them with a double slash (//). This way they will be ignored the next time you run the macro. If the problem disappears, then you know it must be within one of the commands commented out. Should there be no improvement in the situation, then you can easily take out the "comment" marks (//) without having to retype the entire command line.

When All Else Fails ...

If you have no success with any of the preceding techniques, try "stepping through" the macro one command at a time. This involves turning on the STEP mode feature. Although the STEP mode feature is not new to WordPerfect 6.0, it has been substantially enhanced from its same-named cousin in WordPerfect 5.1.

When turned on, the STEP command allows you to step through each command or keystroke in a macro. The WordPerfect 5.1 STEP command displayed cryptic command numbers in place of the actual macro command being executed at the time. This, coupled with the limitation of displaying only a single letter of any menu prompt at a time, made it almost useless as a diagnostic tool.

The STEP command in WordPerfect 6.0 is far superior. First of all, there are no more cryptic command numbers. Rather, the STEP command displays the full command line (including commenting, if used) in a dialog box at the bottom of the screen. Figure 45.6 shows the initial screen when the STEP command has been added to the top of the MEMO4.WPM macro.

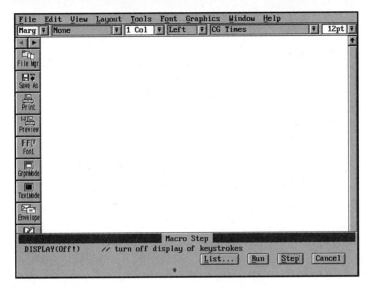

Figure 45.6. The *STEP* command with MEMO4.WPM.

Four option buttons are available in STEP mode:

▲ **Step** "walks" you through the macro, one command at a time. The ability to see the full command line being executed at the moment should provide a much greater capability to isolate thorny runtime or logic errors.

 Note: The command line displayed during the STEP(On!) process is the command *about* to be executed, not the command which has just been executed.

▲ **Run** turns off the STEP command and runs the remainder of the macro at full speed.

▲ **Cancel** forces a QUIT command in the macro and returns you immediately to the main document window.

▲ **List** is an exciting new feature which provides a complete listing of all variables, as well as their contents, currently in memory. This was impossible to do in WordPerfect 5.1 and is a tremendous asset for analyzing and troubleshooting macros. Figure 45.7 shows a listing of variables during a run of the MEMO4.WPM toward the end of the macro, just before the subject line is completed.

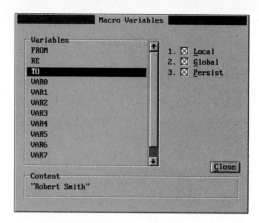

Figure 45.7. The Macro Variables dialog box (MEMO4.WPM).

On the left is a listing of all currently active variables. The Content section at the bottom of the dialog box displays the contents of the variable name (if any) currently highlighted by the cursor bar. On the right side is a control panel on which to indicate the variable types you wish to see displayed.

You will notice a series of variables VAR0, VAR1, ...VAR9 in the list. These variables are always active when WordPerfect is running and are, therefore, classified as persistent. You can confirm this by deselecting the display of local and global variables on the right side of the dialog box. (Click the appropriate boxes or type the number of the item.) Your listing should look like the one shown in Figure 45.8.

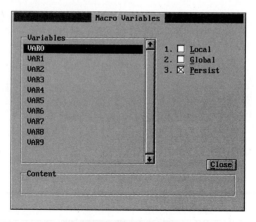

Figure 45.8. The MEMO4.WPM persistent variable list.

Conversely, you can limit your display to only local variables (those created during the current macro routine) to help isolate a problem (see Figure 45.9).

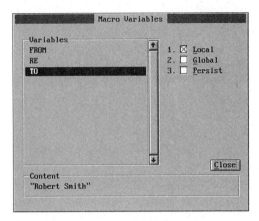

Figure 45.9. The MEMO4.WPM local variable list.

Commenting in Macros

Comments are text in a macro which is ignored by the macro. They are a means of documenting the goings on within a macro section by section, line by line, or a combination of both. It is critical to add comments throughout more complex macros to describe exactly what is going on or why you chose the particular command sequence you chose. (Maybe because of a problem an alternative command sequence was giving you earlier on in the design of the macro.)

Comments are very easy to add. To insert one, simply move your insertion point to where you wish to place a comment, and type two forward slashes (/ /) and then the comment. A comment must be followed by a hard return. That is, should you wish to type several sentences of commenting, you need to end each line with a hard return and begin the next with a new comment delimiter (/ /).

> **Note:** Comments do not affect the speed of your macros. Although they increase the size of the actual macro document, they are ignored by the compiler and, therefore, are not included in the code which is actually executed when the macro is run.

As an example of commenting in a macro, Figure 45.10 shows the MEMO4.WPM discussed in the preceding chapter without any comments (a view of only the first screen). Figure 45.11 shows the same macro with liberal commenting throughout.

Figure 45.10. MEMO4.WPM without comments.

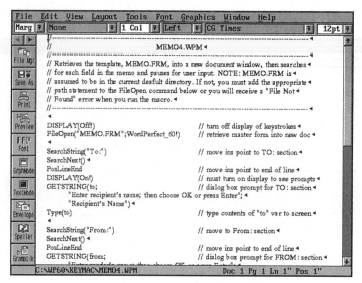

Figure 45.11. MEMO4.WPM with comments.

Macros Included with WordPerfect 6.0

WordPerfect 6.0 ships with several predefined macros, button bars, and keyboard files. Below is a list of the macros which are included with the software program (at the time of this writing), along with a description of what each macro does. A number of the macros are included within the predefined keyboard files and button bars.

The macros are quite sophisticated in that they utilize the full range of programming commands available with WordPerfect 6.0, only a subset of which has been covered in these chapters. Studying their construction will, in fact, be quite helpful in your effort to gain insight into how some of these more advanced features can be utilized.

ALLFONTS.WPM: This macro types out a list of all fonts available in the currently selected printer driver in their respective typefaces. Once launched, it requires no further input from the user. As it may take some time to assemble the listing, a dialog with progress bar is displayed on-screen while the macro is processing. Figure 45.12 shows a partial view of the listing for an HP LaserJet Series III printer driver (HP3.PRS).

Figure 45.12. A partial printout of ALLFONTS.WPM.

 Caution: The list is inserted at the location of your insertion point when the macro is run. Do not run this macro from within a document unless you wish to have the list inserted there.

BULLET.WPM: This macro inserts a bullet character at the beginning of the current paragraph or at the beginning of each of a series of blocked paragraphs. Upon running the macro you are presented with two choices: insert bullet and change bullet. Selecting the change bullet option will display a dialog box list of eight different bullet styles from which to choose. Once a bullet is selected, it is inserted at the beginning of the current paragraph (the insertion point can be located anywhere within the paragraph), followed by a left indent code.

Note: If you change the bullet selection from its initial default (small dot), that change is permanently written to the macro. The next time you run the macro, even after having exited WordPerfect, that change will remain the new default. This default is, in fact, stored in the form of a macro which is NESTed whenever the BULLET macro is run. It is stored in your WordPerfect 6.0 program files directory and is named WP{WP}BL.WPM. Although you could edit this file directly in order to change the default bullet style, it is actually much easier to simply run the macro and have it make the change for you.

CALC.WPM: This macro pops up a calculator on-screen and is similar in functionality to the same-named macro that shipped with WordPerfect 5.1, including inserting any calculations you make at the current location of your insertion point on-screen.

EDITCODE.WPM: This macro allows you to easily edit any code in WordPerfect 6.0. While in Reveal Codes, place your cursor on the code you wish to edit and run this macro. You will be brought into the appropriate menu where you may then make changes to the code. It is designed to run with the predefined MACROS.WPK keyboard (as Ctrl+E).

EXITALL.WPM: This macro returns you to the main document window from any dialog box, editing submenu or the like. It avoids the multiple keystrokes or mouse clicks necessary to exit out of some of these substructures. It is designed to run with the predefined MACROS.WPK keyboard (as Alt+X).

GLOSSARY.WPM: Also included in the predefined MACROS.WPK keyboard file (as Ctrl+G), this macro allows you to create and expand a custom list (glossary) of abbreviations. For example, you could create a glossary entry that expands the abbreviation *vty* to *Very truly yours*, or the abbreviation *fdic* to *Federal Deposit Insurance Corporation*.

To use the macro, you type an abbreviation and run the macro. If the abbreviation is in your custom list, it will be expanded to its long form. If it is not found in your custom list, the macro will pop up a Glossary Definition dialog box and prompt you to add it to the list. From within this dialog box you have the capability to create, edit, and delete individual abbreviations and their expanded forms. You are limited, though, by the dialog box entry window, to a maximum of 40 characters for the expanded version of the abbreviation.

> **Tip:** Your custom list of abbreviations is stored in the form of a macro located in your WordPerfect 6.0 program directory and named WP{WP}GL.WPM. The file is a simple listing of each abbreviation (defined as a global variable) and its expanded form, with each entry separated by a hard page break. Although you are limited to a 40-character maximum within the macro dialog box, you can add an entry directly into this macro with an expanded form as long as 254 characters (at the time of this writing), and it will be incorporated into the GLOSSARY macro next time you run it. Expansions longer than 254 characters will produce a `String too long` error on compilation.

INITCAPS.WPM: This macro capitalizes the first letter of the current word. Your insertion point may be located anywhere on the word or on the space immediately following the word. Not all words will be capitalized, because this macro uses the same exception list as is referenced by the `ConvertCaseInitial Caps` product command used when you block a section of text and switch it to initial caps. This file, located in your WordPerfect 6.0 program directory and named WPUS.ICR, is a WordPerfect 6.0 document you can retrieve and directly edit.

LIBRARY.WPM: This macro is in fact a collection of subroutines (hence the name, *LIBRARY*) referenced by several of the other predefined macros. Each subroutine can be independently run or `NEST`ed from within another macro.

> **Tip:** Browsing through the LIBRARY.WPM file would be a good way to better familiarize yourself with some of the more advanced features of the macro programming language. It is well documented (as are all the predefined macros) and can serve as a model for commenting and indentation within a complex macro.

MEMO.WPM: This macro prompts you to create either a memo, letter, or fax cover sheet. It is quite interactive and will prompt you through the entire process. It has a built-in address database lookup so that you can easily store, edit, and delete your most frequently accessed names and addresses. This way, when you create any of the three documents on the main menu, you don't have to retype the full name and address, but can access the name and address through the internal database.

MOD_ATRB.WPM: This macro pops up a custom dialog box to help you with searching for and/or replacing paired attribute codes. Options on the dialog box include search, replace, backward search, extended search (inside of headers, footers, footers, and so on), confirm modification, and replace original attribute. It can be found on the MACROS.WPK keyboard as Alt+R.

NOTECNV.WPM: This macro, also found on the MACROS.WPK keyboard as Alt+N, displays a simple dialog box with the option to convert footnotes to endnotes or endnotes to footnotes in a document. When run, it converts the appropriate notes to the other format from the current position of your insertion point forward in the document. That is, if you wish to convert all notes from one format to the other, position your insertion point at the top of the document *before* you run the macro. Should you wish to convert only a portion of your notes, you should first block the section of the document and then run the macro. Only notes within the blocked section of text will then be converted.

PLEADING.WPM: This macro prompts you with a custom dialog box, Create Pleading Paper. You may select from the various options on the menu to create a style for pleading papers. The style code is then inserted into your document on-screen or into a blank document to create the pleading paper.

> **Tip:** Once you have configured the setup of the pleading style to reflect your particular format, save the style file to disk so that you may retrieve it when creating new pleadings.

SPACETAB.WPM: This macro helps you convert spaces in a document to tabs. It opens up a custom dialog box where you may select the minimum and maximum number of spaces required to search for in the replace operation, whether to search backward or forward, and whether to confirm each replacement. It can be a very handy macro to help with documents which have been brought into WordPerfect 6.0 from ASCII or other formats which do not have tabs. It can be found on the MACROS.WPK keyboard as Alt+S.

Macro Keystroke to Token Conversion Utility

WordPerfect 6.0 ships with a utility for converting macros in 5.0/5.1 format to WordPerfect 6.0 format. For those of you who have struggled with the problems in converting WordPerfect 5.1 macros into WordPerfect for Windows format, this conversion utility is a great improvement over the conversion utility provided with WordPerfect for Windows. Whereas the conversion "hit rate" for the Windows utility was abysmally low, the "hit rate" for the 6.0 utility is around 90 percent. That is, about 90 percent of your macros will convert without the need to make *any* changes in WordPerfect 6.0 before being able to run them.

The utility is an executable file which must be run from the DOS prompt (or batch file). The filename is MCV.EXE and it is located in your WordPerfect 6.0 program directory. The following startup switches are available from the command line, most of which are self-explanatory:

> /b assumes block on at start of each macro
> /h gives this help message
> /l-logfile creates logfile of all screen messages
> /o (override mode) replaces existing file(s) without confirmation
> /q removes outside quote marks from strings in expressions
> /s uses short, token names

In addition, you may use wildcard specifications for both the source and destination path/filenames. Extensions need not be included, because the WPM extension is assumed on both sides of the conversion.

If the bulk of your WordPerfect 5.1 macros are keystroke-based or use programming commands that do not involve menuing and/or prompting commands (CHAR, TEXT, PROMPT, STATUSPROMPT and {^P} positioning codes), you can most likely convert them and literally run them in WordPerfect 6.0 with almost no modification. If, however, your macros involve any of the 5.1 menuing and/or prompting commands, you may want to rethink how you do your prompting/menuing in the WordPerfect 6.0 environment, because its menuing style (sculpted dialog boxes) is quite different from WordPerfect 5.1 (single line menus at the bottom of the screen or full-screen menus with number/letters as mnemonic choices).

For macros to appear as a seamless extension of WordPerfect, they should really be designed to integrate with WordPerfect's particular style of menuing and prompting. Most of the macros I design in WordPerfect 5.1 are done with prompting and menuing that mimics 5.1's own interface style. Granted, this is an aesthetic question, but one which I believe makes a great deal of difference.

Let's look at an example of a macro which converts flawlessly into WordPerfect 6.0 but which, because of the question of the user interface style, I would not use in WordPerfect 6.0 without modification.

Line Spacing Menu Macro (ALTL.WPM)

This is a simple macro which prompts the user with a line spacing menu. In WordPerfect 5.1, this is designed to avoid the repetition of going into the Format menu, selecting Line Format and Line Spacing, typing in the actual number, pressing Enter, and then exiting back out to the document screen. Alt+L (as shown in Figure 45.13) presents the user with a selection of standard line spacing choices. The user presses either a number or letter of choice, and the line spacing code is entered at the current cursor position. It is a simple but effective macro.

Figure 45.13. ALTL.WPM in WordPerfect 5.1.

Figure 45.14 shows the same macro converted with MCV.EXE in WordPerfect 6.0 text mode. No modifications were made to the macro after conversion. The prompt and functionality of the macro are literally identical. The user presses Alt+L and selects either a number or letter of choice. In fact, it is hard to tell that we are in WordPerfect 6.0 at all.

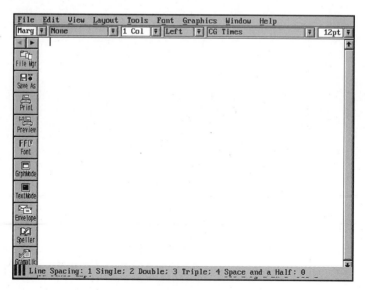

Figure 45.14. ALTL.WPM in WordPerfect 6.0 Text mode.

You can view the same macro in WordPerfect 6.0 Graphics mode. It does not blend in at all with the graphical environment, and it literally cuts off a portion of the button bar on the left side. It would make more sense to design this kind of macro with the MENULIST command discussed in the previous chapter. The resulting dialog box would "blend in" better with WordPerfect 6.0's other menuing and prompting conventions.

Let's look at the actual coding of the macro (unaltered) after conversion in Listing 45.1.

Listing 45.1. ALTL.WPM contents after conversion.

```
//Description: Line Spacing Menu

SAVESTATE PERSISTALL
AutoCodePlacement(OFF!) WP51CursorMovement(ON!) VARERRCHK(OFF!)

CANCEL(OFF!)                       //speeds things up
ONCANCEL(end)
DISPLAY(OFF!)

SHOWPOSITION(0; -1) SHOWCODE(ClrLine!) SHOWATTRON(ReverseOff!)
SHOWTEXT("███ Line Spacing: 1 S")      SHOWATTROFF(Bold!)
SHOWTEXT("ingle; ") SHOWATTRON(Bold!)   SHOWTEXT("2 D")
SHOWATTROFF(Bold!)    SHOWTEXT("ouble; ")
SHOWATTRON(Bold!)     SHOWTEXT("3 T")      SHOWATTROFF(Bold!)
SHOWTEXT("riple; ")  SHOWATTRON(Bold!)   SHOWTEXT("4")
SHOWATTROFF(Bold!)   SHOWTEXT(" Space and a ")
SHOWATTRON(Bold!)    SHOWTEXT("H")        SHOWATTROFF(Bold!)
SHOWTEXT("alf: 0")   SHOWCODE(PosLeft!)
CHAR(line)           ASSIGN(line; NTOC(line) )

CASE(line)
  CASEOF 1: GO( single)      CASEOF "s": GO( single)
  CASEOF "S": GO( single)    CASEOF 2: GO( double)
  CASEOF "d": GO( double)    CASEOF "D": GO( double)
  CASEOF 3: GO( triple)      CASEOF "t": GO( triple)
  CASEOF "T": GO( triple)    CASEOF 4: GO( spacehalf)
  CASEOF "h": GO( spacehalf) CASEOF "H": GO( spacehalf)
  CASEOF NTOC(-8160) : GO(     end)
ENDCASE
  GO(end)

LABEL(single)
LineSpacing(1.0)

GO(end)

LABEL(spacehalf)
LineSpacing(1.5)
```

continues

Listing 45.1. continued

```
GO(end)

LABEL(double)
LineSpacing(2.0)

GO(end)

LABEL(triple)
LineSpacing(3.0)

GO(end)
//  Remove variable from memory
LABEL(end)
ASSIGN(line; "") DISCARD(line)
RETURN                        //end of macro

//eof
```

The actual menu prompt section beginning with SHOWPOSITION(0; -1) is really quite a mess! The original 5.1 TEXT command and bolding codes were translated into a morass of positioning and attribute on/off codes in the 6.0 language. It would be very difficult to edit this macro and add, for example, a fifth option on the menu for line spacing = 2.5.

A better method is to throw out the positioning and attribute commands and replace them with the simpler and yet more powerful MENULIST command. Listing 45.2 shows the same macro revamped for use with the programming commands more appropriate to the WordPerfect 6.0 environment (note that there is a change in the menu design).

Listing 45.2. ALTL.WPM contents after revisions.

```
CANCEL(OFF!)                          //speeds things up
ONCANCEL(end)
DISPLAY(OFF!)

MENULIST(line;
  {"Single";"Double";"Triple";"Space and a Half"};
  "Line Spacing")

SWITCH(line)
  CASEOF 1: GO(single)
  CASEOF 2: GO(double)
  CASEOF 3: GO(triple)
  CASEOF 4: GO(spacehalf)
```

```
    DEFAULT : GO(end)
ENDSWITCH

LABEL(single)
LineSpacing(1.0)
GO(end)

LABEL(spacehalf)
LineSpacing(1.5)
GO(end)

LABEL(double)
LineSpacing(2.0)
GO(end)

LABEL(triple)
LineSpacing(3.0)
GO(end)

LABEL(end)
RETURN                          //end of macro

//eof
```

The messiness of the SHOWPOSITION and SHOWATTROFF/SHOWATTRON coding of the conversion is replaced by a single MENULIST command, which not only simplifies the coding of the macro, but also makes it much more legible. In addition, the resulting dialog box prompt is more in tune with WordPerfect 6.0's new prompting style. The CASE command was also simplified in that there was no longer any need to have multiple options in the CASEOF section; only numbers are possible selections with the MENULIST command.

Conclusion

I hope that this representative macro has demonstrated two things to you:

▲ (On the positive side) That the MCV.EXE macro conversion utility in WordPerfect 6.0 really does do an almost perfect job of translating WordPerfect 5.0/5.1 macro commands into WordPerfect 6.0. And it does so with little, if any, post-conversion cleanup.

▲ (On the negative side) That this utility does a *literal* translation of the 5.1 macro commands and prompts, and that this is not necessarily the best way to approach macro programming in the 6.0 environment. The functionality translates very well (keystroke compatibility, and so on), but the user interface does not.

You should really evaluate each macro you have in WordPerfect 5.1 with an eye toward the user interface design. In those instances where you are using prompts and menus in your WordPerfect 5.1 commands, I would strongly recommend building those prompts and menus from scratch with the native WordPerfect 6.0 commands. You will end up with a more refined and finished product, which is more seamlessly integrated with the new interface and functionality of WordPerfect 6.0.

by William Robertson

Putting It All Together

This chapter brings together everything discussed in the previous chapters and looks toward some of your day-to-day work with WordPerfect 6.0 and creating macros to make those tasks easier to accomplish. Use these macros, not only as routines in your daily work, but also as examples of integrating some of the features discussed in previous chapters (as well as others not discussed) to solve practical problems in WordPerfect 6.0. Although you may wish to input these macros from scratch, all macros in this chapter, as well as those discussed in Chapter 47, "Basic Merge," are available on the enclosed disk. Also enclosed is a button bar, 60SUPER.WPB, with a button for each of the macros included here.

Transposing Two Characters

How often do you make the mistake of transposing two characters when you type a word? This simple macro transposes the two characters in between the current insertion point. If the insertion point isn't between two characters (either no character or a code to the left or right), it prompts the user with an error message.

To use this macro, place the insertion point between the two characters you wish to switch and do one of the following:

▲ Click the Flipchr button on the 60SUPER button bar (if Button Bar is currently selected)

▲ Choose Tools, Macro, Play or press Alt+F10. Type the name flipchr and choose OK or press Enter.

The macro reverses the order of the two characters on either side of the insertion point. Listing 46.1 shows the macro. Following the listing are comments that describe FLIPCHR's construction:

Listing 46.1. FLIPCHR.WPM.

```
1     //------------------------------------------------
2     // FLIPCHR.WPM
3     //------------------------------------------------
4     // Transpose two characters. User must place the insertion
      // point
5     // between the two characters to be transposed before
      // running
6     // this macro.
7     //------------------------------------------------
8
9     USE("LIBRARY")        // Predefined 6.0 macro library
10    DISPLAY(Off!)         // Turn off display
11    IF(?DocBlank)         // Check whether document is blank
12         RETURN
13    ENDIF
14
15    // Next check whether there is a character to the left of
      // the
16    // insertion point
17    IF(?LeftChar="")
18        Msg="Must have a character left of the insertion
      // point!"
19        GO(Error)
20    ENDIF
21
22    // Next check if there is a character at the insertion
23    // point
24    IF(?RightChar="")
25        Msg="Must have a character at the insertion point!"
26        GO(Error)
27    ENDIF
28
29    // Check current state of Reveal Codes and turn off,
30    // if necessary
31    rcstate=?RevealCodesActive
```

```
32      IF(rcstate)
33          RevCodes(Off!)
34      ENDIF
35
36                              // Transpose the two characters
37      DelCharNext             // Delete char/code at insertion point
38      PosCharPrev             // Move backward one character
39      Undel(1)                // Undelete char/code just deleted
40
41      // Turn Reveal Codes on if off at the beginning of macro
42      IF(rcstate)
43          RevCodes(On!)
44      ENDIF
45      RETURN                  // End of macro (w/o error)
46
47      LABEL(Error)
48          BEEP
49          Message(msg)            // Procedure from "library.wpm"
50          RETURN                  // End of macro (with error)
51
52      // End of macro
```

Description of FLIPCHR.WPM

▲ Lines 1–7: These lines are initial comment lines that give the name of the macro and explain in general terms what it does. Note that comments are preceded by two slashes (//) and end with a hard return. Comments can be placed on a line by themselves (as in this example) or they may be placed at the end of a line (as in 36–39). Indentation and blank spaces don't affect the functioning of the macro, but are there to make the macro easier to read.

▲ Line 9: The USE command (not discussed in previous chapters) tells WordPerfect 6.0 to make a macro containing a library of routines available to this macro while running. With USE you can develop a modular set of routines (FUNCTIONs and PROCEDUREs) that you can call up from within any macro you write. This is a technique similar in approach to other high-level programming languages, such as C or Clipper.

▲ Line 10: This turns off the display of keystroke movements during the running of the macro. This, in fact, speeds up the processing of the macro.

▲ Lines 11–13: This IF clause checks to see whether the macro is being run from within a blank document. If so, execution is immediately stopped, and the user is prompted with an error message.

▲ Lines 17–20: This IF clause checks to see whether there is a character immediately to the left of the insertion point. If there is no character (beginning of document) or noncharacter (a code), an error message is stored in the variable msg and control is passed on to the error routine, error, near the bottom of the macro.

▲ Lines 24–27: This IF clause is exactly the same construction as the previous one, except that it checks for a character at the insertion point.

▲ Lines 31–34: First, the variable rcstate is assigned to the current Reveal Codes in the document (On=1; Off=0). The IF clause turns off Reveal Codes if they are currently active.

▲ Lines 37–39: These three command lines do the actual transposing of characters. The character to the right of the insertion point is deleted, the insertion point is moved backward one character, and then the deleted character is undeleted.

▲ Lines 42–44: This IF clause turns Reveals Codes back on, depending on the state of the variable rcstate.

▲ Line 45: Control is passed back to whatever routine called this macro. In contrast to the QUIT command, which unequivocally terminates the macro, the RETURN command is more flexible in that it returns control to a parent macro if the current macro has been NESTed by parent macro. It will terminate the macro also if macro was launched from a document window

▲ Lines 47–50: This LABEL (or subroutine) displays an error message to the user when either a valid character to the left or at the current insertion point isn't found. Line 49 calls a PROCEDURE from the LIBRARY.WPM set of routines that ship with WordPerfect 6.0.

Transposing Two Words

This macro is similar to the FLIPCHR macro, except that it will transpose the order of two adjacent words rather than characters.

To use this macro, place the insertion point between the two words you wish to switch and do one of the following:

1. Click the Flipwrd button on the 60SUPER button bar (if Button Bar is currently selected).

2. Choose Tools, Macro, Play or press Alt+F10. Type the name flipwrd and choose OK or press Enter.

The macro reverses the order of the two words on either side of the insertion point (see Listing 46.2).

Listing 46.2. FLIPWRD.WPM.

```
1    //----------------------------------------------------------
2    //      FLIPWRD.WPM
3    //----------------------------------------------------------
4    // Transpose two words. User must place the insertion point
5    // between the two words to be transposed before running
6    // this macro.
7    //----------------------------------------------------------
8
9    USE("LIBRARY")              // Predefined 6.0 macro library
10   DISPLAY(Off!)              // Turn off display
11   IF(?DocBlank)             // Check whether document is blank
12        RETURN
13   ENDIF
14
15   // Next check whether there is a character to the left of
16   // the insertion point
17   IF(?LeftChar="")
18        Msg="No word to the left of the insertion point!"
19        GO(Error)
20   ENDIF
21
22   // Next check if there is a character at the insertion
23   // point
24   IF(?RightChar="")
25        Msg="No word to at the insertion point!"
26        GO(Error)
27   ENDIF
28
29   // Check current state of Reveal Codes and turn off,
30   // if necessary
31   rcstate=?RevealCodesActive
32   IF(rcstate)
33        RevCodes(Off!)
34   ENDIF
35
36                              // Transpose the two words
37   BlkOn(WordMode!)          // Block current word
38   DelCharNext               // Delete block
39   PosWrdPrev                // Move back one word
40   Undel(1)                  // Undelete char/code just deleted
41
42   // Turn Reveal Codes back on, if off at the
43   // beginning of macro
44   IF(rcstate)
45        RevCodes(On!)
```

continues

Listing 46.2. continued

```
46    ENDIF
47    RETURN                          // End of macro (w/o error)
48
49    LABEL(Error)
50        BEEP
51        Message(msg)                // Procedure from "library.wpm"
52        RETURN                      // End of macro (with error)
53
54    // End of macro
```

Note: The macro can't recognize words separated by a hard return [HRt] code. In general, it isn't likely to work at the beginning of a line (unless that line is in the middle of a paragraph).

Description of FLIPWRD.WPM

With the exception of Lines 37–40, this macro is identical to the FLIPCHR macro already described.

▲ Lines 37–40: The product command in line 37 blocks the current word the insertion point is on. It is then deleted, the insertion point is moved backward one word, and the deleted word is undeleted.

Special Characters Menu

The macro shown in Listing 46.3 is a simple but good example of how to use the MENULIST command coupled with calls to subroutines (called LABELs). Although the MENULIST command is limited to the display of nine selections maximum, it has a sophisticated look for a relatively easy construction design. To run this macro, do one of the following:

1. Click the Spchar button on the 60SUPER button bar (if Button Bar is currently selected).

2. Choose Tools, Macro, Play or press Alt+F10. Type the name spchar and choose OK or press Enter.

Listing 46.3. SPCHAR.WPM.

```
1     //----------------------------------------------------------
2     //     SPCHAR.WPM
3     //----------------------------------------------------------
4     // Displays a menu of special characters to choose from.
      // Simple
5     // use of the MENULIST (limited to 9 selections) and LABEL
6     // commands.
7     //----------------------------------------------------------
8               *
9     USE("LIBRARY")            // Predefined 6.0 macro library
10    DISPLAY(Off!)            // Turn off display
11
12    IF (?BlockActive)        // Text selected
13        Msg="Text can't be selected when running macro!"
14        GO(Error)
15    ENDIF
16
17    MENULIST(spchar;
18        {"Section";
19        "Paragraph";
20        "Section w/hard sp";
21        "Paragraph w/hard sp";
22        "Registered";
23        "Copyright";
24        "Trademark";
25        "British Pound";
26        "Japanese Yen"};
27        "Special Character Menu")
28
29    SWITCH(spchar)                // evaluate each of the 9 choices
30        CASEOF 1: TypeChar(4;6)
31        CASEOF 2: TypeChar(4;5)
32        CASEOF 3: GO(sectsp)
33        CASEOF 4: GO(parasp)
34        CASEOF 5: TypeChar(4;22)
35        CASEOF 6: TypeChar(4;23)
36        CASEOF 7: TypeChar(4;41)
37        CASEOF 8: TypeChar(4;11)
38        CASEOF 9: TypeChar(4;12)
39    ENDSWITCH
40
41    LABEL(End)               // End of macro (w/o error)
42        RETURN
43
```

continues

Listing 46.3. continued

```
44   LABEL(sectsp)              // Section symbol w/hard space
45       TypeChar(4;6)
46       HSpace
47       GO(End)
48
49   LABEL(parasp)              // Paragraph symbol w/hard space
50       TypeChar(4;5)
51       HSpace
52       GO(End)
53
54   LABEL(Error)               // Error message if text selected
55       BEEP
56       Message(msg)                 // Procedure from "library.wpm"
57       RETURN                       // End of macro (with error)
58
59   // End of macro
```

Description of SPCHAR.WPM

▲ Lines 1–7: These are the usual introductory comment lines that name and describe the macro in general terms.

▲ Lines 9–10: The USE and DISPLAY commands are the same as they are in all other macros in this chapter.

▲ Lines 12–15: This IF clause checks whether the macro is being run while the block is active (text selected or not). If so, an error message is passed to the LABEL(*Error*) and execution is stopped immediately.

▲ Lines 17–27: These lines are the core of the MENULIST command. The variable spchar is assigned the result of one of the selections below it. Note that although it isn't necessary, each selection has been indented and placed on a separate line for greater clarity.

▲ Lines 29–39: These lines process the result of whatever item was selected from the menu displayed on screen (including nothing selected). For each possible selection, there is a corresponding CASEOF statement. Notice that selection numbers 3 and 4 require a GO command, which directs execution to jump to a LABEL subroutine later in the macro. This is needed because codes (in this instance, [HSpace]) can't be placed inside either the TypeChar() or Type() product commands. These commands allow only text as parameters. If no selection is made, none of the CASEOF statements are processed, and the macro continues at line 40.

▲ Lines 41–42: This LABEL routine marks the official end of the macro and is referred to by several routines. It consists of a single command, RE-TURN. The RETURN command is used rather than the QUIT command, because it's more flexible. A `QUIT` command doesn't always terminate macro execution. The `RETURN` command returns control to a parent macro (if the macro was originally `NEST`ed by another macro). If no parent exists, the macro terminates, just like the `QUIT` command. The `RETURN` command, therefore, offers the option of designing macros that are modular in nature and that can be easily `NEST`ed by other macros. Use QUIT only when you want to terminate a macro 100 percent of the time.

▲ Lines 44–47: This subroutine types the section symbol, followed by a hard space and directs the macro to continue with the subroutine *End*.

▲ Lines 49–52: This subroutine is the same as in lines 44–47, except that the paragraph symbol is typed, followed by a hard space.

▲ Lines 54–57: This subroutine displays an error message to the user if the block is active when the macro is run. Line 55 calls a PROCEDURE from the LIBRARY.WPM set of routines that ship with WordPerfect 6.0.

Counting Words in a Document

WordPerfect's Spell Check feature counts the total number of words in your document or within a selected block of text. Spell Check isn't capable of counting the number of occurrences of a *specific* word or phrase, however. This macro allows you to type a word or phrase, and it informs you of the number of occurrences found. To run this macro, do one of the following:

1. Click the Wordcnt button on the 60SUPER button bar (if Button Bar is selected).

2. Choose Tools, Macro, Play or press Alt+F10. Type the name wordcnt and choose OK or press Enter.

Listing 46.4. WORDCNT.WPM.

```
1    //---------------------------------------------------------------
2    //    WORDCNT.WPM
3    //---------------------------------------------------------------
4    // Prompts user for a word or phrase and then counts the
     // number
5    // of occurrences of that word or phrase throughout the
     // document
6    // or a range of selected text. Macro finishes with a prompt
7    // telling user how many times word/phrase was located.
```

continues

Listing 46.4. continued

```
8     //-----------------------------------------------------------
9
10    USE("LIBRARY")            // Predefined 6.0 macro library
11    DISPLAY(Off!)             // Turn off display
12
13    IF(?DocBlank)             // Check whether document is blank
14        Msg="Cannot run this macro from a blank document!"
15        GO(Error)
16    ENDIF
17
18    IF (?BlockActive)         // Check whether text has been
      selected
19        block=1                       // Set flag for later
20        Copy                          // Copy selected text
21        FileNew                       // Open new document window
22        Paste                         // Paste in new document window
23    ELSE
24        block=0                       // Set flag for later
25    ENDIF
26
27    GETSTRING(srchstr;
28        "Type a word or phrase, then press ENTER";
29        "Count Word or Phrase";50)
30    count=0                   // Initialize counter
31    PosDocVryTop              // Move insertion point to top of
doc
32    ONNOTFOUND(NoMore)        // Set condition for when search
      fails
33
34    // This subroutine is the principal routine of the macro.
35    // The word or phrase input as "srchstr" is searched for.
36    // Each time it is found, the variable "count" is incremented
37    // by 1. When the search fails, the ONNOTFOUND command kicks
in.
38    LABEL(SrchNext)
39        SrchStr(srchstr)
40        SrchNext()
41        count=count+1
42        GO(SrchNext)
43
44    LABEL(NoMore)             // Assign singular or plural prompt
45        IF(count=1)
46        occur="time"
47            ELSE
48        occur="times"
49            ENDIF
50        // First check whether block was active at beginning of
          // macro.
```

```
51          // If so, SrchNext looping was done in a new document
            // window.
52          // Close window and return to original document/original
53          // insertion point position.
54          IF(block)
55                Close
56     ENDIF
57
58          // This next section beeps, then displays a prompt with
            // info
59          // on how many times "srchstr" was found. Message is
            // calling
60          // a PROCEDURE from the WP60 LIBRARY.WPM file.
61          BEEP
62          Message("'" + srchstr +  "' was located " + count + " "
+
63               occur + " in this document.")
64          RETURN                    // End of macro (w/o error)
65
66     LABEL(Error)                   // Error message if text selected
67          BEEP
68          Message(msg)              // Procedure from "library.wpm"
69          RETURN                    // End of macro (with error)
70
71     // End of macro
```

Description of WORDCNT.WPM

▲ Lines 1–8: These are the usual introductory comment lines that name and describe the macro in general terms.

▲ Lines 10–11: The USE and DISPLAY commands are the same as for all other macros in this chapter.

▲ Lines 13–16: This IF clause checks whether the macro is being run from within a blank document. If so, execution is immediately stopped, and the user is prompted with an error message.

▲ Lines 18–25: This next IF clause checks whether the block is active at the time the macro is run. If so, the selected text is copied and pasted into a new document window. The search routines are then run on that section of text in the new document window rather than the full document on screen in the original document window.

▲ Lines 27–32: This section begins with a prompt for the word or phrase on which user wishes to perform the search/count operation. The count variable is initialized at 0 (to avoid an undefined variable error). The insertion point is then moved to the very top of the document (either original or selected text in new document window), and a condition is set for when the last occurrence of the search string is reached (ONNOTFOUND).

▲ Lines 34–42: This is the principal routine of the macro. Each time the search string defined by the GETSTRING prompt is located, the variable count is incremented by 1 and the process is begun again. When the search string fails (no more occurrences), the ONNOTFOUND condition already specified kicks in and breaks out of the loop.

▲ Lines 44–49: Depending on the number of occurrences of the search string, this initial section defines whether the word *time* needs to be singular or plural in the final prompt to the user.

▲ Lines 50–56: This next section is run only if the block was active when the macro was initially run (block = 0). If so, the new document window is closed, and the insertion point is returned to the original document.

▲ Lines 58–64: This last section beeps and composes the final prompt that informs the user of how many occurrences of the search string were located.

▲ Lines 66–69: This LABEL (or subroutine) displays an error message to the user if the macro is run from a blank document. Line 68 calls a PROCEDURE from the LIBRARY.WPM set of routines that ship with Word-Perfect 6.0.

Page X of Y

WordPerfect 6.0 can place a page number code inside a header or footer so that the appropriate page number prints at the top or bottom of every page. It doesn't have the capability to place the page number in the format Page X of Y yet, however. The handy macro shown in Listing 46.5 places the format Page X of Y inside a Header A code on every page, except the first. It is easily revised to place the coding inside a Header B or Footer A or B code. To run this macro, do one of the following:

1. Click the Pagexy button on the 60SUPER button bar (if Button Bar is currently selected).

2. Choose Tools, Macro, Play; or press Alt+F10. Type in the name pagexy and choose OK or press Enter.

Listing 46.5. PAGEXY.WPM.

```
1    //--------------------------------------------------------
2    //
3    //--------------------------------------------------------
```

```
4    // This macro will create a Header A code with the numbering
5    // style "Page X of Y" If a Header A already exists, it will
6    // prompt the user with an error message.
7    //----------------------------------------------------------
8
9    USE("LIBRARY")              // Predefined 6.0 macro library
10   DISPLAY(Off!)               // Turn off display
11
12   IF(?DocBlank)               // Check whether document is blank
13        Msg="Cannot run this macro from a blank document!"
14        GO(Error)
15   ENDIF
16
17   // Go to bottom of document and assign page number to vari
     // able
18   PosDocVeryBottom
19   lastpg=?Page
20
21   // Go back to top of document and search for Header A code
22   ONNOTFOUND(Create)
23   PosDocVeryTop
24   SearchString("[Header A]")
25   SearchNext()
26
27   // If we reach this point, it is because a [Header A] code
28   // already exists. Warn user and terminate macro.
29   Msg="Header A already exists!"
30   Msg="Please examine document before rerunning macro."
31   GO(Error)
32
33   LABEL(Create)
34        HeaderA(Create!)            // Create [Header A] code
35        Center
36        Type("Page ")
37        PageNumberDisplayFormat
38        Type(" of " + lastpg)
39        HardReturn
40        SubstructureExit
41        Suppress(HeaderA!)
42        RETURN                      // End of macro (w/o error)
43
44   LABEL(Error)
45        BEEP
46        Message(msg)                // Procedure from "library.wpm"
47        RETURN                      // End of macro (with error)
48
49   // End of macro
```

Note: The variable Y is assigned from the last page of the document, so this macro won't work properly if there are multiple sections to the document, each one with a new page number 1.

Description of PAGEXY.WPM

▲ Lines 1–7: These are the usual introductory comment lines that name and describe the macro in general terms.

▲ Lines 9–10: The USE and DISPLAY commands are the same as for all other macros in this chapter.

▲ Lines 12–15: This IF clause checks whether the macro is being run from within a blank document. If so, execution is immediately stopped, and the user is prompted with an error message.

▲ Lines 17–19: The insertion point is moved to the bottom of the document, where the variable lastpg is assigned to the current page number.

▲ Lines 21–25: The insertion point is then moved back to the top of the document. A search is made for an existing [Header A] code. If found, the coding in Lines 27–31 is executed, and the user is prompted with an error message. Otherwise, the LABEL(Create) is executed.

▲ Lines 33–42: This section creates the [Header A] code and places the appropriate wording for Page X of Y inside, followed by a single hard return. The [Header A] code is also suppressed for the first page.

▲ Lines 44–47: This LABEL (or subroutine) displays an error message to the user if the macro is run from a blank document. Line 44 calls a PROCEDURE from the LIBRARY.WPM set of routines that ship with WordPerfect 6.0.

Merge

by Marilyn Horn Claff

Basic Merge

This chapter presents the fundamental concepts of merge and provides step-by-step instructions for common merge operations. You'll learn two ways to create a data file, as well as how to create a form file. You'll then perform a merge to produce a mailing consisting of letters, envelopes, and labels. If your needs are simple, this chapter probably covers all the merge skills you need.

Understanding Merge Concepts

It's no accident that although other word processing systems use terms like *Mail Merge* or *Print Merge*, WordPerfect calls its merge feature simply *Merge*. In WordPerfect, as you'll see in later chapters, merging goes far beyond mass mailings, and merge results are not necessarily sent directly to the printer. With WordPerfect's Merge, you can assemble one-of-a-kind documents, such as legal contracts from boilerplate documents, format a company phone directory from a list of names and phone numbers, or create an interactive fax cover sheet that pauses for you to fill it in.

Merging in WordPerfect involves three basic steps:

▲ Preparing a file, called a data file, that contains the variable information that will be plugged into the form document.

▲ Preparing the form document that contains special codes to tell WordPerfect where to insert the variable data.

▲ Beginning the merge.

> **Note:** Earlier versions of WordPerfect called form documents *Primary Merge Files* and data files *Secondary Merge Files*.

WordPerfect merges a copy of the form document with each entry, or record, in the data file. Unlike most other word processors, which send the merged data directly to the printer, WordPerfect by default creates a single, unnamed document for the merge output in an unused document window. Each new merged document is appended to this unnamed document. As the merge takes place, WordPerfect automatically allows the correct amount of space for the data, wrapping lines and flowing the document onto a new page if necessary. When the merge is complete, you can edit, print, or save the merged document.

> **Note:** If you prefer to merge to the printer instead of sending the merged output to an empty document window, you can choose that as an option from the Run Merge dialog box (see Chapter 48, "Intermediate Merging").

Creating the Data File

The first step in performing a merge is to create a data file. A data file is a structured list of similar items. All the information relating to a single item in the list is called a *record*. For example, if you are sending a letter to the alumni of your school requesting contributions for a new computer lab, all the information in your file that pertains to a single alumnus or alumna constitutes a record.

Each record is comprised of one or more *fields*. A field is simply a piece of information within a record. For each person in your alumni data file, you have similar pieces of information: name, address, year of graduation, and amount of last contribution.

The fields must be in the same order for each record. For example, if the name field is the first field in one record, it must be the first field in every record for the merge to work properly. If you are missing a piece of information for a record, such as the year of graduation, the record must contain a blank field. In most cases, all the records in a data file should have the same number of fields. (WordPerfect allows you to use a variable number of fields per record in advanced merge applications, but don't concern yourself with that here.)

The most important step in creating a data file comes before you actually begin entering data: planning. It's essential to consider how you'll use the data file in future merges you may perform, as well as the one at hand. You need to decide what data you need to provide for each record and how you should divide it into fields. Changing the number and order of the fields is difficult to do after you've entered your data.

> **Tip:** Standardize your field names as much as possible. If you use the same field names in all your data files containing those fields, you'll be able to mix and match data and form files more easily.

If you're lazy, or if you're doing a one-time-only "quick-and-dirty" merge, you'll probably want to use as few fields as possible. By minimizing the number of fields, you can cut out some steps and speed up the data entry. If there's even a remote chance that you'll need to reuse the data file in another merge, be careful about cutting corners. Using too few fields is a very common error. What you gain in ease of use and productivity, you lose in flexibility. The more fields you define, the more flexibility you'll have.

Look at the alumni list. The lazy way to set it up would be to have just three fields:

- ▲ Name and address
- ▲ Year of graduation
- ▲ Amount of last donation

If you combine the name and address in a single field, you'll be limited to addressing each person as "Dear Sir or Madam." You could separate the name and address into two fields, but you still have a problem: your salutation would still sound unnatural.

Your letters would read "Dear Mr. Franklin Smith" and "Dear Ms. Elizabeth Jenkins."

> **Tip:** The length of a field can vary from record to record. For example, an address field could contain from 0-5 lines in a typical data file. There are no absolute limits for the length of fields, the number of fields per record, or the number of records per data file. There are limits for the number of *named* fields per record, however.

The solution is to break the name field down further. At a minimum, you'll need a first name and a last name field. You might also want to have a title field (Mr., Ms., or Dr.). If you care about making a good impression (and if you're serious about fund-raising, you do), you should also have a salutation field so you can write more personal salutations such as "Dear Frank" or "Dear Buffy." The salutation field should contain the version of the name that you'll use after the word *Dear* in your form letter.

Tip: Using an informal salutation ("Dear Hillary") to someone whom you've never met, or a formal salutation ("Dear Ms. Clinton") to someone you know well sounds false and is sure to offend the recipient. The best way to avoid this potential problem is to include a separate salutation field in your data file. That way, you can choose the most appropriate greeting for each person in the list on a case-by-case basis.

The next step is to decide how to handle the address. You'll probably want to take advantage of lower postal rates for presorted and bar-coded mail, so make things easy for yourself by putting the zip code in a field by itself. Now consider the rest of the address: will you ever need to sort or select people on your list by city or state? If the answer is yes, make these separate fields also. If not, you can leave the address, except for the zip code, as a single field.

Note: In some cases, you can sort or select records by city and state without making these separate fields, but it's trickier and you're more likely to run into problems. There's even a way to sort and select by the last word in a field, so you can sort and select by zip code even if the zip code is not defined as a separate field. But why make life difficult?

Now that you've planned your data file, create it. Start by choosing Tools, Merge, Define; or press Shift+F9. The Merge Codes dialog box, shown in Figure 47.1, is displayed.

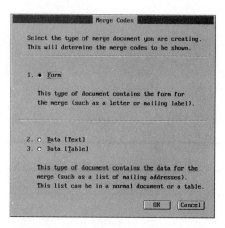

Figure 47.1. The initial Merge Codes dialog box. (This dialog box only appears the *first* time you select merge codes in a form or data file.)

Note: If you are in a merge file (either a form or a data file), WordPerfect skips the Merge Codes dialog box. If your screen does not look like Figure 47.1, try again from an empty document window.

The Form file option is selected when you open the Merge Codes dialog box, but you'll start by creating a data file, because you need to have a data file in order to create a form file. Notice that the Merge Codes dialog box offers a choice between two types of data files: Data [Text] and Data [Table]. These methods are equivalent, and in many cases it doesn't matter which method you use. I'll create a data file in each format and then offer a few tips to help you decide which method to use for your own data.

Creating the Data File as Text

If you choose the option to create the data file as text, you'll create the data file as a regular WordPerfect document and insert special WordPerfect merge codes to mark the end of each field and record. This method is essentially the same method that earlier versions of WordPerfect use.

From the Merge Codes dialog box, choose Data [Text]. The Merge Codes (Text Data File) dialog box, shown in Figure 47.2, appears.

Figure 47.2. The Merge Codes (Text Data File) dialog box.

Defining Field Names

The next step is to define the field names. The Field Names option lets you assign names to each field so that you don't have to refer to them by number in your form file. Although field names are optional, working with field names is much easier than working with field numbers, especially if you have more than a few fields.

Tip: Another reason for using field names instead of field numbers is that you can merge multiple data files whose fields are in a different sequence with the same form file. If you used numbered fields in the data file, you would have to edit the form file if the order of the fields changed in one of the data files. As long as the fields are named properly, WordPerfect doesn't care what order they are in.

Procedure 47.1. Changing field names.

1. Choose Field Names. The Field Names dialog box, shown in Figure 47.3, appears.

Figure 47.3. The Field Names dialog box.

2. In the Field Name text box, type the name of the first field that you plan to use in your data file, and press Enter. For example, type Last Name and press Enter. The name disappears from the Field Name text box and is inserted in the Field Name list box.

Tip: For merging, the order of the field names in your data file is completely immaterial; however, it's a good idea to make your first field the field by which you are most likely to sort. For example, if the data file contains names and addresses of individuals, make your first field the last name field, because you are most likely to sort the list by last name. You can sort the data file by any field, but because WordPerfect uses the first field as its default sort key, putting the sort field first saves you a step each time you sort.

720

Procedure 47.2. Defining field names.

1. Add the remaining field names: First Name, Address, City, State, Zip Code, Class, and Last Gift.

> **Note:** WordPerfect allows a maximum of 255 named fields in a text data file, but you can use even more fields if you reference the additional fields by number.

> **Note:** It doesn't matter whether you use upper- or lowercase letters for the field names ("zip code," "Zip Code," and "ZIP CODE" are all the same name to WordPerfect). Field names can contain spaces, but the spaces count. In other words, WordPerfect considers "Zip Code" and "ZipCode" to be different names.

2. After you have added the last field name to the list, press Enter in the empty Field Name text box. The focus of the dialog box moves to the OK button.

3. Examine the list of field names. If you need to make any changes, choose Field Name List. The four options below the Field Name List, previously grayed out, become active. Using these options, you can insert a new field name above the highlighted name, add a new field name to the end of the list, edit a field name, or delete a field name from the list.

4. When you have finished editing the field name list, choose OK and press Enter to return to your document and begin entering the data.

Changing Field Names

What if you need to edit the field names after you have closed the Field Names dialog box? If you redisplay the Field Names dialog box, it comes up blank, and you would have to reenter all the names from scratch. You'd also have to delete the original Field Names code, along with the end record code and hard page break in your document.

There's an easier way to handle this situation, although it may not be apparent depending on how you've set your preferences.

3. From the document editing window, choose Tools, Merge, Define; or press Shift+F9 to display the Merge Codes (Text Data File) dialog box.

4. Change the Display of Merge Codes to Show Full Codes, if it is not already set that way. (If the display is set to either of the other options, Show Codes as Icons or Hide Codes, you won't be able to edit the field name list.)

The FIELDNAMES merge code should be visible at the beginning of your document, followed by a list of the field names in parentheses, an ENDRECORD code, and a hard page break. The field names are separated by semicolons. Your screen should resemble Figure 47.4.

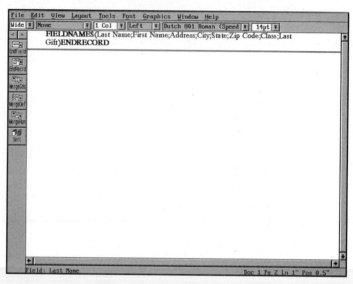

Figure 47.4. The field names merge code.

5. Move the insertion point to the closing parenthesis and type a semicolon and the name of the field to be added. For example, type ;Salutation. (If you have not already entered data in the file, you could insert the new field name between two other field names instead of at the end of the list.) Move the insertion point to the beginning of the file by pressing Home, Home, up arrow. This action causes WordPerfect to execute the field names code and update the list of field names so they display correctly on the status line. Then, move your insertion point to the end of the file, after the hard page break, so you can enter the data.

Entering Data

Defining merge field names is the first step in creating the data text file. WordPerfect treats the FIELDNAMES command as a special record in your data file. Like all merge records in a text data file, the field names record ends with the merge command ENDRECORD and a hard page break. Unless you turned off the merge code display, you should see the ENDRECORD code and the hard page break on-screen. Your insertion point should be after the hard page break, and the prompt on the left side of the status line should say Field: Last Name.

Note: If you do not define field names for your data file, the status line prompt says `Field: n`, where n represents the number of the field.

Tip: Because WordPerfect separates records in a text data file by hard page breaks, the page number on the status line is a handy indication of the number of the record you are working on. (Just subtract one from the page number if you are using field names.)

Procedure 47.3. Entering data for your first record.

To enter the data for your first record, follow these steps:

1. Type the last name.
2. Do *not* type a space or press Enter after typing the name.
3. Press F9 to insert the `ENDFIELD` code.

Note: You must enter merge codes such as `ENDFIELD` and `ENDRECORD` through the shortcut keys or dialog boxes; you cannot type them from the keyboard as regular text.

The cursor moves to the next line, and the message on the status line changes to `Field: First Name`.

4. Continue to enter data for each field according to the prompt on the status line. After entering each field, press F9 to insert the `ENDFIELD` code.

Tip: Alternatively, you can enter the `ENDFIELD` code by pressing Shift+F9, f. This key combination could be helpful if you've remapped your F9 key.

After you enter your last defined field, notice that the status prompt changes to `Field: 10`. You could enter additional unnamed fields if you wanted; WordPerfect does not require all the fields to be named. In the example, the change to a field number in the prompt is a visual clue that you have entered all the fields that you defined for the record.

5. To mark the end of the record, press Shift+F9, e. WordPerfect inserts an `ENDRECORD` field and a hard page break. The status line changes to `Field: Last Name`, and you are all set to enter your next record.

6. Enter the remaining records.
7. Save the file as TEXT.DF.

 Tip: Get into the habit of saving your data file frequently as you work.

 Tip: You could eliminate a step by creating a macro that inserts the ENDRECORD code and hard page break and then saves your file.

Printing a Text Data File

If you try to print your text data file as a regular file, you'll run into a problem. The merge codes will print correctly (if they have not been reduced to icons or hidden), but because you added a hard page break between each record, you'll print only one record per page, a great waste of paper. As in WordPerfect 5.1, you could eliminate the hard page breaks before printing, but this involves an extra step.

Fortunately, WordPerfect 6.0 has an easy solution to this problem. Simply press Shift+F9 to display the Merge Codes (Text Data File) dialog box, and choose Print. WordPerfect will print a blank line in place of every hard page break.

Creating the Data File as a Table

Using a table is another way to enter your merge data. With the table method, each record is a row, and each field in the record is a cell. You may prefer this method because it eliminates the need to enter special merge codes in your data file. You're also less likely to enter fields in the wrong order.

To create a data file as a table, follow these steps:

Procedure 47.4. Creating a data file as a table.

1. From a blank screen, press Tools, Merge, Define; or press Shift+F9 to display the Merge Codes dialog box.
2. Choose Data [Table]. The Merge Codes (Table Data File) dialog box appears. (See Figure 47.5.)
3. Choose Create a Table with Field Names. The Field Names dialog box appears. You can define a maximum of 25 fields per record in a data table file.

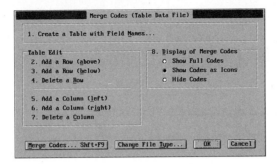

Figure 47.5. The Merge Codes (Table Data File) dialog box.

4. Enter the field names as described in the previous section and choose OK to return to the editing window.

WordPerfect creates a two-row table with a column for each field that you defined, as shown in Figure 47.6. The first row in the table contains the field names, one per column. The second row is blank.

5. Enter the fields for your first record, one field per cell.

6. After typing the last field in the last cell of the row, press Tab to expand the table by one row.

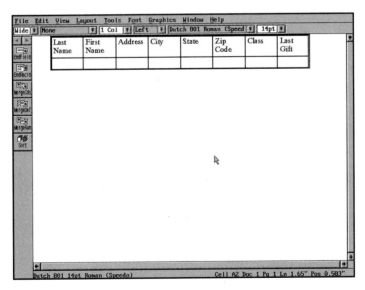

Figure 47.6. The table data file with field names.

Tip: If the text wraps in the middle of a field, it won't hurt anything, but it may make your data harder to read. To avoid word wrap, try adjusting the column widths, reducing the left and right margins, or using a smaller point size or a landscape page.

7. Enter the remaining records.
8. Save the file as TABLE.DF.

Changing the Format of a Data Table

Because a data table is a regular WordPerfect table, you can use any of the table editing options in the Table Edit dialog box to change the format of the table. (With the insertion point in the table, choose Layout, Tables, Edit; or press Alt+F11.) For many common operations, there's an easier way: press Shift+F9 to display the Merge Codes (Table Data File) dialog box (see Figure 47.5). WordPerfect remembers that you are in a table data file and skips the Merge Codes dialog box.

From this dialog box, you can insert rows before or after the current row or delete the current row. Similarly, you can insert columns before or after the current column or delete the current column.

Changing the Field Names in a Data Table

Changing the field names in a data table is a straightforward operation because the field names are regular text, not special merge codes as in data text files. Simply edit the text in the cells of the first row.

Choosing Between Data Text and Data Table Files

Now that you've learned how to create data text and data table files, you're probably wondering which method you should use for your own data.

The advantages of table data files are obvious. Table data files eliminate the need for the ENDFIELD and ENDRECORD merge codes required by the text data files. The ENDFIELD and ENDRECORD codes are cumbersome to enter and tend to clutter the screen. True, WordPerfect has options to reduce merge codes to icons or to hide them from view, but then you cannot tell at a glance if your data file is formatted correctly. With tables, you can usually tell immediately if the data records were entered correctly, because corresponding fields are aligned in columns.

Another advantage to using tables is that adding and deleting records is easier—you just insert or delete rows. With text data files, you could use WordPerfect's Page Delete feature to delete records, but there is no easy way to insert new records. More importantly, with a table data file, you don't have to worry about inadvertently creating a record with the wrong number of fields; with a text file, this mistake is very easy to make because the file is unstructured. The burden of formatting a record correctly in a text data file rests entirely on the shoulders of the user.

Tables also make it easy to add or remove fields from every record by simply inserting or deleting a column. Performing the same operation in a text data file would require complex macros that would be difficult and time-consuming to write.

Note: The table method may not work well if any of your merge fields are long, because a table cell cannot be split over a page break.

Why, then, would anyone ever choose to enter data using the text file format? For one thing, a text data file allows up to 255 named fields. (The number of fields in a text file has no absolute limit, but only the first 255 can be named.) By contrast, the maximum number of fields in a table data file is only 25. (Table fields are always named; WordPerfect has no option for skipping this step.) The practical number of fields in a table data file is even smaller because the columns will be too narrow to enter text without wrapping. If the text wraps, it will still merge correctly, but it becomes very difficult to enter and proofread data on-screen.

A second reason for using the text data format is that this is the format WordPerfect uses when you import WordPerfect 5.1 merge files, or when you convert ASCII delimited files to WordPerfect format. (It's possible to use ASCII delimited files without converting, as you'll see in the next chapter.)

Finally, editing and printing a table is always slower than editing and printing regular text. If you have a slow computer or a large data file, you may prefer to create your merge data file as a text file to get better performance. Some users may find that tables are so much easier to use that speed doesn't matter.

Because WordPerfect does not provide any way to convert between table and text data files, users need to make the correct choice before entering data. (*SuperBook* readers don't need to worry about this problem because we've provided macros on the disk included with this book that convert text files to table files and vice versa.)

Creating the Form File

After creating your data file, you need to create your form file. A form file is a WordPerfect document that contains merge codes to tell WordPerfect where to insert the fields from the data file.

727

Note: To insert Merge codes in a document, you must choose them from a dialog box or use a shortcut key. Although the codes look like regular text, you cannot enter them by typing the commands from the keyboard.

From a blank screen, press Tools, Merge, Define; or press Shift+F9. Choose Form (the default), and the Merge Codes (Form File) dialog box appears (see Figure 47.7).

Figure 47.7. The Merge Codes (Form File) dialog box.

Entering the Merge Date Code

Because you are creating a standard business letter, you'll start by entering the DATE merge code for the current date. As you can see from Figure 47.7, the date code is not listed among the Common Merge Codes. To insert the date code, you must open the All Merge Codes dialog box by pressing Shift+F9 (see Figure 47.8).

Figure 47.8. The All Merge Codes dialog box.

728

Tip: To open the All Merge Codes dialog box directly from the editing screen (after you have opened a form file), press Shift+F9 twice.

The All Merge Codes dialog box displays an alphabetical list of all of WordPerfect's merge programming commands. The dialog box is in Name Search mode, which means that if you begin to type the name of a command, WordPerfect searches for the closest match and highlights that name. To jump to the DATE command, type d in the text entry box (see Figure 47.8). Because DATE is the first command beginning with the letter *d*, WordPerfect highlights it. (If WordPerfect does not highlight the command that you want, continue typing the remaining letters in the name of the command until the command is highlighted.) Notice that the description below the command list box changes to Current date. Click Select or press Enter to insert the DATE code in your form document.

If WordPerfect's Display Merge Codes option is set to Show Full Codes (the default setting), the date code appears in your document as the word *DATE*. When you perform the merge, the date code is replaced by text representing the current date.

Tip: The merge DATE code uses your default date format, unless you insert a code for a different date format ahead of the merge DATE code in the form document. To enter a date format code, choose Tools, Date, Format; or press Shift+F5. Then select a date format from the twelve predefined date formats, or choose Edit to define a custom date format.

To insert additional space between the date and the inside address, press Enter twice.

Entering the Field Names

Now you are ready to enter the field name codes for the elements that make up the inside address.

Procedure 47.5. Entering field name codes.
1. Press Shift+F9 to display the Merge Codes (Form File) dialog box.
2. Choose Field from the five items in Common Merge Codes list. WordPerfect displays the Parameter Entry dialog box shown in Figure 47.9.
3. If you know the exact name for the field that you wish to insert, type it in the text entry box.
4. If you don't know the exact name, press F5 to list field names.

729

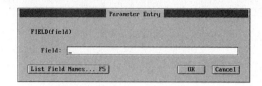

Figure 47.9. The Parameter Entry dialog box.

Because you have not yet selected a data file to use with the form file you are creating, a dialog box prompts you to Select Data File for Field Names (see Figure 47.10).

Figure 47.10. The Select Data File For Field Names dialog box.

5. Type TEXT.DF and press Enter or click Select.

6. If the data file is not in the current directory, type the full path name. The screen returns to the Parameter Entry dialog box (see Figure 47.9).

7. Press F5 to display a list of field names. WordPerfect displays the List Field Names dialog box shown in Figure 47.11.

Figure 47.11. The List Field Names dialog box.

8. Move the highlight bar to the FIRST NAME field and choose Select or press Enter. WordPerfect inserts FIELD(First Name) into your document at the cursor position.

Note: Merge codes may appear in one of three different ways, depending on how you set Display of Merge Codes in View, Screen Setup or in the Merge Codes dialog box for a form or data file.

9. Type a space after inserting the FIRST NAME field, then insert the LAST NAME field by pressing Shift+F9, selecting Field, and either typing Last Name or pressing F5 to display the Field Name List and choosing Last Name from the list.

10. On the same line, type , Class of followed by a space and the CLASS field name.

11. Press Enter to move the insertion point to the next line. Then insert the ADDRESS field name and press Enter.

12. Press Enter to move the insertion point to the next line. Then insert the CITY field name, type a comma and a space, insert the STATE field name, type a space, and insert the ZIP (code) field name.

13. Press Enter twice. Then type Dear followed by a space and insert the SALUTATION field name and a colon, and press Enter twice.

Now type the body of the letter:

You ought to be ashamed of yourself, **FIELD(First Name)**, you penny-pinching cheapskate. The class of **FIELD(Class)** is the stingiest one in the illustrious history of our beloved Alma Mater, and you, **FIELD(First Name)**, are no exception. Your wretched donation of **FIELD(Last Gift)** doesn't even cover the amount we spent on you last year for our fundraising campaign.

You must certainly be aware that we are in dire need of funds for the following worthy causes:

Won't you consider making a donation commensurate with the value of your education?

Sincerely,

Priscilla P. Pringle

Chairperson, Annual Fund

Spell-check the letter and save it as FUNDRAIS.FF. Your form letter should look like Figure 47.12.

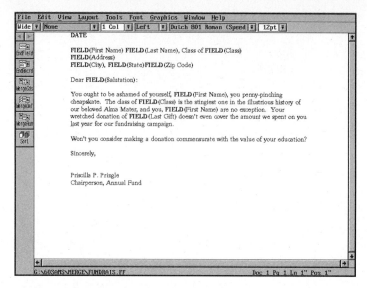

Figure 47.12. The FUNDRAIS.FF Merge Form file.

You're ready to merge!

Performing the Merge

To perform the actual merge, begin with the form letter still on your screen.

Procedure 47.6. Performing the merge.

1. Choose Tools, Merge, Run; or press Ctrl+F9.

2. From the Merge/Sort dialog box, choose Merge.

   The Run Merge dialog box appears, as shown in Figure 47.13.

   The first two text entry boxes on the Run Merge dialog box are drop-down file list boxes that display the last four form files and data files that you used.

3. To use the form file that is already on your screen, press Tab to move the focus from the Form File text box to the Data File text box.

   As soon you move the insertion point to the Data File text box, the words *(Current Document)* appear in the Form File text box.

4. Enter the name of the data file, or press the down arrow to display a list of the last four data files you have used.

> **Note:** The last four files for the form file and the data file text boxes are separate from the Open Document file list.

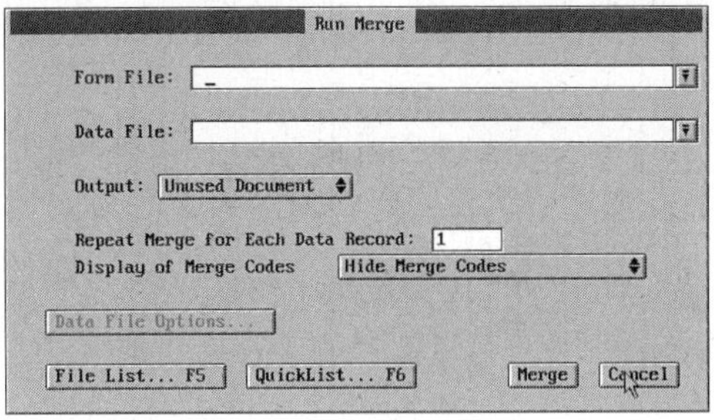

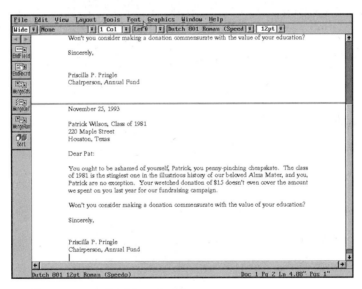

Figure 47.13. The Run Merge dialog box.

Note that the output option button is set for Unused Document.

Choose Merge, and you're done. When the merge is finished, the insertion point will be at the end of the last letter. Your screen should look like the one shown in Figure 47.14.

Figure 47.14. The completed fundraising merge.

Merging the Same Files

You're probably thinking that what you've just done is too much work, and you're right. Fortunately, although a lot of steps are required to set up your first merge, doing a merge with existing files is simple.

733

Starting from a blank screen, follow these steps:

Procedure 47.7. Merging existing files.
1. Select Tools, Merge, Run; or press Ctrl+F9. The Run Merge dialog box appears.
2. Select Form File and choose a form file from the drop-down list.
3. Select Data File and choose a data file from the drop-down list.
4. Select Merge.

Formatting Considerations for Merge Files

To make your merge as efficient as possible, as well as to avoid potential problems, you need to pay special attention to how you format your form file. If necessary, review the distinction between placing formatting codes at the beginning of the form file and placing the formatting codes in Document Initial Codes. As much of your formatting as possible should be placed in Document Initial Codes. This way, the formatting codes won't be repeated at the beginning of every merged letter, as they would be if they were placed at the beginning of the letter itself. Although you may not have formatting problems if you place the codes in the document itself instead of in Document Initial Codes, the resulting extra codes will cause editing and printing in WordPerfect to slow down because the extra codes must be interpreted by WordPerfect's formatter, even if they are redundant.

by Marilyn Horn Claff

Intermediate Merging

In this chapter, you'll learn to use more advanced merge features that enable you to handle most routine merge tasks. This chapter presents four main topics:

▲ How to create an interactive merge.

▲ How to merge with a data file in ASCII delimited format.

▲ How to take advantage of merge options that don't require programming.

▲ How to select records for merging.

Merge from the Keyboard (Interactive Merge)

So far, you've performed a basic merge that combines data from a file with a form letter. In WordPerfect, you can also perform a merge without a data file. Merging from the keyboard is a technique to make merging interactive. Instead of taking data fields from a data file, WordPerfect pauses for you to type the information at the keyboard, saving you the step of creating a data file.

Merging from the keyboard is useful when you are creating only a single document or a small number of documents at a time, when the document you are creating needs to be customized each time, when you know that you will not need to reuse the data, or when human interaction is required for intelligent decision-making. Memos, fax cover sheets, and certificates of service are good applications for merging from the keyboard because they follow a standard format, yet must be customized each time. Moreover, the data that is merged into these forms is largely unique and cannot be pulled in from a pre-existing data file. If you don't plan to reuse the data, taking the time to create a data file usually does not make sense.

WordPerfect even allows you to combine merging from the keyboard with merging from a data file. You'll look at an example of a combination merge later in this chapter.

Pausing for Input from the User

Creating a form file that you can use interactively in a merge from the keyboard is a snap. To create a form file that can be used interactively, just use the KEYBOARD() merge code wherever you want the merge to pause for user input. Like all merge codes, KEYBOARD() must be selected from the Merge Codes dialog box; you cannot type it into your document directly.

Note: The KEYBOARD() code takes the place of two merge codes in WordPerfect 5.1: {KEYBOARD} and {INPUT}message.

In this example, you'll convert a standard memo to an interactive form file, instead of creating the form file from scratch. (The original memo is called MEMO.ORG on the *Super Book* disk.) To create an interactive form file, follow these steps:

Procedure 48.1. Creating an interactive form file.

1. Open MEMO.ORG (see Figure 48.1). Move the insertion point to the word *Whomever* and delete the remainder of the line.

Note: Use Ctrl+right arrow to move the insertion point to the beginning of the next word. To delete from the insertion point to the remainder of the line, press Ctrl+End.

2. Press Shift+F9 to display the Merge Codes dialog box. Choose Form, then OK. WordPerfect displays the Merge Codes (Form File) dialog box shown in Figure 48.2.

3. Choose Keyboard. The Keyboard merge code instructs WordPerfect to pause for input during a merge. The merge resumes when the user presses F9.

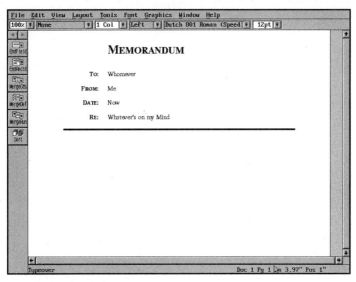

Figure 48.1. MEMO.ORG Standard Memo.

4. At the Parameter Entry dialog box, enter the prompt for the To: field. For example, type Enter name of recipient and press F9 (see Figure 48.3).

This prompt is displayed on the status line when the merge is paused at the Keyboard code. The prompt parameter is optional.

Figure 48.2. The Merge Codes (Form File) dialog box.

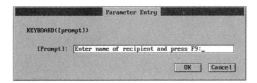

Figure 48.3. The Parameter Entry dialog box: entering a prompt for the keyboard.

Tip: If the context makes the required input clear, you don't need to enter a prompt message for the Keyboard command. It's a good idea, however, to include at least one prompt in each form file to remind the user to press the F9 key to resume the merge.

5. Move the insertion point to the word *Me*, delete the remainder of the line, and insert your own name.

6. Move the insertion point to the word *Now*, delete the remainder of the line, and insert merge date code by pressing Shift+F9, Shift+F9, d and choosing Select. (See Chapter 47, "Basic Merge," for a discussion of the merge date code.)

7. Move the insertion point to the word *Whatever's* and delete the remainder of the line.

8. Press Shift+F9 and choose Keyboard.

9. At the Parameter Entry dialog box (see Figure 48.3), enter the prompt for the Re: field. For example, type Enter subject and press F9.

10. Save the memo as MEMO.FF. Your memo should look like the one shown in Figure 48.4.

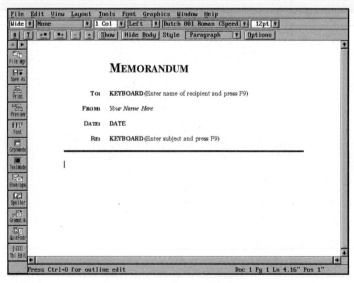

Figure 48.4. MEMO.FF Form File for merge from the keyboard.

Tip: It's a good idea to use identifying filename extensions, such as FF for "Form File" and DF for "Data File," so that you'll be able to tell which files are merge files simply by viewing a list of your files.

Running the Merge from the Keyboard

You start a merge from the keyboard the same way that you start a regular merge.

Procedure 48.2. Starting a merge from the keyboard.

1. Choose **Tools**, **Merge**, **Run**; or press Ctrl+F9 and select Merge. The Run Merge dialog box appears, as shown in Figure 48.5.

Note: The Run Merge dialog box has two versions. This is the shorter version. The longer version is shown in Figure 48.12.

Figure 48.5. The Run Merge dialog box (short version).

2. At the **F**orm File text entry box, enter the name of the form file. For example, type MEMO.FF.

3. To use a form file on the current screen, press Backspace to delete the current setting. WordPerfect inserts the words *(Current Document)* to indicate that it will use the document on the screen.

Note: The drop-down file list displays a list of the last four merge form files that you have used. If the file you need is not listed and you do not remember its name, press F5 to display the file list for the

> current directory, or press F6 to display the QuickList dialog box. You can also choose Clipboard to select the contents of the Shell Clipboard for the form file, the data file, or both. Shell enables you to use up to 80 separate clipboards.

4. At the **D**ata File prompt, leave the text entry box blank.

5. Choose Merge.

   WordPerfect pauses at the first KEYBOARD code. In MEMO.FF, the first KEYBOARD code is at the To: field. If you entered an optional prompt in the Parameter Entry dialog box, the prompt is displayed on the status line of the screen (see Figure 48.6).

> **Note:** If you are using WordPerfect's default settings, the merge codes are not displayed during the merge.

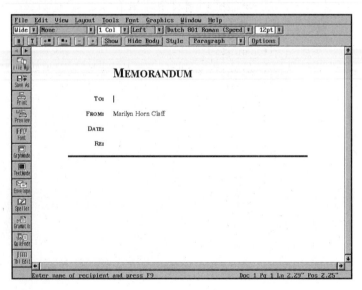

Figure 48.6. MEMO.FF. Pausing for input at the keyboard merge code.

6. Enter the name of the recipient and press F9.

   The F9 key is used in data files to indicate the end of a field, and in merge from the keyboard to indicate the end of the user's response.

   When you press F9, the insertion point jumps to the next KEYBOARD code. Notice that when the insertion point moves past the DATE code, the DATE code is replaced by the text for today's date.

7. The insertion point pauses at the next KEYBOARD code. Enter the subject of the memo and press F9.

   When you press F9 after the last KEYBOARD code, WordPerfect moves the insertion point to the end of the form file.

> **Tip:** If you would like WordPerfect to beep when it is waiting for a keyboard response, add the BEEP merge code immediately before the KEYBOARD code. With the form file on your screen, press Shift+F9, Shift+F9 to display the merge codes list. Choose BEEP and then Select.

Stopping a Merge from the Keyboard

WordPerfect provides two methods for interrupting a merge from the keyboard. Press Shift+F9 when the merge is paused for input. WordPerfect displays a Merge Running dialog box with three options, as shown in Figure 48.7.

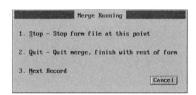

Figure 48.7. Stopping a merge from the keyboard.

Each option corresponds to a command in the merge programming language. **S**top interrupts the merge at the current location in the form file. The remainder of the form file is truncated. **Q**uit interrupts the merge at the same location, but the remainder of the form file is read into the document. The third option, **N**ext Record, has nothing to do with stopping the merge. Next Record allows you to skip a record in the data file.

An easier method is to press Exit (F7). WordPerfect responds with a dialog box asking Exit Merge? Choose Yes if you wish to exit the merge, or choose No or Cancel to continue. Exiting the merge is the equivalent of using the Stop option. The merge is halted, and the remainder of the form file is ignored,

Note: To interrupt a regular merge, just press Cancel (Escape), or, if Cancel has been disabled through the merge language, press Ctrl+Break. If you press Cancel during a merge from the keyboard, WordPerfect treats it like Undelete, a feature which can be quite handy.

Combining Merge from the Keyboard and Merge from a File

You can combine merging from a data file and from the keyboard. This technique is useful when some of the data you need for the merge, such as names and addresses, is already available in a data file format.

To combine these two types of merge, create a form file that uses any combination of FIELD() and KEYBOARD() codes. Start the merge and enter the names of both the form file and the data file. When WordPerfect encounters a FIELD code, it takes the data from the data file. When WordPerfect encounters a KEYBOARD code, it pauses for you to enter the data from the keyboard and press F9.

Macros Versus Merging from the Keyboard

Now that you've seen how to set up a merge from the keyboard, you may have been struck by the similarity between merging from the keyboard and running a macro. Both techniques allow you to display messages for the user, pause for input, and (as you'll see in the chapters on merge programming and merge projects) use conditional logic to make decisions. The question arises, then, of which to use.

From the point of view of functionality, the two techniques are interchangeable, and the technique you choose is strictly a question of personal preference. From the point of view of the programmer (that's you), merge from the keyboard is often a better choice. The primary reason for this is that it's much easier, even for an accomplished macro programmer, to set up a merge from the keyboard than it is to write an interactive macro. Merge files are also easier to edit than macros (even in WordPerfect 6.0). Finally, merge is better suited to handle large blocks of text than a macro is.

Merging with Exported Database and ASCII Files

If you have more than a couple hundred records in your data file, you should consider entering your data into a database program instead of keeping it in a WordPerfect data file. Database programs provide many advantages over a WordPerfect data file: they are more efficient, faster, and offer data validation features. You may also decide to use a database program instead of a data file if you need relational capabilities.

One minor problem with storing your data in a database program is that WordPerfect cannot merge directly with a database, not even with WordPerfect Corp's own DataPerfect. You can, however, merge with the data from virtually any database program by exporting the data from the database in a format that WordPerfect understands. This requires an extra step, but it is generally not difficult to do.

Exporting to a WordPerfect Merge File

First, check to see what export options your database offers. Because Word-Perfect is so popular, some database programs are capable of exporting data in WordPerfect format. If your database program provides an option to export the data as a WordPerfect merge file (any version), this is your best bet for several reasons:

▲ WordPerfect merges are faster and more efficient if the data files are in WordPerfect format.

▲ Exporting to another format may impose restrictions on your data. For example, WordPerfect's merge file format permits an unlimited number of fields per record, and individual fields may be any length and span multiple lines. Other merge formats may limit the number of fields per record or the length of individual fields.

▲ You eliminate a step when you perform the merge, compared to merging with a non-WordPerfect file.

▲ You can add field names to a WordPerfect data file so that you can use field names instead of field numbers in your form file.

743

Exporting to a Delimited ASCII File (DOS Delimited Text)

ASCII files are the *lingua franca* of the binary world. ASCII, an acronym for *American Standard Code for Information Interchange*, is a 7-bit code consisting primarily of alphanumeric characters and a few control characters that represent basic formatting, such as tabs, line feeds, carriage returns, and form feeds. ASCII does not support any of the extended characters (accented characters or line draw characters) or text enhancements.

Virtually every database program can export its data in a format known as ASCII-delimited (or comma-delimited) format. This techie-sounding term simply means that the character set is ASCII, and that fields and records in the file are delimited by special markers. Usually, the end of a record is marked with a Carriage Return-Line Feed combination, and individual fields in a record are separated by commas. Each field is enclosed in quotation marks (see Figure 48.8).

Figure 48.8. An ASCII-delimited data file.

WordPerfect provides built-in support for ASCII-delimited files. WordPerfect can merge directly with ASCII-delimited files (or DOS-delimited text files, as WordPerfect calls them). If your database uses other characters as delimiters, you can change WordPerfect's settings on either a one-time-only or a permanent basis. In WordPerfect, you can specify the format for a delimited text file in two places:

▲ Setup

▲ Run Merge

Changing Delimited Text Options in Setup

To view or change your current settings for delimited text files, choose File, Setup; or press Shift+F1. Then choose Environment, Delimited Text Options. WordPerfect displays the Setup Delimited Text Options dialog box, as shown in Figure 48.9.

Figure 48.9. The Setup Delimited Text Options dialog box.

The Delimited Text options that you select in Setup become your default settings for merging with delimited text files. (You can choose other settings on a one-time basis from the Run Merge dialog box.) Because these settings are standard, you should rarely need to change them. There are four options for delimited text files:

▲ **F**ield Delimiter	The field delimiter is the character or character sequence that marks the end of each field in the data file. By default, the field delimiter is set to a comma.
▲ **R**ecord Delimiter	The record delimiter is the character or character sequence that marks the end of each record. By default, the record delimiter is set to [CR][LF], or carriage return and line feed combination.
▲ Field **E**ncapsulate Character	The field encapsulate character is used to mark the beginning and end of fields that contain the field delimiter. By default, the field encapsulate character is set to a double quote.

For example, if the field delimiter is defined as a comma, and the field encapsulate character is defined as double quotes, each field that contains a comma, such as `Mobile, Alabama`, would be enclosed in quotation marks. The quotation marks serve to tell WordPerfect not to treat the comma in that field as a field delimiter. The quotation marks are stripped out during the merge.

▲ **Strip Characters**   Strip characters are additional charac-
                                          ters that should be stripped out of the
                                          data file during the merge. By default,
                                          this option is blank.

Because you may want to use special ASCII codes for these options, this dialog box
contains a button called Codes that is greyed out unless your insertion point is in
one of the text entry boxes. To insert a code, choose Codes or press F5, and choose
one of the following codes from the list: Tab, Line Feed, Form Feed, or Carriage
Return.

Using a Delimited
Text File in Run Merge

WordPerfect makes it easy to merge with a delimited text file. From the Run Merge
dialog box, enter the name of the form file in the Form File box and the name of the
delimited text file in the Data File box. WordPerfect recognizes that the data file
is not in WordPerfect format and displays the File Format dialog box shown in
Figure 48.10.

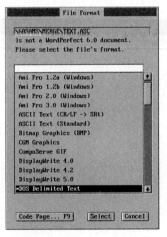

Figure 48.10. The File Format dialog box.

From the File Format list, choose DOS Delimited Text and then Select. The
Delimited Text Options dialog box appears, shown in Figure 48.11. If you're using
a standard ASCII-delimited file, the settings should be correct. Change the settings
if necessary. To make the new settings your default, choose Save Setup Options.
Notice that the title of the dialog box changes from Delimited Text Options to
Setup Delimited Text Options. Choosing Save Setup Options in this dialog box is
equivalent to changing your Delimited Text Options in File, Setup, Environment.
When you have entered the correct Delimited Text Options, choose OK.

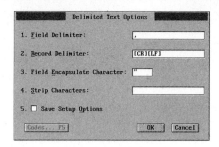

Figure 48.11. The Delimited Text Options dialog box.

WordPerfect now displays the Run Merge dialog box, shown in Figure 48.12. Notice that the Run Merge dialog box is an expansion of the Run Merge dialog box that you saw when you began this process (see Figure 48.5). Ignore for now the additional merge options that appear in this dialog box (we'll cover them later in this chapter) and choose Merge to begin the merge.

Advanced Menu Options

Unlike WordPerfect 5.1, which required knowledge of WordPerfect's merge programming language to take advantage of its powerful merge capabilities, WordPerfect 6.0 offers a wide range of sophisticated merge features that you can choose from dialog boxes. No longer must you struggle with the merge programming language just to accomplish everyday merge tasks such as printing multiple copies, suppressing blank lines and page breaks, or selecting records. The merge language is still available and even more powerful than before, but you'll need to use it less.

Output Options

WordPerfect offers four output options on the Run Merge dialog box. You can choose to send the output to the following:

▲ Current Document
▲ Unused Document
▲ Printer
▲ File

By default, WordPerfect does not automatically send the result of a merge to the printer. Instead, it creates a file with the output in an unused document window. This design gives you an opportunity to look over the merge output before you print, and it is responsible for saving a lot of trees. If you are merging a large number of records, however, sending the output to a document window or to a file

747

may be a poor idea because you may not have enough memory or disk space to hold such a large file. Instead, send the merge directly to the printer.

> **Tip:** It's always a good idea to do a test run of 5–7 records before you merge your entire list. You could output the text results to the current document or an unused document window, examine them, and then output the entire merge directly to the printer. (See Chapter 49, "Advanced Merge Topics," for an easy way to perform a test merge.)

With nine document windows available in WordPerfect, you'll probably always have a free editing window available for your merge results. WordPerfect also allows you to send the merge results to a file. This feature is useful if you don't have a free editing window or if you don't want to merge directly to the printer.

Repeating the Merge for Each Data Record

One particularly nice feature that is new to WordPerfect 6.0 is that you can repeat the merge for each data record a specified number of times. Just enter the number of copies you want in the Repeat Merge for Each Data Record box on the Run Merge dialog box. WordPerfect generates the specified number of copies for you.

Just to be sure that you appreciate how easy this is, here is what you would have had to do in WordPerfect 5.1 to accomplish the same objective:

▲ Write a FOR loop using the merge programming language. This solution is great if you're a programmer, but not everyone is.

or

▲ Use the Print Multiple Copies feature. Again, this solution worked, but if you happened to be printing labels, the copies would not be grouped together on a page, and you wasted labels if the last sheet wasn't full.

or

▲ Repeat the merge. Not only would you tie up your computer this way, but you would waste a lot of time afterward collating the copies that went together.

Displaying Merge Codes

Working with merge codes is far easier in WordPerfect 6.0 than in previous versions, thanks largely to three display options: Hide Codes, Show Full Codes, and Show Codes as Icons. As with so many other WordPerfect options, you can change the settings for the Display of Merge Codes in several different places:

▲ **View, Screen** Setup, Display of **M**erge Codes

This setting is your default setting for all new merge files you create. WordPerfect's default is Show Full Codes.

▲ Merge Codes dialog boxes for Form Files, Text Data Files, and Table Data Files

This setting controls the display of merge codes as you edit the file. You can set the Display of Merge Codes on a file-by-file basis.

▲ Run Merge dialog box

This setting controls the display of merge codes during the actual merge. The default for Display of Merge Codes in the Run Merge dialog box is Hide Codes.

> **Tip:** Take advantage of being able to have different settings for editing and merging. While editing your merge files, you might prefer to set your defaults to either Show Full Codes or Show Codes as Icons, depending on the complexity of the merge files. When you actually perform the merge, you might prefer to change the setting to Hide Codes to keep the display clean and uncluttered.

From any of the Merge Codes dialog boxes, you can choose Show Full Codes (the default) to display both the code and any parameters it may have, for example: FIELD(Last).

> **Tip:** If you need to edit one of the parameters for a merge code, you must use the Show Full Codes option. For example, to change the field name code in your document from FIELD(Last) to FIELD(LastName) without deleting and reinserting the code, turn on the Show Full Codes option, move the insertion point inside the parentheses, and edit the field name.

To tell where the codes are located in your document, but with less clutter than Show Full Codes, choose Show Codes as Icons.

The Show Codes as Icons feature has a nice side effect: the code and its parameters are replaced by a single icon. This means that the merge code behaves like a single character, so you can move it easily.

Or, you can choose Hide to hide the codes altogether. If you hide the merge codes, you can see them only in Reveal Codes. During the merge, the prompts and messages still display on the status line, just as they would with the other display options.

Data File Options

Until you select your data file in the Run Merge dialog box, the Data File Options button is greyed out. If you choose this option after selecting a data file, the Run Merge dialog box expands to its long form, and four new merge capabilities are available (see Figure 48.12).

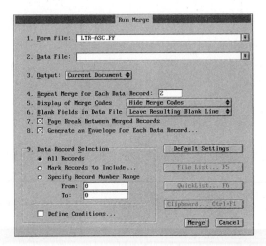

Figure 48.12. The Run Merge dialog box (expanded version).

 Note: Figure 48.5 illustrates the short version of the Run Merge dialog box, and Figure 48.12 shows the expanded version.

Eliminating Blank Lines

In a data file, having blank fields is not unusual. Not everyone on your list has a company name or a title, or phone numbers or zip codes may be missing. Depending on how the fields are used in the form file, blank fields may result in unwanted blank lines when you perform the merge.

There are several ways to handle blank lines in a WordPerfect merge, but the easiest by far is to simply change the setting for the Blank Fields in Data File option on the expanded Run Merge dialog box from Leave Resulting Blank Line to Remove Resulting Blank Line. This setting applies to all the blank lines resulting from blank fields in the merge. If you need to remove some blank lines but leave others, see Chapter 49 for other techniques for handling blank fields.

Eliminating Page Breaks Between Merged Records

WordPerfect's merge is optimized to let you create form letters with as few merge codes as possible. If you are generating form letters, you begin each new letter on a new page. WordPerfect has therefore set the merge default to automatically insert a page break between merged records.

If you are using merge to generate some other type of document, such as a phone list or a legal contract, you'll need to eliminate the page breaks that WordPerfect puts in automatically between merged records. You could insert a merge command in the document, but there's an easier way: just uncheck the Page Break Between Merged Documents option on the expanded Run Merge dialog box.

Generating Envelopes for Each Data Record

Generating envelopes for each letter is a typical merge task. Users of previous versions of WordPerfect had to either run separate merges, one for the letters and one for the envelopes, or chain two primary files together using the merge language. WordPerfect makes this task easier by providing an option to generate envelopes on the Run Merge dialog box.

WordPerfect 6.0 handles this requirement through an option on the expanded Run Merge dialog box. Simply check the option Generate an Envelope for Each Data Record. WordPerfect displays the Envelope dialog box shown in Figure 48.13. Choose Mailing Address. With the insertion point in the Mailing Address text entry box, insert the merge fields for the address as you want it to appear on the envelope. To insert the field codes, choose one of these techniques:

> **Note:** The Merge Envelope dialog box looks almost identical to the regular Envelope dialog box.

▲ If the List Field Names button is not greyed out, choose that option to pick the field names from the list of field names defined in the attached data file.

▲ Press Shift+F9 to display the Merge Codes (Form File) dialog box.

▲ Before opening the Run Merge dialog box, copy the inside address of the letter in your form file to the Shell Clipboard, or use WordPerfect's Move feature to copy it to the move buffer. Then in the Mailing Address box, paste it into the box, codes and all. Edit as necessary.

751

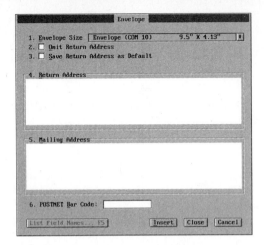

Figure 48.13. The Envelope dialog box (merge version).

▲ (Optional) WordPerfect can create a Postnet bar code from a 5-, 9-, or 11-digit zip code. To print the bar code on the envelope, choose the Postnet Bar Code option. Choose List Field Codes, or press F5 to display a list of merge field codes. Choose the code that contains the zip code; then choose Select. WordPerfect places the bar code above the address.

▲ Choose Insert. WordPerfect returns to the Run Merge dialog box.

▲ Choose Merge.

WordPerfect generates all the letters as defined in your form file, and then generates the matching envelopes.

Data Record Selection

Very often, you may need to do a restricted mailing. Suppose, for example, that you are running for city council and you want to send a mailing only to those voters who live in your district. Your database, however, contains the names and addresses of everyone in the city. If you can come up with a set of guidelines for your mailing, you can tell WordPerfect to restrict the mailing to people who meet those guidelines—all without programming.

Note: WordPerfect's powerful Sort and Select feature, covered in Chapter 51, "Sorting," works with paragraphs, lines, merge data files, and tables. Use Sort and Select if you need to sort a data file, or if you need to select records without performing a merge.

Note: In addition to selecting records by choosing dialog box options, you can select records during a merge by using the advanced programming language.

WordPerfect's Data Record Selection feature is available on the expanded Run Merge dialog box (see Figure 48.12). To display the expanded Run Merge dialog box, choose Tools, Merge, Run; or press Ctrl+F9. Enter the names of your form file and data file and choose Data File Options. The dialog box expands. One of the new options on the expanded dialog box is Data Record Selection.

Notice that the Data Record Selection group contains a set of three radio buttons and one check box option. The radio buttons are labeled as follows:

▲ All Records
▲ Mark Records to Include
▲ Specify Record Number Range

Note: As in Windows, radio buttons are mutually exclusive; only one of the three radio buttons can be selected at a time.

All Records, the default setting, needs no explanation. The other two options let you restrict the records either by marking them from a list or by choosing a numeric range.

Understanding Marked Records

Think of the Mark Records to Include as WordPerfect's *eeny, meeny, miney, mo* feature. If you select data records with this option, you are, in effect, picking the records you need one-by-one from a list. Although this isn't a very efficient way to work, it's the way that most people think. How many times have you created a party list by picking names from your guest book? This approach is a lifesaver when it's not possible to come up with a more objective set of selection rules (such as a zip code range or date of last purchase).

When you choose the Mark Records to Include feature, WordPerfect displays the List Field Names dialog box (see Figure 48.14) with an alphabetical list of the field names for the data file you selected in the Run Merge dialog box.

Select the field you wish to use as your key field, and press Enter. WordPerfect now displays the data file sorted by the key field (see Figure 48.15).

753

Figure 48.14. The List Field Names dialog box.

Mark the records you wish to include in the merge. To mark an individual record, highlight the record and choose Mark, or press *. To unmark a marked record, highlight the record and choose Unmark, or press *. (The asterisk is a toggle.) To mark all records, choose Mark All Records, or press Home, * (with no records selected). To unmark all marked records, choose Unmark All Records, or press Home, *. When you have finished marking records, choose OK.

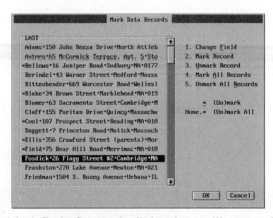

Figure 48.15. The Mark Data Records dialog box with records sorted by key field.

Selecting Records by a Numeric Range

Sometimes being able to select records by a numeric range is convenient. For example, if your data file is very large, you might want to do several smaller merges by selecting a numeric range of records. You can specify a starting and a stopping number. For example, you could choose to merge with records 1500-3000.

If the starting number is set to 0, WordPerfect starts at the beginning of the data file. If the ending number is set to 0, WordPerfect will continue merging to the end of the data file.

Setting Conditions

In addition to choosing one of the three methods you have just seen for selecting data records (all, selected, or a numerical range), you can also specify selection conditions. This is where selecting records can get just a little tricky.

When you select Define Conditions, WordPerfect displays a Define Conditions for Record Selection dialog box, shown in Figure 48.16.

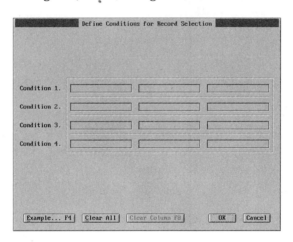

Figure 48.16. The Define Conditions for Record Selection dialog box.

This dialog box allows you to set up to four selection conditions. Each condition is represented by a row. Each row has three columns representing data fields. Records that match the conditions defined in this dialog box are selected for the merge.

 Note: There are no mnemonics for this dialog box, only numbers.

For example, going back to the alumni data file from Chapter 47, you could select all the alumni who graduated between 1970 and 1990 as one condition, and everyone (regardless of graduation date) who donated more than $100 as their last gift as a second condition.

To get started, choose 1 for the first condition. WordPerfect displays the Field Name List dialog box. Choose a field name. In this example, choose class. The field name becomes the title for the column. Now enter a value for that selection condition. In the first example, you want to select everyone who graduated between 1970 and 1990, so type 1970-1990 in the Year column and press Enter.

To enter the second example, choose 2. Use the Tab key to move the insertion point to the next column. As soon as you move to an untitled column, WordPerfect

755

presents the field names list. You want to select by the value of the Last Gift field, so choose Last Gift from the field names list. Notice that the second column is now labeled Last Gift. You want to select every record in which the value of the last gift was greater than $100, so enter >100 here.

Notice that the two selection conditions are defined independently of each other. When you perform the merge, WordPerfect will select all alumni who graduated between 1970-1990, and all alumni who donated more than $100 last year, regardless of when they graduated. If you wanted to combine these two selection criteria so that you selected alumni who graduated between 1970-1990 *and* donated more than $100, you would have had to define these conditions on the same row.

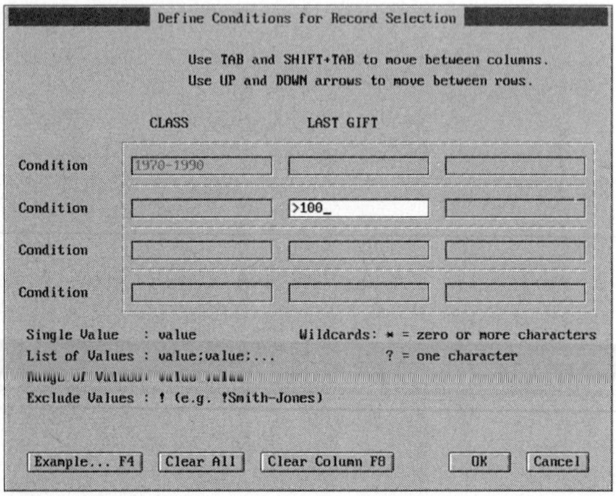

Figure 48.17. The Define Conditions for Record Selection dialog box. The first condition selects everyone who graduated between 1970 and 1990. The second condition selects everyone who donated more than 100 dollars, regardless of their graduation date. Because these conditions are defined on separate rows, they are independent of each other. To select only those graduates between 1970 and 1990 who donated more than 100 dollars, define the conditions on the same row.

Choose OK to return to the Run Merge dialog box, and Merge to begin the merge.

Resetting WordPerfect's Merge Options to the Defaults

The options in the Run Merge dialog box are "sticky"—when you change them, WordPerfect remembers the settings the next time you open the dialog box. If you would like to return to WordPerfect's original default merge settings, just choose Default Settings. WordPerfect's defaults for merge are as follows:

▲ Output merge to an unused document
▲ Repeat the merge once for each data record
▲ Hide merge codes during the merge
▲ Leave blank lines resulting from empty fields
▲ Separate merged records with a page break
▲ Do not generate envelopes
▲ Include all records

by Marilyn Horn Claff

Advanced Merge Topics

WordPerfect's powerful merge language makes it possible to perform complex merge operations. Although the merge language may seem intimidating at first, it's really not difficult to understand and use, even if you have little or no programming background. In this chapter, we'll examine some of the more useful merge language commands in the context of solving typical merge problems. We'll also discuss alternatives to the merge programming commands when they exist. Finally, we'll provide tips for debugging your merges and for improving their speed and efficiency. In the chapter that follows, we'll provide more extensive examples of how merge commands can work together with other WordPerfect features to help automate your work.

Handling Blank and Nonblank Fields

Your data file is bound to contain blank fields. Blank fields present a problem because they may result in unwanted—and unsightly—blank lines in your final document when you run the merge. You may, therefore, want to instruct WordPerfect to suppress blank lines resulting from blank fields. You also may need to perform different actions depending on whether certain fields are blank or nonblank. WordPerfect offers three different approaches to handling blank fields.

Tip: To display a list of common merge codes, press `Shift+F9` in a form or data file. To display the complete list, press `Shift+F9` twice.

Run Merge Dialog Box Option

If your only concern with blank fields is to avoid gaping holes in your merged document, the simplest solution, as we have seen in the previous chapter, is to change the setting on the Run Merge dialog box for Blank Lines in Data File from Leave Resulting Blank Line (the default setting) to Remove Resulting Blank Line. Because this option applies to the entire merge, if you need to suppress some blank lines but print others, you'll need to look for a different solution. Another disadvantage of this solution is that, although the setting is "sticky," it's not permanent, so you must remember to check it each time you run the merge for the first time in each editing session.

 Note: "Sticky" settings remain in effect for that particular merge file during the remainder of the editing session (until you exit WordPerfect). If you need to remerge the same files later in the same editing session, you don't need to reset the Run Merge options. WordPerfect does not provide a way to change these settings permanently.

Using a Question Mark at the End of the Field Parameter

A second solution to the problem of blank fields is to include a question mark at the end of a field name, within the closing parenthesis. For example, when you enter the company field name in the Parameter Entry dialog box, type Company? rather than Company. The resulting merge code in your form document appears as `FIELD(Company?)`.

The question mark technique is handy when the fields that may be blank occur on a line by themselves in the form file:

```
FIELD(Title) FIELD(First) FIELD(Last)
FIELD(Position?)
FIELD(Company?)
FIELD(Address)
FIELD(City), FIELD(State) FIELD(Zip)
```

WordPerfect's *IFBLANK* and *IFNOTBLANK*

The third and most powerful technique for handling blank fields is to use the merge commands `IFBLANK` and `IFNOTBLANK`. The syntax for both commands is:

`IFBLANK(field)`

text or merge command to be done if `FIELD(field)` is blank

`ENDIF`

> **Note:** This example is formatted for clarity. To avoid introducing additional blank lines in your merge document, you need to put the entire statement on one line, comment out the hard return codes, or use the `Codes()` command. For detailed information about formatting merge language statements, see "Formatting Merge Statements."

Suppose, for example, that you want to ship to a customer's shipping address if it is different from his business address:

`IFBLANK(shipping address)FIELD(business address)ENDIF`

`IFNOTBLANK` is the opposite. A typical use for `IFNOTBLANK` is to include a particular field and, often, some additional text if the field is not blank. For example, the company field in your address file may be blank; if it is not blank, you want to include the company field followed by a hard return code:

`FIELD(title) FIELD(first) FIELD(last)`

`IFNOTBLANK(company)FIELD(company)`

`ENDIF FIELD(address)`

Notice that in the preceding example, the closing `ENDIF` command is placed on the line below the `FIELD(company)` code, and is followed by the address field on the same line. This way, the hard return code following the company field is included only if the company field is not blank.

As with the `IF` command, you can use `ELSE` with both `IFBLANK` and `IFNOTBLANK` to introduce an alternative:

`IFNOTBLANK(shipping address)FIELD(shipping address)ELSE`
`FIELD(mailing address)`
`ENDIF FIELD(city)`

In the preceding example, all the merge commands in the `IFNOTBLANK` statement except the `ENDIF` command are placed on one line and wrap to the next line. To make this example easier to read, format it like this:

```
IFNOTBLANK(shipping address)COMMENT(
     )FIELD(shipping address)COMMENT
ELSE COMMENT(
     )FIELD(mailing address)COMMENT
ENDIF FIELD (city)
```

The COMMENT codes instruct WordPerfect to skip the hard return and tab codes before each address field. See "Formatting Merge Statements" later in this chapter.

Controlling Page Breaks

Unless you instruct it otherwise, WordPerfect always inserts a page break between each merged record. As we saw in Chapter 48, "Intermediate Merging," you can suppress page breaks between merged records with an option on the Run Merge dialog box. This setting affects the entire merge. Generally, if you are using merge to do a mass mailing, the default setting will be correct; if you are using merge to create a list, such as a phone list, you'll need to change it. Here is a list of the most common merge situations in which you would want to suppress the page break:

▲ When you are creating a list, such as a phone list

▲ When you are merging into a table (one record per row)

▲ When you are nesting other form files in your main form file

▲ When you use the merge PRINT command in your form document

Note: If you choose Printer on the Run Merge dialog box for your merge output, WordPerfect handles the page breaks correctly even if you don't change the Run Merge setting for Page Break Between Merged Records. If you merge to the printer using the PRINT merge command, you also must change the page break setting with the PAGEOFF command.

WordPerfect's merge language includes two commands, PAGEON and PAGEOFF, to help you control page breaks in a merge. There are three main situations in which you'll need to use these commands in your form file rather than change the page break option on the Run Merge dialog box:

▲ If you need to suppress page breaks selectively

▲ If you're using the merge PRINT command

▲ If you don't want to set the Run Merge page break option each time you run the merge for the first time in a new session

Note that the PAGEON and PAGEOFF commands in the document override the Run Merge dialog box setting.

A typical application for the PAGEOFF command is merging names and phone numbers into a phone list. For example, to create a single-spaced phone list with the name on the left and the phone number flush right, insert the PAGEOFF code, immediately followed by the field Last, a comma, a space, and the field First. Then press Alt+F6 to insert a flush right code (or press Alt+F6 twice to insert a flush right with dot leaders code), and insert the field Phone. Press Enter at the end of the line to insert a [HRt] code. (There needs to be one [HRt] code so that each name and phone number is on a new line.)

PAGEOFF FIELD(Last), FIELD(First)FIELD(Phone)

> **Note:** The PAGEOFF command is placed on the same line as the fields so that the output appears as single spaced. If you put the PAGEOFF code on the line above, use a COMMENT() code around the hard return, unless you want the list to be double spaced.

The resulting phone list looks like this:

Adams, Marian	693-4972
Bellows, Evelyn	445-8695
Blake, Karen	651-6870
Bloom, Tom	864-6799

Without the PAGEOFF command (or changing the Run Merge option), each name and phone number is printed on a separate page. You can use PAGEOFF and PAGEON codes as many times as you like in your form file.

Sending Merge Output to the Printer

If you're doing a large merge, or if you're remerging files that are well tested, you'll probably want to merge directly to the printer. As with so many other features, WordPerfect provides two ways to do this. The first method is to change the Output option on the Run Merge dialog box. The second is to include the merge command PRINT at the end of the form file. The PRINT command instructs WordPerfect to print the merged data up to that point.

When you use the Output option to direct the output to the printer, WordPerfect suppresses the page break that is normally generated automatically between merged records. When you use the PRINT command, however, WordPerfect inserts a page break between merged documents unless you instruct it not to by including a PAGEOFF command before the PRINT command. If you use the PRINT command without a preceding PAGEOFF command, you'll get an extra blank page between each merged record. You should, therefore, get into the habit of using PAGEOFF whenever you use the PRINT command. The PAGEOFF command can be anywhere in the form file as long as it comes before the PRINT command, but your form files are easier to proofread if you put the PAGEOFF command immediately before the PRINT command at the end of the form file:

PAGEOFF PRINT

> **Note:** You could also change the page break option on the Run Merge dialog box, but it makes more sense to include the PAGEOFF command in the form file, so you don't risk forgetting it. Either use both Run Merge options, or insert both merge commands in your form file.

Inserting the Date

WordPerfect users often are puzzled by the fact that WordPerfect's merge language includes a special DATE code, because WordPerfect provides two regular date commands (choose **T**ools, **D**ate; then, select **T**ext or **C**ode). The Date Text command inserts the date as text, just as though you typed it. The Date Code command inserts a date code that is automatically updated each time you retrieve the document. You might think of the merge DATE code as a combination of the other date commands: DATE is a code that is replaced by text during the merge.

You probably would never use the Date Text command to date a form file, because you would have to edit the form file each time you ran the merge. You could use the Date Code command in some cases, but it's always preferable to use the merge Date command. That way, if you later retrieve the output file, it contains the actual date on which it was created. This is especially important if you are using merge to generate contracts, wills, or other kinds of document assembly. If you are merging a batch of letters directly to the printer, there's no advantage to using the merge DATE command rather than the regular [Date] code.

One change in WordPerfect 6.0 greatly increases the versatility of the DATE command in merges. If you change the date format, WordPerfect 6.0 inserts a code in your document that designates the date format rather than change an environment setting. This makes it possible to use a particular date format in your merge, without worrying about whether it is different from the global environment setting or about having to run a macro. It also means that you can have multiple date formats in the same document, a feature that we'll use in our Certificate of Service merge form in Chapter 50, "Merge Projects."

Postnet Bar Codes

WordPerfect's capability to create 5-, 7-, and 11-digit postnet bar codes is unique among word processors. Again, you can use either an option on the Run Merge dialog box or the merge language to include bar codes in a merge.

To generate matching envelopes with the option on the Run Merge dialog box, simply check the bar code option on the envelope dialog box and tell WordPerfect which field contains the zip code. WordPerfect creates a bar code from that field over the recipient's address. (For more detailed instructions, see Chapter 48.)

If you are generating a batch of envelopes without letters, or if you want to include bar codes on labels, post cards, or the letter itself (for example, if you're doing a self-mailer or using a window envelope), you won't be able to use the Run Merge option. Instead, you'll need to use the POSTNET(string) merge command at the point in the form file where you want the bar code to be inserted. This command takes a single parameter, which may be either a string (series of characters) or a field name. For example, to place the bar code over the address, your form file might look like this:

```
POSTNET(FIELD(ZIP))
FIELD(FIRST) FIELD(LAST)
FIELD(ADDRESS)
FIELD(CITY), FIELD(STATE) FIELD(ZIP)
```

Tip: You cannot insert a FIELD code directly into the Parameter Entry dialog box for the POSTNET command, but here's a trick that makes it easier to enter the POSTNET command with a FIELD name as its parameter. First, insert the FIELD code into your document, using the name of the zip code field as its parameter. In your document, you should see:

```
FIELD(ZIP)
```

Now block the field code and press Shift+F9 twice to display the All Merge Codes dialog box. Highlight the POSTNET code and choose Select. At the Parameter Entry dialog box for the POSTNET code, leave the String text entry box blank and choose OK. The POSTNET code is inserted in your document with FIELD(ZIP) as its parameter:

```
POSTNET(FIELD(ZIP))
```

Tip: It's better to create a separate form file for your envelopes than to use the Run Merge envelope option. The Run Merge envelope settings are difficult to edit and are lost when you exit WordPerfect.

Chaining, Nesting, Substituting and Combining Files

WordPerfect provides seven related commands that enable you to chain, nest, substitute, and combine form files and data files:

```
CHAINDATA(filename)
CHAINFORM(filename)
NESTDATA(filename)
NESTFORM(filename)
SUBSTDATA(filename)
SUBSTFORM(filename)
DOCUMENT(filename)
```

Chaining switches control to the chained file, without returning to the original file. Chaining is used more often to chain data files than to chain form files. If you have a very large data file, dividing it into smaller data files that are chained together is one way to make the data more manageable. When all the data from the first data file has been merged, WordPerfect switches control to the second data file, and so on.

With chaining, control is not returned to the original file. No matter where you insert the CHAINDATA or CHAINFORM code in your document, chaining takes place only after the original merge has been completed. If there is more than one chain code, WordPerfect acts on the last one encountered in the file; the others are ignored.

Nesting switches to another data or form document and returns control to the original file. The nesting occurs at the point in the document where the nest code occurs. Because nesting returns control to the calling document, you can have multiple nest codes in a document. The RETURN command is not needed in a nested file because control is automatically returned to the parent document. Nesting is a convenient way to reuse the same merge routines in multiple form files. Nesting is often used in document assembly merges.

Substituting incorporates aspects of both chaining and nesting. As with chaining, substituting does not return control to the calling document. You can, therefore, have only one active substitute code in a document. Like nesting, substituting switches control to the substituted document at the point in the document where

766

the substitute code is encountered. The SUBSTDATA command can be used to attach a data file to a form file so that you don't have to remember its name. See "Using Loops in a Merge" later in this chapter.

The Document command simply inserts the named document at the point in the primary file where the DOCUMENT code is located. The main difference between DOCUMENT and NESTFORM is that the NESTFORM command processes any merge codes in the nested file. If a file inserted with the DOCUMENT command contains merge commands, the commands are not processed.

Chaining, Nesting, and Embedding Macros

To more fully automate your merges, you can combine merging and macros. Macros are an extremely useful tool in many merge applications. For example, macros can perform formatting tasks, insert graphics in documents, calculate math and table formulas, or do a search and replace. WordPerfect provides three different ways to use macro commands in conjunction with merging:

CHAINMACRO(macroname)

As with chained files, a chained macro runs only on completion of the merge. You can have only one chained macro per merge. No matter where the CHAINMACRO code is located in the file, WordPerfect does not act on it until after the merge is complete. If you need to run a macro once for each iteration, use the NESTMACRO command instead.

NESTMACRO(macroname)

The NESTMACRO command causes WordPerfect to run a macro at the point where the NESTMACRO code is located during a merge. You can have any number of NESTMACRO commands in a merge file. You do not need to use a RETURN command at the end of the nested macro because command is automatically returned to the parent document when the macro is finished.

You do not need to include the macro filename extension .WPM in the CHAINMACRO or NESTMACRO commands.

EMBEDMACRO(macro statements)

WordPerfect 6.0 enables you to embed macro statements in your merge files with the EMBEDMACRO command. When WordPerfect encounters this code during a merge, it compiles and plays the embedded macro commands. This feature provides the functionality of a macro without requiring a separate macro file. You could use the EMBEDMACRO command to embed the macro statements to create a dialog box.

Prompting and Getting Input from the User

WordPerfect's merge language includes a variety of tools for displaying prompts and getting input from the user. These tools include two kinds of prompt commands and four commands that get input from the user.

PROMPT(message)

The PROMPT command displays a prompt on the status line. Prompts can be up to 80 characters long and are usually followed by a WAIT command. (WAIT measures time in tenths of a second.) Without the WAIT command, the prompt is displayed too quickly to read. The syntax for the PROMPT command is as follows:

```
PROMPT(Error! Check setup and start over.)
WAIT(30)
```

STATUSPROMPT(message)

STATUSPROMPT is similar to PROMPT, except that it displays its message on the status line indefinitely, until you reset the STATUSPROMPT with another message or clear it. To clear the status prompt, use the STATUSPROMPT command with no parameters.

KEYBOARD(prompt)

The KEYBOARD command is the primary command used in merging from the keyboard to get input directly from the user. KEYBOARD takes a message as its optional parameter. When WordPerfect encounters the KEYBOARD command in a form file, it pauses for user input. The merge continues when the user presses F9 to move to the next place in the form file where user input is required, or to the end of the form file if there are no more commands requiring user input. Whatever the user types in response to the KEYBOARD command is inserted directly into the document. The KEYBOARD command often is used with the BEEP command to alert the user that input is needed.

Here is an example of KEYBOARD:

```
BEEP KEYBOARD(Enter name of defendant; then press F9)
```

To keep the screen display from appearing too cluttered, you may want to include a DISPLAYSTOP command after the KEYBOARD command. For more examples, see "Merging from the Keyboard" in Chapter 48 and several of the merge projects in Chapter 50.

768

LOOK(var)

The LOOK command tests for a single keypress from the user and assigns it to a variable (see "Using Variables" later in this chapter). Subsequent commands in the file can analyze the value of the variable and branch to different routines based on its value. If no key is pressed, the variable is deleted and execution continues. Unlike CHAR, LOOK does not display a message on the screen or pause for input. LOOK is often used to check for a keypress in a loop.

GETSTRING(var(;prompt)(;title))

The GETSTRING command is one of the most useful commands in the merge language. GETSTRING displays a dialog box with an optional prompt and an optional title, and pauses for input from the user (see Figure 49.1). The user may enter up to 127 characters, which are then assigned to the variable. The GETSTRING dialog box includes OK and Cancel buttons.

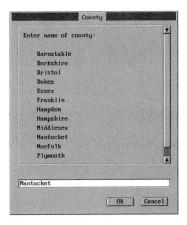

Figure 49.1. The GETSTRING dialog box as it appears during a merge.

To enter the GETSTRING command, press Shift+F9, Shift+F9 in a form file; then choose GETSTRING. Enter the name of the variable. The variable name is the only required parameter. Then enter the prompt message and the title if desired.

Note that although the GETSTRING parameter entry box (see Figure 49.2) does not enable you to enter a hard return in the Parameter Entry dialog box, you can insert [HRt] codes in the prompt message by editing the GETSTRING parameters at the document level. If your GETSTRING prompt extends over multiple lines, WordPerfect expands the dialog box. For example, to create the County dialog box shown in Figure 49.1, edit the prompt text so that it appears as shown in Figure 49.3.

Figure 49.2. The Parameter Entry dialog box for the *GETSTRING* command.

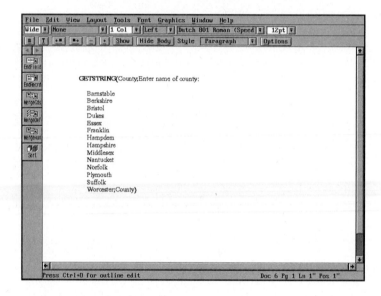

Figure 49.3. Using a multiline prompt with the GetString command.

CHAR(var(;prompt)(;title))

The CHAR command works just like GETSTRING, except that CHAR accepts only a single character as input. You do not need to choose OK or press Enter after typing the character. Like the GETSTRING command, the CHAR dialog box includes OK and Cancel buttons and a vertical scrollbar. CHAR is convenient for displaying multiline prompts, such as a menu of numbered items (see Figure 49.4).

Using Variables

A variable is a memory location where different values are stored. You can manipulate the contents of a variable if you know its name. WordPerfect has two types of merge variables, global (the default) and local. Local variables are visible only in the file in which they are defined. Global variables are visible to more than one file and remain in memory even after the merge has been completed, unless you clear them (see "Clearing Variables" later in this chapter).

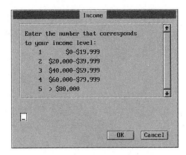

Figure 49.4. Using CHAR to display multiline prompts.

> **Tip:** Variable names are not case-sensitive and may be up to 30 characters long. You cannot have two local variables or two global variables with the same name, but you can use the same name for a local and a global variable. You should not use the same name for a local variable and a label.

Why Use Variables

If you haven't done any merge programming, you may be wondering how to use variables in a merge. As in macros, variables are useful for storing responses from the user. Merge statements then can test the responses and branch to different parts of the merge according to the results of the tests. The merge can use the CHAR command to ask a yes/no question or to display a menu of items, and perform different actions based on the responses.

Similarly, the merge can use the GETSTRING command to prompt the user for a client code, which is stored as a variable named c_code. The merge then can compare the c_code variable against the c_code field in a data file. When it finds a match, the merge retrieves that client's name and address from the data file and ends the merge. You also can use variables to store the results of integer calculations. After performing the calculation, you can insert the contents of the variable directly into your form file.

> **Note:** The merge language cannot handle calculations involving numbers with decimal places.

771

Still another way to use merge variables is to set the value of items that change throughout a document. By asking one question, you can make multiple changes in the document. This technique is not difficult, and it is faster and more foolproof than using a series of search and replace operations to do the same thing. As you become more familiar with merge and try some of the projects in the next chapter, you are certain to come up with your own ideas for using variables in merges.

How Are Variables Assigned?

Variables are assigned in two ways. One way is to use a merge command that requires a response from the user. In the previous sections, we saw three merge commands that get user input and assign it to a variable: GETSTRING, CHAR, and, less commonly, LOOK. The second way is to use a merge statement that performs the assignment without user intervention. The ASSIGN and ASSIGNLOCAL commands are examples of this method.

ASSIGN and *ASSIGNLOCAL*

The only difference between ASSIGN and ASSIGNLOCAL is the scope of the variables they create. The syntax for the two commands is identical:

```
ASSIGN(var;expr)
```

```
ASSIGNLOCAL(var;expr)
```

The expression expr is assigned to the variable var. An expression may be a text string, another variable, a numeric statement, a statement of comparison, or a combination of these. For example, to assign the phrase "Supreme Judicial Court" to the variable court, use the following statement:

```
ASSIGN(court;Supreme Judicial Court)
```

The following statement assigns the sum of the Guests and Staff variables to a local variable called Total:

```
ASSIGNLOCAL(Total);VARIABLE(Guests) + VARIABLE(Staff))
```

Notice in the preceding example that the variable Total is represented by the word itself in the statement, not by the command VARIABLE(var), as the other two variables are. This apparent inconsistency is explained by the fact that because the first parameter of the ASSIGN commands can be only a variable, there is no need to use the VARIABLE() command. Conversely, the VARIABLE commands are required in the expression parameter because the expression is ambiguous without them.

772

VARIABLE(var)

The primary purpose of the VARIABLE command is to insert the contents of a variable into your document. For example, to insert the variable Total into your document, use this command:

```
VARIABLE(Total)
```

When the form is processed, the variable code is replaced by the contents of the variable, just as FIELD(field) codes are replaced by the contents of the field.

Variables can be used to good effect in message prompts. The following example uses the variable Amount Due in the message displayed by the CHAR command:

```
CHAR(Answer;Amount due = VARIABLE(Amount Due).
Send notice? Y N;Deadbeat)
```

> **Caution:** You cannot insert the VARIABLE or the hard return code (to force a line break in the prompt) while you are in the Parameter Entry dialog box for the CHAR command; you must insert them by editing the CHAR command at the document level.

When the CHAR command is processed, the dialog box appears like the one shown in Figure 49.5.

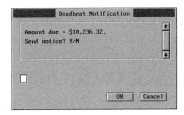

Figure 49.5. Using the Amount Due variable in the *CHAR* prompt.

You can also use variables in expressions. The following example checks to see whether the Days Late variable is less than 90; if so, it uses the NEXTRECORD command to skip that record. (You could use a field rather than a variable code here.)

```
IF(VARIABLE(Days Late)<90)
   NEXTRECORD
ENDIF
```

IFEXISTS(name)

The `IFEXISTS(name)` command simply tests to see whether a variable by that name exists. Like all other commands beginning with `IF`, you must end the statement with an `ENDIF` command. In the following example, the variable `ATTORNEY` is inserted if it has been defined; if not, the merge prompts the user to enter the name of the attorney.

 Note: The `CODES()` command in the `IFEXISTS` example serves to suppress the hard return and tab codes that are used to make the statement more readable. See "Formatting Merge Statement" in this chapter for more details.

```
CODES(IFEXISTS(attorney)
     VARIABLE(attorney)
ELSE
     GETSTRING(attorney;Enter name of attorney;Prosecuting Attor-
ney)
     VARIABLE(attorney)
ENDIF)
```

Clearing Variables

Local variables are cleared when the merge ends or in the case of nested files, when control is returned to the previous level. Global variables are not cleared until you exit WordPerfect, unless you explicitly clear them. To clear a variable, assign an empty value to it. The following example clears the variable `PLAINTIFF`:

```
ASSIGN(plaintiff;)
```

System Variables

WordPerfect includes a number of predefined system variables that hold information about the current document and environment. Although you cannot change the value of a system variable, you can evaluate its value and insert it in your merge document, if desired. For example, you could test to see whether you are in a table with the following command:

```
IF(SYSTEM(InTable)=-1)
     COMMENT(You're in a table)
     ...
ELSE
     COMMENT(You're not in a table)
     ...
ENDIF
```

Note: If a merge expression equals −1, it is true; if it equals 0, it is false.

Conditional Statements

WordPerfect's merge language includes several conditional commands, including IF, SWITCH, and CASEOF.

IF and Related Statements

Of the conditional commands, the IF statement is the most important. The IF statement tests a condition. If it is true, it executes a statement (which may be a null or empty statement); if it is false, it skips the statement. The IF statement always must end with the ENDIF command and may include an optional ELSE command, which is used to introduce an alternative. In the following example, the merge checks to see whether the outstanding balance is greater than zero. If it is, it includes a plea to pay up; if not, it includes a compliment to the customer:

```
IF(FIELD(balance)>0)

Please send your payment promptly. We've enclosed a postage-
paid envelope for your convenience. Mail it today, before you
forget!

ELSE

Thank you for your patronage. You are one of our most valued
customers.

ENDIF
```

The three related commands, IFBLANK, IFNOTBLANK, and IFEXISTS, use the same syntax. All the commands in this group may be nested; just be sure to include an ENDIF command for each IF, IFBLANK, IFNOTBLANK, or IFEXISTS command.

SWITCH and *CASEOF*

The SWITCH and CASEOF statements enable you to evaluate efficiently several possible values. The following example evaluates the state field. If the state field contains the values Massachusetts, New York, or New Jersey, it nests the files MA.FF, NY.FF, or NJ.FF, respectively. If the state field contains any other value, the merge nests the ANYSTATE.FF file.

```
SWITCH(FIELD(state))
  CASEOF(Masschusetts)
    NEST(MA.FF)
```

775

```
      CONTINUE
CASEOF(New York)
   NEST(NY.FF)
   CONTINUE
CASEOF(New Jersey)
   NEST(NJ.FF)
   CONTINUE
DEFAULT
   NEST(ANYSTATE.FF)
ENDSWITCH
```

Using Loops in a Merge (*LABEL/GO, WHILE, FORNEXT, FOREACH*)

Loops are a powerful technique for repeating programming routines. The merge language provides four different looping constructs:

▲ `LABEL(label)`
`GO(label)`

Using a GO command to return to a LABEL is the simplest way to create a loop. The loop is executed once for each record in the data file. When the merge reaches the end of the data file, an error condition is created, and the loop ends.

▲ `WHILE(expr)`
`ENDWHILE`

The `WHILE` command is used to repeat a set of merge statements as long as the expression is true. When the expression is no longer true, the loop ends.

▲ `FOR(var;start;stop[;step])`
`ENDFORNEXT`

The `FORNEXT` command executes a set of merge statements a prescribed number of times. The `FORNEXT` loop is repeated once for each value between the start and stop values, as incremented by the optional step value. (If the step value is not provided, it is assumed to be 1.)

▲ `FOREACH(var;expr1;...;exprN)`
`ENDFOR`

The `FOREACH` command executes a set of merge statements *n* times, once for each expression in the series of expressions in its parameter list. In the following example, the merge commands are executed once for each letter of the alphabet:

```
FOREACH(letter;a;b;c;d;e;f;g;h;i;j;k;l;m;n;o;p;q;r;s;t;u;v;w;x;y;z)
...
ENDFOR
```

Converting Case

The merge language contains four separate commands that convert the case of the supplied expression.

CAPS(expr)

The CAPS command capitalizes the first letter of each word in the expression. For example, the result of

```
CAPS(If anything can go wrong, it will.)
```

is

```
If Anything Can Go Wrong, It Will.
```

Unfortunately, CAPS does not use the Initial Case Resource exception list WPUS.ICR, so you won't get exactly the same results you would by blocking the expression and choosing Switch, Convert Case, Initial Caps.

Also, unlike the regular Initial Caps feature, CAPS does not convert any uppercase letters to lowercase. If you need to convert an uppercase string to mixed case in a merge, use the TOLOWER command first, and then the CAPS command.

FIRSTCAP(expr)

The FIRSTCAP command capitalizes the first letter of the first word in the expression. Like CAPS, it does not convert any uppercase letters to lowercase.

```
FIRSTCAP(a penny saved is a Penny earned)
```

becomes

```
A penny saved is a Penny earned.
```

In this example, the initial a is capitalized by the FIRSTCAP command. The P in Penny is capitalized because it was capitalized in the original expression.

TOUPPER(expr)

TOUPPER converts an expression to uppercase. For example:

```
TOUPPER(a friend in need is a friend indeed)
```

777

becomes

```
A FRIEND IN NEED IS A FRIEND INDEED
```

TOLOWER(expr)

TOLOWER converts an expression to lowercase. For example:

```
TOLOWER(A STITCH IN TIME SAVES NINE)
```

becomes

```
a stitch in time saves nine
```

Formatting Your Merge Documents

When you create a form file, you should consider two formatting issues. First, you need to understand the basics of WordPerfect formatting codes and how you can apply them most efficiently and avoid formatting problems. Second, you need to understand how to format the merge codes so that it is easy to follow the logic of your merge, without inserting unwanted formatting into the merged document.

Using Formatting Codes Efficiently in a Merge

As you learned in Workshop III, "Formatting," WordPerfect's formatting codes may be placed either in the body of your document or in Document Initial Codes. The body of the document is the part of your document that is visible on your editing screen. Document Initial Codes is a special place in your document that is part of the normally invisible file header (also called the document prefix). In some kinds of documents, it doesn't make a great deal of difference whether you insert codes into the body of the document or into the Document Initial Codes area. For merge form files, however, it is much more efficient to place as much of the formatting as possible in Document Initial Codes. If the formatting codes are in Document Initial Codes, they are not repeated with each iteration of the merge, and WordPerfect is capable of processing and printing the document more efficiently.

Suppose, for example, you need to use five formatting codes in a form file that you plan to merge with a data file of 250 records. If you place the formatting codes in Document Initial Codes, WordPerfect has to analyze and act on them only once. If you place them in the body of the document, WordPerfect has to analyze and act on them *once for each record*. In this case, WordPerfect must process 5×250, or 1,250 codes, as opposed to only five if you had placed them in Document Initial Codes. The more formatting codes you use and the more records in your data file, the greater the difference in efficiency between placing the codes in Document Initial Codes and in the body of the document.

Avoiding Formatting Problems in Merged Documents

One common formatting problem in merged documents is that the first merged record is formatted correctly, but all subsequent records are not. If this happens to you, it is because you changed your formatting in the middle of the form file, but never set it back to its original settings. For example, suppose your form file uses the default tab settings of every half inch. At the end of the letter, you reset the tabs for a signature block. When you merge the form with your data file, the first letter formats correctly, but all subsequent letters are a mess.

The reason for this is that after resetting the tabs at the bottom of the letter, WordPerfect did not encounter another tab set code to reset the tabs back to their original settings. To rectify the problem, if you change any formatting midway through the form file, just be sure you include a corresponding code at the beginning of the form file to set it back to the original setting. This is one exception to the rule that all formatting codes should be placed in Document Initial Codes.

An even better way to handle this situation is to block the part of the document that uses different formatting settings, and then apply the formatting, such as a font, tab set, or margin change to the block. By blocking the text before applying the formatting, WordPerfect inserts a pair of *revertible* codes at the beginning and end of the block. If you delete either code of the pair, the corresponding code is deleted with it. If you use revertible codes, you don't have to worry about resetting the formatting at the beginning of the form file.

Formatting Fields in Your Form File

Often, you may want to format a particular field differently from the rest of the form file. This is easy to do in WordPerfect. Just select the `FIELD(field)` code in the form file and apply the formatting you want. For example, you may want to make the company name bold when you use it on an envelope. In Reveal Codes, the company field would look like this:

```
[Bold on][MRG:FIELD]Company[mrg:field][Bold Off]
```

You also can apply Block Protect to parts of your form file to keep text together on a page. This is especially handy, for example, if there is a chance that your form file may overflow onto a second page. To avoid stranding the closing for the letter on a page by itself, block the last paragraph, the closing, and the signature block and apply block protect.

779

Formatting Merge Statements

Normally, when you create a form file, every text character is processed by the merge. As a consequence, every hard return, tab, and space character contributes to the format of the final document. When you enter complex merge statements in a form file, you are faced with a quandary. If you are careful not to use any unnecessary [HRt] or [Tab] codes, your merge document will be impossible to read. If you use [HRt] and [Tab] codes to make the merge statements more readable, you'll probably introduce unwanted blank lines and extra tabs in your final merged document.

Fortunately, there are two solutions to this problem. One is simply to use the COMMENT() command to prevent formatting characters from having any effect in your final document. This is less than ideal, however, because the COMMENT codes themselves contribute to the screen clutter. In the following example, two COMMENT codes are used to suppress the [HRt][Tab] code combinations.

```
IFNOTBLANK(shipping address)COMMENT(
     )FIELD(shipping address)COMMENT(
ELSE COMMENT(
     )FIELD(mailing address)COMMENT(
ENDIF
```

A better solution is to use the CODES(merge codes) command to surround the entire statement. When the CODES command is in effect, WordPerfect ignores everything that is not a merge code. The IFNOTBLANK example we saw previously would appear like this:

```
CODES(
IFNOTBLANK(shipping address)
     FIELD(shipping address)
ELSE
     FIELD(mailing address)
ENDIF
)
```

If you need to include regular text or formatting codes within the CODES command, use the INSERT(text). For example, the INSERT command was used in the following example to include the words FIRST CLASS or THIRD CLASS and a blank line above the shipping address:

```
CODES(
IF(FIELD(class)"="first")
     INSERT(FIRST CLASS
)
ELSE
     INSERT(THIRD CLASS
)
ENDIF
FIELD(shipping address
)
```

Controlling the Merge Display

Normally, WordPerfect does not display the merge in progress on the screen in order to optimize performance. While the merge is in progress, it provides a prompt on the status line that reads: Merging Record: n, where n is the number of the record that is being merged. If you want to see the merge in progress, you can include a REWRITE code in your document to display the merged text up to that point.

If you are merging from the keyboard, WordPerfect automatically displays the form file up to 1,000 characters past the point where it has paused for user input. This enables the user to see the context for the text he or she is entering. In some cases, this display may appear cluttered, especially if there are many merge codes in the form file. To control how much of the document is visible when you merge from the keyboard, use a DISPLAYSTOP command at each point in the form file where you want to limit the display.

Tip: See Chapter 48 for a discussion of display options for merge codes.

Debugging Tips

▲ Run a test merge of 7 to 10 records before doing a large merge. The easiest way to do this is to specify a record number range in the Data File Options option group on the expanded Run Merge dialog box. You can also insert a stop code in the data file after the last record you want to merge and remove it after you finish testing.

▲ Be sure your field names in your form file match the spellings of the field names in your data file. Capitalization doesn't count, but spaces do.

▲ A merge ends when an error condition, such as reaching the end of the data file, is created. If your merge should continue after the end of the data file has been reached, use an ONCANCEL command.

▲ Avoid using spaces between an ENDFIELD code and the hard return that follows it. If you do, you'll get an extra blank line each time you use that field.

▲ If you use the PRINT command, you'll almost certainly need the PAGEOFF command. If you're getting an extra blank page after each merged record, you probably need to use the PAGEOFF command.

▲ Unneeded blank lines at the end of a form file are another reason for blank pages between merged records. The blank lines may be just enough to cause the document to flow onto the next page when the merged data is inserted.

▲ Ending a form file with an unneeded hard page code results in extra blank pages.

▲ If your merge seems to skip every other record in the data file, you probably have an unnecessary NEXTRECORD code in your form file.

Merge Tips

▲ Work in Text mode for greater speed.

▲ Use only your printer's built-in fonts for greater speed when merging to the printer.

▲ Although WP can merge with files in 5.x format, performance is faster if the merge files are converted to 6.0 format first. To convert older merge files to 6.0 format, open and save them in WordPerfect 6.0.

▲ Although WordPerfect can merge directly with ASCII delimited files, merging is faster with data files in WordPerfect format. To convert an ASCII delimited file to WordPerfect merge format, open it from the file manager. WordPerfect prompts you to choose a file format for the file you are opening. Choose DOS Delimited Text, rather than ASCII Text (Standard); change the delimiter characters if necessary; and then save the file in WordPerfect 6.0 format.

Data File Tips

▲ Normally, you shouldn't have formatting commands in your data file.

▲ Use the FIELDNAMES command to name your fields. Working with named fields is much easier than working with numbered fields.

▲ There is no absolute limit to the number of fields and records you can have in a data file. You can only have 255 named fields in a text data file and only 25 named fields in a table data file.

▲ Use a text data file if you have more than 7 to 8 fields, if you have a large number of records, or if you have a slow computer.

▲ Use a table data file if you value ease of use over speed and if you can display most fields without wrapping.

▲ There is no limit to the length of a field in a text data file. Fields in a table data file must fit within a single table cell. Corresponding fields do not have to have the same number of lines.

▲ Put the field that you are most likely to use as a sort key first. For example, if you are most likely to sort your data file by the LAST NAME field, that should be Field 1.

▲ Divide the data into separate fields for the most flexibility.

▲ The `END FIELD` code after the last field, immediately before an `END RECORD` code is optional. Both methods are permissible, but you should be consistent.

▲ You may use the data fields in any order and as many times as you like in the form file. You don't need to use every field from the data file in your merge.

Form File Tips

▲ Put as many of your formatting codes as possible in Document Initial Codes. This way, they are processed only once for the entire merge, rather than once for each data record. Most formatting codes can be placed in Document Initial Codes, but merge codes cannot.

▲ If you need to change formatting for a section of a document, block it and apply the formatting to the block. This causes WordPerfect to use Revertible Codes for that block.

▲ Spell check your form file before merging.

▲ To cancel a merge, press Cancel (Escape) or Ctrl+Break. To cancel a merge from the keyboard, press Exit (F7); or Shift+F9, S (Stop); or Shift+F9, Q.

▲ Use the Merge button bar on the supplementary disk to make it easier to enter merge commands.

▲ If you use graphics, use the "Image on Disk" option to reduce the size and memory requirements for the merged document.

▲ Don't forget that you can merge data into headers, footers, text boxes, endnotes, and footnotes. Merging into a header is a great way to personalize a multipage letter or memo.

▲ If you are using page numbering and you are not merging to the printer, remember to use a `[Pg Num Set]` code on the first page of your form file to reset the page number to one.

▲ Use Block Protect and Conditional End of Page in your form file to control page breaks.

▲ Whenever you expect to reuse your form files, it's worth the effort to include merge language commands rather than enter the equivalent options on the Run Merge dialog box.

by Marilyn Horn Claff

Merge Projects

Now that you understand merge fundamentals and know how to use some of WordPerfect's merge programming commands, the fun begins! The projects in this chapter build on the skills you learned in Chapters 47, "Basic Merge," 48, "Intermediate Merging," and 49, "Advanced Merge Topics," so review those chapters if you have any difficulty with the merge features used in these projects. The projects also incorporate a wide range of formatting features that were covered in earlier sections, so you may need to brush up on your formatting skills as well.

The goal of this chapter is to help you understand how to "pull it all together" to solve real-life problems with Merge. All of the projects require the use of WordPerfect's merge language, but don't let that be an obstacle. Sample files for all of these projects are included on the *Super Book* disk, so you can actually try them to see how they work before you attempt to apply these ideas to your own merge projects. When you see how easy it can be to handle potentially tricky situations, you'll appreciate the power and scope of WordPerfect's merge language.

Fundraising Letter

Sooner or later, nearly everyone has to do a mass mailing. Fortunately, it doesn't have to be a traumatic experience. Once you set up a basic form file for your letter, you can use it as a model for future letters.

Note: All the files you'll need to try these projects are included on the *Super Book* disk. Use the install program on the disk to install them to your hard disk. Then copy into your document directory all the files listed for each project. If the files aren't in your current directory, you'll have to include a full pathname for each file in the Run Merge dialog box, and you'll have to modify the files that use merge commands that refer other files by name.

WordPerfect Features Used

```
IF...[ELSE...]ENDIF statements
```
`DOCUMENT()` merge command to insert document
Merge into a header
`CHAINFORM()` merge command to chain to envelope form file
`POSTNET()` merge command to create a bar code on the envelope

Files Used

```
FUNDRAIS.FF (main form file for letter)
ENVELOPE.FF (form file for envelope)
AUMNI.DF (alumni data file)
WORTHY.LST (document with list of projects)
```

Your first project is to create a fundraising letter and matching envelopes. This project illustrates how to use the `DOCUMENT()` command to pull in another document, techniques for handling multipage form letters, and an easy way to create matching envelopes with bar codes.

1. Open FUNDRAIS.FF (on the *Super Book* disk) and examine the formatting and merge codes (see Figure 50.1).

2. Now merge FUNDRAIS.FF with ALUMNI.DF (also on the *Super Book* disk).

Tip: FUNDRAIS.FF is already on your screen, so tell WordPerfect that you want to use the current document as your form file by leaving blank the Form File text entry box on the Run Merge dialog box. When you press Tab to move the insertion point to the Data File text entry box, WordPerfect displays the words *(Current Document)* in the Form File text entry box.

3. We've used the `IFNOTBLANK...ENDIF` construct twice in this letter, as well as on the corresponding envelope. In plain English, the merge statement following the name in the inside address reads, "If the Class field isn't blank, include the phrase *Class of* and the contents of the Class field.

   The body of the letter contains an `IFNOTBLANK...ELSE...ENDIF` statement that translates "If the Class field isn't blank, include the phrase *The Class of* and the class contents of the Class field; otherwise, if the Class field is blank, include the phrase *your class.*

4. The `DOCUMENT(filename)` merge code pulls the named file into the letter. Here, it includes a list of worthy causes for your fundraising dollars.

   To make the list stand out, we changed the margins immediately before and after the `DOCUMENT()` code. These margin changes were inserted as *revertible* codes by blocking the `DOCUMENT()` code before choosing **L**ayout, **M**argins and entering the new values. Revertible codes apply only to that particular section of the document. You can tell the codes are revertible because they begin with a plus or a minus character (see Figure 50.1).

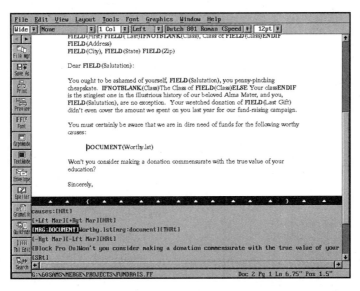

Figure 50.1. Revertible margins codes surrounding the DOCUMENT command.

If you delete either code in a pair of revertible codes, the corresponding code is deleted with it. Because the codes are revertible, changing the margins in the first part of the document (before the revertible codes) is reflected automatically in the last part of the document (after the revertible codes).

If the inserted file includes any formatting codes, those codes carry over to affect the subsequent formatting of the main document, until WordPerfect encounters formatting codes that override them.

Normally, in a form file, you should include as much of your formatting as WordPerfect allows in Document Initial Codes, rather than at the beginning of the document, because this technique minimizes the number of codes in the final merged document. However, if you need to change format settings—such as margins, fonts, or tabs—midway through the form file, you must either use revertible codes for a section of the document or reset those formatting codes at the beginning of the document. For example, if you change your left margin from 1 inch to 1.5 inches in the middle of page one, you need to include a margin code for a 1 inch margin at the top of page one, even if it agrees with your Document Initial Codes setting. When WordPerfect reads in the form file for the next record, it carries over the format settings that were in effect at the end of the last form file instead of reading the default settings from Document Initial Codes. Inserting formatting codes at the beginning of the form file forces WordPerfect to return to those settings when it performs the next merge iteration.

5. If you examine the fundraising form letter carefully, you'll see that it incorporates several useful techniques for working with multipage form letters, such as headers that begin on page two, page numbering, and intelligent page breaks. Most merge letters are only a single page, but if your letter is longer, you could run into problems if you aren't careful. Fortunately, these problems are easy to solve.

One common mistake involves page numbering. Unless you're merging to the printer and if you use page numbering in a merge document, you must remember to reset the page number to one on the first page. By default, WordPerfect merges to the screen, creating a single large file from the merged records. If you don't reset the page number to 1 at the beginning of the form file, your letters will be numbered consecutively. This problem shows up more frequently in multipage merges because page numbering is rarely used in single-page documents.

Tip: If you are merging to the printer, you don't need to reset the page numbering because every merged record is treated like a new document.

6. One of WordPerfect's strengths, and best-kept secrets, is its capability of merging into a header or footer. Why not customize your merge documents by inserting the recipient's name in the header? Most other word processors can't do this (and most WordPerfect users don't know that WordPerfect can do this), so you might even fool people into thinking that you actually wrote them a customized letter.

To merge into a header, insert merge commands in the header (see Figure 50.2). (Figure 50.4 shows the header after merging.)

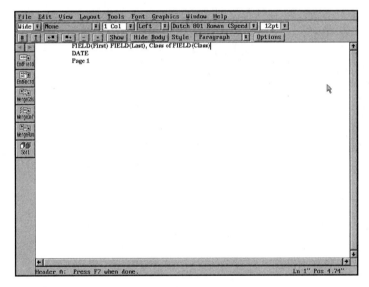

Figure 50.2. Header with merge codes.

Tip: Not only can you merge into headers and footers, but you can also merge into footnotes, endnotes, and text boxes. To make the name and date bold in the completed merge, block the merge commands and choose Bold.

7. Orphaned signature blocks are unacceptable in any letter. Style books recommend that you keep a minimum of two lines of text on the page with the signature block. Your merged letters will look more professional if you set up your form file to automatically insert the page breaks where you want them. To avoid stranded signature blocks, use Block Protect around the last paragraph and closing.

Note: Widow/Orphan Protect and Conditional End of Page are two other ways to help control page breaks. Widow/Orphan Protect prevents single lines of paragraphs from being isolated at the top or bottom of a page. Conditional End of Page keeps a specified number of lines together on a page and is used primarily to keep headings with their following text. Both these features can be used in merge form files. Place the Widow/Orphan Protect code in Document Initial Codes.

Tip: Avoid using Hard Page breaks in form files, especially if the length of the letter could vary from page to page.

8. Although WordPerfect 6.0 has a menu option for creating matching envelopes during a merge, the procedure requires several steps and must be done from scratch each time. A better option is to include a command to chain to an envelope form file. Once you set up an envelope form file, you can chain to it from any form file (provided you used the same field names). In this project, we used a special version of our envelope form file because we wanted to include the recipients' graduation year on the envelope.

Note: No matter where the CHAINFORM() command is located in the form file, chaining occurs only after the merge of original form and data files has been completed.

Matching Envelopes

1. To create matching envelopes for the fundraising letter, we've chained to an envelope form file called ENVELOPE.FF. Because we didn't include a CHAINDATA command specifying a new data file, WordPerfect reuses the ALUMNI.DF data file.

2. Note the use of the IFNOTBLANK...ENDIF command to handle possible blank CLASS fields. In English, this statement means, "If the CLASS field isn't empty, include a comma, a space character, the phrase *Class of*, and the contents of the CLASS field."

Note: The first line of the envelope address looks as though it's too long to fit on one line, but this is due only to the space occupied by the merge codes. If you find the extra space taken by the merge codes disconcerting, you can either hide the merge codes or display them as icons. If you display the merge codes as icons, each code is represented by a solid diamond character and takes the space of a single character. See Chapter 47 for details.

3. To reduce postage costs, we've used the POSTNET(zip) merge command to create bar codes from the contents of the zip field. WordPerfect can automatically create bar codes from 5-, 9-, and 11-digit numbers. If the field used with the POSTNET() command doesn't contain a 5-, 9-, or 11-digit number, WordPerfect ignores it.

 Tip: If you look at a bar code in Reveal Codes, you can see the number from which it was created. For example, you would see [Bar Code:60666] for a bar code created from the 60666 zip code.

Figures 50.3, 50.4, and 50.5 show the completed two-page letter and envelope.

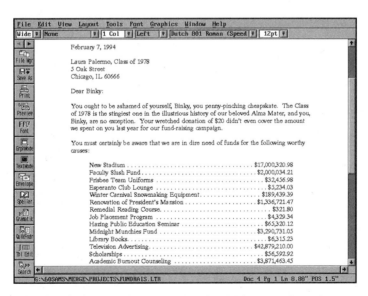

Figure 50.3. Merge letter as displayed in Graphics mode.

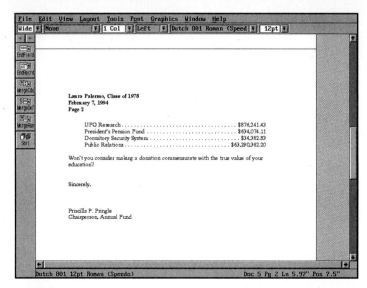

Figure 50.4. Merged letter as displayed in Page mode, showing header.

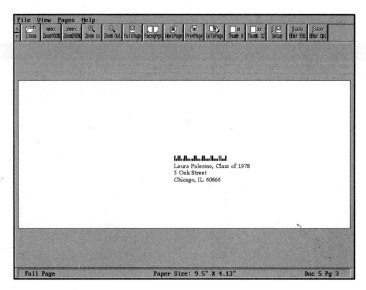

Figure 50.5. Merged envelope.

4. To create alternate letters and envelopes, don't use the CHAINFORM() command or the Run Merge envelope command. Both of these methods create the envelopes after all the letters have been merged. Instead, use a

NESTFORM() command to nest an envelope form file or create an envelope as the last page of your letter form file. (See the next project, the confirmation letter, for an example of a nested envelope form file.) Be sure to include a paper size/type code at the beginning of your letter so that WordPerfect does not print the letter.

Confirmation Letters and Envelopes

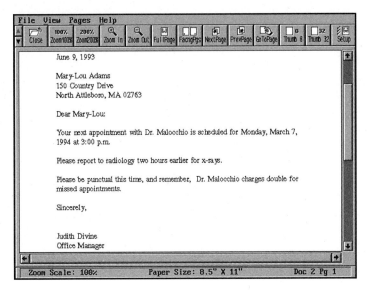

Figure 50.6. CONFIRM.LTR.

WordPerfect Features Used

▲ Combine merging from the keyboard with merging from a file

▲ Attach the data file to the primary file with SUBSTDATA command

▲ Use a WHILE loop to look up a specific record in the data file

▲ Use GETSTRING command to get multicharacter response

▲ Use CHAR command to get single character response

▲ Use TOUPPER and TOLOWER to simplify variable checking

▲ Use NESTFORM to nest a form file that creates an envelope

▲ Use the CODES command so that [HRt] and [Tab] codes can be used to format merge commands without affecting the appearance of the merged document

Files Used

CONFIRM.FF—main form file for letter
ENVELOPE.FF—form file for envelope
PATIENTS.DF—patient data file

The third project is a confirmation letter for an appointment. You're more likely to write confirmation letters singly or in small batches, so we've set them up as a merge from the keyboard. This merge pauses for you to enter the date and time for the appointment.

The most important rule in word processing is "Never retype anything if you can possibly avoid it." We've assumed that you already have a data file which contains the recipient's name, address, and identifying code. All that's missing is the date and time for the appointment. You only need to use the date and time information once, so it wouldn't make sense to add it to your data base unless you needed to prepare a large batch (that is, several dozen or more) of these letters at a time.

Our approach to this problem, then, is to combine merging with a file and merging from the keyboard. That way, you can use your existing data file of names and addresses, but you'll be able to customize each letter easily by typing information directly into the letter during a pause.

Try the merge to see how it works from the user's perspective. After you complete the merge, read the detailed analysis of the files.

1. To start, choose Merge; or press Ctrl+F9. The Run Merge dialog box appears. In the Form File text entry box, type CONFIRM.FF. Leave the Data File box blank and choose Merge.

> **Note:** You don't need to enter the name of the data file in the Run Merge dialog box because it's included in the letter form file. (See the following analysis of the CONFIRM.FF form file.) This technique is convenient if you know that you will always use the same data file with a particular form file. Note that if you enter the name of a data file in the Run Merge dialog box, WordPerfect ignores it in favor of the name of the data file provided in the form file.

2. The Patient Code dialog box appears. Enter a patient code and choose OK. The patients' codes for this practice example are:

CL-2150
PE-5085
TQ-6791
WX-3478

It doesn't matter whether you enter the code in upper- or lowercase because we've allowed for both. If you don't enter a valid code, the merge ends.

> **Note:** The codes are listed in the dialog box for the merge file on the disk.

3. For greater efficiency with longer data files, assume that the data file has been sorted by the key field (patient code, in this case) and that if you need to select multiple records, you'll select them in alphabetical order. If you don't make these assumptions, you would have to begin searching for a match at the beginning of the data file instead of at the current record. If you don't enter a patient code in order, WordPerfect won't be able to find that record unless you restart the merge. Restarting the merge forces WordPerfect to begin searching the data file from the beginning.

> **Note:** Selecting records by the patient code field works because each patient code is unique. Using the last-name field would make this merge easier for the user, but more complicated to set up. To choose a record by the last-name field, you need to test at least one other field in the data file because the last name isn't a unique identifier.

4. WordPerfect displays the beginning of the letter, beeps, and pauses for you to type the date for the appointment. No dialog box appears this time because we used the KEYBOARD command to pause for data. The KEYBOARD command enables you to type data directly into your document. A message on the status line reminds you what to do (enter the date of the appointment and press F9). Because the KEYBOARD prompt is so subtle compared to the dialog boxes used by the GETSTRING and CHAR commands used elsewhere in this merge, we preceded the KEYBOARD command with a BEEP command to alert you that WordPerfect is waiting for you to do something.

Type the date for the appointment and press F9 to continue the merge to the next merge code that requires user input.

Tip: In a data file, F9 enters an ENDFIELD code. In a form file, F9 ends a pause and continues the merge.

Note: When WordPerfect pauses at a KEYBOARD command, you can use most editing and formatting features, including Undelete, Speller, Thesaurus, Document Information, Block, and even Grammatik.

5. WordPerfect pauses so that you can enter the time for the appointment. After you press F9 again, WordPerfect displays a dialog box asking whether x-rays are required. If you answer affirmatively, the merge inserts a sentence in the letter reminding the user to report to Radiology two hours before his or her appointment. Because we used the CHAR command here, you only need to type a single character.

6. WordPerfect completes the letter, creates a matching envelope complete with bar code, and sends the letter and envelope to the printer. The envelope is created from a nested form file. Unlike the fundraising letter in the previous project, we don't use a CHAINFORM command to create the envelope. Instead, we use the NESTFORM command because we want to generate an envelope immediately after the letter is completed.

7. The merge now asks you whether you need to send another confirmation letter. If you answer y or Y, WordPerfect begins the process over, starting the next search from the point in the data file where the last match was found. If you answer n or N, the merge ends.

   Now watch it work. Open CONFIRM.FF, the main form file.(See Figure 50.7.)

8. CODES, the first merge code, tells WordPerfect to ignore everything in parentheses but the merge codes. The CODES command allows you to use [HRt] and [Tab] codes to format the merge commands so that they're easier to read.

9. SUBSTDATA(patients.df) tells WordPerfect to substitute the PATIENTS.DF data file. If you entered the name of a data file in the Run Merge dialog box, WordPerfect would ignore it and use the data file named by the SUBSTDATA file. The SUBSTDATA technique is very handy when you expect always to use the same data file with a particular form file.

10. Note the LABEL(begin) code. After the first letter and envelope are completed, the merge loops back to this label and continues to create letters and envelopes for other patients. We deliberately placed the label after the SUBSTDATA code. (We explain why a bit later.)

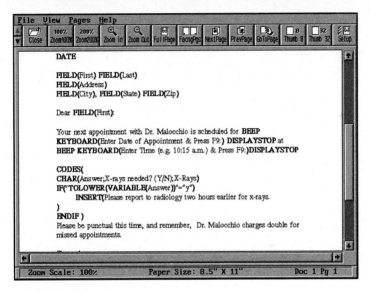

Figure 50.7. CONFIRM.FF.

11. The `GETSTRING` command prompts the user to type the patient code. which is saved as a variable named `P_Code`. The syntax for the `GETSTRING` command is

    ```
    GETSTRING(var[;prompt][;title])
    ```

    The only required parameter for `GETSTRING` is the variable. The message prompt and the title for the dialog box are optional. (For more information about the `GETSTRING` command, see Chapter 49.)

12. We used a trick here to create a multiline message in the `GETSTRING` dialog box. When you enter a `GETSTRING` command (Shift+F9, Shift+F9, g, Enter), you can't enter a multiline prompt in the Parameter Entry dialog box. After you close the Parameter Entry dialog box, however, you can edit the `GETSTRING` command and insert `[HRt]` codes in the prompt, as in this example in which the prompt is displayed on five lines:

    ```
    GETSTRING(P_Code;Enter patient code:
    CL-2150
    PE-5085
    TQ-6791
    WX-3478;Patient Code)
    ```

    We've placed the title parameter (Patient Code) on the same line as the last patient code in our list; if we had placed the `;Patient Code` on a new line, there would have been an extra blank line after the last patient code in the list.

13. The next statement is a `WHILE` loop that instructs WordPerfect to compare the variable `p_code` to the field `p_code` in the data file. The basic merge statement looks like this:

```
WHILE("VARIABLE(P_Code)"!="FIELD(P_Code)")
NEXTRECORD
ENDWHILE
```

In English, this means, "While the variable `p_code` is not equal to the field `p_code`, get the next record." As long as the two don't match, WordPerfect continues to get the next record and recompare the variable `P_Code` with the `Field P_Code`. When WordPerfect encounters a match, the `WHILE` loop ends.

14. To eliminate the possibility of a mismatch due to a difference in case, we added the `TOUPPER` command to convert the contents of the variable `P_Code` and the contents of the field `P_Code` to uppercase:

```
WHILE("TOUPPER(VARIABLE(P_CODE))"!="TOUPPER(FIELD(P_CODE))")
NEXTRECORD
ENDWHILE
```

15. Because we're comparing text strings (sequences of characters) rather than numerical values, we need to use quotation marks around each expression we're comparing.

It doesn't matter whether you use double (") or single (') quote characters as long as each pair on each side of the equation matches. In other words, you can say

```
WHILE("VARIABLE(last)"='Jones')....
```

or

```
WHILE('VARIABLE(last)'="Jones")....
```

16. In the body of the letter, you'll find a combination of `BEEP` and `KEYBOARD` commands to alert the user and pause for input. We added the `DISPLAYSTOP` codes to prevent the merge codes and text that follow the `DISPLAYSTOP` codes from being displayed while the merge is stopped for user input. Suppressing these codes and text helps eliminate extraneous clutter on the screen.

17. The `CODES` statement is similar to the one used at the beginning of the file. The only difference here is the use of the `INSERT` command to insert the sentence, "Please report to radiology two hours earlier for x-rays." followed by a `[HRt]` code. If you simply type this text within the `CODES` parentheses, WordPerfect would have ignored it.

18. The `CHAR` command is like the `GETSTRING` command, except that it pauses for a single keystroke which is assigned to a variable called `ANSWER`. We then use an `IF` statement to see whether the contents of the variable `ANSWER` is equal to *y* or *Y*. Rather than test both cases in the `IF` statement,

we use `TOLOWER(VARIABLE(answer))` to convert the variable `ANSWER` to lowercase before testing its value.

19. At the end of the letter, we inserted a regular Hard Page break to separate the letter from the envelope, which is created for the letter because of the `NESTFORM` command in the next and final statement. As we did with the other two complex merge statements, we used the `CODES` command with the final merge statement so that we could format the commands for readability.

20. The `NESTFORM` command nests the ENVELOPE.FF to create a matching envelope. Because PATIENTS.DF uses the same field codes as ALUMNI.DF does, you can use the same envelope form file.

> **Note:** ENVELOPE.FF includes an `IFNOTBLANK` statement that refers to the class field in ALUMNI.DF, but because PATIENTS.DF doesn't have a field by this name, the statement is ignored.

After the `NESTFORM` statement, we included a `REWRITE` code to force WordPerfect to update the screen, followed by a `PRINT` command to send all the merged data at that point to the printer. Omitting this command would create a file that consists of a letter and envelope for each patient code that we selected. Finally, we ask the user if he or she wants to do another letter:

```
CHAR(Answer;Do another? (Y/N);Repeat)
IF("TOLOWER(VARIABLE(Answer))"!="y")
        STOP
ELSE
        GO(Begin)
ENDIF
```

If the answer is *y* or *Y*, the merge loops back to the Begin label and restarts. If the answer is anything else, a `STOP` command ends the merge immediately. (We could also have used the `QUIT` command in this case, since we are at the end of the rest of the form file.) We must use an explicit `QUIT` or `STOP` command in order to end the merge, because as long as the record pointer is not at the end of the data file, WordPerfect would restart the merge from the beginning if we answered with anything other than "y" or "Y", in which case WordPerfect transfers control to the Begin label. If the answer is anything else, the merge ends. Note that the label Begin comes after the `SUBSTDATA` command. This may seem like a trivial point, but it actually has important consequences. If the `SUBSTDATA` command occurred after the label, each time you restart the merge, WordPerfect would start from the beginning of the data file. By placing the label after the `SUBSTDATA` command, WordPerfect begins the search for the next patient code at the current pointer location in the data file rather than at the beginning. Provided that you sort the data file before you run this merge and that you enter the patient codes in sequence, this technique is far faster than starting at the beginning of the data file each time you search for a patient code.

Mailing Labels

WordPerfect Features Used

▲ Merge into labels

▲ Center all pages to center the address on each label

▲ Use Document Initial Codes to avoid printing one address per sheet of labels

Files Used

S_LABELS.FF - form file for labels

PATIENTS.DF - data file with names and addresses

The third and last mailing project involves creating a batch of mailing labels. We use the Avery Name Badge labels (5095), which have four labels per sheet.

If you've mastered basic merge letters and envelopes, there are no new merge commands to learn. We included this project to show you how to format your labels easily and to avoid typical label traps. To re-create the S_Labels.ff form file, follow these instructions:

1. Insert the following formatting codes into the Document Initial Codes section of your form file.

```
[Labels Form:Avery 5095 Name Badge]
[Paper Sz/Typ:8.5" x 11",Avery Name Badge 5095]
[Lft Mar:0.5"]
[Rgt Mar:0.5"]
[Centr Pgs:On]
```

Tip: To view labels side-by-side on your editing screen, you must work in Page mode. In Graphics mode, labels appear as a series of pages. You may prefer to work in Graphics mode because it is considerably faster than Page mode.

When you choose a label size, WordPerfect inserts two codes in your document, a `[Labels Form]` code and a `[Paper Sz/Typ]` code.

Change the left and right margin to 3/4" (instead of 0") so that the addresses don't print too far to the left.

Use WordPerfect's Center Pages feature to center all pages. WordPerfect treats each label like a page, so all the addresses are centered vertically on the label.

> **Note:** WordPerfect's two center page features—Center Page (one page only) and Center Pages—center your text vertically in the live area of the page, not between the physical edges of the page and not necessarily between the top and bottom margins. The live area of the page is the text area between the header, or top margin if there is no header, and the footer, or the bottom margin if there is no footer. Therefore, if you want text to appear perfectly centered on a page of labels, make your page symmetrical. The top and bottom margins should be equal, and if you use a header, you should create a footer that takes up the same amount of space as the header.

2. Change the Document Initial Font to Swiss 721 Roman (Speedo), Bitstream's version of Helvetica.

3. Add the merge fields that you need.

4. Place the `POSTNET` merge command above the address to create a bar code. `POSTNET` takes the name of the zip code fields as its parameter.

5. To make the name stand out, block the `FIELD(First)` and `FIELD(Last)` and bold the line. Because the merge codes are boldfaced, the text that replaces them during the merge are boldfaced as well.

6. After you run the merge, a sheet of four labels will look like the ones in Figure 50.8.

> **Tip:** For an example of a fancier label format, see Workshop XIII, "Projects."

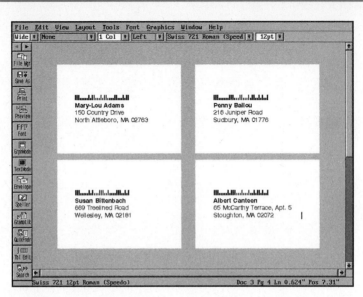

Figure 50.8. Merged labels, as displayed in Page mode.

Advanced Features

by Cathy Wallach

Sorting

Sorting allows you to arrange information in alphabetical or numeric order. This function gives WordPerfect database-like features, much in the same way that the Tables function gives WordPerfect spreadsheet-like features. WordPerfect's Select feature is a component of Sort; it allows you to extract specific information from a file. The combination of Sort and Select gives WordPerfect powerful capabilities.

The more planning you give to setting up your lists, the more powerful and flexible your sort and select functions can be. Perhaps you run a small business and want to mail a brochure only to those customers who have ordered from you within the last six months. If you've included this information in your mailing list, you'll be able to select only these names and sort them by zip code for a bulk mailing. WordPerfect can perform these two steps in one operation.

How WordPerfect 6.0 Performs Database Functions

WordPerfect 6.0 views and organizes text for sorting just as a database would. In a database, related information is grouped into *records*. A company name, address, phone number, and contact is one example of a record. Each record is divided into *fields*. In the previous

example, company name would be one field, phone number another, and so on. WordPerfect sorts and selects records based on the contents of the fields.

WordPerfect allows you to sort by specific words within a field, a task which most database applications cannot do without special programming. You can also perform a numeric sort, which specifically ignores dollar signs and recognizes negative numbers. You can sort in either ascending order (A to Z and lowest to highest numbers) or descending order (Z to A and highest to lowest numbers). New to 6.0 is the capability to perform both an ascending and descending sort in the same pass. For example, you can sort a list of salespersons alphabetically by territory, and within that territory you can sort numerically from highest to lowest sales volume figures. Also new is the capability to sort parallel columns.

Types of Records

WordPerfect 6.0 can perform sorts on five different types of records—line, paragraph, merge data file, tables, and parallel columns. WordPerfect determines the way in which records and fields are identified within the file and automatically assigns the appropriate record type. The table below shows how WordPerfect defines and subdivides each type of record.

Record Type	Definition of Record	Field Separators Within That Record Type	
Line	Text ending with a hard return	Fields:	Tabs, indents
		Words:	Spaces, forward slashes (/), hard hyphens (dashes)
Paragraph	Text ending with two or more hard returns	Lines:	Hard returns
		Fields:	Tab, indents
		Words:	Spaces, forward slashes (/), hard hyphens (dashes)
Merge Data File		Fields:	Text ending with an ENDFIELD code
	ENDRECORD code	Lines:	Hard returns
		Words:	Spaces, forward slashes (/), hard hyphens (dashes)
Table	Rows of cells	Cells:	[Cell] code
		Lines:	Hard returns
		Words:	Spaces, forward slashes (/), hard hyphens (dashes)

Record Type	Definition of Record	Field Separators Within That Record Type	
Parallel Column	Rows of columns	Columns:	`[HCol]` code
		Lines:	Hard returns
		Words:	Spaces, forward slashes (/), hard hyphens (dashes)

Caution: When you create a file for sorting, it is vital to be consistent. Your sort will not work correctly if you have different numbers of fields within records, or if the type of information within fields or lines varies from one record to another. For example, if the zip code is the last entry of the last line in field four in some records, it must have that position in all records for a sort on zip code to work properly.

The Sort Source and Destination Dialog Box

The first Sort dialog box you will see is the Sort Source and Destination dialog box shown in Figure 51.1. The only time you will not see this box is if your cursor is in a table or a parallel column, or if you have blocked text. In those three cases, WordPerfect assumes you want to sort the column, table, or blocked text.

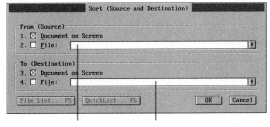

Source File   Destination File

Figure 51.1. The Sort (Source and Destination) dialog box.

807

Sorting a File on Disk and Specifying a Destination File

Most of the time, you will be sorting from the file on-screen and will want the input to also appear on-screen. In that case, you will accept the defaults of the Sort Source and Destination Box and by selecting OK.

However, at times you may want to start your sort from a blank document screen and have the sort procedure retrieve a document, the source file, for you. You may also want to perform a sort that does not change your file but outputs the results to an off-screen file that WordPerfect refers to as a destination file. Designating an output file is particularly useful when you use the Select procedure. To sort a file from disk or to output to a destination file, follow Procedures 51.1 and 51.2.

 Note: You cannot sort a source file from disk if it was a parallel column or a table.

Procedure 51.1. Sorting a file from disk.

1. Choose Tools, Sort; or press Ctrl+F9, Sort. The Sort (Source and Destination) dialog box appears.

 Caution: Be sure to open a new document before you select a source file on disk that you want to output to screen. If you already have a doc-ument on-screen, the sorted source file will be added to the document on-screen at the cursor position.

2. Select File.

3. Type the name of the file you wish to sort, including the path if the file is not in the current default directory. If you don't know the filename, you may use F5 for File List or F6 for QuickList.

 Tip: You can also press the down arrow key or select the down arrow to the right of the filename box to see a list of the last three files you have sorted. Pressing the down arrow will only display files that have been sorted from disk, not from the screen. WordPerfect will remember these files from session to session.

4. Select OK. The file you've chosen will appear on-screen above the Sort dialog box.

5. Be sure to check Record Type and change Sort Keys if necessary. (These steps are shown in Procedures 51.3 and 51.4.)

6. When WordPerfect has finished sorting, the resulting file on-screen will be untitled. You can save it with the same name as the original file, thus replacing the original, or you can save it with a new name.

Procedure 51.2. Specifying a destination file.

1. To specify a file on disk for the output, select File from the Sort (Source and Destination) dialog box.

2. Type a name for the Destination File.

3. If a file with the same name exists, you will be asked if you want to replace the file. Select Yes if you want to overwrite the existing file; otherwise, Select No and type in a different name for the destination file.

Tip: You can search for an existing destination filename in the same ways you search for a source file.

Note: If you specify a file on disk as your destination, the sort will take place off-screen and you will not see the results until you open the destination file.

The Sort Dialog Box

Once you have selected a source and destination file, whether on-screen or from disk, you will see the Sort dialog box, as shown in Figure 51.2. This is where you give WordPerfect all of the necessary information to perform the sort.

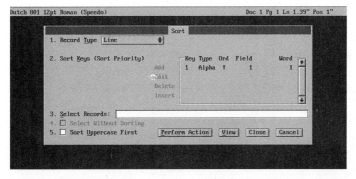

Figure 51.2. The Sort dialog box.

▲ **1. Record Type.** The Record Type is based on the format of the file to be sorted.

▲ **2. Sort Keys (Sort Priority).** Here is where you specify the pieces of information within each record by which you want to sort.

▲ **3. Select Records.** This option allows you to choose only those records that meet certain criteria.

▲ **4. Select Without Sorting.** Use this to select only certain records without changing their order. This option is greyed out until you have entered a selection statement.

▲ **5. Sort Uppercase First.** If you have two listings of the same word or words, one uppercase and one lowercase, WordPerfect will put the lowercase example first in your sort unless you select this choice.

▲ **Perform Action.** Executes the sort.

▲ **View.** Moves your cursor into the text of your document, allowing you to scroll through all the text.

▲ **Close.** Closes the Sort dialog box, saving any changes you've made.

▲ **Cancel.** Closes the Sort dialog box without saving changes.

Line Sorts

A line sort is performed on text where every record ends with a hard return (HRt). This can be as simple as putting a list of names in alphabetical order or as complex as alphabetizing a list of employees by department and, in the same sort operation, putting them in ascending numerical order by salary.

Line Sort on the First Word of the Line

The simplest type of sort is a line sort on the first word of each line. This is WordPerfect's default if you're in a file where each line ends with a hard return. You can perform this type of sort without any option changes. To perform a line sort that will alphabetize the list below by last name, follow the steps in Procedure 51.3.

Clinton, Maggie
Spleid, Kevin
Avery, Angela
Wallach, Robert Lee
Smith, Robert B.
Cary, Linda

Caution: Always save your file before performing a sort. Do not rely on the UNDO feature. If you are running under tight memory constraints and your machine freezes or you get a Windows General Protection Fault, UNDO will not do you any good!

Caution: If you have any soft returns (SRts) in your file, WordPerfect treats them as though they were hard returns and sorts these lines also. Therefore, your sort will not work as intended.

Procedure 51.3. Performing a simple line sort.

1. Choose Tools, Sort; or press Ctrl+F9, Sort. The Sort (Source and Destination) dialog box appears (see Figure 51.1).
2. To sort the file that's on-screen and to see the outcome on-screen, simply select OK to confirm WordPerfect's default choices.
3. The Sort dialog box appears (see Figure 51.3).
4. If each record in your file ends with one HRt, the Record Type will be Line. If the Record Type defaults to something other than Line, choose Record Type and choose Line.

Note: Record Type will read Paragraph if you have any double HRts (or SRts) between lines. When you select Line as the Record Type, be aware that blank lines will be sorted to the beginning of the file.

5. Because you are sorting from A to Z and by the first word of each line, simply select Perform Action, the highlighted choice.
6. You will see a display while WordPerfect is sorting that tells you the number of records examined, selected, and transferred (meaning sorted).

Note: The box may not be on-screen long enough for you to read if the sort is not complex and the document is small.

7. If the results are satisfactory, save your file. If not, Choose Edit, Undo (or press Ctrl+Z), then try again. If Undo doesn't work for any reason, simply exit without saving, reopen the file and try the sort again.

> **Caution:** Any codes that you have on a line will sort with that line. Put codes that you want to affect the entire document in Document Initial Codes.

Changing Options for a Line Sort

You may want to sort your list by something other than the first word in each line. You specify to WordPerfect exactly which information, and in what order, you wish to sort by defining Sort Keys (Sort Priority) from within the Sort dialog box. Key Number 1, which WordPerfect refers to as Key1, designates your top sort priority, Key Number 2 (Key2) your second, and so on.

WordPerfect provides nine possible levels of sort. Key Number 1 is automatically assigned to the first key you define. Editing from the Sort Key box also allows you to set whether the sort on that key is alpha or numeric, and whether it is ascending or descending. The current settings are displayed in the Sort Keys settings box in the Sort dialog box. Sort Keys are retained throughout a session, but not when you exit WordPerfect.

- ▲ **Key Number.** This is where you set the sort priority.
- ▲ **Type.** Select this to choose either an alpha or numeric sort for this key number.
- ▲ **Order.** This is where you indicate either an ascending or descending sort.
- ▲ **Line** allows you to designate the line within the field, paragraph, cell, or column of each record to be sorted.
- ▲ **Field** designates the number of the field within each line, paragraph, or merge data record to be sorted.
- ▲ **Word** designates the word within each line, cell, field, or column.

Sorting by the Last Word in a Line

Let's say that you have the same list of names as above, but with the first name first:

Maggie Clinton
Kevin Spleid
Angela Avery
Robert Lee Wallach
Robert B. Smith
Linda Cary

In order to alphabetize this list by last name you need to sort on the last word of the line. However, if we were to sort by word 2, we would get Robert Lee Wallach before Kevin Spleid and Robert B. Smith before Linda Cary. Fortunately, WordPerfect provides a simple way to sort on the last word, as described in Procedure 51.4.

Procedure 51.4. Sorting on the last word in a line.
1. From the Sort dialog box, choose Sort Keys. A highlighting bar is positioned in the Sort Keys box.
2. Select edit key number 1.
3. Select Word and enter -1. This causes the sort to be performed on the last word in field 1, which is the only field in this file of records.
4. Choose OK.
5. Press F7 or Esc to exit the Sort Keys box.
6. Choose Perform Action.

Caution: Be sure to check your key definitions each time you sort. Once you have changed a key definition, the new definition remains in effect until you change it or until you exit WordPerfect.

Tip: To properly sort last names followed by Jr., Esq., M.D., and so on, separate these titles from the last names with a hard space (Home, space). The hard space forces WordPerfect to view Wallach, Jr. as one word instead of two. If you haven't used hard spaces while typing the list you will need to search and replace all "Esq." with "[Hard Space]Esq." Do the same for Jr., III, and so on. You can create a macro to automate this procedure. You will still need to scroll through your file to make sure you didn't miss anything.

Sorting Other Fields in a Line Sort

With more complex lists you may want to sort on several fields with different priorities and you may want your sort to be descending rather than ascending. The following list is an example of a more complex line sort list, one with multiple fields:

Sales	Joyce Reynolds	150,000
Support	James Wallach	110,000
Distribution	Myra Smith	35,000

Sales	Linda Cary	75,000
Distribution	Robert Lee	46,000
Sales	Robert Montgomery	135,000
Support	William Robertson	85,000

The employee's department, at the left margin, is Field 1. The Name field, following the first tab code, is Field 2. The employee's salary, following the second tab code, is Field 3. Each field after the first is identified by a tab code in front of it.

Caution: Be sure to set appropriate tabs before you type your list. If you use WordPerfect's default tab setting, you may need to hit the Tab key more than once to line up a particular field. Because WordPerfect identifies each field by the number of tab codes preceding it, additional tab codes will make WordPerfect's field count inaccurate and the sort will not work properly.

To sort this list by salary, follow the instructions in Procedure 51.5.

Procedure 51.5. Sorting by another field.

1. From the Sort dialog box choose Sort Keys and Edit.
2. From the Edit Sort Key dialog box select Field.
3. Since salary is Field 3, enter 3.
4. This is a Numeric Sort, so select Type and choose Numeric.
5. Choose OK.
6. Press F7 or Esc to exit the Sort Keys Menu box.
7. Choose Perform Action.

Your list is now sorted in ascending order by salary.

Caution: Be sure to change the Sort Type to numeric. If you do not, 110,000 will end up before 75,000, because WordPerfect looks at the first letter or number if the Sort Type is alpha. It is also essential to change the Sort Type to numeric if there are dollar signs before some of the numbers, or the sort may not work properly.

814

Defining Two Sort Keys and Changing Sort Order

You may want to sort the list above list in other ways. Suppose you wanted to sort alphabetically by department, then within each department by salary from highest to lowest. In this sort you would have two sort priorities: department is your first, salary is your second. Because WordPerfect refers to sort priorities as sort keys, you must now define two sort keys. Define department as Key1 and salary as Key2. As part of your Key2 definition you will change sort order from ascending to descending. To do this, follow the steps in Procedure 51.6.

Procedure 51.6. Sorting on two keys in different order.

1. From the Sort dialog box choose Sort Keys and Edit.

2. Check to make sure that Key1 is already correctly defined as an ascending sort for Field 1, Word 1, the department field. If not, make the appropriate changes.

3. To define your second sort priority, the salary field, select Add. The Edit Sort Key dialog box for Key2 comes up. Key2 is greyed out because when you add a key definition, WordPerfect automatically makes it the last key in the list.

4. From the Edit Sort Key dialog box select Type. Choose Numeric.

5. Select Order. Choose Descending.

6. Select Field. Since salary is Field 3, enter 3.

7. Select OK.

8. Press F7 or Esc to exit the Sort Keys Menu box.

9. Choose Perform Action.

Your list is now sorted as shown below, with department alphabetized first and then, within each department, salaries in descending numerical order.

Distribution	Myra Lee	46,000
Distribution	Mary Smith	35,000
Sales	Joyce Reynolds	150,000
Sales	Robert Montgomery	135,000
Sales	Linda Cary	75,000
Support	James Wallach	110,000
Support	William Robertson	85,000

Tip: If you want a dollar sign ($) to precede the first number on your list, put it in after sorting to make sure the dollar sign remains at the top of the list.

Blocking Text and Sorting

The preceding list should have a heading, indicating that column 1 is Department, column 2 is Name, and column 3 is Salary. When you give the Sort command, WordPerfect sorts the entire file. However, you would not want the heading line to be sorted with the list. To sort only part of this file, block the text you want sorted and then activate Sort. You will not see the Sort (Source and Destination) dialog box. Instead, you will be taken directly to the Sort dialog box.

You would block from the first character of the first line to be sorted to the last character of the last line, as shown in Figure 51.3.

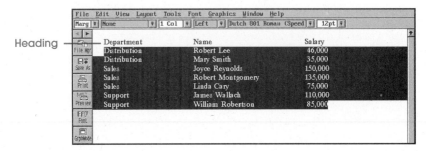

Figure 51.3. A blocked list for sorting.

Inserting, Renumbering, and Deleting Sort Keys

If you want to Insert a new Sort Key to take priority over the existing key definitions, follow Procedure 51.7.

Procedure 51.7. Inserting a sort key definition.

1. From the Sort dialog box select Sort **K**eys (Sort Priority). You will then see a highlighted bar in the sort key description box and the **A**dd, **E**dit, **I**nsert, and **D**elete choices will no longer be greyed out. Edit will be marked for selection.

2. Move the highlighted bar to the Key Number above which you want to insert a key.

3. Select **I**nsert. You are brought into the Edit Sort Key dialog box.

4. Enter the new key definition.

5. Close the box by selecting OK.

The new key will be given priority over the key previously highlighted. WordPerfect automatically renumbers the keys that follow.

To change a Sort Key number, you must have more than one sort key defined. Follow Procedure 51.8 to renumber existing keys.

Procedure 51.8. Renumbering a sort key.

1. From the Sort dialog box select Sort Keys (Sort Priority).
2. Move the highlighted bar to the Key Number you want to change.
3. Select Edit.
4. From the Edit Sort Key dialog box select Key Number.
5. Type in the new Key Number.
6. Press Enter.
7. Select OK.

WordPerfect automatically renumbers the other keys. To delete an existing key definition, follow Procedure 51.9.

Procedure 51.9. Deleting a sort key definition.

1. From the Sort dialog box select Sort Keys (Sort Priority).
2. Move the highlighted bar to the Key Number you want to delete.
3. Select Delete.

Caution: Be careful when deleting! You will not be prompted for confirmation, and Undo is not active while the Sort dialog box is open.

Performing a Paragraph Sort

The ability to perform a paragraph sort is valuable for sorting such text files as bibliographies where every record (author name, book title, publisher, and date) ends with two HRts.

Tip: If your bibliography has been formatted with a single HRt between entries, search and replace every HRt with two HRts and then perform the sort. When you are done with the sort, search and replace every double HRt with a single HRt.

To sort a file such as the one that follows, use the steps in Procedure 51.10.

Bibliography of Sams books:

Patrick, David; et al. *Word for Windows 2 Super Book*, Sams Publishing, 1992.

McFedries, Paul; et al. *Microsoft Excel 4 Super Book*, Sams Publishing, 1992.

Moskowitz, David; et al. *OS/2 2.1 Unleashed*, Sams Publishing, 1993.

Goodman, John M. *Memory Management for All of Us, Deluxe Edition*, Sams Publishing, 1993.

Oliver, Dick. *FractalVision: Put Fractals to Work for You*, Sams Publishing, 1992.

Perry, Greg. *Absolute Beginner's Guide to Programming*, Sams Publishing, 1993.

Wodaski, Ron. *Multimedia Madness*, Sams Publishing, 1992.

Gibbs, Mark. *Absolute Beginner's Guide to Networking*, Sams Publishing, 1993.

Procedure 51.10. Performing a paragraph sort.

1. From the Sort dialog box make sure your Record Type is Paragraph. WordPerfect should default to this when in the file above.

2. Make sure that Key1 is defined correctly for author. It will be defaulted correctly unless you have changed the Keys for a previous sort. Key1 will be Word 1 of Line 1 in Field 1.

3. Choose **Perform Action**. The book list will be sorted alphabetically by author.

Suppose you have two books by the same author and want to sort by title within each author. You can separate the book title from the author with a tab code. Author is then Field 1 and book title becomes Field 2. For the book title field, set a tab far enough from the left margin to accommodate the longest author name.

When you're ready for your final printing, do a global replacement of all tabs in your list with two hard spaces. By using hard spaces, if you add more titles later on you can do a global replace of two hard spaces with tabs and you can sort the list again.

Tip: New to WordPerfect 6.0 is the capability to sort on a negative line number within a paragraph. To sort on the last line of each paragraph, you would define that Key as Line -1.

Sorting a ToDo List

You can also use a paragraph sort as a useful way to sort ToDo lists. For simple purposes, this can substitute for a Personal Information Manager (PIM). Design a

ToDo list with a priority code for each item at the left margin. Use your first tab stop to specify a field (Field 2) for the person involved in each activity. Set a second tab stop (for Field 3) to mark the beginning of your activity description field. To sort by the priority code first, define Key1 as the first word of the first field. To sort by person second, define Key2 as the first word of the second field. In this way you can simply add items as you find out about them and then sort them into group priorities and list the people you must deal with for each.

Performing a Merge Sort

One very powerful application of Sort is to sort a merge data file. Here every field ends with an ENDFIELD code and an HRt code and every record ends with an ENDRECORD code and an HPg (hard page break) code. WordPerfect enables you to sort quite complex merge files in many ways. The following is an example of a name and address merge data file:

```
Cathy WallachENDFIELD
President
Perfect Access, Inc.ENDFIELD
301 East 66th StreetENDFIELD
New York, New York 10021
ENDRECORD
— — — — — — — — — — — — — — — — — — — — — — — — — —
Kevin SpleidENDFIELD
Spleid ComputersENDFIELD
145 East 62nd Street
New York, New York 10021ENDFIELD
ENDRECORD
— — — — — — — — — — — — — — — — — — — — — — — — — —
Linda BrickmanENDFIELD
Director of Communications
A. Public CompanyENDFIELD
90 West 102nd Street
New York, NY 10025ENDFIELD
ENDRECORD
— — — — — — — — — — — — — — — — — — — — — — — — — —
Mark HallENDFIELD
ENDFIELD
875 Fulton Street
New York, NY 10038ENDFIELD
ENDRECORD
```

We could have separated the address lines into different fields, but this was not necessary because the zip code is the only part of the address we will want to sort. The key for zip code is easily defined, as shown in Procedure 51.11.

When your insertion point is in a merge data file on-screen, the record type defaults to Merge Data File. You will also see a new entry for Line in the Sort Keys description box. This refers to lines within fields, not within the record.

819

Procedure 51.11. Sorting a merge data file by zip code.

1. From the Sort Dialog box, choose Sort Keys and Edit to edit Key 1.
2. From the Edit Sort Key dialog box select Field and enter 3.
3. Further identify zip code as Word -1 in Line -1 of Field 3.
4. Choose OK.
5. Press F7 or Esc to exit the Sort Keys menu box.
6. Choose Perform Action. Your list is sorted by zip code.

The preceding file has also been set up with one field for both title and company name. Frequently you'll have a merge data file in which most records have the company name and a few records contain both a company name and title. You don't want to create a separate field for the title because so few records require it. Therefore, company name will sometimes be Line 1 within Field 2 and at other times will be Line 2 within Field 2. You would still be able to sort by company name by using a negative line number, Line -1, in the key definition, as shown in the preceding procedure. Records that have neither a title nor a company name will be sorted to the top of the list.

Performing a Table Sort

Because WordPerfect's Table function is so adaptable, you will often use it to enter data you may later want to sort. WordPerfect defines every row in a table as a record. Every cell in a row is the equivalent of a field and cells are numbered from left to right beginning with Cell 1. You can further divide each cell into lines and words (see Table 51.1).

Table 51.1. Dividing cells into lines and words.

Name	Job Title	Years with Firm	Bonus
Fred Silver	Vice President	1	$500
Sylvia Poorth	President	5	$2000
Nancy Hamilton	Secretary	3	$1000
Gordon James	CEO	5	$2500
Betsy White	Sales Manager	4	$1500

To sort this table by bonus amount, from highest to lowest, follow Procedure 51.12.

Procedure 51.12. Sorting a table.

1. With your insertion point in the table, access the Sort function. You will not get the Sort Source and Destination dialog box when your insertion point is in a table.
2. You will be brought to the Table Sort dialog box.
3. Select Sort Keys.
4. Select Edit to edit Key1.
5. Select cell and change the number to 4. Press Enter.
6. Select Type and choose Numeric.
7. Select Order and choose Descending.
8. Select OK.
9. Press F7 and Enter to Perform Action.

Your sorted table will look like Table 51.2.

Table 51.2. A sorted table.

Name	Job Title	Years with Firm	Bonus
Gordon James	CEO	5	$2500
Sylvia Poorth	President	5	$2000
Betsy White	Sales Manager	4	$1500
Nancy Hamilton	Secretary	3	$1000
Fred Silver	Vice President	1	$500

WordPerfect is smart enough not to sort a header row with the rest of the table. It's therefore a good idea to define title rows as header rows, rather than leaving them as regular rows, because then you don't have to block the table.

If you do need to block a portion of a table to sort it, you must end your block in the last cell of the last row you want to sort, even though it will appear as though the last cell in the row is not blocked. If you extend your block to the beginning of the next row, that row will be sorted also. Blocking in a table is particularly useful when you have a formula in a row and don't want to include that in your sort.

WordPerfect 6.0 has changed from 5.1 in how it deals with "ownership" of the outside lines of a table. If you have a double border for your table and the bottom row ends up in the middle of your table after a sort, you no longer end up with a double line in the middle of your table. However, if you have double lines elsewhere in the table, they will "travel" with the sorted row.

Note: You cannot sort "spanned columns" in tables (i.e., where cells have been joined in the rows you want to sort).

 Note: Cell names do not "travel" with the sorted rows. This is deliberate so that when you sort named cells that are referenced in formulas, the formulas will work as they did before the sort.

Performing a Parallel Column Sort

Tables and parallel columns perform similar functions. You may decide for yourself when one or the other is preferable. Just as you can sort tables, you can sort parallel columns. In parallel columns every row of columns is a record. Each column is the equivalent of a field. Columns are numbered from left to right beginning at Column 1. When your insertion point is in a parallel column, WordPerfect will default the record type to Parallel Column.

To sort the following parallel columns in descending order by the prices in column three, follow the instructions in Procedure 51.13.

Computer	486-DX, 340M hard disk, 3.5-inch floppy, 8M RAM, CD-ROM Drive	$2500.00
Inkjet Printer	2 pages per minute	495.00
Inkjet Cartridges	Black	12.95
Cable	Parallel	9.70
Box Computer Paper	For inkjet printer, single sheets, 500 per box	15.95
Ergonomic Keyboard	Enhanced; specially design with ergonomic considerations in mind	189.00

Procedure 51.13. Sorting parallel columns.

1. With your cursor in a column, access the Sort function.
2. You will be brought to the Parallel Columns Sort dialog box.
3. Select Sort Keys.
4. Select Edit for Key1.
5. Select Column and change the number to 3. Press Enter.

6. Select Type and change to Numeric.

7. Select Order and choose Descending.

8. Select OK.

9. Press F7 and Enter to **P**erform Action.

Selecting Records

There will be times when you want to specify only certain records within a list. WordPerfect's powerful Select feature allows you to isolate records that meet certain criteria. For example, you may be planning a short seminar to which you would like to invite customers that live or work nearby. If you had a list formatted like the one on page 819 (under "Sorting a Merge File"), you could select all the customers from zip code 10021 by following Procedure 51.14.

Caution: Be sure to save your file before using the Select function. Once you have performed the Select function, all you will see on your screen are the selected records, not your original file. To save the resulting file, give it a new name. If you save under the same name, your original file will be overwritten. The safest way to protect yourself against losing data is to specify a destination file before you begin the Select process.

A Simple Select

Because the Select statement refers to a key number, to select records you must first define keys. Additionally, you will want the resulting list sorted by last name for easy reference. Therefore, we need to define a second key by which WordPerfect will sort the records that have been selected (see Procedure 51.14).

Procedure 51.14. Performing a simple select.

1. From the Sort Dialog box choose Sort **K**eys and **E**dit to edit Key 1.

2. From the Edit Sort Key dialog box select **F**ield. Type 3 and press Enter.

3. Further identify zip code as Word -1 in Line -1 of Field 3.

4. Choose OK.

5. Choose **A**dd to add Key 2. From the Edit Sort Key dialog box select **F**ield, type 1, and press Enter.

6. Further identify the last name as Word -1 in Line 1 of Field 1.

7. Choose OK.

8. Press F7 or Esc to exit the Sort Keys menu box.

9. Choose Select Records. A box appears for you to type in your selection statement, as shown in Figure 51.4.

Note: You can also press the Tab key while your cursor is in the Sort Keys selection box to take you directly to the Select Records box.

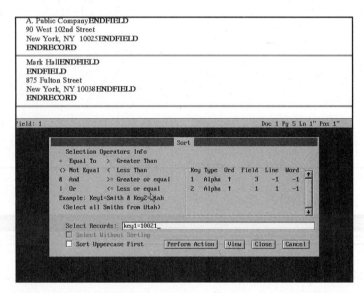

Figure 51.4. The Selection Box.

10. For your selection statement, type `Key1=10021` and press Enter to exit the box. Note that there are no spaces between any elements of this statement. "`Key`" does not need to be capitalized.

11. Choose Perform Action. Only those records with a zip code equal to 10021 will appear on your screen. The records are also sorted alphabetically by last name.

12. Save the resulting file with a new name, or, as mentioned earlier, your original file will be overwritten with this truncated version.

Note: New to WordPerfect 6.0 is the capability to insert a hard space in a selection statement. Also new is the ability to include parentheses as part of the string to match. For example, you can search for and distinguish between an area code such as (212) and the number 212.

Selecting Records with the Global Key

You may want to search records for every occurrence of a word that cannot be assigned to a key number.

For example, perhaps you work for a legal systems integrator and hear of a new software product that simplifies certain forms used in patent law. You want to send a mailing to all clients who practice patent law. Your mailing list may be set up like the one shown later in this chapter, with fields for attorney name, practice areas, firm name, and firm address. There is no way to define a key for "patent," since it can appear anywhere in the practice area field.

You want to select those records that contain "patent" no matter where it appears. WordPerfect allows you to designate a global select key, which it calls *Keyg*. Selecting with the global key is the only time you do not need to define a key before performing Select.

Follow Procedure 51.15 to select all records from the following list with the word *patent* anywhere in the record.

```
Katherine Smith, Esq.ENDFIELD
Patent, trademark, TaxENDFIELD
Law Firm of Smith & SmithENDFIELD
1345 Noteworthy Lane
Seattle, Washington 98121ENDFIELD
ENDRECORD
— — — — — — — — — — — — — — — — — — — — — —
Jonathan Cohen, Esq.ENDFIELD
Personal Injury, Medical MalpracticeENDFIELD
Cohen, Waldman & SmithENDFIELD
56 Seventh Avenue
New York, New York 10001ENDFIELD
ENDRECORD
— — — — — — — — — — — — — — — — — — — — — —
Linda Fredericks, Esq.ENDFIELD
Trademark, PatentENDFIELD
Zinger & LarsonENDFIELD
One Marvin Lane
Ft. Lauderdale, Florida 33303ENDFIELD
ENDRECORD
— — — — — — — — — — — — — — — — — — — — — —
George Klion, Esq.ENDFIELD
Trusts and Estates, Patent, MatrimonialENDFIELD
Singer, Klion & WallachENDFIELD
1100 Washington Street
Cleveland, Ohio 11417ENDFIELD
ENDRECORD
```

Procedure 51.15. Selecting with the global key.

1. From the Sort dialog box, choose Select Records.

2. In the selection box, type `keyg=patent`.

3. Choose Perform Action. The document on-screen now consists of only those records with the word *patent* somewhere in them.

Caution: Be aware that when you use Keyg, WordPerfect will find all occurrences of the text string. Therefore, if searching for *bank*, WordPerfect would also select all records containing *bankrupt*. Using spaces in your select statement to isolate the word will not work because there may be `HRts`, `COMMAS`, or `ENDFIELD` codes surrounding the word rather than spaces. Therefore, check your resulting file.

Note: The global key will only work properly with the =operator. Do not use it with the other operators described in the following discussion of selection operators.

Selection Operators

In the previous example we made a simple selection, using = as our sole selection operator. However, you can create more complex selection statements. WordPerfect's selection operators allow you to specify records that meet more than one criteria, such as those for everyone in your company who works part-time and is not covered by health insurance. You can also select records where specific fields are greater or less than a specified value.

Note: The selection operators in WordPerfect 6.0 are more logical than they were in 5.1. For example, you now use ¦, rather than +, to indicate or. WordPerfect has also added Help for selection operators.

Following is a list of WordPerfect's selection operators and what they mean:

▲ ¦ (OR) selects records that meet the conditions of either key. You can use the ¦ connector when you want to find more than one possible match for the same key. For example, `Key1=Jones¦Smith¦Brown` will select all records where Key1 equals `Jones`, `Smith`, or `Brown`. You must use ¦, not the word `OR`, in your selection statement.

▲ & (AND) selects records that fill the criteria for both keys. You must use two different keys with the & operator because one key cannot equal two quantities at one time. An example of proper use of the & operator would be the select statement Key1=Jones & Key3=WordPerfect. This would find everyone named Jones at WordPerfect. Note that there is a space before and after the & operator. You must use &, not the word AND, in your selection statement.

▲ = selects records that exactly match the designated key.

▲ <> selects records that do not match the designated key.

▲ > selects records that contain information greater than the designated key. For example, if Key3>25, WordPerfect selects records where Key3 is more than 25.

▲ < selects records with information less than the amount in the designated key. (The greater-than and less-than operators can be used to indicate position in the alphabet as well as with numbers. For example, if Key1<France, WordPerfect selects records where Key1 comes before France in the alphabet.)

▲ >= selects records with information greater than or equal to the designated key.

▲ <= selects records with information less than or equal to the designated key.

Selection Statement Order

If you have several operators in your selection statement, WordPerfect reads it from left to right. For example, the following statement selects everyone born in 1960 with the name of Alpert and then adds everyone named Morgan no matter what the birth year.

```
Key2=1960 & Key1=Alpert ¦ Morgan
```

It does not matter whether or not you use spaces before and after the ¦ operator. Use parentheses to change the selection order. For example, the next statement selects the records in the parentheses first (everyone named Alpert or Morgan) then selects only those Alperts or Morgans born in 1960.

```
Key2=1960 & (Key1=Alpert ¦ Morgan)
```

Note: In WordPerfect 5.1, you would have had to type the above statement as Key2=1960 & (Key1=Alpert ¦ Key1=Morgan), repeating Key1=. This is not necessary in WordPerfect 6.0.

Sorting and Selecting Dates

The simplest and most flexible way to enter dates is to separate the month, day, and year with forward slashes: 11/23/93. If you prefer hyphens, you must use hard hyphens, called dashes: 11-23-93. (Press Home, hyphen for a dash. See the following Note.) WordPerfect interprets either forward slashes or hard hyphens as word separators and thus sees the date as three separate words, enabling you to define different keys to isolate the year, month, and day. Therefore, to get an accurate date sort, you have to define three keys. See Procedure 51.16 for an example of how to use dates in a sort and select.

> **Note:** The way in which Sort treats hard hyphens is not at all intuitive. In normal text editing, WordPerfect uses hard hyphens to keep words together (i.e., to prevent separation by a line break). In the Sort feature, WordPerfect uses hard hyphens to separate words. Additionally, regular hyphens are interpreted as word separators in the Edit mode, but not in the Sort mode.
>
> If your file has dates that have been formatted with regular hyphens, you will need to perform a search and replace to replace these with hard hyphens or slashes in order to do a date sort.

Selecting and Sorting Using Date Sort

Suppose you keep a table of your client invoices in WordPerfect. Your table might look like the following, which includes client names, descriptions of work done, billing dates, and amounts due.

Client	Work Done	Invoice Date	Amount Due
Angela Clark	Basic through advanced WordPerfect 5.1 DOS training	6/19/93	2,500
The Confident Company	WordPerfect 6.0 DOS desktop publishing	4/12/93	1,500
Mary Gold	Intermediate WordPerfect 5.2 Windows training	12/24/92	1,250
Jack Allman	Advanced WordPerfect 5.2 Windows training	7/10/93	500

By using a selection operator for one key and sorting on a different key, you can see all clients who owe you $1,000 or more, listed in order from oldest past due to most recent (see Procedure 51.16).

Procedure 51.16. Selecting and sorting using date sort.

1. From the Sort dialog box, edit Key1 to be the key on which you want to perform your primary sort. Because this is the year in the Invoice Date field, your choices will be Cell 3, Line 1, Word 3. Define Type as Numeric. Select OK.

2. We need to do a second level of sort on the month. Add Key2 and define it as Cell 3, Line 1, Word 1. Define Type as Numeric. Select OK.

3. Our third sort level is the day. Add Key3 and define it as Cell 3, Line 1, Word 2. Define Type as Numeric. Select OK.

4. For the Select statement you need to define Key4 as the amount due. Add Key4 and define it as Cell 4, Line 1, Word 1. Define Type as Numeric. Select OK.

5. Press Tab to enter the Select Records box.

6. Type the following Select statement: Key4>=1000.

7. Press Enter.

8. Choose Perform Action.

9. The file on your screen will contain only the selected records and will be sorted in order by date. It will look like the table that follows. Save the file with a new name.

Client	Work Done	Invoice Date	Amount Due
Mary Gold	Intermediate WordPerfect 5.2 Windows training	12/24/92	1,250
The Confident Company	WordPerfect 6.0 DOS desktop publishing	4/12/93	1,500
Angela Clark	Basic through advanced WordPerfect 5.1 DOS training	6/19/93	2,500

Tip: If you want to get really sophisticated and select only invoices that are 30 days past due, you can convert the date formats in the table to Julian dates using the table function MDY(). Then calculate the current date with MDY() and subtract 30 to get a 30-days-past-

> due date. Select records where the invoice date is less than the past-due date. In this case, it would only require one key to define the date, because it is in Julian format and is a single number.

Other Tips

Language: if you want WordPerfect to sort by the rules of another language, insert a language code at the top of the document or in Document Initial Codes. If you sort a block of text, WordPerfect uses the language code closest to the top of the block.

Notebook Files: you can retrieve a WordPerfect Notebook file directly into WordPerfect 6.0 and perform Sort and Select. You can also sort a Notebook file as a source file on disk. Sort type will default to a Merge Data File and you proceed with the sort as with any Merge Data File. If the text format of the Notebook file is WordPerfect 5.1 or 5.0, the Notebook file will come in looking just like a WordPerfect 6.0 Merge Data File. However, if you have set the text format of the Notebook file to be WordPerfect 4.2, you cannot sort directly from disk, and you will get the error message `Not a prefixed file` if you try to do so. You must retrieve the file into WordPerfect 6.0, telling it that the file is in 4.2 format. You can then perform the sort.

by Milan Keeney

Using Math in WordPerfect 6.0

Like the previous version of WordPerfect, WordPerfect 6.0 includes a Math feature. Although this feature is not as powerful as the Tables feature, it can be very useful for adding columns of numbers and displaying their totals.

Math: An Overview

WordPerfect's Math feature uses tabular columns to separate numbers into Numeric, Total, Text, and Calculation columns. Numeric columns are used to add lists of numbers. Total columns display totals from the column to the left; normally, Total columns are placed after Numeric columns to show emphasis on the totals. Text columns contain text and are not used in calculating values in other columns. Calculation columns are a special type of column containing formulas that compile numbers from several Numeric and Total columns.

Accessing the Math Screen

You can access the Math feature from either the Tools option on the pull-down menu or from the keyboard by pressing Alt+F7 and choosing Math. If you want to do more than add simple columns of numbers, you need to change the default column type.

Defining Columns

Procedure 52.1. Changing column definitions.

1. Choose Tools or press Alt+F7. Then select Math.

2. Choose Define from the Columns/Tables dialog box. The Math definition screen appears (see Figure 52.1).

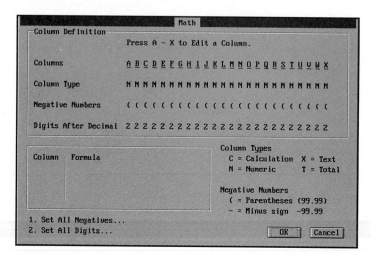

Figure 52.1. The Math screen.

You can define up to 24 math columns. By default, the columns are set up as type Numeric.

Numeric Columns: Numeric columns are used for adding columns of numbers and deriving totals, subtotals, and grand totals. This is the most common type of Math column.

Total Columns: Total columns can be used to display totals, subtotals, and grand totals from the column to the left. Normally, you place a Total column to the right of each numeric column.

Calculation Columns: Calculation columns are a special type of column that allows you to input a formula that includes values from other columns. A formula in a Calculation column will display a value derived from numbers on the same row in other columns.

Text Columns: Text columns are designed for entering labels and text. Numbers entered into a Text column will not be calculated.

You can define as many of each type of column as you want. Math columns start with the first tab stop. The left margin is not a column. It can be used for row labels.

Naming Columns

You can define a column heading for each Math column. The names should be entered before the [Math:On] code in your document. You can turn on Reveal Codes to see where the [Math:On] code appears in the document.

Defining Rows

Each carriage return in a Math section is a row. You can assign each row a name. The space between the first tab stop and the left margin is not used by Math. You can enter row names in this area. Row names are for your benefit and are not required for the Math feature to work.

Enabling Math

After you have defined your column types, you need to enable the Math feature. To enable Math, choose Tools or press Alt+F7. Select 3 or Math. Select 1 or Math On. An *X* will appear in the Math On option.

When Math is enabled, all tab stops are treated as Math columns. When you are finished using Math, you can turn it off. A [Math:On] code is placed in the document at the insertion point when you turn Math on. A [Math:Off] code is placed in the document at the insertion point when you turn Math off. When Math is on, the tab stops are columns and each line represents a new row. In this way, you can think of Math as a table that is 24 columns wide with as many rows as there are lines between the [Math:On] code and the [Math:Off] code.

Parts of a Math Column

Each Math column definition is made of three parts: a column type, a negative number indicator, and the designation of the number of digits to carry numbers past the decimal point.

Changing Column Definitions

From the Math menu, you can change any of the settings for a particular column. You also can set the negative number indicator for all columns and the number of digits all columns will show after the decimal point.

Setting the Column Type

By default, all Math columns are defined as type Numeric. You can select any of the four column types for each column. Procedure 52.2 describes how to set the Column Type.

Procedure 52.2. Setting the column type.

1. From the Math screen, choose the letter, A-X, that corresponds to the column you want to change.

2. Select 1 or Column Type and select the number 1-4 that corresponds to the column type you want to select. If you are defining a Calculation column, you will be prompted to enter a formula (see Figure 52.2).

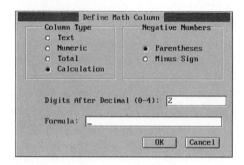

Figure 52.2. Defining a Calculation column.

Setting the Negative Number Indicator

Math has two display formats available when displaying negative numbers. Negative numbers can be displayed using either a minus sign (-), or parentheses "()". Use the following steps to change the negative number indicator for each column.

1. From the Define Math Column screen choose 2 or Negative Number. Option 1 Parentheses will cause all negative numbers in this column to be displayed in parentheses. For example, negative 5 will be displayed as (5.00).

2. If you want negative numbers to appear with a hyphen in front of them (e.g., -5.00), select 2 Minus Sign.

Digits After the Decimal

By default, WordPerfect will display two digits after the decimal point. This is normally sufficient if you are planning to add numbers representing dollars and cents, but you can have the program display between 0 and 4 digits after the decimal.

To change the decimal display, select 3 or Digits from the Define Math Column screen. Select the number of digits you want displayed after the decimal point.

Global Math Display Settings

Normally, you will want to maintain the same display conventions throughout your document. You can set the Negative Number Indicator and the Digits After the Decimal for all columns in Math at one time.

Negative Number Indicator

You can change all the columns to a negative number display other than the default. To change the negative number display for all columns in Math, choose option 1 from the Math screen. Select either 1 **Parentheses** or 2 **Minus Sign**. Setting the negative number indicator here sets it for all 24 columns. You need to individually reset any columns that you do not want to display the global setting.

Digits After the Decimal

You can change the number of digits after the decimal for all columns at one time. From the Math screen, choose 2. Select the number of digits you want to appear after the decimal. The range of valid choices is 0 to 4. Next select OK. Changing the number of digits here updates every column in the table to this value. You need to individually edit any columns where you want a setting that is different from the global one.

Formulas

The Math screen displays any columns that are defined as Calculation columns and the formulas associated with those columns.

A Formula column allows you to do math on several columns at one time. When you are setting up a formula, refer to other columns by their letter designator as defined in the Math setup screen.

Functions in Formulas

The following functions are valid in a Math formula:

+	Addition
-	Subtraction
*	Multiplication
/	Division
()	Parentheses

Use parentheses to separate functions. The formula string can be up to 30 characters long. In a formula, WordPerfect evaluates expressions within parentheses first. For example, the formula $A*(B+C)$ is evaluated as the sum of B and C times the value in column A.

Functions in Columns

The following functions are available when using Math:

+	Adds numbers across Numeric Columns
+/	Averages numbers across Numeric Columns
=	Adds totals across Total Columns
=/	Averages numbers across Total Columns

Math Examples

Let's set up a sample Math definition and try out some of the features we have described. Procedure 52.3 describes setting up the column headings for a simple expense report.

Procedure 52.3. Setting the column heading.

1. Move to the place in your document that you want to create the expense report.
2. Change your tab settings to 1". (Note: numbers that extend beyond the next tab settings will give incorrect totals.)
3. Set up your column headings. With the insertion point at the left margin, press Tab to move to the first tab stop and type the word Monday.
4. Press Tab again and type the word Tuesday.
5. Repeat this process for the days Wednesday through Friday.
6. After typing Friday, press Tab again and type in the word Totals. These will be the column headings (see Figure 52.3).
7. From the menu bar choose Tools, or press Alt+F7. Then choose Math, and select Define.
8. Choose F to modify the sixth column.
9. Select 1 or Type. Change the type from Numeric to Calculation.
10. In the formula box, type in the formula A+B+C+D+E, then select OK.
11. Select OK to return to the Math screen. You will see the formula you entered appear in the formula box in the lower-left corner of the screen.
12. Select OK to return to the Columns/Tables dialog box. The Math On command is highlighted.

13. Select OK to return to the document screen. Press Enter to position to the insertion point at the left margin on the line following the column headings.

14. Select Tools and Math, or Alt+F7 and 3 or Math, and select Math On. Press Enter or select OK to turn on the Math feature. Select OK again to return to the document screen. The word *Math* appears in the lower-left corner of your screen to remind you that the Math feature is currently enabled.

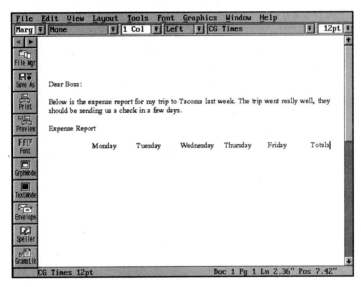

Figure 52.3. The column headings.

You are now ready to add the row information to your document. The tabular column on the left margin is not used in Math calculation. Procedure 52.4 describes how to enter row names into the tabular column.

Procedure 52.4. Adding row names.

1. Move the insertion point to the left margin on the line below the column headings. Type the word Travel and press Enter.

2. Type the words Car Rental and press Enter.

3. Type the word Meals and press Enter.

4. Type the word Totals and press Enter.

Next, fill in actual numbers for each of the categories you have identified.

5. Position the insertion point at the end of the word *Travel* and then press Tab.

6. Type the number 250.00. This represents a $250 charge on Monday.

7. Move the insertion point to the end of the word *Rental* and press Tab. The insertion point should now be positioned under the number *250.00*.

8. Type the number 35.00 and press Tab.

9. Repeat Step 8 four times. The number *35.00* should appear in each of the columns that are labeled with a day of the week.

10. Move the insertion point to the end of the word *Meals* and press Tab.

11. Follow the procedure in Steps 8 and 9 to enter the value 25.00 for meals on each day (see Figure 52.4).

Now that the dollar values are entered into each column, you are ready to add them up. Procedure 52.5 describes the steps needed to calculate the totals.

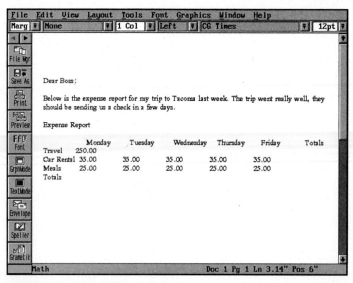

Figure 52.4. Entering the dollar values.

Procedure 52.5. Calculating totals.

1. Move the insertion point to the end of the row titled Travel. If the insertion point is not under the Column title Totals, press Tab until it is.

2. Repeat Step 1 for the rows titled Car Rental and Meals. (Note: the Totals row and the Totals column should both be empty at this point.)

3. Move the insertion point to the row titled Totals and position it after the word *Totals*.

4. Press Tab to move the insertion point to the first tab stop. (The first tab stop is the column titled Monday.)

5. Press the plus (+) key to total the numbers in this column. (The column will not be totaled until you choose Calculate from the Columns/Tables dialog box.)

6. Press Tab to move the insertion point to the Tuesday column. Press the plus (+) key.

7. Repeat Step 6 for the Wednesday, Thursday, and Friday columns. (Do *not* place a plus (+) sign in the Totals column. The formula entered earlier will take care of this column.)

You have now entered all of the information necessary for your expense report. Your screen does not yet show any of the totals. To display the totals, tell the program to Calculate Math. Choose Tools or press Alt+F7. Then choose Math and select Calculate. WordPerfect displays the Please Wait dialog box while it performs the calculations.

You can go back and change numbers in the columns by moving the insertion point to the number, deleting it, and typing a new number. Anytime you change a number, you will need to repeat the calculation step.

53

by Milan Keeney

Equation Editor

WordPerfect 6.0 includes an equation editor. You can use the equation editor to create and edit mathematical formulas, equations, and any kind of reference that includes special characters normally used in science. The WordPerfect Equation editor is simple to use and makes creating and editing formulas a painless process.

What is Equation Editor and Why Would You Want to Use It?

Have you ever tried to create a complicated formula using a word processor? Creating a formula like the quadratic equation, $ax^2 + bx + c = 0$, is fairly simple. However, if you want to express this equation in terms of x (see Figure 53.1), it's almost easier to write the equation by hand than trying to produce it with normal word processing functions.

WordPerfect 6.0's Equation editor makes the process of creating an equation almost as easy as typing normal text. Scientists, mathematicians, statisticians, and anyone who has a need to include mathematical formulas and functions in publishable material will find the WordPerfect 6.0 equation editor extremely helpful.

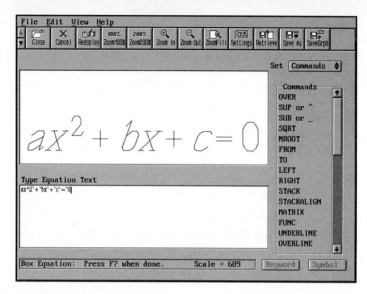

Figure 53.1. A quadratic equation.

Accessing the Equation Editor

Equations are a type of graphic, and therefore you access the Equation editor from the Create Graphics Box screen (see Figure 53.2). Procedure 53.1 explains how to access the equation editor.

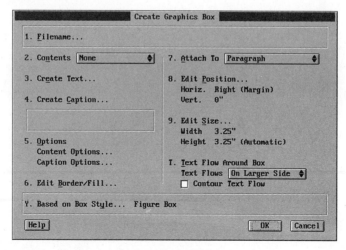

Figure 53.2. The Create Graphics Box screen.

Procedure 53.1. Accessing the Equation editor.

1. From the Create Graphics Box, select Contents or 2 to display the Contents pop-up list.
2. Select Equation from the Contents pop-up list.
3. Select Based on Box Style or Y to display the Graphics Box Styles screen.
4. Select Equations Box to return to the Create Graphics Box screen.
5. Select Create Equation to bring up the Equation editor (see Figure 53.3).

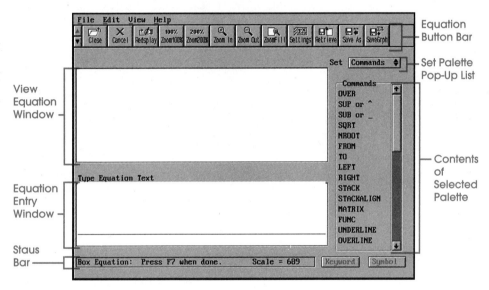

Figure 53.3. The Equation Editor screen.

Equation Palette Sets: What Are They and How Are They Used?

The Equation editor includes eight different palettes. Select the Equation Palette pop-up list to see the eight palette choices (see Figure 53.4). Each palette is a set of a functions or symbols used when creating an equation.

Large Palette

The Large palette contains a set of mathematical, scientific, bracket, and brace symbols. These symbols have both a large and small equivalent available.

Figure 53.4. The equation palette pop-up list.

Figure 53.5. The Large Equation palette.

The following table lists the elements included in the Large Equation palette. The elements are listed from upper-left to lower-right.

SUM	SMALLSUM
INT	SMALLINT
OINT (Contour Integral)	SMALLOINT (Small Contour Integral)
PROD	SMALLPROD
COPROD (Coproduct)	SMALLCOPROD
CAP (Intersection)	BIGCAP
CUP (Union)	BIGCUP
UPLUS (Multiset Union)	BIGUPLUS
SQCAP (Square Intersection)	BIGSQCAP
SQCUP (Square Union)	BIGSQCUP
OR	BIGVEE (Big Logical Or)
AND	BIGWEDGE (Big Logical And)
OPLUS (Circle Plus)	BIGOPLUS
OMINUS (Circle Minus)	BIGOMINUS
OTIMES (Circle Multiply)	BIGOTIMES
ODIV (Circle Divide)	BIGODIV

ODOT (Circle Dot)	BIGODOT
((left parenthesis)	) (right parenthesis)
[(left bracket)	] (right bracket)
LDBRACK (Left Double Bracket)	RDBRACK (Right Double Bracket)
LBRACE	RBRACE
LFLOOR	RFLOOR
LCEIL	RCEIL
LANGLE	RANGLE
LINE (Vertical Line)	DLINE (Double Vertical Line)

Symbols Palette

The Symbols palette contains a group of frequently used symbols such as >
(greater than), < (less than), and = (equal).

Figure 53.6. The Symbols Equation palette.

The following table lists the elements included in the Symbols Equation palette.
The elements are listed from upper-left to lower-right.

prime	double prime
triple prime	INF (INIFINITY)
PARTIAL (Partial Derivative)	GRAD (Gradient)
TIMES	DIV (Division Sign)
+- (PLUSMINUS)	-+ (MINUSPLUS)
CDOT (Center Dot)	XOR (Logical Exclusive Or)
<= (Less Than or Equal To)	>= (Greater Than or Equal To)
<< (Much Less Than)	>> (Much Greater Than)
LLL (Much Much Less)	GGG (Much Much Greater)
!= (Not Equal)	NOT (Logical Not)
PREC (Precedes)	SUCC (Succeeds or Follows)

PRECEQ (Precedes Or Equals)
SUCCEQ (Succeeds Or Equals)
== (Equivalent)
NEQUIV (Not Equivalent)
SIM (Similar)
SIMEQ (Similar Or Equal)
APPROX (Approximately Equal)
CONG (Congruent)
PROPTO (Proportional To)
DOTEQ (Equal by Definition)
PARALLEL
PERP (Perpendicular To)
FORALL
EXISTS
THEREFORE
BECAUSE
IDENTICAL
DSUM (Direct Sum)
QEQUAL (Questioned Equality)
IMAGE
RIMAGE (Reverse Image)
ISO (Isomorphic)
NISO (Not Isomorphic)
ASYMEQ (Asymptotically Equivalent)

NASYMEQ (Not Asymptotically Equal)
SMILE
FROWN
BETWEEN
WREATH (Wreath Product)
TOP
ASSERT
MASSERT (Mirrored Assertion)
MODELS
ANGLE
MSANGLE (Measured Angle)
SANGLE (Spherical Angle)
RTANGLE (Right Angle)
DEG (Degree)

Greek Palette

Not surprisingly, the Greek palette contains Greek symbols—both uppercase and lowercase. In addition to the basic Greek symbol set, some variants are included.

Figure 53.7. The Greek Equation palette.

The following table lists the elements included in the Greek Equation palette. The elements are listed from upper-left to lower-right.

alpha	beta	gamma	delta
epsilon	varepsilon	zeta	eta
theta	vartheta	iota	kappa
lambda	mu	nu	xi
omicron	pi	varpi	rho
varrho	sigma	varsigma	tau
upsilon	phi	varphi	chi
psi	omega	ALPHA	BETA
GAMMA	DELTA	EPSILON	ZETA
ETA	THETA	IOTA	KAPPA
LAMBDA	MU	NU	XI
OMICRON	PI	RHO	SIGMA
TAU	UPSILON	PHI	CHI
PSI	OMEGA		

Arrows Palette

The Arrows palette contains a wide range of arrow symbols including single and double arrows. It also contains a variety of shapes such as circles, squares, diamonds, triangles, and stars. You can display these shapes in either fill-in style or hollow style.

Figure 53.8. The Arrows Equation palette.

The following table lists the elements included in the Arrows Equation palette. The elements are listed from upper-left to lower-right.

Left Arrow	Right Arrow
Up Arrow	Down Arrow
Left & Right Arrow	Up & Down Arrow

Two Left Arrows	Two Right Arrows
Left & Right Arrows	Right & Left Arrows
Double Left Arrow	Double Right Arrow
Double Up Arrow	Double Down Arrow
Double Left & Right Arrow	Double Up & Down Arrow
Northeast Arrow	Southeast Arrow
Southwest Arrow	Northwest Arrow
Curly Right Arrow	Left Harpoon Up
Left Harpoon Down	Right Harpoon Up
Right Harpoon Down	Left & Right Harpoons
Right & Left Harpoons	Up Harpoon Left
Up Harpoon Right	Down Harpoon Left
Down Harpoon Right	Hook Left Arrow
Hook Right Arrow	Maps To
Triangle Left	Triangle Right
Triangle Up	Triangle Down
Small Triangle Left	Small Triangle Right
Big Triangle Up	Big Triangle Down
Solid Triangle Left	Solid Triangle Right
Solid Triangle Up	Solid Triangle Down
Defined As	Corresponds To
Bowtie	Solid Star
Big Solid Star	Diamond
Solid Diamond	Hollow Diamond
Big Circle	Circle
Small Circle	Small Solid Circle
Square	Solid Square

Sets Palette

The Sets palette contains symbols frequently used in set theory such as subset, member, double union and double intersection. It also includes relational operands such as not similar, not greater than, and does not follow, as well as some Fraktur and other special letters.

The following table lists the elements included in the Sets Equation palette. The elements are listed from upper-left to lower-right.

SETMINUS	SUBSET (Proper Subset)
SUPSET (Proper Superset)	Reflex Subset
Reflex superset	Subset But Not Equal
Superset But Not Equal	SQSUBSET (Square Proper Subset)
SQSUPSET (Square Proper Superset)	Square Reflex Subset

Square Reflex Superset	Square Subset, Not Equal To
Square Superset, Not Equal To	IN
NOTIN (Not a Member)	OWNS (Contains As a Member)
EMPTYSET	Double Union
Double Intersection	Double Subset
Double Superset	Not Subset
Not Superset	Not Reflex Subset
Not Reflex Superset	Square Not Subset
Square Not Superset	Square Not Reflex Subset
Square Not Reflex Superset	Not Less Than
Not Less Than or Equal To	Not Greater Than
Not Greater Than or Equal To	Not Similar
Not Similar or Equal To	Not Congruent
Not Approximately Equal To	Does Not Precede
Neither Precedes Nor Equals	Does Not Follow
Neither Follows Nor Equals	Not Parallel
Does Not Divide	There Never Exists
REAL (R Fraktur)	IMAGE (Imaginary—I Fraktur)
C Fraktur	Z Fraktur
Weierstrass	Capital Weierstrass
Planck's Constant	Laplace Transform
Script E	Fourier Transform
Complex Number	Integer
Natural Number	Real Number
MHO	ANGSTROM

Figure 53.9. The Sets Equation palette.

Other Palette

The Other palette contains common diacritical marks such as ^ (hat) and ~ (tilde), as well as a few ellipses.

Figure 53.10. The Other Equation palette.

The following table lists the elements included in the Other Equation palette. The elements are listed from upper-left to lower-right.

VEC (Vector Above: x VEC)	BAR (Overline: x BAR)
HAT (Above: x HAT)	ACUTE (Acute Accent: x ACUTE)
GRAVE (Grave Accent: x GRAVE)	BREVE (Breve Accent: x BREVE)
DOT (Dot Above: x DOT)	DDOT (Double Dot Above: x DDOT)
DDDOT (Triple Dot Above: x DDDOT)	CIRCLE (Circle Above: x CIRCLE)
TILDE (Tilde Above: x TILDE)	DYAD (Dyad Above: x DYAD)
DOTSAXIS (Ellipsis—centered)	DOTSLOW (Ellipsis—on baseline)
DOTSVERT (Ellipsis—vertical)	DOTSDIAG (Ellipsis—diagonal)
CHECK (Check Above: x CHECK)	

Functions Palette

The Functions palette contains mathematical functions such as sin (sine), cot (cotangent), exp (exponent), and lim (limit).

The following table lists the elements included in the Functions Equation palette.

cos	sin	tan	arccos
arcsin	arctan	cos	sin
tan	cot	cot	sec
cosec	exp	log	ln

lim   liminf   limsup   min
max   ged   arc   det
mod

Set [Functions ▲▼]

┌─Commands─────┐
│ cos   │
│ sin   │
│ tan   │
│ arccos   │
│ arcsin   │
│ arctan   │
│ cosh   │
│ sinh   │
│ tanh   │
│ cot   │
│ coth   │
│ sec   │
│ cosec   │
│ exp   │
│ log   │
└──────────────┘

Figure 53.11. The Functions Equation palette.

Commands Palette

The Commands palette contains a list of commands used to arrange format equations appropriately. The items in the Command palette don't appear as part of the displayed equation. They are used while you create the equation text which tells the program how to display the formula you are entering. The following list describes the available commands and lists an example of how they are used.

. (period): The period is used with the LEFT and RIGHT commands to indicate that there is no matching delimiter. In other words, it allows you to use either the LEFT or RIGHT command instead of having to use both as a pair.
Example: `stack{56x # 34Y}~ left>~12z right.`
Result:

' (backward accent): The backward accent is used to insert a space one-quarter the size of a normal space. You can combine backward accents to create a half or three-quarter space.

Example: `a'='{{v^2} over R}`

Result:

$$a = \frac{v^2}{R}$$

{ } (left and right French braces): The left and right French braces are used to group parts of an equation. They are always used in a pair. WordPerfect displays a syntax error if you leave one part of a pair out.

Example: `a'='sqrt { {a_x}^2'+'{a_y}^2}`

Result:

$$a = \sqrt{a_x^2 + a_y^2}$$

 # (pound sign): The pound sign is used to put hard returns into an equation (the Equation editor does not wrap equations for you). The pound sign is also used to indicate line breaks in the `MATRIX`, `STACK`, and `STACKALIGN` commands.

Example: `stack {phantom+2#+3# overline {phantom+5}}`

Result:

$$\begin{array}{c} 2 \\ +3 \\ \hline 5 \end{array}$$

& (ampersand): The ampersand is used with two other functions from the Command palette. With the `MATFORM` or `MATRIX` commands, the ampersand separates columns. With the `STACKALIGN` command, the

ampersand indicates which character you want to use to align the stack.
Example: `stackalign {25.&53 # 103.&96 # 1.&34 # 9.&5 } over underline {underline {140.33}}`
Result:

```
  25.53
 103.96
   1.34
   9.5
 140.33
```

\ (backward slash): The backward slash is used to indicate that the command or symbol following the backward slash should be treated as text rather than as a command.
Example: `\tangent'='{y over x}`
Result:

$$tangent = \frac{y}{x}$$

~ (tilde): The tilde inserts a full space. You can combine tildes to create larger separations.
Example: `tan ~theta '='{{a_y}over{a_x}}`
Result:

$$\tan \theta = \frac{a_y}{a_x}$$

ALIGNC: The `ALIGNC` command is used to center a group of information in a matrix column or a piece of information in a subgroup.
Example: `x'='{{-b'+-'sqrt{b^2'-'4ac}}over alignc {2a}}`
Result:

$$X = \frac{-b \pm \sqrt{b^2 - 4ac}}{2a}$$

ALIGNL: The `ALIGNL` command is used to align a group of information in a matrix column on the left of the column or to align a piece of information in a subgroup on the left margin of the subgroup.
Example: `x'='{{-b'+-'sqrt{b^2'-'4ac}}over alignl {2a}}`
Result:

$$X = \frac{-b \pm \sqrt{b^2 - 4ac}}{2a}$$

ALIGNR: The `ALIGNR` command is used to align a group of information in a matrix column on the right of the column or to align a piece of information in a subgroup on the right margin of the subgroup.
Example: `x'='{{-b'+-'sqrt{b^2'-'4ac}}over alignr {2a}}`
Result:

$$X = \frac{-b \pm \sqrt{b^2 - 4ac}}{2a}$$

BINOM: The `BINOM` command is used to create a binomial expression.
Example: `binom a b over binom x y'='{1 over z}`
Result:

$$\frac{\binom{a}{b}}{\binom{x}{y}} = \frac{1}{z}$$

BINOMSM: The `BINOMSM` command is used to create a binomial expression in a smaller font size.
Example: `binomsm a b over binomsm x y'='{1 over z}`
Result:

$$\frac{\binom{a}{b}}{\binom{x}{y}} = \frac{1}{z}$$

BOLD: The `BOLD` command is used to bold information in an equation.
Example: `bold a'='a_x bold i'+'a_x bold j'+'a_2 bold k`
Result:

$$a = a_x\bar{i} + a_x\bar{j} + a_2k$$

FROM: The `FROM` command is used with the `TO` command to give the beginning and ending limits for a symbol such as derivative or summation symbols.
Example: `int from 0 to INF {x^n e^{-ax}~dx'='{n\!} over {a^{n+1}}}`
Result:

$$\int_0^\infty x^n e^{-ax}\,dx = \frac{n!}{a^{n+1}}$$

FUNC: The `FUNC` command is used to display equation information in non-italic fonts.
Example: `func a 'TIMES 'func b'='- func b'times' func a'='left line"'matrix {matform{alignl & alignc & alignr} func i & func j & func k # a_x & a_y & a_z # b_x & b_y & b_z"} right line`
Result:

$$a \times b = -b \times a = \begin{vmatrix} i & j & k \\ a_x & a_y & a_z \\ b_x & b_y & b_z \end{vmatrix}$$

HORZ: The `HORZ` command is used to manually move information left and right. Use a percentage of the font size to specify the distance to move the information. Positive numbers move the information to the right, and negative numbers move the information to the left.

Example: `~{k{horz -160 vert -110 scalesym 300 _ }} over T`

Result:

ITAL: The `ITAL` command is used to italicize commands that would otherwise be displayed in normal type such as the summation, sine, and cosine symbols.

Example: `B'=' ital {left( {pi r^2} over {pi R^2} right)}`

Result:

$$B = \left[\frac{\pi r^2}{\pi R^2} \right]$$

LEFT: The `LEFT` and `RIGHT` commands are used to create delimiters for subgroups. `LEFT` and `RIGHT` must always be used together.

Example: `1 over lambda '='R left({{1 over I^2}'-'{1 over {u^2}}} right)`

Result:

$$\frac{1}{\lambda} = R\left(\frac{1}{I^2} - \frac{1}{u^2}\right)$$

LINESPACE: The LINESPACE command is used to adjust the vertical spacing in a stack or matrix. This command must be placed before the STACK or MATRIX commands for it to take effect.

Example: LINESPACE 300 stack {x'='LINESPACE 150 stack {b^3'+'y # a^3'+'z}}

Result:

$$X = \frac{b^3 + y}{a^3 + z}$$

LONGDIV: The LONGDIV command displays a long division character.

Example: x^2'longdiv{x^8}

Result:

$$x^2 \overline{\smash{\big)} x^8}$$

LONGDIVS: The LONGDIVS command displays a square-shaped long division character rather than the normal character.

Example: x^2'longdivs{x^8}

Result:

$$x^2 \overline{\left| x^8 \right.}$$

MATFORM: The MATFORM is used to specify the alignment format in matrix columns. It's only used with the MATRIX command. The number of alignments specified after the MATFORM command should match the number of columns in the matrix. The first alignment is matched with the first column, the second with the second column, and so on.

Example: `func a 'TIMES 'func b'='- func b'times' func a'='left line"'matrix {matform{alignl & alignc & alignr} func i & func j & func k # a_x & a_y & a_z # b_x & b_y & b_z"} right line`

Result:

$$a \times b = -b \times a = \begin{vmatrix} i & j & k \\ a_x & a_y & a_z \\ b_x & b_y & b_z \end{vmatrix}$$

MATRIX: The MATRIX command allows you to create a matrix. Use the pound sign (#) to separate rows and the ampersand (&) to separate columns within the matrix.

Example: `func a 'TIMES 'func b'='- func b'times' func a'='left line"'matrix {matform{alignl & alignc & alignr} func i & func j & func k # a_x & a_y & a_z # b_x & b_y & b_z"} right line`

Result:

$$a \times b = -b \times a = \begin{vmatrix} i & j & k \\ a_x & a_y & a_z \\ b_x & b_y & b_z \end{vmatrix}$$

NROOT: The NROOT command is used to create a nth root expression where *n* is a number or letter.

Example: `nroot 3 x`

Result:

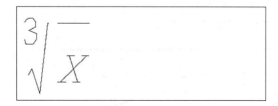

OVER: The `OVER` command is used to place one expression or subgroup in an equation over another expression or subgroup.

Example: `a'=' {v^2} over R`

Result:

$$a = \frac{v^2}{R}$$

OVERLINE: The `OVERLINE` command places a bar (or line) over the expression it's used with.

Example: `p'+'overline p~ _~4 pi^+'+' 4 pi^-`

Result:

$$p + \overline{p} \longrightarrow 4\pi^+ + 4\pi^-$$

OVERSM: The `OVERSM` command is used like the `OVER` command, except that the information following the `OVERSM` command is placed in the next smaller font size.

Example: `T'='{ 1 oversm v}'='{{2 pi m} oversm {qB}}`

Result:

$$T = \frac{1}{v} = \frac{2\pi\,m}{qB}$$

PHANTOM: The `PHANTOM` command is used to put similar non-displaying characters in a stacked equation in order to align the rest of the characters properly. The character immediately following the `PHANTOM` command takes the proper amount of space for the font specified, but the character doesn't display.

Example: `stack {phantom+2#+3# overline {phantom+5}}`

Result:

$$\begin{array}{r} 2 \\ +3 \\ \hline 5 \end{array}$$

SCALESYM: The `SCALESYM` command is used to scale any character by a percentage of the current font size.

Example: `~{k{horz -160 vert -110 scalesym 300 _ }} over T`

Result:

$$\dfrac{\triangle\hspace{-0.5em}\rule[0.4em]{0.6em}{0.4pt}}{T}$$

SQRT: The `SQRT` command is used to place a square root symbol over the expression following the command.

Example: `a'=' sqrt{{a^2}_x'+'{a^2}_y}`

Result:

STACK: The `STACK` command is used to place a list of expressions in a vertical list.

Example: `stack {phantom+2#+3# overline {phantom+5}}`

Result:

$$\begin{array}{r} 2 \\ +3 \\ \hline 5 \end{array}$$

STACKALIGN: **The** STACKALIGN **command is used to align a 'list of expressions or equations on a specified symbol. You must use the ampersand (&) command to specify the symbol you want the expressions to align on. Example:** `stackalign {25.&53 # 103.&96 # 1.&34 # 9.&5 } over underline {underline {140.33}}`
Result:

$$
\begin{array}{r}
25.53 \\
103.96 \\
1.34 \\
\underline{9.5} \\
\underline{140.33}
\end{array}
$$

SUB or _: **The** SUB **or** _ **commands are used to subscript an expression. Example:** `tan theta'='{{a_y} over{a sub x}}`
Result:

$$
\tan\theta = \frac{a_y}{a_x}
$$

SUP or ^: **The** SUP **or** ^ **commands are used to superscript an expression. Example:** `a^2'+'b sup 2'='c^2`
Result:

$$
a^2 + b^2 = c^2
$$

TO: **The** TO **command is used with the** FROM **command to give the beginning and ending limits for a symbol such as the derivative or summation symbols. Example:** `int from 0 to INF {x^n e^{-ax}~dx'='{n\!} over {a^{n+1}}}`
Result:

$$\int_0^\infty x^n e^{-ax} \, dx = \frac{n!}{a^{n+1}}$$

UNDERLINE: The `UNDERLINE` command places a bar (underline) below an expression.

Example: `stackalign {25.&53 # 103.&96 # 1.&34 # 9.&5 } over underline {underline {140.33}}`

Result:

```
  25.53
 103.96
   1.34
   9.5
 140.33
```

VERT: The `VERT` command is used to manually move information up and down. Use a percentage of the font size to specify the distance to move the information. Positive numbers move the information up, and negative numbers move the information down.

Example: `~{k{horz -160 vert -110 scalesym 300 _ }} over T`

Result:

Formatting Equations

Now take a look at how some of these commands work. I'll use my previous example of the quadratic equation to show how to create an equation. Procedure 53.2 explains the steps necessary to create the quadratic equation.

Procedure 53.2. Creating an equation.

1. From the Equation Editor screen, move the insertion point to the Type Equation Text box.
2. Type `ax^2'+'bx'+'c'='0`.
3. Select Redisplay from the button bar or press F9 or Alt+F3 to display the equation in the upper window (see Figure 53.12).

$$ax^2 + bx + c = 0$$

Figure 53.12. Quadratic equation #1.

Notice that the formatting commands (^ and ') don't display in the upper window. Also, the Equation editor sizes your equation so it fits in the display window.

Viewing Equations

Any time you make a change to the expression in the Type Equation Text window, you must refresh the display in the upper window. Do this by selecting Redisplay from the button bar or by pressing F9 or Alt+F3. WordPerfect displays an equation in your document based on what is in the Type Equation Text window, *not* what is in the upper display window.

Spacing

As shown in the example, the format of the information in the Type Equation Text window is different than the format of the formula in the upper display window. You can add regular spaces using the space bar, and by pressing Enter to add lines in the Type Equation Text window, but these items will not display in the upper display window.

You can use the ' (backward accent) and ~ (tilde) to add spaces to the formula that appears in the upper display window. You can add hard returns by using the # (pound) sign.

Sizing

The Equation editor displays your formula in the largest font possible that still allows the entire formula to be displayed in the upper display window. To change the size of the formula in your document, either increase or decrease the size of the equation graphics box.

Displaying Numbers

Characters in the equation display window appear in an italic font. If you want to include real values in your equation, you will generally want them to display as non-italic characters. Use the FUNC command to make characters display in a non-italic font.

For example, if you want to put a real number in your quadratic equation in place of the variables a, b, and c, type FUNC 7x^2'+'FUNC 5x'+'FUNC 11'='FUNC 0. The equation would look like the one shown in Figure 53.13.

$$7x^2 + 5x + 11 = 0$$

Figure 53.13. Quadratic equation #2.

Captions on Equations

Often, you will want to assign a caption to an equation that appears in your document. For example, you might want to identify the quadratic equation that you have created.

You can add captions to an equation in the same way you add captions to a graphic. From the Create Graphics Box screen, select Create Caption or 4 to access the Caption Editor screen (see Figure 53.14).

Type in the text for your caption and exit the Caption Editor screen. The caption appears on your Create Graphics Box screen.

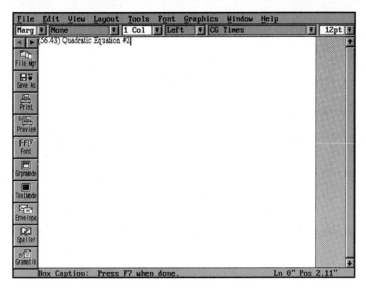

Figure 53.14. The Caption Editor screen.

Saving/Retrieving Equations (Text or Image)

Your equation essentially exists as two separate objects. First, it exists in a text form as the information you typed into the Type Equation Text window. Second, it exists as a graphic image. See Procedure 53.3 for the steps to save the text portion of your equation.

Procedure 53.3. Saving an equation as text.

1. Position the insertion point in the Type Equation Text window.
2. Select Save As or press F10.
3. Enter a filename in the Filename Entry field and select OK.

To save your equation as a graphics file, refer to Procedure 53.4.

Procedure 53.4. Saving an equation as a graphic.

1. From the Equation editor, select the File menu and choose Save as Image.
2. Select the Format drop-down list and choose WordPerfect Graphics 2.0.
3. Enter a filename in the Save Image dialog box and select OK.

Refer to Procedure 53.5 to learn how to retrieve an equation that has been saved as a text file.

Procedure 53.5. Retrieving an equation saved as a text file.

1. From the Create Graphics Box screen, set the Contents to Equation and set the Based on Box Style to Equation Box.
2. Select Filename or 1 and choose the Retrieve option.
3. Type in the name of the equation you want to retrieve or choose it from the File Manager or Quicklist.

Refer to Procedure 53.6 to learn how to retrieve an equation that has been saved as a graphics file.

Procedure 53.6. Retrieving an equation saved as a graphic image.

1. Position the insertion point at the place in your document you want the equation to appear.
2. Select Graphics from the menu and choose Retrieve.
3. Type the name of the file containing the graphic image using the File Manager or Quicklist.

Examples of Equations

The following examples show how to use some of the equation editor functions to create equations.

Quadratic Equation

Example: `x'='{-b +- sqrt {b^2—4ac}} over {2a}`
Result:

$$X = \frac{-b \pm \sqrt{b^2 - 4ac}}{2a}$$

Rotation Inertia Equation

Example: `I'=' INT r^2dm`
Result:

$$I = \int r^2\, dm$$

Probability Function

Example: `p'(E')'='1 over { e^{(E'-'E_F)/kT}"+"1}`
Result:

$$p(E) = \frac{1}{e^{(E-E_F)/kT} + 1}$$

Integral Function

Example: `INT from 0 to inf x^{2n}e^{-ax^2}dx"="{(2n-1)} over {2^{n+1}a^n} sqrt {pi over a}`
Result:

$$\int_0^\infty x^{2n} e^{-ax^2}\, dx = \frac{(2n-1)}{2^{n+1}a^n} \sqrt{\frac{\pi}{a}}$$

by Marilyn Horn Claff

Special Characters and Foreign Languages

WordPerfect 6.0 provides unparalleled support for special characters and foreign languages. In this chapter, we'll explore how to insert special characters in your documents and how to work with documents in foreign languages.

Special Characters

Computers in the IBM PC family are limited to a character set of only 256 characters, which are stored in the computer's video ROM. When IBM introduced the IBM PC in 1982, it extended the basic 128-character ASCII character set to 256 characters. The PC's character set became known as the IBM Character Set or as the Extended ASCII character set. (ASCII, pronounced askee, stands for American Standard Code for Information Interchange.) Virtually all DOS programs use the IBM Character set. Programs designed to run under Windows use a related 256-character set called the ANSI character set. (ANSI stands for American National Standards Institute.) The first 128 characters of the ASCII and ANSI characters sets are identical, but they differ in how they assign the remaining 128 characters, known as the "upper 128" characters.

WordPerfect has overcome the 256-character limitation of the IBM Character Set by creating its own character sets, called WordPerfect character sets, which include more than 1,600 different characters. You can print all of the characters in the WordPerfect character sets, including Greek, Russian (Cyrillic and Georgian), Hebrew, and Arabic characters on any printer that is capable of printing graphics.

There are two main methods for entering WordPerfect characters into your documents—the WordPerfect Characters dialog box and the Compose key. You can also assign these characters to buttons on your button bar or to a custom keyboard layout, or you can enter them with a macro. In addition, you can insert characters in the IBM Extended Character Set by entering their ASCII numeric codes.

ASCII Characters

Fewer than half of the characters in the ASCII character set are represented on a standard computer keyboard. To enter non-keyboard characters in the ASCII character set, you must hold down the Alt key and enter a numeric code on the numeric keypad. For example, the ASCII codes for the paragraph and section symbols are 20 and 21, respectively. To enter the section symbol, follow the steps in Procedure 54.1.

Procedure 54.1. Entering the section symbol.

1. Hold down the Alt kcy.
2. Type the ASCII code on the numeric keypad. In this example, type 21 to enter the code for the section symbol.
3. Release the Alt key.
4. The § symbol is inserted in your document at the cursor position.

Note that it doesn't matter whether Num Lock is on; holding down the Alt key puts the keypad in numeric mode temporarily. (The Num Lock light status does not change when you press the Alt key.)

Entering the ASCII numeric codes on the keypad is not the easiest way to enter ASCII characters in your document, but it is convenient when you already know the ASCII code and don't want to look up its WordPerfect character-set equivalent.

WordPerfect's 15 Character Sets

WordPerfect provides 15 character sets, numbered 0-14, with a total of 2,715 characters. Fourteen of the character sets are predefined. Character Set 11 is reserved for use as a user-defined character set.

Character Set 0 (ASCII)

Character set 0 contains characters from the basic ASCII character set. Note that their WordPerfect numbers are similar to their ASCII numeric codes. For example, the ASCII code for the space character is 32, and its WordPerfect code is 0,32. All of the characters in Character Set 0 are available directly from the keyboard, so unless you are using a non-European-language version of WordPerfect, you'll never need to enter these characters by their WordPerfect codes. Because the characters in Character Set 0 behave differently from the characters in the other WordPerfect character sets, we will use the term *WordPerfect Character Set* to refer to character sets 1-13, and the terms *WordPerfect Characters* and *Special Characters* to refer to the characters in those characters sets.

The first time you open the WordPerfect Characters dialog box in a session, WordPerfect displays Character Set 0. After that, it defaults to the character set of the last character you chose from the WordPerfect Characters dialog box.

Character Sets 1-13

With the exception of the user-defined character set, all of the characters in the WordPerfect character sets are displayed in both Graphics and Page mode. In Text mode, most of the characters in set 1-13 are represented by a small solid square character. (See the section called "Working in Text Mode" later in this chapter for tips on working with special characters in Text mode.)

Table 54.1. WordPerfect Character Sets.

#	Name	Characters	Total
0	ASCII	32-126	94
1	Multinational	0-241	242
2	Phonetic (IPA)	0-144	145
3	Box Drawing	0-87	88
4	Typographic	0-101	102
5	Iconic Symbols	0-254	255
6	Math/Scientific	0-237	238
7	Math/Scientific Extension	0-228	229
8	Greek	0-218	219
9	Hebrew	0-118	119
10	Cyrillic and Georgian	0-249	250

continues

Table 54.1. continued

#	Name	Characters	Total
11	Japanese Kana	0-62	63
12	User-Defined	0-254	255
13	Arabic 1	0-195	196
14	Arabic Script	0-219	220

Each character in character sets 1-13 is represented in WordPerfect as a two-part numeric code. For example, the trademark symbol is represented by the code 4,41. The first number indicates the number of the character set. The second number indicates the number of the character within that character set. When you place your cursor on a special character in Reveal Codes, the code expands to show the WordPerfect character number. (See Figure 54.1.) This feature is especially handy when you are working in Text mode.

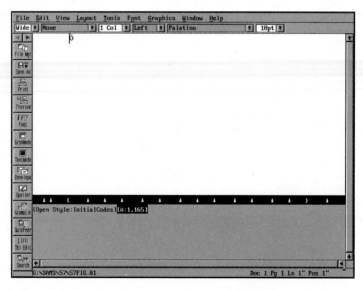

Figure 54.1. Special character as seen in Reveal Codes.

Note: WordPerfect Characters use four bytes of memory, compared to only one byte for characters in the ASCII character set. You'll find that you can enter fewer WordPerfect characters than ASCII characters in dialog boxes that limit the length of your input. Also, you cannot use WordPerfect Characters in DOS filenames.

Entering Special Characters

WordPerfect provides two methods for entering special characters in your documents: the WordPerfect Characters dialog box and the Compose key. For characters that you use frequently, consider assigning the character to a button bar, a macro, or to a custom keyboard layout. (See Chapters 43, "Getting Started with Macros," and 44, "Introduction to the Macro Programming Language.")

Tip: The *Super Book* disk contains keyboard layouts for French, Spanish, German, and Russian.

Entering Special Characters from the WordPerfect Characters Dialog Box

If you want to see what a character looks like before you insert it, or if you don't like memorizing numeric codes, you'll prefer to enter special characters through the WordPerfect Characters Dialog Box (see Figure 54.2).

Figure 54.2. The WordPerfect Characters dialog box.

To enter a character from the WordPerfect Characters dialog box, follow the steps in Procedure 54.2.

Procedure 54.2. Entering a WordPerfect special character.

1. Choose Font, WP Characters; or press Ctrl+W.
2. If you know the numeric WordPerfect Character code or mnemonic shortcut for the character you want, enter it in the Number text entry box.

   To enter a numeric code, type the character set number, followed by a comma and the number for the character in that character set. For example, to enter the numeric code for the Spanish question mark, type: 4,8. To enter a mnemonic shortcut, type the two characters without a comma. For example, to enter the mnemonic shortcut for the Spanish question mark, type: ??.

> **Note:** For a list of WordPerfect's mnemonic shortcuts, see the section called "Mnemonic Shortcuts" later in this chapter.

3. Click Insert or press Enter.
4. If you don't know either the numeric code or the mnemonic shortcut, click on the word Set or press Tab, Enter. The list box expands to display the names of all of the WordPerfect character sets.
5. Choose the character set you want by highlighting the name, then click or press Enter. WordPerfect displays the new character set in the dialog box.
6. Double-click on the character you want, or press c to move the cursor into the character set box. Use the cursor keys to highlight the character you want, then press Enter.

When you open the WordPerfect Character dialog box for the first time, WordPerfect displays Character Set 0 (ASCII), with the first character (0,32—the space character) highlighted. If you choose a character, the next time you open the WordPerfect Characters dialog box, WordPerfect displays that character set in the Characters box, and highlights the numeric code for that character in the Number text entry box.

Entering Special Characters with the Compose Key (Ctrl+A or Ctrl+2)

If you're a fast typist or you have a good memory, you may prefer to use WordPerfect's Compose key to enter special characters. The Compose dialog box displays more quickly and is less obtrusive than the WordPerfect Characters dialog box. Unlike the WordPerfect Characters dialog box, the Compose dialog box does not remember the code for the last character you entered. To enter a special character using the Compose dialog box, follow the steps in Procedure 54.3.

Procedure 54.3. Entering a WordPerfect character with Compose.

1. Press Ctrl+A. The Compose dialog box appears (see Figure 54.3).

Figure 54.3. The Compose dialog box.

> **Tip:** You can also press Ctrl+2 (the regular 2 on the top row of the keyboard), plus a mnemonic combination or a numeric code to enter a special character. Unlike Ctrl+A, the Ctrl+2 key combination does not display a prompt.

2. Type the two letters that make up the Compose mnemonic. For example, to enter ñ, type n˜ .

3. Click OK or press Enter.

> **Note:** You can also type the WordPerfect numeric code for the character. For example, to enter ñ, type 1,57 and choose OK.

> **Tip:** You can use either the numeric method or the mnemonic method with both the Compose key and the WordPerfect Characters dialog box.

875

Mnemonic Shortcuts for WordPerfect Characters (Compose)

For most users, the very thought of memorizing even a handful of WordPerfect numeric codes is daunting. Fortunately, WordPerfect has provided easily remembered shortcuts for many of the special characters. Here's the rule: whenever a special character appears to be made up of two regular characters, you can usually just type those two characters in the text entry box instead of the numeric code. For example, the character á looks like a combination of *a* and the ' character, so type a' or 'a in the dialog box. This feature is called Compose; however, it works exactly the same in the WordPerfect Characters dialog box as it does with the Compose key.

Compose works with two categories of special characters, called digraphs and diacriticals. Digraphs are characters that are made up of two separate characters, such as æ. Diacriticals are special characters, such as accent marks and cedillas, that indicate how to pronounce a character. Note that the order of the characters does not matter.

Digraphs

The following is a table that includes shortcut keys that WordPerfect provides for digraphs:

Table 54.2. Shortcut keys in WordPerfect.

Combination	Character	Code	Description	Combination	Character	Code	Description
n-	–	4,33	En Dash	ij	ij	1,139	ij Digraph
m-	—	4,34	En Dash	f-	ƒ	4,14	Florin/Guilders
--	—	4,34	Em Dash	<<	«	4,9	Left Double Guillemet
==	≡	6,14	Equivalent	>>	»	4,10	Right Double Guillemet
~ ~	≈	6,13	Approximately Equal	oe	œ	1,167	oe Digraph
<=	≤	6,2	Less than or Equal	OE	Œ	1,166	OE Digraph
>=	≥	6,3	Greater than or Equal	P¦	¶	4,5	Paragraph
+-	±	6,1	Plus or Minus	Pt	₧	4,13	Pesetas
*.	•	4,3	Small Solid Bullet	L-	£	4,11	Pound Sterling
**	●	4,0	Medium Solid Bullet	Rx	℞	4,43	Prescription
*o	○	4,45	Small Hollow Bullet	rx	℞	4,43	Prescription
*O	○	4,1	Medium Hollow Bullet	ro	®	4,22	Registered Trade Mark
ao	å	1,35	a with a Ring	RO	®	4,22	Registered Trade Mark
a=	ª	4,15	a Underscore	SM	℠	4,42	Servicemark
o=	º	4,16	o Underscore	sm	℠	4,42	Servicemark
ae	æ	1,37	ae Digraph	TM	™	4,41	Trademark
AE	Æ	1,36	AE Digraph	tm	™	4,41	Trademark
c/	¢	4,19	Cent	??	¿	4,8	Upside down ?
CO	©	4,23	Copyright	!!	¡	4,7	Upside down !
co	©	4,23	Copyright	Y=	¥	4,12	Yen
ox	¤	4,24	General Currency Symbol	/2	½	4,17	One Half
ss	ß	1,23	German Double-S	/4	¼	4,18	One Quarter
IJ	IJ	1,138	IJ Digraph				

Note that you must use the same case that is used in the examples. The trademark symbol, for example, can be entered as tm or as TM, but not as Tm or tM.

Diacriticals

The following keyboard characters represent diacritical marks that can be used to create Special Characters with Compose:

Table 54.3. Keyboard Characters representing diacritical marks.

Character	Name	Diacritical Mark	Example
'	Left Quote	Acute	á
`	Right Quote	Grave	à
"	Quotes	Umlaut	ä
^	Caret	Circumflex	â
v	Letter v	Caron	č
,	Comma	Cedilla	ç
:	Colon	Center Dot	l·
;	Semicolon	Ogonek	ą
-	Dash	Crossbar	đ
.	Period	Dot above	i
@	At Symbol	Ring	å
/	Slash	Slash	ø
\	Backslash	Stroke	ł
_	Underscore	Macron	ā
~	Tilde	Tilde	ã

As with digraphs, the order in which you enter the two characters does not matter.

User-Defined Characters Sets

WordPerfect reserves Character Set 12 as a user-defined character set. Unlike the predefined character sets, the user-defined characters do not display on your screen in any of WordPerfect's editing modes. Instead, WordPerfect represents them with a small hollow box character in Graphics and Page modes, and as a small solid box when you are in Text mode.

If you use many different user-defined characters in the same document, you'll have difficulty keeping them straight. Remember that you can determine the WordPerfect character number for a special character by looking at it in Reveal Codes. (The cursor must be directly on the code in order for it to expand to show its numeric value.)

Bullet Characters

WordPerfect offers a large assortment of bullet characters in Character Set 4, Typographic Symbols. Four of the more common bullet characters (small solid, medium solid, small hollow, and medium hollow) have Compose shortcuts. (See the preceding section on digraphs in this chapter.)

Because bullets are so common, WordPerfect provides two other methods for entering bullet characters that you may find even easier than using Compose: outline styles and a macro.

Entering Bullets with Outline

To enter bullets using outline, change to the Bullets outline style by choosing it from the Outline bar. If the Outline bar is not displayed, open the Outline dialog box, select Tools, Outline, Outline Style, and choose the Bullets style. (See Chapter 55, "Outlining," for detailed instructions for using outlining.) If you use the Bullets outline style frequently, consider adding the [Outline:Bullets] code to your Initial Codes Setup so that you can skip this step in the future.

To insert a bullet, just click on the number symbol # on the Outline bar; or press Ctrl+T. A bullet style code, consisting of a bullet character and an Indent code, is inserted in your document. Each time you press Enter, a new bullet style code is inserted. To switch back to regular text, click the T symbol on the Outline bar; or press Ctrl+T. Ctrl+T toggles between outline mode and regular text, making it easy to intersperse bulleted and unbulleted paragraphs.

 Tip: If you don't like the predefined Bullets outline style, you can customize it by editing the Bullets Outline Style.

Entering Bullets with the Bullet Macro

WordPerfect provides a macro called BULLET.WPM that inserts a bullet character and an Indent code at the insertion point. If you select Change Bullet Character, you can choose from seven different bullet characters, or you can choose any character you like. To select a custom character, choose User Defined. Then press

878

Ctrl+W to display the WP Characters dialog box, or press Ctrl+A if you know the Compose mnemonic or the WP character number (see Figure 54.4).

Figure 54.4. The Bullet macro.

The Bullet macro remembers what character you chose for your bullet from one session to the next. (See Chapter 43 for instructions on how to use macros.)

 Tip: To take best advantage of the Bullet macro, add it to your button bar or to your custom keyboard.

Scientific and Math Characters

Two of the WordPerfect character sets are devoted to scientific and math characters. Character Set 6 contains normal size math and scientific characters. Character Set 7 contains oversize math and scientific characters.

 Tip: WordPerfect comes with an Equation keyboard that assigns many of the most common math and scientific characters to Alt and Ctrl key combinations. You don't need to be in the Equation editor to use this keyboard.

See Chapters 52, "Using Math in WordPerfect 6.0," and 53, "Equation Editor," for information about using the scientific and math characters in the Equation editor.

Printing Special Characters

You can print all of the WordPerfect Special Characters on any printer that is capable of printing graphics. This means that you can print the special characters on almost any laser, dot matrix, or inkjet printer, even if you do not have any fonts that include those characters. The reason WordPerfect is able to print all of the characters is that it creates them graphically from your WP.DRS file. This process is slow, however, so if you often write in a non-European language, or if you use a large number of special symbols in your documents, you should consider purchasing a font that includes those characters. A well-designed commercial font will provide higher text quality and greater printing speed than WordPerfect's graphically produced characters. Also, your printer may not have enough memory to print characters graphically. If only some of the special characters print, it is an indication that your printer does not have sufficient memory.

Whether WordPerfect prints the special characters graphically depends on your printer settings for Text and Graphics Quality. If Graphics Quality is set to Do Not Print, the special character will not print graphically no matter what the Text Quality setting is. Similarly, if the Text Quality is set to Do Not Print, the special characters will not print graphically, no matter what the Graphics Quality setting is. In all other cases, WordPerfect uses the higher of the two settings. The following table illustrates various printing scenarios.

Table 54.4. WordPerfect Printing Scenarios.

| Text Quality | Graphics Quality | | | |
	High	Medium	Draft	Do Not Print
High	Yes—High	Yes—High	Yes—High	No
Medium	Yes—High	Yes—Medium	Yes—Draft	No
Draft	Yes—High	Yes—Medium	Yes—Draft	No
Do Not Print	No	No	No	No

Working in Text Mode

Ideally, if you use many special characters, you will be able to work in Graphics or Page mode so that you'll be able to see the characters as they will print. If you must use a slow computer, or if your document is especially large or complex, you may need to work in Text mode.

Except for characters that are also part of the IBM Character Set, most of the special characters will display as small solid squares when you are in Text mode. There are two ways to determine what character the square box represents: examine the character in Reveal Code or look at it in Print Preview.

If the special character that you are using is similar to one of the keyboard characters, WordPerfect displays the closest match, rather than a box character. For example, if you choose an e with a horizontal bar above it (long e), WordPerfect displays the letter e.

Depending on your video adapter, you may be able to display 512 unique characters in Text mode instead of the standard 256. The capability to display 512 characters in Text mode is one of WordPerfect's best-kept secrets. To change to a 512-character set, first change to Text mode, then choose File, Setup; or press Shift+F1. Then choose Display, Text Mode Screen Type/Colors, Color Schemes. The next step is the tricky one: choose Create. You cannot modify an existing color scheme to use a 512-character set because the opportunity to choose a different screen font is only offered when you first create a color scheme. At the prompt, type a name for your new color scheme. When you press Enter, the insertion point moves into the Screen Font box. Choose 512 Characters, 8 Colors, then choose OK, OK. Then choose Select to make that color scheme/screen font the active one; then choose Close, Close to return to your document.

WordPerfect's 512-character set displays more of the Multinational Character Set characters, as well as Typographic Symbols, including the characters in Figure 54.5.

	WordPerfect Characters that display in 512-Character Text Mode	
Number	Character	Description
4,22	®	Registered Trademark
4,23	©	Copyright Symbol
4,41	™	Trademark
4,31	”	Right Double Quote (like 99)
4,32	“	Inverted Double Quote (like 66)
4,42	SM	Servicemark
4,63	„	Base Double Quote

Figure 54.5. WordPerfect Characters in 512 Character Text mode.

Creating Overstrike Characters

You should only rarely need WordPerfect's powerful Overstrike feature, because virtually every character you'll need is provided in one of the WordPerfect Character Sets. Whenever possible, use a WordPerfect character rather than create a character with overstrike. Special characters give more predictable results if you change the typeface or point size, and they convert better if you save your document in a different format. Special characters also work better with the Speller and words containing special characters can be added to your dictionary. Think of overstrike as a last resort.

WordPerfect's Overstrike feature allows you to overstrike multiple characters. Overstrike characters are treated as a single code, so the characters stay together. Just to make things interesting, you can include special characters and all font attributes, including all attributes for size, position, and appearance. For example, you could overstrike superscripted and subscripted em dash characters and apply large and bold attributes:

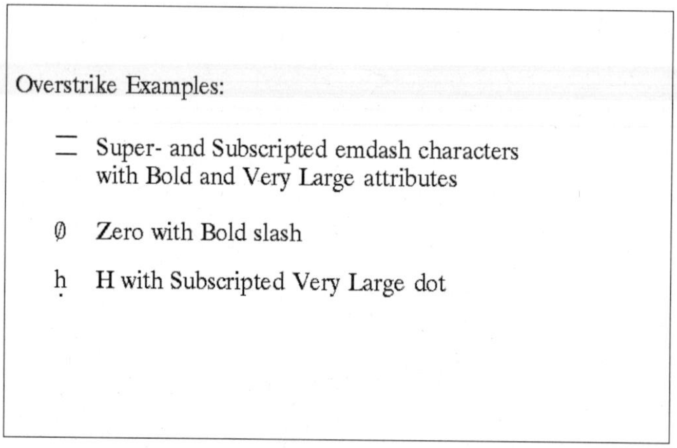

Overstrike Examples:

‾ Super- and Subscripted emdash characters
with Bold and Very Large attributes

Ø Zero with Bold slash

ḥ H with Subscripted Very Large dot

Figure 54.6. Overstrike Characters with special characters.

To create an overstrike, follow the steps in Procedure 54.4.

Procedure 54.4. Creating an overstrike character.

1. Choose Layout; or press Shift+F8.
2. Then choose Character, Create Overstrike.
3. The Create Overstrike dialog box appears (see Figure 54.7).

Figure 54.7. The Create Overstrike Dialog Box.

4. Choose Overstrike Characters.
5. Enter the text in the text entry box without any spaces. Add font attributes as you go by clicking Attributes; or press Ctrl+F8. Select the font attributes you want from the list in the dialog box.

> **Note:** You cannot apply font attributes to selected text in the text edit box. You must insert the attribute code, type the text, and turn off the attribute.

6. Choose OK when done.

WordPerfect inserts the overstrike character in your document. If you are working in Graphics or Page mode, WordPerfect displays the overstrike character as it will print. If you are working in Text mode, WordPerfect displays the overstrike character as the closest character. If no similar character exists, WordPerfect inserts a box character.

Once you have created an overstrike, you can edit it at any time by choosing Layout; or pressing Shift+F8. Then choose Character, Edit Overstrike. You can also search for an overstrike, or search for it and replace it with a different overstrike.

Foreign Language Support

WordPerfect 6.0 has exceptionally strong support for foreign language and multilingual word processing. WordPerfect is available in 27 language versions, including all major Western European languages and most Eastern European languages. You can either purchase WordPerfect in the language version in which you plan to work, or you can purchase additional foreign language modules that work with the language version you already have. Some languages are available only as add-on modules.

WordPerfect's "Package Language" and Language Modules

WordPerfect uses the term *package language* to indicate the language that your version of WordPerfect uses. The package language determines the direction in which text is entered (left-to-right or right-to-left) and the language for the manual, on-screen menus, and help files. Unless you have used language codes in your document, the package language also determines the language for the dictionary, hyphenation, thesaurus, and footnote continuation messages, as well as the sorting order, dates, and default currency formatting.

A language module is an add-on package that provides support for a second language. The contents of the language modules vary from language to language. All language modules include a dictionary and hyphenation support, and many languages, including French, German, and Spanish, also include a thesaurus. Non-English modules usually include one or more keyboard definitions. Modules for languages such as Hebrew and Arabic provide support for right-to-left editing. If the language uses a non-Roman alphabet, the language module may also include a character map. Language modules do not include the WordPerfect program files, nor do they include the files necessary to display the menus, dialog boxes, help, and tutorial files in the second language.

Working in a Bilingual Environment

In a bilingual or multilingual environment, it makes sense to provide menus, help, and tutorial files in the language with which each user is most comfortable. This can be most easily accomplished by installing the package version of WordPerfect for each language that is used.

If you have more than one package language, you can save disk space by installing one complete language package, plus the additional files from the other language package that are required for running WordPerfect in the second language. Just install the second language package into the same directories as the first package. Because the menus files, help files, speller, thesaurus, and hyphenation files are named differently for each language, they can co-exist in the same directories.

Provided that all of the required files are present, each user can choose which language to use as a default language regardless of which language has been chosen by the other users on the network.

Note: The only bilingual version of WordPerfect is the Canadian version. WordPerfect offers two package languages: Canadian French and Canadian English. Each package contains dictionary,

hyphenation, and thesaurus files for both languages. Users purchase the package language of their primary language, because that
is the language of the manual, menus, and help files.

Changing the Environment Language

WordPerfect calls the default language the Environment Language. The Environment Language is the language used for File Manager, menus, dialog boxes, and
help files, as well as the language for WordPerfect features such as the footnote
continuation message. The Environment language also determines the language
for the date, the speller, and the thesaurus if there are no language codes. If you
have more than one package language installed, you can change the Environment
Language in Setup by following Procedure 54.5.

Procedure 54.5. Changing the Environment Language.

1. Choose File, Setup; or press Shift-F1.
2. Choose Environment, then Language.

   The Available Environment Languages box appears, with a list of the
   languages that have been installed on your system.
3. Select the language that you wish to use as a default and choose OK.
4. Choose OK again, then Close.

Language Codes

WordPerfect has assigned a two-character abbreviation for each language that it
supports. Currently, there are 32 predefined language codes (including 4 for
English, and 2 each for French, German, and Portuguese). This abbreviation is
used in many of the filenames for files included with WordPerfect. For example,
the U.S. English version's dictionary file is named WPUS.LEX, and the Canadian
French dictionary is named WPCF.LEX.

Why Use Language Codes?

Language codes enable WordPerfect to keep track of the languages you are using
in your document. Each time you change to a different language, you should insert
a language code for that language in your document. When you change back to
your original language, you insert another language code for that language. If
there are no language codes in your document, WordPerfect assumes that you are
using the package language.

The language codes determine the default format for the date and time, which dictionary and thesaurus WordPerfect uses in that section of the document, and even the sorting order if the language, such as Spanish or Swedish, uses a different sorting order from that of English. If the language code is inserted in Document Initial Codes, it also determines the language for the footnote continuation string.

Inserting Language Codes

To insert a language code in your document, follow the steps in Procedure 54.6.

Procedure 54.6. Inserting a language code.

1. Choose Layout; or press Shift+F8. The name of the current language is displayed in the text box.
2. Choose Other, then Language. A dialog box listing the predefined language codes appears (see Figure 54.8).

Figure 54.8. The Select Languages dialog box.

The languages that appear in the Select Language dialog box are the ones that are defined in your Language Resource file. (See the section "Language Resource Files" in this chapter.)

3. Highlight the name of the language to which you are switching, and press Enter or click OK. Choose OK again, then Close.

WordPerfect inserts a [Lang:XX] code in your document (XX represents the two-letter language code). Note that WordPerfect does not insert the language code if it is identical to the language code in effect in the document.

If the language you wish to use is not listed, move the insertion point to the Other Language Code text entry box, and type a two-letter abbreviation for that language. For example, if your document contains a passage in Old English, you could use OE. When WordPerfect encounters the [Lang:OE] code during a spell check, it automatically changes to the WPOE.LEX dictionary, if it exists. If the dictionary file does not exist, WordPerfect gives you an error message and allows you to skip that section of the document during the spell check.

Tip: It's a good idea to block-define the passage in the foreign language before changing the language code. That way, WordPerfect makes the language code a revertible code and returns to the original document language at the end of the block.

Tip: The *Super Book* disk includes a macro called LANGUAGE.WPM that toggles between U.S. English and a second language. Edit the macro so that it chooses the second language you use the most, and add the macro to your button bar.

Tip: If you frequently edit in a foreign language, consider using a customized keyboard. Several foreign language keyboards, including French, Spanish, German, and Russian, are provided on the *Super Book* disk.

WordPerfect Character Maps

Because WordPerfect Characters take four bytes instead of one, your foreign language documents can become quite large. WordPerfect addresses this problem with a feature called Character Maps. Character Maps map the special characters that the language module requires to characters in the IBM Extended Character set. Unless you purchase an additional language module, your copy of WordPerfect uses only the character map for the package language. If you purchase a language module with a character map, your documents will be significantly smaller than if you simply inserted the same special characters using the WordPerfect Default Map. To change to a different Character Map, follow the steps in Procedure 54.7.

Procedure 54.7. Changing the WordPerfect Character Map.
1. Choose Layout, or press Shift+F8.
2. Choose Document.
3. Choose Character Map, then select the character map you want.

Note: The File Size number indicates the size of the current document. Changing to a different Character Map changes the size of the document.

Language Resource File

WordPerfect stores the settings for the languages it supports in a file called WP.LRS, located in your \WP60 directory. The WP.LRS file is a WordPerfect 6.0 data file that you can edit in WordPerfect. Each language is a record with 18 fields containing information primarily about how the time and date should be displayed in that language. If you work with an unsupported language, you can add a record to the WP.LRS file containing information about that language to facilitate working with dates and table currency formats.

Caution: Edit the WP.LRS file carefully. Do not remove any merge codes or change the number of lines in the file.

The record format of the WP.LRS file is as follows:

Language Resource File Format (WP.LRS)

Field	Lines	Contents
1	Line 1	2-letter language code
	Line 2	Name of Language
2	Line 1	a.m.
	Line 2	p.m.
	Lines 3-14	Date Format Codes
	Line 9	a.m.
	Line 10	p.m.
3	Lines 1-12	Names of months
4	Lines 1-12	Names of months (abbreviated)
5	Lines 1-7	Name of days
6	Lines 1-7	Names of days (abbreviated)
7	Line 1	Footnote continuation message (first page)
8	Line 2	Footnote continuation message (subsequent pages)
9	Line 1	Date format for File Manager (1=dmy;2=mdy;3=ymd)
10	Lines 1-2	Date separator characters for File Manager

Field	Lines	Contents
11	Line 1	Time format (12- or 24-hours) for File Manager
12	Line 1	Valid time separation character for File Manager
	Lines 2-3	A.M. and P.M. abbreviation for 12-hour format
13	Line 1	Thousands separator character for File Manager
14	Line 1	Not applicable (Figure)
15	Line 1	Not applicable (Table)
16	Line 1	Not applicable (ordinal numbers 1-4)
17	Line 1	Date separators
	Line 2	Time separators
18		Table Currency:
	Line 1, char 1	0=currency symbol before number 1=symbol after number
	Line 1, char 2,	0=no space between symbol and number 1=space
	Line 1, char 3,	Currency abbreviation
	Line 2	CR (if CR/DR Symbol selected for negative number)
	Line 3	DR (if CR/DB Symbol selected for negative number) DB

Note: Fields 14-16 do not apply to WordPerfect 6.0. They are included because they are used by other WordPerfect Corporation products which share the same language resource file.

The fields that you are most likely to change are the date and time fields (fields 2-6). Changes to the File Manager fields (9-13) affect only the package or the environment language. You must exit and restart WordPerfect for changes to the File Manager fields to take effect.

Using the Speller and Thesaurus in Multilingual Documents

WordPerfect handles the spell checking of multilingual documents logically. If you insert language codes each time you change languages, whenever you spell check, WordPerfect will automatically use the correct dictionaries for each language without prompting you. If you don't have a dictionary for any of the languages in your document, WordPerfect gives you a warning message that that dictionary is not found and asks you if you want to skip that language or cancel the spell check.

Similarly, if you use language codes each time you change languages, WordPerfect automatically chooses the correct thesaurus for the current language, if it is available.

Unfortunately, WordPerfect does not offer a setup option to eliminate the prompt that tells you a particular language dictionary is not found. If you frequently write in languages for which you do not have the language module, consider disabling the Speller in those sections of your documents, instead of (or in addition to) using the language codes.

> **Note:** The option to disable the Speller also disables Grammatik, but this step is not necessary, because the English version of Grammatik is smart enough to skip sections of the document that are marked with a code for a different language.

To disable the Speller and Grammatik, simply follow the steps in Procedure 54.8.

Procedure 54.8. Disabling the Speller and Grammatik.

1. From the **Tools** menu, choose Writing Tools, or press Alt+F1.
2. Check the box beside Disable Speller/Grammatik (in this part of the document).

WordPerfect inserts a `[Speller/Grammatik:Off]` code in your document. To re-enable the Speller and Grammatik later in the document, uncheck the box.

Using Grammatik with Foreign Language Documents

Currently, Grammatik does not automatically switch between languages, even if you have versions of Grammatik for those languages. If you use language codes in your document, the English version of Grammatik skips over foreign language

890

sections of your document. You can also disable Grammatik (along with the Speller) for sections of your document, as described previously.

If you have installed an additional language module that includes a version of Grammatik for that language, there are two rules that you must follow in order to use it in place of the English version:

1. Place the language code for that language in Document Initial Codes.

   or

2. Start Grammatik with your insertion point in a section of the document that has been marked with a language code for that language.

Hyphenation

WordPerfect handles hyphenation differently depending on the language. For languages such as English that do not follow clear rules and have many special cases, WordPerfect uses a word-based dictionary. For languages that are very regular, such as Finnish, WordPerfect uses a hyphenation algorithm with a list of exceptions.

Initial Caps Conversion

WordPerfect 6.0 offers three types of case conversion: all uppercase, all lowercase, and initial caps. According to the style books, it is incorrect to capitalize filler words such as prepositions, conjunctions, and pronouns. WordPerfect therefore provides an exception list, called WPXX.ICR, for each language that is installed (where XX is the two-letter language code). The ICR file is simply a WordPerfect document that contains a list of exceptions that should not be capitalized, unless they are at the beginning of a sentence. You can create similar exception lists for each of the foreign languages for which you have installed the add-on language module.

> **Tip:** By using an undocumented trick, you can use the Initial Caps conversion feature with European languages even if you don't have the language module. Just create the WPXX.ICR file as described above, then make a copy of the WPCC60US.DTL file (located in the WP60 directory) with the name WPCC60XX.DTL, where XX stands for the language code for the language you are using. For example, if you are writing in Italian, name the file WPCC60IT.DTL.

Footnote Continuation Messages

The Language Resource file (WP.LRS file) determines the footnote continuation messages. WordPerfect assumes that footnote continuation messages should be written in the primary language of the document, not in the language used in the footnote. WordPerfect therefore uses the Environment Language for the footnote continuation messages, unless there is a language code for a different language in Document Initial Codes.

Caution: Simply inserting a language code at the beginning of the document does not affect the footnote continuation messages. You must insert the language code in Document Initial Codes to override the Environment Language.

Sorting

Language codes affect the sort sequence in WordPerfect. Languages such as Spanish and Swedish sort in a different sequence than English. WordPerfect uses the language code in effect to determine the correct sorting order.

Entering Dates in Foreign Languages

Some of WordPerfect's foreign language features require the presence of a language module. One feature that you can use even without purchasing any language modules is the date feature. Simply insert a language code for the language in which you would like to enter the date, then follow the steps described in Procedure 54.9.

Procedure 54.9. Entering the date in another language.

1. Choose Tools, Date; or press Shift+F5.
2. (Optional.) Change the date format by choosing Date Format. A list of twelve formats appears. The date formats show the current date in the currently selected language. These formats are determined by the contents of Lines 3-14 in field 2 in WP.LRS.
3. Choose a predefined date or choose Edit, then choose OK.
4. Choose Insert Date Text or Insert Date Code, then choose OK.

International Currencies

WordPerfect's Tables feature makes it easy to work with international currencies. By defining a cell, a group of cells, or a column for a particular national currency, you eliminate the step of inserting the currency symbol for each cell. To change the national currency for a cell or column, follow the steps in Procedure 54.10.

Procedure 54.10. Changing the currency symbol in a table.

1. From the Tables Edit menu, choose Cell or Column.
2. Choose Number Type and select Currency.
3. Select Options.
4. If desired, check the Align Currency Symbol box.
5. Choose Select.... The International Currencies list appears.
6. Highlight the currency you wish to use, then choose Select, then choose OK twice.
7. Finish formatting the table and choose Close.

Long Documents

by Paul McFedries

Outlining

Probably because they were forced upon us in high school English class, outlines have developed a reputation as one of those chores that should be avoided at all costs. Most writers I know would rather have a root canal than work up an outline.

This reputation is undeserved, because an outline is the best way to introduce some badly needed organization to your long documents and to prevent them from becoming rambling and incoherent. Besides, WordPerfect 6.0 is chock full of new outlining features that make working with outlines a breeze. This chapter takes you through all these features and shows you how to incorporate them into your documents.

What Is an Outline?

Most documents have titles, headings, and subheadings that determine the underlying organizational structure of the document. An *outline* is simply a summary of this structure that lets you see, at a glance, how the document is set up. If things don't look right, you can then use the outline structure to easily reorganize the document. Figure 55.1 shows an example of a document outline.

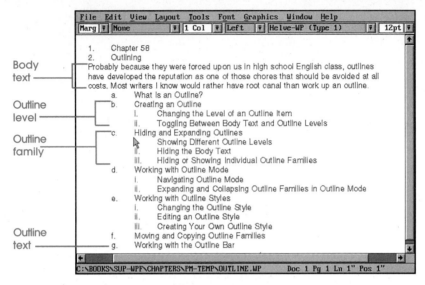

Figure 55.1. A typical WordPerfect outline.

As you can see in Figure 55.1, outlines have four major parts:

▲ **Body text**. Any text that is not part of the outline itself.

▲ **Outline text**. Any text that is part of the outline. This usually consists of a letter, number, or bullet (depending on which outline style you use), followed by some descriptive text. Also called an *outline item*.

▲ **Outline level**. The relative position of the outline text in the outline hierarchy (heading, subheading, and so on). WordPerfect lets you use up to eight levels and identifies each level with a unique numbering style (such as 1, i, A, or a).

▲ **Outline family**. An outline level and all of its subordinate levels.

Creating an Outline

A WordPerfect outline is really just normal text preceded by a paragraph style code. You could enter these codes yourself, but the Outline feature is easier because it adds the codes automatically and makes the proper adjustments if you move or delete outline elements (as you'll see later in this chapter). Follow the steps in Procedure 55.1 to create an outline.

Note: To see how the Outline feature does its job, turn on Reveal Codes (by pressing Alt+F3) before starting Procedure 55.1.

Procedure 55.1. Creating an outline.

1. Select Tools, Outline, or press Ctrl+F5.

2. Select Begin New Outline. WordPerfect displays the Outline Style List dialog box.

3. Highlight the style you want and choose Select. WordPerfect returns you to the document, displays a paragraph number, and indents the insertion point.

4. Type the outline text for this level and press Enter. WordPerfect displays the next paragraph number in the series and again indents the insertion point.

5. If necessary, adjust the outline level by selecting Tools, Outline (or by pressing Ctrl+F5) and then selecting either Next Level or Previous Level. WordPerfect adjusts the outline level accordingly.

> **Tip:** To adjust the outline level quickly, place the insertion point to the left of the outline text and press Tab to move to the next level, or Shift+Tab to move to the previous level.

6. Repeat Steps 4 and 5 until your outline is complete.

7. When you are finished, select Tools, Outline, or press Ctrl+F5. Then select End Outline.

Changing the Level of an Outline Item

As you saw in Procedure 55.1, you can change the level of an outline item by pressing Tab or Shift+Tab. Occasionally, you may need to change an item to a specific level number, and the Tab/Shift+Tab method won't do the job (because you may not be sure which level you're on). Procedure 55.2 shows you how to do this.

Procedure 55.2. Changing the level of an outline item.

1. Place the insertion point on the item you want to change.

2. Select Tools, Outline, Outline Options; or press Ctrl+F5. The Outline dialog box appears.

3. In the Insert Outline Level (1-8) text box, enter the new level number you want to use (enter a number between 1 and 8).

4. Select OK. WordPerfect adjusts the level number of the item.

Toggling Between Body Text and Outline Levels

An outline should contain only your document's headings and subheadings, not the actual text of the document (the body text). If you need to insert some body text while creating an outline, you need to briefly drop out of the current outline level. To do this, select Tools, Outline, or press Ctrl+F5. Then select Change to Body Text. WordPerfect removes the paragraph style code so that you can enter your regular text.

To return to your outline, select Tools, Outline, or press Ctrl+F5. Then select Change to Outline Level.

Tip: An easier way to toggle between body text and outline levels is to press Ctrl+T.

Hiding and Expanding Outlines

When working with your outlines, you will often want to expand or hide the outline headings to give you greater or lesser detail. You may also need to hide the entire outline so you can see just the body text or, conversely, you might want to temporarily get rid of the body text so you can see a clean, uncluttered outline. The following sections show you how to do all this and more.

Showing Different Outline Levels

In most outlines, the individual outline levels represent specific elements of the document. These might be chapter titles, paragraph headings, section descriptions, and so on. If you need to see just those levels up to and including the chapter titles in your outline, for example, you can tell WordPerfect to restrict its outline display. Procedure 55.3 gives you the steps to follow.

Procedure 55.3. Showing different outline levels.

1. Select Tools, Outline, Outline Options; or press Ctrl+F5. The Outline dialog box appears.
2. Select the Show Levels option. WordPerfect displays the Show dialog box.
3. Select the maximum outline level that you want displayed. WordPerfect returns you to the document and adjusts the outline levels accordingly.

Hiding the Entire Outline

Many people prefer not to look at the outline while they enter a document's body text. If you, too, would prefer a less cluttered screen, follow the steps in Procedure 55.4 to hide your outline.

Procedure 55.4. Hiding an outline.
1. Select Tools, Outline, Outline Options; or press Ctrl+F5. WordPerfect displays the Outline dialog box.
2. Select the Hide Outline option. WordPerfect returns you to the document and displays only the body text.
3. To redisplay the outline, follow the steps in Procedure 55.3 and select the appropriate outline level that you want to see.

Hiding the Body Text

As you will see later in this chapter, outlines are useful for making major structural changes to a document (such as cutting and copying entire outline families). You will find, though, that hiding the body text and dealing with just the outline itself is almost always easier. Procedure 55.5 gives you the details.

Procedure 55.5. Hiding a document's body text.
1. Select Tools, Outline, Outline Options; or press Ctrl+F5. The Outline dialog box appears.
2. Select the Hide Body Text option. WordPerfect returns you to the document and displays only the outline.
3. To restore the body text, redisplay the Outline dialog box and select the Show Body Text option.

> **Tip:** Another way to hide the body text is to select Tools, Outline and then select the Hide Body Text command. If you want to display the body text instead, select the Show Body Text command.

Hiding or Showing Individual Outline Families

In WordPerfect, an outline *family* is any outline item (including the number, letter, or bullet, and the outline text) and any other outline items subordinate to the item (including body text). If you like, you can hide (*collapse*) or show (*expand*) the subordinate items of any family in your outline. Procedure 55.6 takes you through the necessary steps:

Procedure 55.6. Hiding or showing individual outline families.

1. Place the insertion point in the highest level of the family you want to hide or show.
2. Select Tools, Outline, Outline Options; or press Ctrl+F5. WordPerfect displays the Outline dialog box.
3. If you want to collapse the family, select the - Hide Family option. To expand the family, select the + Show Family option. WordPerfect redisplays the document with the outline adjusted.

Tip: An alternative method for hiding or showing outline families is to select Tools, Outline and then select either Hide Family or Show Family, as appropriate.

Working with Outline Mode

WordPerfect's Outline mode gives you an easier way to work with individual outline families. Just press Ctrl+O, and WordPerfect places plus (+) and minus (-) signs to the left of each outline level (as shown in Figure 55.2). A plus sign means that the outline family represented by that level is currently collapsed; the minus sign means that the family is expanded.

Note: When you enter Outline mode, WordPerfect automatically displays the Outline bar. I'll discuss how to use the Outline bar at the end of this chapter.

Expanding and Collapsing Outline Families in Outline Mode

One of the advantages of Outline mode is that it makes expanding or collapsing outline families easy. All you do is highlight the family you want to work with and then press either plus (+) to expand the family or minus (-) to collapse it.

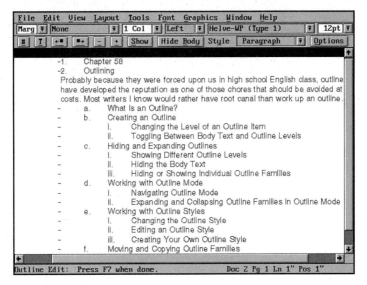

Figure 55.2. WordPerfect's Outline mode.

 Note: When expanding or contracting outline families, make sure you use the plus and minus signs on your keyboard's numeric keypad. (The ones in the alphanumeric keypad won't work.)

Working with Outline Styles

With outlines, the important thing is usually the enhanced organization they provide. As a result, it doesn't matter to most people what style they use for their outlines. However, at times a client might request a particular style, or your profession (such as law) may demand it.

WordPerfect comes with no less than seven predefined outline styles. Each one is characterized in two ways:

▲ **Number format**. This refers to the numbers, letters, or bullets used to identify each level.

▲ **Level style**. This is the formatting that is automatically applied to each level.

Table 55.1 summarizes the predefined styles.

Table 55.1. WordPerfect's predefined outline styles.

Style	Number Format	Level Style
Bullets	Various graphic markers (such as -, *, +, and x)	Level 1–Level 8
Headings	None	Heading 1–Heading 8
Legal	1, 1.1, 1.1.1, etc.	Legal 1–Legal 8
Legal 2	1, 1.01, 1.01.01, etc.	Legal 1–Legal 8
Numbers	1. a. i. (1) (a) (i) 1) a)	None
Outline	I. A. 1. a. (1) (a) i) a)	Level 1–Level 8
Paragraph	1. a. i. (1) (a) (i) 1) a)	Level 1–Level 8

Changing the Outline Style

You pick a style when you first start an outline, but you can easily change horses in midstream. Procedure 55.7 tells you how.

Procedure 55.7. Changing the outline style.

1. Select Tools, Outline, Outline Options, or press Ctrl+F5. WordPerfect displays the Outline dialog box.
2. Select the Outline Style option. The Outline Style List appears.
3. Highlight the style you want to use, and choose the Select option. WordPerfect returns you to the document and applies the new style.

Editing an Outline Style

If WordPerfect's predefined styles aren't quite up to snuff, you can easily edit any of the styles so that they work the way you want them to. Procedure 55.8 shows you the steps to follow.

Procedure 55.8. Editing an outline style.

1. Select Tools, Outline, Outline Options; or press Ctrl+F5. WordPerfect displays the Outline dialog box.
2. Select the Outline Style option. The Outline Style List appears.
3. Highlight the style you want to change and then select Edit. The Edit Outline Style dialog box appears.

4. Use the options in the Edit Outline Style dialog box to make your changes to the style. (You can, if you like, make changes to the level styles from this dialog box. See Chapter 39, "Styles," for details.)

5. When you are done, select OK to return to the Outline Style List dialog box.

Creating Your Own Outline Style

Instead of just editing an existing outline style, you can easily create your own styles. Procedure 55.9 shows you the steps to follow.

Procedure 55.9. Creating your own outline style.

1. Select Tools, Outline, Outline Options; or press Ctrl+F5. The Outline dialog box appears.

2. Select the Outline Style option. WordPerfect displays the Outline Style List.

3. Select Create. The Create Outline Style dialog box appears.

4. Enter a name for the style, and select OK. WordPerfect displays the Edit Outline Style dialog box.

5. Use the options in the Edit Outline Style dialog box to define your style.

6. When you are done, select OK to return to the Outline Style List dialog box.

Tip: If you want a style that is only slightly different from one of the predefined styles, highlight the appropriate style, select Copy, select a destination, and then enter a name for the new style. You can now edit the new style.

Moving and Copying Outline Families

One of the most useful features of outlines is the capability to easily move or copy large chunks of text throughout a document (or even to another document). Yes, you can use the normal cut, copy, and paste commands to do this, but the advantage of outlines is that you can collapse families and hide body text. This makes it easier to navigate through the document, and you don't even have to select a block. Procedure 55.10 tells you everything you need to know.

Procedure 55.10. Moving and copying outline families.

1. Place the insertion point inside the family you want to work with.

2. Select Tools, Outline, Outline Options; or press Ctrl+F5. The Outline dialog box appears.

3. If you're moving the family to a new location, select the Move Family option. If you are making a copy, select the Copy Family option. If you want to delete the family from the document, select the Cut Family option. WordPerfect returns you to the document.

4. If you're moving or copying the family, position the insertion point where you want the family to appear and then press Enter.

Working with the Outline Bar

If you think you will be using the Outline feature a lot, you should get familiar with the Outline bar. This tool gives you easy access to many of the outline features covered in this section. Figure 55.2 shows the Outline bar.

Here is a summary of the controls you will find in the Outline bar:

#	Converts body text to an outline level
T	Converts the current outline level to body text
<-n	Moves each item in the current family up one outline level
n->	Moves each item in the current family down one outline level
-	Collapses the current outline family
+	Expands the current outline family
Show	Displays the Show dialog box to let you specify the maximum outline level to show
Hide Body/Show Body	Toggles the display of the outline's body text
Style	Selects the current outline style
Options	Displays the Outline dialog box

To display the Outline bar, select View, Outline Bar.

by Diane Clayton

QuickMarks, Bookmarks, Comments, and Hidden Text

You know the "little yellow sticky notes" that are so helpful when working with paper documents? Now you can put them (or something very similar) in your WordPerfect documents. They're called QuickMarks, Bookmarks, Comments, and Hidden Text.

You can write "comments" about the document and insert them wherever you choose. These comments are for your eyes only. They won't print. However, you can (if you choose) change them to regular text.

Hidden text is a new feature in WordPerfect 6.0 that allows you to create blocks of text that can be seen on-screen and printed with the document, or "hidden" from both screen and print.

QuickMarks

QuickMarks are automatic bookmarks. You can only have one of them at a time. They're intended to create a quick, easy reference point in a document.

Caution: Because you are limited to one at a time, creating a second QuickMark removes any previous QuickMark.

Creating a QuickMark

To create a QuickMark, place the cursor at the desired spot, then access the Edit menu and choose Bookmark. (The Bookmark screen is shown in Figure 56.1). Highlight QuickMark and press Enter.

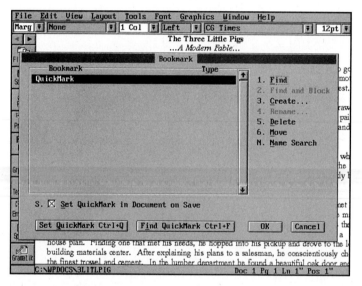

Figure 56.1. The Bookmark Screen.

Tip: Pressing Shift+F12 is a quick way to get to the Bookmark screen.

After you've created a QuickMark, if you look at your document in Reveal Codes you'll see a code that looks like the one shown in Figure 56.2.

If you move your cursor to the code, it expands as shown in Figure 56.3 to show the name of the mark, which in this case is "QuickMark."

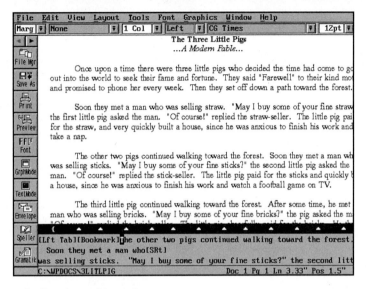

Figure 56.2. A *(Bookmark)* code.

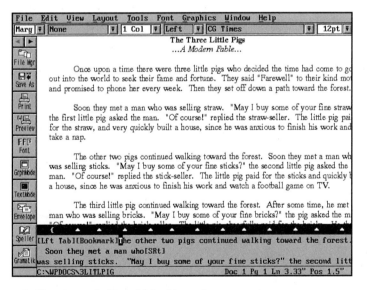

Figure 56.3. A *(Bookmark:QuickMark)* code.

Tip: Now here's the *really* quick way to set a QuickMark: just press Ctrl+Q. If you want to set a QuickMark, and at the same time save the document, press Ctrl+F12. (Pressing Ctrl+F12 will replace the previous document, without asking for confirmation.)

Automatic QuickMarks

Whenever you save a document, WordPerfect places a QuickMark in the document wherever the cursor was located.

However, remember that you can only have one QuickMark, so this feature removes any QuickMark that you previously placed. If you don't want Automatic Bookmarks, you can turn this option off. Just deselect the option Set QuickMark in Document on Save from the bottom of the Bookmark screen.

Finding QuickMarks

To locate a QuickMark, return to the Bookmark screen and highlight QuickMark, then choose Find. (Because this is the default, you can just press Enter.) Your cursor will move to the position just to the right of the Bookmark-QuickMark code.

Tip: The easy way to find a QuickMark is to press Ctrl+F!

Bookmarks

Bookmarks are like QuickMarks, but they are a little more durable. You can have an unlimited number of them, as long as each has a unique name.

Creating a Bookmark

To create a bookmark, first place the cursor in the desired location, then access the Bookmark screen and choose Create. The Bookmark Name field shows the text that occurs right after the cursor (see Figure 56.4).

You can use that text as the "name" of the bookmark—just press Enter. If you prefer to give your bookmark a different name, type the name you choose and press Enter. It's not necessary to delete the text in the name field—as soon as you begin typing, it disappears.

The Bookmark code appears in the document at the cursor location. If you move the cursor to the code, it expands to show the full name of the bookmark.

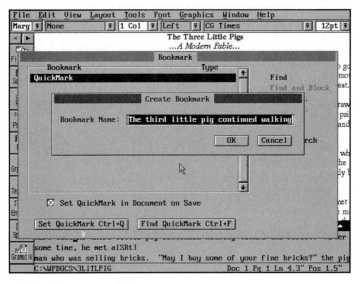

Figure 56.4. The Bookmark Name field.

Finding a Bookmark

To locate any of the bookmarks you have set, go to the Bookmark screen. All bookmarks used in the document will be listed, as shown in Figure 56.5. Highlight the bookmark you want and press Enter (or choose Find). The cursor will move to the position immediately after the bookmark you have chosen. If you used the suggested text for the name of the bookmark, the cursor moves to the first character of that text.

Tip: If you have a long list of Bookmarks, you can use Name Search to move quickly to the mark you want.

Placing Marks Around a Block of Text

If you block a section of text before creating either a QuickMark or a Bookmark, you place marks at both ends of the block. The code at the beginning is +Bookmark-Bookmark; the code at the end is +Bookmark-Bookmark. When the cursor is moved to either code, it expands to show the name of the mark.

911

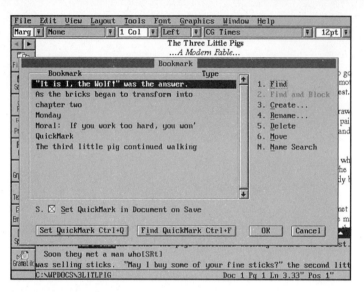

Figure 56.5. A list of Bookmarks in this document.

When you choose this mark from the Bookmark screen, a new option is available to you: Find and Block. Choosing this option not only returns your cursor to the beginning of the text, but also reblocks the section. This capability to find and reblock text is particularly nice if you have a block of text that is to be copied and moved to several other documents. If you prefer, you can choose Find to move to the marker without reblocking.

Find and Block is not available for marks that do not include blocked text.

Editing Marks

You can use the options on the Bookmark screen to do the following:

▲ Rename a Bookmark—highlight the mark and choose Rename, then type the new name and press Enter. (You cannot rename a QuickMark.)

▲ Delete a Bookmark or a QuickMark—highlight the mark and choose Delete, then respond Yes to the confirmation question.

▲ Move the Bookmark or QuickMark to a new location—highlight the mark and choose Move. The mark will be moved to the position in front of the cursor.

Tip: You can remove all bookmarks (including the QuickMark) from your document using WordPerfect's Search and Replace feature. Just choose Bookmark from the list of codes to search for and press Enter when asked for a replacement string.

Comments

Using Comments is an effective way to write reminder notes to yourself or insert supplemental information into a document. The Comment will show on your screen in either Text or Graphics mode, but it will not print.

You can place an unlimited number of Comments in a document. Adding a Comment does not take up any "room" in your document—it doesn't add characters or lines. If you look in reveal codes, all you will see is a single code: Comment. Deleting that code deletes the entire Comment from your document.

You can use any attributes you want when creating a Comment, such as bold or underline. You can even choose a different font for the Comment. When you return to the document, you return to the font that was in effect before the Comment was created, and any attributes that you selected are turned off.

You can use graphics, styles, tables or columns within a comment, and you can use the Thesaurus. You can use the WordPerfect Speller when you are creating a comment (the Speller menu will substitute "Comment" for "Document" as choice #3). Any comments will also be included when Speller checks a document.

Note: Don't confuse Comments with the new feature in WordPerfect 6.0 called "Hidden Text." Hidden Text can be displayed, printed, or hidden. (This feature is discussed later in this chapter.)

Creating a Comment

First place the cursor where you want the Comment to appear.

Caution: If your cursor is in the middle of a word, the Comment box splits the word.

Choose the **L**ayout menu, then select Comment, Create. An alternate method is to press Ctrl+F7. This takes you to the Notes screen, where you can also select Comment, Create (see Figure 56.6).

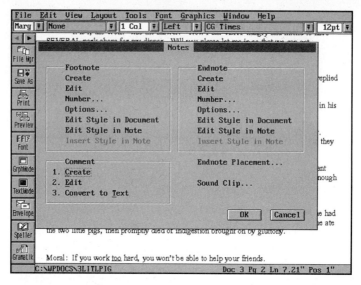

Figure 56.6. The Notes screen.

You will then see a blank screen with a message in the lower-left corner that says `Comment: Press F7 when done`.

Enter the information you want included in the comment. If you choose, you can retrieve previously created text into the comment. When you are done, press Exit to return to your document. You will see the Comment in a box on your screen (see Figure 56.7).

Editing a Comment

To edit a Comment, your cursor must be located *after* the Comment. If there are several Comments in a document, WordPerfect edits the most recent Comment.

To edit a Comment, choose Comment, Edit from either the **Layout** or **Notes** menu. Make any wanted changes to the comment, then press F7 to return to the document.

Converting Comments to Text

Sometimes writers will choose to create unfinished text in Comment form so that it will not be printed with the document. This way, after editing the text into final form, it can be converted into text.

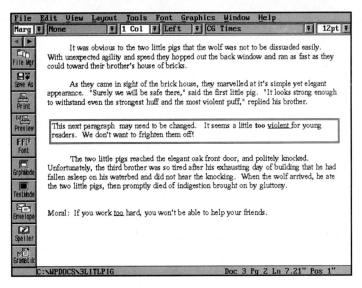

Figure 56.7. A document with Comment.

 Note: If you want a printed copy of your Comments, you must first convert them to text.

To convert a comment to text, place the cursor after the comment, then choose Convert to Text from the Comment menu. The text will appear in the same location where the Comment code was previously located.

 Caution: The text will appear wherever the code occurred. You may need to add spaces or lines to place it correctly. If the comment contains an open code (such as a font change), converting the comment to text will make that code affect the following text.

Converting Text to Comments

To change text to Comment form, first block the text then choose Comment, Create. A Comment code will appear in the document in place of the blocked text.

Hiding Comments

By default, Comments appear on-screen in either Text or Graphics mode. You can, if you choose, "hide" the comments in a document. Choose View, Screen Setup, then deselect Display Comments. The comments code will remain in the document, but the comment text will not be visible. When you want the comments to be seen, choose View, Screen Select and select Display Comments.

Hidden Text

Hidden Text, although similar to Comments, is a separate, new feature in WordPerfect 6.0. Both Hidden Text and Comments can be created from existing text, and both can be converted to regular text. However, there are several distinct differences:

▲ Hidden Text can be displayed, treated (edited) like regular text, and printed with the document, then hidden again. Comments can't do this.

▲ If displayed, Hidden Text affects page numbering. Comments do not affect numbering.

▲ When Hidden Text appears in a document, it looks like regular text. Comments are enclosed in a box.

Tip: A great use for Hidden Text is to hide the answers to tests. Hide the answers on the copy you print for the students (display them on the answer key)!

Creating Hidden Text

Place your cursor in the place you want the hidden text to occur, then press Alt+F5. At the Mark menu, select Hidden Text, and you'll see the Hidden Text menu shown in Figure 56.8.

When you see the Hidden Text menu, there will be two choices:

▲ **H**idden Text
▲ **S**how All Hidden Text

When you are creating hidden text, Show All Hidden Text must be selected before you can access the Hidden Text option! Select both options, then press Enter to return to your document. Type the text you want to be hidden. When you are done, return to the Hidden Text menu and deselect Hidden Text.

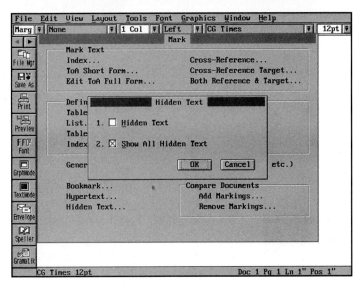

Figure 56.8. The Hidden Text menu.

The text you have typed will appear in your document. If you look in Reveal Codes, you will see a `Hidden On` code at the beginning of the text, and a `Hidden Off` code at the end of it.

You can also turn previously created text into hidden text. Just block it, go to the Hidden Text menu, and choose Hidden Text. The codes will appear at each end of the block.

> **Tip:** When you are working with blocked text, it is not necessary to select Show All Hidden Text first.

Hiding and Displaying Hidden Text

It's not possible to selectively hide or display hidden text. All Hidden Text in a document will be hidden or displayed at the same time. Cursor position is not important when you hide/display text.

From the Hidden Text menu, select Show All Hidden Text if you want Hidden Text displayed.

To hide all Hidden Text, deselect Show All Hidden Text. When text is hidden, a `Hidden` code appears in the document. If you move your cursor to that code, you will be able to read the hidden text in Reveal Codes.

917

Converting and Deleting Hidden Text

If Hidden Text is hidden, deleting the Hidden code in Reveal Codes deletes the text.

If Hidden Text is displayed, deleting either the Hidden On or Hidden Off code converts the text to regular text. You can use Search to locate Hidden On or Hidden Off codes.

Caution: If you are using any of the Writing Tools (Speller, Thesaurus, Grammatik or Document Information) your Hidden Text must first be displayed before it can be included. Also, the Search feature will not examine Hidden Text if it is not displayed.

by Diane Clayton

Footnotes and Endnotes

Footnotes and endnotes provide information about sources, additional information, and references pertaining to your text. Footnotes appear at the bottom of the page where the reference occurs. Endnotes are grouped together at the end of the document. Reference numbers or letters in the text refer to the appropriate note.

Numbering of footnotes and endnotes is automatic. Footnotes and endnotes can be edited and moved. When they are moved, WordPerfect automatically renumbers them.

Creating a Footnote/Endnote

To create a note, position the cursor where you want the reference number to occur. From the Layout menu, choose either Footnote or Endnote, then select Create. (The Layout/Footnote screen is shown in Figure 57.1.) The Endnote screen is identical to the Footnote screen, with the exception of one additional option (Placement), which is discussed later in this chapter.

Footnotes/endnotes can also be created from the Notes screen, which is accessed by pressing Ctrl+F7 (see Figure 57.2). Choose Footnote or Endnote to highlight the desired menu, then select Create.

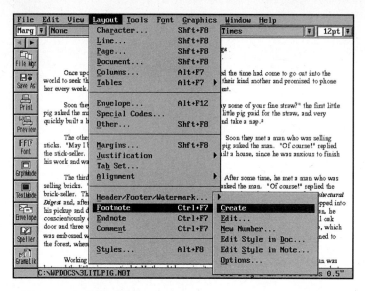

Figure 57.1. The Layout/Footnote screen.

Either of the methods previously described will take you to a blank screen with a message in the lower-left corner that says Footnote: (or Endnote:) Press F7 when done.

At this point you can type the note, retrieve a file that has previously been created, or paste text that has been cut from another location. When you are done, press Exit to return to the document. You will see the reference number in your document, which will match the number of the note you have just created. If you look in Reveal Codes, you will see a [Footnote] or [Endnote] code (see Figure 57.3). Moving the cursor to the code causes the code to expand (see Figure 57.4). The information shown in the expanded code is discussed later in this chapter.

Note: In order to see the actual note, you must be in Page mode or use Print Preview.

Editing a Footnote/Endnote

You can delete a footnote or endnote by deleting the [Footnote] or [Endnote] code. You can move the note to a different place in the document by cutting and pasting the code.

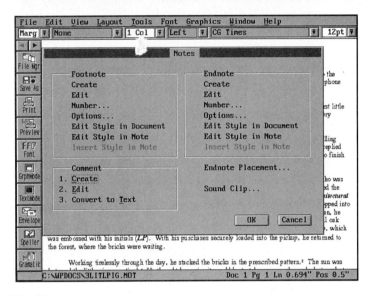

Figure 57.2. The Notes screen.

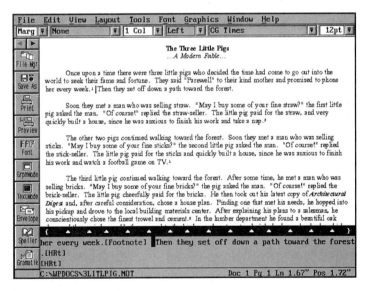

Figure 57.3. The Footnote code.

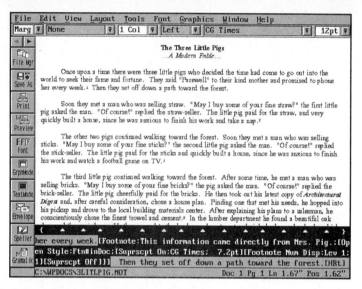

Figure 57.4. The expanded Footnote code.

Tip: A quick way to move a note is to delete the code, move the cursor to the desired location, and press Cancel, Restore to place the code in the new position.

To edit an existing note, choose Footnote or Endnote from either the **Layout** or **Notes** (Ctrl+F7) menu, then choose Edit. Enter the number of the note you want to edit and press Enter. Make the desired changes to the note, then press Exit. You will be returned to the document screen. Your cursor will have moved to the position immediately following the footnote/endnote code.

Tip: When you are editing a footnote or endnote, you can move to the previous or next note by pressing Home, Page Up or Home, Page Down.

Footnote and Endnote Numbering Method

The default for both footnotes and endnotes is to use an Arabic number (such as 1, 2, or 3). This can be confusing if both footnotes and endnotes are used in a document. You can choose alternate numbering methods for either footnotes or endnotes.

Place the cursor where you want the new numbering method to begin. From the Footnote or Endnote menu, choose Number. You will see a Set...Number menu similar to that shown in Figure 57.5. (The Footnote Number and Endnote Number menus are identical.)

If you choose Number Method, you will be able to choose:

▲ Lower Letters such as a, b, c

▲ Upper Letters such as A, B, C

▲ Lower Roman such as i, ii, iii

▲ Upper Roman such as I, II, III

▲ Characters such as *, **, *** (as described below)

When you choose Characters, the chosen character will be used once for the first note, twice for the second note, three times for the third note, and so on. You can use up to five characters, which will each be used in the pattern just described.

If you choose Characters as a numbering method, the Set...Number menu will have a new choice, Characters, which lets you pick the character that will be used. An asterisk is the default, but any WordPerfect character can be entered as a numbering character.

The menu choice, Display in Document, inserts the current note number at the cursor.

(The other choices on this menu, New Number, Increment Number, and Decrement Number, are discussed later in this chapter in the section about restarting footnote or endnote numbering.)

Footnote Formatting Options

You can change the format of footnotes by changing the options. Place the cursor in front of all footnotes that are to be affected by the option changes. Choose Footnote Options from either the Layout or the Notes menu. The available options, which are shown in Figure 57.5, are discussed below. Select or deselect any changes, then press Exit to return to the document.

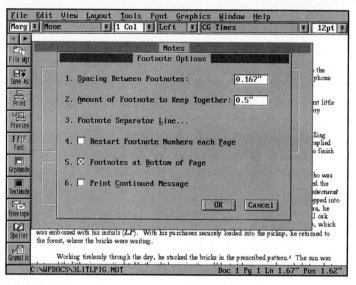

Figure 57.5. Footnote options.

▲ **S**pacing Between Footnotes

The default value is based on the size of the font the footnote will use. To change it, enter the preferred value.

▲ **A**mount/to Keep Together

This shows the minimum amount of each footnote that will print on a page. If less than this amount is available, the note will begin printing on the following page.

▲ Footnote Separator **L**ine

As a default, WordPerfect prints a two-inch line at the bottom of the page between the text and the footnotes. You can change the appearance of this line if you choose. A second menu (as shown in Figure 57.6) lets you change Line Style (from a list of ten options), Line Alignment, Line Length, and the amount of space above and below the line.

▲ Restart/Numbers each **P**age

Selecting this option causes footnote numbers to begin with "1" on every page.

▲ Footnotes at **B**ottom of Page

If this option is off, footnotes will begin immediately below the last line of text on the page.

924

▲ Print **C**ontinued Message

If this option is on, the last footnote line on each page and the first footnote line on the following page will include the message
`continued...`

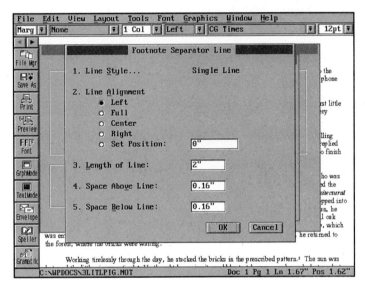

Figure 57.6. The Footnote Separator Line menu.

Endnote Formatting Options

You don't have as many options for changing the format of endnotes as you do for Footnotes, but you can change the amount of space between endnotes and the minimum amount of an endnote to keep together on a page. Choose Endnote Options from either the Layout or the Notes menu. (See Figure 57.7.) Select or deselect any changes, then press Exit to return to the document.

Endnote Placement Options

As a default, WordPerfect prints all your endnotes at the end of your document. However, you may choose to have them placed somewhere else—for example, at the end of each chapter. In this case, position your cursor where you want the endnotes to be, then choose Endnote Placement from the Layout or Notes menu.

Next, you will be asked, "Restart Endnote Numbering?" Responding "Yes" causes the next group of endnotes to begin with number one. If you respond "No," the current numerical sequence continues.

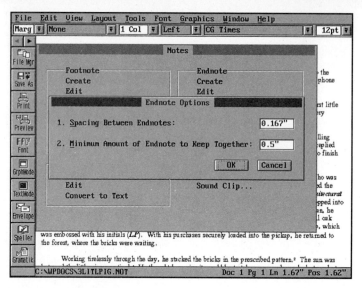

Figure 57.7. Endnote options.

Then, if you are in Text or Graphics mode, you will see a comment box on your screen showing where your endnotes will print. In Page mode, you will see the actual endnotes. A hard page break will separate your endnotes from the rest of your document.

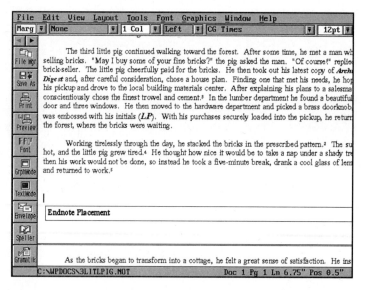

Figure 57.8. An example of a document with Endnote Placement added.

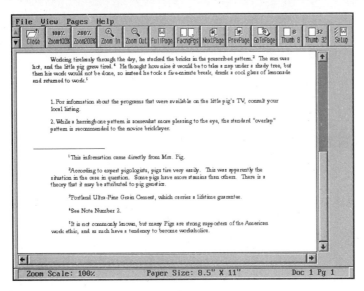

Figure 57.9. Print Preview of Previous Page.

Restarting Footnote or Endnote Numbering

It is possible that you might want to restart the number sequence for footnotes or endnotes when you begin a new chapter or section. In this case, place the cursor where you want the new number sequence to begin. From the Set...Number menu discussed in the previous section about Note Numbering Methods, choose New Number. This option allows you to enter the desired number for the following note. To reset the sequence, choose 1.

Caution: The New Number must match the Numbering Method being used. If you choose a method other than numbers, when you enter a new number, it is converted to the appropriate method. (For example, entering "3" results in "c" if you have chosen lowercase letters.) However, if you have chosen "Number" as your method, you can't use "a" as a new number. An attempt to do so results in an error message on the screen.

If you want to increase or decrease the note number, there are two other choices on this menu:

Increment Number, which increases the Footnote/Endnote number by one.

Decrement Number, which decreases the Footnote/Endnote number by one.

Formatting Note Numbers and Notes

Default formats for note numbers and notes are included in the WordPerfect program's Main System Styles. (See Chapter 39, "Styles," for more details on Styles.)

The default formats for note numbers and notes are as follows:

Footnotes/Endnote numbers (in the document) (a superscripted note number)

The Footnote itself (a Tab, followed by a superscripted note number, followed by the note)

The Endnote itself (a superscripted number followed by a period, followed by the note)

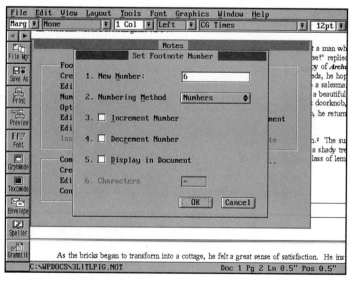

Figure 57.10. Set Footnote Number.

These defaults can be changed to include any WordPerfect formatting codes, such as attributes (bold, underline) and spacing (tab, indent, and so on). Changes affect all occurrences of footnote and/or endnote note numbers or notes in the document, regardless of cursor position.

To change the format of all note numbers, choose Footnote or Endnote, then choose Edit Style in Document. You will see a screen similar to the one shown in Figure 57.11. Add or change any codes you want, then press Exit to return to the document. If you are asked for confirmation, choose OK.

Changing the format is not really as difficult as it might appear. For example, if you want to change the format for footnote numbers from superscripted numbers to bold, subscripted, redlined numbers, follow these steps (the results are shown in Figure 57.12):

▲ Go to the Edit Style in Document screen (see Figure 57.11).

▲ Delete the [Superscript On] code. (The [Superscript Off] code will be automatically deleted.

▲ Select Font, Font Appearance, Bold, then Appearance, Redline.

▲ Select Position, Subscript.

▲ Move the cursor past the [Footnote Num Disp] code and select Font, Appearance. Then deselect Bold and Redline to turn off the attribute codes.

▲ Select Position, Normal.

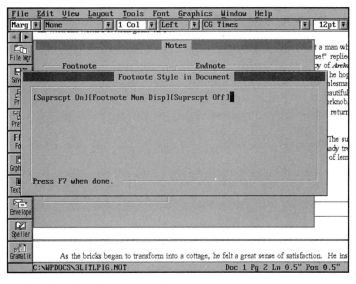

Figure 57.11. Edit Style in Document.

Tip: If you accidentally erase the [Footnote Num Disp] code, you can replace it by choosing Footnote, Number, then pressing Display in Document.

To change the format of all footnotes or endnotes, choose Footnote or Endnote, then choose Edit Style in Note. Make any desired changes as described above, then press Exit to return to the document. If you are asked for confirmation, choose OK.

To copy the edited style for future use, see the section on copying styles in Chapter 39.

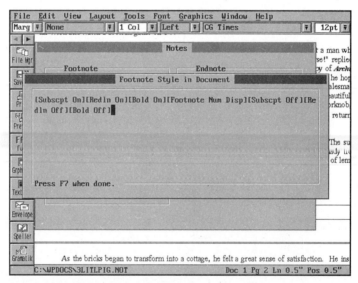

Figure 57.12. After Editing Styles in Document.

Miscellaneous Hints about Footnotes and Endnotes

You can use Speller when you are creating or editing a note. Footnotes and endnotes will automatically be included when a document is spell checked.

You can use footnotes in a table, but they can't occur in a table header row. If you create a footnote in a header row, it automatically is changed to an endnote.

Footnotes can be used in columns. They appear at the bottom of the column in which the reference number occurs.

If you use the Master Document feature, footnotes and endnotes are numbered consecutively throughout the document, unless you choose to restart numbering.

Footnotes and endnotes will be printed in the font chosen as the document's initial font. If you want the document and the notes to be in different fonts, select a font at the beginning of the document. You can use Styles to change endnote or footnote fonts.

by Diane Clayton

Page, Chapter, and Volume Numbering

WordPerfect offers many choices for numbering pages. You can choose standard Arabic numbers or either lowercase or uppercase Roman numerals. You can even number your pages with letters! You can include text with any page numbers, if you choose. You can place your page numbers in any of eight locations on the page margins, or within the text of your document, and you can prevent a page number from printing on any specified page.

WordPerfect 6.0 has added the ability to use two separate sets of page numbers, both of which will automatically increase with the document. These new "secondary page numbers" allow you to use two different sets of page numbers in a document. For example, a newsletter could show the pages for the current issue, plus the total pages for the year.

In addition, there are two more levels for numbering pages. These levels, called "Chapter" and "Volume," make it easy to number sections and subdivisions of long documents and/or to create complex page numbering schemes.

There are also two new features called "Subdivided Pages" and "Print as Booklet" that allow you to assign two page numbers to each physical page. (See Chapter 17, "Page Formatting," and Chapter 18, "Advanced Formatting Features," for more information about creating booklets.)

Note: Page numbers do not appear in Text or Graphics mode. You can see them in Page mode, or by using Print Preview.

Creating Page Numbers

To create a page number, first position the cursor anywhere on the page where you want the page numbers to begin.

 Tip: The Auto Code Placement feature (new with WordPerfect 6.0) places the page numbering code at the beginning of the page.

Next, access the Page Format screen either by selecting Page from the Layout screen or by pressing Shift+F8, then choosing Page. Either of these methods gives you the Page Format screen, which is shown in Figure 58.1. Now, choose Page Numbering to see the screen shown in Figure 58.2.

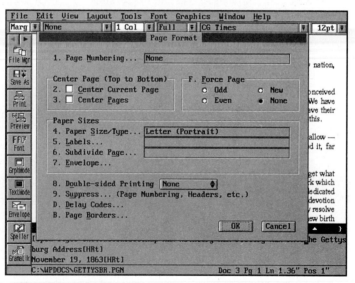

Figure 58.1. The Page Format screen.

Number Position

The first choice on the Page Numbering screen is Page Number **P**osition. When you select it, you'll see the screen shown in Figure 58.3. This screen gives you a lot of options. For example, in order to print the page number in the top-right corner of every page, you can enter 3 or Top Right.

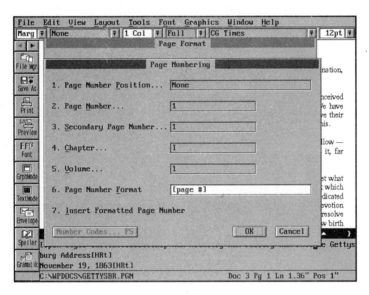

Figure 58.2. The Page Numbering screen.

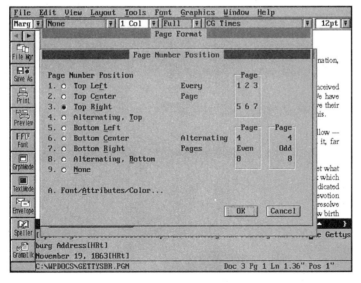

Figure 58.3. Page Number Position options.

The choices on this screen are exclusive. You can only select one. Making a second choice cancels the first. Notice that the last item on the list is "None." Choose it if you do not want page numbers to print.

The choices "4" and "8" refer to "alternating" pages. These selections are appropriate when your document is going to be printed on both sides of the paper (duplex). For example, "4" puts the page number at the top, outside corner of each page (the left corner of even-numbered pages, and the right corner of odd-numbered pages).

Placing Page Numbers in a Document

The choices just discussed place the page number in the top or bottom margin of the text. You also have the capability to place either the fully formatted page number or just the page number at any point in your text.

Place the cursor where you want the number to appear and then access the Page Numbering screen.

To insert the formatted page number, choose Insert Formatted Page Number. A [Formatted Pg Num] code, which will produce the formatted number, (including any Chapter/Volume and Secondary Numbers and any added text), will be inserted in the document. If the code is moved to a different page, the numbers will be updated.

Tip: A quick way to insert a Formatted Page Number at the cursor is to press Ctrl+P.

To insert a page number without formatting codes, choose Page Number, then Display in Document, and press Enter until you return to the document. A [Pg Num Disp] code will be placed in your document, and the current page number will be shown. If you want to display a secondary page number, chapter number, or volume number, first choose that item from the Page Numbering screen, then choose Display in Document from the resulting Set Number screen. The appropriate number (and code) will appear at the cursor.

Number Format

The default method of page numbering uses standard Arabic numbers, such as 1, 2, and 3. If you prefer, you can choose from four other numbering methods:

Lowercase letters such as a, b, and c
Uppercase letters such as A, B, and C
Lowercase Roman numerals such as i, ii, and iii
Uppercase Roman numerals such as I, II and III

To change the page numbering method, choose Page Number from the Page Numbering screen, then choose Numbering Method. Selecting this will let you pick your numbering method, from the screen shown in Figure 58.4.

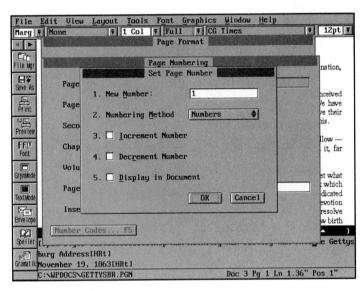

Figure 58.4. Numbering methods.

To include text with your page numbers, go to the Page Numbering screen and choose Page Number Format. The default will be the page number code [page #]. To add the word *Page* in front of the code, just type it in. (Be sure to include a space.)

To change fonts or attributes of page numbers, choose Font/Attributes/Color from the Page Number Position screen shown in Figure 58.3. Choose the desired font or attribute, then press Enter to return to your document.

Setting/Resetting Numbers

It is often necessary to reset page numbers. You may want to return to page 1 at the beginning of a new section. Or, in the event that you are inserting pages from another source into your document (i.e., illustrations) you may want to skip page numbers.

For example, if you plan to insert four pages of illustrations after page 19, your text page numbers might jump from 19 to 24. In that case, you could reset page number 20 to the number that should appear after the illustrations (i.e., 24).

Setting new page numbers is accomplished from the Set Page Number screen shown in Figure 58.5. (Access this screen by choosing Number from the Page

Numbering menu.) From the Set Page Number screen, you can choose New Number, and enter the desired value.

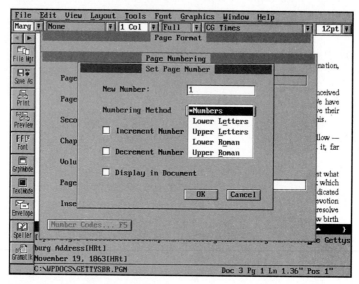

Figure 58.5. The Set Page Number screen.

You can also use Increment Number or Decrement Number to increase or decrease the current number.

> **Tip:** If you have chosen a numbering method other than "Numbers," the New Number you enter will be automatically converted to the proper number for the Numbering Method you have selected. For example, if you are using uppercase Roman numerals, and you enter 47 as a New Page Number, it will appear as XLVII!
>
> However, if you have chosen "Numbers" for your numbering method, entering anything other than an Arabic number will result in an error message that says `Numbering value entered does not match numbering method`.

Forcing Odd/Even Pages

One of the choices on the Page Format screen is Force Page. This option will cause WordPerfect to insert a page break (and new page number) if necessary. This is useful when you want to be sure that each chapter begins on a new page, or that each section of a long document begins on an odd-numbered page. To force a page, place the cursor anywhere in the paragraph where you want the new page to begin.

Caution: Remember that WordPerfect defines a paragraph as a group of characters that end with a hard return code [HRt]. If your "paragraph" contains a [HRt], the [Force] will be inserted at that point.

Tip: Traditionally, chapters and sections of long documents begin on odd-numbered pages, so that they will be on the right-hand side of an open book.

To force a page, place the cursor anywhere in the paragraph where you want the new page to begin. From the Page Format screen, choose Force Page, then select Odd or Even. A "temporary hard page" code [THPg] will be inserted at the beginning of the paragraph. WordPerfect checks to see if the page in question is already "odd" or "even." If it is not already correct, a page break is inserted to make it correct. Also, a [Force] code is placed at the beginning of the paragraph. If changes are made to the document later, the proper page placement is assigned.

If you choose Force Page: New, both a [THPg] and a [Force:New] code is inserted at the beginning of the paragraph. Unless the paragraph is already the first one on a page, a page break is inserted.

Chapter, Volume, and Secondary Page Numbering

Working with long documents often makes it necessary to identify not only a page within a document but also a chapter or section within that document. WordPerfect 6.0 now provides the capability to assign multiple numbering methods to a document. For example, a page might be identified as "Vol. II, Chapter 8, Page 37."

Chapter and volume numbers can add two additional levels to a numbering scheme. However, although page numbers increment (increase) automatically, chapter/volume numbers must be incremented manually. In other words, it is up to the writer to insert the information that "Chapter II" begins at a certain point. This is done by inserting a [Chap Num Set] code in the document, as explained below.

Once this code is placed at the beginning of each chapter, incrementing a chapter will cause all following chapters to be incremented. For example, if the writer decides to insert a new Chapter II, the old Chapter II will automatically become Chapter III, Chapter III will become Chapter IV, and so on. Volume numbers work in the same way that Chapter numbers work, based on a [Vol Num Set] code.

Sometimes there is a need to use two sets of page numbers in a document. For example, in a newsletter or report, you might want to number the pages in a current issue and at the same time to number pages from the beginning of a year or reporting period. Secondary page numbers make it possible to include both number series. Secondary page numbers work identically to page numbers. Both will automatically increment as the document increases in length, and each type of number can be reset.

Including Chapter, Volume, and/or Secondary Page Numbers

Position your cursor in the Page Number Format box in the desired place, then press F5. You'll see the Page Number Codes screen shown in Figure 58.6. Select the desired entry and press Enter.

Note: All forms of page numbers will appear at the same place in the document, which is determined by page number position as discussed above. If you have used chapter, volume, or secondary numbers, they will all print in the same location that page numbers print.

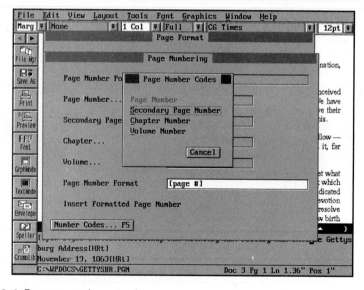

Figure 58.6. Page number codes.

The following codes appears in the Page Number Format box for each selection:

Selection	*Code*
Page Number	[page #]
Secondary Page Number	[scndy pg #]
Chapter Number	[chpt #]
Volume Number	[vol #]

To include text with the codes, type the text where you want it to appear.

> **Tip:** If the formatting you select is lengthy, only a portion of it will show in the box on-screen. Use the right and left arrow keys to move to the ends of the line of text and codes.

Changing Chapter, Volume, and/or Secondary Page Numbers

The Page Numbering screen gives all information about the numbering patterns currently in use for your document. Page Number Format shows which of the four numbering methods will be included. The numbers following "Page Number," "Secondary Page Number," "Chapter," and "Volume" show the current setting for each. To change an item, select it. Each choice produces a screen identical (except for title) to the Set Page Number screen shown in Figure 58.5.

An Example of Multiple Page Numbers

In the following example, Page Number Format has been set as follows:

Vol. [vol #]; Ch. [chpt #], Pg. [scndy pg #] (Issue Page [page #])

(Notice that text, spaces, and punctuation have been added to the codes.)

Page Number refers to the current issue page and reflects the document page. Numbering style = numbers.

Secondary Page Number has been set to a number representing total pages to date. Numbering style = numbers.

Chapter has been set to 3. Since the numbering method for Chapter has been set to Upper Roman, it has been converted to III.

Volume has been set to 4. Since the numbering method for Volume has been set to Upper Letters, it has been converted to D.

Page Number Position has been set at Top Right. Page Number Attributes have been set to Bold.

The Page Numbering screen, with the options mentioned above, is shown in Figure 58.7. The resulting document page is shown in Figure 58.8.

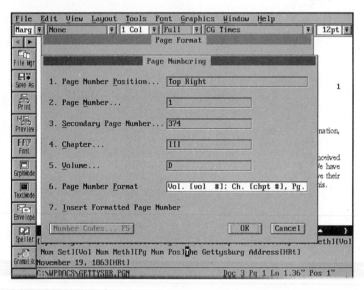

Figure 58.7. The Page Numbering screen.

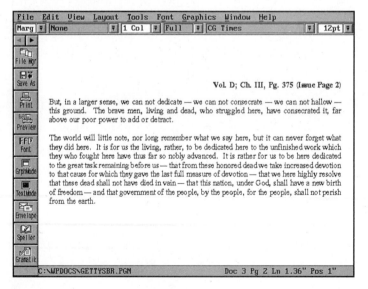

Figure 58.8. A document with multiple page numbers.

by Diane Clayton

Cross Referencing

When you want to refer to another part of your document, using WordPerfect's Cross Reference feature can help. You can refer to another page (using page number, secondary page number, chapter number, or volume number), a location in an outline (such as II.B.3.a), a footnote or endnote, or you can refer to an equation, figure, table, text or user box.

Cross Referencing has two elements:

- ▲ The *reference* occurs in the document where another location is mentioned. (For example, "As shown on page 47, . . .") Each reference is tied to a target name.
- ▲ The *target* is the place to which the reference points. (In the preceding example, the target is page 47.) Each target must have a unique name.

Both references and targets are marked in a document. A final step, called *generating*, ties the two together, based on the names used by reference and target.

Marking References

In order to mark a reference, put your cursor where you want the reference to occur, after any introductory text such as *see page*. From the **Tools** menu, choose Cross-Reference and then select Reference (see Figure 59.1). This takes you to the Mark Cross-Reference screen, shown in Figure 59.2.

Note: An alternate way to reach the Mark Cross-Reference screen is to press Alt+F5 (which produces the Mark menu), Mark Text, and then Cross-Reference.

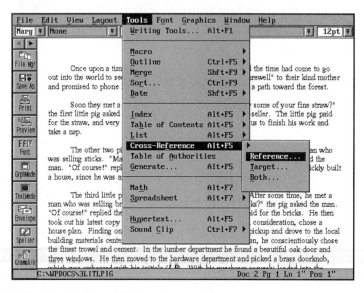

Figure 59.1. The Tools, Cross-Reference menus.

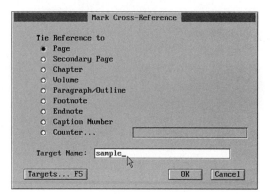

Figure 59.2. The Mark Cross-Reference screen.

On the Mark Cross-Reference screen, the default to which the reference is tied is the page number on which the target occurs. You have the option to refer instead to a different reference type. Your choices include three other types of page numbers: secondary page numbers, chapters, and volumes (see Chapter 58, "Page, Chapter, and Volume Numbering," for more information on these features). You can tie the reference to an outline level or a footnote/endnote number, you can tie it to a caption number (on a graphics box), or you can tie it to the counter that numbers graphics boxes. For more information on setting up counters, see Chapter 14, "Using Character Formatting."

Next, you need to select a target name. You can enter up to 31 characters, including spaces. If you have previously marked any targets, pressing F5 will list them. (F5 is active only after choosing Target Name.) To use any of the listed targets, select it and press Enter. After you enter or select a target name, press Enter to return to the document.

The reference appears in your document as a question mark (?). In Reveal Codes, you will see a `[Ref]` code. (The reference type will follow the word *Ref* in the code.) Moving your cursor to the code expands the code to show the target name.

Marking Targets

If the target is text, place your cursor anywhere in that text. If the target is a graphics box, place the cursor just after the box code.

From the **T**ools menu, choose Cross-Reference and then select Target. You will see the Mark Cross-Reference Target screen shown in Figure 59.3.

Note: An alternative way to reach the Mark Cross-Reference Target screen is to press Alt+F5, Mark Text, and then Cross-Reference Target.

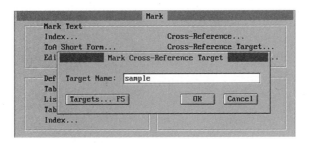

Figure 59.3. The Mark Cross-Reference Target screen.

The name of the last reference you marked will show in the Target Name box. Press Enter to accept this name, or type a different name.

Caution: In order for a reference and a target to tie together, they must have identical names. Check your spelling!

Tip: Pressing F5 lists any targets you have already marked. You can select any of these targets by highlighting it and pressing Enter.

The target will *not* appear in your document. In Reveal Codes, you will see a [Target] code. Moving your cursor to the code expands the code to show the target name.

Marking Both Reference and Target

Often it is easiest to mark both the reference and the target at the same time. From the Tools menu, choose Cross-Reference and then select Both. Except for the title, the screen will be identical to the Mark Cross-Reference screen. When you press Enter, you return to your document and the following message appears at the bottom of the screen: Position cursor and press Enter to insert target.

Caution: While this message is on your screen, all other functions are suspended. You can't do anything except position the cursor and press Enter.

As soon as you press Enter, you will see the reference (?) appear in your document. Both the [Ref] and [Target] codes will be placed at the proper spots. Your cursor will be directly after the [Ref] code.

Caution: Marking both will not work when the reference is in a header/footer or in a graphics box caption.

Generating Cross-References

After all references and targets are marked, it is necessary to generate the cross-references. Choose Generate from either the Tools menu or the Mark menu. You'll see the Generate screen shown in Figure 59.4. Press Enter to begin the process.

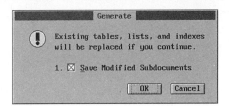

Figure 59.4. The Generate screen.

> **Tip:** Don't be alarmed by the message that says `Existing tables, lists, and indexes will be replaced if you continue`. Each time you generate, new tables, lists, and indexes are created. Replacing those that already exist is exactly what you want to do!

If you are using subdocuments, you may want to deselect Save Modified Subdocuments. (For more information, see Chapter 64, "Master Documents.")

Multiple References and Targets

One reference can point to multiple targets. For example, you could have a reference that says "See the charts on pages 14, 17, and 45." In this example, only one reference would be marked. The targets, all of which would have the same name, would be marked on pages 14, 17, and 45.

One target can be used by several references. Use the same target name when creating multiple references. For example, "See page 42" could occur at several places in the document. Only one target would be marked. And yes, multiple references can point to multiple targets.

Compound References

You can also create compound references, such as "See Figure 19 on page 47." In this example, mark two separate references. For the first, use a Reference Type of Counter, Figure Box. (The code in the document would be `[Ref Count]`.)

For the second reference, use a Reference Type of Page. (The code in the document would be `[Ref Page]`.) Both references should use the same target name. After marking the references, the text would say `See Figure ? on page ?`.

947

Only one target would be created, just to the right of the code for the figure that is being targeted. After generating, the proper figure number and page number would be inserted into the text.

Page X of Y

You can use cross-referencing to create a page numbering method where each page number tells the total number of pages in the document. The following example produces such a method. Before beginning, make sure that page numbers are not being used in the document (the Page Number Position must be set to None).

- ▲ Move the cursor to the end of the document. Create a target named End. The code `[Target(end)]` will appear in Reveal Codes.

- ▲ Move to the top of the document. Access the Page Numbering menu, which is discussed in Chapter 58. Change Page Number Format to include the word *Page* in front of the `[page #]` code, and the word *of* after the code. (Don't forget to include spaces on each side of the `[page #]` code!) The result will look like this: `Page [page #] of`. Press Enter and then return to the document screen. You will have inserted a `[Pg Num Fmt]` code.

- ▲ Now create a header or footer. When you are at the Header or Footer screen, press Ctrl+P to insert the formatted page number. You'll see `Page 1 of` in your header/footer.

- ▲ Insert a blank space after the `[Formatted Pg Num]` code in the header, and then create a reference using the target name End (which will be the default name shown on the screen). Your header/footer will change to `Page 1 of ?`. In Reveal Codes, you will see a `[Ref Pg]` code.

- ▲ Exit the header/footer menu by pressing F7. Now generate the cross reference. In Page mode or Print Preview, you'll see your page numbers now include the total number of pages in the document (e.g., `Page 1 of 7`).

 Caution: If you add new text to the bottom of the document, be sure to reposition the End target so it is on the last page.

60

by Diane Clayton

Creating a Table of Contents

A table of contents for your WordPerfect document will include any text that you choose to identify as a heading or subheading. After marking the text to be included, generating the table of contents will automatically list the proper page numbers for the marked text. When text is added or removed, a few simple steps will update the page numbers shown in the table of contents.

Every table of contents entry is assigned a "level number." Main headings (such as chapter names) are level 1 entries. Each main heading will print in a column at the left side of the table of contents page, followed by the number of the document page where it can be found. Each subsequent level will appear as an indented subheading under the heading, also followed by a page number. You can use up to five levels of headings and subheadings, and you can choose from five numbering modes for each of them.

There are three steps used to create a table of contents:

1. Mark the text that is to be included in the table of contents.
2. Define the location and format for the table of contents.
3. Generate the table of contents.

Tip: The table of contents for this book uses chapter numbers/names as headings, and sections within those chapters (such as "Marking Text") as level 2 headings.

Tip: If you want to include a chart or picture in your table of contents, you can mark the caption in the Graphics box. You can also mark text that appears in a table.

Marking Text

To mark the text, first block the text that is to be included in the table. Then, from the Tools menu, choose Table of Contents and then Mark (see Figure 60.1). You'll see the Mark Table of Contents screen shown in Figure 60.2.

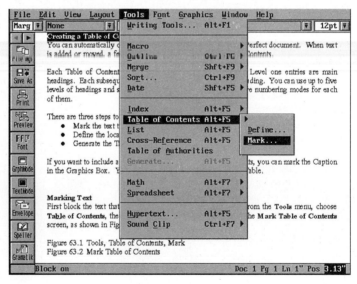

Figure 60.1. Selecting Tools, Table of Contents, Mark.

Figure 60.2. The Mark Table of Contents dialog box.

An alternate way to reach the Mark Table of Contents screen is to block text, press Alt+F5 (see Figure 60.3), and then choose Table of Contents.

Figure 60.3. The Mark Text dialog box.

> **Caution:** Text must be blocked before it can be marked. If text has not been blocked, Mark will not be available as a choice on the Table of Contents menu, and pressing Alt+F5 will produce a different screen!

The level number for the blocked text is entered on the Table of Contents screen. The first time you access this screen, the default is level 1. If this level is correct, press OK. If you want to show the text at a different level, enter the appropriate number and then press Enter. On subsequent Table of Contents screens, the default will be the last level you entered.

> **Caution:** Be sure you don't mark a level that you haven't defined! See the section "Defining a Table of Contents" later in this chapter for more information about levels.

After marking text, a `[Mrk Txt ToC Begin]` code is placed at the beginning of the block, and a `[Mrk Txt ToC End]` code is placed at the end of the block. If you move your cursor to either code, you'll see a colon followed by the level number of the entry. Deleting either code deletes both codes, and the text will no longer be marked for the table of contents.

> **Caution:** Be careful *not* to include any codes (such as bold, underline, or hard return) when you block text to be marked for a table of contents. Any codes that are included with the text will be copied to the table of contents, and the corresponding entries in the table will then be bold or underlined, or followed by a hard return!

Defining a Table of Contents

Defining the table of contents tells the program where you want the table to appear and how you want it to look. First, place the cursor where you want the table.

Tip: The table of contents usually appears at the beginning of the document, on a separate page, right after the title page (if any). If you want it to be on a separate page, press Ctrl+Enter and then move your cursor into the blank page before proceeding.

If you want a title on the page, type it and then press Enter several times. Then, from the **T**ools menu, choose Table of Contents and then Define. You'll see the Define Table of Contents screen shown in Figure 60.4.

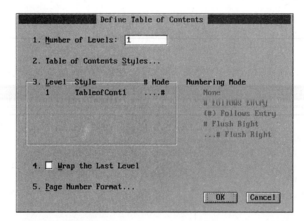

Figure 60.4. The Define Table of Contents screen.

Note: You can also reach the Table of Contents screen by pressing Alt+F5 and then Define, Table of Contents.

Select Number of Levels, type the appropriate number for your table, and then press Enter. You'll see an entry for each level under Level Style. The default numbering mode will be shown for each level. (Changing Numbering Mode is discussed later in this chapter in the "Format Options" section.)

Caution: The number of levels in your definition will determine how many levels will be generated for your table of contents. Levels that are marked but not defined will be ignored. For example, if you mark levels 1, 2, and 3, but define your table with only 2 levels, none of the third-level marks will be shown in your table of contents.

Wrap the Last Level determines the way the last level in your table will be formatted. Page Number Format enables you to use a different format for page numbers in the table of contents. Both options are discussed in detail later in this chapter, under "Format Options."

When you are satisfied with the selections on the Define Table of Contents screen, select OK to return to your document. A [Def Mark] code is placed at the position of the cursor. Moving the cursor to that code in Reveal Codes causes it to expand, showing you that it's for a Table of Contents, followed by the number of levels and the numbering mode selected.

Caution: The table of contents is generated where the [Def Mark] code occurs. If the code is accidentally duplicated in a document, two tables will be generated!

Tip: If you want to suppress the printing of page numbers on the table of contents page, select Format (Shift+F8), **P**age, **S**uppress, **P**age Numbering.

You may want to reset the page numbers so the page following the table of contents is page 1. If so, move the cursor to that page and select Format, **P**age, **P**age Numbering, **P**age Number.

Generating a Table of Contents

After you define the table of contents and mark the text to include in it, you can generate the table. This option is available on the **T**ools menu, or you can press Alt+F5 to access the **M**ark screen. Choosing Generate from either place produces the Generate screen. Press OK to generate your table of contents.

Tip: Unless the `[Def Mark]` code has been accidentally deleted, generating automatically replaces any existing table of contents. You do not have to delete any information (this is also true for lists and indexes).

Tip: After you generate the table of contents, you can edit the text. (For example, you can delete `[Bold]` codes that were accidentally marked with the text.) However, if it is necessary to generate a second time, the codes (and their effect) will return. To really fix the problem, fix the source of the problem; return to the text and move the Mark codes so they do not include the attribute codes.

Reveal Codes will show that a `[Begin Gen Txt]` has been inserted at the beginning of the table, and an `[End Gen Txt]` code has been inserted at the end. Each line entry in the table is preceded by a `[Para Style:Table...]` code, which describes the level and options used. These options are generated by system styles, which determine the defaults.

Tip: The System Styles for Tables of Contents are as follows:

Level 1	TableofCont1	Hard return, an indent, and a back tab
Level 2	TableofCont2	Two indents and a back tab
Level 3	TableofCont3	Three indents and a back tab
Level 4	TableofCont4	Four indents and a back tab
Level 5	TableofCont5	Five indents and a back tab

If you want to change these styles, choose Styles from the Layout menu. From the Style List menu, choose Options and then select List System Styles. Highlight the style for the table of contents level you want to change and then press Edit. Make any desired changes, then press Enter to return to the document.

Format Options

By changing numbering modes, page number format, and wrap options, you can change the appearance of your table of contents to fit your personal needs.

Numbering Modes

The table of contents can display page numbers in five different ways. You can select any of these numbering modes for each level of your table of contents:

1. **None**: No page numbers appear; marked items are shown as present in the document only.

2. **# Follows Entry**: Each entry in the table is followed by a space, and then the page number appears.

3. **(#) Follows Entry**: Each entry in the table is followed by a space, and then the page number appears in parentheses.

4. **# Flush Right**: The page number appears at the right margin following the entry in the table.

5. **...# Flush Right**: The page number, preceded by dot leaders, appears at the right margin following the entry in the table.

The default numbering mode for all five possible levels is flush right with dot leaders. To change any numbering mode, select Level from the Define Table of Contents screen. Highlight the level you want to change and then press the highlighted number or letter from the list of numbering modes. The selected numbering mode will be displayed in the # Mode column following each Level.

> **Note:** If you have chosen Wrap the Last Level (described in the next section), the last two numbering modes will not be available for the final level.

Changing Page Number Format in a Table of Contents

As a default, the page numbers shown in the table of contents will be the same as those shown in page numbering throughout the document. However, you have the option to design a different page number format for your table of contents.

> **Note:** Now that WordPerfect has the capability to create page numbers that include chapter, volume, and secondary page information, the capability to use a different format for the table of contents is even more valuable.

If you want to design a page numbering scheme for your table of contents, choose Page Number Format from the Define Table of Contents screen. The default on this screen is Same as Document. Choose Different from Document and your cursor

955

will move into the format box, as shown in Figure 60.5. You can type any text you want. Pressing F5 lists the available page number codes, shown in Figure 60.6. (For more information on using complex page numbers, see Chapter 59, "Cross Referencing.")

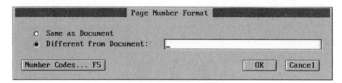

Figure 60.5. The Page Number Format screen.

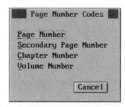

Figure 60.6. The Page Number Codes dialog box.

Wrap the Last Level

If you select Wrap the Last Level from the Define Table of Contents screen, several things happen—but they will affect only the last level of your table of contents. ("Last Level" is the number specified when you defined the Number of Levels.) In order to see the changes, it is necessary to understand the standard format.

Each entry in a table of contents appears on an individual line. Level 1 entries are separated by a blank line; there are no blank lines between other levels.

When an entry in a table of contents is longer than one line, it wraps to the next line. When Wrap is off, text is indented to the next tab stop, beginning with the second line. The page number follows the final line.

When Wrap the Last Level has been selected, multiple last-level headings appear in a continuous line, rather than on separate lines. If more than one line is required to list all entries, each line begins at the same tab stop—they will not be indented further. Also, the two choices of numbering mode that use "Flush Right" are not available for the last level.

The following example shows the effect of using Wrap the Last Level on a simple, three-level table of contents (both tables use default numbering modes):

```
TABLE OF CONTENTS, Wrap = OFF
Signs Spring has arrived1
Flowers2
Flowering Trees2
Daffodils5
Forsythia5
Animals9
Migrating11
Hibernating12
TABLE OF CONTENTS, Wrap = ON
Signs Spring has arrived1
Flowers2
Flowering Trees (2); Daffodils (5); Forsythia (5)
Animals9
Migrating (11); Hibernating (12)
```

by Diane Clayton

Creating a Table of Authorities

Like a table of contents, a table of authorities is a list of the contents of a document, designed to help the reader locate items in the document. When the document is a legal brief, a table of authorities lists the citations included and can separate them into appropriate sections, such as cases and statutes. Each section of the table of authorities is sorted alphabetically, and each can have a different format.

There are four steps to creating a table of authorities:

1. Designing the table
2. Marking the authorities to be included
3. Defining each section of the table
4. Generating the table

Designing a Table of Authorities

The first step in creating a table of authorities is to decide what sections need to be included and the format you want for those sections. Sections vary with the document, but can usually be identified as the document is created.

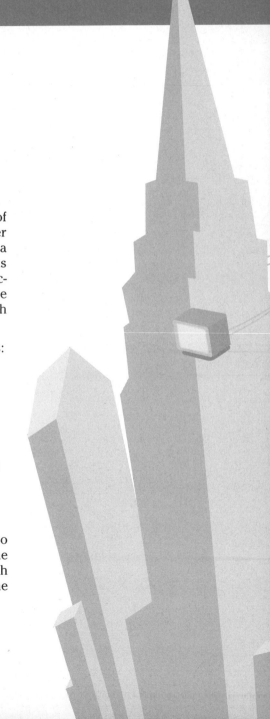

Note: A master document that contains a table of authorities includes all citations found in subdocuments.

Examples of sections included in a table of authorities might be cases, regulations, statutes, and U.S. Constitutional provisions.

Tip: Although you can design a table of authorities after all items are marked, it may be easier to mark items if major sections are decided beforehand.

Mark Text—Full Form

Authorities to be listed in the table can be located in the document, in footnotes, endnotes, graphics boxes, or captions.

The first time each authority is cited, it is marked as a "full form" authority. Detailed information is entered and edited in the form it will appear in the table. A "short form" is then assigned to the authority, and subsequent markings can use the short form. Because references are often cited many times in a legal brief, being able to use a nickname simplifies future referencing.

To create a full form mark, block the first occurrence of the authority. From the **Tools** menu, choose Table of Authorities, and then select Mark Full. You see a ToA Full Form screen similar to the one shown in Figure 61.1.

Note: If you block text, press Alt+F5, and choose Table of Authorities, you will go directly to the ToA Full Form screen. Note that with either method, you must first block the text.

On the ToA Full Form screen, select Section Name and type the name of the section where the authority is to be listed. (If you have already created a section, F5 produces a list from which you can select a section.)

Choose Short Form and enter the nickname for this authority.

Tip: A common practice is to use the first name of the citation as a short form name. However, remember that each short form name must be used with only one full form reference.

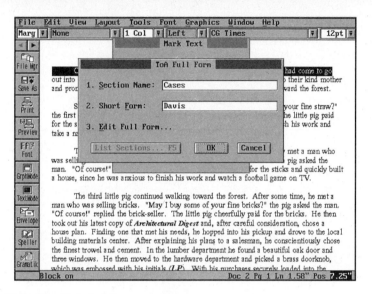

Figure 61.1. The ToA Full Form screen.

Next, choose Edit Full Form. You see the text that you blocked. Edit it into the form you want to appear in your table. You can add or delete text and codes, such as bold and underline. If you want the reference to appear on several lines, add hard returns as necessary. When you are satisfied with the appearance of the text, press Exit to return to the document. Reveal Codes shows that you have inserted a [ToA...Full Form] code into your document, which also lists the section and short form names associated with it. The code is located at the beginning of the text that was blocked; nothing will be visible in the document.

> **Note:** Editing the material in the full form reference will only change the way it appears in the table of authorities. The material in the document will not change.

Mark Text—Short Form

After you mark a full form entry, move your cursor to any other place in the document where that authority is referenced. It isn't necessary to block any text.

> **Tip:** Use Search to find other references to the authority you have marked.

When your cursor is located at a second reference, select Tools, Table of Authorities, and then choose Mark Short. You'll see the Mark ToA Short Form screen shown in Figure 61.2. Type the short name in the Short Form field or press F5, List Short Forms. Select an entry from the list. Choose OK and Close until you return to the document. When you are in Reveal Codes, the [ToA] code inserted in your document expands (when the cursor is moved to it) to show the short form name. Continue this process until all references are marked.

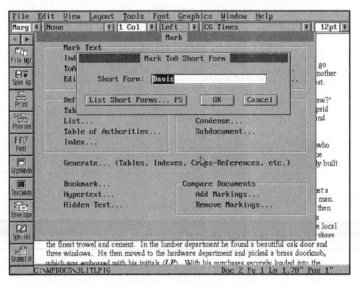

Figure 61.2. The Mark ToA Short Form screen.

Note: The Mark ToA Short Form screen can also be accessed by pressing Alt+F5, and then Mark Text, ToA Short Form.)

Defining a Table of Authorities

Place the cursor at the location where you want the table of authorities to appear. Press Ctrl+Enter if the table is to begin on a new page. Type a heading, such as TABLE OF AUTHORITIES, and then press Enter several times.

Type the name of the first section you want in the table (for example, CASES) and press Enter to create a blank line. Choose Define from the Tools, Table of Authorities menu. You see the Define Table of Authorities screen, as shown in Figure 61.3.

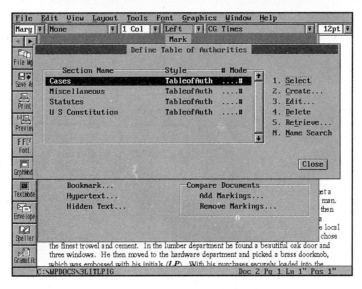

Figure 61.3. The Define Table of Authorities screen.

To create a section, choose Create to see the Create Table of Authorities screen shown in Figure 61.4.

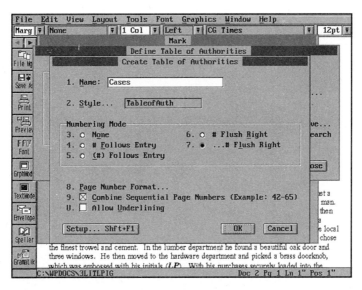

Figure 61.4. The Create Table of Authorities screen.

Enter the name of the section. Select a numbering mode option and a page number format for your table.

963

Note: Numbering modes and Page Number Format are discussed in detail under "Format Options" in Chapter 60, "Creating a Table of Contents."

When a reference appears on several sequential pages, you can choose to have those pages combined by selecting Combine Sequential Page Numbers. For example, with this option selected, pages would print as 59-63, rather than individually (59, 60, 61, 62, 63). The default setting for this option is On.

If you want underlining to appear in the table of authorities, select Allow Underlining. The default setting for this option is Off.

Tip: If you want to change the default settings for sequential pages and underlining, press Shift+F1, Setup.

System Styles for tables of authorities can be selected, created, edited, or reset to defaults. (For more information, see Chapter 39, "Styles.")

Table of Authorities definitions can be changed by highlighting the section name and pressing Edit. When you are satisfied with the options you have created, press Enter until you return to your document, then press Enter several times to create a few blank lines. Type the name of the next section you want to include in your table, followed by Enter.

Now return to the Define Table of Authorities screen and repeat the process just described. Each time you create a name and return to the document, a [Def Mark] code is placed in your document. In Reveal Codes, that code will expand to show the ToA section name and its numbering method.

You can, if you choose, retrieve section definitions from other documents. Choose Retrieve, and then type the name of another document. You can locate the document by using F5 (File List) or F6 (QuickList).

Generating a Table of Authorities

After all text is marked, and the table of authorities has been defined, you can generate the table. This is done in an identical manner to generating a table of contents, list, or index. Choose Generate from the Tools menu or the Mark menu. Respond OK to the warning message that previous tables and lists will be replaced. Your table of authorities appears at the location where it was defined.

62

by Diane Clayton

Indexes and Lists

An index keeps track of selected words and phrases used in a document. A list keeps track of items such as figures, illustrations, and equations. Both create references for the reader, showing page numbers where the word/phrase or list item can be located. Both can be easily created and maintained, using very similar processes. In each case you follow three basic steps:

1. Mark the text to be included
2. Define the index or list
3. Generate

There are a few differences in marking and defining an index and a list. Generating is identical for both.

Creating an Index

An index lists included items in alphabetical order and usually appears at the end of the document. It can include words and phrases, with headings and sub-headings. You can choose where the index will be located, and how the page numbers will be shown. Individual items can be marked in the text for inclusion in an index, and/or a concordance file can be used.

Marking Text

First, block the word or phrase that is to be included in the index. Then, from the **T**ools menu, choose Index, then Mark. You'll see the Mark Index screen shown in Figure 62.1. The blocked text will be displayed in the Heading box.

 Tip: Using styles can make the job of marking lists/indexes easier. For more information, see Chapter 39, "Styles."

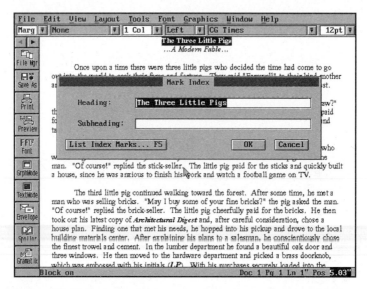

Figure 62.1. The Mark Index screen.

 Note: If you have blocked text, you can press Alt+F5 to access the Mark Text menu, then choose Index to access the Mark Index screen. If text is not blocked, Alt+F5 will give you the Mark menu instead, and you will need to select Mark Text, then Index to see the Mark Index screen.

You can edit (insert or delete) text in the Heading box. If you begin typing, the existing text will disappear. If you want to add to the existing text, move your cursor before entering any characters. The text you type will be shown in the Index; the page number will refer to the position of the text that was blocked.

 Tip: If you want to index a single word, it is not necessary to block it. If no text is blocked, the word at (or to the left of) the cursor will be shown in the Heading box and will be processed as if it had been blocked.

You can also include a subheading in the entry. If you type new information in the Heading field, pressing Enter will move the blocked text to the Subheading box (see Figure 62.2). You can accept that text by pressing Enter, or you can add or delete text. Like headings, the subheading will be printed in the index, and the page number that follows it will refer to the location of the blocked text.

Figure 62.2. A Subheading.

Tip: Because an index prints alphabetically, the use of headings and subheadings is an effective way to control the location of items in your index. Items can be grouped under similar headings or sub-headings, and will then appear together in the index.

At the bottom of the Mark Index screen is a message saying that pressing F5 will List Index Marks. This option will show you a list of all items you have previously marked for the index, including both heading and subheading, as shown in Figure 62.3. You can use Name Search to move to the appropriate Index Mark, then choose Select Complete Mark (which will repeat both heading and subheading) or Select Heading Only.

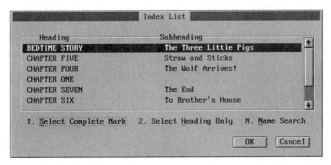

Figure 62.3. The Index List screen.

Pressing Tab will move through the choices on the Mark Index screen. When you are satisfied, choose OK to return to your document. An [Index] code will be placed at the beginning of the blocked text. In Reveal Codes, the code will expand to show the text or heading/subheading included. (If you change your mind, press Cancel and no codes will be inserted.)

Note: If you indexed a single word without blocking text, the [Index] code will appear immediately to the left of the cursor.

Concordance Files

Because an index often is designed to list every occurrence of an item (word or phrase), it would be tedious and time-consuming to have to mark each time that item is found in the document. A concordance file is a separate WordPerfect document that contains a list of words/phrases. When an index is generated, every time an item from the concordance file is found in the document, it will be listed in the index.

Tip: A concordance and individually marked items can be used together. To determine which method to use, ask yourself if *every* occurrence should be included in the index. If the answer is yes, put the item in the concordance. If the answer is no, mark only the occurrences that *should* be listed.

To create a concordance, open a blank document. Type each item you want included on a separate line. Save the document, with whatever filename you choose. The concordance file can be retrieved, modified, and saved as needed. A sample concordance file is shown in Figure 62.4.

Tip: The index will generate faster if you sort the entries in the concordance file alphabetically before saving it. If you need help with sorting a file, see Chapter 51, "Sorting."

Defining an Index

Move your cursor to the end of the document, then press Ctrl+Enter to create a new page. Type a heading for your index if you want, then press Enter a few times to create blank lines between the title and the list itself. Then, from the **Tools** menu, choose Index, then Define. You'll see the Define Index screen shown in Figure 62.5.

Note: If you prefer, you can reach the Define Index screen by pressing Alt+F5, then Define, Index.

Figure 62.4. A sample concordance file.

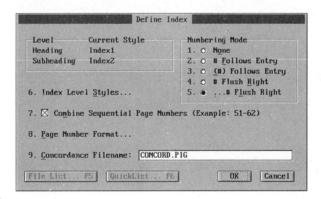

Figure 62.5. The Define Index screen.

The first five choices on this screen are about Numbering Mode, which refers to the way the page numbers will be displayed. The default is Flush Right with dot leaders (choice 5). If you want to change it, press the highlighted number or letter. These choices are available:

1. **None**: no page numbers will appear.
2. **# Follows Entry**: page numbers will appear after each entry.
3. **(#) Follows Entry**: page numbers in parentheses will appear after each entry.

4. # Flush Right: page numbers will appear at the right margin.

5. ...# Flush Right: page numbers will appear at the right margin, preceded by dot leaders.

Choice 6 on the Define Index screen refers to index styles. "Index1" is the default for headings; "Index2" is the default for subheadings. You can edit these styles, choose a different style from the list that will appear if you press Select, or design your own. You can also choose Reset to Default to return to the original Index Level Style. (For more information on styles, see Chapter 39.)

Choice 7 on this screen is Combine Sequential Page Numbers. If this option is chosen, an item that appears on pages 7, 8, 9, and 10 will be shown as "7-10" in the Index. If the option is not checked, pages will be listed individually.

Choice 8 is Page Number Format. Selecting it will access the Page Number Format. If you want the page numbers in the Index to be the same as the page numbers in the document, the default selection Same as Document is correct. If you want a different format, select Different from Document. Type any desired text and/or make any changes to number codes. To access additional number codes (chapter, volume, or secondary page), press F5, select the desired code, and press Enter.

Choice 9 asks you to enter the Concordance Filename. If you created a concordance for this document, enter the name (and path, if necessary) here. When your cursor is in the Concordance Filename box, you have access to both File List (F5) and QuickList (F6), and can select a file from either list.

When you are satisfied with the choices on the Define Index screen, press OK to return to the document. A [Def Mark] code will be at the position of the cursor. In Reveal Codes, the code will expand to show details of the Index.

 Caution: If you are using the Master Documents feature, be sure the [Def Mark] code is in the master document instead of a subdocument.

A sample index is shown in Figure 62.6.

Creating a List

Like an index, a list refers the reader to pages in a document. Lists, however, are concerned with items such as figures, illustrations, and equations rather than words. Several lists can be created for a single document, and they can be identified either by numbers or names. Lists can occur anywhere in the document.

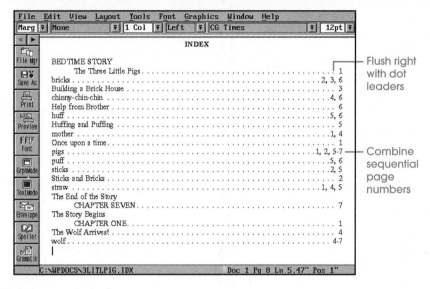

Figure 62.6. A sample index.

Marking the Text

Block the text you want included in the list. Then, from the **T**ools menu, choose List, and then Mark. You'll see the Mark Text for List screen.

> **Caution:** Text that is not blocked cannot be marked for a list.

> **Note:** If you prefer, you can press Alt+F5 to access the Mark Text menu, then choose List to access the Mark Index screen. Be sure to block the text first. Otherwise you'll see the Mark menu instead, and Lists are not a choice on that menu.

The Mark Text for List screen asks for List Name. If you have previously worked with a list during this session of WordPerfect, the last list name will be displayed. If not, you will see the number "1." You can use this for a list name, or you can enter a name or number of your choice. Pressing F5 will show you all currently defined lists. You can highlight any name on this list, and press Enter to select it.

After you have specified the proper List Name, press OK to return to the document. [Mrk Txt List Begin] and [Mrk Txt List End] codes will have been

971

placed at the ends of the blocked text. In Reveal Codes, either code will expand to show the name or number of the list. Deleting either code will also remove the other.

Tip: You don't need to mark captions on any graphics boxes. When you define your list, one of the options is to Include Graphics. You'll see how to do this in a forthcoming section.

Defining a List

Place your cursor where you want the list. If you want it to be on a separate page, press Ctrl+Enter, then move your cursor into the blank page. If you want a title for the list, type it, then press Enter several times to create blank lines between the title and the list.

Now, from the **Tools** menu, choose List, then Define. You'll see the Define List screen shown in Figure 62.7.

Note: If you prefer, you can reach the Define List screen by pressing Alt+F5, then Define, List.

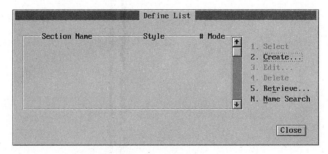

Figure 62.7. The Define List screen.

If you have previously marked list items in this document, you will see the List Names you used. If you define your list prior to marking, the screen will be blank. You can either create a new list definition or retrieve a list definition from another document.

Creating a List

Create will take you to the Create List screen shown in Figure 62.8. Enter a name or number for your list, and press Enter. You can then select the options shown on the screen.

```
┌─────────────────████ Create List ████─────────────────┐
│                                                        │
│   Name:    ┌────────────────────────┐                  │
│            └────────────────────────┘                  │
│                                                        │
│   Style... ┌────────┐                                  │
│            │List    │                                  │
│            └────────┘                                  │
│   ┌─Numbering Mode──────────────────────────────────┐  │
│   │  ○ None              ○ # Flush Right             │  │
│   │  ○ # Follows Entry   ● ...# Flush Right          │  │
│   │  ○ (#) Follows Entry                             │  │
│   └─────────────────────────────────────────────────┘  │
│                                                        │
│   Page Number Format...                                │
│                                                        │
│   Include Graphics... ┌─────────────────┐              │
│                       └─────────────────┘              │
│                            ┌────┐ ┌──────┐             │
│                            │ OK │ │Cancel│             │
│                            └────┘ └──────┘             │
└────────────────────────────────────────────────────────┘
```

Figure 62.8. The Create List screen.

Numbering Mode, Page Number Format, and Style are similar to the options discussed in the section called "Defining an Index," earlier in this chapter.

The remaining choice allows you to include captions for all kinds of graphics boxes: equation, figure, table, text, or user-defined. It is not necessary to mark the text in the captions. To use this option, enter a name for your list on the Create List screen, then select Include Graphics. You'll see the Graphics Box Counters screen shown in Figure 62.9. The graphics box types will be listed. Highlight the type you want to include in the list you are defining, and press Enter to select it.

Figure 62.9. Graphics box counters.

Tip: A list can include only one type of graphic box, unless you mark them individually. Because you can have several types of graphics boxes in a document, you can organize your illustrations into "groups" and create a separate list for each group.

Note: When text is marked before a list is defined, list names are created with default options. If you want to change options, select the name of the list and press Edit. You will see the Edit List screen, which (except for title) is identical to the Create List screen.

Retrieving a List

If you want to retrieve a list definition from another document, choose Retrieve from the Define List dialog box, and you will see the Retrieve Definition screen shown in Figure 62.10. Type the name of another file that has list definitions you would like to use in the current document. (Instead of entering a filename, you can press F5 to see a File List, or F6 to see a QuickList. Select the file you want and press Enter.)

The Retrieve Definition screen will show all the list definitions that occur in the document you named. However, you may not want to use all those lists in the current document. An asterisk (*) in front of a list name indicates it will be copied to the new document. You can select or deselect a list name by placing/removing the asterisk, with either the spacebar or the asterisk key. Pressing Home before you press the asterisk will remove all marks that exist, or, if none exist, place marks on all list names.

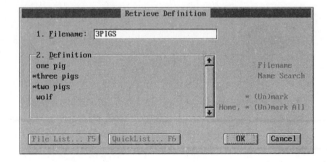

Figure 62.10. Retrieve Definition.

Generating an Index or List

This part is simple. After you have marked and defined your index and/or list, choose Generate from either the Tools or the Mark menu. You'll see the Generate screen shown in Figure 62.11; press OK to continue.

Figure 62.11. The Generate screen.

Each time you generate, you will replace all existing tables, lists and indexes. While the generation is in progress, you will see a screen, which will list any concordance file used, then show the index or list being built, generated, and condensed. At the end of the generation, you will be returned to the document. A [Begin Gen Txt] code will be at the beginning of the index or list, and an [End Gen Txt] code will be at the end of it. Each item will be preceded by a [Para Style ...] code. The cursor will be on the first character of the index or list.

by Diane Clayton

Document Comparison

When you want to see exactly what differences exist between two documents, the Compare Documents feature can help. With this feature, the document on your screen is compared to another document (which you specify) on disk. At the end of the process, your screen shows a composite of the two documents. Areas of difference are marked with redline and/or strikeout attributes to identify the words, phrases, sentences, or paragraphs where the two documents differ. This feature can be used to find editing changes that have been made since a document was last saved, or to compare the current document to a document with a different filename.

Concept and Options

After the comparison, text that appears in the same place in both documents appears as it normally does. Text that differs is marked with codes that make it easy to identify both on-screen and on a printed copy. Two marking patterns are used by Compare Documents:

▲ If text appears in the document on-screen, but it doesn't appear in the document on disk, it is marked with *redline*. The codes [Redln On] and [Redln Off] appear at each end of the text.

▲ If text appears in the document on disk, but it doesn't appear in the document on-screen, it is copied to the screen and marked with strikeout. The codes `[StkOut On]` and `[StkOut Off]` appear at each end of the text.

Tip: You can use Compare Documents to compare changes in footnotes and endnotes and in tables. However, it can't be used to locate changes in comments, headers and footers, or graphics boxes.

In addition, text that appears in both documents but in different places is identified through messages. THE FOLLOWING TEXT WAS MOVED appears before the text, and THE PRECEDING TEXT WAS MOVED appears after the text. Both messages are marked with Strikeout codes.

Word, Phrase, Sentence, and Paragraph Comparisons

Options enable you to compare the two documents (and show the results) by word, phrase, paragraph, or sentence. (The example later in this chapter shows comparing by word. When you compare by phrase, any discrepancy causes the entire phrase to be marked. The other options cause the entire sentence or paragraph to be marked.)

In order to understand this option, it's important to know how WordPerfect defines each of these terms:

▲ A *word* is a collection of characters that ends with a space or with any of the marks that indicate the end of a phrase or a sentence.

▲ A *phrase* is a collection of characters that ends with a comma, colon, semicolon, or any of the marks that indicate the end of a sentence.

▲ A *sentence* is a collection of characters that ends with a period, question mark, exclamation point, or either of the marks that indicate the end of a paragraph.

▲ A *paragraph* is a collection of characters that ends with a hard return or a hard page break.

Procedure 63.1. Comparing documents.

1. Retrieve the most recent version of the document.

978

Caution: Because the Compare function adds codes to your document, it would be wise to save the document on your screen under another name (such as "temp") before proceeding.

2. From the **File** menu, choose Compare Documents, then select Add Markings. You will see the Compare Documents screen shown in Figure 63.1.

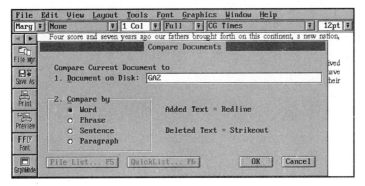

Figure 63.1. The Compare Documents screen.

Note: Compare Documents/Add Markings are also choices on the Mark menu, which you see if you press Alt+F5. The Mark menu is shown in Figure 63.2.

3. Select Word, Phrase, Sentence, or Paragraph to indicate your choice of methods for comparing the two documents. (Descriptions of these options appear in the preceding section.)

4. The name shown as Document on Disk on the Compare Documents menu is the name of the current document. If you want to compare the document on-screen to the version of the document that was last saved, press OK.

If you want to compare the document on-screen with a different document, enter the filename (including path, if necessary) or select it from the File List or QuickList, then choose OK.

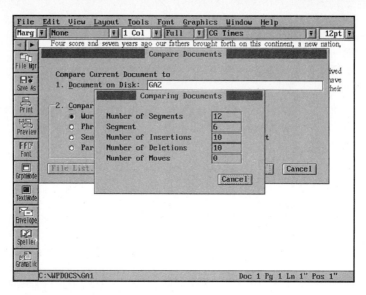

Figure 63.2. The Mark menu.

Analyzing the Results

During the comparison, you see the Comparing Documents screen shown in Figure 63.3. This screen reflects the number of segments to be compared, the current segment, and the number of insertions, deletions, and moves found. When the comparison is finished, you are automatically returned to your document.

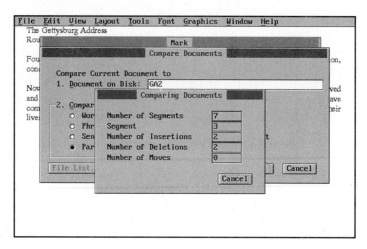

Figure 63.3. Comparing documents.

At the end of the comparison, the text on your screen includes information from both documents, plus the identifying redline/strikeout codes. Remember that REDLINE means the text occurs in the document on-screen but not in the document on disk, and that STRIKEOUT means the text does not occur in the on-screen document.

In the example shown next, the text in Figure 63.4 was on-screen. It was compared with the text in Figure 63.5 using Compare by Word. The results appear in Figure 63.6.

Figure 63.4. Document on-screen.

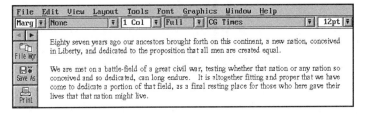

Figure 63.5. Document on disk.

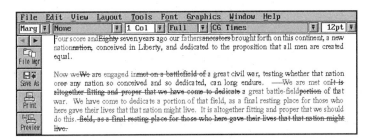

Figure 63.6. After comparing documents.

An example of a screen showing text that has been moved is shown in Figure 63.7.

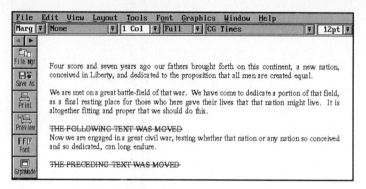

Figure 63.7. Text that has been moved.

Options for Printing Redlined Text

When you print your document, redlined text usually prints with a shaded background or a different font, depending on the printer you use. If you prefer, this can be changed to an indicator character that prints in the margin of all lines that contain redlined text.

From the Layout menu, choose Document. The first choice on the Redline Method screen is Printer Dependent, which refers to the default. The other choices enable you to place an indicator at either side of the document text or on alternate sides of odd and even pages. The Redline Character default is a vertical bar (|). If you choose an option other than Printer Dependent for the Redline Method, you also can change the Redline Character to any WordPerfect character.

Figure 63.8 shows a Print Preview after comparing two documents. Redline Method has been changed to Left, and Redline Character has been changed to a question mark (?).

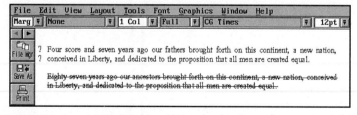

Figure 63.8. Redline character ? in the left margin.

Removing the Markings

After you've analyzed the differences shown on-screen, you have several options. Select Remove Markings from the Mark menu or from the Compare Documents box of the File menu. You will see the dialog box shown in Figure 63.9.

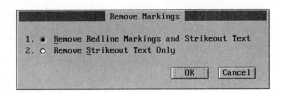

Figure 63.9. Remove markings.

This screen offers you two choices:

▲ **Remove Redline Markings and Strikeout Text** removes all redline and strikeout codes. It also removes the strikeout text that was copied from the document on disk. The document on-screen appears in its original form.

▲ **Remove Strikeout Text Only** removes strikeout codes and the text that was copied from the document on disk. Text that is unique to the document on-screen is still enclosed in Redline codes.

Choose the desired option and select OK. You can continue working on your document or save it for future use.

by Paul McFedries

Master Documents

This chapter shows you how to manage large projects using WordPerfect's Master Document feature. You will learn how to set up and maintain both a master document and its associated subdocuments, and you will also learn how to incorporate other WordPerfect features (such as footnotes and tables of contents) into your master documents.

Understanding Master Documents

Most WordPerfect documents are small (a page or two) and therefore easily manageable. But many projects—such as dissertations, detailed reports, and full-length books—can run to dozens or even hundreds of pages. You could try stuffing these projects into a single document, but you will only make things harder for yourself.

▲ **Searching**. The longer the document, the more time it will take you to find the text you need (this is true of both scrolling and using the Search feature).

▲ **Editing**. Whether you are cutting, copying, or searching and replacing, editing large documents can be a nightmare.

▲ **Speed**. Huge documents (especially if you are running WordPerfect in Graphics mode) are just plain slower than smaller ones. Everything from opening to saving to spell checking seems to take forever.

▲ **Memory**. A finite amount of memory is a fact of computing life. Beefy documents take up large chunks of precious RAM and can cause WordPerfect to balk at some features (such as Graphics mode or opening other files at the same time).

The solution is to break your large projects into a number of smaller documents (called *subdocuments*) that are easier (and faster) to manage. In a book, for example, you could create a subdocument for each chapter. You can then track the project as a whole by setting up a *master document* that includes codes referencing each of the subdocuments. When you've finished working with the subdocuments, you can use the master document to assemble (or *expand*) the entire project, print everything out, or even create a table of contents or index.

Creating a Master Document

A master document is just a basic WordPerfect document like any other. The difference is that it consists almost entirely of codes that serve to link it with its associated subdocuments. If needed, you can also include codes for page numbers, footnotes, a table of contents, and more.

You can use either of the following two methods to create a master document:

▲ Add a new subdocument link to the master document each time you complete a subdocument.

▲ Wait until you have completed all your subdocuments and then add each of the subdocument links to the master document.

Note: WordPerfect doesn't mind if you include a link to a nonexistent file in a master document. However, unless you are sure about the filenames you will be using for your subdocuments, I recommend waiting until you have created a subdocument before including a link to it in a master document.

Caution: Formatting codes in a subdocument take precedence over the same codes imbedded in the master document. This means that document formats such as the base font, margins, or justification will default to whatever settings are used in your subdocuments. To be safe, remove all such formatting from the subdocuments and include it only in the master document, as explained later in this chapter.

Whichever method you choose, follow the steps in Procedure 64.1 to create a master document.

Procedure 64.1. Creating a master document.

1. Open (or create) the file you want to use for the master document.
2. Place the insertion point where you want the next subdocument link to appear.
3. Select File, Master Document; or press Alt+F5. Then select Subdocument. The Include Subdocument dialog box appears, as shown in Figure 64.1.

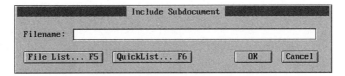

Figure 64.1. The Include Subdocument dialog box.

4. Enter the name of the file you want to link with the master document (or select it from the File List or QuickList) and then select OK. WordPerfect returns you to the document and displays a box representing the new subdocument link.
5. Repeat Steps 2-4 for any other subdocument links you want to include in the master document.

Figure 64.2 shows a master document with several subdocument links.

> **Tip:** If you want each subdocument to appear on a new page, be sure to include a hard page break (Ctrl+Enter) between each subdocument link in the master document.

Working with Subdocument Links

Another advantage to master documents is that they make rearranging the various chapters or sections of a project much easier. In a single large file, you would have to find the chapter you want to move, block it, find the new position, and then paste it there. A master document saves you all that legwork, because subdocument links are just [Subdoc] codes imbedded in the master document. This means that they can be quickly included in a block, cut or copied, and then pasted just like any other code.

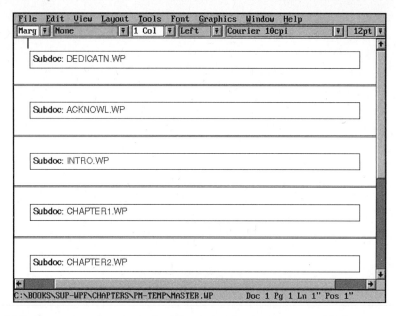

Figure 64.2. A master document with several subdocument links.

Note: To make sure you are working with the right codes, you may want to select Reveal Codes (Alt+F3) before working with subdocument links in this way.

Formatting the Master Document

As explained earlier, subdocument formatting codes take precedence over master document codes. (The exception to this is with initial codes—master document initial codes always override subdocument initial codes.) To be sure you get consistent formatting throughout your expanded document, include codes for things like your base font, margins, and justification at the beginning of the master document and exclude them from the subdocuments.

Tip: To avoid cluttering the beginning of your master document, include any formatting codes in the master documents initial codes section. See Chapter 11, "Default Settings," for details.

988

Caution: Be careful when using styles in a master document, because they will override any styles with the same name in a subdocument. To avoid problems, either use styles with unique names or else make sure that styles with the same name contain the same formatting codes.

Expanding a Master Document

Once you've completed your subdocuments and inserted the appropriate links in the master document, you need to gather all the subdocuments together in order to print the entire project or generate a table of contents. This process is called *expanding* the master document, and the steps are outlined in Procedure 64.2.

Procedure 64.2. Expanding a master document.

1. With the master document displayed, select File, Master Document; or press Alt+F5. Then select Expand. WordPerfect displays the Expand Master Document dialog box shown in Figure 64.3.

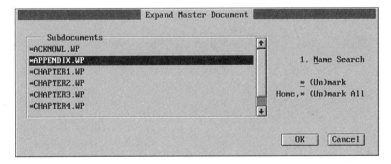

Figure 64.3. The Expand Master Document dialog box.

2. The Subdocuments box contains a list of all the subdocuments with links in the master document. The ones with asterisks beside them will be included when you expand the master document (all the documents have asterisks at first). If you want to exclude any subdocuments from the expansion, highlight each one and press either * or the spacebar.

3. When you are ready, select OK. WordPerfect will ask if you want to expand the marked subdocuments. Select Yes.

4. If WordPerfect can't find one of the subdocuments with a link in the master document, the Subdocument Not Found dialog box appears, and it displays the name of the file. Select Skip to ignore this file or New Filename to change the name of the file. If you choose the latter, WordPerfect displays the Include Subdocument dialog box for you to enter the name of the file.

Note: If WordPerfect can't find a subdocument during an expansion and you select the New Filename option, WordPerfect replaces the old subdocument link in the master document with the new subdocument you select.

During the expansion, WordPerfect gathers all the marked subdocuments and starts inserting them into the master document. Each subdocument box is replaced by two boxes that mark the beginning and end of the subdocument, as shown in Figure 64.4.

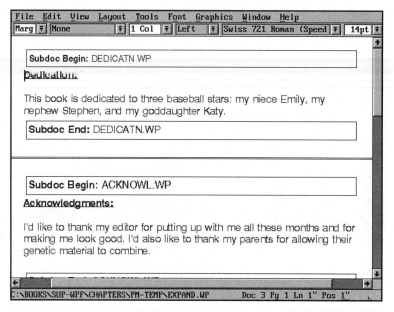

Figure 64.4. A master document expanded to include its linked subdocuments.

With the master document expanded, you can proceed to edit the subdocument text, create a table of contents or index (explained at the end of this chapter), or print out the entire project (the Subdoc comment boxes are not included in the printout).

Note: If the subdocuments are in a different WordPerfect format (such as 5.1), they are converted to the 6.0 format when they are retrieved into the master document.

Caution: If you try to save an expanded master document, WordPerfect asks if you want to condense the document first (condensing is explained in the next section). Saving a master document with expanded subdocuments just wastes disk space, so you should always condense it first.

Condensing a Master Document

When you've finished working with an expanded master document, you need to remove the subdocuments in order to save disk space and memory. This process is called *condensing*, and Procedure 64.3 shows you the appropriate steps.

Procedure 64.3. Condensing a master document.

1. Display the master document and select File, Master Document; or press Alt+F5. Then select Condense. WordPerfect displays the Condense Master Document dialog box shown in Figure 64.5.

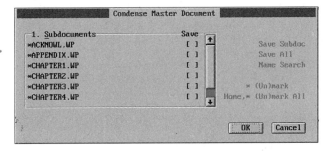

Figure 64.5. The Condense Master Document dialog box.

2. For each subdocument you don't want condensed, highlight it and press either * or the spacebar.

3. If you made any changes to the subdocuments and you want to save these changes to the appropriate files, highlight each changed sub-document and select Save Subdoc, or else select Save All to save all your changes.

4. When you are ready, select OK. When WordPerfect asks if you want to condense the marked subdocuments, select Yes.

Tip: While a subdocument is highlighted, you can activate the Save check box by pressing Enter or double-clicking the document name.

Tips for Working with Master Documents

For the most part, you work with master documents the same way you work with any WordPerfect document. However, a few features work slightly differently in a master document, and there are also some advantages to working with an expanded master document instead of the separate subdocuments. The topics in this section give you a few tips for working with master documents.

Using Search and Replace

WordPerfect's Search and Replace feature is generally faster with smaller documents, but this isn't always the case. For example, if you have to replace a word or phrase throughout all of a project's subdocuments, it can take forever to open the appropriate file, perform the search and replace, close (and save) the document, and then open another.

Instead of all this rigmarole, you should expand the master document, perform the search and replace once, and then condense the master document. (Make sure you tell WordPerfect to save all your changes to the subdocument files.)

Spelling and Grammar Checking

Like Search and Replace, Speller and Grammatik are normally faster with smaller subdocuments. However, running these utilities on an expanded master document does provide some efficiencies. In Speller, for example, you can elect to skip a word throughout the entire document. If you do this in an expanded master document, WordPerfect skips the word in all the subdocuments. Similarly, in Grammatik you can skip certain rule classes or phrases.

Again, once you have finished with the expanded master document, condense it and save your subdocument changes.

Adding Footnotes and Endnotes

Recall that subdocument formatting codes override those in the master document. This, of course, applies to footnotes and endnotes, so you need to make some decisions about where you want your notes to appear and what options you want to use.

If you want all your footnotes and endnotes to have the same format, make sure you include the appropriate codes at the beginning of the master document and that you remove any codes that might be in the subdocuments.

Footnote and Endnote Numbers

If you want your footnote or endnote numbers to run consecutively throughout the subdocuments, you don't need to do anything special. Just create the footnotes or endnotes in the subdocuments, and WordPerfect will adjust the numbers appropriately when you expand the master document.

However, at times you might want to restart the notes at 1 for each chapter or section. In this case, for each subdocument, you need to place the insertion point at the beginning of the file and tell WordPerfect to start the footnote or endnote numbering at 1. (See Chapter 57, "Footnotes and Endnotes," for details.)

Endnote Placement

If your project includes endnotes, you need to think about where you want them placed. You have two choices:

▲ You can place all the endnotes in one place (at the end of the master document, for example). In this case, position the insertion point where you want the endnotes to appear, and then add an endnote placement code.

▲ You can place them at the end of each chapter or section. To do this, position the insertion point at the end of each subdocument and add an endnote placement code.

Adding Numbered Elements

When adding numbered elements, such as page or paragraph numbers, use the master document to insert the appropriate codes. If you have subdocuments that require different numbering arrangements (for example, you might want an introduction to have lowercase Roman numerals and the main chapters to have regular numbers), simply insert the proper number codes just before the [Subdoc] codes in the master document.

Note: If you want to include chapter numbers, these are also best handled in the master document. This way, if you need to rearrange your chapters, you don't need to worry about changing the chapter numbers. (However, when cutting or copying a subdocument link, turn on Reveal Codes to make sure you don't accidentally include the chapter number code in the block.)

Generating Features

You can use a master document to generate features such as indexes, tables of contents, lists, or tables of authorities that cover all the linked subdocuments. You follow more or less the same steps that were outlined in the appropriate chapters earlier in this Workshop. However, Procedure 64.4 lists the basic steps to follow to generate one of these features in a master document.

Procedure 64.4. Generating features in a master document.

1. For each subdocument, mark the text you want to use for the feature.
2. Open the master document and position the insertion point where you want the feature to appear.
3. Define the appearance of the feature (include a title, if desired).
4. Generate the feature. If the master document was not expanded, WordPerfect expands it before generating the feature and then condenses it when it is done.

Projects

Title of Paper Here

by

Your Name Here

Date Here (I set Font to Relative Size: Large)

by Susan Hafer

Designing Academic Papers

WordPerfect is a superb choice for academic writing for many reasons:

- ▲ Excellent support for long documents, including features such as master documents, bookmarks, and flexible page numbering
- ▲ Footnotes, endnotes, cross-referencing, table of contents, and lists
- ▲ Approximately 1,700 special characters that print on any graphics-capable printer
- ▲ Redefinable keyboards
- ▲ Collapsible outliner
- ▲ Macros to help automate repetitive work
- ▲ Styles to simplify formatting
- ▲ Additional language modules available from WP Corp
- ▲ Equation editor
- ▲ Tables with built-in spreadsheet functions
- ▲ Graphics support

 We've provided a sample academic paper, ACADEMIC.PRO, on the *Super Book* disk. It is not a real paper with real text, but a sample document designed to show you how to use the macros and styles to set up a typical (more or less) academic document that includes a title page, preface page, body, and bibliography. To make the macros and features more accessible (for mouse users, at least), we've provided a button bar that you can use as is or customize for your own use.

All the macros and styles in this project are suggestions only. You may create your own or modify the ones used here to suit your own tastes and needs. (Your institution or discipline may have strict rules for formatting scholarly papers.)

Special Instructions

1. Copy the macros (*.WPM) to your personal or shared macro directory.
2. Copy ACADEMIC.WPB to your personal or shared macro directory.
3. Copy ACADEMIC.STY to your personal or shared styles directory.
4. Copy ACADEMIC.PRO to your document directory.
5. From the View menu, choose Button Bar Setup; highlight the ACADEMIC button bar, and choose Select.

WordPerfect 6.0 Features Used

Macros (TITLEPAG.WPM, PREFACE.WPM, BIBLIOGR.WPM, SORTBIB.WPM)
Styles (found in the Style Library ACADEMIC.STY)
Page Border, with Shaded Fill
Page Header
Fancy page numbering (using Roman numerals, resetting page numbers, inserting a formatted page number in a page header)
Relative Font Size
Footnote System Style
Paragraph Margins (rather than hanging indents)

Files Used

```
ACADEMIC.PRO
ACADEMIC.STY
ACADEMIC.WPB
TITLEPAG.WPM
PREFACE.WPM
SORTBIB.WPM
BIBLIOGR.WPM
```

Fonts Used

ROMAN-WP (Type 1)

The Title Page

A macro, TITLEPAG, creates a title page similar to the one shown at the beginning of this project. This macro does the following:

▲ Turns on center justification.

▲ Inserts an Advance from Top of Page code approximately 1/3 of the way from the top page, turns on the Very Large font attribute, prompts you to enter the title for the paper (using the macro INPUT command), and sets the font back to normal.

▲ Inserts two hard returns, turns on the Large font attribute, prompts you to enter your name, and sets the font back to normal.

▲ Inserts an Advance from Top of Page code to move the insertion point to 8 inches from the top of the page, and prompts you for the name of the professor, the course title, and the name of the school, and then inserts the date text.

▲ Turns on a Page Border using a shaded fill (Layout, Page, Page Borders, Border Style, Thin Thick, Fill Style, 10% Shaded).

▲ Uses a delay code to turn off the border and to set the justification to left beginning on the next page.

Caution: When you use Advance codes instead of pressing Enter to move to a new vertical position, the page border and fill do not display correctly in Graphics or Page mode. The page looks correct in Print Preview and prints correctly. Despite the screen glitches, it's better to use Advance because it's more precise and the text won't drift. Another solution would be to put the title and other information in text boxes anchored to the page, but that involves more steps both to create and to edit.

Use the following steps to create a page border yourself:

1. Press Shft+F8; or select Layout. Select Page. The Page Format dialog box appears.

2. Select Page Borders. The dialog box looks much like the one shown in Figure 65.1.

3. Select Border Style. A dialog box similar to the one shown in Figure 65.2 appears.

4. Select the Border Style you would like to use for this page. For this example, we used Thin Thick.

5. Back in the Create Page Border dialog box, select Fill Style. A dialog box similar to the one shown in Figure 65.3 appears.

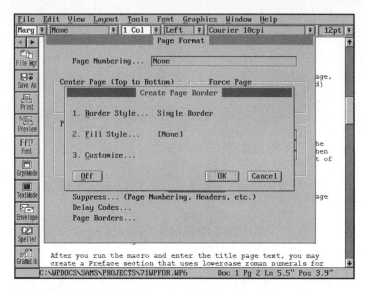

Figure 65.1. The Create Page Border dialog box.

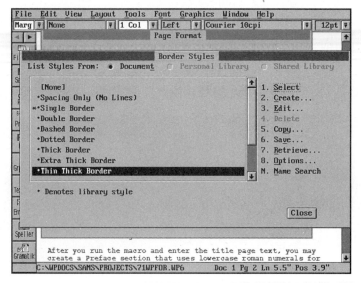

Figure 65.2. The Border Style dialog box.

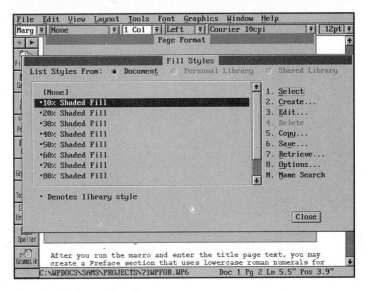

Figure 65.3. The Fill Style dialog box.

6. Select the Fill Style you would like to use, if any. For this example, we used 10% Fill Shading.

7. Press Home, F7 to exit all layers of dialog boxes and return to your document with the new page border style turned on, or choose Off, then Home, F7 to return to your document without turning the page border style on.

Tip: If you have a slow printer, eliminate the border fill.

To run the TITLEPAG macro, press Alt+F10, type the word TITLEPAG, and press Enter. If the ACADEMIC button bar is active, just click the Preface button. After you run the TITLEPAG macro and enter the title page text, you may create a preface section that uses lowercase Roman numerals for page numbers (i, ii, iii, iv, v, and so on).

Caution: Because the PREFACE macro sets up the page numbering for the entire document, as well as for the preface section, you may want to run the PREFACE macro and then delete the preface page if you won't be using it.

Preface

If you have a preface in your paper, use the macro PREFACE, which does the following:

- ▲ Sets the page number to page 1
- ▲ Sets the Page Numbering Method to lowercase Roman numerals
- ▲ Sets the Page Number Position to bottom-center
- ▲ Sets the Page Number Format to include the word *Page* before the [page #] code
- ▲ Centers the line (Shift+F6)
- ▲ Selects a Font of Relative Size Large
- ▲ Types the title Preface
- ▲ Selects a Font of Relative Size Normal
- ▲ Inserts two hard returns (press Enter twice)
- ▲ Inserts a hard page Break (Ctrl+Enter)
- ▲ On this next page, resets Page Number to 1
- ▲ Changes Page Number Method to Numbers
- ▲ Changes Page Number Position to Top Right
- ▲ Uses Page Format Suppress to make page numbers appear on the bottom center of the page, just for this page
- ▲ Goes back up a line, into the preface page

To run the PREFACE macro, press Alt+F10, type the word preface, and press Enter. If the ACADEMIC button bar is active, just click the Preface button. After running the macro, you can begin entering the preface text. The first page will be numbered i, the next ii, the next iii, the next iv, and so on. Figure 65.4 shows an example.

When you are ready to begin typing the main body of the document, just move the cursor past the hard page, and page numbering will begin at page 1. The first page of the paper will have its page number at the bottom-center of the page, and subsequent pages will have page numbers at the top-right corner of the page.

To use the Suppress method to have the current page of any document print the page number in the bottom-center, regardless of where it prints page numbers for the rest of the document, use the following steps:

1. Place the cursor anywhere on the page, if Automatic Code Placement is turned on, or place the cursor at the top of the current page if ACP is off. (If you aren't sure, you might play it safe and use Goto (Ctrl+Home), up arrow to move the cursor to the top of the current page.)

2. Select Layout; or press Shft+F8 for Format.

3. Select Page, Suppress.

4. Select Print Page Number at Bottom Center.

5. Press Home, F7 to exit all layers of dialog boxes and return to your document.

6. If you used Goto, up arrow to go to the beginning of the current page, you may want to now use Goto, Goto (Ctrl+Home, Ctrl+Home) to return the cursor to its previous location.

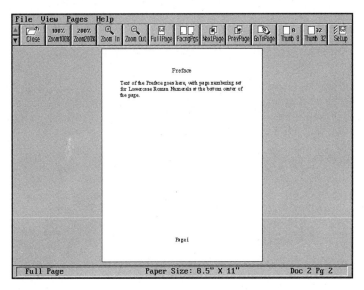

Figure 65.4. The sample preface page in the sample file ACADEMIC.PRO.

Indented Quotes

As you type a paper, you may want to include indented quotes. One of the styles in ACADEMIC.STY, called QUOTE, does the following:

▲ Selects Line Format and sets Spacing to 1 (single) in case your document is doublespaced

▲ Uses a Double Indent (Shft+F4) code to indent the paragraph equally from both the left and right margins

Note: This can also be done using Paragraph Margins, similar to the approach used later in this chapter for the bibliography format. You must press Shift+F4 for each new paragraph. Like Indent, Double Indent affects only the current paragraph. The amount of the indentation depends on your tab settings.

▲ Selects a small font (using the Small Relative Size attribute)

▲ Inserts two hard returns when you press Enter to end the quote (one hard return is defined as a Style Off Code and the other is inserted by the Enter key you press to turn off the style)

To use the QUOTE Style, insert a blank line between the body of the text and the quote you are about to type, then press Style (Alt+F8) and select Quote. Type the quotation and press Enter to end it. Alternatively, if the quotation has already been typed into the paper, move the insertion point anywhere in the paragraph. Then select the Quote Style from the Style List dialog box, or from the pull-down list of paragragh styles on the ribbon.

Tip: Because the Quote style was defined as a Paragraph style, you don't need to block existing text to apply the style. As with other paragraph styles (such as the Bibliography style described later in this chapter), you can select the Quote style from your ribbon, once you have used it in your document (or if you copied it to your document from a style library).

Tip: Experiment with other options for the Quote style. For example, add italics or insert the code to disable Speller and Grammatik (Tools, Writing Tools, Disable Speller/Grammatik). If your quotations are usually longer than a single paragraph, consider defining the Quote style as a Character style or changing the Enter Key Action to Off/On so that the Quote style is turned off and back on when you press Enter. (See Chapter 39, "Styles," for more information about these options.)

The sample quotation in ACADEMIC.PRO is shown in Figure 65.5.

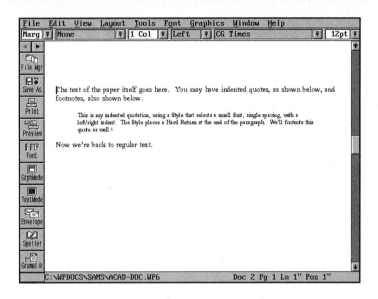

Figure 65.5. A sample quotation paragraph using the Quote Style.

Changing the Footnote System Style to Use a Small Font

In WordPerfect 6.0, the appearance of your footnotes is governed by a special kind of style called the Footnote System Style, which is based on your InitialCodes style. (See Chapter 39 for more information about regular and system styles.) By changing the Footnote System Style, you can reformat all of your footnotes in a single operation.

Note: The following instructions explain how to change the Footnote System Style for the current document. To change the appearance of your footnotes in all new documents, see "Copying Your Footnote Style to Your Personal Style Library" later in this chapter.

Caution: The footnote style, like several other system styles, is based on the InitialCodes style (the same as your Document Initial Codes).

This means that your footnotes use the justification, margins, font, and other formatting settings set in Document Initial Codes and Initial Font, unless you change your Footnote style. Footnotes do not use the formatting settings in the body of your document (except by coincidence).

You may want your footnotes to appear in a font slightly smaller than the font used in the main body of the document. In Figure 65.5 just shown, you can see a footnote number at the end of the sample quotation. Figure 65.6 shows the footnote text itself, using a Font of **R**elative Size Small.

You could also change the size to a precise point size by choosing Size from the Font dialog box. The advantage using a relative font size is that it will always be in proportion to the size of your base font.

Tip: The default for the Small attribute is 80 percent of your current base font. You can change the size ratios for Small and other relative sizes in the **F**ont, Setup dialog box.

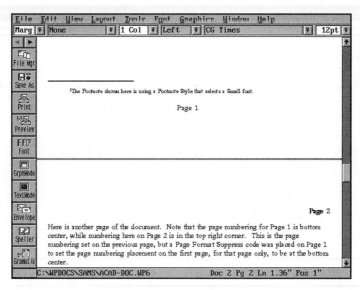

Figure 65.6. A footnote using a Small size attribute for the footnote text.

To set all footnotes in the current document to use a Small font, complete the following steps:

1. Press Notes (Ctrl+F7) and select Footnote; or select Layout, Footnote.
2. Select Edit Style in Note.
3. Move to the end of all the codes in the dialog box. You should see something similar to what is shown in Figure 65.7.

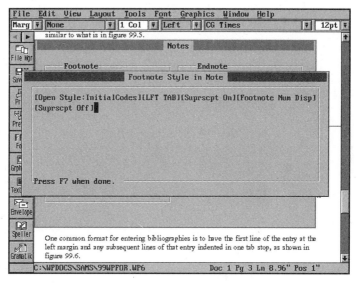

Figure 65.7. Changing the style of footnote text for this document.

4. Press Font (Ctrl+F8) and select Relative Size; or select Font, Size/Position.
5. Select Small. Press Exit (F7) to exit the dialog box. If you used the Footnote function key in Step 1, press Exit or Enter to return to your document.

Copying Your Footnote Style to Your Personal Style Library

You may want to use your customized footnote style in other documents. To do this, you must copy the footnote style from your current document to your personal style library. First, make sure that you have set up a personal style library in Setup, as explained in Chapter 39. Then complete the following steps:

1. Press Layout, Styles (Ctrl+F8), then Options.
2. Choose List System Styles and choose OK.
3. Highlight the Footnote style. Notice that there is no bullet in the Type column. The absence of the bullet indicates that this style has been customized.
4. Select Copy.

5. In the Copy Styles dialog box, choose Personal Library

6. Choose Close to return to your document.

Bibliography

One common format for bibliographies is to indent all but the first line of the entry, as shown in Figure 65.8.

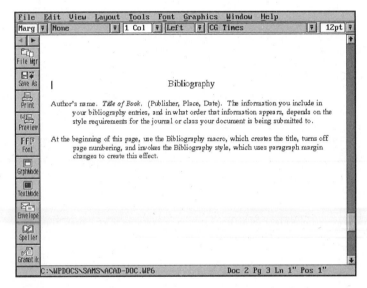

Figure 65.8. A sample bibliography format, using the Bibliography Style in ACADEMIC.STY.

Earlier versions of WordPerfect achieved this look with a hanging indent. WordPerfect 6.0 also has hanging indents, but an easier approach is to use WordPerfect's new paragraph margin settings (Layout, Margins, Left Margin Adjustment 0.5", and First Line Indent 0.5").

> **Tip:** To create a hanging paragraph without changing your paragraph margins, press Indent (F4), BackTab (Shift+Tab) at the beginning of the paragraph.

There are three important advantages to using the Margins features instead of Hanging Indent:

▲ Paragraph Margins are not dependent on your tab settings, as are Indents, Double Indents, and Hanging Indents.

▲ Editing pargraphs that use Hanging Indents can be tricky because the Indent and BackTab codes can get separated from the text. Another problem is that if you delete one of the codes by mistake, there's no intuitive way to fix it.

▲ Even more important for a bibliography, you can sort the bibliographic entries easily if you use paragraph margins. Sorting paragraphs that use hanging indents is tricky.

Caution: Due to one of WordPerfect's idiosyncrasies, you cannot sort a bibliography easily if you used a paragraph style (such as our Bibliography style) in which the Enter Key Action defined as Off/On, so we've provided a macro called SORTBIB.WPM that does this for you. To run the SORTBIB macro, press Alt+F10, type the word `sortbib`, and press Enter. If the ACADEMIC button bar is active, just click the Sortbib button.

The Bibliography Style in ACADEMIC.STY uses Paragraph Margins. This style is defined as a paragraph style because bibliographic entries are always a single paragraph. The Enter Key Action is defined as Off/On, which means that when you press Enter, the Bibliography style is turned off and immediately turns the Bibliography style back on. This option is ideal for when you need to format a series of similar paragraphs, as in a bibliography. Once you turn the Bibliography style on, simply type an entry, press Enter, type the next entry, press Enter, and so on, without worrying about the formatting.

Note: The BIBLIOGR.WPM macro, included on the disk, inserts the word *Bibliography* centered in a large font on a new page, enters two hard returns, and turns on the Bibliography style. If you use this macro, just type each bilbiographic entry and press Enter to start the next one. The SORTBIB.WPM macro, also on the disk, uses the word *Bibliography* to determine what part of the file to sort.

When you are finished entering bibliographic entries, turn off the style by choosing Style (Ctrl+F8), then selecting the None style, or by choosing the None style from the ribbon.

Tip: Because the Bibliography style is defined as a paragraph style, you can apply it to an existing paragraph without blocking the paragraph.

1993		OCTOBER			1993	
Sunday	Monday	Tuesday	Wednesday	Thursday	Friday	Saturday
					1	2
3	4	5	6	7	8	9
10	11	12	13	14	15	16
17	18	19	20	21	22	23
24	25	26	27	28	29	30
31						

by Marilyn Horn Claff

Monthly Calendar

Keeping track of your time and activities is a challenge. A calendar that shows you a full month at a glance can be a great help, but it doesn't take long before a handwritten calendar has so many corrections and changes that it's impossible to read. With our calendar template and macro, you can easily generate a new blank calendar in a matter of seconds. The finished calendar is a table, so it's easy to edit.

WordPerfect 6.0 Features Used

Landscape page
Table
Paragraph styles

Files Used

MONTHCAL.PRO
MONTHCAL.WPM (macro)

Fonts Used

Davida Bold   (included on the *Super Book* disk)
Swiss Bold
Dutch Roman (which comes with WordPerfect)

Creating the Calendar Template

To create the monthly calendar, we'll create a calendar template as a table. Because the number of weeks in a month varies from four to six, we designed the calendar template to consist only of the title rows and the row that represents the first week. A macro prompts the user for the month and the year, determines the starting day of the week and the number of days in that month, and expands the table to the correct number of rows. The user doesn't have to do any calculations or delete any empty rows.

Tip: If the table cells are too small for your notes, use endnotes to attach notes to specific days.

First, from the Format Page dialog box, set your page to landscape and turn on Center Current Page. Because the number of weeks in a month varies from four to six, we chose to use a macro to expand the number of rows to accommodate the correct number of days for that month so the user doesn't have to delete any empty rows.

1. To duplicate our template, create a table with three rows and seven columns (see Figure 66.1).

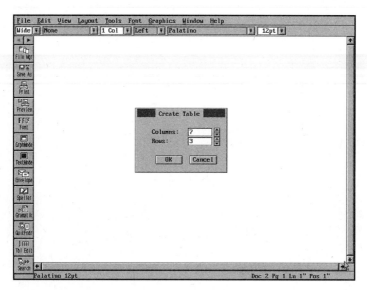

Figure 66.1. The Table dialog box with seven columns and three rows.

2. In Table Edit mode, block the entire table and change the Line Style to Single and the Border Style to Single.

3. Block the five center cells in the first row and join them.

4. Block all the cells in the second row and change the shading to 10 percent.

5. While still in Table Edit mode, block all the cells in the first two rows and change the justification and vertical alignment to Center.

6. Block the cells in the first row and change the Cell Attribute Size to Extra Large. The changes you make at the Cell Attribute dialog box apply to all the blocked cells. (You aren't using the bold attribute here because you'll be using a bold font.)

7. Block the cells in the second row and change the Cell Attribute Appearance to Bold.

8. Next, change the row options for each of the three table rows. From the Table Edit mode, choose Row to display the Row Format dialog box (see Figure 66.4).

   a. Change the Lines of Text option for the first row to Single.

   b. Change the Row Height for the second row to Fixed and 0.3". Change the Lines of Text option to Single (see Figure 66.2).

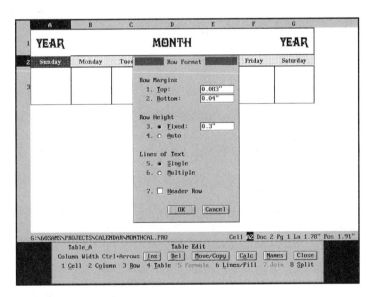

Figure 66.2. The Row format dialog box.

   c. Change the Row Height for the third row to Fixed and 1".

9. Change the width of the table columns to 1.1". The easiest way to change multiple column widths is to block at least one cell from each column before choosing Column. The settings you change at the Column Format dialog box apply to all the blocked columns (see Figure 66.3).

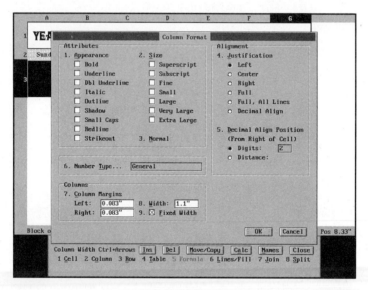

Figure 66.3. Column format dialog box.

10. Change the Table Position to Center.

    Press F7 to exit to the regular editing screen.

11. In the first and third cells of the first row, type the word year. In the second cell of the first row, type the word month.

12. Starting and ending with the insertion point in the first row, bold the three words and choose Font. From the Font dialog box, change the typeface to Davida Bold and the point size to 13 pt. These font codes are inserted as revertible codes.

13. In the second row, type the names of the days of the week.

14. Starting and ending with the insertion point in the second row, block the names of the week and change the typeface to Swiss Bold and the point size to 12 pt. These codes are inserted as revertible codes.

15. In Table Edit mode, lock the cells in the second row and exit back to the main editing screen.

From the **Layout, Page** dialog box, choose Center Current Page.

Note: If Auto Code Placement is On, you don't have to move the insertion point to the beginning of the document before choosing this option.

Creating the Styles

We've used a Paragraph style called Number to format the date numbers. The Number style is linked to another Paragraph style called DayText, which controls the remainder of the cell. To create the Number and DayText styles, perform the following steps:

1. Create the Number paragraph style that changes the typeface to Davida Bold, the point size to 13 pt. and include a flush right code. The Number style should be linked to the DayText style. (In WordPerfect, you can't add the linking information unless the linked style already exists.) Your completed Number style definition should look like the one shown in Figure 66.4.

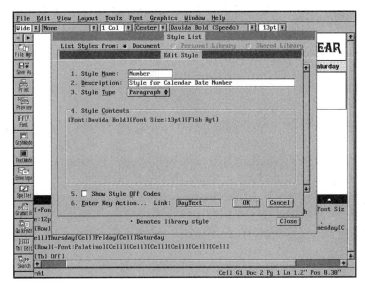

Figure 66.4. Number style.

2. Create the DayText paragraph style that changes the typeface to Dutch Roman and the point size to 10.5 pt. The Enter key should be defined as Off/On. Your completed DayText style definition should look like the one shown in Figure 66.5.

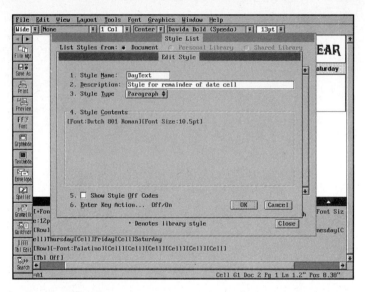

Figure 66.5. DayText style.

When you exit from the Style List dialog box, your calendar template should look like the one shown in Figure 66.6.

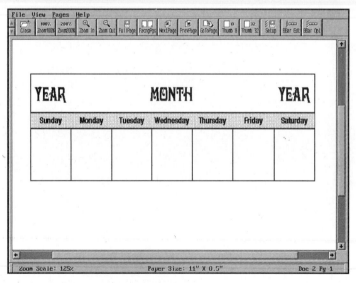

Figure 66.6. Print Preview of the template.

Save your table template as MONTHCAL.PRO and clear your screen.

Running the MONTHCAL Macro

The Monthcal macro included on the *SuperBook* disk retrieves the MONTHCAL.PRO file from the current directory, prompts you for the year and the month, and constructs a calendar that starts on the correct day of the week and includes the appropriate number of days for that month.

To use the Monthcal macro, complete the following steps:

1. Copy MONTHCAL.WPM to your macro directory. Be sure that the MONTHCAL.PRO calendar template is in your current directory.

2. Run the macro by choosing **Tools**, **Macro**, **Play** or press Alt+F10. Then enter the name of the macro (MONTHCAL).

3. The macro retrieves the MONTHCAL.PRO template and prompts you for the year. Enter the year and choose OK (see Figure 66.7).

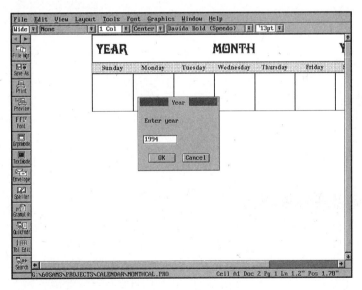

Figure 66.7. MONTHCAL macro prompting for the year.

4. The macro prompts you for the month. Select the month that you want and choose OK (see Figure 66.8).

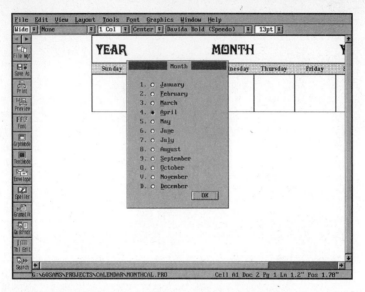

Figure 66.8. MONTHCAL macro prompting for month.

> **Note:** MONTHCAL suggests the current year and month as its defaults.

5. Sit back and wait. In a few seconds (or minutes, depending on the speed of your computer), you'll have a calendar that looks like the one shown in Figure 66.9.

To add appointments or other information to your calendar, follow these steps:

1. Move your insertion point to the cell for the appropriate date.

2. If your insertion point is on a number (as it will be if you moved into that cell from the cell above or from the cell to the left), press the down arrow to move to the line below the number in the same cell. (If you moved into the cell from the cell below or to the right, the insertion point should already be on the line below the number.)

3. Type the appointment text. If you have more than one item per day, when you press Enter, the DayText style will be turned off and back on again, so all of the items are formatted the same way.

4. Use the regular table navigation keys to move to the next cell where you need to enter an appointment. The styles used in one cell will not affect the text in adjacent cells.

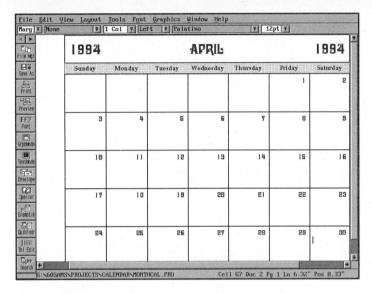

Figure 66.9. The completed calendar.

Note: Because the Number style is a paragraph style linked to the DayText paragraph style, as soon as you move the insertion point below the number, anything you type will be formatted by the DayText style.

Note: We've set up the table so that the rows have a fixed height. If you need to be able to expand the cell to accommodate longer notes, open the MONTHCAL.PRO file, move your insertion point into the third row, choose Table Edit mode (Alt+F11), then choose Row. In the Row Format dialog box, change the row height to Auto. Then choose Close to return to your regular editing screen.

Student of the Year
awarded to
Your Name
For outstanding achievement
at Boston Latin High School
during the 1993-1994 academic year
Date

_____   _____
Date   Principal

by Marilyn Horn Claff

Certificate

Awards and certificates are a popular desktop publishing project that you can do easily with WordPerfect. We've created a sample certificate (shown at the beginning of this project) that you can modify or turn into a "merge from the keyboard" that pauses for you to fill in the name, date, and other variable information. Certificates are a good application for merging from the keyboard because you may have to do several at once. If you need to print more than a dozen, you'll probably want to modify the file for a regular merge with a data file containing a list of award recipients.

WordPerfect 6.0 Features Used

> Open style
> Landscape page
> Page border
> Font size (revertible code)
> Advance down
> Parallel columns
> Graphics lines
> Merge keyboard command

Files Used

CERTIF.PRO
CERTIF.FF

Fonts Used

EnglishTowne Normal

We've kept this certificate simple. We use only one typeface, EnglishTowne, in various sizes. If you plan to print your certificate on special certificate paper, eliminate the page border.

Creating the Certificate Style

We've created an Open style called Certificate that contains the basic formatting for the certificate. You could use direct formatting instead of a style, but you'll find it easier to create multiple certificates if you use a style.

1. Choose Layout, Styles or press Alt+F8. Then choose Create and enter Certificate as the style name. WordPerfect defaults to paragraph styles, so change the style type to Open. Then choose OK.

2. At the Edit Style dialog box, enter the description for the title, and then choose Style Contents.

3. Choose Layout, Page to open the Page Format dialog box.

4. Change the paper size type to [Paper Sz/Typ:11" x 8.5", Letter(Landscape)].

5. From the Page Format dialog box, add a page border.

   Choose Page Borders.

   From the Create Page Border dialog box, choose Border Style.

   From the Border Styles dialog box, choose Thick Thin Border.

   The Thick Thin border, one of WordPerfect's predefined border options, has a thick outside line and a thin inside line (see Figure 67.1).

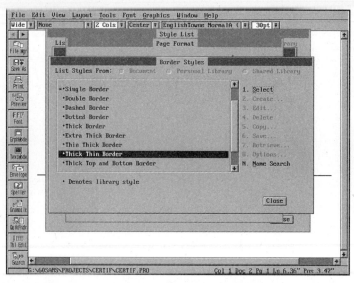

Figure 67.1. Selecting the Thick/Thin page border style.

6. From the Page Format dialog box, choose Center Current Page.

7. From the Line Format dialog box, choose Center Justification and set the Line spacing to 1.1. Changing the line spacing to 1.1 increases the line spacing by 10 percent.

8. From the Font dialog box, choose EnglishTowne Normal and change the point size to 30 (see Figure 67.2).

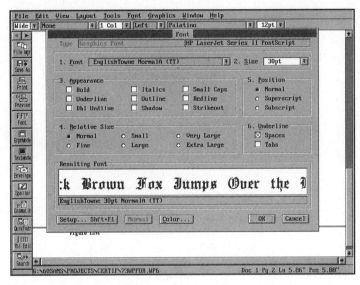

Figure 67.2. The Font dialog box.

9. Exit from the Style Contents box. Your Certificate style definition should look like the one shown in Figure 67.3.

10. Choose OK, and then Select to select the Certificate style.

Creating a Certificate

1. Now type the text of the certificate, changing it to fit your situation.

```
AWARD TITLE
awarded to
NAME
For outstanding achievement
at INSTITUTION
during the 1993-1994 academic year
DATE
```

Press Enter twice after the DATE. Your screen should look like the one shown in Figure 67.4.

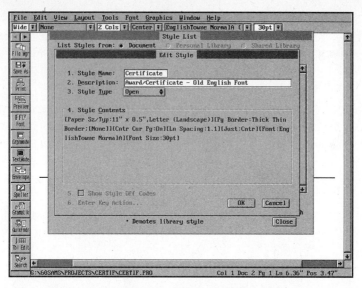

Figure 67.3. Certificate style definition (the Style Edit dialog box).

 Tip: Avoid embarrassment—don't forget to check spelling in your document. It's too easy to miss typos with an ornate font like EnglishTowne.

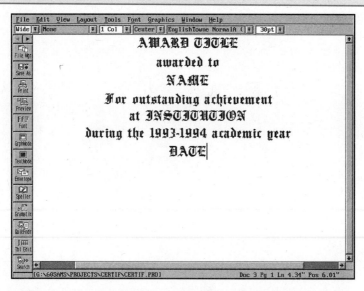

Figure 67.4. The text for the certificate before changing font sizes.

2. Your next step is to change the size of the text for the Award Title, Name, and Date lines. Instead of using relative font sizes, such as Large or Very Large, set precise size using WordPerfect's Font Size feature. For each of these lines, do the following:

Block the line of text (see Figure 67.5).

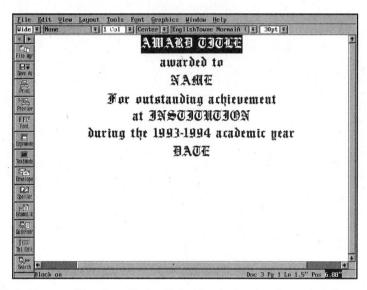

Figure 67.5. The certificate with text blocked prior to changing the point size.

 Note: The point size affects the amount of space inserted by a hard return. To duplicate this certificate exactly, highlight just the text, without the hard return at the end of the line. If you include the hard return character, the spacing in your certificate will be different from our example.

Choose Font, then Size. Type the new point size and choose OK.

Make the Award Title and the Date 48 points and the Name 54 points.

When you change the format for a block of text, WordPerfect inserts revertible codes. Revertible codes affect only the blocked text. At the end of the block, the formatting reverts to the settings that are in effect before the block.

All the text that we didn't block remains at its original size of 30 points. (This point size is set in the Certificate style.)

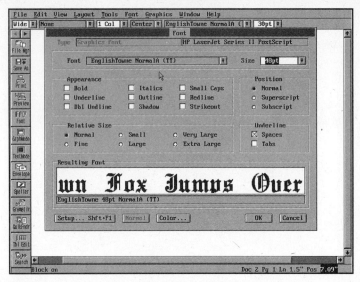

Figure 67.6. The Font dialog box with size highlighted.

Creating the Signature Lines

There are many possible ways to create signature lines in WordPerfect, but the following technique works especially well for side-by-side lines.

1. Choose Layout, Columns.

2. For the Column Type, choose Parallel with Block Protect.

   Block Protect isn't necessary in a one-page document, but it could be important in a document with a long series of signature lines.

3. Change the distance between columns to 1.5 inches (see Figure 67.7).

   Choose OK to accept the changes and turn on columns.

4. Now add a graphics line to the left column.

   Choose Graphics, Graphics Lines, Create.

   Choose OK to accept the default settings. Because WordPerfect's default setting for horizontal position is Full, you have a graphics line that extends the width of your column. (If you later change the column margins, the length of the line adjusts to the new margins.)

   Press Enter to insert a hard return. The insertion point is now beneath the line. Center justification is still in effect, so anything you type is centered (see Figure 67.9).

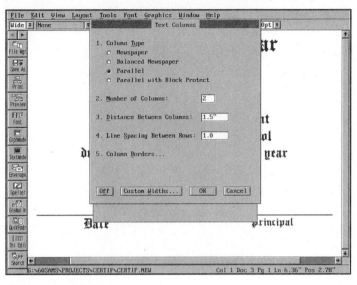

Figure 67.7. Setting up parallel columns for the signature lines.

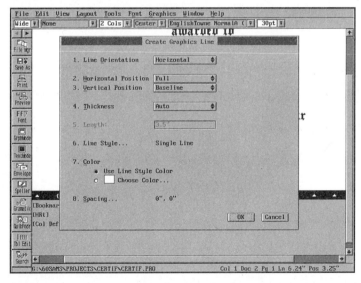

Figure 67.8. Graphics line.

Type the word Date and press Ctrl+Enter to insert a hard column break ([HCol]) and move the insertion point to the right column.

Figure 67.9. The signature line.

Repeat Step 4.a to add a graphics line to the right column.

Press Enter and type the title of the person who will be signing the certificate.

You're done! Your certificate should look like the one shown in Figure 67.10.

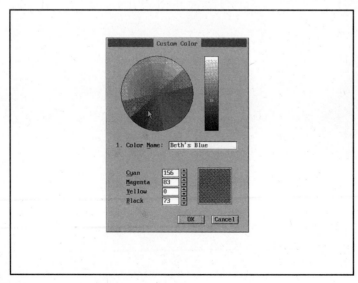

Figure 67.10. The completed certificate.

Note: The Thick Thin Border may display as a single thick border on the screen. If you zoom in on the border in Print Preview, you should be able to distinguish two separate lines, as shown in Figure 67.11.

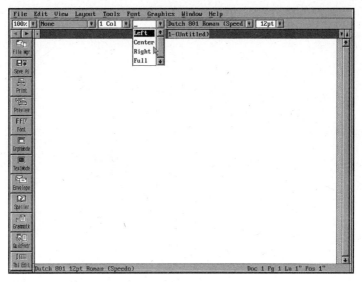

Figure 67.11. Zooming in on the certificate border in Print Preview.

Using the Certificate for a Merge from the Keyboard

Modifying the certificate so you can use it as a merge from the keyboard is easy:

Note: A version of the certificate set up for a merge from the keyboard is provided on the *Super Book* disk as CERTIF.FF.

1. Move the insertion point to the first line where you want the merge to pause. (For example, move to the NAME line.)
2. Press Alt+F3 to turn on Reveal Codes. Delete the text without deleting any formatting codes.

3. Press Shift+F9 to display the Merge Codes dialog box, choose Form, and then choose OK.

> Note: The next time you press Shift+F9 in this document, WordPerfect skips this dialog box and goes directly to the Merge Codes (Form File) dialog box.

4. At the Merge Codes (Form File) dialog box, choose Keyboard (see Figure 67.12).

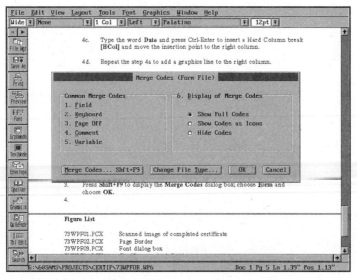

Figure 67.12. The Merge Codes (Form File) dialog box.

5. At the Parameter Entry dialog box, enter the text that you would like displayed on the status line as a prompt for the user. If you don't want a prompt, just choose OK (see Figure 67.13).

> Tip: It's a good idea to include at least one prompt message to remind the user to press F9 to continue. You might also precede the KEYBOARD command with a BEEP command to get the user's attention.

1030

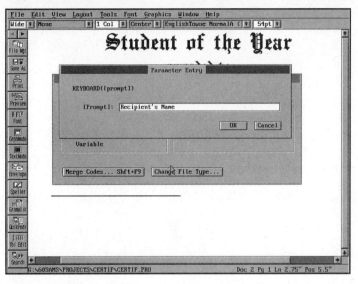

Figure 67.13. The KEYBOARD Parameter Entry dialog box.

 Note: Because it's clear from the context what text is required, you may not wish to include a prompt. If you do include a prompt, the form file appears to wrap lines incorrectly because the merge codes are taking space, but the final document won't be affected. If this spacing bothers you, change the display of merge codes to display as icons or hidden.

6. Repeat Steps 4 and 5 for each place where you want the merge to pause and save the file as CERTIF.FF.

7. To run the merge, from a clear screen, press Ctrl+F9 and choose Merge.

8. In the Run Merge dialog box, enter CERTIF.FF, the name of the certificate merge file in the Form File box. Leave the Data File box blank and choose Merge.

9. When the merge reaches a KEYBOARD code, it pauses for you to enter text. To resume the merge, press F9.

For more detailed information about merging from the keyboard, see Chapter 48, "Intermediate Merging."

PRESS RELEASE

Computer Novices of America, Inc.   Contact: John Witloss
3001 Executive Office Towers   Phone: 617-555-5555
Boston, MA 02101   Fax: 617-555-5556

FOR IMMEDIATE RELEASE

Computer Phobia Awareness Day

Boston, MA—November 11, 1993—In response to an intense public awareness campaign by the Boston Chapter of Computer Novice of America, Inc., Governor William Weld declared January 14th, 1994 to be the first annual Computer Phobia Awareness Day.

Lorem ipsum dolor sit amet, consectetu minimim veniami quis nostrud exercitatum tyriusmod tempor incidunt ut labore et eiusmod nonumy diam sed. Ectamen nedue enim haec et sinc novere eronylar at ille pellit sensar lupi expeting. In motuon sit et parvo eos et eccu delenit aigue duos dolor et moles. Ipsum dolor sit amet, consectetu minimim veniami quis nostrud exercitatum tyriusmod tempor incidunt ut labore et eisumod nonumy diam sed.

In motuon sit et parvo eos at eccu delenit aigue duos dolor et moles. Ipsum dolor sit amet, consectetu minimim veniami quis nostrud exercitatum tyriusmod tempor incidunt ut labore et eius nonumy diam sed.

Parvos eos at eccu delenit aigue duos dolor et moles. Ipsum dolor sit amet, consectetu minimim veniami quis nostrud exercitatum tyriusmod tempor incidunt ut labore et iami quis nostrud exercitatum tyriusmod incidunt ut labore et eisumod diam sed. Ectamen nedue enim meiusmod nonumy.

— END —

by Marilyn Horn Claff

Press Release

A press release should grab the reader's attention and provide key information in an easily assimilated format. Our press release uses an oversized title in a distinctive display font (Bitstream's Umbra Regular, included on the *Super Book* disk) with a paragraph border for additional emphasis. The contact information is presented clearly and simply in a slightly larger than usual font. Two black bars with reversed type set off the body of the press release. Bold, italic, and small cap attributes impart a sense of urgency and importance to the words, *For Immediate Release*. The second black bar highlights the word *End*, the traditional closing for press releases.

WordPerfect 6.0 Features Used

> Paragraph Borders and Fills
> Paragraph Styles
> Reversed Type (paragraph)
> Small Caps
> Letterspacing
> Table lines
> Table Column Margins

File Used

> PRESSREL.PRO

Fonts Used

> Umbra Regular (on disk)
> Swiss 721 Bold Italic (which comes with WordPerfect)
> Dutch 801 Roman (which comes with WordPerfect)

Creating the Press Release Styles

When you send out a press release, always use a consistent format so your readers recognize it as yours. The easiest way to achieve consistency in WordPerfect is to use the Styles feature. Styles provide other advantages as well:

▲ Styles reduce production time

▲ Styles help reduce WordPerfect's "code clutter"

▲ Styles make it possible to reformat documents easily

We will create three paragraph styles for our press release:

▲ Title

▲ Story Title

▲ Bar

The Title style controls the formatting for the words *Press Release*, the Story Title style controls the formatting for the title of the story, and the Bar style controls the formatting for the two black bars at the beginning and the end of the story.

Rather than create an Open style to set up the press release, we've opted to change our Document Initial Codes for this document. It's always a good idea to put as many of the formatting codes as possible in Document Initial Codes, because this technique gets the codes out of your way.

In WordPerfect 6.0, Document Initial Codes are treated like an Open style. Instead of changing our Press Release Document Initial Codes from the Layout menu, change them by modifying the InitialCodes style from the Style List dialog box. This method is more convenient, because we have to open the Style List dialog box to create our paragraph styles anyway. We'll make three changes to your InitialCodes style:

▲ Change justification to Full

▲ Change hyphenation to On

▲ Turn on Widow/Orphan Protect

WordPerfect's default justification is Left, which gives a ragged right margin. We've changed justification to Full because a ragged right margin does not look good with a symmetrical layout such as this one with its paragraph borders, flush right text, and centered titles. Whenever you use full justification, it's a good idea to also turn on hyphenation to avoid "rivers" of white space.

We've turned on Widow/Orphan Protection to keep WordPerfect from stranding single lines of paragraph text at the bottom or the top of pages.

1. Change the InitialCodes style:

   Press Alt+F8 to open the Style List dialog box (see Figure 68.1).

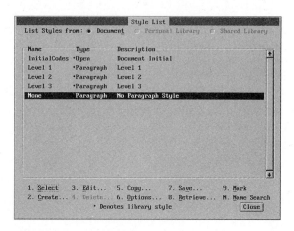

Figure 68.1. The Style List dialog box.

2. Select the InitialCodes style, choose Edit, then choose Style Contents.

3. From the Line Format dialog box (choose Layout; or press Shift+F8; then choose Line Format), change justification to Full and hyphenation to On.

4. Choose OK, then choose Other. Check the **Widow/Orphan Protect** box.

5. Choose OK, then Close. WordPerfect inserts the following codes into the InitialCodes Style:

   [Just:Full]
   [Hyph:On]
   [Widow/Orph:On]

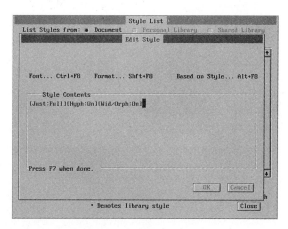

Figure 68.2. InitialCodes style with codes.

6. Press F7 twice to return to the Style List dialog box.

Now we'll create the paragraph styles for the Title, Story Title, and the reverse print bars. Although they take a little more effort to set up initially than direct formatting, paragraph styles are much easier to work with than direct formatting, because the codes "stick" to the paragraphs to which the styles are applied. (See the Styles section for more information about paragraph styles.)

To create the Title style, follow these steps from the Style List dialog box:

1. Choose Create and enter Title as the style name. WordPerfect defaults to paragraph styles, so you don't have to change the style type. Because you haven't entered any formatting codes in your document, ignore the Create from Current Paragraph checkbox, then choose OK.

2. At the Edit Style dialog box, enter the description for the title:

   Umbra 60pt., Thick Border, Centered

   Then choose Style Contents (see Figure 68.3).

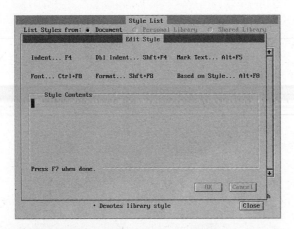

Figure 68.3. The Style Contents box with formatting options.

Notice the list of formatting options that appears above the Style Contents box.

3. From the Font menu (Font or Ctrl+F8), change the font to [Font:Umbra Regular] and the point size to [Font Size:60pt] (see Figure 68.4).

4. Next, add a thick paragraph border to the Title style. From the Layout menu (Layout or Shift+F8), choose Line. The Line Format dialog box appears. Choose Paragraph Borders.

5. From the Create Paragraph Border dialog box, choose Border Style.

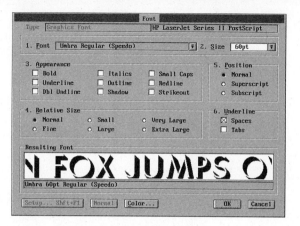

Figure 68.4. The Font dialog box (Umbra 60pt).

6. Highlight the Thick Border style and choose Select. WordPerfect returns to the Create Paragraph Border.

   Leave the Fill Style set to [None] and choose OK. WordPerfect inserts a [Para Border:Thick Border;[None]] code in the Style Contents box.

7. Press Center(Shift+F6). WordPerfect inserts a [Centr on Mar] code.

8. Press Exit or click F7 when done.

9. Now change the Enter Key Action to Off.

   Your screen should look like the Style Contents box shown in Figure 68.5.

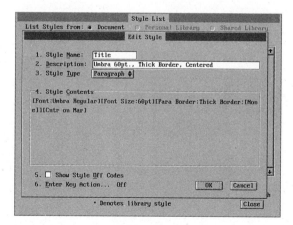

Figure 68.5. The completed Title Style.

10. Choose OK to return to the Style List dialog box to create the Bar style.

11. Follow the same general procedure to create the Bar style. In the Bar Style Contents box, press Shift+F6 to insert a [Centr on Mar] code.

12. Next, choose Font or press Ctrl+F8 to open the Font dialog box. Make the following changes:

```
[Font:Swiss 721 Bold Italic]
[FontSize:16pt]
[Sm Cap On]
```

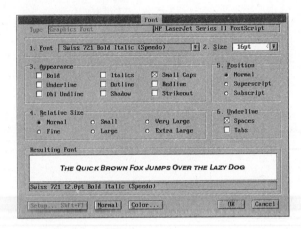

Figure 68.6. The Font dialog box.

13. From the Font dialog box, choose Color... to display the Color Selection dialog box.

14. Select White as the font color and choose Close. The Font dialog box should appear (see Figure 68.7).

15. The last step to create the Bar style is to add a paragraph border and change the background shading to 100 percent fill. With the insertion point still in the Style Contents box, choose Layout, Line Format, then Paragraph Borders. From the Create Paragraph Border dialog box, choose Fill Style dialog box, select 100% shaded fill (see Figure 68.8).

16. Choose OK twice, then Close to return to the Style Contents box. Your style should contain the following code:

```
[Para Border:Single Border;100% Shade Fill]
```

17. Press Exit or click F7 to exit the Style Contents dialog box.

18. Change the Enter Key Action to Off.

(Your completed Bar style should look like the one shown in Figure 68.9.)

Figure 68.7. The Font dialog box with reversed print.

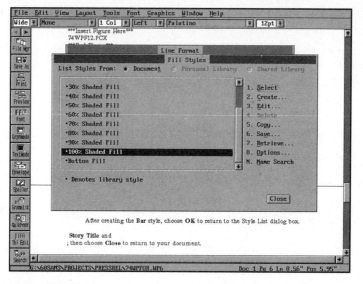

Figure 68.8. The Fill Style.

Note: Not all printers are capable of printing white on blank print. If the reversed text does not print correctly, you may still be able to print if you choose the Print Jobs Graphically option on the Print/Fax dialog box.

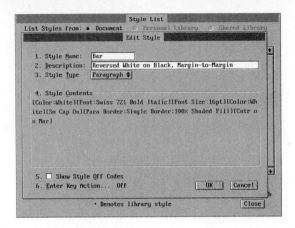

Figure 68.9. The completed Bar style.

19. After creating the Bar style, choose OK to return to the Style List dialog box.

You can now create your final style, the Story Title style. Fortunately, this style is much simpler than the others. Follow the same general procedure to create the Story Title style.

1. From the Style Contents box, choose Layout, Line Format, and change justification to Center.

   (Use Center Justification instead of Center Line in case the press release titles are more than one line.)

2. Choose Font or press Ctrl+F8 to open the Font dialog box. Choose Very Large.

3. Exit the Style Contents box.

4. Change the Enter Key Action to Off.

   (The Style Title style should look like the one shown in Figure 68.10.)

5. Choose OK then Close to return to your document.

Next, change the Document Initial Font to Dutch Roman 801, 12pt. Choose Layout, Document, Initial Font.

Now all the preliminary work is done and you're ready to create the press release.

1. At the main editing screen, type the words *PRESS RELEASE*, and turn on the Title style. If you use a mouse and have the ribbon displayed, click on the Title style from the drop-down style list (see Figure 68.11).

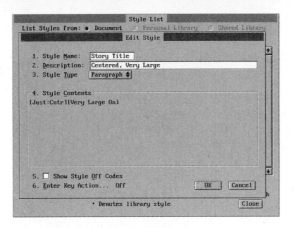

Figure 68.10. The complete Story Title Style.

Figure 68.11. Apply the Title style from the ribbon.

2. We've used a table with the lines and borders turned off for the contact information because tables have many more formatting options than columns.

   Create a table (Alt+F7, Tables, Create). Enter 2 for the number of columns and 1 for the number of rows (see Figure 68.12).

Figure 68.12. The Create Table dialog box.

3. Turn off all of the table lines. In Table Edit mode, block the entire table and choose Lines/Fill. In the Default Table Lines dialog box, change the Line Style to [None]. In the Table Border Fill dialog box, change the Border Style to [None].

4. Set the left margin of the left column and the right margin of the right column to 0" (see Figure 68.13).

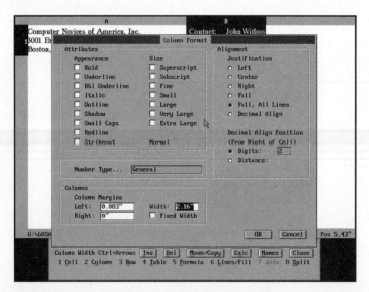

Figure 68.13. The Table Column margins for the left columns. Set the left margin of the left table column margin and the right margin of the right table column to 0" so that the table text is flush with the document margins.

Note: If you don't change the leftmost and rightmost table column margins to 0", the table text appears to be indented.

5. Change the Table Position to Full.

6. Change the cell attributes for both cells to Large.

7. Choose Close to exit Table Edit mode.

8. Type the contact address in the cell on the left and the contact person's name and phone number in the cell on the right. To enter a tab in a table cell, press Ctrl+A, then Tab.

9. Press Alt+F11 to return to Table Edit mode.

10. Use Ctrl+left arrow and Ctrl+right arrow to change the width of the column on the right until it is as narrow as you can make it without causing the text to wrap.

11. Change the column justification for the column on the right to Full, All Lines and choose OK. Press Close to return to the regular editing screen.

12. Insert two hard returns below the table and type the words *For Immediate Release*. With the insertion point anywhere in the paragraph, apply the Bar style to that paragraph. Move the insertion point to the end of the line and press Enter three times.

13. Type the title for your press release and apply the Story Title style.

14. Press Enter twice. Type the city and date, block them, and apply the Bold attribute.

15. To create the em dashes, press Ctrl+A, m-.

16. Type your press release or use WordPerfect's Retrieve into Current Document feature to insert an existing document.

17. At the end of the press release, press Enter twice, type the word - - End - - and apply the Bar style.

That's it! Save your press release. When you need to write another press release, make a copy of this one, delete everything between the two bar styles, and type in the new text.

		DATE	INVOICE
		6/17/94	1095

BILL
TO:

Mr. Sam R. Hooligan
977 Linden Drive
Chicago, IL 60601

Invoice

67	Widgets	23	$	1,541.00
176	What Knots	31	$	5,984.00
60	Gizmos	10	$	600.00
			$	0.00
			$	0.00
			$	0.00
			$	0.00
			$	0.00
			$	0.00
			$	0.00
			$	8,125.00

by Marilyn Horn Claff

Invoice

Although our invoice looks simple, it incorporates a great many WordPerfect features (see the figure on the first page of this project). The body of the invoice is obviously a table, but you may be surprised to learn that the entire invoice is actually a single table. We created it this way for two reasons: first, we wanted the address box to line up neatly with the description column, and secondly, it's much easier to move the insertion point through a single table than through two separate tables separated by regular text.

WordPerfect 6.0 Features Used:

Table formatting
Table header rows
Table calculations
Table locked cells
Table currency format
Date format code
Reversed type
Small caps
Letterspacing
Revertible codes
Advance
Hypertext macro button

Files Used

INVOICE.PRO

CALC_INV.WPM (macro)

Fonts Used

Dutch Roman
Swiss Bold

Copy INVOICE.PRO to your macro directory.

Creating the Invoice Template

If you need to print invoices at all, you probably need to print them on a regular basis. We've built as much of the formatting as possible into the invoice template so that you can just enter your data and calculate the total (using the linked CALC_INV macro) without worrying about formatting. To re-create our invoice template, use the following steps:

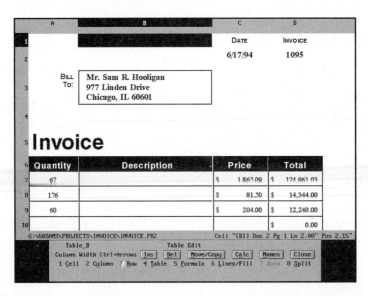

Figure 69.1. A view of an Invoice from the Table Edit dialog box (this illustrates that the billing information is part of the same table).

1. Open a new document window and change the left and right margins to .75 inches in Document Initial Codes. The narrowed margins allow a wider table.

2. You'll probably print your invoices on preprinted letterhead. Leave additional space at the top of the first page using Advance from Top of Page to begin printing 2 inches (or whatever distance you want) from the top of the page. Choose Layout, Other, Advance. In the Advance dialog box, choose Vertical Position and enter 2". WordPerfect inserts a [VAdvFromTop:2"] code in your document. This technique makes it easy

to print the first page on letterhead and the second and subsequent pages on plain paper, without having to use delay codes or worry about where the page breaks will fall (see Figure 69.2).

Figure 69.2. The Advance dialog box.

Tip: When you work in Graphics or Page mode, WordPerfect moves the insertion point when you use an Advance code. In Text mode, you must rely solely on the status line to see your actual position.

3. Create a table with 4 columns and 17 rows. The first part of the table provides billing information (see Figure 69.3).

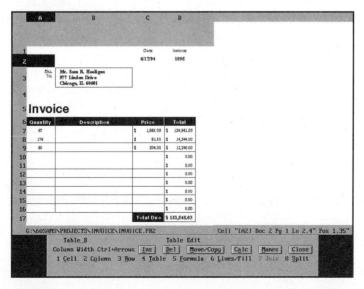

Figure 69.3. Table Edit mode showing 4 columns and 17 rows.

4. For each column, starting from left to right, choose Column to display the Column Format dialog box. Change the columns widths to:

Column 1   1.2"
Column 2   3.2"
Column 3   1.3"
Column 4   1.3"

and check the Fixed Width box so that the widths of the columns won't be affected by changes in other columns or in the document margins. Then choose Table. From the Table Format dialog box, change the Table Position to Full. Press Exit (F7) or choose Close to exit Table Edit mode.

Tip: To make two or more adjacent columns equal in width, block at least one cell from each before choosing Column. To make all columns equal in width, select Table to display the Format Table dialog box, and change the column width.

5. At the main editing screen, enter the text labels in the following cells:

C1   Date
D1   Invoice
A3   Bill To:
A5   Invoice

6. Press Alt+F11 to return to Table Edit mode. Choose Cell to display the Cell Format dialog box. Change the cell attributes to Bold and Small Caps for the cells containing the labels Date, Invoice, and Bill To. Change the Number Type to Text. Change the cell justification for the Date and Invoice label cells to Center, and the cell justification for the Bill To label cell to Right (see Figure 69.4).

Figure 69.4. Cell formatting options.

Note: After you are satisfied that the formatting is the way you want it, you can return to the Cell Format dialog box to lock cells that aren't used for data entry.

Note: By changing the cell type for these cells to Text, you won't add them to your calculated values by mistake. Nothing could be more embarassing than overbilling a client by the amount of his or her invoice number. (If you want to format the cell as a number, but not include the cell contents in your calculations, choose Ignore When Calculating.)

Tip: Whenever possible, use the built-in table formatting options, rather than the regular formatting codes. To use the built-in table formatting, choose options from the Table Edit dialog boxes. Using the built-in options helps to reduce code clutter and makes it less likely that the user will inadvertently change or undo the formatting because there are no codes to delete. Since the built-in formatting options apply only to entire cells, if you need to apply a certain attribute for only part of a cell, you must use the regular formatting codes.

7. In Table Edit mode, highlight cell C2 and choose Cell to display the **Cell Format** dialog box. Change the Number **T**ype to Date, then choose Select Date Format. Choose the second date format (Month/Day/Year), then choose OK twice to return to the Table Edit dialog box. By changing the date format for the cell, if you insert either a date text or date code in the date cell, the date is formatted correctly no matter what your default date setting is (see Figure 69.5).

Note: It's better to use the Date Text command rather than the Date Code command to insert the current date in your invoices (you will be able to tell when you wrote them). Because the Date Code always displays the current date, if you need to reprint an invoice at a later date, you wouldn't be able to tell when it was originally written.

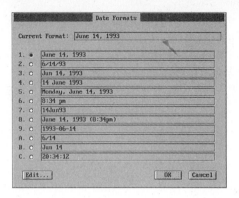

Figure 69.5. The Date format dialog box.

8. In Table Edit mode, block the cells in the fifth row and choose Join. Answer Y when WordPerfect prompts, `Join cells?`

9. In Table Edit mode, turn off the Border for the entire table. Choose Lines/Fill. At the Table Lines dialog box, choose Border/Fill. The Table Border/Fill dialog box, changes the Border Style to None.

9. In Table Edit mode, block the first five lines of the table and turn off the cell lines. Highlight the address cell and turn the cell lines back on for that cell to make it stand out. Because the billing address row is defined as multiline (the default), the box expands as you add more lines of text (see Figure 69.6).

10. Turn off the Left and Bottom lines for the first two cells in the last row.

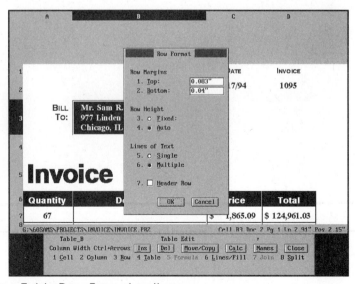

Figure 69.6. Table Row Format options.

11. In the document screen, block the word *Invoice* and change the typeface to Swiss Bold and the point size to 36. By blocking before changing the typeface and size, these formatting options are treated as revertible codes. In Reveal Codes, the On portion of a revertible code displays with a preceding plus (+) character and the Off portion with a minus (-) character. If you delete either the On or the Off code of a pair of revertible codes, its mate is deleted with it.

12. To create the reversed type, create a character style called Reverse that does the following:

▲ Changes the font color to white

▲ Changes the base font to Swiss Bold

▲ Changes the font size to Large

▲ Changes the letterspacing to 115 percent

13. To change letterspacing, choose Layout, Other, Printer Functions, Word Spacing and Letterspacing. Then choose Letterspacing, % of Optimal and enter 115%. Then press Home, Exit (F7) to return to your document (see Figure 69.7).

Tip: Use the Home, F7 key combination to exit from a dialog box, several layers deep, directly to your document editing screen. (Alas, the Home, F7 combination does not work from all dialogs.)

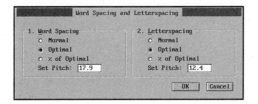

Figure 69.7. The Word Spacing and Letterspacing dialog box.

Note: Reversed type is not as readable as black-on-white, so use it carefully. To improve readability, we chose a bold version of sans serif font (Swiss Bold), increased the font size to large, and increased the letterspacing to 115 percent.

Caution: If the reversed type does not print correctly on your printer, you need to change one of the Output Options settings on the Print/Fax dialog box. Check the Print Job Graphically option. Your document will take longer to print with this option, but you'll be able to use light text against a dark background.

14. Block the cells in the title row and turn on the Reverse style. Be careful to begin and end the block with the insertion point in that row, so when you later lock the cells, the formatting is locked with them. If either the Style On or the Style Off codes is in an unlocked cell, it's possible to remove the formatting by deleting the style code.

15. Change the Fill Style for the title row and the Total Due cell to 100 percent shaded (see Figure 69.8).

    (Your text should appear in reverse.)

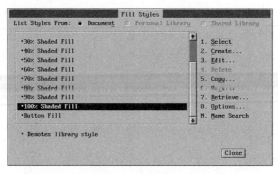

Figure 69.8. Fill Style—100 percent shaded.

16. Change the justification for the cells in the title row and the Total Due label cell to Centered.

17. Make the title row a table header row. Table header rows repeat on each page of a multipage table.

 Tip: In WordPerfect 6.0, any row can be a header row. In previous versions of WordPerfect, table header rows had to be at the beginning of the Table.

18. Change the column justification of the Quantity column to Center, the Description column to Left, and the Price and Total columns to Decimal Align.

1052

19. Change the Number Style Format for the Price and Total columns to Accounting. The Accounting format inserts the dollar sign at the left side of the cell and aligns the numbers on the decimal point.

20. Change the attributes for the last cell in the Total Column to Bold and Large.

21. Turn off the lines on the left and bottom sides of the first two cells in the last row of the table.

22. Change all of the cells except the cells in the Quantity, Price, and Total columns to Ignore when calculating.

 Note: This step is very important. If you omit it, you could add the invoice number to your total, unless you define the Number Type for the invoice number cell as Text.

23. Lock all the cells except the cells where you will enter data (the cells for the date, invoice number, billing address, and the cells in the Quantity, Description, Price and Total columns). Locking cells where no data entry is required makes it easier to fill out the invoice because the cursor skips over locked cells. A second benefit of locked cells is that users cannot inadvertently change the formatting.

24. Name the first column *Quantity* and the third column *Price*. (Figure 69.9)

25. In the first data entry cell in the Total column, enter the table formula Quantity*Price and copy it down to all but the last cell (see Figure 69.10).

26. In the last cell of the Total column, enter the formula + to total the cells above it.

Save the invoice form and enter your data. To calculate the total, click on the left side of the Total Due cell in the last row. This cell contains a hypertext button with a link to a macro called CALC__INV.WPM that calculates the total. (We placed the hypertext button in a table cell for aesthetic reasons. If the hypertext button were placed outside the table, the button would either have to be invisible, or it would print as it appears on-screen, which would not be acceptable on a real invoice. By placing the button in a table cell, it does not stand out, yet we can tell the user a precise location to click.)

To insert a hypertext macro, choose Tools, Hypertext, Create Link. Then choose Run Macro as the Hypertext Action, and Button as the Hypertext Appearance (see Figure 69.11).

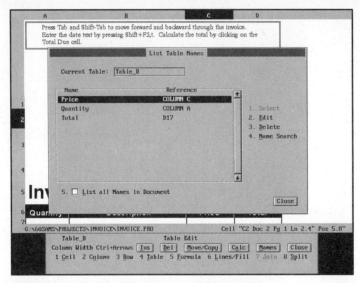

Figure 69.9. Name the columns Price and Quantity.

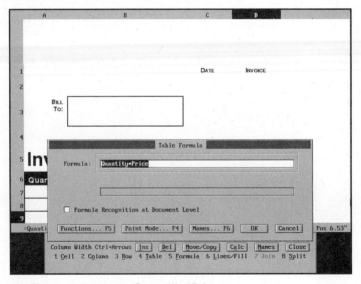

Figure 69.10. The cell formula Quantity*Price.

Caution: Although WordPerfect allows hypertext buttons in tables, it is very finicky about how they are inserted. The hypertext button should be the first code in the cell. If you edit this cell, be very careful not to change the order of the hidden codes.

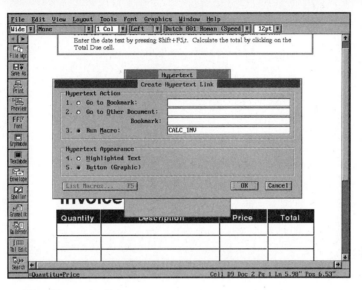

Figure 69.11. The Hypertext screen.

Use the following steps to calculate the total without using a macro:

1. With the insertion point in the table, press Alt+F11 to enter Table Edit mode.

2. Choose Calc, then Close; or press Exit (F7) to return to the regular editing screen.

To make tables to calculate, write a macro that uses the Calculate All option from the Tables/Columns dialog box to calculate all of the tables in a document.

> **Note:** Important! Your insertion point must be in the table in order to calculate, unless you use the Calculate All option from the Columns/Tables dialog box.

> **Note:** All of the cells with formulas display $ 0.00 when you calculate the results. You can delete these characters with the Delete key. When WordPerfect asks you if you want to replace the formula, answer N. If you choose Y, WordPerfect replaces the formula with nothing, and you won't be able to do additional calculations involving those cells.

Just desserts
from apple pie to zabaglione

May 16, 1994

Joe Fatso
Broadway
Fat City, Euphoria

Dear Sir:

We would be delighted to cater your wedding. Our menus are full of calories, but don't take our word for it. We would be delighted to cater your wedding. Our menus are full of calories, but don't take our word for it. We would be delighted to cater your wedding. Our menus are full of calories, but don't take our word for it. We would be delighted to cater your wedding. Our menus are full of calories, but don't take our word for it. We would be delighted to cater your wedding. Our menus are full of calories, but don't take our word for it.

We would be delighted to cater your wedding. Our menus are full of calories, but don't take our word for it. We would be delighted to cater your wedding. Our menus are full of calories, but don't take our word for it. We would be delighted to cater your wedding. Our menus are full of calories, but don't take our word for it. We would be delighted to cater your wedding. Our menus are full of calories, but don't take our word for it. We would be delighted to cater your wedding. Our menus are full of calories, but don't take our word for it.

We would be delighted to cater your wedding. Our menus are full of calories, but don't take our word for it. We would be delighted to cater your wedding. Our menus are full of calories, but don't take our word for it. We would be delighted to cater your wedding. Our menus are full of calories, but don't take our word for it. We would be delighted to cater your wedding. Our menus are full of calories, but don't take our word for it. We would be delighted to cater your wedding. Our menus are full of calories, but don't take our word for it.

We would be delighted to cater your wedding. Our menus are full of calories, but don't take our word for it. We would be delighted to cater your wedding. Our menus are full of calories, but don't take our word for it. We would be delighted to cater your wedding. Our menus are full of calories, but don't take

2888 Big Rock Candy Mountain Road, Sublimity, Oregon 97385
Tel. 555-873-3877   & & & & &   Fax 555-873-3878

Just desserts   Tel. 555-873-3877   Fax 555-873-3878

our word for it. We would be delighted to cater your wedding. Our menus are full of calories, but don't take our word for it. We would be delighted to cater your wedding. Our menus are full of calories, but don't take our word for it.

We would be delighted to cater your wedding. Our menus are full of calories, but don't take our word for it. We would be delighted to cater your wedding. Our menus are full of calories, but don't take our word for it. We would be delighted to cater your wedding. Our menus are full of calories, but don't take our word for it. We would be delighted to cater your wedding. Our menus are full of calories, but don't take our word for it. We would be delighted to cater your wedding. Our menus are full of calories, but don't take our word for it.

We would be delighted to cater your wedding. Our menus are full of calories, but don't take our word for it. We would be delighted to cater your wedding. Our menus are full of calories, but don't take our word for it. We would be delighted to cater your wedding. Our menus are full of calories, but don't take our word for it. We would be delighted to cater your wedding. Our menus are full of calories, but don't take our word for it. We would be delighted to cater your wedding. Our menus are full of calories, but don't take our word for it.

We would be delighted to cater your wedding. Our menus are full of calories, but don't take our word for it. We would be delighted to cater your wedding. Our menus are full of calories, but don't take our word for it. We would be delighted to cater your wedding. Our menus are full of calories, but don't take our word for it. We would be delighted to cater your wedding. Our menus are full of calories, but don't take our word for it. We would be delighted to cater your wedding. Our menus are full of calories, but don't take our word for it.

We would be delighted to cater your wedding. Our menus are full of calories, but don't take our word for it. We would be delighted to cater your wedding. Our menus are full of calories, but don't take our word for it. We would be delighted to cater your wedding. Our menus are full of calories, but don't take our word for it. We would be delighted to cater your wedding. Our menus are full of calories, but don't take our word for it. We would be delighted to cater your wedding. Our menus are full of calories, but don't take our word for it.

by Marilyn Horn Claff

Letterhead

With the WordPerfect's formatting capability and the right fonts, you can create surprisingly professional-looking letterheads right from WordPerfect. While snobs may turn up their noses at the very idea, a computer-generated letterhead makes good sense, especially if you are lucky enough to have a printer that can print at 600dpi or higher.

WordPerfect 6.0 Features Used

> Open Style
> Delay Codes
> Footer
> Header
> Advance

Files Used

LETTERHD.PRO
LETTERHD.STY
ALTL.WPM

Fonts Used

FormalScript (included on the *Super Book* disk)

The best argument for computer-generated letterheads is the dearth of printer bins in most business office printers. A typical business needs at least four bins (for plain paper, first and second sheet letterhead, and envelopes), but the majority of laser printers have only one or two. It's therefore up to you to make sure the correct paper is loaded in the printer before you print. If you share a printer with other users, another print job may intervene, and despite your precautions, your print job will print on the wrong paper. Creating your letterhead in WordPerfect and sending it to the printer along with your documents is one sure way to guarantee that your document will print with letterhead and that you won't waste paper (and time) because your document printed on the wrong paper.

Faxing directly from WordPerfect is another reason to create your letterhead on your computer. Without a computer version of your letterhead, documents faxed from your computer won't look professional and official.

Even if you are faxing from a traditional fax machine, you should create a computer version of your letterhead to avoid wasting expensive printed stationery. Most faxes are sent at only 100 dpi or 200 dpi. At that resolution, it's impossible for the recipient to tell whether the original document was produced on printed or computer-generated letterhead.

Our "Just desserts" letterhead is made up of three elements: a logo at the top of page 1, a footer that prints only at the bottom of page 1, and a header that begins on page 2. We've created an open style that includes all of the formatting and text that comprise the letterhead. All you need to do to use the letterhead is to turn on the Letterhead style at the beginning of the first page of your letter.

Because it's important to see what our letterhead looks like as we create it, we'll first create a regular document with all of the formatting elements that comprise the letterhead. When we're finished, we'll copy the text and formatting codes into an Open style. Then we'll copy the completed style definition to our default style library, so it will be readily available. Finally, we'll create a macro that turns on the Letterhead style and inserts the date text.

Creating the Logo for the First Sheet

1. From the Margin Format dialog box, change the top and bottom margins to 0.5".

2. From the Page Format dialog box, suppress Header A.

3. From the Header/Footer/Watermark dialog box, change the Space Below Header and the Space Above Footer to .2" (see Figure 70.1).

4. Change the typeface to FormalScript 421 Regular and the size to 80 point (see Figure 70.2).

5. Change the justification to Full, **All** Lines. This setting stretches the text horizontally to fill the available space between margins.

6. Type Just desserts and press Enter.

7. Change the point size to 30 points.

8. Change the justification to **Left**.

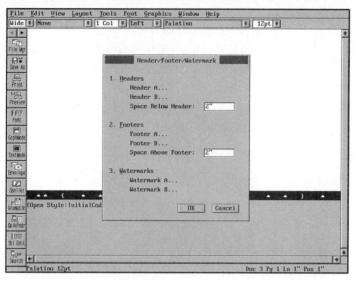

Figure 70.1. Changing the space below the header and above the footer.

Figure 70.2. The Font dialog box—FormalScript 80pt.

9. In the Advance Dialog box, enter Right 0.4" (see Figure 70.3).
10. In the Advance Dialog box, enter Up 0.15".
11. Type from apple pie to zabaglione and press Enter.

12. Change the font to Swiss 721 Roman and the size to 12 point. This font will be the base font for the body of your letter.

13. Change the left margin to 1.4". This will be the left margin for your letter.

14. Advance from the top of the page 2.5". This setting controls where the beginning of your letter will start.

Now we'll create the footer for the first sheet.

Creating the Address Footer for the First Sheet

1. Open a Footer window.

2. While in the Footer window, change the typeface to FormalScript 421 Regular and the font size to 13.5 points.

3. Change the left and right margins to 1.4".

4. Change the justification to Full, All Lines.

5. Type the following two lines of text (see also the opening image of this chapter):

```
2888 Big Rock Candy Mountain Road, Sublimity, Oregon 97385
Tel. 555-079-3077      & & & & &      Fax 555-873-3878
```

Note: To type the second line, type the phone number at the left margin, press Center (Shift+F6), type the ampersands (separated by spaces), and press Flush Right (Alt+F6).

Now that we've created the footer, we need to use a delay code so WordPerfect turns it off beginning on page 2. Use the following steps to create the delay code:

1. Choose Layout, Page, Delay Codes.

2. At the Delay Codes dialog box, choose 1 for the Number of Pages to Delay Codes. This setting causes the delay codes to begin on the next page.

3. In the Delay Codes dialog box, change the bottom margin to 1" and turn off footer A. WordPerfect inserts two codes in the box (see Figure 70.3):

```
[Bot Mar:1"]
[FooterA:Off;]
```

4. Press or click F7 to return to the main editing screen.

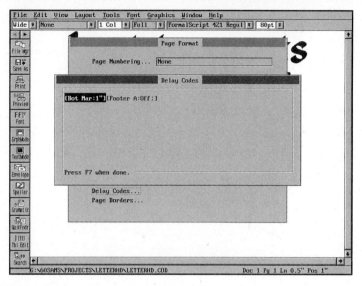

Figure 70.3. The Delay Codes box.

Creating the Letterhead Header

The second sheet of the letterhead is handled by a header that is suppressed on page one. Use the following steps to create the header:

1. From the Layout menu, choose Header/Footer/Watermark. Choose Header A, All Pages, Create.

2. Change the left margin to 1.4.

3. Change the typeface to FormalScript 421 Regular and the point size to 36pt.

4. To allow the *j* to jut into the left margin area, insert an Advance code to advance left 0.15".

5. Type the words `just desserts`.

6. On the same line, change the point size to 13.5.

7. Type seven spaces and the phone number. (We're using spaces here because nothing has to line up under the phone number.)

8. Press Flush Right (Alt+F6) and type the fax number.

9. Press F7 to return to your document.

Creating the Letterhead Style

To be able to use the letterhead we've created easily, we'll turn it into a style:

1. Move your insertion point to the very beginning of the document, before all codes (Home, Home, Home, up arrow).
2. Turn on Block (F12) and move the insertion point to the bottom of the document (Home, Home, down arrow).
3. Press Move (Ctrl+F4) and choose Copy and Paste.
4. Press Style (Alt+F8) and choose Create.
5. Enter Letterhead for the style name and change the style type to Open Style (see Figure 70.4).

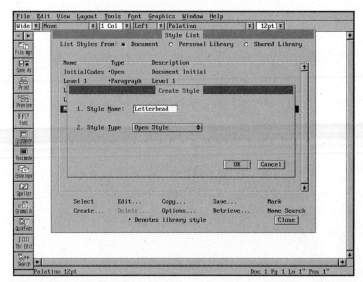

Figure 70.4. Create open style.

6. Enter a description for the style.
7. Choose Style Contents and press Enter to retrieve the block. Then press F7 to exit the Style Contents box.

Your screen should look like the one shown in Figure 70.5.

Press OK to return to the Style list.

8. In order to use your style with other documents, you must copy or save it to another style library:

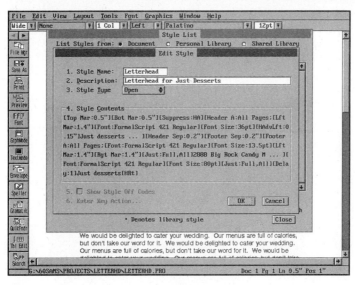

Figure 70.5. The Style contents of Letterhead style.

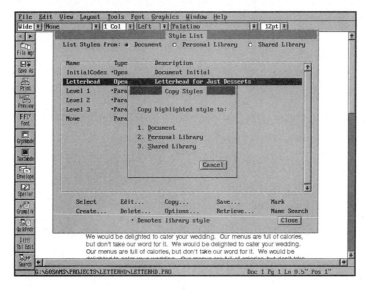

Figure 70.6. Style Copy.

9. Choose Copy to copy the Letterhead style to your personal style library (see Figure 70.6).

or

10. Choose Save to save your styles to a new style library (see Figure 70.7).

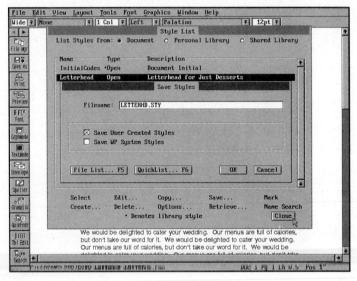

Figure 70.7. Style Save.

Creating the Letterhead Macro

To use your Letterhead style, first make sure that the style library containing your letterhead style is defined as your personal or shared style library. Then record a macro that does the following:

1. Opens the Style dialog box.
2. Chooses Personal Library or Shared Library.
3. Turns on the Letterhead style.
4. Inserts the date text.
5. Inserts two hard returns.

We've included a macro called ALTLZ.WPM on the *Super Book* disk that performs these tasks and provides an error message if the Letterhead style is not available in the personal style library.

fax

to:

attn:

from:

of:

voice:

fax:

pages: including this one

date:

time:

subject:

notes:

by Marilyn Horn Claff

Fax Cover Sheet

Fax cover sheets need to convey a lot of information in a form that is still legible after transmission. We've used oversized fonts and a table with the lines turned off to create a cover sheet that looks good, has plenty of room for writing, and is easy to fill out. We've included a simple macro that opens the FAXCOVER.PRO file and inserts the date and time for you. Add your name, company, fax and voice numbers to the cover sheet and save it. When you need to send out a fax, you'll be able to complete the cover sheet in no time at all.

WordPerfect 6.0 Features Used
Tables
Paragraph Style
Revertible Codes
Date Format

Files Used

FAXCOVER.PRO
FAXCOVER.WPM

Fonts Used

Mister Earl Normal (included on the *Super Book* disk)

Create the Table

1. Start by creating a table with two columns and twelve rows (see Figure 71.1).

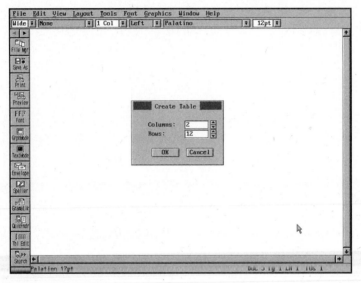

Figure 71.1. Create Table dialog box.

2. While still in Table Edit mode, block the entire table and turn off all the lines and borders. Choose Lines/Fill, Default Line, Line Style. Change the Line Style to [None] (see Figure 71.2).

3. From the Table/Lines dialog box, choose Border/Fill and change the border to [None] (see Figure 71.3). Exit from Table Edit mode.

4. Type the word fax in the first cell. Block it and change the typeface to Mister Earl Regular and the point size to 120 (see Figure 71.4).

> **Note:** When you change a typeface or font size when Block is active, the font codes are inserted as *revertible* codes. At the end of the block, the formatting reverts to the settings in effect before the beginning of the block. Because we were careful to use only revertible codes and paragraph styles for font changes in the left column, we've ensured that the text in the right column reverts to your Document Initial Font.

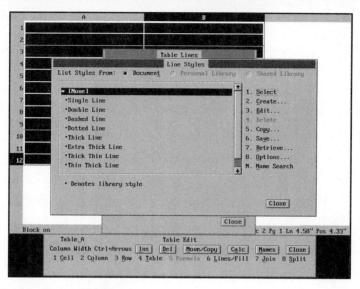

Figure 71.2. Line Style dialog box.

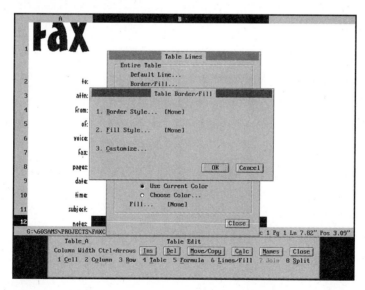

Figure 71.3. Border Style dialog box.

Figure 71.4. The Font dialog box.

5. Press Alt+F11 to return to Table Edit mode. Use Ctrl+right arrow and Ctrl+left arrow to adjust the width of the left column. Make the column as narrow as you can. (If the column is too narrow for the text, the text will either wrap to the next line or disappear, depending on how your options are set.)

6. Change the column justification for the left column to Right. Exit from Table Edit mode.

7. Add the following text labels to the cells in the left column:

   to:
   attn:
   from:
   of:
   voice:
   fax:
   pages:
   date:
   time:
   subject:
   notes:

8. Next, create a paragraph style called FaxHeader to format the text labels. The FaxHeader style changes the base font to Mister Earl Regular and the font size to 16 points and increases the letterspacing to 110 percent to

improve readability. Your completed FaxHeader style should look like the one shown in Figure 71.5.

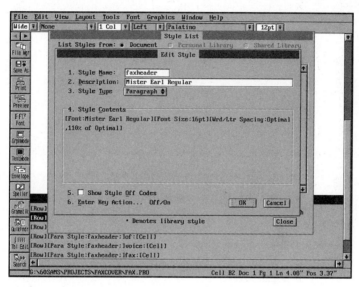

Figure 71.5. FaxHeader style.

 Note: We chose a paragraph style for the labels because paragraph styles are automatically turned off at the end of a cell.

9. We'll use a trick to apply the FaxHeader style to all of the cells in the left column in one step. Normally, you have to apply the style cell by cell, because WordPerfect does not provide a command to block a single column. Because the cells in the column on the right are still empty, however, the paragraph style doesn't have any effect on them. With the cells highlighted as shown in Figure 71.6, choose the FaxHeader style from the pull-down paragraph style list on the ribbon, or choose FaxHeader from the Style List dialog box.

10. Type a space and the words `including this one` in the cell to the right of the pages cell.

11. Move your insertion point into the cell with the word `date:` and change the date format to include the day of the week, the month, the date, and the year (see Figure 71.7). This date format determines the date format for the cell in the column on the right.

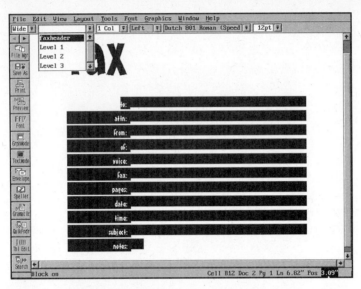

Figure 71.6. Block with the pull-down style menu.

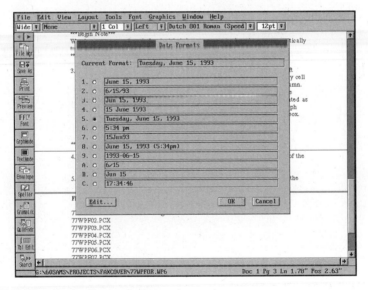

Figure 71.7. The Date Format dialog box.

12. Move your insertion point into the cell with the word `time:` and change the date format to display the hours and minutes (see Figure 71.8). This date format determines the time format for the cell in the column on the right.

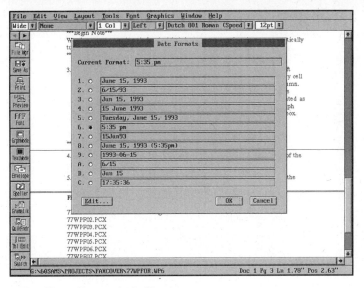

Figure 71.8. The Time Format dialog box.

13. In Table Edit mode, block all the cells in the left column and turn on cell lock. Then move the insertion point to the first cell in the right column (opposite the word fax) and lock it. Exit from Table Edit mode.

14. Add your name, company name, voice, and fax number in the appropriate cells. Turn on Table Edit mode and lock those cells so the insertion point skips over them in the regular editing screen.

15. Still in Table Edit mode, move the insertion point to the cell where the date will go and name the cell date (see Figure 71.9).

16. Move the insertion point down one row and name the cell time. (The fax macro uses the cell names to find the correct cells to insert the date and time.)

17. Save your fax cover sheet with the name FAX.PRO.

18. To fill in the fax cover sheet, run the fax macro included on the *Super Book* disk. The macro fills in the date and time using the date text feature, moves the insertion point up to the first empty field, and ends. Fill in the cells and press Tab to move to the next cell, or Shift+Tab to move back to the previous cell. Because all the cells except the data entry cells are locked, filling out the cover sheet is quick and easy.

Note: The fax macro assumes that the fax cover sheet FAX.PRO is in the current directory.

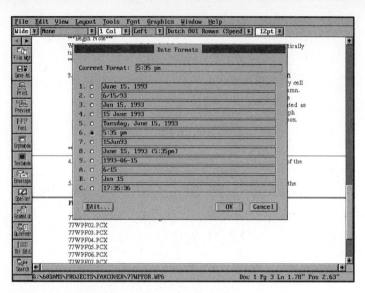

Figure 71.9. The Date Format dialog box.

You're invited

to a dinner party
in honour of
the 50th wedding anniversary
of Mr. and Mrs. Samuel Smith
given by their daughter Trixie
at the Rolling Acres Country Club
Seaside, New Hampshire
on July 15, 1995
at 7:00 pm

rsvp 555-234-9987

by Marilyn Horn Claff

Invitation

Use WordPerfect to create simple, yet elegant party invitations. We've used Subdivide Page to divide a landscape sheet of 8.5-inch by 11-inch paper into four quadrants, or logical pages. The cover text is rotated 180 degrees on the first quadrant and the inside text is placed on the fourth.

WordPerfect 6.0 Features Used
Landscape Page
Subdivided Page
Open Style
Text Box with Rotated Text

Files Used
INVITE.PRO

Fonts Used
FormalScript 421 Regular

Note: WordPerfect can rotate any graphics font on any printer capable of printing graphics (laser, inkjet, or dot matrix). If you choose one of your printer's built-in or cartridge fonts, you can rotate text only if the printer can perform the font rotation—most printers cannot. As long as you choose one of the fonts that comes with WordPerfect or on the *Super Book* disk, and you have a graphics-capable printer, you'll be able to rotate text.

Creating the Invitation Style

Start by creating an Open style called Invitation that will contain most of the formatting information. Once you have created the Invitation style, you can copy the style to your personal or shared style library so you can reuse the same settings for other invitations. To create the Title style, follow these steps:

1. Choose Layout, Styles; or press Alt+F8. Then choose Create and enter Invitation as the style name. WordPerfect defaults to paragraph styles, so change the style type to Open. Then choose OK.

2. At the Edit Style dialog box, enter the description for the title, then choose Style Contents.

3. Choose Layout, Page to open the Page Format dialog box.

4. Change the paper size type to [Paper Sz/Typ:11" x 8.5", Letter(Landscape)].

5. Choose Subdivide Page. At the Subdivide Page dialog box, enter 2 as the number of columns and rows and choose OK.

6. From the Font menu (Font or Ctrl+F8), change the font to [Font:FormalScript 421 Regular] and the point size to [Font Size:16pt] (see Figure 72.1).

7. From the Layout, Page dialog box, choose Center Pages.

8. From the Layout, Line dialog box, change the justification to Center and the line spacing to 1.2. Changing the line spacing to 1.2 increases the spacing between lines of text by 20 percent.

9. From the Layout, Margins dialog box, change the left, right, top, and bottom margins to 0.5".

10. Your screen should look like the Style Contents box shown in Figure 72.2.

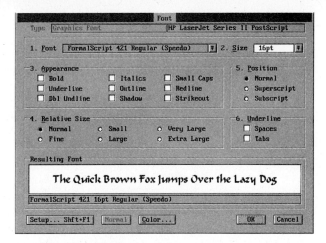

Figure 72.1. The Font dialog box.

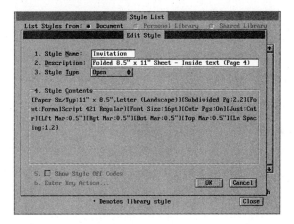

Figure 72.2. The Edit Style dialog box—shows all codes.

11. Press Exit or click F7 when done to exit the Style Contents box. Then choose OK to return to the Style List dialog box, and choose Select to turn on the Invitation style.

Creating the Invitation

1. We'll create the inside page first. The inside page will be the lower-right quadrant, or page 4. Press Ctrl+Enter three times to insert three hard page breaks, then type the text for the inside page of your invitation:

```
to a dinner party
in honour of
the 50th wedding anniversary
of Mr. and Mrs. Samuel Smith
given by their daughter Trixie
at the Rolling Acres Country Club
Seaside, New Hampshire
on July 15, 1995
at 7:00 pm
rsvp 555-234-9987
```

2. Block the `rsvp` line and choose Font, Relative Size, Small (see Figure 72.3).

Figure 72.3. The text of the invitation.

Creating the Invitation's Cover

1. Move your cursor to the first page. To rotate text in WordPerfect, the text must be placed in a graphics box, so choose Graphics, then Graphics Boxes, then Create to display the Create Graphics Box dialog box.

2. At the Create Graphics Box dialog box, you need to make several changes:

   2.a. Change Contents to Text.

   2.b. Change Based on Box Style to User. (User boxes do not have borders.)

2.c. Change **A**ttach To to **P**age.

2.d. Change Edit **P**osition to **F**ull Page.

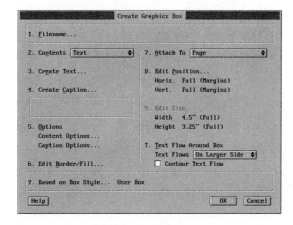

Figure 72.4. The Create Graphics dialog box—new settings.

Caution: The Full Page button only appears in the Edit Position dialog box if you first changed the Attach to setting to Page instead of Paragraph (default).

3. Still in the Create Graphics Box dialog box, choose Create Text.

4. In the editing window that appears, change the font and point size to FormalScript 721 Regular and 48 pt.

Note: Unless you've changed the BoxText system style, WordPerfect uses the Document Initial Font as your starting font. WordPerfect does not use your document font in a text box (unless it happens to be the same as your Document Initial Font). When you change a font in a text box, you don't need to change it back at the end of the text because font changes in text boxes do not affect the rest of the document.

5. Type the text for the front of the invitation (see Figure 72.5):

You're invited!

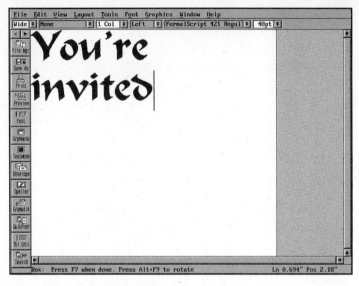

Figure 72.5. The user box with text.

6. Choose Alt+F9 to rotate the text. The Graphics dialog box appears (Figure 72.6).

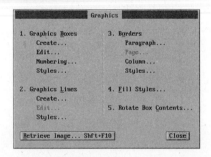

Figure 72.6. The Graphics dialog box.

7. Choose Rotate Box Contents (see Figure 72.7).

8. Choose 180° Rotation, then OK. Notice that the text does not appear rotated in this editing window.

9. Press or click F7 to return to the main editing screen. Your text should be rotated as shown in Figure 72.8.

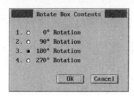

Figure 72.7. The Rotate Contents dialog box—180.

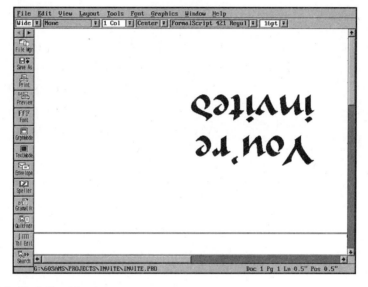

Figure 72.8. Rotated text.

10. Choose Print Preview to see your completed invitation. Your invitation should look like the one shown in Figure 72.9.

That's it! Save your invitation. When you need to design a new invitation, use this invitation style as your starting point.

Tip: To reuse your Invitation style, copy it to your personal or shared style library from the Style List dialog box.

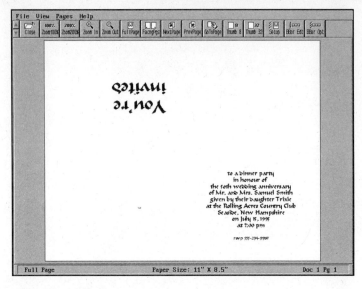

Figure 72.9. Print Preview.

Pygmalion Image Consultants
1001 Renovation Place, Boston, MA 02116

Mary-Lou Adams
150 Country Drive
North Attleboro, MA 02763

We'll make you over in our own image.

Pygmalion Image Consultants
1001 Renovation Place, Boston, MA 02116

Anne Appleby
65 Linden Street
Stoughton, MA 02072

We'll make you over in our own image.

Pygmalion Image Consultants
1001 Renovation Place, Boston, MA 02116

Penny Ballou
216 Juniper Road
Sudbury, MA 01776

We'll make you over in our own image.

Pygmalion Image Consultants
1001 Renovation Place, Boston, MA 02116

Suzanne Black
6 Spruce Road
Sudbury, MA 01776

We'll make you over in our own image.

Pygmalion Image Consultants
1001 Renovation Place, Boston, MA 02116

Susan Bush
669 Treelined Road
Wellesley, MA 02181

We'll make you over in our own image.

Pygmalion Image Consultants
1001 Renovation Place, Boston, MA 02116

Albert Canteen
65 McCarthy Terrace, Apt. 5
Stoughton, MA 02072

We'll make you over in our own image.

Pygmalion Image Consultants
1001 Renovation Place, Boston, MA 02116

Alan Flynn
354 White River Road
Arlington, MA 02174

We'll make you over in our own image.

Pygmalion Image Consultants
1001 Renovation Place, Boston, MA 02116

Jean-Paul Hatfield
89 Orchard Park
Boston, MA 02117

We'll make you over in our own image.

Pygmalion Image Consultants
1001 Renovation Place, Boston, MA 02116

Nancy Spector
200 Main Street
Cambridge, MA 02138

We'll make you over in our own image.

Pygmalion Image Consultants
1001 Renovation Place, Boston, MA 02116

Antonio Witherspoon
340 Tremont Street
Boston, MA 02117

We'll make you over in our own image.

by Marilyn Horn Claff

Shipping Labels

If you run a business, you probably take great pains to project the right image. Don't ruin it by using ordinary mailing labels generated in Courier by a database program! Here's a label design that looks good, is easily readable, and manages to squeeze in an advertising slogan to boot.

WordPerfect 6.0 Features Used
Labels
Page borders
Paragraph borders
Headers
Footers
Center all pages
Merge

Files Used

LABELS.PRO
LABELS.FF
PEOPLE.DF

Fonts Used
Swiss Bold (included with WordPerfect)
Dutch Roman (included with WordPerfect)

Mister Earl (included on the *Super Book* disk)

The company name and slogan are in Mister Earl, one of the Bitstream fonts on the *Super Book* disk, and the return address is in Swiss Bold. The recipient's address prints in your Initial Font, unless you include a font code in the document. We used Avery 5163 Shipping Labels, and added a rounded page border to emphasize the shape of the labels.

WordPerfect considers labels, like subdivided pages, as *logical pages.* A logical page is a subdivision of the physical page. In this case, the physical page is the full sheet of labels. Logical pages behave like regular pages in most ways: headers, footers, watermarks, page borders, page numbering, and page centering all affect logical pages. We've taken advantage of this design by using page borders to put a border around each individual label and by using a header and footer to repeat the company address and slogan on each label. We've also used WordPerfect's Center All Pages command to center the recipient's address between the header and footer on each label.

We've set up our labels as a merge form file (see Workshop X, "Merge"). If your names and addresses aren't in merge format, you can still use labels. Just separate each name and address with a hard page break and follow the formatting instructions.

Caution: Complex labels like these may not print on your printer. If you experience a printing problem, try these steps before you give up:

▲ Substitute built-in fonts for the graphics fonts we've used.

▲ Remove the graphics border and/or line.

▲ Add more memory to your printer if possible.

▲ If you have a PostScript printer, increase the time-out value by downloading a PostScript program to your printer. Using an ASCII editor, modify the TIMEOUT.PS file in your \WPC60DOS directory so that the numbers on the `setdefaulttimeouts` line are `0 0 0`. These values instruct the printer to wait an infinite amount of time for a print job, instead of giving up after a minute (or whatever your time-out value currently is). Then from DOS, copy the TIMEOUT.PS file to your printer, using the following syntax:

```
copy timeout.ps lpt1
```

▲ Check to make sure that you have an up-to-date printer driver for your printer. WordPerfect printer drivers are available from

WordPerfect Corp., from the WordPerfect Corp. bulletin board, and from the WordPerfect forum on CompuServe. If none of these suggestions helps, you may have to simplify your document format.

Creating the Labels

To eliminate code clutter in our label document, we'll put as much of the formatting as we can in Document Initial Codes. This step not only makes the complex labels document easier to work with because the codes are out of your way, but it ensures that you'll be able to merge sucessfully with this document.

1. Change your Document Initial Font to the font that you plan to use for the addresses of the recipients. We've used Dutch Roman 11.5 point.

2. Choose Layout, Document, Document Initial Codes.

3. Choose Layout, Page and Labels.

4. From the Labels dialog box, choose Avery 5163 Shipping (see Figure 73.1).

Note: If you do not see a list of predefined labels at the Labels dialog box, check your setup. The default label definitions are contained in a file called WP_WP_US.LAB, which WordPerfect looks for in the shared printer directory.

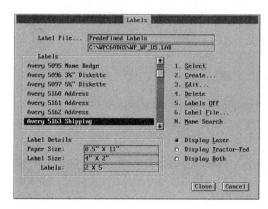

Figure 73.1. The Labels dialog box.

WordPerfect returns you to the Page Format dialog box.

5. Choose Center Pages.

6. Choose Page Borders.

7. From the Create Page Borders dialog box, choose Customize.

8. From the Customize Page Borders, change the Based on Border Style to Dashed Border.

> **Tip:** You may want to customize the dashed border. For example, you could increase the thickness of the line and the space between dashes.

9. Choose Spacing. WordPerfect displays the Border Spacing dialog box.
10. Turn off Automatic Spacing and choose Outside, Set All to set the amount of white space outside the border on all sides. Enter 0.15" as the amount. The dialog box should look like the one shown in Figure 73.2.

Figure 73.2. The Border Spacing dialog box.

Choose OK to return to the Customize Page Borders dialog box.
11. Choose Corners. Select Rounded and enter 0.2" as the radius value.

> **Note:** The lower the radius value, the less rounded the corner.

12. Press Close, and then OK twice to return to the Format dialog box.
13. While still in Document Initial Codes, choose Layout Margins to display the Margins dialog box. Change the left and right margins to 0.35" and the top and bottom margins to 0.25" (or your printer's minimum margins; see Figure 73.3). Press OK to return to the Format dialog box.

> **Note:** Remember, headers, footers, and other page elements are based on the settings in Document Initial Codes and on the Document Initial Font.

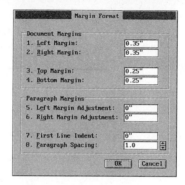

Figure 73.3. The Margin Format dialog box.

14. While still in Document Initial Codes, choose Layout, Header/Footer/
    Watermark and change the Space Below Header and the Space Above
    Footer to 0.1" (see Figure 73.4).

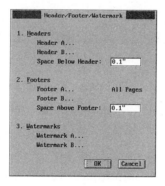

Figure 73.4. The Header/Footer/Watermark dialog box.

You should still be in Document Initial Codes. Now you need to create the header
and footer. In WordPerfect 6.0, you can create headers and footers in Document
Initial Codes. By creating them in Document Initial Codes, they won't clutter up the
text area of the document, and the merging will be more efficient, because the
codes won't be repeated on each label.

Creating the Header

1. Choose Layout, Header/Footer/Watermark. Then choose Headers, Header
   A, and then Create.
2. In the Header A editing window, change the justification to Center.
3. Change the typeface to Mister Earl and the point size to 14 pts.

4. Type Pygmalion Image Consultants and press Enter.

5. Change the typeface to Swiss 721 Bold and the point size to 10 pts.

6. Type 1001 Renovation Place, Boston, MA 02116.

7. From the Format, Line dialog box, choose Paragraph Borders.

8. Choose Customize, Lines, and then Select All. Choose [None] to turn off all four borders.

9. Choose Bottom and select Single Line. Choose Select and then Close to return to the Customize Paragraph Border dialog box (see Figure 73.5). Press Home, F7 to exit from all dialog boxes.

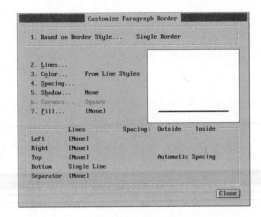

Figure 73.5. The Customize Paragraph Border dialog box.

Creating the Footer

1. From Document Initial Codes, choose Layout, Header/Footer/Watermark.

2. Create Footer A.

3. In the Footer A editing window, change the typeface to Mister Earl Regular and the point size to 12 pt.

4. Press Center (Shift+F6).

5. Type We'll make you over in our own image.

6. Press or click F7 to exit from Footer A. Then exit from Document Initial Codes.

Setting the Margins for the Label Addresses

So far, we've placed all our formatting codes in Document Initial Codes. One exception is the margins for the label text, which should go in the document area.

If we set the margins in Document Initial Codes, the margin settings would affect the header and footer, because the system styles for the header and footer include a copy of the Document Initial Codes. To avoid editing both the header and footer, insert the margin settings in the document area.

1. Change the left margin to 1".
2. Change the right margin to 0.8".

Tip: Rather than set equal margins for the addresses, make the right margin a little smaller than the left to allow for occasional long lines. If you made both margins narrower, most of the addresses would appear to be too far to the left.

Adding the Merge Codes

The final step is to add the merge field codes for your data file.

1. Press Shift+F9, choose Form, and then Field.

   The next time you press Shift+F9, WordPerfect doesn't prompt you for the type of merge file.

2. Enter the name of the merge field in the Parameter Entry dialog box.

3. Repeat Step 2 for each field that you need. Remember to use spaces and punctuation marks between fields as necessary.

Tip: If you have a merge form file, such as a letter with an inside address or an envelope, already set up with the names of the fields you need, you can save a few steps by copying the merge codes into your label file.

4. To merge with the PEOPLE.DF data file on the *Super Book* disk, use the following field names:

```
FIELD(FIRST) FIELD(LAST)
FIELD(ADDRESS)
FIELD(City), FIELD(State) FIELD(Zip)
```

Note: If the display of merge codes is set up to Show Full Codes, the merge fields for the address will probably split across two labels. Although the files will merge correctly, you may find this display annoying, If so, there's an easy solution: change the merge display to either Show as Icons or Hide Codes In Page mode, the address label with the codes displayed as icons appears in Figure 73.6.

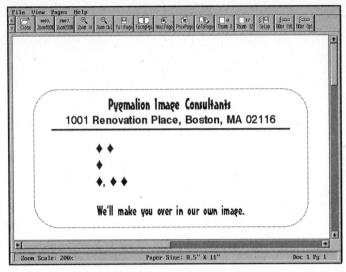

Figure 73.6. The label showing codes displayed as icons.

   5. Save the file as LABELS.FF.

Merging

To merge the labels with the sample data file, press Merge (Ctrl+F9). Enter LABELS.PF as the name of the form file and PEOPLE.DF as the name of the data file, and select Merge. Your finished merge should look like the one shown in Figure 73.7.

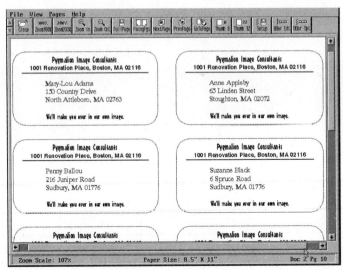

Figure 73.7. The finished merge.

Titles

1-2-3 In Business	$29.95
(0-672-22803-3) *Jun-91*	
1-2-3 Bible	$29.95
(0-672-22763-0) *Nov-91*	
1-800-Help with Wind. 3.1	$24.95
(0-672-30246-2) *Jun-92*	
Absolute Beginner's Guide to Programming	$19.95
(0-672-30269-1) *Jan-93*	
Active Filter Cookbook	$24.95
(0-672-21168-8) *May-75*	
Advanced C++	$39.95
(0-672-30158-X) *Nov-92*	
Advanced Digital Audio	$39.95
(0-672-22768-1) *Sep-91*	
Advanced C Tips and Tech	$29.95
(0-672-48417-X) *May-88*	
Advanced C	$39.95
(0-672-30168-7) *Oct-92*	
Audio System Design & Inst	$59.95
(0-672-22677-3) *May-90*	
Basic Electricity & DC Cir	$29.95
(0-672-27023-4) *1986*	
Basic AC Circuits	$29.95
(0-672-27025-0) *1986*	
BBO MS-DOS 5	$24.95
(0-672-48499-4) *Jun-91*	
BBO MS Windows 3	$24.95
(0-672-22708-8) *Jul-90*	
BBO DOS	$24.95
(0-672-22680-4) *Jul-89*	
Best Book of Lotus 2.3, 4/E	$26.95
(0-672-30010-9) *Jun-91*	
Best Book of Lotus 3.1	$27.95
(0-672-22713-4) *Jan-91*	
Best Book of Paradox 3	$24.95
(0-672-22704-5) *Feb-90*	
Best Book of Peachtree	$24.95
(0-672-22743-6) *Apr-90*	

Best Book of Prof Write/File	$22.95
(0-672-22726-6) *Mar-90*	
Best Book of Word for the MAC	$24.95
(0-672-48445-5) *Oct-89*	
Best Book of Word for Windows	$22.95
(0-672-48468-4) *Apr-90*	
Best Book of WordStar 6, 2/E	$24.95
(0-672-48495-1) *Dec-90*	
Best Book of WordPerfect 5.0	$21.95
(0-672-48423-4) *May-88*	
Best Book of WordPerfect 5.1	$26.95
(0-672-48467-6) *Dec-89*	
Best Book of Lotus 2.2, 3/E	$26.95
(0-672-22640-5) *Sep-89*	
Best Book of Works 2.0 for PC	$22.95
(0-672-22710-X) *Mar-90*	
Best Book of PFS: First Choice	$24.95
(0-672-22663-4) *Aug-90*	
Best Book of Animator	$29.95
(0-672-22735-5) *Apr-90*	
Best Book of Harvard Graphics	$24.95
(0-672-22740-1) *Feb-91*	
Best Book of FoxPro	$24.95
(0-672-22769-X) *Dec-90*	
Best Book of AutoCAD 11	$34.95
(0-672-22725-8) *Feb-91*	
Beyond Nintendo	$9.95
(0-672-48483-8) *Jun-90*	
Borland C++ Prog. Gd to Grap.	$29.95
(0-672-30201-2) *Jun-91*	
Borland C++ 3 OOP	$39.95
(0-672-30004-4) *Mar-92*	
Borland C++ 3.1 Obj-Orin Programming 2E	$39.95
(0-672-30140-7) *Jul-92*	
Bus. Guide to LANs	$24.95
(0-672-22728-2) *Feb-90*	
C Programming for Unix	$29.95
(0-672-48518-4) *Dec-93*	
C Programmer's Guide to Serial Comm	$29.95
(0-672-22584-0) *Mar-87*	

by Marilyn Horn Claff

Booklet

If you've ever tried to create a camera-ready booklet with two pages per printed sheet using page numbering, you know what a nightmare it can be to try to get the pages in the correct order and with the correct page numbers. Until WordPerfect 6.0, booklet printing was best done with a pair of scissors and a photocopy machine.

Fortunately, if you have WordPerfect 6.0, booklet printing couldn't be simpler. To print a booklet in WordPerfect 6.0, just set up your document for two subdivided pages per physical page, and choose Booklet Printing from the Multiple Pages dialog box when you print. WordPerfect rearranges the pages for you and (eventually) prints them in the correct order. If you have an 8-page document, for example, WordPerfect prints logical pages 8 and 1, 6 and 3, 2 and 7, and 4 and 5 on 4 sheets of pages. After printing the fronts of the sheets, WordPerfect even prompts you to refeed the sheets so that you can print the backs

WordPerfect 6.0 Features Used

- Subdivided Pages
- Booklet Printing
- Open Styles
- Page Border
- Paragraph Border
- Delay Codes
- Rotated Text
- Graphics Boxes
- Advanced Merge Commands

Files Used

```
BOOKLET.PRO (booklet project - blank except for the titles and footers)
BOOKLET.SAM (sample completed booklet)
BOOKLET.FF (merge form file)
TITLES.DF (merge data file)
```

Fonts Used

> Dutch Roman (included with WordPerfect)
> Futura Extra Bold
> Helvetica Narrow

So far, so good. The difficulty you are likely to encounter with booklet printing is no longer in arranging and numbering the pages, but in working with all of the other features you'll be tempted to use in your booklet. Will you be happy without a front cover? If you have a front cover, should the first page of text begin on the back of the cover, or on the next odd page? Will you be satisfied with simple page numbering, or do you require headers and/or footers? If you use a header or footer, you'll probably want different headers and footers on left and right pages. What about the back cover? If you'll be mailing your booklet, you may want to create a mailing panel, and that means rotating the text, as well as turning off page numbering, headers, footers, and page borders.

In this chapter, we'll show you how to create a 16-page pamphlet complete with front, inside, and back covers, page borders, and alternating footers. We'll explain why we formatted our booklet the way we did, and give you some pointers that may help you avoid potential pitfalls.

We constructed our booklet as a merge form file so that we could merge in a list of book titles from a database. Merging a list into an existing file requires a simple looping technique. We also used the SUBSTDATA command so that we wouldn't have to enter the name of the data file each time we run the merge.

> **Note:** You could simply retrieve an existing document instead of merging in a data file.

For this project, we used two fonts which you may not have, Futura Extra Bold and Helvetica Narrow, because we wanted to create a rough approximation of the Sams logo. If you don't have these fonts, WordPerfect will substitute other fonts, most likely Helve-WP and Swiss in bold and regular weights, when you open the sample files.

Caution: The Booklet project is quite complex and involves many advanced (and obscure) features. We've tried to explain the less obvious aspects of these features, but you'll need to be comfortable with the fundamentals of the program in order to follow the project through to the end.

We've separated the discussion of how to set up and print a booklet from the discussion of the more advanced formatting options, so that you can skip the advanced sections if you're a beginner or if you don't have the patience to deal with all these codes (see "Formatting Your Document as a Booklet" and "Printing Your Document as a Booklet" in this chapter). Now let's begin!

Formatting Your Document as a Booklet

To get started, we need to change a few formatting settings in Document Initial Codes, save our settings as a document template, retrieve a file into the current document, and adjust the formatting to make best use of the paper.

Changing Document Initial Codes and Font

To format a document as a 5.5-inch by 8.5-inch booklet, you need to change three settings in Document Initial Codes.

Tip: You can make these changes in either Document Initial Codes (Layout, Document, Document Initial Codes) or in the InitialCodes style, which is actually just another way to access Document Initial Codes. To change the InitialCodes style, choose Layout, Styles, select Initial Codes from the Style List dialog box, and choose Edit.

▲ From Layout, Document, change the Initial Font to Dutch Roman 10 point. The Initial Font is used as the default in headers, footers, graphics boxes, footnotes, and endnotes, so it is important to set it.

▲ From the Layout, Page Format dialog box, change the Paper Size/Type to Letter (Landscape).

▲ From the Page Format dialog box, choose Subdivide Page and change the number of columns to 2; leave the number of rows at 1 (see Figure 74.1).

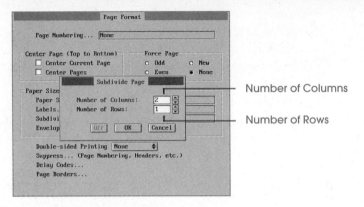

Figure 74.1. The Subdivide Page dialog box.

Tip: If you are using the keyboard, you can increment or decrement the counters by holding down the Alt key and pressing the dedicated up and down arrows.

As with labels, when you use the Subdivide Page feature, each division of the page (called a logical page) behaves like an actual (or physical) page. Headers, footers, page numbering, page borders, center page, watermarks, and footnotes all apply to logical pages just as they do to physical pages.

▲ Change your margins from the default 1" to something more appropriate for your booklet. We've used 0.5" for our left and right margins, 0.4" for our bottom margin, and 0.6" for our top margin.

Caution: If you plan to use headers, footers, endnotes, or footnotes, it's important to change the margins settings in Document Initial Codes, because the InitialCodes style is automatically included in each of these substructures. If you change your margins in the document area instead of in Document Initial Codes, you'll also have to change them in your headers, footers, endnotes, and footnotes, or edit the system styles for each of that substructure.

Saving Your Document as a Document Template

Even though you don't have any text on your screen, save what you've done so far. Name your document BOOKLET.TPL. This file will become your booklet template.

> **Tip:** A document template is an empty document that contains only formatting codes and boilerplate text. Document templates make it easier to format complex documents. When you are satisfied that your booklet template is formatted the way you want your booklets to appear, use the DOS `ATTRIB` command to make it read-only so you won't overwrite it by mistake.

Retrieving a Document into the Current Document

Now press Retrieve (Shift+F10) twice to change the Open Document method to Retrieve into Current Document, enter the name of the file containing the text for your booklet, and choose OK.

Immediately save your document under a new name so you don't overwrite your template-in-progress.

Making the Best Use of Paper in a Booklet

Booklets are based on page layouts that are multiples of four (two pages/two sides). If your document is not an even multiple of four, you'll have one or more blank sides. If you have two or more unwanted blank pages and are concerned about the environment, paper and mailing costs, or even printing and folding time, you may want to adjust the formatting of your booklet so that the page count is an even multiple of four.

Conversely, if there is just no way that your booklet can be squeezed onto less paper, you might as well take better advantage of the paper that you are already using (and paying for). A booklet that is crammed full, with minimal margins and white space, yet ends with three blank pages, is visually offensive.

Condensing a Booklet

Here are some tips for condensing your booklet into less space, or for stretching it out:

▲ The best trick for condensing more text into fewer pages is to change the line spacing to slightly less than one. I like to use 0.95. If you change the line spacing at the beginning of a document, the effect is cumulative. You'll be surprised at how much space this can save.

▲ Use the paragraph spacing feature on the Margins dialog box to use less space between paragraphs. (Set it to less than 1 if you are in the habit of pressing Enter twice between paragraphs, or to more than one if you press Enter only once between paragraphs.)

▲ Change to a smaller point size font or to a different typeface.

▲ Tighten the word spacing and letterspacing (Layout, Other Format, Printer Functions).

▲ Use a smaller paragraph indent. (Change your tab settings or use the First Line Indent feature on the Paragraph Margins dialog box.)

▲ Change the Space Below Header, the Space Above Footer, the Spacing Between Footnotes, and the Spacing Between Endnotes to less than the default (0.167 inches for all). If you are using a separator line for footnotes, reduce the space above and below the line. Use a smaller point size for footnotes and endnotes. (See the advanced discussion below for instructions for changing the spacing above a footer.)

▲ Eliminate the title page if you don't need it.

▲ Edit to fit. (This is called *copyfitting* and is the traditional and time-honored solution to the problem.)

▲ As a last resort, turn off Widow/Orphan Protect if it is on.

Stretching Out a Booklet

It's always easier to stretch out your document than to condense it. In addition to reversing the advice given above, here are a few ideas that you may not have considered:

▲ Leave a blank page after the title page. (You should do this anyway. See the BOOKLET.PRO file below.)

▲ Include a Table of Contents page if the booklet is long enough to warrant it.

▲ Add a mailing panel.

▲ Add page borders, headers, footers, and/or page numbering.

▲ Insert more frequent subject headings. Subject headings not only take up space, they provide useful information to the reader.

▲ Use call-outs to emphasize text.

▲ Use graphics.

▲ Use bulleted lists and indented quotations.

▲ Include extra space or a hard page break between sections.

Printing Your Document as a Booklet

Now that you have a bare-bones booklet with text, you're almost ready to print. Before printing, examine your document in Print Preview. Print Preview doesn't understand booklet printing, but it can at least help you determine if you're on the right track.

 Note: The reason Print Preview doesn't show you your booklet as it will print is that the booklet printing feature is an option you choose at print time, not a code that is inserted in your document.

Print Preview

If you work in Page mode, you'll be able to see your subdivided pages side-by-side in sequential order as you edit, along with headers, footers, and page numbering and other features that WordPerfect does not display in Graphics or Text mode. You'll probably find, however, that Page mode is just too pokey for editing a complex file such as a booklet. You'll probably prefer to work in Graphics mode, and to switch to Print Preview when you need to see a display that will be closer to the printed version. Print Preview is the most accurate way to see your document in WordPerfect since it shows elements not visible even in Page mode, such as watermarks and rounded corners for borders. Print Preview also offers a zoom feature and thumbnail views of your document.

Like Page mode, Print Preview can only display pages in their natural order. If you view a document formatted as subdivided pages or as labels, Print Preview displays the pages in the order in which they occur in the document. Logical pages 1 and 2 are displayed side-by-side, then pages 3 and 4, and so on (see Figure 74.2).

If you print a document as a booklet, WordPerfect arranges the pages in booklet order. One consequence of this is that the right- and left-hand pages are switched from the way they are displayed in Print Preview. When you view a booklet in Print Preview, keep this in mind and try to mentally swap the left- and right-hand pages. Setting up page numbering, headers, and footers, or boxes with rotated text can be confusing if you don't.

Duplex Printing

Some printers, such as the Hewlett-Packard LaserJet IIID and IIISI, can print on both sides of the page automatically. This feature is called duplex or double-sided printing. In WordPerfect 6.0, you can insert a special code in your documents that tells the printer to use the duplex option if it is available. If duplexing is not available for your printer, WordPerfect ignores the code.

To insert the duplex code, from the **Layout, P**age Format dialog box, choose Double-Sided Printing and select Long Edge if the document will be bound on the long edge of the paper, or Short Edge if the document will be bound on the short edge of the paper. If duplex printing is on, you can choose None to turn it off (see Figure 74.3).

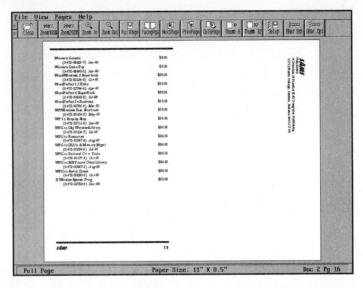

Figure 74.2. Subdivided Pages as shown in Print Preview. The page on the left is actually a right-hand page, and the page on the right is a left-hand page.

Tip: If you want to use duplex printing to print your booklet, choose Long Edge, because you are printing in Landscape.

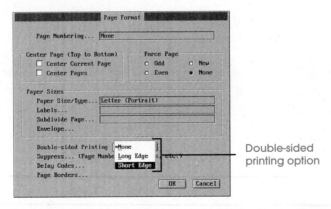

Figure 74.3. The Double-Sided Printing option on the Page Format dialog box.

In Reveal Codes, the duplex code appears as [Dbl-Sided Print].

Note: WordPerfect allows you to insert the duplex printing code in your document even if the currently selected printer driver is not capable of duplex printing. This way, you can prepare a document for duplex printing, even if your own printer is not capable of double-sided printing.

 Note: In previous versions of WordPerfect, you selected duplex printing by choosing a specially defined paper size/type. The method used in WordPerfect 6.0 is much simpler.

Choosing Booklet Printing on the Print/Fax Dialog Box

To print your document as a booklet, choose Multiple Pages, then Print as Booklet from the Print/Fax dialog box (Figure 74.4).

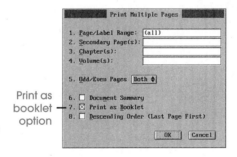

Print as booklet option

Figure 74.4. The Print Multiple Pages dialog box, with Print as Booklet selected.

If you chose double-sided printing, WordPerfect automatically prints the entire document as a double-sided booklet. Even if you did not insert the double-sided printing code, WordPerfect assumes that you want to print the pages back-to-back and prints the front sides of the pages. It then prompts you to reinsert the pages manually and even tells you exactly which page to insert.

 Caution: Unfortunately, there are a couple of problems with this design. First, there appears to be no way to print the entire job single-sided, using the continuous feed option. You might want to do this if you plan to have your booklet photocopied or offset printed. Second, if you are on a network, WordPerfect prompts you to reinsert pages that are still in the print queue. (The network does not release the print job to the printer until it is complete.) Finally, even if you intend to print your booklet back-to-back, there is apparently no option to print all of the front sides, flip them, and print all of the back sides. This would be more convenient than feeding the reverse sides manually one by one. It's possible that WordPerfect Corporation will enhance this feature in an interim release, especially if the feature proves to be popular.

If you used page numbering in your document, the page numbers will print correctly when you print it as a booklet. Remember to turn page numbering off for the appropriate pages (for example, the front cover, inside cover, and back cover). If you turn page numbering off for certain pages, you'll probably need to reset your page number afterward.

Caution: Booklet printing is extraordinarily slow, compared to printing a document in the normal page order. Be prepared to wait, especially if your document is more than 16 pages or if you have a slow (or even average) computer.

Tip: You can speed up printing considerably by using your printer's built-in or cartridge fonts instead of WordPerfect's graphics fonts. If your printer has both a PostScript and a PCL mode, switch to PCL mode for faster printing.

If you don't need fancy formatting, that's all you need to know to print your documents as booklets.

Creating the Front Cover

Our front cover is not difficult, but it requires a great many steps. Here's a rundown of how to re-create it:

1. Set Page Number Position to None. Turn off all page numbers, headers, footers, and watermarks.
2. Set the typeface to Dutch 801 Roman and the font size to 10 points.

3. Turn on Widow/Orphan Protect.

4. Clear all tabs, then set a single tab stop at 0.3" from the margin.

5. Set the Spacing Above Footer to 0". We don't need to allow any space because the custom paragraph border used in the footers has 0.2 inches of space on the outside (i.e., above the line).

Create the two Sams logos. We created the one at the top of the page as regular text. In order to anchor the logo at the bottom of the page, we put it inside a graphics box.

6a. To create the first logo, type the words *SAMS* and *PUBLISHING* each on a line by itself. Block the word *SAMS* and choose Futura Extra Bold as your typeface, change the point size to 26, and choose Italics. Now block the *A* in *SAMS* and make it Large.

Block the word *PUBLISHING* and choose Helvetica Narrow and 13 point.

Block both lines and change the Line Spacing to 0.8". This reduces the space between lines by 20 percent. Because both lines are set in all caps, the default spacing is too much.

Note: The only way to determine the correct point sizes for a logo such as this one is by trial and error.

Note: We blocked the text before applying the formatting so the codes would be inserted as *revertible* codes. Revertible codes apply only to the selected text and behave like paired codes.

6b. To create the logo at the bottom of the page, create a graphics box based on the User Box Style (no borders, no shading) (see Figure 74.5). Attach the box to the bottom of the page and make it the width of the page. Change the contents to text and the Content options to left-aligned and top.

Choose Edit Text and enter the following text:

```
SAMS
PUBLISHING
A Division of Prentice Hall Computer Publishing
11711 North College, Carmel, Indiana 46032 USA
```

Format this logo as you did the first one, making the word *Sams* 18 points and *PUBLISHING* 9 points.

Advance down 2 points (0.028 inches) to provide a little extra space below the logo, and change the font to Dutch Roman 9.5 points.

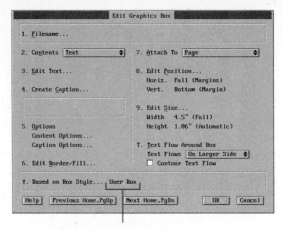

Based on "user box" style

Figure 74.5. The Edit Graphics dialog box.

7. Create the custom border that we will attach to all the pages (except the last) beginning on page three. The same border is also used in the footers. (You'll use this border in a delay code, but you must create it before you open the Delay Codes box.)

To create the custom border, choose Graphics, Borders, Styles, then choose Create. At the prompt, enter Top Rule, the name for your custom border (see Figure 74.6).

New Border Style Name

Figure 74.6. The New Border Style Name dialog box.

Select Lines. At the Border Line Styles dialog box, choose Select All and choose [None]. Then choose Top Line, then Create.

At the Create Line Style dialog box, enter 3Pt. Rule as the name of your new line style. Then choose Thickness and enter 3p. WordPerfect converts the points to inches and enters 0.042" (see Figure 74.7). Choose OK to accept.

After WordPerfect displays the Border Line Styles dialog box, you are back at the Create Border Style dialog box. All that remains to do is to change the outside and inside spacing for your border style. Choose

Spacing. The Border Spacing dialog box appears (see Figure 74.8). Deselect the Automatic Spacing box. Enter 0.2" for the Outside Spacing for the Top border, and 0.1" as the Inside Spacing for the Top Border. Choose OK.

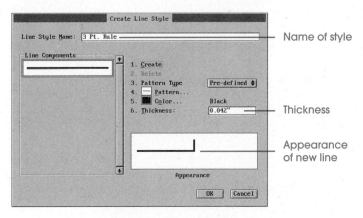

Figure 74.7. The Create Line Style dialog box.

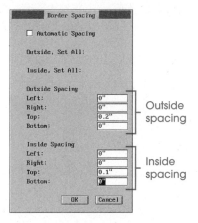

Figure 74.8. The Border Spacing dialog box.

Now you should return to the Create Border Style dialog box. Choose OK. At the Border Styles dialog box, choose Close.

 Tip: After all of that effort to define a single line and border style, you'll want to copy your style to your personal or shared style library. At the Border Styles dialog, choose Copy. At the prompt Copy Highlighted Style to, choose Personal Library or Shared Library.

> **Tip:** Although you can customize the predefined line and border styles, it's better to create your own so that you know at a glance which styles you've customized and which use the default settings.

8. Now create a delay code for formatting that will take effect on page three:

Choose **L**ayout, **P**age Format, then **D**elay Codes. Enter a value of 2. In the Delay Codes box that appears, enter a code to reset the page number to 1, turn on a page border using the Top Rule style that you just created, and create Footer A and Footer B to print on odd and even pages.

The footers should contain a font code to change to Futura Extra Bold 12 point and a paragraph border that uses the custom border Top Rule. The footers each contain a version of the Sams logo and the page number. To create the logo, type the word SAMS, italicize it, block the letter *A*, and apply the Large attribute. The footer for the even pages should have the page number on the left and the log on the right; the footer for the odd pages should be the reverse. (When you look at your formatted footers in Print Preview, they will look wrong, because WordPerfect displays the left-hand page on the right and vice versa. See Figure 74.9.)

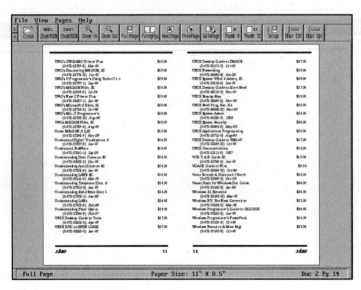

Figure 74.9. Footers as they appear in Print Preview.

> **Note:** The footers inherit the settings from Document Initial Codes and Initial Font, unless they are overridden by the footer styles or formatting codes in the footer themselves.

The remainder of the cover is very straightforward:

9. Type the title, block it, and change the justification to Center. Block it again and change the point size to 24 point. Block it a third time and turn on kerning. (**K**erning is hidden on the **L**ayout, Format **O**ther, **P**rinter Functions dialog box.)

> **Note:** We did not use kerning for the entire document because it slows down printing and is not really noticeable except at larger point sizes.

10. Type the date for the catalog, block it, and choose Italics. Then center the line.

Creating the Inside Cover

You could leave the inside cover blank, but we've chosen to insert a copyright notice at the bottom of the page. We used an Advance from Top of Page command to position it exactly 7.5 inches from the top of the page. This is a much better way to position the text than using hard returns, because with Advance, the text will stay in place. We could have also put the text in a page box, as we did with the Sams logo and address on the first page.

Creating the Back Cover

The back cover is a mailing panel with rotated text. We used an Open Style to create the mailing panel so it is easy to turn it on where we want to.

> **Note:** Our first approach was to create the back panel by using a delay code. One serious flaw with that approach is that once you enter a number of pages to skip, you cannot change the number. (You can copy the codes from one delay code dialog box to another, but that workaround is clumsy.) If you won't always have the same number of pages in your booklet, don't use this method.

The Open Style technique is not automatic; the user must remember to insert a hard page break and to turn on the style. Even so, the Open Style method works better than the Delay Codes method because if does not require any editing if the length of your document changes.

Once we determined how to get the graphics box on the right page, we then created a text box and entered the text. The only difficult aspect of rotating the text was figuring out what direction to move the text. This was made more confusing by the fact that WordPerfect displays even-numbered pages on the right side of the screen in Print Preview.

Use the following steps to create the back panel:

1. Create an open style called LastPage that turns off page borders and footers and contains a graphics box the size of the panel. Anchor the box to the page and change the contents to Text.

2. From the Edit Graphics Box dialog box, choose Edit Text and type the following text:

   SAMS
   PUBLISHING
   A Division of Prentice Hall Computer Publishing
   11711 North College, Carmel, Indiana 46032 USA

   Format the text as you did on the front cover.

3. At the Edit Graphics Box dialog box, choose Content Options (see Figure 74.10). Change the Horizontal Position of Contents in Box to Right and the Vertical Position of Contents in Box to Top.

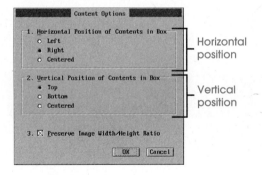

Figure 74.10. The Content Options dialog box.

4. At the Edit Text editing screen, press Alt+F9 to display Graphics dialog box. Choose Rotate Text. At the Rotate Box Contents choose 270 degrees (see Figure 74.11).

Figure 74.11. The Rotate Box Contents dialog box.

To create the back panel, insert a hard page break after your last page, and turn on the LastPage style. Just make sure than the number of the page where you turn on the LastPage style would be a multiple of four, if you counted every page and numbered them consecutively. In our booklet example, the back panel should be on page 14, because we have two unnumbered pages at the beginning of the booklet.

Using Styles in Your Booklet

As you work through this exercise, you'll discover just how complex (and sometimes cumbersome) WordPerfect documents can be. One technique that makes it easier to work with formatting codes is to put all of the formatting (or as much of the formatting as possible) in style definitions. The formatting codes in a style are treated as a single code, so they are easier to work with. Not only do you save time formatting, but you don't have to worry about inadvertently deleting or moving a code.

The BOOKLET.SAM and BOOKLET.FF files on the *Super Book* disk contain the same formatting that we've described in this chapter, but all of the formatting is controlled through styles. Although creating complex styles such as these can be difficult, in the long run, it is worth the effort because styles are so much easier to work with. Only two main styles, BOOKLET and LASTPAGE, are needed. Use the BOOKLET style at the beginning of the document to set up the booklet, and use the LASTPAGE style at the end of the document to format the back panel of the booklet.

 Caution: To make your BOOKLET style foolproof to use, you'll need to include margin and font codes in the footers that are included in the BOOKLET style. This step is not necessary if you modify your Document Initial Codes as we have in our exercise.

Merging with a Data File

To merge a data file into our booklet, include the following merge codes on the page where the data entry begins:

```
SUBSTDATA(TITLES.DF)
LABEL(BEGINTITLES)FIELD(TITLE)        FIELD(PRICE)
(FIELD(IBSN)) FIELD(PUBDATE)
NEXTRECORD GO(BEGINTITLES)
```

The SUBSTDATA command instructs WordPerfect to use the TITLES.DF data file. This is a handy technique to use when you nearly always merge a form file with the same data file. By using this command, you don't need to enter the name of a data file when you start a merge. (In fact, if you do enter the name of a data file at the Run Merge dialog box, WordPerfect ignores it.)

When you perform a regular merge, WordPerfect reads in a new copy of the form file for each record in the data file. When you are merging into a list, as we are here, you don't want to restart the form file for each new record; rather, you just want to continue merging in new records at the current location in the form file. This simple merge statement accomplishes exactly that. We've used the LABEL command to mark the beginning of the fields that we want to merge in for each new record. After the last field, we use the NEXTRECORD command to increment the record pointer in the data file, and use a GO command to go to the beginning of the loop. When WordPerfect reaches the end of the data file, the merge is automatically terminated.

We've used a couple of tricks to improve the appearance of the merged output and to reduce the amount of editing that may be required.

- ▲ We blocked the FIELD(TITLE) and FIELD(PRICE) and bolded the merge codes, so that the resulting titles and prices will be bold.
- ▲ We put parentheses around the ISBN field, so the resulting ISBN code in the document is enclosed in parentheses.
- ▲ We italicized the PUBDATE field.
- ▲ We block-protected the text from the FIELD(TITLE) to the FIELD(PUBDATE), so in the merge output, each record stays together on a page.

 Caution: Be sure to begin the block protect and bold codes after the label, or these features will not work correctly.

Tips, Tricks, and Traps

Here are a few tips, tricks, and traps that may help you plan your document.

Page Borders, Headers, and Footers

If your document includes page borders, headers and/or footers, the page borders print above the headers and below the footers. To give the appearance of a page border that prints above the footer, we used a paragraph border above the footer itself.

Delay Codes

Delay codes are extremely useful, but somewhat cumbersome to work with. Once you enter a page number value, you can't adjust it. The best solution is to create a new delay code and copy the codes from one delay code to another.

Another helpful (if undocumented) technique is to retrieve a file into a delay code. Any text in the file is stripped out, and codes that are allowed in delay codes remain. Formatting codes allowed in delay codes include open codes (page formatting, margins, tab settings, graphics boxes, styles, borders, font codes, columns, and so on). Formatting codes not allowed in delay codes include paired codes and codes that only have an effect on the immediate location, such as tabs and indent codes.

Occasionally, you may not be able to enter a specific code in a delay code if that setting is already in effect at your current cursor position. If this should happen to you, exit from the Delay Codes box, change the setting in your document, edit the Delay Codes box, and then change your document back to the original setting.

Working with Styles, Graphics, and Delay Codes

One feature that styles, graphics, and delay codes share is that they allow you to create structures within structures. You can use a delay code in a graphics box, within a style, all within another graphics box, which is in turn included in a style. Keeping track of where you are is not always easy. To simplify formatting, try to develop your design initially without nesting these features. Once you are satisfied that the formatting codes will do what you want them to do, copy them into styles, graphics boxes, or delay codes.

Appendixes

by Beth Fitzherbert

Installation and System Requirements

WordPerfect 6.0 is the most powerful word processing software for the DOS environment to date. Unfortunately, to handle that power, WordPerfect users need more powerful computers than they did for previous versions. Older PCs without at least an 80286 processor won't be able to handle WordPerfect 6.0. (Maybe it's time for that hardware upgrade?)

Minimum System Configuration

The minimum system configuration is:

- ▲ Personal computer with an 80286 processor
- ▲ 480K free conventional memory
- ▲ DOS 3.0 or higher
- ▲ Hard disk with 7M disk space for minimal installation (includes only WordPerfect program files, font files, and printer files)

Recommended System Configuration

If you have a more powerful PC than the system described in the following list, all the better. The recommended system configuration is:

▲ Personal computer with an 80386 processor

▲ 520K free conventional memory

▲ DOS 5.0

▲ Hard disk with 16M disk space for complete installation (includes minimal installation above plus graphics, writing tools, sound, learning, and more)

▲ VGA or higher resolution graphics adapter and monitor

Optional System Features

Optional recommended system features are:

▲ Mouse

▲ Fax device

▲ Sound board

▲ Disk cache, expanded memory, or extended memory

Installation

When you've determined that your computer meets the system requirements, you're ready to begin installation by following the steps in the Procedure below.

Procedure A.1. Beginning installation.

1. Start your computer.
2. Insert the Install 1 disk in drive A: or drive B:.
3. At a DOS prompt, enter a:install. Or, enter b:install if you're using drive B:. The installation program loads.
4. Answer Yes or No when WordPerfect asks if you can see colors on your screen. This informs WordPerfect whether your monitor can display color. The Installation menu appears, as shown in Figure A.1.

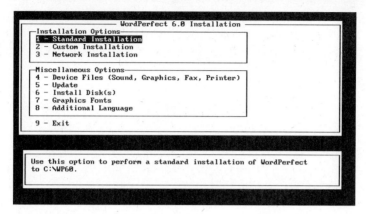

Figure A.1. The Installation menu.

Installation Basics

WordPerfect 6.0 offers four installation options:

▲ **Standard**. Choose this option if you want to install the entire program and accept WordPerfect's default locations for its files. This option is a good choice if you've never installed WordPerfect before or if you want to install the complete program as quickly as possible.

▲ **Custom**. With this option, you can specify which groups of WordPerfect files you want to install and where you want WordPerfect to put them. For example, you can choose not to install the Learning files to save some disk space, or you can put your graphics files in a different directory than the one WordPerfect has chosen.

When you use the Custom option, however, you don't have to change any file locations or other settings at all. Custom installation can install the full program just as the Standard option does—it just takes a few more steps.

Under the Custom installation option, you can also choose to perform a Minimal installation of WordPerfect. In this case, only the WordPerfect program files, font files, and printer files are installed. If you are low on disk space, you might consider this option. To perform a Minimal installation, choose Custom from the Installation menu. When WordPerfect asks you to identify which groups of files you want to install, the first option on the menu at the bottom of the screen is Minimal. Minimum disk space required for a Minimal installation is 7M.

> **Caution:** Be aware that if you perform a minimal installation, you won't be able to use many of WordPerfect's features. This includes features such as Speller or the new graphics files.

▲ **Network**. If you want to use WordPerfect 6.0 on a network, choose this installation option. All copies of WordPerfect 6.0 are network-ready—you don't need a special set of disks to install it on a network—but you should install it using the Network option. To handle shared files and individual user files properly, WordPerfect requests information about your network during installation.

You can install WordPerfect from a 3.5-inch floppy drive or a 5.25-inch floppy drive, either of which is drive A: or drive B:. WordPerfect installs to the default location C:\WP60 unless you specify otherwise.

WordPerfect installs its files in one main directory, a shared product directory, and two directories for fonts. It also creates subdirectories for secondary file groups in the main program directory. You don't have to create any of these directories or subdirectories before running the installation program— WordPerfect creates them for you as it installs.

If you're a WordPerfect 5.1 user, be aware that some of the files you've tailored for specific uses will not work with WordPerfect 6.0. You can use documents, styles, macros (if you convert them), and graphics from Version 5.1 in WordPerfect 6.0, but generally, your printer files and keyboard layouts won't work.

Standard Installation

The Standard installation option is the quickest way to install the entire WordPerfect 6.0 program. Follow the steps in Procedure A.2 to install using the Standard option.

If you choose not to install printer drivers, sound board drivers, or additional graphics drivers, you can run the installation program again or use the Setup feature in WordPerfect to install them later.

Procedure A.2. Using Standard installation.

1. Select Standard from the Installation menu. The locations from which and to which WordPerfect installs its files appear.

2. Do you want to change these directories? Answer:

    No to accept the current settings. If you answer no without changing the Install from location or the Install to location, WordPerfect installs from the drive where the Install 1 disk is and installs to C:\WP60.

Yes to specify the Install from and Install to locations. When these locations are correct, answer No.

3. Disk Space Recommendations. Look at the disk space available on the drive you're installing to and compare it to the space required for complete and minimal installations (see Figure A.2). Confirm that you have enough disk space for a complete installation. (Remember that you'll also need space for your documents). Answer Yes to continue the installation.

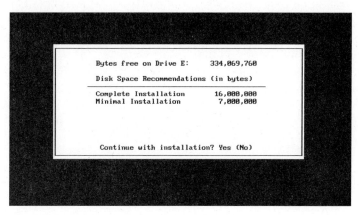

Figure A.2. WordPerfect tells you the amount of disk space you have available to help you choose an installation option.

If disk space is a little tight and you don't mind omitting some file groups to save room, you might consider starting the installation again using the Custom installation option. You can always run the installation program again later to add the files you decide to skip this time.

4. Replace Existing Files. Select an option to tell WordPerfect what to do if it finds a file with the same name as one it's trying to copy:

Choose any option. If you're installing WordPerfect 6.0 for the first time, you don't need to worry about this situation occurring because you have no existing WordPerfect files.

Always. If you're updating a previous installation of WordPerfect 6.0 and want to confirm each file replacement, choose this option.

Never. If you're updating a previous installation of WordPerfect 6.0 and don't mind if WordPerfect overwrites all your old files, choose this.

Smart prompting. If you're updating a previous installation and want WordPerfect to prompt you when it finds a file you might not want replaced (such as customized macros or dictionary files), choose this option. It's the default selection and is usually the best choice.

5. Add program directory to path? Answer:

Yes if you want WordPerfect to add its program directory to the PATH statement in your AUTOEXEC.BAT file. AUTOEXEC.BAT is a file of instructions that your computer reads each time you turn on or restart your computer. The PATH statement tells DOS where to look when you command it to start a program. When WordPerfect 6.0 is in your PATH statement, you can start WordPerfect from any directory.

No if you don't mind changing to the WordPerfect directory each time you want to start WordPerfect. You can also add WordPerfect to your PATH statement later.

6. Install additional Graphics Drivers? Answer:

Yes if your graphics card and monitor are capable of resolutions higher than 640 x 480. WordPerfect installs a standard EGA/VGA driver automatically, but if your hardware has better resolution, you may want to take advantage of it. Select the correct driver for your graphics card from the list (see Figure A.3). If your graphics card isn't listed, a driver for it may be available in the future. Contact WordPerfect Corporation for more information.

 Note: When you answer Yes to the question "Install additional drivers?" while installing graphics or other drivers, WordPerfect prompts you to install additional drivers until you answer No.

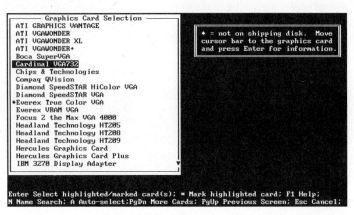

Figure A.3. Selecting a graphics driver.

No if you want to use the standard EGA/VGA driver that WordPerfect installs. You can add another driver later by running the installation program again or by using the Setup feature in WordPerfect.

7. Install Printer Drivers? Answer:

Yes if you want to print documents in WordPerfect. Find your printer on the Printer Selection list and select it to install its driver. If your printer isn't listed, the box entitled IF YOUR PRINTER IS NOT LISTED on the right side of the screen suggests possible emulations for different types of printers. Press F1 for more help, and consult the manual, dealer, or manufacturer of your printer for more information on other printers your printer can emulate.

No if you do not want to print in WordPerfect or if you do not want to add printer drivers at this time. You can add printers later by running the installation program again or by using Printer Setup in WordPerfect.

> **Tip:** Don't forget to add drivers for printers you use with WordPerfect 6.0 at other places, such as your home or office. WordPerfect can reformat documents for any printer, but sometimes the appearance of a document changes when it's reformatted. If you have the driver for your office printer installed and selected on your copy of WordPerfect 6.0 at home, you can work on office documents as they will look when printed at the office.

8. Insert the other WordPerfect 6.0 disks in your floppy drive as WordPerfect prompts you for them.

9. Do you want to install any Fax Files? Answer:

Yes if you have a fax device and you want to use it with WordPerfect. Now select your fax device type from the Fax Device Options menu to install the correct fax driver files.

No if you do not have a fax device or do not want to use your fax device with WordPerfect.

10. Install Sound Drivers? Answer:

Yes if you have a sound board and want to use sound clips in your WordPerfect documents. Find your sound board on the Sound Driver Selection list and select it to install its driver.

No if you don't have a sound board or if you don't want to use sound clips in WordPerfect documents.

11. Continue to insert your WordPerfect 6.0 disks as WordPerfect prompts you for them until you see the message `Loading WordPerfect to complete printer selection`.

12. Enter your registration number when WordPerfect prompts you for it. You're not required to enter it, but you'll have it handy if you need it.

13. WordPerfect prompts you to make port and default font selections, then installation is complete. If WordPerfect made changes to your AUTOEXEC.BAT file, restart your computer now so the changes can take effect.

Custom Installation

Use the Custom option if you want more control over how WordPerfect is installed on your computer. With the Custom option, you can specify the locations of each of WordPerfect's file groups, or omit some file groups if your disk space is limited. Choose this installation option if you want to perform a minimal installation.

If you choose not to install printer drivers, sound board drivers, or additional graphics drivers, you can run the installation program again or use the Setup feature in WordPerfect to install them later.

Procedure A.3. Using Custom installation.

1. Select Custom from the Installation menu. The Custom Installation menu appears.

2. Select the first option if you want to change where you're installing WordPerfect from. The default is the drive from which you started the Install program.

    Select the second option to display the Location of Files menu. Here you can specify where you want to install each of WordPerfect's file groups. The default location for the program files is C:\WP60. When you've made your changes, select Exit to return to the Custom Installation menu.

3. When you've completed your selections for installing from and to, select the option Continue Installation. The Disk Space Required box appears. WordPerfect asks, Continue with installation? Answer Yes to continue. A list of the file groups and the disk space each requires appears, as shown in Figure A.4.

> **Note:** When you change the drive and path of the program files, WordPerfect automatically changes the drive and paths of the other file groups accordingly.

4. Highlight each file group you want to omit from the installation and press Enter to toggle between selecting the group and deselecting it, as shown in Figure A.5.

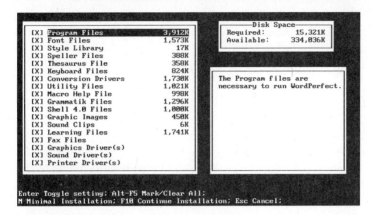

Figure A.4. The File Selection dialog box.

Figure A.5. By omitting files that aren't necessary, you can save some disk space.

In the box on the right of the File Selection dialog box, WordPerfect describes the file group and tells you whether the group is required to run the program. Notice that WordPerfect keeps a running tally of disk space available and disk space required in the upper-right corner of the screen. If you want to perform a minimal installation, choose Minimal from the menu at the bottom of the screen. Press Alt+F5 to toggle between selecting all files and deselecting all files. When you've completed your selections, press F10 to continue.

5. Replace Existing Files. Select an option to tell WordPerfect what to do if it finds a file with the same name as one it's trying to copy:

Choose any option. If you're installing WordPerfect for the first time, you don't need to worry about this situation because you have no existing WordPerfect files.

Always. If you're upgrading from a previous version and want to confirm each file replacement, choose this option.

Never. If you're upgrading from a previous version and don't mind if WordPerfect overwrites all of your old files, choose this option.

Smart prompting. If you're upgrading from a previous version and want WordPerfect to prompt you when it finds a file you might not want replaced (such as customized macros or dictionary files), choose this option. It's the default selection and is usually the best choice.

6. Add program directory to path? Answer:

Yes if you want WordPerfect to add its program directory to the PATH statement in your AUTOEXEC.BAT file. AUTOEXEC.BAT is a file of instructions that your computer reads each time you turn on or restart your computer. The PATH statement tells DOS where to look for files when you start a program. When WordPerfect 6.0 is in your PATH statement, you can start WordPerfect from any directory.

No if you don't mind changing to the WordPerfect directory each time you want to start WordPerfect. You can also add WordPerfect to your PATH statement later.

7. Graphics Driver Selection. If your graphics card and monitor are capable of resolutions higher than 640 x 480, choose the correct driver for your graphics card. If you don't choose a graphics driver, WordPerfect installs a standard EGA/VGA driver automatically. If your graphics card isn't listed, a driver for it may be available in the future. Contact WordPerfect Corporation for more information. Press Esc if you don't want to install an additional graphics driver.

8. Printer Selection. Select the printer drivers you want to install. If your printer isn't listed, the box entitled IF YOUR PRINTER IS NOT LISTED on the right side of the screen suggests possible emulations for different types of printers. Press F1 for more help, and consult the manual, dealer, or manufacturer of your printer for more information on other printers your printer can emulate. Press Esc if you don't want to install a printer driver at this time.

Tip: Don't forget to add drivers for printers you use with WordPerfect 6.0 at other places, such as your home or office. WordPerfect can reformat documents for any printer, but sometimes the appearance of a document changes when it's reformatted. If you have the driver for your office printer installed and selected on your copy of

> WordPerfect 6.0 at home, you can work on office documents as they will look when printed at the office.

9. Insert the other WordPerfect 6.0 disks in your floppy drive as WordPerfect prompts you for them.

10. Sound Board Selection. If you have a sound board and you want to use sound clips in your WordPerfect documents, find your sound board on the Sound Driver Selection list (see Figure A.6) and select it to install its driver. Press Esc if you don't want to install a sound board driver.

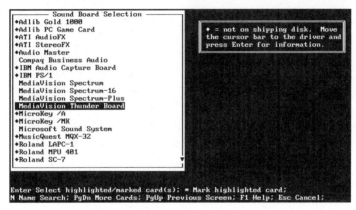

Figure A.6. The Sound Driver Selection list.

11. Do you want to install any Fax Files? Answer:

    Yes if you have a fax device and you want to use it with WordPerfect. Now select your fax device type from the Fax Device Options menu to install the correct fax driver files.

    No if you do not have a fax device or do not want to use your fax device with WordPerfect.

12. Continue to insert the other WordPerfect 6.0 disks as the installation program prompts you for them until `Loading WordPerfect to complete printer selection` appears.

13. Enter your registration number when WordPerfect prompts you for it. You're not required to enter it, but you'll have it handy if you need it. Your registration number appears in Help under **WP** Info.

14. WordPerfect prompts you to make port and default font selections, then installation is complete. If WordPerfect made changes to your AUTOEXEC.BAT file, restart your computer now so the changes can take effect.

Minimal Installation

A minimal installation requires approximately 7M and includes only the program files, font files, and printer files. If you're short on disk space, this option may be for you. You can always run the installation program again to add more file groups. To perform a minimal installation, follow Procedure A.2 and select Minimal in Step 3. The Minimal installation option is illustrated in Figure A.7.

Figure A.7. The Minimal installation option is in the File Selection dialog box when you select Custom Installation.

Network Installation

If you presently use a previous version of WordPerfect on your network, you'll want to install WordPerfect 6.0 in a new directory. If network disk space is tight, make a backup copy of your present installation of WordPerfect, delete the present installation, then install WordPerfect 6.0 in its place.

Follow the steps in Procedure A.4 to perform your network installation. Also note the section "Network Issues" later in this appendix.

Procedure A.4. Using Network Installation.

1. Select Network from the Installation menu. The Network Installation menu window appears.

2. Select the first option if you want to change where you're installing WordPerfect from.

   Select the second option to display the Location of Files menu. Here you can specify where you want to install each of WordPerfect's file groups.

The default location for the program files is `C:\WP60`. When you've made your changes, select Exit to return to the Network Installation menu.

3. When you've completed your selections for installing from and to, select Continue Installation. The Disk Space Required box appears. WordPerfect asks, Continue with installation? Answer Yes to continue. A list of the file groups and the disk space each requires appears, as shown in Figure A.4.

> **Note:** When you change the location of the program files, WordPerfect automatically changes the locations of the other file groups accordingly.

4. Highlight any file groups you want to omit from the installation and press Enter to toggle between selecting the group and deselecting it. In the box to the right of the list of file groups, WordPerfect describes the file group and tells you whether the group is required to run the program. Notice that WordPerfect keeps a running tally of disk space available and disk space required in the upper-right corner of the screen. Press Alt+F5 to toggle between selecting all files and deselecting all files. When you've completed your selections, press F10 to continue.

5. Select your LAN type from the dialog box shown in Figure A.8.

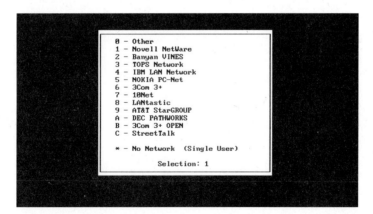

Figure A.8. Selecting your network type.

6. Enter a network drive and directory for the master setup file and user setup files. Setup files are files that contain each user's personal preferences, such as screen colors, default margins, initial font, and other settings that allow users to customize WordPerfect for their individual work environments.

7. Graphics Driver Selection. Select a graphics driver for each monitor and graphics card on your network. If your graphics cards and monitors are capable of resolutions higher than 640 x 480, users may want to take advantage of them. If you don't select graphics drivers, WordPerfect installs a standard EGA/VGA driver automatically. If your graphics cards aren't listed, drivers for them may be available in the future. Contact WordPerfect Corporation for more information. Press Esc if you don't want to install additional graphics drivers.

8. Printer Selection. Select a printer driver for each type of printer on your network. Figure A.9 shows the Printer Selection dialog box.

Figure A.9. The Printer Selection dialog box.

If any of your printers aren't listed, the box entitled IF YOUR PRINTER IS NOT LISTED on the right side of the screen suggests possible emulations for different types of printers. Press F1 for more help, and consult the manual, dealer, or manufacturer of your printers for more information on other printers your printers can emulate.

9. Insert the other WordPerfect 6.0 disks in your floppy drive as WordPerfect prompts you for them.

10. Sound Board Selection. If any PCs on your network are equipped with sound boards, users may want to use sound clips in their WordPerfect documents. Find your sound boards on the Sound Driver Selection list and select them to install their drivers. Press Esc if you don't want to install any sound board drivers.

11. Do you want to install any Fax Files? Answer:

Yes if you have a fax device and you want to use it with WordPerfect. Now select your fax device type from the Fax Device Options menu to install the correct fax driver files.

No if you do not have a fax device or do not want to use your fax device with WordPerfect.

12. Continue to insert the other WordPerfect 6.0 disks as the installation program prompts you for them until `Loading WordPerfect to complete printer selection` appears, and WordPerfect launches.

13. Enter your registration number when WordPerfect prompts you for it. You're not required to enter it, but you'll have it handy if you need it.

14. WordPerfect prompts you to make port and default font selections, then installation is complete. Refer to the section "Network Issues" in this appendix and your WordPerfect 6.0 manual for more information on using WordPerfect 6.0 on a network.

Miscellaneous Options

The Miscellaneous Options portion of the Installation menu offers options for installing graphics fonts, language modules, and additional device drivers for sound boards, graphics, fax boards, and printers (see Figure A.10).

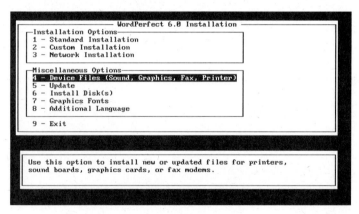

Figure A.10. Miscellaneous installation options.

To use Miscellaneous Options, you may need disks other than those in the original set that was packaged with WordPerfect. For example, WordPerfect 6.0 supports more than 900 output devices (such as printers and plotters), so it's possible that the driver for your output device isn't normally shipped with the program. Contact WordPerfect Corporation to obtain the disk you need.

Language modules, which are used with the Speller feature, contain dictionaries and thesauruses for languages other than American English. You can purchase language modules from WordPerfect Corporation. If you want to install device drivers that you didn't install when you initially installed WordPerfect, have your WordPerfect disks or disks with the appropriate drivers handy. To install more graphics fonts, you'll need the disks with the fonts you want to install.

Installing Additional Device Drivers

Use the steps in the following procedure to install additional device drivers.

Procedure A.5. Installing additional device drivers.

1. Select Device Files (Sound, Graphics, Fax, Printer) on the Installation menu.
2. Type the drive and directory location of the driver you want to install. (You can install the additional drivers from a hard drive if that's where they're located—just enter the drive and path.)
3. Type the location of your WordPerfect program.
4. If you're installing a driver from a disk other than those in the original WordPerfect 6.0 set, insert the disk now.
5. Select the type of driver you want to install from the Install: Device menu shown in Figure A.11. If you didn't enter a hard drive location in Step 2 or insert a disk in Step 4, WordPerfect prompts you to insert one of the disks in its original set.

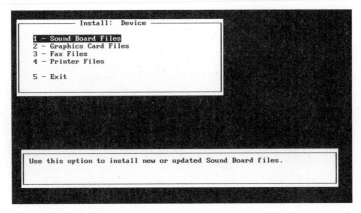

Figure A.11. Selecting a type of driver to install.

6. Follow the prompts to install the driver. The screens and menus are similar to those you followed when you installed WordPerfect. If you're installing a driver for a fax board, WordPerfect asks you to identify the type of your fax device.

Update and Install Disk(s)

Use the Update option to update your copy of WordPerfect from the Install and Program disk sets (usually provided for interim releases of WordPerfect). Use the Install Disk(s) option to install compressed files such as printer .ALL files and additional WordPerfect font files from disks.

Installing Graphics Fonts

You can use any of WordPerfect's graphics fonts, your printer's fonts, or fonts from third-party sources such as Bitstream and Adobe with WordPerfect 6.0. The Graphics Fonts option installs third-party fonts already installed on your hard disk to your font resource file WP.DRS. If the additional fonts you want to install are from WordPerfect Corporation, use the Install Disk(s)—not the Graphic Fonts option—to install the fonts from the disks.

> **Note:** WP.DRS from other versions of WordPerfect do not work with Version 6.0.

To install additional fonts, you can use WordPerfect's Font Installer from the Fonts menu in WordPerfect or from the Installation menu, but the fonts first must be installed on your hard drive according to the font manufacturer's installation instructions. To install the fonts for WordPerfect, first be sure that you've installed a printer in WordPerfect.

During font installation, WordPerfect first prompts you for the type of fonts you want to install, as shown in Figure A.12.

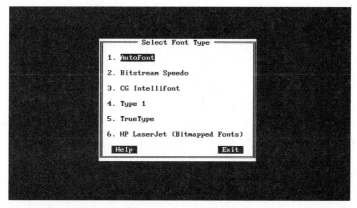

Figure A.12. Selecting the type of fonts to install.

Next, WordPerfect prompts you for the location of your printer files and the location of the third-party fonts installed on your hard disk. Then, WordPerfect asks you to select your printer. Finally, mark the fonts you want to install. Then select Exit. Your graphics and printer font files are updated when you exit Font Installer.

Installing Additional Languages

The language of your copy of WordPerfect 6.0 is American English, but if you work with documents in other languages and want to be able to spell check them, you can purchase Language Modules for the languages you need from WordPerfect Corporation.

When you receive your Language Module disks, select the Additional Languages from the Installation menu to install the files.

Startup Options

Startup options are often used to configure WordPerfect for your particular type of hardware, or to perform a special function. You can use as many startup options as you need and in any combination that you choose.

When running stand-alone, startup options are invoked from the DOS command line when you start WordPerfect. To use startup options, type:

```
wp <startup options>
```

For example: `wp /du /mono /tx`

In the example, the parameter /du disables use of upper memory blocks, and WordPerfect is commanded to emulate monochrome mode (/mono) and to operate in text mode (/tx).

Certain startup options are necessary for WordPerfect to run on a network, as described in the next section, "Network Issues." For detailed explanation of network startup options and a complete list of all startup options, consult your WordPerfect manual.

Network Issues

When running WordPerfect 6.0 on a network, you should be aware of the following issues unique to network environments.

File Access and Attributes

Protecting the integrity of WordPerfect's files while allowing users access to the program is essential in a network environment. Make all WordPerfect directories accessible to all users on the network, but mark these files read-only using a network utility such as Novell NetWare's FLAG command or the DOS ATTRIB command. Refer to Table A.1 for list of read-only files.

Table A.1. Files that should be marked read-only.

Directory	Extensions	
\WP60		
	*.EXE	*.FRS
	*.FIL	*.TRS
	*.CRS	*.ORS
\WPCDOS60		
	*.EXE	*.TRS
	*.FIL	*.HLP
	*.DRS	*.MOR
	*.THS	*.PHR
	*.LEX	*.WPS
	*.HYD	

Also, be sure that users have read-write access to the directory that contains their individual setup (.SET) files.

Depending on your users' level of knowledge and the way they use the network, you may choose to allow read-write access to some types of files in WordPerfect. Printer files are an example. To set up a paper size for a certain type of label or non-standard size paper for use with a network printer, a user must have read-write access to the .PRS file (the printer definition file) for that printer. You can allow users read-write access to those files so they can set their own paper sizes, or you can keep the files read-only and set up new paper sizes for users on request. If you do allow users read-write access to printer definition files or macro files, and so on, be sure to maintain a backup copy of the original file.

Tip: If you grant users unlimited read-write access to printer files, you may spend considerable time cleaning up files, yet if you insist on making changes involving printer files yourself, you may find

> yourself occupied more with adjusting paper sizes than running your LAN. A compromise might be to mark the files read-only, but allow users read-write access for a limited time—perhaps for an hour or two—when they need to set a paper size or make other changes that modify the .PRS files. That way, you'll have more control over who's changing the files and when, but you won't be spending time making the changes yourself.
>
> Another option is to anticipate every possible paper size and type your users might need and set up the .PRS files accordingly. You can then mark your .PRS files read-only for safety and still give each user access to all paper sizes and types.

Environment Settings for Networks

During installation, WordPerfect creates an environment file for your network called WP{WP}.ENV that identifies the type of network you use and where your .SET files are located. The program reads the environment file each time you start WordPerfect. The network and .SET file path are defined by two startup options in the environment file, */nt* and */ps*. You can include other network startup options in it, also. If you use a Novell network, your basic WP{WP}.ENV file might look like this:

```
/nt=1
/ps=w:\wp60\setup
```

If you need to edit the path for .SET files or make other changes to your WP{WP}.ENV file, you can do so using a DOS text editor.

More information on network startup options is in the "Network Startup Options" section in this appendix and your WordPerfect 6.0 manual.

Network Startup Options

Certain startup options are particularly useful when you use WordPerfect on a network. You can use any network startup option on the command line, and you can insert some (but not all) options in your environment file (WP{WP}.ENV). Network startup options are shown in the following list.

/d-*path*>: Redirects overflow files and temporary buffer files to the specified directory. This path must be unique for each concurrent user, and each user must have read, write, and create access in the specified directory.

1138

/nt=<*network #*>: Tells WordPerfect what networking software you're using.

/pf=<*path*>: Redirects temporary print queue files to the specified path.

/ps=<*path*>: Directs WordPerfect to use the .SET file in the specified path.

/sa: Runs WordPerfect in standalone mode, even if it's on a network.

/u=<*user initials*>: Allows WordPerfect to run on a network. Creates unique temporary files for each user.

/u@=<*userid*>: Overrides the user name provided by the network when WordPerfect cannot find **/u=<*user initials*>** or USERID.FIL.

Setup Files on a Network

A network installation of WordPerfect has two types of setup (.SET) files, a master setup file and individual user setup files. Using a master setup file, you can set defaults for your LAN's copy of WordPerfect—such as initial font, the date format, or a style for tables of contents—according to your organization's needs. A user setup file takes its settings from the master setup file when the user enters WordPerfect for the first time. Thereafter, the user can make changes that are saved in his or her personal setup file, but which leave the master setup file intact.

The master setup file is W{WP__}.SET. User setup files are named W*xxxxx*.SET, where *xxxxx* is a string of up to five characters that identify the user (usually the user's initials) and is created when the user enters WordPerfect for the first time. The user must enter WordPerfect using the same initials to use the same .SET file. Create a master setup file *before* any users start WordPerfect.

> **Tip:** One way to ensure that users always use their own setup files is to use the /u startup option in each user's AUTOEXEC.BAT file or, on a Novell network, in each user's login script. For more information, see the "Network Startup Options" section in this appendix, or consult your WordPerfect 6.0 manual.

To create your master setup file, start WordPerfect by entering wp/u={wp. Note the use of the /u startup option with {wp, the supervisor initials. Set up WordPerfect with the settings appropriate for your users' needs.

The NWPSETUP Utility

Once you've created a master setup file and users have created their setup files by entering WordPerfect, you can use the NWPSETUP utility to update all .SET file settings simultaneously. NWPSETUP also lets you update .SET files by groups if you have different groups in your organization that need their own unique settings for WordPerfect. If you have a user who's already set up in WordPerfect the way you want the entire LAN to be set up, NWSETUP lets you select that user's .SET file to be the master setup file. This saves you the time of selecting each setting yourself. The NWPSETUP menu is illustrated in Figure A.13.

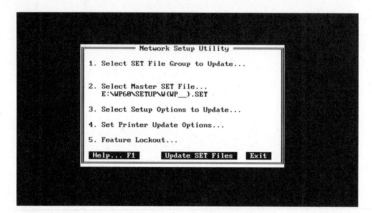

Figure A.13. The NWPSETUP menu.

To run NWPSETUP, change to your setup file directory, and enter NWSETUP at the DOS prompt. Before you run NWSETUP, be sure that all users have exited WordPerfect. Setup files of users who are still in WordPerfect when you run NWPSETUP won't be updated.

Network Printers

While you're creating your master setup file, follow Procedure A.6 to set up your network printers.

Procedure A.6. Setting up a network printer.

1. Select File, then Print/Fax; or press Shift+F7.
2. Choose Select. Check to be sure that each printer on the network has its own printer definition (.PRS file).

 Note: Each time you select and configure a printer, you're creating a printer definition—a .PRS file—for that printer. Create a .PRS file for each printer on the network, even if they are identical in make and model—they probably aren't identical in where they're located or in how users use them. Use Copy to duplicate previously created .PRS files if necessary.

3. Select a printer definition name, Edit, then Description.

4. Enter a unique name for the printer. The best way to name the printer is by its location or by a user who sits nearby (for example, FRONT2 or RON_PRINTER).

5. Select Network Port and specify a port. (If you use Novell NetWare, choose Server, a server name, Queue, and enter a queue name. Choose Suppress Top of Form if you want to suppress the top of the form that NetWare includes at the end of print jobs.) Choose OK.

6. Edit the printer definition by specifying the printer's font cartridges, sheet feeders, and so on.

7. Repeat this procedure for each printer on your network.

B

by Beth Fitzherbert

Customizing WordPerfect 6.0

Setup and Environment

A comfortable work environment is more than sitting in an ergonomically designed chair and typing on a keyboard positioned at the correct height. It's also the ease with which you can command your computer and what you want to see on-screen. In addition to the setup options you may be accustomed to seeing in previous versions of WordPerfect, WordPerfect 6.0 offers new ways to customize your work environment for comfort and efficiency. The way documents are displayed, the layout of the keyboard, and the way your mouse moves can all be adjusted to make WordPerfect easier to use.

The Setup feature is located on the File menu. Use it whenever you want to change your preferences for the options described in the following pages. Your setup configuration is saved in a file that WordPerfect reads each time you enter the program, so your settings remain in effect until you change them.

For the following Setup options, select File, Setup; or press Shift+F1. The Setup menu in shown in Figure B.1.

Note: If you use WordPerfect on a network, your setup preferences are stored in a file separate from those of other users. Changes you make in Setup won't affect other network users.

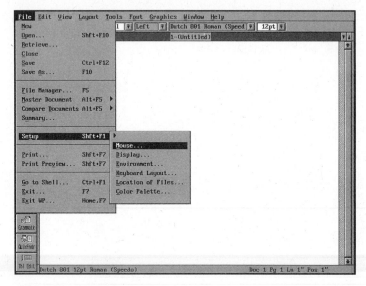

Figure B.1. The Setup menu.

Mouse

Choose **Mouse** to select the correct driver for your mouse and specify the speed of your mouse's response when you move it or double-click it.

Mouse Type

Select **Type** from the Mouse menu and look for your type of mouse on the list. Choose the generic mouse type, Mouse Driver (MOUSE.COM), if your mouse isn't listed. If no mice are listed, WordPerfect cannot locate your mouse drivers; select **Directory** on the Setup Mouse Type menu and enter the correct path for the location of the mouse drivers. If your mouse doesn't work after you've selected a mouse type, try using **Auto** Select to allow WordPerfect to choose a mouse driver for you.

Port

Your mouse may be connected to a serial port on the back of your computer, which means that your port setting should be COM1 or COM2. Modems, printers, and other peripheral devices often connect to your computer through COM1 or COM2, so your mouse must use whichever port is available. The Port setting option is available only if you use a serial mouse.

Double-Click Interval

The Double-click Interval is the amount of time (in 100ths of a second) between the two clicks in a double-click. If you're a quick clicker, you may want to set this number lower than the default value. If you're new to using a mouse or if you're just more comfortable with slower clicks, you may want to set this number higher.

Acceleration Factor

The Acceleration factor is the speed the pointer moves on the screen as you move the mouse. Select a value from 0 to 100 for this setting. The easiest way to discover your choices for the speed settings is to set each at different speeds a few times and try them out.

Left-Handed Mouse

The last option in the Mouse dialog box, Left-handed Mouse, can be helpful if you use your mouse with your left hand. It reverses the buttons on your mouse so that the action button, normally the far-left button, is the far-right button.

Display

Display lets you specify the Graphics mode or Text mode screen type appropriate for your monitor and graphics card. You can also choose the colors you want to use in Graphics mode or Text mode.

Screen Type

It's important to select a screen type that's compatible with your monitor and graphics card. For example, if your monitor's maximum resolution is 680 x 480 and you try to set your screen type at 1024 x 768, you'll likely encounter problems, depending on your monitor and graphics card.

To select a screen type for graphics mode, select Graphics Mode Screen Type/ Colors, Screen Type. A list of graphics mode screen types is shown in Figure B.2. WordPerfect selects a default screen type during installation, but you should select the one that exactly matches your monitor and graphics card for optimum performance. If your screen type is not listed, use the Auto Select option to allow WordPerfect to choose a screen type.

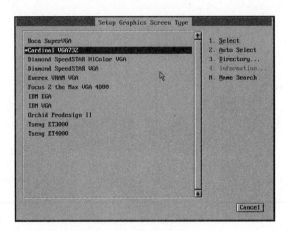

Figure B.2. A list of Graphics mode screen types.

If no screen types are listed, WordPerfect cannot find its graphics driver files. Choose Directory to enter the path for the location of the graphics driver files.

WordPerfect automatically selects your text mode screen type; you probably won't need to make changes to the text mode screen type setting. If you do, refer to the preceding paragraph on selecting the graphics mode screen type.

Screen Colors

People often have strong opinions on screen colors. Fortunately, you have plenty to choose from in WordPerfect 6.0—256 colors to choose from in graphics mode, and 256 color combinations in text mode. You can specify the color of nearly every object on your screen. Remember that screen colors are only used to display text and objects on your screen—they don't affect the appearance of your printed documents.

Graphics Mode Screen Colors

You can select one of the color schemes WordPerfect has created, create your own from scratch or edit one of the available schemes.

Procedure B.1. Working with Screen Colors, Graphics Mode.

1. Select **F**ile, Se**t**up, **D**isplay, **G**raphics Mode Screen Type/Colors, then **C**olor Schemes.

2. Choose **C**reate and enter a name for a new color scheme. Or, select a color scheme and choose **E**dit. The Edit Graphics Screen Colors dialog box is displayed in Figure B.3. A list of screen elements is shown on the left, and a sample of the current color scheme is shown on the right.

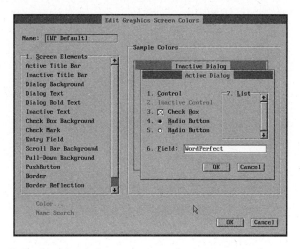

Figure B.3. The Edit Graphics Screen Colors dialog box.

Note: You can't edit the color schemes provided by WordPerfect, but you can copy, rename, and then edit the copies.

3. Look at the sample and decide which colors you want to change. Select the screen element you want to change from the list. For example, choose Dialog Background.

4. Now select the Color option that appears below the list to view a palette of colors (use the scroll bar or the cursor keys to view all 256 colors).

5. Select the color you want for the background of your dialog boxes. When you select OK, your choice is displayed in the sample. Continue choosing colors until you arrive at the color combination you want.

Procedure B.2. Working with Screen Colors, Text mode.

1. In Text mode, select **F**ile, Se**t**up, **D**isplay, **T**ext Mode Screen Type/Colors, then **C**olor Schemes.

2. To create a new color scheme, select Create. If you're creating a new scheme, WordPerfect prompts you to name it and select the type of font for which you want to change colors. Or, select a color scheme and choose Edit. To create a new color scheme based on one of the schemes provided by WordPerfect, such as Gettysburg, select the scheme, copy it, then choose Edit.

3. In the Edit Text Screen Colors dialog box, choose Text Attributes or Menus & Dialogs. (If you changed screen colors in a previous version of WordPerfect, Text Attributes may look familiar.) As shown in Figure B.4, a list of text attributes such as Bold and Redline, or menus and dialogs attributes such as PushButton and Dialog Text appear under Attributes. A sample of the current color scheme is shown on the right.

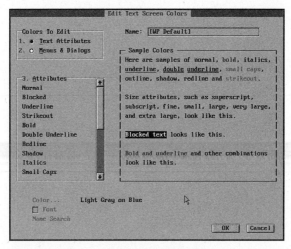

Figure B.4. The Edit Text Screen Colors dialog box.

4. Select Attributes, then choose the attribute you want to change. When you select an attribute from the list, the Color option below the list shows the current color setting for that attribute.

5. Select Color to change the setting. From the screen of color combinations that appears, select the one you want, then select OK.

Environment

Environment settings are settings that determine some of the ways you want WordPerfect to work as you create and edit documents. To change Environment settings, choose Setup, Environment. The Environment dialog box is shown in Figure B.5.

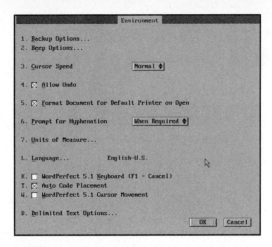

Figure B.5. The Environment dialog box.

Backup Options

WordPerfect has two document backup options, Timed Document Backup and Original Document. You may choose to use both, one, or neither. The WordPerfect default settings are Timed Document Backup on at a backup time interval of ten minutes and Original Document off. The backup options are shown in Figure B.6.

Timed Document Backup

When activated, Timed Document Backup automatically saves any open document to a temporary file while you work. When you exit WordPerfect properly (by selecting Exit on the File menu), the temporary file is deleted. The purpose of Timed Document Backup is to save your document in emergency situations such as a power loss or a PC lock up. This feature is especially good insurance when you've typed steadily for several minutes without remembering to save the document yourself.

Check the Timed Document Backup box to activate this feature.

 Caution: Timed Document Backup is not a substitute for the Save feature. Under normal circumstances, if you want to save your document, you must select Save from the File menu, name the document, and save it. Don't assume that Timed Document Backup has saved your document and then exit WordPerfect without saving it yourself—you'll lose all of your work!

Minutes Between Backup

Timed Document Backup saves open documents periodically on an interval of minutes that you specify. The less time between intervals, the less work you might lose. If you're a fast typist, you may want to set **M**inutes Between Backup at five or ten minutes. If you're a slow typist or if you pause frequently while you work, an interval of 15 or 20 minutes may be sufficient. You know that Timed Document Backup is working if you see the Timed Backup box flash on your screen.

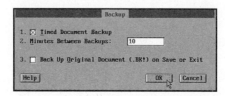

Figure B.6. WordPerfect's two backup options are Timed Document Backup and Backup Original Document.

If a power loss or other catastrophe stops WordPerfect, Timed Document Backup saves the backup copy of your document in the directory that you've named as your backup directory in Setup under **L**ocation of Files. The names of the Timed Document Backup files are WP{WPC}.BK1 for the document that was open on the Document 1 screen at the time the power loss occurred, WP{WPC}.BK2 for the document that was open on the Document 2 screen, and so on. If you have six documents open, WordPerfect makes six backup files. Each file is current as of the last timed backup interval that occurred. When you re-enter WordPerfect, the Backup File Exists dialog box displays and asks you to rename, delete, or open any existing backup files. You cannot rename the backup file to an existing filename.

Caution: You can open the backup file to check its contents, but once you do, you should rename it or delete it. If you want to save the file, you must rename it, because WordPerfect overwrites the file the next time it performs a Timed Document Backup if the file is still named WP{WPC}.BK1, WP{WPC}.BK2, and so on.

Backup Original Document

If you activate Backup Original Document, each time you save a document, Backup Original Document also saves the document as it existed the last time you saved it. Backup Original Document files have the filename extension .BK! and are saved in the backup directory specified in Location of Files under Setup. If you often make changes to a document, save it, and then wish you had the original version of the file back, try using the Original Backup feature.

Check Back Up **O**riginal Document (.BK!) on Save or Exit to activate the Backup Original Document feature.

Beep Options

Select Beep Options to tell WordPerfect to do the following:

▲ **Beep on Error**. WordPerfect beeps when an error occurs that causes an error dialog box to appear on-screen. The default setting is Off.

▲ **Beep on Hyphenation**. This setting causes a beep to sound when the Position Hyphen box appears. The default setting is On.

▲ **Beep on Search Failure**. After searching for the character string you specify and finding no match, WordPerfect beeps when it displays the message String not found. The default setting is Off.

Cursor Speed

Cursor Speed controls how fast the cursor moves across the screen when you use the arrow keys. Available speeds are 15, 20, 30, 40, and 50 characters per second.

Allow Undo

Check this box to activate the Undo feature. Undo allows you to undo the last formatting or editing change you made to your document.

Format Document for Default Printer on Open

When enabled, this option reformats any document for your current printer when you open the document. Different printers often handle fonts, margins, and other characteristics of your document's formatting quite differently, and you may or may not want the document to change. The default setting for this option is On.

When this option is disabled, WordPerfect looks in your list of installed printers for the printer for which the document was last formatted. If it cannot find the printer, it formats the document for the current printer.

Prompt for Hyphenation

This setting controls what WordPerfect does when a word needs to be hyphenated and hyphenation is turned on:

▲ **Never**. This option tells WordPerfect to follow the current hyphenation dictionary. If WordPerfect cannot find the word there, it wraps the whole word to the next line.

▲ **When Required**. This option also tells WordPerfect to hyphenate the word according to the hyphenation dictionary. However, for this option, if WordPerfect cannot find the word, it prompts you to position the hyphen. This is the default setting.

▲ **Always**. Select this option if you want WordPerfect to stop each time it encounters a word that needs a hyphen and prompt you to position the hyphen.

Units of Measure

You can set WordPerfect's units of measure for display and entry of numbers in dialog boxes with one unit of measure and to display information on the status line with another. Inches displayed with the " symbol is the default unit of measure, but you can also choose inches displayed with i, centimeters, millimeters, points, 1200ths of an inch, or WordPerfect Version 4.2 units (lines and columns).

Tip: WordPerfect can convert units of measure to decimals for you. In setting a margin, for example, if you enter 1 5/8" in the Margins dialog box, WordPerfect automatically converts 1 5/8 to its rounded decimal equivalent, 1.63.

Language

If you create documents in languages other than United States English and have installed the WordPerfect dictionaries for those languages, WordPerfect refers to them in performing certain functions such as sorting and spell-checking. Use the Language option to select the language you want WordPerfect to use.

You can use one language for an entire document, or you can change languages within a document. Changing your language setting does not change the language WordPerfect uses in menus, Help, or other features.

WordPerfect 5.1 Keyboard

The default keyboard for WordPerfect 6.0 is the CUA, or common user access keyboard. Some users of WordPerfect, however, may prefer to use the Version 5.1

keyboard, in which F1 is Cancel, F3 is Help, and Esc is Repeat. Check this box to activate the WordPerfect 5.1 keyboard. (For more information on the CUA keyboard and keyboard layouts, see the section on keyboard layouts in this appendix.)

Auto Code Placement

Auto Code Placement allows WordPerfect to choose the most logical position for a particular code. For example, a page numbering code usually affects an entire document, so WordPerfect automatically places page numbering codes at the top of the document.

Delimited Text Options

You can export and import data from and to most database and spreadsheet programs by formatting the data as DOS delimited text. A delimiter is a character, such as a comma, that's used to separate fields and records of data for exporting. In the Setup dialog box, you can specify how you want WordPerfect to handle delimited text.

Keyboard Layout

In WordPerfect, you can select different keyboards designed especially for certain tasks. The ability to change keyboard layouts is a useful tool that many people use to their advantage.

You can select a different keyboard layout at any time, and your choice remains in effect until you change it. The characters in documents you type with one keyboard layout do not change if you open them with a different keyboard selected. In fact, you can change keyboard layouts within a document as often as necessary.

To select, create, or edit a keyboard layout, select File, Setup, Keyboard.

Types of Keyboard Layouts

WordPerfect 6.0 installs four different keyboard layouts when you install the program. The default keyboard layout when you install WordPerfect using the standard installation option is Original.

To see the key assignments for the keyboard you've selected, (except Original) choose Map in the Keyboard Layout dialog box. Use the cursor keys to move around the rows of keys. The key action and a description of the key's current function appear at the bottom of the Keyboard Map dialog box, as shown in Figure B.7.

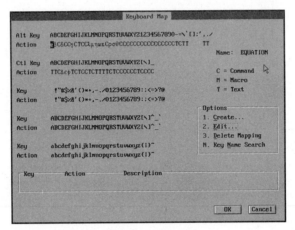

Figure B.7. The Keyboard Map dialog box.

The types of keyboard layouts shipped with WordPerfect are.

▲ **CUAWPW52**. This is the common user access (CUA) keyboard layout. *Common user access* refers to the standard keyboard layout adopted by many software companies. The idea is that if, for example, F5 is the key that commands the computer to print in one program, it should be the key for the print command in all other programs, even if they're produced by different companies.

The CUA keyboard does vary somewhat from program to program, however, because different programs function differently. For example, database software performs different functions than word processing software, so many keys have assignments for commands that aren't in word processing programs. Despite unavoidable inconsistencies, industry-wide use of a standard keyboard layout significantly decreases the amount of time it takes software users to learn new programs.

▲ **Equation**. This keyboard is mapped to help you use the Equations feature more efficiently.

▲ **Macros**. This keyboard is mapped especially for use with the Macros feature.

▲ **Original**. When you install WordPerfect 6.0, Original is the default selection.

Working with Keyboard Layouts

You can use the keyboard layouts supplied by WordPerfect, or you can create your own keyboard layout. For example, you can create a new keyboard layout that has special characters used in foreign languages, such as ñ in Spanish or ç in French. If you frequently work with documents written in a language other than English, creating a keyboard designed especially for that language is the easiest way to insert special characters.

Perhaps some words that you use frequently in documents are difficult to type, such as a company name that's spelled in an unusual way. By editing your keyboard, you can assign the entire company name to one key.

Procedure B.3. Creating keyboard layouts.

1. Choose File, Setup, Keyboard Layout, and Create. Then enter a name for the new keyboard. The Edit Keyboard dialog box appears.
2. Select Create. The Create Key dialog box is displayed in Figure B.8.

Figure B.8. The Create Key dialog box.

3. Press the key or key combination you want to define and enter a description of the key's function.
4. Choose the Action Type:

   ▲ **Text**. Select this if the key will be used for inserting text. Enter the text you want to assign to the key in the text field.

   ▲ **Command**. Select this if the key will be used for a single command. A dialog box containing all available keyboard commands displays. Select the appropriate command.

   ▲ **Macro**. Select this if the key will be used to invoke a macro. You can create and edit macros using this option.

Repeat Steps 2 through 4 until you've finished assigning the keys you want.

Procedure B.4. Editing keyboard layouts.

1. Choose File, Setup, then Keyboard Layout. Select the keyboard layout you want to edit and choose Edit in the Keyboard Layout dialog box. The Edit Keyboard dialog box appears.

2. Select the key you want to edit. Select Edit. The Edit Key dialog box appears.

3. Press the key or key combination you want to redefine and enter a description of the key's new function. Choose a new Action Type if necessary. Repeat Steps 2 and 3 for each key you want to reassign. If you're editing a key, you probably don't want to change the key or key combination.

> **Tip:** To assign special characters from WordPerfect character sets (such as foreign language characters) to a keyboard layout, select Text as the Action Type. You can then press Ctrl+W to display the WordPerfect characters sets. Select the character you want, then select Insert to add it to the action text field.

You can edit any keyboard layout unless you use WordPerfect on a network. Always make a copy of the layout before editing it, so you have the original if you need it.

If you're on a network, the keyboard files are shared by users on the network and may be marked as read-only. This means that you can use the files, but you cannot change them. If you try to edit this type of file, WordPerfect alerts you that the file is a read-only file. You can edit keyboard layouts that you create. Network users should contact their LAN administrator for help with creating customized keyboard layouts.

Location of Files

The Location of Files option shows you where the program files, graphics files, and other types of files used by WordPerfect 6.0 are located. The Location of Files dialog box is illustrated in Figure B.9.

If you chose the custom installation option or installed WordPerfect 6.0 on a network, the file locations you specified at that time appear in Location of Files. If you chose the standard installation option, WordPerfect automatically chose most of your file locations for you. Some file locations, such as the location of backup files, are left blank for you to specify.

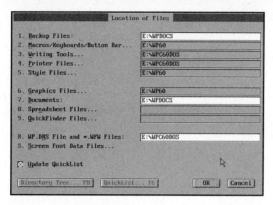

Figure B.9. The Location of Files dialog box.

Tip: If you want to specify a new directory path in Location of Files but forgot to create a directory first, go ahead and enter the path. WordPerfect creates the directory for you as long as the path to it is valid.

Caution: While it runs, the WordPerfect program looks for the files it needs according to the locations shown in the Location of Files dialog box. Some people start out using the WordPerfect default locations for files and later decide to group files such as macros or graphics files in separate subdirectories. That's fine, but if you decide to move files or rename directories, be sure to make the appropriate changes in the Location of Files dialog box so WordPerfect can find the files.

Personal and Shared Paths

When you select a file type in the Location of Files dialog box, many of the file types let you specify a personal or shared path for the files, as shown in Figure B.10. If you're not using WordPerfect on a network, you don't need to be concerned with this—all the locations of your files appear as personal paths. If you do use WordPerfect on a network, however, this enhancement saves you some of the frustration that network users of previous versions of WordPerfect experienced when trying to write their own macros or create their own styles and still have easy access to the shared styles and macros.

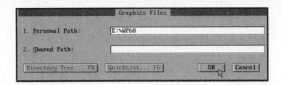

Figure B.10. You can specify both personal and shared paths if you use WordPerfect on a network.

As you may know, shared program files on networks are often marked read-only to prevent users from changing or deleting them. In previous versions of WordPerfect, all macro files, styles, keyboard layouts, and other similar files— files created with certain features to be used as tools—were stored in single, shared directories. People could use the files, but they couldn't edit them, and because their access to the directory itself was restricted, often they couldn't create their own styles, and so on.

In WordPerfect 6.0, instead of being thwarted by read-only files, you can save your own macros, keyboard layouts, styles, and other handy tools in your own directories that are located on your personal paths. You can still use the shared files, too.

Most of the options in the Location of Files dialog box offer space for a shared path and a personal path. An exception is Writing Tools, which asks for a Main path and a Supplementary path. Writing Tools includes WordPerfect's dictionaries. All WordPerfect users have been able to create personal, or supplementary, dictionary files for some time.

Color Printing Palette

If you have access to a color printer, you may want to customize color palettes. WordPerfect comes with two color palettes. You can use them as they are, or you can edit them. You can also create your own palettes.

To go to the Color Palette, choose File, Setup, Color Palette.

Color Display Units

Three types of color display units are available: RGB, which is red-green-blue; CMYK, which is cyan-magenta-yellow-black; and HLS, which is hue-luminosity-saturation.

When you adjust red, green, and blue using the RGB system or cyan, magenta, yellow, and black using the CMYK system, you're specifying the amounts of each color to use. In the HSL system, hue is the ratio of the colors that combine to make the custom color. Saturation is the purity of the color, and luminosity is the lightness or darkness of the hue.

Procedure B.5. Creating and editing color palettes.

1. To create a new color palette, select Create in the Color Printing Palettes dialog box, then enter a name for your palette.

2. Select the palette you just named, and choose Edit. To edit an existing palette, select it, then select Edit in the Color Printing Palettes dialog box. If you're creating your own color palette, WordPerfect provides a list of colors in a basic palette that you can edit, add to, or delete from. If you're editing a palette, the colors in the currently selected palette appear on the list.

3. To create a new color for a palette, select Create and enter a name for the color. Then "mix" the color using the hue and saturation color wheel and the lumination color bar or by entering the amounts of each color of the color display unit you selected. The color wheel and the lumination color bar are shown in Figure B.11. To edit a color on the palette, select the color, then choose Edit.

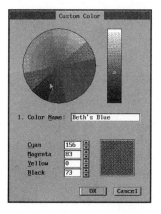

Figure B.11. Use the color wheel and the lumination color bar to "mix" your colors for a color printing palette.

The changes you make to the basic palette stay in your palettes. The default palette remains unchanged for the next time you want to create a palette.

Screen Setup

WordPerfect 6.0 provides many more options for screen displays than previous versions of WordPerfect. Whether you prefer your screen full of colorful buttons or virtually empty with only spartan necessities showing, you'll appreciate the flexibility the screen display options offer.

To change screen settings, choose View, Screen Setup.

Screen Options

Under Screen Options in the Screen Setup dialog box, you can control the objects that are within the document screen. Customize your screen by selecting or deselecting these options:

▲ **Pull-Down Menus**. As in previous versions of WordPerfect since 5.0, you can choose to use pull-down menus or not. In the default setting, pull-down menus are turned on.

▲ **Alt Key Activates Menus**. Also as in previous versions, you can activate the pulldown menus with the Alt key. This option is turned off in the default settings.

> **Note:** Remember that the Alt key is used in hotkey combinations in some TSR (terminate-and-stay-resident) programs (TSRs are programs that stay in memory so you can start them from inside another program by pressing a key combination known as a "hotkey"), so using the Alt key to pull down menus in WordPerfect may create conflicts when you try to use some TSRs.

▲ **Ribbon**. The ribbon is a thin bar between the menu bar and the button bar that gives you quick access to zoom options, outline levels, number of columns, justification, fonts, and point sizes. You can use the ribbon only if you use a mouse. The ribbon works in Graphics mode and Text mode. See Figure B.12 for an illustration of the ribbon.

▲ **Outline Bar**. The Outline Bar provides you with convenient access to the Outline feature's tools and options. You can use the Outline bar in Graphics mode and Text mode.

▲ **Button Bar**. The button bar, which you can also activate through the View menu, lets you assign all of your favorite commands to handy buttons. The button bar is available in both Graphics mode and Text mode.

▲ **Display Characters**. In a WYSIWYG environment in which you're using proportional fonts and working in graphics mode, determining the number of spaces between words or the number of lines between paragraphs is sometimes difficult. A character such as a less-than symbol (<) can show hard carriage returns and a dash or a period can show your spacing clearly. An example is illustrated in Figure B.13.

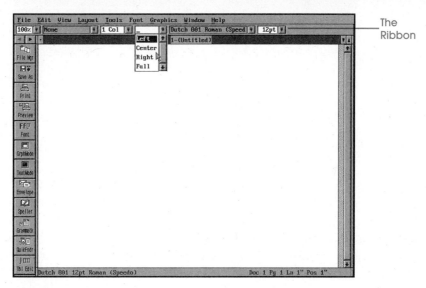

Figure B.12. The ribbon lets you access fonts and other often-used tools.

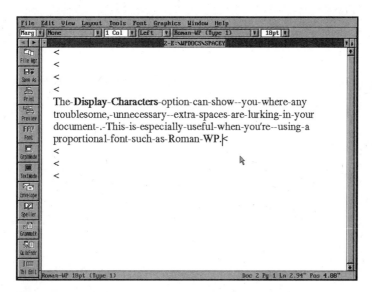

Figure B.13. Use the Display Characters option to help you count lines and see unnecessary spacing.

▲ **Display of Merge Codes**. Use this option to control the display of merge codes in documents. The default setting is Show Full Codes, but you may find that displaying the codes detracts from the document's actual appearance.

1161

▲ **Window Options**. This option controls the appearance of the window surrounding the document screen. Framed Window clearly shows the boundaries of the document on-screen. The scroll bars are helpful for moving through your document quickly. If you've entered comments about the document, such as the author and the date it was created, Display Comments shows them. The Status Line option lets you select the information that you want to appear on the status line, which is the bottom line on your screen.

 Note: Like the button bar, outline bar, and the ribbon, the scroll bars are available in both Graphics and Text mode.

▲ **Reveal Codes**. Use this option to customize Reveal Codes. When you check the Display Details box, Reveal Codes includes details such as column measurements and graphics filenames in your codes. If you find Reveal Codes a little intimidating because of the amount of seemingly undecipherable information it displays, you may prefer to switch this option off for codes-only display. Window Percentage is the amount of screen space Reveal Codes occupies when active. The default setting is 25 percent.

▲ **Zoom**. You can set your default Zoom value by selecting one of these options.

Button Bars

A handy new feature in WordPerfect is the button bar. If you find plodding through pulldown menus tiresome, using a button bar with your mouse saves time and patience. To turn button bar on, select View, Button Bar. The button bar feature is also located in Screen Setup under View. Figure B.14 illustrates a button bar.

Button bars allow you to assign the commands you use most often to buttons that are displayed on-screen. To use a command on the button bar, just click its button. For example, to turn off columns without using the button bar, choose Layout, then Columns, then Columns Off. That's three steps. If you've assigned Columns Off to a button on the button bar, however, just click the Columns Off button with your mouse and Columns is off.

WPMAIN is the name of the default button bar. WordPerfect comes with six other button bars already set up for you. You can use them as they are, edit them, or create your own from scratch. Nearly any WordPerfect command can be assigned to a button—you can even assign other button bars to a button.

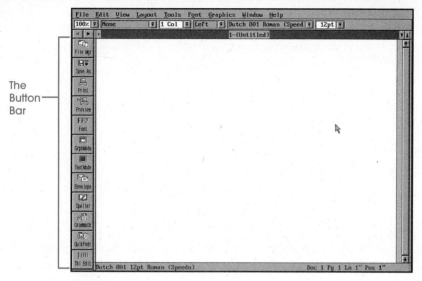

The
Button
Bar

Figure B.14. The button bar.

To select the current button bar, choose View, Button Bar Setup, then Select. A list of available button bars appears, as illustrated in Figure B.15. Select the button bar you want to use.

Tip: Consider creating a button bar styled for each type of document or project you do in WordPerfect, and then assign each of those button bars to a button. You have quick access to every feature you need for everything you do, simply by clicking once or twice on the button bar.

Procedure B.6. Editing button bars.

1. Choose View, Button Bar Setup, then Edit or Select. If you choose Select, choose Edit from the Select Button Bar dialog box. A list of the current button bar commands and a list of options appear. You can add commands to the button bar by selecting one of the first four options:

   ▲ **Add Menu Item.** Select this option to assign buttons by browsing through the pulldown menus. Using your mouse, just pull menus down and choose on the features that you want to add to the button bar. Select OK or press F7 when you've made all of your selections.

▲ **Add Feature**. Select this option to assign buttons from a list of all features that can be assigned to the button bar. A partial list of available features is shown in Figure B.16. Highlight a feature, then choose Select.

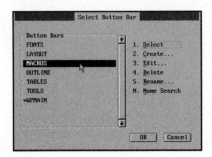

Figure B.15. A partial list of the features you can assign to buttons on the button bar.

▲ **Add Macro**. Select this option to assign a macro to a button. Highlight a macro name, then choose Select.

▲ **Add Button Bar**. Select this option to assign a button bar to a button. Highlight a button bar name, then choose Select.

Note: Certain commands such as Zoom, Justification, and Alignment cannot be assigned to buttons themselves, but their follow-on commands can. For example, you can't assign Zoom to a button, but you can assign 150 percent, Page Width, or the other options on the Zoom menu to buttons.

2. To delete a button, highlight the button and choose Delete Button.

3. To move a button, select the button and choose Move Button. Now go back to the button list and select the button that you want positioned after the button you're moving. Choose Paste Button, and the button is inserted in its new place. The buttons are listed in the order they appear on-screen, which may be left to right or top to bottom, depending on how you've told WordPerfect to display them.

4. Choose OK when you're finished.

Procedure B.7. Creating button bars.

1. Choose View, Button Bar Setup, then Select. A list of the available button bars appears.

2. Choose Create, give your new button bar a name, then select your buttons as described previously.

3. Choose OK when you're finished.

> **Tip:** A quick way to create a new button bar is to edit an existing one that already has most of the buttons you want. Be sure to rename the existing button bar first so you'll still have an unchanged copy. (On a network, the button bar files that come with WordPerfect, such as WPMAIN.WPB, are probably marked read-only so network users cannot change or rename them. Network users can change and rename button bars they've created themselves, however.)

Button Bar Display Options

Not only can you choose what commands go on your button bars, but you can also tell WordPerfect how you want them displayed on-screen:

▲ Horizontally across the top or bottom

▲ Vertically on the left or right

▲ Pictures and text showing

▲ Text-only showing

▲ Pictures-only showing

One of many ways you can set up your button bar on-screen is illustrated in Figure B.16.

To customize your button bar display, choose View, Button Bar Setup, then Options.

Often, because of the size of the screen, not all the buttons on a button bar can be displayed at once. When there are more buttons than fit on-screen, click the small arrows to the left or top of the button bar to access all the buttons.

> **Tip:** Some ways of arranging your button bars allow more buttons to display at one time. A setup of text-only buttons down the right or left side of the screen can display the most buttons at once.

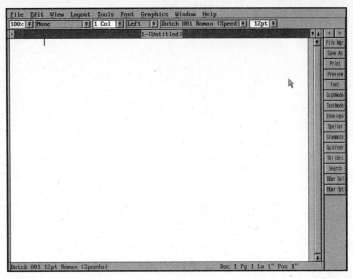

Figure B.16. An example of a vertical, text-only button bar positioned on the right.

Custom Dictionaries

In addition to beeps, button bars, and backup files, you can control the way Speller and its dictionaries work.

To find Speller Setup, select Tools, Writing Tools, then Speller. Setup is in the lower-left corner of the Speller dialog box. Press Shift+F1 to access it.

Chain Dictionaries

The term *main dictionary* refers to a dictionary shipped with WordPerfect or purchased from WordPerfect Corporation for use with the Speller feature. If you purchased WordPerfect in the United States, the main dictionary in your software is United States English. You may also have main dictionaries for other languages if you use foreign languages in WordPerfect and have purchased dictionaries for them from WordPerfect Corporation.

Although you always have at least one main dictionary available for spell-checking in WordPerfect, you can chain main and supplemental dictionaries so that WordPerfect can use more than one if necessary.

For example, perhaps your doctoral dissertation examines advances in French medical practices in the time of Napoleon, and you quote various sources in

French throughout the document. If you mark the French text as French and chain WordPerfect's French national dictionary to your United States English main dictionary, WordPerfect can simultaneously spell-check the English and the French using their respective dictionaries. If you've added medical terms to a special supplemental dictionary, WordPerfect can use that dictionary in the spell-check also.

To chain main or supplemental dictionaries, select Chain Main Dictionaries or Chain Supplemental Dictionaries on the Speller Setup menu. A list of chains appears. Select Add Chain, then select the dictionary you want to chain to your main or supplemental dictionary. If WordPerfect can't find the dictionary file, enter the path where the file is located. (Ideally, all of your dictionary files should be located in the same directory.) WordPerfect dictionary files have the filename extension .LEX.

Other options on the Speller Setup menu are:

▲ **Check for Numbers in Words**. Speller checks words with numbers in them just as it checks any other word. You may prefer, however, to deselect this option so WordPerfect will ignore such words.

▲ **Check for Double Words**. Have you ever paused while typing and then started again, accidentally typing the word on which you paused again, so the word appears twice in a row in the sentence? When Check for Double Words is on, Speller alerts you to words that appear two consecutive times.

▲ **Check for Irregular Capitalization**. When this option is turned on, WordPerfect checks for uppercase letters within words, even if they are spelled correctly, such as "apPle" or "emploYment."

▲ **Prompt on Auto-Replace? Disable Document Dictionary**. Each document you create is saved with its own supplemental dictionary. Words that you tell Speller to skip during a spell check are added to the document dictionary if this option is turned off.

Using the Shell

Shell is a popular WordPerfect product that you may know from WordPerfect Office or WordPerfect Library. Simply speaking, Shell is a desktop organizer that lets you assign all of the programs you run on your PC to a menu, which can save you considerable time. When you have all your programs on a menu, you don't have to change directories or type directory paths. Shell also offers features that enhance the menu system such as hot keys that let you access programs with a few keystrokes and a clipboard to cut, copy, and paste text from one program to another. Now developed into Version 4.0, Shell is shipped with your copy of WordPerfect 6.0.

Shell is installed to your WPC60DOS directory when you install WordPerfect 6.0. You can run Shell from there by changing to that directory and typing `shell`, but to take full advantage of Shell's capability, you may want to edit your AUTOEXEC.BAT file so that it loads Shell automatically and displays your menu when you turn on your computer or reboot. And, if you include the WPC60DOS directory in your path, you can start Shell from anywhere in DOS. Your AUTOEXEC.BAT file might look something like this:

```
echo off
path c:\;c:\DOS;c:\wp60;c:\wpc60dos
prompt=$p$g
cd\wpc60dos
shell
```

If you use WordPerfect 6.0 on a network, your network may already be set up with Shell menus. Contact your network administrator for more information.

The rest of this section on using Shell is a brief overview to get you started. To take advantage of all of Shell's functions, be sure to consult the documentation included in your WordPerfect 6.0 package.

Creating Your Initial Menu

When you enter Shell for the first time, it prompts you to create an initial menu using one of four options, as shown in Figure B.17.

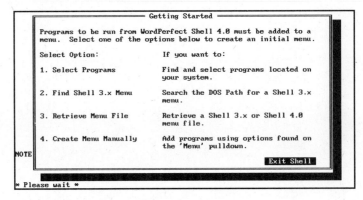

Figure B.17. Getting started with the Initial menu.

If you've never used Shell before, select:

> Option 1, **Select Programs**. Use this option to command Shell to search for the types of programs you want to include on your menu, including program files, macro files, batch files, and others.

Option 4, **Create Menu Manually**. Use this option to add programs manually. If you know where your program files are located, this option is the easier of the two, because you can tell Shell exactly what you want without waiting for it to search for files.

If you've used Shell before and want to use your menu from a previous version, select:

Option 2, **Find Shell 3.x Menu**. This option searches for menu files from previous versions of Shell.

Option 3, **Retrieve Menu File**. Use this option to retrieve a Shell Version 3.x or 4.x menu file.

Starting a Program

When you've created your menu, it appears in the center of the Shell screen. To start a program, double-click a menu item if you have a mouse, or highlight the item using the arrow keys and press Enter.

Switching Between Programs

Shell allows you to run more than one program at a time. To switch from one program to another without exiting the first program, press the second program's hot key, which is Ctrl+Alt+[the program's hotkey]. You can define and edit a program's hotkey by selecting Menu, Add Item or Edit Item, Program, HotKey.

Customizing Your Shell Desktop

You can customize your Shell desktop by selecting File, Setup. In Setup, you can change your screen colors, customize your windows, edit your menus, and choose to display Shell systems windows to help you organize information while you're working in Shell.

File Manager

You can use WordPerfect's File Manager in Shell to find, copy, move, and delete your files as well as the other File Manager tasks to which you may be accustomed if you've used WordPerfect in the past. File Manager in Shell is the same program as File Manager in WordPerfect 6.0. (See Figure B.18 for an illustration of the File Manager screen.)

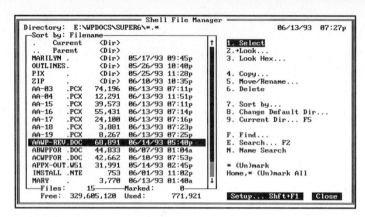

Figure B.18. The Shell File Manager.

Message Board

Shell also offers Message Board, an area where you can store personal or, if you're on a network, shared public messages. Just write a message to yourself or to someone else and post it on a Message Board. This feature is a bit like electronic mail in that you're exchanging messages with people, but you're posting messages instead of sending them. On a network, anyone with access to the directory where you place a shared message board can read the messages there. Figure B.19 shows an example of adding a message to a personal Message Board.

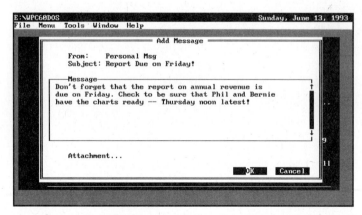

Figure B.19. Adding a message to a personal Message Board.

To set up a personal Message Board, select File, Setup, Location of Files, Messages. Then, if you're on a network, select Personal Directory. To set up a shared

Message Board, select File, Setup, Location of Files, Messages, Shared Directory. Then set up your Message Board user name by selecting Tools, Message Board, User Name.

Clipboards

Clipboards allow you to store information that you can copy and paste between programs or to different locations within the same program. Clipboard information is stored temporarily—it's deleted when you exit Shell. You can create up to 80 different clipboards of information per Shell session.

As a simple example of using Clipboard with WordPerfect Corporation products, suppose you wrote a bulleted list in WordPerfect 6.0 that you wanted to include in a slide for a presentation in WordPerfect Presentations 2.0. Rather than retype the information, you would:

1. Hotkey from Presentations to WordPerfect 6.0.
2. Retrieve the file where the bulleted list is stored and block the text you want to use in the slide.
3. Press Ctrl+F1, which is the Shell key combination for WordPerfect products. Then select Save to save the list to a Clipboard.
4. Hotkey back to Presentations and position the cursor where you want to insert the bulleted list.
5. Press Ctrl+F1 to paste the list into the slide.

That might seem like a lot of steps, but when you get used to following them, you'll be amazed at the time you can save.

You can also use Clipboard with Shell-aware programs; that is, programs that, although they aren't WordPerfect products, are designed to work with the WordPerfect Shell.

Shell Macros

You can also write macros in Shell to automate repetitive tasks. Shell offers two types of macros: Keystroke macros and Advanced macros. Keystroke macros are simply a series of recorded keystrokes that you play back to perform a task. Advanced macros can function that way, and they can include other macro commands and variables. To use Advanced macros, however, you must first load the macro engine.

To create a macro, select Tools, Macros, then Type (if you've loaded the macro engine); or, press Ctrl+Alt+F10. Select the type of macro you want, then select Record to name the macro and record it.

C

by Beth Fitzherbert

What's New in WordPerfect 6.0

What's new in WordPerfect 6.0? When you see it, you'll think that everything is. The new graphical interfaces, button bars, and dialog boxes might fool you, but if you look closer, you'll see that your favorite features are still there. Even though it has a new look, the uncluttered document screen WordPerfect is famous for is still there and still uncluttered. (Of course, if you're new to WordPerfect, you're in for a treat. Welcome!)

WordPerfect 6.0 is much more than the usual features embellished with sculptured boxes and buttons, however. Finally, after all the commotion created by Microsoft Windows, DOS users have a word processor that rivals any of its Windows counterparts in function, appearance, and ease of use. In fact, WordPerfect 6.0 offers many of the same features found in WordPerfect for Windows.

This version introduces more new features and enhancements than ever before in a DOS version of WordPerfect. If you've ever called WordPerfect customer support with a problem or a request, take some of the credit for this new version. WordPerfect Corporation added many of Version 6.0's enhancements—about 650 in all—because 30,000 customers said they wanted the enhancements, or their problems showed that the enhancements were needed.

The buzzword for WordPerfect 6.0 could be *integrated*. As you use the program, you'll see basic database capability in the Merge feature, a variety of spreadsheet functions in Tables, and several enhancements in printing, graphics, and fonts that assert WordPerfect's potential as a full-fledged desktop publishing system. With the Sound Clips feature, WordPerfect is even making moves toward multimedia. WordPerfect 6.0 also supports electronic mail and faxing now. What does all this mean? It means that your favorite word processing software may become your favorite "everything" software. For small business and home computer users, WordPerfect 6.0 is an economical alternative to buying separate database and spreadsheet software. Not everyone needs a full-featured database or spreadsheet program that does complex calculations.

Important to note is that although WordPerfect Corporation has invested considerable time and resources in adding new functions to Version 6.0, it didn't ignore the role that made WordPerfect famous—the most powerful document handler available. From finding files to creating button bars, WordPerfect's enhancements help you spend more time working in your document and less time trudging through menus.

This appendix introduces you to some of the new features and briefly explains them. The features are listed alphabetically, so you can look for a specific feature, or leisurely browse the list if you prefer. Basic instructions for accessing most features are included, so you'll know where to find them in WordPerfect.

New Features and Enhancements

The following sections highlight some of the new features and enhancments in WordPerfect 6.0.

Auto Code Placement

Certain types of codes, such as those for page numbering and margins, are best placed at the beginning of the page, paragraph, or line. Auto Code Placement positions such codes for you automatically. Not only does Auto Code Placement make these codes easier to find in your document, it also deletes unnecessary duplicate codes. No longer will you wonder where all those extra, meaningless bold codes came from! To find Auto Code Placement, select File, Setup, Environment or press Shift+F1, and then select Environment.

Bar Codes

Mail-sorting machines can scan and sort bar-coded envelopes more quickly and accurately than they can sort envelopes without bar codes. When you print an envelope, WordPerfect 6.0 can find the zip code in the address and create a 9- or 11-digit bar code for it, which speeds your letters on their way (WordPerfect prints 5-digit bar codes also, but the U.S. Postal Service much prefers 9- or 11-digit bar codes). To add a bar code, type the 9- or 11-digit zip code in the POSTNET Bar Code box near the bottom of the Envelope dialog box.

Bookmark

In a long document, scrolling through pages and pages of text can take a lot of time. By placing bookmarks on pages throughout a document, you can skip from one bookmark to another almost instantly. To find Bookmark, select Edit, Bookmark.

Borders and Border Styles

Now paragraphs, columns, tables, graphics boxes, and pages can have borders with styles that you design with settings for inside and outside spacing, shading, corners, fills, and line styles. The perimeter lines of tables are borders now, so you can control them more easily. To find Borders, select Graphics, Borders.

Button Bars

Button bars, introduced in WordPerfect for Windows, is one of the most useful features included in this version of WordPerfect. When you assign your favorite and most-used features to buttons, you can access them with one click of your mouse—without having to pull down menus. You can assign macros and even other button bars to button bars, too. To find the Button Bar feature, select View, Button Bar or Button Bar Setup.

WordPerfect Coaches

"Just-in-time learning" has become the training buzzphrase of the nineties. Educators are finally recognizing what successful learners have always known: the best time to master a new skill is when you need it and are ready to use it. This is especially true for adult learners who often insist (and rightly so) that the training be directly relevant to their immediate goals. Much of the effort required to learn a new skill is wasted if you do not apply that skill immediately.

WordPerfect 6.0 incorporates a new and innovative training technology called Coaches that builds on the principles of just-in-time learning. Coaches are a new type of computer-based training that differs from traditional CBT in several important ways.

First, unlike WordPerfect's traditional CBT program, which assumes that you will follow a prescribed set of lessons in a particular order (for the most part, at least), WordPerfect coaches are designed to focus on individual features, so you can pick and choose coach topics in any order you like. Each of the coaches is designed to reduce the topic to its most essential points.

Secondly, WordPerfect coaches allow you to learn a new skill or feature without leaving your current document. If you're in the middle of a project and discover that you need to create a table of contents, a task you've never done before, simply turn on the table of contents coach, and in a matter of minutes, WordPerfect will coach you through the process of creating a table of contents, using your own document as its example. It's not quite the same as having a live instructor by your side, but it's the next best thing.

Third, the coaches are written in a version of the WordPerfect macro language, so consultants, system administrators, third-party developers, and office gurus will be able to create their own coaches to meet the special needs of their users. (If you are interested in developing coaches for others to use, you'll probably want to order the WordPerfect Developers' Toolkit from WordPerfect Corporation.)

WordPerfect 6.0 ships with coaches on the following topics:

Bold, Underline, and Italics
Bookmarks
Bullets
Hypertext
Indent Lines and Paragragraphs
Labels
Outline
Search and Replace
Tables
Table of Contents

Using Coaches

Before you try out any of the coaches, you must set your video driver to use Standard VA mode, 640x480, rather than one of the Super VA modes (800x600 or 1280x786). If you're not sure what video mode you're using, just try to run one of the coaches. If you get an error message that you are using the wrong video mode, follow these steps to change to Standard VA:

1. Choose File, Setup, Display. Note your current settings, so you can set them back later.
2. Choose Graphics Screen Colors, then Screen Type.
3. Choose IBM VA and choose Select.

4. Choose 640x480 16 Color (if you have a color VA) or 640x480 16 Gray (if you have monochrome) and choose Select.

5. Press Home, F7 to exit all dialog boxes.

To use a coach, use the following steps:

1. Choose Help, then Coaches.

2. Choose the coach that you want to try from the Coaches dialog box.

3. WordPerfect begins the coaching session, prompting you for each step.

Follow the instructions on your screen. To quit before the coach is finished, press Escape. That's it!

Collapsible Outlines

You can use the Collapsible Outlines feature to collapse a document into outline form, which is especially useful when working with large documents. You can edit major headings quickly without scrolling through the text, as well as choose which sections of the outline to hide or expand. To find the Outline feature, select Tools, Outline or press Ctrl+F5

Color Printing

If your printer can print graphics and color, you can print color lines, borders, text, fills, and figures in WordPerfect. Your black-and-white presentations will never be the same! Color printing capability for non-Postscript color printers is the new feature most requested by WordPerfect customers.

Color Palette

Not only can you print in color anything on the page, you have 16 million color combinations to choose from when you create color palettes to use in color printing. You can create and name your own custom colors to use in color palettes too. To set up color palettes, select File, Setup, Color Printing Palette or press Shift+F1, then select Color Palette.

Conversion

Use WordPerfect's new conversion utility to convert and retrieve documents from many word processing formats. Select File, Open to open the file or press Shift+F10. WordPerfect prompts you to convert the file to Version 6.0 format.

Delay Codes

With Delay Codes, you can place codes at the beginning of your document and specify where in the document they should take effect. Like Auto Code Placement, Delay Codes helps you place codes in their optimal positions and find them more easily. To find Delay Codes, select Layout, Page, Delay Codes or press Shift+F8, then select Page, Delay Codes.

Document Information

Document Information is a quick-access databank that provides information such as size of your document, its average word length, and number and average length of words and sentences. To find Document Information, select Tools, Writing Tools, Document Info or press Alt+F1, then select Document Info.

Envelopes

Envelope printing is streamlined and enhanced in WordPerfect 6.0. When you select the Envelope feature, WordPerfect automatically finds the address in your letter, enters it in the address field of the envelope, and creates a bar code from the 9- to 11-digit zip code. To find the Envelope feature, select Layout, Page, Envelope. You can also print envelopes in Merge.

Fax Capability

WordPerfect 6.0 supports FaxBIOS technology, which allows you to fax directly from WordPerfect through your local or network fax board or fax modem. No need to print the document first, and no special fax software is required. WordPerfect ships with drivers for Class 1, Class 2, or CAS compliant fax devices. To find Fax Services, select File, Print, Fax Services or press Shift+F7, then select Fax Services.

File Manager Sorting

Because WordPerfect customers requested it almost more than any other enhancement, File Manager can now sort files by date of creation, filename, extension, and size. To find File Manager, select File, File Manager or press F5.

Font Preview Box

In Graphics mode or Page mode, you can preview fonts before you apply them to your text to see exactly what they'll look like. To find Font Preview, select Font. The Font Preview box is in the Font dialog box.

Grammar-Checking

The popular grammar-checking software, Grammatik, is now one of your tools in WordPerfect. You can use Grammatik to check your documents for grammar and punctuation errors in any of several styles, such as business, technical, fiction, or advertising. It also helps you evaluate your writing for clarity, structure, readability, and word usage. To find Grammatik, select Tools, Writing Tools, Grammatik.

Graphics

Mouse users particularly will find the new enhancements to the Graphics feature appealing. You can click on graphics and drag them to move or size them. Your text can automatically wrap around graphics, even those of irregular shape. Creating a graphic is easier than before, and you can add polish to graphics with borders and fill patterns.

Keyboard Setup

You can choose to use the WordPerfect 6.0 keyboard that is mapped according to a *common user access* (CUA) layout, or you can use the WordPerfect 5.1 layout. To change your keyboard layout, select File, Setup, Keyboard Layout or, press Shift+F1, then select Keyboard Layout.

Labels

Label definitions have been redesigned to function separately from the printer definition (.PRS) files, so you can use the same label definition with any printer. In previous versions, label definitions were part of the printer definition files, which meant that if you wanted to use the same label definition for more than one printer, you had to create a label definition for each .PRS file.

Last Open File

Each time you open a file, WordPerfect 6.0 remembers the filename. The next time you want to open that file, press the down arrow key in the Open Document or Retrieve Document dialog boxes. A list of the last four documents you opened appears; you can select a file you used recently without climbing up and down your directory tree. WordPerfect remembers the Last Open File list when you exit WordPerfect or even if you turn off your computer.

Merge

The Merge feature in WordPerfect 6.0 is much more flexible than in the past; it has acquired more database characteristics. Now you can select the type of merge you want by specifying the fields in data files that you want to merge, you can set the criteria by which you want to merge them, and set the range of records you want to include. You can also use a table as a data file. Merge will even print envelopes in corresponding order to your documents. To find the Merge feature, select Tools, Merge or press Shift+F9.

Network Setup Utility

The Network Setup Utility is a program that gives network administrators central control over all network users' setup files. With it, you can set defaults for all users simultaneously by modifying the master .SET file. You can also divide user .SET files into groups and set defaults for groups, depending on each group's specific needs. To use the Network Setup Utility, change to the WPC60DOS directory at a DOS prompt and type NWPSETUP.

Nine Documents Open

In previous DOS versions of WordPerfect, you used the Switch feature to open two documents at once, each on its own document screen. You had to switch screens to move from one document to the other. In WordPerfect 6.0, you can have nine documents open at once and view them all at the same time by displaying them in tiles or in a cascade. Use cut, copy, and paste to move text, codes, and other elements between them. To open up to nine documents at once, select File, Open and open the documents you want (or select New to open windows for new documents). To switch between full-screen views, select Window, and then use the last four options on the Window menu to move between the documents. To display them in tile or cascade arrangement, select Window, then Tile or Cascade.

Outline Bar

The Outline Bar is available in Outline Edit mode. With a click of your mouse on the Outline Bar, you can choose quickly which levels of an outline you want to hide or display. To find the Outline Bar, select View, Outline Bar.

Page Numbering

With WordPerfect 6.0, you can have four levels of page numbers—flexibility you often need in large documents. You can number pages by volume, chapter, and page. You can also select page numbering for secondary pages. To find Page Numbering, select Layout, Page or press Shift+F8, then select Page.

QuickFinder

With QuickFinder's indexing capability, you can search for specific files by their content, using key words and phrases. You can build an index that spans directories and drives, both local and network. To find the QuickFinder feature, select File, File Manager or press F5, F4.

QuickList

To save your having to search through drives and directories for files and then having to remember their locations, use QuickList to assign descriptive names to files or directories. To find the QuickList feature, select File, File Manager or press F5, F6.

QuickMark

When you want to close a document and continue working on it later, insert a QuickMark where the cursor is. Later, when you open the document again, press Ctrl+F to move the cursor to the QuickMark and start working right where you left off. To find the QuickMark feature, select Edit, Bookmark.

Reverse Printing

If documents come out of your printer in reverse order with the last page face-up on top, you can use Reverse Printing to print your documents starting with the last page. No more shuffling paper to get pages in order when your print job is finished!

For Reverse Printing, select File, Print, Multiple Pages, Descending Order or press Shift+F7, then select Multiple Pages, Descending Order.

Ribbon

The ribbon is a bar you can display on your screen that has quick pop-up lists for fonts, justification, and zoom settings. The ribbon is available in Text, Graphics, or Page mode. To turn it on, select View, Ribbon.

Scalable Fonts

In addition to its own collection of scalable fonts, WordPerfect supports Bitstream Speedo, Type 1, CG Intellifont, and TrueType scalable fonts. Once you install these third-party fonts with WordPerfect's new Font Installer utility, you can use Graphics mode to view your text on the screen as it will print.

Scroll Bars

The scroll bars are better designed than their Version 5.1 counterparts, and you can use them to move quickly up and down or side to side in your document. Click a handle and drag it vertically or horizontally to scroll smoothly through a document or click the arrows to move by sections. To turn on Scroll Bars, select View, Horizontal Scroll Bar or Vertical Scroll Bar.

Search and Replace

Search and Replace has always been a time-saver in WordPerfect, and now it has been expanded to include searches for more codes than just bold and underline. Now Search and Replace can search for more specific codes such as styles, margins, and justification. To find Search and Replace, select Edit, then Search or Replace or press F2 for Search or Alt+F2 for Replace.

Sound

Back in the days of WordPerfect 4.2 and 5.0, the idea of adding sound to documents was unheard of. In today's WordPerfect, however, as computers speed toward multimedia environments, you can record a sound clip—perhaps a comment about the file—and insert it in your document. All you need is a compatible sound board. To find the Sound Clip feature, select Tools, Sound Clip or press Ctrl+F7, then select Sound Clip.

Speller

Speller has been enhanced to allow you to link dictionaries, so you can spell-check documents using more than one dictionary at a time. You also can customize Speller for checking numbers in words, double words, and irregular capitalization. To find the Speller feature, select Tools, Writing Tools, Speller, Setup or press Ctrl+F2, Shift+F1.

Spreadsheets

The major enhancement to the Tables feature is the addition of spreadsheet capability. WordPerfect 6.0 offers more than 100 spreadsheet functions. You can import spreadsheets from Lotus 1-2-3, Quattro Pro, Excel, and PlanPerfect. To find the Tables feature, select Layout, Tables or press Alt+F2.

Thumbnails

Consistent formatting is often essential in long documents that have headers and footers, chapter headings, and other organizing elements. WordPerfect 6.0 offers a new feature called Thumbnails that you can use to view from 1 to 255 screens at a time in Print Preview. You can see immediately how one page flows to the next and whether its formatting is consistent. To find the Thumbnails feature, select File, Print Preview or press Shift+F7, then Print Preview.

Undo

Similar to but not the same as Cancel and Restore in previous versions of WordPerfect, Undo reverses the last change made or function executed in a document. To use Undo, select Edit, Undo or press Ctrl+Z.

WYSIWYG Editing

WordPerfect 6.0 has retained its familiar text-mode screen interface while adding WYSIWYG graphics viewing and editing modes for users who have the equipment to support them. WYSIWYG editing means "what you see is what you get" editing; what you see on the screen is what will come out of the printer. To change viewing modes, select View.

WordPerfect 6.0's three different editing modes are as follows:

Graphics. This mode is one of WordPerfect's two *graphical user interface* (GUI) modes. When you view and edit your documents in this mode, you see primary formatting elements such as fonts and margins just as they will appear on the printed page.

Page. Page mode is also a graphics mode, but it shows you everything on the page—not only primary formatting elements, but also page numbering, headers, footers, and so on.

Text. In this mode, your documents look much like they did in Version 5.1. Text mode offers all the dialog boxes, scroll bars, button bars, and pull-down menus that the graphics modes do.

Zoom In, Zoom Out

In Print Preview, you can zoom in up to 1,000 percent to see exactly what will print. To use Zoom in Print Preview, select File, Print Preview, then View or click the Zoom buttons on the Print Preview button bar; or, press Shift+F7, Print Preview, then View.

Zoom Settings

In Graphics and Page modes, you can choose how closely you want to look at your document on the editing screen, from Full Page up to 300 percent. To find Zoom options, select View, Zoom.

The *SuperDisk*

The *SuperDisk* included with this book contains more than 3 megabytes of WordPerfect 6.0 "goodies," including:

- ▲ 5 Bitstream Fonts from the *WordPerfect 6.0 Font Pack*
- ▲ More than 40 pieces of clip art from *Masterclips™—The Art of Business* collection
- ▲ A special version of *QwkScreen™*
- ▲ *!Bang* utility
- ▲ *WPReveal* utility
- ▲ All files from the Projects section of the book
- ▲ Macros, keyboards, graphics and sample files used in the book
- ▲ Spreadsheet, button bar and keyboard reference lists

 Anywhere you see the disk icon (shown to the left of this paragraph), you'll know that the author is discussing a file which is on the *SuperDisk*. If you haven't already installed the *SuperDisk*, see the installation page for instructions (it's the last page in the book).

Bitstream™ Fonts

Bitstream, Inc.
1-800-522-FONT (orders only)

Location: \WPSUPER\FONTS

The five fonts included with the *SuperDisk* are a sample of what you'll find in the WordPerfect 6.0 Font Pack from Bitstream. For a complete list of fonts in the Font Pack, see Bitstream's ad in the back of this book.

Here is a list of the fonts included on the *SuperDisk:*

- ▲ Davida Bold
- ▲ Freehand 471
- ▲ Mister Earl
- ▲ Monterey
- ▲ Umbra

To install these fonts in WordPerfect 6.0, see Chapter 40, "Producing Good Looking Documents."

Masterclips™—The Art of Business

Masterclips, Inc.
5201 Ravenswood Road, Suite 111
Fort Lauderdale, FL 33312
1-800-292-CLIP (orders only)
(305) 983-7440
(305) 967-9452 (fax)

Location: \WPSUPER\MCLIPS

The clip art included on the *SuperDisk* is a sampler from *The Art of Business* collection. This collection is available on disks and CD-ROM, and it contains more than 6,000 full color images, all drawn by professional artists. More than 100 categories are represented, and the images are available in CGM or WPG format.

The full retail package also includes a keyword image browser and a color to black-and-white converter. See the Masterclips ad in the back of the book for more information.

 Note: To use this clip art, you need to specify the location of the images on your hard disk each time you create a graphics box in WordPerfect. If you want the clip art to automatically appear in your default list of graphics files, you must copy the files to the standard WordPerfect 6.0 graphics directory. Unless you changed this during installation of WordPerfect, the standard graphics directory is \WP60\GRAPHICS.

Masterclips also offers *Custom Clips*™, a service for converting your logos or product images into electronic clip art images. These images are hand drawn from your original camera-ready art, which guarantees an exact reproduction of the original.

Your *Custom Clips* can be produced in full color and in black-and-white, in a variety of graphics formats. Contact Masterclips for more information; you can also fax your logo or image for a free estimate.

QwkScreen™

QwkScreen Corporation
252 Lincoln Road
Brooklyn, NY 11225
1-800-671-9974 (orders only)

Location: \WPSUPER\QSCREEN

QwkScreen is an integrated system of keyboard files and macros that transform the raw power and complexity of WordPerfect into a simple and powerful writing tool. This special version of QwkScreen was produced for inclusion in this book.

Setting Up QwkScreen

Before you use QwkScreen for the first time, you need to set up WordPerfect so it knows where the QwkScreen files are located. Follow these steps:

1. Go to the setup menu (Shift-F1).
2. Choose Location of Files.
3. Select Macros/Keyboards/Button Bar....
4. Choose Shared Path.
5. In the space for the path, type \WPSUPER\QSCREEN and press Enter.
6. Press Enter three times to exit the setup menu.

> **Note:** If you are using WordPerfect on a network, and your Shared Path is already being used, you'll need to copy the QwkScreen files into your WordPerfect macros directory. Unless you changed this directory, it is named \WP60\MACROS.

Starting QwkScreen

Now that WordPerfect knows where to find QwkScreen, you can start it by simply pressing Alt+Q. In addition to shortcut keys, QwkScreen adds a number of powerful features to the WordPerfect menus.

Your keyboard will now be set up for QwkScreen. To see a list of the QwkScreen shortcut keys, press Alt+K. Use your right and left arrows while you are viewing this screen, and you'll see additional lists of QwkScreen keys.

Here are just a few of the many functions included in QwkScreen:

▲ One-key copy, move, and delete functions

▲ One-key character formatting

▲ One-key printer's quotes

▲ One-key time and date

▲ QwkOpen of last four documents

▲ Enhanced close, clear, and exit functions

▲ Delete extra spaces tool

▲ Invisible codes cleanup

▲ Convert measurements from English to metric and vice versa

▲ Convert temperatures measurements

▲ Easy insertion of common abbreviations for states, chemical elements, publishing terms, degrees and titles, scholarly references, and more

▲ Easy creation and formatting of tables

▲ Easy selection of common documents styles, such as memo, term paper, letter, and more.

To get a feel for how QwkScreen works, try moving, copying or deleting some text. Use the F11 key to turn the block on, then press Ctrl+M to move the text, Ctrl+C to copy it, or Ctrl+D to delete it. If you blocked the text first, QwkScreen makes these operations quick and easy. If you don't block the text first, QwkScreen presents you with options for what to do next.

> **Note:** If you are using a keyboard with only 10 function keys, you will need the full retail version of QwkScreen. It contains an alternate setup that accommodates this type of keyboard.

To explore QwkScreen further, try the many QwkScreen options that are added to the WordPerfect menus. Press Alt+Z to show the QwkScreen menu bar. Press F1 to open the QwkScreen help system. For more information about upgrading to the full retail version of QwkScreen, see their ad page in the back of this book.

!Bang

PC Techniques
William Claff
7 Roberts Rd.
Wellesley, MA 02181

Location: \WPSUPER\BANG

!Bang provides a variety of powerful and flexible hard-disk management functions in a single command-line driven program. You can use !Bang from the DOS prompt, in batch files, or from WordPerfect Office's shell menu.

Here are just a few of the things that !Bang can do:

▲ Find files on multiple hard disks
▲ Find WordPerfect 5.x and 6.0 files
▲ Find duplicate filenames
▲ Find unique filenames
▲ Find files according to their creation date
▲ Execute the files that are found
▲ Perform actions on the files that are found

The executable file for !Bang is !.EXE. To use !Bang, type !, followed by any command-line options. You'll find information on using !Bang in these files:

!.DOC—the manual, which is formatted for printing.
!BANG.TXT—a quick reference to get you acquainted with the program.

The program includes several options of particular interest to users of WordPerfect. You can restrict the output to WordPerfect 5.x documents, WordPerfect 6.0 files, all WordPerfect files, or particular types of WordPerfect files.

!Bang is distributed as shareware. Registered users receive a copy of the latest release, additional documentation, telephone support, update notification, and minor releases at cost. See the file !BANG.TXT for more information.

WPReveal

PC Techniques
William Claff
7 Roberts Rd.
Wellesley, MA 02181

Location: \WPSUPER\WPREVEAL

The primary use of WPReveal is to extract portions of WordPerfect 6.0 documents that are not easily accessed from WordPerfect itself. For example, you can extract all of the footnotes in a document.

The only required parameter to the WPReveal program is a file specification; you may use wild cards for this file specification, such as *.DOC. WPReveal will process all of the WordPerfect 6.0 documents that match the file specification. The filenames will be displayed on the screen as they are processed.

The default action of WPReveal is to parse the file and to report errors. To extract all or part of a document you must include one or more of the optional command-line switches (Table D.1). These switches cause all or part of the document to be displayed on the screen in a manner similar to reveal codes.

Often you will want to redirect this output to a file. To do this, add > *filename* to the end of the WPReveal command line. This will redirect the output of WPReveal to *filename*, which you specify.

Table D.1. WPReveal command-line switches.

Switch	Action
/?	Display help information
/DOC	Display additional help on document codes
/PREFIX	Display additional help on prefix codes
/UPDATE	Display update form. Redirect to your printer
/WARN	Display warning if file does not conform to WP specification
[code]	Display a portion of a document (see Table D.2)
{code}	Display a portion of the prefix (see Table D.3)
@filename	File containing additional Filespecs and Options

The /DOC switch causes the entire document (except undo information) to be output. Use the parameters in Table D.2 with /DOC to see portions of the document information.

Table D.2. /DOC parameters.

[code]	Action
[*]	Display entire document (except undo codes)
[BOOKMARK]	Display bookmarks
[COMMENT]	Display comment blocks

[code]	*Action*
[ENDNOTE]	Display endnotes
[FONT]	Display font codes
[FOOTNOTE]	Display footnotes
[INDEX]	Display index entries
[MARK TXT LIST]	Display Mark Txt List entries
[MARK TXT TOC]	Display Mark Txt ToC entries
[TARGET]	Display Target codes
[TOA]	Display ToA entries
[UNDO]	Display undo codes (if used with [*])

The /PREFIX switch causes the entire prefix to be displayed. Use the parameters in Table D.3 with /PREFIX to see portions of the document information.

Table D.3. /PREFIX parameters.

{code}	*Action*
{*}	Display entire document prefix
{Bookmark}	Display bookmark prefixes
{Default Initial Font}	Display default initial font
{Form Paper Size/Type}	Display form paper size/type
{Graphics Filename}	Display graphics filename
{List of Fonts}	Display list of fonts used in the document
{Merge Filename}	Display merge filename
{Merge Filetype}	Display merge filetype
{Personal Style Library}	Display personal style library
{Shared Style Library}	Display shared style library
{Sound Clip Description}	Display sound clip description
{Sound Clip Filename}	Display sound clip filename
{Subdocument}	Display subdocument filename
{Summary}	Display extended summary information

WPReveal (© 1988-1993), William Claff and PC Techniques.

Projects

Location: \WPSUPER\PROJECTS

The following is a list of Project files contained on the *SuperDisk*.

Chapter 65: Academic paper files.

ACADEMIC.PRO	Sample academic paper
ACADEMIC.STY	Styles for academic paper
ACADEMIC.WPB	Academic paper button bar
BIBLIOGR.WPM	Macro to create bibliography
PREFACE.WPM	Macro to create preface
SORTBIB.DOC	Documentation for the SortBIB macro
SORTBIB.WPM	Macro to sort bibliographic entries
TITLEPG.WPM	Macro to create title page for paper

Chapter 66: Monthly calendar files.

MONTHCAL.PRO	Template for monthly calendar (requires MONTHCAL.WPM)
MONTHCAL.WPM	Macro to create monthly calendar

Chapter 67: Certificate files.

CERTIF.PRO	Sample certificate
CERTIF.FF	Certificate set up as a merge from the keyboard

Chapter 68: Press release files.

PRESSREL.PRO	Sample press release

Note: If the reverse text does not print correctly on your printer, try the Print Job Graphically option on the print dialog box.

Chapter 69: Invoice files.

INVOICE.PRO	Invoice template
CALC_INV.WPM	Macro to calculate invoice total

Note: If the reverse text does not print correctly on your printer, try the Print Job Graphically option on the print dialog box.

Chapter 70: Letterhead files.

LETTERHD.PRO	Sample letter with letterhead
LETTERHD.STY	Letterhead style
ALTZ.WPM	Macro to create letter

Note: This letterhead style requires Bitstream FormalScript in order to duplicate the appearance of the letterhead pictured in the *WordPerfect 6.0 Super Book*.

Chapter 71: Fax cover sheet files.

FAX.PRO	Template for fax cover sheet
FAX.WPM	Macro to fill in fax cover sheet

Chapter 72: Invitation files.

INVITE.PRO	Sample invitation

Chapter 73: Labels files.

LABELS.PRO	Template for Labels
LABELS.FF	Labels form file for merge
PEOPLE.DF	Sample data file for merging with LABELS.FF

Chapter 74: Booklet files.

BOOKLET.PRO	Template for booklet
BOOKLET.FF	Form file for booklet merge
BOOKLET.SAM	Sample booklet
TITLES.DF	List of Sams book titles in data file format, for merging with BOOKLET.FF

Chapter Files

The authors of the book have created a variety of macros, keyboard files, example documents and styles for your use. These files are arranged by the chapter where the files are discussed. For example, the example merge files from Chapter 53, "Equation Editor," are located in \WPSUPER\CH53.

Reference Files

The authors of this book have created three reference files for your use:

KEYBOARD.REF	Standard WordPerfect keyboard assignments
BUTTONS.REF	Standard WordPerfect button bars assignments
SPSHEET.REF	WordPerfect spreadsheet functions

These files are in WP 6.0 format; they can be viewed, searched or printed from within WordPerfect.

Index

X–Z

Add to Your Sams Library Today with the Best Books for Programming, Operating Systems, and New Technologies

The easiest way to order is to pick up the phone and call

1-800-428-5331

between 9:00 a.m. and 5:00 p.m. EST.
For faster service please have your credit card available.

ISBN	Quantity	Description of Item	Unit Cost	Total Cost
0-672-30269-1		Absolute Beginner's Guide to Programming	$19.95	
0-672-30341-8		Absolute Beginner's Guide to C	$16.95	
0-672-30342-6		Absolute Beginner's Guide to QBasic	$16.95	
0-672-30282-9		Absolute Beginner's Guide to Memory Management	$16.95	
0-672-30326-4		Absolute Beginner's Guide to Networking	$19.95	
0-672-30240-3		OS/2 2.1 Unleashed (Book/Disk)	$34.95	
0-672-30317-5		Your OS/2 2.1 Consultant	$24.95	
0-672-30288-8		DOS Secrets Unleashed (Book/Disk)	$39.95	
0-672-30298-5		Windows NT: The Next Generation	$22.95	
0-672-30248-9		FractalVision (Book/Disk)	$39.95	
0-672-30249-7		Multimedia Madness! (Book/Disk/CD-ROM)	$44.95	
0-672-30310-8		Windows Graphics FunPack (Book/Disk)	$19.95	
0-672-30318-3		Windows Sound FunPack (Book/Disk)	$19.95	
0-672-30040-0		Teach Yourself C in 21 Days	$24.95	
0-672-30324-8		Teach Yourself QBasic in 21 Days	$24.95	
0-672-30259-4		Do-It-Yourself Visual Basic for Windows, 2E	$24.95	
0-672-30349-3		DOS 6 for the Guru Wanna-Be	$18.95	
❏ 3 ½" Disk		Shipping and Handling: See information below.		
❏ 5 ¼" Disk		TOTAL		

Shipping and Handling: $4.00 for the first book, and $1.75 for each additional book. Floppy disk: add $1.75 for shipping and handling. If you need to have it NOW, we can ship product to you in 24 hours for an additional charge of approximately $18.00, and you will receive your item overnight or in two days. Overseas Shipping and Handling: add $2.00 per book, and $8.00 for up to three disks. Prices subject to change. Call for availability and pricing information on latest editions.

11711 N. College Avenue, Suite 140, Carmel, Indiana 46032

1-800-428-5331 — Orders   1-800-835-3202 — FAX   1-800-858-7674 — Customer Service

Book ISBN 0-672-30260-8

What's on the *SuperDisk*

▲ Five decorative fonts from the *Bitstream™ WordPerfect 6.0 Font Pack*

▲ More than 40 pieces of color clip art from the *Masterclips—The Art of Business* collection

▲ A special version of *QwkScreen™*, the program that makes WordPerfect 6.0 easier and faster to use

▲ *Bang*, the file utility that searches for and performs actions on WordPerfect 6.0, 5.1, and 5.0 files

▲ *WPReveal*, a utility that extracts and saves codes, notes, comments, and more from WordPerfect documents

▲ All example projects from the book

▲ A variety of useful macros and button bars

▲ Four foreign language keyboards

▲ A complete reference for WordPerfect's spreadsheet functions

Installing the *SuperDisk*

The software included with this book is stored in a compressed form. To install all the files, you need at least 3.5M of free space on your hard drive.

1. From the DOS prompt, type B:INSTALL and press Enter if the *SuperDisk* is in drive B; type A:INSTALL if the disk is in drive A. The installation program will display an introductory message— press any key to continue with the installation.

2. You'll be given the option to change the drive where the programs will be installed. If you want to change to a drive other than C, press Enter and select from the list of available drives.

3. Choose the Start Installation selection. The program will begin installing the files to your hard drive.

4. When the files have been installed, the file WPSUPER.DOC will be displayed for you to read. It contains information on the files that were installed. Press Esc when you are finished reading.

5. A message will appear when the program is finished—press any key to exit the installation program.

You're now ready to begin using the software from the *SuperDisk!* The files are located in the \WPSUPER directory of your hard drive. Be sure to read Appendix D, "The *SuperDisk*," which contains information on the files and how to use them.